EXPLORATIONS: AN OPEN INVITATION TO BIOLOGICAL ANTHROPOLOGY

EXPLORATIONS: AN OPEN INVITATION TO BIOLOGICAL ANTHROPOLOGY

Editors: Beth Shook, Katie Nelson, Kelsie Aguilera and Lara Braff

American Anthropological Association
Arlington, VA

2019

CC BY-NC 4.0 International, except where otherwise noted

ISBN – 978-1-931303-63-7

www.explorations.americananthro.org

Contents

Preface — vi

Part I. Main Body

1. Introduction to Biological Anthropology — 2
2. Evolution — 29
3. Molecular Biology and Genetics — 58
4. Forces of Evolution — 109
5. Meet the Living Primates — 148
6. Primate Ecology and Behavior — 190
7. Understanding the Fossil Context — 233
8. Primate Evolution — 274
9. Early Hominins — 319
10. Early Members of the Genus Homo — 374
11. Archaic Homo — 403
12. Modern Homo sapiens — 444
13. Race and Human Variation — 489
14. Human Variation: An Adaptive Significance Approach — 516
15. Bioarchaeology and Forensic Anthropology — 546
16. Contemporary Topics: Human Biology and Health — 580

Part II. Appendices

a) Osteology — 623
b) Primate Conservation — 665
c) Human Behavioral Ecology — 695

Preface

Welcome to *Explorations: An Open Invitation to Biological Anthropology*. We (the editors) joined together in 2017 to create this dynamic and comprehensive Open Educational Resource (OER) for biological anthropology. We were motivated by the lack of existing OER in this subdiscipline and by a desire to save our students money on textbooks. We were also inspired by the recent success of *Perspectives: An Open Invitation to Cultural Anthropology* and supported by the editors of *Perspectives* and by the Society for Anthropology in Community Colleges (SACC), a section of the American Anthropological Association that consists of higher-education instructors who promote teaching excellence in anthropology. Together, the four editors bring to this project decades of experience in the classroom and a commitment to creating a resource that speaks to our students, sparking their interest in scientific inquiry and anthropological discoveries.

Global Open Educational Resources Logo by Jonathasmello is used under a CC BY 3.0 License.

This project is also grounded in the wider OER movement that emerged as a response to the skyrocketing costs of traditional textbooks. These costs, along with increased tuition, create serious barriers to student learning and success, especially for students dealing with financial constraints. As anthropologists concerned with social equity, we find that OER can begin to level the playing field within academia by enabling *all* students, regardless of socioeconomic status, to access materials they need to succeed in their courses.

An OER for YOU

Students: This textbook has been created with you and your success in mind. The editors and authors are experienced instructors who hope to engage your curiosity and questions about humankind. It is available to you for FREE!

Instructors: We commend you for making the inspired choice to adopt this textbook written, reviewed, and edited by anthropology instructors. Like other OER, *Explorations* offers you the academic freedom to align course materials with your own pedagogy, course content, and areas of expertise. Rather than conform your course to the chapters of a conventional textbook, you are free to modify, supplement, or add to this textbook. This is why we chose to publish *Explorations* with a Creative Commons Attribution-NonCommercial 4.0 International License (CC BY-NC 4.0), which allows anyone to remix, adapt, transform, and build upon the contents. In other words, you can use this book as it is or alter it by reorganizing, omitting chapters or sections of chapters, assigning only some chapters, or curating chapter selections. The only requirement is that you credit the authors and source, specify the license, and indicate any changes made. In the spirit of open education, this textbook and the content within cannot be used for commercial purposes.

We view *Explorations* as a dynamic text: we encourage your contributions on an ongoing basis. You may contribute by simply spreading the word! This textbook started as a grassroots endeavor that gained momentum by virtue of support from our professional communities, colleagues, and students. You may also contribute substantially by providing feedback, corrections, updated information, or additional research via the form on our website or by sending an email to explorationstextbook@gmail.com. We recognize that biological anthropology is ever-evolving as new discoveries challenge prior understandings to extend knowledge of our species.

Explorations: Mission and Organization

> *Mission Statement: To provide a high-quality introductory biological anthropology textbook that is readable, engaging, and accessible to all students. With chapters written by experienced instructors and subject area specialists, this textbook addresses the question of what it means to be human by exploring the origins, evolution, and diversification of primates, especially that of our species, Homo sapiens.*

Anthropology is the study of humanity, in all its biological and cultural aspects, past and present. It is a four-field discipline comprised of biological anthropology, cultural anthropology, archaeology, and linguistic anthropology. The focus of this book is biological anthropology, which explores who we are from biological, evolutionary, and adaptive perspectives.

We lay the foundation for this inquiry in the first four chapters by introducing the discipline of anthropology, evolutionary theory, molecular biology and genetics, and the forces of evolution. Chapters 5–8 consider evolutionary, biological, and social aspects of our closest living relatives, nonhuman primates, with whom we share millions of years of evolution. We also learn about how fossils provide material insight into our past. Chapters 9–12 describe prior hominin species and the emergence of *Homo sapiens*, us! Finally, the last four chapters (Chapters 13–16) explore human biological variation and the concept of race, bioarchaeology and forensic anthropology, and human biology and health in the past and present. We include further readings on osteology (Appendix A), primate conservation (Appendix B), and human behavioral ecology (Appendix C). To guide your reading, each chapter begins with learning objectives and ends with review questions and a list of key terms.

Acknowledgments

This book is for our students, past, present, and future, who inspire us to be better educators and better anthropologists.

The editors met through the Society for Anthropology in Community Colleges (SACC), which provided, and continues to provide, the collegial context in which this textbook emerged. We thank SACC for its support and seed money to begin this project. We appreciate the American Anthropological Association (AAA) for housing our book on their website, providing our ISBN, and publishing printed copies of this book at low cost. We thank the University of Hawai'i OER initiative for providing access to Pressbooks, the formatting software we used for this project.

We also thank the editors of *Perspectives*: Nina Brown, Laura Tubelle de Gonzalez, and Thomas McIlwraith for their guidance and encouragement.

We are grateful for grants we received to finance this project. The Minnesota State Innovation Grant enabled us to hire professional copy editors and illustrators to ensure a professional product. We appreciate the support and guidance from Stephen Kelly, Minnesota State Open Education and Innovation Program Coordinator. The Academic Senate for California Community Colleges- OER Initiative (ASCCC-OERI) funded the development of our ancillary materials (lecture slides and test banks) to enhance this textbook (see Teaching Resources on our website).

Finally, this book would not be possible without the outstanding voluntary efforts of our 41 authors and 48 reviewers. Thank you!

With appreciation,

Beth, Katie, Kelsie, and Lara

REVIEWERS

- Jessica Amato, Napa Valley College
- Lindsay Barone, DNA Learning Center
- Lisa Becker, Anoka Ramsey Community College
- James Bindon, The University of Alabama
- Samantha Blatt, Idaho State University
- Nina Brown, The Community College of Baltimore County
- Jennifer Byrnes, University of Hawai'i – West O'ahu
- Keith Chan, Grossmont College
- Shannon Clinkinbeard, Sierra College and California State University
- Chico Victoria Clow, Dallas County Community College District
- Katherine Fernandez, Wichita State University
- Monique Fortunato, Cosumnes River College
- Davette Gadison, Tulane University
- Sydney Garcia, San Diego Museum of Man
- Justin Garcia, Millersville University of Pennsylvania
- Kimberly Garza, University of Illinois at Chicago
- Rebecca Gilmour, McMaster University
- Laura Tubelle de Gonzalez, Miramar College
- Kaitlin Hakanson, Klamath Community College
- Carol Hayman, Austin Community College
- Maureen Hickey, Los Angeles Mission College
- Angela Jenks, University of California, Irvine
- Alexandra Klales, Washburn University
- Winsome Lee, Kenyon International Emergency Services

- Chris Maier, Eckerd College
- Katherine McElvaney, University of Houston
- Tad McIlwraith, University of Guelph
- Cara Monroe, University of Oklahoma
- Matthew O'Brien, California State University, Chico
- Kathryn Olszowy, New Mexico State University
- Carolyn Orbann, University of Missouri
- Tanusree Pandit, Panjab University, Educational Institution, Chandigarh
- Amanda Paskey, Cosumnes River College
- Betsy Abrams Rich, Los Angeles Valley College and Santa Monica College
- Benjamin Schaefer, Georgia State University
- Arnie Schoenberg, San Diego City College
- Laure Spake, Simon Fraser University
- Jay VanderVeen, Indiana University South Bend
- Marco Vidal Cordasco, National Research Center on Human Evolution (CENIEH)
- Sandra Wheeler, University of Central Florida
- Kyleb Wild, Grossmont College
- Marlo Willows, Palomar College
- Kristin Wilson, Cabrillo College
- Katrina Worley, American River College
- Heather Worne, University of Kentucky
- Bonnie Yoshida-Levine, Grossmont College
- Aaron Young, University of Arizona
- Melissa Zolnierz, Kansas City University

ILLUSTRATOR

- Mary Nelson

COVER ART

- Stewart Williams

CARTOGRAPHY

- Elyssa Ebding and Geo Place, California State University, Chico
- Chelsea Barron, GeoPlace, California State University, Chico
- Peter Hansen, GeoPlace, California State University, Chico

COPYEDITORS

- Annik Babinski
- Laura Carney
- Mayumi Shimose Poe

PART I
MAIN BODY

Chapter 1: Introduction to Biological Anthropology

Katie Nelson, Ph.D., Inver Hills Community College
Lara Braff, Ph.D., Grossmont College
Beth Shook, Ph.D., California State University, Chico
Kelsie Aguilera, M.A., Leeward Community College

Learning Objectives

- Define anthropology and the main anthropological approaches.
- Describe the origins and early development of anthropology.
- Identify the four subdisciplines of anthropology and specify the focus of each one.
- Define biological anthropology, describe its key questions, and identify major subfields.
- Explain key components of the scientific method.
- Differentiate between hypotheses, theories, and laws.
- Differentiate science from other ways of knowing.

The first time one of the authors [Katie Nelson] heard of biological anthropology, she was a first-year college student at Macalester College in Saint Paul, Minnesota, taking her first-ever anthropology course. Before she enrolled in the class she didn't really know what *anthropology* meant. She knew it had something to do with people, but didn't know how it all fit together. The course description appealed to her, so she signed up. She quickly learned that anthropology was the study of humans and that it was an incredibly broad discipline that included explorations of cultural diversity, human origins, past human societies, and human languages, among a great many other subjects. She had always been interested in learning about people. She enjoyed observing the different ways people interacted in public spaces, like the mall or the zoo. She enjoyed learning Spanish in high school and loved listening to how people who spoke different languages produced different sounds. She was curious about how people inherited unique characteristics from their parents and was especially intrigued by immigration and migration and what caused people to uproot themselves and move to another part of the world. During the second week of class she began to learn about biological anthropology and some of the leading theories for how and why ancient humans left Africa and migrated throughout the world. As she sat in class, she vividly remembers imagining a small group of ancient humans walking barefoot together through the African savannah. She imagined what they wore, what their language sounded like, how they held hands, how they shared food, and so on. She wondered why they were migrating and what they would miss about their homeland. She was hooked on anthropology!

WHAT IS ANTHROPOLOGY?

Why are people so diverse? Some people live in the frigid Arctic tundra, others in the arid deserts of sub-Saharan Africa, and still others in the dense forests of Papua New Guinea. Human beings speak more than 6,000 distinct languages. Some people are barely five feet tall while others stoop to fit through a standard door frame. In some places, people generally have very dark skin, in other places, people are generally pale. In some societies, eating pig is strictly prohibited; in others, pork is a rather ordinary food. What makes people differ from one another? What do we all share in common? How are humans different from other primates? How have primates adapted to different places? How and why did humans develop in the first place? These are some of the questions anthropologists try to answer.

Derived from Greek, the word "anthropos" means "human" and "logy" refers to the "study of." Therefore anthropology, by definition, is the study of humans. Anthropologists are not the only scholars to focus on the human condition; biologists, sociologists, psychologists, and others also examine human nature and societies. However, anthropologists uniquely draw on four key approaches to do their research: **holism**, comparison, dynamism, and fieldwork. Anthropology is an incredibly broad and dynamic discipline. It studies humanity by exploring our past and our present and all of our biological and cultural complexity.

Figure 1.1 Despite the many evident differences among people, humans are among the most genetically similar species.

Holism

Anthropologists are interested in the *whole* of humanity, in how various aspects of biological or cultural life intersect. One cannot fully understand what it means to be human by studying a single aspect of our complex bodies or societies. By using a holistic approach, anthropologists ask how different aspects interact with and influence one another. For example, a biological anthropologist studying monkeys in South America might consider the species' physical adaptations, foraging patterns, ecological conditions, and interactions with humans in order to answer questions about their social behaviors. By understanding how nonhuman primates behave, we discover more about ourselves: after all, as you will learn in this book, humans *are* primates! A cultural anthropologist studying marriage in a small village in India might consider local gender norms, existing family networks, laws regarding marriage, religious rules, and economic requisites in order to understand the particular meanings of marriage in that context. By using a holistic approach, anthropologists appreciate the complexity of any biological, social, or cultural phenomenon.

As we will discuss in more detail, anthropology itself is a holistic discipline, comprised (in the United States) of four major areas of study called **subdisciplines**: cultural anthropology, biological anthropology, linguistic anthropology, and archaeology. We need all four subdisciplines in order to understand the human experience, which involves culture, language, and biological and social adaptations, as well as our history, evolution, and relationship to our closest living relatives: nonhuman primates.

Comparison

Figure 1.2 By using a holistic approach, anthropologists learn how different aspects of humanity interact with and influence one another.

Anthropology is a comparative discipline: anthropologists compare and contrast data in order to understand what all humans have in common, how we differ, and how we have changed over time. The comparative approach can be historical: How do humans today differ from ancient *Homo sapiens*? How has Egyptian society changed since the building of the great pyramids? How is the English language adapting to new modes of communication like smartphones? The comparative approach is also applied to sociocultural phenomena. We can compare the roles of men and women in different societies or different religious traditions within a given society. Some anthropologists compare different primate species, investigating traits shared by all primates (including humans!) or identifying traits that distinguish one primate group from another. Unlike some other disciplines that also use comparative approaches, anthropologists do not just consider our own species or society. Our comparisons span societies, cultures, time, place, and species.

Dynamism

Humans are one of the most dynamic species. Our ability to change, both biologically and culturally, has enabled us to persist over the course of millions of years, and to thrive in many different environments.

Depending on their research focus, anthropologists ask about all kinds of changes: short-term or long-term, temporary or permanent, cultural or biological. For example, a cultural anthropologist might look at how people in a relatively isolated society change in the context of globalization, the process of interaction and interdependence among different nations and cultures of the world. A linguistic anthropologist might ask how a new form of language, like Spanglish, emerges. An archaeologist might ask how climate change influenced the emergence of agriculture. A biological anthropologist might consider how diseases affecting our ancestors led to changes in their bodies. All these examples highlight the dynamic nature of human bodies and societies. While we differ from our ancestors who lived hundreds of thousands of years ago, we share with them this capacity for change.

Fieldwork

Throughout this book, you will read examples of anthropological research that will take you around the world. Anthropologists do not only work in laboratories, libraries, or offices. To collect data, they go to where their data lives, whether it is a city, village, cave, tropical forest, or desert. At their field sites, anthropologists collect data which, depending on subdiscipline, may be interviews with local peoples, examples of language in use, skeletal remains, or human cultural remains like potsherds or stone tools. While anthropologists ask an array of questions and use diverse methods to answer their research questions, they share this commitment to conducting their research out of their offices and in the field.

A Brief History of Anthropology

Imagine only interacting with people who looked, spoke, and acted like you. Now, how would you begin to understand a seemingly new group of people? As people first began to explore the world, they grappled with how to make sense of human differences. Many were adventurers, missionaries, or traders, motivated by a desire to explore, spread their religion, or acquire wealth. All of them were familiar with only one way of life–their own. It was, therefore, through the lens of their own culture that they viewed people they met during their travels.

Figure 1.3 Anthropologist Katie Nelson conducting fieldwork among undocumented Mexican immigrant college students.

Figure 1.4 Caption: Statue of Zhang Qian in Chenggu, China. Zhang Qian is still celebrated today in China as an important diplomat and pioneer of the silk road.

One of the first examples of someone who attempted to systematically study and document cultural differences among different peoples is Zhang Qian (Chang Ch'ien 164 BC – 113 BC). Born in the second century BCE in Hanzhong, China, Zhang was a military officer who was assigned by Emperor Wu of Han to travel through Central Asia, going as far as what is today Uzbekistan. He spent more than 25 years traveling and recording his observations of the peoples and cultures of Central Asia (Wood 2004). The Emperor used this information to establish new relationships and cultural connections with China's neighbors to the West. Zhang discovered many of the trade routes used in the Silk Road and introduced many new cultural ideas, including Buddhism, into Chinese culture.

Figure 1.5 An illustration of Abu Abdullah Muhammad Ibn Battuta in Egypt from Jules Verne's book Discovery of the Earth.

Another early traveler of note was Abu Abdullah Muhammad Ibn Battuta (known most widely as *Ibn Battuta*) (1304-1369). Ibn Battuta was an Amazigh (Berber) Moroccan Muslim scholar. Over a period of nearly 30 years during the fourteenth century, Ibn Battuta's travels covered nearly the whole of the Islamic world, including parts of Europe, sub-Saharan Africa, India, and China. Upon his return to the Kingdom of Morocco, he documented the customs and traditions of the people he encountered in a book called *Tuhfat al-anzar fi gharaaib al-amsar wa ajaaib al-asfar* (A Gift to those who Contemplate the Wonders of Cities and the Marvels of Traveling), but became commonly known as *Al Rihla*, which means "travels" in Arabic (McIntosh-Smith 2003: ix). This book became part of a genre of Arabic literature that included descriptions of the people and places visited along with commentary about the cultures encountered. Some scholars consider *Rihla* to be among the first examples of early pre-anthropological writing.

Later, from the 1400s through 1700s, during the so-called "Age of Discovery," Europeans began to not only explore the world but also colonize it. Europeans exploited natural resources and human labor, exerting social and political control over people they encountered. New trade routes, along with the slave trade, fueled a growing European empire, while forever disrupting previously independent cultures in the Old World. European **ethnocentrism**—the belief that one's own culture is better than others—was used to justify the subjugation of non-European societies.

As European empires expanded, new ways of understanding the world and its people arose. Beginning in the eighteenth century in Europe, the Age of Enlightenment was a social and philosophical movement that privileged science, rationality, and empiricism while critiquing religious authority. This crucial period of intellectual development planted the seeds for many academic disciplines, including anthropology. It gave ordinary people the capacity to learn through observation and experience: *Anyone* could ask questions and use rational thought to discover things about the natural and social world.

For example, Charles Lyell (1797–1875), a geologist, would observe layers of rock and argue that Earth's surface must have changed gradually over long periods of time, such that it could not be only 6,000 years old (as the Young Earth interpretation in the Bible contends). Charles Darwin (1809–1882), a naturalist and biologist, would observe similarities between fossils and living specimens, leading him to argue that all life is descended from a common ancestor. Philosopher John Locke (1632–1704) would contemplate the origins of society itself. He wrote that people lived in relative isolation until they agreed to form a society in which the government would protect their personal property.

These radical ideas about the earth, evolution, and society influenced early social scientists into the nineteenth century. For example, Herbert Spencer (1820–1903), inspired by scientific principles, used biological evolution as a model to understand social evolution: just as biological life evolved from simple to complex multicellular organisms, he postulated that societies "evolve" to become larger and more complex. Lewis Henry Morgan (1818–1881) argued that all societies "progress" through the same stages of development: savagery–barbarism–civilization. Societies were classified into these stages based on their kinship patterns, technologies, subsistence patterns, and so forth. So-called savage societies, ones that used rudimentary tools and foraged for food, were said to be stalled in their mental and moral development.

Figure 1.6 Caption: Charles Darwin, circa 1881.

Ethnocentric ideas, like those of Morgan, were challenged by anthropologists in the early twentieth century in both Europe and the United States. During World War I, Bronislaw Malinowski (1884–1942), a Polish anthropologist, became stranded on the Trobriand Islands, where he started to do **participant-observation** fieldwork: the method of immersive, long-term fieldwork that cultural anthropologists use today. By living with and observing the Trobrianders, he realized that their culture was not "savage," but rather fulfilled the needs of the people. He developed a theory to explain human cultural diversity: Each culture functions to satisfy the specific biological and psychological needs of its people. While this theory has been critiqued for overemphasizing individuals apart from culture, it was an early attempt to view other cultures in more relativistic ways.

Around the same time in the United States, Franz Boas (1858–1942), widely regarded as the founder of American anthropology, developed the cultural relativistic approach: the view that cultures differ but are not better or worse than one another. In his critique of ethnocentric views, Boas insisted that physical and behavioral differences among so-called racial groups in the United States were shaped by environmental and social conditions, not biology. In fact, he argued, culture and biology are distinct realms of experience: Human behaviors are socially learned, contextual, and flexible, not innate. Further, Boas worked to transform anthropology into a professional and **empirical** academic discipline that integrated the four subdisciplines: cultural anthropology, linguistic anthropology, archaeology, and biological anthropology.

Figure 1.7 Franz Boas, circa 1915.

THE SUBDISCIPLINES

Because human experiences are varied and complex, we need a diversified tool kit to study them. Anthropology therefore comprises four subdisciplines: Some are more scientific (like biological anthropology), while others are more humanistic (like cultural anthropology). The scientific subdisciplines tend to use the scientific method to develop theories that explain human origins, evolution, material remains, or behaviors. The humanistic subdisciplines tend to use observational methods and interpretive approaches to understand human beliefs, languages, behaviors, cultures, and social organization. Findings from all four subdisciplines contribute to a multifaceted appreciation of human biocultural experiences, past and present.

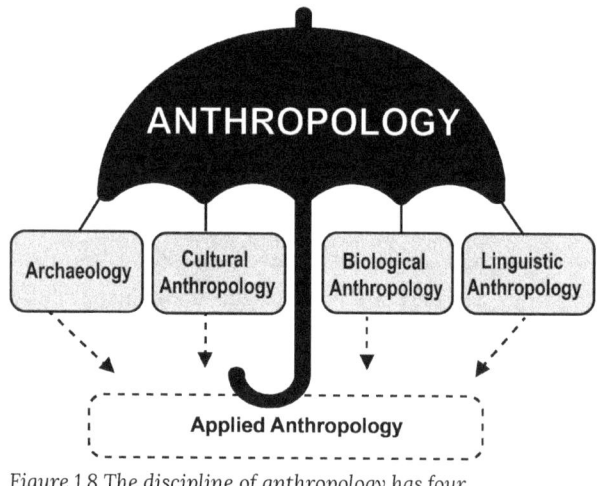

Figure 1.8 *The discipline of anthropology has four subdisciplines as well as an applied dimension.*

Cultural Anthropology

Cultural anthropologists focus on similarities and differences among living societies. They suspend their own sense of what is "normal" in order to understand the perspectives of the people they study (**cultural relativism**). They learn these perspectives through participant-observation fieldwork: a method that involves living with, observing, and learning from the people one studies. Beyond describing another way of life, cultural anthropologists ask broader questions about humankind: Are human emotions universal or culturally specific? Does globalization make us all the same or do we maintain cultural differences? For cultural anthropologists, no aspect of human life is outside their purview: They study art, religion, healing, natural disasters, video gaming, even pet cemeteries. While many cultural anthropologists are intrigued by human diversity, they realize that people around the world share much in common.

One famous American cultural anthropologist, Margaret Mead (1901–1978), conducted several cross-cultural studies of gender and socialization practices. In the early twentieth century in the United States, people wondered if the emotional turbulence of American adolescence was caused by the biology of puberty (and thus natural and universal) or something else. To find out, Mead set off for the Samoan Islands, where she lived for several months getting to know Samoan teenagers. She learned that Samoan adolescence was not angst-ridden (like it was in the United States), but rather a relatively tranquil and happy life stage. Upon returning to the United States, Mead wrote *Coming of Age in Samoa*, a best-selling book that was both sensational and scandalous (Mead 1928). In it, she critiqued U.S. parenting as overly restrictive, and contrasted it to Samoan parenting, which allowed teenagers to freely explore their community and even their sexuality. Ultimately, she argued that nurture (i.e., socialization) more than nature played a key role in the experience of child development.

Figure 1.9 *Margaret Mead, circa 1948.*

Cultural anthropologists do not always travel far to provide insight into human experience. In the 1980s, American anthropologist Philippe Bourgois (1956–) wanted to understand how pockets of extreme poverty persist amid the wealth and overall high quality of life in the United States. To answer this question, he lived with Puerto Rican crack dealers in East Harlem, contextualizing their experiences both historically (in terms of socioeconomic dynamics in Puerto Rico and in the United States) and presently (in terms of social marginalization and institutional racism). Rather than blame crack dealers for their poor choices or blame our society for perpetuating inequality, he argued that both individual choices and social inequality can trap people in the overlapping worlds of drugs and poverty (Bourgois 2003).

Linguistic Anthropology

Language is a defining trait of human beings. While other animals have communication systems, only humans have complex, symbolic languages—more than 6,000 of them! Human language makes it possible to teach and learn, to plan and think abstractly, to coordinate our efforts, and to contemplate even our own demise. Linguistic anthropologists ask questions like: How did language first emerge? How has it evolved and diversified over time? How has language helped us succeed as a species? How does language indicate social identity? How does language influence our views of the world? If you speak two or more languages, you may experience how language affects you. For example, in English, we say: "I love you." But Spanish speakers use different terms—"te amo," "te adoro," "te quiero," and so on—to convey different kinds of love: romantic love, platonic love, maternal love, etc. The Spanish language arguably expresses more nuanced versions of love than the English language

One intriguing line of linguistic anthropological research focuses on the relationships between language, thought, and culture. It may seem intuitive that our thoughts come first; after all, we like to say, "Think before you speak." However, according to the **Sapir-Whorf hypothesis** (also known as linguistic relativity), the language you speak allows you to think about some things and not other things. When Benjamin Whorf (1897-1941) studied the Hopi language, he not only found word-level differences, but also grammatical differences between Hopi and English tenses. He wrote that Hopi has no grammatical tenses to convey the passage of time. Rather, Hopi language only indicates whether or not something has "manifested." Whorf argued that English grammatical tenses (past, present, future) inspire a linear sense of time, while Hopi language inspires a cyclical experience of time (Whorf 1956). Some critics, like German American linguist Ekkehart Malotki (1938-), refute Whorf's theory, arguing that Hopi do have linguistic terms for time and that a linear sense of time is natural and perhaps universal. At the same time, Malotki recognized that English and Hopi tenses differ, albeit in ways less pronounced than Whorf proposed (Malotki 1983).

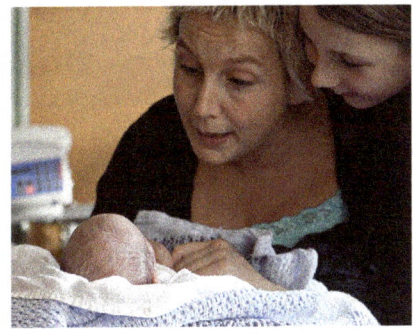

Figure 1.10 From the moment they are born, children learn through language and nonverbal forms of communication.

Other linguistic anthropologists track the emergence and diversification of languages, while others focus on language use in today's social contexts. Still others explore how language is crucial to socialization: children learn their culture and social identities through language and nonverbal forms of communication (Ochs and Schieffelin 2012).

Archaeology

Archaeologists focus on the material past: the tools, food, pottery, art, shelters, seeds, and other objects left behind by people. **Prehistoric archaeologists** recover and analyze these materials to reconstruct the lifeways of past societies that lacked writing. They ask specific questions like: How did people in a particular area live? What did they eat? What happened to them? They ask general questions about humankind: When and why did humans first develop agriculture? How did cities first develop? What type of interactions did prehistoric people have with their neighbors?

One key method that archaeologists use to answer their questions is excavation—a method of careful digging and removing of dirt and stones to uncover material remains while recording their context. Archaeological research spans millions of years from human origins to the present. For example, Kathleen Kenyon (1906-1978), a British archaeologist, was one of few women working in this field in the 1940s. While excavating at Jericho (which dates back to 10,000 BCE), she discovered city structures and cemeteries built during the Early Bronze Age (3,200 yBP in Europe). Based on her findings, she argued that Jericho is the oldest city continuously occupied by different groups of people (Kenyon 1979).

Figure 1.11 Archaeologists, including Kathleen Kenyon, have helped unearth the foundations of ancient dwellings at Jericho.

Historical archaeologists study recent societies using material remains to complement the written record. For example, the Garbage Project, which began in the 1970s, is an archaeological project based in Tucson, Arizona. It involves excavating a contemporary landfill as if it were a conventional dig site. Archaeologists found a difference between what people say they throw out and what is actually in their trash. In fact, many landfills hold large amounts of paper products and construction debris (Rathje and Murphy 1992). This finding has practical implications for creating more environmentally sustainable waste-disposal practices.

Biological Anthropology

Biological anthropology, which will be thoroughly introduced later in this chapter, is the study of human origins, evolution, and variation. Some biological anthropologists focus on our closest living relatives: monkeys and apes. They examine the biological and behavioral similarities and differences between nonhuman primates and human primates (us!). Other biological anthropologists focus on extinct human species, asking questions like: What did our ancestors look like? What did they eat? When did they start to speak? And, how did they adapt to new environments?

Many biological anthropologists explore how human genetic and phenotypic (observable) traits vary in response to environmental conditions. For instance, Nina Jablonski (1953–) asks why darker skin pigmentation is more prevalent in high ultraviolet (UV) contexts (like Central Africa), while lighter skin pigmentation is more prevalent in low UV contexts (like Nordic countries). She explains this pattern in terms of the interplay among skin pigmentation, UV radiation, folic acid, and vitamin D. In brief, UV radiation breaks down folic acid, which is essential to DNA and cell production. Dark skin helps to block UV, thereby protecting the body's folic acid reserves in high-UV contexts. Light skin evolved when humans migrated out of Africa to low-UV contexts, where dark skin blocks too much UV radiation, compromising the body's ability to absorb vitamin D from the sun (vitamin D is essential to calcium absorption and a healthy skeleton). Jablonski shows that the spectrum of skin pigmentation that we see today evolved to balance UV exposure with the bodily need for vitamin D and folic acid (Jablonski 2012).

Figure 1.12 Chimpanzees are the nonhuman primate that is most closely related to humans.

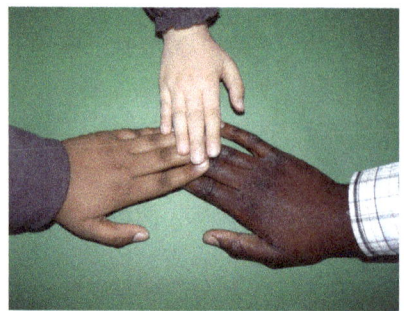

Figure 1.13 Human skin color ranges from dark brown to light pink.

While some biological anthropologists study **hominins** (modern-day humans and human ancestors), others focus on nonhuman primates. For example, Jane Goodall (1934–) has devoted her life to studying wild chimpanzees (Goodall 1996). Beginning in the 1960s when she began her research in Tanzania, Goodall challenged widely held assumptions about the inherent differences between humans and apes. At the time, it was assumed that monkeys and apes lacked the social and emotional traits that made human beings such exceptional creatures. However, Goodall discovered that, like humans, chimpanzees also make tools, socialize their young, have intense emotional lives, and form strong maternal-infant bonds. Her work highlights the value of field-based research in natural settings as it can reveal the complex lives of nonhuman primates. Throughout this book, we will learn about many examples of biological anthropological research that explores our earliest ancestors, our evolution, and our nonhuman primate cousins.

Applied Anthropology

Sometimes considered a fifth subdiscipline, applied anthropology involves the practical application of anthropological theories, methods, and findings to solve real-world problems. Applied anthropologists are employed outside of academic settings, in both the public and private sectors, including business or consulting firms, advertising companies, city government, law enforcement, the medical field, nongovernmental organizations, and even the military.

Applied anthropologists span the subdisciplines. An applied archaeologist might work in cultural resource management to assess a potentially significant archaeological site unearthed during a construction project. An applied cultural anthropologist could work for a technology company that seeks to understand the human-technology interface in order to design better tools.

Medical anthropology is an example of both an applied and theoretical area of study that draws on all four subdisciplines to understand the interrelationship of health, illness, and culture. Rather than assume that disease resides only within the individual body, medical anthropologists explore the environmental, social, and cultural conditions that impact the *experience* of illness. For example, in some cultures, people believe that illness is caused by an imbalance within the community. Therefore, a communal response, such as a group healing ceremony, is necessary to restore the health of the person *and* the group. In other cultures, like mainstream U.S. society, people typically go to a doctor to find the biological cause of an illness and then take medicine to restore the individual body.

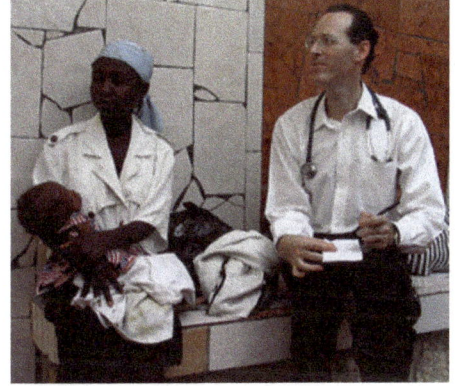

Figure 1.14 Paul Farmer in Haiti (right).

Trained as both a physician and medical anthropologist, Paul Farmer (1959–) demonstrates the potential of applied anthropology. During his college years in North Carolina, Farmer's interest in the Haitian migrants working on nearby farms inspired him to visit Haiti. There, he was struck by the poor living conditions and lack of health care facilities. Eventually, as a physician, he would return to Haiti to treat diseases, like tuberculosis and cholera, that were rarely seen in the United States. As an anthropologist, he would contextualize the suffering of his Haitian patients in relation to the historical, social, and political forces that impact Haiti, the poorest country in the Western Hemisphere (Farmer 2006). Today, he not only writes academic books about human suffering, he also takes action. Through the work of Partners in Health, a nonprofit organization that he cofounded, he has opened health clinics in many resource-poor countries and trained local staff to administer care. In this way, he applies his medical and anthropological training to improve people's lives.

WHAT IS BIOLOGICAL ANTHROPOLOGY?

The focus of this book is the anthropological subdiscipline of biological anthropology, which is the study of the human species from a biological perspective. Biological anthropology uses a scientific and evolutionary approach to answer many of the same questions all anthropologists are concerned with: What does it mean to be human? Where do we come from? Who are we today? Biological anthropologists are concerned with exploring how humans vary biologically, how humans adapt to their changing environments, and how humans have evolved over time and continue to evolve today. Some biological anthropologists also study nonhuman primates to learn about what we have in common and how we differ.

You may have heard biological anthropology referred to by another name—physical anthropology. Physical anthropology is an area of research that dates to as far back as the eighteenth century, when it focused mostly on physical variation among humans. Some early physical anthropologists were also physicians interested in comparing and contrasting human skeletons. These researchers dedicated themselves to measuring bodies and skulls (anthropometry and craniometry) in great detail. Many also acted under the misguided and oftentimes racist belief that human biological races existed and it was possible to differentiate between, or even rank, such races by measuring differences in human anatomy. Most anthropologists today agree that there are no biological human races and that all humans alive today are members of the same species and subspecies, *Homo sapiens sapiens*. We recognize that the differences we can see between peoples' bodies are due to a wide variety of factors, including our environment, our diet, the activities we engage in, and our genetic makeup.

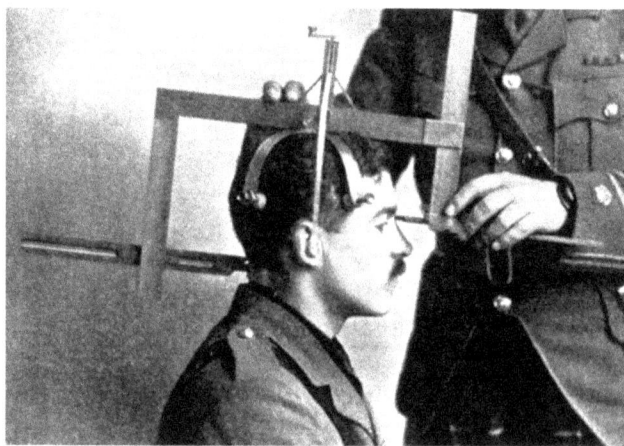

Figure 1.15 An anthropometric device used to measure a subject's head, circa 1913.

The subdiscipline has changed a great deal since these early years. Biological anthropologists no longer set out to identify human differences in order to assign people to groups, like races. The focus is instead understanding how and why human and primate variation developed through evolutionary processes. The name for the subdiscipline has transitioned in recent years to reflect these changes. Many believe the term biological anthropology better reflects the subdiscipline's focus today, which includes genetic and molecular research. Nevertheless, the term physical anthropology is still common.

The Scope of Biological Anthropology

Just as anthropology as a discipline is wide ranging and holistic, so too is the subdiscipline of biological anthropology. There are at least six **subfields** within biological anthropology. Each subfield focuses on a different dimension of what it means to be human from a biological perspective. Through their varied research in these subfields, biological anthropologists try to answer the following key questions:

- What is our place in nature? How are we related to other organisms? What makes us unique?
- What are our origins? What influenced our evolution?
- How and when did we move/migrate across the globe?
- How are humans around the world today different from and similar to each other? What influences these patterns of variation? What are the patterns of our recent evolution and how do we continue to evolve?

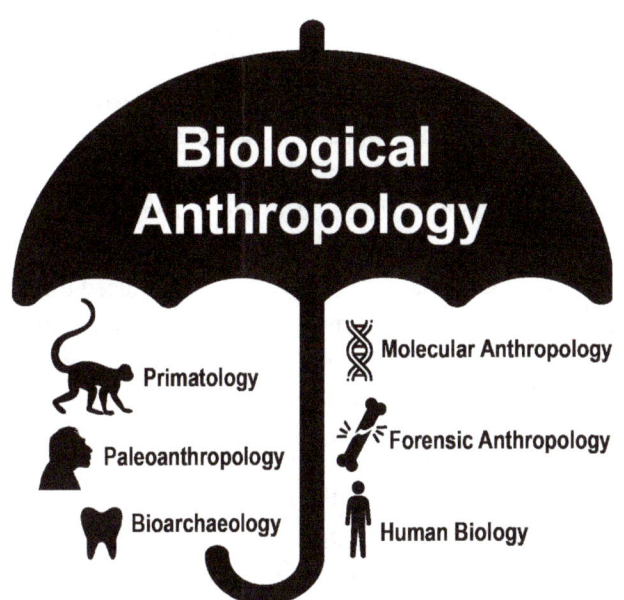

Figure 1.16 Biological anthropology has at least six subfields.

The terms *subfield* and *subdiscipline* are very similar and can be confusing because they are often used interchangeably. In this book we use *subdiscipline* to refer to the four major areas of focus that make up the discipline of anthropology: biological anthropology, cultural anthropology, archaeological anthropology, and linguistic anthropology. When we use the term *subfield* we are referring to the different specializations within biological anthropology. These subfields include primatology, paleoanthropology, molecular anthropology, bioarchaeology, forensic anthropology, and human biology.

Primatology

Primatologists study the anatomy, behavior, ecology and genetics of living and extinct nonhuman primates, including apes, monkeys, tarsiers, lemurs, and lorises, because nonhuman primates are our closest living biological relatives. The research done by primatologists gives us insights into how evolution has shaped our species and primates in general. Through such studies we have learned that all primates share a suite of traits. Primates, for instance, have nails instead of claws, have hands that can grasp and manipulate objects, invest great amounts of time and energy in raising just a few offspring, and have complex social behaviors.

Similar to Jane Goodall's studies of wild chimpanzees, Dian Fossey's research among mountain gorillas provided scientists with some illuminating insights into our primate cousins. She learned, for instance, that gorillas are like humans in that they have families and form strong maternal-infant relationships. Gorillas mourn the death of their group members, and also exhibit behaviors similar to humans such as playing and tickling. Importantly, the work of Dian Fossey, Jane Goodall, Karen B. Strier (see Appendix B), and others focus on primate conservation: They have brought attention to the fact that 60% of primates are currently threatened with extinction (Estrada et al. 2017).

Figure 1.17 Adult male mountain gorillas feeding on insects. Notice how similar his fingers are to your own fingers.

Paleoanthropology

Paleoanthropologists study human ancestors from the distant past to learn how, why, and where they evolved. Because these ancestors lived before there were written records, paleoanthropologists have to rely on various types of physical evidence to come to their conclusions. This evidence includes fossilized remains (particularly fossilized bones), artifacts such as stone tools, and the contexts in which these items are found. Paleoanthropologists have made some monumental discoveries that have shaped the way we understand **hominin** evolution (hominin refers to humans and fossil relatives that are more similar to us than chimpanzees).

Figure 1.18 Donald Johanson and an Australopithicus fossil skull.

One such discovery was made in Ethiopia in 1974 by paleoanthropologist Donald C. Johanson. He found the remains of a 3.2-million-year-old fossilized skeleton he named Lucy (she was named after the Beatles song "Lucy in the Sky with Diamonds," which the archaeologists played repeatedly at the celebration the evening after her discovery). Lucy was a remarkable find because she represented a new hominin species, *Australopithecus afarensis*, and the skeleton was over 40% complete. Like humans, she was **bipedal** (walked on two legs) and likely used tools. However she had a much smaller brain than humans, larger teeth and likely spent time in trees and on the ground. She was, in many ways, a transitional species between humans and earlier primates.

Since the discovery of Lucy, several hundred more *Australopithicus* fossils have been found in Africa, as you will learn more about in chapter nine. From these finds, we know that many *Australopithicus* species flourished for millions of years. Some of these species likely led to our genus (*Homo*), while others appear to have died off. These findings helped us learn that human evolution did not occur in a simple, straight line, but branched out in many directions. Most branches were evolutionary "dead ends." Humans are now the only hominins left living on planet Earth. Paleoanthropologists frequently work together with other scientists such as archaeologists, geologists, and paleontologists to interpret and understand the evidence they find. Paleoanthropology is a dynamic subfield of biological anthropology that contributes significantly to our understanding of human origins and evolution.

Molecular Anthropology

Molecular anthropologists use molecular techniques (primarily genetics) to compare ancient and modern populations and to study living populations of humans and nonhuman primates. By examining DNA sequences in different populations, molecular anthropologists can estimate how closely related two populations are, as well as identify population events, like a population decline, that explain the observed genetic patterns. This information helps scientists trace patterns of migration or identify how people have adapted to different environments over time.

Some exciting work that molecular anthropologists are doing today is studying the genetic material they find in ancient specimens. From this work we have learned, for instance, that many people in the world today have inherited some DNA from Neanderthals and/or a newly discovered species known as Denisovans. This tells us that at some point in our ancient past our modern human ancestors mated with Neanderthals and Denisovans and their genes were passed down to us. Moreover, it is now believed some of these genes helped our human ancestors survive.

From the work of molecular anthropologists we have also learned which genes distinguish us genetically from our closest living relatives: chimpanzees, bonobos, and gorillas. In the case of chimpanzees, our genomes are somewhere between 96% and 99% identical (Prufer et al. 2012; Relethford and Bolnick 2018). Yet that 2-4% contributes to a lot of physical (morphological) and behavioral differences! Molecular anthropology is a field changing quickly as new techniques and discoveries shape our understanding of ourselves and our nonhuman primate cousins.

Bioarchaeology

Bioarchaeologists study human skeletal remains and the soils and other materials found in and around the remains. They use the research methods of skeletal biology, mortuary studies, osteology, and archaeology to answer questions about the lives and lifeways of past populations. Through studying the bones and burials of past peoples, bioarchaeologists search for answers to how people lived and died. For example, bioarchaeologists can estimate the sex, height, and age at which someone died. They can also gather clues about their lifestyle based on the skeleton, since bones respond to muscle use and developed muscle attachments may indicate extensive muscle use. Most bioarchaeologists study not just individuals, but populations, to reveal biological and cultural patterns.

Bioarchaeologists are also interested in learning about ancient people's health and nutrition, the diseases they suffered from and injuries they suffered. They may also look for clues to what people ate by examining the wear and condition of teeth or, in the case of well-preserved specimens, the residue from their last meals. Chemical studies of bones and teeth can also provide information about people's diets as well as where people lived and moved during their lives. Bioarchaeologists can reconstruct human migration and track the growth or decline of populations by looking for patterns of malnutrition, disease, and activities.

Figure 1.19 A model of what Ötzi may have looked like in life.

Not all places are ideal for finding well-preserved human remains. Environments that are very cold, very dry, or devoid of oxygen can preserve corpses for many years, sometimes centuries. In 1991, a group of hikers found the body of a man frozen in the Italian Alps. Because of how well-preserved the body was, the discoverers initially thought he might be a hiker who had died several years prior. However, once bioarchaeologists had a chance to study the body, they discovered the man had died around 5,300 years ago! Nicknamed Ötzi, or the Iceman, bioarchaeologists determined he was wearing leggings, a coat, and shoes made of leather and fur when he died. They also discovered he had an arrow embedded in his left shoulder, suffered from osteoporosis, had multiple tattoo patterns throughout his body and was infected by the bacterium H. pylori, a common human stomach pathogen that likely gave him significant stomach pain. Researchers later found similarities between the strain of H. plyori bacterium that plagued Ötzi and the strains seen today in parts of Central and Southern Asia. Modern-day Europeans have strains of the bacterium that reflect mixtures of both African and Asian strains. This research helped scientists demonstrate that for thousands of years after Ötzi died human groups were migrating all over the world, even returning to Africa and then moving back north again. Research within the subfield of bioarchaeology is continually providing important insights into humanity's past.

Forensic Anthropology

Forensic anthropologists use many of the same techniques as bioarchaeologists to develop a biological profile for unidentified individuals including estimating sex, age at death, height, ancestry, diseases they had, or other unique identifying features. They may also go to a crime or accident scene to assist in the search and recovery of human remains, and/or identify trauma, like fractures, on bones. The popular television program *Bones* told the fictional story of a forensic anthropologist, Dr. Temperance Brennan, who brilliantly interpreted clues from victims' bones and helped solve crimes. While the show includes forensic anthropology techniques and responsibilities, it also includes many inaccuracies. For example, forensic anthropologists generally do not collect trace evidence like hair or fibers, run DNA tests, carry weapons, or solve criminal cases. These researchers play an important role in aiding law enforcement to identify human remains.

Some forensic anthropologists have been called on to interpret the remains of victims of mass murders, such as the case of the town of El Mozote in El Salvador. In December of 1981, during the country's intense civil war, over 1,000 people were brutally killed by the Salvadoran right-wing military in and around a church in the town of El Mozote. Researchers later discovered that the U.S. government, under President Reagan, funded and trained the Special Forces of the Salvadoran Army who perpetrated the massacre. Starting in the mid-1990s, human rights organizations began to investigate the incident as a war crime, and finally, in 2015, a team of forensic anthropologists were called upon to study the bones of the deceased and try to reconstruct what happened at El Mozote and how the victims died (Binford 2016). Their work provided important clues that helped bring some closure to the families and survivors of this horrible incident. It also provided answers to investigators looking to bring accountability to those responsible.

Figure 1.20 A remembrance of the victims of El Mozote Massacre in El Salvador.

Forensic anthropology is considered an "applied" area of biological anthropology, since it is a practical application of anthropological theories, methods, and findings to solve real-world problems. While many forensic anthropologists are also academics and work for colleges and universities, some are employed by other agencies. Forensic anthropology is an active area of applied biological anthropology and a career that is useful all over the world.

Human Biology

Many biological anthropologists do work that falls under the label human biology. This type of research is varied, but tends to explore how the human body is impacted by different physical environments, cultural influences, and nutrition. These include studies of **human variation** or the physiological differences among humans around the world. For instance, some humans have the ability to digest lactase in milk into adulthood, and others lack this ability. Some humans have an enhanced ability to resist malarial infections. Some humans tend to be very tall and lean while others are short and stocky. Still others tend to have dark skin and others lighter brown and even pale skin colors.

Some of these anthropologists study **human adaptations** to extreme environments, which includes individual physiological responses and genetic advantages populations develop to help them live there. For example, people born at very high elevations adapt to life in an environment with decreased oxygen. Research has shown that populations that have lived for many generations at very high elevations, such as those in parts of Tibet, Peru, and Ethiopia, have developed long-term physiological adaptations. These include large lungs and chests and enhanced oxygen respiration and blood circulation systems that help them survive in an environment that otherwise might cause life-threatening hypoxia (oxygen deprivation) (Bigham 2016). Some anthropologists believe Tibetans' adaptation to living in high altitudes, estimated to have occurred in less than 3,000 years, is one of the fastest cases of human evolution in the scientific record!

In addition to studying how humans adapt to their physical environments and vary biologically, some biological anthropologists are interested in how nutrition and disease affect human growth and development. The modern Western diet that is high in processed starches, refined carbohydrates, saturated fats, sugar, and salt is increasingly causing a number of metabolic conditions. As cultural groups around the world begin to replace their traditional diets with these processed food products, they begin to experience a rise in diseases that plague Western societies, such as diabetes, heart disease, and hormonal imbalances. Other biological anthropologists have asked why girls in Western societies have begun to menstruate earlier (sometimes as young as seven years of age). A definitive explanation is still unresolved. Some speculate this may have to do with changes in our diet, while others believe it may also have to do with exposure to chemicals in the environment or other factors. Biological anthropologists engage in a wide range of research that span the breadth of human biological diversity.

The six subfields of biological anthropology—primatology, paleoanthropology, bioarchaeology, molecular anthropology, forensic anthropology, and human biology—all help us understand what it means to be biologically human. From molecular analyses of our cells, to studies of our changing skeleton, to research on our nonhuman primate cousins, biological anthropology helps answer the central question of the larger discipline of anthropology: What does it mean to be human? Despite their different foci, all biological anthropologists share a commitment to using a scientific approach to study how we became the complex, adaptable species we are today.

ANTHROPOLOGISTS AS SCIENTISTS

Biological anthropologists use the scientific method as a way of learning about the world around them. Many people think of science as taking place in a sterile laboratory, and sometimes it does, but in biological anthropology it also occurs many other places, such as at a research station in Ethiopia, a field site in Tanzania, and a town in El Salvador. To understand how information in this field is established, it is important to recognize what science is (and is not) as well as understand how the scientific method actually works.

Recognizing Science

Science combines our natural curiosity with our ability to experiment so we can understand the world around us and address needs in our communities. Thanks to science, meteorologists can predict the weather, it takes only a relatively small number of farmers to grow enough food to feed our large population, our medicine continues to improve, and over 90% of Americans have a cell phone.

Anyone can participate in science—not just academics. In fact, children are often some of the best scientists. An early, well-known psychologist, Jean Piaget (1896–1980), argued that a child is a "little scientist," internally motivated to experiment and explore their world. This can be seen when an infant repeatedly drops a toy to see if the parent will pick it up, or when a four-year-old sincerely asks "why" again and again. Maria Montessori (1870–1952), an Italian doctor and educator, was interested in how children learn. Through her research, she also recognized that children have natural scientific tendencies. Children have a desire to explore their environment, ask questions, use their imaginations, and learn by doing. In 1907, Montessori opened a school to foster children's natural desire to learn this way. This developed a child-centered teaching method that has spread around the world and is being used in over 22,000 schools today. In anthropology and other scientific fields, the process of learning is more formalized, but scientists still benefit from the curiosity that motivates children and still experience the thrill of discovery.

Science represents both a body of knowledge and the process for learning that knowledge (the scientific method). Scientific claims can, at times, be difficult to distinguish from other information. Science also incorporates a broad range of methods to collect data, adding to the difficulty of knowing what science really is. This section of the chapter will address four key characteristics that help define and recognize science: (1) science studies the physical and natural world and how it works, (2) scientific explanations must be testable and refutable, (3) science relies on empirical evidence, and (4) science involves the scientific community.

Figure 1.21 Children are true scientists as they explore and test the world around them through sight and touch.

Science Studies the Physical and Natural World and How It Works

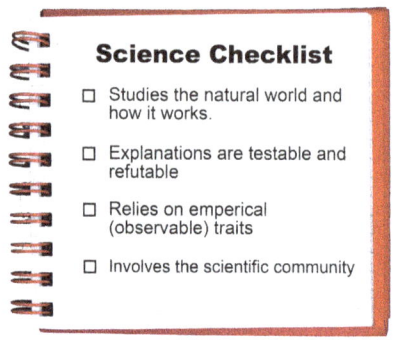

Figure 1.22 Science checklist.

Our physical and natural universe ranges from very small (e.g., electrons) to the very large (e.g., Earth itself and galaxies beyond it). Scientists often design their research to address how and why natural forces influence our physical and natural word. In biological anthropology, we focus our questions on humans as well as primate species, both living and extinct. We ask questions like: What influences a primate's diet? Why do humans walk bipedally? And did Neanderthals and modern humans interbreed?

There are very few questions that are considered off-limits in science. That being said, the scope of scientific investigation is generally focused on natural phenomena and natural processes and excludes the supernatural. People often regard the supernatural, whether it be a ghost, luck, or god, as working outside the laws of the universe, which makes it difficult to study with a scientific approach. Science neither supports nor contradicts the existence of supernatural powers—it simply does not include the supernatural in its explanations.

Scientific Explanations Must Be Testable and Refutable

The goal of scientists is to identify a research question and then identify the best answer(s) to that question. For example, an excavation of a prehistoric cemetery may reveal that many of the people buried there had unhealed fractures when they died, and the lead anthropologist may ask, "Why did this population experience more broken bones than their neighbors?" There might be multiple explanations to address this question, such as a lack of calcium in their diets, participation in dangerous work, or violent conflict with neighbors; these explanations are considered hypotheses. In the past, you might have learned that a hypothesis is an "educated guess," but in science, hypotheses are much more than that. A scientific hypothesis reflects a scientist's knowledge-based experiences and background research. A **hypothesis** is better defined as an explanation of observed facts; hypotheses explain how and why observed phenomena are the way they are.

Scientific hypotheses should generate expectations that are testable. For example, if the best explanation regarding our prehistoric population was that they were experiencing violent conflict with their neighbors, we should expect to find clues, like weapons or protective walls around their homes, in the anthropological record to support this. Alternatively, if this population did not experience violent conflict with their neighbors, we may eventually be able to gather enough evidence to rule out (refute) this explanation. An important part of science is rigorous testing. Science does not prove any hypothesis. However, a strong hypothesis is one that has strong supporting evidence and has not yet been disproven.

Science Relies on Empirical Evidence

The word "empirical" refers to experience that is verified by observation (rather than evidence that derives primarily from logic or theory). In anthropology, much evidence about our world is collected by observation through fieldwork or in a laboratory. The most reliable studies are based on accurately and precisely recorded observations. Scientists value studies that explain exactly what methods were used, so their data collection and analysis processes are reproducible. This allows for other scientists to expand the study or provide new insights into the observations.

Science Involves the Scientific Community

Contrary to many Hollywood science fiction films, good science is not carried out in isolation in a secret basement laboratory but rather is done as part of a community. Scientists pay attention to what others have done before them, present new ideas to each other, and publish in scientific journals. Most scientific research is collaborative, bringing together researchers with different types of specialized knowledge to work on a shared project. Today, thanks to technology, scientific projects can bring together researchers from different backgrounds, experiences, locations, and perspectives. Most big anthropological questions—"Where did modern humans develop?" "What genetic changes make us uniquely human?" "How did cooperative behavior evolve?"—cannot be addressed with one simple study, but are tested with different lines of evidence and by different scientists over time.

Working within a scientific community supports one of the most valuable aspects of science: that science is self-correcting. Science that is openly communicated with others allows for a system with checks and balances: competing explanations can be proposed and questionable studies can be reevaluated. Ultimately, the belief is that through science the best explanations will stand the test of time.

How Science Works: The Scientific Method

Most students have learned the scientific method as a simple linear, or perhaps circular, process. Textbooks may phrase each step differently, but students usually recognize that the process begins with making observations about the natural world. Another important step is the selection or development of a scientific hypothesis. From the hypothesis a set of predictions can be made, which are then tested by experimentation or by making additional observations. Scientific predictions are often phrased as "if... then..." statements, such as "If hypothesis A is true, then this experiment will show outcome B." The results of a scientific study should then either support or reject the hypothesis.

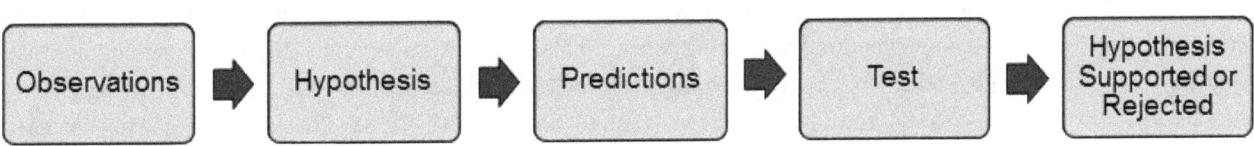

Figure 1.23 Simple depiction of the scientific method.

This relatively simple version of the scientific method is valuable as it highlights the key aspects that should be present in any scientific research experiment or scientific paper. However, this simplistic view of the scientific method does not accurately represent the dynamic and creative side of science, nor does it highlight the complex steps that are incorporated into a scientist's routine.

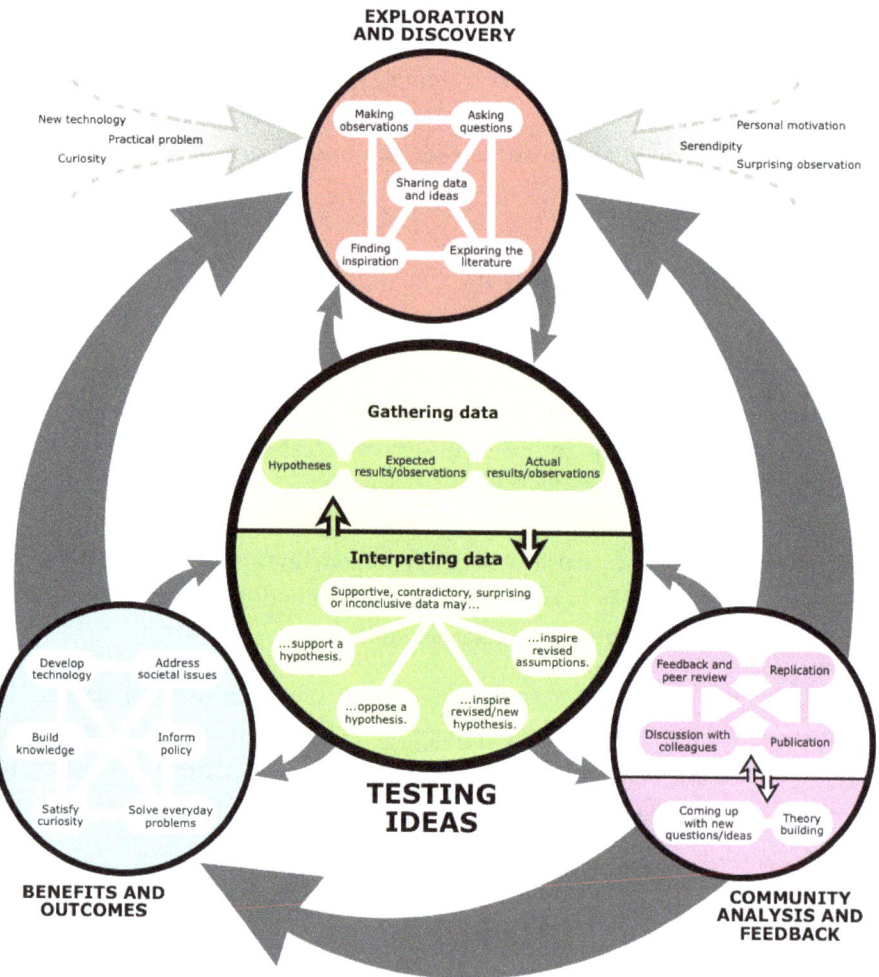

Figure 1.24 Complex flow of the scientific method.

Figure 1.24 provides an alternative representation of the scientific method that emphasizes the many paths to scientific discovery. While still incorporating the key components of making observations, testing ideas, and interpreting results, this chart shows that scientific ideas have many possible starting points and influences, and scientists often repeat steps and circle back around. Gathering evidence does not always rest on experiments in the laboratory. Evaluating data is not always clear-cut, and results are sometimes surprising or inconclusive. Many important discoveries were in fact made by mistake. For example, engineer Percy Spencer accidentally melted a chocolate bar in his pocket with a magnetron, which became the first microwave, and Spencer Silver invented the adhesive for 3M Post-it ® notes while trying to develop a strong glue. The real scientific process is more similar to the philosophy of the animated television character Ms. Frizzle from *The Magic School Bus*, "Take chances, make mistakes, get messy."

Two key components lacking in the simple version of the scientific method are exploration and discovery. There are many reasons that a scientist might choose a particular research question: they may be motivated by personal experience, struck by something they read about, or inspired by a student's question in class. Often scientific research reveals more questions than answers, so experienced researchers rarely lack problems to solve. But identifying a research question is just part of the process; most scientists spend more time exploring the literature, sharing ideas, asking questions, and planning their research project than conducting the test itself.

Science itself is a social enterprise that is influenced by cultural issues and values, as well as funding priorities. For example, corporations are the biggest funders of scientific research, followed next by government agencies like the National Science Foundation (which often fund research done by academics at colleges and universities). Those organizations have great influence on what is considered valuable research at any given time. For example, there are many diseases that the World Health Organization (WHO) has classified as "neglected tropical diseases," including dengue, leprosy, rabies, and hookworm, that affect an estimated 1 billion people, mostly in impoverished areas. These debilitating diseases can be as deadly as diseases that receive more attention, like AIDS and tuberculosis, but these tropical diseases receive comparatively little funding when it comes to research, drug development, and health care development (Farmer et al. 2013).

Also very important to the scientific process are interactions within the scientific community. Scientific collaboration can take place through informal discussion over a cup of coffee, but also includes more formal interactions, such as presenting at conferences and engaging in **scholarly peer review**. Scholarly peer review is the process where an author's work must pass the scrutiny of other experts in the field before being published in a journal or book. This helps keep scientists accountable for ethically responsible research projects and papers. Additionally, presenting data at conferences and in articles and books allows researchers to potentially receive critical feedback from academic peers and others to test these ideas and further the field of science toward identifying the best explanations.

Hypotheses, Theories, and Laws

Scientific investigation occurs at many levels, from investigating individual cases (for example, "What is causing this child's mysterious illness?") to understanding processes that affect most of us ("What is the ideal amount of sleep for an adult?"). All of these questions are important and will generate different types of testable scientific explanations. So far, we have used the term "hypothesis" to describe these scientific explanations for why observed phenomena are the way they are. Hypotheses are typically explanations that address a narrow set of phenomena, such as (in anthropology), a particular population or primate species.

In science, a **theory** is an explanation of observations that addresses a *wide* range of phenomena. Like hypotheses, theories also explain how or why something occurs, rely on empirical evidence, and are testable and able to be refuted. Because the term theory is often used casually outside of science, you may hear people try to dismiss a scientific claim as "just a theory." In science there are often multiple competing theories, but over time some are eliminated, leaving the theory or theories that best explain the most evidence. Scientific theories that have stood the test of time are thus supported by many lines of evidence and are usually reliable. Some well-tested theories accepted by most scientists include the theory of general relativity, which explains the law of gravitation and its relation to other forces, and evolutionary theory, which describes how heritable traits can change in a population over time.

While scientific hypotheses and theories share many characteristics, laws are quite different. A **law** is a prediction about what will happen given certain conditions, *not* an explanation for how or why it happens. A law is not a "mature" version of a theory. For example, Newton's universal law of gravity allows us to predict the gravitational force (F) between any two objects using the equation $F = G(m_1 m_2)/r^2$, but it does not explain *why* gravity works. Laws are often mathematical, and some well-known laws include Newton's three laws of motion and laws of genetic inheritance. Laws are important, and their discovery often promotes the development of theories.

To demonstrate how important laws can be—and show how unusual things can inspire scientific discoveries—we can use the story of the ancient Greek mathematician and inventor Archimedes. Archimedes' buoyancy principle is a law that is useful for many things, including density calculations and designing ships. Purportedly, he made this discovery when he noticed the water level rise in the bathtub when he climbed in it. Realizing its importance, he is said to have shouted "Eureka" and proceeded to run naked through the city of Syracuse. While this is a fun story (that may or may not be true), it does remain that scientific laws, alongside scientific hypotheses and theories, do have a very important role in the scientific process and in generating scientific explanations about our natural world.

Figure 1.25 Archimedes is portrayed here having just discovered his Principle of Buoyancy. The vignette is by Count Giammaria Mazzuchelli (1707-1765).

WAYS OF KNOWING: SCIENCE, FAITH, AND ANTHROPOLOGY

In anthropology, we recognize that there are many ways people have of knowing things. Human knowledge is very diverse. For instance, you might know that fingernails are softer than metal because as a child you accidentally stapled through your fingernail while doing an art project (a coauthor of this chapter once experienced this). This would be an example of knowledge you gained through experience. You might also know that inserting a knife into an electrical outlet is dangerous and could harm your health. Hopefully you know this not from personal experience, but through instruction from parents, teachers, and others in your social group. The degree to which humans rely on and benefit from the experiential knowledge of others is an important characteristic of what makes us human!

A unified way of knowing that is shared by a group of people and is used to explain and predict phenomena is called a **knowledge system**. Human knowledge systems are diverse and reflect the wide range of cultures and societies throughout the world and through time.

Science and religion are both knowledge systems and it is useful to understand how they differ. The type of knowledge gained from science is oftentimes called scientific **understanding**. As we have explored in the previous section, scientific understanding can change and relies on evidence and rigorous, repeated testing. Religious ways of knowing are called **belief**, which is different from scientific understanding because it does not require repeated testing or validation (although it can rely on observations and experiences). Instead, religious belief relies on trust and **faith**.

Since the beginning of the discipline, anthropologists have been interested in understanding religion because it can be important to understanding human cultures. However, religion (as well as magic, witchcraft, and other faith-based traditions) has proven notoriously difficult to define from an anthropological perspective, partly because there are so many religious practices and beliefs throughout the world that play different roles in people's lives. For instance, some religions have multiple supernatural deities or gods, such as Hinduism, while others have hardly any supernatural elements, such as Buddhism. Some have beliefs that relate to energies and powers found in certain objects, animals, and people, while others place faith in ancestors and collective cultural heritage. Some religions provide instruction on nearly every day-to-day activity a person does, while others provide merely a rough framework for how one should act and behave. Emile Durkheim (1858-1917), an early social scientist, offered a definition of religion as "a unified set of beliefs and practices relative to sacred things, that is to say, things set apart and forbidden—beliefs and practices which unite [into] one single moral community, all those who adhere to them" (Durkheim 2008).

Different individuals, cultures and societies may place more value on one type of knowing than another, although most use a combination that includes science and religion. In fact, in the early twentieth century, Bronisław Malinowski (1884-1942), an important early anthropologist, concluded that all societies use religion and science in some way or another. These are common ways that humans have of knowing our world.

In contemporary societies such as the United States, science and (some) religions conflict on the topic of human origins. Nearly every culture and society has a unique origin story that explains where they came from and how they came to be who they are today. These stories are often integrated into the culture's religious belief system. Many anthropologists are interested in faith-based origin stories and other beliefs because they show us how a particular group of people explain the world and their place in it. Anthropologists also value scientific understanding as the basis for how humans vary biologically and change over time. In other words, anthropologists value the multiple knowledge systems of different groups and use them to understand the human condition in a broad and inclusive way.

It is also important to note that scientists often depend on the local knowledge of the people they work with to help them understand elements of the natural or physical world that science has not yet investigated. Many groups, including **indigenous** peoples, know about the world through prolonged relationships with the environment. Indigenous knowledge systems—those ways of knowing about and explaining the world that are specific to an indigenous community or group—are informed by their own empirical observation of a specific environment and passed down over generations.

While religion and indigenous knowledge systems may play a complementary role in helping anthropologists understand the human condition, they are distinct from science. The anthropological subdiscipline of biological anthropology is based on scientific ways of knowing about humans and human origins. In this text we will exclusively explore what science tells us about how humans came to be and why we are the way we are today. Therefore, you do not need to *believe* in evolution to master this material, because belief is not a scientific way of knowing. For this textbook, you only need to *understand* the scientific perspective(s) of evolution.

Throughout our lives, each of us work to reconcile and integrate into our worldview the different ways we have of knowing things. This is part of our lifelong intellectual journey. It is also, in our opinion, one of the most exciting parts of learning. We are pleased you have joined us on this journey of knowledge about humanity and yourself! Welcome!

Review Questions

- What are some key approaches to anthropological research?
- How has the discipline of anthropology changed over time?
- What are some similarities and differences between the subdisciplines? How does the "fifth subdiscipline" of applied anthropology fit within the larger discipline of anthropology?
- What are some subfields of biological anthropology and what do those anthropologists study?
- What is science? What is the scientific method? How does science compare to other ways of knowing?

Key Terms

Belief (religious): A firmly held opinion or conviction typically based on spiritual apprehension rather than empirical proof.

Bipedal: Habitually using only two legs to walk.

Cultural relativism: The anthropological practice of suspending judgment and seeking to understand another culture on its own terms sympathetically enough so that the culture appears to be a coherent and meaningful design for living.

Empirical: Evidence that is verifiable by observation or experience instead of relying primarily on logic or theory.

Ethnocentrism: The opinion that one's own way of life is natural or correct and the only true way of being fully human.

Faith (religious): Complete trust or confidence in the doctrines of a religion, typically based on spiritual apprehension rather than empirical proof.

Historical archaeologists: Archaeologists who excavate and analyze material remains to supplement a society's written records.

Holism: The idea that the parts of a system interconnect and interact to make up the whole.

Hominins: Species that are regarded as human, directly ancestral to humans, or very closely related to humans.

Human variation: The range of forms of any human characteristic, such as body shape or skin color.

Human adaptation: The ways in which human bodies, people, or cultures change, often in ways better suited to the environment or social context.

Hypothesis: Explanation of observed facts; explains how and why observed phenomena are the way they are. Scientific hypotheses rely on empirical evidence, are testable, and are able to be refuted.

Indigenous: Refers to people who are the original settlers of a given region and have deep ties to that place. Also known as First Peoples, Aboriginal Peoples, or Native Peoples, these populations are in contrast to other groups who have settled, occupied, or colonized the area more recently.

Knowledge system: A unified way of knowing that is shared by a group of people and is used to explain and predict phenomena.

Law: A prediction about what will happen given certain conditions; typically mathematical.

Participant observation: A research method common in cultural anthropology that involves living with, observing, and participating in the same activities as the people one studies.

Prehistoric archaeologists: Archaeologists who survey, excavate, and analyze material remains to study civilizations that lacked written records.

Sapir-Whorf hypothesis: The principle that the language you speak allows you to think about some things and not other things. This is also known as the linguistic relativity hypothesis.

Scholarly peer review: The process where an author's work must pass the scrutiny of other experts in the field before being published in a journal or book.

Subdiscipline: These refer to the four major areas that make up the discipline of anthropology: biological anthropology, cultural anthropology, archaeology, and linguistic anthropology.

Subfield: In this book, subfield refers to the different specializations within biological anthropology, including primatology, paleoanthropology, molecular anthropology, bioarchaeology, forensic anthropology, and human biology.

Theory: An explanation of observations that typically addresses a wide range of phenomena.

Understanding (scientific): Knowledge accumulated by systematic scientific study, supported by rigorous testing and organized by general principles.

About the Authors

Katie Nelson, Ph.D.

Inver Hills Community College, knelson@inverhills.edu, www.kanelson.com

Katie Nelson

Katie Nelson is an instructor of anthropology at Inver Hills Community College. Her research focuses on migration in human history and citizenship(s), identity, belonging and state mechanisms of migrant control in the contemporary United States, Mexico, and Morocco.

She received her B.A. in anthropology and Latin American studies from Macalester College, her M.A. in anthropology from the University of California, Santa Barbara, an M.A. in education and instructional technology from the University of Saint Thomas, and her Ph.D. fromCIESAS Occidente (Centro de Investigaciones y Estudios Superiores en Antropología Social –Center for Research and Higher Education in Social Anthropology), based in Guadalajara, Mexico.

Katie views teaching and learning as central to her practice as an anthropologist and as mutually reinforcing elements of her professional life. She is the former chair of the Teaching Anthropology Interest Group (2016-2018) of the General Anthropology Division of the American Anthropological Association and currently serves as the online content editor for theTeaching and Learning Anthropology Journal. She has contributed to several open access textbook projects, both as an author and an editor, and views the affordability of quality learning materials as an important piece of the equity and inclusion puzzle in higher education.

Lara Braff, Ph.D.

Grossmont College, Lara.Braff@gcccd.edu

Lara Braff

Lara Braff is an instructor of anthropology at Grossmont College, where she teaches cultural anthropology and biological anthropology courses. She received her B.A. in anthropology and Spanish from the University of California at Berkeley and both her M.A. and Ph.D. in comparative human development from the University of Chicago, where she specialized in medical anthropology. Her research has focused on social identities and disparities in the context of reproduction and medicine in Mexico and the U.S..

Lara's concerns about the social ramifications of inequality have guided her research projects, teaching practices, and involvement with open access projects like this textbook. Recently, motivated by the desire to make college more affordable and accessible to all students, she has been serving as co-coordinator of Grossmont College's Open Educational Resources (OER) and Zero Textbook Cost (ZTC) degree initiatives.

Beth Shook, Ph.D.

California State University, Chico, bashook@csuchico.edu

Beth Shook

Beth Shook is a lecturer in the anthropology department at California State University, Chico. She received her B.A. in anthropology and in molecular biology from Cornell College (in Mount Vernon, Iowa) and her M.A. and Ph.D. in anthropology from the University of California, Davis. While she is broadly trained in anthropology, her research has been in molecular anthropology and research interests have focused on prehistory, history, and contemporary concerns of indigenous North Americans.

Beth enjoys teaching courses in multiple subdisciplines, as well as mentoring graduate students in teaching. Additionally, she coleads Chico State's Affordable Learning Solutions (CAL$) program, is committed to programs that prioritize diversity, and serves on the Society for Anthropology in Community Colleges (SACC) Executive Board as vice president for Membership and Development & Regional Networks chair.

Kelsie Aguilera, M.A.

Leeward Community College, kelsieag@hawaii.edu

Kelsie Aguilera

Kelsie Aguilera is an assistant professor of anthropology at Leeward Community College. Located on the island of O'ahu, Leeward Community College is part of the University of Hawai'i System and holds a special commitment to Native Hawaiian education. At Leeward, Kelsie teaches anthropology courses in all of the subdisciplines and serves on the Open Educational Resources committee. Committed to the open-door mission of community colleges, she previously taught anthropology at Miami-Dade College.

Kelsie received her B.A. in anthropology from the University of Miami and her M.A. in anthropology from Binghamton University. She serves as treasurer on the executive board of the Society for Anthropology in Community Colleges (SACC) and continues to work hard toward making anthropology accessible and relevant for her students.

For Further Exploration

American Anthropological Association website: https://www.americananthro.org/

Partners in Health: https://www.pih.org/

Understanding Science. 2018. University of California Museum of Paleontology. 3 January. http://www.understandingscience.org.

Anticole, Matt. What's the difference between a scientific law and theory? TedEd Lesson. https://ed.ted.com/lessons/what-s-the-difference-between-a-scientific-law-and-theory-matt-anticole#watch

References

Bigham, Abigail W. 2016. "Genetics of Human Origin and Evolution: High-Altitude Adaptations." Current Opinion in Genetics & Development 41: 8–13.

Binford, Leigh. 2016. The El Mozote Massacre: Human Rights and Global Implications. Tucson: University of Arizona Press.

Bourgois, Phillippe. 2003. In Search of Respect. Cambridge: Cambridge University Press.

Durkheim, Emile. 2008. The Elementary Forms of Religious Life. Translated by Carol Cosman and Edited by Mark S. Cladis. New York: Oxford University Press.

Farmer, Paul. 2006. AIDS and Accusation: Haiti and the Geography of Blame. Berkeley: University of California Press.

Farmer, Paul, Matthew Basilico, Vanessa Kerry, Madeleine Ballard, Anne Becker, Gene Bukhman, Ophelia Dahl, et al. "Global Health Priorities for the Early Twenty-first Century." In Reimagining Global Health: An Introduction, edited by Paul Farmer, Jim Yong Kim, Arthur Kleinman, and Matthew Basilico, 302–339. Berkeley: University of California Press.

Goodall, Jane. 1996. My Life With the Chimpanzees. Aladdin Press.

Jablonski, Nina. 2012. Living Color: The Biological and Social Meaning of Skin Color. Berkeley: University of California Press.

Kenyon, Kathleen. 1979. Archaeology in the Holy Land. New York: W.W. Norton & Co. Malotki, Ekkehart. 1983. Hopi Time. The Hague: Mouton.

McIntosh-Smith, Tim. 2002. The Travels of Ibn Battutah. London: Picador.

Mead, Margaret. 1928. Coming of Age in Samoa. Oxford: Morrow.

Ochs, Elinor, and Bambi B. Schieffelin. 2012. "The theory of language socialization." In The Handbook of Language Socialization. Edited by Alessandro Duranti, Elinor Ochs, and Bambi Schieffelin, 1–21. Malden, MA: Wiley-Blackwell.

Prüfer, Kay, Kasper Munch, Ines Hellmann, Keiko Akagi, Jason R. Miller, Brian Walenz, Sergey Koren, et al. 2012. "The Bonobo Genome Compared with the Chimpanzee and Human Genomes." Nature 486 (June): 527–531.

Rathje, William, and Cullen Murphy. 1992. Rubbish!: The Archaeology of Garbage. New York: HarperCollins.

Relethford, John, and Deborah Bolnick. 2018. Reflections of our Past: How Human History Is Revealed in our Genes. 2nd ed. New York: Routledge.

Whorf, Benjamin. 1956. Language, Thought, and Reality. Cambridge: MIT Press.

Wood, Frances. 2004. The Silk Road: Two Thousand Years in the Heart of Asia. Berkeley: University of California Press.

Acknowledgment

We are grateful to Lahcen Mourad, J.D., Moroccan Arabic educator and scholar, for sharing insights from his scholarship on the legacy of Ibn Battuta and his influence on the early development of the social sciences.

Figure Attributions

Figure 1.1 Untitled by Mission de l'ONU au Mali – UN Mission in Mali/Gema Cortes is under a CC BY-NC-SA 2.0 License; Untitled in Middle East by Mark Fischer is used under a CC-BY-SA 2.0 License; Smiling Blonde Girl by Egor Gribanov from St. Petersburg, Russia is under aCC BY 2.0 License; Steppe Gobi Desert Mongolia Nomadic Man Travel at MaxPixel has been designated to the public domain (CC0).

Figure 1.2 Holism original to Explorations: An Open Invitation to Biological Anthropology by Mary Nelson is under a CC BY-NC 4.0 License.

Figure 1.3 Untitled by Luke Berhow is under a CC BY-NC 4.0 License.

Figure 1.4 Statue of Zhang Qian in Chenggu by Debi Lander is used with permission.

Figure 1.5 Ibn Batuta en Égypte by Léon Benett is in the public domain.

Figure 1.6 Charles Darwin Standing by unknown photographer is in the public domain.

Figure 1.7 FranzBoas by unknown photographer is in the public domain. This image is from the collection of the Canadian Museum of Civilization, Negative 79-796.

Figure 1.8 Subdisciplines of anthropology original to Explorations: An Open Invitation to Biological Anthropology by Mary Nelson is under a CC BY-NC 4.0 License.

Figure 1.9 Margaret Mead – Image from page 47 of "A brief expedition into science at the American Museum of Natural History" (1969) by Internet Archive Book Images is in the public domain.

Figure 1.10 Babytalk by Torbein Rønning is under a CC BY-NC-ND 2.0 License.

Figure 1.11 Jerycho8 by A. Sobkowski has been designated to the public domain (CC0).

Figure 1.12 Chimpanzees by Klaus Post is under a CC BY 2.0License.

Figure 1.13 Untitled at pxhere.com has been designated to the public domain (CC0).

Figure 1.14 PEF-with-mom-and-baby–Quy-Ton-12-2003 1-1-310 by Cjmadson is under a CC BY 3.0 License.

Figure 1.15 Head-Measurer of Tremearne (side view) by A.J.N. Tremearne, Man 15 (1914): 87-88 is in the public domain.

Figure 1.16 Subfields of biological anthropology original to Explorations: An Open Invitation to Biological Anthropology by Mary Nelson is under a CC BY-NC 4.0 License.

Figure 1.17 Mountain gorilla finger detail.KMRA by Kurt Ackermann (English Wikipedia username KMRA) is under a CC BY 2.5 License.

Figure 1.18 Donald Johanson 2009 by Julesasu has been designated to the public domain (CC0 1.0).

Figure 1.19 Oetzi the Iceman Rekonstruktion 1 by Thilo Parg is under a CC BY-SA 3.0 License.

Figure 1.20 Untitled by Presidencia El Salvadorhas been designated to the public domain (CC0 1.0).

Figure 1.21 Child Scientists by Beth Shook is under a CC BY-NC 4.0 License.

Figure 1.22 Science Checklist original to Explorations: An Open Invitation to Biological Anthropology is under a CC BY-NC 4.0 License.

Figure 1.23 Simple depiction of the scientific method original to Explorations: An Open Invitation to Biological Anthropology is under a CC BY-NC 4.0 License.

Figure 1.24 Complex Science Flowchart (2018) by Understanding Science, University of California Museum of Paleontology is used by permission and available here under a CC BY-NC 4.0 License.

Figure 1.25 Eureka! Archimede by Giammaria Mazzucchelli is in the public domain.

Chapter 2: Evolution

Jonathan Marks, Ph.D., University of North Carolina at Charlotte

Learning Objectives

LEARNING OBJECTIVES

- Discuss differing perspectives about how the human species descended from a primate ancestor.
- Discuss pre-Darwinian perspectives on the nature of the earth and evolution.
- Explain the process of natural selection.
- Describe what is meant by the "biopolitics of heredity".
- Examine and correct several misconceptions about human evolution.
- Discuss Darwin's theory and contributions to our understanding of evolution.

THE SCIENCE OF WHO WE ARE AND WHERE WE COME FROM

As we discussed at the end of Chapter 1, all peoples tell stories about their ancestors. Scientific stories about our ancestors are constrained by the assumptions of science, which developed out of 17th-century European philosophy. The first of these scientific assumptions is that the universe is divisible into (a) the natural world of matter and law and (b) the supernatural world of spirit and miracle, and we can focus our attention solely on the former. The second is that miracles, or capricious suspensions of the laws of nature, are not explanatory in the natural world; rather, historical processes are. The third is that we learn about nature by principally collecting data, under controlled circumstances, so that anyone, anywhere, can come to the same conclusions. We call such fundamental cultural assumptions like these **epistemes**, and we can label these as naturalism, rationalism, and empiricism, respectively. Our fourth assumption is that maximum accuracy is the only goal of a good scientific explanation. All of these are quite unusual cross-culturally; after all, the basis of most polite conversation universally is the assumption that maximum accuracy is *not* desirable. For example, when someone in the United States asks how you are, they generally *do not really want to know*, and if you insist on telling them, they will probably think you are a freak and not talk to you again.

Nevertheless, as these particular epistemic assumptions began to dominate European scholarly research in the 1600s, traditional ideas about how the world works began to fall away. Many of these ideas had theological implications. For example, it was generally believed by medieval European scholars that Heaven was a place up in the sky, and it was fundamentally different from Earth; after all, Heaven is where God lives. Things on Earth tend to move in straight lines, but in the sky they move in circles. Things on Earth decay; things in the sky seem to be eternal. Things here are ugly and uneven; things in the sky are perfect crystalline spheres. Things on Earth are made of four elements (earth, air, fire, and water), but things in the sky partake of a fifth element, the quintessence, which gives them those different properties. Nevertheless, by 1700 it was clear that the same basic rules of gravity and motion govern things up in Heaven and here on Earth. An apple falls from a tree by virtue of exactly the same laws of matter and motion that keep the moon revolving around the earth, as Isaac Newton showed.

The earth itself is a body in space revolving around the sun, just as the other planets in the solar system do. Things up in the sky and down here on Earth really aren't so different, after all.

Scholars began trying to reconstruct the history of the earth naturalistically. Around 1700 Thomas Burnet speculated that perhaps a comet smashed into the earth, which set off the Great Flood related in the Bible. At about the same time, the English anatomist Edward Tyson published the first anatomical study of the animal we now call a chimpanzee, demonstrating that it was physically more similar to us than to any other creature known. He even counted up its similarities: the chimpanzee resembled humans in 48 ways, but monkeys in only 34 ways (see Figure 2.1).

Figure 2.1 Tyson's "orang-outang".

PRE-DARWINIAN INTELLECTUAL TRENDS

Three general problems were especially vexing to pious Christian biologists of the 1700s. First, **extinction**—the loss of a species from the face of the earth—became grudgingly accepted as a fact, even though it seemed to diminish the power and wisdom of God, by making His creation and plan more transient than had traditionally been imagined. Yet not only was there extinction in the present (notably, a bird known as the dodo, hunted and eaten by Dutch colonists on the island of Mauritius, the only place it lived), but there was extinction in the past as well—and a lot of it, the evidence of which was being recovered as fossils. Moreover, the extinctions implied by the fossils were not contemporaneous—the extinctions were patterned, as if different kinds of creatures had lived and died at different times, embedded in distinct geological formations. What might that mean?

The second problem involved a great discovery by the Swedish biologist Carl Linnaeus. Where animal species had traditionally been linearly conceptualized in terms of how similar to humans they are—forming a "Great Chain of Being"—Linnaeus identified a distinctly different pattern. After all, there was no clear basis on which to say that an elk is more like a human than a tiger or a walrus is. Linnaeus, rather, argued that species should be arranged not according to how similar they are to us but, rather, by how similar they are to one another. In so doing, Linnaeus found that warm-blooded, hairy, lactating vertebrates formed a natural group that he named "Mammalia" in 1758 (in contrast to, say, fish or birds). Within that group was a cluster of species he called "Primates," and among them, according to our physical features, was our own species, which he named *Homo sapiens*. These physical correspondences among diverse kinds of creatures later came to be known as **homology**. But why did such a pattern of nested similarities exist, and what did it mean?

Figure 2.2A Ring-tailed Lemur. *Figure 2.2B Ruffed Lemur.* *Figure 2.2C Red Ruffed Lemur.* *Figure 2.2D Blue-eyed black lemur.*

The third problem involved the relationship between **adaptation** and biogeography. Even through the Bible doesn't exactly say so, it was understood that animals are adapted to their surroundings because God made them that way. The Bible does say that all living species of animals started out together in the same place—the mountains of Ararat, where

Noah's Ark landed. Yet those animals would not have been adapted to Ararat; so how did polar bears get to the Arctic, koalas to Australia, and bison to the Great Plains, where they are each well adapted, without going extinct first? How could all the lemurs have ended up in Madagascar and nowhere else (see Figure 2.2)? An explanation for adaptation that was historical, rather than miraculous, would be very valuable.

These were the questions that dominated the field of natural history by the beginning of the 1800s. But of course the big questions of the day weren't even about fossils or polar bears at all but, rather, about the biopolitics of slavery. Were all people of one stock, the descendants of **Adam and Eve**? That would seem to afford a moral argument against treating some people as property, if we are all brothers and sisters under the skin, and would seem to accord well with the biblical narrative as well. This position, however, required the development of a biological theory to explain how Adam and Eve's descendants could have morphed into the diverse peoples of the world. In other words, if you imagined Adam and Eve to be white, then how did black people arise? (Or vice versa.) This position, known as **monogenism**, was biblical, socially progressive, and generated the earliest modern evolutionary theories—microevolutionary, to be sure, but theories intended to explain the naturalistic production of difference, or what we would now call evolution.

Others believed that Africans and Europeans shared no common ancestry at all, being the products of separate creations by God. Perhaps in Adam and Eve, the Bible was merely recounting His most recent creation, but the peoples of the rest of the world were fundamentally and unalterably different and had always been so. This position, known as **polygenism**, was attractive to those looking to rationalize slavery as well as to radical intellectuals who did not feel constrained by biblical literalism. Paradoxically, however, in holding that peoples are as they always have been and could never change, the polygenists had more intellectual continuity with modern-day creationists.

By the mid-1800s, the discovery of stone tools in the ground implied a remote period in ancient Europe when the ancestors lived like the "**savages**" who still used stone tools, whom Europeans were encountering in more remote places of the world. This in turn implied an ancient European "stone age" before the invention of metals, which, like many of the new discoveries, was not part of the information in the Bible. It was increasingly becoming apparent that a long time ago, very primitive Europeans had lived with some extinct animals, like woolly mammoths. They even drew pictures of the extinct animals on the walls of their caves (see Figure 2.3).

Figure 2.3 Cave painting in the Grotte de Rouffignac.

Figure 2.4 Trilobite fossil.

Further, even a Stone Age seemed relatively recent in the larger context of the new geology. All those extinct fossil remains were being found in geological formations far more ancient than any known human evidence (see Figure 2.4). Just how ancient was not very clear, but judging by the pace of geological processes we can see today, those processes seem to have been going on for a very, very long time. You simply can't get fossilization or fossil fuels made in the ground over the few thousands of years of biblical time. The most rational interpretation of the geological evidence, argued the pious Scottish lawyer/geologist Charles Lyell is that the earth is very, very old—thus stimulating a revolution in both geological and ethnological time. Lyell himself argued that the earth was very old in the 1830s but waffled on how old the human species was until the 1860s.

Finally, educated Europeans were taking their biblical stories more and more loosely, as the field of biblical studies matured. The Bible was being understood as a collection of sacred Jewish and early Christian writings composed at different times and selected from a much larger corpus. Thomas Jefferson had privately distinguished between the things Jesus probably said and did and the things Jesus probably did not say and do. In 1835, a German biblical scholar named David Strauss scandalously interpreted the life of Christ without miracles; his work was published in English in 1846, translated by the aspiring novelist Marian Evans (aka George Eliot). We should focus, argued Strauss, on the meaning of the stories of the Bible, not on whether they really happened or not, for their meaning lies in their narrative content, not in their historicity. This launched a revolution in the area of biblical scholarship.

THE TRANSMUTATION HYPOTHESIS

The publication of *The Origin of Species* by Charles Darwin in 1859 became an intellectual flash point in European intellectual life (Darwin 1859). It was focused on a significantly narrow point: Where do new species, adapted to their surroundings, come from? The Bible says God made all species. However, the Bible also says that God made all languages at the foot of the **Tower of Babel**; and yet, half a century of historical linguistics had showed clearly that such was not the case (French and Spanish had only been different languages, having diverged from Vulgar Latin, for a matter of a few centuries), and nobody seemed to get too upset about it.

Moreover, the suggestion that species came from other species was not all that radical. The celebrated French naturalist Lamarck had said as much in 1809 and an anonymous 1844 English bestseller called *Vestiges of the Natural History of Creation* had sensationalized it—to the consternation of both theologians and naturalists. Indeed, by the 1850s European biologists were very confident that cells were fundamental units of life and that the only way you could get new cells was from old cells. While this begged the question of where the first cell came from, it nevertheless was not too much of a stretch to see species as fundamental units of life as well and to ask whether new ones arose miraculously, or just from older species. The idea that species had their beginnings in other, older, similar species was known as "**the transmutation hypothesis**."

Charles Darwin had come to think about the origin of species upon returning from a long voyage around the world in the early 1830s on the *H.M.S. Beagle*. In South America, Darwin had observed that the unusual species he saw alive there were very similar to the unusual extinct animals in the same area. This suggested some sort of historical continuity between them—**descent with modification**, he called it. The problem was how to make sense historically, rather than miraculously, of the particular adaptations that differentiate species. The engine of adaptation, Darwin realized, was competition. This did not necessarily entail face-to-face competition but simply the fact that not all members of a species are equally likely to survive and breed. Which ones are more likely? The ones that randomly are a bit more in sync with their environment. Those creatures will disproportionately thrive and breed, and the next generation of the species will come to look just a bit more like them, on the average. The core of Darwin's thought is thus a two-step process: the random generation of variation, and the nonrandom process by which the environment subtly favors organisms with certain features to thrive and breed.

The biology that Darwin learned in college had invoked a famous simile: a species is like a watch, meticulously crafted by a wise watchmaker, implying a heavenly species-maker. Darwin substituted a more powerful simile, arguing that a species is actually like a breed or strain of animals, rather than like a watch. But we know that a breed or strain of animals arises naturally, historically, by the actions of breeders who select certain features to characterize populations.

Whether dogs, pigeons, or roses, the properties of living beings can change, and have changed, in quite dramatic ways by virtue of human activity in rather short periods of time. If people could make beagles and greyhounds and bulldogs by selecting the progenitors of particular stocks, then maybe nature could work to select progenitors as well, although more subtly and over vastly longer periods of time (see Figure 2.5).

Darwin called this principle **"natural selection"** and planned to write a long book about it someday. But in 1858 he received a manuscript from a fellow naturalist, Alfred Russel Wallace, who had come up with quite similar ideas to his own while working in the Malay archipelago. Darwin's friend, the geologist Charles Lyell, had papers by Darwin and Wallace read into the record, *The Transactions of the Linnaean Society*, July 1, 1858, so they could share credit for the discovery, and Darwin set about to publish the work he had done on natural selection. The result was called *On the Origin of Species by Means of Natural Selection, or the Preservation of Favoured Races in the Struggle for Life*, published on November 24, 1859.

Figure 2.5A Beagle.

Figure 2.5B Bulldog.

Figure 2.5C Greyhound.

Darwin's central thesis was that the differences among breeds or strains or varieties of animals and plants were the same kinds of differences that exist between species, only smaller and formed over short periods of time. The origin of new species lay in the long-term biases of survival and reproduction in older species. The result was a convincing naturalistic explanation for adaptation. Moreover, it finally explained the nested pattern of similarities among species that Linnaeus had discovered a century earlier but couldn't explain. Those nested patterns were the legacy of common ancestries; they were literally family resemblances.

Darwin was especially careful to omit any discussion of people from his book. He wanted the discussion to be about the general process; consequently he wrote just a single line, near the end, about people: "Light will be thrown on the origin of man and his history" (Darwin 1859, 488). He was willing to acknowledge the possibility that life had "been originally breathed into a few forms or into one," but he was satisfied with having described the mechanism by which adaptive change has taken place in the organic world since then—in parallel with Isaac Newton, who famously refused to speculate on where gravity came from, focusing instead only on how it works (Darwin 1859, 490).

People, however, were bound to be the central issue. A British scholar named Herbert Spencer had also come up with a similar idea, which he called "survival of the fittest" and he convinced Darwin that his phrase was synonymous with "natural selection." And of course, who was more fit than wealthy, British white men? This confusion of human history (that is, the construction of social and political hierarchies) for evolutionary biology would prove to be a consistent irritation for students of human diversity and ancestry. Indeed, this issue eventually led Darwin and Wallace to part ways. Wallace asked: if natural selection does not produce useless organs, then why does the "savage" have a brain as big as a civilized European's, if the savage doesn't use it? This seeming paradox led Wallace into spiritualism and the possibility that all species of organisms had evolved…but human intelligence had had a little divine help. Darwin wrote him, "I hope you have not murdered too completely your own and my child" (Darwin, 1869). In 1871, the early British anthropologist Edward Tylor formally separated the evolution and study of "culture" from the biological properties of people. Of course the so-called "savage's" brain was as good as the European's, and he does use it fully, but it was filled with different information—"knowledge, belief, art, morals, law, custom, and any other capabilities and habits acquired by man as a member of society" (Tylor 1871, 1). Furthermore, this cultural information was the product of historical process, not miracle. This understanding marks the beginning of modern anthropology.

Within the academy, there was not too much reaction against the proposition that humans had descended with modification from an ape stock, and had then differentiated from that stock over the eons as a result of the differential preservation of favorable variations. The heart of Darwinism as applied to humans is simply ape ancestry and adaptive divergence.

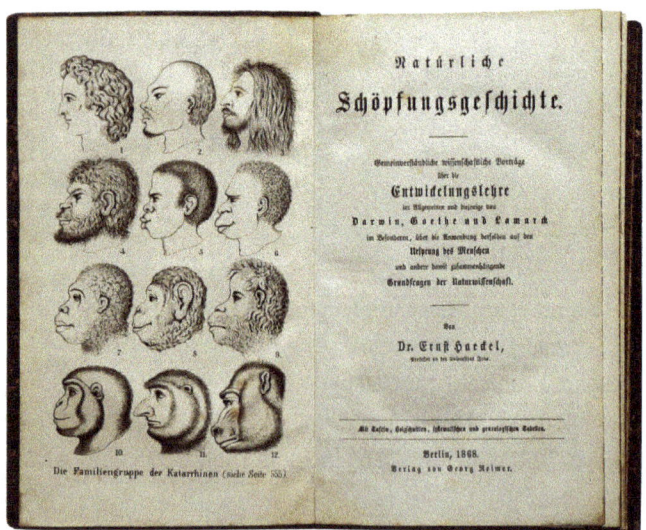

Figure 2.6 The frontispiece to Ernst Haeckel's (1868) popular German book on Darwinism. The English translation lacked this illustration.

But the early Darwinians were faced with a dilemma—in 1860, there was no fossil evidence linking humans to apes. The German biologist Ernst Haeckel solved this problem by fatefully arguing that we don't need a fossil record to link us to the apes, because Europeans are linked to the apes through the nonwhite peoples of the world. He envisioned 12 different species of living peoples, each at different distances from the apes, thus sacrificing the full humanity of most people on the altar of Darwinism (see Figure 2.6). Scientists of the 1860s thought the full humanity of Africans was less important than evolution, Today that is morally repugnant. While Darwin and his English colleagues did not agree with these details, they nevertheless saw Haeckel as an ally in the broader struggle to get evolution accepted. With hindsight, we can judge this to be a morally questionable decision: Today we would hopefully universally consider the full humanity of Africans to be more important than whether humans are descended from apes, and thoroughly repudiate anyone who denied it.

POST-DARWINIAN THEORIES AND DISPUTES

The immediate theoretical weakness of Darwinism lay in its reliance upon a pool of undirected variation for nature to select from. The dominant theory of heredity at the time was known as **blending inheritance**, in which a child is a blend of the parents—like paint, if mom is red and dad is blue, then the child is purple (see Figure 2.7). The problem is that any descendants of purple child will never be as different as blue mom and red dad. You can't recover the original blue and red from purple paint—which simply means that for people, variation is lost every generation. How can natural selection work if you lose variation every generation?

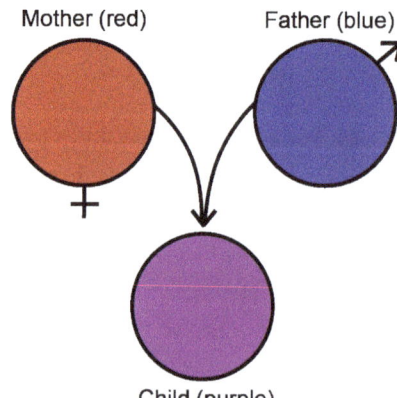

Figure 2.7 Blending inheritance in color.

Darwin fell back on a principle developed by Lamarck known as the "**inheritance of acquired characteristics**" or "use and disuse of organs." Here, whatever attributes you develop over the course of your life—muscles, a tan, compassion, bad breath—can be stably passed on to your children, somehow. That way, variation can be reintroduced every generation, by virtue of this new pool of acquired characters. Unfortunately, an influential school of German biologists in the 1880s, led by August Weismann, had identified just two types of cells in bodies: reproductive or germ cells, and somatic or body cells. It was the germ cells that formed the next generation; the somatic cells, which form the body, comprise merely an evolutionary dead-end to aid in the transmission of the germ-line. Life could thus be seen as a continuous series of germ-cells, with adult bodies as transient receptacles grown up around them every generation. (On this basis, the English writer Samuel Butler quipped that a hen is just an egg's way of making another egg.) But how, then, could information about your elbow or your cerebral cortex during the course of your life get into your germ cells? There didn't seem to be a way, so that generation called themselves "neoDarwinians" to express their belief in natural selection minus the inheritance of acquired characteristics.

The entire problem was rendered moot with the discovery in 1900 of Gregor Mendel's work on heredity in peas from 35 years earlier. Mendel showed that heredity didn't actually work like the blending of paints at all. When you isolated particular traits, you saw that offspring were not midway between their parents; rather, they were like one or the other parent. The offspring of a plant with green peas and one with yellow peas was green, not chartreuse. The offspring of a plant with wrinkled peas and one with round peas was round, not wrinkly-round. This suggested, rather, that heredity worked like interacting particles that came into new combinations but fundamentally retained their structural integrity every generation. Unlike paints, you could indeed recover the original variants under this model; variation wasn't lost every generation.

Mendelian genetics soon created new problems for Darwinism, however. The new geneticists were focused on discrete binary states of existence, like Mendel's peas: green/yellow, wrinkled/round, tall/short, in experimental populations. But the old Darwinian naturalists were working with quantitative variations in real populations—many of them intermediate, not extreme, in form. So, the Mendelians had a robust theory of heredity that had difficulty explaining natural patterns of variation, and the Darwinians had a robust theory of biological change that had difficulty accommodating discontinuous variation. One solution might be to reconceptualize all variation as fundamentally binary; the American geneticist Charles Davenport, for example, argued with considerable success that there were two kinds of people—smart and stupid—and that the stupid people simply had the **allele** for "feeblemindedness." This actually had a major and regrettable impact on American science and social policy in the 1920s.

A better solution came with the invention of population genetics, in works published around 1930 by the British geneticists Ronald Fisher and J. B. S. Haldane and the American geneticist Sewall Wright. In this model, a **gene** has small but cumulative effects. If we reduce a body to its genetic composition or **genotype**, and we reduce a species to its cumulative genetic composition, or **gene pool**, we can mathematically model the ways in which the gene pool can be transformed. There are rather few ways to accomplish it, and each has characteristic and predictable effects.

Figure 2.8 George Gaylord Simpson (1983). Photo courtesy of Jonathan Marks.

This became the first part of the **Synthetic Theory of Evolution**, the extension of Mendelian genetics to population genetics and the formal mathematical study of how gene pools may be transformed through time. The second part involved the study of how species diversify in addition to simply changing, and it entailed integrating speciation and geography in the story of how animal species have come to be. The primary scholars involved were the Russian-American fruit fly geneticist Theodosius Dobzhansky, the German-American ornithologist Ernst Mayr, and the American paleontologist George Gaylord Simpson (see Figure 2.8).

By the 1960s, then, biologists had a robust theory to explain the history of life. Genetic or genotypic changes (known to be encoded in molecules of DNA) cause changes in the physical appearance or **phenotype**. The environment sorts out these changes, and their proportion within a species rises or falls with the nature and stringency of the environment. Selection could now be reduced to the favoring of certain genotypes over alternatives, which can make populations genetically adaptively different from one another. **Genetic drift**, or stochastic (random) changes to the gene pool, makes populations genetically different from one another nonadaptively—that is to say, in ways that don't track the environment. The genetic contact of populations, or **gene flow**, makes populations more similar to one another. Disrupting gene flow acts to divide gene pools, which is in turn stabilized by the development of reproductive barriers between the populations. These processes can be directly studied within living species and can be extrapolated and can adequately explain the differences we find among species.

MOLECULAR EVOLUTION

The Evolutionary Synthesis successfully reduced evolution to genetics, but until the 1980s it was not possible to study the DNA sequence of the genes directly. Various surrogate measures had been employed for decades. For example, not only is blood a powerful metaphor for heredity, but also it contains genetically controlled immunological properties that can be used to study evolution. It was known in this way by the 1920s that the blood of human and chimpanzee were more similar to one another than were the blood of horse and donkey (see Figure 2.9). By the mid-1960s, it was well established that the blood of human and chimpanzee were more similar to one another than either was to the blood of an orangutan. With greater precision, the actual amino acid sequences of some proteins could be established and compared across species.

Figure 2.9A Horse.

It quickly became clear that while genetic differences appear generally to track anatomical differences—that is, the closest relatives of species inferred from their hemoglobin (the blood protein that carries gases) are generally the same as those inferred from their teeth—they nevertheless don't match well quantitatively. Thus, while humans are very easily distinguishable from gorillas physically and mentally, their hemoglobins only have two differences—the other 285 amino acids composing the protein match up perfectly. With less than one percent difference in the structure of their hemoglobin, yet striking differences in anatomical form, communication, and behavior, there seems to be a paradox in their biochemical versus anatomical relationships. This led to some thoughtless early inferences from biochemists, such as suggesting that humans are merely variant gorillas, from the viewpoint of hemoglobin. (But if we do not appear to be variant gorillas from any other viewpoint, then perhaps the viewpoint of hemoglobin—or molecular genetics more broadly, so went the counter-argument—is a foolish one to adopt.)

Figure 2.9B Donkey.

We now appreciate that anatomical variation tracks adaptive divergence of the species (obvious differences between humans and apes relate to locomotion, cognition, sound production, heat dissipation, etc.). But genetic variation more closely tracks the time since the species diverged from one another. By the late 1960s, molecular data were being used to test an important hypothesis about human evolution. Where physical anthropologist Sherwood Washburn thought that humans and African apes probably shared a common ancestor as recently as three to five million years ago, paleoanthropologist David Pilbeam felt that they had separated far earlier than that. Armed with the well-dated (but poorly reconstructed) dental remains of a 14-million-year-old fossil called *Ramapithecus*, Pilbeam argued that

Figure 2.10 Dentition of Ramapithecus.

Ramapithecus was a part of the human lineage, which in turn had to be at least that old (Figure 2.10). But Washburn's colleagues, Allan Wilson and Vincent Sarich, showed in 1967 that (1) the biochemical changes they measured were changing in a clocklike manner and (2) given the small amount of biochemical difference detectable between human and chimpanzee, the species separated no more than five million years ago. Thus, (3) *Ramapithecus* could not be on the human line 14 million years ago, because there was no separate human line 14 million years ago!

We now see *Ramapithecus* differently, as part of the orangutan lineage, and we find that genetic or molecular evolution does indeed tend to track time, rather than adaptive divergence. The reason is that most of the genome's DNA falls between genes and does not actually code for anything. Consequently, **mutations** that occur to most of the DNA do not have discernible effects on the body and are thus nonadaptive. Only a small bit of the DNA, it seems, actually builds the organism and encodes its adaptations; and even today, the processes by which it does so are vaguely understood.

When we compare actual DNA sequences across species, we consequently find striking patterns. Notably, we almost always find more difference across species in DNA *between* genes than in DNA *within* genes (see Figure 2.11). Where you might find two percent difference between species in the base sequence of a gene, you will find three percent difference in the DNA outside of that gene. Mutations are just as likely to arise within a gene as outside of a gene, yet when you compare species, you find more differences between genes. This suggests that the DNA between genes can tolerate changes without significantly harming the organism, because that DNA is not expressed, while DNA within genes cannot tolerate mutations quite as readily, so they get weeded out. Why? Because the genes do indeed function; consequently, random changes in a gene are far more likely to compromise that function than to improve it. Imagine trying to adjust the fuel injector in your car with a hammer. There is a small probability that you might hit it in just the right way to improve its performance, but chances are good that you would make it worse. Similarly, a random change to an already-functioning molecule is far more likely to make it work worse than to make it work better. That is why mutations can give you cancer, not superpowers. And by compromising the health of its bearer, such a mutation would be "weeded out" by natural selection (See the discussion in Chapters 3 and 4).

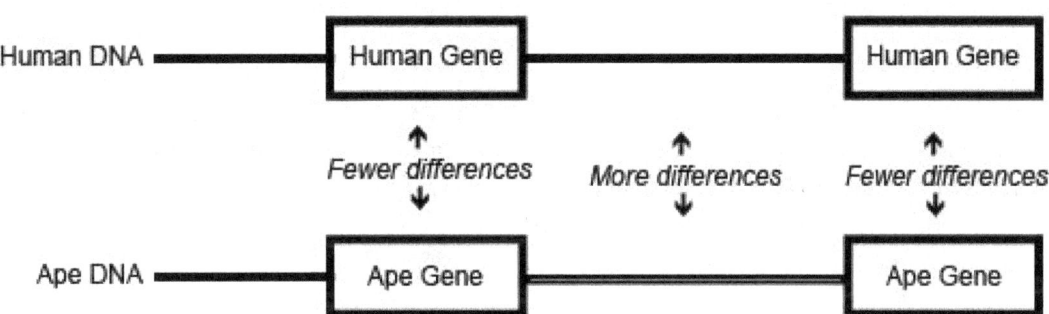

Figure 2.11 DNA comparisons yield more difference between than within genes.

This interpretation is supported when we examine the DNA differences simply *within* genes across species. While most mutations to the gene's coding sequence must affect the structure of the protein it codes for, a few do not. We call these "**synonymous mutations**," and when we compare genes across species, we almost always find far more of them than we find of the mutations that do indeed change the structure of the gene product. So even though synonymous mutations are a small proportion of mutations, they predominate in cross-species comparisons of genes. And for exactly the same reason: synonymous DNA mutations are less likely to be weeded out, because they are unexpressed and are thus invisible to the environment.

This helps to explain why the genetics seems to track time while the anatomy seems to track adaptation. If most mutations are neutral, with no net effect on the fitness of the organisms that possess them, then (as statisticians calculated in the 1960s) they will spread through a population rarely and in proportion to the rate at which they arise. The mutation rate is a constant, so consequently, over time, neutral mutations will spread and come to differentiate populations in proportion to the time since those gene pools have been separated from one another. Bodily difference, by contrast, interacts with the environment in important ways, and its evolution will track that interaction. Thus, biologists often envision evolution working on different hierarchical "levels": a genetic or molecular level and an anatomical level.

Yet how do we simultaneously accommodate the knowledge that (1) genetics and anatomy are different levels, with one tracking time and the other adaptive divergence, and that (2) the genes somehow cause the anatomy? The disconnect lies in the recognition that we still do not know how our one-dimensional DNA nucleotide sequence encodes a four-dimensional animal. This was the unfulfilled promise of the Human Genome Project in the 1990s: This Project produced the complete DNA sequence of a human cell in the hopes that it would reveal how human bodies are built and how to cure them when they are built poorly; however, that information has remained elusive. Presumably the knowledge of how organisms are produced from DNA sequences will one day permit us to reconcile the discrepancies between the patterns we see in anatomical and molecular evolution.

ORGANISMAL AND MULTILEVEL EVOLUTION

By the 1980s, the acknowledgment that even though genes cause bodies, genes and bodies evolve with different rates and patterns, led to a renewed focus on how bodies change. The Evolutionary Synthesis of the 1930s–1970s had reduced organisms to their genotypes and species to their gene pools, which provided valuable insights about the processes of biological change, but it was only a first approximation. Animals are in fact reactive and adaptable beings, not passive and inert genotypes. Nor are species simply gene pools; rather, they are clusters of socially interacting and reproductively compatible organisms.

So, accepting that evolutionary change is fundamentally genetic change, how do bodies nevertheless function and evolve? And accepting that speciation is ultimately a division of the gene pool, how do groups of animals nevertheless come to see one another as potential mates or competitors for mates, as opposed to just other creatures in the environment? Are there evolutionary processes that are not explicable by population genetics? These questions were raised in the 1980s by paleontologist Stephen Jay Gould, the leading evolutionary biologist of the late 20th century, to progress beyond the reductive assumptions that had guided the earlier generation.

Gould spearheaded a movement to identify and examine higher-order processes and features of evolution that were not adequately explained by population genetics. For example, extinction, which was such a problem for biologists of the 1600s, could now be seen as playing a more complex role in the history of life than population genetics had been able to model. The crucial recognition was that there are two kinds of extinctions, each with different consequences: background extinctions and mass extinctions. Background extinctions are those that reflect the balance of nature, because in a competitive Darwinian world, some things go extinct and other things take their place. Ecologically, your species may be adapted to its niche, but if another species comes along that's better adapted to the same niche, eventually your species will go extinct. It sucks, but it is the way of all life: you come into existence, you endure, and you pass out of existence. But mass extinctions are quite different. They reflect not so much the balance of nature as the wholesale disruption of nature: many species from many different lineages dying off at roughly the same time—presumably as the result of some kind of rare ecological disaster. The situation may not be survival of the fittest as much as survival of the luckiest. The result, then, would be an ecological scramble among the survivors. Having made it through the worst, the survivors could now simply divide up the new ecosystem amongst themselves, since their competitors were gone. Something like this may well have happened about 65 million years ago, with mammals surviving and dinosaurs not. Something like this may be happening now, due to human expansion and environmental degradation. Note, though, that there is only a limited descriptive role here for population genetics: the phenomena we are describing are about organisms and species in ecosystems.

Another question involved the properties of species that might not be reducible to the properties of their gene pools. For example, there are upwards of 15 species of gibbons but only two of chimpanzees. Why? There are upwards of 20 species of guenons but fewer than ten of baboons. Why? Are there genes for that? It seems unlikely. Gould suggested that species, as analytic units of nature, might have properties that are not reducible to the genes in their cells. For example, characteristic rates of speciation and extinction might be emergent properties of their ecologies and histories, and not properties of the genes. Consistent biases of speciation rates might well produce patterns of macroevolutionary diversity that are difficult to explain genetically and that need to be understood ecologically. Gould called such biases in speciation rates **species selection**—a higher-order process that invokes competition between species, in addition to the classic Darwinian competition between individuals.

One of Gould's most important studies involved the very nature of species. In the classical view, a species is continually adapting to its environment until it changes so much that it is a different species than it was at the beginning of this sentence (Eldredge and Gould 1972). That implies that the species is a fundamentally unstable entity through time, continuously changing to fit in. But suppose, argued Gould along with paleontologist Niles Eldredge, a species is more fundamentally stable through time and only really adapts as it is being founded? Then we might expect to find in the fossil record long equilibrium periods—a few million years or so—in which species don't seem to change much, punctuated by relatively brief periods in which they change a bit and then stabilize again as new species. They called this idea **punctuated equilibria**, and it helps to explain certain features of the fossil record, notably the existence of small anatomical "gaps" between closely related fossil forms (see Figure 2.12). Its significance, once again, lies in the fact that although it incorporates genetics, it is not really a theory of genetics but a theory of groups of bodies in deep time.

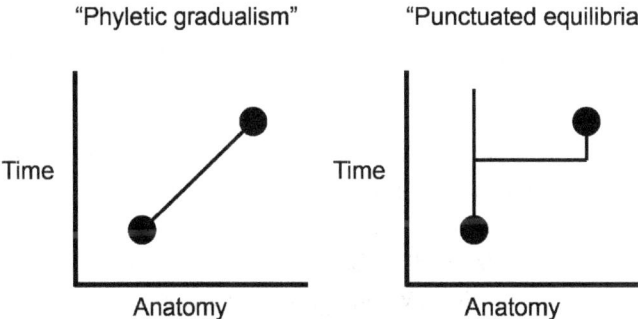

Figure 2.12 Different ways of conceptualizing the evolutionary relationship between an earlier and a later species.

In response to the call for a theory of the evolution of form, the field of **evo-devo**—the intersection of evolutionary and developmental biology—arose. The central focus here is on how changes in form and shape arise. An embryo matures by the stimulation of certain cells to divide, forming growth fields. The interactions and relationships among these growth fields generate the structures of the body. The genes that regulate these growth fields turn out to be very highly conserved across the animal kingdom. This is because they repeatedly turn on and off the most basic genes guiding the animal's development, and thus any changes to them would be catastrophic. Indeed, these genes were first identified by producing a bizarre mutant fruit fly that grew a pair of legs where its antennae were supposed to be.

Certain genetic changes can alter the fates of cells and the body parts that they build; meanwhile, other genetic changes can simply affect the rates at which neighboring groups of cells grow and divide, thus producing physical bumps or dents in the developing body. The result of altering the relationships among these fields of cellular proliferation in the growing embryo is allometry, or the differential growth of body parts. As an animal gets larger—either over the course of its life or over the course of macroevolution—it often has to change shape in order to live at a different size. Many important physiological functions depend on properties of geometric area: the strength of a bone, for example, is proportional to its cross-sectional area. But area is a two-dimensional quality, while growing takes place in three dimensions—as an increase in mass or volume. As an animal expands, its bones necessarily weaken, because volume expands faster than area does. Consequently a bigger animal has more stress on its bones than a smaller animal does and must evolve bones even thicker than they would be by simply scaling the animal up proportionally. In other words, if you expand a mouse to the size of an elephant, it will nevertheless still have much thinner bones than the elephant does. But those giant mouse bones will unfortunately not be adequate to the task. Thus, a giant mouse would have to change aspects of its form to maintain function at a larger size (see Figure 2.13).

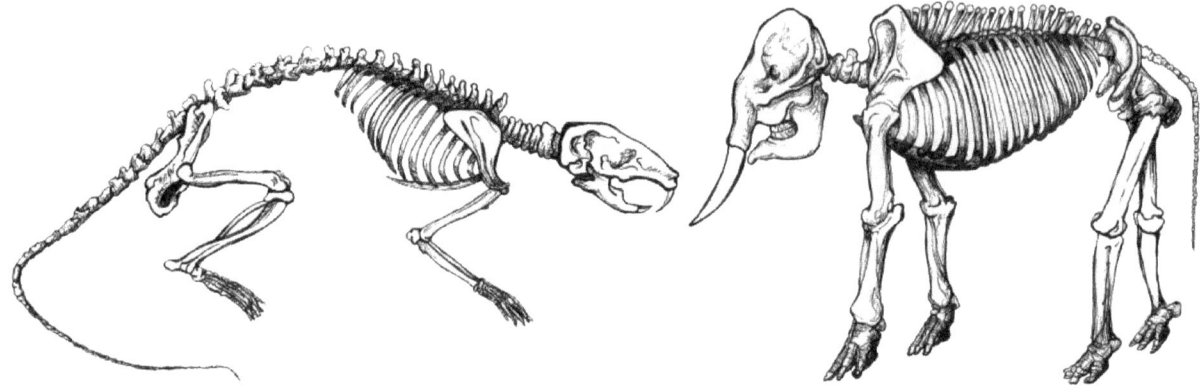

Figure 2.13 Mouse (left) and elephant skeletons (right). Notice the elephant's bones are more robust when the two animals are the same size.

Physiologically, we would like to know how the body "knows" when to turn on and off the genes that regulate growth to produce a normal animal. Evolutionarily, we would like to know how the body "learns" to alter the genetic on/off switch (or the genetic "slow down/speed up" switch) to produce an animal that looks different. Moreover, since organisms differ from one another, we would like to know how the developing body distinguishes a range of normal variation from abnormal, pathological variation. And finally, how does abnormal variation eventually become normal in a descendant species?

Gould here invoked the work of a British geneticist named Conrad H. Waddington, who thought about genetics less reductively than his colleagues. Without isolating specific DNA sites and analyzing their function, Waddington instead studied the inheritance of an organism's reactivity–its ability to adapt to the circumstances of its life. In a famous experiment, he grew fruit fly eggs in an atmosphere containing ether. Most died, but a few survived somehow by developing a weird physical feature: a second thorax, with a second pair of wings. Waddington bred these flies and soon developed a stable line of flies who would reliably develop a second thorax when grown in ether. Then he began to lower the concentration of ether, while continuing to selectively breed the flies that developed the strange appearance. Eventually he had a line of flies that would stably develop the "bithorax" phenotype even when there was no ether; it had become the "new normal." The flies had genetically assimilated the bithorax condition.

Waddington was thus able to mimic the inheritance of acquired characteristics: what had been a trait stimulated by ether a few generations ago was now a normal part of the development of the descendants. Waddington recognized that he had performed a selection experiment on genetic variants, yet he had not selected for particular traits but, rather, for the physiological tendency to develop particular traits when appropriately stimulated. He called that tendency **plasticity** and its converse, the tendency to stay the same even under weird environmental circumstances, **canalization**. Waddington had initially selected for plasticity, the tendency to develop the bithorax phenotype under weird conditions, and then, later, for canalization, the developmental normalization of that weird physical trait. Although Waddington had high stature in the community of geneticists, evolutionary biologists of the 1950s and 1960s regarded him with suspicion because he was not working within the standard mindset of reductionism, which saw evolution as the spread of genetic variants that coded for favorable traits.

Waddington also recognized that cells had two types of inheritance patterns. Through mitosis, one cell becomes two cells that contain the same genetic information as one another and as the original cell. The faithful transmission of the DNA base sequences is genetic transmission. And yet, genetically identical nerve cells, skin cells, and white blood cells faithfully transmit their identities as nerve cells, skin cells, and white blood cells to their descendant cells, in spite of being genetically identical (see Figure 2.14). White blood cells only make more white blood cells, never nerve cells—even though they have exactly the same DNA sequence. Waddington called this kind of cellular inheritance **epigenetic**.

Figure 2.14 Five kinds of cells that all have the same DNA sequence yet look different.

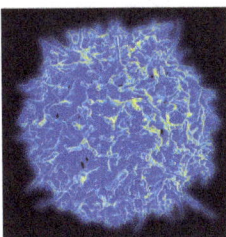 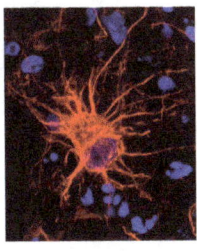 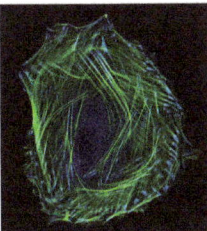 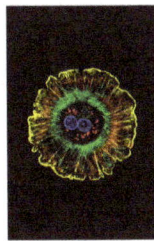 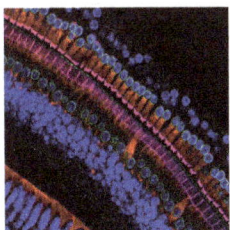

Figure 2.14A Healthy Human T cell. *Figure 2.14B Human brain cell.* *Figure 2.14C Embryonic smooth muscle.* *Figure 2.14D Human liver cell.* *Figure 2.14E Human hair cells in the ear.*

The Human Genome Project in the 1990s generated a great deal of public interest in analyzing the human DNA sequence from the standpoint of medical genetics. Some of the rhetoric was extravagant in trying to sell the public on the idea of investing a lot of money and resources in sequencing the human genome: showing the genetic basis of heritable traits, curing genetic diseases, and learning what it means ultimately to be biologically human. However, the human DNA sequence was not actually able to answer those questions, and interest began to shift from genetic information to epigenetic information: the modification of DNA structure, but not the base sequence, and the stable multi-generational inheritance of that modification.

This interest in genetics built upon decades of research in human biology, which saw the human body as highly adaptable, as controlled anthropometric studies of immigrant communities begun by anthropologists like Franz Boas and Harry Shapiro had been showing since the early 20th century. The growing human body adjusts itself to the conditions of life, such as diet, sunshine, high altitude, hard labor, population density, how babies are carried—any and all of which can have subtle but consistent effects upon its development. There can thus be no normal human form, only a context-specific range of human forms. What the human biologists called human adaptability, evolutionary biologists called developmental plasticity, and evidence quickly began to mount for its cause being epigenetic modifications to DNA.

Evolution is about how descendants come to differ from ancestors. Inheritance from parent to offspring is still the critical elementary process. But in the 21st century, the intimate relationship between evolution and inheritance has been broadened to include not merely genetic inheritance patterns but epigenetic inheritance patterns as well. We also recognize two other forms of intergenerational transmission and inheritance, which also have consequences for evolution. In addition to genetic and epigenetic variation as sources of heritable physical differences among organisms that can lead to biases in survival and reproduction, we can also model the effects of behavioral variation. Here the transmitted information is not in the DNA at all and is thus not transmitted across generations (intergenerationally). Instead, this information is transmitted horizontally (intragenerationally), permitting more rapid ways for organisms to adjust to the environment. Finally, humans are unique in that we are the only species that horizontally transmits an arbitrary set of rules to govern communication, social interaction, and thought. This shared information is symbolic and has resulted in what we recognize as "culture": an imaginary world of names, words, pictures, classifications, revered pasts, possible futures, spirits, dead ancestors, unborn descendants, in-laws, politeness, taboo, justice, beauty, and story, all accompanied by a material world of tools. This is a fourth, symbolic or cultural mode of transmission.

Consequently our post-Synthesis ideas about evolution tend to see the evolutionary processes as hierarchically organized and not restricted to simply the differential transmission of DNA sequences into the next generation. While that is indeed a significant part of evolution, the organism and species are nevertheless crucial to understanding how those DNA sequences get transmitted and cannot be taken for granted. Nor can we take for granted the complex roles played by the transmission of epigenetic, behavioral, and symbolic information in perpetuating our genes, bodies, and species. In the case of human evolution, one can readily see that symbolic information and cultural adaptation are far more central to our lives and our survival today than DNA and genetic adaptation. It is thus misleading to think of humans passively occupying an environmental niche. Rather, humans are actively engaged in constructing our own niches, as well as adapting to them and using them to adapt. The complex interplay between a species and its active engagement in creating its own ecology is known as **niche construction**.

THE BIOPOLITICS OF HEREDITY

Perhaps the hardest lesson about human evolution to learn is that it is intensely political. Indeed, to see it from the opposite side, as it were, the history of creationism is essentially a history of legal decisions: most famously, *Tennessee vs. John T. Scopes* (1925), in which a schoolteacher was prosecuted for violating a law in Tennessee that prohibited the teaching of human evolution in public schools, where public school teachers were required by law to teach creationism. More recently, *McLean vs. Arkansas* (1982) dispatched "scientific creationism"; and *Kitzmiller vs. Dover (Pennsylvania) Area School District* (2005), dispatched "intelligent design." In some cases, people see unbiblical things in evolution, although most Christian theologians are easily able to reconcile science to the Bible. In other cases, people see immoral things in evolution, although there is morality and its opposite everywhere. And some people see evolution as an aspect of alt-religion, usurping the authority of science in schools to teach the rejection of the Christian faith, which would be unconstitutional.

Clearly, the position that there is no politics here is untenable. But is the politics in evolution an aberration or is it somehow embedded in the science, even if we don't see it? In the early 20th century, scientists commonly promoted the view that science and politics were separate—science was a pure activity, only rarely corrupted by politics. And yet as early as World War I, the politics of nationalism made a hero of the German chemist Fritz Haber for inventing poison gas. And of course in World War II, German doctors and American physicists were recruited to the war effort and helped to end many civilian lives for different sides. So we now think of the apolitical scientist as a self-serving myth that functions merely to absolve scientists of responsibility for their politics. The history of science shows how every generation of scientists has used evolutionary theory to rationalize political and moral positions. In the very first generation of evolutionary science, Darwin's *Origin of Species* (1859) is today far more readable than his *Descent of Man* (1871). The reason is that Darwin consciously purged *The Origin of Species* of any discussion of people, as we noted earlier. And when he finally got around to people, in *The Descent of Man*, he simply imbued them with the quaint Victorian prejudices of his age, and the result often makes you want to cringe every few pages. There is plenty of politics in there—sexism, racism, and colonialism at the very least—and that is simply because *you cannot talk about people apolitically*.

One immediate faddish deduction from Darwinism, popularized by Herbert Spencer as "survival of the fittest," held that unfettered competition led to advancement in nature, and also in human history, and since the poor were losers in that struggle, anything that made their lives easier would go against the natural order. This position later came to be known ironically as "Social Darwinism." Spencer was challenged by fellow Darwinian Thomas Huxley ("Man's Place in Nature"), who agreed that struggle was the law of the jungle but observed that we don't live in jungles any more. The obligation to make lives better for others is a moral, not a natural, fact. We simultaneously inhabit a natural universe of descent from apes and a moral universe of injustice and inequality, and science is not well served by ignoring the latter.

Concurrently, the German biologist Ernst Haeckel's 1868 popularization of Darwinism was translated into English a few years later as *The History of Creation*. As we saw earlier, Haeckel was determined to convince his readers that they were descended from apes, even in the absence of fossil evidence attesting to it. When he made non-Europeans into the missing links that connected his readers to the apes, and depicted them as ugly caricatures, he knew precisely what he was doing. Indeed, when the degrading racial drawings were deleted from the English translation of his book, the text nevertheless made his arguments quite clear. And a generation later, when the Americans had not yet entered the Great War in 1916, a biologist named Vernon Kellogg visited the German High Command as a neutral observer and found that the officers knew a lot about evolutionary biology, which they had gotten from Haeckel and which rationalized their military aggressions. Kellogg went home and wrote a bestseller about it, called *Headquarters Nights* (1917). World War I would have been fought with or without evolutionary theory, but as a source of scientific authority, evolution—even if a perversion of the Darwinian theory—had very quickly attained global geopolitical relevance.

Scientific racism, the recruitment of science for the evil political ends of racism, proved remarkably impervious to evolution. Before Darwin, there was creationist scientific racism, and after Darwin, there was evolutionist scientific racism. And there is still scientific racism, self-justified by recourse to evolution, which means that scientists have to be politically astute and sensitive to the uses of their work.

More commonly, however, the politics in the evolutionary science is subtle. This is in large part an expression of the advancement of science. We recognize the biases of our academic ancestors and modify our scientific stories accordingly. But we can never be free of our own cultural biases, which are invisible to us, as much as our predecessors' biases were invisible to them. In some cases, the most important cultural issues resurface in different guises each generation, like scientific racism.

Consider this: Are you just your ancestry, or can you transcend it? If that sounds like a weird question, it was actually quite important to a turn-of-the-20th-century European society in which an old hereditary aristocracy was under increasing threat from a rising middle class. And that is why the very first English textbook of Mendelian genetics concluded with the thought that "permanent progress is a question of breeding rather than of pedagogics; a matter of gametes, not of training … the creature is not made but born." (Punnett 1905, 60). *Translation: Not only do we now know a bit about how heredity works, but it's also the most important thing about you. Trust me, I'm a scientist.*

Yet evolution is about how descendants come to differ from ancestors. Do we really know that your heredity, your DNA, your ancestry, is the most important thing about you? That you were born, not made? After all, we do know that you could be born a slave or a peasant, and come from a long line of slaves or peasants, and yet not have slavery or peasantry be the most important thing about you. Whatever your ancestors were may constrain what you can be but probably should not, as a moral precept. But now we can also begin to see that ancestry is not a strictly biological concept. Human ancestry is biopolitics, not biology.

Evolution is fundamentally a theory about ancestry and yet ancestors are, in the broad anthropological sense, sacred—and often far more meaningful symbolically than biologically. Just a few years after *The Origin of Species*, the British politician and writer Benjamin Disraeli declared himself to be on the side of the angels, not the apes, and to "repudiate with indignation and abhorrence those new-fangled theories" (Monypenny 1920, 105) He turned his back on an ape ancestry and looked to the angel; yet, he did so as a prominent Jew-turned-Anglican, who had personally transcended his humble roots and risen to the pinnacle of the Empire. Ancestry was certainly important, and Disraeli was famously proud of his, but it was also certainly not the most important thing, not the primary determinant of his place in the world. Indeed, quite the opposite: Disraeli's life was built on the transcendence of many centuries of Jewish poverty and oppression in Europe. Humble ancestry was there to be superseded and nobility was there to be earned; Disraeli would later become the Earl of Beaconsfield. Clearly, "are you just your ancestry" is not a value-neutral question, and "the creature is not made, but born" is not a value-neutral answer.

The idea that the most important thing about you is your ancestry became popular twice in 20th century science. The first time was at the beginning of the century, when the **eugenics** movement in America called attention to feeble-minded stocks–which usually referred to the poor or immigrants (see Figure 2.15). This movement culminated in Congress restricting the immigration of feeble-minded races (notably Jews and Italians) in 1924, and the Supreme Court declaring it acceptable for states to sterilize their feeble-minded citizens involuntarily in 1927. When the Nazis picked up and embellished these ideas, Americans fell away from them during World War II.

Figure 2.15 Eugenic and Health Exhibit, Fitter Families exhibit and examination building, Kansas State Free Fair.

The second time that ancestry became paramount was as part of a successful attempt to drum up public support for the Human Genome Project in the 1990s. Public support for sequencing the human genome was encouraged by a popular science campaign that featured books titled *The Book of Man*, *The Human Blueprint*, and *The Code of Codes*. These books generally promised cures for genetic diseases and a deeper understanding of the human condition. We can certainly identify progress in molecular genetics over the last couple of decades since the human genome was sequenced, but that progress has notably not been accompanied by cures for genetic diseases, nor by deeper understandings of the human condition.

Even at the most detailed and refined levels of genetic analysis, we still don't have much of an understanding of the actual basis by which things seem to "run in families." While the genetic basis of simple, if tragic, genetic diseases have become well-known–such as sickle-cell anemia, cystic fibrosis, and Tay-Sachs' Disease–we still haven't found the ostensible genetic basis for traits that are thought to have a strong genetic component. For example, a recent genetic summary found over 600 genetic sites that contributed to height, yet nevertheless still explained only about 16 percent of the variation in height, which we know strongly runs in families (Wood et al., 2014).

Partly in reaction to the reductionistic hype of the Human Genome Project, the study of epigenetics has now become the subject of great clinical and evolutionary interest. One famous natural experiment involves a Nazi-imposed famine in Holland over the winter of 1944-1945. Children born during and shortly after the famine experienced a higher incidence of certain health problems as adults, many decades later. Apparently, certain genes had been down-regulated early in development and remained that way throughout the course of life. Indeed, this modified regulation of the genes in response to the severe environmental conditions may have been passed on to their children.

Obviously one's particular genetic constitution may play an important role in one's life trajectory. But overvaluing that role may have important social and political consequences. In the first place, genotypes are rendered meaningful in a cultural universe. Thus, if you live in a strongly patriarchal society and are born without a Y chromosome (since human males are chromosomally XY and females XX), your genotype will indeed have a strong effect upon your life course. So even though the variation is natural, the consequences are political. The mediating factors are the cultural ideas about how people ought to be treated, and the role of the state in permitting people to develop and thrive. More broadly, there are implications for public education if variation in intelligence is genetic. There are implications for the legal system if criminality is genetic. There are implications for the justice system if sexual preference, or sexual identity, is genetic. There are implications for the development of sports talent if that is genetic. And yet, even for the human traits that are more straightforward to measure and that are known to be strongly heritable, the DNA base sequence variation only seems to explain a little.

Genetic determinism or **hereditarianism** is the idea that "the creature is made, not born"–or, in a more recent formulation by James Watson, that "our fate is in our genes." One of the major implications drawn from genetic determinism is that the feature in question must inevitably express itself; therefore, we can't do anything about it. Therefore, we might as well not fund the social programs designed to ameliorate economic inequality and improve people's lives, because their courses are fated genetically. And therefore, they don't deserve better lives.

All of the "therefores" in the preceding paragraph are open to debate. What is important is that the argument relies on a very narrow understanding of the role of genetics in human life, and it misdirects the causes of inequality from cultural to natural processes. By contrast, instead of focusing on the genes and imagining them to place an invisible limit upon social progress, we can study the ways in which your DNA sequence does *not* limit your capability for self-improvement or fix your place in a social hierarchy. In general, two such avenues exist. First, we can examine the ways in which the human body responds and reacts to environmental variation: human adaptability and plasticity. This line of research began with the anthropometric studies of immigrants by Franz Boas in the early 20th century and has now expanded to incorporate the epigenetic inheritance of modified human DNA. And second, we can consider how human lives are shaped by the social histories, and especially the structural inequalities within the societies in which they grow up.

Although it arises and is refuted every generation, the radical hereditarian position (genetic determinism) perennially claims to speak for both science and evolution. It does not. It is the voice of a radical fringe–perhaps naive, perhaps evil. It is not the authentic voice of science or of evolution. Indeed, keeping Charles Darwin's name unsullied by protecting it from association with bad science often seems like a full-time job. Culture and epigenetics are very much a part of the human condition, and their roles are significant parts of the complete story of human evolution.

ADAPTATION AND ADAPTATIONISM

Charles Darwin explained in material, naturalistic terms how animals adapt to their environments. The most fit, it seems, have survived over eons of the history of life on earth to co-create ecosystems full of animals and plants. Our own bodies are full of evident adaptations: eyes for seeing, ears for hearing, feet for walking on.

But what about hands? Feet are adapted to be primarily weight-bearing structures (rather than grasping structures, as in the apes) and that is what we primarily use them for. But we use our hands in many ways: for fine-scale manipulation, greeting, pointing, stimulating a sexual partner, writing, throwing, and cooking, among other uses. So which of these uses express what hands are "for," when all of them express what hands do?

There is an important lesson in recognizing that what things do in the present is not a good guide to understand why they came to exist. Gunpowder was invented for entertainment–and only later adopted for killing people. The Internet was invented to decentralize computers in case of a nuclear attack–and only later adopted for social media. The apes have short thumbs and use their hands in locomotion; our ancestors stopped using their hands in locomotion by about six million years ago and had fairly modern-looking hands by about two million years ago. We can speculate that a combination of selection for abstract thought and dexterity led to evolution of the human hand, with its capability for tool-making that exceeds what apes can do (see Figure 2.16). But let's face it–how many tools have you made today?

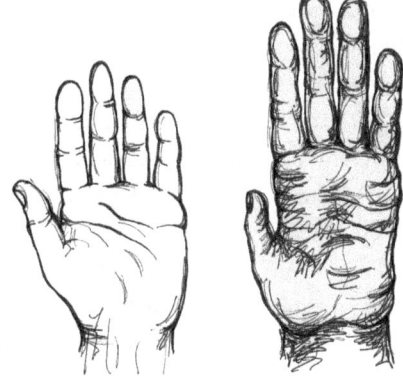

Figure 2.16 Chimpanzee hand (right) compared to a human hand (left).

Consequently, we are obliged to see the human foot as having a purpose to which it is adapted and the human hand as having multiple purposes, most of which are different from what it originally evolved for. Paleontologists Stephen Jay Gould and Elisabeth Vrba suggested that an original use be regarded as an adaptation, and the additional uses be called "**exaptations**." Thus, we would consider the human hand to be an adaptation for tool-making and an exaptation for writing. So how do we know whether any particular feature is an adaptation, like the walking foot, rather than an exaptation, like the writing hand? Or more broadly, how can we reason rigorously from what a feature does to what it evolved for?

The answer to the question "what did this feature evolve for?" is an origin myth. This origin myth contains three assumptions: (1) that features can be isolated and decontextualized as evolutionary units; (2) that there is a reason for the existence of any particular feature; and (3) that such a reason can be discerned.

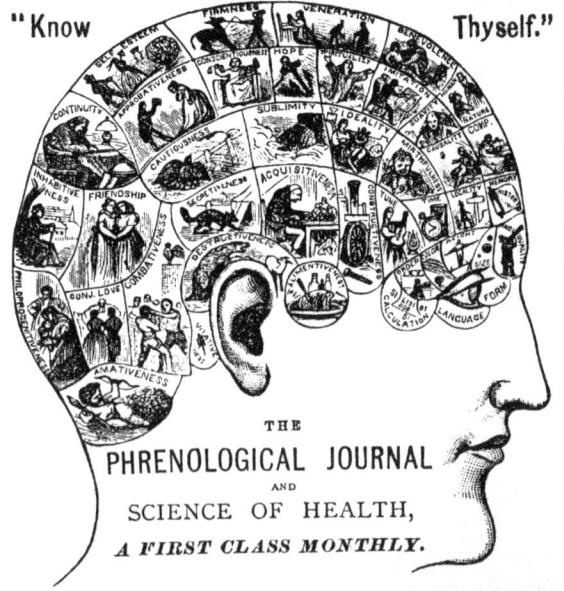

Figure 2.17 According to the early 19th century science of phrenology, units of personality could be reliably mapped onto units of the head.

The first assumption was appreciated a century ago as the "unit-character problem." Are the units by which the body grows and evolves the same as units we name? Clearly not; we have genes and we have noses, and we have genes that affect noses, but we don't have "nose genes." What, then, is the relationship between the evolving elements that we see, identify, and name and the elements that actually biologically exist and evolve? It is hard to know, but we can use the history of science as a guide to see how that fallacy has been used by earlier generations. Back in the 19th century, the early anatomists argued that since the brain contained the mind, they could map different mental states (acquisitiveness, punctuality, sensitivity) on to parts of the brain. Someone who was very introspective, say, would have an enlarged introspection part of the brain, a cranial bulge to represent the hyperactivity of this mental state. The anatomical science was known as **phrenology**, and it was predicated on the false assumption that units of thought or personality or behavior could be mapped to distinct parts of the brain and physically observed (see Figure 2.17). This is the fallacy of reification, imagining that something named is something real.

The second assumption, that everything has a reason, has long been recognized as a core belief of religion. Our desire to impose order and simplicity on the workings of the universe, however, does not constrain it to obey simple and orderly causes. Magic, witchcraft, spirits, and divine agency are all powerful explanations for why things happen. Consequently, it is probably not a good idea to lump natural selection in with those. Sometimes things do happen for a reason, of course, but other times things happen as byproducts of other things, or for very complicated and entangled reasons, or for no reason at all. What phenomena have reasons and thereby merit explanation? Chimpanzees have very large testicles, and we think we know why: their promiscuous sexual behavior triggers intense competition for high sperm count. But chimpanzees also have very large ears, and we don't even try to explain them (see Figure 2.18). Why not? Why should there be a reason for chimp testicles but not for chimp ears? What determines the kinds of features that we try to explain, as opposed to the ones that we do not? Again, the assumption that any specific feature has a reason is metaphysical; that is to say, it may be true in any particular case, but to assume it in all cases is gratuitous.

Figure 2.18 Chimpanzees have big ears, although we don't know why.

And third, the possibility of knowing what the reason for any particular feature is, assuming that it has one, is a challenge for evolutionary epistemology (the theory of how we know things). Consider the big adaptations of our lineage: bipedalism and language. Nobody doubts that they are good and they evolved by natural selection, and we know how they work. But why did they evolve? If talking and walking are simply better than not talking and not walking, then why did they evolve in just a single branch of the ape lineage in the primate family tree? We don't know what bipedalism evolved for, although there are plenty of speculations: walking long distances, running long distances, cooling the head, seeing over tall grass, carrying babies, carrying food, wading, threatening, counting calories, sexual display. Neither do we know what language evolved for, although there are speculations: coordinating hunting, gossiping, manipulating others. But it also possible that bipedality is simply the way that a small arboreal ape travels on the ground, if it isn't in the treetops. Or that language is simply the way that a primate with small canine teeth and certain mental propensities comes to communicate. If that were true, then there might be no reason for bipedality or language: having the unique suite of preconditions and a fortuitous set of circumstances simply set them in motion, and natural selection elaborated and explored their potentials. Possibly, walking and talking solved problems that no other lineage had ever solved; but even if so, the fact remains that rest of the species in the history of life have done pretty well without having solved them.

It is certainly very optimistic to think that all three assumptions (that organisms can be meaningfully atomized, that everything has a reason, and that we can know the reason) would be simultaneously in effect. Indeed, just as there are many ways of adapting (genetically, epigenetically, behaviorally, culturally), there are also many ways of being nonadaptive, which would imply that there is no reason at all for the feature in question.

First, there is the element of randomness of population histories. There are more cases of sickle-cell anemia among sub-Saharan Africans than other peoples, and there is a reason for it: carriers of sickle-cell anemia have a resistance to malaria, which is more frequent in parts of Africa (as discussed in Chapters 4 and 14). But there are more cases of a blood disease called variegated porphyria, a rare genetic metabolic disorder, in the Afrikaners of South Africa (descendants of mostly Dutch settlers in the 17th century) than in other peoples, and there is no reason for it. Yet we know the cause: One of the founding Dutch colonial settlers had the allele, and everyone in South Africa with it today is her descendant. But that is not a reason, that is simply an accident of history.

Second, there is the potential mismatch between the past and the present. The value of a particular feature in the past may be changed as the environmental circumstances change. Our species is diurnal, and our ancestors were diurnal. But beginning around a few hundred thousand years ago, our ancestors could build fires, which extended the light period, which was subsequently further amplified by lamps and candles. And over the course of the 20th century, electrical power has made it possible for people to stay up very late when it is dark—working, partying, worrying—to a greater extent than any other closely related species. In other words, we evolved to be diurnal, yet we are now far more nocturnal than any of our recent ancestors or close relatives. Are we adapting to nocturnality? If so, why? Does it even make any sense to speak of the human occupation of a nocturnal ape niche, despite the fact that we empirically seem to be doing just that? And if so, does it make sense to ask what the reason for it is?

Third, there is a genetic phenomenon known as a selective sweep, or the hitchhiker effect. Imagine three genes—A, B, and C—located very closely together on a chromosome. They each have several variants, or alleles, in the population. Now, for whatever reason, it becomes beneficial to have one of the B alleles, say B4; this B4 allele is now under strong positive selection. Obviously, we will expect future generations to be characterized by mostly B4. But what was B4 attached to? Because whatever A and C alleles were adjacent to it will also be quickly spread, simply by virtue of the selection for B4. Even if the A and C alleles are not very good, they will spread because of the good B4 allele between them. Eventually the linkage groups will break up because of genetic crossing-over in future generations. But in the meantime, some random version of genes A and C are proliferating in the species simply because they are joined to superior allele B4. And clearly, the A and C alleles are there because of selection—but not because of selection *for* them!

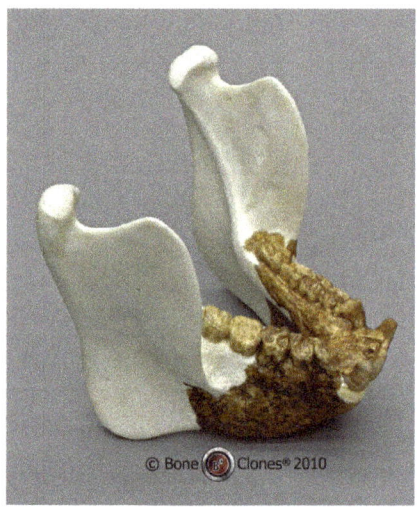

Figure 2.19 Lower jaw of Gigantopithecus.

Fourth, why does the jaw of the Miocene ape *Gigantopithecus* contain a first molar the size of a quarter? Was there something special about the enlarged molar? No, it had enormous jaws and teeth, and the first molar is simply one of them. This is the correlation of parts, the problem with atomizing the organism and imagining the parts to be existing and evolving independently. There is no reason for *Gigantopithecus* to have a large molar; there may well have been a reason that *Gigantopithecus*'s jaws (and, inferentially, head and body) were huge, but framing questions about the size of one tooth will never produce the correct answer (see Figure 2.19).

Fifth, some features are simply consequences of other properties rather than adaptations to external conditions. We already have noted the phenomenon of allometric growth, in which some physical features have to outgrow others simply to maintain function at an increased size. Can we ask the reason for the massive brow ridges of *Homo erectus*, or are brow ridges simply what you get when you have a conjunction of thick skull bones, a large face, and a sloping forehead—and, thus, again would have a cause but no reason?

Sixth, some features may be underutilized and on the way out. What is the reason for our two outer toes? They aren't propulsive, they don't do anything, and sometimes they're just in the way. Obviously they are there because we are descended from pentadactyl tetrapod ancestors. Is it possible that a million years from now, we will just have our three largest toes, just as the ancestors of the horse lost their digits in favor of a single hoof per limb? Or will our outer toes find another use, such as stabilizing the landings in our personal jet-packs? For the time being, we can just recognize vestigiality as another nonadaptive explanation for the presence of a given feature.

Finally, Darwin himself recognized that many obvious features do not help an animal survive. Some things may instead help an animal breed. The peacock's tail feathers do not help it eat, but they do help it mate. There is competition, but only against half of the species; Darwin called this **sexual selection**. Its result is not a fit to the environment but, rather, a fit to the opposite sex. In some species, that is literally the case, as the male and female genitalia have specific ways of anatomically fitting together. The specific form is less important than the specific match, so inquiring about the reason for a particular form of the reproductive anatomy may be misleading. The specific form may be effectively random, as long as it fits the opposite sex and is different from the anatomies of other species. Nor is sexual selection the only form of selection that can affect the body differently from natural selection. Competition might also take place between biological units other than organisms—perhaps genes, perhaps cells, or populations, or species. The spread of cultural things, such as head-binding or cheap refined fructose or forced labor, can have significant effects upon bodies, which are also not adaptations produced by natural selection. They are often adaptive physiological responses to stresses but not the products of natural selection.

Clearly, with so many paths available by which a physical feature might have naturalistically arisen without specifically having been the object of natural selection, it is unwise to simply assume that any individual trait is an adaptation. And that generalization applies to the best-known, best-studied, and most materially based evolutionary adaptations of our lineage. But our cultural behaviors are also highly adaptive, so what about our most familiar social behaviors? Patriarchy, hierarchy, warfare—are these adaptations? Do they have reasons? Are they good for something?

This is where some sloppy thinking has been troublesome. What would it mean to say that patriarchy evolved by natural selection in the human species? If, on the one hand, it means that the human mind evolved by natural selection to be able to create and survive in many different kinds of social and political regimes, of which patriarchy is one (or several), then biological anthropologists will readily agree. If, on the other hand, it means that patriarchy itself evolved by natural selection, that implies that patriarchy is genetically determined (since natural selection is a genetic process) and out-reproduced the alleles for other, more egalitarian, social forms. This in turn would imply that patriarchy is an adaptation and therefore of some beneficial value in the past as well as an ingrained part of human nature today. This would be bad news, say, if you harbored ambitions of dismantling it. Dismantling patriarchy in that case would be to go against nature, a futile gesture. In other words, this latter interpretation would be a naturalistic manifesto for a conservative political platform: don't try to dismantle the patriarchy, because it is within us, the product of evolution—suck it up and live with it.

Here, evolution is being used simply as a political instrument for transforming the human genome into an imaginary glass ceiling against equality. There is thus a convergence between the pseudo-biology of crude adaptationism (the idea that everything is the product of natural selection) and the pseudo-biology of hereditarianism. Naturalizing inequality is not the business of evolutionary theory, and it represents a difficult moral position for a scientist to adopt, as well as a poor scientific position.

MISCONCEPTIONS ABOUT HUMAN EVOLUTION

At root, human evolutionary theory consists of two propositions: (1) that the human species is descended from other similar species and (2) that natural selection has been the primary agency of biological adaptation. Pretty much everything else is subject to some degree of contestation. To conclude this chapter, let us call attention to some of the major corrections we would like to apply to popular misunderstandings of human micro- and macroevolution.

- There is no separation of culture from science, or facts from values, in human evolution.

    As we have seen, the scientific study of who we are and where we come from is not biology. It is a branch of anthropology that overlaps in crucial ways with biology, and yet it also traffics in the world of politics, cultures, moral codes, and histories. This is not to say that other sciences can necessarily be free of culture but simply that it is easier to be objective about boron than about your ancestors. Narratives about ancestors are invariably sacred stories, and biological anthropologists incur an unusual responsibility in being the scientific custodians of our ancestors' stories-writing and validating their stories, shepherding them through history.

- Equality is not identity.

    The great geneticist Theodosius Dobzhansky emphasized the distinction between equality (a political state) and identity (a biological state). Sameness/difference is unrelated to equal/unequal, under our system of government. No matter what kind of person you are, you are entitled to equality. Consequently all discussions of race or sex are irrelevant to questions of rights: All citizens are entitled to equal rights. The difficulty is how to guarantee that all receive them, which is a political issue, because obviously there is a great deal of inequality in America. Patterns of social inequality are not grounded in human biological variation. It has become a moral challenge for the nation and for science to better understand this fact, particularly as critiques of equality are too often accompanied by pseudo-biological arguments.

- All humans are equally close to apes, despite the attempt of some people to question the essential humanity of certain populations by suggesting that some people are more apelike than others.

    The suggestion that some groups of humans are more naturally apelike than others is a recurrent slander of the modern age. Apelike is obviously a synonym for subhuman; and the symbolic association of apes with African peoples is actually a pre-Darwinian slur, from centuries before evolutionary theory was developed. All humans are equally distantly related from the chimpanzee, but some humans, especially people of color, have been symbolically dehumanized throughout modern history by associating them with apes. Consequently, such a comparison is no longer considered funny.

- Competition can take many forms other than overt aggression.

    Some biologists use Darwinism as a way of rationalizing war, arguing that even though war sucks, it is the very competition among political entities that leads to social advances in human history. But even Darwin knew that it wasn't necessarily the case, and it remains a problematic moral position. Darwin's intellectual inspiration here was actually the Scottish economist Adam Smith, whose 1776 book *The Wealth of Nations* is the foundation of modern capitalism. Smith argued that people simply acting in their own best interests in competition with one another would naturally form complex thriving economic systems, which would function to the mutual prosperity of all, as if guided by an "invisible hand." The competition was neither cutthroat nor physical. Today we recognize competition as potentially occurring in many ways and between several different kinds of things, from DNA segments to cultural artifacts. Physical aggression is one way humans have interacted competitively, but there is nothing particularly Darwinian in the attempt to identify merit in war. A conscientious scientist is more interested in ways to avert it.

- There is no "person of the future."

    We do the great bulk of our adapting culturally, although our gene pool is continually being tweaked by diseases and demographic trends. But of course we cannot predict future environments for our descendants to adapt to, culturally or naturally. The idea that our species is simply a way station for the next great step in evolution betrays teleological thinking about history–that is, the idea that history is preset and that there is a path down which we are proceeding. But there is no path; there is only the present and possible solutions to the problems of the present. Consequently, there is no way to know what a "person of the future" might look like. No lateral toes? Maybe. No wisdom teeth? Maybe. A brain the size of a basketball? Not without radically restructuring the maternal anatomy and the birth process. Perhaps with the colonization of other planets, our own species will undergo novel forms of selection and a great deal of founder effect or genetic drift. But their products are inherently unpredictable.

- Evolution is more like a tree than like an escalator.

    Darwin thought of evolution as producing separate branches, like those of a tree, with the tips representing living species. But the word *evolution* implies to many people an unfolding, a development along a path–this is what the word meant initially to Darwin, who avoided it in the first edition of *The Origin of Species*. Teleological theories of evolution have indeed been proposed from time to time, but if we see evolution as divergence rather than improvement, then we reject teleology. When creationists ask, "If we evolved from monkeys, then why are there still monkeys?" they are imagining evolution as a teleological process. The pre-Darwinian evolutionist Lamarck imagined that in the face of extinction a species could survive by changing into something a little higher up on the Great Chain of Being. In such a world, monkeys might constantly be evolving into people, but that is not a branching, Darwinian world. Rather, we would say that our monkey ancestor diverged and eventually became an ape-like creature but did so without necessarily exterminating monkeys in the process. Interestingly, genomics is now revealing that speciation is commonly less complete than we used to imagine, and ostensibly discrete branches sometimes come together. This might call for a new metaphor to describe human evolution, such as the roots of a tree, rather than its branches.

- Bible scholarship does not conflict with science.

    Contemporary scholars recognize that the Bible is a collection of traditional stories and tales, culled from a larger set of writings from various times and places and later collected into a single volume. They have meant, and continue to mean, different things to different communities. For many centuries, scholars have studied what the texts mean, assuming that the Bible's meanings are neither obvious nor literal but relevant to the lives of worshippers in any specific time and place and denomination. Consequently, there can be no "true meaning" of the Bible, only the most useful and appropriate meaning for the particular community. Biblical literalism is a very recent phenomenon, independent of the centuries-old humanistic traditions of biblical scholarship, and it demands a very selective and arbitrary approach to the texts chosen to be taken literally. The creationist today thus rejects not merely modern scientific scholarship but modern biblical scholarship as well. Nevertheless, many Jewish, Catholic, and Protestant scholars, as well as scholars from other religious traditions in the modern age, are actively engaged in understanding what it means to lead a fulfilled life in a post-Darwinian world.

Now that you've finished this chapter on evolution, you are equipped to go into the post-Darwinian world armed with an understanding of the true intentions of Darwin's work, and where his findings part from past and current racist misinterpretations of his theories. You understand that politics is often inseparable from biology, no matter the best intentions toward objectivity of the scientist.

Review Questions

- How is the study of your ancestors biopolitical, not just biological? Does that make it less scientific or differently scientific?
- What was gained by reducing organisms to genotypes and species to gene pools? What is gained by reintroducing bodies and species into evolutionary studies?
- How do genetic or molecular studies complement anatomical studies of evolution?
- How are you reducible to your ancestry? If you could meet your ancestors from the year 1700 (and you would have well over a thousand of them!), would their lives be meaningfully similar to yours? Would you even be able to communicate with them?
- The molecular biologist François Jacob argued that evolution is more like a tinkerer than like an engineer. In what ways do we seem like precisely engineered machinery, and in what ways do we seem like jerry-rigged or improvised contraptions?

Key Terms

Adam and Eve: According to the Bible (Genesis 2–3), the first two people are Adam (man) and Eve (life). They inhabit The Garden of Eden, with a Tree of Life and a Tree of the Knowledge of Good and Evil in the center. They are instructed not to eat the fruit of the latter tree, but they do so anyway and are subsequently cursed and expelled from the garden. This forms the basis for the traditional origin myth of Jews, Muslims and Christians.

Adaptation: A fit between the organism and environment.

Allele: A genetic variant.

Blending Inheritance: Heredity conceptualized as a mixture of fluids. Its opposite would be particulate inheritance, where heredity is regarded as the interaction of discrete elements and provides the basis of Mendelian genetics.

Canalization: The tendency of a growing organism to be buffered toward normal development.

Descent with Modification: Darwin's term for what we now call "evolution," in which animals and plants look different from their ancestors.

Epigenetics: The study of how genetically identical cells and organisms (with the same DNA base sequence) can nevertheless differ in stably inherited ways.

Epistemes: Fundamental cultural ideas, which organize the world and help to render it meaningful. Similar to paradigm.

Eugenics: An idea that was popular in the 1920s that society should be improved by breeding better kinds of people.

Evo-devo: The study of the origin of form; a contraction of "evolutionary developmental biology."

Exaptation: An additional beneficial use for a biological feature.

Extinction: The loss of a species from the face of the earth.

Founder Effect: The reduced genetic diversity that results when a population is descended from a small number of ancestors.

Gene: A stretch of DNA with an identifiable function (sometimes broadened to include any DNA with recognizable structural features as well).

Gene Flow: Geographical movement of genes, due to the contact of populations.

Gene Pool: Hypothetical summation of the entire genetic composition of population or species.

Genetic Drift: Random, short-term perturbations to the gene pool, with nonadaptive effects.

Genotype: Genetic constitution of an individual organism.

Hereditarianism: The idea that genes or ancestry is the most crucial or salient element in a human life. Generally associated with an argument for natural inequality on pseudo-genetic grounds.

Homology: Correspondence of parts between species due to the mutual inheritance of a primordial form from a common ancestor.

Inheritance of Acquired Characteristics: The idea that you pass on the features that developed during your lifetime, not just your genes; also known as Lamarckian inheritance.

Monogenism: The idea that all people share a common single origin.

Mutation: An alteration to the base sequence of DNA.

Natural Selection: A consistent bias in survival and fertility, leading to the over-representation of certain features in future generations and an improved fit between an average member of the population and the environment.

Niche Construction: The active engagement by which species transform their surroundings in favorable ways, rather than passively inhabiting them.

Noah's Ark: According to the Bible (Genesis 6–9), God decides to destroy all life because of the wickedness of people, but he saves a righteous man named Noah, his three sons, and their wives. They build a large boat and preserve pairs of all the animals; the boat eventually lands "on the mountains of Ararat" and the world is subsequently repopulated. Other ancient cultures also have cognate myths about a flood, boat-builder, and animal-saver, with differing details.

Phenotype: Observable manifestation of a genetic constitution, expressed in a particular set of circumstances.

Plasticity: The tendency of a growing organism to react developmentally to its particular conditions of life.

Polygenism: The idea that different peoples have different origins.

Phrenology: The 19th century anatomical study of bumps on the head as an indication of personality and mental abilities.

Punctuated Equilibria: The idea that species are stable through time and are formed very rapidly relative to their duration. (The opposite, that species are unstable and constantly changing through time, is called phyletic gradualism.)

Savage: A dehumanizing term used by pre-modern European scholars to suggest that other cultures were primitive, violent, immoral, and illogical.

Sexual Selection: Natural selection arising through preference by one sex for certain characteristics in individuals of the other sex.

Synonymous Mutation: A change in the DNA sequence that codes for amino acids in a protein sequence, but does not change the encoded amino acid.

Synthetic Theory of Evolution: Explains the evolution of life in terms of genetic changes occurring in the population that leads to the formation of new species.

Species Selection: A postulated evolutionary process in which selection acts on an entire species population, rather than individuals.

Teleological: The explanation of phenomena in terms of the purpose they serve rather than of the cause by which they arise.

Tower of Babel: According to the Bible (Genesis 11), all people once spoke a single language and decided to cooperate to build a giant tower that would stretch into the heavens. For this arrogance, they are made to speak different languages and must give up building the tower. The story's setting is generally thought to refer to the ancient ziggurats of Babylonia.

Transmutation Hypothesis: The nineteenth century idea that life forms were spontaneously generated and not descended from a common ancestor.

About the Author

Jonathan Marks

University of North Carolina at Charlotte, Jmarks@uncc.edu

Jonathan Marks

Jonathan Marks is Professor of Anthropology at the University of North Carolina at Charlotte. He has published many books and articles on broad aspects of biological anthropology. In 2006 he was elected a Fellow of the American Association for the Advancement of Science. In 2012 he was awarded the First Citizen's Bank Scholar's Medal from UNC Charlotte. In recent years he has been a Visiting Research Fellow at the ESRC Genomics Forum in Edinburgh, at the Max Planck Institute for the History of Science in Berlin, and a Templeton Fellow at the Institute for Advanced Study at Notre Dame. His work has received the W. W. Howells Book Prize and the General Anthropology Division Prize for Exemplary Cross-Field Scholarship from the American Anthropological Association as well as the J. I. Staley Prize from the School for Advanced Research. Two of his books are called *What It Means to Be 98% Chimpanzee* and *Why I Am Not a Scientist*, but actually he is about 98 percent scientist and not a chimpanzee.

For Further Exploration

Ackermann, Rebecca Rogers, Alex Mackay, and Michael L. Arnold. 2016. "The Hybrid Origin of 'Modern' Humans." *Evolutionary Biology* 43 (1): 1–11.

Bateson, Patrick, and Peter Gluckman. 2011. *Plasticity, Robustness, Development and Evolution*. New York: Cambridge University Press.

Cosans, Christopher E. 2009. *Owen's Ape and Darwin's Bulldog: Beyond Darwinism and Creationism*. Bloomington, IN: Indiana University Press.

Desmond, Adrian, and James Moore. 2009. *Darwin's Sacred Cause: How a Hatred of Slavery Shaped Darwin's Views on Human Evolution*. New York: Houghton Mifflin Harcourt.

Dobzhansky, Theodosius, Francisco J. Ayala, G. Ledyard Stebbins, and James W. Valentine. 1977. *Evolution*. San Francisco: W.H. Freeman and Company.

Fuentes, Agustín. 2017. *The Creative Spark: How Imagination Made Humans Exceptional*. New York: Dutton.

Gould, Stephen J. 2003. *The Structure of Evolutionary Theory*. Cambridge, MA: Harvard University Press.

Haraway, Donna J. 1989. *Primate Visions: Gender, Race, and Nature in the World of Modern Science*. New York: Routledge.

Huxley, Thomas. 1863. *Evidence as to Man's Place in Nature*. London: Williams & Norgate.

Jablonka, Eva, and Marion J. Lamb. 2005. *Evolution in Four Dimensions: Genetic, Epigenetic, Behavioral, and Symbolic Variation in the History of Life*. Cambridge, MA: The MIT Press.

Kuklick, Henrika, ed. 2008. *A New History of Anthropology*. New York: Blackwell.

Laland, Kevin N., Tobias Uller, Marcus W. Feldman, Kim Sterelny, Gerd B. Muller, Armin Moczek, Eva Jablonka, and John Odling-Smee. 2015. "The Extended Evolutionary Synthesis: Its Structure, Assumptions and Predictions." *Proceedings of the Royal Society, Series B*, 282 (1813): 20151019.

Lamarck, Jean Baptiste. 1809. *Philosophie Zoologique*. Paris: Dentu.

Landau, Misia. 1991. *Narratives of Human Evolution*. New Haven: Yale University Press.

Lee, Sang-Hee. 2017. *Close Encounters with Humankind: A Paleoanthropologist Investigates Our Evolving Species*. New York: W. W. Norton.

Livingstone, David N. 2008. *Adam's Ancestors: Race, Religion, and the Politics of Human Origins*. Baltimore: Johns Hopkins University Press.

Marks, Jonathan. 2015. *Tales of the Ex-Apes: How We Think about Human Evolution*. Berkeley, CA: University of California Press.

Pigliucci, Massimo. 2009. "The Year in Evolutionary Biology 2009: An Extended Synthesis for Evolutionary Biology." *Annals of the New York Academy of Sciences* 1168: 218–228.

Simpson, George Gaylord. 1949. *The Meaning of Evolution: A Study of the History of Life and of Its Significance for Man*. New Haven: Yale University Press.

Sommer, Marianne. 2016. *History Within: The Science, Culture, and Politics of Bones, Organisms, and Molecules*. Chicago: University of Chicago Press.

Stoczkowski, Wiktor. 2002. *Explaining Human Origins: Myth, Imagination and Conjecture*. New York: Cambridge University Press.

Tattersall, Ian, and Rob DeSalle. 2019. *The Accidental Homo sapiens: Genetics, Behavior, and Free Will*. New York: Pegasus.

References

Darwin, Charles. 1859. *On the origin of species by means of natural selection, or, the preservation of favoured races in the struggle for life*. London: J. Murray.

Darwin, Charles. 1869. *Correspondence Project*. "Letter no. 6684," accessed on 11 July 2019, http://www.darwinproject.ac.uk/DCP-LETT-6684

Eldredge, N., and S. J. Gould. 1972. "Punctuated equilibria: an alternative to phyletic gradualism." In *Models in Paleobiology*, ed.by T. J. Schopf, 82-115. San Francisco: W. H. Freeman.

Haeckel, Ernst. 1868. *Natürliche Schöpfungsgeschichte*. Berlin: Reimer.

Kellogg, Vernon. 1917. *Headquarters Nights*. Boston: The Atlantic Monthly Press.

Monypenny, William Flavelle, and George Earle Buckle. 1929. *The Life of Benjamin Disraeli, Earl of Beaconsfield. Volume II. 1860–1881*. London: John Murray.

Punnett, R. C. 1905. *Mendelism*. Cambridge: Macmillan and Bowes.

Tylor, Edward B. 1871. *Primitive Culture*. London: John Murray.

Wood, Andrew R. et al. 2014. Defining the role of common variation in the genomic and biological architecture of adult human height. *Nature Genetics* 46:1173-1186.

Figure Attributions

Figure 2.1 Affe-tyson by Benutzer:Bradypus, originally called "Orang-Outang" (but in fact a chimpanzee) by Edward Tyson, is in the public domain.

Figure 2.2A Ring-tailed lemur portrait 2 by Francis C. Franklin is used under a CC-BY-SA-3.0 License.

Figure 2.2B Lemur (39490547425) by Mathias Appel has been designated to the public domain (CC0).

Figure 2.2C Lemur (26992319228) by Mathias Appel has been designated to the public domain (CC0).

Figure 2.2D Blue-eyed black lemur by Clément Bardot is used under a CC BY-SA 4.0 License.

Figure 2.3 Grotte de Rouff mammut by cave painter is in the public domain.

Figure 2.4 Queensland State Archives 2436 Trilobite fossil at the Queensland Museum Brisbane c 1927 by Agriculture And Stock Department, Publicity Branch is in the public domain.

Figure 2.5A Pet (pet-dog-animals-cute-animal-dogs-3635986/) by Somo_Photography has been designated to the public domain (CC0).

Figure 2.5B English bulldog (2705136) by mk817 has been designated to the public domain (CC0) .

Figure 2.5C ItalianGreyhound by Just chaos is used under a CC BY 2.0 license.

Figure 2.6 Ernst Haeckel – Natürliche Schöpfungsgeschichte, 1868 by Foto H.-P.Haack Das Foto darf gebührenfrei verwendet werden, sofern der Urheber mit "Foto H.-P.Haack" vermerkt wird. is used under a CC BY-SA 3.0 DE license.

Figure 2.7 Blending inheritance in color original to Explorations: An Open Invitation to Biological Anthropology by Mary Nelson is under a CC BY-NC 4.0 License.

Figure 2.8 George Gaylord Simpson (1983) photo courtesy of Jonathan Mark is under a CC BY-NC 4.0 License.

Figure 2.9A Horse (pferd-tier-säugetier-reiten-153500) by openclipart-vectors-30363 has been designated to the public domain (CC0).

Figure 2.9B Donkey by papapishu has been designated to the public domain (CC0).

Figure 2.10 Dentition of Ramapithecus – Fossil – Human Evolution Gallery – Indian Museum – Kolkata 2014-04-04 4499 by Biswarup Ganguly is under a CC BY-NC 4.0 License.

Figure 2.11 Human and ape DNA comparisons original to Explorations: An Open Invitation to Biological Anthropology is under a CC BY-NC 4.0 License.

Figure 2.12 Phyletic gradualism vs. punctuated equilibria original to Explorations: An Open Invitation to Biological Anthropology is under a CC BY-NC 4.0 License.

Figure 2.13 Mouse and elephant skeletons original to Explorations: An Open Invitation to Biological Anthropology is under a CC BY-NC 4.0 License.

Figure 2.14A Healthy human t cell by NIAID is under a CC BY 2.0 License.

Figure 2.14B Star shaped brain cells (astrocytes) by NIH (Pasca Lab, Stanford University) is under a CC BY-NC 2.0 License.

Figure 2.14C Embryonic smooth muscle cell by NIH (National Institute of Dental and Craniofacial Research, National Institutes of Health) is under a CC BY-NC 2.0 License.

Figure 2.14D Human liver cell by NIH (Donna Beer Stolz, University of Pittsburgh) is under a CC BY-NC 2.0 License.

Figure 2.14E Hair cells: the sound-sensing cells in the ear by NIH (Henning Horn, Brian Burke and Colin Stewart, Institute of Medical Biology, Agency for Science, Technology, and Research, Singapore) is under a CC BY-NC 2.0 License.

Figure 2.15 Gallery 14: Eugenics Exhibit at the Kansas State Free Fair, 1920 ID (ID 16328) by Cold Spring Harbor (Courtesy American Philisophical Society) is under a CC BY-NC-ND 3.0 License.

Figure 2.16 Human and chimpanzee hand original to Explorations: An Open Invitation to Biological Anthropology is under a CC BY-NC 4.0 License.

Figure 2.17 Phrenology; Chart (slide number 5278, photo number: L0000992) by Wellcome Collection, original from The Phrenological Journal (Know Thyself), print from Dr. E. Clark is under a CC BY 4.0 license.

Figure 2.18 Chimpanzee head sketch by Roger Zenner, original by Brehms Tierleben (1887), is in the public domain.

Figure 2.19 Gigantopithecus blacki Jaw Only "Reconstruction" by ©BoneClones is used by permission and available here under a CC BY-NC 4.0 License.

Chapter 3: Molecular Biology and Genetics:

Hayley Mann, M.A., Binghamton University

Xazmin Lowman, Ph.D., University of California, Irvine

Malaina Gaddis, Ph.D.

> *Learning Objectives*
>
> - Define terms useful to molecular biology and genetics.
> - Explain and identify the purpose of both DNA replication and the cell cycle.
> - Identify key differences between mitosis and meiosis.
> - Outline the process of protein synthesis including transcription and translation.
> - Use principles of Mendelian inheritance to predict genotypes and phenotypes of future generations.
> - Explain complexities surrounding patterns of genetic inheritance and polygenic traits.
> - Discuss challenges to and bioethical concerns of genetic testing.

I [Hayley Mann] started my Bachelor's degree in 2003, which was the same year the Human Genome Project released its first draft sequence. I initially declared a genetics major because I thought it sounded cool. However, upon taking an actual class, I discovered that genetics was *challenging*. In addition to my genetics major, I signed up for biological anthropology classes and soon learned that anthropology could bring all those molecular lessons to life. For instance, we are composed of cells, proteins, nucleic acids, carbohydrates, and lipids. Anthropologists often include these molecules in their studies to identify how humans vary; if there are meaningful differences, they propose theories to explain them.

Since the release of the first human genome sequence, the field of *genetics* has grown into *genomics*. Researchers now address these complex questions on a large scale. To process "big data," some scientists have moved to working on a computer full time doing computational biology. As you learned in Chapter 1, molecular anthropologists use genetics to compare ancient and modern populations as well as study nonhuman primates. Molecular anthropologists must also stay current with advancing technology (you will learn about the results of some of this genomic research as it has been applied to fossils in Chapters 11 and 12). If you wish to be part of this dynamic field, then take advantage of available campus laboratory classes and internships and also never stop reading scientific papers.

This chapter provides the basics for understanding human variation and how the evolutionary process works. A few advanced genetics topics are also presented because biotechnology is now commonplace in health and society. Understanding the science behind this remarkable field means you will be able to participate in bioethical and anthropological discussions as well as make more informed decisions regarding genetic testing.

CELLS AND MOLECULES

Molecules of Life

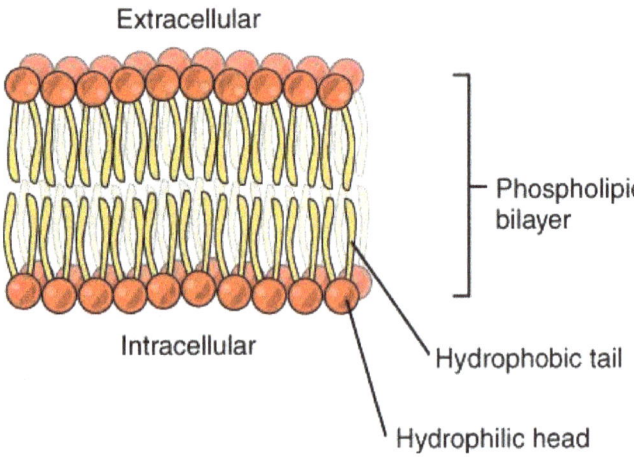

Figure 3.1 Phospholipid molecules forming a bilayer with their hydrophobic tails and hydrophilic heads.

Organisms are composed of four basic types of molecules that are essential for cell structure and function: proteins, lipids, carbohydrates, and nucleic acids. **Proteins** are strings of amino acids that are often folded into complex 3-D shapes. The structure of **lipids** can be described as having a hydrophilic (water-loving) head and a hydrophobic (water-repelling) tail (Figure 3.1). When lipids are chained together, they form more-complex molecules called fats and triglycerides. **Carbohydrates** are composed of carbon and hydrogen atoms that can be broken down to supply energy for an organism. Lastly, **nucleic acids** carry genetic information about a living organism.

Probably the most familiar nucleic acid is **deoxyribonucleic acid (DNA)**. DNA comprises a **sugar phosphate backbone and nucleotides** (Figure 3.2). (More details on the physical structure of DNA and what information DNA nucleotides provide will be discussed later.) Anthropologists can analyze sequences of DNA nucleotides and determine how different organisms are related to each other, since they all have their own unique DNA *genetic code*. In the case of humans, forensic scientists can identify individuals by analyzing 20 different short **DNA sequences** known as "CODIS Core Loci." Another nucleic acid is called **ribonucleic acid (RNA)**. One type of RNA molecule is responsible for chaining amino acids together in order to build proteins (Figure 3.3 and Figure 3.4). How RNA synthesizes amino acids into proteins will be reviewed further on in the chapter.

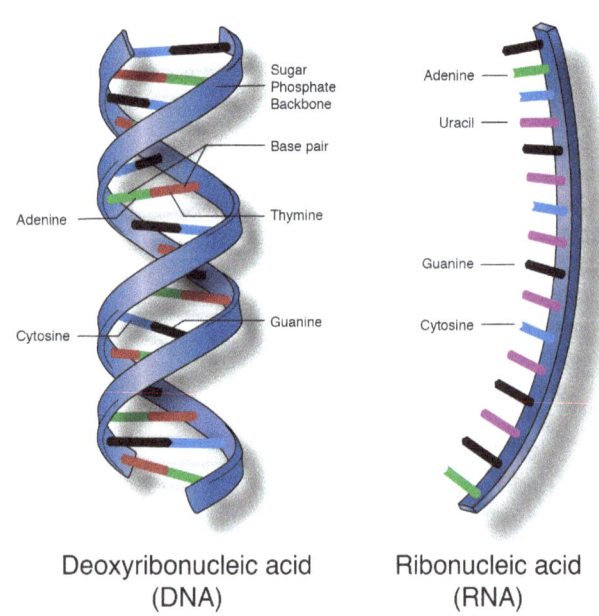

Figure 3.2 Structural components that form double-stranded nucleic acid (DNA) or single-stranded nucleic acid (RNA).

Molecular Biology and Genetics | 59

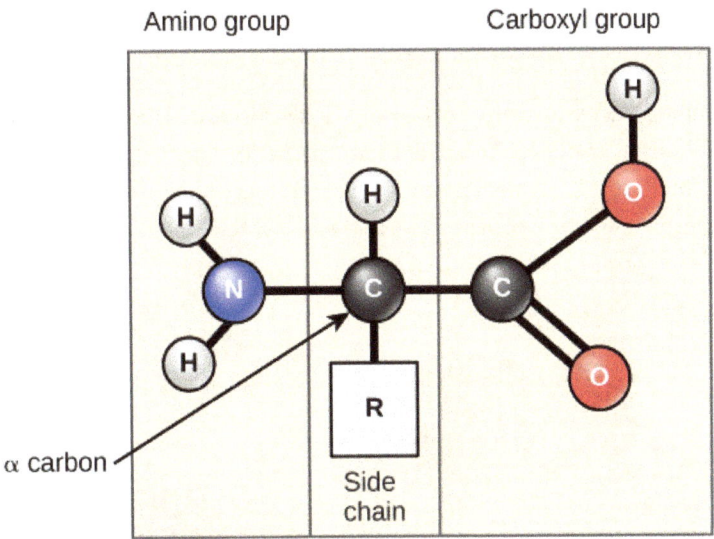

Figure 3.3 Chemical elements that characterize an amino acid. C: carbon; N: Nitrogen; O: Oxygen; H: Hydrogen.

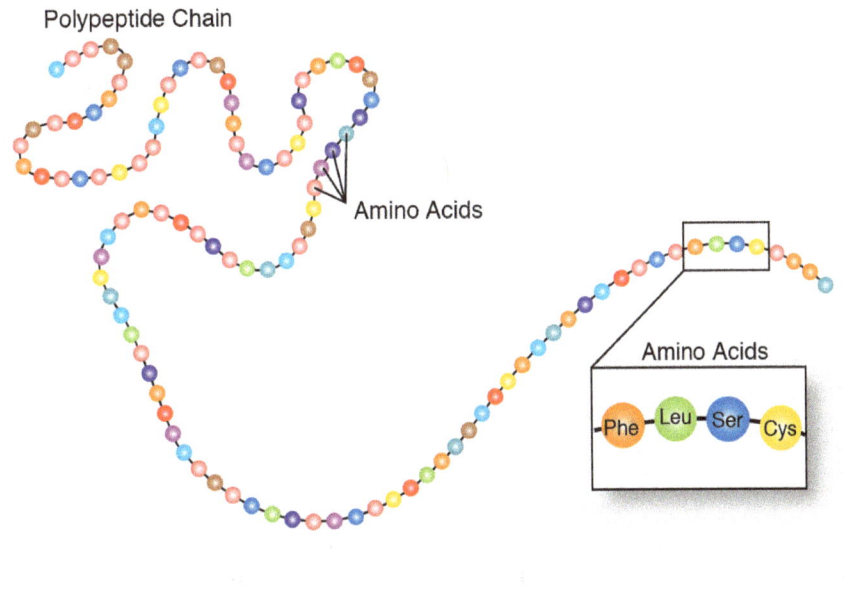

Amino Acids

Ala: Alanine	Gln: Glutamine	Leu: Leucine	Ser: Serine
Arg: Arginine	Glu: Glutamic acid	Lys: Lysine	Thr: Threonine
Asn: Asparagine	Gly: Glycine	Met: Methionine	Trp: Tryptophane
Asp: Aspartic acid	His: Histidine	Phe: Phenylalanine	Tyr: Tyrosisne
Cys: Cysteine	Ile: Isoleucine	Pro: Proline	Val: Valine

Figure 3.4 Amino acids (20 different types) strung together form a polypeptide chain.

Cells

In 1665, Robert Hooke observed slices of plant cork using a microscope. Hooke noted that the microscopic plant structures he saw resembled *cella*, meaning "a small room" in Latin. Approximately two centuries later, biologists recognized the cell as being the most fundamental unit of life and that all life is composed of cells. Cellular organisms can be characterized as two main cell types: **prokaryotes** and **eukaryotes**.

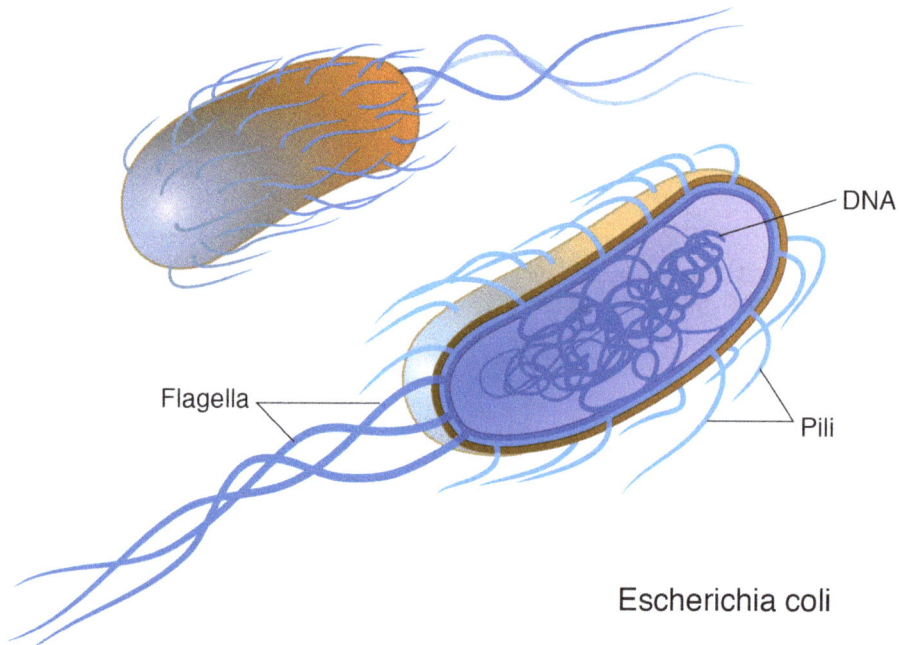

Figure 3.5 A representation of the single-celled body of E. coli bacteria.

Prokaryotes include bacteria and archaea, and they are composed of a single cell. Additionally, their DNA and **organelles** are not surrounded by individual membranes. Thus, no compartments separate their DNA from the rest of the cell (Figure 3.5). It is well known that some bacteria can cause illness in humans. For instance, *Escherichia coli* (*E. coli*) and *Salmonella* contamination can result in food poisoning symptoms. Pneumonia and strep throat are caused by *Streptococcal* bacteria. *Neisseria gonorrhoeae* is a bacterial sexually transmitted disease. Although bacteria are commonly associated with illness, not all bacteria are harmful. For example, researchers are studying the relationship between the **microbiome** and human health. The bacteria that are part of the healthy human microbiome perform beneficial roles, such as food digestion, boosting the immune system, and even making vitamins (e.g., B12 and K).

Archaea, the other type of prokaryotic organism, were once believed to be closely related to bacteria. However, it was determined through genetic analysis that archaea have their own distinct evolutionary lineage so biologists reclassified them into their own taxonomic domain. Archaea were discovered living in extreme environments and are therefore known as "extremophiles." For example, archaea can be found in high temperatures, such as Old Faithful Geyser in Yellowstone National Park.

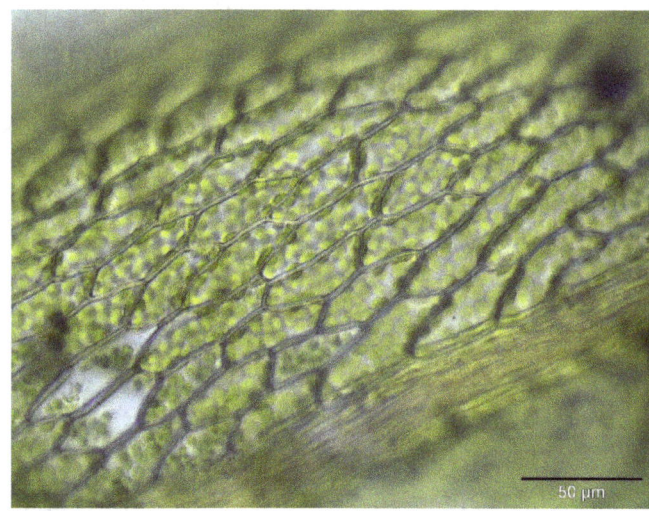

Eukaryotes can be single-celled or multicelled in their body composition. In contrast to prokaryotes, eukaryotes possess membranes that surround their DNA and organelles. An example of a single-celled eukaryote is the microscopic algae found in ponds (phytoplankton), which can produce oxygen from the sun. Yeasts are also single-celled, and fungi can be single- or multicellular. Plants and animals are all multicellular.

Figure 3.6 A microscopic view of plant cell membranes.

Although plant and animal cells have a surprising number of similarities, there are some key differences. For example, plant cells possess a thick outer cell membrane made of a fibrous carbohydrate called cellulose (Figure 3.6). Animal and plant cells also have different **tissues**. A tissue is an aggregation of cells that are morphologically similar and perform the same task. For most plants, the outermost layer of cells forms a waxy cuticle that helps to protect the cells and to prevent water loss. However, humans have skin, the outermost cell layer of which is mostly composed of a tough protein called keratin. Overall, humans have a diversity of tissue types (e.g., cartilage, brain, and heart).

Animal Cell Organelles

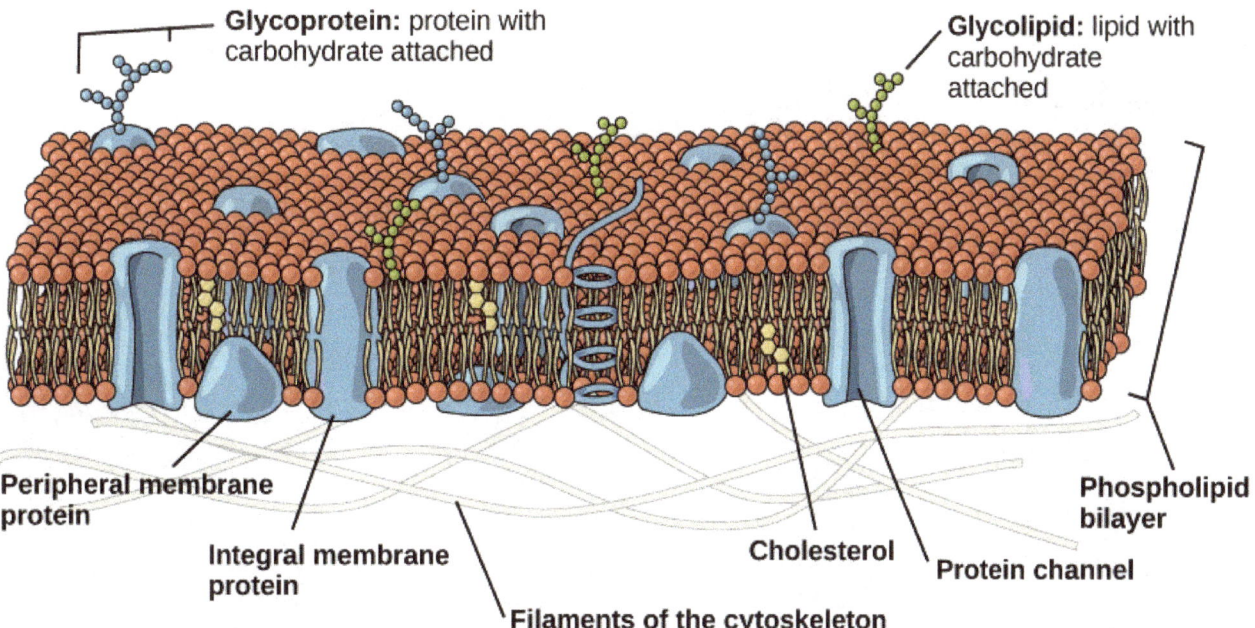

Figure 3.7 A phospholipid bilayer with membrane-bound carbohydrates and proteins.

An animal cell is surrounded by a double membrane called the **phospholipid bilayer** (Figure 3.7). A closer look reveals that this protective barrier is made of lipids and proteins that provide structure and function for cellular activities. For example, lipids and proteins embedded in the cell's membrane work together to regulate the passage of molecules and ions (e.g., H_2O and sodium) into and out of the cell. **Cytoplasm** is the jelly-like matrix inside of the cell membrane. Part of the cytoplasm comprises organelles, which perform different specialized tasks for the cell (Figure 3.8). An example of an organelle is the **nucleus**, where the cell's DNA is located (Figure 3.9). The double membrane that encloses the nucleus is known as the **nuclear envelope**; its purpose is to regulate molecules into and out of the nucleus and serve as a barrier to protect DNA integrity.

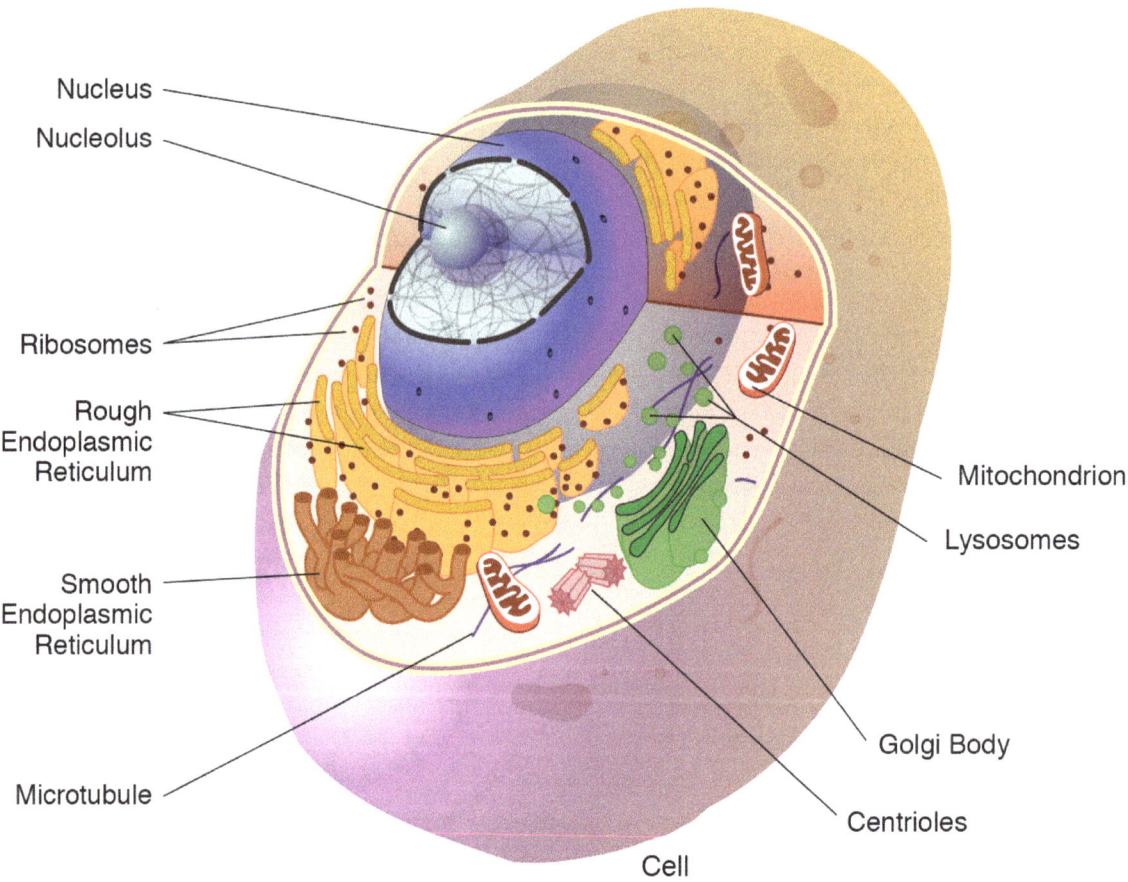

Figure 3.8 An animal cell with membrane-enclosed organelles.

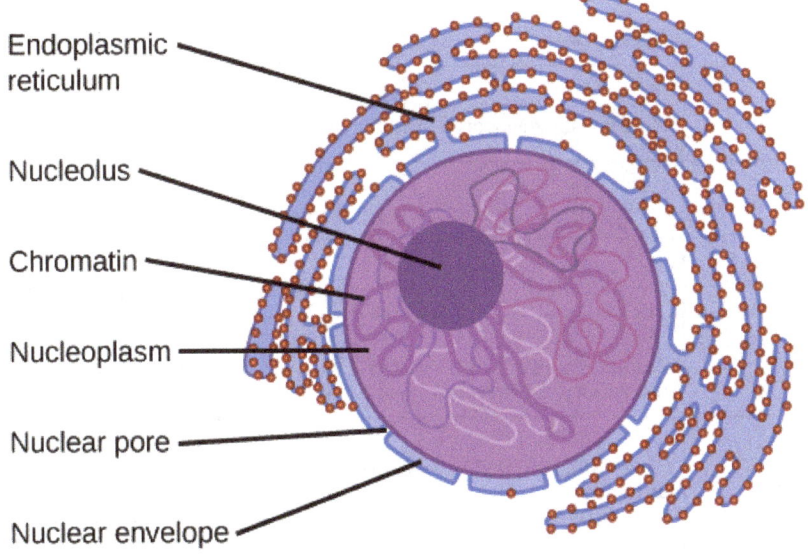

Figure 3.9 A membrane-enclosed nucleus of an animal cell.

Another important organelle is the **mitochondrion** (Figure 3.10). Mitochondria are often referred to as "powerhouse centers" because they produce energy for the cell in the form of **adenosine triphosphate (ATP)**. Depending on the species and tissue type, multicellular eukaryotes can have hundreds to thousands of mitochondria in each of their cells. Scientists have determined that mitochondria played an important role in the evolution of the eukaryotic cell. Mitochondria were once *symbiotic* prokaryotic organisms (i.e., helpful bacteria) that transformed into cellular organelles over time. Because mitochondria used to be separate organisms, this explains why mitochondria also have their own DNA, called **mitochondrial DNA (mtDNA)**. All organelles have important physiological functions, and when they cannot perform their role optimally, it can result in disease. For example, there are mitochondrial diseases for which cells have abnormally less mitochondria. In humans, this leads to various neurological symptoms and disorders. Figure 3.11 lists other organelles found in the cell and their specialized cellular roles.

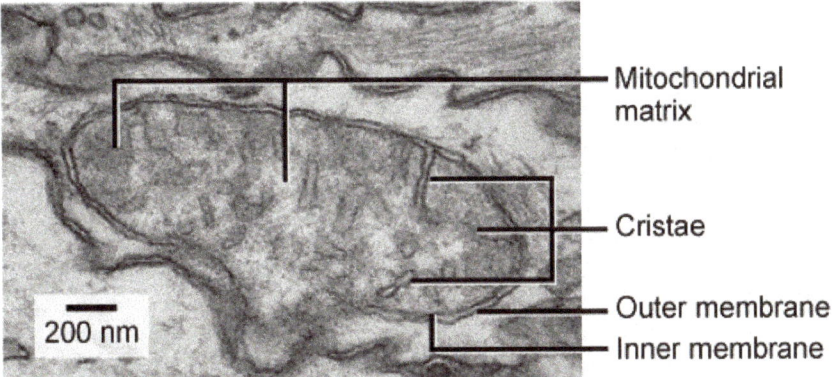

Figure 3.10 Microscopic view of an animal mitochondrion organelle.

Cell structure	Description
Cytoplasm	Fluid substance located inside of cell membrane that contains organelles
Nucleopore	Pores in the nuclear envelope that are selectively permeable
Nucleus	Contains the cell's DNA and is surrounded by the nuclear envelope
Nucleolus	Resides inside of the nucleus and is the site of ribosomal RNA (rRNA) transcription, processing, and assembly
Mitochondrion	Responsible for cellular respiration, where energy is produced by converting nutrients into ATP
Ribosome	Located in the cytoplasm and also the membrane of the rough endoplasmic reticulum. Messenger RNA (mRNA) binds to ribosomes and proteins are synthesized
Endoplasmic reticulum (ER)	Continuous membrane with the nucleus that helps transport, synthesize, modify, and fold proteins. Rough ER has embedded ribosomes, whereas smooth ER lacks ribosomes
Golgi body	Layers of flattened sacs that receive and transmit messages from the ER to secrete and transport proteins within the cell
Lysosome	Located in the cytoplasm and contains enzymes to degrade cellular components
Microtubule	Involved with cellular movement including intracellular transport and cell division
Centrioles	Assist with the organization of mitotic spindles which extend and contract for the purpose of cellular movement during mitosis and meiosis

Figure 3.11 Names of organelles and their cellular functions.

INTRODUCTION TO GENETICS

Genetics is the study of heredity. Parents pass down their genetic traits to their offspring. Although children resemble their parents, traits often vary in appearance or molecular function. For example, two parents with normal color vision can sometimes produce a son with red-green colorblindness. Patterns of genetic inheritance will be discussed in a later section. Molecular geneticists study the biological mechanisms responsible for creating variation between individuals, such as DNA **mutations** (see Chapter 4), cell division, and genetic regulation.

Molecular anthropologists use genetic data to test anthropological questions. Although their interests are diverse, areas of molecular anthropology research include the following: human origins, dispersals, evolution, adaptation, demography, health, disease, behavior, and animal domestication. In addition to conducting research in a laboratory, molecular anthropologists also work in the field with different communities of people. Some anthropologists also study DNA from individuals who have been deceased for decades—even hundreds or thousands of years. The study of **ancient DNA (aDNA)** has led to the development of specialized laboratory techniques. Over time, the DNA in skeletons of ancient individuals becomes degraded (i.e., less intact), which is why careful methodological considerations must be taken. A recent example of an aDNA study is provided in Special Topic: Native American Immunity and European Diseases, and another will be presented in Chapter 10.

SPECIAL TOPIC: FOCUS ON NATIVE AMERICAN IMMUNITY AND EUROPEAN DISEASES—A STUDY OF ANCIENT DNA

Figure 3.12a Tsimshian Native Americans of the Pacific Northwest Coast.

Beginning in the early 15th century, Native Americans progressively suffered from high mortality rates as the result of colonization from foreign powers. European-borne diseases such as measles, tuberculosis, influenza, and smallpox are largely responsible for the population collapse of indigenous peoples in the Americas. Many Europeans who immigrated to the New World had lived in large sedentary populations, which also included coexisting with domestic animals and pests. Although a few prehistoric Native American populations can be characterized as large agricultural societies (especially in Mesoamerica), their overall culture, community lifestyle, and subsistence practices were markedly different from that of Europeans. Therefore, because they did not share the same urban living environments as Europeans, it is believed that Native Americans were susceptible to old-world diseases.

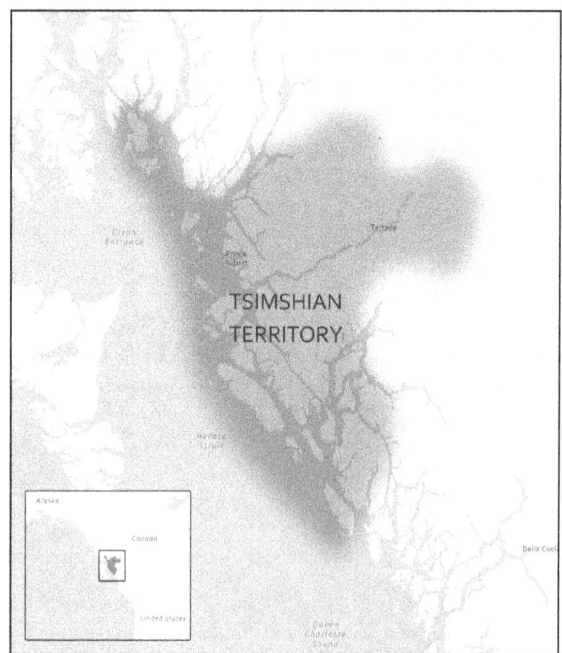

In 2016, a *Nature* article published by John Lindo and colleagues was the first to investigate whether pre-contact Native Americans possessed a genetic susceptibility to European diseases. Their study included Tsimshians, a First Nation community from British Columbia (Figure 3.12). The DNA from both present-day and ancient individuals (who lived between 500 and 6,000 years ago) was analyzed. The research team discovered that a change occurred in the genetic region HLADQ-1, which is a member of the major histocompatibility complex (MHC) immune system molecules. These molecules are responsible for detecting and triggering an immune response against pathogens. Lindo and colleagues (2016) concluded that HLADQ-1 helped Native Americans adapt to their local environmental ecology. However, when European-borne epidemics occurred in the Northwest during the 1800s, a certain HLADQ-1 DNA sequence associated with ancient Tsimshian immunity was no longer adaptive.

Figure 3.12b Tsimshian territory in present-day British Columbia.

As the result of past selective pressures from European diseases, present-day Tsimshians have a different frequency of HLADQ-1 sequences. The precise role that HLADQ-1 plays in immune adaptation still requires further investigation. But overall, this study serves as an example of how studying ancient DNA from the remains of deceased individuals can help provide insight into living human populations and historical events.

DNA Carries Hereditary Information

Surprisingly, the study of inheritance preceded the discovery of DNA. For a period of time, it was believed that proteins carried the hereditary information passed from parents to offspring. Then, in 1944, Oswald Avery, Colin MacLeod, and Maclyn McCarty discovered an association between extracted nucleic acids and the success of their bacterial genetic experiments. Specifically, they demonstrated that DNA was the molecule responsible for the genetic transformation of their pneumonia bacterial strains. Although this was revolutionary work at the time, the field of molecular biology did not fully embrace their findings (it has also been suggested that they were overlooked for a Nobel Prize). It was eventually accepted by the scientific community that DNA is the hereditary material of an organism, especially after the chemical structure of DNA was revealed.

DNA Structure

The 1953 discovery of the molecular structure of DNA was one of the greatest scientific achievements of all time. Using X-ray crystallography, Rosalind Franklin (Figure 3.13) provided the image that clearly showed the double helix shape of DNA. However, due to a great deal of controversy, Franklin's colleague and outside associates received greater publicity for the discovery. In 1962, James Watson, Francis Crick, and Maurice Wilkins received a Nobel Prize for developing a biochemical model of DNA. Unfortunately, Rosalind Franklin had passed away in 1958 from ovarian cancer. In current times, Franklin's important contribution and her reputation as a skilled scientist are widely acknowledged.

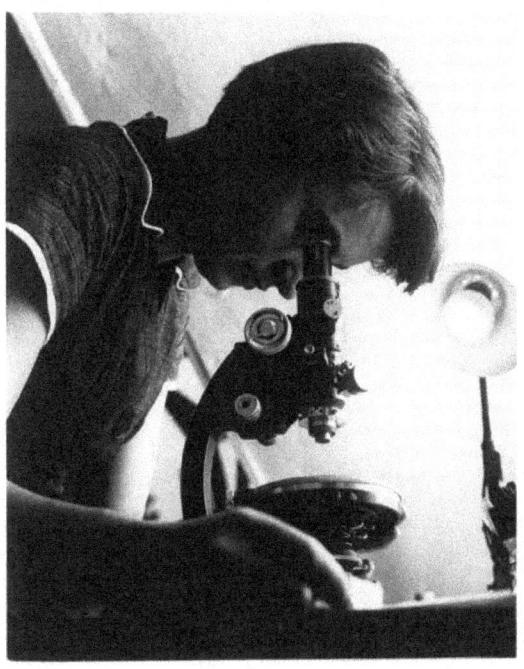

Figure 3.13 Chemist and X-ray crystallographer Rosalind Franklin.

The double helix shape of DNA can be described as a twisted ladder (refer back to Figure 3.2). More specifically, DNA is a double-stranded molecule with its two strands oriented in opposite directions (i.e., antiparallel). Each strand is composed of nucleotides with a sugar phosphate backbone. There are four different types of DNA nucleotides: adenine (A), thymine (T), cytosine (C), and guanine (G). The two DNA strands are held together by nucleotide **base pairs**, which have chemical bonding rules. The complementary base-pairing rules are as follows: A and T bond with each other, while C and G form a bond. The chemical bonds between A–T and C–G are formed by "weak" hydrogen atom interactions, which means the two strands can be easily separated. A DNA sequence is the order of nucleotide bases (A, T, G, C) along only one DNA strand. If one DNA strand has the sequence CATGCT, then the other strand will have a complementary sequence GTACGA. This is an example of a short DNA sequence. In reality, there are approximately three billion DNA base pairs in human cells.

DNA Is Highly Organized Within the Nucleus

If you removed the DNA from a single human cell and stretched it out completely, it would measure approximately two meters (about 6.5 feet). Therefore, DNA molecules must be compactly organized in the nucleus. To achieve this, the double helix configuration of DNA undergoes coiling. An analogy would be twisting a string until coils are formed and then continuing to twist so that secondary coils are formed, and so on. To assist with coiling, DNA is first wrapped around proteins called **histones**. This creates a complex called **chromatin,** which resembles "beads on a string" (Figure 3.14). Next, chromatin is further coiled into a **chromosome**. Another important feature of DNA is that chromosomes can be altered from tightly coiled (chromatin) to loosely coiled (**euchromatin**). Most of the time, chromosomes in the nucleus remain in a euchromatin state so that DNA sequences are accessible for regulatory processes to occur.

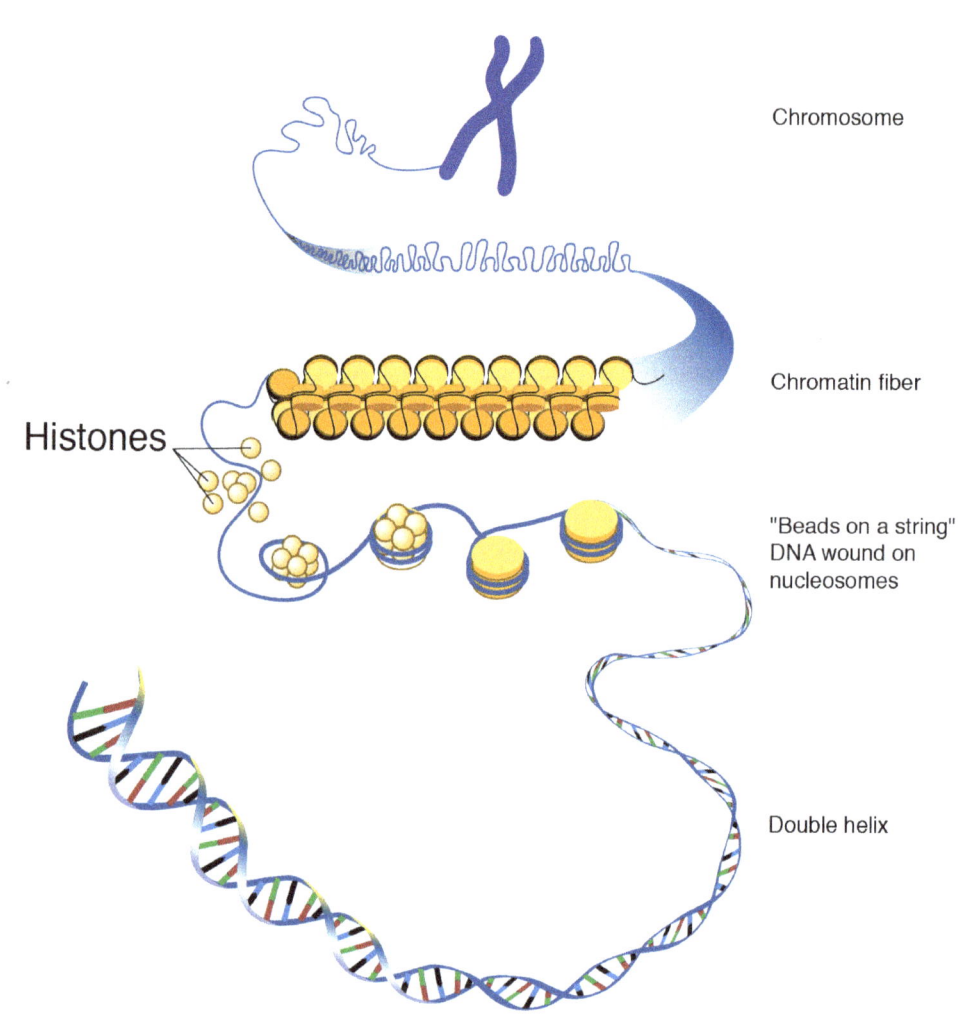

Figure 3.14 The hierarchical organization of chromosomes.

Human body cells typically have 23 pairs of chromosomes, for a total of 46 chromosomes in each cell's nucleus (Figure 3.15). An interesting fact is that the number of chromosomes an organism possesses varies, and this figure is not dependent upon the size or complexity of the organism. For instance, chimpanzees have a total of 48 chromosomes, while hermit crabs have 254. Chromosomes also have a distinct physical structure, including **centromeres** (the "centers") and **telomeres** (the ends) (Figure 3.16). Because of centromeres, chromosomes are described as having two different "arms," where one arm is long and the other is shorter. Centromeres play an important role during cell division, which will be discussed in the next section. Telomeres are located at the ends of chromosomes and they help protect the chromosomes from degradation after every round of cell division. However, our telomeres become shorter as we age, and if chromosome telomeres become too short, then the cell will stop dividing. Therefore, the link between the regulation of telomere length and cellular aging is of great interest to researchers.

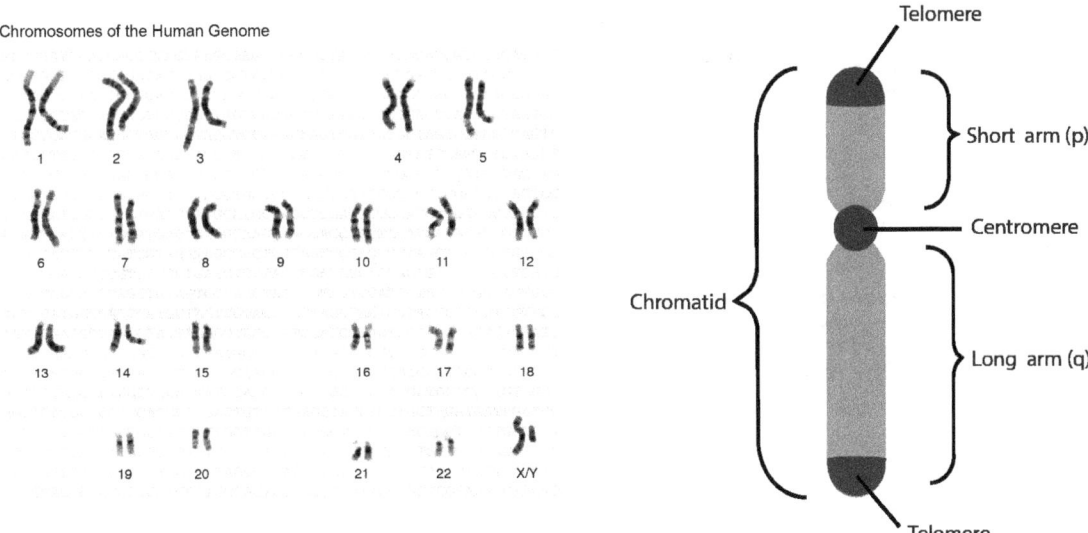

Figure 3.15 The 23 human chromosome pairs.

Figure 3.16 The regions of a chromosome.

DNA REPLICATION AND CELL DIVISION

For life to continue and flourish, cells must be able to divide. Tissue growth and cellular damage repair are also necessary to maintain an organism throughout its life. All these rely on the dynamic processes of **DNA replication** and the **cell cycle**. The mechanisms highlighted in this section are tightly regulated and represent only part of the life cycle of a cell.

DNA Replication

DNA replication is the process by which new DNA is copied from an original DNA template. It is one phase of the highly coordinated cell cycle and requires a variety of enzymes with special functions. Specifically, enzymes carry out the structural and high-energy reactions associated with replicating a double helical molecule. The creation of a complementary DNA strand from a template strand is described as **semi-conservative replication**. The result of semi-conservative replication is two separate double-stranded DNA molecules, each of which is composed of an original "parent" template strand and a newly synthesized "daughter" DNA strand.

DNA replication progresses in three steps referred to as **initiation, elongation,** and **termination**. Initiation denotes the start of DNA replication by recruiting enzymes to specific sites along the DNA sequence. For example, the double helix of DNA presents structural challenges for replication, so an initiator enzyme, called **helicase**, "unwinds" DNA by breaking the hydrogen bonds between the two parent strands. The unraveling of the helix into two separated strands creates a fork, which is the active site of replication machinery (Figure 3.17). Once both strands are separated, the parent template strands are exposed, meaning they can be read and replicated.

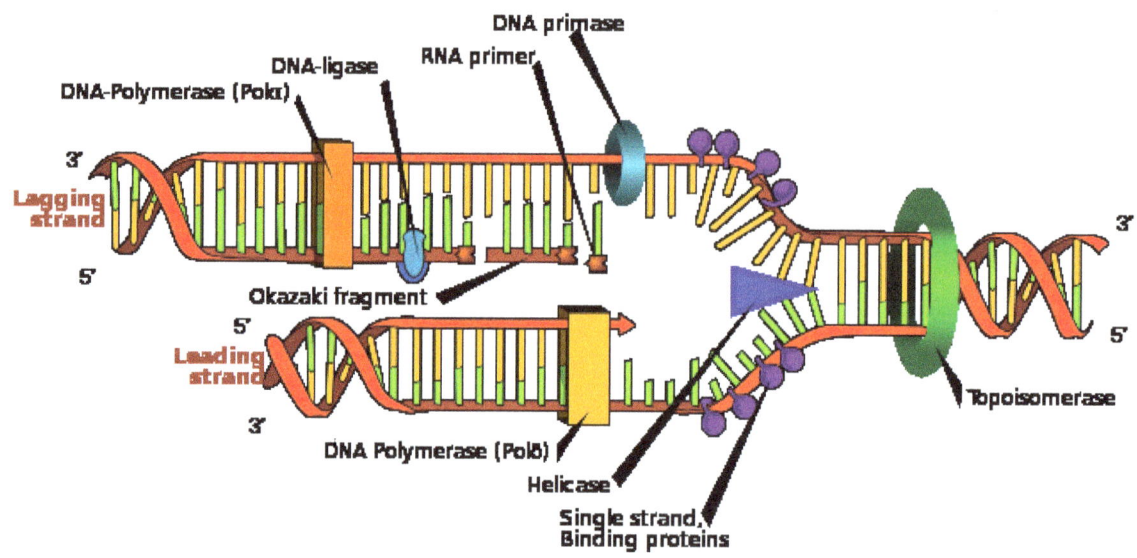

Figure 3.17 The different enzymes associated with DNA replication.

Elongation describes the assembly of new DNA daughter strands from parent strands. The two parent strands can further be classified as **leading strand** or **lagging strand** and are distinguished by the continuous or discontinuous direction of replication, respectively. A short fragment of RNA nucleotides acts as a **primer**, which binds to the parent DNA strand that will be copied. The leading strand receives one primer and the lagging strand receives several. Elongation proceeds with help from enzymes called **DNA polymerases**, which read parent template strands in a specific direction. Complementary nucleotides are added, and the newly formed daughter strand will grow. The direction in which replication proceeds depends on whether it is the leading or lagging strand. On the leading parent strand, a DNA polymerase will create one continuous strand. Because the lagging parent strand requires several primers, disjointed strands (called **Okazaki fragments**) will be generated. Other enzymes will fill in the missing nucleotide gaps between the disconnected lagging strand Okazaki fragments.

Finally, termination refers to the end of DNA replication activity. It is signaled by a stop sequence in the DNA, which is recognized by machinery at the replication fork. The end result of DNA replication is that the number of chromosomes are doubled so that the cell can divide into two.

DNA Mutations

DNA replication should result in the creation of two molecules with identical DNA nucleotide sequences. Although DNA polymerases are quite precise during DNA replication, copying mistakes are estimated to occur every 10^7 DNA nucleotides. Variation from the original DNA sequence is known as a mutation. The different types of mutations will be discussed in greater detail in Chapter 4. Briefly, mutations can result in single nucleotide changes as well as the insertion or deletion of nucleotides and repeated sequences. Depending on where they occur, mutations can be **deleterious** (harmful). For example, mutations may occur in regions that control cell cycle regulation, which can result in cancer (see Special Topic: The Cell Cycle and Immortality of Cancer Cells). Many other mutations, however, are not harmful to an organism.

Regardless of their effect, the cell attempts to reduce the frequency of mutations that occur during DNA replication.

To accomplish this, there are polymerases with proofreading capacities that can identify and correct mismatched nucleotides. These safeguards reduce the frequency of DNA mutations so that they only occur every 10^9 nucleotides.

SPECIAL TOPIC: THE CELL CYCLE AND IMMORTALITY OF CANCER CELLS

DNA replication is part of a series of preparatory phases that a cell undergoes prior to cell division, collectively known as **interphase** (Figure 3.18). During interphase, the cell not only doubles its chromosomes through DNA replication, but it also increases its metabolic capacity to provide energy for growth and division. Transition into each phase of the cell cycle is tightly controlled by proteins that serve as checkpoints. If a cell fails to pass a checkpoint, then DNA replication and/or cell division will not continue. Some of the reasons why a cell may fail at a checkpoint is DNA damage, lack of nutrients to continue the process, or insufficient size. In turn, a cell may undergo **apoptosis**, which is a mechanism for cell death.

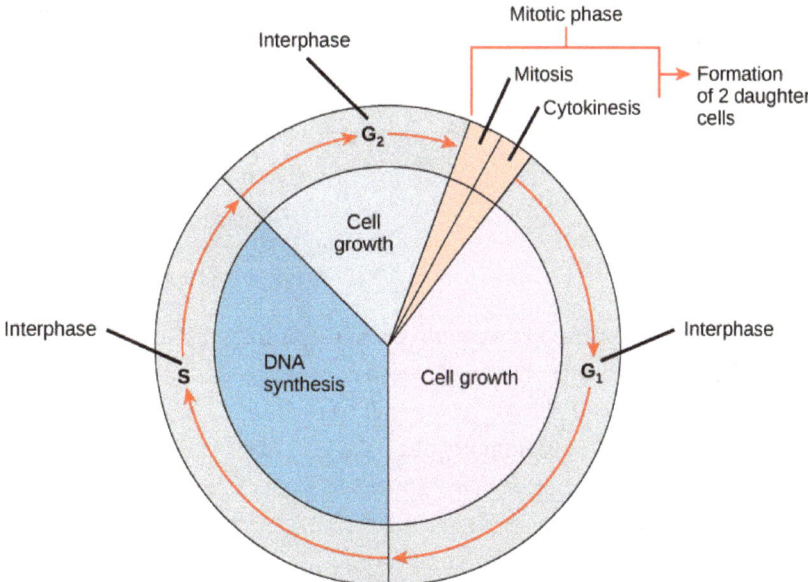

Figure 3.18 The phases and checkpoints of the cell cycle.

Unchecked cellular growth is a distinguishing hallmark of cancer. In other words, as cancer cells grow and proliferate, they acquire the capacity to avoid death and replicate indefinitely. This uncontrolled and continuous cell division is also known as "immortality." As previously discussed, most cells lose the ability to divide due to shortening of telomeres on the ends of chromosomes over time. One way in which cancer cells retain replicative immortality is that the length of their telomeres is continuously protected. Chemotherapy is often used to treat cancer by targeting cell division, which halts the propagation of genetically abnormal cells. Another therapeutic approach that continues to be investigated is targeting telomere activity to stop the division of cancer cells.

Researchers have exploited the immortality of cancer cells for molecular research. The oldest immortal cell line is HeLa cells (Figure 3.19), which was harvested from Henrietta Lacks, an African-American woman diagnosed with cervical cancer in 1955. At that time, extracted cells frequently died during experiments, but surprisingly, HeLa cells continued to replicate. Propagation of Lacks's cell line has significantly contributed to medical research, including ongoing cancer research and helping to test the polio vaccine in the 1950s. Unfortunately, Lacks had not given her consent for her tumor biopsy to be used in cell culture research. Moreover, her family was unaware of the extraction and remarkable application of her cells for two decades. The history of HeLa cell origin was first revealed in 1976. The controversy voiced by the Lacks family was included in an extensive account of HeLa cells published in Rebecca Skloot's 2010 book, *The Immortal Life of Henrietta Lacks*. A film based on the book was also released in 2017.

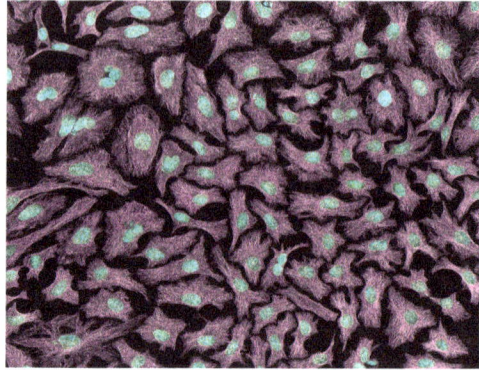

Figure 3.19 A microscopic slide of HeLa cancer cells.

Mitotic Cell Division

The body and its various tissues are comprised of **somatic cells**. Organisms that contain two sets of chromosomes in their somatic cells are called **diploid** organisms. Humans have 46 chromosomes and they are diploid because they inherit one set of chromosomes ($n = 23$) from each parent. As a result, they have 23 matching pairs of chromosomes, which are known as **homologous chromosomes**. These homologous pairs vary in size and are generally numbered from largest (chromosome 1) to smallest (chromosome 22), as seen in Figure 3.15, with the exception of the 23rd pair, which is made up of the sex chromosomes (X and Y). Typically, the female sex is XX and the male sex is XY. Individuals inherit an X chromosome from their mother and an X or Y from their father.

In order to grow and repair tissues, somatic cells must divide. As discussed previously, a cell must first replicate its genetic material for cell division to occur. During DNA replication, each chromosome produces double the amount of genetic information. The duplicated arms of chromosomes are known as **sister chromatids**, and they are attached at the centromeric region. To elaborate, the number of chromosomes stays the same ($n = 46$); however, the amount of genetic material is doubled in the cell as the result of replication.

Mitosis is the process of somatic cell division that gives rise to two diploid daughter cells. Figure 3.20 shows a brief overview of mitosis. Once DNA and other organelles in the cell have finished replication, mitotic spindle fibers (microtubules) assist with chromosomal movement by attaching to the centromeric region of each chromosome. Specifically, the spindle fibers physically align each chromosome at the center of the cell. Next, the spindle fibers divide the sister chromatids and move each one to opposite sides of the cell. At this phase, there are 46 chromosomes on each side of the cell. The cell can now divide into two fully separated daughter cells.

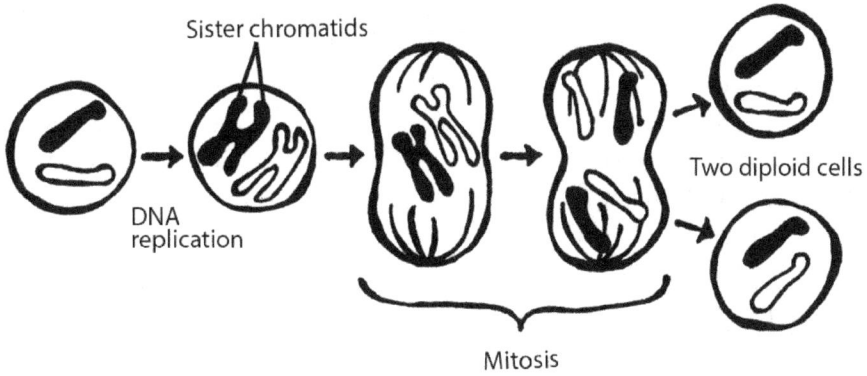

Figure 3.20 Steps of mitotic cell division.

Meiotic Cell Division

Gametogenesis is the production of **gametes** (sperm and egg cells); it involves two rounds of cell division called **meiosis**. Similar to mitosis, the parent cell in meiosis is diploid. However, meiosis has a few key differences, including the number of daughter cells produced (four cells, which require two rounds of cell division to produce) and the number of chromosomes each daughter cell has (Figure 3.21). During the first round of division (known as meiosis I), each chromosome ($n = 46$) replicates its DNA so that sister chromatids are formed. Next, with the help of spindle fibers, homologous chromosomes align near the center of the cell and sister chromatids physically swap genetic material. In other words, the sister chromatids of matching chromosomes cross over with each other at matching DNA nucleotide positions. The occurrence of homologous chromosomes crossing over, swapping DNA, and then rejoining segments is called **genetic recombination**. The "genetic shuffling" that occurs in gametes increases organismal genetic diversity by creating new combinations of genes on chromosomes that are different from the parent cell. Genetic mutations can also arise during recombination. For example, there may be an unequal swapping of genetic material that occurs between the two sister chromatids, which can result in deletions or duplications of DNA nucleotides. Once genetic recombination is complete, homologous chromosomes are separated and two daughter cells are formed.

The daughter cells after the first round of meiosis are **haploid**, meaning they only have one set of chromosomes ($n = 23$). During the second round of cell division (known as meiosis II), sister chromatids are separated and two additional haploid daughter cells are formed. Therefore, the four resulting daughter cells have one set of chromosomes ($n = 23$), and they also have a genetic composition that is not identical to the parent cells nor to each other.

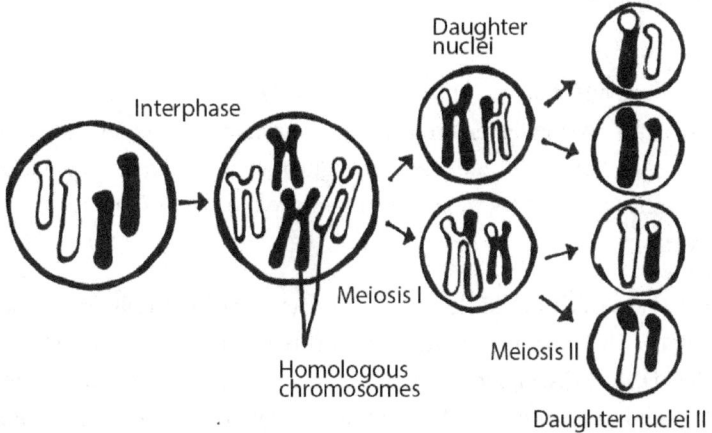

Figure 3.21 Meiotic cell division.

Although both sperm and egg gamete production undergo meiosis, they differ in the final number of viable daughter cells. In the case of spermatogenesis, four mature sperm cells are produced. Although four egg cells are also produced in oogenesis, only one of these egg cells will result in an ovum (mature egg). During fertilization, an egg cell and sperm cell fuse, which creates a diploid cell that develops into an embryo. The ovum also provides the cellular organelles necessary for embryonic cell division. This includes mitochondria, which is why humans, and most other multicellular eukaryotes, have the same mtDNA sequence as their mothers.

Chromosomal Disorders

During mitosis or meiosis, entire deletions or duplications of chromosomes can occur due to error. For example, homologous chromosomes may fail to separate properly, so one daughter cell may end up with an extra chromosome while the other daughter cell has one less. Cells with an unexpected (or abnormal) number of chromosomes are known as **aneuploid**. Adult or embryonic cells can be tested for chromosome number (**karyotyping**). Aneuploid cells are typically detrimental to a dividing cell or developing embryo, which can lead to a loss of pregnancy. However, the occurrence of individuals being born with three copies of the 21st chromosome is relatively common; this genetic condition is known as Down Syndrome. Moreover, human males and females can be born with aneuploid sex chromosome conditions such as XXY, XXX, and XO (referring to only one X chromosome).

PROTEIN SYNTHESIS

At the beginning of the chapter, we defined *proteins* as strings of **amino acids** that fold into complex 3-D shapes. There are 20 standard amino acids that can be strung together in different orders in humans, and the result is that proteins can perform an impressive amount of different functions. For instance, muscle fibers are proteins that help facilitate movement. A special class of proteins (immunoglobulins) help protect the organism by detecting disease-causing pathogens in the body. Protein hormones, such as insulin, help regulate physiological activity. Blood hemoglobin is a protein that transports oxygen throughout the body. **Enzymes** are also proteins, and they are catalysts for biochemical reactions that occur in the cell (e.g., metabolism). Larger-scale protein structures can be visibly seen as physical features of an organism (e.g., hair and nails).

Transcription and Translation

Coding nucleotides in our DNA provide instructions on how to make proteins. Making proteins, also known as **protein synthesis**, can be broken down into two main steps referred to as **transcription** and **translation**. Protein synthesis relies on many molecules in the cell including different types of regulatory proteins and RNAs for each step in the process. Although there are many different types of RNA molecules that have a variety of functions within the cell, we will mainly focus on **messenger RNA (mRNA)**.

A **gene** is a segment of DNA that codes for RNA, and genes can vary in length from a few hundred to as many as two million base pairs in length. The purpose of transcription is to make an RNA copy of that genetic code (Figure 3.22). Unlike double-stranded DNA, RNA molecules are single-stranded nucleotide sequences (refer back to Figure 3.2). Additionally, while DNA contains the nucleotide thymine (T), RNA does not—instead, its fourth nucleotide is uracil (U). Uracil is complementary to (or can pair with) adenine (A), while cytosine (C) and guanine (G) continue to be complementary to each other. For transcription to proceed, a gene must first be turned "on" by the cell (see Special Topic: Genetic Regulation of the Lactase (LCT) Gene for a more detailed discussion of gene regulation). The double-stranded DNA is then separated, and one side of the DNA strand is used as a template where complementary RNA nucleotides are strung together. For example, if a DNA template is TACGGATGC, then the newly constructed mRNA sequence will be AUGCCUACG. Sometimes the end product needed by the cell is that transcribed RNA, but for protein synthesis constructing the RNA (specifically pre-messenger RNA, or pre-mRNA) is just the first step.

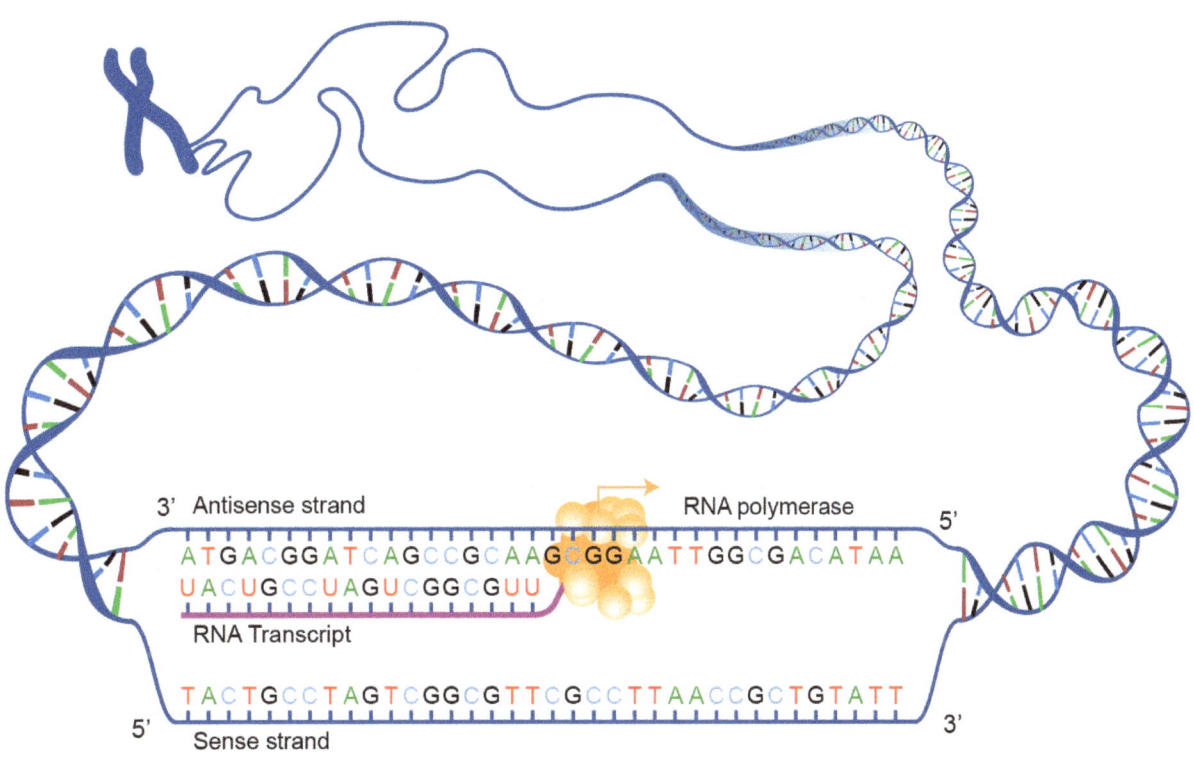

Figure 3.22 RNA polymerase catalyzing DNA transcription.

Genes contain segments called **introns** and **exons**. Exons are considered "coding" while introns are considered "noncoding"—meaning the information they contain will not be needed to construct proteins. When a gene is first transcribed into pre-mRNA, introns and exons are both included (Figure 3.23). However, once transcription is finished, introns are removed in a process called **splicing**. During splicing, a protein/RNA complex attaches itself to the pre-mRNA and removes introns and then connects the remaining exons, thus creating a shorter mature mRNA.

76 | Molecular Biology and Genetics

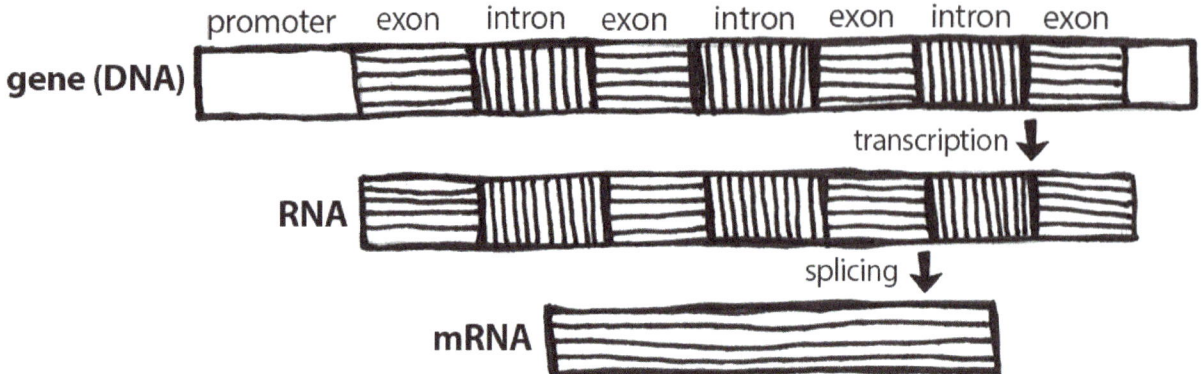

Figure 3.23 RNA processing is the modification of RNA, including the removal of introns, called splicing, between transcription and translation.

The process by which mRNA is "read" and amino acids chained together to form new proteins is called translation. During translation, mature mRNA is transported outside of the nucleus where it is bound to a **ribosome** (Figure 3.24). The nucleotides in the mRNA are read as triplets, which are called **codons**. Each codon corresponds to an amino acid, and this is the basis for building a protein. Continuing with our example from above, the mRNA sequence AUG-CCU-ACG codes for three amino acids. Using a codon table (Figure 3.25), AUG is a codon for methionine (Met), CCU is proline (Pro), and ACG is threonine (Thr). Therefore, the protein sequence is Met-Pro-Thr. Methionine is the most common "start codon" (AUG) for the initiation of protein translation in eukaryotes. As the ribosome moves along the mRNA, the growing amino acid chain exits the ribosome and folds into a protein (Figure 3.26). When the ribosome reaches a "stop" codon (UAA, UAG, or UGA), the ribosome stops adding new amino acids, detaches from the mRNA, and the protein is released. Folded proteins can then be used to complete a structural or functional task.

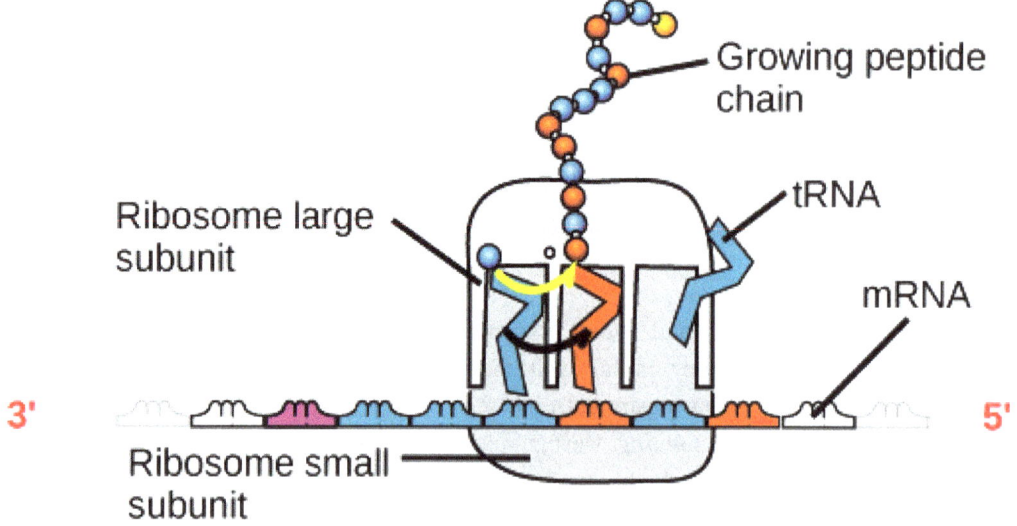

Figure 3.24 Translation of mRNA into an amino acid.

Molecular Biology and Genetics | 77

RNA codon table

1st position	2nd position U	2nd position C	2nd position A	2nd position G	3rd position
U	Phe Phe Leu Leu	Ser Ser Ser Ser	Tyr Tyr stop stop	Cys Cys stop Trp	U C A G
C	Leu Leu Leu Leu	Pro Pro Pro Pro	His His Gln Gln	Arg Arg Arg Arg	U C A G
A	Ile Ile Ile Met	Thr Thr Thr Thr	Asn Asn Lys Lys	Ser Ser Arg Arg	U C A G
G	Val Val Val Val	Ala Ala Ala Ala	Asp Asp Glu Glu	Gly Gly Gly Gly	U C A G

Amino Acids

Ala: Alanine
Arg: Arginine
Asn: Asparagine
Asp: Aspartic acid
Cys: Cysteine
Gln: Glutamine
Glu: Glutamic acid
Gly: Glycine
His: Histidine
Ile: Isoleucine
Leu: Leucine
Lys: Lysine
Met: Methionine
Phe: Phenylalanine
Pro: Proline
Ser: Serine
Thr: Threonine
Trp: Tryptophane
Tyr: Tyrosine
Val: Valine

Figure 3.25 This table can be used to identify which mRNA codons (sequence of three nucleotides) correspond with each of the 20 different amino acids. For example, if the codon is CAU, the first position is "C" and you would look in that corresponding row, the second position is "A" and you would look in that column. "U" is the third position—narrowing the row and indicating that the CAU codon corresponds with the amino acid "histidine" (abbreviated "His"). The table also indicates the most common "start codon" (AUG) that correlates with Methionine, and the three "stop" codons (UAA, UAG, or UGA).

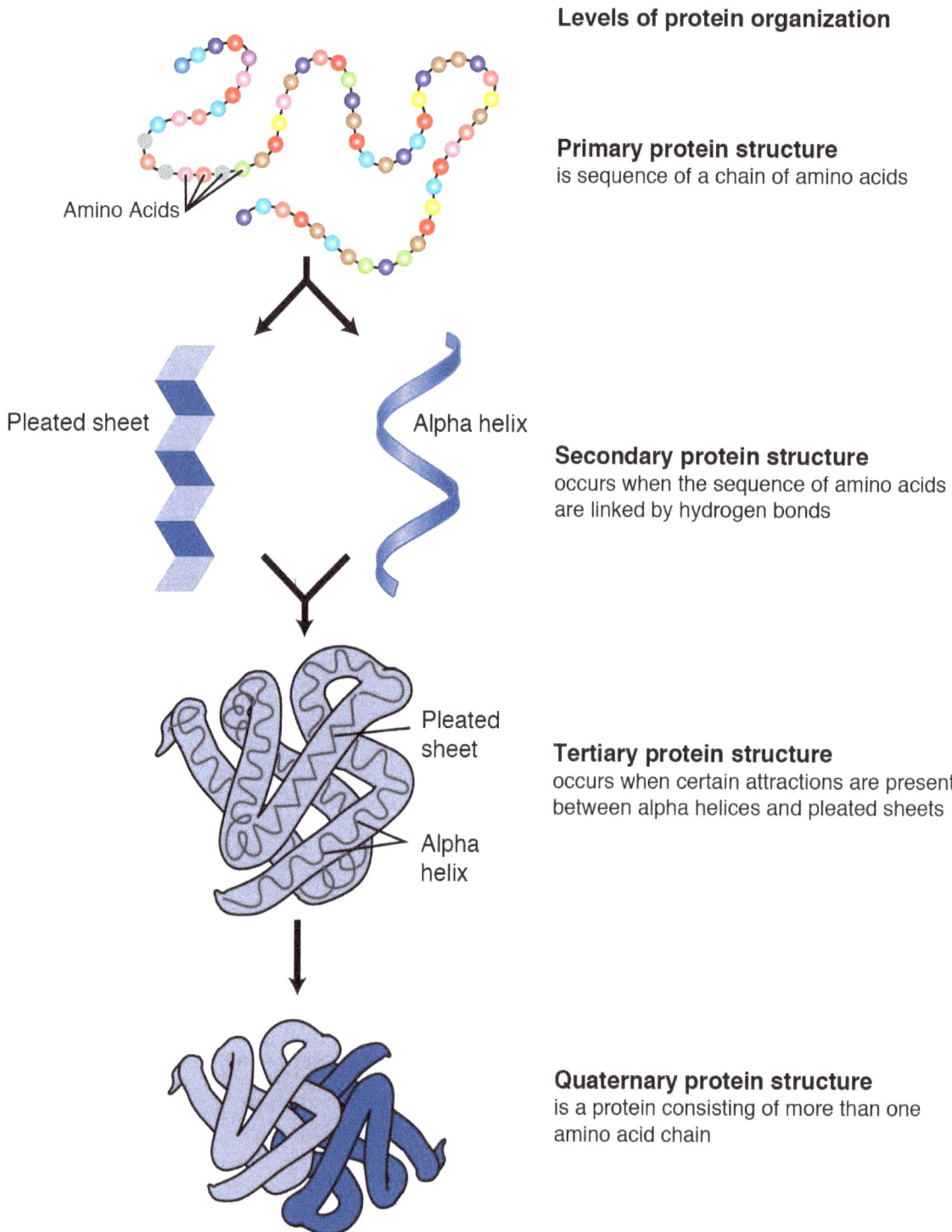

Figure 3.26 Indicates levels of protein organization from the simple amino acid chain that is then folded and organized into more complex protein structures.

Molecular Biology and Genetics | 79

SPECIAL TOPIC: GENETIC REGULATION OF THE LACTASE (*LCT*) GENE

The LCT gene codes for a protein called lactase, an enzyme produced in the small intestine. It is responsible for breaking down the sugar "lactose" found in milk. Lactose intolerance occurs when not enough lactase enzyme is produced and, in turn, digestive symptoms occur. To avoid this discomfort, individuals may take lactase supplements, drink lactose-free milk, or avoid milk products altogether.

The LCT gene is a good example of how cells regulate protein synthesis. The **promoter** region of the LCT gene helps regulate whether it is transcribed or not transcribed (i.e., turned "on" or "off," respectively). Lactase production is initiated when a regulatory protein known as a **transcription factor** binds to a site on the LCT promoter. **RNA polymerases** are then recruited; they read DNA and string together nucleotides to make RNA molecules (Figure 3.22). An LCT pre-mRNA is synthesized (made) in the nucleus, and further chemical modifications flank the ends of the mRNA to ensure the molecule will not be degraded in the cell.

Next, RNA processing occurs. A spliceosome complex removes the introns and connects exons to form the mature mRNA. Once the LCT mRNA is transported outside of the nucleus, it is bound to a ribosome, which is a multi-protein complex that includes **ribosomal RNA (rRNA)**. The ribosome of eukaryotes has two main subunits: the smaller bottom subunit that binds to the mRNA and the larger top subunit that contains **transfer RNA (tRNA)** binding sites (see Figure 3.24). Each tRNA has a nucleotide anticodon that recognizes an mRNA codon. When a tRNA binds to an mRNA codon in the ribosome, the tRNA transfers the corresponding amino acid. rRNA ensures the newly added amino acid is linked in the correct order. The growing protein then folds into the lactase enzyme, which can break down lactose.

Most animals lose their ability to digest milk as they mature due to the decreasing transcriptional "silence" of the LCT gene over time. However, some humans have the ability to digest lactose into adulthood (also known as "lactase persistence"). This means they have a genetic mutation that leads to continuous transcriptional activity of *LCT*. Lactase persistence mutations are common in populations with a long history of pastoral farming, such as northern European and North African populations. It is believed that lactase persistence evolved because the ability to digest milk was nutritionally beneficial. More information about lactase persistence will be covered in Chapter 14.

MENDELIAN GENETICS AND OTHER PATTERNS OF INHERITANCE

Gregor Johann Mendel (1822–1884) is often described as the "Father of Genetics." Mendel was a monk who conducted pea plant breeding experiments in a monastery located in the present-day Czech Republic (Figure 3.27). After several years of experiments, Mendel presented his work to a local scientific community in 1865 and published his findings the following year. Although his meticulous effort was notable, the importance of his work was not recognized for another 35 years. One reason for this delay in recognition is that his findings did not agree with the predominant scientific viewpoints on inheritance at the time. For example, it was believed that parental physical traits "blended" together and offspring inherited an intermediate form of that trait. In contrast, Mendel showed that certain pea plant physical traits (e.g., flower color) were passed down separately to the next generation in a statistically predictable manner. Mendel also observed that some

Figure 3.27 Statue of Mendel located at the Mendel Museum located at Masaryk University in Brno, Czech Republic.

parental traits disappeared in offspring but then reappeared in later generations. He explained this occurrence by introducing the concept of "dominant" and "recessive" traits. Mendel established a few fundamental laws of inheritance, and this section reviews some of these concepts. Moreover, the study of traits and diseases that are controlled by a single gene is commonly referred to as **Mendelian genetics**.

Mendelian Genetics

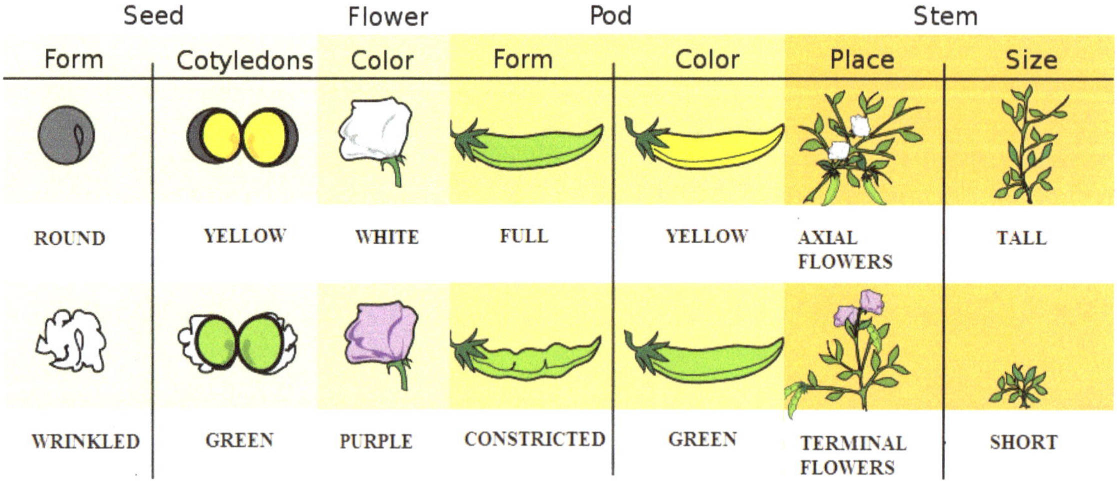

Figure 3.28 Various phenotypic characteristics of pea plants resulting from different genotypes.

The physical appearance of a trait is called an organism's **phenotype**. Figure 3.28 shows pea plant (*Pisum sativum*) phenotypes that were studied by Mendel, and in each of these cases the physical traits are controlled by a single gene. In the case of Mendelian genetics, a phenotype is determined by an organism's **genotype**. A genotype consists of two gene copies, wherein one copy was inherited from each parent. Gene copies are also known as **alleles** (Figure 3.29), which means they are found in the same gene location on homologous chromosomes. Alleles have a nonidentical DNA

Molecular Biology and Genetics | 81

sequence, which means their phenotypic effect can be different. In other words, although alleles code for the same trait, different phenotypes can be produced depending on which two alleles (i.e., genotypes) an organism possesses. For example, Mendel's pea plants all have flowers, but their flower color can be purple or white. Flower color is therefore dependent upon which two color alleles are present in a genotype.

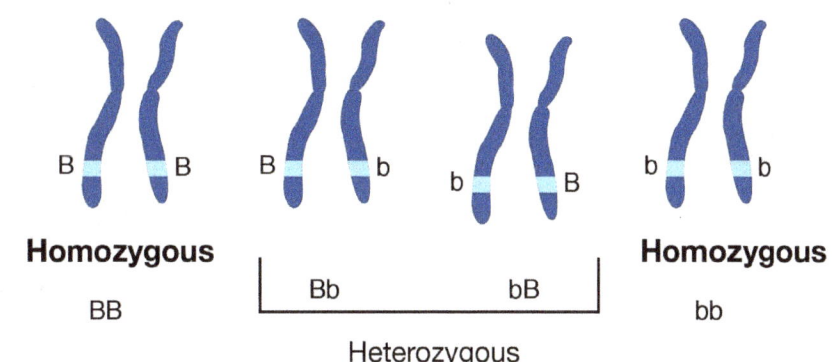

Figure 3.29 Homologous chromosome pairs showing the different homozygous and heterozygous combinations that can exist from two different alleles (B and b).

A Punnett square is a diagram that can help visualize Mendelian inheritance patterns. For instance, when parents of known genotypes mate, a Punnett square can help predict the ratio of Mendelian genotypes and phenotypes that their offspring would possess. Figure 3.30 is a Punnett square that includes two **heterozygous** parents for flower color (Bb). A heterozygous genotype means there are two different alleles for the same gene. Therefore, a pea plant that is heterozygous for flower color has one purple allele and one white allele. When an organism is **homozygous** for a specific trait, it means their genotype consists of two copies of the same allele. Using the Punnett square example (Figure 3.30), the two heterozygous pea plant parents can produce offspring with two different homozygous genotypes (BB or bb) or offspring that are heterozygous (Bb).

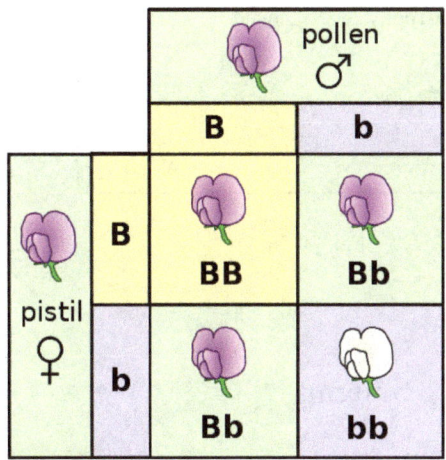

Figure 3.30 Punnett square depicting the possible genetic combinations of offspring from two heterozygous parents.

A pea plant with purple flowers could be heterozygous (Bb) or homozygous (BB). This is because the purple color allele (B) is **dominant** to the white color allele (b), and therefore it only needs one copy of that allele to phenotypically express purple flowers. Because the white flower allele is **recessive**, a pea plant must be homozygous for the recessive allele in order to have a white color phenotype (bb). As seen by the Punnett square example (Figure 3.30), three of four offspring will have purple flowers and the other one will have white flowers.

The *Law of Segregation* was introduced by Mendel to explain why we can predict the ratio of genotypes and phenotypes in offspring. As discussed previously, a parent will have two alleles for a certain gene (with each copy on a different homologous chromosome). The Law of Segregation states that the two copies will be segregated from each other and will each be distributed to their own gamete. We now know that the process where that occurs is meiosis.

Offspring are the products of two gametes combining, which means the offspring inherits one allele from each gamete for most genes. When multiple offspring are produced (like with pea plant breeding), the predicted phenotype ratios are more clearly observed. The pea plants Mendel studied provide a simplistic model to understand single-gene genetics. While many traits anthropologists are interested in have a more complicated inheritance (e.g., are informed by many genes), there are a few known Mendelian traits in humans. Additionally, some human diseases also follow a Mendelian pattern of inheritance (Figure 3.31). Because humans do not have as many offspring as other organisms, we may not recognize Mendelian patterns as easily. However, understanding these principles and being able to calculate the probability that an offspring will have a Mendelian phenotype is still important.

Mendelian disorder	Gene	Mendelian disorder	Gene
Alpha Thalassemia	HBA1	Maple Syrup Urine Disease: Type 1A	BCKDHA
Androgen Insensitivity Syndrome	AR	Mitochondrial DNA Depletion Syndrome	TYMP
Bloom Syndrome	BLM	MTHFR Deficiency	MTHFR
Canavan Disease	ASPA	Oculocutaneous Albinism: Type 1	TYR
Cartilage-Hair Hypoplasia	RMRP	Oculocutaneous Albinism: Type 3	TYRP1
Cystic Fibrosis	CFTR	Persistent Mullerian Duct Syndrome: Type I	AMH
Familial Chloride Diarrhea	SLC26A3	Polycystic Kidney Disease	PKHD1
Fragile X Syndrome	FMR1	Sickle-cell anemia	HBB
Glucose-6-Phosphate Dehydrogenase Deficiency	G6PD	Spermatogenic failure	USP9Y
Hemophilia A	F8	Spinal Muscular Atrophy: SMN1 Linked	SMN1
Huntington disease	HTT	Tay-Sachs Disease	HEXA
Hurler Syndrome	IDUA	Wilson Disease	ATP7B

Figure 3.31 Human diseases that follow a Mendelian pattern of inheritance.

Example of Mendelian Inheritance: The ABO Blood Group System

In 1901, Karl Landsteiner at the University of Vienna published his discovery of ABO blood groups. This was a result of conducting blood immunology experiments in which he combined the blood of individuals who possess different blood cell types and observed an agglutination (clotting) reaction. The presence of agglutination implies there is an incompatible immunological reaction, whereas no agglutination will occur in individuals with the same blood type. This work was clearly important because it resulted in a higher survival rate of patients who received blood transfusions.

Blood transfusions from someone with a different type of blood causes agglutinations, and the resulting coagulated blood can not easily pass through blood vessels, resulting in death. Accordingly, Landsteiner received the Nobel Prize (1930) for explaining the ABO blood group system.

Blood **cell surface antigens** are proteins that coat the surface of red blood cells, and **antibodies** are specifically "against" or "anti" to the antigens from other blood types. Thus, antibodies are responsible for causing agglutination between incompatible blood types. Understanding the interaction of antigens and antibodies helps to determine ABO compatibility amongst blood donors and recipients. In order to better understand blood phenotypes and ABO compatibility, blood cell antigens and plasma antibodies are presented in Figure 3.32. Individuals that are blood type A have A antigens on the red blood cell surface, and anti-B antibodies, which will bind with B antigens should they come in contact. Alternatively, individuals with blood type B have B antigens and anti-A antibodies. Individuals with blood type AB have both A and B antigens but do not produce antibodies for the ABO system. This does not mean type AB does not have any antibodies, just that anti-A or anti-B antibodies are not produced. Individuals who are blood type O have nonspecific antigens but produce both anti-A and anti-B antibodies.

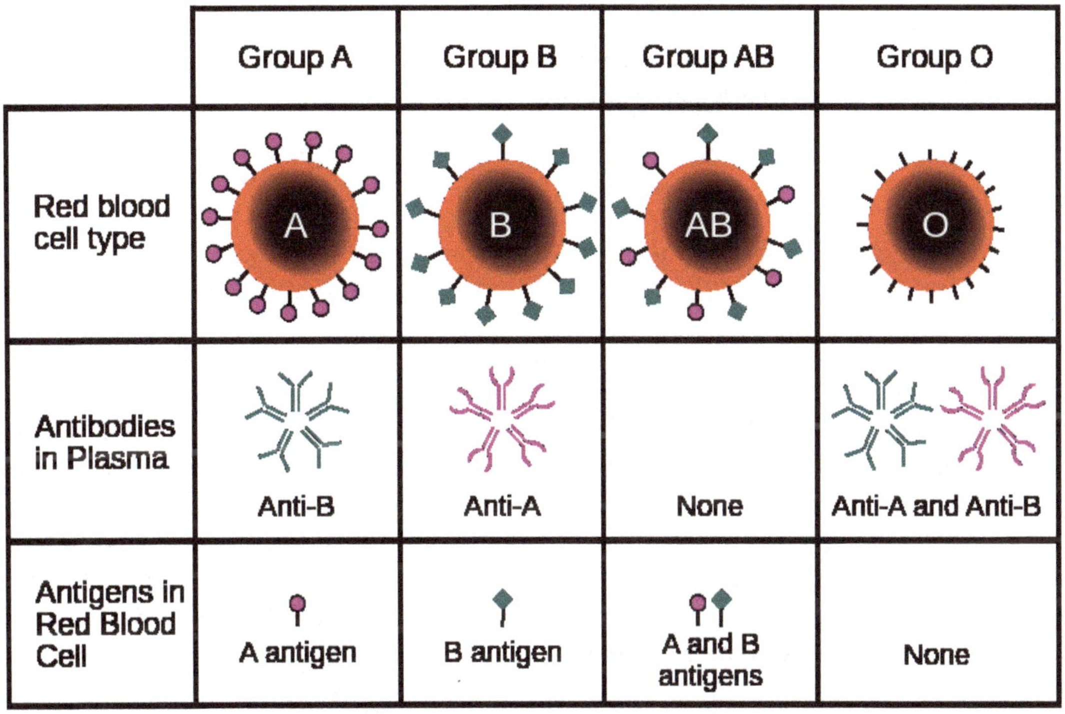

	Group A	Group B	Group AB	Group O
Red blood cell type	A	B	AB	O
Antibodies in Plasma	Anti-B	Anti-A	None	Anti-A and Anti-B
Antigens in Red Blood Cell	A antigen	B antigen	A and B antigens	None

Figure 3.32 The different ABO blood types with their associated antibodies and antigens.

Figure 3.33 shows a table of the ABO allele system, which has a Mendelian pattern of inheritance. Both the A and B alleles function as dominant alleles, so the A allele always codes for the A antigen, and the B allele codes for the B antigen. The O allele differs from A and B, because it codes for a nonfunctional antigen protein, which means there is no antigen present on the cell surface of O blood cells. To have blood type O, two copies of the O allele must be inherited, one from each parent, thus the O allele is considered recessive. Therefore, someone who is a heterozygous AO genotype is phenotypically blood type A and a genotype of BO is blood type B. The ABO blood system

	A	B	O
A	AA	AB	AO
B	AB	BB	BO
O	AO	BO	OO

Figure 3.33 The different combinations of ABO blood alleles (A, B, and O) to form ABO blood genotypes.

also provides an example of **codominance**, which is when the effect of both alleles is observed in the phenotype. This is true for blood type AB: when an individual inherits both the A and B alleles, then both A and B antigens will be present on the cell surface.

Also found on the surface of red blood cells is the rhesus group antigen, known as "Rh factor." In reality, there are several antigens on red blood cells independent from the ABO blood system, however, the Rh factor is the second most important antigen to consider when determining blood donor and recipient compatibility. Rh antigens must also be considered when a pregnant mother and her baby have incompatible Rh factors. In such cases, a doctor can administer necessary treatment steps to prevent pregnancy complications and hemolytic disease, which is when the mother's antibodies break down the newborn's red blood cells.

An individual can possess the Rh antigen (be Rh positive) or lack the Rh antigen (be Rh negative). The Rh factor is controlled by a single gene and is inherited independently of the ABO alleles. Therefore, all blood types can either be positive (O+, A+, B+, AB+) or negative (O-, A-, B-, AB-).

Individuals with O+ red blood cells can donate blood to A+, B+, AB+, and O+ blood type recipients. Because O- individuals do not have AB or Rh antigens, they are compatible with all blood cell types and are referred to as "universal donors." Individuals that are AB+ are considered to be "universal recipients" because they do not possess antibodies against other blood types.

Mendelian Patterns of Inheritance and Pedigrees

A pedigree can be used to investigate a family's medical history by determining if a health issue is inheritable and will possibly require medical intervention. A pedigree can also help determine if it is a Mendelian recessive or dominant genetic condition. Figure 3.34 is a pedigree example of a family with Huntington's disease, which has a Mendelian dominant pattern of inheritance. In a standard pedigree, males are represented by a square and females are represented by a circle. When an individual is affected with a certain condition, the square or circle is filled in as a solid color. With a dominant condition, at least one of the parents will have the disease and an offspring will have a 50% chance of inheriting the affected chromosome. Therefore, dominant genetic conditions tend to be present in every generation. In the case of Huntington's, some individuals may not be diagnosed until later in adulthood, so parents may unknowingly pass this dominantly inherited disease to their children.

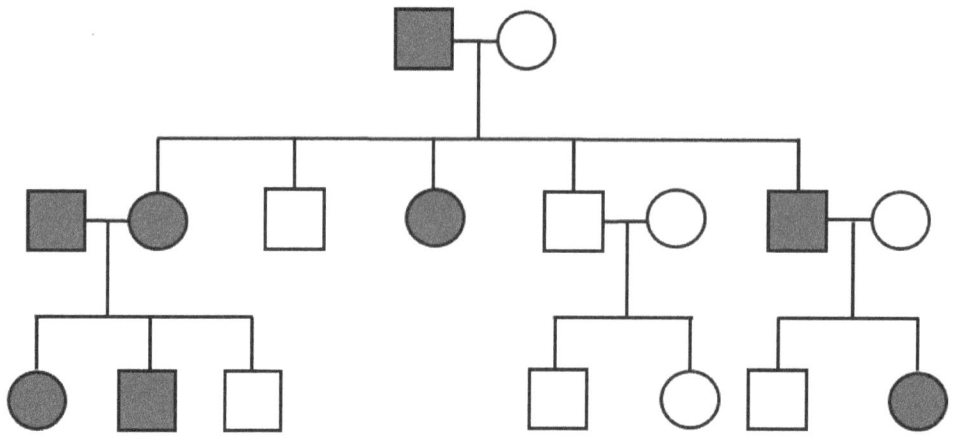

Figure 3.34 A three-generation pedigree depicting an example of dominant Mendelian inheritance like Huntington's.

Because the probability of inheriting a disease-causing recessive allele is more rare, recessive medical conditions can skip generations. Figure 3.35 is an example of a family that carries a recessive cystic fibrosis mutation. A parent that is heterozygous for the cystic fibrosis allele has a 50% chance of passing down their affected chromosome to the next generation. If a child has a recessive disease, then it means both of their parents are **carriers** (heterozygous) for that condition. In most cases, carriers for recessive conditions show no serious medical symptoms. Individuals whose family have a known medical history for certain conditions sometimes seek family planning services (see the Genetic Testing section).

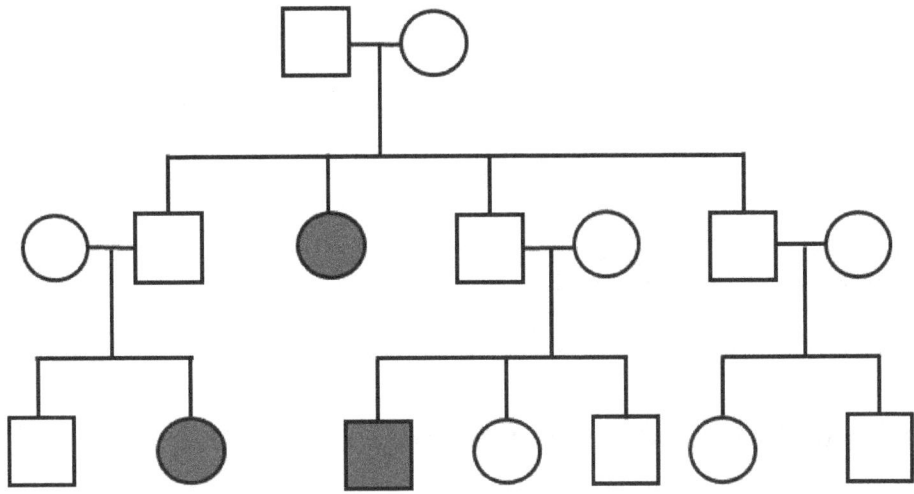

Figure 3.35 A three-generation pedigree depicting an example of recessive Mendelian inheritance like cystic fibrosis.

Pedigrees can also help distinguish if a health issue has an **autosomal** or **X-linked** pattern of inheritance. As previously discussed, there are 23 pairs of chromosomes and 22 of these pairs are known as **autosomes**. The provided pedigree examples (Figure 3.34–35) are autosomally linked genetic diseases. This means the genes that cause the disease are located on one of the chromosomes numbered 1 to 22. Disease causing genes can also be X-linked, which means they are located on the X chromosome.

Figure 3.36 depicts a family in which the mother is a carrier for the X-linked recessive disease Duchenne Muscular Dystrophy (DMD). The mother is a carrier for DMD, so daughters and sons will have a 50% chance of inheriting the pathogenic DMD allele. Because females have two X chromosomes, females will not have the disease (although in rare cases, female carriers may show some symptoms of the disease). On the other hand, males who inherit a copy of an X-linked pathogenic DMD allele will typically be affected with the condition. Males are more susceptible to X-linked conditions because they only have one X chromosome. Therefore, when evaluating a pedigree, if a higher proportion of males are affected with the disease, this could suggest the disease is X-linked recessive. Finally, Y-linked traits are very rare because compared to other chromosomes, the Y chromosome is smaller and only has a few active (transcribed) genes.

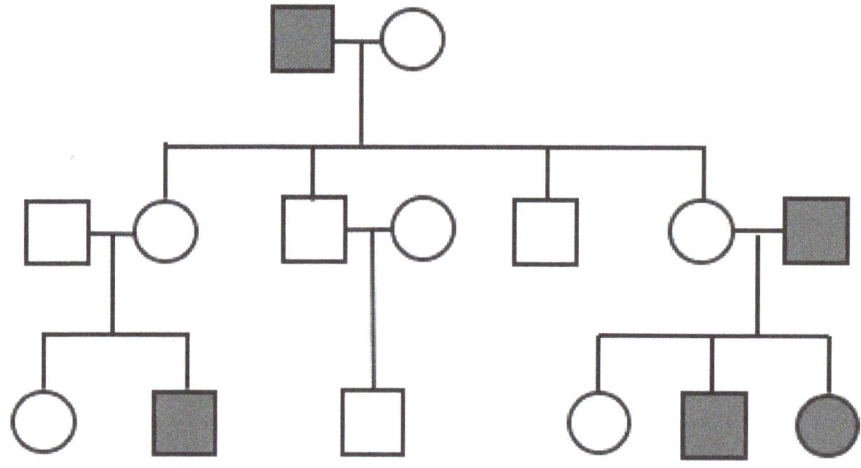

Figure 3.36 A three-generation pedigree depicting an example of X-linked Mendelian inheritance like Duchenne Muscular Dystrophy (DMD).

Complexity Surrounding Mendelian Inheritance

Figure 3.37 Snap dragons with different genotypes resulting in different flower color phenotypes.

Pea plant trait genetics are relatively simple compared to what we know about genetic inheritance today. The vast majority of genetically controlled traits are not strictly dominant or recessive, so the relationship among alleles and predicting phenotype is often more complicated. For example, a heterozygous genotype that exhibits an intermediate phenotype of both alleles is known as incomplete dominance. In snapdragon flowers, the red flower color (R) is dominant and white is recessive (r). Therefore, the homozygous dominant RR is red and homozygous recessive rr is white. However, because the R allele is not completely dominant, the heterozygote Rr is a blend of red and white, which results in a pink flower (Figure 3.37).

An example of incomplete dominance in humans is the enzyme β-hexosaminidase A (Hex A), which is encoded by the gene HEXA. Patients with two dysfunctional HEXA alleles are unable to metabolize a specific lipid-sugar molecule (GM2 ganglioside); because of this, the molecule builds up and causes damage to nerve cells in the brain and spinal cord. This condition is known as Tay-Sachs disease, and it usually appears in infants who are three to six months old. Most children with Tay-Sachs do not live past early childhood. Individuals who are heterozygous for the functional type HEXA allele and one dysfunctional allele have reduced Hex A activity. However, the amount of enzyme activity is still sufficient, so carriers do not exhibit any neurological phenotypes and appear healthy.

Some genes and alleles can also have higher **penetrance** than others. Penetrance can be defined as the proportion of individuals who have a certain allele and also express an expected phenotype. If a genotype always produces an expected phenotype, then those alleles are said to be fully penetrant. However, in the case of incomplete (or reduced) penetrance, an expected phenotype may not occur even if an individual possesses the alleles that are known to control a trait or cause a disease.

A well-studied example of genetic penetrance is the cancer-related genes BRCA1 and BRCA2. Mutations in these genes can affect crucial processes such as DNA repair, which can lead to breast and ovarian cancers. Although BRCA1 and BRCA2 mutations have an autosomal dominant pattern of inheritance, it does not mean an individual will develop cancer if they inherit a pathogenic allele. Several lifestyle and environmental factors can also influence the risk for developing cancer. Regardless, if a family has a history of certain types of cancers, then it is often recommended that genetic testing be performed for individuals who are at risk. Moreover, publically available genetic testing companies are now offering health reports that include BRCA1/2 allele testing (see the Genetic Testing section).

POLYGENIC TRAITS

While Mendelian traits tend to be influenced by a single gene, the vast majority of human phenotypes are **polygenic traits**. The term *polygenic* means "many genes." Therefore, a polygenic trait is influenced by many genes that work together to produce the phenotype. Human phenotypes such as hair color, eye color, height, and weight are examples of polygenic traits. **Complex diseases** (e.g., cardiovascular diseases, Alzheimer's, and Schizophrenia) also have a polygenic basis.

Human hair color is an example of a polygenic trait. Hair color is largely determined by the type and quantity of a pigment called melanin, which is produced by a specialized cell type within the skin called melanocytes. The quantity and ratio of melanin pigments determine black, brown, blond, and red hair colors. MC1R is a well-studied gene that encodes a protein expressed on the surface of melanocytes that is involved in the production of eumelanin pigment. Typically, people with two functional copies of MC1R have brown hair. People with reduced functioning MC1R allele copies tend to produce pheomelanin, which results in blond or red hair. However, MC1R alleles have variable penetrance, and studies are continually identifying new genes (e.g., TYR, TYRP1, SLC24A5, and KITLG) that also influence hair color. Individuals with two non-functioning copies of the gene TYR have a condition called oculocuteaneous albinism—their melanocytes are unable to produce melanin so these individuals have white hair, light eyes, and pale skin.

In comparison to Mendelian disease, complex diseases tend to be more prevalent in humans. Complex diseases can also run in families, but they often do not have a clear pattern of inheritance. Geneticists may not know all of the genes involved with a given complex disease. In addition to different gene combinations, complex diseases are also influenced by environment and lifestyle factors. Moreover, how much each of these determinants contribute to a disease phenotype can be difficult to decipher. Therefore, predicting medical risk is often a significant challenge. For instance, cardiovascular diseases (CVDs) continue to be one of the leading causes of death around the world. Development of CVDs has been linked to malnutrition during fetal development, high fat and sedentary lifestyles, smoking/drug usage, adverse socioeconomic conditions, and various genes. Human environments are diverse, and public health research including the field of Human Biology can help identify risk factors and behaviors associated with chronic diseases. Large-scale genetic studies can also help elucidate some of these complex relationships.

GENOMICS AND EPIGENETICS

The **genome** is all of the genetic material for an organism. In the case of humans, this includes 46 chromosomes and mtDNA. The human genome contains approximately three billion base pairs of DNA and has regions that are both noncoding and coding. Scientists now estimate that the human genome contains 20,000–25,000 protein-coding genes, with each chromosome containing a few hundred to a few thousand genes. As our knowledge of heredity increases, researchers have begun to realize the importance of **epigenetics**, or changes in gene expression that do not result in a change of the underlying DNA sequence. Epigenetics research is also crucial for unraveling gene regulation, which involves complex interactions between DNA, RNA, proteins, and the environment.

Genomics

The vast majority of the human genome is noncoding, meaning there are no instructions to make a protein or RNA product in these regions. Historically, noncoding DNA was referred to as "junk DNA" because these vast segments of the genome were thought to be irrelevant and non-functional. However, continual improvement of DNA **sequencing** technology along with world-wide scientific collaborations and consortia have contributed to our increased understanding of how the genome functions. Through these technological advances and collaborations, we have since discovered that many of these noncoding DNA regions are involved in dynamic genetic regulatory processes.

Genomics is a diverse field of molecular biology that focuses on genomic evolution, structure and function; gene mapping; and **genotyping** (determining the alleles present). Evolutionary genomics determined that humans and chimpanzees share a significant portion of shared DNA sequence (about 98.8%). Given the phenotypic differences between humans and chimpanzees, having a DNA sequence difference of 1.2% seems surprising. However, a lot of genomics research is also focused on understanding how noncoding genomic regions influence how individual genes are turned "on" and "off" (i.e., regulated). Therefore, although DNA sequences are identical, regulatory differences in noncoding genetic regions (e.g., promoters) are believed to be largely responsible for the physical differences between humans and chimpanzees.

Further understanding of genomic regulatory elements can lead to new therapies and personalized treatments for a broad range of diseases. For example, targeting the regulatory region of a pathogenic gene to "turn off" its expression can prevent its otherwise harmful effects. Such molecular targeting approaches can be personalized based on an individual's genetic makeup. Genome-wide association studies (GWAS) seek to determine genes that are linked to complex traits and diseases and typically require significant computational efforts. This is because millions of DNA sequences must be analyzed and GWAS sometimes include thousands of participants. During the beginning of the genomics field, most of the large-scale genomics studies only included North American, European, and East Asian participants and patients. Researchers are now focusing on increasing ethnic diversity in genomic studies and databases. In turn, accuracy of individual disease risk across all human populations will be improved and more rare-disease-causing alleles will be identified.

Epigenetics

All cells within your body have the same copy of DNA. For example, a brain neuron has the same DNA blueprint as does a skin cell on your arm. Although these cells have the same genetic information, they are considered specialized. The reason all cells within the body have the same DNA but different morphologies and functions is that different subsets of genes are turned "on" and "off" within the different cell types. A more precise explanation is that there is differential expression of genes among different cell types. In the case of neuronal cells, a unique subset of genes are active that allow them to grow axons to send and receive messages. This subset of genes will be inactive in non-neuronal cell types such as skin cells. Epigenetics is a branch of genetics that studies how these genes are regulated through mechanisms that do not change the underlying DNA sequence. Special Topics: Epigenetics and X Chromosome Inactivation details a well-known example of epigenetic regulation.

The prefix *epi* means "on, above, or near," and epigenetic mechanisms such as **DNA methylation** and histone modifications occur on, above, or near DNA. The addition of a methyl group ($-CH_3$) to DNA is known as DNA methylation (Figure 3.38). DNA methylation and other modifications made to the histones around which DNA are wrapped are thought to make chromatin more compact. This DNA is inaccessible to transcription factors and RNA polymerases, thus preventing genes from being turned on (i.e., transcribed). Other histone modifications have the opposite effect by loosening chromatin, which makes genes accessible to transcription factors.

It is important to note that environmental factors can alter DNA methylation and histone modifications and also that these changes can be passed from generation to generation. For example, someone's **epigenetic profile** can be altered during a stressful time (e.g., natural disasters, famine, etc.), and those regulatory changes can be inherited by the next generation. Moreover, our epigenetic expression profile changes as we age. For example, certain places in our genome become "hyper" or "hypo" methylated over time. Identical twins also have epigenetic profiles that become more different as they age. Researchers are only beginning to understand what all of these genome-wide epigenetic changes mean. Scientists have also discovered that changes in epigenetic modifications can alter gene expression in ways that contribute to diseases. It is also important to note that, unlike DNA mutations (which permanently change the nucleotide sequence), epigenetic changes can be easily reversed. A lot of research now focuses on how drugs can alter or modulate changes in DNA methylation and histone modifications to treat diseases such as cancer.

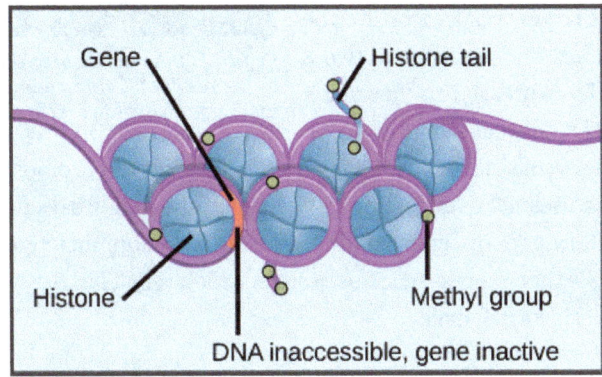

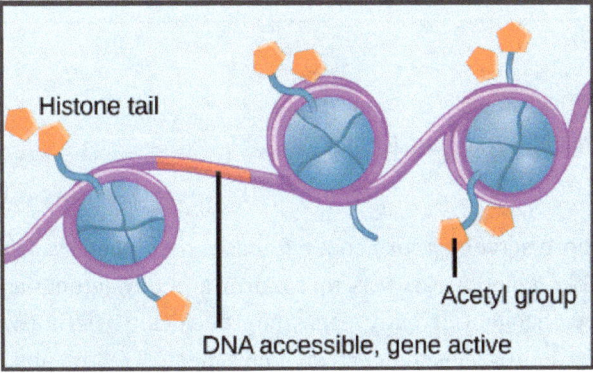

Figure 3.38 *Different types of epigenetic histone tail modifications that can tighten (top) and loosen (bottom) the chromatin of DNA.*

SPECIAL TOPIC: EPIGENETICS AND X CHROMOSOME INACTIVATION

Mary Lyon was a British geneticist that presented a hypothesis for X chromosome inactivation (called the *Lyon hypothesis*) based on her work and other studies of the day. Females inherit two X chromosomes, one from each parent. Males have one functional X chromosome; however, this does not mean females have more active genes than males. During the genetic embryonic development of many female mammals, one of the X chromosomes is inactivated at random, so females have one functional X chromosome. The process of X chromosome inactivation in females occurs through epigenetic mechanisms, such as DNA methylation and histone modifications. Recent studies have analyzed the role of a long noncoding RNA called X-inactive specific transcript (XIST), which is largely responsible for the random silencing of one of the X chromosomes. The presence of two X chromosomes is the signal for XIST RNA to be expressed so that one X chromosome can be inactivated. However, some cells may have an active paternal X chromosome while other cells may have an active maternal X chromosome. This phenomenon is easily seen in calico and tortoiseshell cats (Figure 3.39). In cats, the gene that controls coat color is found on the X chromosome. During early embryo development, random inactivation of X chromosomes gives rise to populations of cells that express black or orange, which results in the unique coat patterning. Therefore, calico cats are typically always female.

Figure 3.39 *A multicolored coat pattern as the result of X chromosome inactivation during development.*

GENETIC TESTING

In order to assist with public health efforts, newborn screening for genetic diseases have been available in the United States for over 50 years. One of the first available genetic tests was to confirm a phenylketonuria (*PKU*) diagnosis in infants, which is easily treatable with a dietary change. Currently, each state decides what genes are included on newborn screening panels and some states even have programs to help with infant medical follow-ups.

There are now hundreds of laboratories that provide testing for a few thousand different genes that can inform medical decisions for infants and adults. What has made this industry possible are the advancements in technology and decreased cost to patients. Moreover, genetic testing has been made available publicly to anyone without the assistance of medical professionals.

Polymerase Chain Reaction (PCR) and Sanger Sequencing

One of the most important inventions in the genetics field was **polymerase chain reaction (PCR)**. In order for researchers to visualize and therefore analyze DNA, the concentration must meet certain thresholds. In 1985, Kary Mullis developed PCR, which can amplify millions of copies of DNA from a very small amount of template DNA (Figure 3.40). For example, a trace amount of DNA at a crime scene can be amplified and tested for a DNA match. Also, aDNA is typically degraded, so a few remaining molecules of DNA can be amplified to reconstruct ancient genomes. The PCR assay uses similar biochemical reactions to our own cells during DNA replication.

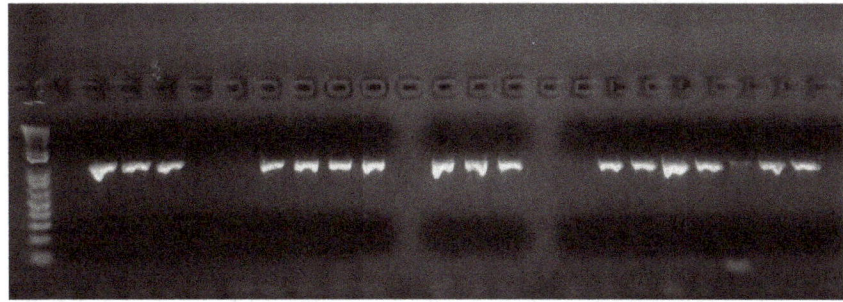

Figure 3.40 Gel electrophoresis used to visualize DNA after PCR amplification.

In **Sanger sequencing**, PCR sequences can be analyzed at the nucleotide level with the help of fluorescent labeling. Several different types of alleles and genetic changes can be detected in DNA by using this analysis. Figure 3.41 shows someone who is heterozygous for a single nucleotide allele. These methods continue to be used extensively alongside larger-scale genome technologies.

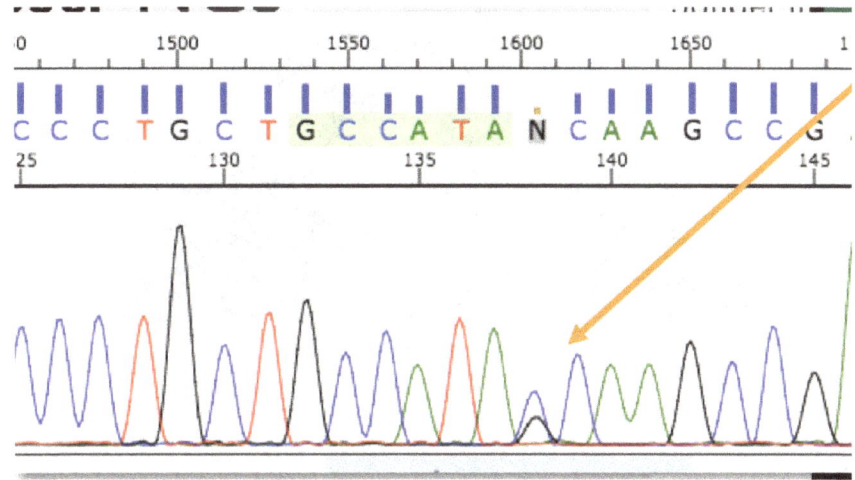

Figure 3.41 Sanger sequencing results showing a heterozygous DNA nucleotide.

Genetic Biotechnology and Clinical Testing

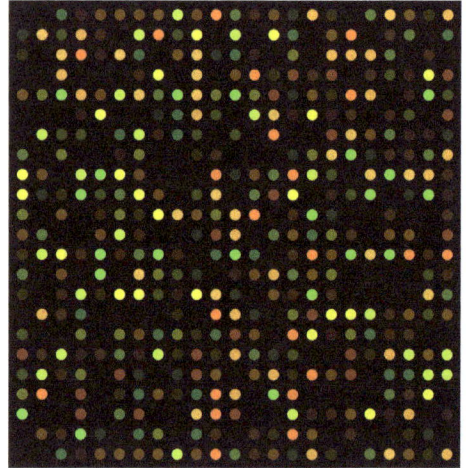

Figure 3.42 Microarray chip with fluorescent labeled probes that hybridize with DNA to detect homozygous and heterozygous nucleotides throughout the genome.

Genetic innovations are transforming the healthcare industry. However, the different types of technology and the results of these tests often include a learning curve for patients, the public, and medical practitioners. **Microarray technology**, when DNA samples are genotyped (or "screened") for specific alleles, has been available for quite some time (Figure 3.42). Presently, microarray chips can include hundreds of alleles that are known to be associated with various diseases. The microarray chip only binds with a DNA sample if it is "positive" for that particular allele and a fluorescent signal is emitted, which can be further analyzed.

If a patient is suspected of having a rare genetic condition that cannot be easily diagnosed or the diagnosis is entirely unknown, whole genome sequencing may be recommended by a doctor. **Next-generation sequencing (NGS)** is a newer technology that can screen the entire genome by analyzing millions of sequences within a single machine run (Figure 3.43). However, sequencing the entire genome yields a significant amount of data and information. Therefore, clinical NGS genetic testing typically only includes a small subset of the genome known to have pathogenic disease-causing mutations.

Figure 3.43 Next-generation sequencing machines.

There is a diversity of clinical genetics tests available to assist patients with making medically informed decisions about family planning and health, including assistance with *in vitro* fertilization (IVF) procedures and embryo genetic screening. To ensure accuracy, it is highly important that all clinical laboratories are continually regulated. The Clinical Laboratory Improvement Amendments (CLIA) are United States federal standards that all human laboratory testing clinics must follow. A major benefit provided by some clinical genetic testing companies is access to genetic counselors, who have specialized education and training in medical genetics and counseling. Both partners are usually tested to see if there is a risk for passing on a disease to a child. Counselors use their skillset to aid patients and doctors with risk assessment for genetic diseases and interpretation of genetic testing results. Genetic counselors also guide and support patients when making impactful medical decisions.

Direct-to-Consumer (DTC) Genetic Testing

People with this result have a slightly increased risk of developing celiac disease. Lifestyle and other factors can also affect your risk.

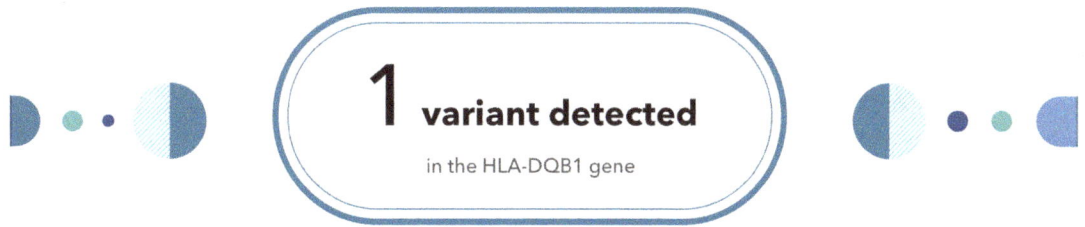

Figure 3.44 *A positive result for a genetic allele associated with an increased risk for celiac disease.*

Genetic testing that is performed without the guidance of medical professionals is called direct-to-consumer (DTC) genetic testing. Companies that sell affordable genome sequencing products to the public continue to increase in number and popularity. These companies have marketing campaigns typically based on the notion of "personal empowerment," which can be achieved by "knowing more about your DNA." For example, if you are identified as having a slightly increased risk for developing celiac disease (Figure 3.44), then you may be motivated to modify your dietary consumption by removing gluten from your diet. Another scenario is that you could test positive for a known pathogenic BRCA1 or BRCA2 allele. In this case, you may want to follow up with additional testing from a medical facility, which could lead to life-altering decisions. DNA sequencing products for entertainment purposes are also available. For example, by having your "Vinome" analyzed, you can discover if you are more predisposed to liking Pinots as your favorite wine. Additionally, an individual and their partner can be genotyped to predict what physical characteristics their baby might inherit.

DTC testing typically lacks genetic counselor services and regulations are not as strict. This has led to some controversies including company genetic products that provide health information. The company 23andMe was the first on the market to offer DTC health testing, and in 2013, the U.S. Food and Drug Administration (FDA) intervened. 23andMe worked toward complying with FDA regulations and then gained approval to offer testing on a few medically related genes. In 2017, 23andMe offered a "Late-Onset Alzheimer's Disease" genetic risk report. Such offerings have been criticized because customers could receive results they may not fully be able to interpret. In turn, this could increase the stress of participants (sometimes called the "burden of knowing") and could also lead to unnecessary medical intervention. In order to address this issue, 23andMe now provides disclaimers and also interactive learning modules that customers must complete if they wish to view certain genotyping results. However, individuals who tested positive for a disease-causing allele have also been able to successfully seek medical help. The potential for harm and the proposed benefits of DTC testing continue to be a topic of debate and investigation.

Ancestry percentage tests are also widely popular (Figure 3.45). Customers are genotyped and their alleles are assigned to different groups from around the world (Chapter 4 will discuss human biological variation in further detail). However, the scientific significance and potential harm of ancestry percentage tests have been called into question. For example, most alleles tested are not exclusive to one population, and populations may be defined differently depending on the testing companies. If an allele is assigned to the "Irish" population, there is a good chance that the allele may have evolved in a different cultural group or region that pre-dates the formation of the country Ireland. In other words, genetic variation often pre-dates the origins the population and geographical names of the region used by genetic testing companies. Another critique is that someone's identity need not include biological relationships. Individuals also have the option to find and connect online with individuals with whom they share portions of their genome, which has resulted in both positive and negative outcomes. Another interesting consideration is that law enforcement is currently developing forensic techniques that involve mining DTC genomic databases for the purpose of identifying suspects linked to crimes. Regardless of these various considerations, there are now millions of individuals worldwide who have "unlocked the secrets" of their DNA, and the multi-billion dollar genomics market only continues to grow.

As you have seen in this chapter, DNA provides instructions to our cells, which results in the creation and regulation of proteins. Understanding these fundamental mechanisms is important to being able to understand how the evolutionary process works (see Chapter 4) and how humans vary from one another (see Chapters 13 and 14). It is also the advancement in genetic technologies–including ancient DNA studies, genomics, and epigenetics–that has led to new anthropological understandings about our biological relationships to other living (extant) and extinct primates. Many of these genetic discoveries will be covered in the chapters to come.

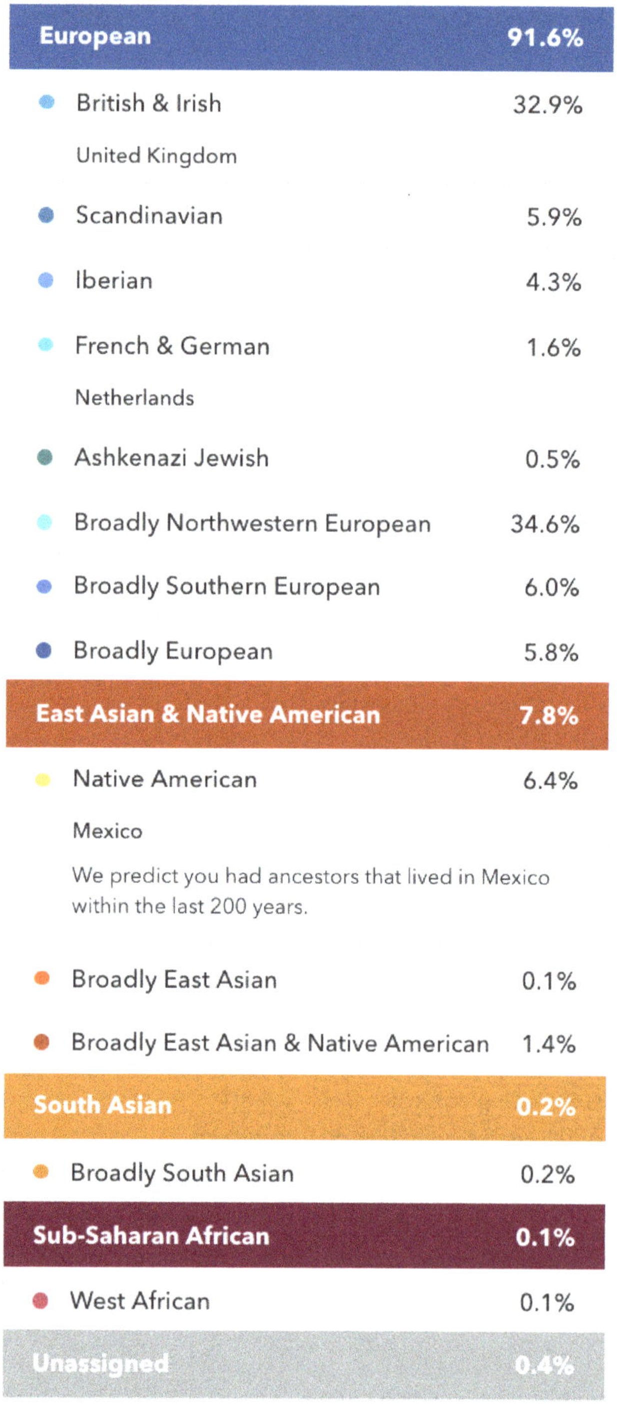

European	91.6%
British & Irish	32.9%
United Kingdom	
Scandinavian	5.9%
Iberian	4.3%
French & German	1.6%
Netherlands	
Ashkenazi Jewish	0.5%
Broadly Northwestern European	34.6%
Broadly Southern European	6.0%
Broadly European	5.8%
East Asian & Native American	**7.8%**
Native American	6.4%
Mexico	
We predict you had ancestors that lived in Mexico within the last 200 years.	
Broadly East Asian	0.1%
Broadly East Asian & Native American	1.4%
South Asian	**0.2%**
Broadly South Asian	0.2%
Sub-Saharan African	**0.1%**
West African	0.1%
Unassigned	0.4%

Figure 3.45 An example of ancestry percentage results provided to customers.

Review Questions

- What is the purpose of DNA replication? Explain in a few sentences what happens during DNA replication. When do DNA mutations happen? And how does this create phenotypic variation (i.e., different phenotypes of the same physical trait)?
- Using your own words, what are homologous chromosomes and sister chromatids? What are the key differences between mitosis and meiosis?
- Determine if the pedigree diagram below represents an autosomal dominant, autosomal recessive, or X-linked recessive pattern of inheritance. You should write the genotype (i.e., AA, Aa, or aa) above each square to help you (note: there may sometimes be two possible answers for a square's genotype). Please also explain why you concluded that particular pattern of inheritance.

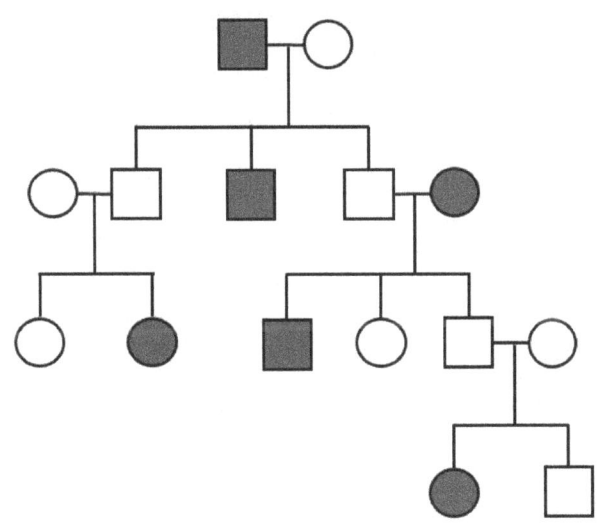

Figure 3.46

- Use base pairing rules to transcribe the following DNA template sequence into mRNA: **GTAAAGGTGCTGGCCATC**. Next, use the protein codon table (Figure 3.25) to translate the sequence. In regard to transcription, explain what the significance is of the first and last codon/protein in the sequence.
- In your opinion, what do you think the benefits are of direct-to-consumer (DTC) genetic testing? What are the drawbacks and/or greater ethical concerns? Do you think benefits outweigh concerns?
- Imagine that you submit your DNA sample to a genetic testing company and among the various diseases for which they test, there is an allele that is associated with late-onset Alzheimer's disease. You have the option to view your Alzheimer's result or to not view your result. What do you do and why?

Key Terms

Adenosine triphosphate (ATP): A high-energy compound produced by mitochondria that powers cellular processes.

Allele: A non-identical DNA sequence found in the same gene location on a homologous chromosome, or gene copy, that codes for the same trait but produces a different phenotype.

Amino acids: Organic molecules that are the building blocks of protein. Each of the 20 different amino acids have their own unique chemical property. Amino acids are also chained together to form proteins.

Ancient (aDNA): DNA that is isolated from organic remains often dating from hundreds to thousands of years ago. Also, aDNA is typically degraded (i.e., damaged) due to exposure to the elements such as heat, acidity, and humidity.

Aneuploid: A cell with an unexpected amount of chromosomes. The loss or gain of chromosomes can occur during mitotic or meiotic division.

Antibodies: Immune-related proteins that can detect and bind to foreign substances in the blood such as pathogens.

Apoptosis: A series of molecular steps that is activated leading to cell death. Apoptosis can be activated when a cell fails checkpoints during the cell cycle; however, cancer cells have the ability to avoid apoptosis.

Autosomal: Refers to a pattern of inheritance where an allele is located on an autosome.

Base pairs: Chemical bonding between nucleotides, like adenine (A) and thymine (T) or cytosine (C) and guanine (G) in DNA; or (A) and uracil (U) in RNA

Carbohydrate: Molecules composed of carbon and hydrogen atoms that can be broken down to supply energy.

Carrier: An individual who has a heterozygous genotype that is typically associated with a disease.

Cell cycle: A cycle the cell undergoes with checkpoints between phases to ensure that DNA replication and cell division occur properly.

Cell surface antigen: A protein that is found on a red blood cell's surface.

Centromere: A structural feature that is defined as the "center" of a chromosome and which creates two different arm lengths. Term also refers to the region of attachment for microtubules during mitosis and meiosis.

Chromatin: DNA wrapped around histone complexes. During cell division, chromatin becomes a condensed chromosome.

Chromosome: DNA molecule that is wrapped around protein complexes, including histones.

Codominance: The effects of both alleles in a genotype can be seen in the phenotype.

Codons: A sequence that comprises three DNA nucleotides that together code for a protein.

Complex diseases: A category of diseases that are polygenic and are also influenced by environment and lifestyle factors.

Cytoplasm: The "jelly-like" matrix inside of the cell that contains many organelles and other cellular molecules.

Deleterious: A mutation that increases an organism's susceptibility to disease.

Deoxyribonucleic acid (DNA): A molecule that carries the hereditary information passed down from parents to offspring.

DNA can be described as a "double helix'" shape. It includes two chains of nucleotides held together by hydrogen bonds with a sugar-phosphate backbone.

Diploid: Refers to an organism or cell with two sets of chromosomes.

DNA methylation: Methyl groups bind DNA, which modifies the transcriptional activity of a gene by turning it "on" or "off."

DNA polymerase: Enzyme that adds nucleotides to existing nucleic acid strands during DNA replication. These enzymes can be distinguished by their processivity (e.g., DNA replication).

DNA replication: Cellular process in which DNA is copied and doubled.

DNA sequence: The order of nucleotide bases. A DNA sequence can be short, long, or representative of entire chromosomes or organismal genomes.

Dominant: Refers to an allele for which one copy is sufficient to be visible in the phenotype.

Elongation: The assembly of new DNA from template strands with the help of DNA polymerases.

Enzymes: Proteins responsible for catalyzing (accelerating) various biochemical reactions in cells.

Epigenetic profile: The methylation pattern throughout a genome—that is, which genes (and other genomic sites) are methylated and unmethylated.

Epigenetics: Changes in gene expression that do not result in a change of the underlying DNA sequence. These changes typically involve DNA methylation and histone modifications. These changes are reversible and can also be inherited by the next generation.

Euchromatin: Loosely coiled chromosomes found within the nucleus that is accessible for regulatory processing of DNA.

Eukaryote: Single-celled or multicelled organism characterized by a distinct nucleus, with each organelle surrounded by its own membrane.

Exon: Protein-coding segment of a gene.

Gametes: Haploid cells referred to as an egg and sperm that will fuse together during sexual reproduction to form a diploid organism.

Gene: Segment of DNA that contains protein-coding information and various regulatory (e.g., promoter) and noncoding (e.g., introns) regions.

Genetic recombination: A cellular process that occurs during meiosis I in which homologous chromosomes pair up and sister chromatids on different chromosomes physically swap genetic information.

Genome: All the genetic information of an organism.

Genotype: The combination of two alleles that code for or are associated with the same gene.

Genotyping: A molecular procedure that is performed to test for the presence of certain alleles or to discover new ones.

Haploid: Cell or organism with one set of chromosomes ($n = 23$).

Helicase: A protein that breaks the hydrogen bonds that hold double-stranded DNA together.

Heterozygous: Genotype that consists of two different alleles.

Histones: Protein that DNA wraps around to assist with DNA organization within the nucleus.

Homologous chromosomes: A matching pair of chromosomes wherein one chromosome is maternally inherited and the other is paternally inherited.

Homozygous: Genotype that consists of two identical alleles.

Incomplete dominance: Heterozygous genotype that produces a phenotype that is a blend of both alleles.

Initiation: The recruitment of proteins to separate DNA strands and begin DNA replication.

Interphase: Preparatory period of the cell cycle when increased metabolic demand allows for DNA replication and doubling of the cell prior to cell division.

Introns: Segment of DNA that does not code for proteins.

Karyotyping: The microscopic procedure where the number of chromosomes in a cell is determined.

Lagging strand: DNA template strand that is opposite to the leading strand. Therefore, DNA replication proceeds discontinuously, generating Okazaki fragments.

Leading strand: DNA template strand in which replication proceeds continuously.

Lipids: Fatty acid molecules that serves various purposes in the cell, including energy storage, cell signaling, and structure.

Meiosis: The process that gametes undergo to divide. The end of meiosis results in four haploid daughter cells.

Mendelian genetics: A classification given to phenotypic traits that are controlled by a single gene.

Messenger RNA (mRNA): RNA molecule that is transcribed from DNA. Its tri-nucleotide codons are "read" by a ribosome to build a protein.

Microarray technology: A genotyping procedure that utilizes a microarray chip, which is a collection of thousands of short nucleotide sequences attached to a solid surface that can probe genomic DNA.

Microbiome: The collective genomes of the community of microorganisms that humans have living inside of their body.

Mitochondrial DNA (mtDNA): Circular DNA segment found in mitochondria that is inherited maternally.

Mitochondrion: Specialized cellular organelle that is the site for energy production. It also has its own genome (mtDNA).

Mitosis: The process that somatic cells undergo to divide. The end of mitosis results in two diploid daughter cells.

Mutation: A nucleotide sequence variation from the template DNA strand that can occur during replication. Mutations can also happen during recombination.

Next-generation sequencing: A genotyping technology that involves producing millions of nucleotide sequences (from a single DNA sample) that are then read with a sequencing machine. It can be used for analyzing entire genomes or specific regions and requires extensive program-based applications.

Nuclear envelope: A double-layered membrane that encircles the nucleus.

Nucleic acid: A complex structure (like DNA or RNA) that carries genetic information about a living organism.

Nucleotide: The basic structural component of nucleic acids, which includes DNA (A, T, C, and G) and RNA (A, U, C, and G).

Nucleus: Double-membrane cellular organelle that helps protect DNA and regulation of nuclear activities.

Okazaki fragment: Short DNA strands derived from DNA replication on the lagging strand. They were discovered by Reiji and Tsuneko Okazaki in the 1960s.

Organelle: A structure within a cell that performs specialized tasks that are essential for the cell. There are different types of organelles with their own function.

Pathogenic: A genetic mutation (i.e., allele) that has a harmful phenotypic disease-causing effect.

Penetrance: The proportion of how often the possession of an allele results in an expected phenotype. Some alleles are more penetrant than others.

Phenotype: The physical appearance of a given trait.

Phospholipid bilayer: Two layers of lipids that form a barrier due to the properties of a hydrophilic (water-loving) head and a hydrophobic (water-repelling) tail.

Polygenic trait: A phenotype that is controlled by two or more genes.

Polymerase chain reaction (PCR): A molecular biology procedure that can make copies of genomic DNA segments. A small amount of DNA is used as a starting template and is then used to make millions of copies.

Primer: A primer is a small sequence of nucleotides that bind DNA to start the process of DNA replication or PCR.

Prokaryote: A single-celled organism characterized by lack of a nucleus and membrane-enclosed organelles.

Promoter: The region of a gene that initiates transcription. Transcription factors can bind and DNA methylation may occur at a promoter site, which can modify the transcriptional activities of a gene.

Protein: Chain of amino acids that fold into a three dimensional structure that allow a cell to function in a variety of ways.

Protein synthesis: A multi-step process by which amino acids are strung together by RNA machinery read from a DNA template.

Recessive: Refers to an allele whose effect is not normally seen unless two copies are present in an individual's genotype.

Ribonucleic acid (RNA): Single-stranded nucleic acid molecule. There are different RNAs found within cells and they perform a variety of functions, such as cell signaling and involvement in protein synthesis.

Ribosomal RNA (rRNA): A ribosome-bound molecule that is used to correctly assemble amino acids into proteins.

Ribosome: An organelle in the cell found in the cytoplasm or endoplasmic reticulum. It is responsible for reading mRNA and protein assemblage.

RNA polymerase: An enzyme that catalyzes the process of making RNA from a DNA template.

Sanger-sequencing: A process that involves the usage of fluorescently labeled nucleotides to visualize DNA (PCR fragments) at the nucleotide level.

Semi-conservative replication: DNA replication in which new DNA is replicated from an existing DNA template strand.

Sequencing: A molecular laboratory procedure that produces the order of nucleotide bases (i.e., sequences).

Sister chromatids: During DNA replication, sister chromatids are produced on the chromosome. In cell division, sister chromatids are pulled apart so that two cells can be formed. In meiosis, sister chromatids are also the sites of genetic recombination.

Somatic cells: Diploid cells that comprise body tissues and undergo mitosis for maintenance and repair of tissues.

Splicing: The process by which mature mRNAs are produced. Introns are removed (spliced) and exons are joined together.

Sugar phosphate backbone: A biochemical structural component of DNA. The "backbone" consists of deoxyribose sugars and phosphate molecules.

Telomere: A compound structure located at the ends of chromosomes to help protect the chromosomes from degradation after every round of cell division.

Termination: The halt of DNA replication activity that occurs when a DNA sequence "stop" codon is encountered.

Tissue: A cluster of cells that are morphologically similar and perform the same task.

Transcription: The process by which DNA nucleotides (within a gene) are copied, which results in a messenger RNA molecule.

Transcription factors: Proteins that bind to regulatory regions of genes (e.g., promoter) and increase or decrease the amount of transcriptional activity of a gene, including turning them "on" or "off."

Transfer RNA (tRNA): RNA molecule involved in translation. Transfer RNA transports amino acids from the cell's cytoplasm to a ribosome.

Translation: The process by which messenger RNA codons are read and amino acids are "chained together" to form proteins.

X-linked: Refers to a pattern of inheritance where the allele is located on the X or Y chromosome.

About the Authors

Hayley Mann, M.A.

Binghamton University, hmann3@binghamton.edu

Hayley Mann received her bachelor's degree in Genetics from the University of California, Davis, and continued her graduate studies in Biological and Molecular Anthropology at the California State University, Sacramento. She is currently a Ph.D. candidate at Binghamton University, where her dissertation focus is on studying genetic variation of Pacific Islanders (Republic of Vanuatu) and also changes in health as the result of colonization. Hayley also works in clinical genomics and specializes in various DNA-sequencing methodologies.

Hayley Mann

Xazmin Lowman, Ph.D.

University of California, Irvine, xlowman@uci.edu

Xazmin Lowman received her bachelor's degree in Physiology from the University of Arizona. She pursued her doctorate in cancer biology at the University of Minnesota, where she studied how blood cancers evade cell death. Currently, her scientific interests have led to a postdoctoral fellowship at the University of California, Irvine, where she studies how solid tumors adapt to metabolic stress. Beyond figuring out the mechanisms that drive cancer, she enjoys traveling to learn of other cultures and share her own upbringing on the Navajo reservation.

Xazmin Lowman

Malaina Gaddis, Ph.D.

malainagaddis@gmail.com

Malaina Gaddis studied biology at Brigham Young University in Utah and then earned a Ph.D. in genetics and molecular and cellular biology at the University of Southern California. During her Ph.D. studies, she investigated small molecule inhibitors that alter epigenetic modifications and gene expression in cancer cells. Following her Ph.D., she focused on the business side of the biotech industry by completing a master's degree in bioscience management at the Keck Graduate Institute. Malaina is especially interested in using genomics to further genetic testing and personalized treatment and currently works as a genome variation scientist.

Malaina Gaddis

For Further Exploration

Websites

National Human Genome Research Institute https://www.genome.gov/

Genetics Home Reference https://ghr.nlm.nih.gov/

Genetics Generation http://knowgenetics.org/

yourgenome https://www.yourgenome.org/

Cardiovascular Disease: Genes are Important, but Health-Related Behaviors and Lifestyle Choices Can Make or Break Your Health http://ehrweb.aaas.org/ehr/books/3_howard.html

Gene Sequencing Speeds Diagnosis of Deadly Newborn Diseases http://www.pbs.org/wgbh/nova/next/body/newborn-gene-sequencing/

Carl Zimmer's Game of Genomes https://www.statnews.com/feature/game-of-genomes/season-one/

Illumina Sequencing by Synthesis https://www.youtube.com/watch?v=fCd6B5HRaZ8

Articles

Aartsma-Rus, Annemieke, Ieke B. Ginjaar, and Kate Bushby. 2016. "The Importance of Genetic Diagnosis for Duchenne Muscular Dystrophy." *Journal of Medical Genetics* 53 (3): 145-151.

Acuna-Hidalgo, Rocio, Joris A. Veltman, and Alexander Hoischen. 2016. "New Insights into the Generation and Role of De Novo Mutations in Health and Disease." *Genome Biology* 17 (241): 1-19.

Albert, Benjamin, Susanna Tomassetti, Yvonne Gloor, Daniel Dilg, Stefano Mattarocci, Slawomir Kubik, Lukas Hafner, and David Shore. 2019. "Sfp1 Regulates Transcriptional Networks Driving Cell Growth and Division through Multiple Promoter-Binding Modes." *Genes & Development* 33 (5-6): 288–293.

Almathen, Faisal, Haitham Elbir, Hussain Bahbahani, Joram Mwacharo, and Olivier Hanotte. 2018. "Polymorphisms in Mc1r and Asip Genes Are Associated With Coat Color Variation in the Arabian Camel." *Journal of Heredity* 109 (6): 700–706.

Ballester, Leomar Y., Rajyalakshmi Luthra, Rashmi Kanagal-Shamanna, and Rajesh R. Singh. 2016. "Advances in Clinical Next-Generation Sequencing: Target Enrichment and Sequencing Technologies." *Expert Review of Molecular Diagnostics* 16 (3): 357–372.

Baranovskiy, Andrey G., Vincent N. Duong, Nigar D. Babayeva, Yinbo Zhang, Youri I. Pavlov, Karen S. Anderson, and Tahir H. Tahirov. 2018. "Activity and Fidelity of Human DNA Polymerase Alpha Depend on Primer Structure." *Journal of Biological Chemistry* 293 (18): 6,824–6,843.

Brezina, Paulina R., Raymond Anchan, and William G. Kearns. 2016. "Preimplantation Genetic Testing for Aneuploidy: What Technology Should You Use and What Are the Differences?" *Journal of Assisted Reproduction and Genetics* 33 (7): 823-832.

Bultman, Scott J. 2017. "Interplay Between Diet, Gut Microbiota, Epigenetic Events, and Colorectal Cancer." *Molecular Nutrition & Food Research* 61 (1):1-12.

Cutting, Garry R. 2015. "Cystic Fibrosis Genetics: From Molecular Understanding to Clinical Application." *Nature Reviews Genetics* 16 (1): 45–56.

D'Alessandro, Giuseppina., and Fabrizio d'Adda di Fagagna. 2017. "Transcription and DNA Damage: Holding Hands or Crossing Swords?" *Journal of Molecular Biology* 429 (21): 3,215–3,229.

De Craene, Johan-Owen, Dimitri L. Bertazzi, Séverine Bar, and Sylvie Friant. 2017. "Phosphoinositides, Major Actors in Membrane Trafficking and Lipid Signaling Pathways." *International Journal of Molecular Sciences* 18 (3): 1-20.

Deng, Lian, and Shuhua Xu. 2018. "Adaptation of Human Skin Color in Various Populations." *Hereditas* 155 (1): 1-12.

Dever, Thomas E., Terri G. Kinzy, and Graham D. Pavitt. 2016. "Mechanism and Regulation of Protein Synthesis in Saccharomyces Cerevisiae." *Genetics* 203 (1): 65–107.

Eme, Laura, Anja Spang, Jonathan Lombard, Courtney W. Stairs, and Thijs J. G. Ettema. 2017. "Archaea and the Origin of Eukaryotes." *Nature Reviews Microbiology* 15 (12): 711–723.

Gomez-Carballa, Alberto, Jacobo Pardo-Seco, Stefania Brandini, Alessandro Achilli, Ugo A. Perego, Michael D. Coble, Toni M. Diegoli, *et al.* 2018. "The Peopling of South America and the Trans-Andean Gene Flow of the First Settlers." *Genome Research* 28 (6): 767–779.

Gvozdenov, Zlata, Janhavi Kolhe, and Brian C. Freeman. 2019. "The Nuclear and DNA-Associated Molecular Chaperone Network." *Cold Spring Harbor Perspectives in Biology*. New York:Cold Spring Harbor Laboratory Press.

Harkins, Kelly M., and Anne C. Stone. 2015. "Ancient Pathogen Genomics: Insights Into Timing and Adaptation." *Journal of Human Evolution* 79: 137–149.

Jackson, Maria, Leah Marks, Gerhard H. W. May, and Joanna B. Wilson. 2018. "The Genetic Basis of Disease." *Essays in Biochemistry* 62 (5): 643–723.

Lenormand, Thomas., Jan Engelstadter, Susan E. Johnston, Erik Wijnker, and Christopher R. Haag. 2016. "Evolutionary Mysteries in Meiosis." *Philosophical Transactions of the Royal Society B* 371: 1–14.

Levy, Shawn E., and Richard M. Myers. 2016. "Advancements in Next-Generation Sequencing." *Annual Review of Genomics and Human Genetics* 17: 95–115.

Lu, Mengfei, Cathryn M. Lewis, and Matthew Traylor. 2017. "Pharmacogenetic Testing Through the Direct-to-Consumer Genetic Testing Company 23andme." *BMC Medical Genomics* 10 (47): 1–8.

Ly, Lundi, Donovan Chan, Mahmoud Aarabi, Mylene Landry, Nathalie A. Behan, Amanda J. MacFarlane, and Jacquetta Trasler. 2017. "Intergenerational Impact of Paternal Lifetime Exposures to Both Folic Acid Deficiency and Supplementation on Reproductive Outcomes and Imprinted Gene Methylation." *Molecular Human Reproduction* 23 (7): 461–477.

Ma, Wenxiu, Giancarlo Bonora, Joel B. Berletch, Xinxian Deng, William S. Noble, and Christine M. Disteche. 2018. "X-Chromosome Inactivation and Escape From X Inactivation in Mouse." *Methods in Molecular Biology* 1,861: 205–219.

Machiela, Mitchell J., Weiyin Zhou, Eric Karlins, Joshua N. Sampson, Neal D. Freedman, Qi Yang, Belynda Hicks, *et al.* 2016. "Female Chromosome X Mosaicism Is Age-Related and Preferentially Affects the Inactivated X Chromosome." *Nat Commun* 7: 1–9. doi: 10.1038/ncomms11843.

Mahdavi, Morteza, Mohammadreza Nassiri, Mohammad M. Kooshyar, Masoume Vakili-Azghandi, Amir Avan, Ryan Sandry, Suja Pillai, Alfred K. Lam, and Vinod Gopalan. 2019. "Hereditary Breast Cancer; Genetic Penetrance and Current Status With BRCA." *Journal of Cellular Physiology* 234 (5): 5,741–5,750.

McDade, Thomas W., Calen P. Ryan, Meaghan J. Jones, Morgan K. Hoke, Judith Borja, Gregory E. Miller, Christopher W. Kuzawa, and Michael S. Kobor. 2019. "Genome-Wide Analysis of DNA Methylation in Relation to Socioeconomic Status During Development and Early Adulthood." *American Journal of Physical Anthropology* 169 (1): 3–11.

Migeon, Barbara R. 2017. "Choosing the Active X: The Human Version of X Inactivation." *Trends in Genetics* 33 (12): 899–909.

Myerowitz, Rachel. 1997. "Tay-Sachs Disease-Causing Mutations and Neutral Polymorphisms in the Hex a Gene." *Human Mutation* 9: 195–208.

Onufriev, Alexey V. and Helmut Schiessel. 2019. "The Nucleosome: From Structure to Function Through Physics." *Current Opinion in Structural Biology* 56: 119–130.

Quillen, Ellen E., Heather L. Norton, Esteban J. Parra, Frida Lona-Durazo, Khai C. Ang, Florin M. Illiescu, Laurel N. Pearson, *et al.* 2019. "Shades of Complexity: New Perspectives on the Evolution and Genetic Architecture of Human Skin." *American Journal of Physical Anthropology* 168 (67): 4–26.

Raspelli, Erica and Roberta Fraschini. 2019. "Spindle Pole Power in Health and Disease." *Current Genetics* 65 (4): 851-855.

Ravinet, M., R. Faria, R. K. Butlin, J. Galindo, N. Bierne, M. Rafajlovic, M. A. F. Noor, B. Mehlig, and A. M. Westram. 2017.

"Interpreting the Genomic Landscape of Speciation: A Road Map for Finding Barriers to Gene Flow." *Journal of Evolutionary Biology* 30 (8): 1,450–1,477.

Regev, Aviv, Sarah A. Teichmann, Eric S. Lander, Ido Amit, Christophe Benoist, Ewan Birney, Bernd Bodenmiller, *et al.* 2017. "The Human Cell Atlas." *Elife* 6e27041: 1-30. doi: https://doi.org/10.7554.eLife.27041.

Roberts, Andrea L., Nicole Gladish, Evan Gatev, Meaghan J. Jones, Ying Chen, Julia L. MacIsaac, Shelley S. Tworoger, *et al.* 2018. "Exposure to Childhood Abuse Is Associated With Human Sperm DNA Methylation." *Translational Psychiatry* 8 (194): 1-11.

Roger, Andrew J., Sergio A. Muñoz-Gómez, and Ryoma Kamikawa. 2017. "The Origin and Diversification of Mitochondria." *Current Biology* 27 (21): R1177–R1192.

Ségurel, Laure and Céline Bon. 2017. "On the Evolution of Lactase Persistence in Humans." *Annual Review of Genomics and Human Genetics* 18: 297–319.

Sheth, Bhavisha P. and Vrinda S. Thaker. 2017. "DNA Barcoding and Traditional Taxonomy: An Integrated Approach for Biodiversity Conservation." *Genome* 60 (7): 618–628.

Snedeker, Jonathan, Matthew Wooten, and Xin Chen. 2017. "The Inherent Asymmetry of DNA Replication." *Annual Review of Cell and Developmental Biology* 33: 291–318.

Sullivan-Pyke, Chantae and Anuja Dokras. 2018. "Preimplantation Genetic Screening and Preimplantation Genetic Diagnosis." *Obstetrics and Gynecology Clinics of North America* 45 (1): 113–125.

Szostak, Jack W. 2017. "The Narrow Road to the Deep Past: In Search of the Chemistry of the Origin of Life." *Angewandte Chemie International Edition* 56 (37): 11,037–11,043.

Tessema, Mathewos, Ulrich Lehmann, and Hans Kreipe. 2004. "Cell Cycle and No End." *Virchows Archiv European Journal of Pathology* 444 (4): 313–323.

Tishkoff, Sarah A., Floyd A. Reed, Alessia Ranciaro, Benjamin F. Voight, Courtney C. Babbitt, Jesse S. Silverman, Kweli Powell, *et al.* 2007. "Convergent Adaptation of Human Lactase Persistence in Africa and Europe." *Nature Genetics* 39 (1): 31–40.

Visootsak, Jeannie and John M. Graham, Jr. 2006. "Klinefelter Syndrome and Other Sex Chromosomal Aneuploidies." *Orphanet Journal of Rare Diseases* 1:42 doi: 10.1186/1750-1172-1-42.

Yamamoto, Fumi-ichiro, Henrik Clausen, Thayer White, John Marken, and Sen-itiroh Hakomori. 1990. "Molecular Genetic Basis of the Histo-Blood Group Abo System." *Nature* 345: 229–233.

Zlotogora, Joël. 2003. "Penetrance and Expressivity in the Molecular Age." *Genetics in Medicine* 5: 347–352.

Zorina-Lichtenwalter, Katerina, Ryan N. Lichtenwalter, Dima V. Zaykin, Marc Parisien, Simon Gravel, Andrey Bortsov, and Luda Diatchenko. 2019. "A Study in Scarlet: MC1R as the Main Predictor of Red Hair and Exemplar of the Flip-Flop Effect." *Human Molecular Genetics* 28 (12): 2,093-2,106.

Zwart, Haeh. 2018. "In the Beginning Was the Genome: Genomics and the Bi-Textuality of Human Existence." *New Bioethics* 24 (1): 26–43.

References

Lindo, John, Emilia Huerta-Sánchez, Shigeki Nakagome, Morten Rasmussen, Barbara Petzelt, Joycelynn Mitchell, Jerome S. Cybulski, et al. 2016. "A Time Transect of Exomes From a Native American Population Before and After European Contact." *Nature Communications* 7: 1–11. doi: 10.1038/ncomms13175.

Skloot, Rebecca. 2010. *The Immortal Life of Henrietta Lacks.* New York: Crown Publishing Group.

Wolfe, George C., dir. 2017. *The Immortal Life of Henrietta Lacks.* HBO Films, April 22, 2017. TV Movie.

Figure Attributions

Figure 3.1 Phospholipid Bilayer (Anatomy & Physiology, Chapter 3.1, Figure 2) by OpenStax is used under a CC BY 4.0 License.

Figure 3.2 Nucleic Acid by NIH National Human Genome Research Institute is in the public domain.

Figure 3.3 Amino acids (Biology 2e, Figure 3.22) by OpenStax is used under a CC BY 4.0 License.

Figure 3.4 Amino Acids by NIH National Human Genome Research Institute is in the public domain.

Figure 3.5 Bacteria by NIH National Human Genome Research Institute is in the public domain.

Figure 3.6 Bryum capillare lamina by Kristian Peters [Fabelfroh 13:07, 2007 (UTC)] is used under a CC BY-SA 3.0 License.

Figure 3.7 Cell Membrane (Anatomy & Physiology, Figure 3.4) by OpenStax is used under a CC BY 4.0 License.

Figure 3.8 Organelle by NIH National Human Genome Research Institute is in the public domain.

Figure 3.9 Nucleus (Biology 2e, Figure 4.11) by OpenStax is used under a CC BY 4.0 License.

Figure 3.10 Mitochondrion through an electron microscope (Biology 2e, Figure 4.14) by OpenStax is used under a CC BY 4.0 License.

Figure 3.11 Cell Structure table original to Explorations: An Open Invitation to Biological Anthropology by Hayley Mann, Xazmin Lowman, and Malaina Gaddis is under a CC BY-NC 4.0 License.

Figure 3.12a A group of Tsimshian people having a tea party in a tent, Lax Kw'alaams (formerly Port Simpson), B.C., c. 1890 by unknown photographer at Online MIKAN no. 3368729 Library and Archives Canada (C-060817). Copyright is expired.

Figure 3.12b Tsimshian Territory map original to Explorations: An Open Invitation to Biological Anthropology by Elyssa Ebding at GeoPlace, California State University, Chico is under a CC BY-NC 4.0 License.

Figure 3.13 Rosalind Franklin from the personal collection of Jenifer Glynn by MRC Laboratory of Molecular Biology is used under a CC BY-SA 4.0 License.

Figure 3.14 Histone by NIH National Human Genome Research Institute is in the public domain.

Figure 3.15 Genome by NIH National Human Genome Research Institute is in the public domain.

Figure 3.16 Chromosome original to Explorations: An Open Invitation to Biological Anthropology by Katie Nelson is under a CC BY-NC 4.0 License.

Figure 3.17 DNA replication zh by LadyofHats has been designated to the public domain (CC0).

Figure 3.18 Cell cycle (Biology 2e, Figure 10.5) by OpenStax is used under a CC BY 4.0 License.

Figure 3.19 HeLa-III by National Institutes of Health (NIH) is in the public domain.

Figure 3.20 Mitosis original to Explorations: An Open Invitation to Biological Anthropology by Mary Nelson is under a CC BY-NC 4.0 License.

Figure 3.21 Meiosis original to Explorations: An Open Invitation to Biological Anthropology by Mary Nelson is under a CC BY-NC 4.0 License.

Figure 3.22 Transcription by NIH National Human Genome Research Institute is in the public domain.

Figure 3.23 Protein synthesis original to Explorations: An Open Invitation to Biological Anthropology by Mary Nelson is under a CC BY-NC 4.0 License.

Figure 3.24 Ribosome (Biology 2e, Figure 3.34) by OpenStax is used under a CC BY 4.0 License

Figure 3.25 Codon Table by NIH National Human Genome Research Institute, accessed August 13, 2018 is in the public domain.

Figure 3.26 Protein by NIH National Human Genome Research Institute is in the public domain.

Figure 3.27 Mendel's statue by Coeli has been designated to the public domain (CC0).

Figure 3.28 Mendels peas by Mariana Ruiz LadyofHats has been designated to the public domain (CC0 1.0).

Figure 3.29 Homozygous by NIH National Human Genome Research Institute is in the public domain.

Figure 3.30 Punnett square mendel flowers by Madeleine Price Ball (Madprime) is used under a CC BY-SA 3.0 License.

Figure 3.31 Mendelian disorders table original to Explorations: An Open Invitation to Biological Anthropology by Hayley Mann, Xazmin Lowman, and Malaina Gaddis is under a CC BY-NC 4.0 License.

Figure 3.32 Blood types by Shahinsahar is used under a CC BY-SA 3.0 License.

Figure 3.33 ABO Blood Genotypes original to Explorations: An Open Invitation to Biological Anthropology by Katie Nelson is under a CC BY-NC 4.0 License.

Figure 3.34 Mendelian dominant pattern of inheritance original to Explorations: An Open Invitation to Biological Anthropology by Beth Shook is under a CC BY-NC 4.0 License.

Figure 3.35 Cystic fibrosis, Mendelian recessive pattern of inheritance, original to Explorations: An Open Invitation to Biological Anthropology by Beth Shook is under a CC BY-NC 4.0 License.

Figure 3.36 X-linked recessive pattern of inheritance original to Explorations: An Open Invitation to Biological Anthropology by Beth Shook is under a CC BY-NC 4.0 License.

Figure 3.37 Antirrhinum a.k.a. Snap dragon at lalbagh 7112 by Rameshng is used under a CC BY-SA 3.0 License.

Figure 3.38 Epigenetic Control (Biology 2e, Figure 16.7) by OpenStax is used under a CC BY 4.0 License.

Figure 3.39 "Rue" the calico cat by Hayley Mann is under a CC BY-NC 4.0 License.

Figure 3.40 PCR electrophoresis gel by Hayley Mann is under a CC BY-NC 4.0 License.

Figure 3.41 Sanger sequencing with heterozygous result by Hayley Mann is under a CC BY-NC 4.0 License.

Figure 3.42 DNA microarray by Guillaume Paumier (user:guillom) is used under a CC BY-SA 3.0 License.

Figure 3.43 Illumina Hiseq 2,000 sequencers, BGI Hong Kong sequencing room by Scotted400 is used under a CC BY 3.0 License.

Figure 3.44 Positive carrier result for celiac disease allele by Hayley Mann is under a CC BY-NC 4.0 License.

Figure 3.45 DNA ancestry percentage test results by Hayley Mann is under a CC BY-NC 4.0 License.

Figure 3.46 Pedigree original to Explorations: An Open Invitation to Biological Anthropology by Beth Shook is under a CC BY-NC 4.0 License.

Chapter 4: Forces of Evolution

Andrea J. Alveshere, Ph.D., Western Illinois University

> *Learning Objectives*
>
> - Describe the history and contributions of the Modern Synthesis.
> - Define populations and population genetics as well as the methods used to study them.
> - Identify the forces of evolution and become familiar with examples of each.
> - Discuss the evolutionary significance of mutation, genetic drift, gene flow, and natural selection.
> - Explain how allele frequencies can be used to study evolution as it happens.
> - Contrast micro- and macroevolution.

It's hard for us, with our typical human life spans of less than 100 years, to imagine all the way back, 3.8 billion years ago, to the **origins of life**. Scientists still study and debate how life came into being and whether it originated on Earth or in some other region of the universe (including some scientists who believe that studying evolution can reveal the complex processes that were set in motion by God or a higher power). What we do know is that a living single-celled organism was present on Earth during the early stages of our planet's existence. This organism had the potential to reproduce by making copies of itself, just like bacteria, many amoebae, and our own living cells today. In fact, with today's genetic and genomic technologies, we can now trace genetic lineages, or **phylogenies**, and determine the relationships between all of today's living organisms—eukaryotes (animals, plants, fungi, etc.), archaea, and bacteria—on the branches of the **phylogenetic tree of life** (Figure 4.1).

Looking at the common sequences in modern genomes, we can even make educated guesses about what the genetic sequence of the first organism, or **universal ancestor** of all living things, would likely have been. Through a wondrous series of mechanisms and events, that first single-celled organism gave rise to the rich diversity of species that fill the lands, seas, and skies of our planet. This chapter explores the mechanisms by which that amazing transformation occurred and considers some of the crucial scientific experiments that shaped our current understanding of the evolutionary process.

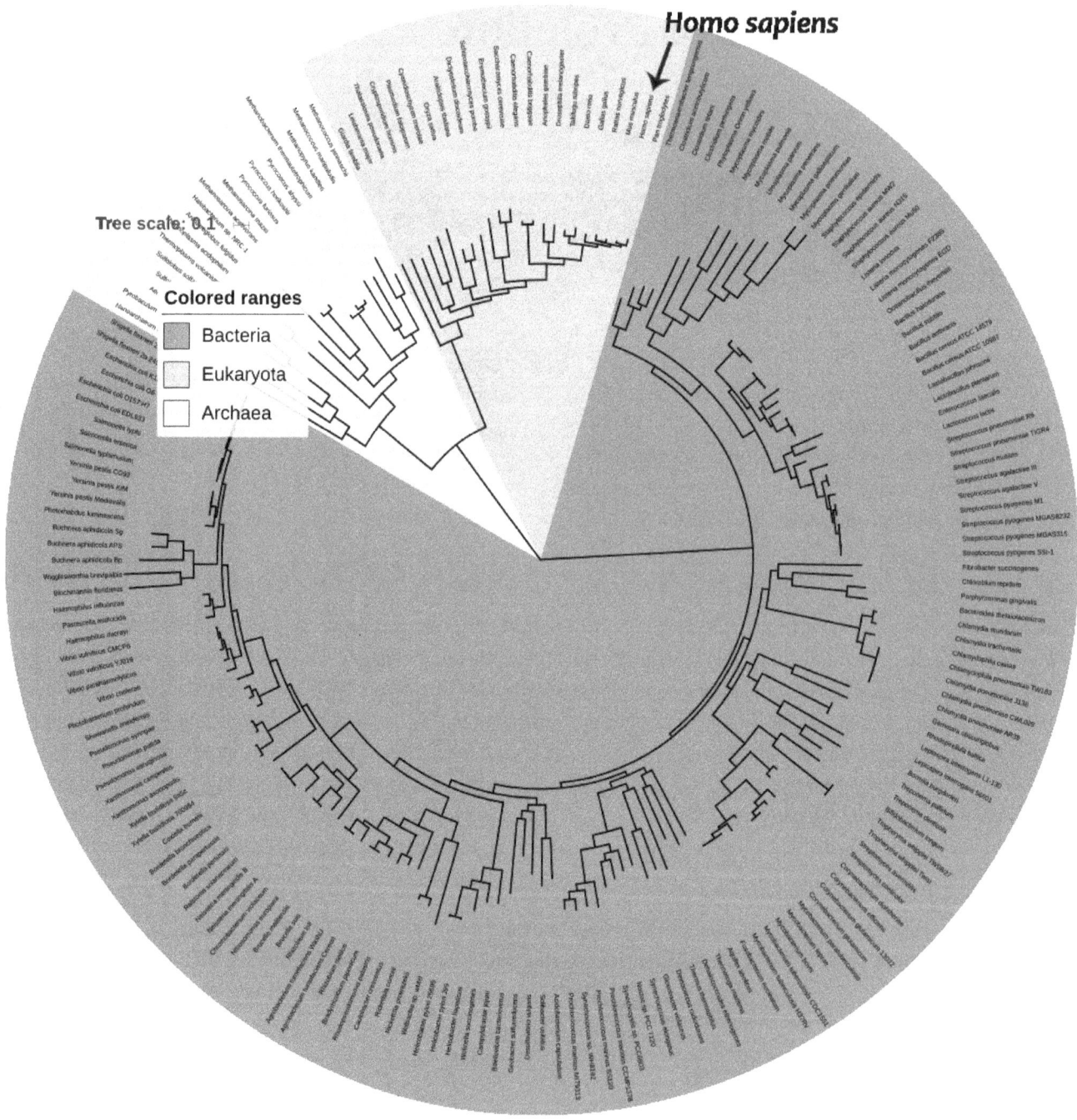

Figure 4.1 Phylogenetic tree of life.

THE MODERN SYNTHESIS

Historical Framework

When learning about biological sciences today, we always recognize the contributions of Charles Darwin and Gregor Mendel, so it may be surprising to learn that for a time, before we arrived at today's understanding of genetics and inheritance, both Darwin's and Mendel's work fell out of favor. Neither Darwin's theory of natural selection, nor Mendel's particulate inheritance were individually sufficient to fully explain all the phenomena being observed in the natural world. It would take many decades, and many careful scientific experiments to solve the puzzle of evolution.

Rethinking Darwin

As noted in Chapter 2, Darwin's 1859 book On the Origin of Species made a big splash; however, as other researchers began doing what scientists do—testing whether or not the concept of natural selection could consistently account for the variation seen in organisms—they began to find many exceptions. One reason for this is that, as we now know, natural selection is only one of the forces of evolution. Another challenge was a general lack of understanding about how variation is initiated and how inheritance works. Many scientists of the day subscribed to the concept known as **Lamarckian inheritance**, which posited that offspring would inherit characteristics that were acquired during their parents' lifetimes (Figure 4.2).Darwin himself, in 1868, promoted an idea called **pangenesis**, which combines the Lamarckian idea of inheriting acquired characteristics with the idea that particles from different parts of the body make their way to the sex cells. Alfred Russell Wallace, evolution. Another researcher, August Weismann, also rejected the idea that acquired characteristics could be passed on. Weismann (1892) devised an experiment to directly test whether offspring inherited acquired characteristics: he cut the tails off mice, bred them, and then waited eagerly to find out if the offspring had tails. All the baby mice were born with tails intact, demonstrating Lamarckian inheritance of acquired characteristics to be incorrect (Figure 4.3).

Figure 4.2B The Modern Synthesis perspective: The ancestral population had a range of variation in neck length. Those individuals with the longest necks would be the most likely to survive to pass on their longer-neck alleles to future generations.

Figure 4.2A The Lamarckian hypothesis: If a short-necked parent often stretched its neck to reach higher branches, each generation of offspring would be born with somewhat longer necks.

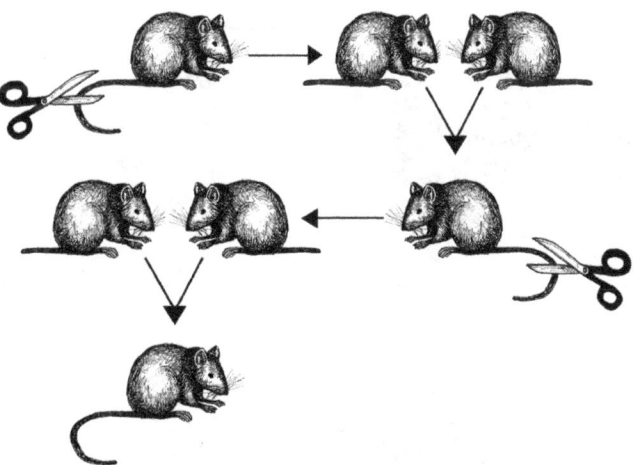

Figure 4.3 Weismann's mouse-tail experiment showing that offspring do not inherit traits that the parents acquired during their lifetimes.who had arrived at the concept of natural selection independently of Darwin, rejected Lamarckian

Forces of Evolution | 111

Rediscovering Mendel

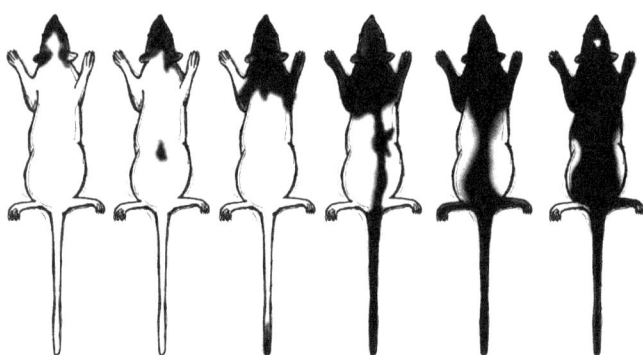

Figure 4.4 *The continuous range of variation observed in hooded rat coat patterns after five generations.*

In 1900, two scientists named Hugo de Vries and Carl Correns, who were independently studying the mechanisms of inheritance, rediscovered Gregor Mendel's work. Mendel's pea plant experiments provided the concepts of dominant and recessive traits, which explained retention of certain characteristics in a way that Darwin's idea, blending inheritance, didn't. The debate that unfolded was between the **Mutationists**, who believed that variation was caused by mutations in distinct, inherited cells, and **Biometricians**, who believed that individual mutations of discrete hereditary units could never account for the continuous spectrum of variation seen in many traits. One set of experiments that helped resolve this debate was a five-year study carried out by William Castle and John Phillips on laboratory rats (Castle and Phillips 1914). The dominant coat color was the gray wild type, and the piebald or "hooded" color was recessive. He cross-bred the rats multiple ways for five generations and proved that he could achieve a continuous range of variation; in fact, he even achieved coat pattern variations that were more extreme than the original maximums of the parent groups (Figure 4.4).

Another scientist, Thomas Hunt Morgan, conducted studies in which he induced genetic mutations in populations of the fruit fly, *Drosophila melanogaster* (Figure 4.5). His work demonstrated that most mutations merely increased variation within populations, rather than creating new species (Morgan 1911).

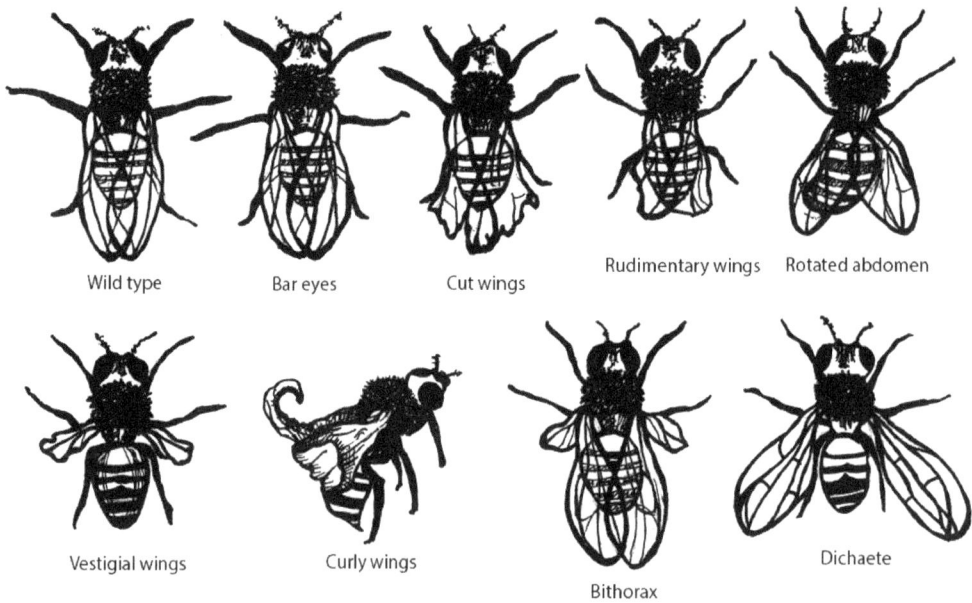

Figure 4.5 *Examples of mutations producing phenotypic variation in a single species of fruit fly.*

112 | Forces of Evolution

Tying It All Together

While the biggest leap forward in understanding how evolution works came with the joining (synthesis) of Darwin's concept of natural selection with Mendel's insights about particulate inheritance, there were some other big contributions that were crucial to making sense of the variation that was being observed. R.A. Fisher (1919) and John Burdon Sanderson Haldane (1924) developed and tested mathematical models for evolutionary change that provided the tools to study variation and became the basis for the study of population genetics. Sewall Wright (1932) and Theodosius Dobzhansky (1937) performed studies that revealed the existence of **chromosomes** as carriers of collections of genes. Edmund Brisco Ford (1949) conducted studies on wild butterflies that confirmed Fisher's mathematical predictions and also led to his definition of the concept of **polymorphisms** to describe alternative phenotypes, or multiple forms of a trait. Ford (1942) also correctly predicted that human blood type polymorphisms were maintained in the population because they were involved in disease resistance. Julian Huxley's 1942 book, *Evolution: The Modern Synthesis*, provided an easy-to-read summary of the evolutionary studies that had come before. It was with this book that the term **Modern Synthesis** was first used to describe the integration of Darwin's, Mendel's, and subsequent research into a unified theory of evolution. In appealing to the general public, Huxley's book also found new success establishing a wide acceptance of the process of evolution.

POPULATION GENETICS

Defining Species and Populations and the Variations Within Them

One of the major breakthroughs in understanding the mechanisms of evolutionary change came with the realization that evolution takes place at the level of populations, not within individuals. In the biological sciences, a **population** is defined as a group of individuals of the same species who are geographically near enough to one another that they can breed and produce new generations of individuals. **Species** are organisms whose individuals are capable of breeding because they are biologically and behaviorally compatible to produce viable, fertile offspring. **Viable offspring** are those offspring who are healthy enough to survive to adulthood. **Fertile offspring** can reproduce successfully to have offspring of their own. Both conditions must be met for individuals to be considered part of the same species. As you can imagine, these criteria complicate the identification of distinct species in fossilized remains of extinct populations. In those cases, we must examine how much phenotypic variation is typically found within a comparable modern-day species, and then determine whether the fossilized remains fall within the expected range of variation for a single species.

Some species have subpopulations that are regionally distinct. These are classified as separate **subspecies** because they have their own unique phenotypes and are geographically isolated from one another, but if they do happen to encounter one another, they are still capable of successful interbreeding.

There are many examples of sterile hybrids that are offspring of parents from two different species. For example, horses and donkeys can breed and have offspring together. Depending on which species is the mother and which is the father, the offspring are either called mules, or hennies. Mules and hennies can live full life spans but are not able to have offspring of their own. Likewise, tigers and lions have been known to mate and have viable offspring. Again, depending on which species is the mother and which is the father, these offspring are called either ligers or tigons. Like mules and hennies, ligers and tigons are unable to reproduce. In each of these cases, the mismatched set of chromosomes that the offspring inherit still produce an adequate set of functioning genes for the hybrid offspring, but, once mixed and divided in meiosis, the gametes don't contain the full complement of genes needed for survival in the third generation.

For the purpose of studying evolution, we recognize populations by their even smaller units: genes. Each individual, for genetic inheritance purposes, carries a collection of genes that can be passed down to future generations. For this reason, in population genetics, we think of populations as **gene pools**, which refers to the entire collection of genetic material in a breeding community that can be passed on from one generation to the next.

Remember, a **gene** is the basic unit of information that encodes the proteins needed to grow and function as a living organism. Each gene can have multiple **alleles**, or variants, each of which may produce a slightly different protein. For example, there are brown- or blue-pigment alleles for eye color (green is a slight variant of the brown type). The set of alleles that an individual inherits for a given gene is known as the **genotype** (e.g., inheriting both brown and blue eye pigments gives a genotype of B*b*); while the observable traits that are produced by a genotype is known as the **phenotype** (e.g., a B*b* individual exhibiting the dominant brown eye trait). For genes carried on our human chromosomes (our nuclear DNA), we inherit two copies of each, one from each parent. This means we may carry two of the same alleles (a **homozygous genotype**; eye pigment genotypes BB or *bb*) or two different alleles (a **heterozygous genotype**; eye pigment genotype B*b*) for each nuclear gene. Only one of each of our alleles will get passed on to each of our children (the other will come from the child's other parent). This means that children often inherit new genotypes and likely express unique phenotypes, compared to their parents. A common example is when two brown-eyed parents (who happen to be heterozygous for the pigment alleles) have a blue-eyed baby (genotype *bb*; who has inherited the recessive *b* alleles from both parents).

Defining Evolution

In order to understand evolution, it's crucial to remember that evolution is always studied at the population level. Also, if a population were to stay exactly the same from one generation to the next, it would not be evolving. So evolution requires both a population of breeding individuals and some kind of a genetic change occurring within it. Thus, the simple definition of **evolution** is a change in the allele frequencies in a population over time. What do we mean by allele frequencies? **Allele frequencies** refer to the ratio, or percentage, of one allele (one variant of a gene) compared to the other alleles for that gene within the study population. By contrast, **genotype frequencies** are the ratios or percentages of the different homozygous and heterozygous genotypes in the population. Because we carry two alleles per genotype, the total count of alleles in a population will usually be exactly double the total count of genotypes in the same population (with the exception being rare cases in which an individual carries a different number of chromosomes than the typical two; e.g., Down syndrome results when a child carries three copies of Chromosome 21).

THE FORCES OF EVOLUTION

Today, we recognize that evolution takes place through a combination of mechanisms: mutation, genetic drift, gene flow, and natural selection. These mechanisms are called the "forces of evolution" and together they can account for all the genotypic variation observed in the world today. Keep in mind that each of these forces was first defined and then tested–and re-tested–through the experimental work of the many scientists who contributed to the Modern Synthesis.

Mutation

The first force of evolution we will discuss is mutation, and for good reason: Mutation is the original source of all the genetic variation found in every living thing. Let's try again to imagine all the way back in time to the very first single-celled organism, floating in Earth's primordial sea. Based on what we observe in simple, single-celled organisms today, that organism probably spent its lifetime absorbing nutrients and dividing to produce cloned copies of itself. While the numbers of individuals in that population would have grown (as long as the environment was favorable), nothing would have changed in that perfectly cloned population. There would not have been variety among the individuals. It was only through a copying error—the introduction of a **mutation**, or change, into the genetic code—that each new allele was introduced into the population.

When we think of genetic mutation, we often first think of **deleterious mutations**—the ones associated with negative effects such as the beginnings of cancers or heritable disorders. The fact is, though, that every genetic adaptation that has helped our ancestors survive since the dawn of life is directly due to a **beneficial mutation**—a changes in the DNA that provided some sort of advantage to a given population at a particular moment in time. For example, a beneficial mutation allowed chihuahuas and other tropical-adapted dog breeds to have much thinner fur coats than their cold-adapted cousins the northern wolves, malamutes, and huskies.

Every one of us has genetic mutations. Yes, even you. The DNA in some of your cells today differs from the original DNA that you inherited when you were a tiny, fertilized egg. Mutations occur all the time in the cells of our skin and other organs, due to chemical changes in the nucleotides. Exposure to the UV radiation in sunlight is one common cause of skin mutations. Interaction with UV light causes **UV crosslinking**, in which adjacent thymine bases bind with one another (Figure 4.6). Many of these mutations are detected and corrected by **DNA repair mechanisms**, enzymes that patrol and repair DNA in living cells, while other mutations may cause a new freckle or mole or, perhaps, an unusual hair to grow. For people with the **autosomal recessive** disease **xeroderma pigmentosum**, these repair mechanisms do not function correctly, resulting in a host of problems, especially related to sun exposure, including severe sunburns, dry skin, heavy freckling, and other pigment changes.

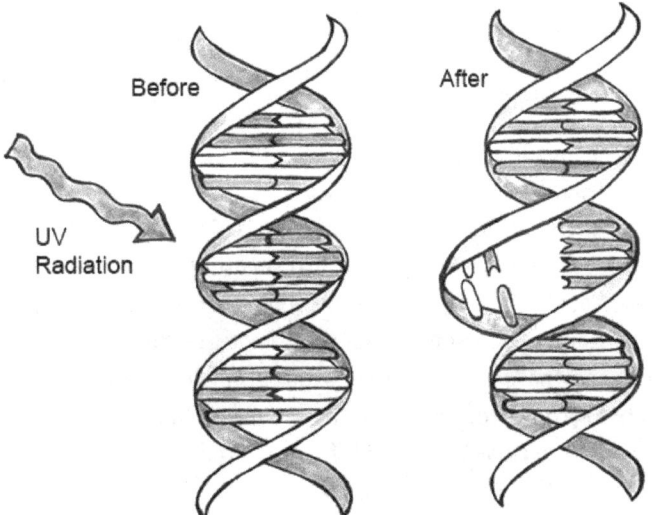

Figure 4.6 A crosslinking mutation in which a UV photon induces a bond between two thymine bases.

Most of our mutations exist in **somatic** cells, which are the cells of our organs and other body tissues. Those will not be passed on to future generations and so will not affect the population over time. Only mutations that occur in the **gametes**, the reproductive cells (i.e., the sperm or egg cells), will be passed on to future generations. When a new mutation pops up at random in a family lineage, it is known as a **spontaneous mutation**. If the individual born with this spontaneous mutation passes it on to his offspring, those offspring receive an **inherited mutation**. Geneticists have identified many classes of mutations and the causes and effects of many of these.

Point Mutations

A **point mutation** is a single-letter (single-nucleotide) change in the genetic code resulting in the substitution of one nucleic acid base for a different one. As you learned in Chapter 3, the DNA code in each gene is translated through three-letter "words" known as **codons**. So depending on how the point mutation changes the "word," the effect it will have on the protein may be major or minor, or may make no difference at all. One of the most common causes of point mutations is a chemical change called cytosine methylation. In **cytosine methylation**, a methyl group is added to a cytosine base, which further converts to thymine after hydrolytic deamination (water-induced removal of an amine group; Figure 4.7). If this mutation is not detected before replication, half of the daughter cells will inherit a thymine (T) in the sequence where a cytosine (C) is usually located. This is one of the most common causes of the autosomal dominant disorder neurofibromatosis type 1 (NF1), discussed in Case Study #1 (see below).

If a mutation does not change the resulting protein, then it is called a **synonymous mutation**. Synonymous mutations do involve a letter (nucleic acid) change, but that change results in a codon that codes for the same "instruction" (the same amino acid or stop code) as the original codon. Mutations that do cause a change in the protein are known as **non-synonymous mutations**. There are several classes of non-synonymous mutations, which are defined by their effects on the encoded protein: missense, nonsense, and splice site mutations (Figure 4.8).

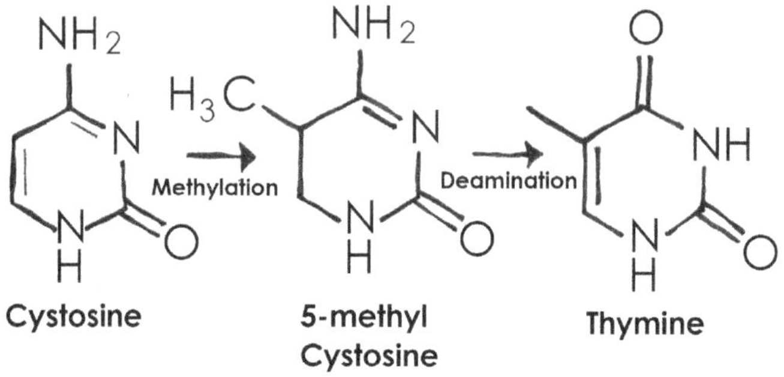

Figure 4.7 The mechanism by which a cytosine-to-thymine point mutation can occur.

A **missense mutation** produces a change in a single amino acid. In this case, the protein is assembled correctly, both before and after the point mutation, but one amino acid, encoded by the codon containing the point mutation, is incorrect. This may impact how the finished protein functions by, for example, preventing it from folding correctly and/or disrupting an enzyme binding site. **Nonsense mutations** convert codons that encode amino acids into stop codons, meaning that the protein will be assembled correctly up until the codon containing the mutation and then assembly will be prematurely terminated. Depending on where in the gene the nonsense mutation falls, this may have a major or very minor impact. A **splice site mutation** changes the genetic code so that the process of removing the intron sequences from the mRNA is disrupted. This can result in the erroneous inclusion of an intron sequence or the exclusion of one of the exons that should have been retained.

Mutation Type	Illustration	Result
No mutation (normal DNA)	Template DNA strand: A A A A T A C G T G C A / mRNA: U U U U A U G C A C G U / Normal peptide: Phe—Tyr—Ala—Arg	Normal protein produced
Synonymous (silent) mutation	Mutated template DNA strand: A A G A T A C G T G C A / Mutated mRNA: U U C U A U G C A C G U / Phe—Tyr—Ala—Arg	Normal protein produced
Missense mutation	Mutated template DNA strand: A A A A T A C C T G C A / Mutated mRNA: U U U U A U G G A C G U / Phe—Tyr—Gly—Arg	Slight difference in amino acid sequence
Nonsense mutation	Mutated template DNA strand: A A A A T T C G T G C A / Mutated mRNA: U U U U A A G C A C G U / Phe—Stop codon	Protein terminates early

Chart continued on next page

Mutation Type	Illustration	Result
Frameshift insertion	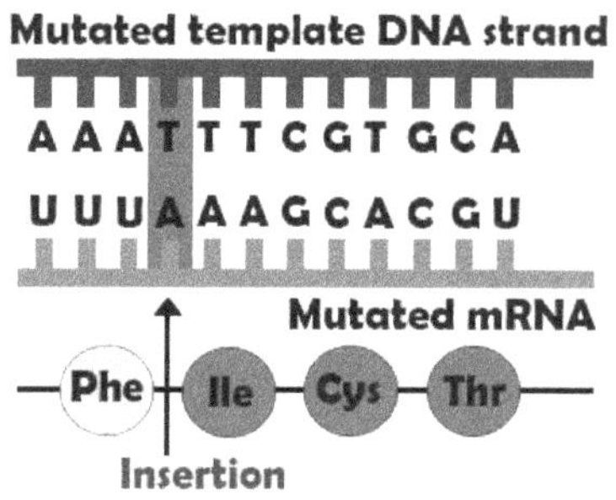 Mutated template DNA strand: AAAT TCGTGCA / UUUAAAGCACGU; Mutated mRNA: Phe–Ile–Cys–Thr (Insertion)	Major difference in amino acid sequence
Frameshift deletion	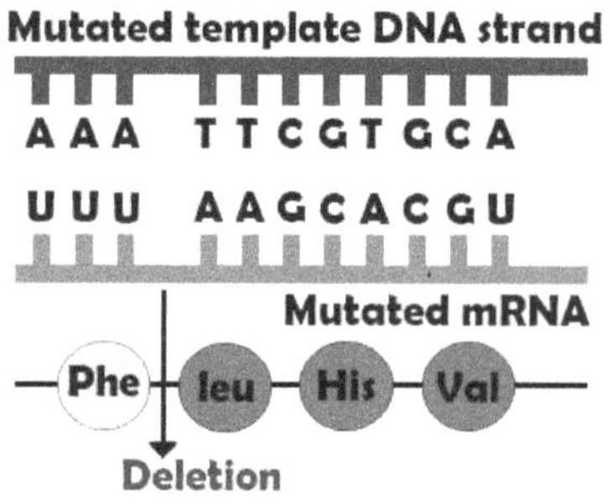 Mutated template DNA strand: AAA TTCGTGCA / UUU AAGCACGU; Mutated mRNA: Phe–Leu–His–Val (Deletion)	Major difference in amino acid sequence

Figure 4.8 Examples and results of point and frameshift mutations.

Insertions and Deletions

In addition to point mutations, another class of mutations are **insertions** and **deletions**, or **indels**, for short. As the name suggests, these involve the addition (insertion) or removal (deletion) of one or more coding sequence letters (nucleic acids). These typically first occur as an error in DNA replication, wherein one or more nucleotides are either duplicated or skipped in error.

Frameshift mutations are types of indels that involve the insertion or deletion of any number of nucleotides that is not a multiple of three. Because these indels are not consistent with the codon numbering, they "shift the reading frame," causing all the codons beyond the mutation to be misread. These mutations can create extensive changes to the protein sequence, potentially not only causing it to lose function but also possibly creating new enzyme-binding sites, leading to new interactions between the protein and other components of the cellular environment. Like point mutations, small indels can also disrupt splice sites. Entire codons or sets of codons may also be removed or added if the indel is a multiple of three nucleotides.

Transposable Elements, or **transposons**, are fragments of DNA that can "jump" around in the genome. There are two types of transposons: Class I transposons, or **retrotransposons**, which are transcribed from DNA into RNA and then "reverse transcribed," to insert the copied sequence into a new location in the DNA; and Class II transposons, or DNA transposons, which do not involve RNA– instead, **DNA transposons** are clipped out of the DNA sequence itself and inserted elsewhere in the genome. Because transposable elements insert themselves into (and, in the case of Class II transposons, remove themselves from) existing DNA sequences, they are frequent gene disruptors. At certain times, and in certain species, it appears that transposons became very active, likely accelerating the mutation rate (and thus, the genetic variation) in those populations during the active periods.

Chromosomal Alterations

The final major category of genetic mutations are changes at the chromosome level: crossover events, nondisjunction events, and translocations. **Crossover events** occur when DNA is swapped between homologous chromosomes while they are paired up during meiosis I. Crossovers are thought to be so common that some DNA swapping may happen every time chromosomes go through meiosis I. Crossovers don't necessarily introduce new alleles into a population, but they do make it possible for new combinations of alleles to exist on a single chromosome that can be passed to future generations. This also enables new combinations of alleles to be found within siblings who share the same parents. Also, if the fragments that cross over don't break at exactly the same point, they can cause genes to be deleted from one of the homologous chromosomes and duplicated on the other.

Nondisjunction events occur when the homologous chromosomes (in meiosis I) or sister chromatids (in meiosis II and mitosis) fail to separate after pairing. The result is that both chromosomes or chromatids end up in the same daughter cell, leaving the other daughter cell without any copy of that chromosome. Most nondisjunctions at the gamete level are fatal to the embryo. The most widely known exception is Trisomy 21, or Down syndrome, which results from an embryo that inherits three copies of Chromosome 21: two from one parent (due to a nondisjunction event) and one from the other. **Trisomies** (triple chromosome conditions) of Chromosomes 18 (Edwards syndrome) and 13 (Patau syndrome) are also known to result in live births, but the children usually have severe complications and rarely survive beyond the first year of life. Sex chromosome trisomies (XXX, XXY, XYY) and X chromosome **monosomies** (inheritance of an X chromosome from one parent and no sex chromosome from the other) are also survivable and fairly common. The symptoms vary but often include atypical sexual characteristics, either at birth or at puberty, and often result in sterility. The X chromosome carries unique genes that are required for survival; therefore, Y chromosome monosomies are incompatible with life.

Chromosomal translocations involve transfers of DNA between non-homologous chromosomes. This may involve swapping large portions of two or more chromosomes. The exchanges of DNA may be balanced or unbalanced. In **balanced translocations**, the genes are swapped, but no genetic information is lost. In **unbalanced translocations**, there is an unequal exchange of genetic material resulting in duplication or loss of genes. Translocations result in new chromosomal structures called **derivative chromosomes**, because they are derived or created from two different chromosomes. Translocations are often found to be linked to cancers and can also cause infertility. Even if the translocations are balanced in the parent, the embryo often won't survive unless the baby inherits both of that parent's derivative chromosomes (to maintain the balance).

Case Study #1: Neurofibromatosis Type 1 (NF1)

Neurofibromatosis Type 1, also known as **NF1**, is a surprisingly common genetic disorder, affecting more people than cystic fibrosis and muscular dystrophy combined. Even more surprising, given how common it is, is how few people have heard of it. One in every 3,000 babies is born with NF1, and this holds true for all populations worldwide (Riccardi 1992). This means that, for every 3,000 people in your community, there is likely at least one community member living with this disorder. Approximately half of these cases are due to spontaneous mutations—that is, the person is the first in their family to have the disorder. The other half of the NF1 cases are inherited from a parent with this disorder. NF1 syndrome is an **autosomal dominant** condition, which means that everyone born with a mutation in the gene, whether inherited or spontaneous, has a 50:50 chance of passing the NF1 syndrome on to each of their children.

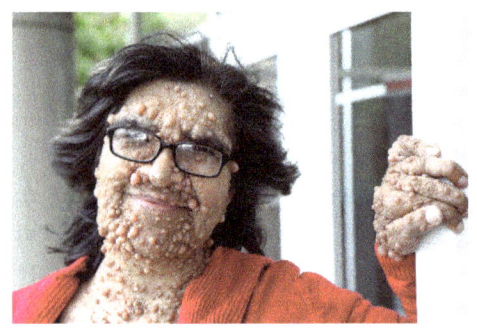

Figure 4.9 Photo of a woman with many cutaneous neurofibromas, a common symptom of Neurofibromatosis Type 1.

The NF1 disorder results from disruption of the NF1 gene on Chromosome 17. Studies of individuals with NF1 have identified over 3,000 different mutations within the gene (including small and large indels, point mutations, and translocations). The NF1 gene is one of the largest known genes, containing at least 60 **exons** (protein-encoding sequences) in a span of about 300,000 nucleotides. It encodes a correspondingly large protein called neurofibromin. Neurofibromin is a fascinating protein, and we are still learning about all its functions.

Studying the symptoms in people who have mutations in an NF1 gene can provide important insights. There are two other types of Neurofibromatosis (Type 2 and Schwannomatosis) that involve some of the same symptoms but are much less common than NF1 and are not due to mutations in the same gene (or even the same chromosome).

We know that neurofibromin plays an important role in preventing tumor growth because, when a mutation occurs causing the NF1 disorder, one of the most common symptoms is the growth of **benign** (non-cancerous) tumors, called **neurofibromas**. Neurofibromas sprout from nerve sheaths—the tissues that encase our nerves—throughout the body. There is no way to predict where the tumors will occur, or when or how quickly they will grow, although only about 15% turn malignant (cancerous).

Figure 4.10A Photo of a man with large plexiform neurofibroma, another symptom of Neurofibromatosis Type 1.

The two types of neurofibromas that are typically most visible are **cutaneous neurofibromas**, which are spherical bumps on, or just under, the surface of the skin (Figure 4.9), and **plexiform neurofibromas**, growths involving whole branches of nerves, often giving the appearance that the surface of the skin is "melting" (Figure 4.10).

Figure 4.10B Childhood photo of the same man, illustrating the progressive nature of the NF1 disorder.

Unfortunately, although research is ongoing, there is currently no cure for NF1. Surgical removal of neurofibromas risks paralysis, due to the high potential for nerve damage, and often results in the tumors growing back even more vigorously. This means that patients are often forced to live with disfiguring and often painful neurofibromas. People who are not familiar with NF1 often mistake neurofibromas for something contagious. This makes it especially hard for people living with NF1 to get jobs working with the public or even to enjoy spending time away from home. Raising public awareness about NF1 and its symptoms can be a great help in improving the quality of life for people living with this condition.

Figure 4.11 Child with café-au-lait macules (birthmarks) typical of the earliest symptoms of NF1.

Babies who have NF1 rarely have neurofibromas, which often begin to grow during puberty. One of the first symptoms of NF1 in a small child is usually the appearance of **café-au-lait spots**, or **CALS**, which are flat, brown birthmark-like spots on the skin (Figure 4.11). CALS are often light brown, like the color of coffee with cream, which is the reason for the name, although the shade of the pigment depends on a person's overall complexion. Some babies are born with CALS, but for others the spots appear within the first few years of life. Having six or more CALS larger than five millimeters (mm) across is a strong indicator that a child may have NF1 (the required size increases to 15 mm for diagnosis after puberty).

A second sign is always needed to confirm a clinical diagnosis of NF1. The second sign often comes in the form of freckles in unusual areas, such as the groin or underarms, or with the first appearance of neurofibromas. Other common symptoms include gliomas (tumors) of the optic nerve, which can cause vision loss; thinning of bones and failure to heal if they break (often requiring amputation); low muscle tone (poor muscle development, often delaying milestones such as sitting up, crawling, and walking); hearing loss, due to neurofibromas on auditory nerves; and learning disabilities, especially those involving spatial reasoning. Approximately 50 % of people with NF1 have some type of speech and/or learning disability and often benefit greatly from early intervention services. Intellectual disability, however, is not common with NF1, so most people with NF1 live independently as adults. Many people with NF1 live full and successful lives, as long as their symptoms can be managed.

Based on the wide variety of symptoms, it's clear that neurofibromin plays important roles in many biochemical pathways. While everyone who has NF1 will exhibit some symptoms during their lifetime, there is a great deal of variation in the types and severity of symptoms, even between individuals from the same family who share the exact same NF1 mutation. It seems crazy that a gene with so many important functions would be so susceptible to mutation. Part of this undoubtedly has to do with its massive size—a gene with 300,000 nucleotides has ten times more nucleotides available for mutation than does a gene of 30,000 bases. This also suggests that the mutability of this gene might provide some benefits, which is a possibility that we will revisit later in this chapter.

Genetic Drift

The second force of evolution is commonly known as genetic drift. This is an unfortunate misnomer, as this force actually involves the drifting of alleles, not genes. **Genetic drift** refers to *random* changes ("drift") in allele frequencies from one generation to the next. The genes are remaining constant within the population; it is only the alleles of the genes are changing in frequency. The random nature of genetic drift is a crucial point to understand: it specifically occurs when none of the variant alleles confer an advantage.

Let's imagine far back in time, again, to that first population of living cells, subsisting and occasionally dividing, in the primordial sea. Many generations have passed, and mutations have created distinct chromosomes. The cells are now amoeba-like, larger than many of their tiny bacterial neighbors, who have long since become their favorite source of nutrients. A mutation occurs in one of the cells that changes the texture of the cell membrane from a relatively smooth surface to a highly ruffled one. This has absolutely no effect on the cell's quality of life or ability to reproduce. In fact, eyes haven't evolved yet, so no one in the world at the time would even notice the difference. The cells in the population continue to divide, and the offspring of the ruffled cell inherit the ruffled membrane. The frequency (%) of the ruffled allele in the population, from one generation to the next, will depend entirely on how many offspring that first ruffled cell ends up having, and the random events that might make the ruffled alleles more common or more rare (such as population bottlenecks and founder effects, discussed below).

Sexual Reproduction and Random Inheritance

Tracking alleles gets a bit more complicated in our primordial cells when, after a number of generations, a series of mutations have created populations that reproduce sexually. These cells go through an extra round of cell-division (meiosis) to create haploid gametes. The combination of two gametes, each containing half a set of homologous chromosomes, is required to produce each new diploid offspring. In the earlier population, which reproduced via **asexual reproduction**, a cell either carried the smooth allele or the ruffled allele. With **sexual reproduction**, a cell inherits one allele from each parent, so there are homozygous cells that contain two smooth alleles, homozygous cells that contain two ruffled alleles, and heterozygous cells that contain one of each allele. If the new, ruffled allele happens to be dominant (and we'll imagine that it is), the heterozygotes will have ruffled cell phenotypes, but will have a 50:50 chance of passing on a smooth allele to each offspring.

In sexually reproducing populations (including humans and many other animals and plants in the world today), that 50:50 chance of inheriting one or the other allele from each parent plays a major role in the random nature of genetic drift.

Population Bottlenecks

A **population bottleneck** occurs when the number of individuals in a population drops dramatically due to some random event. The most obvious, familiar examples are natural disasters. Tsunamis and hurricanes devastating island and coastal populations and forest fires and river floods wiping out populations in other areas are all too familiar. When a large portion of a population is randomly wiped out, the allele frequencies (i.e., the percentages of each allele) in the small population of survivors are often much different from the frequencies in the pre-disaster, or "parent," population. If such an event happened to our primordial ocean cell population—perhaps a volcanic fissure erupted in the ocean floor and only the cells that happened to be farthest from the spewing lava and boiling water survived—we might end up, by random chance, with a surviving population that had mostly ruffled alleles, in contrast to the parent population, which had only a small percentage of ruffles.

One of the most famous examples of a population bottleneck is the prehistoric disaster that led to the extinction of dinosaurs, the **Cretaceous–Paleogene extinction** event (often abbreviated K-Pg; previously K-T). This occurred approximately 66 million years ago. Dinosaurs and all their neighbors were going about their ordinary routines when a massive asteroid zoomed in from space and crashed into what is now the Gulf of Mexico, creating an impact so enormous that populations within hundreds of miles of the crash site were likely immediately wiped out. The skies filled with dust and debris, causing temperatures to plummet worldwide. It's estimated that 75% of the world's species went extinct as a result of the impact and the deep freeze that followed (Jablonski and Chaloner 1994). The populations that emerged from the K-Pg extinction were markedly different from their pre-disaster communities. Surviving mammal populations expanded and diversified, and other new creatures appeared. The ecosystems of Earth filled with new organisms and have never been the same (Figure 4.12).

Figure 4.12 The Cretaceous–Paleogene extinction event. Fall of the dinosaurs and rise of the mammals.

Much more recently in geological time, during the colonial period, many human populations experienced bottlenecks as a result of the fact that imperial powers were inclined to slaughter communities who were reluctant to give up their lands and resources. This effect was especially profound in the Americas, where indigenous populations faced the compounded effects of brutal warfare, exposure to new bacteria and viruses (against which they had no immunity), and ultimately segregation on resource-starved reservations. The populations in Europe, Asia, and Africa had experienced regular gene flow during the 10,000-year period in which most kinds of livestock were being domesticated, giving them many generations of experience building up immunity against zoonotic diseases (those that can pass from animals to humans). In contrast, the residents of the Americas had been almost completely isolated during those millennia, so all these diseases swept through the Americas in rapid succession, creating a major loss of genetic diversity in the indigenous American population. It is estimated that between 50% and 95% of the indigenous American populations died during the first decades after European contact, around 500 years ago (Livi-Bacci 2006).

An urgent health challenge facing humans today involves human-induced population bottlenecks that produce antibiotic-resistant bacteria. **Antibiotics** are medicines prescribed to treat bacterial infections. The typical prescription includes enough medicine for ten days. People often feel better after less than ten days and sometimes decide to quit taking the medicine ahead of schedule. This is often a big mistake. The antibiotics have quickly killed off a large percentage of the bacteria—enough to reduce the symptoms and make you feel much better. However, this has created a bacterial population bottleneck. There are usually a small number of bacteria that survive those early days. If you take the medicine as prescribed for the full ten days, it's quite likely that there will be no bacterial survivors. If you quit early, though, the survivors—who were the members of the original population who were most resistant to the antibiotic—will begin to reproduce again. Soon the infection will be back, possibly worse than before, and now all of the bacteria are resistant to the antibiotic that you had been prescribed.

Other activities that have contributed to the rise of antibiotic-resistant bacteria include the use of antibacterial cleaning products and the inappropriate use of antibiotics as a preventative measure in livestock or to treat infections that are viral instead of bacterial (viruses do not respond to antibiotics). In 2017, the World Health Organization published a list of twelve antibiotic-resistant pathogens that are considered top priority targets for the development of new antibiotics (World Health Organization 2017).

Founder Effects

Founder effects occur when members of a population leave the main or "parent" group and form a new population that no longer interbreeds with the other members of the original group. Similar to survivors of a population bottleneck, the newly founded population often has allele frequencies that are different from the original group. Alleles that may have been relatively rare in the parent population can end up being very common due to founder effect. Likewise, recessive traits that were seldom seen in the parent population may be seen frequently in the descendants of the offshoot population. One striking example of founder effect was first noted in the Dominican Republic in the 1970s. During a several-year period, eighteen children who had been born with female genitalia and raised as girls suddenly grew penises at puberty. This culture tended to value sons over daughters, so these transitions were generally celebrated. They labeled the condition **guevedoces**, which translates to "penis at twelve," due to the average age at which this occurred. Scientists were fascinated by the phenomenon.

Genetic and hormonal studies revealed that the condition, scientifically termed **5-alpha reductase deficiency,** is an autosomal recessive syndrome that manifests when a child having both X and Y sex chromosomes inherits two nonfunctional (mutated) copies of the SRD5A2 gene (Imperato-McGinley and Zhu 2002). These children develop testes internally, but the 5-alpha reductase 2 steroid, which is necessary for development of male genitals in babies, is not produced. In absence of this male hormone, the baby develops female-looking genitalia (in humans, "female" is the default infant body form, if the full set of the necessary male hormones are not produced). At puberty, however, a different set of male hormones are produced by other fully functional genes. These hormones complete the male genital development that did not happen in infancy. This condition became quite common in the Dominican Republic during the 1970s due to founder effect—that is, the mutated SRD5A2 gene happened to be much more common among the Dominican Republic's founding population than in the parent populations [the Dominican population derives from a mixture of indigenous Native American (Taino) peoples, West Africans, and Western Europeans]. Five-alpha reductase syndrome has since been observed in other small, isolated populations around the world.

Founder effect is closely linked to the concept of inbreeding, which in population genetics does not necessarily mean breeding with immediate family relatives. Instead, **inbreeding** refers to the selection of mates exclusively from within a small, closed population—that is, from a group with limited allelic variability. This can be observed in small, physically isolated populations but also can happen when cultural practices limit mates to a small group. As with founder effect, inbreeding increases the risk of inheriting two copies of any nonfunctional (mutant) alleles.

The Amish in the United States are a population that, due to their unique history and cultural practices, emerged from a small founding population and have tended to select mates from within their groups. The **Old Order Amish** population of Lancaster County, Pennsylvania, has approximately 50,000 current members, all of whom can trace their ancestry back to a group of approximately 80 individuals. This small founding population immigrated to the United States from Switzerland in the mid-1700s to escape religious persecution. Keeping to themselves, and selecting mates almost exclusively from their own communities, the Amish have become familiar with far more recessive traits than are seen in their parent population.

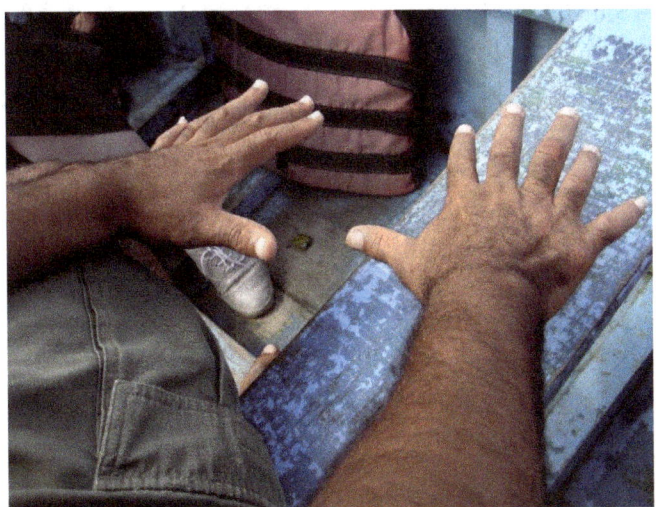

Figure 4.13 Photo of a man with polydactyly.

One of the genetic conditions that has been observed much more frequently in the Lancaster County Amish population is **Ellis-van Creveld syndrome**, which is an autosomal recessive disorder characterized by short stature (dwarfism), polydactyly [the development of more than five digits (fingers or toes) on the hands or feet], abnormal tooth development, and heart defects (see Figure 4.13). Among the general world population, Ellis-van Creveld syndrome is estimated to affect approximately 1 in 60,000 individuals; among the Old Order Amish of Lancaster County, the rate is estimated to be as high as 1 in every 200 births (D'Asdia et al. 2013). One of the great insights that has come from the study of founder effects is that a limited gene pool carries a much higher risk for genetic diseases. Genetic diversity in a population tends to greatly reduce these risks.

Gene Flow

The third force of evolution is traditionally called gene flow. As with genetic drift, this is a misnomer, because it refers to flowing alleles, not genes. (All populations of the same species share the same genes; it is the alleles of those genes that may vary.) **Gene flow** refers to the movement of alleles from one population to another. In most cases, gene flow can be considered synonymous with migration between populations.

Returning again to the example of our primordial cell population, let's imagine that, after the volcanic fissure opened up in the ocean floor, wiping out the majority of the parent population, two surviving populations developed in the waters on opposite sides of the fissure. Ultimately, the lava from the fissure grew into a chain of islands that continued to provide a physical barrier between the populations, even after the lava had cooled.

In the initial generations after the eruption, due to founder effect, isolation, and random inheritance (genetic drift), the population to the west of the islands contained a vast majority of the ruffled membrane alleles while the eastern population predominantly carried the smooth alleles. Ocean currents in the area typically flowed from west to east, sometimes carrying cells (facilitating gene flow) from the western (ruffled) population to the eastern (smooth) population. Due to the ocean currents, it was almost impossible for any cells from the eastern population to be carried westward. Thus, for inheritance purposes, the western (ruffled) population remained isolated. In this case, the gene flow is uni-directional (going only in one direction) and unbalanced (only one population is receiving the new alleles).

Admixture

Among humans, gene flow is often described as **admixture**. In forensic cases, anthropologists and geneticists are often asked to estimate the ancestry of unidentified human remains to help determine whether they match any missing persons' reports. This is one of the most complicated tasks in these professions because, while "race" or "ancestry" involves simple checkboxes on a missing person's form, among humans today there are no truly distinct genetic populations. All modern humans are members of the same fully breeding-compatible species, and all human communities have experienced multiple episodes of gene flow (admixture), leading all humans today to be so genetically similar that we are all members of the same (and only surviving) human subspecies: Homo sapiens sapiens.

Gene flow between otherwise isolated non-human populations is often termed **hybridization.** One example of this involves the hybridization and spread of **Africanized honey bees** (a.k.a., "killer bees") in the Americas. All honey bees worldwide are classified as Apis mellifera. Due to distinct adaptations to various environments around the world, there are 28 different subspecies of Apis mellifera.

During the 1950s, a Brazilian biologist named Warwick E. Kerr experimented with hybridizing African and European subspecies of honey bees to try to develop a strain that was better suited to tropical environments than the European honey bees that had long been kept by North American beekeepers. Dr. Kerr was careful to contain the reproductive queens and drones from the African subspecies, but in 1957, a visiting beekeeper accidentally released 26 queen bees of the subspecies Apis mellifera scutellate from southern Africa into the Brazilian countryside. The African bees quickly interbred with local European honey bee populations. The hybridized bees exhibited the more aggressively defensive behavior of the African strain, fatally or near-fatally attacking many humans and livestock that ventured too close to their hives. The Africanized bees spread throughout South America and reached Mexico and California by 1985. By 1990, permanent colonies had been established in Texas, and by 1997, 90% of trapped bee swarms around Tucson, Arizona, were found to be Africanized (Sanford 2006).

Another example involves the introduction of the **Harlequin ladybeetle**, Harmonia axyridis, native to East Asia, to other parts of the world as a "natural" form of pest control. Harlequin ladybeetles are natural predators of some of the aphids and other crop-pest insects. First introduced to North America in 1916, the "biocontrol" strains of Harlequin ladybeetles were considered to be quite successful in reducing crop pests and saving farmers substantial amounts of money. After many decades of successful use in North America, biocontrol strains of Harlequin ladybeetles were also developed in Europe and South America in the 1980s.

Over the seven decades of biocontrol use, the Harlequin ladybeetle had never shown any potential for development of wild colonies outside of its native habitat in China and Japan. New generations of beetles always had to be reared in the lab. That all changed in 1988, when a wild colony took root near New Orleans, Louisiana. Either through admixture with a native ladybeetle strain, or due to a spontaneous mutation, a new allele was clearly introduced into this population that suddenly enabled them to survive and reproduce in a wide range of environments. This population spread rapidly across the Americas and had reached Africa by 2004. In Europe, the invasive, North American strain of Harlequin ladybeetle admixed with the European strain (Figure 4.14), causing a population explosion (Lombaert et al. 2010). Even strains specifically developed to be flightless (to curtail the spreading) produced flighted offspring after admixture with members of the North American population (Facon et al. 2011). The fast-spreading, invasive strain has quickly become a disaster, out-competing native ladybeetle populations (some to the point of extinction), causing home infestations, decimating fruit crops, and contaminating many batches of wine with their bitter flavor after being inadvertently harvested with the grapes (Pickering et al. 2004).

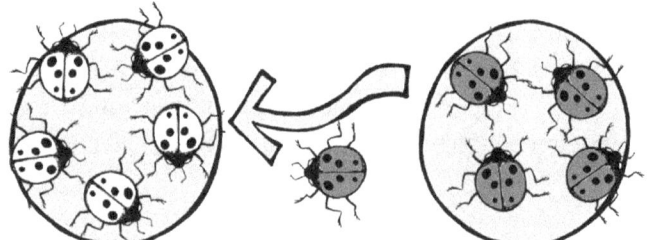

Figure 4.14 Gene flow between two populations of ladybeetles (ladybugs).

Natural Selection

The final force of evolution is natural selection. This is the evolutionary process that Charles Darwin first brought to light, and it is what the general public typically evokes when considering the process of evolution. **Natural selection** occurs when certain phenotypes confer an advantage or disadvantage in survival and/or reproductive success. The alleles associated with those phenotypes will change in frequency over time due to this selective pressure. It's also important to note that the advantageous allele may change over time (with environmental changes) and that an allele that had previously been benign may become advantageous or detrimental. Of course, dominant, recessive, and codominant traits will be selected upon a bit differently from one another. Because natural selection acts upon phenotypes rather than the alleles themselves, deleterious (disadvantageous) recessive alleles can be retained by heterozygotes without any negative effects.

In the case of our primordial ocean cells, up until now, the texture of their cell membranes has been benign. The frequencies of smooth to ruffled alleles, and smooth to ruffled phenotypes, has changed over time, due to genetic drift and gene flow. Let's now imagine that the Earth's climate has cooled to a point that the waters frequently become too cold for survival of the tiny bacteria that are the dietary staples of our smooth and ruffled cell populations. The way amoeba-like cells "eat" is to stretch out the cell membrane, almost like an arm, to encapsulate, then ingest, the tiny bacteria. When the temperatures plummet, the tiny bacteria populations plummet with them. Larger bacteria, however, are better able to withstand the temperature change.

The smooth cells were well-adapted to ingesting tiny bacteria but poorly suited to encapsulating the larger bacteria. The cells with the ruffled membranes, however, are easily able to extend their ruffles to encapsulate the larger bacteria. They also find themselves able to stretch their entire membrane to a much larger size than their smooth-surfaced neighbors, allowing them to ingest more bacteria at a given time and to go for longer periods between feedings. The smooth and ruffled traits, which had previously offered no advantage or disadvantage while food was plentiful, now are subject to natural selection. During the cold snaps, at least, the ruffled cells have a definite advantage. We can imagine that the western population that has mostly ruffled alleles will continue to do well, while the eastern population, which has a much smaller proportion of ruffled alleles, will gradually shift toward a higher frequency of ruffled alleles in future generations.

Figure 4.15 Dark and light peppered moth variants and their relative camouflage abilities on clean (top) and sooty (bottom) trees.

A classic example of natural selection involves the study of an insect called the **peppered moth** (*Biston betularia*) in England during the Industrial Revolution in the 1800s. Prior to the Industrial Revolution, the peppered moth population was predominantly light in color, with dark (pepper-like) speckles on the wings. The "peppered" coloration was very similar to the appearance of the bark and lichens that grew on the local trees (Figure 4.15). This helped to camouflage the moths as they rested on a tree, making it harder for moth-eating birds to find and snack on them. There was another phenotype that popped up occasionally in the population. These individuals were heterozygotes that carried an overactive, dominant pigment allele, producing a solid black coloration. As you can imagine, the black moths were much easier for birds to spot, making this phenotype a real disadvantage. The situation changed, however, as the Industrial Revolution took off. Large factories began spewing vast amounts of coal smoke into the air, blanketing the countryside, including the lichens and trees, in black soot. Suddenly, it was the light-colored moths that were easy for birds to spot and the black moths that held the advantage. The frequency of the dark pigment allele rose dramatically. By 1895, the black moth phenotype accounted for 98% of observed moths (Grant 1999).

Thanks to new environmental regulations in the 1960s, the air pollution in England began to taper off. As the soot levels decreased, returning the trees to their former, lighter color, this provided the perfect opportunity to study how the peppered moth population would respond. Repeated follow-up studies documented the gradual rise in the frequency of the lighter-colored phenotype. By 2003, the maximum frequency of the dark phenotype was 50% and in most parts of England had decreased to less than 10% (Cook 2003).

Directional, Balancing/Stabilizing, and Disruptive/Diversifying Selection

Natural selection can be classified as directional, balancing/stabilizing, or disruptive/diversifying, depending on how the pressure is applied to the population (Figure 4.16).

Both of the above examples of natural selection involve **directional selection**: the environmental pressures are favoring one phenotype over the other and causing the frequencies of the associated advantageous alleles (ruffled membranes, dark pigment) to

gradually increase. In the case of the peppered moths, the direction shifted three times: first, it was selecting for lighter pigment; then, with the increase in pollution, the pressure switched to selection for darker pigment; finally, with reduction of the pollution, the selection pressure shifted back again to favoring light-colored moths.

Balancing selection (a.k.a., stabilizing selection) occurs when selection works against the extremes of a trait and favors the intermediate phenotype. For example, humans maintain an average birth weight that balances the need for babies to be small enough not to cause complications during pregnancy and childbirth but big enough to maintain a safe body temperature after they are born. Another example of balancing selection is found in the genetic disorder called sickle cell anemia, which is featured in Case Study #2 (see below).

Disruptive selection (a.k.a., diversifying selection), the opposite of balancing selection, occurs when both extremes of a trait are advantageous. Since individuals with traits in the mid-range are selected against, disruptive selection can eventually lead to the population evolving into two separate species. Darwin believed that the many species of finches (small birds) found in the

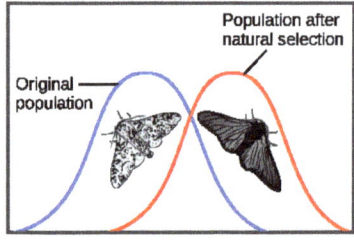
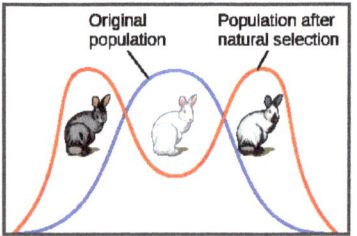

Figure 4.16 Caption: (a) Balancing/Stabilizing, (b) Directional, and (c) Disruptive/Diversifying Selection.

remote Galapagos Islands provided a clear example of disruptive selection leading to speciation. He observed that seed-eating finches either had large beaks, capable of eating very large seeds, or small beaks, capable of retrieving tiny seeds. The islands did not have many plants that produced medium-size seeds. Thus, birds with medium-size beaks would have trouble eating the very large seeds and would also have been inefficient at picking up the tiny seeds. Over time, Darwin surmised, this pressure against mid-size beaks may have led the population to divide into two separate species.

Case Study #2 : Sickle Cell Anemia

Sickle cell anemia is an autosomal recessive genetic disorder that affects millions of people worldwide. It is most common in Africa, countries around the Mediterranean Sea, and eastward as far as India. Populations in the Americas that have high percentages of ancestors from these regions also have high rates of sickle cell anemia. In the United States, it's estimated that 72,000 people live with the disease, with one in approximately 1,200 Hispanic-American babies and one in every 500 African-American babies inheriting the condition (World Health Organization 1996).

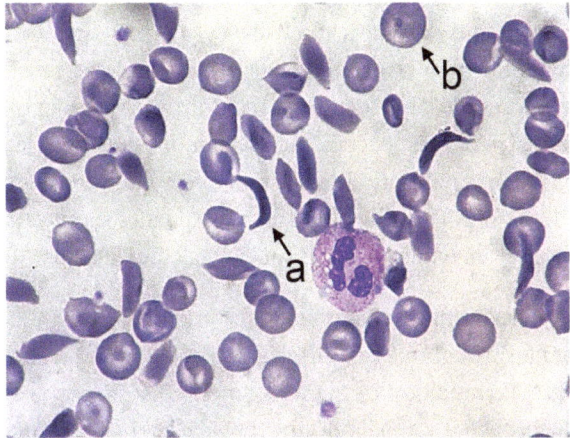

Figure 4.17 Sickle Cell Anemia. Arrows indicate (a) sickled and (b) normal red blood cells.

Sickle cell anemia affects the hemoglobin protein in red blood cells. Normal red blood cells are somewhat doughnut-shaped—round with a depression on both sides of the middle. They carry oxygen around the bloodstream to cells throughout the body. Red blood cells produced by the mutated form of the gene take on a stiff, sickle-like crescent shape when stressed by low oxygen or dehydration (Figure 4.17). Because of their elongated shape and the fact that they are stiff rather than flexible, they tend to form clumps in the blood vessels, inhibiting blood flow to adjacent areas of the body. This causes episodes of extreme pain and can cause serious problems in the oxygen-deprived tissues. The sickle cells also break down much more quickly than normal cells, often lasting only 20 days rather than the 120 days of normal cells. This causes an overall shortage of blood cells in the sickle cell patient, resulting in low iron (anemia) and problems associated with it such as extreme fatigue, shortness of breath, and hindrances to children's growth and development.

The devastating effects of sickle cell anemia made its high frequency a pressing mystery. Why would an allele that is so deleterious in its homozygous form be maintained in a population at levels as high as the one in twelve African-Americans estimated to carry at least one copy of the allele? The answer turned out to be one of the most interesting cases of balancing selection in the history of genetic study.

While looking for an explanation, scientists noticed that the countries with high rates of sickle cell disease also shared a high risk for another disease called **malaria**, which is caused by infection of the blood by a *Plasmodium* parasite. These parasites are carried by mosquitoes and enter the human bloodstream via a mosquito bite. Once infected, the person will experience flu-like symptoms that, if untreated, can often lead to death. Researchers discovered that many people living in these regions seemed to have a natural resistance to malaria. Further study revealed that people who carry the sickle cell allele are far less likely to experience a severe case of malaria. This would not be enough of a benefit to make the allele advantageous for the sickle cell homozygotes who face shortened life spans due to sickle cell anemia. The real benefit of the sickle cell allele goes to the heterozygotes.

People who are heterozygous for sickle cell carry one normal allele, which produces the normal, round, red blood cells, and one sickle cell allele, which produces the sickle-shaped red blood cells. Thus, they have both the sickle and round blood cell types in their bloodstream. They produce enough of the round red blood cells to avoid the symptoms of sickle cell anemia, but they have enough sickle cells to provide protection from malaria.

When the *Plasmodium* parasites infect an individual, they begin to multiply in the liver, but then must infect the red blood cells to complete their reproductive cycle. When the parasites enter sickle-type cells, the cells respond by taking on the sickle shape. This prevents the parasite from circulating through the bloodstream and completing its life cycle, greatly inhibiting the severity of the infection in the sickle cell heterozygotes compared to non-sickle-cell homozygotes. See chapter 14 for more discussion of sickle cell anemia.

Sexual Selection

Sexual selection is an aspect of natural selection in which the selective pressure specifically affects reproductive success (the ability to successfully breed and raise offspring) rather than survival. Sexual selection favors traits that will attract a mate. Sometimes these sexually appealing traits even carry greater risks in terms of survival.

A classic example of sexual selection involves the brightly colored feathers of the peacock. The **peacock** is the male sex of the peafowl genera *Pavo* and *Afropavo*. During mating season, peacocks will fan their colorful tails wide and strut in front of the peahens in a grand display. The peahens will carefully observe these displays and will elect to mate with the male that they find the most appealing. Many studies have found that peahens prefer the males with the fullest, most colorful tails. While these large, showy tails provide a reproductive advantage, they can be a real burden in terms of escaping predators. The bright colors and patterns as well as the large size of the peacock tail make it difficult to hide. Once predators spot them, peacocks also struggle to fly away, with the heavy tail trailing behind and weighing them down (Figure 4.18). Some researchers have argued that the increased risk is part of the appeal for the peahens: only an especially strong, alert, and healthy peacock would be able to avoid predators while sporting such a spectacular tail.

Figure 4.18 Showy peacock tail advantages (impressing peahens) and disadvantages (becoming easier prey).

It's important to keep in mind that sexual selection relies on the trait being present throughout mating years. Reflecting back on Case Study #1, the examination of the NF1 genetic disorder, some might find it surprising that half of the babies born with NF1 inherited it from a parent. Given how disfiguring the symptoms can become, and the fact that the disorder is autosomal dominant and fully penetrant (meaning it has no unaffected carriers), it may seem surprising that sexual selection doesn't exert more pressure against the mutated alleles. One important factor is that, while the neurofibromas typically begin to appear during puberty, they usually emerge only a few at a time and may grow very slowly. Many NF1 patients don't experience the more severe or disfiguring symptoms until later in life, long after they have started families of their own.

Some researchers prefer to classify sexual selection separately, as a fifth force of evolution. The traits that underpin mate selection are entirely natural, of course. Research has shown that subtle traits, such as the type of pheromones (hormonal odors related to immune system alleles) someone emits and how those are perceived by the immune system genotype of the "sniffer," may play crucial and subconscious roles in whether we find someone attractive or not (Chaix et al. 2008).

SPECIAL TOPIC: THE REAL PRIMORDIAL CELLS—*DICTYOSTELIUM DISCOIDEUM*

The amoeba-like primordial cells that were used as recurring examples throughout this chapter are inspired by actual research that is truly fascinating. In 2015, Gareth Bloomfield and colleagues reported on their genomic study of the social amoeba **Dictyostelium discoideum** (a.k.a., "slime molds," although technically they are amoebae, not molds). Strains of these amoebae have been grown in research laboratories for many decades and are useful in studying phagocytosis and micropinocytosis—the mechanisms that amoeboid single-celled organisms use to ingest food and liquid. For simplification of our examples in this chapter, our amoeba-like cells remained ocean dwellers. Wild *Dictyostelium discoideum*, however, live in soil and feed on soil bacteria by growing ruffles in their membranes that reach out to encapsulate the bacterial cell. Laboratory strains, however, are typically raised on liquid media (agar) in Petri dishes, which is not suitable for the wild-type amoebae. It was widely known that the laboratory strains must have developed mutations in one or more genes to allow them to ingest the larger nutrient particles in the agar and larger volumes of liquid, but the genes involved were not known.

Bloomfield and colleagues performed genomic testing on both the wild and the laboratory strains of *Dictyostelium discoideum*. Their discovery was astounding: every one of the laboratory strains carried a mutation in the NF1 gene, the very same gene associated with Neurofibromatosis Type 1 (NF1) in humans. The antiquity of this massive, easily mutated gene is incredible. It originated in a common ancestor to humans and these amoebae and has been retained in both lineages ever since. As seen in *Dictyostelium discoideum*, breaking the gene can be advantageous. Without a functioning copy of the neurofibromin protein, the cell membrane is able to form much larger feeding structures, allowing the NF1 mutants to ingest larger particles and larger volumes of liquid. For these amoebae, this may provide dietary flexibility that functions somewhat like an insurance policy for times when the food supply is limited.

Dictyostelium discoideum are also interesting in that they typically reproduce asexually, but under certain conditions, one cell will convert into a "giant" cell, which encapsulates surrounding cells, transforming into one of three sexes. This cell will undergo meiosis, producing gametes that must combine with one of the other two sexes in order to produce viable offspring. This ability for sexual reproduction may be what allows *Dictyostelium discoideum* to benefit from the advantages of NF1 mutation, while also being able to restore the wild type NF1 gene in future generations.

What does this mean for humans living with NF1? Well, understanding the role of the neurofibromin protein in the membranes of simple organisms like *Dictyostelium discoideum* may help us to better understand how it functions and malfunctions in the sheaths of human neurons. It's also possible that the mutability of the NF1 gene confers certain advantages to humans as well. Alleles of the NF1 gene have been found to reduce one's risk for alcoholism (Repunte-Canonigo et al. 2015), opiate addiction (Sanna et al. 2002), Type 2 diabetes (Martins et al. 2016), and hypomusicality (a lower-than-average musical aptitude; Cota et al. 2018). This research is ongoing and will be exciting to follow in the coming years.

STUDYING EVOLUTION IN ACTION

The Hardy-Weinberg Equilibrium

This chapter has introduced you to the forces of evolution, the mechanisms by which evolution occurs. How do we detect and study evolution, though, in real time, as it happens? One tool we use is the **Hardy-Weinberg Equilibrium**: a mathematical formula that allows estimation of the number and distribution of dominant and recessive alleles in a population. This aids in determining whether allele frequencies are changing and, if so, how quickly over time, and in favor of which allele? It's important to note that the Hardy-Weinberg formula only gives us an estimate based on the data for a snapshot in time. We will have to calculate it again later, after various intervals, to determine if our population is evolving and in what way the allele frequencies are changing. To learn how to calculate the Hardy-Weinberg formula, see the Special Topic box at the end of the chapter.

Interpreting Evolutionary Change

Once we have detected change occurring in a population, we need to consider which evolutionary processes might be the cause of the change. It is important to watch for non-random mating patterns, to see if they can be included or excluded as possible sources of variation in allele frequencies.

Non-Random Mating

Non-Random Mating (also known as Assortative Mating) occurs when mate choice within a population follows a non-random pattern. **Positive assortative mating** patterns result from a tendency for individuals to mate with others who share similar phenotypes. This often happens based on body size. Taking as an example dog breeds, it is easier for two Chihuahuas to mate and have healthy offspring than it is for a Chihuahua and a St. Bernard to do so. This is especially true if the Chihuahua is the female and would have to give birth to giant St. Bernard pups.

Negative assortative mating patterns occur when individuals tend to select mates with qualities different from their own. This is what is at work when humans choose partners whose pheromones indicate that they have different and complementary immune alleles, providing potential offspring with a better chance at a stronger immune system.

Among domestic animals, such as pets and livestock, assortative mating is often directed by humans who decide which pairs will mate to increase the chances of offspring having certain desirable traits. This is known as **artificial selection**.

Among humans, in addition to phenotypic traits, cultural traits such as religion and ethnicity may also influence assortative mating patterns.

Micro- to Macroevolution

Microevolution refers to changes in allele frequencies within breeding populations, that is, within single species. **Macroevolution** involves changes that result in the emergence of new species, the similarities and differences between species and their phylogenetic relationships with other taxa. Consider our example of the peppered moth which illustrated microevolution over time, via directional selection favoring the peppered allele when the trees were clean and the dark pigment allele when the trees were sooty. Imagine that environmental regulations had cleaned up the air pollution in one part of the nation, while the coal-fired factories continued to spew soot in another area. If this went on long enough, it's possible that two distinct moth populations would eventually emerge—one containing only the peppered allele and the other only harboring the dark pigment allele.

When a single population divides into two or more separate species, it is called **speciation**. The changes that prevent successful breeding between individuals who descended from the same ancestral population may involve chromosomal rearrangements, changes in the ability of the sperm from one species to permeate the egg membrane of the other species, or dramatic changes in hormonal schedules or mating behaviors that prevent members from the new species from being able to effectively pair up.

There are two types of speciation: allopatric and sympatric. **Allopatric speciation** is caused by long-term **isolation** (physical separation) of subgroups of the population (Figure 4.19). Something occurs in the environment—perhaps a river changes its course and splits the group, preventing them from breeding with members on the opposite riverbank. Over many generations, new mutations and adaptations to the different environments on each side of the river may drive the two subpopulations to change so much that they can no longer produce fertile, viable offspring, even if the barrier is someday removed.

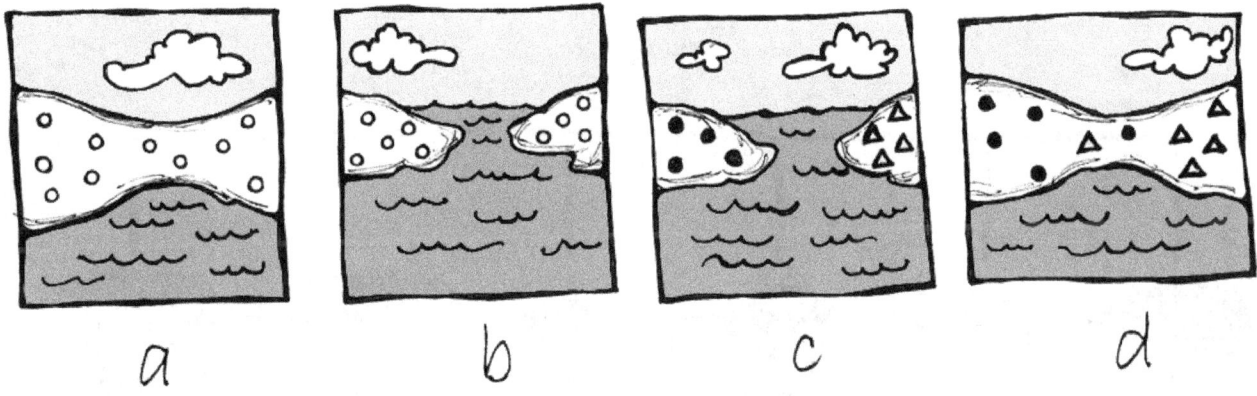

Figure 4.19 Isolation leading to speciation: (a) original population before isolation; (b) a barrier divides the population and prevents interbreeding between the two groups; (c) time passes, and the populations become genetically distinct; (d) after many generations, the two populations are no longer biologically or behaviorally compatible, thus can no longer interbreed, even if the barrier is removed.

Sympatric speciation occurs when the population splits into two or more separate species while remaining located together *without* a physical barrier. This typically results from a new mutation that pops up among some members of the population that prevents them from successfully reproducing with anyone who does not carry the same mutation. This is seen particularly often in plants, as they have a higher frequency of chromosomal duplications.

One of the quickest rates of speciation is observed in the case of adaptive radiation. **Adaptive radiation** refers to the situation in which subgroups of a single species rapidly diversify and adapt to fill a variety of ecological niches. An **ecological niche** is a set of constraints and resources that is available in an environmental setting. Evidence for adaptive radiations is often seen after population bottlenecks. A mass disaster kills off many species, and the survivors have access to a new set of territories and resources that were either unavailable or much coveted and fought over before the disaster. The offspring of the surviving population will often split into multiple species, each of which stems from members in that first group of survivors who happened to carry alleles that were advantageous for a particular niche.

The classic example of adaptive radiation brings us back to Charles Darwin and his observations of the many species of finches on the Galapagos Islands. We are still not sure how the ancestral population of finches first arrived on that remote Pacific Island chain, but they found themselves in an environment filled with various insects, large and tiny seeds, fruit, and delicious varieties of cactus. Some members of that initial population carried alleles that gave them advantages for each of these dietary niches. In subsequent generations, others developed new mutations, some of which were beneficial. These traits were selected for, making the advantageous alleles more common among their offspring. As the finches spread from one island to the next, they would be far more likely to find mates among the birds on their new island. Birds feeding in the same area were then more likely to mate together than birds who have different diets, contributing to additional assortative mating. Together, these evolutionary mechanisms caused rapid speciation that allowed the new species to make the most of the various dietary niches (Figure 4.20).

Figure 4.20 Darwin's finches demonstrating Adaptive Radiation.

In today's modern world, understanding these evolutionary processes is crucial for developing immunizations and antibiotics that can keep up with the rapid mutation rate of viruses and bacteria. This is also relevant to our food supply, which relies, in large part, on the development of herbicides and pesticides that keep up with the mutation rates of pests and weeds. Viruses, bacteria, agricultural pests, and weeds have all shown great flexibility in developing alleles that make them resistant to the latest medical treatment, pesticide, or herbicide. Billion-dollar industries have specialized in trying to keep our species one step ahead of the next mutation in the pests and infectious diseases that put our survival at risk.

SPECIAL TOPIC: CALCULATING THE HARDY-WEINBERG EQUILIBRIUM

In the Hardy-Weinberg formula, p represents the frequency of the dominant allele, and q represents the frequency of the recessive allele. Remember, an allele's frequency is the proportion, or percentage, of that allele in the population. For the purposes of Hardy-Weinberg, we give the allele percentages as decimal numbers (e.g., 42% = 0.42), with the entire population (100% of alleles) equaling 1. If we can figure out the frequency of one of the alleles in the population, then it is simple to calculate the other. Simply subtract the known frequency from 1 (the entire population). Therefore: $1 - p = q$ and $1 - q = p$

The Hardy-Weinberg formula is $p^2 + 2pq + q^2$, where

p^2 represents the frequency of the homozygous dominant genotype;

$2pq$ represents the frequency of the heterozygous genotype; and

q^2 represents the frequency of the homozygous recessive genotype.

It is often easiest to determine q^2 first, simply by counting the number of individuals with the unique, homozygous recessive phenotype (then dividing by the total individuals in the population to arrive at the "frequency"). If we can do this, we simply need to calculate the square root of the homozygous recessive phenotype frequency. That gives us q. Remember, $1 - q$ equals p, so now we have the frequencies for both alleles in the population. If we needed to figure out the frequencies of heterozygotes and homozygous dominant genotypes, we'd just need to plug the p and q frequencies back into the p^2 and $2pq$ formulas.

Let's imagine we have a population of ladybeetles that carries two alleles: a dominant allele that produces red ladybeetles and a recessive allele that produces orange ladybeetles. Since red is dominant, we'll use R to represent the red allele, and r to represent the orange allele. Our population has ten beetles, and seven are red and three are orange (Figure 4.21). Let's calculate the number of genotypes and alleles in this population.

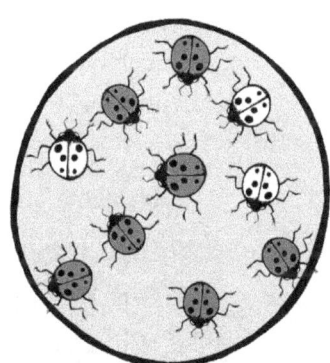

Figure 4.21 Ladybug population with a mixture of dark (red) and light (orange) individuals.

We have three orange beetles of our ten, 3/10 = .30 (30%) frequency, and we know they are homozygous recessive (rr). So:

rr = .3; therefore, $r = \sqrt{.3} = .5477$

R = 1 − .5477 = .4523

Using the Hardy-Weinberg formula:

$1 = .4523^2 + 2 \times .4523 \times .5477 + .5477^2 = .20 + .50 + .30 = 1$

Thus, the genotype breakdown is 20% RR, 50% Rr, and 30% rr

(2 red homozygotes, 5 red heterozygotes, and 3 orange homozygotes).

Since we have 10 individuals, we know we have 20 total alleles: 4 red from the RR group, 5 red and 5 orange from the Rr group, and 6 orange from the rr group, for a grand total of 9 red and 11 orange (45% red and 55% orange, just like we estimated in the $1 - q$ step).

Reminder: The Hardy-Weinberg formula only gives us an estimate for a snapshot in time. We will have to calculate it again later, after various intervals, to determine if our population is evolving and in what way the allele frequencies are changing.

Review Questions

- Devise an argument explaining how we know that the Pangenesis model for evolution is incorrect. Provide examples from the text of experiments that helped prove this wrong.
- You inherit a house from a long-lost relative that contains a fancy aquarium, filled with a variety of snails. The phenotypes include large snails and small snails; red, black, and yellow snails; and solid, striped, and spotted snails. Devise a series of experiments that would help you determine how many snail species are present in your aquarium.
- Imagine a population of common house mice (*Mus musculus*). Draw a comic strip illustrating how mutation, genetic drift, gene flow, and natural selection might transform this population over several (or more) generations.
- The many breeds of the single species of domestic dog (*Canis familiaris*) provide an extreme example of microevolution. Discuss why this is the case. What future scenarios can you imagine that could potentially transform the domestic dog into an example of macroevolution?
- The ability to roll one's tongue (lift the outer edges of the tongue to touch each other, forming a tube) is a dominant trait. In small town of 1,500 people, 500 can roll their tongues. Use the Hardy-Weinberg formula to determine how many individuals in the town are homozygous dominant, heterozygous, and homozygous recessive.
- Match the correct force of evolution with the correct real-world example:

  a. Mutation   i. 5-alpha reductase deficiency

  b. Genetic Drift   ii. Peppered Moths

  c. Gene Flow   iii. Neurofibromatosis Type 1

  d. Natural Selection   iv. Africanized Honey Bees

Key Terms

5-alpha reductase deficiency: An autosomal recessive syndrome that manifests when a child having both X and Y sex chromosomes inherits two non-functional (mutated) copies of the SRD5A2 gene, producing a deficiency in a hormone necessary for development in infancy of typical male genitalia. These children often appear at birth to have female genitalia, but they develop a penis and other sexual characteristics when other hormones kick in during puberty.

Adaptive radiation: The situation in which subgroups of a single species rapidly diversify and adapt to fill a variety of ecological niches.

Admixture: A term often used to describe gene flow between human populations. Sometimes also used to describe gene flow between non-human populations.

Africanized honey bees: A strain of honey bees that resulted from the hybridization of African and European honey bee subspecies. These bees were accidentally released into the wild in 1957 in Brazil, and have since spread throughout South and Central America and into the United States. Also known as "killer bees," they tend to be very aggressive in defense of their hives and have caused many fatal injuries to humans and livestock.

Allele frequency: The ratio, or percentage, of one allele compared to the other alleles for that gene within the study population.

Alleles: Variant forms of genes.

Allopatric speciation: Speciation caused by long-term isolation (physical separation) of subgroups of the population.

Antibiotics: Medicines prescribed to treat bacterial infections.

Artificial selection: Human-directed assortative mating among domestic animals, such as pets and livestock, designed to increase the chances of offspring having certain desirable traits.

Asexual reproduction: Reproduction via mitosis, whereby offspring are clones of the parents.

Autosomal dominant: A phenotype produced by a gene on an autosomal chromosome that is expressed, to the exclusion of the recessive phenotype, in heterozygotes.

Autosomal recessive: A phenotype produced by a gene on an autosomal chromosome that is expressed only in individuals homozygous for the recessive allele.

Balanced translocations: Chromosomal translocations in which the genes are swapped, but no genetic information is lost.

Balancing selection: A pattern of natural selection that occurs when the extremes of a trait are selected against, favoring the intermediate phenotype (a.k.a., stabilizing selection).

Beneficial mutations: Mutations that produce some sort of an advantage to the individual.

Benign: Non-cancerous. Benign tumors may cause problems due to the area in which they are located (e.g., they might put pressure on a nerve or brain area), but they will not release cells that aggressively spread to other areas of the body.

Biometricians: A group of early biological scientists who believed that individual mutations of discrete hereditary units could never account for the continuous spectrum of variation seen in many traits.

Café-au-lait spots (CALS): Flat, brown birthmark-like spots on the skin, commonly associated with Neurofibromatosis Type 1.

Chromosomal translocations: The transfer of DNA between non-homologous chromosomes.

Chromosomes: Molecules that carry collections of genes.

Codons: Three-nucleotide units of DNA that function as three-letter "words," encoding instructions for the addition of one amino acid to a protein or indicating that the protein is complete.

Cretaceous–Paleogene extinction: A mass disaster caused by an asteroid that struck the earth approximately 66 million years ago and killed 75% of life on Earth, including all terrestrial dinosaurs. (a.k.a., K-Pg Extinction, Cretatious-Tertiary Extinction and K-T Extinction).

Crossover events: Chromosomal alterations that occur when DNA is swapped between homologous chromosomes while they are paired up during meiosis I.

Cutaneous neurofibromas: Neurofibromas that manifest as spherical bumps on or just under the surface of the skin.

Cytosine methylation: A type of point mutation in which a cytosine nucleotide is converted to a thymine. A methyl group is added to a cytosine base, changing it to 5-methyl cytosine, which further converts to thymine after hydrolytic deamination (water-induced removal of an amine group).

Deleterious mutation: A mutation producing negative effects to the individual such as the beginnings of cancers or heritable disorders.

Deletions: Mutations that involve removal of one or more nucleotides from a DNA sequence.

Derivative chromosomes: New chromosomal structures resulting from translocations.

***Dictyostelium discoideum*:** A species of social amoebae that has been widely used for laboratory research. Laboratory strains of *Dictyostelium discoideum* all carry mutations in the NF1 gene, which is what allows them to survive on liquid media (agar) in Petri dishes.

Directional selection: A pattern of natural selection in which one phenotype is favored over the other, causing the frequencies of the associated advantageous alleles to gradually increase.

Disruptive selection: A pattern of natural selection that occurs when both extremes of a trait are advantageous and intermediate phenotypes are selected against (a.k.a., diversifying selection).

DNA repair mechanisms: Enzymes that patrol and repair DNA in living cells.

DNA transposons: Transposons that are clipped out of the DNA sequence itself and inserted elsewhere in the genome.

Ecological niche: A set of constraints and resources that are available in an environmental setting.

Ellis-van Creveld syndrome: An autosomal recessive disorder characterized by short stature (dwarfism), polydactyly [the development of more than five digits (fingers or toes) on the hands or feet], abnormal tooth development, and heart defects. Estimated to affect approximately one in 60,000 individuals worldwide, among the Old Order Amish of Lancaster County, the rate is estimated to be as high as one in every 200 births.

Evolution: A change in the allele frequencies in a population over time.

Exons: The DNA sequences within a gene that directly encode protein sequences. After being transcribed into messenger RNA, the introns are clipped out, and the exons are pasted together prior to translation.

Fertile offspring: Offspring that can reproduce successfully to have offspring of their own.

Founder effect: A type of genetic drift that occurs when members of a population leave the main or "parent" group and form a new population that no longer interbreeds with the other members of the original group.

Frameshift mutations: Types of indels that involve the insertion or deletion of any number of nucleotides that is not a multiple of three. These "shift the reading frame" and cause all codons beyond the mutation to be misread.

Gametes: The reproductive cells, produced through meiosis (a.k.a., germ cells or sperm or egg cells).

Gene: A sequence of DNA that provides coding information for the construction of proteins.

Gene flow: The movement of alleles from one population to another. This is one of the forces of evolution.

Gene pool: The entire collection of genetic material in a breeding community that can be passed on from one generation to the next.

Genetic drift: Random changes in allele frequencies within a population from one generation to the next. This is one of the forces of evolution.

Genotype: The set of alleles that an individual has for a given gene.

Genotype frequencies: The ratios or percentages of the different homozygous and heterozygous genotypes in the population.

Guevedoces: The term coined locally in the Dominican Republic for the condition scientifically known as 5-alpha reductase deficiency. The literal translation is "penis at twelve."

Hardy-Weinberg Equilibrium: A mathematical formula ($p^2 + 2pq + q^2$) that allows estimation of the number and distribution of dominant and recessive alleles in a population.

Harlequin ladybeetle: A species of ladybeetle, native to East Asia, that was introduced to Europe and the Americas as a form of pest control. After many decades of use, one of the North American strains developed the ability to reproduce in diverse environments, causing it to spread rapidly throughout the Americas, Europe, and Africa. It has hybridized with European strains and is now a major pest in its own right.

Heterozygous genotype: A genotype comprising two different alleles.

Homozygous genotype: A genotype comprising an identical set of alleles.

Hybridization: A term often used to describe gene flow between non-human populations.

Inbreeding: The selection of mates exclusively from within a small, closed population.

Indels: A class of mutations that includes both insertions and deletions.

Inherited mutation: A mutation that has been passed from parent to offspring.

Insertions: Mutations that involve addition of one or more nucleotides into a DNA sequence.

Introns: DNA sequences within a gene that do not directly encode protein sequences. After being transcribed into messenger RNA, the introns are clipped out, and the exons are pasted together prior to translation.

Isolation: Prevention of a population subgroup from breeding with other members of the same species due to a physical barrier or (in humans) a cultural rule.

Lamarckian inheritance: An early model for inheritance that predicted that offspring inherit characteristics acquired during their parents' lifetimes. This has now been proven incorrect.

Macroevolution: Changes that result in the emergence of new species, the similarities and differences between species, and their phylogenetic relationships with other taxa.

Malaria: A frequently deadly mosquito-borne disease caused by infection of the blood by a Plasmodium parasite.

Malignant: Cancerous. Malignant tumors grow aggressively and their cells may metastasize (travel through the blood or lymph systems) to form new, aggressive tumors in other areas of the body.

Microevolution: Changes in allele frequencies within breeding populations—that is, within a single species.

Missense mutation: A point mutation that produces a change in a single amino acid.

Modern Synthesis: The integration of Darwin's, Mendel's, and subsequent research into a unified theory of evolution.

Monosomies: Conditions resulting from a non-disjunction event, in which a cell ends up with only one copy of a chromosome. In humans, a single X chromosome is the only survivable monosomy.

Mutation: A change in the nucleotide sequence of the genetic code. This is one of the forces of evolution.

Mutationists: A group of early biological scientists who believed that variation was caused by mutations in distinct, inherited cells.

Natural selection: An evolutionary process that occurs when certain phenotypes confer an advantage or disadvantage in survival and/or reproductive success. This is one of the forces of evolution.

Negative assortative mating: A pattern that occurs when individuals tend to select mates with qualities different from their own.

Neurofibromas: Nerve sheath tumors that are common symptoms of Neurofibromatosis Type 1.

Neurofibromatosis Type 1: An autosomal dominant genetic disorder affecting one in every 3,000 people. It is caused by mutation of the NF1 gene on Chromosome 17, resulting in a defective neurofibromin protein. The disorder is characterized by neurofibromas, café-au-lait spots, and a host of other potential symptoms.

NF1: An abbreviation for Neurofibromatosis Type 1. When italicized, NF1 refers to the gene on Chromosome 17 that encodes the neurofibromin protein.

Nondisjunction events: Chromosomal abnormalities that occur when the homologous chromosomes (in meiosis I) or sister chromatids (in meiosis II and mitosis) fail to separate after pairing. The result is that both chromosomes or chromatids end up in the same daughter cell, leaving the other daughter cell without any copy of that chromosome.

Non-random mating: A scenario in which mate choice within a population follows a non-random pattern (a.k.a., Assortative Mating).

Nonsense mutation: A point mutation that converts a codon that encodes an amino acid into a stop codon.

Non-synonymous mutation: A point mutation that causes a change in the resulting protein.

Old Order Amish: A culturally isolated population in Lancaster County, Pennsylvania, that has approximately 50,000 current members, all of whom can trace their ancestry back to a group of approximately eighty individuals. This group has high rates of certain genetics disorders including Ellis-van Creveld syndrome.

Origins of life: How the first living organism came into being.

Pangenesis: An early model for inheritance that combines the Lamarckian idea of inheriting acquired characteristics with the idea that particles from different parts of the body make their way to the sex cells. This has now been proven to be incorrect.

Peacock: The male sex of the peafowl, famous for its large, colorful tail, which it dramatically displays to attract mates. (The female of the species is known as a peahen.)

Peppered moth: A species of moth found in England that has light and dark phenotypes. During the Industrial Revolution, when soot blackened the trees, the frequency of the previously rare dark phenotype dramatically increased, as lighter-colored moths were easier for birds to spot against the sooty trees. After environmental regulations eliminated the soot, the lighter-colored phenotype gradually became most common again.

Phenotype: The observable traits that are produced by a genotype.

Phylogenetic tree of life: A family tree of all living organisms, based on genetic relationships.

Phylogenies: Genetically determined family lineages.

Plasmodium: A genus of mosquito-borne parasite. Several Plasmodium species cause malaria when introduced to the human bloodstream via a mosquito bite.

Plexiform neurofibromas: Neurofibromas that involve whole branches of nerves, often giving the appearance that the surface of the skin is "melting."

Point mutation: A single-letter (single-nucleotide) change in the genetic code, resulting in the substitution of one nucleic acid base for a different one.

Polymorphisms: Multiple forms of a trait; alternative phenotypes within a given species.

Population: A group of individuals who are genetically similar enough and geographically near enough to one another that they can breed and produce new generations of individuals.

Population bottleneck: A type of genetic drift that occurs when the number of individuals in a population drops dramatically due to some random event.

Positive assortative mating: A pattern that results from a tendency for individuals to mate with others who share similar phenotypes.

Retrotransposons: Transposons that are transcribed from DNA into RNA, and then are "reverse transcribed," to insert the copied sequence into a new location in the DNA.

Sexual reproduction: Reproduction via meiosis and combination of gametes. Offspring inherit genetic material from both parents.

Sexual selection: An aspect of natural selection in which the selective pressure specifically affects reproductive success (the ability to successfully breed and raise offspring).

Sickle cell anemia: An autosomal recessive genetic disorder that affects millions of people worldwide. It is most common in Africa, countries around the Mediterranean Sea, and eastward as far as India. Homozygotes for the recessive allele develop the disorder, which produce misshapen red blood cells that cause iron deficiency, painful episodes of oxygen-deprivation in localized tissues, and a host of other symptoms. In heterozygotes, though, the sickle cell allele confers a greater resistance to malaria.

Somatic cells: The cells of our organs and other body tissues (all cells except gametes) that replicate by mitosis.

Speciation: The process by which a single population divides into two or more separate species.

Species: Organisms whose individuals are capable of breeding because they are biologically and behaviorally compatible to produce viable, fertile offspring.

Splice site mutation: A mutation that changes the genetic code so that the correct area to be modified for mRNA splicing is not recognized by the appropriate enzymes.

Spontaneous mutation: A mutation that occurs due to random chance or unintentional exposure to mutagens. In families, a spontaneous mutation is the first case, as opposed to mutations that are inherited from parents.

Subspecies: A distinct subtype of a species. Most often, this is a geographically isolated population with unique phenotypes; however, it remains biologically and behaviorally capable of interbreeding with other populations of the same species.

Sympatric speciation: When a population splits into two or more separate species while remaining located together without a physical (or cultural) barrier.

Synonymous mutation: A point mutation that does not change the resulting protein.

Transposable elements: Fragments of DNA that can "jump" around in the genome.

Transposon: Another term for "transposable element."

Trisomies: Conditions in which three copies of the same chromosome end up in a cell, resulting from a non-disjunction event. Down syndrome, Edwards syndrome, and Patau syndrome are trisomies.

Unbalanced translocations: Chromosomal translocations in which there is an unequal exchange of genetic material resulting in duplication or loss of genes.

Universal ancestor: The first living organism, from which all living things are descended.

UV crosslinking: A type of mutation in which adjacent thymine bases bind to one another in the presence of UV light.

Viable Offspring: Offspring that are healthy enough to survive to adulthood.

Xeroderma pigmentosum: An autosomal recessive disease in which DNA repair mechanisms do not function correctly, resulting in a host of problems, especially related to sun exposure, including severe sunburns, dry skin, heavy freckling, and other pigment changes.

About the Author

Andrea Alveshere

Western Illinois University, a-alveshere@wiu.edu, http://www.wiu.edu/cas/anthropology/faculty-staff/alveshere.php

Dr. Alveshere at the summit of Monk's Mound at the Cahokia Mississippian site in Collinsville, Illinois. Note the St. Louis, Missouri, skyline in the background.

Dr. Andrea Alveshere is an assistant professor of anthropology and chemistry at Western Illinois University. Her research focuses on relationships between humans and their environments, including questions of diet and health; cultural and biological adaptations; genetic disorders such as Neurofibromatosis Type 1 (NF1); effects of environmental factors on the preservation of bones, plant remains, and the molecules within them; and the comparative utility of various field and laboratory techniques to produce informative archaeological, nutritional, and forensic data.

Dr. Alveshere earned her B.A. in anthropology at the University of Washington with an emphasis in archaeology and an undergraduate research focus on the analysis of skeletal remains and geoarchaeological deposits. At the University of Minnesota, she completed her Ph.D. in anthropology, with a minor in human genetics. Her graduate thesis investigated factors that influence the preservation and detection of DNA in ancient and forensic specimens.

In addition to her academic experience, Dr. Alveshere worked for several years as a forensic scientist in the DNA/Biology section of the Minnesota Bureau of Criminal Apprehension Forensic Science Laboratory. She leads the WIU Archaeological Field School, which is offered every other summer, and has also conducted archaeological excavations in Israel, South Africa, and throughout the Midwestern United States.

For Further Exploration

Explore Evolution. HHMI's Biointeractive. https://www.hhmi.org/biointeractive/evolution-collection

Teaching Evolution Through Human Examples. Smithsonian Museum of Natural History. http://humanorigins.si.edu/education/teaching-evolution-through-human-examples

References

Bloomfield, Gareth, David Traynor, Sophia P. Sander, Douwe M. Veltman, Justin A. Pachebat, and Robert R. Kay. 2015. "Neurofibromin Controls Macropinocytosis and Phagocytosis in Dictyostelium." eLife 4:e04940.

Castle, W. E., and J. C. Phillips. 1914. Piebald Rats and Selection: An Experimental Test of the Effectiveness of Selection and of the Theory of Gametic Purity in Mendelian Crosses. Carnegie Institute of Washington, No. 195. Washington, DC: Carnegie Institute of Washington.

Chaix, Raphaëlle, Chen Cao, and Peter Donnelly. 2008. "Is Mate Choice in Humans MHC-Dependent?" PLoS Genetics 4 (9): e1000184.

Cook, Laurence M. 2003. "The Rise and Fall of the Carbonaria Form of the Peppered Moth." The Quarterly Review of Biology 78 (4): 399–417.

Cota, Bruno Cézar Lage, João Gabriel Marques Fonseca, Luiz Oswaldo Carneiro Rodrigues, Nilton Alves de Rezende, Pollyanna Barros Batista, Vincent Michael Riccardi, Luciana Macedo de Resende. 2018. "Amusia and Its Electrophysiological Correlates in Neurofibromatosis Type 1." Arquivos de Neuro-Psiquiatria 76 (5): 287-295.

Darwin, Charles. 1859. On the Origin of Species by Means of Natural Selection, or the Preservation of Favoured Races in the Struggle for Life. London: John Murray.

D'Asdia, Maria Cecilia, Isabella Torrente, Federica Consoli, Rosangela Ferese, Monia Magliozzi, Laura Bernardini, Valentina Guida, et al. 2013. "Novel and Recurrent EVC and EVC2 Mutations in Ellis-van Creveld Syndrome and Weyers Acrofacial Dyostosis." European Journal of Medical Genetics 56 (2): 80–87.

Dobzhansky, Theodosius (1937). Genetics and the Origin of Species. Columbia University Biological Series. New York: Columbia University Press.

Facon, Benoît, Laurent Crespin, Anne Loiseau, Eric Lombaert, Alexandra Magro, Arnaud Estoup. 2011. "Can Things Get Worse When an Invasive Species Hybridizes? The Harlequin Ladybird Harmonia axyridis in France as a Case Study." Evolutionary Applications 4 (1): 71–88.

Fisher, Ronald A. (1919). "The Correlation Between Relatives on the Supposition of Mendelian Inheritance." Transactions of the Royal Society of Edinburgh 52 (2): 399–433.

Ford, E. B. 1942. Genetics for Medical Students. London: Methuen.

Ford, E. B. 1949. Mendelism and Evolution. London: Methuen.

Grant, Bruce S. 1999. "Fine-tuning the Peppered Moth Paradigm." Evolution 53 (3): 980–984.

Haldane, J. B. S. 1924. "A Mathematical Theory of Natural and Artificial Selection (Part 1)." Transactions of the Cambridge Philosophical Society 23:19–41.

Huxley, Julian. 1942. Evolution: The Modern Synthesis. London: Allen & Unwin.

Imperato-McGinley, J., and Y.-S. Zhu. 2002. "Androgens and Male Physiology: The Syndrome of 5 Alpha-Reductase-2 Deficiency." Molecular and Cellular Endocrinology 198: 51–59.

Jablonski, David, and W. G. Chaloner. 1994. "Extinctions in the Fossil Record [and Discussion]." Philosophical Transactions of the Royal Society of London B: Biological Sciences 344 (1,307): 11–17.

Livi-Bacci, Massimo. 2006. "The Depopulation of Hispanic America After the Conquest." Population Development and Review 32 (2): 199–232.

Lombaert, Eric, Thomas Guillemaud, Jean-Marie Cornuet, Thibaut Malausa, Benoît Facon, and Arnaud Estoup. 2010. "Bridgehead Effect in the Worldwide Invasion of the Biocontrol Harlequin Ladybird." PLoS ONE 5 (3): e9743.

Martins, Aline Stangherlin, Ann Kristine Jansen, Luiz Oswaldo Carneiro Rodrigues, Camila Maria Matos, Marcio Leandro Ribeiro Souza, Juliana Ferreira de Souza, Maria de Fátima Haueisen Sander Diniz, et al. 2016. "Lower Fasting Blood Glucose in Neurofibromatosis Type 1." Endocrine Connections 5 (1): 28–33.

Morgan, T. H. 1911. "Random Segregation Versus Coupling in Mendelian Inheritance." Science 34 (873): 384.

Pickering, Gary, James Lin, Roland Riesen, Andrew Reynolds, Ian Brindle, and George Soleas. 2004. "Influence of Harmonia axyridis on the Sensory Properties of White and Red Wine." American Journal of Enology and Viticulture 55 (2): 153–159.

Repunte-Canonigo Vez, Melissa A. Herman, Tomoya Kawamura, Henry R. Kranzler, Richard Sherva, Joel Gelernter, Lindsay A. Farrer, Marisa Roberto, and Pietro Paolo Sanna. 2015. "NF1 Regulates Alcohol Dependence-Associated Excessive Drinking and Gamma-Aminobutyric Acid Release in the Central Amygdala in Mice and Is Associated with Alcohol Dependence in Humans." Biological Psychiatry 77 (10): 870–879.

Riccardi, Vincent M. 1992. Neurofibromatosis: Phenotype, Natural History, and Pathogenesis. Baltimore: Johns Hopkins University Press.

Sanford, Malcolm T. 2006. "The Africanized Honey Bee in the Americas: A Biological Revolution With Human Cultural Implications, Part V—Conclusion." American Bee Journal 146 (7): 597–599.

Sanna, Pietro Paolo, Cindy Simpson, Robert Lutjens, and George Koob. 2002. "ERK Regulation in Chronic Ethanol Exposure and Withdrawal." Brain Research 948 (1–2): 186–191.

Weismann, August. 1892. Das Keimplasma: Eine Theorie der Vererbung [The Germ Plasm: A Theory of Inheritance]. Jena: Fischer.

World Health Organization. 1996. "Control of Hereditary Disorders: Report of WHO Scientific meeting (1996)." WHO Technical Reports 865. Geneva: World Health Organization.

World Health Organization. 2017. "Global Priority List of Antibiotic-Resistant Bacteria to Guide Research, Discovery, and Development of New Antibiotics." Global Priority Pathogens List, February 27. Geneva: World Health Organization. https://www.who.int/medicines/publications/WHO-PPL-Short_Summary_25Feb-ET_NM_WHO.pdf

Wright, Sewall. 1932. "The Roles of Mutation, Inbreeding, Crossbreeding, and Selection in Evolution." Proceedings of the Sixth International Congress on Genetics 1 (6): 356–366.

Acknowledgment

Many thanks to Dr. Vincent M. Riccardi for sharing his vast knowledge of neurofibromatosis and for encouraging me to explore it from an anthropological perspective.

Figure Attributions

Figure 4.1 Tree of life SVG by Ivica Letunic: Iletunic, retraced by Mariana Ruiz Villarreal: LadyofHats, has been designated to the public domain (CC0). This item has been modified (made grayscale, rotated, labels added).

Figure 4.2A Lamarckian Evolution original to Explorations: An Open Invitation to Biological Anthropology by Mary Nelson is under a CC BY-NC 4.0 License.

Figure 4.2B Modern Synthesis original to Explorations: An Open Invitation to Biological Anthropology by Mary Nelson is under a CC BY-NC 4.0 License.

Figure 4.3 Weismann's mouse-tail experiment original to Explorations: An Open Invitation to Biological Anthropology by Mary Nelson is under a CC BY-NC 4.0 License.

Figure 4.4 Castle's Hooded Rat Experiment original to Explorations: An Open Invitation to Biological Anthropology by Mary Nelson is under a CC BY-NC 4.0 License.

Figure 4.5 Morgan's Mutant Fruit Flies original to Explorations: An Open Invitation to Biological Anthropology by Mary Nelson is under a CC BY-NC 4.0 License.

Figure 4.6 UV-induced Thymine dimer mutation original to Explorations: An Open Invitation to Biological Anthropology by Mary Nelson is under a CC BY-NC 4.0 License.

Figure 4.7 Cytosine-to-thymine point mutation original to An Open Invitation to Biological Anthropology by Mary Nelson is under a CC BY-NC 4.0 License.

Figure 4.8 Point and frameshift mutations original to An Open Invitation to Biological Anthropology by Mary Nelson is under a CC BY-NC 4.0 License.

Figure 4.9 Woman with cutaneous neurofibromas (syptom of NF1) by Rick Guidotti of Positive Exposure is used by permission and available here is under a CC BY-NC 4.0 License.

Figure 4.10a Man with plexiform neurofibroma (syptom of NF1) is used by permission from Ashok Shrestha and available here is under a CC BY-NC 4.0 License.

Figure 4.10b Childhood photo of the same man with NF1 disorder is used by permission from Ashok Shrestha and available here is under a CC BY-NC 4.0 License.

Figure 4.11 Child with café-au-lait macules (birthmarks) typical of the earliest symptoms of NF1 by Andrea J. Alveshere is under a CC BY-NC 4.0 License.

Figure 4.12 The Cretaceous–Paleogene extinction event original to Explorations: An Open Invitation to Biological Anthropology by Mary Nelson is under a CC BY-NC 4.0 License.

Figure 4.13 6 Finger by Wilhelmy is under a CC BY-SA 4.0 License.

Figure 4.14 Ladybug Gene Flow original to Explorations: An Open Invitation to Biological Anthropology by Mary Nelson is under a CC BY-NC 4.0 License.

Figure 4.15 Peppered moths c2 by Khaydock is under a CC BY-SA 3.0 License.

Figure 4.16 Biology (ID: 185cbf87-c72e-48f5-b51e-f14f21b5eabd@9.17) by CNX OpenStax is used under a CC BY 4.0 License.

Figure 4.17 Sickle-cell smear 2015-09-10 by Paulo Henrique Orlandi Mourao, contrast modified and labels added by Katie Nelson, CC BY-SA 4.0.

Figure 4.18 Peacock tail advantage and disadvantages soriginal to Explorations: An Open Invitation to Biological Anthropology by Mary Nelson is under a CC BY-NC 4.0 License.

Figure 4.19 Isolation Leading to Speciation original to Explorations: An Open Invitation to Biological Anthropology by Mary Nelson is under a CC BY-NC 4.0 License.

Figure 4.20 Darwin's finches original to Explorations: An Open Invitation to Biological Anthropology by Mary Nelson is under a CC BY-NC 4.0 License.

Figure 4.21 Ladybug mix original to Explorations: An Open Invitation to Biological Anthropology by Mary Nelson is under a CC BY-NC 4.0 License.

Chapter 5: Meet the Living Primates

Stephanie Etting, Ph.D., Sacramento City College

> *Learning Objectives*
>
> - Learn how primates are different from other mammals.
> - Understand how studying non-human primates is important in anthropology.
> - Identify different types of traits that we use to evaluate primate taxa.
> - Describe the major primate taxa using their key characteristics.
> - Understand your place in nature by learning your taxonomic classification.

One of the best parts of teaching anthropology for me is getting to spend time at zoos watching primates. What I also find interesting is watching people watch primates. I have very often heard a parent and child walk up to a chimpanzee enclosure and exclaim "Look at the monkeys!" The parent and child often don't know that a chimpanzee is not a monkey, nor are they likely to know that chimpanzees share more than 98% of their DNA with us. What strikes me as significant is that, although most people do not know the difference between a monkey, an ape, and a lemur, they nonetheless recognize something in the animals as being similar to themselves. What people probably mean when they say "monkey" is actually "primate," a term that refers to all organisms classified within the Order Primates and also the subject of this chapter. You may be wondering why a field dedicated to the study of humans would include the study of non-human animals. Because humans are primates, we share a wide range of behavioral and morphological traits with the other species who also fall into this group. In Chapter 2, you learned about the nature of Linnaean classification, the system we use for organizing life-forms. Here, we focus on the organization and diversity within the Order Primates. The term *Order Primates* dates back to 1758 when, in his tenth edition of *Systema Naturae*, Carolus Linnaeus put humans, "simia" (monkeys and apes), "lemurs" (lemurs and colugos), and some bats into one of eight groups of mammals. Linnaeus was wrong in including colugos (now in Order Dermoptera) and bats (now in Order Chiroptera), but the grouping of humans with the then-known non-human primates was significant in that by doing so Linnaeus formally recognized the affinities between humans and these non-human taxa. In fact, acknowledgment of similarities between humans and non-humans dates back far earlier than Linnaeus (see the Special Topic box), yet it was only more recently that we attained the genetic data to back up our intuition.

WHAT IS A PRIMATE?

Primates are one of at least twenty Orders belonging to the Class Mammalia. All members of this class share certain characteristics, including, among other things, having fur or hair, producing milk from mammary glands, and being warm-blooded. There are three types of mammals: monotremes, marsupials, and placental mammals. Monotremes are the most primitive of the mammals, meaning they have retained more ancient traits than marsupials or placental mammals, and so, monotremes are characterized by some unusual traits. Monotremes, which include echidnas and duck-billed platypuses, lay eggs rather than give birth to live young. Once the young hatch, they lap up milk produced from glands on the mother's abdomen rather than latch onto nipples. Marsupial mammals are those, like kangaroos and koalas, who internally gestate for a very short period of time and give birth to relatively undeveloped young. Joeys, as these newborns are called, complete their growth externally in their mother's pouch where they suckle. Lastly, there are placental mammals. Placental mammals internally gestate for a longer period of time and give birth to fairly well-developed young who are then nursed. Primates, including ourselves, belong to this last group. Among the diversity of mammalian orders alive today, primates are very likely one of the oldest. One genetic estimate puts the origin of primates at approximately 91 million years ago (mya), predating the extinction of the dinosaurs (Bininda-Emonds et al. 2007). Today, the Order Primates is a diverse group of animals that includes lemurs and lorises, tarsiers, monkeys of the New and Old Worlds, apes, and humans, all of which are united in sharing a suite of anatomical, behavioral, and life history characteristics. Before delving into the specific traits that distinguish primates from other animals, it is important to first discuss the different types of traits that we will encounter.

Types of Traits

When evaluating relationships between different groups of primates, we use key traits that allow us to determine which species are most closely related to one another. Traits can be either primitive or derived. **Primitive** traits are those that a taxon has because it has inherited the trait from a distant ancestor. For example, all primates have body hair because we are mammals and all mammals share an ancestor hundreds of millions of years ago that had body hair. This trait has been passed down to all mammals from this shared ancestor, so all mammals alive today have body hair. **Derived** traits are those that have been more recently altered. This type of trait is most useful when we are trying to distinguish one group from another because derived traits tell us which taxa are more closely related to each other. For example, humans walk on two legs. The many adaptations that humans possess which allow us to move in this way evolved after humans split from the Genus *Pan*. This means that when we find fossil taxa that share derived traits for walking on two legs, we can conclude that they are likely more closely related to humans than to chimpanzees and bonobos.

There are a couple of other important points about primitive and derived traits that will become apparent as we discuss primate diversity. First, the terms *primitive* and *derived* are relative terms. This means that depending on what taxa are being compared, a trait can be either one. For example, in the previous section, body hair was used as an example for a primitive trait among primates. All mammals have body hair because we share a distant ancestor who had this trait. The presence of body hair therefore doesn't allow you to distinguish whether monkeys are more closely related to apes or lemurs because they all share this trait. However, if we are comparing mammals to birds and fish, then body hair becomes a derived trait of mammals. It evolved after mammals diverged from birds and fish, and it tells us that all mammals are more closely related to each other than they are to birds or fish. The second important point is that very often when one lineage splits into two, one taxon will stay more similar to the last common ancestor in retaining more primitive traits, whereas the other lineage will usually become more different from the last common ancestor by developing more derived traits. This will become very apparent when we discuss the two suborders of primates, Strepsirrhini and Haplorrhini. When these two lineages diverged, strepsirrhines retained more primitive traits (those present in the ancestor of primates) and haplorrhines developed more derived traits (became more different from the ancestor of primates).

There are two other types of traits that will be relevant to our discussions here: generalized and specialized traits. **Generalized traits** are those characteristics that are useful for a wide range of things. Having **opposable thumbs** that go in a different direction than the rest of your fingers is a very useful, generalized trait. You can hold a pen, grab a branch, peel a banana, or text your friends all thanks to your opposable thumbs. **Specialized traits** are those that have been modified for a specific purpose. These traits may not have a wide range of uses, but they will be very efficient at their job. Hooves in horses are a good example of a specialized trait. Horses cannot grasp objects with their hooves, but hooves allow horses to run very quickly on the ground on all fours. You can think of generalized traits as a Swiss Army knife, useful for a wide range of tasks but not particularly good at any of one them. That is, if you're in a bind, then a Swiss Army knife can be very useful to cut a rope or fix a loose screw, but if you were going to build furniture or fix a kitchen sink, then you'd want specialized tools for the job. As we will see, most primate traits tend to be generalized.

Primate Suite of Traits

The Order Primates is distinguished from other groups of mammals in having a suite of characteristics. This means that there is no individual trait that you can use to instantly identify an animal as a primate; instead, you have to look for animals that possess a collection of traits. What this also means is that each individual trait we discuss may be found in non-primates, but if you see an animal that has most or all of these traits, there is a good chance it is a primate.

One area in which the Order Primates is most distinguished from other organisms regards traits related to our senses, especially our vision. Compared to other animals, primates rely on vision as a primary sense. Our heavy reliance on vision is reflected in many areas of our anatomy and behavior. All primates have eyes that face forward with convergent (overlapping) visual fields. This means that if you cover one eye with your hand, you can still see most of the room with your other one. This also means that we cannot see on the sides or behind us as well as some other animals can. In order to protect the sides of the eyes from the muscles we use for chewing, all primates have at least a **postorbital bar,** a bony ring around the outside of the eye (Figure 5.1). Some primate taxa have more convergent eyes than others, so those primates need extra protection for their eyes. As a result, animals with greater orbital convergence will have a **postorbital plate** or **postorbital closure** in addition to the bar (Figure 5.1). The postorbital bar is a derived trait of primates, appearing in our earliest ancestors, which you will read more about in Chapter 8.

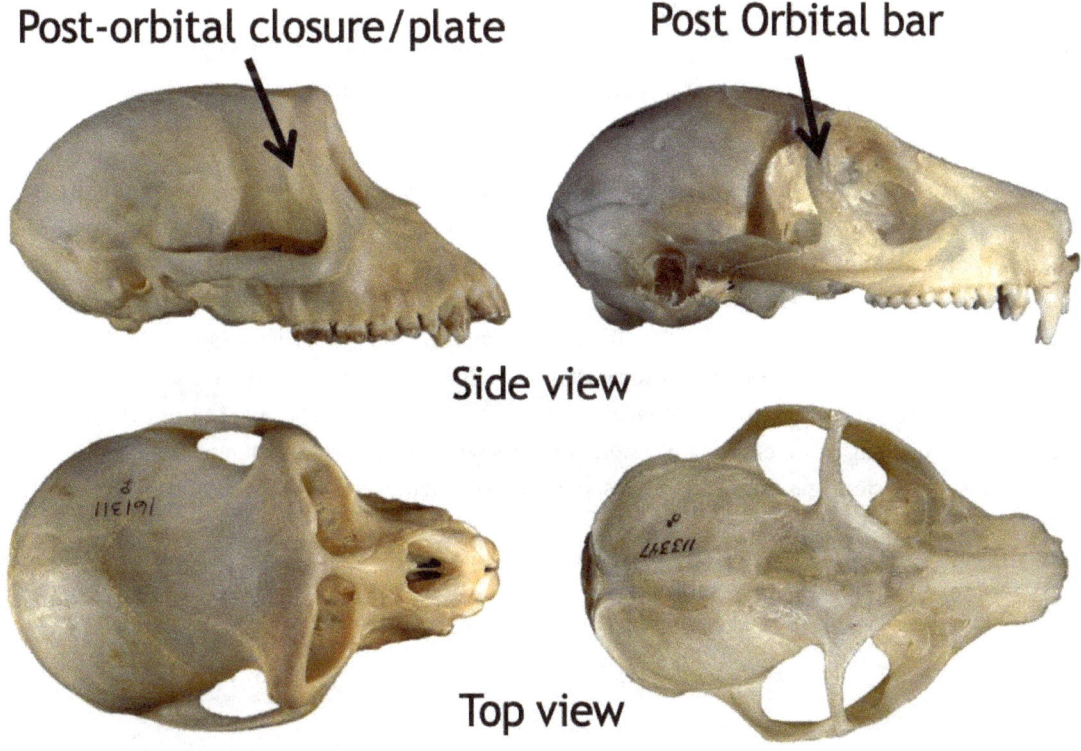

Figure 5.1 All primates have some form of bony protection around their eyes. Some have a postorbital bar only (right), but many have full postorbital closure, also called a postorbital plate, that completely protects the back of the eye socket (left).

Another important and distinctive trait of our Order is that many primates have **trichromatic color vision**, the ability to distinguish reds and yellows in addition to blues and greens. Interestingly, birds, fish, and reptiles are **tetrachromatic** (they can see reds, yellows, blues, greens, and even ultraviolet), but most mammals, including some primates, are only **dichromatic** (they see only in blues and greens). It is thought that the nocturnal ancestors of mammals benefited from seeing better at night rather than in color, and so dichromacy is thought to be the primitive condition for mammals. There is a lot of interest in why some primates would re-evolve trichromacy. Some theories revolve around food, arguing that the ability to see reds/yellows may allow primates who can see these colors to better detect young leaves (Dominy and Lucas 2001) or ripe fruits (Regan et al. 2001) against an otherwise green, leafy background. Color vision has also been suggested to be useful for detecting predators, especially big cats (Pessoa et al. 2014). Another theory emphasizes the usefulness of trichromacy in social and mate-choice contexts (Changizi et al. 2006). Thus far there is no consensus, as trichromatic color vision can be useful in many circumstances. There is also the added complication that sometimes dichromacy is more advantageous, as animals who are dichromatic are usually better at seeing through camouflage to find hidden items like foods or predators (Morgan et al. 1992). Therefore, investigating the evolution of color vision continues to be an interesting and ongoing area of research.

Primates also differ from other mammals in the size and complexity of our brains. All primates have brains that are larger than you would expect when compared to other mammals of the same size. On average, primates have brains that are twice as big for their body size as you would expect when compared to other mammals. Not unexpectedly, the visual centers of the brain are larger in primates and the wiring is different from that in other animals, reflecting our reliance on this sense. The neocortex, which is used for higher functions like consciousness and language in humans, as well as sensory perception and spatial awareness, is also larger in primates relative to other animals. In non-primates this part of the brain is often smooth, but in primates it is made up of many folds which increase the surface area. It has been proposed that the more complex neocortex of primates is related to diet, with fruit-eating primates having larger relative brain sizes than leaf-eating primates, due to the more challenging cognitive demands required to find and process fruits (Clutton-Brock and Harvey 1980). An alternative hypothesis argues that larger brain size is necessary for navigating the complexities of primate social life, with larger brains occurring in species who live in larger, more complex groups relative to those living in pairs or solitarily (Dunbar 1998). There seems to be support for both hypotheses, as large brains are a benefit under both sets of selective pressures.

The primate visual system uses a lot of energy, so primates have compensated by cutting back on other sensory systems, particularly our sense of smell. Compared to other mammals, primates have relatively reduced snouts. This is another derived trait of primates that appears even in our earliest ancestors. As we will discuss, there is variation across primate taxa in how much snouts are reduced. Those with a better sense of smell usually have poorer vision than those with a relatively dull sense of smell. The reason for this is that all organisms have a limited amount of energy to spend on running our bodies, so we make **evolutionary trade-offs**, because energy spent on one trait must mean cutting back on energy spent on another. With regards to primate senses, primates with better vision (more convergent eyes, better visual acuity, etc.) are spending more energy on vision and thus will have poorer smell (and a shorter snout). Primates who spend less energy on vision (less convergent eyes, poorer visual acuity, etc.) will have a better sense of smell (and a longer snout).

Primates also differ from other animals in our hands and feet. The Order Primates is a largely **arboreal** taxonomic group, which means that most primates spend a significant amount of their time in trees. As a result, the hands and feet of primates have evolved to move around in a three-dimensional environment. Primates have the generalized trait of **pentadactyly**– possessing five digits (fingers and toes) on each limb. Many non-primates, like dogs and horses, have fewer digits because they are specialized for high-speed, **terrestrial** (on the ground) running. Pentadactyly is also a primitive trait, one that dates back to the earliest four-footed animals. Primates today have opposable thumbs and, except humans, opposable big toes (Figure 5.2). **Opposable thumbs/toes** are a derived trait that appeared in the earliest primates about 55 million years ago. Having thumbs and big toes that go in a different direction from the rest of the fingers and toes allow primates to be excellent climbers in trees but also allow us to manipulate objects. Our ability to manipulate objects is further enhanced by the flattened nails on the backs of our fingers and toes that we possess in the place of the claws and hooves that many other mammals have. On the other side of our digits, we have sensitive **tactile pads** that allow us to have a fine sense of touch. Primates use this fine sense of touch for handling food and, in many species, grooming themselves and others. In primates, grooming is an important social currency, through which individuals forge and maintain social bonds. You will learn more about grooming in Chapter 6.

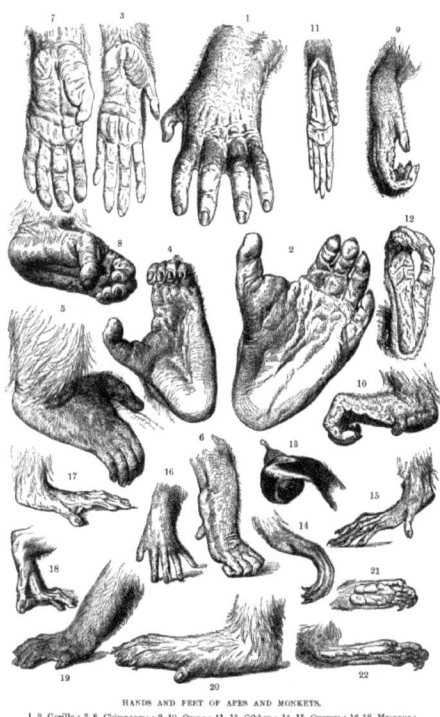

Figure 5.2 These drawings of the hands and feet of different primates clearly show the opposable thumbs and big toes, pentadactyly, flattened nails, and tactile pads that are characteristic of our Order.

Animals with large brains usually have extended life history patterns, and primates are no exception. **Life history** refers to the pace at which an organism grows, reproduces, ages, and so forth. Some animals grow very quickly and reproduce many offspring in a short time frame, but do not live very long. Other animals grow slowly, reproduce few offspring, reproduce infrequently, and live a long time. Primates are all in the "slow lane" of life history patterns. Compared to animals of similar body size, primates grow and develop more slowly, have fewer offspring per pregnancy, reproduce less often, and live longer. Primates also invest heavily in each offspring, a subject you will learn more about in the next chapter. With a few exceptions, most primates only have one offspring at a time. There is a group of small-bodied monkeys in the New World who regularly give birth to twins, and some lemurs are able to give birth to multiple offspring at a time, but these primates are the exception rather than the rule. Primates also reproduce relatively infrequently. The fastest-reproducing primates will produce offspring about every six months, while the slowest, the orangutan, reproduces only once every seven to nine years. This very slow reproductive rate makes the orangutan the slowest-reproducing animal on the planet! Primates are also characterized by having long lifespans. The group that includes humans and large-bodied apes has the most extended life history patterns among all primates, with some large-bodied apes estimated to live up to 58 years in the wild (Robson et al. 2006).

Lastly, primates share some behavioral and ecological traits. Primates are very social animals, and all primates, even those that search for food alone, have strong social networks with others of their species. Indeed, social networks in primates have been shown to be crucial in times of stress and to enhance reproductive success (Silk et al. 2009). Unlike many animals, primates do not migrate. This means that primates stay in a relatively stable area for their whole life, often interacting with the same individuals for their long lives. The long-term relationships that primates form with others of their species lead to complex and fascinating social behaviors, which you will read about in Chapter 6. Finally, non-human primates show a clear preference for tropical regions of the world. Most primates are found between the Tropic of Cancer and the Tropic of Capricorn, with only a few taxa living outside of these regions. You can see a summary of the primate suite of traits in Figure 5.3.

Primate suite of traits
Convergent eyes
Post-orbital bar
Many have trichromatic color vision
Short snouts
Opposable thumbs and big toes
Pentadactyly
Flattened nails
Tactile pads
Highly arboreal
Large brains
Extended life histories
Live in the tropics

Figure 5.3 Primate Traits at a Glance: This table summarizes the suite of traits that differentiate primates from other mammals.

KEY TRAITS USED TO DISTINGUISH BETWEEN PRIMATE TAXA

When trying to place primate species into specific taxonomic groups, we use a variety of dental characteristics, locomotor adaptations, and behavioral adaptations. Differences in these characteristics across groups reflect constraints of evolutionary history as well as variation in adaptations.

Dental Characteristics

Teeth may not seem like the most exciting topic with which to start, but we can learn a tremendous amount of information about an organism from its teeth. First, teeth are vital to survival. Wild animals do not have the benefit of knives and forks, and so rely primarily on their teeth to process their food. Because of this, teeth of any species have evolved to reflect what that organism eats and so tell us directly about their diet. Second, variation in tooth size, shape, and number tells us a lot about an organism's evolutionary history. Some taxa have more teeth than others or different forms of teeth than others. Furthermore, differences in teeth between males and females can tell us about competition over mates (see Chapter 6). Lastly, teeth preserve really well in the fossil record. Enamel is hard, and there is little meat on jaws so carnivores and scavengers often leave them behind. Because of this, very often we find a lot of fossil jaws and teeth, and so we need to be able to learn as much as we can from those pieces.

If you've ever seen the jaws of a shark, dinosaur, or crocodile, you were probably struck by how sharp their teeth were and by the sheer number of teeth they had. What you probably didn't think about was that they also only have one type of tooth, referred to as **homodont**. In fact, one of the ways that mammals differ from other organisms is that we have multiple types of teeth (**heterodont**) that we use in different ways. We have **incisors**, which we use for slicing; we have **premolars** and **molars**, which we use for grinding up our food; and we have **canines**, which most primates (not humans) use as weapons against predators and each other. The sizes of canines vary across species and can often be **sexually dimorphic**, with male canines usually being larger than those of females. Non-human primates often **hone**, or sharpen, their canines by gnashing the teeth together to sharpen the sides. The upper canine sharpens on the first lower premolar and the lower canine sharpens on the front of the upper canine. As canines get larger, they require a space to fit in order for the jaws to close. This space between the teeth is called a **diastema** (Figure 5.4).

Figure 5.4 This open-mouthed Hamadryas baboon clearly demonstrates the diastema between his upper canine and front teeth. This space is taken up by his lower canine when he closes his mouth.

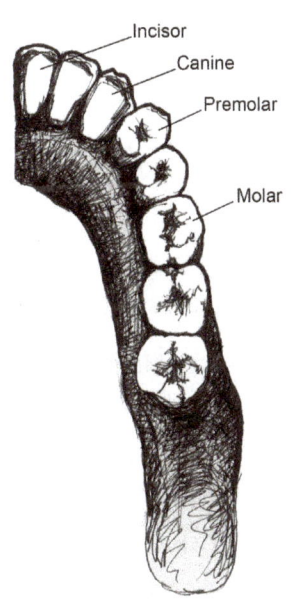

Figure 5.5 This drawing shows half of the human mandible. With the four types of teeth labeled, you can determine that the dental formula is 2:1:2:3.

As discussed before, primate taxa can vary in the numbers and forms of teeth they have. We determine the number of each type of tooth an organism has by its **dental formula**. The dental formula tells you how many incisors, canines, premolars, and molars are in each quadrant of the mouth (half of the top or bottom). For example, Figure 5.5 shows half of the lower teeth of a human. You can see that in half of the mandible, there are two incisors, one canine, two premolars, and three molars. This dental formula is written as 2:1:2:3. (The first number represents the number of incisors, followed by the number of canines, premolars, and molars). Some early fossil primates had a dental formula of 2:1:4:3, but among the living primates, none have more teeth than can be found in a 2:1:3:3 dental formula. Many have fewer teeth, however, and some have a different dental formula on the top than they do on the bottom.

To determine the dental formula, you need to be able to identify the different types of teeth. You can recognize incisors because they often look like spatulas with a flat, blade-like surface. Premolars and molars can be differentiated by the number of **cusps** that they have. Cusps are the little bumps (which in some species can be quite sharp) that you can feel with your tongue on the surface of your back teeth. Premolars are smaller than molars and, in primates, often have one or two cusps on them. Molars are bigger, with a larger chewing surface, and so have more cusps. Depending on the species of primate and whether you're looking at upper or lower teeth, molars can have between three and five cusps. There is even one extinct primate (*Oreopithecus*) who had six cusps on its molars. Molar cusps can also vary between taxa in how they are arranged, as you will learn more about later in this chapter. Canines are often easy to distinguish because they are usually much longer and more conical than the other teeth. This is not always the case, however, as you will see when you read about the teeth of lemurs and lorises.

Teeth also tell us directly about an organism's diet. Primates are known to eat a wide range of plant parts, insects, gums, and, rarely, meat. While all primates eat a variety of foods, what differs among primates are the proportions of each of these food items in the diet. That is, two primates living in the same forest may be eating the same foods but in vastly different proportions, and so we would categorize them as different dietary types. The most common dietary types among primates are those whose diets consist primarily of fruit (**frugivores**), those who eat mostly insects (**insectivores**), and those who eat primarily leaves (**folivores**). Fewer primates are **gummivores**, who specialize in eating gums and saps, so we will not discuss the adaptations for this dietary type in great detail.

Frugivores

Plants want animals to eat their fruits because, in doing so, animals eat the seeds of the fruit and then disperse them far away from the parent plant. Because plants want animals to eat the fruit, plants often "advertise" fruits by making them colorful and easy to spot, full of easy-to-digest sugars that make them taste good—and, often, easy to chew and digest (not being too fibrous or tough). For these reasons, frugivores often do not need a lot of specialized traits to consume a diet rich in fruits (Figure 5.6a). Their molars usually have a broad chewing surface with low, rounded cusps (referred to as **bunodont** molars). Frugivores also often have large incisors for slicing through the outer coatings on fruit. Primates that eat fruit tend to have stomachs, colons, and small intestines that are intermediate in terms of size and complexity between insectivores and folivores (Chivers and Hladik 1980). They are also usually of intermediate body size between the other two dietary types. Because fruit does not contain protein, frugivores must supplement their diet with protein from insects and/or leaves. Some frugivorous primates get protein by eating seeds and so have evolved to have thicker enamel on their teeth to protect them from excessive wear.

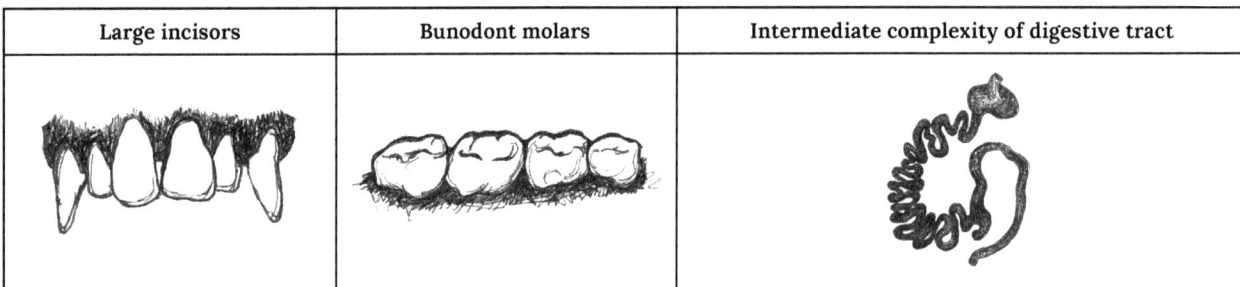

Figure 5.6a Frugivores are characterized by large incisors, bunodont molars, and digestive tracts that are intermediate in complexity between the other two dietary types.

Insectivores

Insects can be difficult to find and catch but are not typically difficult to chew. As a result, insectivorous primates usually have small molars with pointed cusps that allow them to puncture the exoskeleton of the insects (Figure 5.6b). Once the outer shells of the insects are punctured, insects are not difficult to digest, so insectivores have simple stomachs and colons and a long small intestine. Nutritionally, insects provide a lot of protein and fat but are not plentiful enough in the environment to support large-bodied animals, so insectivores are usually the smallest of the primates.

Sharp, pointed molars	Simple digestive tract

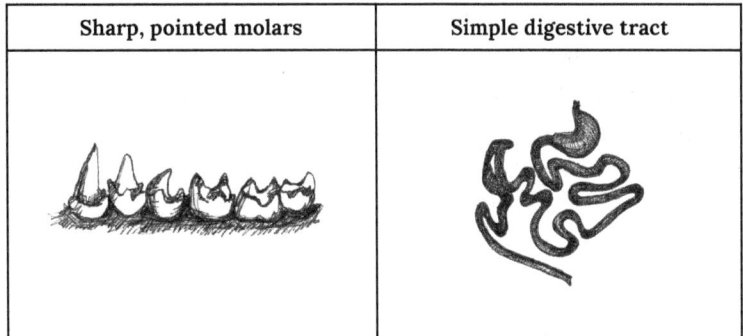

Figure 5.6b Insectivores need sharp, pointed molar cusps in order to break through the exoskeletons of insects. Insects are easy to digest, so these primates have simple digestive tracts.

Folivores

Unlike with fruits, plants do not want animals to eat their leaves. Leaves are the way plants get their energy from the sun, therefore, plants evolved to make their leaves very difficult for animals to eat. Leaves often have toxins in them, taste bitter, are very fibrous and difficult to chew, and are made of large cellulose molecules that are difficult to break down into usable sugars. Because of these defenses, animals who eat leaves need a lot of specialized traits (Figure 5.6c). Folivorous primates have broad molars with high, sharp cusps connected by **shearing crests**. These molar traits allow folivores to physically break down fibrous leaves when chewing. Folivores then have to chemically break down cellulose molecules into usable energy, so these animals need specialized digestive systems. Some folivores have complex stomachs with multiple compartments, but all leaf eaters have large, long intestines and special gut bacteria that can break up cellulose. Folivores are usually the largest bodied of all primates, and they spend a large portion of their day digesting their food, so they are often less active than frugivores or insectivores.

Smaller incisors	High, sharp molar cusps with shearing crests	Complex digestive tract

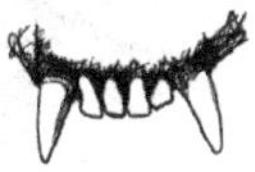

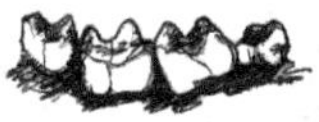

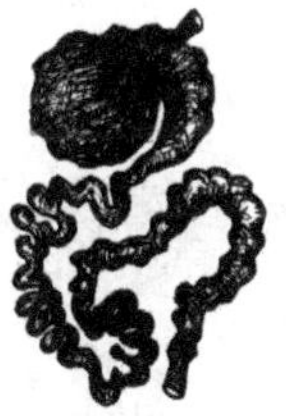

Figure 5.6c In order to derive energy from leaves, folivores have smaller incisors, high, sharp molar cusps connected by shearing crests and complex digestive tracts filled with specialized bacteria.

Behavioral Adaptations

Chapter 6 is entirely dedicated to primate behavior, so only broad differences related to taxonomic classification will be discussed here. These differences include variations in activity patterns, social grouping, and habitat use. Primate groups often differ in **activity patterns**—that is, whether they are active during the day (**diurnal**), at night (**nocturnal**), or through the 24-hour period (**cathemeral**). We also see variations among primate groups in social groupings: some taxa are primarily solitary, others live in pairs, and still others live in groups of varying sizes and compositions. Lastly, some taxa are primarily arboreal while others are more terrestrial.

Locomotor Adaptations

Figure 5.7 An example of a vertical clinger and leaper. Note the longer legs than arms, long lower back and long fingers and toes. This vertical clinger and leaper doesn't have a tail, but most have long tails as well.

Finally, primate groups vary in their adaptations for different forms of **locomotion**, or how they move around. Living primates are known to move by vertical clinging and leaping, quadrupedalism, brachiation, and bipedalism. **Vertical clinging and leaping** is when an animal grasps a vertical branch with its body upright, pushes off with long hind legs and then lands on another vertical support branch (Figure 5.7). Animals who move in this way usually have longer legs than arms, long fingers and toes, and smaller bodies. Vertical clinger leapers also tend to have elongated ankle bones, which serve as a lever to help them push off with their legs and leap to another branch.

Figure 5.8 Here are examples of a typical quadrupedal primate. Note that the arms and legs are about the same length and the back is long and flexible. This is a terrestrial quadruped so the arms and legs are relatively long and the tail is shorter.

Quadrupedalism is the most common form of locomotion among primates (Figure 5.8). The term *quadrupedal* means to walk on all fours. Animals that move in this way usually have legs and arms that are about the same length and typically have a tail for balance. Arboreal quadrupeds usually have shorter arms and legs and longer tails, while terrestrial quadrupeds have longer arms and legs and, often, shorter tails. These differences relate to the lower center of gravity needed by arboreal quadrupeds for balance in trees and the longer tail required for better balance when moving along the tops of branches. Terrestrial quadrupeds have longer limbs to help them cover more distance more efficiently. You will learn more specific anatomical features of quadrupedalism later in the chapter.

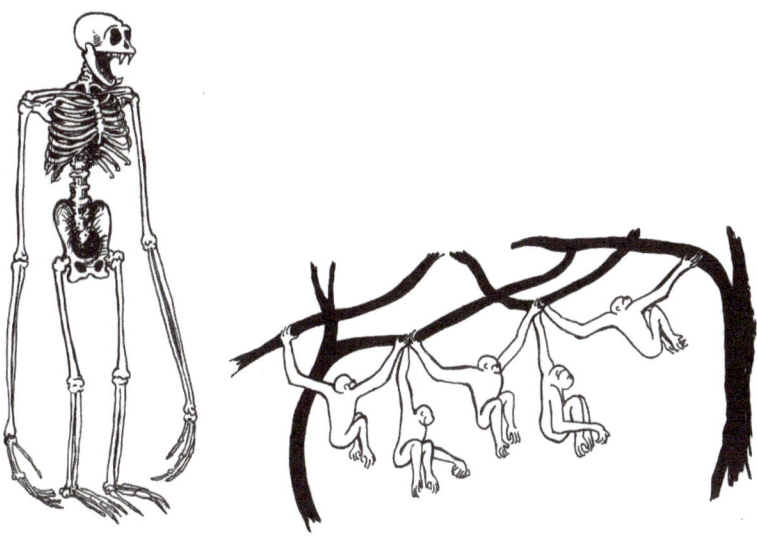

Figure 5.9 These are examples of a typical brachiator. Note the longer arms than legs, short back, and lack of a tail. You will read about more details of their anatomy later in the chapter.

The third form of locomotion seen in primates is **brachiation**, the way of moving you used if you played on "monkey bars" as a child. Brachiation involves swinging below branches by the hands (Figure 5.9). To be an efficient brachiator, a primate needs to have longer arms than legs, flexible shoulders and wrists, a short lower back, and no tail. You will learn more about the specifics of these traits when you learn about apes later in this chapter. Some primates move via **semi-brachiation**. These taxa also swing below branches but do not have all of the same specializations as brachiators. They have flexible shoulders, but their arms and legs are about the same length, useful because they are quadrupedal when on the ground. Semi-brachiators also use long **prehensile tails** as a third limb when swinging (Figure 5.10). The underside of the tail has a tactile pad, resembling your fingerprints, for better grip.

Figure 5.10 Spider monkeys, like the one shown here, are considered semi-brachiators who can swing below branches but use their tails as a third limb. On the ground they move via quadrupedal locomotion.

Lastly, humans move around on two feet, called **bipedalism**. Some primates will occasionally travel on two feet but do so awkwardly and never for long distances. Among mammals, only humans have evolved to walk with a striding gait on two legs as a primary form of locomotion. To move bipedally, humans need many specialized adaptations that will be discussed in detail in later chapters.

PRIMATE DIVERSITY

As we begin exploring the different taxa of primates, it is important to keep in mind the hierarchical nature of taxonomic classification (discussed in Chapter 2) and how this relates to the key characteristics that will be covered. Figure 5.11 summarizes the major taxonomic groups of primates. If you locate humans on the chart, you can trace our classification and see all of the categories getting more and more inclusive as you work your way up to the Order Primates. What this means is that humans will have the key traits of each of those groups. It is a good idea to refer to the figure to orient yourself as we discuss each taxon.

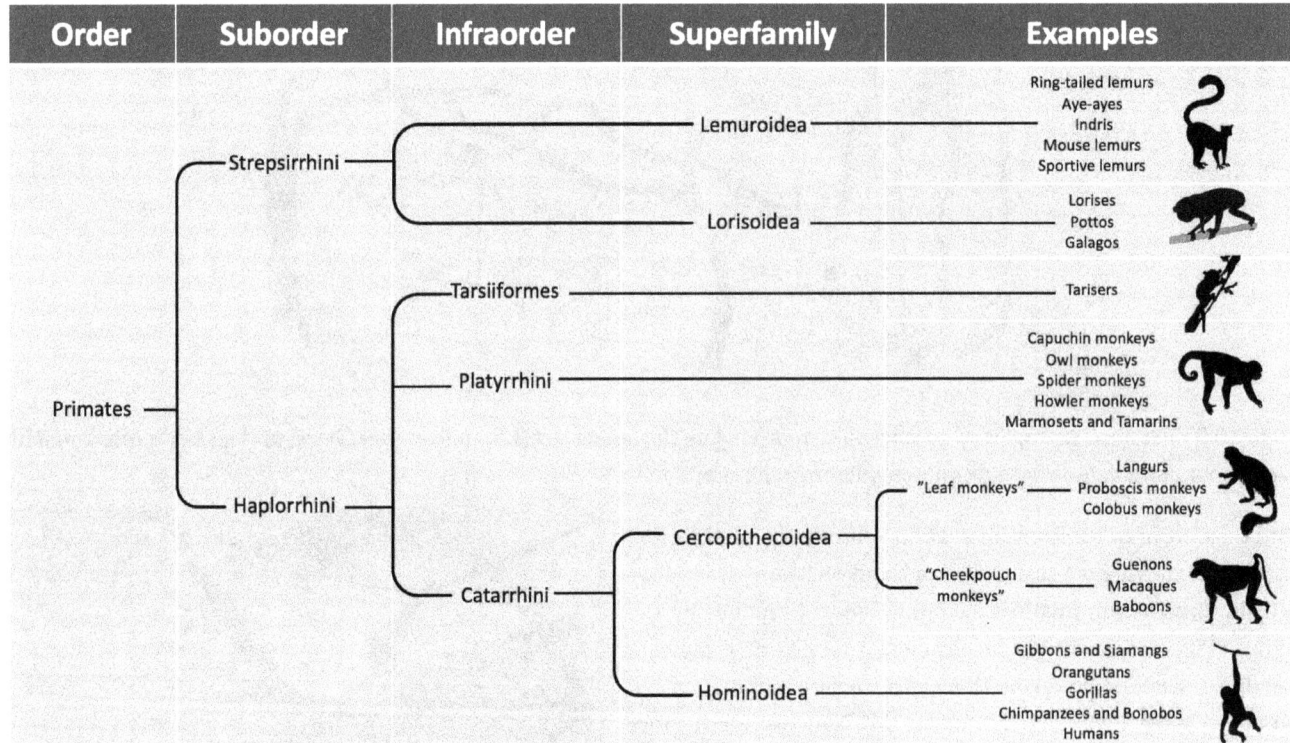

Figure 5.11 This taxonomy chart shows the major groups of primate taxa. Be sure to refer back to this chart as you read through the primate groups so that you can see how each group is related to one another.

Ways of Organizing Taxa

Our goal in taxonomic classification is to place taxa into categories that reflect their clade relationships. A **clade** is a grouping of organisms that reflect a branch of the evolutionary tree, a grouping based on relatedness. Clade relationships are determined using derived traits shared by groups of taxa as well as genetic similarities. An example of a clade would be a grouping that includes humans, chimpanzees, bonobos, and gorillas. These taxa are in what is referred to as the **African clade** of hominoids. The African clade grouping reflects the fact that humans, chimpanzees, bonobos, and gorillas all share a more recent ancestor with each other than any of them do with other species—that is, we are on the same branch of the evolutionary tree. We know members of the African clade are most closely related based on derived morphological traits as well as genetic similarities. In this grouping, we exclude the orangutan, which is considered a member of the **Asian clade** of hominoids.

Meet the Living Primates

Figure 5.12 Grades vs. Clades: Grouping orangutans, gorillas, chimpanzees and bonobos but excluding humans is a grade classification based on overall similarity in appearance and lifestyle among the apes. We are most interested in groupings based on evolutionary relationships, so we use the clade classification in which humans are grouped with gorillas, chimpanzees, and bonobos. This grouping reflects our evolutionary relationships.

In contrast, **grades** are groupings that reflect levels of adaptation or overall similarity and not necessarily actual evolutionary relationships. An example of a grade would be placing orangutans, gorillas, bonobos, and chimpanzees into a group, and excluding humans. Grouping in this way is based on the superficial similarities of the apes in being large-bodied, having lots of body hair, living in tropical forests, using trees, and so on. According to these criteria, humans seem to be the unusual ones in that we differ in our morphology, behavior, and ecology. Separating humans from the other large-bodied apes is the system that was used historically. We now know that grouping orangutans, gorillas, bonobos, and chimpanzees and excluding humans does not accurately reflect our true evolutionary relationships (Figure 5.12), and because our goal in taxonomic classification is to organize animals to reflect their evolutionary relationships, we prefer to use clade classifications.

Suborder Strepsirrhini

Figure 5.13 The foot of a ring-tailed lemur showing its grooming claw on the second digit.

The Order Primates is subdivided into Suborder Strepsirrhini and Suborder Haplorrhini, which, according to molecular estimates, split about 70–80 million years ago (Pozzi et al. 2014). The strepsirrhines include the groups commonly called lemurs, lorises, and galagos (Figure 5.14). Strepsirrhines differ from haplorrhines in many ways, most of which involve retaining primitive traits from the last common ancestor of primates. All of the traits discussed below are primitive traits, but strepsirrhines do have two key derived traits that evolved after they diverged from the haplorrhines. The two derived traits are the **grooming claw** (Figure 5.13), which is on the second digit of each foot, and the **tooth comb** (or **dental comb**), located on the lower, front teeth (Figure 5.15). In most strepsirrhines, there are six teeth in the toothcomb—the four incisors and the two canines. Other than the tooth comb, the teeth of strepsirrhines are fairly simple in not being particularly large or distinctive relative to haplorrhines.

Figure 5.14 (Clockwise from top right) sifaka, black-and-white ruffed lemur, loris, galago, slender loris, mouse lemur, aye-aye, and ring-tailed lemur.

Compared to haplorrhines, strepsirrhines rely more on nonvisual senses. Strepsirrhines have longer snouts than haplorrhines and get their name because they all have wet noses (**rhinariums**) like cats and dogs. The long snout and rhinarium reflect strepsirrhines' greater reliance on olfaction relative to haplorrhines. Indeed, many strepsirrhines use **scent marking**, rubbing scent glands or urine on objects in the environment to communicate with others. Additionally, many strepsirrhines have mobile ears that they use to locate insect prey and predators. As discussed earlier, there are trade-offs in sensory systems, so while strepsirrhines have a better sense of smell than haplorrhines, their visual adaptations are more primitive. Strepsirrhines have less convergent eyes than haplorrhines, and therefore all have postorbital bars whereas haplorrhines have full postorbital closure (Figure 5.1). All strepsirrhines have a **tapetum lucidum**, a reflective layer at the back of the eye that reflects light and thereby enhances the ability to see in low-light conditions. It is the same layer that causes your dog or cat to have "yellow eye" when you take photos of them with the flash on. It is thought to be primitive among mammals as a whole.

Strepsirrhines also differ from haplorrhines in some aspects of their ecology and behavior. The majority of strepsirrhines are solitary, traveling alone to search for food, although some taxa are more social. Most strepsirrhines are also nocturnal and arboreal. Strepsirrhines are, on average, smaller than haplorrhines, and so many more of them have a diet consisting of insects and fruit, with few taxa eating primarily leaves. Lastly, most strepsirrhines are good at leaping, with several taxa specialized for vertical clinging and leaping. In fact, among primates, all but one of the vertical clinger leapers are in the Suborder Strepsirrhini.

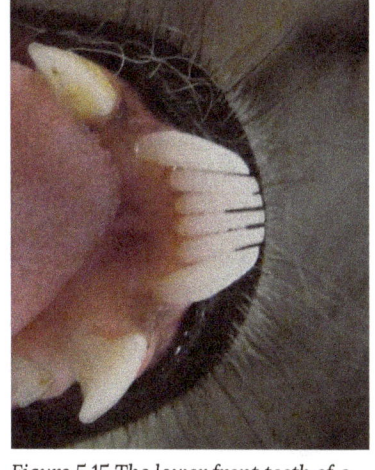

Figure 5.15 The lower front teeth of a ring-tailed lemur showing a tooth comb. Note that there are six teeth in the tooth comb, four incisors and two canines. The teeth that superficially look like canines are actually premolars.

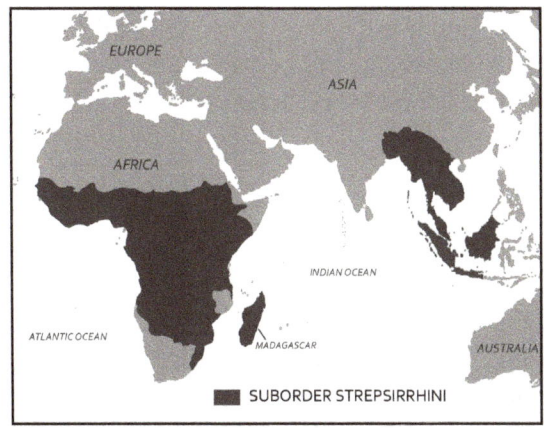

Figure 5.16 Geographic distribution of living strepsirrhines. Lemurs live only on the island of Madagascar, while their relatives the lorises and galagos live across Central Africa and South and Southeast Asia.

Strepsirrhines can be found all across the Old World: in Asia, Africa, and on the island of Madagascar (Figure 5.16). The Suborder Strepsirrhini is divided into two groups: (1) the lemurs of Madagascar and (2) the lorises, pottos, and galagos of Africa and Asia. By molecular estimates, these two groups split about 65 million years ago (Pozzi et al. 2014).

Lemurs of Madagascar

Madagascar is an island off the east coast of Africa, and it is roughly the size of California, Oregon, and Washington combined. It has been separated from Africa for about 130 million years and from India for about 85 million years, which means it was already an island when strepsirrhines got there approximately 60–70 million years ago. Only a few mammal species ever reached Madagascar, and so when lemurs arrived they were able to flourish into a variety of forms.

The lemurs of Madagascar are much more diverse compared to their mainland counterparts, the lorises and galagos. Malagasy strepsirrhines display a variety of activity patterns. While many species are nocturnal, plenty of others are diurnal or cathemeral. They range in body size from the smallest of all primates, the mouse lemur, some species of which weigh a little over an ounce (Figure 5.14), up to the largest of all strepsirrhines, the indri, which weighs up to about 20 pounds (Figure 5.17). Lemurs include species that are insectivorous, frugivorous, and folivorous. A couple of members of this group have specialized in more unusual diets for primates. These include the gummivorous fork-marked lemurs as well as bamboo lemurs, who are able to

Figure 5.17 Indris, the largest of the lemurs. These folivorous lemurs are vertical clingers and leapers and live in pairs.

metabolize the cyanide in bamboo. The most unusual lemur is the aye-aye, which you can see depicted in Figure 5.14. This nocturnal lemur exhibits traits not seen in any other primate, including having rodent-like front teeth that grow continuously and a long-bony middle finger that it uses to fish grubs out of wood. It has a very large brain compared to other strepsirrhines, which it fuels with a diet that includes bird's eggs and other animal matter. Based on genetic estimates and morphological studies, it is believed that aye-ayes were the first lemurs to separate from all of the other strepsirrhines and so have been evolving on their own since around the time strepsirrhines got to Madagascar (Matsui et al. 2009).

Lemurs are also diverse in terms of behavior. Many Malagasy strepsirrhines are solitary foragers, but some live in pairs, others in small groups, some in larger groups, and some, like the red-ruffed lemur, are now known to live in complex social groups that are unlike what we see in any other primates (Vasey 2006). It is also among the lemurs that we see some of the best vertical clingers and leapers. Many lemurs are quadrupedal, but even the quadrupedal lemurs are quite adept at leaping. Malagasy strepsirrhines also exhibit a few unusual traits. They are highly seasonal breeders, often mating only during a short window, once a year (Wright 1999). Female ring-tailed lemurs, for example, only come into estrus one day a year for a mere six hours. Malagasy strepsirrhines are also unusual in that females are socially dominant. In most primates, males dominate females because they are typically larger and exhibit greater aggression, but in lemur groups, males and females are usually the same size and females have priority access to resources over males.

Lorises, Pottos, and Galagos of Asia and Africa

Unlike the lemurs of Madagascar, lorises, pottos, and galagos live in areas where they share their environments with monkeys and apes, who often eat similar foods. Lorises live across South and Southeast Asia, while pottos and galagos live across Central Africa. Because of competition with larger-bodied monkeys and apes, mainland strepsirrhines are more restricted in the niches they can fill in their environments and so are not as diverse as the lemurs of Madagascar.

Figure 5.18 This slow loris, like all others in this taxonomic group, is solitary and nocturnal, with a diet heavy in insects and fruit.

All strepsirrhines in Africa and Asia are nocturnal and solitary. Their body sizes don't range as greatly as the lemurs, and neither do their diets. For the most part, the diet of lorises, pottos, and galagos consist of fruits and insects. A couple of species eat more gum, but overall the diet of this group is fairly narrow when compared to the Malagasy lemurs. Lorises and pottos are known for being slow, quadrupedal climbers, moving quietly through the forests to avoid being detected by predators (Figure 5.18). Because they are not fast moving, these strepsirrhines have developed alternative defenses against predators. Lorises, for example, eat a lot of caterpillars, which makes their saliva slightly toxic. Loris mothers will then bathe their young in this toxic saliva, thus making the babies unappealing to predators. In comparison to the slow-moving lorises and pottos, galagos are active quadrupedal runners and leapers that scurry about the forests at night. Galagos make distinctive calls that sound like a baby crying, which has led to their nickname "bushbabies." Figure 5.19 summarizes the key differences between these two groups of strepsirrhines.

	 Lemurs	 Lorises, Pottos and Galagos
Geographic range	Madagascar	South and Southeast Asia, Central Africa
Activity patterns	Diurnal, nocturnal or cathemeral	Nocturnal
Dietary types	Insectivore, frugivore or folivore	Insectivore, frugivore
Social groupings	Solitary, pairs, or small to large groups	Solitary
Forms of locomotion	Vertical clinger leapers, quadrupedal	Slow quadrupedal climbers and active quadrupedal runners

Figure 5.19 Strepsirrhini at a glance: This table summarizes the key differences between the two groups of strepsirrhines.

Suborder Haplorrhini

When the strepsirrhini and haplorrhini split from one another, strepsirrhines retained more primitive traits (those likely present in the last common ancestor), while haplorrhines became quite different, developing many derived traits. Thus, all of the traits discussed below are considered derived traits.

As mentioned earlier, the visual systems of haplorrhines are more developed than those of strepsirrhines. Many haplorrhines are trichromatic and, with one exception that will be discussed shortly, all have full postorbital closure (Figure 5.1). This increase in bony closure around the eye protects the more convergent eyes that haplorrhines possess. Haplorrhines also evolved to have a **fovea**, a depression in the retina at the back of the eye containing concentrations of cells that allow us to see things very close up in great detail. The heavier reliance on vision over olfaction is also reflected in the shorter snouts ending with the **dry nose** (no rhinarium) of haplorrhines. All but two genera of living haplorrhines are active during the day, so this group lacks the tapetum lucidum which is so useful to nocturnal species. On average, haplorrhines also have larger brains relative to their body size when compared with strepsirrhines.

The Haplorrhini differ from the Strepsirrhini in aspects of ecology and behavior as well. Haplorrhines are generally larger than strepsirrhines, and so we see many more species that are folivorous and frugivorous, and fewer that are insectivorous. This dietary difference is reflected in the teeth of haplorrhines, which are broader with more surface area for chewing. The larger body size of this taxon also influences locomotion. Only one haplorrhine is a vertical clinger and leaper. Most members of this suborder are quadrupedal, with one subgroup specialized for brachiation. A few haplorrhine taxa are **monomorphic**, meaning males and females are the same size, but many members of this group show moderate to high sexual dimorphism in body size and canine size. Haplorrhines also differ in social behavior. All but two haplorrhines live in groups, which is very different from the primarily solitary strepsirrhines. Differences between the two suborders are summarized in Figure 5.20.

	 Suborder Strepsirrhini	 Suborder Haplorrhini
Sensory adaptations	Rhinarium Longer snout Eyes less convergent Post-orbital bar Tapetum lucidum Mobile ears	No rhinarium Short snout Eyes more convergent Post-orbital plate No tapetum lucidum Many are trichromatic Fovea
Dietary differences	Mostly insectivores and frugivores, few folivores	Few insectivores, mostly frugivores and folivores
Activity patterns and Ecology	Mostly nocturnal, few diurnal or cathemeral Almost entirely arboreal	Only two are nocturnal, rest are diurnal Many arboreal taxa, also many terrestrial taxa
Social groupings	Mostly solitary, some pairs, small to large groups	Only two are solitary, all others live in pairs, small to very large groups
Sexual dimorphism	Minimal to none	Few taxa have little/none, many taxa show moderate to high dimorphism

Figure 5.20 Suborders at a glance: This table summarizes the key differences between the two primate suborders.

Suborder Haplorrhini is divided into three infraorders: Tarsiiformes, which includes the tarsiers of Asia; Platyrrhini, which includes the New World monkeys of Central and South America; and Catarrhini, a group that includes the Old World monkeys and apes of Asia and Africa, as well as humans. According to molecular estimates, tarsiers split from the other haplorrhines close to 70 million years ago, and platyrrhini split from catarrhini close to 46 million years ago (Pozzi et al. 2014).

Infraorder Tarsiiformes of Asia

Figure 5.21 Tarsiers are the only living representatives of this Infraorder.

Today, the Infraorder Tarsiiformes includes only one genus, Tarsius (Figure 5.21). Tarsiers are small-bodied primates that live in Southeast Asian forests (Figure 5.22) and possess an unusual collection of traits that have led to some debate about their position in the primate taxonomy. They are widely considered members of the haplorrhine group because they share several key derived traits with monkeys, apes, and humans,

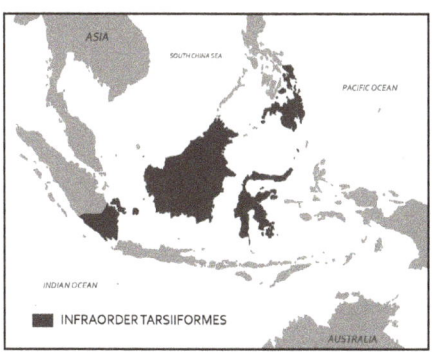

Figure 5.22 Tarsiiformes can be found in tropical forests of Southeast Asia.

including dry noses, a fovea, not having a tapetum lucidum, and having eyes that are close together. Tarsiers also have some traits that are more like strepsirrhines and some that are unique. Tarsiers are the only haplorrhine that are specialized vertical clinger leapers, a form of locomotion only otherwise seen in some strepsirrhines. Tarsiers actually get their name because their ankle (tarsal) bones are elongated to provide a lever for vertical clinging and leaping. Tarsiiformes are also small, with most species weighing between 100 and 150 grams. Like strepsirrhines, tarsiers are nocturnal, but because they lack a tapetum lucidum, tarsiers compensate by having enormous eyes. In fact, each eye of a tarsier is larger than its brain. These large eyes allow enough light in for tarsiers to still be able to see well at night without the reflecting layer in their eyes. To protect their large eyes, tarsiers have a partially closed postorbital plate that is somewhat intermediate between the postorbital bar of strepsirrhines and the full postorbital closure of other haplorrhines (Figure 5.23). Tarsiers have different dental formulas on their upper and lower teeth. On the top, the dental formula is 2:1:3:3, but on the bottom it is 1:1:3:3. Other unusual traits of tarsiers include having two grooming claws on each foot and the ability to rotate their heads around 180 degrees, a trait useful in locating insect prey. The tarsier diet is considered **faunivorous** because it consists entirely of animal matter, making them the only primate not to eat any vegetation. They are also only one of two living haplorrhines to be solitary, the other being the orangutan. Most tarsiers are not sexually dimorphic, like strepsirrhines, although males of a few species are slightly larger than females.

Two alternative classifications have emerged due to the unusual mix of traits that tarsiers have. Historically, tarsiers were grouped with lemurs, lorises, and galagos into a suborder called Prosimii. This classification was based on tarsiers, lemurs, lorises, and galagos all having grooming claws and similar lifestyles (e.g., small, nocturnal, more leaping locomotion, diet heavy in insects, more solitary). Monkeys, apes, and humans were then separated into a suborder called the Anthropoidea. These suborder groupings were based on grade rather than clade. Today, most people use Suborders Strepsirrhini and Haplorrhini, which are clade groupings based on the derived traits that tarsiers share with monkeys, apes, and humans (e.g., more postorbital closure, fovea, no tapetum

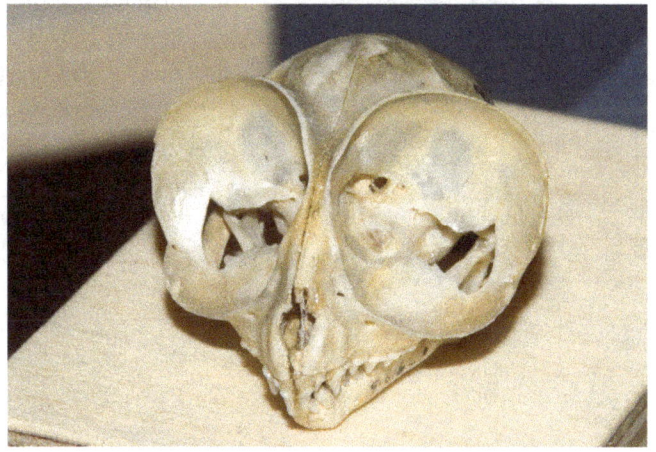

Figure 5.23 Skull of a tarsier showing very large eye sockets and partially closed postorbital plates.

lucidum, dry nose). The Strepsirrhini/Haplorrhini dichotomy is also supported by the genetic evidence that indicates tarsiers are more closely related to monkeys, apes, and humans (Jameson et al. 2011). Figure 5.24 summarizes the unusual mix of traits seen in tarsiers.

Like Strepsirrhini	Unique	Like Haplorrhini
Very small Nocturnal Highly insectivorous Solitary Vertical clinger-leapers Little/no sexual dimorphism	Two grooming claws 2:1:3:3/1:1:3:3 dental formula Do not eat vegetation Can rotate their heads nearly 180 degrees	Almost full PO closure More convergent eyes No tapetum lucidum No rhinarium Genetic evidence Fovea

Figure 5.24 Tarsiers at a glance: Tarsiers have a mix of traits that lead to debate about their classification. Some of their traits superficially resemble strepsirrhines, but they share many derived traits with haplorrhines. They also possess unique characteristics that are unlike any other primates.

Infraorder Platyrrhini of Central and South America

Figure 5.25 Geographic distribution of the platyrrhines across Central and South America. New World monkeys are the only naturally occurring non-human primates in the Americas.

The platyrrhines, also commonly called New World monkeys, are the only non-human primates in Central and South America (Figure 5.25) and so, like the lemurs of Madagascar, have diversified into a variety of forms in the absence of competition. Infraorder Platyrrhini get their name from their distinctive nose shape. "Platy" means flat and "rhini" refers to noses and, indeed, New World monkeys have noses that are flat and wide, with nostrils that are far apart, facing outward, and usually round in shape (Figure 5.26). This nose shape is very different from what we see in catarrhines, the group that includes Old World monkeys, apes, and humans.

On average, Platyrrhini are smaller and less sexually dimorphic than catarrhines, and they have retained the more primitive primate dental formula of 2:1:3:3. Platyrrhines are also all highly arboreal, whereas many Old World monkeys and apes spend significant time on the ground. The New World monkeys also differ in having less well-developed vision. This is reflected in the wiring in the visual system of the brain but also in their **polymorphic color vision**. The genes that enable individuals to distinguish reds and yellows from blues and greens are on the X

Figure 5.26 A capuchin monkey demonstrating a typical platyrrhine nose shape with round nostrils pointing outward on a flat nose.

Meet the Living Primates | 167

chromosome. Different genes code for being able to see different wavelengths of light so to distinguish between them you need to be heterozygous for seeing color. In New World monkeys, each X chromosome carries the genes for seeing one wavelength. This means that male platyrrhines (having only one X chromosome) are always dichromatic. Female platyrrhines can be dichromatic (if they are homozygous for the same version of the color vision gene) or trichromatic (if they are heterozygous) (Kawamura et al. 2012). We currently know of two exceptions to this pattern among platyrrhines. Owl monkeys, which are nocturnal, are **monochromatic**, meaning that they cannot distinguish any colors. The other exception are Howler monkeys, which have evolved to have two color vision genes on each X chromosome. This means that both male and female howler monkeys are able to see reds and yellows. As we will discuss, all Old World monkeys, apes, and humans are trichromatic.

Platyrrhines include the smallest of the monkeys, the marmosets and tamarins (Figure 5.27). These small monkeys, all of which weigh less than 1 kilogram, live in cooperative family groups, wherein usually only one female reproduces and everyone else helps carry and raise the offspring. They are unusual primates in that they regularly produce twins. The diet of marmosets and tamarins largely consists of gums and saps, so these monkeys have evolved claw-like nails that enable them to cling to the sides of tree trunks like squirrels as well as special teeth that allow them to gnaw through bark. They also have one fewer molar than other platyrrhines, giving them a dental formula of 2:1:3:2.

The largest of the platyrrhines are a family that include spider monkeys, woolly spider monkeys, woolly monkeys, and howler monkeys (Figure 5.28). This group of monkeys can weigh up to 9–15 kg and have evolved prehensile tails that can hold their entire body weight. It is among this group that we see semi-brachiators, like the spider monkey (Figure 5.10). To make them more efficient in this form of locomotion, spider monkeys evolved to not have thumbs so that their hands work more like hooks that can easily let go of branches while swinging. Howler monkeys are another well-known member of this group, earning their name due to their loud calls, which can be heard for miles away. To make these loud vocalizations, howler monkeys have a specialized vocal system that includes a large larynx and hyoid bone. Howler monkeys are the most folivorous of the platyrrhines and are known for spending a large portion of their day digesting their food.

There are many other monkeys in the New World, including the gregarious capuchins (Figure 5.26) and squirrel monkeys, the pair-living titi monkeys, and the nocturnal owl monkeys. There are also the seed-eating monkeys such as saki monkeys and uakaris. In many areas across Central and South America, multiple different species of platyrrhine will share the forests, and some species will even travel together in associations that you will learn about in Chapter 6. According to molecular evidence, the diversity of platyrrhines that we see today seems to have originated about 25 million years ago (Schneider and Sampaio 2015). Figure 5.29 summarizes the key traits of platyrrhines relative to the other infraorders of Haplorrhini.

Figure 5.27 (Clockwise from top-right) golden-headed lion tamarin, pygmy marmoset, Goeldi's monkey, bare-eared marmoset, emperor tamarin, and common marmoset.

Figure 5.28 (Clockwise from top right) howler monkey, woolly monkey, woolly spider monkey, and spider monkey.

Platyrrhini traits
Flat nose with rounded nostrils pointing to the side
Highly arboreal
Less sexually dimorphic on average
2:1:3:3 dental formula*
Polymorphic color vision*

*Figure 5.29 Platyrrhini at a glance: Summary of the key traits we use to distinguish platyrrhines. Traits indicated with an * are those with exceptions detailed in the text.*

Infraorder Catarrhini of Asia and Africa

Infraorder Catarrhini includes Old World monkeys, apes, and humans. Non-human catarrhines are found all over Africa and South and Southeast Asia, with some being found as far north as Japan. The most northerly and southerly catarrhines are from the superfamily that includes the Old World monkeys. In contrast, apes are less tolerant of drier, more seasonal environments and so have a relatively restricted geographic range.

Figure 5.30 A Wolf's guenon demonstrating a typical catarrhine nose with teardrop-shaped nostrils close together and pointed downward.

When compared to the other haplorrhine infraorders, catarrhines are distinguished by several characteristics. Catarrhines have a distinctive nose shape, with teardrop-shaped nostrils that are close together and point downward (Figure 5.30). Old World monkeys, apes, and humans also have one fewer premolar than most other primates, giving us a dental formula of 2:1:2:3 (Figure 5.31). On average, catarrhines are the largest and most sexually dimorphic group of primates. Gorillas are the largest of all living primates, with males weighing up to 220 kg. The most sexually dimorphic of all primates are mandrills. Mandrill males not only have much more vibrant coloration than mandrill females but also have larger canines and can weigh up to three times more (Setchell et al. 2001). The larger body size of catarrhines is related to the more terrestrial lifestyle of many members of this infraorder. In fact, the most terrestrial of living primates can be found in this group. Among all primate taxa, vision is the most developed in catarrhines. Catarrhines independently evolved the same adaptation as howler monkeys in having each X chromosome with sufficient genes to distinguish both reds and yellows, so all catarrhines are trichromatic. Trichromatic color vision is particularly useful to catarrhines, which are all diurnal.

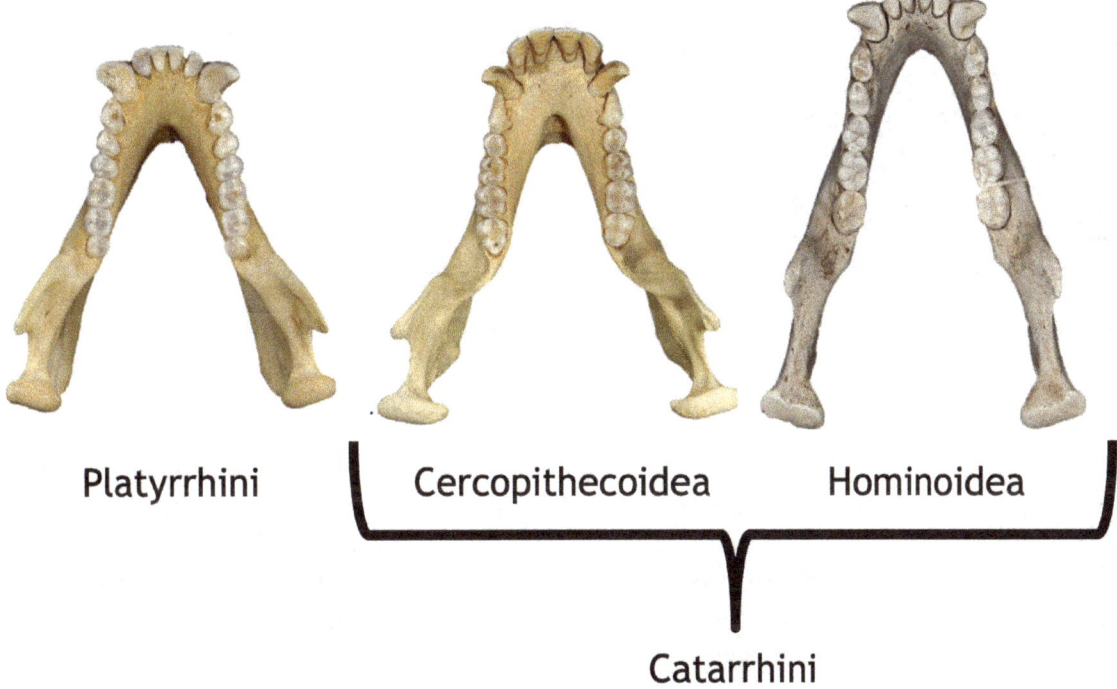

Figure 5.31 Catarrhines are distinguished in that they only have two premolars compared to the three premolars seen in most other primate taxa, including the platyrrhines shown here for comparison. In these images you can also see one of the derived traits of cercopithecoids, their bilophodont molars, which differ from the more primitive Y-5 molars that apes and humans have.

Infraorder Catarrhini is divided into two superfamilies: Superfamily Cercopithecoidea, which includes Old World monkeys, and Superfamily Hominoidea, which includes apes and humans. Molecular estimates place the split between cercopithecoids and hominoids at about 32 million years ago (Pozzi et al. 2014), which fits well with the fossil record showing evidence of the lineages by about 25 million years ago (see Chapter 8 on primate evolution).

Superfamily Cercopithecoidea of Africa and Asia

Compared to hominoids, Old World monkeys have a more primitive quadrupedal body plan (discussed later in Figure 5.39), but they do have a couple of derived traits shared by all members of this group. Cercopithecoidea have **bilophodont** molars ("bi" meaning two, "loph" referring to ridge, and "dont" meaning tooth). Referring back to Figure 5.31, you will see how the molars of cercopithecoids have four cusps arranged in a square pattern and have two ridges connecting them. It is thought that this molar enabled Old World monkeys to eat a wide range of foods, thus allowing them to live in habitats that apes cannot. The other key derived trait that all cercopithecoids share is having **ischial callosities** (Figure 5.32). The ischium is the part of your pelvis that you are sitting on right now (see Appendix A: Osteology). In Old World monkeys, this part of the pelvis has a flattened surface that, in living animals, will have callused skin over it. These function as seat pads for cercopithecoids, who often sit above branches when feeding and resting.

Figure 5.32 The second derived trait of cercopithecoids are their ischial callosities, shown here on a crested black macaque.

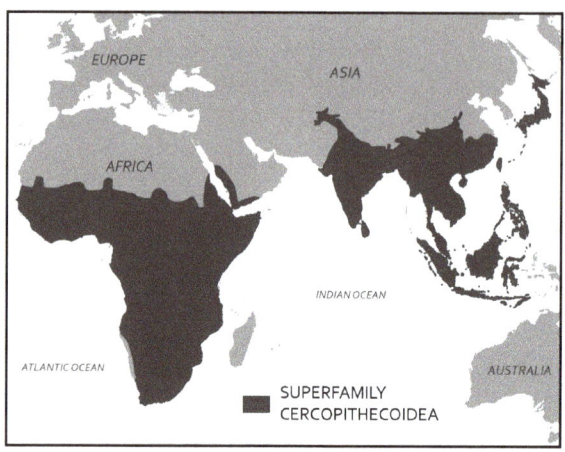

Figure 5.33 Geographic distribution of the Old World monkeys. Catarrhines have the widest geographic distribution due to the success of cercopithecoid monkeys who are found all across Africa and Asia.

Figure 5.34 Silver leaf monkey infants are born with orange fur, dramatically contrasting the adult coat color of their mothers. After a few months, the infants gradually change color to that of their parents.

The cercopithecoid monkeys are the most geographically widespread group of non-human primates (Figure 5.33). Since their divergence from hominoids, this monkey group has increased in numbers and diversity. In part, their success over hominoids is due to the faster reproductive rates of cercopithecoids relative to hominoids. On average, Old World monkeys will reproduce every one to two years, whereas hominoids will reproduce once every four to nine years, depending on the taxon.

Cercopithecoidea is split into two groups, the leaf monkeys and the cheek-pouch monkeys. Both groups coexist in Asia and Africa; however, the majority of leaf monkey species live in Asia with only a few taxa in Africa. In contrast, only one genus of cheek-pouch monkey lives in Asia, and all the rest of them in Africa. As you can probably guess based on their names, the two groups differ in terms of diet. Leaf monkeys are primarily folivores, with some species eating a significant amount of seeds. Cheek-pouch monkeys tend to be more frugivorous or omnivorous, with one taxon, geladas, eating primarily grasses. The two groups also differ in some other

Figure 5.35 Proboscis monkeys are one of several "odd-nosed" leaf monkeys. Male proboscis monkeys, like the one shown here, have large, pendulous noses. Female proboscis monkey noses are much smaller; in this species nose size is a sexually dimorphic trait.

Meet the Living Primates | 171

interesting ways. Leaf monkeys tend to produce infants with **natal coats**—infants whose fur is a completely different color from their parents (Figure 5.34). Leaf monkeys are also known for having odd noses (Figure 5.35), and so they are sometimes called "odd-nosed monkeys." Cheek-pouch monkeys are able to pack food into their cheek pouches (Figure 5.36), thus allowing them to move to a location safe from predators or aggressive individuals of their own species where they can eat in peace.

Figure 5.36 This bonnet macaque has filled its cheek pouches with food. This adaptation is useful in transporting food to a safer location to eat.

SPECIAL TOPIC: PRIMATES IN CULTURE AND RELIGION

Figure 5.37 Because of important monkey-like figures in the Hindu religion, macaques are protected in India and often live near temples where they are fed by local peoples.

In the introduction to this chapter, I mentioned the innate affinity that humans have toward non-human primates even when we do not fully understand our exact relationship to them. In fact, recognition of similarities between humans and other primates is very ancient, dating back far earlier than Linnaeus. For many of us, we only ever get to see primates in zoos and animal parks, but in many areas of the world, humans have coexisted with these animals for thousands of years. In areas where humans and primates have a long, shared history, non-human primates often play key roles in creation myths and cultural symbolism.

Hamadryas baboons feature significantly in Ancient Egyptian iconography. Ancient Egyptian deities and beliefs transformed over time, as did the role of hamadryas baboons. Early on, baboons were thought to represent dead ancestors, and one monkey deity, called Babi or Baba, was thought to feed off of dead souls. Later, baboons became the totem animal for Thoth, the deity of science, writing, wisdom, and measurement, who also wrote the book of the dead. Sunbathing hamadryas baboons led ancient Egyptians to associate them with Ra, the sun god, who was the son of Thoth. During mummification, human organs were removed and put into canopic jars, one of which was topped with the head of the baboon-headed god, Hapi. Hamadryas baboons were also often kept as pets, as depicted in hieroglyphics, and occasionally mummified as well.

On Madagascar, indris and aye-ayes play roles in the creation myths and omens of local people. There are many myths regarding the origins of indris and their relationship to humans, including one where two brothers living in the forest separated, with one brother leaving the forest and becoming a human while the other stayed in the forest to become the indri. Indris are considered sacred and are therefore protected, due to their similarities to humans in having long legs, no tail, and upright posture. Unfortunately, the aye-aye is not treated with the same reverence. Aye-ayes, due to their unusual appearance, are thought to be omens of death. They are usually killed when encountered because it is believed that someone will die if an aye-aye points at them.

In India, monkeys play a key role in the Hindu religion. Hanuman, who resembles a monkey, is a key figure in the Ramayana. Hanuman is thought to be a guardian deity, and so local monkeys like Hanuman langurs and macaques are protected in India (Figure 5.37). In Thailand, where Hinduism is also practiced, the Hindu reverence for monkeys extends to "monkey feasts," where large quantities of food are spread out in gratitude to the monkeys for bringing good fortune.

The people of Japan have coexisted with Japanese macaques for thousands of years, and so monkeys play key roles in both of the major Japanese religions. In the Shinto religion, macaques are thought of as messengers between the spirit world and humans and monkey symbols are thought to be good luck. The other major religion in Japan is Buddhism, and monkeys play a role in symbolism of this religion as well. The "Three Wise Monkeys" who see no evil, speak no evil, and hear no evil derive from Buddhist iconography of monkeys.

In the New World, monkeys feature often in Mayan and Aztec stories. In the Mayan creation story, the Popol Vuh, the "hero brothers" are actually a howler monkey and a spider monkey, who represent ancestors of humans in the story. In the Aztec religion, spider monkeys are associated with the god of arts, pleasure, and playfulness. A spider monkey is also represented in a Peruvian Nazca geoglyph, a large design made on the ground by moving rocks.

In many of these regions today, the relationships between humans and non-human primates are complicated. The bushmeat and pet trades make these animals valuable at the expense of many animals' lives, and in some areas, non-human primates have become pests who raid crop fields and consume valuable foods. All of this has led to the development of a new subarea of anthropology called **Ethnoprimatology**, which involves studying the political, economic, symbolic, and practical relationships between humans and non-human primates. This field highlights the particular challenges for humans of having to coexist with animals with whom we share so much in common. It also provides insight into some of the challenges facing primate conservation efforts (see Appendix A: Primate Conservation).

Superfamily Hominoidea of Africa and Asia

The Superfamily Hominoidea of Africa and Asia (Figure 5.38) includes the largest of the living primates, apes and humans, but our superfamily differs from other primates in some other key ways as well. When compared to cercopithecoids, hominoids have more primitive teeth. Whereas Old World monkeys have bilophodont molars, hominoids have **Y-5 molars**, which feature five cusps separated by a "Y"-shaped groove pattern (Figure 5.31). The Y-5 molar was present in the common ancestors of hominoids and cercopithecoids, thus telling us it is the more primitive molar pattern of the two. Where hominoids differ the most from other primates, however, is in our body plans. This is due to the unusual form of locomotion that hominoids are adapted for, brachiation (Figure 5.39).

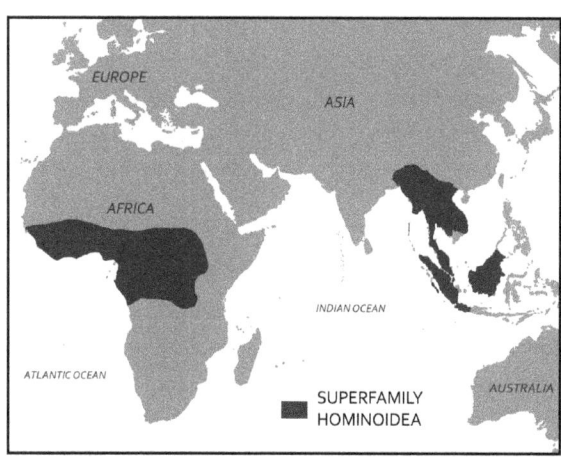

Figure 5.38 Geographic distribution of apes across Central and West Africa, and Southeast Asia. Hominoids overlap geographically with cercopithecoid monkeys but have a lower tolerance for seasonal environments and so are found only in tropical forests across these regions.

	Quadrupedalism	Brachiation
Arm length vs. leg length	About equal	Arms are longer
Shoulder position	More on the front	Out to the side
Ribcage shape	Deep front-to-back Narrow side-to-side	Shallow front-to-back Wide side-to-side
Length of lower back	Long	Short
Collar bone length	Short	Long
Ulnar olecranon process	Long	Short
Ulnar styloid process	Long	Short
Tail	Short to long	None

Figure 5.39 Quadrupedalism vs. brachiation: Summary of the key anatomical differences between a quadrupedal primate and one adapted for brachiation. To view and compare these traits using photos of bones, check out the interactive skeletal websites listed under the "Further Explorations" section at the end of this chapter.

To successfully swing below branches, many changes to the body needed to occur. The arms of a hominoid are much longer than the legs in order to increase reach, and the lower back is shorter and less flexible to increase control when swinging. The torso, shoulders, and arms of hominoids have evolved to increase range of motion and flexibility

(Figure 5.9). The clavicle, or collar bone, is longer in order to stabilize the shoulder joint out to the side, thus enabling us to rotate our arms 360 degrees. Our rib cages are wider side to side and shallower front to back than those of cercopithecoids and we do not have tails, as tails are useful for balance when running on all fours but not useful when swinging. Hominoids also have modified ulnae, one of the two bones in the forearm (see Appendix A: Osteology). At the elbow end of the ulna, hominoids have a short **olecranon process**, which allows for improved extension in our arms. At the wrist end of the ulna, hominoids have a short **styloid process**, which enables us to have very flexible wrists, a trait critical for swinging. Both the olecranon process and styloid process are long in quadrupedal animals who carry much of their weight on their forelimbs when traveling and who therefore need greater stability rather than flexibility in those joints.

Apes and humans also differ from other primates in behavior and life history characteristics. Hominoids all seem to show varying degrees of female dispersal at sexual maturity. Dispersal refers to leaving the area or group where an individual was born. As you will learn about in Chapter 6, it is more common that males leave. Indeed, some apes show males dispersing in addition to females, but the broader tendency for female dispersal in hominoids is a bit unusual among primates. Our superfamily is also characterized by the most extended life histories of all primates. All members of this group live a long time and take a long time to grow and start reproducing. Hominoids also reproduce much less frequently compared to cercopithecoid monkeys. The slow pace of this life history is likely related to why hominoids have decreased in diversity since they first evolved. In the past, hominoids were tremendously diverse in both geography and adaptations. Today, there are only five types of hominoids left: gibbons and siamangs, orangutans, gorillas, chimpanzees and bonobos, and humans.

Infraorder Catarrhini
Downward facing, tear-drop shaped nostrils, close together
Arboreal and more terrestrial taxa
On average, largest primates
On average, most sexually dimorphic taxonomic group
2:1:2:3 dental formula
All trichromatic

Superfamily Cercopithecoidea	**Superfamily Hominoidea**
Wide geographic distribution	Tropical forests of Africa and Asia
Bilophodont molars	Y-5 molars
Ischial callosities	Adaptations for brachiation
Reproduce every 1-2 years	Reproduce every 4-9 years

Figure 5.40 Catarrhini at a glance: Summary of key traits of the Infraorder Catarrhini as well as the characteristics used to distinguish between the two superfamilies within this group.

Family *Hylobatidae* of Southeast Asia

Figure 5.41 Siamangs are the largest of the Hylobatidae family. They are all black and, as you can see inflated in this photo, have a throat sac that they use to give loud calls.

The number of genera in this group has been changing in recent years, but the taxa included can broadly be discussed as gibbons and siamangs. Both are found across Southeast Asian tropical forests. These are the smallest of the hominoids and so are sometimes referred to as the "lesser apes." Gibbons weigh, on average, about 13 pounds and tend to be more frugivorous, whereas siamangs are about twice the size of gibbons and are more folivorous. Unlike the larger-bodied apes (orangutans, chimps, bonobos, and gorillas) who make nests to sleep in every night, gibbons and siamangs will develop callused patches on their ischium resembling ischial callosities. There are many different gibbon species that vary in their coloration and markings. Siamangs, however, are all black with big throat sacs that are used in their exuberant vocalizations (Figure 5.41). Both gibbons and siamangs live in pairs with very little sexual dimorphism, although males and females do differ in coloration in some species.

Pongo of Southeast Asia

Figure 5.42a A female orangutan and her infant.

Figure 5.42b A flanged adult male. Male orangutans are about twice the size of females, and in these photos you can also see the sexual dimorphism in coat length, cheek flanges and throat sac in the male.

The Genus *Pongo* refers to orangutans. These large red apes are found on the islands of Borneo and Sumatra in Southeast Asia. There are two well-known species of orangutan, one on each island. Recently, a third, very rare species was discovered in Southern Sumatra (Nater et al. 2017). Orangutans are highly frugivorous but will supplement their diet with leaves and even bark when fruit is less available. As mentioned earlier, orangutans are the only diurnal, solitary taxon among primates and are extremely slow to reproduce, producing only one offspring about every seven to nine years. They are highly sexually dimorphic (Figure 5.42), with fully developed, "flanged" males being approximately twice the size of females. These males have large throat sacs; long, shaggy coats; and cheek flanges. The skulls of male orangutans often feature a **sagittal crest**, which is believed to function as both additional attachment area for chewing muscles but also in sexual competition (Balolia et al. 2017). An unusual feature of orangutan biology is **male bimaturism**. Male orangutans are known to delay maturation until one of the more dominant, flanged males disappears. The males that delay maturation are called "unflanged" males, and they can remain in this state for their entire life. Unflanged males resemble females in their size and appearance and will sneak copulations with females while avoiding the bigger, flanged males. Flanged and unflanged male orangutans represent alternative reproductive strategies, both of which successfully produce offspring (Utami et al. 2002).

Gorilla of Africa

There are several species of gorillas that can be found across Central Africa. Gorilla males, like orangutan males, are about twice the size of female gorillas (Figure 5.43). When on the ground, gorillas use a form of quadrupedalism called **knuckle-walking**, where the fingers are curled under and the weight is carried on the knuckles. Male gorillas have a large sagittal crest and larger canines compared with females. Adult male gorillas are often called "silverbacks" because when they reach about twelve to thirteen years old, the hair on their backs turns silvery gray. Gorillas typically live in groups of one male and several females. Gorillas are considered folivorous, although they can be more frugivorous depending on fruit seasonality (Remis 1997).

Figure 5.43a A female gorilla and her offspring.

Figure 5.43b A silverback male. Male gorillas are about twice the size of females, but also differ from females in having a large sagittal crest, and silver back, which appears as they mature.

Pan of Africa

Figure 5.44 *Bonobo, Pan paniscus. You can see the distinctive hair-part on this bonobo.*

The Genus *Pan* includes two species: *Pan troglodytes* (the common chimpanzee) and *Pan paniscus* (the bonobo). These species are separated by the Congo River, with chimpanzees ranging across West and Central Africa and bonobos located in a restricted area south of the Congo River. Chimpanzees and bonobos both have broad, largely frugivorous diets and similar social groups. The two species differ morphologically in that bonobos are slightly smaller, have their hair parted down the middle of their foreheads, and are born with dark faces (Figure 5.44). In contrast, chimpanzees do not have the distinctive parted hair and are born with light faces which darken as they mature (Figure 5.45). Chimpanzees and bonobos live in a grouping called a fission-fusion community, which you will learn more about in Chapter 6. Both species are moderately sexually dimorphic, with males about 20% larger than females. When on the ground, chimpanzees and bonobos knuckle-walk like gorillas do.

Figure 5.45 *A common chimpanzee, Pan troglodytes, female and her offspring. Note the pink face of the youngest individual. Bonobos are born with dark-skinned faces, but chimpanzees are born with pink faces that darken with age.*

Homo

The last member of the Hominoidea to discuss is our own taxon, *Genus Homo*. Humans differ from apes in many aspects of our morphology, behavior, and life history, all of which you will be learning about in later chapters. One of the objectives of this chapter, however, and of biological anthropology in general, is to understand our place in nature. This means looking for the aspects of human biology that lead us to place humans within the taxonomic diversity we have just discussed. To accomplish this, we not only consider how humans are different from other species but also examine the traits that unite us with the other primates, our similarities—that is our focus here.

There are clear similarities between humans and the other apes in our morphology and life history. Like other hominoids, humans lack a tail and possess upper-body adaptations for brachiation. While our lower body has been modified for a bipedal gait, we are still able to swing from branches or "monkey bars," or throw a fastball, all thanks to our mobile shoulder joint. Humans, like other hominoids, also have a Y-5 cusp pattern on our molars. As discussed earlier, all hominoids have an extended life history, taking a long time to grow and develop, and have a long life span. Humans, too, exhibit these same characteristics. Lastly, while humans show a great deal of variation across cultures, many human societies show patterns of female dispersal in which males stay in the group into which they were born while females leave (Burton et al. 1996).

Among the hominoids, humans show particular affinities with other members of the African Clade, *Pan* and *Gorilla*. Humans share over 96% of our DNA with gorillas (Scally et al. 2012), and over 98% with *Pan* (Ebersberger et al. 2002). Even without this strong genetic evidence, the African Clade of hominoids share many morphological similarities. These shared traits include eye sockets that are slightly farther apart and are more square or rounded compared to the closely placed, ovoid eyes of orangutans. Also, the cheekbones of the African clade sweep backward compared to the more flattened orangutan cheekbones. Today, *Pan* and *Gorilla* knuckle-walk when on the ground, and it has been suggested that the last common ancestor of chimpanzees, bonobos, gorillas, and humans shared this trait (Richmond et al. 2001).

Our closest living relatives today are chimpanzees and bonobos. Because of our close relationship, humans share many additional traits in common with *Pan*. Humans, chimpanzees, and bonobos all live in similar social groups that are characterized by territoriality and male cooperation, among other things. Chimpanzee males are well-known to cooperate in hunting, a common trait across human societies as well. As you will learn more about in the next chapter, chimpanzee populations have also been observed to make and use tools for different purposes, not unlike what humans do.

LEARNING FROM PRIMATES

While primates are fascinating animals in their own right, we study non-human primates in anthropology with the ultimate goal of understanding more about our own biology and evolutionary history. The close relationship between humans and non-human primates makes them excellent for studying humans via **homology,** looking at traits that are shared between two taxa because they inherited the trait from a common ancestor. Consider, for example, the characteristics discussed in the previous section that are shared by humans and *Pan*. Since both taxa exhibit these traits, they are likely *homologous*, meaning these shared traits were probably present in the last common ancestor of humans and *Pan* approximately 6-8 million years ago .

Non-human primates also make excellent comparators for learning about humans via **analogy** (sometimes called convergent evolution, parallel evolution, or homoplasy). Many non-human primates live in environments or social groups similar to those in which our ancestors lived and therefore exhibit similar behavioral and morphological traits as what we see in humans. For example, baboons and humans share the trait of having long legs. In humans, this is because about 1.7 million years ago, our ancestors moved into open savanna habitats, like those baboons live in today, and longer legs enabled them to move over long distances more efficiently. Baboons independently evolved longer arms and legs for the same reason—to be able to cover more ground, more efficiently, in an open habitat. This means that having long legs is an *analogous* trait in baboons and humans—that is, this adaptation evolved independently in the two species but for the same purpose.

Conclusion

The Order Primates is a diverse and fascinating group of animals united in sharing a suite of characteristics—visual specialization, grasping hands and feet, large brains, and extended life histories—that differentiates us from other groups of mammals. In this chapter, we surveyed the major taxonomic groups of primates, discussing where humans fit among our close relatives as well as discovering that primates are interesting animals in their own right. We discussed a range of key traits used to distinguish between the many taxa of living primates, including dietary, locomotor, and behavioral characteristics. Because of our long, shared evolutionary history with these animals, non-human primates provide a crucial resource for understanding our current biology. In the next chapter, you will discover the fascinating and complex social behaviors of non-human primates which provide further insight into our evolutionary biology.

> ## Review Questions
>
> - Why does the field of anthropology, a field dedicated to the study of humans, include the study of non-human animals? What important things can we learn from non-human primates in anthropology?
> - One of the important goals of an introductory biological anthropology course is to teach you about your place in nature. What is the full taxonomic classification of humans, and what are some of the traits we have of each of these categories?
> - When you have seen primates in person, did you observe any facial expressions, behaviors, or physical traits that seemed familiar to you? If so, which ones and why?
> - Why is it important to try to place taxa into a clade classification rather than groupings based on grade? Can you think of an example?
> - Draw out a tree showing the major taxonomic group of primates described here, making sure to leave room in between each level. Underneath each taxon, list some of the key features of this group so that you can compare traits between groups.

Key Terms

Activity pattern: Refers to the time of day an animal is typically active.

African clade: A grouping that includes gorillas, chimpanzees, bonobos, humans, and their extinct relatives.

Analogy: When two or more taxa exhibit similar traits that have evolved independently, the similar traits evolve due to similar selective pressures. (Also sometimes called convergent evolution, parallel evolution, or homoplasy.)

Arboreal: A descriptor for an organism that spends most of its time in trees.

Asian clade: A grouping that includes orangutans and their extinct relatives.

Bilophodont: Molar pattern of cercopithecoid monkeys in which there are usually four cusps that are arranged in a square pattern and connected by two ridges.

Bipedalism: Walking on two legs.

Brachiation: A form of locomotion in which the organism swings below branches using the forelimbs.

Bunodont: Low, rounded cusps on the cheek teeth.

Canines: In most primates, these are the longest of the teeth, often conical in shape and used as a weapon against predators or others of their species.

Cathemeral: Active throughout the 24-hour period.

Clade: A grouping based on ancestral relationships; a branch of the evolutionary tree.

Cusps: The bumps on the chewing surface of the premolars and molars, which can be quite sharp in some species.

Dental formula: The number of each type of tooth in one quadrant of the mouth, written as number of incisors: canines: premolars: molars.

Derived trait: A trait that has been recently modified, most helpful when assigning taxonomic classification.

Diastema: A space between the teeth, usually for large canines to fit when the mouth is closed.

Dichromatic: Being able to see only blues and greens.

Diurnal: Active during the day.

Dry nose: The nose and upper lip are separated and the upper lip can move independently; sometimes referred to as a "hairy" or "mobile" upper lip.

Ethnoprimatology: A subarea of anthropology that studies the complexities of human-primate relationships in the modern environment.

Evolutionary trade-off: When an organism, which is limited in the time and energy it can put into aspects of its biology and behavior, is shaped by natural selection to invest in one adaptation at the expense of another.

Faunivorous: Having a diet consisting of animal matter: insects, eggs, lizards, etc.

Frugivore: Having a diet consisting primarily of fruit.

Folivore: Having a diet consisting primarily of leaves.

Fovea: A depressed area in the retina at the back of the eye containing a concentration of cells that allow us to focus on objects very close to our face.

Generalized trait: A trait that is useful for a wide range of tasks.

Grade: A grouping based on overall similarity in lifestyle, appearance, and behavior.

Grooming claw: A claw present on the second pedal digit in strepsirrhines.

Gummivore: Having a diet consisting primarily of gums and saps.

Heterodont: Having different types of teeth.

Homodont: Having only one type of tooth.

Homology: When two or more taxa share characteristics because they inherited them from a common ancestor.

Hone: When primates sharpen their canines by wearing them on adjacent teeth.

Incisors: The spatula-shaped teeth at the front of the mouth.

Insectivore: Having a diet consisting primarily of insects.

Ischial callosities: A flattened area of the ischium on the pelvis over which calluses form; functioning as seat pads for sitting and resting atop branches.

Knuckle-walking: A form of quadrupedal movement used by *Gorilla* and *Pan* when on the ground, where the front limbs are supported on the knuckles of the hands.

Life history: Refers to an organism's pace of growth, reproduction, lifespan, etc.

Locomotion: How an organism moves around.

Male bimaturism: Refers to the alternative reproductive strategies in orangutans in which males can delay maturation, sometimes indefinitely, until a fully mature, "flanged" male disappears.

Molars: The largest teeth at the back of the mouth; used for chewing; in primates, these teeth usually have between three and five cusps.

Monochromatic: Being able to see only in shades of light to dark, no color.

Monomorphic: When males and females of a species do not exhibit significant sexual dimorphism.

Natal coat: Refers to the contrasting fur color of baby leaf monkeys compared to adults.

Nocturnal: Active at night.

Olecranon process: Bony projection at the elbow end of the ulna.

Opposable thumb or **opposable big toe:** Having thumbs and toes that go in a different direction from the rest of the fingers, allows for grasping with hands and feet.

Pentadactyly: Having five digits or fingers and toes.

Polymorphic color vision: A system in which individuals of a species vary in their abilities to see color. In primates, it refers to males being dichromatic and females being either trichromatic or dichromatic.

Postorbital bar: A bony ring that surrounds the eye socket, open at the back.

Postorbital closure/plate: A bony plate that provides protection to the side and back of the eye.

Prehensile tail: A tail that is able to hold the full body weight of an organism, which often has a tactile pad on the underside of the tip for improved grip.

Premolars: Smaller than the molars, used for chewing. In primates, these teeth usually have one or two cusps.

Primitive trait: A trait that has been inherited from a distant ancestor.

Quadrupedalism: Moving around on all fours.

Rhinariums: Wet noses; produced when the nose is connected to the upper lip.

Sagittal crest: A bony ridge along the top/middle of the skull, used for attachment of chewing muscles.

Scent marking: The behavior of rubbing scent glands or urine onto objects as a way of communicating with others.

Semi-brachiation: A form of locomotion in which an organism swings below branches using a combination of forelimbs and prehensile tail.

Sexually dimorphic: When a species exhibits sex differences in morphology, behavior, hormones, and/or coloration.

Shearing crests: Sharpened ridges that connect cusps on a bilophodont molar.

Specialized trait: A trait that has been modified for a specific purpose.

Styloid process of ulna: A bony projection of the ulna at the end near the wrist.

Tactile pads: Sensitive skin at the fingertips for sense of touch. Animals with a prehensile tail have a tactile pad on the underside of the tail as well.

Tapetum lucidum: Reflecting layer at the back of the eye that magnifies light.

Terrestrial: Spending most of the time on the ground.

Tetrachromatic: Having the ability to see reds, yellows, blues, greens, and ultraviolet.

Tooth comb or **dental comb:** A trait of the front, lower teeth of strepsirrhines in which, typically, the four incisors and canines are long and thin and protrude outward.

Trichromatic color vision: Being able to distinguish yellows and reds in addition to blues and greens.

Vertical clinging and leaping: A locomotor pattern in which animals are oriented upright while clinging to vertical branches, push off with hind legs, and land oriented upright on another vertical branch.

Y-5 molar: Molar cusp pattern in which five molar cusps are separated by a "Y"-shaped groove pattern.

About the Author

Stephanie Etting

Sacramento City College

Stephanie Etting

Dr. Stephanie Etting became hooked on biological anthropology as a freshman at UC Davis when she took the "Introduction to Biological Anthropology" course. She obtained her Ph.D. in anthropology in 2011 from UC Davis, where she studied anti-predator behavior toward snakes in rhesus macaques, squirrel monkeys, and black-and-white ruffed lemurs. While in graduate school, Dr. Etting discovered her love of teaching and, since finishing her dissertation, has taught at UC Berkeley; Sonoma State University; UC Davis; California State University, Sacramento; and Sacramento City College. In addition to her interests in primate behavior, Dr. Etting is also very interested in primate evolution and functional anatomy.

For Further Exploration

Animal Diversity Web: https://animaldiversity.org/accounts/Primates/specimens/ This website is hosted by the Zoology Department at the University of Michigan. It has photographs of skulls, teeth, hands, arms, and feet of many primate species.

eSkeletons: http://www.eskeletons.org This website is hosted by the Department of Anthropology at University of Texas, Austin. It is an interactive website where you can compare specific bones from different species of primates.

Fleagle, John G. 2013. Primate Adaptation and Evolution. Third edition. San Diego: Academic Press.

Fuentes, Agustín, and Kimberley J. Hockings. 2010. "The Ethnoprimatological Approach in Primatology." American Journal of Primatology 72 (10): 841–847.

Rowe, Noel. 1996. Pictorial Guide to the Living Primates. Charlestown, VA: Pogonias Press.

Whitehead, Paul F., William K. Sacco, and Susan B. Hochgraf. 2005. A Photographic Atlas for Physical Anthropology. Englewood, CO: Morton Publishing.

References

Balolia, Katharine L., Christophe Soligo, and Bernard Wood. 2017. "Sagittal Crest Formation in Great Apes and Gibbons." Journal of Anatomy 230 (6): 820–832.

Bininda-Emonds, Olaf R., Marcel Cardillo, Kate E. Jones, Ross D. E. MacPhee, Robin M. D. Beck, Richard Grenyer, Samantha A. Price, Rutger A. Vos, John L. Gittleman, and Andy Purvis. 2007. "The Delayed Rise of Present-Day Mammals." Nature 446 (7,135): 507–512.

Burton, Michael L., Carmella C. Moore, John W. M. Whiting, A. Kimball Romney, David F. Aberle, Juan A. Barcelo, Malcolm M. Dow, et al.. 1996. "Regions Based on Social Structure." Current Anthropology 37 (1): 87–123.

Changizi, Mark A., Qiong Zhang, and Shinsuke Shimojo. 2006. "Bare Skin, Blood and the Evolution of Primate Colour Vision." Biology Letters 2 (2): 217–221.

Chivers, David J., and C. M. Hladik. 1980. "Morphology of the Gastrointestinal Tract in Primates: Comparisons With Other Mammals in Relation to Diet." Journal of Morphology 166 (3): 337–386.

Clutton-Brock, T. H., and Paul H. Harvey. 1980. "Primates, Brains, and Ecology." Journal of Zoology 190 (3): 309–323.

Dominy, Nathaniel J., and Peter W. Lucas. 2001. "Ecological Importance of Trichromatic Vision to Primates." Nature 410 (6,826): 363–366.

Dunbar, Robin I. M. 1998. "The Social Brain Hypothesis." Evolutionary Anthropology 6 (5): 178–190.

Ebersberger, Ingo, Dirk Metzler, Carsten Schwarz, and Svante Pääbo. 2002. "Genomewide Comparison of DNA Sequences Between Humans and Chimpanzees." American Journal of Human Genetics 70 (6): 1,490–1,497.

Jameson, Natalie M., Zhoucheng Hou, Kirsten N. Sterner, Amy Weckle, Morris Goodman, Michael E. Steiper, and Derek Wildman. 2011. "Genomic Data Reject the Hypothesis of a Prosimian Primate Clade." Journal of Human Evolution 61 (3): 295–305.

Kawamura, Shoji, Chihiro Hiramatsu, Amanda D. Melin, Colleen M. Schaffner, Filippo Aureli, and Linda Marie Fedigan.

2012. "Polymorphic Color Vision in Primates: Evolutionary Considerations." In Post-Genome Biology of Primates, edited by H. Irai, H. Imai, and Y. Go, 93–120. Tokyo: Springer.

Matsui, Atsushi, Felix Rakotondraparany, Isao Munechika, Masami Hasegawa, and Satoshi Horai. 2009. "Molecular Phylogeny and Evolution of Prosimians Based on Complete Sequences of Mitochondrial DNAs." Gene 441 (1–2): 53–66.

Morgan, M. J., A. Adam, and J. D. Mollon. 1992. "Dichromats Detect Colour-Camouflaged Objects That Are Not Detected by Trichromats." Proceedings of the Royal Society London B: Biological Sciences 248 (1,323): 291–295.

Nater, Alexander, Maja P. Mattle-Greminger, Anton Nurcahyo, Matthew G. Nowak, Marc De Manuel, Tariq Desai, Colin Groves, et al. 2017. "Morphometric, Behavioral, and Genomic Evidence for a New Orangutan Species." Current Biology 27 (22): 3,487–3,498.

Pessoa, Daniel Marques Almeida, Rafael Maia, Rafael Cavalcanti de Albuquerque Ajuz, Pedro Zurvaino Palmeiro Melo Rosa De Moraes, Maria Helena Constantino Spyrides, and Valdir Filgueiras Pessoa. 2014. "The Adaptive Value of Primate Color Vision for Predator Detection." American Journal of Primatology 76 (8): 721–729.

Pozzi, Luca, Jason A. Hodgson, Andrew S. Burrell, Kirstin N. Sterner, Ryan L. Raaum, and Todd R. Disotell. 2014. "Primate Phylogenetic Relationships and Divergence Dates Inferred From Complete Mitochondrial Genomes." Molecular Phylogenetics and Evolution 75: 165–183.

Regan, B. C., C. Julliot, B. Simmen, F. Viénot, P. Charles-Dominique, and J. D. Mollon. 2001. "Fruits, Foliage and the Evolution of Primate Colour Vision." Philosophical Transactions of the Royal Society of London B: Biological Sciences 356 (1,407): 229–283.

Remis, Melissa J. 1997. "Western Lowland Gorillas (Gorilla gorilla gorilla) as Seasonal Frugivores: Use of Variable Resources." American Journal of Primatology 43 (2): 87–109.

Richmond, Brian G., David R. Begun, and David S. Strait. 2001. "Origin of Human Bipedalism: The Knuckle-Walking Hypothesis Revisited." American Journal of Physical Anthropology 116 (S33): 70–105.

Robson, Shannen L., Carel P. van Schaik, and Kristen Hawkes. 2006. "The Derived Features of Human Life History." In The Evolution of Human Life History, edited by Richard R. Paine and Kristen Hawkes, 17–44. Santa Fe: SAR Press.

Scally, Aylwyn, Julien Y. Dutheil, LaDeana W. Hillier, Gregory E. Jordan, Ian Goodhead, Javier Herrero, Asger Hobolth, et al. 2012. "Insights Into Hominid Evolution From the Gorilla Genome Sequence." Nature 483 (7,388): 169–175.

Schneider, Horacio, and Iracilda Sampaio. 2015. "The Systematics and Evolution of New World Primates: A Review." Molecular Phylogenetics and Evolution 82 (B): 348–357.

Setchell, Joanna M., Phyllis C. Lee, E. Jean Wickings, and Alan F. Dixson. 2001. "Growth and Ontogeny of Sexual Size Dimorphism in the Mandrill (Mandrillus sphinx)." American Journal of Physical Anthropology 115 (4): 349–360.

Silk, Joan B., Jacintha C. Beehner, Thore J. Bergman, Catherine Crockford, Anne L. Engh, Liza R. Moscovice, Roman M. Wittig, Robert M. Seyfarth, and Dorothy L. Cheney. 2009. "The Benefits of Social Capital: Close Social Bonds Among Female Baboons Enhance Offspring Survival." Proceedings of the Royal Society of London B: Biological Sciences 276 (1,670): 3,099–3,104.

Utami, Sri Suci, Benoît Goossens, Michael W. Bruford, Jan R. de Ruiter, and Jan A. R. A. M. van Hooff. 2002. "Male Bimaturism and Reproductive Success in Sumatran Orang-utans." Behavioral Ecology 13 (5): 643–652.

Vasey, Natalie. 2006. "Impact of Seasonality and Reproduction on Social Structure, Ranging Patterns, and Fission–Fusion

Social Organization in Red Ruffed Lemurs." In Lemurs: Ecology and Adaptation, edited by Lisa Gould and Michelle L. Sauther, 275–304. Boston: Springer.

Wright, Patricia C. 1999. "Lemur Traits and Madagascar Ecology: Coping With an Island Environment." American Journal of Physical Anthropology 110 (S29): 31–72.

Acknowledgements

The author would very much like to thank the editors for the opportunity to contribute to this textbook, along with two anonymous reviewers who provided useful feedback on earlier drafts of this chapter. She would also like to thank Karin Enstam Jaffe for her support and encouragement during the writing of this chapter. Most of all, the author would like to thank all of the Introduction to Biological Anthropology students that she has had over the years who have listened to her lecture endlessly on these animals that she finds so fascinating and who have helped her to hone her pedagogy in a field that she loves.

Figure Attributions

Figure 5.1 Post-orbital bar/Post-orbital closure a derivative work original to Explorations: An Open Invitation to Biological Anthropology by Stephanie Etting is under a CC BY-NC-SA 4.0 License. [Includes Otolemur crassicaudatus (greater galago) by Animal Diversity Web, CC BY-NC-SA 3.0; Macaca fascicularis (long-tailed macaque) by Animal Diversity Web, CC BY-NC-SA 3.0.]

Figure 5.2 PrimateFeet by Richard Lydekker, original from The Royal Natural History 1:15 (1893), is in the public domain.

Figure 5.3 Primate suite of traits table by Stephanie Etting original to Explorations: An Open Invitation to Biological Anthropology is under a CC BY-NC 4.0 License.

Figure 5.4 Ha,ha,ha …. (14986571843) by Rolf Dietrich Brecher from Germany is under a CC BY-SA 2.0 License.

Figure 5.5 Four types of human teeth original to Explorations: An Open Invitation to Biological Anthropology by Mary Nelson is under a CC BY-NC 4.0 License.

Figure 5.6a Frugivore characteristics original to Explorations: An Open Invitation to Biological Anthropology by Mary Nelson is under a CC BY-NC 4.0 License.

Figure 5.6b Insectivore characteristics original to Explorations: An Open Invitation to Biological Anthropology by Mary Nelson is under a CC BY-NC 4.0 License.

Figure 5.6c Folivore characteristics original to Explorations: An Open Invitation to Biological Anthropology by Mary Nelson is under a CC BY-NC 4.0 License.

Figure 5.7 Vertical clinger and leaper locomotion original to Explorations: An Open Invitation to Biological Anthropology by Mary Nelson is under a CC BY-NC 4.0 License.

Figure 5.8 Terrestrial quadrupedal primate original to Explorations: An Open Invitation to Biological Anthropology by Mary Nelson is under a CC BY-NC 4.0 License.

Figure 5.9 Brachiator original to Explorations: An Open Invitation to Biological Anthropology by Mary Nelson is under a CC BY-NC 4.0 License.

Figure 5.10 Ateles-fusciceps 54724770b by LeaMaimone is under a CC BY 2.5 License.

Figure 5.11: Primate taxonomy chart a derivative work original to Explorations: An Open Invitation to Biological Anthropology by Stephanie Etting is under a CC BY-NC 4.0 License. [Includes Lemur catta Linnaeus, 1759 by Roberto Díaz Sibaja, CC BY 3.0; Lorisoidea original to Explorations: An Open Invitation to Biological Anthropology by Katie Nelson, CC BY-NC 4.0; Tarsiiformes original to Explorations: An Open Invitation to Biological Anthropology by Mary Nelson, CC BY-NC 4.0; Cebinae Bonaparte, 1831 by Sarah Werning, CC BY 3.0; Colobus guereza Ruppell, 1835 by Yan Wong from drawing in The Century Dictionary (1911) (flipped horizontally), designated to the public domain (CC0); Papio cynocephalus by Owen Jones, designated to the public domain (CC0); animals silhouette wolf elephant (2755766) by mohamed_hassan, Pixabay License.]

Figure 5.12 Grades vs. clades comparison a derivative work original to Explorations: An Open Invitation to Biological Anthropology by Stephanie Etting is under a CC BY-NC 4.0 License. [Includes Orangutan on a tree (Unsplash) by Dawn Armfield darmfield, public domain (CC0 1.0); Gorilla Profile (17997840570) by Charlie Marshall from Bristol UK, United Kingdom, modified (cropped), CC BY 2.0 License; Chimpanzee (14679767561) by Magnus Johansson, modified (cropped), CC BY-SA 2.0; Pointing finger (1922074) by truthseeker08, Pixabay License.]

Figure 5.13 Lemur catta toilet claw by Alex Dunkel (Maky) is used under a CC BY 3.0 Licesnse.

Figure 5.14 Extant Strepsirrhini a derivative work by Mark Dumont is under a CC BY-SA 3.0 License. [Includes Katta család by Veszprémi Állatkert, CC BY-SA 3.0; Aye-aye at night in the wild in Madagascar by Frank Vassen, CC BY 2.0; Diademed ready to push off by Michael Hogan, designated to the public domain (CC0); Juvenile Black-and-White Ruffed Lemur, Mantadia, Madagascar by Frank Vassen, CC BY 2.0; Microcebus murinus -Artis Zoo, Amsterdam, Netherlands-8a by Arjan Haverkamp, CC BY 2.0; Slow Loris by Jmiksanek, CC BY-SA 3.0; Slender Loris by Kalyan Varma (Kalyanvarma), CC BY-SA 4.0; Garnett's Galago (Greater Bushbaby) by Mark Dumont, CC BY 2.0].

Figure 5.15 Lemur catta toothcomb by Alex Dunkel (Maky) is used under a CC BY 3.0 licesnse.

Figure 5.16 Geographic distribution of living strepsirrhines original to Explorations: An Open Invitation to Biological Anthropology by Elyssa Ebding at GeoPlace, California State University, Chico is under a CC BY-NC 4.0 License.

Figure 5.17 Indri indri 0003 by Christophe Germain is used under a CC BY-SA 4.0 License.

Figure 5.18 Nycticebus coucang 002 by David Haring / Duke Lemur Center is used under a CC BY-SA 3.0 License.

Figure 5.19 Strepsirrhines at a glance a derivative work original to Explorations: An Open Invitation to Biological Anthropology by Stephanie Etting is under a CC BY-NC-SA 4.0 License. [Includes Ringtailed Lemurs in Berenty by David Dennis, CC BY-SA 2.0; Komba ušatá by Petr Hamerník, CC BY-SA 4.0.]

Figure 5.20 Suborders at a glance a derivative work original to Explorations: An Open Invitation to Biological Anthropology by Stephanie Etting is under a CC BY-NC-SA 4.0 License. [Includes Black-and-White Ruffed Lemur, Mantadia, Madagascar by Frank Vassen, CC BY 2.0; Crab eating macaque face by Bruce89, CC BY-SA 4.0.]

Figure 5.21 Tarsier Sanctuary, Corella, Bohol (2052878890) by yeowatzup is used under a CC BY 2.0 License.

Figure 5.22 Infraorder Tarsiiformes of Asia map original to Explorations: An Open Invitation to Biological Anthropology by Elyssa Ebding at GeoPlace, California State University, Chico is under a CC BY-NC 4.0 License.

Figure 5.23 Tarsier skull by Andrew Bardwell from Cleveland, Ohio, USA is used under a CC BY-SA 2.0 License.

Figure 5.24 Tarsiers at a glance table original to Explorations: An Open Invitation to Biological Anthropology by Stephanie Etting is under a CC BY-NC 4.0 License.

Figure 5.25 Infraorder Platyrrhini map original to Explorations: An Open Invitation to Biological Anthropology by Elyssa Ebding at GeoPlace, California State University, Chico is under a CC BY-NC 4.0 License.

Figure 5.26 CARABLANCA – panoramio by Manuel Velazquez is used under a CC BY 3.0 License.

Figure 5.27 Callitrichinae genus a derivative work by Miguelrangeljris is used under a CC BY-SA 3.0 License. [Includes Weißbüschelaffe_(Callithrix_jacchus) by Raymond, CC BY-SA 4.0; Leontopithecus chrysomelas (portrait) by Hans Hillewaert, CC BY-SA 4.0; Emperor_Tamarin_portrait_2_edit1 by Brocken Inaglory, CC BY-SA 4.0; Dværgsilkeabe_Callithrix_pygmaea by Malene Thyssen (User Malene), GNU Free Documentation License; Mico_argentatus_(portrait) by Hans Hillewaert, CC BY-SA 4.0; Titi Monkey by Jeff Kubina.CC BY-SA 2.0].]

Figure 5.28 Atelidae Family a derivative work by User:Miguelrangeljr is used under a CC BY-SA 3.0 License. [Includes Ateles marginatus (Sao Paulo zoo) by Miguelrangeljr, CC BY-SA 3.0; Alouatta caraya male by Miguelrangeljr, CC BY-SA 3.0; Brachyteles hypoxanthus2 by Paulo B. Chaves, CC BY 2.0; Lagothrix lagotricha (walking) by Hans Hillewaert, CC BY-SA 3.0.]

Figure 5.29 Platyrrhini at a glance table original to Explorations: An Open Invitation to Biological Anthropology by Stephanie Etting is under a CC BY-NC 4.0 License.

Figure 5.30 Wolf's Guenon Picking Up Food (19095137693) by Eric Kilby from Somerville, MA, USA, is used under a CC BY-SA 2.0 License.

Figure 5.31 Platyrrhini vs. Catarrhini dentition a derivative work original to Explorations: An Open Invitation to Biological Anthropology by Stephanie Etting is under a CC BY-NC-SA 4.0 License. [Includes Cebus apella (brown capuchin) at Animal Diversity Web by Phil Myers, Museum of Zoology, University of Michigan-Ann Arbor, CC BY-NC-SA 3.0; Lophocebus albigena (gray-cheeked mangaby) at Animal Diversity Web by Phil Myers, Museum of Zoology, University of Michigan-Ann Arbor, CC BY-NC-SA 3.0; Symphalangus syndactylus (siamang) at Animal Diversity Web by Phil Myers, Museum of Zoology, University of Michigan-Ann Arbor, CC BY-NC-SA 3.0.]

Figure 5.32 Sulawesi trsr DSCN0572 v1 by T. R. Shankar Ramanis used under a CC BY-SA 3.0 License.

Figure 5.33 Superfamily Cercopithecoidea map original to Explorations: An Open Invitation to Biological Anthropology by Elyssa Ebding at GeoPlace, California State University, Chico is under a CC BY-NC 4.0 License.

Figure 5.34 Silverleaf Monkey (Kuala Lumpur) by Andrea Lai from Auckland, New Zealand is used under a CC BY 2.0 License.

Figure 5.35 Proboscis monkey (Nasalis larvatus) male head by Charles J Sharp creator QS:P170,Q54800218 is used under a CC BY-SA 4.0 License.

Figure 5.36 Bonnet macaque DSC 0893 by T. R. Shankar Raman is used under a CC BY-SA 4.0 License.

Figure 5.37 Macaque India 4 by Thomas Schoch is used under a CC BY-SA 3.0 License.

Figure 5.38 Superfamily Hominoidea map original to Explorations: An Open Invitation to Biological Anthropology by Elyssa Ebding at GeoPlace, California State University, Chico is under a CC BY-NC 4.0 License.

Figure 5.39: Quadrupedalism vs. Brachiation table original to Explorations: An Open Invitation to Biological Anthropology by Stephanie Etting is under a CC BY-NC 4.0 License.

Figure 5.40 Catarrhini at a glance a derivative work original to Explorations: An Open Invitation to Biological

Anthropology by Stephanie Etting is under a CC BY-NC 4.0 License. [Includes Duskyleafmonkey1 by Robertpollai, CC BY 3.0 AT; Male Bornean Orangutan – Big Cheeks by Eric Kilby from Somerville, MA, USA, CC BY-SA 2.0.]

Figure 5.41 Shout (373310729) by su neko is used under a CC BY-SA 2.0 License.

Figure 5.42a Orang Utan (Pongo pygmaeus) female with baby (8066259067) by Bernard DUPONT from FRANCE is used under a CC BY-SA 2.0 Licence.

Figure 5.42b Orangutan -Zoologischer Garten Berlin-8a by David Arvidsson is used under a CC BY 2.0 License.

Figure 5.43a Enzo naomi echo by Zoostar is used under a CC BY 3.0 License.

Figure 5.43b Male gorilla in SF zoo by Brocken Inaglory is used under a CC BY-SA 3.0 License.

Figure 5.44 Bonobo male Jasongo 15yo Twycross 582a (2014 11 14 01 04 18 UTC) by William H. Calvin is used under a CC BY-SA 4.0 License.

Figure 5.45 Chimpanzees in Uganda (5984913059) by USAID Africa Bureau uploaded by Elitre is in the public domain.

Chapter 6: Primate Behavior and Ecology

Karin Enstam Jaffe, Ph.D., Sonoma State University

Learning Objectives

- Describe the behavioral variation that exists within the Primate Order and how primate behavior and morphology are influenced by diet, predation, and other ecological factors.
- Explain why primates live in groups.
- Distinguish primate social systems from mating systems.
- Contrast male and female reproductive and parental investment strategies.
- Describe the ways in which primates communicate.
- Evaluate the evidence for primate cultural variation.

Nonhuman primates (from now on simply referred to as "primates") are our closest living relatives, and their behavior is often strikingly similar to our own. If you've ever seen a female monkey at your local zoo cooing over her newborn baby (Figure 6.1a) or watched a video of a tufted capuchin monkey using rocks as a hammer and anvil to crack open a nut to access the edible kernel inside (Figure 6.1b), then you know how interesting they can be.

Figure 6.1a A female Japanese macaque nursing her infant.

Figure 6.1b A juvenile capuchin monkey in Serra da Capivara, Brazil, uses a stone as a tool to open a seed.

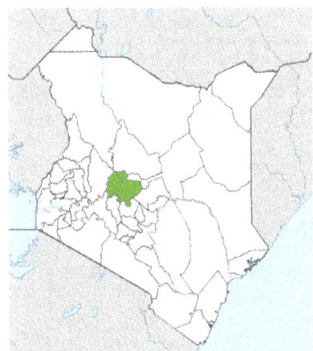

Figure 6.2 Map of Kenya with Laikipia District, where the author conducted her fieldwork, highlighted.

I have been fascinated by primates since I was a young child. In the summer of 1996, I went with my dissertation advisor, Dr. Lynne A. Isbell, to her field site in Laikipia, Kenya (Figure 6.2) with the intention of studying the play behavior of juvenile patas monkeys. One day we were following our patas study group when several females and juveniles began giving high-pitched "nyow" alarm calls. I was awestruck as I watched the entire group take off at breakneck speed. Patas monkeys are, after all, the fastest primate, capable of running 20 miles per hour for short distances. It did not even occur to me that they had sounded an alarm and then run away from *something*—until my advisor pointed to the lioness hidden in the grass at the base of a tree. (We slowly backed away and got in our car.) My research interests changed in that moment: I wanted to study primate antipredator behavior, the strategies primates use to escape from predators. I would spend two years at that same field site collecting data on anti-predator behavior of patas monkeys and vervets, two closely related species who occupy different habitats. Patas monkeys (Figure 6.3a) live far from rivers, in habitats composed of short trees spaced far apart (Figure 6.3b). These trees have little to no overlapping canopy, so climbing one to escape a lion in pursuit can result in a literal dead end. In contrast, vervets (Figure 6.4a) spend most of their time along rivers, with access to tall trees with overlapping canopies

(Figure 6.4b) that provide good escape routes from terrestrial predators. But they also venture into patas habitats, the short trees with canopies that do not overlap. I wanted to know: How would the structure of these habitats affect the responses of vervets and patas monkeys to alarm calls that signal the approach of a terrestrial predator like a lion? Not surprisingly, when vervets are near the river, they climb the tall trees to seek refuge from such predators. But not patas monkeys. These "cheetahs of the primate world" are more likely to take off running (as I had seen them do that summer), even bypassing nearby trees. Their physical adaptations for speed, like their long legs, combined with the lack of arboreal escape routes, makes fleeing on the ground their best option. But what do vervets do when they are away from the river and the safety of their tall trees? Is their behavior "hard-wired" so that their response to an alarm call is the same, regardless of the habitat? Or do they assess key aspects of their habitat, like tree height and canopy cover, and alter their behavior? Although they cannot run as fast, when they hear an alarm call they run back toward the river, by-passing the short trees, just like the patas do (Enstam and Isbell 2002). The implication is clear: these monkeys, our close relatives, with their highly developed intelligence and ability to learn, *do* assess key features of their habitat and use this information to alter their behavior and maximize their chance of escape.

Figure 6.3a and 6.3b A female patas monkey with infant (left). A patas habitat in Laikipia, Kenya (right).

Figure 6.4a and 6.4b A female vervet (left). A vervet habitat in Laikipia, Kenya (right).

The branch of science that focuses on the study of primate behavior is called **primatology**, and people, like myself, who study primates (Figure 6.5) are called **primatologists**. Primatologists come from many different disciplines and study primate behavior for different reasons. Biologists study primates as examples of evolutionary theories like natural selection or parental investment. Primate intelligence is of interest to psychologists who want to learn more about the underlying cognitive principles involved in deceptive or cooperative behavior and to linguists interested in the principles of communication and language. Ecologists studying conservation issues examine how primates are affected by deforestation, poaching, or illegal animal trade. Biological anthropologists, like myself, who study primates are interested in their social complexity and ecological and behavioral variation. Because both humans and most nonhuman primates live in groups, biological anthropologists study primates to better understand the evolution of social behavior and its costs and benefits. Because primates are our closest living relatives, we study them to gain insights into how our human ancestors may have behaved as well as to better understand our own behavior.

Figure 6.5 The author observing patas monkeys in Laikipia, Kenya.

ECOLOGY

The more than 600 species and subspecies of living primates are highly diverse in their dietary preferences and the habitats they occupy. These aspects of primate ecology have significant impacts on every part of a primate's life, including their morphology, physiology, and body size as well as their interactions with other individuals inside and outside their social group. They even play a role in determining whether a primate lives in a group or is **solitary** and lives alone. A primate's habitat determines the food to which they have access and the community of other species with whom they interact, including predators.

Primate Diets

Diet may be the most important variable influencing variation in primate morphology, behavior, and ecology, and primate diets are highly varied. Some primatologists separate **foraging**, the act of finding and handling food, from **feeding**, the act of consuming food, while others combine these into one category. Most primates are **omnivores** who ingest a variety of foods in order to obtain appropriate levels of protein, carbohydrates, fats, and fluids, but one type of food often makes up the majority of each species' diet. Because you learned about the dental and digestive adaptations experienced by **frugivores** (who feed primarily on fruit), **folivores** (whose diet consists mostly of leaves), and **insectivores** (who eat mainly insects) in Chapter 5, we will not discuss them here. Instead, we will focus on the relationship between diet and body size and the variation in food **abundance** (how much is available in a given area) and **distribution** (how it is spread out).

Body Size and Diet

Figure 6.6a A spectral tarsier eating a grasshopper.

Figure 6.6b A mountain gorilla eating leaves.

As you learned in Chapter 5, insects are a high-quality food. Full of easily digestible protein and high in calories, insects are an excellent source of nutrients, meeting most of a primate's dietary needs. Although all primates will eat insects if they come upon them, those species that rely most heavily on insects tend to be the smallest. If insects are such a high-quality food, why aren't all primates insectivores? The answer is that larger primates simply cannot capture and consume enough insects every day to survive. This is because the **basal metabolic rate** (BMR), or the rate at which energy is used to maintain the body while at rest, increases more slowly than body size. The result? Heavier animals must consume *absolutely more food*, but they have a slower metabolism so they need *fewer calories per unit of body weight*. Because of their small size (less than 150 g), tarsiers do not need to consume large amounts of food each day, but their high metabolic rate means they convert food into energy very quickly. This is only possible by consuming food that is easily digestible, like insects. It does not matter to a tarsier that a grasshopper only weighs 300 mg, because the tarsier itself is so small that one grasshopper is a good-size meal (Figure 6.6a). However, an adult male gorilla, who may weigh up to 200 kilograms, cannot possibly consume enough insects to meet its caloric needs. And it does not need to. Because of their large body size, gorillas have a much lower metabolic rate than tarsiers, so they can consume low-quality food, like leaves, and take their time digesting it, so long as they get enough (Figure 6.6b). Fortunately for gorillas, leaves are plentiful, as we will see in the next section. Most medium-size primates are highly frugivorous. Whether they supplement their high-fruit diet with insects or leaves also depends on their size. Smaller frugivores tend to supplement with insects, while larger frugivores tend to supplement with leaves.

Food Abundance and Distribution

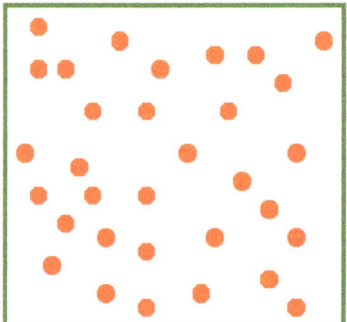

Figure 6.7a Food is abundant when there is a lot of it in a given area.

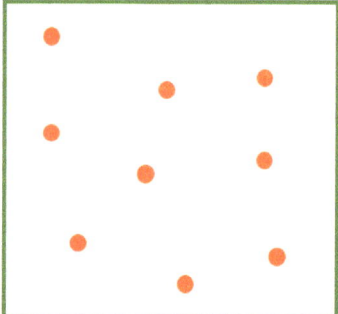

Figure 6.7b Food is scarce when there is not much of it in a given area.

Nutrients (see Chapter 5) and food quality are not the only dietary considerations primates must make. They must also ensure that they consume more calories than they burn. The abundance and distribution of food affect energy expenditure and calorie intake because they determine how far animals must travel in search of food and how much they must compete to obtain it. Abundance refers to *how much food* is available in a given area while distribution refers to *how food is spread out*. Food abundance is either plentiful (Figure 6.7a) or scarce (Figure 6.7b). Food is distributed in one of three

Primate Ecology and Behavior | 193

ways: uniformly (Figure 6.8a), in clumps (Figure 6.8b), or randomly (Figure 6.8c). In general, higher-quality foods, like fruit and insects, are less abundant and have patchier distributions than lower-quality foods, like leaves. In a rainforest, like the Amazon, every tree has leaves, so they are abundant and uniformly distributed (Figure 6.9a). Folivores do not have to travel very far to find food so they do not burn many calories searching for food. In comparison to leaves, fruit is scarce and clumped (Figure 6.9b). Because not every tree contains fruit, it is less plentiful than leaves. In addition, in a rainforest, a single tree with fruit may be surrounded by many trees without fruit. To a frugivore, this one fruit tree is a clump of fruit. Frugivores who do not eat leaves must travel farther distances in search of food because they can only feed in some trees (i.e., those producing fruit). Frugivores burn more calories searching for food than folivores, so it is a good thing that fruit is such a high-quality food. Lastly, insects are scarce, and due to their mobile nature, most are randomly distributed (Figure 6.9c). This combination makes it impossible for larger primates to rely on insects for a significant part of their diet.

Figure 6.8a Food has a uniform distribution when it is spread out evenly in the environment.

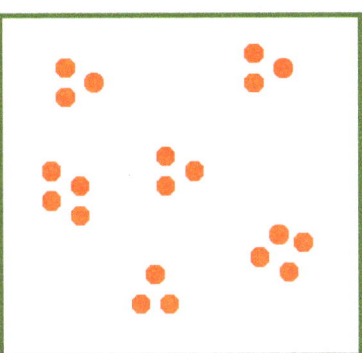

Figure 6.8b Food has a clumped distribution when it is found in patches.

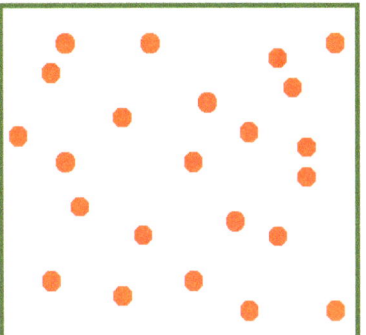

Figure 6.8c Food is randomly distributed when it has neither uniform nor clumped distribution.

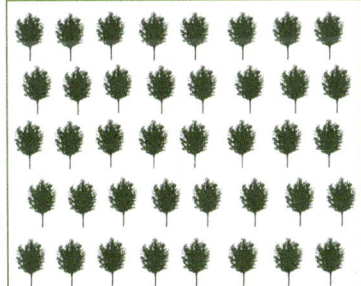

Figure 6.9a For folivores living in a rainforest like the Amazon, food is abundant and everywhere. In this drawing, every tree has edible leaves.

Figure 6.9b For frugivores, only trees producing fruit contain food so food is scarce and found in clumps. In this drawing, only the four fruit trees contain food.

Figure 6.9c Insects are generally scarce and randomly distributed because they are highly mobile. In this drawing, only the insects on the trees are edible.

It is important to remember that species preferences for specific *types* of food may cause it to exist in abundance or distribution that is different than the general patterns we've discussed here. For example, for folivores who prefer young (i.e., immature) leaves, their food supply is patchier and less abundant than it appears to a researcher looking at the lush green carpet of the Amazon forest because only *some* leaves are immature at any point in time. During fruiting season, when many trees are producing fruit, fruit may be temporarily abundant and less clumped. Similarly, some insects, like termites in a termite mound (Figure 6.10), are found in clumps, similar to the way a single fruit tree is a "clump" of fruit surrounded by trees with no fruit.

Competition for Food

When a resource that is important for survival or reproduction is scarce, individuals will compete to obtain that resource. This is a central tenet of Charles Darwin's theory of evolution by natural selection (see Chapter 2). Because female primates (like all mammals) devote a lot of energy to offspring production and care (discussed in detail in the "Parental Investment" section of this chapter), especially while pregnant and nursing, they compete for access to food, *so long as the food is worth competing for*. Competition between primates takes two forms: Individuals engage in direct competition (e.g., fighting) over resources that are large and worth defending (fruit is a good example of a food resource over which primates will fight) or individuals engage in indirect competition (e.g., eating food before another individual gets to it), which occurs when a resource is small or not worth defending. Primates often engage in indirect competition for insects, like grasshoppers, that are eaten quickly (Figure 6.6a). Primates may engage in direct and/or indirect competition with members of their own group or with members of other groups.

Figure 6.10 Individual insects are usually scarce and randomly distributed in the environment. A notable exception are termite mounds, like this one in Tanzania, where, inside the mound, insects are abundant and clumped.

Effects of Food Abundance and Distribution on Interactions Between and Within Groups

The amount, or abundance, of food determines the nature of competition *between* different groups (Isbell 1991). Between-group competition is seen in terms of changes to home range size and nature of interactions between groups. A group's **home range** is the area over which the group moves in search of food. Groups that defend the boundary of their home range are said to occupy a **territory**. Consider a patch of forest covered in leaves (e.g., Figure 6.9a). If you are a folivore, every tree is a dinner table. When your group size increases, your home range does not expand because there is more than enough food for everyone, and it is a waste of energy to travel farther than you need to. And as long as your group does not expand its home range, you will not encroach on the trees of neighboring groups. This keeps competitive interactions between groups of folivores to a minimum. Now imagine you are a frugivore. Unlike leaves, not every tree has fruit on it. Maybe only two or three trees are in fruit at any given time, so fruit is scarce (Figure 6.9b). Thus, if your group size increases, it is likely that the few fruit trees available in your current home range will not be able to feed everyone. If that's the case, then your group will need to expand its home range in search of additional fruit trees, which are in the home ranges of neighboring groups. Home-range expansion is also often accompanied by fighting between groups as members attempt to keep intruders away from valuable, scarce food resources.

While food abundance determines interactions between groups, food distribution determines the interactions between individuals *within* a group (Isbell 1991). Competition within a group is marked by changes in day-range length and the presence of dominance hierarchies. **Day-range length** measures the distance a group must travel in a single day in search of food. A **dominance hierarchy** reflects the place of each individual in the group in comparison to others. An individual's place in the hierarchy, or "rank," determines their priority of access to resources. If food is evenly distributed (as with leaves; Figure 6.9a), individuals can spread out while feeding so that their day-range length does not increase when their group size increases. Likewise, because leaves are "everywhere," there is little benefit to females engaging in interactions that determine "priority of access" to resources, so dominance hierarchies are uncommon among folivores. However, if food is clumped (as with fruit; Figure 6.9b), individuals in groups must feed in more cohesive units (i.e., all in one fruit tree). When group size increases, the group must travel farther each day in order to visit enough fruit trees to feed all group members. Likewise, when food is clumped, individuals have the opportunity to monopolize it and keep others from feeding. Under such circumstances, females benefit from competing with one another for "priority of access" to the resource, and dominance hierarchies result.

The fact that food abundance and food distribution vary independently helps us understand the complex nature of between-group and within-group interactions (Isbell 1991). For example, both olive baboons and patas monkeys feed on scarce resources, and both species engage in competition with other groups and expand their home-range size when food is in short supply. But olive baboons' food is clumped while patas monkeys' is dispersed, so the interactions within groups are very different. Female baboons have a strong dominance hierarchy, and the distance they travel each day increases with group size. Patas monkeys have a weak dominance hierarchy, and when group size increases, individuals spread out while feeding and daily travel distance does not increase.

Community Ecology

Figure 6.11a A patas monkey.

Figure 6.11b A vervet.

In addition to interactions with other members of their own group and other groups of **conspecifics** (members of the same species), primates are members of broader ecological communities composed of other species, including other primates, predators, and even humans. When two species (or populations) occupy the same geographic area, they are **sympatric**. The patas monkeys and vervets that I studied in Kenya, along with olive baboons and Senegal bush babies, are sympatric and form a **primate community** (Figure 6.11a–d). However, vervets (Figure 6.11b) and muriquis of Brazil (Figure 6.12) are **allopatric**, meaning their geographic ranges do not overlap. Some habitats support highly diverse primate communities consisting of 10 or more species (Figure 6.13). How can so many species of primate occupy the same area and avoid competition? Sympatric species *do* sometimes compete with each other.

Figure 6.11c An olive baboon.

Observations of one species displacing another at a food site is a sign of competition between the two species. When this happens, usually it is the large-bodied species that supplants the small-bodied species. The exception is when the small-bodied species significantly outnumbers the larger-bodied one. The **competitive exclusion principle** states that two species that compete for the exact same resources cannot coexist. This means that two species cannot occupy the same **niche**—cannot seek to meet their needs for food and shelter in the exact same way. Because tropical rainforests are highly variable, with many habitats and many sources of food and shelter, there are many different niches for multiple species

Figure 6.11d A Senegal bush baby.

Figure 6.12 A muriqui mother an infant.

to exploit, and large primate communities result (Figure 6.13). In non-rainforest habitats, like Kenya's open woodland, which is home to four species (Figure 6.11a–d), there are fewer niches for multiple species to occupy. Regardless of habitat type, sympatric species avoid competition through **niche partitioning** (using the environment differently). Niche partitioning includes differences in diet, ranging behavior, and habitat use. In Laikipia, Kenya, bush babies reduce competition with vervets by feeding more heavily on insects. They further reduce competition by being nocturnal while vervets are diurnal. Even though bush babies (Figure 6.11d) and vervets (Figure 6.11b) do sometimes eat the same food, since they eat at different times of day they rarely, if ever, interact.

Site	Primate Community
Krau Game Reserve, Malaysia	white-handed gibbon, siamang, dusky leaf monkey, mitered leaf monkey, long-tailed macaque, pigtail macaque, slow loris
Manu National Park, Peru	black spider monkey, red howler monkey, brown capuchin, white-fronted capuchin, South American squirrel monkey, owl monkey, dusky titi monkey, common woolly monkey, monk saki monkey, Goeldi's marmoset, emperor tamarin, saddleback tamarin, pygmy marmoset
Beza Mahafaly Reserve, Madagascar	ring-tailed lemur, Verreaux's sifaka, white-footed sportive lemur, reddish-gray mouse lemur
Kibale National Park, Uganda	Ugandan mangabey, L'Hoest's monkey, Ugandan red colobus monkey, vervet monkey, olive baboon, blue monkey, grey-cheeked mangabey, potto, galago, black and white colobus monkey, chimpanzee

Figure 6.13 Examples of primate communities.

Predation

Figure 6.14a Opportunistic hunting of a lizard by a lion-tailed macaque

Figure 6.14b Adult male chimpanzee in Gombe Stream National Park, Tanzania with dead bushbuck.

An important aspect of primate communities is the predators that also occupy them. As discussed in the "Primate Diets" section, all primates incorporate some insects into their diet, and so they may be themselves considered predators in this respect. In this section, we will limit our discussion to predation of and by **vertebrates** (animals with an internal spinal column or backbone). Many primates incorporate some vertebrate prey into their diet. Often, predation by primates is opportunistic, occurring because the prey happen to be in the right place at the right time. I've observed vervets opportunistically killing lizards by smashing them against a rock

Primate Ecology and Behavior | 197

or tree trunk and eating them (much as this lion-tailed macaque has done; Figure 6.14a). In some parts of their range (including Gombe Stream National Park and Mahale Mountain National Park, both in Tanzania), chimpanzees are described as opportunistic hunters, with the vast majority of hunts occurring after a chance encounter with prey (Figure 6.14b; Boesch and Boesch 1989). Other primates are more deliberate predators, and some even work together to increase their chances of success. Cooperative hunting has been observed in white-faced capuchins and some chimpanzee populations. White-faced capuchins hunt more often during the dry season, when other food is scarce, and sometimes work together to chase, surround, and capture small mammals like young squirrels or coatis (Fedigan 1990). The chimpanzees of Taï National Park in Côte d'Ivoire take deliberate, cooperative hunting to the next level. Unlike their Tanzanian counterparts, they form hunting parties to search for red colobus monkeys and, once located, anticipate the prey's movement and coordinate with other hunters to drive, isolate, and capture prey (Boesch 2002). Since hunting-party size correlates with hunting success, it is not surprising that sharing the spoils of a successful hunt is more common in Taï chimpanzees who rely on others for success (Boesch and Boesch 1989).

All primates are susceptible to predation by mammalian **carnivores** (animals whose diet consists primarily of animal tissue) (Figures 6.15a–d), birds of prey (Figures 6.15e-f), and/ or reptiles (Figure 6.15g), although the specific predators differ based on geography and primate body size. Smaller primates fall prey to a wider range of predators than larger primates, and some habitats contain a greater diversity of predators. Primates use a variety of anti-predator tactics to avoid and/or escape predation. Perhaps the best way to avoid predation is to avoid being detected by predators in the first place, and some primates use **crypsis** to great effect.

Figure 6.15a African leopard.

Nocturnal primates are often small and solitary or live in very small groups. If you are already hard to see because you are active at night, moving quietly in small groups is a good strategy to avoid detection by predators. The slow loris of Southeast Asia exemplifies this strategy (Figure 6.16). Nocturnal and solitary, the slow loris moves slowly (as its name suggests) and quietly as its primary strategy to avoid predation (Wiens and Zitzmann 2003). If detected, however, the slow loris will attempt to escape by releasing its grip and falling off the branch or biting in defense.

Figure 6.15b Jaguar of Latin America.

Figure 6.15c Tiger of Asia.

Interestingly, the slow loris is the only venomous primate. The venom is formed when the slow loris combines oil from a gland on its arm with its saliva (Nekaris et al. 2013). It can either apply the venom to its head for protection or store it in the mouth to deliver through a bite. Slow loris bites are painful and take a long time to heal. In extreme cases, individuals who are bitten may go into shock and die. It is not as easy for diurnal primates to avoid

Figure 6.15d Fossa of Madagascar.

detection by predators, and most (but not all) diurnal primates, like Hanuman langurs, have larger body sizes and live in groups (Figure 6.17). Indeed, anti-predator behavior, including vigilance, alarm calling, and mobbing, may be one of the primary benefits primates get from living in groups; we will discuss these behaviors in a later section, entitled "Why do Primates Live in Groups?"

Figure 6.15e Martial eagle of Africa.

Figure 6.15f Harpy eagle of Latin America.

Figure 6.15g South African python.

Figure 6.16 The slow loris is a solitary nocturnal primate.

Figure 6.17 Hanuman langurs are group-living diurnal primates.

SPECIAL TOPIC: PRIMATE CONSERVATION

Figure 6.18a Deforestation of Bornean rainforest for conversion to palm oil plantations.

Figure 6.18b Men in Madagascar hunt and kill a white-fronted brown lemur for bushmeat.

There are over 600 species and subspecies of primates on the planet today, and almost half of them live under the threat of extinction. While there are many threats to primates, habitat destruction and hunting are the leading causes of population decline (Figure 6.18a–b). Primate populations have withstood small-scale forest clearing and low levels of hunting by local human groups for hundreds of years. However, the recent, intense pressure of expanding human populations on many primate habitats is resulting in rapid population declines for many species. The majority of primates live in tropical habitats, and the loss of tropical forest, whether due to logging or farming, is the single greatest factor contributing to the decline of primate populations across the planet. Between 1973 and 2010, almost 100,000 km2 of orangutan habitat was cleared for palm oil plantations in Borneo (Figure 6.18a). During this same time, the orangutan population decreased from almost 300,000 to 100,000, an average loss of more than 5,000 orangutans every year. As of 2017, that number may be as low as 60,000 (Schwitzer et al. 2017). If this rate of loss is not curtailed, the Bornean orangutan will go extinct in less than 15 years. Hunting, whether for bushmeat (Figure 6.18b), trophies, or the pet trade, has had devastating effects on many primate populations. Even though Grauer's gorillas are legally protected, they are highly prized for bushmeat because they are relatively easy to track and shoot, and their large body size yields significant amounts of meat. Survey work has revealed that the Grauer gorilla population has declined significantly since the 1990s, due almost entirely to illegal hunting. The gorilla population in Kahuzi-Biega National Park, in Democratic Republic of Congo (DRC), is estimated to have declined 87% since 1994 (Schwitzer et al. 2017).

As consumers and concerned citizens, all of us are learning how to use our wallets to combat habitat and species loss. We do not buy palm oil or products made with palm oil in an effort to save orangutans. We donate to conservation organizations doing important on-the-ground work in Democratic Republic of Congo and other conservation hot-spots. We educate ourselves as well as our friends, families, and communities about the plight of endangered primates. Primatologists, too, contribute to conservation efforts. No longer is primatology research restricted to the "ivory tower" of academia. Current and future primatologists have the opportunity to affect real change in primate conservation (Chapman and Peres 2001). Whether understanding the mechanisms that determine species abundance, predicting the effects of human activity on species survival, documenting patterns of environmental change, understanding the effects of species removal in broader contexts, or evaluating different approaches to conservation, information gained from

> primate studies offers some of the best hope we have for a future that continues to include our closest living relatives. You can learn more about primate conservation in Appendix B.

SOCIALITY, RESIDENCY PATTERNS, AND DISPERSAL

The majority of mammal species are solitary, with individuals living alone, except for mothers and dependent offspring. However, most primate species live in groups. Primate groups vary in size, composition, and cohesiveness. Gibbons and siamangs of Southeast Asia and titi monkeys of South America form long-term pair bonds with groups consisting of an adult male and female with their dependent young. Ukaris of South America and ring-tailed lemurs of Madagascar both live in groups of up to 35 individuals containing multiple adult males and females, juveniles, and infants. Gorilla troops typically number between eight and 10 individuals, consisting of multiple females, juveniles, and infants but only one adult male, the silverback. Some primate groups (like gorillas, ukaris, and ring-tailed lemurs) are stable and cohesive over long periods, except for the **dispersal** of some individuals who leave the group. Others, like chimpanzees and spider monkeys, have more fluid social systems, called **fission-fusion**, where groups break up and reunite based on differences in food availability throughout the year. In this section, we'll examine why primates live in groups and who stays, who goes, and why.

Why Do Primates Live in Groups?

Because group living is relatively unusual among mammals but quite common among primates, a central question for primatologists is: Why do primates live in groups? The answer is that primates live in groups when the benefits of feeding competition and/or predation avoidance exceed the costs.

Feeding Competition

As discussed in the previous section, when species feed on high-quality, scarce food (like fruit), larger groups mean there are more individuals competing for access to the resource. The result of this competition takes the form of dominance hierarchies and increased day-range length. A dominance hierarchy is the result of aggressive and submissive interactions, but once established, a dominance hierarchy functions to reduce levels of aggression because all individuals "know their place." Female vervets illustrate the costs and benefits of different dominance ranks (Whitten 1983). Dominant (high-ranking) females spend more time feeding and eat more ripe fruit than subordinates (low-ranking), so they consume more nutrients. This affects their health and **fitness** (an individual's reproductive success relative to that of other individuals; Whitten 1983). Dominants weigh more, start reproducing earlier, and produce more offspring than subordinates do. So why do subordinate females remain in the group? The answer is that larger groups are more successful in competition with other groups. In a long-term study of vervets in Kenya's Amboseli National Park, larger vervet groups had larger and better home ranges, which importantly included access to permanent sources of water. The result? Females in larger groups had shorter **interbirth intervals** (the average length of time between one birth and the next) and higher average infant and female survival rates than the smallest group. In terms of competition for resources, the benefits of being a member of a larger vervet group (even a low-ranking member) outweigh the costs (Cheney and Seyfarth 1987).

Predator Avoidance

While D. L. Cheney and R. M. Seyfarth (1987) found that larger vervet groups had higher average infant and female survival rates, *causes* of mortality differed based on group size. Unlike the small group, mortality in larger groups was almost entirely due to predation, and this highlights another set of costs and benefits of group living. Larger groups are more conspicuous than smaller groups. This is one of the reasons that primates who rely on crypsis to avoid predation (like the slow loris; Figure 6.16) are often solitary. However, some anti-predator behaviors, like shared vigilance duties, alarm calling, and mobbing, are responses to predators that are only available to group-living species (like Hanuman langurs; Figure 6.17). Whether or not a primate is group-living or solitary, it engages in some form of **vigilance**, or watchful behavior to detect potential danger. Often, researchers cannot determine whether vigilance is intended to detect predators or potential competing conspecifics (with predator detection as a side benefit). However, because vigilance interferes with other important behaviors like feeding, resting, or being social, primates who live in groups benefit from sharing the cost of vigilance and reaping the rewards of early predator detection. When a predator is detected, an alarm call is given. We will discuss the information communicated through alarm calls in greater detail in the "Communication" section, but in short, they serve one of two functions: (1) to alert members of the group to the presence of a predator or (2) to alert the predator that it has been detected. In some species, **mobbing** (the act of cooperatively attacking or harassing a predator) accompanies alarm calls. Mobbing involves two or more individuals making repeated advances on a predator, often while vocalizing and/or displaying. The point of mobbing is to drive off or distract the predator long enough for others to escape. Primates have been observed mobbing several species of predators, including chimpanzees, leopards, and eagles, but snakes are the most common targets. Although mobbing often occurs as the predator is approaching, in some cases, it occurs *after* a predator has attacked and escalates to a counter-attack. A group of Coquerel's sifaka mobbed a Madagascar ground boa that had grabbed and was constricting an adult female. The attack, which consisted of loud alarm calls, along with multiple individuals biting and scratching the snake's body and head, resulted in the snake releasing the female sifaka, who survived (Gardner et al. 2015). Similar reports of mobbing resulting in the rescue of a group member from the coils of a boa constrictor have also been reported for white-faced capuchins and moustached tamarins. Such examples clearly illustrate the benefits of group living.

Polyspecific Associations

In regions with a large number of sympatric primate species (Figure 6.13), interactions between species are bound to occur. Often interactions are competitive (more on this in the "Competition for Food" section). However, **polyspecific associations** are different. These are associations between two or more different species in which at least one species changes its behavior to maintain the association. Polyspecific associations have been documented in many New World and Old World primate communities. While some associations are short in duration, others can be semi-permanent. In these cases, species are found more often in association than not. As discussed above, decades of research indicates that primates obtain benefits from living in groups with conspecifics. So why do some primates form associations with other species instead of increasing the size of their own group? Although the specific costs and benefits of polyspecific associations differ in each case, in general, species that form these associations gain foraging or anti-predator benefits while avoiding within-group competition for food that occurs in a larger group of conspecifics.

There are many possible foraging benefits of polyspecific associations. In some cases, one species gains access to a food resource that is otherwise inaccessible. In Manu National Park, in Peru, brown capuchins chase smaller squirrel monkeys away from scarce resources. Despite this, squirrel monkeys maintain the association because the capuchins can crack open palm nuts that squirrel monkeys cannot. Squirrel monkeys then feed on kernels dropped by the capuchins (Terborgh 1984). In Brazil, saddle-back tamarins obtain a slightly different foraging benefit by associating with moustached tamarins. The larger (in body and group size) moustached tamarins flush insects from the upper canopy as they forage. The fleeing insects are captured at high rates by saddle-back tamarins foraging below them (Peres 1992). In other cases, associated species avoid competition for food. In Makokou, Gabon, associations form between greater spot-nosed guenons, moustached guenons, and crowned guenons, despite the fact that these closely related species have very similar diets. Instead of competing for food, the species benefit from reduced indirect competition. Because they encounter food sites together, they avoid visiting a site that might have been depleted by one of the other species if they were foraging separately (Gautier-Hion et al. 1983).

In other cases, the benefit of polyspecific associations is predator avoidance. Like foraging benefits discussed above, anti-predator benefits are variable. In some cases, one species may be particularly good at detecting a specific type of predator and may alert the other species to its presence. In Makokou, Gabon, the guenon species discussed above play different alarm call roles when associated (Gautier-Hion et al. 1983). Moustached guenons, who spend more time close to the ground, are usually the first to alarm call at terrestrial predators. Crowned guenons, who spend more time high in the forest canopy, are most likely to detect aerial predators. Because both species give an alarm call familiar to the other species in the association, everyone benefits from increased predator detection. Sometimes associations result in proactive defense against predators. In the Una Biological Reserve in Bahia, Brazil, a mixed-species group of golden-headed lion tamarins and black-tufted ear marmosets was observed jointly mobbing an ocelot (Raboy et al. 2008). In Taï National Park in Côte d'Ivoire, putty-nosed guenons join Diana monkeys in coordinated mobbing of crowned eagles (Eckardt and Zuberbühler 2004).

Dispersal: Who Goes, Who Stays, and Why?

Whether primates live in groups or are solitary, some individuals must disperse, or leave the place or group of their birth. In the solitary orangutan, females spend about seven years caring for each highly dependent offspring. But once mature, offspring of both sexes leave their mother's home range. If this did not happen, orangutans would not be solitary. In group-living species, one or both sexes must disperse at sexual maturity. Which sex disperses depends on the relative costs and benefits to each. In most primate species, males are the dispersing sex because the benefits of dispersal, including increased access to mates and reduced competition from other males, outweigh the costs. For most female primates, the opposite is true: they usually benefit from remaining **philopatric**, or in the group of their birth. This allows them to maintain strong social alliances so that they can compete successfully against other groups for food. In species where females are typically philopatric, like vervets and macaques, female dispersal only occurs under extreme circumstances, such as when group size falls to precariously low levels. Despite the patterns discussed below, it is important to remember that there is considerable variation in dispersal and numerous exceptions to any rule. Although uncommon, female dispersal has been observed in typically female philopatric species like capuchins and baboons. Likewise, female philopatry has been recorded in species like chimpanzees and muriquis, whose females typically disperse. These exceptions underscore the high degree of behavioral variation and flexibility displayed by primates.

Costs of Dispersal

Transferring into a new group can be fraught with difficulties. Members of both sexes may experience aggression from same-sex members of their chosen group because they are viewed as potential competitors. Aggression toward transferring individuals has been documented in multiple species, and aggression directed toward transferring males is almost universal and can be lethal (Isbell and Van Vuren 1996). During my fieldwork in Kenya, a subadult male patas monkey who had recently dispersed attempted to return to the group into which he was born, which happened to be our study group. The resident male attacked him and severely wounded him. We did not see the subadult male again and assume he died. Transferring females can also experience aggression. Female red howler monkeys are often prevented from joining established groups and can be injured by resident females when they attempt to do so (Crockett and Pope 1988). Even if new group mates are not aggressive, the dispersing individual has lost all alliances with members of their old group and must expend time and energy developing relationships with members of the new group. New group members are often lower in the dominance hierarchy and may produce fewer offspring and suffer from greater mortality. Individuals who disperse into an unfamiliar home range must contend with a lack of ecological knowledge. For species who feed on clumped and seasonal resources like fruit, the lack of knowledge about food sites in a new area can be a significant cost. Lack of knowledge about predators can also put dispersing individuals at greater risk, as appears to be the case for vervets. When their trees deteriorated, vervets in Amboseli National Park, in Tanzania, began to shift home ranges. Use of unfamiliar areas correlated with an increase in vervet disappearances. Most were suspected to have died from leopard predation, probably due to a lack of knowledge about escape routes and refuges in unfamiliar areas (Isbell et al. 1990). Individuals who lose both social allies and knowledge of a specific area when they disperse may suffer even higher costs (Isbell and Van Vuren 1996).

Benefits of Dispersal

If the costs are so high, why do individuals disperse at all? The answer to this question depends on whether we look at the immediate cause of dispersal or the reproductive consequences over the long term. In the short term, the *cause* of dispersal is often eviction by same sex members of the group, as occurs in gibbons, ring-tailed lemurs, red howler monkeys, and other species. In Hanuman langurs, the resident male may be kicked out by bachelor males who invade heterosexual groups during the breeding season. In other cases, maturing individuals may choose to leave their group because they are attracted to individuals in another group. This explanation is supported by the observation that most transfers by males between groups occur during the breeding season, when females are sexually **receptive**, or ready to mate. Among hamadryas baboons of Ethiopia, one cause of female dispersal is abduction of juvenile females by adult males. The male incorporates the female into his harem and mates with her when she reaches adulthood (Swedell and Schreier 2006). In chimpanzees, females disperse because males gain significant benefits from remaining in their **natal group** (the group into which they are born). These benefits include hunting cooperatively and patrolling the community boundary together (Lutz et al. 2016; Stumpf et al. 2009). Other explanations for dispersal are related to enhancing **reproductive success**, or one's genetic contribution to future generations, often measured through number of offspring produced. A male may disperse to enter a group with fewer same-sex individuals, so as to avoid competition for mates. Likewise, dispersing into a group with more members of the opposite sex can increase an individual's mating opportunities. Perhaps the most common explanation for dispersal of at least one sex from the perspective of reproductive success is to avoid **inbreeding**, or mating with close relatives. When close relatives mate, the likelihood that the offspring will inherit two copies of a recessive gene increases. If the trait that these recessive genes code for is harmful, then such matings can result in **inbreeding depression**, or reduced fitness of the population. Evidence for inbreeding avoidance as an explanation for dispersal includes the fact that **natal dispersal**, or dispersal out of the group of one's birth, takes place at sexual maturity and that at least one sex always disperses.

REPRODUCTIVE STRATEGIES

It is important to recognize that primate reproductive strategies have evolved to maximize individual reproductive success. These strategies are divided into those dealing with offspring production and care (parental investment) and those that maximize mating success (sexual selection). Because the reproductive physiology of male and female primates differs (males produce sperm and cannot gestate or lactate; females produce eggs and gestate and lactate), males and females differ with regard to parental investment and sexual selection strategies. Female strategies, on the one hand, focus on obtaining the food necessary to sustain a pregnancy and choosing the best male(s) to father offspring. Male strategies, on the other hand, focus on obtaining access to receptive females.

Parental Investment

Biologically speaking, **parental investment** is any time or energy a parent devotes to the current offspring that enhances its survival (and eventual reproductive success) at the expense of the parent's ability to invest in the next offspring (Trivers 1972). Female primates invest more heavily in offspring than males. Even before conception, females produce energy-laden eggs, and will be responsible for sustaining a fertilized egg until it implants in the uterus. After that, they invest in pregnancy and lactation (Figure 6.1a). Because all of this investment is energetically expensive, female primates can only produce one offspring (or litter) at a time. A species' interbirth interval is determined by the length of time necessary to maximize each offspring's survival without jeopardizing the female's ability to produce the greatest number of offspring possible. If a female invests too little (i.e., weans an offspring too early), she may give birth to many offspring, but very few (if any) of them will survive. If she invests too much (i.e., nurses an offspring even though it could be weaned), she ensures the survival of that individual offspring but will not be able to produce very many during her lifetime. To maximize her reproductive success, a female must invest *just* long enough to ensure the greatest number of offspring survive to reproduce.

We often think of maternal care as a natural, instinctive behavior. Yet this is not the case. Zoos, for example, almost always have nurseries where infants are cared for by zookeepers if their mothers will not care for them. These exhibits are among the most popular because the babies are so cute and so much fun to watch. And the caretaking positions in zoo nurseries are often among the most coveted by zoo personnel for the same reasons. But if maternal behavior is instinctive, why do zoo nurseries even exist? The answer is that in many species, including primates, maternal behavior is not purely instinctual; it is dependent on **social learning** (behavior learned by observing and imitating others), as well. Captive female primates, including gorillas and chimpanzees, who have not had the opportunity to observe their mother or other females care for infants do not know how to care for their own offspring. Although it is preferred that the mother care for her infant, in cases when she will not, humans must step in to ensure the offspring survives. When hand-rearing by humans is necessary, the infant is returned to the group as soon as possible in the hopes that it will learn species-typical behavior from its mother and other conspecifics. Observations such as these indicate that maternal behavior is learned, not innate, and that maternal care is critically important to the social and psychological development of young primates.

Although females invest more in offspring than males, there are some conditions under which males will invest. Male investment takes many forms, ranging from carrying or grooming infants to sharing food with them, to protecting them from **infanticide** (killing of infants of one's own species) or predators, to simply tolerating their presence. A male who has some degree of **paternity certainty**, or confidence that he is the father, is more likely to invest in an offspring than a male who does not because any investment in the offspring *may* increase his own reproductive success. Males appear to use a very simple rule, "Have I recently mated with this infant's mother?", to determine their paternity certainty. For example, male mantled howler monkeys only care for infants they may have fathered while Hanuman langur males protect and never attack infants who might be their own (Borries et al. 1999; Clarke et al. 1998). During my fieldwork in Kenya, I observed the first suspected case of infanticide in patas monkeys (Enstam et al. 2002), committed by the only resident male over a 10-year study period who took over the group too late in the breeding season to have fathered any of the offspring. It is certainly not a perfect rule, and males may sometimes invest in an offspring they did not father. However, this is less costly than killing your own infant.

Sexual Selection

Sexual selection, or selection for traits that maximize mating success, comes in two forms. **Intrasexual selection** is selection for traits that enhance the ability of members of one sex to compete amongst themselves ("*intra*sexual" = within one sex). **Intersexual selection** is selection for traits that enhance the ability of one sex to attract the other ("*inter*sexual" = between the sexes). Intrasexual selection most often operates on males. In the wild, adult females are either pregnant or lactating for most of their adult lives. So the ratio of sexually available males to sexually receptive females (the **operational sex ratio**) usually includes more males than females. The result? Receptive females are a scarce resource over which males compete. Intrasexual selection favors traits that make a male a better competitor (i.e., a winner). Competition between males (hereafter referred to as male-male competition) can take many forms but comes in two main categories: direct competition and indirect competition (just like competition between females for food). Intersexual selection also tends to operate on males, selecting traits that make a male more attractive to females. Females, in turn, choose among potential fathers. Because female primates invest more in offspring production and care than males (see the "Parental Investment" section), they pay a significantly higher cost if the offspring dies before maturity or reaches maturity but does not reproduce. Thus, it benefits a female primate to be choosy, and this requires males to display traits that tell a female why she should choose *him*, and not another male, as her mate.

Intrasexual Selection: Competition for Mates

Figure 6.19a Hamadryas baboons are sexually dimorphic. The male (left) is much bigger than the female (center) and also has different colored fur.

Figure 6.19b In the Simien Mountains of Ethiopia, an adult male gelada baboon displays his large canines.

If females live together in groups, a male (or males) may be able to monopolize access to them. Under such circumstances, intrasexual selection favors traits like large body size (Figure 6.19a) and large canines, which increase a male's competitive ability in fights with other males. Because females don't possess these same traits, males and females of some species look different, which is called **sexual dimorphism** (Figure 6.19a). We will discuss sexual dimorphism in greater detail in the next section. In some species, a single, highly competitive male is able to defend a group of females from other males. Males may use vocalizations, displays, or physical combat to defend their group of females from extra-group males. In other species, it is impossible for a single male to monopolize a group of females. In these species, groups contain multiple females and multiple males. In combat between two males, the stronger, larger male is more likely to win, all else being equal. However, when groups contain multiple males, males have the opportunity to form **coalitions**, or temporary alliances to cooperate in an effort to enhance their competitive ability.

Figure 6.20a An adult male orangutan displaying secondary sexual characteristics including cheek phalanges and a throat sac.

If one male cannot keep another from mating with a female, indirect competition occurs. Indirect competition can take many forms, but in all cases, the males do not interact; they may, in fact, never even see each other. **Sperm competition** occurs when multiple males mate with the same female in relatively close succession. Under such circumstances,

Figure 6.20b An adult male orangutan in a state of arrested development who has not developed secondary sexual characteristics associated with adult males.

the male that produces the greatest quantity of long-lived sperm should have a better chance of fertilizing the female's egg. Evidence for sperm competition comes from correlations between mating system and testes weight, which is used as a proxy for sperm production (Harcourt et al. 1981). Take chimpanzees and gorillas as an example. Chimpanzees live in groups with multiple adult males and females while gorilla troops contain one adult male (the silverback) and multiple females (for more information on social and mating systems, see the next section). Because male chimpanzees cannot keep others from mating with females, producing greater quantities of sperm is perhaps their best way to ensure paternity. Male gorillas who are able to monopolize a group of females (through direct competition with other males) do not need to compete with sperm, and so they do not need to produce it in large amounts. Therefore, although male gorillas are much larger in body size, male chimpanzees have larger testicles to produce more sperm. In other species, males engage in alternative mating strategies. Orangutans are socially solitary, but a single large adult male's territory overlaps the territories of multiple females. The male actively keeps other males out and away from the females. A non-territorial male may compete directly with a territorial male, but this is dangerous and can result in serious injury. Some males avoid this by delaying the development of **secondary sexual characteristics**, or traits associated with sexual maturity. In orangutans, these traits include large cheek phalanges, a throat sac, and large body size (Figure 6.20a). Males that do not develop these traits look like juveniles (Figure 6.20b) and seem to use their non-threatening appearance to sneak into the territories of fully developed males to mate with females. The mechanism that results in the two male morphologies is not well understood, but males lacking secondary sexual characteristics have lower testosterone levels (Marty et al. 2015). Lastly, males may compete indirectly by committing infanticide. Infanticide occurs in many primate species, including red howler monkeys, chacma baboons, crab-eating macaques, diademed sifakas, ring-tailed lemurs, Hanuman langurs, and mountain gorillas. If a male kills a competitor's infant, the mother will resume ovulation more quickly, providing the infanticidal male with an opportunity to father her next infant. Thus, under the right circumstances, an infanticidal male benefits by removing his competitor's genes from the gene pool while adding his own to it.

Figure 6.21a An emperor tamarin carrying twins.

Figure 6.21b A common marmoset family with twins.

Although more rare than male-male competition, sometimes females compete for mates. The callitrichids, the primate family that includes marmosets and tamarins, are unusual in their reproductive pattern. Breeding females often give birth to twins (Figure 6.21a–b), sometimes producing litters twice a year. Another interesting characteristic of callitrichid reproductive behavior is the fact that often only one female reproduces, a phenomenon that is achieved through **reproductive suppression** (Digby et al. 2011). The mechanisms differ across species but generally involve the prevention of reproduction by subordinate females through physiological and/or behavioral means. These subordinate females are often the older daughters of the breeding female. In some species, the dominant female emits chemicals that delay ovulation in subordinates. In others, she physically breaks up matings between males and subordinate females. Regardless of the exact mechanism, the goal is the same: to limit the opportunities for subordinate females to become pregnant. But why? Although a breeding female can give birth to triplets or quadruplets, it is rare for more than two offspring from each litter to survive. Even ensuring the survival of twins is more than the mother can manage by herself. To maximize her offsprings' survival, she needs all group members, including other (reproductive-age) females, to care for her offspring instead of focusing on their own. It is clear that this strategy helps the breeding female's reproductive success. But why would her reproductive-age daughters "agree" to stay in their natal group and help mom raise their siblings instead of dispersing to another group and breeding themselves? If a subordinate female cannot find a group to transfer into as the breeding female, she has two options: stay in her natal group and raise younger siblings, or transfer to another group as a subordinate and raise the offspring of a female to whom she is not related. Because she shares genes with her siblings (50% if they are full siblings, 25% if they are half siblings), some of the subordinate female's genes get passed down if her siblings survive and reproduce. On the one hand, fewer of the female's genes get passed down through siblings (called **indirect fitness**) than if she had produced her own offspring (called **direct fitness**). But, on the other hand, she passes on more genes by raising her siblings than if she helped to raise the offspring of a female to whom she was not related. Not surprisingly, subordinate females rarely leave their natal group unless a breeding position opens in another group.

Intersexual Selection: Mate Choice

As we discussed at the beginning of this section, female primates are choosy because it is more costly for them (in terms of reproductive success) if they produce an offspring that either does not survive or that survives but cannot or does not reproduce. But *what* is it that they are choosing in males? Like all other examples of primate behavior and ecology, there is both species-level and individual-level variation in female choice. In many animals, including humans, females choose a male who can provide important resources, such as food, paternal care, or protection. Examples of such direct benefits are rare in primates, since most females do not require males to supply them these resources. Female mountain gorillas and chacma baboons, however, may choose males based on who can protect them from infanticidal males (Henzi and Barrett 2003; van Schaik and Kappeler 1997). More commonly, female primates obtain indirect (i.e., genetic) benefits from choosing one male over another. Often the specific criteria by which females select mates is unknown. However, if a female chooses a healthy (as indicated by traits like a plush coat, bright coloration, or large body size) or older male, she may obtain genes for her offspring that code for health or longevity. If a male's rank is determined by competitive ability that has a genetic component, females who choose such males may acquire these genes (and qualities) for their offspring. Females in some species appear to prefer new immigrants, sometimes even "sneaking" copulations with males who are not established members of their groups. Such a preference may provide their offspring with novel genes and increase genetic variation (for more about the importance of genetic variation, see Chapter 4). Lastly, female choice does not necessarily imply that females are choosing only *one* male with whom to mate. In many species, females actively choose to mate with multiple males. The most likely explanation for this phenomenon is an attempt to avoid infanticide by ensuring that multiple males think they are possibly the father. This is called **paternity confusion**. In such cases, females may not be choosing mates based on direct (resource-based) or indirect (genetic) benefits but, rather, ensuring that any male who might be in close proximity to her infant after birth will not kill it.

Female choice is often more subtle than male-male competition, so it can be more difficult to study. However, as more research is conducted, we better understand the ways that female primates exert their choice. In many species, females actively solicit sexual interactions with some males and not others. In other cases, females reject advances by some males and not others. Grey-cheeked mangabeys in Kibale National Park, Uganda, exert female choice in multiple ways (Arlet et al. 2007; Smith 1994). They present their hindquarters (which signals interest in mating) significantly more to high-ranking and immigrant males; they refuse to mate with some males; and most mate with multiple males when they are receptive. These results indicate that rather than being passive actors who accept matings with eager males, female primates actively participate in choosing amongst suitors.

Social and Mating Systems

Sometimes the terms *social system* and *mating system* are used interchangeably, but there are important differences between the two terms. A **social system** describes the typical number of males and females of all age classes that live together. A **mating system** describes which male(s) and female(s) mate. Two species can have the same social system but a different mating system and vice versa. For example, the mating system of both orangutans and mountain gorillas is **polygyny**–that is, one male mating with multiple females–but the social systems of these two great apes is very different. The home range of one large adult male orangutan overlaps the home ranges of many females, with whom he mates, but they do not travel together as a cohesive group (Figure 6.22a). Mountain gorillas travel in cohesive one-male, multi-female groups consisting of a silverback male, multiple females, and their dependent young, and the silverback male mates with the females of his group (Figure 6.22b). So how is it that two species can have the same mating system and different social systems or, alternately, the same social system and different mating systems? It all depends on how food, females, and males are distributed.

We can understand primate social and mating systems by thinking of layers of a map. The first layer is food distribution. Because female reproductive success is limited by access to food, females "map onto food" and form the second layer of the map. If food exists in large clumps that can feed multiple individuals (like fruit), females can also exist in "clumps" (i.e., groups) and will benefit from doing so because living in groups helps with defense of food sources. Finally, because male reproductive success is limited by access to females, males "map onto females" forming the third layer of the map. If females live in cohesive groups, one or a few males have the opportunity to monopolize them. If females are widely distributed, it is more difficult (sometimes impossible) for males to monopolize multiple females.

Key: ▪ = adult male; • = adult female; open black circle represents the outline of the male's home range (solitary species) or group's home range; open red circle represents individual female home ranges (solitary species). Illustrations by Karin Enstam Jaffe.

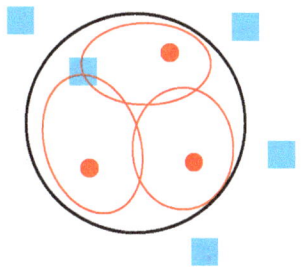

Figure 6.22a *Polygyny in a solitary species, like orangutans.*

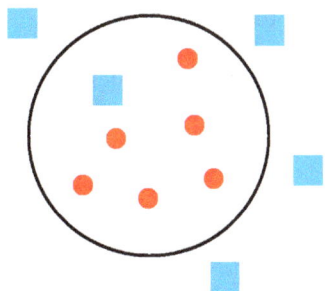

Figure 6.22b *Polygyny in a group-living species with a single-male, multi-female social group, like mountain gorillas.*

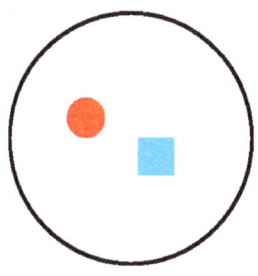

Figure 6.22c *Monogamy in species that form family groups, like gibbons.*

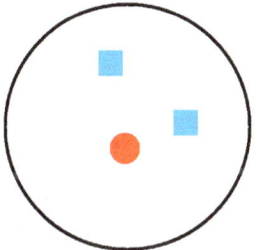

Figure 6.22d *Polyandry in species like tamarins and marmosets.*

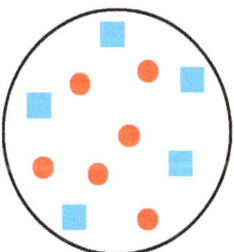

Figure 6.22e *Polygamy in species that live in multi-male, multi-female groups, like vervets.*

When Females Are Solitary

When food is distributed in such a way that females are unable to live in close proximity to each other, they must spread out to avoid too much competition. A male may choose to guard one female, try to monopolize multiple females by himself, cooperate with other males to monopolize multiple females, or cooperate with other males to help raise the offspring of an individual female. The difference in these male strategies is illustrated by the gibbon, orangutan, chimpanzee, and tamarin.

Both gibbon and orangutan females eat fruit found in relatively small patches that does not support groups, so females of both species are solitary. However, the way in which males map onto the distribution of females is quite different. A male gibbon guards a single female, resulting in a **monogamous** mating system (Figure 6.22c). A pair of gibbons form a long-term bond that includes defending a territory and relatively high paternity certainty that results in male care of offspring. Mated pairs defend their territory by calling together in a patterned vocalization called a duet. These coordinated vocalizations tell other gibbons that the territory is occupied and to stay away. Because most males get a mate, male-male competition is relaxed, and there is little pressure for males to develop large body size or weaponry to use in competition with other males. Thus, it is not surprising that male and female gibbons exhibit **sexual monomorphism**, meaning that males and females are similar in body size and often look alike. Because males and females both exclude same-sex competitors, the social group consists of an adult male, an adult female, and their dependent offspring, sometimes referred to as a family group.

Like gibbons, orangutan females are also solitary. But unlike gibbon males, who cannot monopolize access to multiple females, a male orangutan has a very large home range that overlaps the home ranges of two or more females (Figure 6.22a). The females do not regularly travel with each other or the male, but he mates with them, resulting in a polygynous mating system but a solitary social system. Because some males monopolize multiple females, many male orangutans do not have access to females. Male-male competition is intense, and males benefit from large body size, weaponry, and other traits that increase their competitiveness. The result is significant sexual dimorphism. Male orangutans are twice the size of females and have large canines, cheek phalanges, and throat sacs (Figure 6.20a) that help them defend their home range (and females) through direct (fighting) and indirect (territorial vocalizations) competition with other males. As we discussed in the previous section, the competition is so intense that some males remain in a state of arrested development (Figure 6.20b).

Chimpanzees have a fluid social system referred to as fission-fusion. When food is plentiful, female chimpanzees of the same community travel together within their community territory. When food is scarce, the group "fissions" and females travel independently, with their dependent offspring, in their own range but still within the community territory. Because male chimpanzees are philopatric and related to one another, they share more genes in common than males in other primate species who are unrelated. The high degree of relatedness results in high levels of cooperation (see the discussion of chimpanzee cooperative hunting in the "Why Do Primates Live in Groups?" section) and reduced sexual competition between males. Even males who do not father their own offspring have some genes passed on by male relatives who do (this is another example of indirect fitness). Male chimpanzees do compete to be at the top of the dominance hierarchy so as to obtain priority of access to females. However, no male in the community is excluded from mating with community females, so chimpanzees practice **polygamy** as a mating system (in which multiple males mate with multiple females), even though females are solitary for some of the year. Competition between males is relaxed because they are related and all get to mate. This results in reduced sexual dimorphism. Unlike orangutan males, male chimpanzees are only about 25% heavier than females. But like orangutans, male chimpanzees compete indirectly, particularly through sperm competition.

Although there are many examples of multiple males living in groups with multiple females (we'll discuss some examples below), it is rare for multiple males to live with a *single breeding female*, a mating system referred to as **polyandry** (Figure 6.22d). Yet this is the pattern we often see in the callitrichids: tamarins and marmosets. As we discussed in the "Parental Investment" section, due to their rapid reproductive rate and propensity for twinning (Figure 6.21a–b), breeding females need help from all group members to raise their offspring, and they suppress reproduction in other females in their group, effectively making *breeding females* solitary. In some callitrichid species, the dominant male fathers most or all of the offspring, but the males in the group are relatives so they benefit genetically, similar to chimpanzee males (Baker et al. 1993). In other species, males are not related, but the breeding female mates with all the males in the group, so every male has a chance of being the father of the offspring (Díaz-Muñoz 2011). In both cases, males help rear offspring because they cannot afford not to do so. Although social systems differ across tamarin and marmoset species, and even across populations of the same species, polyandry is common among callitrichids but extremely rare in other primates.

SPECIAL TOPIC: WOMEN IN PRIMATOLOGY: MEET "THE TRIMATES"

While many STEM (Science, Technology, Engineering, and Math) fields have traditionally been, and continue to be, dominated by men, primatology has a long history of significant research conducted by women. This is due, in part, to the fact that three of the most well-known primatologists are women, making it clear that this is a field in which women can excel. In the early 1960s, British paleoanthropologist Louis Leakey (see Chapters 9 and 10 for more about Louis Leakey's work) was looking for students to study the great apes in hopes of shedding light on the behavior of our early ancestors. He chose Jane Goodall (Figure 6.23a) to study chimpanzees, Dian Fossey (Figure 6.23b) to study mountain gorillas, and Birute Galdikas (Figure 6.23c) to study orangutans. These three women, sometimes referred to as Leakey's "Trimates," have transformed our understanding of ape (and primate) behavior through their work.

Figure 6.23a Jane Goodall is a primatologist, anthropologist, conservationist and activist. Her research on the Gombe chimpanzees spans over half a century.

Arriving at the Gombe Stream Reserve in Tanzania in 1960, Jane Goodall (Figure 6.23a) was the first scientist to conduct a long-term study of wild nonhuman primates. Until then, most field studies lasted less than a year. By 1961, she had made two astounding observations that forced us to reconsider what differentiates humans from the rest of the primate order: She observed chimpanzees eating a colobus monkey, the first reported evidence of meat eating in our closest relatives (she later observed them hunting and killing other mammals and sharing the meat) and also discovered that chimpanzees make and use tools by stripping leaves off twigs to "fish" for termites. After several decades of study, her work has produced long-term data on chimpanzee mating strategies, mother-infant bonds, and aggression within and between communities. When her study group, the Kasakela community, fissioned in the mid-1970s, she observed males of the larger community attack and kill those of the smaller one. This behavior, which Goodall compared to human warfare, is now known to be typical of wild chimpanzees and is another behavior we share with our closest relatives. In the mid-1980s, Goodall transitioned from field researcher to conservationist and activist, advocating for the humane use of nonhuman animals (Stanford 2017).

In 1967, Dian Fossey (Figure 6.23b) began her long-term study of mountain gorillas and founded the Karisoke Research Center in Rwanda. Through patience and hard work, Fossey habituated several groups of gorillas to the presence of human observers, and their research over several decades has formed the foundation of our understanding of gorilla social behavior, ecology, and life history. Gaining the gorillas' trust was difficult as they were fearful of humans they had known only as poachers. Censuses of the Virunga gorilla population in the 1970s by Fossey and her colleagues estimated a population of fewer than 300. This represented a decline of 40% from the previous decade. The primary causes of this decline were habitat loss and illegal hunting. Fossey's advocacy for mountain gorilla conservation kicked into high gear when, at the end of 1977, poachers killed her favorite gorilla, Digit, as he protected his group. A year later, poachers attacked one of her main study groups and killed several gorillas as they tried to kidnap an infant to sell to a zoo. Her efforts to publicize the killings led to the development of conservation programs that ultimately saved the mountain gorilla. By the end of the 1980s, the population had begun to recover and continues to increase. Tragically, Dian Fossey was murdered in her research cabin at Karisoke in December 1985; the case remains unsolved (Stewart 2017).

Figure 6.23b Dian Fossey was a primatologist and conservationist. She studied mountain gorillas in Rwanda for almost 20 years, until her murder in 1985.

Figure 6.23c Birute Galdikas is an anthropologist, primatologist, and conservationist. Her research and rescue work on behalf of orangutans spans 40 years.

Birute Galdikas (Figure 6.23c) began her study of orangutans in Kalimantan, Borneo, in 1971 and set up a field station called Camp Leakey. Hers was the first long-term study conducted on the Bornean orangutan. Her research still continues, and over 150,000 hours of observational data have been collected by Galdikas and her colleagues, focusing on the life histories of individual orangutans. While conducting her behavioral research, Galdikas discovered that the pet trade and habitat loss were adversely affecting the orangutan population. She began working with the Indonesian government to confiscate orangutans that had been removed from the wild illegally, many of whom ended up as pets. Taking these orphaned orangutans back to Camp Leakey, Galdikas's conservation efforts began to extend beyond advocacy and into rehabilitation and forest preservation (Bell 2017). If you would like to learn more about primate conservation, please see Appendix B.

When Females Live in Groups

When females live together, either because their food is abundant (in the case of folivores) or because their food is distributed in large patches that are worth defending (in the case of frugivores), males have the opportunity to monopolize multiple females. Sometimes a single male is able to monopolize a group of females. Other times, a male may not be able to exclude other males from the group.

Generally speaking, when female groups are small and cohesive, it tends to be easier for a single male to monopolize a group of females. Mountain gorillas, hanuman langurs, red howler monkeys, and patas monkeys are examples of single-male, multi-female groups, which consist of one adult resident male, multiple adult females, and their dependent offspring. The mating system for single-male, multi-female groups is polygyny (Figure 6.22b). Because a relatively small number of males monopolize all the breeding females, there are many adult males who do not have mates. As with orangutans, this results in strong competition between males, resulting in sexual dimorphism where males are much larger than females. In mountain gorillas, fights between silverbacks can be intense. Males can use their large canines to cause serious wounds that may even result in death (Fossey 1983).

When a single male cannot monopolize a group of females, often because the group consists of many females that may be spread out over a wide area, the result is a multi-male, multi-female group consisting of multiple adult males, multiple adult females, and their dependent offspring (Figure 6.22e). Olive baboons, ring-tailed lemurs, and squirrel monkeys are examples of primate species with this type of social system. Because a single male cannot exclude others in the group from mating, the mating system in multi-male, multi-female groups is polygamy, but that does not mean that all males have equal reproductive success. When multiple males live in a group, they often form a dominance hierarchy that determines their priority of access to females in the group. This is similar to the way a female dominance hierarchy determines a female's priority of access to food. Because their place in the hierarchy can affect their reproductive success, males in multi-male groups engage in male-male competition, but because it is rare for males to be excluded from mating altogether, the level of competition, and degree of sexual dimorphism, is less extreme than what we see in polygynous species.

COMMUNICATION

In its most basic form, communication occurs when one individual (the sender) emits a signal that conveys information, which is detected by another individual. We have discussed several aspects of primate sociality in this chapter, all of which require the communication of information between individuals. But, *how* does a female chimpanzee communicate her sexual availability? *How* does a vervet monkey communicate the approach of a leopard or that a python is nearby? *How* does a dominant (or subordinate) macaque signal its place in the dominance hierarchy? *How* do solitary, nocturnal primates, like the slow loris, communicate information about themselves to conspecifics?

Forms of Communication

Primate communication comes in four forms: vocal, visual, olfactory, and tactile. Species vary in their reliance on each. Because it is difficult to see others in the dark, and because nocturnal primates avoid predators by remaining quiet, species like the slow loris and the aye-aye rely heavily on scent-marking to communicate with conspecifics. Diurnal species tend to rely more heavily on visual and vocal forms of communication.

Vocal Communication

Primates use sound to claim and maintain a territory, make contact with other group members, or to communicate danger or threats, among other things. Loud calls are designed to travel great distances and are used in territorial defense by many primate species including indris, orangutans, gibbons, howler monkeys, and siamangs. In dense forest, where visual communication can be difficult, loud calls can be useful in signaling to conspecifics that a group or individual occupies a specific area. Howler monkeys are named for their loud calls, or "roars," which can be heard one kilometer or more away (Schön Ybarra 1986). Howler group roars may act to maintain distance between neighboring groups or keep extra-group males from entering the home range (Schön Ybarra 1986; Sekulic 1982).

Other vocalizations are intended to communicate with individuals in one's own group. These include vocalizations given as part of threat displays or dominance interactions, as well as contact calls that provide information about location to other group members. Baboons have a rich repertoire of vocalizations for communicating with other group members (Fischer et al. 2008; Ransom 1981). Adult males give specific vocalizations during threat displays and physical confrontations. Subordinates "screech" when retreating from a dominant individual, signaling submission. Since baboons rely on membership in their group for finding food and detecting predators, a baboon separated from his group will vocalize in an attempt to regain contact. Young baboons emit their own contact calls when separated from their mothers.

Alarm-calling behavior is widespread in primates. Often, alarm calls serve to notify conspecifics of potential danger, as is the case with vervet monkeys (Figures 6.4a, 6.11b). Research by Dorothy Cheney, Robert Seyfarth, and others has shown that: (1) vervets classify predators based on hunting style; (2) alarm calls convey information to other vervets about that hunting style; and (3) other vervets respond in ways appropriate for evading that type of predator (Seyfarth et al. 1980a). When a vervet gives a "leopard" alarm call [directed at mammalian carnivores like leopards (Figure 6.15a) and dogs], monkeys on the ground climb the nearest tree, while monkeys already in trees stay there or climb higher. Since most mammalian carnivores hunt on the ground, getting into, and staying in, a tall tree is the best option for escape. When the distinct "snake" alarm call is given, vervets stand on their hind legs and look down at the ground. Since snakes, like pythons (Figure 6.15g) are not pursuit predators, locating them so as to avoid them is the best strategy. Lastly, when an "eagle" alarm call is given, vervets look up or run into bushes, both of which are useful responses for avoiding hawks and eagles (Figure 6.15e), which attack from above. Vervets clearly understand the meaning of each type of alarm call, as they respond appropriately even when they do not see the actual predator (Seyfarth et al.1980b). Such **semantic communication**, which involves the systematic use of signals to refer to objects in the environment, was once believed to be unique to humans. It may be a precursor to the symbolic capacities of human language.

Research on other African monkeys indicates that some species use alarm calls to signal to the predator that it has been detected. Diana monkeys, Campbell's guenons, and sooty mangabeys of the Taï forest give alarm calls to leopards but not chimpanzees (Zuberbühler et al. 1997). Because leopards (Figure 6.15a) are stealth predators, they rely on the element of surprise to sneak up on their prey. Alarm calling at leopards appears to tell the leopard that it has been seen and therefore its chance of success will be low. Leopards are more likely to stop hunting after an alarm call has been emitted. Unlike leopards, chimpanzees are pursuit predators and may even use alarm calls to locate potential prey. With such a predator, prey are better off remaining as silent as possible so as not to alert the predator to their location (Boesch and Boesch 1989; Zuberbühler et al. 1999).

Visual Communication

Visual signals are an important component of nonhuman primate behavior, alone or in combination with other forms

Visual Communication

Visual signals are an important component of nonhuman primate behavior, alone or in combination with other forms of communication. Some visual signals are common to all nonhuman primates. For example, **piloerection**, or raising one's hair or fur, is used in aggressive interactions to make an individual appear larger than it actually is. The females of many Old World primate species, including macaques, baboons, and chimpanzees, signal sexual receptivity through changes in the size, shape, and, often, color of their hindquarters, called a **sexual swelling** (Figure 6.24a). The sexual swelling reaches its maximum size at ovulation. When females are not receptive, either because they are pregnant or are nursing, they do not display a sexual swelling (Figure 6.24b). Thus, its presence or absence signals a female's reproductive state. In some species, females use other visual cues to indicate sexual receptivity. Common marmoset females solicit mating through tongue-flicking displays directed at males, while female patas monkeys engage in a more elaborate visual display. When soliciting mating, the female crouches in front of the male and looks back at him while blowing air into her cheeks; she also may drool and curl her tail (Chism et al. 1984).

Figure 6.24a This female hamadryas baboon displays a sexual swelling.

Figure 6.24b A female hamadryas baboon with infant (foreground); note the lack of a sexual swelling (a male is behind her).

Figure 6.25 A male mandrill yawning.

Figure 6.26 A male gelada baboon lip flip.

Monkeys and apes also use a diversity of facial expressions in visual communication. Showing your teeth in a "smile" sends a signal of friendship in humans. Displaying teeth in this way is a sign of anxiety or fear in Old World monkeys. That male mandrill you see "yawning" at your local zoo is actually displaying his teeth to signal tension or threaten a rival (Figure 6.25). Male gelada baboons use "lip flips," in which the gums and teeth are exposed by flipping the upper lip up over the nostrils (Figure 6.26), and "raised eyelids," in which the pale eyelids are exposed by pulling the scalp back as threatening gestures (Aich et al. 1990). Submissive males respond by fleeing or presenting their hindquarters. In the Smithsonian Channel video[1], male gelada baboons use the lip flip in competition with other males.

Figure 6.27 A male mandrill.

Primates also communicate through color. In some species, facial coloration provides information about individual health or status to conspecifics. Mandrills are a good example of this. Female mandrill faces are brighter during ovulation, which may function to communicate reproductive state to males (Setchell et al. 2006). Redness of male mandrill faces is correlated with androgen levels. Thus, facial coloration can, on the one hand, communicate information about competitiveness to other males and information about reproductive fitness to females (Figure 6.27; Setchell et al. 2008). On the other hand, the variation in facial coloration among New World monkeys, ranging from very simple (Figure 6.28a) to highly complex color patterns (Figure 6.28b), appears to be linked to **species recognition**, or the ability to distinguish conspecifics from other species. Species with more complex facial color patterns tend to be those that are sympatric with a larger number of other primate species. In such circumstances, distinct facial coloration and patterning may help individuals recognize conspecifics and reduce the chances of mating with another species (Santana et al. 2012).

Figure 6.28a and 6.28b A ukari displaying bold but simple facial coloration (left). Figure 6.28b A white-bellied spider monkey displaying a complex facial color pattern (right).

1. Smithsonian Channel. June 9, 2017. "Why These Vegetarian Monkeys Have Sharp Predator Teeth." Accessed July 25, 2019. https://www.youtube.com/watch?time_continue=145&v=aC6iYj_EBjY

Olfactory Communication

All primates use scent to communicate. Females secrete chemicals from their **anogenital** region (the area of the anus and genitals) that provide males with information about their reproductive state. In some species, like macaques and chimpanzees, this olfactory signal is enhanced by a sexual swelling (a visual signal; see Figure 6.24a and discussion above). Olfactory communication is particularly important for New World monkeys, lemurs, and lorises. Male and female squirrel monkeys engage in "urine washing," in which an individual urinates on its hands and feet and then uses them to spread urine all over its body. The function of urine washing may include marking trails for other group members to follow, self-cleaning or controlling body temperature, dominance displays, enhanced grasping ability while climbing, or communicating reproductive state (Boinski 1992). During aggressive interactions with other males, male ring-tailed lemurs rub their tails with scent from glands on their wrists and chests. They then waive their tails toward their opponent, who responds with his own "stinky tail" display, physical aggression, or by fleeing (Jolly 1966). Both sexes use their anogenital scent glands to mark substrates (like saplings, fallen trees, or tree trunks) in their group's territory (Jolly 1966). Males also leave visual and scent marks during "spur marking," in which they impregnate a substrate with scent from their wrist gland after using a thorny "spur" near the gland to cut into it (Figure 6.29). Because substrate marking behavior occurs where the ranges of two groups overlap, and increases during the mating season, the primary function is believed to reinforce territorial boundaries (Mertl-Millhollen 1988).

Figure 6.29 A male ring-tailed lemur uses spur marking to deposit scent on a young tree at Berenty Reserve in Madagascar.

Tactile Communication

Tactile communication, or touch, is very important in all primate species. Physical contact is used to comfort and reassure, is part of courtship and mating, and is used to establish dominance and alliances. Grooming is an important and clearly enjoyable form of tactile communication for all primates (Figure 6.30a–d). Not only does grooming serve to clean the skin and fur, removing parasites and debris, but it is an important **affiliative** (non-aggressive) behavior that helps reinforce social bonds, repair relationships, and cement alliances. Among chimpanzees, subordinates groom dominants in an effort to receive benefits such as protection, acceptance, and reciprocal grooming. When yellow baboon females engage in more grooming activity (as both givers and receivers), their offspring have an increased chance of surviving to one year (Silk et al. 2003). Although the mechanism behind this relationship is unknown, close associations with group members may provide females and their young offspring with protection from harassment or access to valuable resources that enhance infant survival. Social integration, as exemplified by grooming, is of significant adaptive value to primates.

Figure 6.30a A group of Japanese macaques grooming each other.

Figure 6.30b Tufted capuchins grooming.

Figure 6.30c A group of gelada baboons grooming.

Figure 6.30d Black-and-white ruffed lemurs groom each other.

THE QUESTION OF CULTURE

It may be surprising in a chapter on nonhuman primates to see a discussion of culture. After all, culture is considered by many, including cultural anthropologists, to be a distinguishing characteristic of humans. Indeed, some anthropologists question claims of culture in primates and other animals. Definitions of animal culture focus on specific behaviors that are unique to one population. Anthropological definitions of *human culture* emphasize shared ideology (e.g., values, morals, beliefs) and symbols, not just behavior. Using this definition, some cultural anthropologists view primates as lacking culture because of the absence of symbolic life (e.g., religion). However, the longer we study primate groups and populations, the more insight we gain into primate behavioral variation. If we define **culture** as the transmission of behavior from one generation to the next through social learning, then we must view at least some of the behavioral variation we see in primates as forms of **cultural tradition,** or a distinctive pattern of behavior shared by multiple individuals in a social group that persists over time (Whitten 2001).

Examples of Culture in Primates

Chimpanzee Culture

Due to both their high level of intelligence and the large number of long-term studies on several different populations, chimpanzees provide the best example of cultural tradition in primates. Research on a variety of animals, including fish, rodents, birds, and monkeys indicate the transmission of a single behavior pattern through social learning, resulting in cultural variation. But chimpanzees, along with orangutans, are the only species other than humans to express cultural variation in *multiple* behavioral patterns. Examining behavioral variation across chimpanzee study sites, researchers have identified over 40 cultural traditions, or distinct behavioral patterns, in chimpanzees (Whiten 2011). These cultural traditions span the gamut from population-specific prey preferences to tool-use techniques, hunting strategies, and social behaviors.

It is not just the sheer number of cultural traditions that make chimpanzee culture so fascinating. It is that each chimpanzee community displays a unique cultural profile defined by a subset of the known traditions. For example, in Tanzania, chimpanzees fish for termites by poking twigs (which they've stripped) into termite mounds. But in Gambia, they use modified twigs to extract honey from holes in trees. In Fongoli, Sénégal, chimpanzees use sticks as "spears" that they stab into tree cavities to hunt for galagos (Figure 6.31). Multiple chimpanzee populations use use a "hammer and anvil" to crack open nuts, but the techniques differ. In some populations, chimps place a nut on a large flat rock and use a stone "hammer" to crack it open; in others, they use pieces of wood. Chimpanzees in Guinea use three stones for nut cracking: one as the anvil, the second one as the hammer, and a third as a wedge to secure the anvil (McGrew 1998). The National Geographic video "Chimps and Tools" (n.d.)[2] provides a glimpse into some of the known variation in chimpanzee tool use. Because the cultural traditions are so diverse and unique, if a researcher can observe enough of a chimpanzee's behavior, that individual can be assigned to a specific community, much in the same way a human being can be associated with a specific culture based on his or her behavior (Whiten 2011).

Figure 6.31 Tool-assisted hunting by a chimpanzee at Fongoli, Sénégal. An adult male chimpanzee uses a tree branch with a modified end to (a–c) stab into a cavity within a hollow tree branch that houses a galago. He ultimately captures the galago as (d) his adolescent brother looks on.

So how do chimpanzee cultures develop, and how does cultural transmission occur? Although we do not know for sure how chimpanzee cultural traditions develop initially, it is possible that different groups invent, either accidentally or deliberately, certain behaviors that other individuals copy. There is little evidence currently to support the idea that chimpanzees actively teach one another a new behavior, so it appears that they learn through observation and practice. This lack of teaching is one reason that some primatologists call the traditions in chimpanzees (and other primates) "pre-culture." However, immigration between communities does appear to be an important avenue of cultural transmission in

---

2. National Geographic. n.d. "Chimps and Tools." Accessed July 25, 2019.
   https://video.nationalgeographic.com/video/00000144-0a1e-d3cb-a96c-7b1fadbd0000

chimpanzees, much as it is between human cultures. Immigrants (typically females) may bring cultural traditions to their new community, which residents observe and learn. Conversely, immigrants may observe and learn a cultural tradition practiced in their new community (Whiten 2011).

Cultural Transmission in Macaques

Figure 6.32 *Japanese macaques using the Jigokudani Hot Spring in Nagano Prefecture, Japan.*

Two monkey species are well known for behavioral variation that has been called "pre-cultural" by some primatologists: Japanese macaques and capuchins. The transmission of unique foraging behaviors through a provisioned group of Japanese macaques on Koshima Island is well known (McGrew 1998). In an effort to keep the monkeys nearby, researchers provided them with piles of sweet potatoes. A juvenile female named Imo spontaneously washed a muddy sweet potato in a stream. This new food-processing technique first spread among other juveniles and then gradually to older individuals. Within 30 years, it had spread across generations, and 46 of 57 monkeys in the group engaged in the behavior. Another example comes from a group living far to the north, in the snowy forests of Honshu. Researchers threw apples into hot springs to record the monkeys' behavior. Not only did the monkeys enter the springs to retrieve the apples, but over multiple years, they learned to immerse themselves in the hot springs to keep warm when not foraging (McGrew 1998; Figure 6.32; watch Japanese macaques using hot springs in the National Geographic video "Meditative Snow Monkeys Hang Out in Hot Springs" (n.d.)[3]. Some primatologists discount the significance of these (pre)cultural traditions since they began as a result of humans providing food to the monkeys and are therefore not "natural" behaviors. However, the behaviors have changed over time, even though the underlying provisioning either did not change or ceased altogether (McGrew 1998). For example, although sweet potato washing started in freshwater, it gradually shifted to seawater, apparently to add salt for flavor. Thirty years after the behavior started, the most common form involved dipping the potato into salt water, even if it was clean. Similarly, female macaques entering the hot springs initially left their young infants at the edge, but today juveniles play and even swim underwater in the hot springs. These examples share several characteristics with human culture, including invention or modification of behavior, transmission of behavior between individuals, and the persistence of the behavior across generations (McGrew 1998).

CONCLUSION

Primates are socially complex and extremely intelligent. Highly adaptable, they display significant variation in diet, habitat, and behavior. By studying primates in their natural habitats, we learn how their behavior and morphology are influenced by ecology, including the foods they eat and the other species with which they live. As our closest living relatives, primates provide important insights into the evolution of human social behavior, language, and culture. These are topics you will learn about in later chapters of this book.

---

3. National Geographic. n.d. "Meditative Snow Monkeys Hang Out in Hot Springs." Accessed July 25, 2019. https://video.nationalgeographic.com/video/short-film-showcase/ 00000149-d415-de71-a9eb-dc9539210000

Review Questions

- If anthropology is the study of humans, why do some anthropologists study primates?
- What is the nature of interactions between primates and other members of their broader ecological communities, including other species of primates?
- What is the difference between a social system and a mating system? Describe the variety of social and mating systems observed in primates. How do primatologists use the distribution of food, females, and males to understand this variation, including the fact that two species can have the same mating system but different social systems? Compare and contrast male and female mating strategies. Why and how, do females choose a potential mate? Why and how do males compete for potential mates?
- What are the costs and benefits of group living? If living in a group is beneficial for most primates, why do some individuals disperse and leave their group? How do the costs and benefits of dispersal differ for males and females?
- Discuss the variation in primate communication. How is communication between primates similar to and different from communication between humans?
- What is the evidence for cultural variation in primates? How do primatologists think cultural transmission occurs in primates? How do you think this process compares to cultural transmission in humans?

Key Terms

Abundance: How much food is available in a given area.

Affiliative: A description of non-aggressive social interactions and associations between individuals.

Allopatric: Two or more species that do not overlap in geographic distribution.

Anogenital: Relating to the anus and genitals.

Basal metabolic rate: The rate at which an individual uses energy when at rest.

Carnivores: Organisms whose diet consists primarily of animal tissue.

Coalition: A temporary group composed of two or more individuals who work together to achieve a common goal. It is often used in reference to male-male competition, such as when two less-competitive males join forces against a more-competitive male.

Competitive exclusion principle: The idea that two species that compete for the exact same resources cannot coexist.

Conspecifics: Members of the same species.

Culture: The transmission of behavior from one generation to the next through observation and imitation.

Cultural tradition: A distinctive pattern of behavior shared by multiple individuals in a social group, which persists over time and is acquired through social learning.

Crypsis: The ability to avoid detection by other organisms.

Day-range length: The distance traveled in a day.

Direct fitness: An individual's genetic contribution to future generations that is due to offspring production.

Dispersal: To leave one's group or area. This may or may not involve entering another group.

Distribution: How food is spread out.

Dominance hierarchy: The ranked organization of individuals established by the outcome of aggressive-submissive interactions.

Feeding: The act of consuming food.

Fission-fusion: Societies in which group composition is flexible, such as chimpanzee and spider monkey societies. Individuals may break up into smaller feeding groups (fission) and combine into larger groups (fusion).

Fitness: An individual's reproductive success relative to other members of the same species.

Foraging: The act of searching for food.

Folivores: Organisms whose diet consists primarily of leaves.

Frugivores: Organisms whose diet consists primarily of fruit.

Home range: The area a group or individual uses over a given period of time (often over a year).

Inbreeding: Reproduction between relatives.

Inbreeding depression: Harmful genetic effects of breeding between relatives.

Indirect fitness: An individual's genetic contribution to future generations that is due to the reproduction of non-descent relatives.

Infanticide: The killing of infants of one's own species.

Insectivores: Organisms whose diets consist primarily of insects.

Intrasexual selection: Selection for traits that enhance the ability of members of one sex to compete amongst themselves.

Interbirth interval: The length of time between successive births.

Intersexual selection: The selection for traits that enhance the ability of the members of one sex to attract the attention of the other.

Mating system: A way of describing which male(s) and female(s) mate.

Mobbing: Cooperatively attacking or harassing a predator.

Monogamous: A mating system in which one male mates with one female.

Natal group: The group into which an organism is born.

Natal dispersal: Emigrating from the group into which one is born.

Niche: The role of a species in its environment; how it meets its needs for food, shelter, etc.

Niche partitioning: The process by which potentially competing species reduce competition by using the environment differently.

Omnivores: Organisms whose diet consists of plant and animal matter.

Operational sex ratio: The ratio of sexually active (or available) males to sexually active (or available) females.

Parental investment: Any time or energy a parent devotes to the current offspring that enhances its survival (and eventual reproductive success) at the expense of the parent's ability to invest in the next offspring.

Paternity certainty: Confidence in which male fathered an offspring.

Paternity confusion: When males are uncertain if they fathered an offspring. This is often a female strategy to reduce the chance of infanticide.

Philopatric: Remaining in the group of one's birth.

Piloerection: Raising one's hair or fur in an effort to look bigger.

Polyandry: A mating system in which multiple males mate with a single breeding female.

Polygamy: A mating system in which multiple males mate with multiple females.

Polygyny: A mating system in which one male mates with multiple females.

Polyspecific associations: Associations between two or more different species involving behavioral changes by at least one of the associated species.

Primate community: All living organisms that occur in an area that includes primates.

Primatologist: A scientist who studies primate behavior and/or ecology.

Primatology: The scientific field that studies primate behavior and/or ecology.

Receptive: A term used to describe females who are ready for sexual reproduction (i.e., not pregnant or nursing).

Reproductive success: An individual's genetic contribution to future generations.

Reproductive suppression: The prevention or inhibition of reproduction of healthy adults.

Secondary sexual characteristics: Characteristics that appear at time of sexual maturity. These are not directly involved in reproduction, but they provide individuals an advantage in courtship and competition for mates.

Semantic communication: The systematic use of signals to refer to objects in the environment.

Sexual dimorphism: When males and females of a species have different morphological traits.

Sexual monomorphism: When males and females of a species have similar morphological traits.

Sexual selection: The selection for traits that increase mating success. This occurs via intersexual selection and intrasexual selection.

Sexual swelling: Area of the hindquarters that change in size, shape and often color over the course of a female's reproductive cycle, reaching maximum size at ovulation. Occurs in many Old World primate species.

Social learning: The idea that new behaviors can be acquired by observing and imitating others.

Social system: A way of describing the typical number of males and females of all age classes that live together.

Solitary: Living alone.

Species recognition: Recognition of conspecifics.

Sperm competition: Competition between sperm of two or more different males to fertilize the same egg.

Sympatric: Two or more species that overlap in geographic distribution.

Territory: A home range whose boundary is defended from intrusion by conspecifics.

Vertebrates: The group of animals characterized by an internal spinal column or backbone. This includes fish, amphibians, reptiles, birds, and mammals.

Vigilance: Watchful behavior to detect or in response to potential danger, usually in the form of predators or potential competitors.

About the Author

Karin Enstam Jaffe

Sonoma State University, karin.jaffe@sonoma.edu

Karin Enstam Jaffe

Dr. Karin Enstam Jaffe has loved primates since she was five years old. As an undergraduate at U.C. San Diego, she participated in projects studying orangutans, langurs, and Mona monkeys. She earned her Ph.D. in Anthropology from U.C. Davis studying vervet and patas monkey anti-predator behavior. Dr. Jaffe has over 20 years of experience studying primate behavior in Kenya and Grenada and at the San Diego Zoo, San Francisco Zoo, and Safari West Wildlife Preserve in Sonoma County, California. She has been a faculty member in the Anthropology Department at Sonoma State University since August 2002. A dedicated teacher-scholar, Dr. Jaffe has won several teaching, scholarship, and mentoring awards, including SSU's Excellence in Teaching Award, Educational Experience Enhancement Award, and the President's Excellence in Scholarship Award. In addition to teaching, she is a Research Associate at Oakland Zoo, where she has been involved in behavioral enrichment research involving ring-tailed lemurs, chimpanzees, and sun bears, as well as a study of the social network of hamadryas baboons.

For Further Exploration

Fossey, Dian. 1983. *Gorillas in the Mist*. London: Hodder & Stoughton.

Goodall, Jane. 1971. *In the Shadow of Man*. Boston: Houghton Mifflin.

Rowe, Noel, and Marc Myers, eds. 2016. *All the World's Primates*. Charleston, Rhode Island: Pogonias Press.

Strier, Karen B. 2017. *Primate Behavioral Ecology*. 5th ed. New York: Routledge.

Primate Info Net (http://pin.primate.wisc.edu/) is an information service of the National Primate Research Center at the University of Wisconsin, Madison. It includes Primate Factsheets, primate news and publications, a list of primate-related jobs, and an international directory of primatology, among other information.

Primate Specialist Group (http://www.primate-sg.org/) is a collection of scientists and conservationists who work in dozens of African, Asian, and Latin American nations to promote research on primate conservation.

References

Aich, H., R. Moos-Heilen, and E. Zimmermann. 1990. "Vocalizations of Adult Gelada Baboons (*Theropithecus gelada*): Acoustic Structure and Behavioural Context." *Folia Primatologica* 55 (3-4): 109-132.

Arlet, Małgorzata E., Freerk Molleman, and Colin Chapman. 2007. "Indications for Female Mate Choice in Grey-Cheeked Mangabeys *Lophocebus albigena johnstoni* in Kibale National Park, Uganda." *Acta Ethologica* 10 (2): 89-95.

Baker, Andrew J., James M. Dietz, and Devra G. Kleiman. 1993. "Behavioural Evidence for Monopolization of Paternity in Multi-Male Groups of Golden Lion Tamarins." *Animal Behaviour* 46 (6): 1,091-1,103.

Bell, Sarah A. 2017. "Galdikas, Birute." In *The International Encyclopedia of Primatology, Volume A-G*, edited by Agustín Fuentes, 445-446. Malden, Massachusetts: John Wiley & Sons.

Boesch, Christophe. 2002. "Cooperative Hunting Roles Among Taï Chimpanzees." *Human Nature* 13 (1): 27-46.

Boesch, Christophe, and Hedwige Boesch. 1989. "Hunting Behavior of Wild Chimpanzees in the Taï National Park." *American Journal of Physical Anthropology* 78 (4): 547-573.

Boinski, S. 1992. "Olfactory Communication among Costa Rican Squirrel Monkeys: A Field Study." *Folia Primatologica* 59 (3): 127-136.

Borries, Carola, Kristin Launhardt, Cornelia Epplen, Jörg T. Epplen, and Paul Winkler. 1999. "Males as Infant Protectors in Hanuman Langurs (*Presbytis entellus*) Living in Multimale Groups: Defence Pattern, Paternity, and Sexual Behaviour." *Behavioral Ecology and Sociobiology* 46 (5): 350-356.

Chapman, Colin A., and Carlos A. Peres. 2001. "Primate Conservation in the New Millennium: The Role of Scientists." *Evolutionary Anthropology: Issues, News, and Reviews* 10 (1): 16-33.

Cheney, D. L., and R. M. Seyfarth. 1987. "The Influence of Intergroup Competition on the Survival and Reproduction of Female Vervet Monkeys." *Behavioral Ecology and Sociobiology* 21 (6): 375-386.

Chism, J. B., T. E. Rowell, and D. Olson. 1984. "Life History Patterns of Female Patas Monkeys." In *Female Primates: Studies of Women Primatologists*, edited by Meredith Small, 175-190. New York: A.R. Liss.

Clarke, Margaret R., Kenneth E. Glander, and Evan L. Zucker. 1998. "Infant-Nonmother Interactions in Free-Ranging Howlers (Alouatta palliata) in Costa Rica." *International Journal of Primatology* 19 (3): 451–472.

Crockett, Carolyn M., and Theresa Pope. 1988. "Inferring Patterns of Aggression from Red Howler Monkey Injuries." *American Journal of Primatology* 15 (4): 289–308.

Díaz-Muñoz, Samuel L. 2011. "Paternity and Relatedness in a Polyandrous Nonhuman Primate: Testing Adaptive Hypotheses of Male Reproductive Cooperation." *Animal Behaviour* 82 (3): 563–571.

Digby, Leslie J., Stephen F. Ferrari, and Wendy Saltzman. (2007) 2011. "Callitrichines: The Role of Competition in Cooperatively Breeding Species." In *Primates in Perspective*, edited by Christina J. Campbell, AugustÍn Fuentes, Katherine C. MacKinnon, Simon K. Bearder, and Rebecca M. Stumpf, 91–10. Second edition, New York: Oxford University Press.

Eckardt, Winnie, and Klaus Zuberbühler. 2004. "Cooperation and Competition in Two Forest Monkeys." *Behavioral Ecology* 15 (3): 400–411.

Enstam, Karin L., and Lynne A. Isbell. 2002. "Comparison of Responses to Alarm Calls by Patas (Erythrocebus patas) and Vervet (Cercopithecus aethiops) Monkeys in Relation to Habitat Structure." *American Journal of Physical Anthropology* 119 (1): 3–14.

Enstam, Karin L., Lynne A. Isbell, and Thomas W. de Maar. 2002. "Male Demography, Female Mating Behavior, and Infanticide in Wild Patas Monkeys (Erythrocebus patas)." *International Journal of Primatology.* 23 (1): 85–104.

Fedigan, Linda Marie. 1990. "Vertebrate Predation in Cebus capucinus: Meat Eating in a Neotropical Monkey." *Folia Primatologica* 54 (3–4): 196–205.

Fischer, Julia, Kurt Hammerschmidt, Dorothy L. Cheney, and Robert M. Seyfarth. 2008. "Acoustic Features of Female Chacma Baboon Barks." *Ethology* 107 (1): 33–54.

Fossey, Dian. 1983. *Gorillas in the Mist*. London: Hodder & Stoughton.

Gardner, Charlie J., Patrick Radolalaina, Mahandry Rajerison, and Harry W. Greene. 2015. "Cooperative Rescue and Predator Fatality Involving a Group-Living Strepsirrhine, Coquerel's Sifaka (Propithecus coquereli), and a Madagascar Ground Boa (Acrantophis madagascariensis)." *Primates* 56 (2): 127–129.

Gautier-Hion, Annie, René Quris, and Jean-Pierre Gautier. 1983. "Monospecific vs. Polyspecific Life: A Comparative Study of Foraging and Antipredator Tactics in a Community of Cercopithecus Monkeys." *Behavioral Ecology and Sociobiology* 12 (4): 325–335.

Harcourt, A. H., P. H. Harvey, S. G. Larson, and R. V. Short. 1981. "Testis Weight, Body Weight and Breeding System in Primates." *Nature* 293 (5,827): 55–57.

Henzi, Peter, and Louise Barrett. 2003. "Evolutionary Ecology, Sexual Conflict, and Behavioral Differentiation among Baboon Populations." *Evolutionary Anthropology* 12 (5): 217–230.

Isbell, Lynne A. 1991. "Contest and Scramble Competition: Patterns of Female Aggression and Ranging Behavior Among Primates." *Behavioral Ecology* 2 (2): 143–155.

Isbell, Lynne A., Dorothy L. Cheney, and Robert M. Seyfarth. 1990. "Costs and Benefits of Home Range Shifts Among Vervet Monkeys (Cercopithecus aethiops) in Amboseli National Park, Kenya." *Behavioral Ecology and Sociobiology* 27 (5): 351–358.

Isbell, Lynne A., and Dirk Van Vuren. 1996. "Differential Costs of Locational and Social Dispersal and Their Consequences for Female Group-Living Primates." *Behaviour* 133 (1–2): 1–36.

Jolly, Alison. 1966. *Lemur Behavior: A Madagascar Field Study*. Chicago: University of Chicago Press.

Lutz, Clayton L., Duane R. Diefenbach, and Christopher S. Rosenberry. 2016. "Proximate Influences on Female Dispersal in White-Tailed Deer." *Journal of Wildlife Management* 80 (7): 1,218–1,226.

Marty, Pascal R., Maria A. van Noordwijk, Michael Heistermann, Erik P. Willems, Lynda P. Dunkel, Manuela Cadilek, Muhammad Agil, and Tony Weingrill. 2015. "Endocrinological Correlates of Male Bimaturism in Wild Bornean Orangutans." *American Journal of Primatology* 77 (11): 1,170–1,178.

McGrew, W. C. 1998. "Culture in Nonhuman Primates?" *Annual Review of Anthropology* 27 (1): 301–328.

Mertl-Millhollen, Anne S. 1988. "Olfactory Demarcation of Territorial but Not Home Range Boundaries by *Lemur catta*." *Folia Primatologica* 50 (3–4): 175–187.

National Geographic. n.d. "Chimps and Tools." Accessed July 25, 2019. https://video.nationalgeographic.com/video/00000144-0a1e-d3cb-a96c-7b1fadbd0000

National Geographic. n.d. "Meditative Snow Monkeys Hang Out in Hot Springs." Accessed July 25, 2019. https://video.nationalgeographic.com/video/short-film-showcase/00000149-d415-de71-a9eb-dc9539210000

Nekaris, K. Anne-Isola, Richard S. Moore, E. Johanna Rode, and Bryan G. Fry. 2013. "Mad, Bad, and Dangerous to Know: The Biochemistry, Ecology, and Evolution of Slow Loris Venom." *The Journal of Venomous Animals and Toxins Including Tropical Diseases* 19 (1): 21.

Peres, Carlosa. 1992. "Prey-Capture Benefits in a Mixed-Species Group of Amazonian Tamarins, *Saguinus fuscicollis* and *S. mystax*." *Behavioral Ecology and Sociobiology* 31 (5): 339–347. https://doi.org/10.1007/bf00177774.

Raboy, Becky E., Gustavo R. Canale, and James M. Dietz. 2008. "Ecology of *Callithrix kuhlii* and a Review of Eastern Brazilian Marmosets." *International Journal of Primatology* 29 (2): 449–467.

Ransom, Timothy W. 1981. *Beach Troop of the Gombe*. East Brunswick, New Jersey: Bucknell University Press.

Santana, Sharlene E., Jessica Lynch Alfaro, and Michael E. Alfaro. 2012. "Adaptive Evolution of Facial Colour Patterns in Neotropical Primates." *Proceedings of the Royal Society B: Biological Sciences* 279 (1,736): 2,204–2,211.

Schön Ybarra, M. A. 1986. "Loud Calls of Adult Male Red Howling Monkeys (*Alouatta seniculus*)." *Folia Primatologica* 47 (4): 204–216.

Schwitzer, Christoph, Russell A. Mittermeier, Anthony B. Rylands, Federica Chiozza, Elizabeth A. Williamson, Elizabeth J. Macfie, Janette Wallis, and Alison Cotton. 2017. *Primates in Peril: The World's 25 Most Endangered Primates 2016–2018*. Arlington, VA: IUCN SSC Primate Specialist Group (PSG), International Primatological Society (IPS), Conservation International (CI), and Bristol Zoological Society.

Sekulic, Ranka. 1982. "The Function of Howling in Red Howler Monkeys (*Alouatta seniculus*)." *Behaviour* 81 (1): 38–54.

Setchell, Joanna M., Tessa Smith, E. Jean Wickings, and Leslie A. Knapp. 2008. "Social Correlates of Testosterone and Ornamentation in Male Mandrills." *Hormones and Behavior* 54 (3): 365–372.

Setchell, Joanna M., E. Jean Wickings, and Leslie A. Knapp. 2006. "Signal Content of Red Facial Coloration in Female Mandrills (*Mandrillus sphinx*)." *Proceedings of the Royal Society B: Biological Sciences* 273 (1599): 2395–2400.

Seyfarth, R. M., D. L. Cheney, and P. Marler. 1980a. "Monkey Responses to Three Different Alarm Calls: Evidence of Predator Classification and Semantic Communication." *Science* 210 (4,471): 801–803.

Seyfarth, Robert M., Dorothy L. Cheney, and Peter Marler. 1980b. "Vervet Monkey Alarm Calls: Semantic Communication in a Free-Ranging Primate." *Animal Behaviour* 28 (4): 1,070–1,094.

Silk, Joan B., Susan C. Alberts, and Jeanne Altmann. 2003. "Social Bonds of Female Baboons Enhance Infant Survival." *Science* 302 (5,648): 1,231–1,234.

Smith, David Glenn. 1994. "Male Dominance and Reproductive Success in a Captive Group of Rhesus Macaques (*Macaca mulatta*)." *Behaviour* 129 (3): 225–242.

Smithsonian Channel. June 9, 2017. "Why These Vegetarian Monkeys Have Sharp Predator Teeth." Accessed July 25, 2019. https://www.youtube.com/watch?time_continue=145&v=aC6iYj_EBjY

Stanford, Craig B. 2017. "Goodall, Jane." In *The International Encyclopedia of Primatology, Volume A–G*, edited by Agustín Fuentes, 471–472. Malden, Massachusetts: John Wiley & Sons.

Stewart, Kelly. 2017. "Fossey, Dian." In *The International Encyclopedia of Primatology, Volume A–G*, edited by Agustín Fuentes, 432–433. Malden, Massachusetts: John Wiley & Sons.

Stumpf, R. M., M. Emery Thompson, M. N. Muller, and R. W. Wrangham. 2009. "The Context of Female Dispersal in Kanyawara Chimpanzees." *Behaviour* 146 (4–5): 629–656.

Swedell, Larissa, and Amy Schreier. 2006. "Male Aggression toward Females in Hamadryas Baboons: Conditioning, Coercion, and Control." In *Sexual Coercion in Primates and Humans*, edited by Martin N. Muller and Richard W. Wrangham, 244–268. Cambridge, Massachusetts: Harvard University Press.

Terborgh, John. 1984. *Five New World Primates: A Study in Comparative Ecology*. Princeton: Princeton University Press.

Trivers, Robert L. 1972. "Parental Investment and Sexual Selection." In *Sexual Selection and the Descent of Man, 1871–1971*, edited by Bernard Campbell, 136–179. Chicago: Aldine.

van Schaik, Carel P., and Peter M. Kappeler. 1997. "Infanticide Risk and the Evolution of Male-Female Association in Primates." *Proceedings of the Royal Society B: Biological Sciences* 264 (1,388): 1,687–1,694.

Whiten, Andrew. 2011. "The Scope of Culture in Chimpanzees, Humans and Ancestral Apes." *Philosophical Transactions of the Royal Society of London B: Biological Sciences* 366 (1,567): 997–1,007.

Whitten, Patricia L. 1983. "Diet and Dominance among Female Vervet Monkeys (*Cercopithecus aethiops*)." *American Journal of Primatology* 5 (2): 139–159.

Wiens, Frank, and Annette Zitzmann. 2003. "Social Structure of the Solitary Slow Loris *Nycticebus coucang* (Lorisidae)." *Journal of Zoology* 261 (1): 35–46.

Zuberbühler, Klaus, David Jenny, and Redouan Bshary. 1999. "The Predator Deterrence Function of Primate Alarm Calls." *Ethology* 105 (6): 477–490.

Zuberbühler, Klaus, Ronald Noë, and Robert M. Seyfarth. 1997. "Diana Monkey Long-Distance Calls: Messages for Conspecifics and Predators." *Animal Behaviour* 53 (3): 589–604.

Acknowledgements

The author is grateful to the editors for the opportunity to contribute to this open-source textbook. She thanks Stephanie Etting for her encouragement and support during the writing of this chapter. Her suggestions, along with comments made by two anonymous reviewers on an earlier version of this chapter, improved the final version considerably. Finally, she thanks all the primatologists who came before her, especially her advisor, Lynne A. Isbell, for their tireless efforts to understand the behavior and ecology of the living primates. Without their work, this chapter would not have been possible.

Figure Attributions

Figure 6.1a Snow monkey baby milk time by Daisuke tashiro is used under a CC BY-SA 2.0 License.

Figure 6.1b Stone tool use by a capuchin monkey by Tiago Falótico is used under a CC BY-SA 4.0 License.

Figure 6.2 Laikipia location map by Nairobi123 is used under a CC BY-SA 3.0 License.

Figure 6.3a Female patas monkey with infant by Karin Enstam Jaffe is under a CC BY-NC 4.0 License.

Figure 6.3b Patas habitat in Laikipia, Kenya by Karin Enstam Jaffe is under a CC BY-NC 4.0 License.

Figure 6.3a Monkey (27996706462) by Martie Swart from Johannesburg, South Africa is under a CC BY 2.0 License.

Figure 6.4b Vervet habitat in Laikipia, Kenya by Karin Enstam Jaffe is under a CC BY-NC 4.0 License.

Figure 6.5 Karin Enstam Jaffe observing patas monkeys in Laikipia, Kenya by Rebecca Chancellor is under a CC BY-NC 4.0 License.

Figure 6.6a Spectral Tarsier Tarsius tarsier (7911549768) by Bernard DUPONT from FRANCE has been modified (cropped) and is used under a CC BY-SA 2.0 License.

Figure 6.6b Mountain gorilla (Gorilla beringei beringei) eating by Charles J Sharp creator QS:P170,Q54800218 is used under a CC BY-SA 4.0 License.

Figure 6.7 Food abundance and food scarcity by Karin Enstam Jaffe original to Explorations: An Open Invitation to Biological Anthropology is under a CC BY-NC 4.0 License.

Figure 6.8 Food distribution patterns by Karin Enstam Jaffe original to Explorations: An Open Invitation to Biological Anthropology is under a CC BY-NC 4.0 License.

Figure 6.9 Food distribution patterns of folivores, frugivores, and insectivores a derivative work by Karin Enstam Jaffe original to Explorations: An Open Invitation to Biological Anthropology is under a CC BY-NC 4.0 License. [Includes Green fruit tree, Lemon tree, and Ladybug image, all from publicdomainvectors.org designated to the public domain (CC0)].

Figure 6.10 Termite mound-Tanzania by Vierka Maráková, Slovakia (Krokodild) has been designated to the public domain (CC0).

Figure 6.11a Patas Monkey Jr by alex roberts from San Francisco, USA is used under a CC BY-SA 2.0 License.

Figure 6.11b Chlorocebus pygerythrus by Xlandfair at English Wikipedia has been designated to the public domain (CC0).

Figure 6.11c Male Olive Baboon 2 by ryan harvey from Portland, OR is used under a CC BY-SA 2.0 License.

Figure 6.11d Komba ušatá2 by Petr Hamerník is used under a CC BY-SA 4.0 License.

Figure 6.12 Muriquis 3 by Mônica Imbuzeiro is used under a CC BY-SA 4.0 License.

Figure 6.13 Examples of primate communities table original to Explorations: An Open Invitation to Biological Anthropology by Karin Enstam Jaffe is under a CC BY-NC 4.0 License.

Figure 6.14a Lion tailed macaque eating Lizard by Prasadchangarath is used under a CC BY-SA 4.0 License.

Figure 6.14b Gombe Stream NP Beute by Ikiwaner is used under a GNU License.

Figure 6.15a Leopard africa by JanErkamp at the English Wikipedia is used under a CC BY-SA 3.0 License.

Figure 6.15b Jaguar (Panthera onca palustris) male Rio Negro 2 by Charles J Sharp creator QS:P170,Q54800218 is used under a CC BY-SA 4.0 License.

Figure 6.15c Male Tiger Ranthambhore (3646793728) by Koshy Koshy is used under a CC BY 2.0 License.

Figure 6.15d Fosa fotovideo by Bertal is used under a CC BY-SA 3.0 License.

Figure 6.15e Martial eagle (Polemaetus bellicosus) by Charles J Sharp creator QS:P170,Q54800218 is used under a CC BY-SA 4.0 License.

Figure 6.15f Harpy Eagle with wings lifted by Jonathan Wilkins is used under a CC BY-SA 3.0 License.

Figure 6.15g Python natalensis G. J. Alexander by Graham J. Alexander, University of the Witwatersrand has been designated to the public domain (CC0).

Figure 6.16 Slow Loris by Jmiksanek is used under a CC BY-SA 3.0 License.

Figure 6.17 Monkey group by Natureloverperson is used under a CC BY-SA 4.0 License.

Figure 6.18a Deforestation near Bukit Tiga Puluh NP by Aidenvironment (1998) is used under a CC BY-SA 2.0 License.

Figure 6.18b Lemur poaching 004 by author who does not wish to be named for safety reasons is used under a CC BY-SA 3.0 License.

Figure 6.19a Dierenpark Emmen baboon (2679944324) by robin bos from heerenveen, the Netherlands is used under a CC BY 2.0 License.

Figure 6.19b Male Gelada Baboon, Chenek, Simien Mountains (6190375633) by Rod Waddington from Kergunyah, Australia has been modified (cropped) and is used under a CC BY-SA 2.0 License.

Figure 6.20a Azy (orangutan) at the Indianapolis Zoo by Tom Britt is used under a CC BY 2.0 License.

Figure 6.20b Orangutan male (15433476577) by Russ is used under a CC BY 2.0 License.

Figure 6.21a Emperor Tamarin with babies sf by Brocken Inaglory is used under a CC BY-SA 3.0 License.

Figure 6.21b Family of Common Marmoset – REGUA – Brazil MG 9480 (12930855765) by Francesco Veronesi from Italy is used under a CC BY-SA 2.0 License.

Figure 6.22 Social and Mating Systems by Karin Enstam Jaffe original to Explorations: An Open Invitation to Biological Anthropology is under a CC BY-NC 4.0 License.

Figure 6.23a Jane Goodall HK by Jeekc is used under a CC BY-SA 3.0 License.

Figure 6.23b US-223658 Dian Fossey (2925879356) by Mary-Lynn is used under a CC BY 2.0 License.

Figure 6.23c Dr Birute Galdikas by Simon Fraser University – University Communications is used under a CC BY 2.0 License.

Figure 6.24a Sexual swelling in female Hamadryas baboon by Mamoritai is used under a CC BY-SA 2.0 License.

Figure 6.24b Hamadryas baboon at Giza Zoo by Hatem Moushir 36 by Hatem Moushir is used under a CC BY-SA 3.0 License.

Figure 6.25 Mandrill 08 by SuperJew is used under a CC BY-SA 4.0 License.

Figure 6.26 BabouinGeladaAuReveil by BluesyPete is used under a CC BY-SA 3.0 License.

Figure 6.27 Mandrill 09 by SuperJew is used under a CC BY-SA 4.0 License.

Figure 6.28a Uakari by Coada dragos is used under a CC BY-SA 4.0 License.

Figure 6.28b Ateles belzebuth (White-bellied spider monkey) 2 by Ewa is used under a CC BY 2.0 License.

Figure 6.29 Lemur catta 004 by Alex Dunkel (Visionholder) is used under a CC BY-SA 3.0 License.

Figure 6.30a Yakushima macaques grooming each other by Grendelkhan is used under a CC BY-SA 4.0 License.

Figure 6.30b Tufted capuchin monkeys grooming session III by Adrian Soldati is used under a CC BY-SA 4.0 License.

Figure 6.30c Baboons Wunania 012018 by Kim Toogood is used under a CC BY-SA 4.0 License.

Figure 6.30d Black-and-white ruffed lemur 03 by Mattis2412 has been designated to the public domain (CC0 1.0).

Figure 6.31 Pan troglodytes, tool use in Senegal by J. D. Pruetz, P. Bertolani, K. Boyer Ontl, S. Lindshield, M. Shelley, and E. G. Wessling is used under a CC BY 4.0 License.

Figure 6.32 Jigokudani hotspring in Nagano Japan 001 by Yosemite is used under a CC BY-SA 3.0 License.

Chapter 7: Understanding the Fossil Context

Sarah S. King, Ph.D., Cerro Coso Community College

Lee Anne Zajicek, B.A.

Learning Objectives

- Describe how the Age of Wonder advanced scientific inquiry and helped develop modern anthropological methods.
- Identify the different types of fossils and describe how they are formed.
- Discuss relative and chronometric dating methods, the type of material they analyze, and their applications.
- Describe the methods used to reconstruct past environments.

FOSSIL STUDY: AN EVOLVING PROCESS

Mary Anning and the Age of Wonder

Figure 7.1 An oil painting of Mary Anning and her dog, Tray, prior to 1845. The "Jurassic Coast" of Lyme Regis is in the background. Notice that Anning is pointing at a fossil!

Mary Anning (1799–1847) is likely the most famous fossil hunter you've never heard of (Figure 7.1). Anning lived her entire life in Lyme Regis on the Dorset coast in England. As a woman, born to a poor family, with a minimal education (even by 19th-century standards), the odds were against Anning becoming a scientist (Emling 2011, xii). It was remarkable that Anning was eventually able to influence the great scientists of the day with her fossil discoveries and her subsequent hypotheses regarding evolution.

The time when Anning lived was a remarkable period in human history because of the Industrial Revolution in Britain. Moreover, the scientific discoveries of the 18th century set the stage for great leaps of knowledge and understanding about humans and the natural world. Barely a century earlier, Sir Isaac Newton had developed his theories on physics and become the president of the Royal Society of London (Dolnick 2011, 5). In this framework, the pursuit of intellectual and scientific discovery became a popular avocation for many individuals, the vast majority of whom were wealthy men (Figure 7.2).

Figure 7.2 A Walk at Dusk, 1830-1835, by Caspar David Friedrich. The prehistoric world fascinated scholars and was an accepted part of Earth's history, even if explanation defied non-secular thought.

Figure 7.3 The "Jurassic Coast" of Lyme Regis: the home of fossil hunter Mary Anning.

In spite of the expectations of Georgian English society to the contrary, Anning became a highly successful fossil hunter as well as a self-educated geologist and anatomist. The geology of Lyme Regis, with its limestone cliffs, provided a fortuitous backdrop for Anning's lifework. Now called the "Jurassic Coast," Lyme Regis has always been a rich source for fossilized remains (Figure 7.3). Continuing her father's passion for fossil hunting, Anning scoured the crumbling cliffs after storms for fossilized remains and shells. The work was physically demanding and downright dangerous. In 1833, while searching for fossils, Anning lost her beloved dog in a landslide and nearly lost her own life in the process (Emling 2011).

Around the age of 10, Anning located and excavated a complete fossilized skeleton of an ichthyosaurus ("fish lizard"). She eventually found *Pterodactylus macronyx* and a 2.7-meter *Plesiosaurus*, considered by many to be her greatest discovery (Figure 7.4). These discoveries proved that there had been significant changes in the way living things appeared throughout the history of the world. Like many of her peers, including Darwin, Anning had strong religious convictions. However, the evidence that was being found in the fossil record was contradictory to the Genesis story in the Bible. In *The Fossil Hunter: Dinosaurs, Evolution, and the Woman Whose Discoveries Changed the World*, Anning's biographer Shelley Emling (2011, 38) notes, "the puzzling attributes of Mary's fossil [ichthyosaurus] struck a blow at this belief and eventually helped pave the way for a real understanding of life before the age of humans."

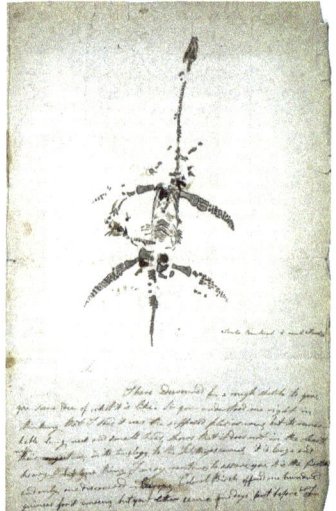

Figure 7.4 Plesiosaurus, illustrated and described by Mary Anning in an undated handwritten letter.

Intellectual and scientific debate now had physical evidence to support the theory of evolution, which would eventually result in Darwin's seminal work, *On the Origin of Species* (1859). Anning's discoveries and theories were appreciated and advocated by her friends, intellectual men who were associated with the Geological Society of London. Regrettably, this organization was closed to women, and Anning received little official recognition for her contributions to the field of natural history and paleontology. Even today, Anning's contributions are largely overlooked, a wrong that will be hopefully corrected. It is clear that Anning's knowledge, diligence, and uncanny luck in finding magnificent specimens of fossils earned her unshakeable credibility and made her a peer to many antiquarians (Emling 2011).

Fossil hunting is still providing evidence and a narrative of the story of Earth. Mary Anning recognized the value of fossils in understanding natural history and relentlessly championed her theories to the brightest minds of her day. Anning's ability to creatively think "outside the box"—skillfully assimilating knowledge from multiple academic fields—was her gift to our present understanding of the fossil record. Given how profoundly Anning has shaped how we, in the modern day, think about the origins of life, it is surprising that her contributions have been so marginalized. Anning's name should be on the tip of everyone's tongue. Fortunately, at least in one sense of the word, it is. The well-known tongue twister, below, was actually written about Mary Anning:

> She sells sea-shells on the sea-shore
>
> The shells she sells are sea-shells, I'm sure
>
> For if she sells sea-shells on the sea-shore
>
> Then I'm sure she sells sea-shore shells.
>
> —T. Sullivan (1908)

Developing Modern Methods

Figure 7.5 Ammonites are very common and date as far back as the early Jurassic with many variations. They are the fossilized remains of extinct water creatures that are characterized by tightly coiled shells. This ammonite has been cut in half to reveal the intricate interior structure and polished.

Prior to the 19th century, the overwhelming majority of Westerners believed that the physical appearances of humans and all living things were unchanged since creation and that "Creation" was the work of "God," as specified by the Holy Scriptures. To even consider that humans and animals might have evolved over time was practically an admission that the Christian God had made mistakes that needed correction in His creation of Earth and all living things (Emling 2011, 38). Thus, the Bible was viewed as a literal and rigid history of the world, and there was no tolerance for the possibility of natural forces in science to bring about change in speciation. To think otherwise was considered heresy and was punishable by excommunication from the Church—or even death. The limited vision imposed by the Church on this matter significantly restricted the way scholars could formulate hypotheses about natural history (Emling 2011, 39). In 1650, Bishop James Ussher made a famous calculation based on his study of the Old Testament that Creation occurred on Sunday (the first day of Creation), October 23, 4004 B.C. (Barr 1984, 575). Ussher's chronology made sense in the face of limited evidence and the historical detail documented in the Bible. Many learned men, including Martin Luther, had made similar calculations using the Bible (Braterman 2013). Other physical evidence, such as prehistoric henges or megaliths, neatly fell into this timeline that the world was, at most, 6,000 years old. A dinosaur bone was discovered shortly after Ussher's chronology had been published, but it was considered to have belonged to a giant human as the term "dinosaur" ("terrible lizard") was not used until 1842. Fossils such as ammonites (Figure 7.5), vertebrae, and belemnites were often found in layers of crumbling cliffs. However, they were not recognized as the fossilized remains of creatures both **extinct** (terminated or vanished) and **extant** (still surviving). Instead, fossils were used in folk medicine or treasured as amulets for luck or protection. Because of a lack of evidence to the contrary and the overwhelming pressure of the Church, natural science was bordering on stagnation, and folklore unofficially explained most poorly understood natural phenomena. Simply put, "scientists were still trying to fit geologic evidence into Biblical chronology" (Einhard 1998).

However, during the Scientific Revolution, Scotsman James Hutton hypothesized about the formation of Earth and provided a much longer timeline of events, which would eventually support the theory of evolution. Hutton's theory of **Deep Time** was crucial to the understanding of fossils. Deep Time gave the history of Earth enough time—4.543 billion years—to encompass continental drift, the evolution of species, and the fossilization process. A second Scotsman, Charles Lyell, propelled Hutton's work into his own theory of **uniformitarianism**, the doctrine that Earth's geologic formations are the work of slow geologic forces. Uniformitarianism was a theory that clashed with the church's doctrine of **catastrophism**, the belief that Earth's formation was due to a set of relatively quick biblical catastrophic events. Noah's flood, as described in the book of Genesis, is an example of a catastrophic event. Lyell's three-volume work, *Principles of Geology* (1830-1833), was influential to naturalist Charles Darwin (see Chapter 2 for more information on Darwin's work). In fact, Lyell's first volume

Figure 7.6 Murexsul (Miocene) This fossil was found at the Naval Weapons Center, China Lake, California, in 1945. The fossil was buried deep in the strata and was pulled out of the ground along with a crashed "Fat Boy" missile after atomic missile testing (S. Brubaker, March 9, 2018, pers. comm).

accompanied Darwin on his five-year voyage around the world on the *HMS Beagle* (1831-1836). The concepts proposed by Lyell gave Darwin an opportunity to apply his working theories of evolution by natural selection and a greater length of time with which to work. These resulting theories were important scientific discoveries and paved the way for the "Age of Wonder," or the second Scientific Revolution (Holmes 2010, xvi).

The work of Anning, Darwin, Lyell, and others laid the foundation for the modern methods we use today. Though anthropology is focused on humans and our primate relatives (and not dinosaurs as many people wrongly assume), you will see that methods developed in paleontology, geology, chemistry, biology, and physics are often applied in anthropological research. In this chapter, you will learn about the primary methods and techniques employed by biological anthropologists to answer questions about **fossils**, the mineralized copies of once-living organisms (Figure 7.6). Ultimately, these answers provide insights into human evolution. Pay close attention to ways in which modern biological anthropologists use other disciplines to analyze evidence and reconstruct past activities and environments.

EARTH: IT'S OLDER THAN DIRT

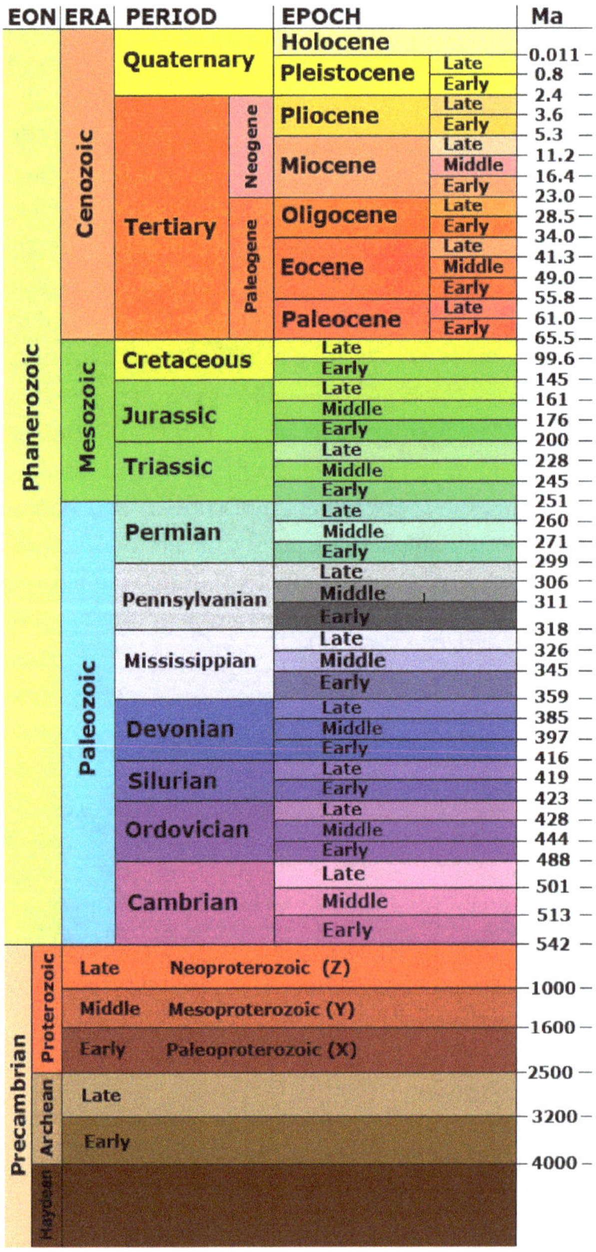

Scientists have developed precise and accurate dating methods based on work in the fields of physics and chemistry. Using these methods, scientists are able to establish the age of Earth as well as approximate ages of the organisms that have lived here. Earth is roughly 4.6 billion years old, give or take a few hundred million years. The first evidence for a living organism appeared around 3.5 billion years ago (**bya**). That is a huge amount of time to conceptualize, and many changes have taken place within that time. The scale of geologic time can seem downright overwhelming. In order to organize and make sense of Earth's past, geologists break up that time into subunits. These subunits are human-made divisions along Earth's timeline in the same way that inches and centimeters are human-made units that are used to divide up distance. The largest subunit is the **eon**. An eon is further divided into **eras**, and eras are divided into **periods**. Finally, periods are divided into **epochs** (see Figure 7.7) (Williams 2004, 37). Currently, we are living in the Phanerozoic eon, Cenozoic era, Quaternary period, and probably the Holocene epoch—though there is considerable academic debate about which epoch we are currently in.

Though these divisions are human-made and, to some extent, arbitrary, they are based on major changes and events recorded in the geologic record. Events like significant shifts in climate or mass extinctions can be used to mark the end of one geologic time unit and the beginning of another. However, it is important to remember that these borders are not real in a physical sense; they are merely helpful organizational guidelines for scientific research. The boundaries are not

Figure 7.8 *The Chooz Nuclear Power, in a valley in Ardennes, France, is a reminder that human activity impacts the planet greatly.*

Figure 7.7 *The geologic time scale showing eons, eras, periods, epochs, and the correlating time frame.*

236 | Understanding the Fossil Context

fixed, and there can be significant debate regarding exact dates and names of particular periods and epochs. For instance, the current epoch has been traditionally known as the **Holocene**. It began around 10 thousand years ago (**kya**) during the warming period after that last major ice age. Some anthropologists argued that it shouldn't be called the Holocene because it might not be a new epoch; perhaps it is simply a warm blip in a larger epoch that includes the Pleistocene. Today, there is lots of evidence to indicate human-driven climate change is warming the world and changing the environmental patterns faster than the natural cyclical processes. This has led some scientists within the stratigraphic community to argue for a new epoch beginning around 1950 with the Nuclear Age called the **Anthropocene** (Monastersky 2015; Waters et al. n.d.). Nobel Laureate Paul Crutzen places the beginning of the Anthropocene much earlier—at the dawn of the Industrial Revolution, with its polluting effects of burning coal (Crutzen and Stoermer 2000, 17–18). Geologist William Ruddiman argues that the epoch began 5,000–8,000 years ago with the advent of agriculture and the buildup of early methane gases (Ruddiman et al. 2008). Regardless of when the Anthropocene started, the major event that marks the boundary is the warming temperatures and mass extinction of nonhuman species caused by human activity (Figure 7.8). Researchers now declare that "human activity now rivals geologic forces in influencing the trajectory of the Earth System" (Steffen et al. 2018, 1).

Geologic Processes

Through the study of fossils, anthropologists are able to learn a great deal about the history of Earth. If you were to closely examine the map of the world, you might notice that the seven continents seem to have outlines that could fit together if rotated and adjusted like puzzle pieces (Figure 7.9). Moreover, the geologic features of those puzzle pieces fit together and reveal many similarities. For instance, the White Cliffs of Dover, England, geologically match La Côte d'Albâtre (the Alabaster Coast) across the English Channel in France (Figures 7.10 and 7.11).

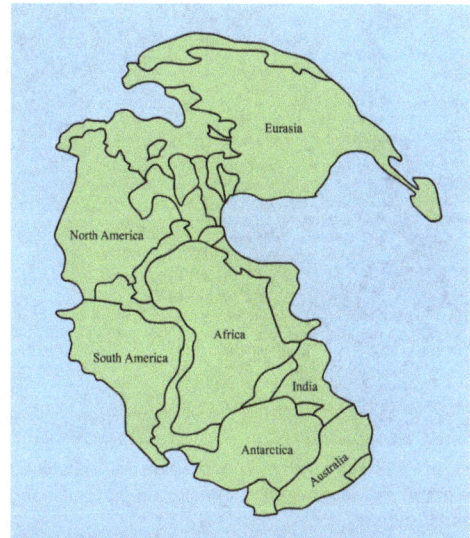

Figure 7.9 Map of Pangea reflecting the way our current continents fit into the landmass.

Figure 7.10 The White Cliffs of Dover, England, with the English Channel in the foreground.

The shapes of the continents are easier to see from above and when looking at a map. From this perspective, it is not a far reach of the imagination to see how the shapes could fit together. However, in 1596, long before the advent of flight or space travel that would give such a perspective to a person studying geography, Abraham Ortelius theorized about the way the continents were shaped. Ortelius came up with the concept that one supercontinent called **Pangea** had existed much earlier in Earth's history (USGS 2012). Approximately 200 million years ago (**mya**), Pangea started to slowly break apart, with the resulting pieces of land shifting and moving through the process of **continental drift**. In the late Triassic (roughly 135 mya), Pangea broke into two supercontinents called Laurasia and Gondwanaland, with additional movement that changed the physical representation of the landmasses and resulted in our current land configuration of seven continents. It is important to remember that continental drift continues to this day and will continue for the life of our planet. In another 250 million years, the map of Earth will look significantly different than it does today.

Figure 7.11 The geologically similar cliffs across the English Channel along La Côte d'Albâtre (Alabaster Coast) in France.

Figure 7.12 The landscape of the San Andreas Fault is scarred by the movement of tectonic plates during earthquakes.

Ortelius's theory made sense in some respects; after all, was it just sheer coincidence that the continents shared such complementary shapes? Yet the problem was that there was no scientific way to explain how continental drift occurred. Remember, too, that up until the late 1700s, the concept of Deep Time did not exist. In the absence of these vital pieces of information, it was impossible to explain what force would have been strong enough or how there was enough time in the history of the world to allow for the movement of huge masses of land to the various corners of the planet. In 1912, an answer was proposed, using the fossil record as evidence. Alfred Wegener used the fossilized remains of a fern, *Glossopteris*, that have been found on nearly every continent. He theorized that the only way this ancient plant could have existed in all of those areas was if the landmasses had been connected at some point in Earth's early history. With this evidence (and much more), Wegener was able to develop his **Tectonic Plate Theory**. Simply put, Earth's landmasses are relatively "thin, brittle fragments floating on top of hot, squishy material" (Murck 2001, p. 16). There is bound to be movement, even of large fragments. Furthermore, there are ridges or shelves in the Atlantic and Pacific Oceans that reflect the shifting of the planet's crust. This theory not only supports the breakup of Pangea but also provides the basis for our current understanding of how earthquakes work. Physicists monitor the movement of tectonic plates for earthquake activity along known fault lines such as the San Andreas in California (Figure 7.12).

Besides the examples provided above, Pangea is also supported by the evidence found in the fauna of the fossil record. At the Gray Fossil Site in Gray, Tennessee, for instance, fossilized remains of the red panda (*Pristinailurus bristoli*) dating back four million years to the late Miocene era have been discovered (Figure 7.13). Red pandas are considered a "living fossil" because they have changed so little in millions of years and because they are represented in the fossil record. Today, red pandas are endangered and found exclusively in China and Nepal. Thus, the existence of the red panda in the Miocene in the Appalachian Mountains but living only in Asia today is clear evidence that the red panda moved freely and that our continents were part of a supercontinent (Wallace and Wang 2004, 556).

Figure 7.13 Fossils of the red panda, a close ancestor of this modern red panda, were found in Gray, Tennessee. The animal is now only found in Asia; specifically, in China and Nepal.

FOSSILS: PRESERVING PREHISTORIC LIFE

Taphonomy

Figure 7.14 Taphonomy focuses on what happens to the remains of an organism, like this coyote, after death.

Most of the evidence of human evolution comes from the study of the dead. To obtain as much information as possible from the remains of once-living creatures, one must understand the processes that occur after death. This is where **taphonomy** comes in (Figure 7.14). Taphonomy can be defined as the study of what happens to an organism after death (Komar and Buikstra 2008, 189; Stodder 2008). It includes the study of how an organism becomes a fossil. However, as you'll see throughout this book, the majority of organisms never make it through the full fossilization process.

Taphonomy is extremely important in biological anthropology, especially in subdisciplines like bioarchaeology (study of human remains in the archaeological record) and zooarchaeology (the study of faunal remains from archaeological sites). It is so important that many scientists have recreated a variety of burial and decay experiments to track taphonomic change in modern contexts. These contexts can then be used to understand the taphonomic patterns seen in the fossil record (uniformitarianism at work; see Reitz and Wing 1999, 122–141).

An example of taphonomic study in action comes from Iron Age England (circa 750 B.C.E. to 43 C.E.). The Iron Age in southern England has a rich and diverse burial record. Since there is no universal or "normative" burial rite, taphonomic study is crucial to figuring out what cultural and ritual processes were operating at this time. Suddern Farm, an Iron Age site in Hampshire, England, includes a cemetery as well as isolated burials outside the cemetery and burials in ritual pits accompanied by the remains of feasting (King 2014, 187).

One of these pit burials, identified as P78, presents an interesting taphonomic case. He was a young adult male approximately 18–25 years old at the time of his death. His remains showed multiple sharp-force and penetrating wounds acquired around the time of his death. There were also carnivore tooth marks on the head of his right femur. These tooth marks provide an important taphonomic clue about how this individual was treated after death. P78 not only met a violent end, but his body was also allowed to lie exposed to the elements and animal scavengers before burial. If an individual is buried immediately, or protected prior to burial, animals do not have the opportunity to gnaw on the bones and flesh (Komar and Buikstra 2008, 196–200). Most Iron Age burials from this site were buried without exposure to scavengers, so P78 stood out as different. He was also buried in a pit when the majority of individuals at Suddern Farm were buried in the cemetery. He was not treated in the same way as the other dead in his community (King 2010, 136–139), and it is useful for us to consider why. P78 may represent a special ritual burial associated with violence or punishment. By better understanding the processes that occur in and to the body after death, we can reconstruct the cultural, biological, and geologic processes that affect remains.

Taphonomic analysis can also give us important insights into the development of complex thought and ritual in human evolution. In Chapter 11, you will see the first evidence of recognized burial practices in hominins. Taphonomy helped to establish whether these burials were simply the result of natural processes or intentionally constructed by humans (Klein 1999, 395; Straus 1989). Deliberate burials often include the body placed in a specific position, such as supine (on the back) with arms crossed over the chest or in a flexed position (think fetal position) facing a particular direction. If bones have evidence of a carnivore or rodent gnawing on them, it can be inferred that the remains were exposed to scavengers after death (as with P78 above). Going back further in time, taphonomic evidence may tell us how our ancestors died. For instance, several australopithecine fossils show evidence of carnivore tooth marks and even punctures from saber-toothed cats, indicating that we weren't always the top of the food chain. The Bodo cranium, a *Homo erectus* cranium from Middle Awash Valley, Ethiopia, shows cut marks made by stone tools, indicating an early example of possible defleshing activity in our human ancestors (White 1986).

Preservation of Biological Remains

As we can only study the evidence that gets left behind in the fossil and archaeological record, preservation is a key topic in anthropological research. This chapter is concerned with the fossil record; however, there are other forms of preserved remains that provide anthropologists with information about the past. You've undoubtedly heard of mummification, likely in the context of Egyptian or South American mummies. However, bog bodies and ice mummies are further examples of how remains can be preserved in special circumstances. It is important to note that fossilization is a process that takes much longer than the preservation of bog bodies or mummies.

The most important element in the preservation of remains is a stable environment. This means that the organism should not be exposed to significant fluctuations in temperature, humidity, and weather patterns. Changes to moisture and temperature cause the organic tissues to expand and contract repeatedly, which will eventually cause microfractures and break down (Stodder 2008). Wetlands are a particularly good area for preservation because they allow for rapid permanent burial and a stable moisture environment. That is why many fossils are found in and around ancient lakes and river systems.

Bog bodies are good examples of wetland preservation. Peat bogs are formed by the slow accumulation of vegetation and silts in ponds and lakes. The conditions are naturally **anaerobic** (without oxygen). Much of the bacteria that causes decay is already present in our gut and can begin the decomposition process shortly after death during putrefaction (Booth et al. 2015). Since oxygen is necessary for the body's bacteria to break down organic material, the decay process is significantly slowed or halted in anaerobic conditions. Throughout western Europe in the Bronze and Iron Ages, individuals were buried in these bogs. When they were found thousands of years later, they resembled recent burials. The hair, skin, clothing, and organs were exceptionally well preserved in addition to the bones and teeth (Eisenbeiss 2016; Ravn 2010). Preservation was so good in fact that archaeologists could identify the individuals' last meals and re-create tattoos found on their skin.

Extreme cold can also halt the natural decay process. A well-known **ice mummy** is Otzi, a Copper Age man found in the Alps (Vidale et al. 2016). As with the bog bodies, his hair, skin, clothing, and organs were all well preserved. Recently, archaeologists were able to identify his last meal (Maixner et al. 2018). It was high in fat, a necessity when trying to survive in the extreme cold.

In the Andes, ancient peoples would bury human sacrifices throughout the high peaks in a sacred ritual called Capacocha (Wilson et al. 2007). The best-preserved mummy to date is called the "Maiden" or "Sarita" because she was found at the summit of Sara Sara Volcano. Her remains are over 500 years old, but she still looks like the 15-year-old girl she was at the time of her death, as if she had slept for 500 years. A Ripina Van Winkle, if you will (Reinhard 2006).

Finally, arid environments can also contribute to the preservation of organic remains. As discussed with waterlogged sites, much of the bacteria that is active in breaking down bodies is already present in our gut and begins the putrefaction process shortly after death. Arid environments deplete organic material of the moisture that putrefactive bacteria need to function (Booth et al. 2015). When that occurs, the soft tissue like skin, hair, and organs can be preserved. It is similar to the way a food dehydrator works to preserve meat, fruit, and vegetables for longterm storage. There are several examples of arid environments spontaneously preserving human remains, including catacomb burials in Austria and Italy (Aufderheide 2003, 170 and 192–205).

FOSSILIZATION

Though much of our knowledge about human evolution relies on evidence derived from fossils, it is important to realize that fossils only represent a tiny fraction of creatures that existed in the past. It would be impossible to calculate the exact amount, but the vast majority of animals that once lived do not make it into the fossil record. The reason for such a small number is that it is extremely difficult for an organism to become a fossil. There are many stages involved and if the process is disturbed at any of the stages, the organism will fail to become a fossil. After all, organisms are set up to deteriorate after we die. Bacteria, insects, scavengers, weather, and environment all aid in the process that breaks down organisms so their nutrients, molecules, and elements can be returned to Earth to maintain ecosystems (Stodder 2008). **Fossilization**, therefore, is the preservation of an organism against these natural decay processes (Figure 7.15).

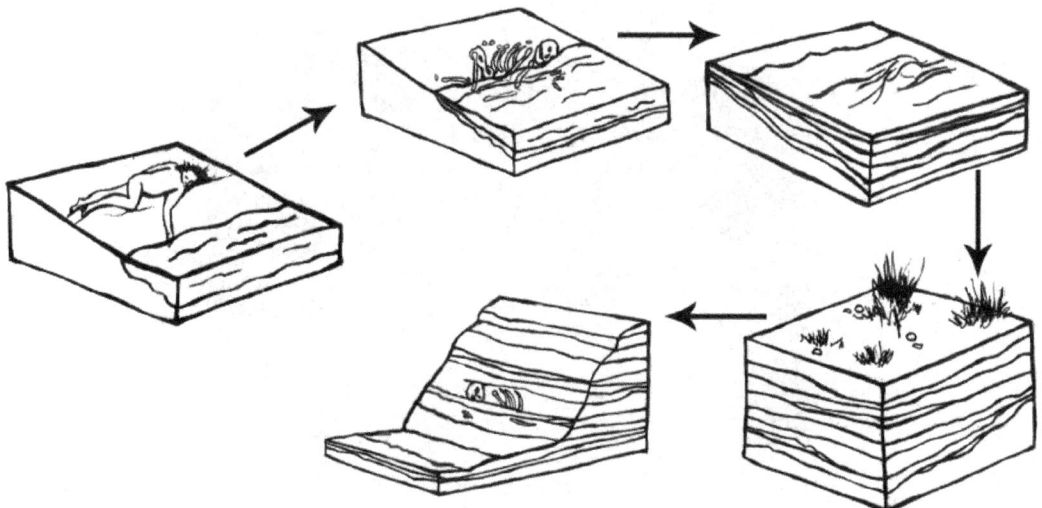

Figure 7.15 A simplified illustration of the fossilization process from the organism's death to its eventual discovery by paleoanthropologists.

For fossilization to occur, several important things must happen. First, the organism must be protected from things like bacterial activity, scavengers, and temperature and moisture fluctuations. Since soft tissue like organs, muscle, and skin are more easily broken down in the decay process, they are less likely to be preserved except in rare circumstances. Bones and teeth, however, last much longer and are more likely to be preserved in the fossil record (Williams 2004, 207).

The next important step in the fossilization process is sediment accumulation. The sediments cover and protect the organism from the environment. They, along with water, provide the minerals that will eventually become the fossil (Williams 2004, 31). Sediment accumulation also provides the pressure needed for mineralization to take place. **Lithification** is when the weight and pressure of the sediments squeeze out extra fluids and replace the voids, that appear in the remains as they decay, with minerals from the surrounding sediments. Finally, we have **permineralization**. This is when the organism is fully replaced by minerals from the sediments. A fossil is really a mineral copy of the original organism (Williams 2004, 31).

Types of Fossils

Plants

Plants make up the majority of fossilized materials. One of the most common plants existing today, the fern, has been found in fossilized form many times. Other plants that no longer exist or the early ancestors of modern plants come in fossilized forms as well. It is through these fossils that we can discover how plants evolved and learn about the climate of Earth over different periods of time.

Another type of fossilized plant is **petrified wood**. This fossil is created when actual pieces of wood—such as the trunk of a tree—mineralize and turn into rock. Petrified wood is a combination of silica, calcite, and quartz, and it is both heavy and brittle. Petrified wood can be colorful and is generally aesthetically pleasing because all the features of the original tree's composition are illuminated through mineralization (Figure 7.16). There are a number of places all over the world where petrified wood "forests" can be found, but there is an excellent assemblage in Arizona, at the Petrified Forest National Park. At this site, evidence relating to the environment of the area some 225 mya is on display.

Figure 7.16 An exquisite piece of petrified wood.

Human/Animal Remains

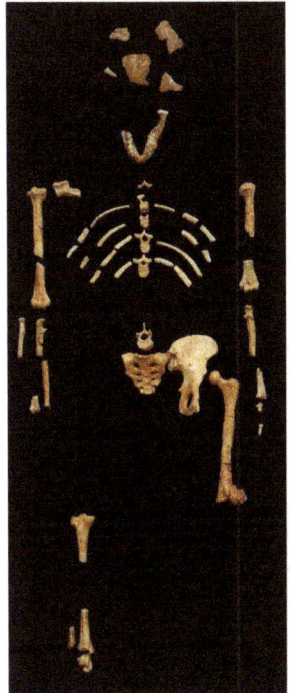

Figure 7.17 "Lucy" (AL 288-1), *Australopithecus afarensis*.

We are more familiar with the fossils of early animals because natural history museums have exhibits of dinosaurs and prehistoric mammals. However, there are a number of fossilized hominin remains that provide a picture of the fossil record over the course of our evolution from primates. The term **hominins** includes all human ancestors who existed after the evolutionary split from chimpanzees and bonobos, some six to seven mya. Modern humans are *Homo sapiens*, but hominins can include much earlier versions of humans. One such hominin is "Lucy" (AL 288-1), the 3.2 million-year-old fossil of *Australopithecus afarensis* that was discovered in Ethiopia in 1974 (Figure 7.17). Until recently, Lucy was the most complete and oldest hominin fossil, with 40% of her skeleton preserved (see Chapter 9 for more information about Lucy). In 1994, an *Australopithecus* fossil nicknamed "Little Foot" (Stw 573) was located in the World Heritage Site at Sterkfontein Caves ("the Cradle of Humankind") in South Africa. Little Foot is more complete than Lucy and possibly the oldest fossil that has so far been found, dating to at least 3.6 million years (Granger et al. 2015). Through tedious excavation, the specific ankle bones of the fossil were extricated from the matrix of concrete-like rock, revealing that the bones of the ankles and feet indicate bipedalism (University of Witwatersrand 2017).

Both the Lucy and Little Foot fossils date back to the Pliocene (5.8 to 2.3 mya). Older hominin fossils from the late Miocene (7.25 to 5.5 mya) have been located, although they are much less complete. The oldest hominin fossil is a fragmentary skull named *Sahelanthropus tchadensis*, found in Northern Chad and dating to circa seven mya (Lebatard et al. 2008).

The fossils of animals can be simple or complex, from worms to mammals. The fossils of primates provide information regarding the backstory of humankind. It is through the discovery, dating, and study of primate and early hominin fossils that we find physical evidence of the evolutionary timeline of humans. Without a complete cranium (or other fossilized remains), it is difficult to tell exactly what was going on in the fossil record. Only a small number of living things will ever become fossilized. Furthermore, it is reasonable to assume that of the existing fossilized remains, many remain hidden in glaciated rock, in caves, or in the ground. (See "Special Topic: Cold Case Naia" for a particularly interesting cave discovery.)

Amber

Figure 7.18 A piece of Baltic amber with an ant trapped inside.

Figure 7.19 A few amber pieces that have been turned into beautiful pendants.

Amber is the fossilized sap of coniferous trees. Sometimes pieces of amber contain inclusions such as air bubbles or insects that become trapped in the sap (Figure 7.18). This beautiful fossil comes in a variety of colors from light gold to orange red to even green. For this reason, amber is frequently polished to a high luster and used in jewelry (Figure 7.19). Raw Baltic amber is also known as succinite and can be over 40 million years old. It comes from the cold Baltic region of northern Europe. Baltic amber is often worn for pain relief by teething infants or individuals with arthritis because succinic acid is released when warmed by body heat. The notoriety of amber increased significantly when it was featured in the highly fictionalized

Understanding the Fossil Context | 243

Jurassic Park film franchise. In the film, they were able to extract dinosaur DNA from the blood inside a fossilized mosquito. Rest assured, at the time of this writing, amber is not being used as the genetic basis for the regeneration of extinct dinosaurs, although the recent discovery of a tick that fed off of dinosaur blood that is trapped in amber has renewed interest in the idea (Pickrell 2017).

Asphalt

Figure 7.20 *This is a recreation of how animals tragically came to be trapped in the asphalt lake at the La Brea Tar Pits.*

Asphalt, a form of crude oil, can also yield fossilized remains. Asphalt is commonly referred to in error as tar because of its viscous nature and dark color. A famous fossil site from California is La Brea Tar Pits in downtown Los Angeles (Figure 7.20). In the middle of the busy city on Wilshire Boulevard, asphalt (not tar) bubbles up through seeps (cracks) in the sidewalk. The La Brea Tar Pits Museum provides an incredible look at the both extinct and extant animals that lived in the Los Angeles Basin 40,000–11,000 years ago. These animals became entrapped in the asphalt during the Pleistocene and perished in place. Even today, in several directions from the museum, small invertebrates such as worms and insects are still being entrapped as the asphalt seeps up from the ground. Ongoing excavations have yielded millions of fossils, including **megafauna** such as American mastodons and incomplete skeletons of extinct species of dire wolves, *Canis dirus*, and the saber-toothed cat, *Smilodon fatalis* (Figures 7.21 and 7.22). Fossilized remains of plants have also been found in the asphalt. Between the fossils of animals and those of plants, paleontologists have a good idea of the way the Los Angeles Basin looked and the climate in the area many thousands of years ago.

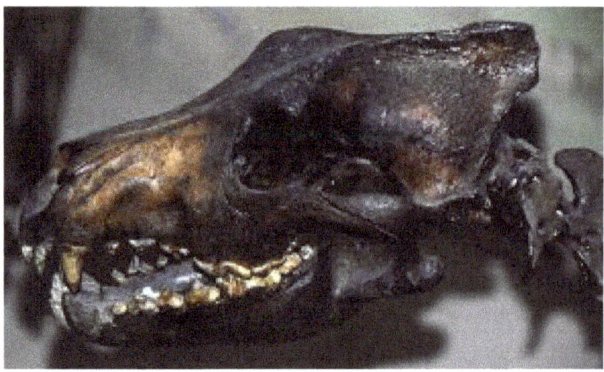

Figure 7.21 *A dire wolf (C. dirus) found at the La Brea Tar Pits.*

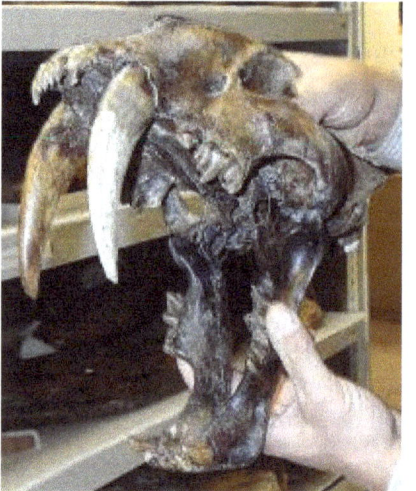

Figure 7.22 *The fearsome jaws of the saber-toothed tiger (Smilodon fatalis) found at the La Brea Tar Pits.*

Igneous Rock

Most fossils are found in sedimentary rock. This type of rock that has been formed from deposits of minerals over millions of years in bodies of water on Earth's surface. Some examples include shale, limestone, and siltstone. Sedimentary rock typically has a layered appearance. However, fossils have been found in igneous rock as well. Igneous rock is volcanic rock that is created from cooled molten lava. It is rare for fossils to survive molten lava, and it is estimated that only 2% of all fossils have been found in igneous rock (Ingber 2012). Part of a giant rhinocerotid skull dating back 9.2 mya to the Miocene was discovered in Cappadocia, Turkey, in 2010. The fossil was a remarkable find because the eruption of the Çardak caldera was so sudden that it simply dehydrated and "baked" the animal (Antoine et al. 2012).

Trace Fossils

Depending on the specific circumstances of weather and time, even footprints can become fossilized. Footprints fall into the category of **trace fossils**, which includes other evidence of biological activity such as nests, burrows, tooth marks, shells. When you consider how quickly our footprints on the ground or in sand disappear, you must also realize how rare it is that footprints can become fossilized. A well-known example of trace fossils are the Laetoli footprints in Tanzania (Figure 7.23). (You can read more about the Laetoli footprints in the Special Topics box at the end of this section.)

Figure 7.23 Just a few of the early hominin footprints that fossilized at Laetoli.

Other fossilized footprints have been discovered around the world. At Pech Merle cave in the Dordogne region of France, archaeologists discovered two fossilized footprints. They then brought in indigenous trackers from Namibia to look for other footprints. The approach worked as many other footprints belonging to as many as five individuals were discovered with the expert eyes of the trackers (Pastoors et al. 2017). These footprints date back 12,000 years (Granger Historical Picture Archive 2018).

Some of the more unappealing but fascinating trace fossils are bezoars and coprolite. Mary Anning found **bezoars**, or hard, concrete-like substances in the intestines of fossilized creatures. Bezoars start off like the hair balls that cats and rabbits accumulate from grooming but become hard, concrete-like substances in the intestines. If an animal with a hairball dies before expelling the hair ball mass *and* the organism becomes fossilized, that mass becomes a bezoar.

You may remember that in the *Harry Potter* books, Professor Snape discusses bezoars on the first day of Potions Class (Rowling 1998, p. 137). Later, the bezoar is crucial in saving Ron Weasley when he's poisoned (Rowling 2005, p. 398).

Anning also found **coprolite**, or fossilized dung. The Dean of Westminster, geologist and paleontologist William Buckland (1784–1856), first recognized the value of coprolite, but it was Anning who provided him with specimens. One of the best collections of coprolites is affectionately known as the "Poozeum." The collection includes a huge coprolite named "Precious" (Figure 7.24). Coprolite, like all fossilized materials, can be **in matrix**—meaning that the fossil is embedded in secondary rock. As unpleasant as it may seem to work with coprolites, remember that the organic material in dung has mineralized or has started to mineralize; therefore, it is no longer soft and is generally not smelly. Also, just as a doctor can tell a lot about health and diet from a stool sample, anthropologists can glean a great deal of information from coprolite about the diets of ancient animals and the environment in which the food sources existed. For instance, 65 million-year-old grass *phytoliths* (microscopic silica in plants) found in dinosaur coprolite in India revealed that grasses had been in existence much earlier than scientists initially believed (Taylor and O'Dea 2014, 133).

Figure 7.24 An extremely large (and yet somehow endearing) coprolite named "Precious".

Pseudofossils

Figure 7.25 A beautiful example of dendrites, a type of pseudofossil. It's easy to see how the black crystals look like plant growth.

Pseudofossils are not to be mistaken for fake fossils, which have vexed scientists from time to time. A fake fossil is an item that is deliberately manipulated or manufactured to mislead scientists and the general public. In contrast, pseudofossils are not misrepresentations but rather misinterpretations of rocks that look like true fossilized remains (S. Brubaker, personal communication, March 9, 2018). Pseudofossils are the result of impressions or markings on rock, or even the way other inorganic materials react with the rock. A common example is dendrites, the crystallized deposits of black minerals that resemble plant growth (Figure 7.25). Other examples of pseudofossils are unusual or odd-shaped rocks that include various concretions and nodules. An expert can examine a potential fossil to see if there is the requisite internal structure of organic material such as bone or wood that would qualify the item as a fossil.

SPECIAL TOPIC: LAETOLI FOOTPRINTS

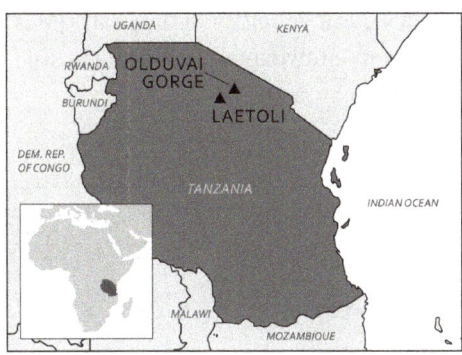

Figure 7.26 Location of Laetoli site in Tanzania, Africa, with Olduvai Gorge nearby.

In 1974, British anthropologist Mary Leakey discovered fossilized animal tracks at Laetoli (Figure 7.26), not far from the important paleoanthropological site at Olduvai Gorge in Tanzania. A few years later, a 27 meter trail of hominin footprints were discovered at the same site. These 70 footprints, now referred to as the Laetoli Footprints, were created when early humans walked in wet volcanic ash. Before the impressions were obscured, more volcanic ash and rain fell, sealing the footprints. These series of environmental events were truly extraordinary, but they fortunately resulted in some of the most famous and revealing trace fossils ever found. Dating of the footprints indicate that they were made 3.6 mya (Smithsonian National Museum of Natural History 2018).

Just as forensic scientists can use footprints to identify the approximate build of a potential suspect in a crime, archaeologists have read the Laetoli Footprints for clues to this early human. The footprints clearly indicate a bipedal hominin who had a foot similar to that of modern humans. Analysis of the gait through computer simulation revealed that the hominins at Laetoli walked similarly to the way we walk today (Crompton 2012). More recent analyses confirm the similarity to modern humans but also indicate that their gait involved more of a flexed limb than that of modern humans (Hatala et al. 2016; Raichlen and Gordon 2017). The relatively short stride implies that the hominin had short legs–unlike the longer legs of later early humans who migrated out of Africa (Smithsonian National Museum of History 2018; see Figure 7.27). In the context of Olduvai Gorge, where fossils of *Australopithecus afarensis* have been located and dated to the same timeframe as the footprints, it is likely that these newly discovered impressions were left by this same hominin.

Figure 7.27 A visit with Lucy at the Natural History Museum in Washington, D.C.

The footprints at Laetoli were made by a small group of as many as three *Australopithecus afarensis*, walking in close proximity, not unlike what we would see on a

Understanding the Fossil Context | 247

modern street or sidewalk. Two trails of footprints have been positively identified with one set of the prints indicating that the individual was carrying something on one side. The third set of prints are much smaller and seem to appear in the tracks left by one of the larger individuals. While scientific methods have given us the ability to date the footprints and understand the body mechanics of the hominin, additional consideration of the footprints can lead to other implications. For instance, the close proximity of the individuals implies a close relationship existed between them, not unlike that of a family. Due to the size variation and the depth of impression, the footprints seem to have been made by two larger adults and possibly one child. Scientists theorize that the weight being carried by one of the larger individuals is a young child or a baby (Masao et al. 2016). Excavation continues at Laetoli today, resulting in the discovery of two more footprints in 2015, also believed to have been made by *Au. afarensis* (Masao et al. 2016).

VOICES FROM THE PAST: WHAT FOSSILS CAN TELL US

Given that so few organisms ever become fossilized, any anthropologist or fossil hunter will tell you that finding a fossil is extremely exciting. But this is just the beginning of a fantastic mystery. With the creative application of scientific methods and deductive reasoning, a great deal can be learned about the fossilized organism and the environment in which it lived, leading to enhanced understanding of the world around us.

Dating Methods

Context is a crucial concept in paleoanthropology and archaeology. Objects and fossils are interesting in and of themselves, but without context there is only so much we can learn from them. One of the most important contextual pieces is the dating of an object or fossil. By being able to place it in time, we can compare it more accurately with other contemporary fossils and artifacts or we can better analyze the evolution of a fossil species or artifacts. To answer the question "How do we know what we know?" you have to know how archaeologists and paleoanthropologists establish dates for artifacts, fossils, and sites.

Dating techniques are divided into two broad categories: relative dating methods and chronometric (sometimes called absolute) dating methods.

Relative Dating

Relative dating methods are the first used because they rely on simple observational skills. In the 1820s, Christian Jürgensen Thomsen at the National Museum of Denmark in Copenhagen developed the "three-age" system still used in European prehistory today (Feder 2017, 17). He categorized the artifacts at the museum based on the idea that simpler tools and materials were most likely older than more complex tools and materials. Stone tools must predate metal tools because they do not require special technology to develop. Copper and bronze tools must predate iron because they can be smelted or worked at lower temperatures, etc. Based on these observations, he categorized the artifacts into Stone Age, Bronze Age, and Iron Age.

The restriction of relative dating is that you don't know specific dates or how much time passed between different sites or artifacts. You simply know that one artifact or fossil is older than another. Thomsen knew that Stone Age artifacts were older than Bronze Age artifacts, but he couldn't tell if they were hundreds of years older or thousands of years older. The same is true with fossils that have differences of ages into the hundreds of millions of years.

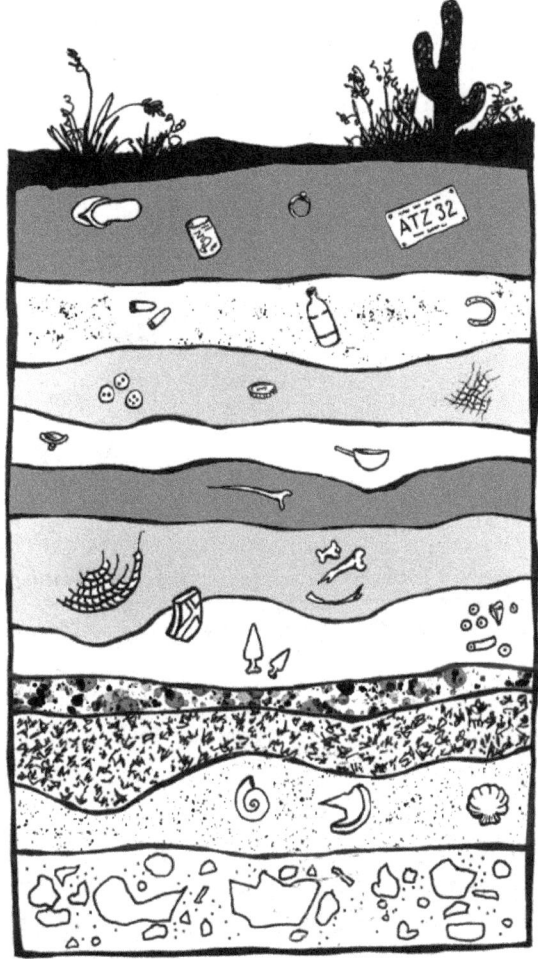

Figure 7.28 An illustration of a stratigraphic cross-section. The objects at a lower strata are older than the one above.

The first relative dating technique is **stratigraphy** (Figure 7.28). You might have already heard this term if you have watched documentaries on archaeological excavations. That's because it is still being used today. It provides a solid foundation for other dating techniques to be used and gives important context to artifacts and fossils found at a site.

Stratigraphy is based on the **Law of Superposition** first proposed by Nicholas Steno in 1669 and further explored by James Hutton (the previously mentioned "Father" of Deep Time). Essentially, superposition tells us that things on the bottom are older than things on the top (Williams 2004, 28). Notice on Figure 7.28 that there are distinctive layers piled on top of each other. It stands to reason that each layer is older than the one immediately on top of it (Hester et al. 1997, 338). Think of a pile of laundry on the floor. Over the course of a week, as dirty clothes get tossed on that pile, the shirt tossed down on Monday will be at the bottom of the pile while the shirt tossed down on Friday will be at the top. Assuming that the laundry pile was undisturbed throughout the week, if the clothes were picked up layer by layer, the clothing choices that week could be reconstructed in the order that they were worn. This concept may seem simple or even obvious, but it is extremely important in archaeology.

Another important relative dating technique is **biostratigraphy**. This form of dating looks at the context of a fossil or artifact and compares it to the other fossils and biological remains (plant and animal) found in the same stratigraphic layers. For instance, if an artifact is found in the same layer as wooly mammoth remains, you know that it must date to around the last ice age, when wooly mammoths were still abundant on Earth. In the absence of more specific dating techniques, early archaeologists could prove the great antiquity of stone tools because of their association with extinct animals. The application of this relative dating technique in archaeology was used at the Folsom site in New Mexico. Ever since Europeans encountered people in the Americas, they wondered how long they had been on the continent. Were they recent arrivals from Asia or had their ancestors been there thousands of years? Biostratigraphy helped answer this question before absolute dating techniques had even been invented. In 1927, at a site in Folsom, New Mexico, a stone spear point was discovered embedded in the rib of an extinct species of bison. Because of the undeniable association between the artifact and the ancient animal, there was proof that people had occupied the North American continent since antiquity (Cook 1928).

Similar to biostratigraphic dating is **cultural dating** (Figure 7.29). This relative dating technique is used to identify the chronological relationships between human-made artifacts. Cultural dating is based on artifact types and styles (Hester et al. 1997, 338). For instance, a pocket knife by itself is difficult to date. However, if the same pocket knife is discovered surrounded by cassette tapes and VHS tapes, it is logical to assume that the artifact came from the 1980s or 1990s like the cassette and VHS tapes. The pocket knife could not be dated earlier than the age of the cassette and VHS tapes because the tapes were made no earlier than the 1980s. In the Thomsen example above, he was able to identify a relative chronology of ancient European tools based on the artifact styles, manufacturing techniques, and raw materials. Cultural dating can be used with any human-made artifacts. Both cultural dating and biostratigraphy are most effective when you are already familiar with the time periods for the artifacts and animals. They are still used today to identify general time periods for sites.

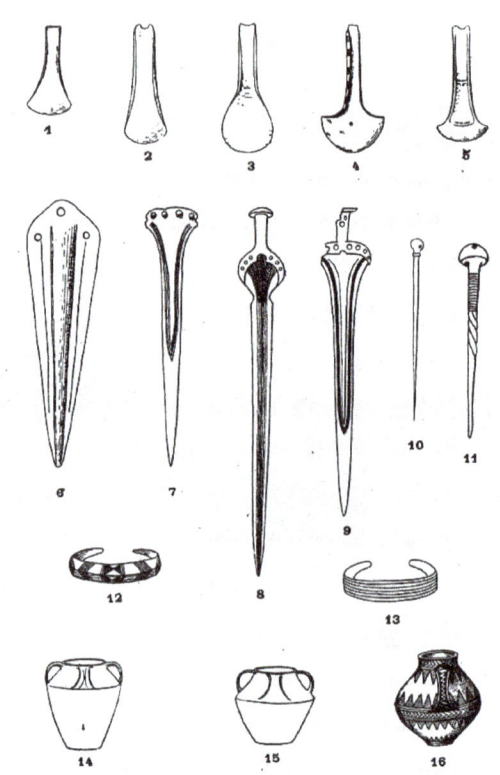

Chemical dating was developed in the 19th century and represents one of the early attempts to use soil composition and chemistry to date artifacts. A specific type of chemical dating is **fluorine dating**, and it is commonly used to compare the age of the soil around artifacts located in close proximity (Cook and Ezra-Cohn 1959). While this technique is based on chemical dating, it only provides the relative dates of items rather than their absolute ages. For this reason, fluorine dating is considered a hybrid form of relative and chronometric dating methods (discussed below).

Figure 7.29 Charts of typology, like these representing items from the Bronze Age, are used to classify artifacts and illustrate cultural material assemblages.

Soils contain different amounts of chemicals, and those chemicals, such as fluorine, can be absorbed by human and animal bones buried in the soil. The longer the remains are in the soil, the more fluorine they will absorb (Cook and Ezra-Cohn 1959). Unfortunately, this absorption rate is highly sensitive to temperature, soil pH, and varying fluorine levels in local soil and groundwater (Haddy and Hanson 1982). This makes it difficult to get an accurate date for the remains or to compare remains between two sites. However, this technique is particularly useful for determining whether different artifacts come from the same burial context. If they were buried in the same soil for the same length of time, their fluorine signatures would match.

Figure 7.30 The Piltdown Man forgery that confused scientists for 40 years.

The fluorine technique was used to identify the famous archaeological forgery, "Piltdown Man" (Figure 7.30). In 1912, Charles Dawson of England "discovered" Piltdown Man, or *Eoanthropus dawsoni*. In addition to bringing worldwide attention to British anthropology, Dawson himself became famous for his discovery. As a fossil specimen, Piltdown Man had a large bulbous cranium like modern humans, but a primitive apelike jaw and teeth. These characteristics helped Dawson convince many in the field of anthropology that his fossil was the "missing link" between apes and humans. Dawson's find also served as incontrovertible evidence for a European origin of human evolution, a hypothesis that favored Western-imposed thought and superiority. Because Dawson's discovery was accepted for over 40 years, many researchers became skeptical of the newer finds coming out of South Afria that did not share the same unique characteristics as *Eoanthropus* (De Groote et al. 2016). However, as more and more of the human African fossils began emerging, scientists began to suspect Piltdown Man was not the missing link as it had been represented and the credibility of *Eoanthropus* was brought into scrutiny.

It was not until after Dawson's death that outside researchers were able to access the remains and conduct independent analysis on them. They noticed that the teeth had odd wear patterns on them. Dawson had filed them down to better fit the mandible to the maxilla. Fluorine analysis determined that the jaw and cranium had different fluorine signatures. Thus, these bones could not have come from the same individual in the same burial environment. It turned out that the cranium was from two, maybe three, medieval humans and the jaw from a modern Bornean orangutan, *Pongo pygmaeus* (De Groote et al. 2016). Furthermore, all of the pieces of the cranium were stained to give a uniform and ancient-looking color. Piltdown Man was a forgery that greatly disrupted legitimate anthropological research and confused the understanding of the fossil record in the early 20th century.

Chronometric Dating

Unlike relative dating methods, **chronometric dating** methods provide specific dates and time ranges. Many of the chronometric techniques we will discuss are based on work in other disciplines such as chemistry and physics. The modern developments in studying radioactive materials are extremely accurate and precise in establishing dates for ancient sites and remains.

Many of the chronometric dating methods are based on the measurement of radioactive decay of particular elements. **Elements** are materials that cannot be broken down into more simple materials without losing their chemical identity (Brown et al. 2018, 48). Each element consists of an **atom** that has a specific number of protons (positively charged particles) and electrons (negatively charged particles) as well as varying numbers of neutrons (particles with no charge). The protons and neutrons are located in the densely compacted nucleus of the atom, but the majority of the volume of an atom is space outside the nucleus around which the electrons orbit (see Figure 7.31).

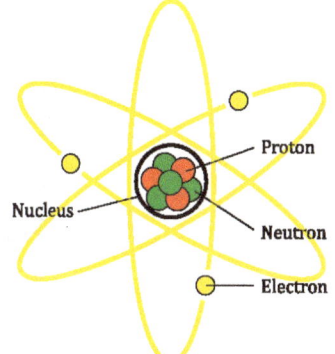

Figure 7.31 *Simplified illustration of an atom.*

Elements are classified based on the number of protons in the nucleus. For example, carbon has six protons, giving it an atomic number 6. Uranium has 92 protons, which means that it has an atomic number 92. While the number of protons in the atom of an element do not vary, the number of neutrons may. Atoms of a given element that have different numbers of neutrons are known as **isotopes**.

The majority of an atom's mass is determined by the protons and neutrons, which have more than a thousand times the mass of an electron. Due to the different numbers of neutrons in the nucleus, isotopes vary by nuclear/atomic weight (Brown et al. 2018, 94). For instance, isotopes of carbon include carbon 12 (^{12}C), carbon 13 (^{13}C), and carbon 14 (^{14}C). Carbon always has six protons, but ^{12}C has six neutrons whereas ^{14}C has eight neutrons. Because ^{14}C has more neutrons, it has a greater mass than ^{12}C (Brown et al. 2018, 95).

Most isotopes in nature are considered **stable isotopes** and will remain in their normal structure indefinitely. However, some isotopes are considered **unstable isotopes** (sometimes called radioisotopes) because they spontaneously release energy and particles, transforming into stable isotopes (Brown et al. 2018, 946; Flowers et al. 2018, section 21.1). The process of transforming the atom by spontaneously releasing energy is called **radioactive decay**. This change occurs at a predictable rate for nearly all radioisotopes of elements, allowing scientists to use unstable isotopes to measure time passage from a few hundred to a few billion years with a large degree of accuracy and precision.

The leading chronometric method for archaeology is **radiocarbon dating** (Figure 7.32). This method is based on the decay of ^{14}C, which is an unstable isotope of carbon. It is created when nitrogen 14 (^{14}N) interacts with cosmic rays, which causes it to convert to ^{14}C. Carbon 14 in our atmosphere is absorbed by plants during photosynthesis, a process by which light energy is turned into chemical energy to sustain life in plants, algae, and some bacteria. Plants absorb carbon dioxide from the atmosphere and use the energy from light to convert it into sugar that fuels the plant (Campbell and Reece 2005, 181–200). Though ^{14}C is an unstable isotope, plants can use it in the same way that they use the stable isotopes of carbon.

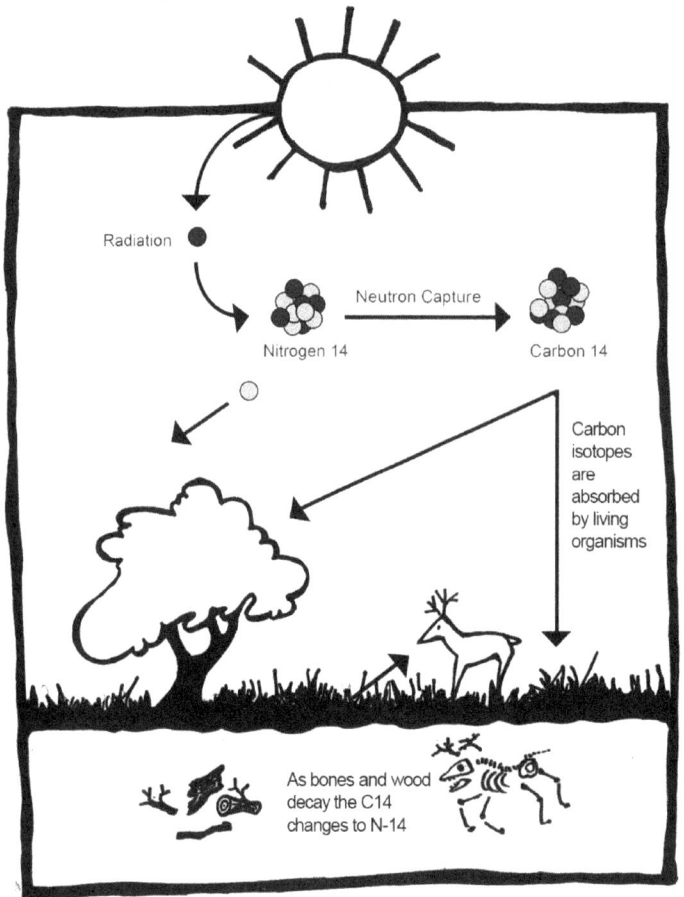

Figure 7.32 A graphic illustrating how 14C is created in the atmosphere, absorbed by living organisms, and ends up in the archaeological record.

Animals get the ^{14}C by eating the plants. Humans take it in by eating plants and animals. Carbon 14 has a half-life of 5,730 years (Hester et al. 1997, 324). That means that in 5,730 years, half the amount of ^{14}C will have converted back into ^{14}N. Because the pattern of radioactive decay is so reliable, we can use ^{14}C to accurately date sites up to 50,000 years old. However, ^{14}C can only be used on the remains of biological organisms. This includes shell, wood, plant material, and bone.

As mentioned before, ^{14}C is unstable and ultimately decays back into ^{14}N. This decay is happening at a constant rate (even now inside your own body!). However, as long as an organism is alive and taking in food, ^{14}C is being replenished in the body. As soon as an organism dies, it no longer takes in new ^{14}C. We can then use the rate of decay to measure how long it has been since the organism died (Hester et al. 1997, 324).

An example of this is the use of ^{14}C to date burials. For instance, at the Iron Age site of Wetwang Slack in East Yorkshire, England, a selection of burials across the site were dated directly with ^{14}C. By choosing a range of burials, archaeologists were able to identify the length of time the cemetery was used as well as different phases of use (Dent 1982). Because we can assume that any artifacts found with the bodies were placed there at the time of burial, we can estimate the age of the artifacts even though the bones were the only things directly dated.

As you will see in the hominin chapters, 50,000 years is only a tiny fragment of human evolutionary history. It is insignificant in the context of the age of our planet. In order to date even older fossils, other methods of dating are necessary. Some of these are also based on radioactive decay.

Potassium-argon (K-Ar) dating and **argon-argon (Ar-Ar) dating** can reach further back into the past than radiocarbon dating. Used to date volcanic rock, these techniques are based on the decay of unstable potassium 40 (^{40}K) into argon 40 (^{40}Ar) gas, which gets trapped in the crystalline structures of volcanic material. It's important to note that this form of dating is not done directly on the fossil in which you are interested. This is where stratigraphy becomes important. The K-Ar method dates the layers around the fossil to give approximate dates for when that fossil was deposited. The benefit of this dating technique is that ^{40}K has a half-life of circa 1.3 billion years, so it can be used on sites as young as 100 kya and as old as the age of Earth. As you will see in later chapters, it is particularly useful in dating early hominin sites in Africa (Michels 1972, 120; Renfrew and Bahn 2016, 155).

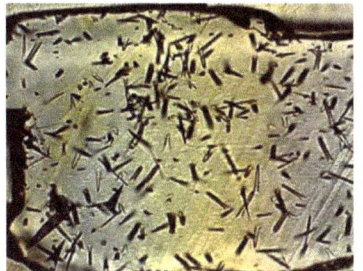

Figure 7.33 Thin section showing damage tracks from fission.

Fission track dating is another useful dating technique for sites that are millions of years old. This is based on the decay of radioactive uranium 238 (^{238}U). The unstable atom of ^{238}U fissions at a predictable rate. The fission takes a lot of energy and causes damage to the surrounding rock (see Figure 7.33). For instance, in volcanic glasses we can see this damage as trails in the glass. Researchers in the lab count the number of fission trails using an optical microscope. As ^{238}U has a half-life of 4,500 million years, it can be used to date rock and mineral material starting at just a few decades and extending back to the age of Earth. As with K-Ar, archaeologists are not dating artifacts directly. They are dating the layers around the artifacts in which they are interested (Laurenzi et al. 2007).

Luminescence dating, which includes thermoluminescence and a related technique called optically stimulated luminescence, is based on the naturally occurring background radiation in soils. Pottery, baked clay, and sediments that include quartz and feldspar are bombarded by radiation from the soils surrounding it. Electrons in the material get displaced from their orbit and trapped in the crystalline structure of the pottery, rock, or sediment. When heated to 500°C (thermoluminescence) or exposed to particular light wavelengths (optically stimulated luminescence) in the laboratory, this energy gets released in the form of light and heat and can be measured (Cochrane et al. 2013; Renfrew and Bahn 2016, 160). You can use this method to date artifacts like pottery and burnt flint directly. When attempting to date fossils, you may use this method on the crystalline grains of quartz and feldspar in the surrounding soils (Cochrane et al. 2013). The important thing to remember with this form of dating is that heating the artifact or soils will reset the clock. The method is not necessarily dating when the object was last made or used but when it was last heated to 500°C or more (pottery) or exposed to sunlight (sediments). Luminescence dating can be used on sites from less than 100 years to over 100,000 years (Duller 2008, 4). As with all archaeological data, context is crucial to understanding the information.

Like thermoluminescence dating, **electron spin resonance dating** is based on the measurement of accumulated background radiation from the burial environment. It is used on artifacts and rocks with crystalline structures, including tooth enamel, shell, and rock–those for which thermoluminescence would not work. The radiation causes electrons to become dislodged from their normal orbit. They become trapped in the crystalline matrix and affect the electromagnetic energy of the object. This energy can be measured and used to estimate the length of time in the burial environment. This technique works well for remains as old as two million years (Carvajal et al. 2011, 115–116). It has the added benefit of being nondestructive, which is an important consideration when dealing with irreplaceable material.

Not all chronometric dating methods are based on unstable isotopes and their rates of decay. There are several other methods that make use of other natural biological and geologic processes. One such method is known as **dendrochronology** (Figure 7.34). It is based on the natural growth patterns of trees. As most of you probably learned in elementary school, trees create concentric rings as they grow. The width of those rings depends on environmental conditions and season. In a perfect world, you can tell the age of a tree by counting the rings. You can also see a record of rainfall, droughts, and forest fires using the rings.

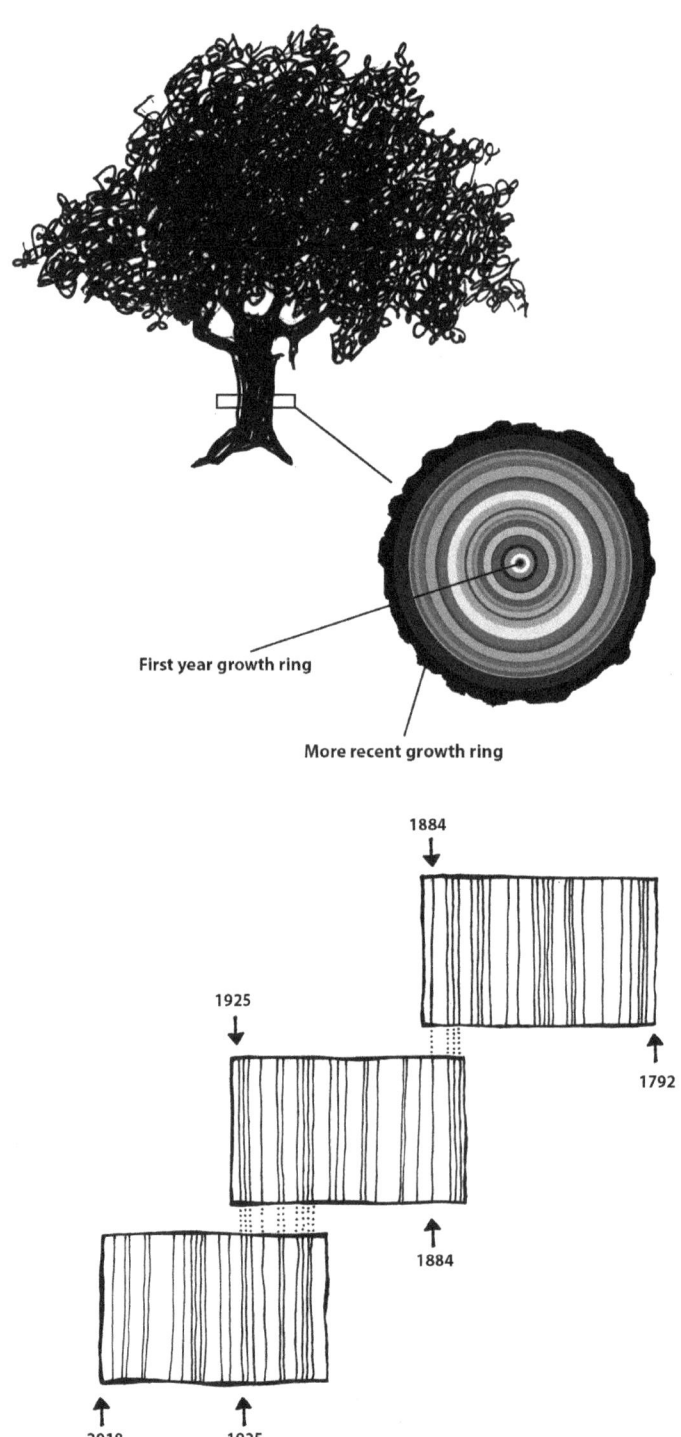

Figure 7.34 Dendrochronology uses the variations in tree rings to create timelines.

Tree rings can be used to date wood artifacts from ancient sites. First, archaeologists need to create a profile of trees in a particular area. They start with modern trees and identify patterns in ring growth. Then, they overlap these patterns with slightly older trees to extend the timeline back. These tree patterns can be overlapped back in time as long as there are intact tree rings available. The Northern Hemisphere chronology stretches backs nearly 14,000 years (Reimer et al. 2013, 1870). Archaeologists can then compare wood artifacts with existing timelines and find where their artifacts fit in the pattern.

This method, however, is not foolproof. Growth can be interrupted so that tree rings do not correspond exactly with the tree's age. Microclimates and tree species variation can also alter growth patterns. However, dendrochronologists can work around these issues using multiple samples, statistical analysis, and calibration with other dating methods. Additionally, for this method to work, the artifact must be preserved well enough to have visible tree rings to analyze. The results of the analysis will tell you an approximate time that the tree lived. To know exactly when the tree was cut down, the outer rings and bark should be present. But despite these limitations, dendrochronology can be a powerful tool in dating archaeological sites (Hillam et al. 1990; Kuniholm and Striker 1987).

Dendrochronology has been in use since the early 20th century (Dean 2009, 25). It has been used successfully to date southwestern U.S. sites such as Pueblo Bonito and Aztec Ruin (Dean 2009, 26). In Europe during the mid-20th century, archaeologists built chronologies that spanned thousands of years. The dendrochronological evidence helped calibrate radiocarbon dates and even provided direct evidence of global warming (Dean 2009, 26–27).

Amino acid racemization (AAR) is a dating method that is used for organic materials such as bones, teeth, and shell. Organic tissues include amino acids that help build their structures. The molecular structure of amino acids occurs in two forms (isomers), "D (dextrorotatory) and L (levorotatory) forms" (Komutrattananont and Mahakkanukrauh 2017). These forms (referred to as enantiomers) have molecular structures that are mirror images of each other under polarized light. During life, most amino acids are in the L-form. However, upon the death of an organism the amino acids flip to the mirror image or D-form. This switch happens at a predictable rate and, like radiocarbon dating, can be a useful measure of time elapsed since the organism's death. Its usable time range extends well beyond that of radiocarbon dating and can be used on remains over a million years old (Renfrew and Bahn 2016, 163). However, AAR is sensitive to temperature, so it is important know the relative temperature fluctuations of the site or the results will not be reliable.

Figure 7.35 *The classroom globe reflecting planet Earth as a perfect sphere with an axis that bisects the points known as Geographic North and Geographic South.*

Finally, we have **paleomagnetic/geomagnetic reversals**. This is a fairly easy concept, but it takes a bit of explanation because it is easy to confuse geographic positions with geomagnetism. Most people are aware that the North Pole occurs at the Arctic Circle and the South Pole occurs at the Antarctic Circle. The typical classroom globe reinforces this concept because it typically has a rod inserted through the middle of the sphere that attaches the globe to its stand (Figure 7.35). The rod is an imaginary axis on which Earth supposedly spins, and because it enters the globe at Latitude 90° N., this point is called Geographic North. The coordinates for the south pole are just the opposite or 90° S., Geographic South.

However, for planet Earth, the poles are actually magnetic fields, and geomagnetic poles are not located at the same places as geographic poles. Just to complicate the matter, magnetic poles move around. Fortunately, scientists have been able to chart these movements since 1899. According to Randy Russell (2007), in the early 20th century, there was about 9 km of movement per year. However, by 1970, the movement sped up significantly, to 41 km per year. The impact of human activity with global warming and the melting of glacial mass loss continues to speed up this movement (Adhikari and Ivins 2016). Eventually, the geomagnetic north and south poles will swap, an event called a paleomagnetic or geomagnetic reversal. As radical as that seems, it's important to remember that these reversals have occurred many times, typically every couple of hundreds of thousands of years over the course of long history of the earth. Obviously, there are implications to reversal. The clearest is that compasses will not work as expected. Animals may become disoriented, at least at first (Drake 2018). Furthermore, some scientists predict an increase in solar flares that will create holes in the ozone layer, likely resulting in increased instances of skin cancer and interference with satellite technology (Valet and Valladas 2010; Wolchover 2012). But it is not all bad news. The beautiful green and purple skies created by the aurora borealis or "Northern Lights" will be increasingly visible at southern latitudes as the geomagnetic reversal progresses (Drake 2018). However, there is a great deal of debate regarding impacts of geomagnetic reversals on the planet and studies are ongoing.

When the poles do reverse, we can identify it in the geologic record by analyzing volcanic rock. Iron minerals in volcanic material align themselves with the poles' positions at the time the volcanic material is still molten. When the material cools and hardens, those minerals are locked into place. They give us a glimpse of the poles' locations at the time the rock cooled (Gubbins 2008). These events can be correlated with other dating methods and are used to identify broad time periods (sometimes lasting tens to hundreds of thousands of years) of particular layers of interest.

Environmental Reconstruction

Another important part of understanding human evolution (and evolution in general) is understanding the way in which an organism's environment affects its survival. As you read in chapter 2, Darwin, Lamarck, Wallace, and others recognized the importance of the environment in shaping the evolutionary course of animal species. To understand what selective processes might be shaping evolutionary change, we must be able to reconstruct the environment in which the organism was living.

One of the ways to do that is to look at the plant species that lived in the same time range as the species in which you are interested. One way to identify ancient flora is to analyze **sediment cores** from water and other protected sources. Pollen gets released into the air and some of that pollen will fall on wetlands, lakes, caves, and so forth. Eventually it sinks to the bottom of the lake and forms part of the sediment. This happens year after year, so subsequent layers of pollen build up in an area, creating strata. By taking a core sample and analyzing the pollen and other organic material, an archaeologist can build a timeline of plant types and see changes in the vegetation of the area (Hester et al. 1997, 284). This can even be done over large areas by studying ocean bed cores, which accumulate pollen and dust from large swaths of neighboring continents.

Another way of reconstructing past environments is by using stable isotopes. Unlike unstable isotopes, stable isotopes remain constant in the environment throughout time. Plants take in the isotopes through photosynthesis and ground water absorption. Animals take in isotopes by drinking local water and eating plants. Stable isotopes can be powerful tools for identifying where an organism grew up and what kind of food the organism ate throughout its life. They can even be used to identify global temperature fluctuations.

Global Temperature Reconstruction

Oxygen isotopes are a powerful tool in tracking global temperature fluctuations throughout time. The isotopes of Oxygen 18 (^{18}O) and Oxygen 16 (^{16}O) occur naturally in Earth's water. Both are stable isotopes, but ^{18}O has a heavier atomic weight. In the normal water cycle, evaporation takes water molecules from the surface to the atmosphere. Because ^{16}O is lighter, it is more likely to be part of this evaporation process. The moisture gathers in the atmosphere as clouds that eventually may produce rain or snow and release the water back to the surface of the planet. During cool periods like **glacial periods** (ice ages), the evaporated water often comes down to Earth's surface as snow. During these periods, snow piles up in the winter but, because of the cooler summers, does not melt off. Instead, the snow gets compacted and layered year after year, eventually resulting in large glaciers or ice sheets covering parts of Earth. Since ^{16}O, with the lighter atomic weight, is more likely to be absorbed in the evaporation process, it gets locked up in glacier formation. The waters left in oceans would have a higher ratio of ^{18}O during these periods of cooler global temperatures (Potts 2012, 154–156; see Figure 7.36).

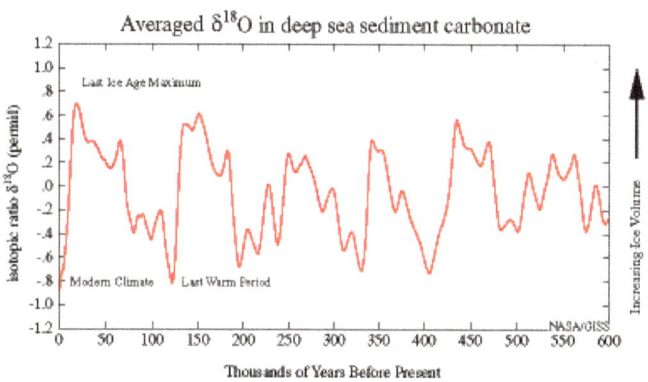

Figure 7.36 *The temperatures of the sea have fluctuated greatly over the course of the history of the planet.*

The microorganisms that live in the oceans, **foraminifera**, absorb the water from their environment and use the oxygen isotopes in their body structures. When these organisms die, they sink to the ocean floor, contributing to the layers of sediment. Scientists can extract these ocean cores and sample the remains of foraminifera for their ^{18}O and ^{16}O ratios. These ratios will give a good approximation of global temperatures deep into the past. Cooler temperatures indicate higher ratios of ^{18}O (Potts 2012, 154–156).

Diet Reconstruction

Stable isotopes can also be used to reconstruct animal diet and migration patterns. The concept is "you are what you eat." Living organisms absorb elements from ingested plants and water. These elements are used in tissues like bones, teeth, skin, hair, and so on. By analyzing the stable isotopes in the bones and teeth of humans and other animals, we can identify the types of food they ate at different stages of their lives as well as where they lived.

Plants take in carbon dioxide from the atmosphere during photosynthesis. We've already discussed this using the example of the unstable isotope ^{14}C; however, this absorption also takes place with the stable isotopes of ^{12}C and ^{13}C. During photosynthesis, some plants incorporate carbon dioxide as a three-carbon molecule (C3 plants) and some as a four-carbon molecule (C4 plants). On the one hand, C3 plants include certain types of trees and shrubs that are found in relatively wet environments and have lower ratios of ^{13}C compared to ^{12}C. C4 plants, on the other hand, include plants from drier environments like savannahs and grasslands. C4 plants have higher ratios of ^{13}C to ^{12}C than C3 plants (Renfrew and Bahn 2016, 312). These ratios remain stable as you go up the food chain. Therefore, you can analyze the bones and teeth of an animal to identify the $^{13}C/^{12}C$ ratios and identify the types of plants that animal was eating.

The ratios of stable nitrogen isotopes ^{15}N and ^{14}N can also give information about the diet of fossilized or deceased organisms. Though initially absorbed from water and soils by plants, the nitrogen ratios change depending on the primary diet of the organism. An animal who has a mostly vegetarian diet will have lower ratios of ^{15}N to ^{14}N, while those further up the food chain, like carnivores, will have higher ratios of ^{15}N. Interestingly, breastfeeding infants have a higher nitrogen ratio than their mothers, because they are getting all of their nutrients through their mother's milk. So nitrogen can be used to track life events like weaning (Jay et al. 2008, 2). A marine versus terrestrial diet will also affect the nitrogen signatures. Terrestrial diets have lower ratios of ^{15}N than marine diets. In the course of human evolution, this type of analysis can help us identify important changes in human nutrition. It can help anthropologists figure out when meat became a primary part of the ancient human diet or when marine resources began to be used. The ratios of stable nitrogen isotopes can also be used to determine a change in status, as in the case of the Llullaillaco children (the "ice mummies") found in the Andes Mountains (Wilson et al. 2007). Although the two younger children had little changes in their diets in the last year of their short lives, the changes in their nitrogen values were significant enough to suggest that the improvement in their diets may have been attributed to the Incas' desire to sacrifice healthy, high-status children" (Faux 2012, 6).

Migration

Stable isotopes can also tell a great deal about where an individual lived and whether they migrated during their lifetime. The geology of Earth varies because rocks and soils have different amounts or ratios of certain elements in them. These variations in the ratios of isotopes of certain elements are called isotopic signatures. They are like a chemical fingerprint for a geographical region. These isotopes get into the groundwater and are absorbed by plants and animals living in that area. Elements like strontium, oxygen, and nitrogen, among others, are then used by the body to build bones and teeth. If you ate and drank local water all of your life, your bones and teeth would have the same isotopic signature as the geographical region in which you lived.

However, most people (and animals) move around during their lifetimes. Isotopic signatures can be used to identify migration patterns in organisms (Montgomery et al. 2005). Teeth develop in early childhood. If the isotopes of teeth are analyzed, these isotopes would resemble those found in the geographic area where an individual lived as a child. Bones, however, are a different story. Bones are constantly changing throughout life. Old cells are removed and new cells are deposited to respond to growth, healing, activity change, and general deterioration. Therefore, the isotopic signature of bones will reflect the geographical area in which an individual spent the last seven to ten years of life. If an individual has different isotopic signatures for their bones and teeth, it could indicate a migration some time during their life after childhood.

Figure 7.37 Stonehenge continues to provide clues to its mysterious existence with recent research using isotope ratios.

Recent work involving stable isotope analysis has been done on the cremation burials from Stonehenge, in Wessex, England (Figure 7.37). Much of the archaeological work at Stonehenge in the past focused on the building and development of the monument itself. That is partly because most of the burials at the monument were cremated remains, which are difficult to study because of their fragmentary nature and the chemical alterations that bone and teeth undergo when heated. The cremation process complicates the oxygen and carbon isotopes. However, the researchers determined that strontium would not be affected by heating and could still be analyzed in cranial fragments. Using the remains of 25 individuals, they compared their strontium signatures to the geology of Wessex and other regions of the UK. Fifteen of those individuals had strontium signatures that matched the local geology. This means that in the last ten or so years of their lives, they lived and ate food from around Stonehenge. However, ten of the individuals did not match the local geologic signature. These individuals had strontium ratios more closely aligned with the geology of west Wales. Archaeologists find this particularly interesting because in the early phases of Stonehenge's construction, the smaller "blue stones" were brought 200 km from Wales in a feat of prehistoric engineering. These larger regional connections show that Stonehenge was not just a site of local importance. It dominated a much larger region of influence and drew people from all over ancient Britain (Snoeck et al. 2018).

SPECIAL TOPIC: COLD CASE NAIA

In 2007, cave divers exploring the Sistema Sac Actun in the Yucatán Peninsula in Mexico (see Figure 7.38) discovered the bones of a 15- to 16-year-old female human along with the bones of various extinct animals from the Pleistocene (Figures 7.39 and 7.40) (Collins et al. 2015). The site was named Hoyo Negro ("Black Hole"). The human bones belonged to a Paleoindian, later named "Naia" after a Greek water nymph. Examination of the partially fossilized remains revealed a great deal about Naia's life, and the radiocarbon dating of her tooth enamel indicated that she lived some 11,000 years ago (Chatters et al. 2014). Naia's arms were not overly developed, so her daily activities did not involve heavy carrying or grinding of grain or seeds. Her legs, however, were quite muscular, implying that Naia was used to walking long distances. Naia's teeth and bones indicate habitually poor nutrition. There is evidence of violent injury during the course of Naia's life from a healed spiral fracture of her left forearm. Naia also suffered from tooth decay and osteoporosis even though she appeared young and undersize. Dr. Jim Chatters hypothesizes that Naia entered the cave at a time when it was not flooded, probably looking for water. She may have become disoriented and fell off a high ledge to her death. The trauma to her pelvis is consistent with such an injury (Watson 2017).

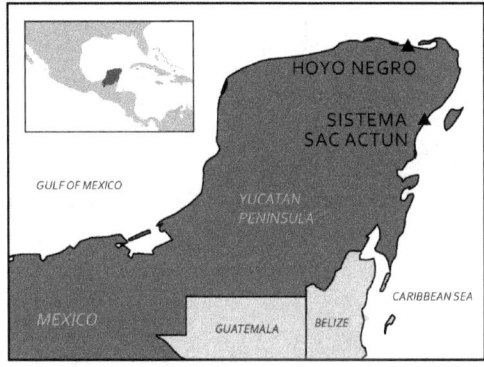

Figure 7.38 Map of Mexico showing the Yucatan Peninsula and the locations of Hoyo Negro and Sistema Sac Actun.

Understanding the Fossil Context | 259

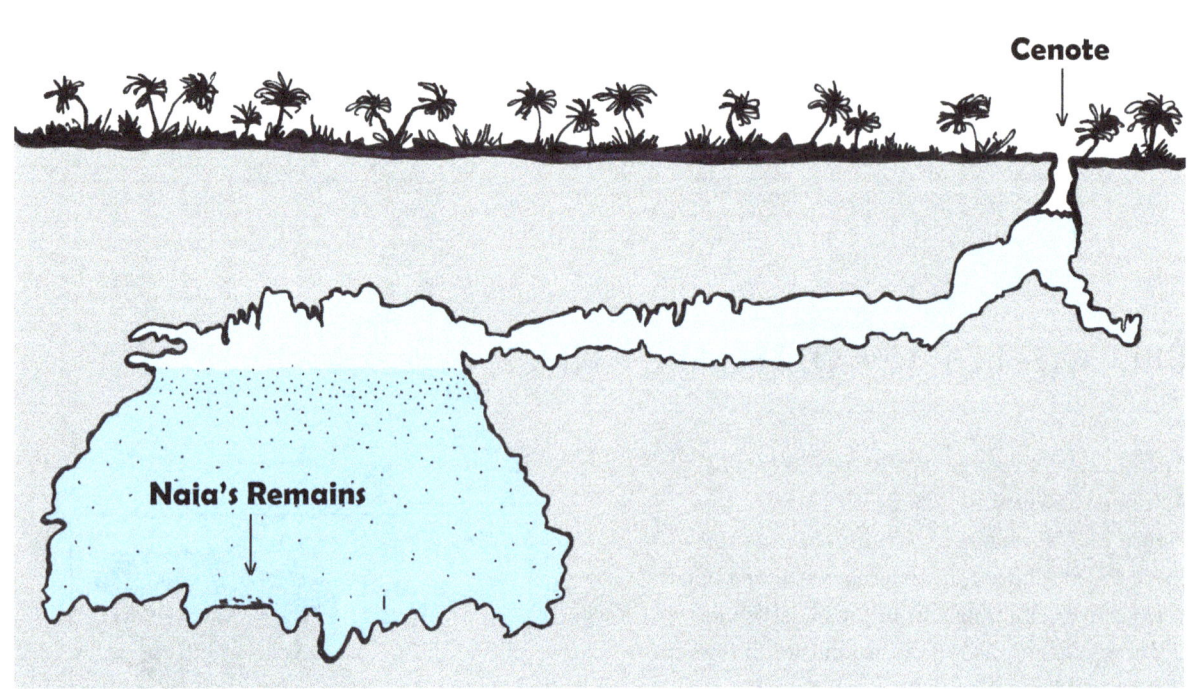

Figure 7.39 A diagram of the Sistema Sac Actun and the Hoyo Negro cenote where Naia rested underwater for roughly 13,000 years.

Although Naia's skeleton is incomplete, it is more complete than any other "New World skeleton" ever found. As divers were able to locate her skull, Naia's physical appearance in life could be interpreted. Surprisingly, in examining the skull, it was determined that Naia did not resemble modern Native Americans. However, the **mitochondrial DNA** (mtDNA) recovered from a tooth indicates that Naia shares her DNA with modern Native Americans whose DNA has been linked conclusively to ancestors in Siberia. This means that Naia proves the theory that there was a migration over the land bridge known as Beringia after the last ice age and that the changes in craniofacial morphology are due to evolution after the migration (Chatters et al. 2014).

SUMMARY

With a timeline that extends back some 4.6 billion years, Earth has witnessed continental drift, environmental changes, and a growing complexity of life. Fossils, the mineralized remains of living organisms, provide physical evidence of life and the environment on the planet over the course of billions of years. Early fossil hunter Mary Anning had a profound influence on the way scholars, including Charles Darwin, interpreted evolutionary history. In order to better understand the fossil record, anthropologists rely on the collaboration of numerous academic fields and disciplines. Anthropologists use a variety of scientific methods, both relative and chronometric, to analyze fossils to determine age, origins, and migration patterns as well as to provide insight into the health and diet of the fossilized organism. While each method has its advantages, disadvantages, and limited applications, these tools enable anthropologists to theorize how all living organisms evolved, including the evolution of early humans into modern humans, *H. sapiens*. The fossil record is far from complete, but our expanding understanding of the fossil context, with exciting new discoveries and improved scientific methods, enables us to document the history of our planet and the evolution of life on Earth.

> ## Review Questions
>
> - In what ways did early paleontologists shape our modern methods of fossil extraction and analysis?
> - What kind of information could you acquire from a single fossil? What could it tell you about the broader environment?
> - What factors would you take into consideration when deciding which dating method to use for a particular artifact?
> - How do stable isotopes help us reconstruct past environments and lifestyles?

Key Terms

Amino acid racemization: A chronometric dating method that measures the ratio of L-form to D-form amino acids in shell, bone, and teeth to establish elapsed time since death.

Anaerobic: An oxygen-free environment.

Anthropocene: The proposed name for our current geologic epoch based on human-driven climate change.

Argon-argon (Ar-Ar) dating: A chronometric dating method that measures the ratio of argon gas in volcanic rock to estimate time elapsed since the volcanic rock cooled and solidified. See also potassium-argon dating.

Atom: A small building block of matter.

Bezoars: Hard, concrete-like substances found in the intestines of fossil creatures.

Biostratigraphy: A relative dating method that uses other plant and animal remains occurring in the stratigraphic context to establish time depth.

Bog bodies: Bodies preserved in the peaty, waterlogged bogs, typically in northern Europe.

Bya: Billion years ago.

Catastrophism: The theoretical perspective that Earth is young and that any changes in the landscape resulted from sudden catastrophic events like volcano eruptions and floods.

Chronometric dating: Dating methods that give estimated numbers of years for artifacts and sites.

Continental drift: The slow movement of continents over time.

Coprolite: Fossilized poop.

Cultural dating: The relative dating method that arranges human-made artifacts in a time frame from oldest to youngest based on material, production technique, style, and other features.

Deep Time: James Hutton's theory that the world was much older than biblical explanations allowed. This age could be determined by gradual natural processes like soil erosion.

Dendrochronology: A chronometric dating method that uses the annual growth of trees to build a timeline into the past.

Electron spin resonance dating: A chronometric dating method that measures the background radiation accumulated in material over time.

Element: Matter that cannot be broken down into smaller matter.

Epochs: The smallest units of geologic time, spanning thousands to millions of years.

Eon: The largest unit of geologic time, spanning billions of years and divided into subunits called eras, periods, and epochs.

Eras: Units of geologic time that span millions to billions of years and that are subdivided into periods and epochs.

Extant: A word used to describe species that are currently alive today.

Extinct: A word used to describe species that are no longer represented by living organisms.

Fission track dating: A chronometric dating method that is based on the fission of ^{283}U.

Fluorine dating: A relative dating method that analyzes the absorption of fluorine in bones from the surrounding soils.

Foraminifera: Single-celled marine organisms with shells.

Fossils: Mineralized copies of organisms or activity imprints.

Fossilization: The process by which an organism becomes a fossil.

Glacial periods: Periods characterized by low global temperatures and the expansion of ice sheets on Earth's surface.

Holocene: The geologic epoch from 10 kya to present. (See the discussion on Anthropocene for the debate on the current epoch name.)

Hominin: The term used for humans and their ancestors after the split with chimpanzees and bonobos.

Ice mummy: A specimen of human remains that is naturally mummified by extreme low temperatures.

In matrix: When a fossil is embedded in a substance, such as igneous rock.

Isotopes: Variants of elements.

Kya: Thousand years ago.

Law of Superposition: The scientific law that states that rock and soil are deposited in layers, with the youngest layers on top and the oldest layers on the bottom.

Lithification: The process by which the pressure of sediments squeeze extra water out of decaying remains and replace the voids that appear with minerals from the surrounding soil and groundwater.

Luminescence dating: The chronometric dating method based on the buildup of background radiation in pottery, clay, and soils.

Megafauna: Large animals such as mammoths and mastodons.

Mitochondrial DNA: DNA located in the mitochondria of a cell that is only passed down from biological mother to child.

Mya: Million years ago.

Paleomagnetic/geomagnetic reversal: Periods in Earth's history when magnetic north and south move significantly from their current positions.

Pangea: A supercontinent that existed during the Paleozoic era.

Periods: Geologic time units that span millions of years and are subdivided into epochs.

Permineralization: When minerals from water impregnate or replace organic remains, leaving a fossilized copy of the organism.

Petrified wood: A fossilized piece of wood in which the original organism is completely replaced by minerals through petrifaction.

Potassium-argon (K-Ar) dating: A chronometric dating method that measures the ratio of argon gas in volcanic rock to estimate time elapsed since the volcanic rock cooled and solidified. See also argon-argon dating.

Pseudofossils: Natural rocks or mineral formations that can be mistaken for fossils.

Radioactive decay: The process of transforming the atom by spontaneously releasing energy.

Radiocarbon dating: The chronometric dating method based on the radioactive decay of ^{14}C in organic remains.

Relative dating: Dating methods that do not result in numbers of years but, rather, in relative timelines wherein some organisms or artifacts are older or younger than others.

Sediment cores: Core samples taken from lake beds or other water sources for analysis of their pollen.

Stable isotopes: Variants of elements that do not change over time without outside interference.

Stratigraphy: A relative dating method that is based on ordered layers or (strata) that build up over time.

Taphonomy: The study of what happens to an organism after death.

Tectonic Plate Theory: The scientific theory that Earth is divided into plates that are capable of movement.

Trace fossils: Fossilized remains of activity such as footprints.

Uniformitarianism: The theoretical perspective that the geologic processes observed today are the same as the processes operating in the past.

Unstable isotopes: Variants of elements that spontaneously change into stable isotopes over time.

About the Authors

Sarah S. King

Cerro Coso Community College

Sarah S. King

Dr. Sarah S. King is an anthropology/sociology professor at Cerro Coso Community College in California. She completed her Ph.D. work at the Division of Archaeological, Geographical and Environmental Sciences at the University of Bradford in West Yorkshire, England. Her thesis was entitled "What Makes War?: Assessing Iron Age Warfare Through Mortuary Behavior and Osteological Patterns of Violence." She also holds anthropology degrees from the University of California, Santa Cruz (B.A. hons., 2004), and the University of New Mexico, Albuquerque (M.A., 2006).

Lee Anne Zajicek

Lee Anne Zajicek

Lee Anne Zajicek is a grandmother and a retired homeschool mother of four children who are assimilating into four-year universities via the California Community College system. Mrs. Zajicek received her B.A. in history at Mary Washington College, in Fredericksburg, Virginia, and most recently has worked on her MLitt in archaeological studies at the University of the Highlands and Islands, in Orkney, Scotland, UK. A former Montessori preschool teacher, Ms. Zajicek currently works as a curation assistant at the Maturango Museum in both history and archaeology.

For Further Exploration

Books

Bjornerud, Marcia. 2006. *Reading the Rocks: The Autobiography of the Earth.* New York: Basic Books.

Brusatte, Steve. 2018. *The Rise and Fall of the Dinosaurs: A New History of a Lost World.* New York: William Morrow.

Dolnick, Edward. 2011. *The Clockwork Universe: Isaac Newton, the Royal Society, and the Birth of the Modern World.* New York: Harper Collins.

Emling, Shelley. 2011. *The Fossil Hunter: Dinosaurs, Evolution, and the Woman Whose Discoveries Changed the World.* New York: St. Martin's Griffin.

Hazen, Robert M. 2013. *The Story of Earth: The First 4.5 Billion Years, From Stardust to Living Planet.* New York: Viking Penguin.

Holmes, Richard. 2010. *The Age of Wonder: The Romantic Generation and the Discovery of the Beauty and Terror of Science.* New York: Vintage.

Horner, Jack, and James Gormer. 2009. *How to Build a Dinosaur.* Boston: Dutton Books.

Murck, Barbara. 2001. *Geology: A Self-Teaching Guide.* New York: John Wiley & Sons.

Palmer, Douglas. 2005. *Earth Time: Exploring the Deep Past From Victorian England to the Grand Canyon.* New York: John Wiley & Sons.

Prothero, Donald R. 2015. *The Story of Life in 25 Fossils: Tales of Intrepid Fossil Hunters and the Wonder of Evolution.* New York: Columbia University Press.

Pyne, Lydia. 2016. *Seven Skeletons: The Evolution of the World's Most Famous Human Fossils.* New York: Viking Books.

Reinhard, Johan. 2006. *Ice Maiden: Inca Mummies, Mountain Gods, and Sacred Sites in the Andes.* Washington, D.C.: National Geographic.

Repcheck, Jack. 2009. *The Man Who Found Time: James Hutton and the Discovery of the Earth's Antiquity.* New York: Basic Books.

Taylor, Paul D. 2014. *A History of Life in 100 Fossils.* Washington, D.C.: Smithsonian Books.

Ward, David. 2002. *Smithsonian Handbooks: Fossils.* Washington, D.C.: Smithsonian Books.

Winchester, Simon. 2009. *The Map That Changed the World: William Smith and the Birth of Modern Geology.* New York: Harper Perennial.

Videos

Andrew, Danielle. 2015. "What Did Neanderthals Sound Like?" Retrieved from *IFL Science*, April 1. http://www.iflscience.com/plants-and-animals/could-neanderthals-have-high-pitched-voices/

Coleman, David, dir. 2012. "Lucy." *Prehistoric Autopsy*, part 3. 52 min. Glasgow, UK: BBC Productions. Video.

College Humor staff. 2015. "If Jurassic Park Were in Different Geologic Eras." *College Humor*, June 26. http://www.collegehumor.com/video/7025308/if-jurassic-park-were-in-different-geological-eras

Smithsonian.com staff. 2018. "Is the Inca Maiden the World's Best-Preserved Mummy?" *Smithsonian.com*, N.d. https://www.smithsonianmag.com/videos/category/history/is-this-the-worlds-best-preserved-mummy/

Townsley, Graham, dir. 2018. *First Face of America*. 53 min. PBS NOVA. http://www.pbs.org/wgbh/nova/evolution/first-face-america.html

Websites

Amber Museum: http://www.ambermuseum.eu/en/

East Tennessee State University Center of Excellence in Paleontology: https://www.etsu.edu/cas/paleontology/

Granger Historical Picture Archive: Granger.com

La Brea Tar Pits Museum: https://tarpits.org

Lyme Regis Philpot Museum: http://www.lymeregismuseum.co.uk

Natural History Museum of London, Mary Anning: http://www.nhm.ac.uk/discover/mary-anning-unsung-hero.html

Pech Merle Cave: http://en.pechmerle.com

Petrified Forest National Park (NE Arizona): https://www.nps.gov/pefo/index.htm

Poozeum: The No. 2 Wonder of the World: http://www.poozeum.com/poop-s-past.html

The Scoop on Poop!: https://www.floridamuseum.ufl.edu/exhibits/scoop/

Smithsonian National Museum of Natural History Department of Paleobiology: https://paleobiology.si.edu/fossiLab/projects.html

Smithsonian National Museum of Natural History Human Origins: http://humanorigins.si.edu

References

Adhikari, Surendra, and Erik R. Ivins. 2016. "Climate-Driven Polar Motion: 2003–2015." *Science Advances* 2(4): e1501693.

Antoine, Pierre-Oliver, Maeva J. Orliac, Gokhan Atici, Inan Ulusoy, Erdal Sen, H. Evren Çubukçu, Ebru Ibayrak, Neşe Oyal, Erkan Aydar, and Sevket Sen. 2012. "A Rhinocerotid Skull Cooked to Death in a 9.2 Mya-Old Ignimbrite Flow of Turkey." *PLoS ONE* 7 (11): e49997.

Aufderheide, Arthur C. 2003. *The Scientific Study of Mummies*. Cambridge, UK: Cambridge University Press.

Barr, James. 1984. "Why the World Was Created in 4004 BC: Archbishop Ussher and Biblical Chronology," *Bulletin of the John Rylands University Library of Manchester* 67: 575–608.

Booth, Thomas J., Andrew T. Chamberlain, and Mike Parker Pearson. 2015. "Mummification in Bronze Age Britain." *Antiquity* 89 (347): 1,155–1,173.

Braterman, Paul S. 2013. "How Science Figured Out the Age of the Earth." Special issue, "Determining the Age of the Earth," *Scientific American*, October 20. https://www.scientificamerican.com/article/how-science-figured-out-the-age-of-the-earth/

Brown, Theodore L., H. Eugene LeMay Jr., Bruce E. Burston, Catherine J. Murphy, Patrick M. Woodward, and Matthew Stoltzfus. 2018. *Chemistry: The Central Science*. New York: Pearson.

Campbell, Neil A. and Jane B. Reece. 2005. *Biology 7th ed.* New York, NY: Pearson

Carvajal, Eduar, Luis Montes, and Ovidio A. Almanza. 2011. "Quaternary Dating by Electron Spin Resonance (ESR) Applied to Human Tooth Enamel." *Earth Sciences Research Journal* 15 (2): 115–120.

Chatters, James C., Douglas J. Kennett, Yemane Asmerom, Brian M. Kemp, Victor Polyak, Alberto Nava Blank, Patricia A. Beddows, et al. 2014. "Late Pleistocene Human Skeleton and mtDNA Link Paleoamericans and Modern Native Americans." *Science* 344 (6,185): 750–754.

Cochrane, Grant W. G., Trudy Doelman, and Lyn Wadley. 2013. "Another Dating Revolution for Prehistoric Archaeology?" *Journal of Archaeological Method and Theory* 20 (1): 42–60.

Collins, S. V., E. G. Reinhardt, D. Rissolo, J. C. Chatters, A. Nava-Blank, and P. Luna-Erreguerena. 2015. "Reconstructing Water Level in Hoyo Negro, Quintana Roo, Mexico, Implications for Early Paleoamerican and Faunal Access." *Quaternary Science Reviews* 124: 68–83.

Cook, Harold J. 1928. "Glacial Age Man in New Mexico." *Scientific American* 139 (1): 38–40.

Cook, S. F., and H. C. Ezra-Cohn. 1959. "An Evaluation of the Fluorine Dating Method." *Southwestern Journal of Anthropology* 15 (3): 276–290.

Crompton, Robin H., Todd C. Pataky, Russell Savage, Kristiaan D'Août, Matthew R. Bennett, Michael H. Day, Karl Bates, Sarita Morse, and William I. Sellers. 2011. "Human-like External Function of the Foot, and Fully Upright Gait, Confirmed in the 3.66 Million Year Old Laetoli Hominin Footprints by Topographic Statistics, Experimental Footprint-Formation and Computer Simulation," *Journal of the Royal Society Interface* 9 (69): 707–719.

Crutzen, Paul J., and Eugene F. Stoermer. 2000. "The 'Anthropocene.'" *Global Change Newsletter* 41: 17–18.

Darwin, Charles. 1859. *On the Origin of Species*. London, UK: John Murray.

Dean, Jeffery S. 2009. "One Hundred Years of Dendroarchaeology: Dating, Human Behavior, and Past Climate." In *Tree-rings, Kings, and Old World Archaeology and Environment: Papers Presented in Honor of Peter Ian Kuniholm*. Edited by S. Manning and M. J. Bruce. Oxford, UK: Oxbow Books.

De Groote, Isabelle, Linus Girdland Flink, Rizwaan Abbas, Silvia M. Bello, Lucia Burgia, Laura Tabitha Buck, Christopher Dean, et al. 2016. "New Genetic and Morphological Evidence Suggests a Single Hoaxer Created 'Piltdown Man.'" *Royal Society Open Science* 3: 160328.

Dent, John S. 1982. "Cemeteries and Settlement Patterns of the Iron Age on the Yorkshire Wolds." *Proceedings of the Prehistoric Society* 48: 437–457.

Dolnick, Edward. 2011. *The Clockwork Universe: Isaac Newton, the Royal Society, and the Birth of the Modern World*. New York: HarperCollins.

Drake, Nadia. 2018. "No, We're Not All Doomed by Earth's Magnetic Field Flip." *National Geographic*, February 7. https://news.nationalgeographic.com/2018/01/earth-magnetic-field-flip-north-south-poles-science/

Duller, G.A.T. 2008. *Luminescence Dating: Guidelines on Using Luminescence Dating in Archaeology*. Swindon, UK: English Heritage.

Eisenbeiss, Sabine. 2016. "Preserved in Peat: Decoding Bodies from Lower Saxony, Germany." *Expedition* 58 (2): 18–21.

Emling, Shelley. 2009. *The Fossil Hunter: Dinosaurs, Evolution, and the Woman Whose Discoveries Changed the World*. New York: St. Martin's Griffin.

Faux, Jennifer L. 2012. "Hail the Conquering Gods: Ritual Sacrifice of Children in Inca Society." *Journal of Contemporary Anthropology* 3 (1): 1–15.

Feder, Kenneth L. 2017. *The Past in Perspective: An Introduction to Human Prehistory*. 7th Ed. New York: Oxford University Press.

Flowers, Paul, Klaus Theopold, Richard Langley, and William R. Robinson. 2018. *Chemistry*. Houston, TX: Openstax, Rice University.

Granger, Darryl E., Ryan J. Gibbon, Kathleen Kuman, Ronald J. Clarke, Laurent Bruxelles, and Marc W. Caffee. 2015. "New Cosmogenic Burial Ages for Sterkfontein Member 2 *Australopithecus* and Member 5 Oldowan." *Nature* 522 (7,554): 85–88.

Granger Historical Picture Archive. 2018. *Cro-Magnon Footprint*. Image no. 0167868. https://www.granger.com/results.asp?image=0167868&itemw=4&itemf=0001&itemstep=1&itemx=11&screenwidth=1085

Gubbins, David. 2008. "Earth Science: Geomagnetic Reversals." *Nature* 452 (7184): 165–167.

Haddy, A., and A. Hanson. 1982. "Research Notes and Application Reports Nitrogen and Fluorine Dating of Moundville Skeletal Samples. *Archaeometry* 24 (1): 37–44.

Hatala, Kevin G., Brigitte Demes, Brian G. Richmond. 2016. "Laetoli Footprints Reveal Bipedal Gait Biomechanics Different From Those of Modern Humans and Chimpanzees," *Proceedings of the Royal Society B* 283: 20160235. http://dx.doi.org/10.1098/rspb.2016.0235

Hester, Thomas R., Harry J. Shafer, and Kenneth L. Feder. 1997. *Field Methods in Archaeology* (7th Ed.). Mountain View, CA: Mayfield Publishing.

Hillam, J., C. M. Groves, D. M. Brown, M. G. L. Baillie, J. M. Coles, and B. J. Coles. 1990. "Dendrochronology of the English Neolithic." *Antiquity* 64 (243): 210–220.

Holmes, Richard. 2010. *The Age of Wonder: How the Romantic Generation Discovered the Beauty and Terror of Science*. New York: Vintage.

Ingber, Sasha. 2012. "Volcano Eruption Baked Rare Rhino Fossil," *National Geographic*. November 30. Accessed July 25, 2018.

Jay, Mandy, B. T. Fuller, Michael P. Richards, Christopher J. Knüsel, and Sarah S. King. 2008. "Iron Age Breastfeeding Practices in Britain: Isotopic Evidence From Wetwang Slack, East Yorkshire." *American Journal of Physical Anthropology* 136 (3): 327–337.

King, Sarah S. 2010. "What Makes War? Assessing Iron Age Warfare through Mortuary Behaviour and Osteological Patterns of Violence." Ph.D. thesis, Department of Archaeological Sciences, University of Bradford.

———. 2014. "Socialized Violence: Contextualizing Violence through Mortuary Behaviour in Iron Age Britain." In *The Routledge Handbook of the Bioarchaeology of Human Conflict*. Edited by Christopher Knüsel and Martin J. Smith. New York: Routledge.

Klein, Richard G. 1999. *The Human Career: Human Biological and Cultural Origins*. Second ed. Chicago: University of Chicago Press.

Komar, Debra A., and Jane E. Buikstra. 2008. *Forensic Anthropology: Contemporary Theory and Practice*. New York: Oxford University Press.

Komutrattananont, P. , and P. Mahakkanukrauh. 2017. "Age Estimation by Using Aspartic Acid Racemization From Purified Elastin of Aorta." *Medicine and Health* 12 (2): 170–178.

Kuniholm, Peter Ian, and Cecil L. Striker. 1987. "Dendrochronological Investigations in the Aegean and Neighboring Regions, 1983–1986." *Journal of Field Archaeology* 14 (4): 385–398.

Laurenzi, Marinella A., Maria Laura Balestrieri, Giulio Bigazzi, Julio C. Hadler Neto, Pedro J. Iunes, Pio Norelli, Massimo Oddone, Ana Maria Osorio Araya, and José G. Viramonte. 2007. "New Constraints on Ages of Glasses Proposed as Reference Materials for Fission-Track Dating." *Geostandards & Geoanalytical Research* 31 (2): 105–124.

Lebatard, Anne-Elisabeth, Didier L. Bourlès, Philippe Duringer, Marc Jolivet, Régis Braucher, Julien Carcaillet, Mathieu Schuster, et al. 2008. "Cosmogenic nuclide dating of *Sahelanthropus tchadensis* and *Australopithecus bahrelghazali*: Mio-Pliocene hominids from Chad." *Proceedings of the National Academy of Sciences* 105 (9): 3,226–3,231.

Leinhard, John H. 1998. "The Age of the Earth: Science, Religion, and Perception." Distinguished Lecture presented for the Shell Distinguished Lecture Series, Shell E&P Technology Company, Houston, May 21. https://www.uh.edu/engines/shell.htm

Lyell, Charles. 1830-1833. *Principles of geology, being an attempt to explain the former changes of the Earth's surface, by reference to causes now in operation*. Volumes 1, 2 and 3. London: John Murray

Maixner, Frank, Dmitrij Turaev, Amaury Cazenave-Gassiot, Marek Janko, Ben Krause-Kyora, Michael R. Hoopmann, Ulrike Kusebauch, et al. 2018. "The Iceman's Last Meal Consisted of Fat, Wild Meat, and Cereals." *Current Biology Report* 28 (14): 2,348–2,355.

Masao, Fidelis T., Elgidius B. Ichumbaki, Marco Cherin, Angelo Barili, Giovanni Boschian, David A. Lurino, Sofia Menconero, Jacopo Moggi-Cecchi, and Giorgio Manzi. 2016. "New Footprints From Laetoli (Tanzania) Provide Evidence for Marked Body Size Variation in Early Hominins." *eLife* 5: e19568. https://elifesciences.org/articles/19568

Michels, Joseph W. 1972. "Dating Methods." *Annual Review of Anthropology* 1: 113–126.

Monastersky, Richard. 2015. "Anthropocene: The Human Age." *Nature* 519 (7,542): 144–147.

Montgomery, Janet, Jane A. Evans, Dominic Powlesland, and Charlotte A. Roberts. 2005. "Continuity or Colonization in Anglo-Saxon England? Isotope Evidence for Mobility, Subsistence Practice, and Status at West Heslerton." *American Journal of Physical Anthropology* 126 (2): 123–138.

Murck, Barbara. 2001. *Geology: A Self-Teaching Guide*. New York: John Wiley & Sons.

Pastoors, Andreas, Tilman Lenssen-Erz, Bernd Breuckmann, Tsamkxao Ciqae, Ui Kxunta, Dirk Rieke-Zapp, and Thui Thao. 2017. "Experience Based Reading of Pleistocene Human Footprints in Pech-Merle." *Quaternary International* 430 (A): 155–162.

Pickrell, John. 2017. Ticks That Fed on Dinosaurs Found Trapped in Amber. *National Geographic*, December 12. https://news.nationalgeographic.com/2017/12/tick-dinosaur-feather-found-in-amber-blood-parastites-science/

Potts, Richard. 2012. "Evolution and Environmental Change in Early Human Prehistory." *Annual Review of Anthropology* 41: 151–167.

Raichlen David A. and Adam D. Gordon. 2017. "Interpretation of Footprints From Site S Confirms Human-like Bipedal Biomechanics in Laetoli Hominins," *Journal of Human Evolution* 107: 134–138.

Ravn, Morten. 2010. "Bronze and Early Iron Age Bog Bodies From Denmark." *Acta Archaeologica* 81 (1): 112–113.

Reimer, Paula J., Edouard Bard, Alex Bayliss, J. Warren Beck, Paul G. Blackwell, Christopher Bronk Ramsey, Caitlin E. Buck, et al. 2013. "INTCAL13 and Marine13 Radiocarbon Age Calibration Curves 0–50,000 Years cal BP." *Radiocarbon* 55 (4): 1,869–1,887.

Reinhard, Johan. 2016. "Frozen Mummies of the Andes." *Expedition* 58 (2): n. pag. https://www.penn.museum/sites/expedition/frozen-mummies-of-the-andes/

Reitz, Elizabeth J., and Elizabeth S. Wing. 1999. Zooarchaeology. Cambridge, UK: Cambridge University Press.

Renfrew, Colin, and Paul Bahn. 2016. *Archaeology: Theories, Methods, and Practice*. Seventh ed. New York: Thames and Hudson.

Repcheck, Jack. 2009. *The Man Who Found Time: James Hutton and the Discovery of the Earth's Antiquity*. New York: Basic Books.

Rowling, J. K. 1998. *Harry Potter and the Sorcerer's Stone*. New York: Scholastic.

Rowling, J. K. 2005. *Harry Potter and the Half-Blood Prince*. New York: Scholastic.

Ruddiman, William F., Zhengtang Guo, Xin Zhou, Hanbin Wu, and Yanyan Yu. 2008. "Early Rice Farming and Anomalous Methane Trends." *Quaternary Science Reviews* 27 (13–14): 1,291–1,295.

Russell, Randy. 2007. Earth's Magnetic Poles. *Windows to the Universe*, August 22. https://www.windows2universe.org/earth/Magnetosphere/earth_magnetic_poles.html

Smithsonian National Museum of Natural History. 2018. Laetoli Footprint Trails. Smithsonian National Museum of History, October 23. http://humanorigins.si.edu/evidence/behavior/footprints/laetoli-footprint-trails

Snoeck, Christophe, John Pouncett, Philippe Claeys, Steven Goderis, Nadine Mattielli, Mike Parker Pearson, Christie Willis, Antoine Zazzo, Julia A. Lee-Thorp, and Rick J. Schulting. 2018. "Strontium Isotope Analysis on Cremated Human Remains From Stonehenge Support[sic] Links With West Wales." *Scientific Reports* 8. https://www.nature.com/articles/s41598-018-28969-8

Steffen, Will, Johan Rockström, Katherine Richardson, Timothy M. Lenton, Carl Folke, Diana Liverman, Colin P. Summerhayes, et al. 2018. "Trajectories of the Earth System in the Anthropocene." *PNAS* 115 (33): 8,252–8,259.

Stodder, Ann L. W. 2008. "Taphonomy and the Nature of Archaeological Assemblages." In *Biological Anthropology of the Human Skeleton*. Edited by M. Anne Katzenberg and Shelley R. Saunders, 71–115. Hoboken, NJ: Wiley Blackwell.

Straus, Lawrence Guy. 1989. "Grave Reservations: More on Paleolithic Burial Evidence." *Current Anthropology* 30 (5): 633–634.

Sullivan, Terry and Harry Gifford. 1908. *She sells sea-shells*. London: Francis, Day, and Hunter.

United States Geological Survey. *Historical Perspectives*. 2012. United States Geological Survey, last updated August 7. https://pubs.usgs.gov/gip/dynamic/historical.html

University of the Witwatersrand. 2017. "Little Foot Takes a Bow: South Africa's Oldest and the World's Most Complete *Australopithecus* Skeleton Ever Found, Introduced to the World." *ScienceDaily*, December 6. https://www.sciencedaily.com/releases/2017/12/171206100104.htm

Valet, Jean-Pierre, Hélène Valladas. 2010. "The Laschamp-Mono Lake Geomagnetic Events and the Extinction of Neanderthal: A Causal Link or a Coincidence?" Quaternary Science Reviews 29(27–28): 3,887–3,893. https://doi.org/10.1016/j.quascirev.2010.09.010

Vidale, M., L. Bondioli, D. W. Frayer, M. Gallinaro, and A. Vanzetti. 2016. "Ötzi the Iceman." *Expedition* 58 (2): 13–17. https://www.penn.museum/sites/expedition/otzi-the-iceman/

Wallace, Steven C., and Xiaoming Wang. 2004. "Two New Carnivores From an Unusual Late Tertiary Forest Biota in Eastern North America." *Nature* 431 (7,008): 556–559.

Waters, Colin N., Jan Zalasiewicz, Anthony D. Barnosky, Alejandro Cearreta, Agieszka Galuszka, Juliana A. Ivar Do Sul, Catherine Jeandel, et al. N.d. "Is the Anthropocene Distinct From the Holocene?" In *Strati 2015 2nd International Congress on Stratigraphy*, Graz, Austria, July 19–23, 2015. Unpublished MS.

Watson, Traci. 2017. "Ancient Bones Reveal Girl's Tough Life in Early Americas." *Nature* 544 (7,648): 15–16.

White, Tim D. 1986. "Cut Marks on the Bodo Cranium: A Case of Prehistoric Defleshing." *American Journal of Physical Anthropology* 69 (4): 503–509.

Williams, Linda D. 2004. *Earth Science Demystified*. New York: McGraw-Hill Professional.

Wilson, Andrew S., Timothy Taylor, Maria Constanza Ceruti, Jose Antonio Chavez, Johan Reinhard, Vaughan Grimes, Wolfram Meier-Augenstein, et al. 2007. "Stable Isotope and DNA Evidence for Ritual Sequences in Inca Child Sacrifice." PNAS 104 (42): 16,456–16,461.

Wolchover, Natalie. 2012. "What If Earth's Magnetic Poles Switch?" Live Science, February 10. https://www.livescience.com/18426-earth-magnetic-poles-flip.html

Acknowledgements

The authors thank the staff of the Maturango Museum, Ridgecrest, California—and, specifically, Debbie Benson, executive director; Alexander K. Rogers, archaeology curator; Sherry Brubaker, natural history curator; and Elaine Wiley, history curator—for their generous help with photography and fossil images. The authors thank Sharlene Paxton, a librarian at Cerro Coso Community College, Ridgecrest, California, for her guidance and expertise with OER and open-source images, and John Stenger-Smith and Claudia Sellers from Cerro Coso Community College, Ridgecrest, California, for their feedback on the chemistry and plant biology content. Finally, the authors thank William and Lauren Zajicek, our community college students, for providing their impressions and extensive feedback on early drafts of the chapter.

Figure Attributions

Figure 7.1 Mary Anning by B. J. Donne from the Geological Society/NHMPL is in the public domain.

Figure 7.2 A Walk at Dusk (object 93.PA.14 at the J. Paul Getty Museum) by Casper David Friedrich (German 1774-1840) is in the public domain and part of the Getty Open Content Program.

Figure 7.3 lyme-regis-coast-sea-cliffs-924431 by jstarj and has been designated under a Pixabay License.

Figure 7.4 Mary Anning Plesiosaurus by Mary Anning (1799-1847) is in the public domain.

Figure 7.5 Ammonite by Sarah S. King and Lee Anne Zajicek is under a CC BY-NC 4.0 License.

Figure 7.6 Murexsul from the Maturango Museum, Ridgecrest, California, by Sarah S. King and Lee Anne Zajicek is under a CC BY-NC 4.0 License.

Figure 7.7 Geologic time scale by United States Geological Survey is in the public domain.

Figure 7.8 Chooz Nuclear Power Plant-9361 by Raimond Spekking is used under a CC BY-SA 4.0 License.

Figure 7.9 Pangaea continents by LucasVB is used under a CC BY-SA 3.0 License.

Figure 7.10 White Cliffs Of Dover 2 by Eleanor Nelson available on www.PublicDomainPictures.net has been designated to the public domain (CC0 1.0).

Figure 7.11 Etretat 07 August 2005 019 by anonymous is used under a CC BY-SA 3.0 License.

Figure 7.12 Aerial-SanAndreas-CarrizoPlain by John Wiley User:Jw4nvc – Santa Barbara, California is used under a CC BY 3.0 License.

Figure 7.13 Red Panda (25193861686) by Mathias Appel has been designated to the public domain (CC0 1.0).

Figure 7.14 Coyote remains by Sarah S. King is under a CC BY-NC 4.0 License.

Figure 7.15 Fossilization process original to Explorations: An Open Invitation to Biological Anthropology by Mary Nelson is under a CC BY-NC 4.0 License.

Figure 7.16 PetrifiedWood at the Petrified Forest National Park by Jon Sullivan has been designated to the public domain (CC0).

Figure 7.17 Lucy blackbg by 120 is used under a CC BY 2.5 License.

Figure 7.18 Amber2 by Anders L. Damgaard (www.amber-inclusions.dk – Baltic-amber-beetle) is used under a CC BY-SA 3.0 License.

Figure 7.19 Amber.pendants.800pix.050203 by Adrian Pingstone (2003) has been designated to the public domain (CC0).

Figure 7.20 Mammoth Tragedy at La Brea Tar Pits (5463657162) by KimonBerlin is used under a CC BY-SA 2.0 License.

Figure 7.21 Canis dirus (dire wolf) (La Brea Asphalt, Upper Pleistocene, La Brea Tar Pits, California, USA) 3 by James St. John is used under a CC BY 2.0 License.

Figure 7.22 Smilodon saber-toothed tiger skull (La Brea Asphalt, Upper Pleistocene; Rancho La Brea tar pits, southern California, USA) 1 by James St. John is used under a CC BY 2.0 License.

Figure 7.23 NHM – Laetoli Fußspuren by Wolfgang Sauber is used under a CC BY-SA 4.0 License.

Figure 7.24 Precious the Coprolite Courtesy of the Poozeum by Poozeum is used under a CC BY-SA 4.0 License.

Figure 7.25 Dendrites from the Maturango Museum, Ridgecrest, California, by Sarah S. King and Lee Anne Zajicek is under a CC BY-NC 4.0 License.

Figure 7.26 Laetoli and Olduvai Gorge sites original to Explorations: An Open Invitation to Biological Anthropology by Elyssa Ebding at GeoPlace, California State University, Chico is under a CC BY-NC 4.0 License.

Figure 7.27 Woman with bronze cast of Au. afarensis at the Natural History Museum in Washington, D.C., by Lee Anne Zajicek is under a CC BY-NC 4.0 License.

Figure 7.28 Stratigraphic cross-section original to Explorations: An Open Invitation to Biological Anthropology by Mary Nelson is under a CC BY-NC 4.0 License.

Figure 7.29 Bronze Age implements, ornaments and pottery (Period II) by Wellcome Collection is used under a CC BY 4.0 License.

Figure 7.30 Sterkfontein Piltdown man by Anrie is used under a CC BY-SA 3.0 License.

Figure 7.31 Atom Diagram by AG Caesar is used under a CC BY-SA 4.0 License.

Figure 7.32 Radiocarbon dating original to Explorations: An Open Invitation to Biological Anthropology by Mary Nelson is under a CC BY-NC 4.0 License.

Figure 7.33 Çjkgfmj by Abdulkadirtiryaki is used under a CC BY-SA 3.0 License.

Figure 7.34 Dendrochronology original to Explorations: An Open Invitation to Biological Anthropology by Mary Nelson is under a CC BY-NC 4.0 License.

Figure 7.35 Blue Globe by Ken Teegardin is used under a CC BY 2.0 License.

Figure 7.36 Oxygen in deep sea sediment carbonate by NASA Goddard Institute for Space Studies, originally from "Science Briefs: Cold Climates, Warm Climates: How Can We Tell Past Temperatures?", is in the public domain.

Figure 7.37 Stonehenge by Sarah S. King is under a CC BY-NC 4.0 License.

Figure 7.38 Hoyo Negro and Sistema Sac Actun, Mexico original to Explorations: An Open Invitation to Biological Anthropology by Elyssa Ebding at GeoPlace, California State University, Chico is under a CC BY-NC 4.0 License.

Figure 7.39 Hoyo Negro cenote original to Explorations: An Open Invitation to Biological Anthropology by Mary Nelson is under a CC BY-NC 4.0 License.

Chapter 8: Primate Evolution

Jonathan M. G. Perry, Ph.D., The Johns Hopkins University School of Medicine

Stephanie L. Canington, B.A., The Johns Hopkins University School of Medicine

> *Learning Objectives*
>
> - Understand the major trends in primate evolution from the origin of primates to the origin of our own species.
> - Learn about primate adaptations and how they characterize major primate groups.
> - Discuss the kinds of evidence that anthropologists use to find out how extinct primates are related to each other and to living primates.
> - Recognize how the changing geography and climate of Earth have influenced where and when primates have thrived or gone extinct.

The first fifty million years of primate evolution was a series of adaptive **radiations** leading to the diversification of the earliest lemurs, monkeys, and apes. The primate story begins in the canopy and understory of conifer-dominated forests, with our small, furtive ancestors subsisting at night, beneath the notice of day-active dinosaurs.

From the archaic **plesiadapiforms** (archaic primates) to the earliest groups of true primates (**euprimates**), the origin of our own order is characterized by the struggle for new food sources and microhabitats in the arboreal setting. Climate change forced major extinctions as the northern continents became increasingly dry, cold, and seasonal and as tropical rainforests gave way to deciduous forests, woodlands, and eventually grasslands. Lemurs, lorises, and tarsiers—once diverse groups containing many species—became rare, except for lemurs in Madagascar where there were no anthropoid competitors and perhaps few predators. Meanwhile, **anthropoids** (monkeys and apes) emerged in the **Old World**, then dispersed across parts of the northern hemisphere, Africa, and ultimately South America. Meanwhile, the movement of continents, shifting sea levels, and changing patterns of rainfall and vegetation contributed to the developing landscape of primate biogeography, morphology, and behavior. Today's primates provide modest reminders of the past diversity and remarkable adaptations of their extinct relatives. This chapter explores the major trends in primate evolution from the origin of the Order Primates to the beginnings of our own lineage, providing a window into these stories from our ancient past.

HOW TO DIAGNOSE A PRIMATE

When you examine the skeleton of a mammal, how do you know if you are looking at a primate? Some physical traits are useful in the **diagnosis** of primates and have been used to make decisions about which living and fossil mammals belong in our definition of the Order Primates. However, primates are hard to diagnose. There is no obvious diagnostic trait of our own order. From the first modern attempts to classify primates, scientists have struggled to come up with traits that are possessed exclusively and universally by primates. In the end, most have generated lists of traits that are of variable utility in making a correct diagnosis.

In the 19th century, British naturalist St. George Jackson Mivart articulated the most famous diagnosis of the Order Primates. This "primate pattern" is a list of the following traits: nails, clavicles, placentation, orbits encircled by bone, three tooth types (i.e., incisors, canines, premolars/molars), posterior lobe of the brain, calcarine fissure of the brain, opposable thumb and/or big toe, nail on the big toe, well-developed cecum, pendulous penis, testes within a scrotum, and two nipples in the pectoral region. Many primatologists have pointed out that no single feature on this list is unique to primates. Also, nails appear twice. Taken together, perhaps it is a useful list. Unfortunately, some of these traits (e.g., three types of teeth) are neither clear nor true of all primates. Other traits, like nipple number and location, are quite variable among primates. Still others, for example the pendulousness of the penis, can be assessed in only males.

Modifications of this approach by subsequent scientists have included lists of trends, like that suggested by Le Gros Clark. Clark's trends emphasize the flexibility and generalized nature of the limbs, mobility and dexterity of the digits, reduction of the snout with elaboration of the visual system, retention of simple teeth, and elaboration of the brain with prolonged period of juvenile dependence. Later, Robert D. Martin emphasized distinctive reproductive characteristics of primates, along with details of cranial anatomy and grasping extremities (Martin 1968, 1990).

Most modern workers have focused on the grasping extremities and flattened nails, as well as branching of the carotid artery supply to the brain and of the formation of the auditory bulla of the cranium. In extant primates, the brain receives its blood supply via two principal routes (one pathway to the back of the brain and one toward the front). For all taxa, the paired vertebral arteries provide most of the blood to the back of the brain. Blood supply to the front, however, is more complex and involves branches of the internal carotid artery (ICA) and external carotid artery (ECA). For haplorhines (tarsiers, **catarrhines**, and **platyrrhines**), the main artery to the front of the brain is a branch of the ICA called the promontory artery (though most human gross anatomy textbooks simply refer to it as the internal carotid artery). In most lemuriforms, this is the job of a second branch of the ICA known as the stapedial artery (which tends to be absent in adult haplorhines). Finally, in lorisiformes and cheirogaleid lemuriformes, the front of the brain is supplied by the ascending pharyngeal artery (a branch of the ECA). These differences provide a valuable method for reconstructing phylogenetic relationships between fossil primates and living taxa.

In all extant primates, the auditory bulla is ossified and is formed by an extension of the petrous part of the temporal bone (or, more simply, petrosal bone). This last trait, a petrosal bulla, is perhaps the best candidate for a universally applicable diagnostic trait of primates. Unfortunately, it is often extremely difficult to assess in an adult cranium and perhaps even more difficult to assess in a fossil that has various cracks and deformities associated with preservation and preparation.

Although taxonomists crave neat and complete lists of traits to aid in sorting animals into bins, the true definition of a phylogenetic group is always one of descent from a common ancestor. The Order Primates is made up of all of the descendants of some common ancestor in the remote past. This last common ancestor probably did not possess all of the traits common to primates today and might have been indistinguishable from other primitive placental mammals living in the Cretaceous Period.

MAJOR HYPOTHESES ABOUT PRIMATE ORIGINS

For many groups of mammals, there is a key feature that led to their success. A good example is powered flight in bats. Primates lack a feature like this. Instead, if there is something unique about primates, it is probably a group of features rather than one single thing. Because of this, anthropologists and paleontologists struggle to describe an ecological scenario that could explain the rise and success of our own order. Three major hypotheses have been advanced to explain the origin of primates and to explain what makes our own order unique among mammals (Figure 8.1); these are described below.

Figure 8.1 Three major hypotheses are A) the arboreal hypothesis, B) the visual predation hypothesis, and C) the angiosperm-primate coevolution hypothesis.

Arboreal Hypothesis

In the 1800s, many anthropologists viewed all animals in relation to humans. That is, animals that were more like humans were considered to be more "advanced" and those lacking humanlike features were considered more "primitive." This way of thinking was particularly obvious in studies of primates.

Thus, when anthropologists sought features that separate primates from other mammals, they focused on features that were least developed in lemurs and lorises, more developed in monkeys, and most developed in apes (Figure 8.2). Frederic Wood Jones, one of the leading anatomist-anthropologists of the early 1900s, is usually credited with the Arboreal Hypothesis of primate origins (Jones 1916). This hypothesis holds that many of the features of primates evolved to improve locomotion in the trees. For example, the grasping hands and feet of primates are well suited to gripping tree branches of various sizes and our flexible joints are good for reorienting the extremities in many different ways. A mentor of Jones, Grafton Elliot Smith, had suggested that the reduced olfactory system, acute vision, and forward-facing eyes of primates are an adaptation to making accurate leaps and bounds through a complex, three-dimensional canopy (Smith 1912). The forward orientation of the eyes in primates causes the visual fields to overlap, enhancing depth perception, especially at close range. Evidence to support this hypothesis includes the facts that many extant primates are arboreal, and the primitive members of most primate groups are dedicated arborealists. The Arboreal Hypothesis was well accepted by most anthropologists at the time and for decades afterward.

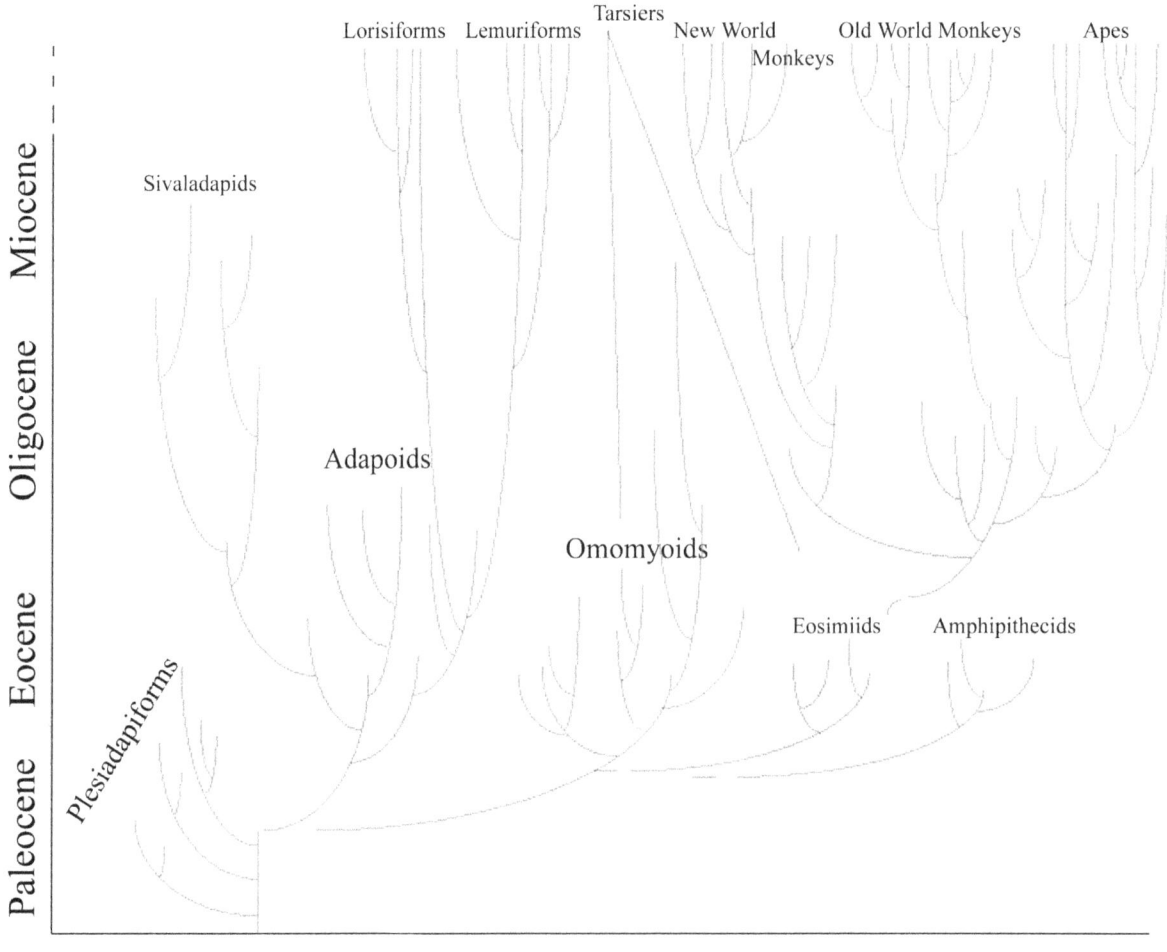

Figure 8.2. Primate family tree showing major groups. Disconnected lines show uncertainty about relationships. Note two lines leading to tarsiers from different possible groups of origin. The timescale is shortened for the epochs since the Miocene.

Visual Predation Hypothesis

In the late 1960s and early 1970s, Matt Cartmill studied and tested the idea that the characteristic features of primates evolved in the context of arboreal locomotion. Cartmill noted that squirrels climb trees (and even vertical walls) very effectively, even though they lack some of the key adaptations of primates. As members of the Order Rodentia, squirrels also lack the hand and foot anatomy of primates. They have claws instead of flattened nails and their eyes face more laterally than those of primates. Cartmill reasoned that there must be some other explanation for the unique traits of primates. He noted that some non-arboreal animals share at least some of these traits with primates; for example, cats and predatory birds have forward-facing eyes that enable visual field overlap. Cartmill suggested that the unique suite of features in primates is an adaptation to detecting insect prey and guiding the hands (or feet) to catch insects (Cartmill 1972). His hypothesis emphasizes the primary role of vision in prey detection and capture; it is explicitly comparative, relying on form function relationships in other mammals and nonmammalian vertebrates. According to Cartmill, many of the key features of primates evolved for preying on insects in this special manner (Cartmill 1974).

Angiosperm-Primate Coevolution Hypothesis

The visual predation hypothesis was unpopular with some anthropologists. One reason for this is that many primates today are not especially predatory. Another is that, whereas primates do seem well adapted to moving around in the smallest, terminal branches of trees, insects are not necessarily easier to find there. A counterargument to the visual predation hypothesis is the angiosperm-primate coevolution hypothesis. Primate ecologist Robert Sussman (Sussman 1991) argued that the few primates that eat mostly insects often catch their prey on the ground rather than in the fine branches of trees. Furthermore, predatory primates often use their ears more than their eyes to detect prey. Finally, most early primate fossils show signs of having been omnivorous rather than insectivorous. Instead, he argued, the earliest primates were probably seeking fruit. Fruit (and flowers) of angiosperms (flowering plants) often develop in the terminal branches. Therefore, any mammal trying to access those fruits must possess anatomical traits that allow them to maintain their hold on thin branches and avoid falling while reaching for the fruits. Primates likely evolved their distinctive visual traits and extremities in the Paleocene (approximately 65 million to 54 million years ago) and Eocene (approximately 54 million to 34 million years ago) epochs, just when angiosperms were going through a revolution of their own—the evolution of large, fleshy fruit that would have been attractive to a small arboreal mammal. Sussman argued that, just as primates were evolving anatomical traits that made them more efficient fruit foragers, angiosperms were also evolving fruit that would be more attractive to primates to promote better seed dispersal. This mutually beneficial relationship between the angiosperms and the primates was termed "coevolution" or more specifically "**diffuse coevolution**."

At about the same time, D. Tab Rasmussen noted several parallel traits in primates and the South American woolly opossum, *Caluromys*. He argued that early primates were probably foraging on both fruits and insects (Rasmussen 1990). As is true of *Caluromys* today, early primates probably foraged for fruits in the terminal branches of angiosperms, and they probably used their visual sense to aid in catching insects. Insects are also attracted to fruit (and flowers), so these insects represent a convenient opportunity for a primarily fruit-eating primate to gather protein. This solution is, in effect, a compromise between the visual predation hypothesis and the angiosperm-primate coevolution hypothesis. It is worth noting that other models of primate origins have been proposed, and these include the possibility that no single ecological scenario can account for the origin of primates.

THE ORIGIN OF PRIMATES

Paleocene: Mammals in the Wake of Dinosaur Extinctions

Placental mammals, including primates, originated in the Mesozoic Era (approximately 251 million to 65.5 million years ago), the Age of Dinosaurs. During this time, most placental mammals were small, probably nocturnal, and probably avoided predators via camouflage and slow, quiet movement. It has been suggested that the success and diversity of the dinosaurs constituted a kind of ecological barrier to Mesozoic mammals. The extinction of the dinosaurs (and many other organisms) at the end of the Cretaceous Period (approximately 145.5–65.5 million years ago) might have opened up these ecological niches, leading to the increased diversity and disparity in mammals of the Tertiary Period (approximately 65.5–2.5 million years ago).

The Paleocene was the first epoch in the Age of Mammals. Soon after the Cretaceous-Tertiary (K-T) extinction event, new groups of placental mammals appear in the fossil record. Many of these groups achieved a broad range of sizes and lifestyles as well as a great number of species before declining sometime in the Eocene (or soon thereafter). These groups were ultimately replaced by the modern orders of placental mammals (Figure 8.3). It is unknown whether these replacements occurred gradually, for example by competitive exclusion, or rapidly, perhaps by sudden geographic dispersals with replacement. In some senses, the Paleocene might have been a time of recovery from the extinction event; it was cooler and more seasonal globally than the subsequent Eocene.

Figure 8.3 Depiction of Eocene flora and fauna in North America.

Plesiadapiforms, the Archaic Primates

The Paleocene epoch saw the emergence of several families of mammals that have been implicated in the origin of primates. These are the plesiadapiforms. Plesiadapiforms are archaic primates, meaning that they possessed some primate features and lacked others. The word *plesiadapiform* means "almost adapiform," a reference to some similarities between some plesiadapiforms and some adapiforms (or adapoids; later-appearing true primates)—mainly in the molar teeth. Because enamel fossilizes better than other parts of the body, the molar teeth are the parts most often found and first discovered for any new species. Thus, dental similarities were often the first to be noticed by early mammalian paleontologists, partly explaining why plesiadapiforms were thought to be primates. Major morphological differences between plesiadapiforms and euprimates (true primates) were observed later when more parts of plesiadapiform skeletons were discovered. Many plesiadapiforms have unusual anterior teeth and most have digits possessing claws rather than nails. So far, no plesiadapiform ever discovered has a postorbital bar (seen in extant strepsirrhines) or septum (as seen in **haplorhines**), and whether or not the **auditory bulla** was formed by the **petrous bone** remains unclear for many plesiadapiform specimens. Nevertheless, there are compelling reasons (partly from new skeletal material) for including plesiadapiforms within the Order Primates.

Geographic and Temporal Distribution

Purgatorius is generally considered to be the earliest primate. This Paleocene mammal is known from teeth that are very primitive for a primate. It has some characteristics that suggest it is a basal plesiadapiform, but there is very little to link it specifically with euprimates (see Clemens 2004). Its ankle bones suggest a high degree of mobility, signaling an arboreal lifestyle (Chester et al. 2015). *Purgatorius* is primitive enough to have given rise to all primates, including the plesiadapiforms. Plesiadapiform families were numerous and diverse during parts of the Paleocene in western North America and western Europe, with some genera (e.g., *Plesiadapis*; see Table 8.1) living on both continents (Figure 8.4). Thus, there were probably corridors for plesiadapiform dispersal between the two continents, and it stands to reason that these mammals were living all across North America, including in the eastern half of the continent and at high latitudes. A few plesiadapiforms have been described from Asia (e.g., *Carpocristes*), but the affinities of these remain uncertain.

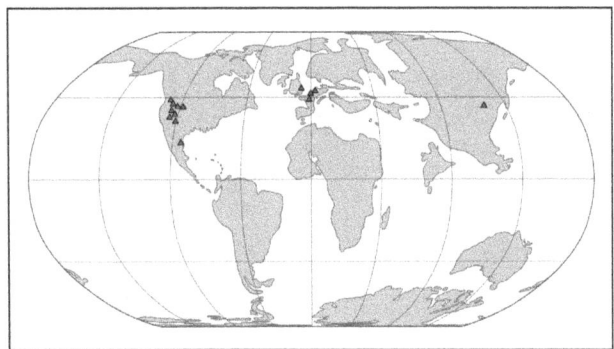

Figure 8.4 Map of the world in the Paleocene, highlighting plesiadapiform localities.

General Morphological Features

Although there is much morphological variation among the families of plesiadapiforms, there are some common features of the group. Most plesiadapiforms were small, the largest being about three kilograms (approximately 7 lbs.; *Plesiadapis cookei*). They had small brains and fairly large snouts, with variable eye size (as deduced from the bony orbits). In general, the eyes faced more laterally than in euprimates. Most plesiadapiforms have large incisors relative to the molars and in some species, the lower incisors (usually one pair) are reminiscent of long daggers or spears. In many plesiadapiforms, the upper central incisors are also very unusual, with small cuspules spaced out like fingers, having some unknown function perhaps related to seizing or cropping food. Many species show reduction and/or loss of the canine and anterior premolars, with the resulting formation of a rodent-like **diastema**; this probably implies a herbivorous diet. The spaces available for the chewing musculature are very large, and most plesiadapiforms probably had very powerful chewing muscles, perhaps capable of processing very tough foods (e.g., leaves). Some families appear to have had very specialized diets, as suggested by unusual tooth and jaw shapes. For example, an enlarged, laterally compressed, blade-like lower premolar appears to have evolved via **convergent evolution** in two different families, the Carpolestidae and the Saxonellidae.

Arguably the most interesting and unusual family of plesiadapiforms is the Carpolestidae. This family contains three major genera and a few minor ones. They are almost exclusively from North America (with a couple of possible members from Asia), and mainly from the Middle and Late Paleocene. Their molars are not very remarkable, being quite similar to those of some other plesiadapiforms (e.g., Plesiadapidae). However, nearly everything else is unusual. Their lower posterior premolars (p4) are laterally compressed and blade-like with vertical serrations topped by tiny cuspules. This unusual dental morphology is termed "**plagiaulacoid**" (Simpson 1933). It is similar to the condition in some living and fossil marsupials, but in marsupials, the blade-like lower tooth slides across a similar-looking blade-like upper tooth. In carpolestids, the blade-like tooth meets upper premolars that look completely different. The upper premolar occlusal surfaces are broad and are covered with many small cuspules; the blade-like lower premolar might have cut across these cuspules, between them, or both.

Many plesiadapiforms have hallmarks of arboreality in the skeleton, though the long bones are rather robust. Instead of having nails, most taxa had sharp claws on most or all of the digits. The extremities show signs that at least some of these archaic primates had grasping abilities comparable to those of primates and some arboreal marsupials. Nearly complete skeletons are known for several North American plesiadapiforms, and these have yielded a tremendous wealth of information on locomotor and foraging habits. Many plesiadapiforms appear to have been well adapted to clinging to vertical substrates (like a broad tree trunk) using their sharp claws, propelling themselves upward using powerful hindlimbs, bounding along horizontal supports, grasping smaller branches, and moving head-first down tree trunks. In carpolestids in particular, the skeleton appears to have been especially well adapted to moving slowly and carefully in small terminal branches. The big toe likely was especially good at grasping (Figure 8.5). There is a single specimen of a flattened nail-bearing distal big toe bone of *Carpolestes simpsoni* (Table 8.1), and this feature suggests affinities with euprimates.

Figure 8.5 *An artistic rendition of Carpolestes simpsoni moving along a small diameter support.*

Debate: Relationship of Plesiadapiforms to True Primates

In the middle of the 20th century, treeshrews (Order Scandentia) were often considered part of the Order Primates, based on anatomical similarities between some treeshrews and primates. For many people, plesiadapiforms represented intermediates between primates and treeshrews, so plesiadapiforms were included in Primates as well.

Later, studies of reproduction and brain anatomy in treeshrews and lemurs suggested that treeshrews are not primates (e.g., Martin 1968). This was soon followed by the suggestion to also expel plesiadapiforms (Martin 1972). Like treeshrews, plesiadapiforms lack a postorbital bar, nails, and details of the ear region that characterize true primates. Many paleoanthropologists were reluctant to accept this move to banish plesiadapiforms (e.g. P. D. Gingerich 1980).

Later, Beard (1990) found that in some ways, the digits of paromomyid plesiadapiforms are actually more similar to those of dermopterans (Order Dermoptera), the closest living relatives of primates, than they are to those of primates themselves (but see Krause 1991). At the same time, Kay and colleagues (1990) found that cranial circulation patterns and auditory bulla morphology in the paromomyid, *Ignacius* (Table 8.1), are more like those of dermopterans than like those of primates.

For many anthropologists, this one-two punch effectively removed plesiadapiforms from the Order Primates. In the last two decades, the tide of opinion has turned again, with many researchers including plesiadapiforms in the Order Primates. New and more complete specimens demonstrate that the postcranial skeletons of plesiadapiforms, including the hands and feet, were primate-like, not dermorpteran-like (Bloch and Boyer 2002, 2007). New fine-grained CT scans of relatively complete plesiadapiform skulls revealed that they share some key traits with primates to the exclusion of other placental mammals (Bloch and Silcox 2006). Most significant was the suggestion that *Carpolestes simpsoni* possessed an auditory bulla formed by the petrosal bone, like in all living primates.

The debate about the status of plesiadapiforms continues, owing to a persistent lack of key bones in some species and owing to genuine complexity of the anatomical traits involved. Maybe plesiadapiforms were the primitive stock from which all primates arose, with some plesiadapiforms (e.g., carpolestids) nearer to the primate **stem** than others.

Geographic and Temporal Distribution

The first universally accepted primates to appear in the fossil record are the earliest members of two groups: the adapoids and the omomyoids. These groups become quite distinct over evolutionary time, filling mutually exclusive niches for the most part. However, at the start of the Eocene, the most primitive adapoids are very similar to the most primitive omomyoids.

Adapoids are called adapiforms or adapids by some and are here considered members of the superfamily **Adapoidea**. Omomyoids (omomyiforms or omomyids, according to some) are members of the superfamily **Omomyoidea**. The adapoids were mainly diurnal and herbivorous, with some achieving larger sizes than any plesiadapiforms (10 kg; 22 lbs.). By contrast, the omomyoids were mainly nocturnal, insectivorous and frugivorous, and small.

Both groups appear suddenly at the start of the Eocene, where they are present in western North America, western Europe, and India (Figure 8.6). If the primate *Altiatlasius* is an omomyoid, then these were also present in the Late Paleocene of North Africa. This wide dispersal of early primates was probably due to the presence of rainforest corridors extending far into northern latitudes.

In North America and Europe, both groups achieved considerable diversity in the Middle Eocene, then mostly died out at the end of that epoch. In some Eocene rock formations in the western United States, adapoids and omomyoids make up a major part of the mammalian fauna. The Eocene of India has yielded a modest diversity of euprimates, some of which are so primitive that it is difficult to know whether they are adapoids or omomyoids (or even early anthropoids).

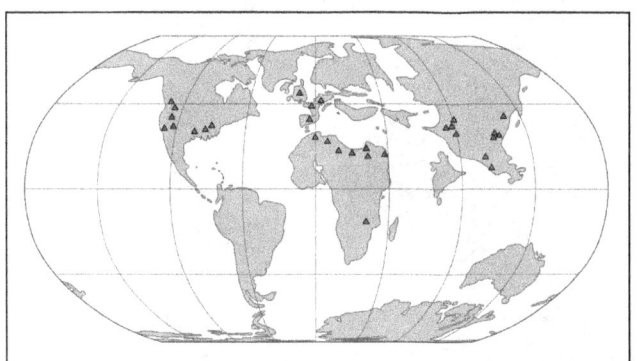

Figure 8.6 Map of the world in the Eocene, highlighting adapoid and omomyoid localities.

Adapoids and omomyoids barely survived the Eocene-Oligocene extinctions, when colder temperatures, increased seasonality, and the retreat of rainforests to lower latitudes led to changes in mammalian biogeography. In North America, one genus originally considered an omomyoid but recently placed in the Adapoidea persisted until the Miocene: *Ekgmowechashala*, from various parts of North America (Rose and Rensberger 1983). This taxon has highly unusual teeth and might have been a late immigrant to North America from Asia. In Asia, one family of adapoids, the Sivaladapidae, retained considerable diversity as late as the Late Miocene. In Africa and Arabia, several fossil primates resembling extant strepsirrhines were present in the Eocene and Oligocene (approximately 34 million to 24 million years ago; Seiffert 2012).

Adapoid Diversity

Adapoids were very diverse, particularly in the Eocene of North America and Europe. They can be divided into six families, with a few species of uncertain familial relationship. As a group, adapoids have some features in common, although much of what they share is primitive. Important features include the hallmarks of euprimates: postorbital bar, flattened nails, grasping extremities, and a petrosal bulla. In addition, some adapoids retain the primitive dental formula of 2.1.4.3; that is, in each quadrant of the mouth, there are two incisors, one canine, four premolars, and three molars. In general, the incisors are small compared to the molars, but the canines are relatively large, with sexual dimorphism in some species. Their snouts are somewhat long, and evidence from cranial specimens suggests that the carotid artery branches that fed the front of the brain were variable and sometimes multiple. Cutting crests on the molars are well developed in some species, and the two halves of the mandible were fused at the midline in some species. Some adapoids were quite small (*Anchomomys* at a little over 100 g), and some were quite large (*Magnadapis* at 10 kg; 22 lbs.). Many had relatively small eyes, and in some the eyes faced somewhat laterally and/or upwardly. Furthermore, the spaces and attachment features for the chewing muscles were truly enormous in some species, suggesting that these muscles were very large and powerful. Taken together, this suggests an overall adaptive profile of diurnal herbivory. The canine sexual dimorphism in some species suggests a possible mating pattern of polygyny, as males in polygynous primate species often compete with each other for mates and have especially large canine teeth. The description that follows provides greater detail for the two best known adapoid families, the Adapidae and the Notharctidae; the additional families are summarized briefly.

The first adapoids to be described belong to the family Adapidae. This family was exclusive to Europe and includes some of the most cranially and postcranially robust primates of the Eocene (Figure 8.7). The first primate fossil ever named was *Adapis*, which was described by Baron Georges Cuvier between 1812 and 1822. Originally it was thought to be an ungulate and was recognized as a primate starting in the 1870s. Many adapids are known from exceptionally complete cranial and postcranial material from France and Switzerland. Unfortunately, most of the best fossils were collected in the 1800s as part of fertilizer mining operations and stratigraphic provenience of those specimens is uncertain. Furthermore, these fossils come from jumbled fissure fills, making it hard to know which bones came from the same animal.

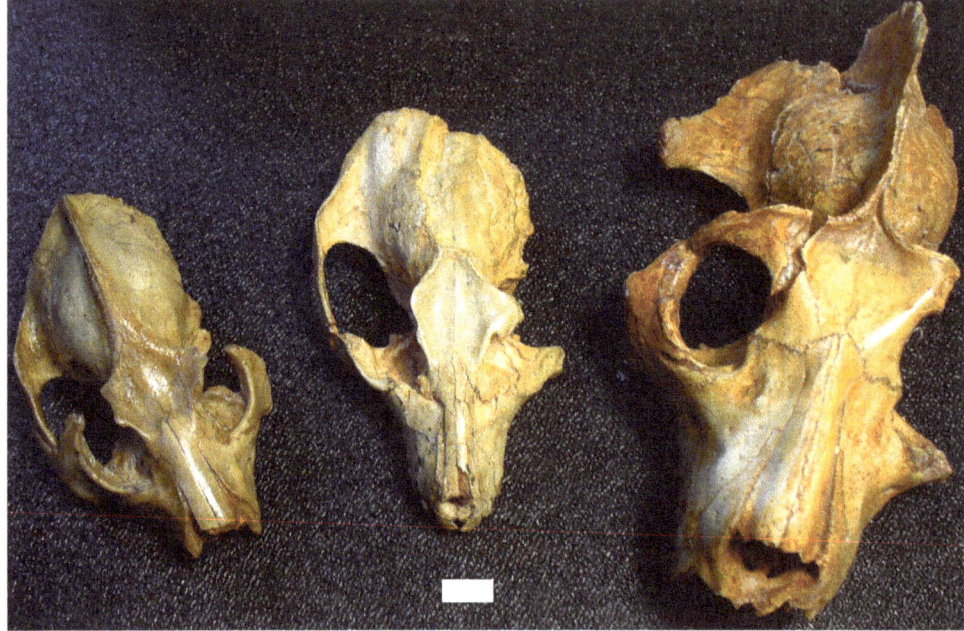

Figure 8.7 Representative crania of adapids (European adapoids) from the natural history museum in Montauban, France. The white scale bar is 1 cm long.

Perhaps the best known adapoids are the Notharctidae from western North America, with a few species from Europe. Collections from Wyoming and Colorado in the United States have yielded many relatively complete skeletons—not to mention thousands of jaws with teeth—of such genera as *Notharctus* (Table 8.1), *Cantius*, and *Smilodectes*. The notharctids have been described as especially lemur-like (Table 8.2) on the basis of their postcranial adaptations for clinging and leaping as well as on the basis of overall cranial resemblance (Gregory 1920). The primitive *Cantius* has representatives in both North America and Europe.

The Cercamoniidae (e.g., *Donrussellia*; Table 8.1) from Europe and Asia includes some of the most primitive adapoids. The Caenopithecidae contains several genera once considered to be in Cercamoniidae, but that share an overall decrease in the length of the snout accompanied by increasing robusticity of the jaws, loss of some premolar teeth, and leaping adaptations. This family must have been very widely dispersed across the northern continents as it has representatives in the Eocene of Europe, North America, Africa, and Asia (Kirk and Williams 2011; Seiffert et al. 2009). It includes the Fayum genera *Aframonius* and *Afradapis* (Table 8.1) as well as *Europolemur*, *Godinotia*, and *Darwinius* (Figure 8.8) from the Messel oil shales in Germany (approximately 47.3 million years ago).

Figure 8.8 Darwinius masillae. The slab on the left is Plate A and the slab on the right is Plate B. The parts of the skeleton in B that are outside of the dashed lines were fabricated.

The Asiadapidae and Sivaladapidae are known from only Asia. Asiadapids are primitive adapoids from India. Postcranial elements are known from the same horizons as the described teeth, but the combination of anatomical traits in these bones makes it difficult to know if they belonged to adapoids or to omomyoids, both of which were present (Dunn et al. 2016; Rose et al. 2018). The Sivaladapidae from India, Pakistan, China, and Thailand (e.g., *Sivaladapis*; Table 8.1), mostly represented by jaws with teeth, persisted well into the Miocene and, in some cases, achieved a large size (4 kg; 8.82 lbs.). The sivaladapids might have evolved from the asiadapids.

Omomyoid Diversity

Like adapoids, omomyoids appeared suddenly at the start of the Eocene and then became very diverse with most species dying out before the Oligocene. Omomyoids are known from thousands of jaws with teeth, relatively complete skulls for about a half-dozen species, and very little postcranial material. Omomyoids were relatively small primates, with the largest being less than three kilograms (approximately 7 lbs.; *Macrotarsius montanus*). All known crania possess a postorbital bar, which in some has been described as "incipient closure." Some—but not all—known crania have an elongated bony ear tube extending lateral to the location of the eardrum, a feature seen in living tarsiers and catarrhines. The anterior teeth tend to be large, with canines that are usually not much larger than the incisors. Often it is difficult to distinguish closely related species using molar morphology, but the premolars tend to be distinct from one species to another. The postcranial skeleton of most omomyoids shows hallmarks of leaping behavior reminiscent of that of tarsiers.

European omomyoids are grouped together in one family, the Microchoeridae. All microchoerids were small, had relatively large eyes, and were probably nocturnal frugivore-insectivores. Some species are known from some of the same classic fissure fill deposits as adapoids. These have yielded beautifully preserved cranial material, especially for the genus *Necrolemur*. The cranial morphology of *Necrolemur* led early paleoanthropologists to suspect they had something to do with the origin of tarsiers, a hypothesis that persists to this day (see Table 8.2). Furthermore, well-preserved ankle bones of *Necrolemur* and other microchoerids are strikingly like the ankle bones of tarsiers (Schmid 1979), suggesting that if there is no special relationship to tarsiers, then at least they were leaping in very similar ways. In North America, omomyoids became very diverse and abundant. In fact, omomyoids from Wyoming are sufficiently abundant and from such stratigraphically controlled conditions that they have served as strong evidence for the gradual evolution of anatomical traits over time (Rose and Bown 1984). These gradual changes have also made it difficult in some cases to establish clear boundaries between species because such boundaries usually rely on discrete differences in anatomical traits. As with European omomyoids, those in North America were probably mainly small, nocturnal, and frugivorous-insectivorous (Strait 2001). The preserved crania in some species (e.g., *Shoshonius*) are very like those of tarsiers (Beard and MacPhee 1994), though lacking the degree of postorbital closure. Crania in some other species (e.g., *Rooneyia*) are quite unusual.

North American omomyoids are grouped into one family, Omomyidae, with two subfamilies: Anaptomorphinae and Omomyinae. The anaptomorphines were mostly smaller and more generalized whereas some omomyines achieved larger sizes (1–2 kg; 2–4 lbs.) and some were more specialized.

Figure 8.9 A map of the world during the earliest Eocene showing one hypothesis for the direction of dispersal of the omomyoid Teilhardina. The image also emphasizes the presence of forest corridors at high latitudes. Smith et al. 2006. National Academy of Sciences.

Teilhardina (Figure 8.9; Table 8.1) is one of the earliest and arguably the most primitive of omomyoids. *Teilhardina* has several species, most of which are from North America, with one from Europe (*T. belgica*) and one from Asia (*T. asiatica*). The species of this genus are anatomically similar and the deposits from which they are derived are roughly contemporaneous. Thus, this small primate likely dispersed across the northern continents very rapidly (Smith et al. 2006).

THE EMERGENCE OF MODERN PRIMATE GROUPS

Origins of Crown Strepsirrhines

Until the turn of this century, very little was known about the origins of the crown (living) strepsirrhines. The Quaternary record of Madagascar contains many amazing forms of lemurs, including giant sloth-like lemurs, lemurs with perhaps monkey-like habits, lemurs with koala-like habits, and even a giant aye-aye (Godfrey and Jungers 2002). However, in Madagascar early Tertiary continental sediments are lacking, and there is no record of lemur fossils before the Pleistocene.

The fossil record of galagos is slightly more informative. Namely, there are Miocene African fossils that are very likely progenitors of lorisids (Simpson 1967). However, these are much like modern galagos and do not reveal anything about the relationship between crown strepsirrhines and Eocene fossil primates (but see below regarding *Propotto*). A similar situation exists for lorises in Asia: there are Miocene representatives, but these are substantially like modern lorises.

In 2003, the description of two new fossil genera from the Birket Qarun locality in the Fayum Basin of Egypt provided the "smoking gun" for the origin of crown strepsirrhines (Seiffert et al. 2003). *Saharagalago* and *Karanisia* are two small primates that bear clear affinities with crown strepsirrhines to the exclusion of other primates. Most striking is a lower canine of *Karanisia* that clearly sat within a strepsirrhine-style **toothcomb**. Recently, several other African primates have been recognized as having strepsirrhine affinities (Seiffert 2012). These include *Azibius* and *Algeripithecus* from Algeria, *Djebelemur* from Tunisia, *Omanodon* and *Shizarodon* from Oman, and *Namaia* from Namibia (see Marivaux et al. 2013). These important fossil primates are mainly known from teeth and jaws. The enigmatic Fayum primate *Plesiopithecus* is known from a single skull that has been compared to aye-ayes and to lorises (Godinot 2006; Simons and Rasmussen 1994a).

The now-recognized diversity of stem strepsirrhines from the Eocene and Oligocene of Afro-Arabia is strong evidence to suggest that strepsirrhines originated in that geographic area. This implies that lorises dispersed to Asia subsequent to an African origin. It is unknown what the first strepsirrhines in Madagascar were like. However, it seems likely that the lemuriform-lorisiform split occurred in continental Africa, followed by dispersal of lemuriform stock to Madagascar. Recent evidence suggests that *Propotto*, a Miocene primate from Kenya originally described as a potto antecedent, actually forms a clade with *Plesiopithecus* and the aye-aye; this might suggest that strepsirrhines dispersed to Madagascar from continental Africa more than once (Gunnell et al. 2018).

The Fossil Record of Tarsiers

Tarsiers are so unusual that they fuel major debates about primate taxonomy. Tarsiers today are moderately diverse but geographically limited and not very different in their ecological habits—especially considering that the split between them and their nearest living relative probably occurred over 50 million years ago. If omomyoids are excluded, then the fossil record of tarsiers is very limited. Two fossil species from the Miocene of Thailand have been placed in the genus *Tarsius*, as has an Eocene fossil from China (Beard et al. 1994). These, and *Xanthorhysis* from the Eocene of China, are all very tarsier-like. In fact, it is striking that *Tarsius eocaenus* from China was already so tarsier-like as early as the Eocene. This suggests that tarsiers achieved their current morphology very early on in their evolution and have remained more or less the same while other primates changed dramatically. Two additional genera, *Afrotarsius* from the Oligocene of Egypt and Libya and *Afrasia* from the Eocene of Myanmar, have also been implicated in tarsier origins, though the relationship between them and tarsiers is unclear (Chaimanee et al. 2012). More recently, a partial skeleton of a small Eocene primate from China, Archicebus achilles (dated to approximately 55.8 million to 54.8 million years ago), was described as the most basal tarsiiform (Ni et al. 2013). This primate is reconstructed as a diurnal insectivore and an arboreal quadruped that did some leaping–but not to the specialized degree seen in living tarsiers. The anatomy of the eye in living tarsiers suggests that their lineage passed through a diurnal stage, so Archicebus (and diurnal omomyoids) might represent such a stage.

Climate Change and the Paleogeography of Modern Primate Origins

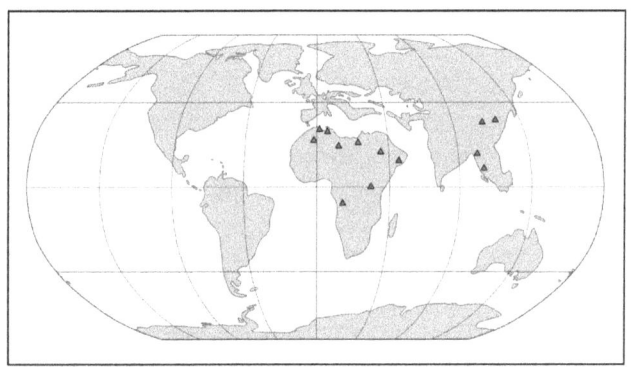

Figure 8.10 Map of key localities of early anthropoids. Note that the landmasses are in their current configuration.

Changing global climate has had profound effects on primate dispersal patterns and ecological habits over evolutionary time. Primates today are strongly tied to patches of trees and particular plant parts such as fruits, seeds, and immature leaves. It is no surprise, then, that the distribution of primates mirrors the distribution of forests. Today, primates are most diverse in the tropics and especially in tropical rainforests. Global temperature trends across the Tertiary have affected primate ranges. Following the Cretaceous-Tertiary extinction event, cooler temperatures and greater seasonality characterized the Paleocene. In the Eocene, temperatures (and probably rainfall) increased globally and rainforests likely extended to very high latitudes. During this time, euprimates became very diverse. With cooling and increased aridity at the end of the Eocene, many primate extinctions occurred in the northern continents and the surviving primates were confined to lower latitudes in South America, Afro-Arabia, Asia, and southern Europe. Among these survivors are the progenitors of the living groups of primates: lemurs and lorises, tarsiers, New World monkeys, Old World monkeys, and apes (Figure 8.10).

Competing Hypotheses for the Origin of Anthropoids

There is considerable debate among paleoanthropologists as to the geographic origins of anthropoids. In addition, there is debate regarding the source group for anthropoids. Three different hypotheses have been articulated in the literature. These are the adapoid origin hypothesis, the omomyoid origin hypothesis, and the tarsier origin hypothesis (Figure 8.11).

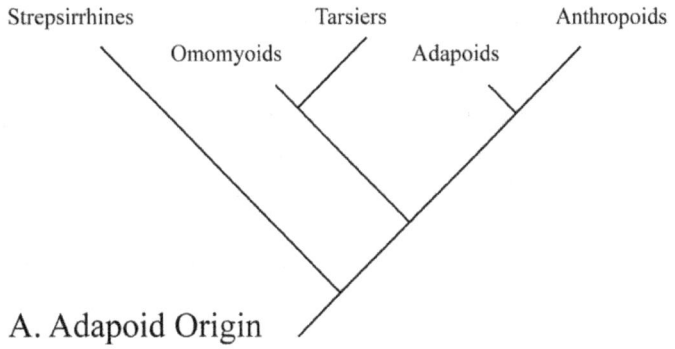

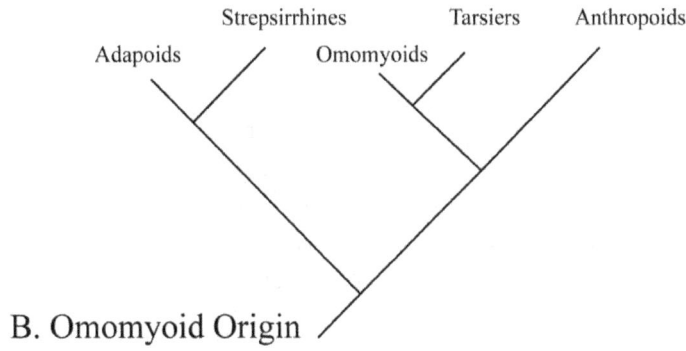

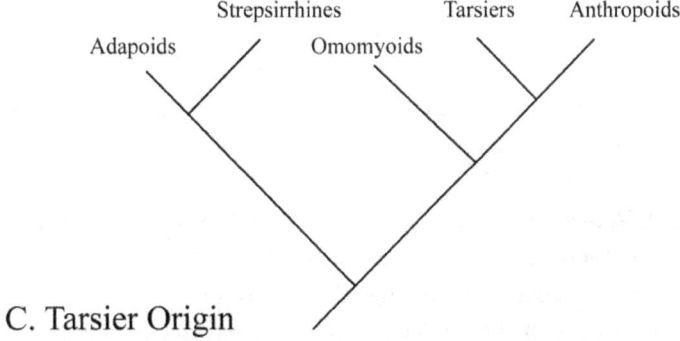

Figure 8.11 Competing trees for anthropoid origins. Branch lengths are not to scale. Note that the position of strepsirrhines is not necessarily specified by the omomyoid origin and tarsier origin models.

Adapoid Origin Hypothesis

Resemblances between some adapoids and some extant anthropoids include fusion of the **mandibular symphysis**, overall robusticity of the chewing system, overall large body size, features that signal a diurnal lifestyle (like relatively small eye sockets), and details of ankle bone morphology. Another feature in common is canine sexual dimorphism, which is present in some species of adapoids (probably) and in several species of anthropoids.

These features led some paleoanthropologists in the last half of the 20th century to suggest that anthropoids arose from adapoid stock (Gingerich 1980; Simons and Rasmussen 1994b). One of the earliest supporters of the link between adapoids and anthropoids was Hans Georg Stehlin, who described much of the best material of adapoids and who compared these Eocene primates to South American monkeys (Stehlin 1912). In more recent times, the adapoid origin hypothesis was reinforced by resemblances between these European adapoids (especially *Adapis* and *Leptadapis*) and some early anthropoids from the Fayum Basin (e.g., *Aegyptopithecus*, see below; Table 8.1).

Unfortunately for the adapoid hypothesis, most of the shared features listed above probably arose independently in the two groups as adaptations to a diet of hard and/or tough foods. For example, fusion of the mandibular symphysis likely evolved as a means to strengthen the jaw against forces that would pull the two halves away from each other, in the context of active chewing muscles on both sides of the head generating great bite forces. This context would also favor the development of robust jaws, large chewing muscles, shorter faces, and some other features shared by some adapoids and some anthropoids.

As older and more primitive anthropoids were found in the Fayum Basin, it became clear that the earliest anthropoids from Africa do not possess these features of jaw robusticity (Seiffert et al. 2009). Furthermore, many adapoids never evolved these features. Fusion of the mandibular symphysis in adapoids is actually quite different from that in anthropoids and probably occurred during juvenile development in the former (Beecher 1983; Ravosa 1996). Eventually, the adapoid origin hypothesis fell out of favor among most paleoanthropologists, although the description of *Darwinius* is a recent revival of that idea (Franzen et al. 2009; but see Seiffert et al. 2009, Williams et al. 2010b).

Omomyoid Origin Hypothesis

Similarities in cranial and hindlimb morphology between some omomyoids and extant tarsiers have led to the suggestion that tarsiers arose from some kind of omomyoid. In particular, *Necrolemur* has many features in common with tarsiers, as does the North American *Shoshonius*, which is known from a few beautifully preserved (although distorted) crania. Tarsiers and *Shoshonius* share exclusively some features of the base of the cranium; however, *Shoshonius* does not have any sign of postorbital closure and it lacks the bony ear tube of tarsiers. Nevertheless, some of the resemblances between some omomyoids and tarsiers suggest that tarsiers might have originated from within the Omomyoidea (Beard 2002; Beard and MacPhee 1994). In this scenario, although living tarsiers and living anthropoids might be sister taxa, they might have evolved from different omomyoids, possibly separated from each other by more than 50 million years of evolution, or anthropoids evolved from some non-omomyoid fossil group. The arguments against the omomyoid origin hypothesis are essentially the arguments *for* the tarsier origin hypothesis (see below). Namely, tarsiers and anthropoids share many features (especially of the soft tissues) that must have been retained for many millions of years or must have evolved convergently in the two groups. Furthermore, a key hard-tissue feature shared between the two extant groups, the postorbital septum, was not present in any omomyoid. Therefore, that feature must have arisen convergently in the two extant groups or must have been lost in omomyoids. Neither scenario is very appealing, although recent arguments for convergent evolution of the postorbital septum in tarsiers and anthropoids have arisen from embryology and histology of the structure (DeLeon et al. 2016).

Tarsier Origin Hypothesis

Several paleoanthropologists have suggested that there is a relationship between tarsiers and anthropoids to the exclusion of omomyoids and adapoids (e.g., Cartmill and Kay 1978; Ross 2000; Williams and Kay 1995). As mentioned, tarsiers and anthropoids today share several traits. These include many soft-tissue features related to the olfactory system such as the loss of a hairless external nose and loss of the median cleft running from the nose to the mouth (possessed by strepsirrhines). Also included are aspects of the visual system such as the loss of a reflective layer at the back of the eye, similarities in carotid circulation to the brain, and mode of placentation. Unfortunately, none of these can be assessed directly in fossils. Some bony similarities between tarsiers and anthropoids include an extra air-filled chamber below the middle ear cavity, reduced bones within the nasal cavity, and substantial postorbital closure; these can be assessed in fossils, but the distribution of these traits in omomyoids does not yield clear answers. Furthermore, several of the similarities between tarsiers and anthropoids are probably due to similarities in the sensory systems, which might have evolved in parallel for ecological reasons. Although early attempts to resolve the crown primates with molecular data were sometimes equivocal or in disagreement with one another, more recent analyses (including those of short interspersed elements) suggest that tarsiers and anthropoids are sister groups to the exclusion of lemurs and lorises (Williams et al. 2010a). However, this does not address omomyoids, all of which are far too ancient for DNA extraction.

The above three hypotheses are not the only possibilities for anthropoid origins. It may be that anthropoids are neither the closest sister group of tarsiers, nor evolved from adapoids or omomyoids. In recent years, two new groups of Eocene Asian primates have been implicated in the origin of anthropoids: the eosimiids and the amphipithecids. It is possible that one or the other of these two groups gave rise to anthropoids. Regardless of the true configuration of the tree for crown primates, the three major extant groups probably diverged from each other quite long ago (Seiffert et al. 2004).

Early Anthropoid Fossils in Africa

Figure 8.12 Egyptian workers sweeping Quarry I in the Fayum Basin (2004). This is a technique called wind harvesting that removes the desert crust and permits wind to blow out fine sediment and reveal fossils.

The classic localities yielding the greatest wealth of early anthropoid fossils are those from the Fayum Basin in Egypt (Simons 2008; Figure 8.12). The Fayum is a veritable oasis of fossil primates in an otherwise rather spotty early Tertiary African record. Since the 1960s, teams led by E. L. Simons have discovered several new species of early anthropoids, some of which are known from many parts of the skeleton and several individuals (Figure 8.13).

The Fayum Jebel Qatrani Formation and Birket Qarun Formation between them have yielded a remarkable array of terrestrial, arboreal, and aquatic mammals. These include ungulates, bats, sea cows, elephants, hyraces, rodents, whales, and primates. Also, many other vertebrates, like water birds, were present. The area at the time of deposition (Late Eocene through Early Oligocene) was probably very wet, with slow-moving rivers, standing water, swampy conditions, and lots of trees (see Bown and Kraus 1988). In short, it was an excellent place for primates.

Figure 8.13 Elwyn Laverne Simons excavating Aegyptopithecus in the Fayum Basin.

General Morphology of Anthropoids

The anthropoids known from the Fayum (and their close relatives from elsewhere in East Africa and Afro-Arabia) bear many of the anatomical hallmarks of extant anthropoids; however, there are primitive forms in several families that lack one or more anthropoid traits. All Fayum anthropoids known from skulls possess postorbital closure, most had fused mandibular symphyses, and most had ring-like **ectotympanic** bones. Tooth formulae were generally either 2.1.3.3 or 2.1.2.3. Fayum anthropoids ranged in size from the very small *Qatrania* and *Biretia* (less than 500 g) to the much-larger *Aegyptopithecus* (approximately 7 kg; 15 lbs.). Fruit was probably the main component of the diet for most or all of the anthropoids, with some of them supplementing with leaves (Kay and Simons 1980; Teaford et al. 1996; Kirk and Simons 2001). Most Fayum anthropoids were probably diurnal above-branch quadrupeds. Some of them (e.g., *Apidium*; Table 8.1) were probably very good leapers (Gebo and Simons 1987), but none show specializations for gibbon-style suspensory locomotion. Some of the Fayum anthropoids are known from hundreds of individuals, permitting the assessment of individual variation, sexual dimorphism, and in some cases growth and development. The description that follows provides greater detail for the two best known Fayum anthropoid families, the Propliopithecidae and the Parapithecidae; the additional families are summarized briefly.

Fayum Anthropoid Families

The Propliopithecidae (e.g., *Pliopithecus*; Table 8.1) include the largest anthropoids from the fauna, and they are known from several crania and some postcranial elements. They have been suggested to be stem catarrhines (Old World Monkeys and apes), although perhaps near the split between catarrhines and platyrrhines. The best known propliopithecid is *Aegyptopithecus*, known from many teeth, crania, and postcranial elements. The crania (Figure 8.14) show substantial morphological variation between individuals, some of which might be due to sexual dimorphism and a polygynous mating system (Simons et al. 2007). *Aegyptopithecus* was large (greater than 7 kg; 15 lbs.) with prominent attachments for the chewing muscles and with low, rounded, and well-buttressed molars. The snout is long and the canines are large. There is only partial development of a bony ear tube (Simons et al. 2007). The known long bones of *Aegyptopithecus* are quite robust, and the skeleton suggests that this animal was a generalized arboreal quadruped with no strong specialization for suspension (Gebo and Simons 1987).

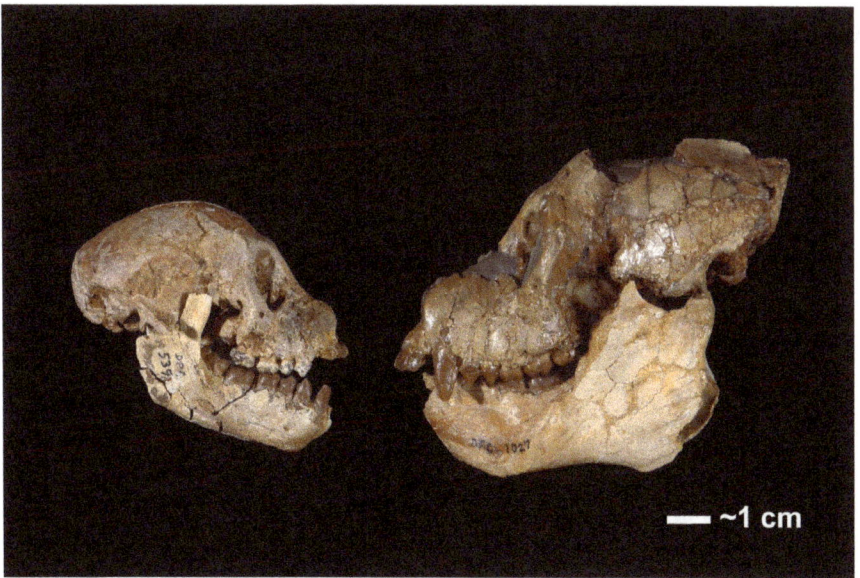

Figure 8.14 Female and male skull material for Aegyptopithecus zeuxis. The female is on the left. The mandibles are not associated with the crania. Simons et al. 2007. Copyright (2007) National Academy of Sciences.

An extremely abundant and unusual family of anthropoids from the Fayum is the Parapithecidae. Parapithecids have the primitive anthropoid tooth formula of 2.1.3.3 and they have very large conules on the upper molars and premolars. The parapithecid *Apidium* is known from many jaws with teeth, crushed and distorted crania, and several skeletal elements. The molars of *Apidium* had low, rounded cusps and thick enamel, suggesting a frugivorous diet. *Apidium* was probably a good leaper, having tightly apposed distal tibia and fibula as well as a narrow distal femur with a deep patellar groove (Fleagle and Simons 1995). *Parapithecus* is known from cranial material including a beautiful, undistorted cranium. This genus shows extreme reduction of the incisors, including complete absence of the lower incisors in *P. grangeri* (Simons 2001). This trait is unique among primates. *Biretia* is a primitive member of the family that has the primitive trait of an unfused mandibular symphysis. Parapithecids were once thought to be the ancestral stock of platyrrhines; however, their platyrrhine-like features are probably just primitive retentions and the most conservative approach is to consider them stem anthropoids.

The Oligopithecidae share the catarrhine tooth formula of 2.1.2.3 as well as having a canine honing complex that involves the anterior lower premolar. The postcranial elements known for the group suggest generalized arboreal quadrupedalism. The best known member, *Catopithecus*, is known from crania that demonstrate a postorbital septum and from mandibles that lack symphyseal fusion (Simons and Rasmussen 1996). The jaws are deep, with broad muscle attachment areas and crested teeth. *Catopithecus* was probably a little less than a kilogram in weight.

The Proteopithecidae had an overall primitive dentition that includes three premolars per quadrant and a generalized skeleton; they are considered stem anthropoids. The best known genus, *Proteopithecus*, is represented by dentitions, crania, and postcranial elements that suggest a diet of mostly fruit and a generalized style of locomotion, including arboreal quadrupedalism with some leaping (Simons and Seiffert 1999). It weighed about a kilogram.

Other genera of putative anthropoids from the Fayum include the very poorly known *Arsinoea*, the contentious *Afrotarsius*, and the enigmatic *Nosmips*. The last of these possesses traits of several major primate **clades** and defies classification (Seiffert et al. 2010).

Early Anthropoid Fossils in Asia

For the last half of the 1900s, researchers believed that Africa was the unquestioned homeland of early anthropoids (see Fleagle and Kay 1994). However, two very different groups of primates from Asia soon began to change that. One was an entirely new discovery (Eosimiidae), and the other was a poorly known group discovered decades prior (Amphipithecidae). Soon, attention on anthropoid origins began to shift eastward (see Ross and Kay 2004, Simons 2004). If anthropoids arose in Asia instead of Africa, then this implies that the African early anthropoids either emigrated from Asia or evolved their anthropoid traits in parallel with living anthropoids.

Eosimiids

First described in the 1990s, the eosimiids are best represented by *Eosimias* (Table 8.1). This "dawn monkey" is known from relatively complete jaws with teeth, a few small fragments of the face, and some postcranial elements (Beard et al. 1994; Beard et al. 1996; Gebo et al. 2000). The lower jaw is distinctive in being very deep relative to its length and breadth, as in some early Fayum anthropoids (Figure 8.15). It also has pointed incisors that are about the same size as the canines. The lower premolars are crowded together and they are set obliquely in the jaw. This last trait, also present

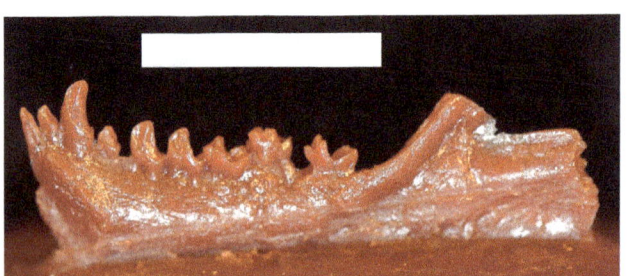

Figure 8.15 Cast of the right half of the mandible of Eosimias centennicus, type specimen. The white scale bar is 1 cm long.

in another eosimiid called *Bahinia*, was described as a shared derived trait with anthropoids, though it is also present in some adapoids (e.g., *Afradapis* from North Africa and *Asiadapis* [Table 8.1] from India). The mandibular symphysis is vertically inclined, as in some anthropoids, but is unfused. Overall, *Eosimias* was small, no heavier than a can of soda pop. *Eosimias* (along with the other less-well-known genera in its family) bears some resemblance to tarsiers as well as anthropoids. The shared features with anthropoids are mainly jaw shape and details of dental morphology. Unfortunately, no good crania are known for this family and the anatomy of, for example, the posterior orbital margin could be very revealing as to higher-level relationships.

Amphipithecids

Amphipithecids are small- to medium-size primates (up to 10 kg; 22 lbs.). Most are from the Eocene Pondaung Formation in Myanmar (Early–Middle Eocene), but one genus is known from Thailand. They were first discovered in the 1910s, and all of the specimens discovered in the first half of the 20th century were fragmentary jaws with teeth that were mostly worn down. Nevertheless, some dental similarities with anthropoids were noted early on. These include deep jaws and wide basins that separate low molar cusps. Starting in the 1970s, intensive collecting efforts in Myanmar yielded new material for the best known genera *Pondaungia* and *Amphipithecus* (Ciochon and Gunnell 2002; Table 8.1). Soon, another genus was discovered: *Myanmarpithecus*. It bears some resemblance to the other genera but has longer molar crests, suggesting a higher degree of folivory (Kay et al. 2004). Another amphipithecid, *Siamopithecus* from Thailand, has very rounded molars and was probably a seed-eater (Figure 8.16). In addition to teeth and jaws, some cranial fragments, ankle material, and ends of postcranial bones have been found for *Pondaungia*. There are important resemblances between the postcranial bones of *Pondaungia* and those of adapoids, suggesting adapoid affinities for the amphipithecidae. This would imply that the resemblances with anthropoids in the teeth are convergent, based on similarities in diet (see

Ciochon and Gunnell 2002). Unfortunately, the association between postcranial bones and teeth is not definite. With other primates in these faunas (including eosimiids), one cannot be certain that the postcranial bones belong with the teeth. Perhaps, as suggested by some, some of the bones belong to a sivaladapid (or asiadapid) and others belong to an early anthropoid (Beard et al. 2007; Marivaux et al. 2003). Additional well-associated material of amphipithecids would help to clear up this uncertainty.

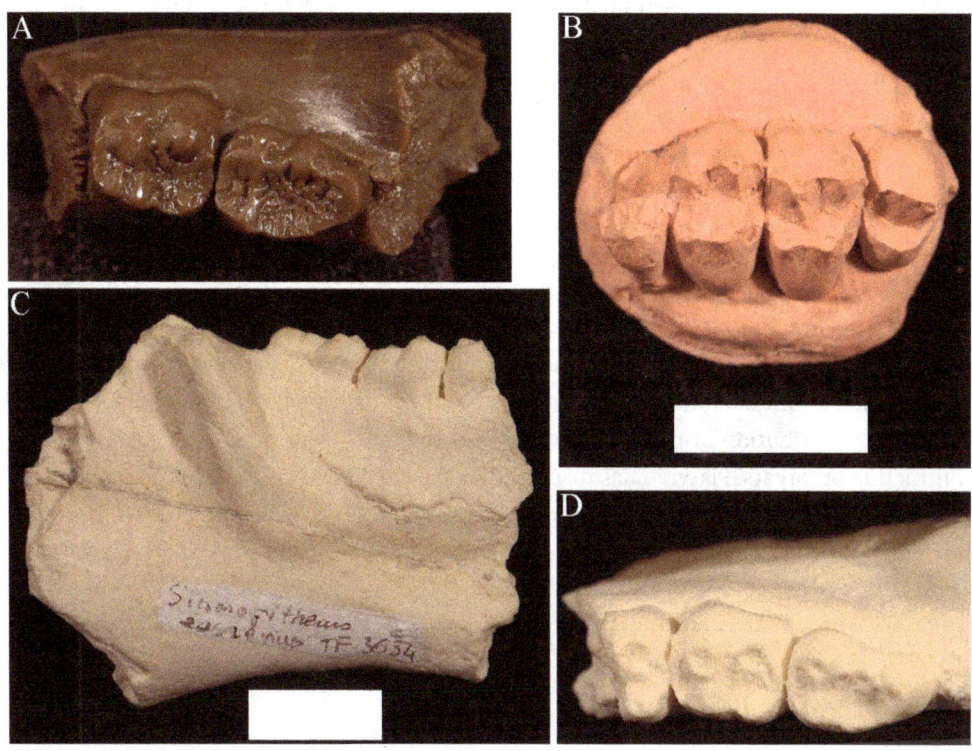

Figure 8.16 Casts of representative amphipithecid material. A, Pondaungia cotteri right lower jaw fragment with m2 and m3. B, Siamopithecus eocaenus right upper jaw fragment with p4-m3. C, S. eocaenus right lower jaw fragment with partial m1, m2, and m3 in lateral view; note the great depth of this jaw. D, same as in C, but occlusal view. White scale bars are 1 cm long; the scale is the same for A, B, and D.

Platyrrhine Dispersal to South America

Today there is an impressive diversity of primates in South and Central America. These are considered to be part of a single clade, the Platyrrhini. Primates colonized South America sometime in the Eocene from an African source. In the first half of the 20th century, the source of platyrrhines was a matter of major debate among paleontologists, with some favoring a North American origin (e.g., Simpson 1940).

Part of the reason for this debate is that South America was an island in the Eocene. Primates needed to cross open ocean to get there from either North America or Africa, although the distance from the former was shorter. Morphology yields clues to platyrrhine origins. The first known primates in South America have more in common morphologically with African primates than with North American ones. At the time, anthropoids were popping up in North Africa, whereas the only euprimates in North America were adapoids and omomyoids. Despite lacking a bony ear tube, early platyrrhines shared a great deal with other anthropoids, including full postorbital closure and fusion of the mandibular symphysis.

The means by which a population of small North African primates managed to disperse across the Atlantic and survive to colonize South America remains a mystery. The most plausible scenario is one of rafting. That is, primates must have been trapped on vegetation that was blown out to sea by a storm. The vegetation then became a sort of life raft, which eventually landed ashore, dumping its passengers in South America. Rodents probably arrived in South America in the same way (Antoine et al. 2012).

Once ashore, platyrrhines must have crossed South America fairly rapidly because the earliest-known primates from that continent are from Peru (Bond et al. 2015). Soon after that, platyrrhines were in Bolivia, namely *Branisella*. By the Miocene, platyrrhines were living in extreme southern Argentina and were exploiting a variety of feeding niches. The Early Miocene platyrrhines were all somewhat primitive in their morphology, but some features that likely arose by ecological convergence suggest (to some) relationships with extant platyrrhine families. This has led to a lively debate about the pattern of primate evolution in South America (Kay 2015; Kay and Fleagle 2010; Rosenberger 2010). By the Middle Miocene, clear representatives of modern families were present in a diverse fauna from La Venta, Colombia (Wheeler 2010). The Plio-Pleistocene saw the emergence of giant platyrrhines as well as several taxa of platyrrhines living on Caribbean islands (Cooke et al. 2016).

The story of platyrrhines seems to be one of amazing sweepstakes dispersal, followed by rapid diversification and widespread geographic colonization of much of South America. After that, dramatic extinctions resulted in the current, much smaller geographic distribution of platyrrhines. These extinctions were probably caused by changing climates, leading to the contraction of forests. Platyrrhines dispersed to the Caribbean and to Central America, with subsequent extinctions in those regions that might have been related to interactions with humans. Unlike anthropoids of the Old World, platyrrhines do not seem to have evolved any primarily terrestrial forms and so have always been highly dependent on forests.

SPECIAL TOPIC: JONATHAN PERRY AND PRIMATES OF THE EXTREME SOUTH

Many primates are very vulnerable to ecological disturbance because they are heavily dependent on fruit to eat and trees to live in. This is one reason why so many primates are endangered today and why many of them went extinct due to climatic and vegetational changes in the past. Jonathan Perry's paleontological research focuses on primates that lived on the edge of their geographic distribution. This research has taken him to two extremes in the Americas: extreme southern Patagonia and the Canadian prairies.

Santa Cruz Province in Argentina is as far south as primates have ever lived. The Santa Cruz fauna of the Miocene has yielded a moderate diversity of platyrrhines, each with slightly different dietary adaptations. These include *Homunculus* (Table 8.1), first described by Florentino Ameghino in 1891 (Figure 8.17). Recent fieldwork by Perry and colleagues in Argentina has revealed several skulls of *Homunculus* as well as many parts of the skeleton (Kay et al. 2012). The emerging profile of this extinct primate is one of a dedicated arboreal quadruped that fed on fruits and leaves. Many of the foods eaten by *Homunculus* must have been very tough and were probably covered and impregnated with grit; we suspect this because the cheek teeth are very worn down, even in young individuals, and because the molar tooth roots were very large, presumably to resist strong bite forces (Perry et al. 2010, 2014).

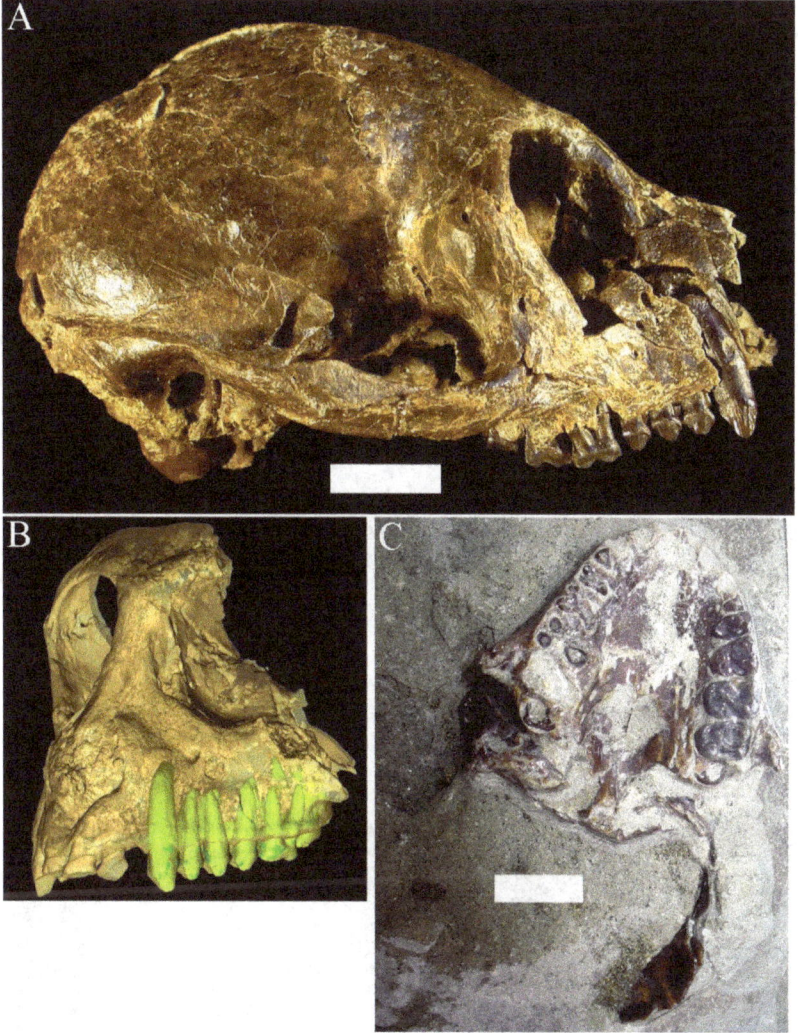

Figure 8.17 Representative specimens of Homunculus patagonicus. A, adult cranium in lateral view. B, adult cranium surface reconstructed from microCT scans, with the teeth segmented out. C, juvenile cranium. White scale bars are 1cm long.

Perry began working in Argentina while a graduate student at Duke University. He participated as a field assistant in a team led by his Ph.D. advisor, Richard F. Kay, and Argentine colleagues Sergio F. Vizcaíno and M. Susana Bargo. Most of the localities examined belong to a suite of beach sites known since the 1800s and visited by many field parties from various museums in the early 1900s. Since 2003, their international team of paleontologists from the U.S. and Argentina has visited these localities every single year (Figure 8.18). Over time, new fossils and new students have led to new projects and new approaches, including the use of microcomputed tomography (microCT) to visualize and analyze internal structures of the skeleton.

Figure 8.18 Field localities in Argentina and Canada. A, Cañadon Palos locality, coastal Santa Cruz Province, Argentina. B, Swift Current Creek locality, southwest Saskatchewan, Canada.

PLANET OF APES

Geologic Activity and Climate Change in the Miocene

The Miocene Epoch was a time of mammalian diversification and extinction, global climate change, and ecological turnover. In the Miocene, there was an initial warming trend across the globe with the expansion of subtropical forests, followed by widespread cooling and drying with the retreat of tropical forests and replacement with more open woodlands and eventually grasslands. It was also a time of major geologic activity. On one side of the globe, South America experienced the rise of the Andes Mountains. On the other side, the Indian subcontinent collided with mainland Asia, resulting in the rise of the Himalayan Mountains. In Africa, volcanic activity promoted the development of the East African Rift System. Critical to the story of ape evolution was the exposure of an intercontinental landbridge between East Africa and Eurasia, permitting a true planet of apes (Figure 8.19).

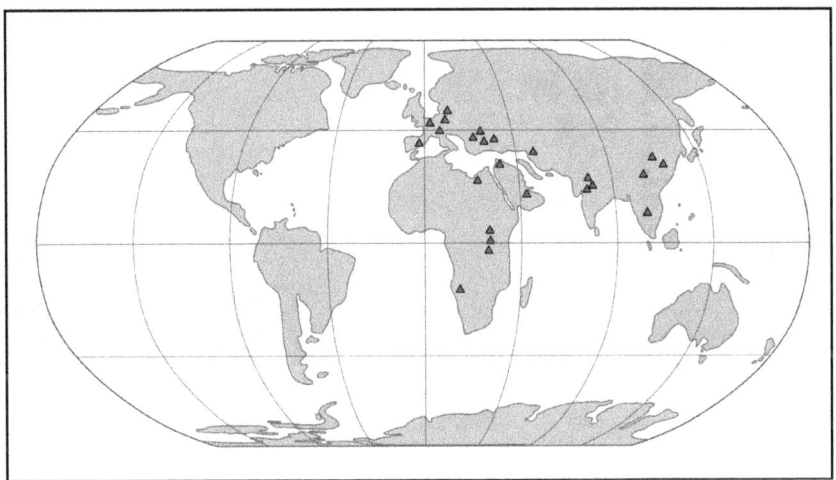

Figure 8.19 Map of the world in the Miocene, highlighting fossil ape localities.

Geographic Distribution: Africa, Asia, Europe

The world of the Miocene had tremendous ape diversity compared to today. The earliest records of fossil apes are from Early Miocene deposits in Africa. However, something dramatic happened around 16 million years ago. With the closure of the ancient Tethys Sea, the subsequent exposure of the *Gomphotherium* Landbridge, and a period of global warming, the Middle-Late Miocene saw waves of emigration of mammals (including primates) out of Africa and into Eurasia, with evidence of later African re-entry for some (Harrison 2010). Some of the mammals that dispersed from Africa to Eurasia and back were apes. Though most of these early apes left no modern descendants, some of them gave rise to the ancestors of modern apes—including **hominins** (Figure 8.20).

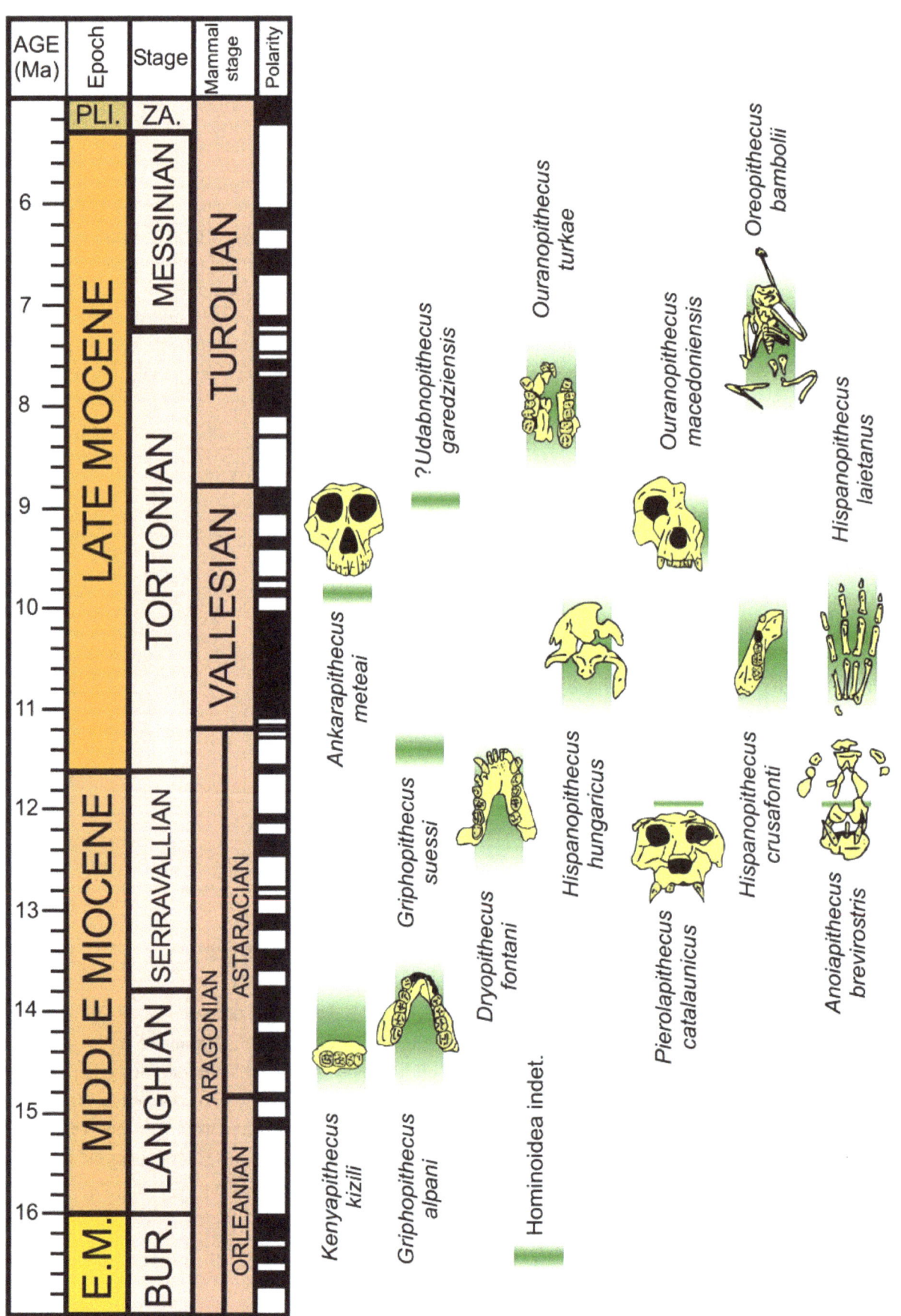

Figure 8.20 Representative Miocene apes set against a geologic time scale. Casanova-Vilar et al. (2011).

Where Are the Monkeys? Old World Monkey Diversity in the Miocene

Whereas the Oligocene deposits in the Fayum of Egypt have yielded the earliest-known catarrhine fossils, the Miocene demonstrates some diversification of Cercopithecoidea. However, compared to the numerous and diverse Miocene apes (see below), monkeys of the Miocene are very rare and restricted to a single extinct family, the Victoriapithecidae (Table 8.1). This family contains the earliest definite Old World monkeys. These monkeys are known from northern and eastern Africa between 20 million and 12.5 million years ago (Miller et al. 2009). The best known early Old World monkey is *Victoriapithecus* (Figure 8.21; Table 8.1), a small-bodied (approximately 7 kg; 15 lbs.), small-brained monkey with a long sloping face and round, narrowly spaced orbits. *Victoriapithecus* shares some cranial features with *Aegyptopithecus*; for example, both have a deep malar region of the zygomatic bone and a well-developed sagittal crest (Benefit and McCrossin 1997; Fleagle 2013). Beginning in the Early Miocene, and certainly by the Middle Miocene, bilophodonty, known to be a hallmark of molar teeth of modern Old World monkeys, was present to some extent. Although this dental feature is often indicative of increased leaf-processing efficiency in modern Old World monkeys, *Victoriapithecus* has been reconstructed as being more frugivorous and perhaps spent more time on the ground (terrestrial locomotion) than in the trees (arboreal locomotion; Blue et al. 2006). The two major groups of Old World monkeys today are cercopithecines and colobines. The earliest records demonstrating clear members of each of these two groups are at the end of the Miocene. Examples include the early colobine *Microcolobus* from Kenya and the early cercopithecine *Pliopapio* from Ethiopia.

Figure 8.21 Skull of Victoriapithecus macinnesi (Musee d'Histoire Naturelle, Paris).

The Story of Us, the Apes

African Ape Diversity

The Early Miocene of Africa has yielded around 14 genera of early apes (Begun 2003). Many of these taxa have been reconstructed as frugivorous arboreal quadrupeds (Kay 1977).

One of the best studied of these genera is the East African *Proconsul* (Family Proconsulidae; Table 8.1), a short-faced ape with generalized dentition and above-branch locomotor behaviors (Begun 2007). Several species have been described, with body mass reconstructions ranging from 17 to 50 kg (approximately 37–110 lbs.). A paleoenvironmental study reconstructed the habitat of *Proconsul* to be a dense, closed-canopy tropical forest (Michel et al. 2014). One of the most interesting questions about this taxon is whether or not it possessed a tail, a lack of which is an important characteristic for distinguishing living apes from Old World monkeys. No caudal vertebrae (tail bones) have been found in direct association with *Proconsul* postcrania, and the morphology of the sacrum is consistent with *Proconsul* lacking a tail (Russo 2016; Ward et al. 1991).

Overall, the African ape fossil record in the Late Miocene is sparse, with seven fossil localities dating between eleven and five million years ago (Pickford et al. 2009). Nevertheless, most species of great apes live in Africa today. Where did the progenitors of modern African apes arise? Did they evolve in Africa or somewhere else? The paucity of apes in the Late Miocene of Africa stands in contrast to the situation in Eurasia. There, ape diversity was high. Furthermore, several Eurasian ape fossils show morphological affinities with modern hominoids (apes). This has suggested to some paleoanthropologists that the ancestors of modern African great apes recolonized Africa from Eurasia toward the end of the Miocene (Begun 2002). However, discoveries of Late Miocene hominoids like the Kenyan *Nakalipithecus* (9.9 million to 9.8 million years ago) and the Ethiopian *Chororapithecus* (10.7 million to 10.1 million years ago) fuel an alternative hypothesis—namely that African hominoid diversity was maintained throughout the Miocene and that one of these taxa might, in fact, be the last common ancestor of extant African apes (Kunimatsu et al. 2007). The previously underappreciated diversity of Late Miocene apes in Africa might be due to poor sampling of the fossil record in Africa.

Eurasian Ape Diversity

With the establishment of the *Gomphotherium* Landbridge (a result of the closure of the Eastern Mediterranean seaway; Rögl 1999), the Middle Miocene was an exciting time for hominoid radiations outside of Africa (see Figure 8.20). Eurasian hominoid species exploited their environments in many different ways in the Miocene. Food exploitation ranged from soft-fruit feeding in some taxa to hard-object feeding in others, in part owing to seasonal fluctuations and the necessary adoptions of fallback foods (DeMiguel et al. 2014). For example, the molars of *Oreopithecus bambolii* (Family Hominidae) have relatively long lower-molar shearing crests, suggesting that this hominoid was very folivorous (Ungar and Kay 1995). Associated with variation in diet, there is great variation in the degree to which cranial features (e.g., zygomatic bone or supraorbital tori) are developed across the many taxa (Cameron 1997); however, Middle Miocene fossils tend to exhibit relatively thick molar enamel and relatively robust jaws (Andrews and Martin 1991).

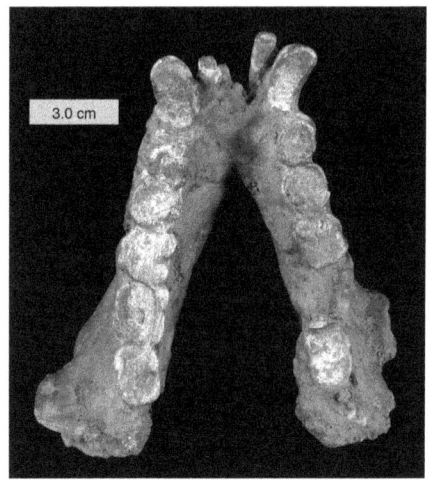

Figure 8.22 Cast of the mandible of Gigantopithecus blacki.

One of the most extreme examples of ape robusticity is the Asian hominoid, *Gigantopithecus* (Table 8.1). Known only from teeth and jaws (e.g., Figure 8.22), this ape probably weighed as much as 270 kg (595 lbs.) and was likely the largest primate ever (Bocherens et al. 2017). Because of unique features of its teeth (including molarized premolars and patterns of wear) and its massive size, it has been reconstructed as a bamboo specialist, somewhat like the modern panda. Small silica particles (phytoliths) from grasses have been found stuck to the molars of *Gigantopithecus* (Ciochon et al. 1990). Recent studies evaluating the carbon isotope composition of the enamel sampled from *Gigantopithecus* teeth suggest that this ape exploited a wide range of vegetation, including fruits, leaves, roots, and bamboo (Bocherens et al. 2017).

In Spain, the cranium with upper dentition, part of a mandible, and partial skeleton of *Pliobates* (Family Pliobatidae), a small-bodied ape (4–5 kg; 9–11 lbs.), was discovered in deposits dating to 11.6 million years ago (Alba et al. 2015). The authors of the study reconstructed this European catarrhine as a frugivore that overlapped in relative brain size with modern cercopithecoids. The fossilized postcrania of *Pliobates* suggest that this ape might have had a unique style of locomotion, including the tendency to walk across the branches of trees with its palms facing downward and flexible wrists that permitted rotation of the forearm during climbing. However, the anatomy of the distal humerus differs from those of living apes in ways that suggest that *Pliobates* was less efficient at stabilizing its elbow while suspended (Benefit and McCrossin 2015). Two other recently described apes from Spain, *Pierolapithecus* and *Anoiapithecus*, are known from relatively complete skeletons. *Pierolapithecus* had a very projecting face and thick molar enamel as well as some skeletal features that suggest (albeit controversially) a less suspensory locomotor style than in extant apes (Moyà-Solà et al. 2004). In contrast to *Pierolapithecus*, the slightly younger *Anoiapithecus* has a very flat face (Moyà-Solà et al. 2009).

Postcranial evidence for suspensory or well-developed orthograde behaviors in apes does not appear until the Late Miocene of Europe. Primary evidence supporting these specialized locomotor modes includes the relatively short lumbar vertebrae of *Oreopithecus* (Figure 8.23) and *Dryopithecus* (Maclatchy 2004). The Late Miocene saw the extinction of most of the Eurasian hominoids in an event referred to as the Vallesian Crisis (Agustí et al. 2003). Among the latest surviving hominoid taxa in Eurasia were *Oreopithecus* and *Gigantopithecus*, the latter of which held out until the Pleistocene in Asia and was probably even sympatric with *Homo erectus* (Cachel 2015).

The Origins of Extant Apes

The fossil record of the extant apes is somewhat underwhelming: it ranges from being practically nonexistent for some taxa (e.g., chimpanzees) to being a little better for others (e.g., humans). There are many possible reasons for these differences in fossil abundance, and many are associated with the environmental conditions necessary for the fossilization of bones. One way to understand the evolution of extant apes that is not so dependent on the fossil record is via molecular evolutionary analyses. This can include counting up the differences in the genetic sequence between two closely related species to estimate the amount of time since these species shared a common ancestor. This is called a molecular clock, and it is often calibrated using fossils of known absolute age that stand in for the last common ancestor of a particular clade. Molecular clock estimates have placed the split

Figure 8.23 Skeleton of Oreopithecus bambolii.

between Hylobatidae and Hominidae between 19.7 million and 24.1 million years ago, followed by an African ape and Asian ape split between 15.7 million and 19.3 million years ago, and, finally, with the more recent radiation of Hylobatidae into its current genera between 6.4 million and 8 million years ago (Israfil et al. 2011).

Lesser Ape Origins and Fossils

Unfortunately, the fossil record for the lesser apes is meager, particularly in Miocene deposits. One possible early hylobatid is *Laccopithecus robustus*, a Late Miocene catarrhine from China (Harrison 2016). Although it does share some characteristics with modern gibbons and siamangs (including an overall small body size and a short face), *Laccopithecus* most likely represents a primitive stem catarrhine and is therefore distantly related to extant apes (Jablonski and Chaplin 2009). A more likely candidate for the hylobatid stem is another Late Miocene taxon from China, *Yuanmoupithecus xiaoyuan* (Table 8.1). Interpretation of its phylogenetic standing, however, is complicated by contradicting dental features—some of them quite primitive—which some believe best place *Yuanmoupithecus* as a stem hylobatid (Harrison 2016). The history of Hylobatidae becomes clearer in the Pleistocene, with fossils representing extant genera.

Great Ape Origins and Fossils

The most extensive fossil record of a modern great ape is that of our own genus, *Homo*. The evolution of our own species will be covered in the next chapter. The evolutionary history of the Asian great ape, the orangutan (*Pongo*), is becoming clearer. Today, orangutans are found only on the islands of Borneo and Sumatra. However, Pleistocene-aged teeth, attributed to *Pongo*, have been found in Cambodia, China, Laos, Peninsular Malaysia, and Vietnam—demonstrating the vastness of the orangutan's previous range (Ibrahim et al. 2013; Wang et al. 2014). *Sivapithecus* from the Miocene of India and Pakistan is represented by many specimens, including parts of the face. *Sivapithecus* is very similar to *Pongo*, especially in the face, and it probably is closely related to ancestral orangutans (Pilbeam 1982). Originally, jaws and teeth belonging to the former genus *Ramapithecus* were thought to be important in the origin of humans (Simons 1961), but now these are recognized as specimens of *Sivapithecus* (Kelley 2002). Postcranial bones of *Sivapithecus*, however, suggest a more generalized locomotor mode—including terrestrial locomotion—than seen in *Pongo* (Pilbeam et al. 1990).

In Africa, the first fossil to be confidently attributed to *Pan*, and known to be the earliest evidence of a chimpanzee, was described based on teeth found in Middle Pleistocene deposits in the Eastern Rift Valley of Kenya (McBrearty and Jablonski 2005). Paleoenvironmental reconstructions of this locality suggest that this early chimpanzee was living in close proximity to early *Homo* in a closed-canopy wooded habitat. Similarly, fossil teeth and mandibular remains attributed to two species of Middle-Late Miocene apes—*Chororapithecus abyssinicus* (from Ethiopia; Suwa et al. 2007) and *Nakalipithecus nakayamai* (from Kenya; Kunimatsu et al. 2007)—have been suggested as basal members of the gorilla clade.

Clearly, more work is needed to fill in the large gaps in the fossil record of the nonhuman great apes. The 20th century witnessed the discovery of many hominin fossils in East Africa, which have been critical for improving our understanding of human evolution. While 21st-century conservationists fight to prevent the extinction of the living great apes, perhaps efforts by 21st-century paleoanthropologists will yield the evolutionary story of these, our closest relatives.

Review Questions

- Compare three major hypotheses about primate origins, making reference to each one's key ecological reason for primate uniqueness.
- Explain how changes in temperature, rainfall, and vegetation led to major changes in primate biogeography over the Early Tertiary.
- List some euprimate features that plesiadapiforms have and some that they lack.
- Contrast adapoids and omomyoids in terms of life habits.
- Describe one piece of evidence for each of the adapoid, omomyoid, and tarsier origin hypotheses for anthropoids.
- Discuss the biogeography of the origins of African great apes and orangutans using examples from the Miocene ape fossil record.

Key Terms

Adapoidea: Order: Primates. One of the earliest groups of euprimates (true primates; earliest records from the early Eocene).

Anthropoids: Group containing monkeys and apes, including humans.

Auditory bulla: The rounded bony floor of the middle ear cavity.

Bilophodonty: Dental condition in which the cusps of molar teeth form ridges (or lophs) separated from each other by valleys (seen, e.g., in modern Old World monkeys).

Catarrhines: Order: Primates; Suborder: Anthropoidea; Infraorder: Catarrhini. Group containing Old World monkeys and apes, including humans.

Clade: Group containing all of the descendants of a single ancestor. A portion of a phylogenetic tree represented as a bifurcation (node) in a lineage and all of the branches leading forward in time from that bifurcation.

Convergent evolution: The independent evolution of a morphological feature in animals not closely related (e.g., wings in birds and bats).

Crown group: Smallest monophyletic group (clade) containing a specified set of extant taxa and all descendants of their last common ancestor.

Diagnosis: The features that allow you to recognize a group.

Diastema: Space between adjacent teeth.

Diffuse coevolution: The ecological interaction between whole groups of species (e.g., primates) with whole groups of other species (e.g., fruiting trees).

Ectotympanic: Bony ring or tube that holds the tympanic membrane (eardrum).

Euprimates: Order: Primates. True primates or primates of modern aspect.

Haplorhines: Group containing catarrhines, platyrrhines, and tarsiers.

Hominins: Modern humans and any extinct relatives more closely related to us than to chimpanzees.

Mandibular symphysis: Fibrocartilaginous joint between the left and right mandibular segments, located in the midline of the body.

Old World: Africa and Eurasia.

Omomyoidea: Order: Primates; Superfamily: Omomyoidea. One of the earliest groups of euprimates (true primates; earliest record in the early Eocene).

Petrosal bone: Petrous portion of the temporal bone. It houses the inner ear apparatus, among other things.

Plagiaulacoid: Dental condition where at least one of the lower cheek-teeth (molars or premolars) is a laterally compressed blade.

Platyrrhines: Order: Primates; Suborder: Anthropoidea; Infraorder: Platyrrhini. Group containing New World monkeys.

Plesiadapiforms: Order: Plesiadapiformes. Archaic primates or primate-like placental mammals (Early Paleocene–Late Eocene).

Stem: Taxa are basal to a given crown group but are more closely related to the crown group than to the closest living sister taxon of the crown group.

Strepsirrhines: Order: Primates; Suborder: Stresirrhini. Group containing lemurs, lorises, and galagos (does not include tarsiers).

Toothcomb: Dental condition found in modern strepsirrhines in which the lower incisors and canines are laterally compressed and protrude forward at a nearly horizontal inclination. This structure is used in grooming.

About the Authors

Jonathan Perry

Jonathan Perry was trained as a paleontologist and primatologist at the University of Alberta, Duke University, and Stony Brook University. His research focuses on the relationship between food, feeding, and craniodental anatomy in primates both living and extinct. This work includes primate feeding behavior, comparative anatomy, biomechanics, and field paleontology. For the past six years, he has taught courses on primate evolution at the undergraduate and graduate level.

Jonathan Perry

Stephanie Canington

Stephanie Canington is a Ph.D. student. Her current research is on the links between food properties, feeding behavior, and jaw morphology in lemurs that live in varying forms of captivity.

Stephanie Canington

For Further Exploration

Beard, Chris 2004. *The Hunt for the Dawn Monkey: Unearthing the Origins of Monkeys, Apes, and Humans.* Berkeley: University of California Press.

Begun, David R. 2010. Miocene Hominids and the Origins of the African Apes and Humans. *Annual Review of Anthropology* 39: 67–84.

Fleagle, John G. 2013. *Primate Adaptation and Evolution*. Third edition. San Diego, CA: Academic Press.

Gebo, Daniel L., ed. 1993. *Postcranial Adaptations in Nonhuman Primates*. Dekalb: Northern Illinois University Press.

Godfrey, Laurie R., and William L. Jungers. 2002. Quaternary Fossil Lemurs. In *The Primate Fossil Record*, edited by Walter C. Hartwig, 97–121. Cambridge: Cambridge University Press.

Godinot, Marc. 2006. Lemuriform Origins as Viewed from the Fossil Record. *Folia Primatologica* 77 (6): 446–464.

Kay, Richard F. 2018. 100 Years of Primate Paleontology. *American Journal of Physical Anthropology* 165 (4): 652–676.

Marivaux, Laurent. 2006. The Eosimiid and Amphipithecid Primates (Anthropoidea) from the Oligocene of the Bugti Hills (Balochistan, Pakistan): New Insight into Early Higher Primate Evolution in South Asia. *Palaeovertebrata, Montpellier* 34 (1-2): 29–109.

Martin, R. D. 1990. *Primate Origins and Evolution, a Phylogenetic Reconstruction*. Princeton: Princeton University Press.

Rose, Kenneth D., Marc Godinot, and Thomas M. Bown. 1994. The Early Radiation of Euprimates and the Initial Diversification of Omomyidae. In *Anthropoid Origins: The Fossil Evidence*, edited by John G. Fleagle and Richard F. Kay, 1–28. New York: Plenum Press.

Ross, Callum F. 1999. How to Carry Out Functional Morphology. *Evolutionary Anthropology* 7 (6): 217–222.

Seiffert, Erik R. 2012. Early Primate Evolution in Afro-Arabia. *Evolutionary Anthropology: Issues, News, and Reviews* 21: 239–253.

Szalay, Frederic S., and Eric Delson. 1979. Evolutionary History of the Primates. New York: Academic Press.

Ungar, Peter S. 2002. Reconstructing the Diets of Fossil Primates. In *Reconstructing Behavior in the Primate Fossil Record*, edited by Joseph Plavcan, Richard F. Kay, William Jungers, and Carel P. van Schaik, 261–296. New York: Kluwer Academic/Plenum Publishers.

References

Agustí, J., A. Sanz de Siria, and M. Garcés M. 2003. Explaining the End of the Hominoid Experiment in Europe. *Journal of Human Evolution* 45 (2): 145–153.

Alba, David M., Sergio Almécija, Daniel DeMiguel, Josep Fortuny, Miriam Pérez de los Ríos, Marta Pina, Josep M. Robles, and Salvador Moyà-Solà. 2015. Miocene Small-Bodied Ape from Eurasia Sheds Light on Hominoid Evolution. *Science* 350 (6,260): aab2625.

Andrews, Peter, and Lawrence Martin. 1991. Hominoid Dietary Evolution. *Philosophical Transactions of the Royal Society of London B: Biological Sciences* 334 (1,270): 199–209.

Antoine, Pierre-Oliver, Laurent Marivaux, Darren A. Croft, Guillaume Billet, Morgan Ganerød, Carlos Jaramillo, Thomas Martin, et al. 2012. Middle Eocene Rodents From Peruvian Amazonia Reveal the Pattern and Timing of Caviomorph Origins and Biogeography. *Proceedings of the Royal Society B: Biological Sciences* 279 (1,732): 1,319–1,326.

Beard, K. Christopher. 1990. Gliding Behaviour and Palaeoecology of the Alleged Primate Family Paromomyidae (Mammalia, Dermoptera). *Nature* 345 (6,273): 340–341.

———. 2002. Basal anthropoids. In *The Primate Fossil Record*, edited by William C. Hartwig, 133–150. Cambridge: Cambridge University Press.

Beard, K. Christopher, and R. D. E. MacPhee. 1994. Cranial Anatomy of *Shoshonius* and the Antiquity of Anthropoidea. In *Anthropoid Origins: The Fossil Evidence*, edited by John G. Fleagle and Richard F. Kay, 55–98. New York: Plenum Press.

Beard, K. Christopher, Laurent Marivaux, Soe Thura Tun, Aung Naing Soe, Yaowalak Chaimanee, Wanna Htoon, Bernard Marandat, Htun Htun Aung, and Jean-Jacques Jaeger. 2007. New Sivaladapid Primates From the Eocene Pondaung Formation of Myanmar and the Anthropoid Status of Amphipithecidae. *Bulletin of Carnegie Museum of Natural History* 39: 67–76.

Beard, K. Christopher, Tao Qi, Mary R. Dawson, Banyue Wang, and Chuankuei Li. 1994. A Diverse New Primate Fauna From Middle Eocene Fissure-Fillings in Southeastern China. *Nature* 368 (6,472): 604–609.

Beard, K. Christopher, Yongsheng Tong, Mary R. Dawson, Jingwen Wang, and Xueshi Huang. 1996. Earliest Complete Dentition of an Anthropoid Primate From the Late Middle Eocene of Shanxi Province, China. *Science* 272 (5,258): 82–85.

Beecher, Robert M. 1983. Evolution of the Mandibular Symphysis in Notharctinae (Adapidae, Primates). *International Journal of Primatology* 4 (1): 99–112.

Begun, David R. 2002. European Hominoids. In *The Primate Fossil Record*, edited by William C. Hartwig, 339–368. Cambridge: Cambridge University Press.

———. 2003. Planet of the Apes. *Scientific American* 289 (2): 74–83.

———. 2007. Fossil Record of Miocene Hominoids. In *Handbook of Paleoanthropology*, edited by Winfried Henke and Ian Tattersall, 921–977. New York: Springer.

Benefit, Brenda R., and Monte L. McCrossin. 1997. Earliest Known Old World Monkey Skull. *Nature* 388 (6,640): 368–371.

———. 2015. A Window Into Ape Evolution. *Science* 350 (6,260): 515–516.

Bloch, Jonathan I., and David M. Boyer. 2002. Grasping Primate Origins. *Science* 298 (5,598): 1,606–1,610.

———. 2007. New Skeletons of Paleocene-Eocene Plesiadapiformes: A Diversity of Arboreal Positional Behaviors in Early Primates. In *Primate Origins: Adaptations and Evolution*, edited by Matthew J. Ravosa and Marian Dagosto, 535–581. New York: Springer.

Bloch, Jonathan I., and Mary T. Silcox. 2001. New Basicrania of Paleocene-Eocene *Ignacius*: Re-evaluation of the Plesiadapiform-Dermopteran Link. *American Journal of Physical Anthropology* 116 (3): 184–198.

———. 2006. Cranial Anatomy of the Paleocene Plesiadapiform *Carpolestes simpsoni* (Mammalia, Primates) Using Ultra High-Resolution X-ray Computed Tomography, and the Relationships of Plesiadapiforms to Euprimates. *Journal of Human Evolution:* 50 (1), 1–35.

Bloch, Jonathan I., Mary T. Silcox, Doug M. Boyer, and Eric J. Sargis. 2007. New Paleocene Skeletons and the Relationship of Plesiadapiforms to Crown-Clade Primates. *Proceedings of the National Academy of Sciences of the United States of America* 104 (4): 1,159–1,164.

Blue, Kathleen T., Monte L. McCrossin, and Brenda R. Benefit. 2006. Terrestriality in a Middle Miocene Context: *Victoriapithecus* from Maboko, Kenya. In *Human Origins and Environmental Backgrounds*, edited by Hidemi Ishida, Russell Tuttle, Martin Pickford, Naomichi Ogihara, and Masato Nakatsukasa, 45–58. New York: Springer.

Bocherens, Hervé, Friedemann Schrenk, Yaowalak Chaimanee, Ottmar Kullmer, Doris Mörike, Diana Pushkina, and Jean-

Jacques Jaeger. 2017. Flexibility of Diet and Habitat in Pleistocene South Asian Mammals: Implications for the Fate of the Giant Fossil Ape *Gigantopithecus*. *Quaternary International* 434 (A): 148-155.

Bond, Mariano, Marcelo F. Tejedor, Kenneth E. Campbell Jr., Laura Chornogubsky, Nelson Novo, and Francisco Goin. 2015. Eocene Primates of South America and the African Origins of New World Monkeys. *Nature* 520 (7,548): 539-541.

Bown, T. M., and M. J. Kraus. 1988. Geology and Paleoenvironment of the Oligocene Jebel Qatrani Formation and Adjacent Rocks, Fayum Depression, Egypt. Professional Paper, 1452. Washington D.C.: U.S. Geological Survey Professional Papers.

Cachel, Susan. 2015. *Fossil Primates*. Vol. 69. Cambridge: Cambridge University Press.

Cameron, David W. 1997. A Revised Systematic Scheme for the Eurasian Miocene Fossil Hominidae. *Journal of Human Evolution* 33 (4): 449-477.

Cartmill, Matt. 1972. Arboreal Adaptations and the Origin of the Order Primates. In *The Functional and Evolutionary Biology of Primates*, edited by Russell Tuttle, 97-122. Chicago: Aldine-Atherton.

---. 1974. Rethinking Primate Origins. *Science* 184 (4,135): 436-443.

Cartmill, Matt, and Richard F. Kay. 1978. Craniodental Morphology, Tarsier Affinities, and Primate Suborders. In *Recent Advances in Primatology: Evolution*, edited by D. J. Chivers and K. A. Joysey, 205-214. London: Academic Press.

Casanovas-Vilar, Isaac, David M. Alba, Miguel Garcés, Josep M. Robles, and Salvador Moyà-Solà. 2011. Updated chronology for the Miocene hominoid radiation in Western Eurasia. *Proceedings of the National Academy of Sciences* 108 (14): 5,554-5,559. https://doi:10.1073/pnas.1018562108

Chaimanee, Yaowalak, Olivier Chavasseau, K. Christopher Beard, Aung Aung Kyaw, Aung Naing Soe, Chit Sein, Vincent Lazzari, et al. 2012. Late Middle Eocene Primate from Myanmar and the Initial Anthropoid Colonization of Africa. *Proceedings of the National Academy of Sciences of the United States of America* 109 (26): 10,293-10,297.

Chester, Stephen G. B., Jonathan I. Bloch, Doug M. Boyer, and William A. Clemens. 2015. Oldest Known Euarchontan Tarsals and Affinities of Paleocene *Purgatorius* to Primates. *Proceedings of the National Academy of Sciences of the United States of America* 112 (5): 1,487-1,492.

Ciochon, Russell L., and Gregg F. Gunnell. 2002. Chronology of Primate Discoveries in Myanmar: Influences on the Anthropoid Origins Debate. *Yearbook of Physical Anthropology* 45: 2-35.

Ciochon, R. L., D. R. Piperno, and R. G. Thompson. 1990. Opal Phytoliths Found on the Teeth of the Extinct Ape *Gigantopithecus blacki*: Implications for Paleodietary Studies. *Proceedings of the National Academy of Sciences of the United States of America* 87 (20): 8,120-8,124.

Clemens, William A. 2004. *Purgatorius* (Plesiadapiformes, Primates?, Mammalia), a Paleocene Immigrant Into Northeastern Montana: Stratigraphic Occurrences and Incisor Proportions. *Bulletin of Carnegie Museum of Natural History* 36: 3-13.

Cooke, Siobhán B., Justin T. Gladman, Lauren B. Halenar, Zachary S. Klukkert, and Alfred L. Rosenberber. 2016. The Paleobiology of the Recently Extinct Platyrrhines of Brazil and the Caribbean. In *Molecular Population Genetics, Evolutionary Biology and Biological Conservation of Neotropical Primates*, edited by Manuel Ruiz-Garcia and Joseph Mark Shostell, 41-89. New York: Nova Publishers.

DeLeon, Valerie B., Timothy D. Smith, and Alfred L. Rosenberger. 2016. Ontogeny of the Postorbital Region in Tarsiers and Other Primates. *Anatomical Record: Advances in Integrative Anatomy and Evolutionary Biology* 299 (12): 1,631-1,645.

DeMiguel, Daniel, David M. Alba, and Salvador Moyà-Solà. 2014. Dietary specialization during the evolution of western Eurasian hominoids and the extinction of European great apes. PLoS ONE 9 (5): e97442. https://doi.org/10.1371/journal.pone.0097442

Dunn, Rachel H., Kenneth D. Rose, Rajendra Rana, Kishore Kumar, Ashok Sahni, and Thierry Smith. 2016. New Euprimate Postcrania From the early Eocene of Gujarat, India, and the Strepsirrhine-Haplorhine Divergence. *Journal of Human Evolution* 99: 25-51.

Fleagle, John G. 2013. Primate Adaptation and Evolution, Third Edition. San Diego, CA: Academic Press.

Fleagle, John G., and Richard F. Kay. 1994. Anthropoid Origins. New York: Plenum Press.

Fleagle, John G., and Elwyn L. Simons. 1995. Limb Skeleton and Locomotor Adaptations of *Apidium phiomense*, an Oligocene Anthropoid from Egypt. American Journal of Physical Anthropology 97 (3): 235-289.

Franzen, Jens Lorenz. 1994. The Messel Primates and Anthropoid Origins. In *Anthropoid Origins: The Fossil Evidence*, edited by John G. Fleagle and Richard F. Kay, 99-122. New York: Plenum Press.

Franzen, Jens Lorenz, Phillip D. Gingerich, Jörg Habersetzer, Jørn Hurum, von Wighart Koenigswald, and B. Holly Smith. 2009. Complete Primate Skeleton From the Middle Eocene of Messel in Germany: Morphology and Paleobiology. PLoS ONE 4 (5): e5723.

Gebo, Daniel L., and Elwyn L. Simons. 1987. Morphology and Locomotor Adaptations of the Foot in Early Oligocene Anthropoids. *American Journal of Physical Anthropology* 74 (1): 83-101.

Gebo, Daniel L., Marian Dagosto, K. Christopher Beard, Tao Qi, and Jingwen Wang. 2000. The Oldest Known Anthropoid Postcranial Fossils and the Early Evolution of Higher Primates. *Nature* 404 (6,775): 276-278.

Gingerich, P. D. 1980. Eocene Adapidae, Paleobiogeography, and the Origin of South American Platyrrhini. In *Evolutionary Biology of the New World Monkeys and Continental Drift*, edited by Russell L. Ciochon and A. Brunetto Chiarelli, 123-138. New York: Plenum Press.

Godfrey, Laurie R., and William L. Jungers. 2002. Quaternary Fossil Lemurs. In *The Primate Fossil Record*, edited by Walter C. Hartwig, 97-121. Cambridge: Cambridge University Press.

Godinot, Marc. 2006. Lemuriform Origins As Viewed From the Fossil Record. *Folia Primatologica* 77 (6): 446-464.

Gregory, William K. 1920. On the Structure and Relations of *Notharctus*, an American Eocene Primate. *Memoirs of the American Museum of Natural History* (N.S.) 3 (2): 45-243.

Gunnell, Gregg F., Doug M. Boyer, Anthony R. Friscia, Steven Heritage, Frederik Kyalo Manthi, Ellen R. Miller, Hesham M. Sallam, Nancy B. Simmons, Nancy J. Stevens, and Erik R. Seiffert. 2018. Fossil Lemurs From Egypt and Kenya Suggest an African Origin for Madagascar's Aye-aye. *Nature Communications* 9 (3,193): 1-12.

Harrison, Terry. 2010. Apes Among the Tangled Branches of Human Origins. *Science* 327 (5,965): 532-534.

———. 2016. The Fossil Record and Evolutionary History of Hylobatids. In *Evolution of Gibbons and Siamang*, edited by Ullrich H. Reichard, Hirohisa Hirai, and Claudia Barelli, 91-110. New York: Springer.

Ibrahim, Yasamin Kh., Lim Tze Tshen, Kira E. Westaway, Earl of Cranbrook, Louise Humphrey, Ross Fatihah Muhammad, Jian-xin Zhao, and Lee Chai Peng. 2013. First Discovery of Pleistocene Orangutan (*Pongo* sp.) Fossils in Peninsular Malaysia: Biogeographic and Paleoenvironmental Implications. *Journal of Human Evolution* 65 (6): 770-797.

Israfil, Hulya, Sarah M. Zehr, Alan R. Mootnick, Maryellen Ruvolo, and Michael E. Steiper. 2011. Unresolved molecular phylogenies of gibbons and siamangs (Family: Hylobatidae) based on mitochondrial, Y-linked, and X-linked loci indicate a rapid Miocene radiation or sudden vicariance event. *Molecular Phylogenetics and Evolution* 58 (3): 447–455.

Jablonski, Nina G., and George Chaplin. 2009. The Fossil Record of Gibbons. In *The Gibbons*, edited by Danielle Whittaker and Susan Lappan, 111–130. New York: Springer.

Jones, F. Wood. 1916. *Arboreal Man*. London: Edward Arnold.

Kay, Richard F. 1977. Diets of Early Miocene African Hominoids. *Nature* 268 (5,621): 628–630.

———. 2015. Biogeography in Deep Time: What Do Phylogenetics, Geology, and Paleoclimate Tell Us about Early Platyrrhine Evolution? *Molecular Phylogenetics and Evolution* 82 (B): 358–374.

Kay, Richard F., and John G. Fleagle. 2010. Stem Taxa, Homoplasy, Long Lineages, and the Phylogenetic Position of *Dolichocebus*. *Journal of Human Evolution* 59 (2): 218–222.

Kay, Richard F., Jonathan M. G. Perry, Michael Malinzak, Kari L. Allen, E. Christopher Kirk, J. Michael Plavcan, and John G. Fleagle. 2012. Paleobiology of Santacrucian Primates. In *Early Miocene Paleobiology in Patagonia: High-Latitude Paleocommunities of the Santa Cruz Formation*, edited by Sergio F. Vizcaíno, Richard F. Kay, and M. Susana Bargo, 306–330. Cambridge: Cambridge University Press.

Kay, Richard F., Daniel O Schmitt, Christopher J. Vinyard, Jonathan M. G. Perry, Nobuo Shigehara, Masanaru Takai, and Naoko Egi. 2004. The paleobiology of Amphipithecidae, South Asian late Eocene primates. *Journal of Human Evolution* 46 (1): 3–25.

Kay, Richard F., and Elwyn L. Simons. 1980. The Ecology of Oligocene African Anthropoidea. *International Journal of Primatology* 1 (1): 21–37.

Kay, Richard F., Richard W. Thorington, and Peter Houde. 1990. Eocene Plesiadapiform Shows Affinities With Flying Lemurs Not Primates. *Nature* 345 (6,273): 342–344.

Kelley, Jay. 2002. The Hominoid Radiation in Asia. In *The Primate Fossil Record*, edited by Walter C. Hartwig, 369–384. Cambridge: Cambridge University Press.

Kirk, E. Christopher, and Elwyn L. Simons. 2001. Diets of fossil primates From the Fayum Depression of Egypt: A Quantitative Analysis of Molar Shearing. *Journal of Human Evolution* 40 (3): 203–229.

Kirk, E. Christopher, and Blythe A. Williams. 2011. New Adapiform Primate of Old World Affinities From the Devil's Graveyard Formation of Texas. *Journal of Human Evolution* 61 (2): 156–168.

Krause, David W. 1991. Were Paromomyids Gliders? Maybe, Maybe Not. *Journal of Human Evolution* 21 (3): 177–188.

Kunimatsu, Yutaka, Masato Nakatsukasa, Yoshihiro Sawada, Tetsuya Sakai, Masayuki Hyodo, Hironobu Hyodo, Tetsumaru Itaya, et al. 2007. A New Late Miocene Great Ape From Kenya and Its Implications for the Origins of African Great Apes and Humans. *Proceedings of the National Academy of Sciences of the United States of America* 104 (49): 19,220–19,225.

Maclatchy, Laura. 2004. The Oldest Ape. *Evolutionary Anthropology: Issues, News, and Reviews* 13 (3): 90–103.

Marivaux, Laurent, Yaowalak Chaimanee, Stéphane Ducrocq, Bernard Marandat, Jean Sudre, Aung Naing Soe, Soe Thura Tun, Wanna Htoon, and Jean-Jacques Jaeger. 2003. The Anthropoid Status of a Primate from the Late Middle Eocene Pondaung Formation (Central Myanmar): Tarsal Evidence. *Proceedings of the National Academy of Sciences of the United States of America* 100 (23): 13,173–13,178.

Marivaux, Laurent, Anusha Ramdarshan, El Mabrouk Essid, Wissem Marzougui, Hayet Khayati Ammar, Renaud Lebrun, Bernard Marandat, Gilles Merzeraud, Rodolphe Tabuce, and Monique Vianey-Liaud. 2013. *Djebelemur*, a Tiny Pre-ToothCombed Primate from the Eocene of Tunisia: A Glimpse into the Origin of Crown Strepsirrhines. PLoS ONE 8 (12): e80778.

Martin, R. D. 1968. Towards a New Definition of Primates. *Man* (N.S.) 3 (3): 377–401.

———. 1972. Adaptive Radiation and Behaviour of the Malagasy Primates. *Philosophical Transactions of the Royal Society B: Biological Sciences* 264 (862): 295–352.

———. 1990. *Primate Origins and Evolution, a Phylogenetic Reconstruction*. Princeton: Princeton University Press.

McBrearty, Sally, and Nina G. Jablonski. 2005. First Fossil Chimpanzee. *Nature* 437 (7,055): 105–108.

Michel, Lauren A., Daniel J. Peppe, James A. Lutz, Stephen G. Driese, Holly M. Dunsworth, William E. H. Harcourt-Smith, William H. Horner, Thomas Lehmann, Sheila Nightingale, and Kieran P. McNulty. 2014. Remnants of an Ancient Forest Provide Ecological Context for Early Miocene Fossil Apes. *Nature Communications* 5: 3,236.

Miller, E. R., B. R. Benefit, M. L. McCrossin, J. M. Plavcan, M. G. Leakey, A. N. El-Barkooky, M. A. Hamdan, M. K. A. Gawad, S. M. Hassan, and E. L. Simons. 2009. Systematics of Early and Middle Miocene Old World Monkeys. *Journal of Human Evolution* 57 (3): 195–211.

Moyà-Solà, Salvadore, David M. Alba, Sergio Almécija, Isaac Casanovas-Vilar, Meike Köhler, Soledad De Esteban-Trivigno, Josep M. Robles, Jordi Galindo, and Josep Fortuny. 2009. A Unique Middle Miocene European Hominoid and the Origins of the Great Ape and Human Clade. *Proceedings of the National Academy of Sciences of the United States of America* 106 (24): 9,601–9,606.

Moyà-Solà, Salvador, Meike Köhler, David M. Alba, Isaac Casanovas-Vilar, and Jordi Galindo. 2004. *Pierolapithecus catalaunicus*, a New Middle Miocene Great Ape from Spain. *Science* 306 (5,700): 1,339–1,344.

Ni, Xijun, Daniel L. Gebo, Marian Dagosto, Jin Meng, Paul Tafforeau, John J. Flynn, and K. Christopher Beard. 2013. The Oldest Known Primate Skeleton and Early Haplorhine Evolution. *Nature* 498 (7,452): 60–64.

Perry, Jonathan M. G., Richard F. Kay, Sergio F. Vizcaíno, and M. Susana Bargo. 2010. Tooth Root Size, Chewing Muscle Leverage, and the Biology of *Homunculus patagonicus* (Primates) From the Late Early Miocene of Patagonia. *Ameghiniana* 47 (3): 355–371.

———. 2014. Oldest Known Cranium of a Juvenile New World Monkey (Early Miocene, Patagonia, Argentina): Implications for the Taxonomy and the Molar Eruption Pattern of Early Platyrrhines. *Journal of Human Evolution* 74: 67–81.

Pickford, Martin, Yves Coppens, Brigitte Senut, Jorge Morales, and José Braga. 2009. Late Miocene Hominoid from Niger. *Comptes Rendus Palevol* 8 (4): 413–425.

Pilbeam, David. 1982. New Hominoid Skull Material from the Miocene of Pakistan. *Nature* 295 (5,846): 232–234.

Pilbeam, David, Michael D. Rose, John C. Barry, and S. M. Ibrahim Shah. 1990. New *Sivapithecus* Humeri From Pakistan and the Relationship of *Sivapithecus* and *Pongo*. *Nature* 348 (6,298): 237–239.

Rasmussen, D. Tab. 1990. Primate Origins: Lessons From a Neotropical Marsupial. *American Journal of Primatology* 22 (4): 263–277.

Ravosa, Matthew J. 1996. Mandibular Form and Function in North American and European Adapidae and Omomyidae. *Journal of Morphology* 229 (2): 171–190.

Rögl, Fred. 1999. Mediterranean and Paratethys Palaeogeography during the Oligocene and Miocene. In *Hominoid Evolution and Climatic Change in Europe*, edited by Jorge Agustí, Lorenzo Rook, and Peter Andrews, 8–22. Cambridge: Cambridge University Press.

Rose, Kenneth D. 1975. The Carpolestidae: Early Tertiary Primates From North America. *Bulletin of the Museum of Comparative Zoology at Harvard University* 147: 1–74.

———. 2006. *The Beginning of the Age of Mammals*. Baltimore: Johns Hopkins University Press.

Rose, Kenneth D., and Thomas M. Bown. 1984. Gradual Phyletic Evolution at the Generic Level in Early Eocene Omomyoid Primates. *Nature* 309 (5,965): 250–252.

Rose, Kenneth D., Rachel H. Dunn, Kishor Kumar, Jonathan M. G. Perry, Kristen A. Prufrock, Rajendra S. Rana, and Thierry Smith. 2018. New Fossils From Tadkeshwar Mine (Gujarat, India) Increase Primate Diversity from the Early Eocene Cambay Shale. *Journal of Human Evolution* 122: 93–107.

Rose, Kenneth D., and John M. Rensberger. 1983. Upper Dentition of *Ekgmowechashala* (Omomyoid Primate) From the John Day Formation, Oligo-Miocene of Oregon. *Folia Primatologica* 41: 102–111.

Rosenberger, Alfred L. 2010. Platyrrhines, PAUP, Parallelism, and the Long Lineage Hypothesis: A Reply to Kay *et al.* (2008). *Journal of Human Evolution* 59 (2): 214–217.

Ross, Callum F. 2000. Into the Light: The Origins of Anthropoidea. *Annual Review of Anthropology* 29: 147–194.

Ross, Callum F., and Richard F. Kay, eds. 2004. Anthropoid Origins: New Visions. New York: Kluwer Academic/Plenum Publishers.

Russo, Gabrielle A. 2016. Comparative Sacral Morphology and the Reconstructed Tail Lengths of Five Extinct Primates: *Proconsul heseloni*, *Epipliopithecus vindobonensis*, *Archaeolemur edwardsi*, *Megaladapis grandidieri*, and *Palaeopropithecus kelyus*. *Journal of Human Evolution* 90: 135–162.

Schmid, Peter. 1979. Evidence of Microchoerine Evolution From Dielsdorf (Zürich Region, Switzerland): A Preliminary Report. *Folia Primatologica* 31 (4): 301–311.

Seiffert, Erik R. 2012. Early Primate Evolution in Afro-Arabia. *Evolutionary Anthropology: Issues, News, and Reviews* 21 (6): 239–253.

Seiffert, Erik R., Jonathan M. G. Perry, Elwyn L. Simons, and Doug M. Boyer. 2009. Convergent Evolution of Anthropoid-like Adaptations in Eocene Adapiform Primates. *Nature* 461 (7,267): 1,118–1,121.

Seiffert, Erik R., Elwyn L. Simons, and Yousry Attia. 2003. Fossil Evidence for an Ancient Divergence of Lorises and Galagos. *Nature* 422 (6,930): 421–424.

Seiffert, Erik R., Elwyn L. Simons, Doug M. Boyer, Jonathan M. G. Perry, Timothy M. Ryan, and Hesham M. Sallam. 2010. A Fossil Primate of Uncertain Affinities From the Earliest Late Eocene of Egypt. *Proceedings of the National Academy of Sciences of the United States of America* 107 (21): 9,712–9,717.

Seiffert, Erik R., Elwyn L. Simons, and Cornelia V. M. Simons. 2004. Phylogenetic, Biogeographic, and Adaptive Implications of New Fossil Evidence Bearing on Crown Anthropoid Origins and Early Stem Catarrhine Evolution. In *Anthropoid Origins: New Visions*, edited by Callum F. Ross and Richard F. Kay, 157–182. New York: Kluwer/Plenum Publishing.

Silcox, Mary T. 2001. A Phylogenetic Analysis of Plesiadapiformes and Their Relationship to Euprimates and to Other

Archontans. Ph.D. dissertation, Center for Functional Anatomy and Evolution, The Johns Hopkins University School of Medicine.

Simons, Elwyn L. 1961. The Phyletic Position of *Ramapithecus*. *Postilla* 57: 1–9.

———. 2001. The Cranium of *Parapithecus grangeri*, an Egyptian Oligocene Anthropoidean Primate. *Proceedings of the National Academy of Sciences of the United States of America* 98 (4): 7,892–7,897.

———. 2004. The Cranium and Adaptations of *Parapithecus grangeri*, a Stem Anthropoid From the Fayum Oligocene of Egypt. In *Anthropoid Origins: New Visions*, edited by Callum F. Ross and Richard F. Kay, 183–204. New York: Kluwer/Plenum Publishing.

———. 2008. Eocene and Oligocene Mammals of the Fayum, Egypt. In *Elwyn Simons: A Search for Origins*, edited by John G. Fleagle and Christopher C. Gilbert, 87–105. New York: Springer.

Simons, Elwyn L., and D. Tab Rasmussen. 1994a. A Remarkable Cranium of *Plesiopithecus teras* (Primates, Prosimii) From the Eocene of Egypt. *Proceedings of the National Academy of Sciences of the United States of America* 91: 9,946–9,950.

Simons, Elwyn L., and D. Tab Rasmussen. 1994b. A Whole New World of Ancestors: Eocene Anthropoideans From Africa. *Evolutionary Anthropology* 3 (4): 128–139.

———. 1996. Skull of *Catopithecus browni*, an Early Tertiary Catarrhine. *American Journal of Physical Anthropology* 100 (2): 261–292.

Simons, Elwyn L., and Erik R. Seiffert. 1999. A Partial Skeleton of *Proteopithecus sylviae* (Primates Anthropoidea): First Associated Dental and Postcranial Remains of an Eocene Anthropoidean. *Comptes Rendus de l'Académie des Sciences, Paris* 329 (12): 921–927.

Simons, Elwyn L., Erik R. Seiffert, Timothy M. Ryan, and Yousry Attia. 2007. A Remarkable Female Cranium of the Early Oligocene Anthropoid *Aegyptopithecus zeuxis* (Catarrhini, Propliopithecidae). *Proceedings of the National Academy of Sciences of the United States of America* 104 (21): 8,731–8,736.

Simpson, George Gaylord. 1933. The "Plagiaulacoid" Type of Mammalian Dentition: A Study of Convergence. *Journal of Mammalogy* 14 (2): 97–107.

———. 1940. Review of the Mammal-Bearing Tertiary of South America. *Proceedings of the American Philosophical Society* 83 (5): 649–709.

———. 1967. The Tertiary Lorisiform Primates of Africa. *Bulletin of the Museum of Comparative Zoology at Harvard University* 136: 39–62.

Smith, G. Elliot. 1912. The Evolution of Man. *Smithsonian Institute Annual Report* 2012: 553–572.

Smith, Thierry, Kenneth D. Rose, and Philip D. Gingerich. 2006. Rapid Asia–Europe–North America Geographic Dispersal of Earliest Eocene Primate *Teilhardina* During the Paleocene-Eocene Thermal Maximum. *Proceedings of the National Academy of Sciences of the United States of America* 103 (30): 11,223–11,227.

Stehlin, Hans G. 1912. Die säugetiere des schweizerischen Eocaens. Siebenter teil, erst hälfte: *Adapis*. *Abhandlungen der Schweizerischen Paläontologischen Gesellschaft* 38: 1,165–1,298.

Strait, Suzanne G. 2001. Dietary Reconstruction of Small-Bodied Omomyoid Primates. *Journal of Vertebrate Paleontology* 21 (2): 322–334.

Sussman, Robert W. 1991. Primate Origins and the Evolution of Angiosperms. *American Journal of Primatology* 23 (4): 209–223.

Suwa, Gen, Reiko T. Kono, Shigehiro Katoh, Berhane Asfaw, and Yonas Beyene. 2007. A New Species of Great Ape From the Late Miocene Epoch in Ethiopia. *Nature* 448 (7,156): 921–924.

Teaford, Mark F., Mary C. Maas, and Elwyn L. Simons. 1996. Dental Microwear and Microstructure in Early Oligocene Primates from the Fayum, Egypt: Implications for Diet. *American Journal of Physical Anthropology* 101 (4): 527–543.

Ungar, Peter S., and Richard F. Kay. 1995. The Dietary Adaptations of European Miocene Catarrhines. *Proceedings of the National Academy of Sciences of the United States of America* 92 (12): 5,479–5,481.

Wang, Cui-Bin, Ling-Xia Zhao, Chang-Zhu Jin, Yuan Wang, Da-Gong Qin, and Wen-Shi Pan. 2014. New Discovery of Early Pleistocene Orangutan Fossils From Sanhe Cave in Chongzuo, Guangxi, Southern China. *Quaternary International* 354: 68–74.

Ward, C. V., A. Walker, and M. F. Teaford. 1991. *Proconsul* Did Not Have a Tail. *Journal of Human Evolution* 21 (3): 215–220.

Wheeler, Brandon C. 2010. Community Ecology of the Middle Miocene Primates of La Venta, Colombia: The Relationship Between Ecological Diversity, Divergence Time, and Phylogenetic Richness. *Primates* 51 (2): 131–138.

Williams, Blythe A., and Richard F. Kay. 1995. The Taxon Anthropoidea and the Crown Clade Concept. *Evolutionary Anthropology* 3 (6): 188–190.

Williams, Blythe A., Richard F. Kay, and E. Christopher Kirk. 2010a. New Perspectives on Anthropoid Origins. *Proceedings of the National Academy of the United States of America* 107 (11): 4,797–4,804.

Williams, Blythe A., Richard F. Kay, E. Christopher Kirk, and Callum F. Ross. 2010b. *Darwinius masillae* Is a European Middle Eocene Stem Strepsirrhine—A Reply to Franzen et al. *Journal of Human Evolution* 59: 567–573.

Tables

Table 8.1. Major Families of Fossil Primates Discussed Here

Broad Group	Family	Example Taxon	Approximate Age for Group [1]
Plesiadapiforms	Paromomyidae	*Ignacius*	Middle Paleocene–Late Eocene
	Carpolestidae	*Carpolestes*	Late Paleocene–Early Eocene
	Plesiadapidae	*Plesiadapis*	Late Paleocene–Early Eocene
Early Euprimates	Asiadapidae	*Asiadapis*	Early Eocene
	Cercamoniidae	*Donrussellia*	Early Eocene
	Omomyidae	*Teilhardina*	Early Eocene
	Caenopithecidae	*Darwinius*	Eocene
	Adapidae	*Notharctus*	Middle Eocene
	Sivaladapidae	*Sivaladapis*	Late Miocene
Early Anthropoids	Eosimiidae	*Eosimias*	Middle Eocene
	Amphipithecidae	*Amphipithecus*	Middle–Late Eocene
	Oligopithecidae	*Catopithecus*	Late Eocene
	Proteopithecidae	*Proteopithecus*	Late Eocene
	Parapithecidae	*Apidium*	Early Oligocene
	Propliopithecidae	*Aegyptopithecus*	Early Oligocene
	Homunculidae	*Homunculus*	Early–Middle Miocene
Later Anthropoids	Proconsulidae	*Proconsul*	Early Miocene
	Victoriapithecidae	*Victoriapithecus*	Middle Miocene
	Pliopithecidae	*Pliopithecus*	Middle–Late Miocene
	Hylobatidae	*Yuanmoupithecus*	Late Miocene
	Hominidae	*Gigantopithecus*	Late Miocene–Pleistocene

[1] Derived from Fleagle (2013).

Table 8.2. Morphological Comparisons Between Early Euprimates and Extant Primates

Group	Similarities to Strepsirrhines	Similarities to Haplorhines
Adapoids	- Ring-shaped tympanic bone - Similar wrist and ankle bones - Similar molars	- Fusion of mandibular symphysis (in some adapoids and in all anthropoids but not in tarsiers) - Similarly small incisors - Sexual dimorphism in some taxa
Omomyoids	- Small and nocturnal - Unfused mandibular symphysis - Postorbital bar	- Large eyes - Tube-like tympanic bone (in some omomyoids and in catarrhines and tarsiers) - Pointy incisors - General skull proportions - Proportions of some ankle bones - "Leaping" femur (tarsiers)

Figure Attributions

Figure 8.1 Hypotheses about primate origins a derivative work by Jonathan M. G. Perry and Stephanie L. Canington is under a CC BY-NC 4.0 License. [Includes Garnett's Galago by Ltshears, CC BY-SA 3.0; Nycticebus bancanus by Gunay M.E., CC BY-SA 4.0; Anja réserve (Madagascar) – 06 by Wayne77, CC BY-SA 4.0].

Figure 8.2 Primate family tree by Jonathan M. G. Perry is under a CC BY-NC 4.0 License.

Figure 8.3 Eocene Jay Matternes by Jay Matternes creator QS:P170,Q16732146 is in the public domain.

Figure 8.4 Paleocene Map with Plesiadapiform Localities original to Explorations: An Open Invitation to Biological Anthropology by Elyssa Ebding at GeoPlace, California State University, Chico is under a CC BY-NC 4.0 License. Localities based on p. 211 of Fleagle, John G. 2013. Primate Adaptation and Evolution, Third Edition. San Diego, CA: Academic Press.

Figure 8.5 CarpolestesCL by Sisyphos23 is used under a CC BY-SA 3.0 License.

Figure 8.6 Eocene Map with Adapoid and Omomyoid Localities original to Explorations: An Open Invitation to Biological Anthropology by Elyssa Ebding at GeoPlace, California State University, Chico is under a CC BY-NC 4.0 License. Localities based on p. 229 of Fleagle, John G. 2013. Primate Adaptation and Evolution, Third Edition. San Diego, CA: Academic Press.

Figure 8.7 Representative crania of adapids (European adapoids) from the Museum d'Histoire Naturelle Victor Brun in Montauban, France original to Explorations: An Open Invitation to Biological Anthropology by Jonathan M. G. Perry is under a CC BY-NC 4.0 License.

Figure 8.8 Darwinius masillae holotype slabs by Jens L. Franzen, Philip D. Gingerich, Jörg Habersetzer1, Jørn H. Hurum, Wighart von Koenigswald, B. Holly Smith. Originally from Franzen et al. 2009. Complete Primate Skeleton from the Middle Eocene of Messel in Germany: Morphology and Paleobiology. *PLoS ONE* 4(5): e5723. doi.org/10.1371/journal.pone.0005723. Used under a CC BY 2.5 License.

Figure 8.9 Paleogeographic map showing hypothetical migration routes of *Teilhardina* by Smith et. al. Originally from Smith, Thierry, Kenneth D. Rose, and Philip D. Gingerich. 2006. Rapid Asia–Europe–North America geographic dispersal of earliest Eocene primate *Teilhardina* during the Paleocene-Eocene Thermal Maximum. Proceedings of the National Academy of Sciences 103 (30): 11,223-11,227. doi:10.1073/pnas.0511296103.

Figure 8.10 Oligocene Map with Key Early Anthropoid Localities original to Explorations: An Open Invitation to Biological Anthropology by Elyssa Ebding at GeoPlace, California State University, Chico is under a CC BY-NC 4.0 License. Localities based on p. 265 of Fleagle, John G. 2013. Primate Adaptation and Evolution, Third Edition. San Diego, CA: Academic Press.

Figure 8.11 Competing Trees for Anthropoid Origins by Jonathan M. G. Perry is under a CC BY-NC 4.0 License.

Figure 8.12 Egyptian workers sweeping Quarry I in the Fayum Basin (2004) by Jonathan M. G. Perry is under a CC BY-NC 4.0 License.

Figure 8.13 Elwyn Laverne Simons excavating Aegyptopithecus in the Fayum Basin used by permission of the Duke Lemur Center, Division of Fossil Primates.

Figure 8.14 Female and male cranium of A. zeuxis by Simons, Elwyn L., Erik R. Seiffert, Timothy M. Ryan, and Yousry Attia. Original from Simons, et al. 2007. A remarkable female cranium of the early Oligocene anthropoid *Aegyptopithecus zeuxis* (Catarrhini, Propliopithecidae). *Proceedings of the National Academy of Sciences of the United States of America* 104 (21): 8,731-8,736. doi.org/10.1073/pnas.0703129104.

Figure 8.15 Cast of the right half of the mandible of *Eosimias centennicus*, type specimen, from K.D. Rose cast collection, photo by Jonathan M. G. Perry is under a CC BY-NC 4.0 License.

Figure 8.16 Casts of representative amphipithecid material from K.D. Rose cast collection, photo by Jonathan M. G. Perry is under a CC BY-NC 4.0 License.

Figure 8.17 Representative specimens of *Homunculus patagonicus* from K.D. Rose cast collection, photo by Jonathan M. G. Perry is under a CC BY-NC 4.0 License.

Figure 8.18a Cañadon Palos Field Locality in Argentina by Jonathan M. G. Perry is under a CC BY-NC 4.0 License.

Figure 8.18b Swift Current Creek locality, Saskatchewan, Canada by Jonathan M. G. Perry is under a CC BY-NC 4.0 License.

Figure 8.19 Miocene Map with Fossil Ape Localities original to Explorations: An Open Invitation to Biological Anthropology by Elyssa Ebding at GeoPlace, California State University, Chico is under a CC BY-NC 4.0 License. Localities based on p. 311 of Fleagle, John G. 2013. Primate Adaptation and Evolution, Third Edition. San Diego, CA: Academic Press.

Figure 8.20 Range chart for Miocene hominoids of Western Eurasia by Casanovas-Vilar, Isaac, David M. Alba, Miguel Garcés, Josep M. Robles, and Salvador Moyà-Solà. Original from Casanovas-Vilar et al. 2011. Updated chronology for the Miocene hominoid radiation in Western Eurasia. *Proceedings of the National Academy of Sciences* 108 (14): 5,554-5,559.

Figure 8.21 Victoriapithecus macinnesi skull photo taken at the Musee d'Histoire Naturelle, Paris by Ghedoghedo is used under a CC BY-SA 3.0 License.

Figure 8.22 Gigantopithecus blacki mandible 010112 by Wilson44691 is used under a CC BY-SA 3.0 License.

Figure 8.23 Oreopithecus bambolii 1 by Ghedoghedo is used under a CC BY-SA 3.0 License.

Chapter 9: Early Hominins

Kerryn Warren, Ph.D., University of Cape Town

Lindsay Hunter, Ph.D., University of Witwatersrand

Navashni Naidoo, M.Sc., University of Cape Town

Silindokuhle Mavuso, M.Sc., University of Witwatersrand

Kimberleigh Tommy, M.Sc., University of Witwatersrand

Rosa Moll, M.Sc., University of Witwatersrand

Nomawethu Hlazo, M.Sc., University of Cape Town

Learning Objectives

- Define what is meant by "hominin".
- Understand what is meant by "derived" and "primitive" traits and why this is relevant for understanding early hominin evolution.
- Understand changing paleoclimates and paleoenvironments during early human evolution, and contextualize them as potential factors influencing adaptations during this time.
- Describe the anatomical changes associated with bipedalism in early hominins and the implications for changes in locomotion.
- Describe the anatomical changes associated with dentition in early hominins and their implication for diet in the Plio-Pleistocene.
- Describe early hominin genera and species, including their currently understood dates and geographic expanses and what we know about them.
- Describe the earliest stone tool techno-complex and what it implies about the transition from early hominins to our genus.

DEFINING HOMININS

It is through our study of our hominin ancestors and relatives that we are exposed to a world of "might have beens": of other paths not taken by our species, other ways of being human. But in order to better understand these different evolutionary trajectories, we must first define the terms we are using. If an imaginary line were drawn between ourselves and our closest relatives, the great apes, **bipedalism** (or habitually walking upright on two feet) is where that line would be. **Hominin,** then, means everyone on "our" side of the line: humans and all of our extinct bipedal ancestors and relatives since our divergence from the **last common ancestor (LCA)** with chimpanzees.

Historic interpretations of our evolution, prior to our finding of early hominin **fossils**, varied. Debates in the mid-1800s regarding hominin origins focused on two key issues:

1. Where did we evolve?
2. Which traits evolved first?

Charles Darwin hypothesized that we evolved in Africa, as he was convinced that we shared greater commonality with chimpanzees and gorillas on the continent (Darwin 1871). Others, such as Ernst Haekel and Eugene Dubois, insisted that we were closer in affinity to orangutans and that we evolved in Eurasia where, until the discovery of the Taung Child in South Africa in 1924, all humanlike fossils (of Neanderthals and *Homo erectus*) had been found (Shipman 2002). Adding to this debate was the discovery of the Piltdown Man in England, which turned out later to be a forgery of a modified orangutan mandible and medieval human skull.

Within this conversation, naturalists and early **paleoanthropologists** (people who study human evolution) speculated as to which human traits came first. These included the evolution of a big brain (**encephalization**), the evolution of the strange way in which we move about on two legs (bipedalism), and the evolution of our strange flat faces and small teeth (indications of dietary change). Original hypotheses suggested that in order to be motivated to change diet and move about in a bipedal fashion, the large brain needed to have evolved first. And, until research picked up in Africa, fossil finds of species mentioned above predominantly had larger heads.

We now know that bipedal locomotion is one of the first things that evolved in our lineage, with early relatives having small brains and more apelike dentition. In this chapter, we will tease out the details of what this looks like in terms of **morphology** (i.e. the study of the form or size and shape of things; in this case, skeletal parts).

We also know that early human evolution occurred in a very complicated fashion. We have multiple species (multiple genera), diverse in the extent to which they move like us and the diets on which they subsist. Specimen finds have been made all along the **East African Rift System** (**EARS**; in Ethiopia, Kenya, Tanzania, and Malawi), in limestone caves in South Africa, and in Chad. Dates of these early relatives range from around 7 million years ago (mya) to around 1 mya, overlapping temporally with members of our genus, *Homo* (Figure 9.1).

Figure 9.1 East Africa Rift System.

Yet there is still so much to understand. Modern debates now look at the relatedness of these species to us and to one another. Discussions regarding which of these species were able to make and use tools continue. Every **site** discovery in the patchy hominin fossil record tells us more about our evolution. New scientific techniques provide us with insight into the diets, environments, and lifestyles of these ancient relatives that was not available to researchers even ten years ago.

A Note on Brain Size

It is worth noting that while brain size expansion is seen primarily in our genus, *Homo*, earlier hominin brain sizes were highly variable between and within taxa, from 300 cc (cranial capacity, cm^3), estimated in *Ardipithecus*, to 550 cc, estimated in *Paranthropus boisei*. The lower estimates are well within the range of variation of nonhuman extant great apes, and body size variability also plays a role in the interpretation of whether brain size could be considered large or small for a particular species or specimen.

Increases in brain size do not necessarily correlate with an increase in intelligence in animals, especially if body size is not taken into consideration. However, the brain is an expensive tissue to build and maintain. Researchers therefore argue that the cost of maintenance must yield some evolutionary benefit. This is more easily understood in hominins where the stone tool record (an indication of behavior and intelligence) is well associated with the species.

Ancestral and Derived Traits

In Chapter 5, you were introduced to ways of organizing living **taxa**. In the past, **taxonomy** was primarily based on morphology (i.e., the physical features of organisms). Today they are tied to known relationships based on molecular **phylogeny** (such as based on DNA) or a combination of the two. This technique is complicated when applied to living taxa, but it becomes immensely more difficult when we seek to categorize ancestor-descendant relationships in long-extinct forms, where molecular information is no longer preserved. In many ways, we find ourselves falling back on morphological comparisons (often on teeth and partially fossilized skeletal material) in the absence of genetic material.

It is here that we turn to the related concepts of **cladistics** and **phylogenetics**. Cladistics groups organisms according to their last common ancestors based on shared **derived traits**. These are traits (in the case of early hominins, morphological) that are evolved, differing from those seen in earlier populations or forms. These new or modified traits or characteristics provide evidence of evolutionary relationships, and organisms with the same derived traits are grouped in the same **clade** (Figure 9.2). For example, if we use feathers as a trait, we can group pigeons and ostriches into the clade "birds." A good example we will see in this chapter is the grouping of what is known as the "Robust Australopithecines," whose cranial and dental features differ from those of other hominins of a similar or earlier time period and can therefore be considered derived.

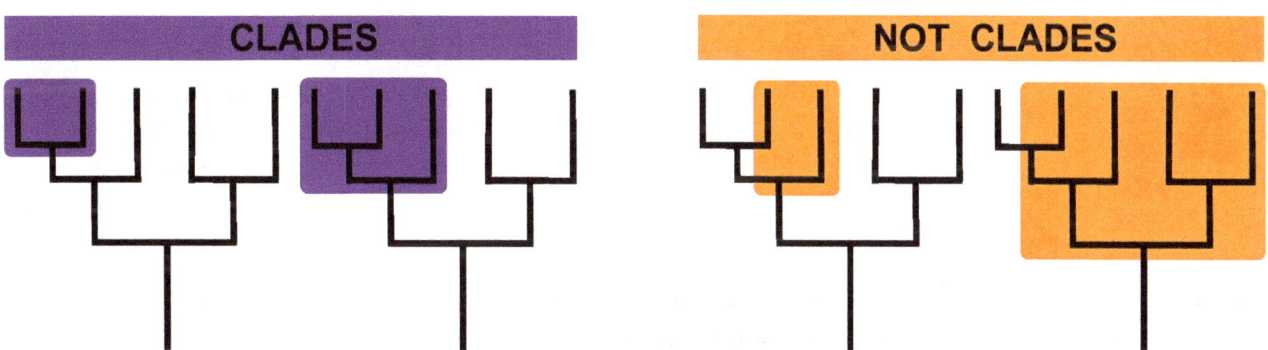

Figure 9.2 *Clades refer to groups of species or taxa that share a common ancestor.*

It is also worth noting that species designations for early hominin specimens are often highly contested. This is, in part, due to the fragmentary nature of the fossil record, the large timescale (in millions of years) with which paleoanthropologists need to work, and because of the difficulty in evaluating whether morphological differences and similarities are due to meaningful phylogenetic or biological differences or subtle differences/variation in niche occupation or time. In other words, do morphological differences indicate different species? How would classifying species in the paleoanthropological record compare with classifying living species today, for whom we can sequence genomes and observe lifestyles?

There are also broader philosophical differences among researchers when it comes to paleo-species designations. Some scientists, known as "**lumpers**," argue that large variability is expected among multiple populations in a given species over time. These researchers will therefore prefer to "lump" specimens of subtle differences into single taxa.

Others, known as "**splitters**," argue that species variability can be measured and that even subtle differences can imply differences in niche occupation that are extreme enough to mirror modern species differences. In general, splitters would consider geographic differences among populations as meaning that a species is **polytypic** (i.e., capable of interacting and breeding biologically but having morphological population differences). This is worth keeping in mind when learning about why species designations may be contested.

This further plays a role in evaluating ancestry. Debates over which species "gave rise" to which continue to this day. It is common to try to create "lineages" of species–determining, in other words, when one species evolves into another over time. We refer to these as **chronospecies**. Constructed hominin phylogenetic trees are routinely variable, changing with new specimen discoveries, new techniques for evaluating and comparing species, and, some have argued, nationalist or biased interpretations of the record. More recently, some researchers have shifted away from "treelike" models of ancestry toward more nuanced metaphors such as the "braided stream," where some levels of interbreeding among species and populations are seen as natural processes of evolution.

Finally, it is worth considering the process of fossil discovery and publication. Some fossils are easily diagnostic to a species level and allow for easy and accurate interpretation. Some, however, are more controversial. This could be because they do not easily preserve or are incomplete, making it difficult to compare and place within a specific species (e.g., the patella or knee bone). Researchers often need to make several important claims when announcing or publishing a find: a secure date (if possible), clear association with other finds, and an adequate comparison among multiple species (both extant and fossil). It is therefore not uncommon for the scientific community to know that an important find was made years before it is scientifically published.

PALEOENVIRONMENT AND HOMININ EVOLUTION

There is so much more to paleoanthropology than digging up and grouping fossil hominins: the discipline seeks to explain and understand the evolution of our ancestors' behavior and morphology. There is no doubt that one of the major drivers (selective pressures) in hominin evolution is the environment. Large-scale changes in global and regional climate, as well as alterations to the environment, are all linked to hominin diversification, dispersal, and extinction (Maslin et al. 2014).

Environmental reconstructions often use modern analogues. Let us take, for instance, the hippopotamus. It is an animal that thrives in environments that have abundant water to keep its skin cool and moist. If the environment for some reason becomes drier, it is expected that hippopotamus populations will reduce. If a drier environment becomes wetter, it is possible that hippopotamus populations may be attracted to the new environment and thrive. Such instances have occurred multiple times in the past, and the bones of some **fauna** (animals, like the hippopotamus) that are sensitive to these changes give us insights into these events.

Reconstructing a **paleoenvironment** relies on a range of techniques, which vary depending on whether research interests focus on local changes or more global environmental changes/reconstructions. For local environments (reconstructing those of a single site or region), looking at the **faunal assemblages** (collections of fossils of other animals found at a site) and comparing them to animals found in certain modern environments allow us to determine if the environments in the past mirror those seen today in the region. Changes in the faunal assemblages, as well as when they occur and how they occur, tell us about past environmental changes. Other techniques are also useful in this regard. **Isotopes** of these fauna, for instance, tell us about the relative diets of individual fauna (e.g., using carbon isotopes to differentiate between species eating more grassland-heavy diets and those consuming bushland/tree-heavy diets) and whether the environment of individual animals was wetter or drier than the present day (e.g., nitrogen isotopes; Kingston & Harrison 2007).

Global climatic changes in the distant past, which fluctuated between being colder and drier and warmer and wetter on average, would have global implications for environmental change (Figure 9.3). These can be studied by using marine core and terrestrial soil data and by comparing these lines of evidence across multiple localities/sites/regions. These techniques allow us to use chemistry (such as nitrogen and oxygen isotopes in shells and sediments) or pollen grains (which show directly the kinds of **flora** surviving in an environment at a specific time period). This means that there are multiple lines of evidence that allow us to visualize global trends over millions of years (although it should be noted that the direction and extent of these changes could differ by geographic region).

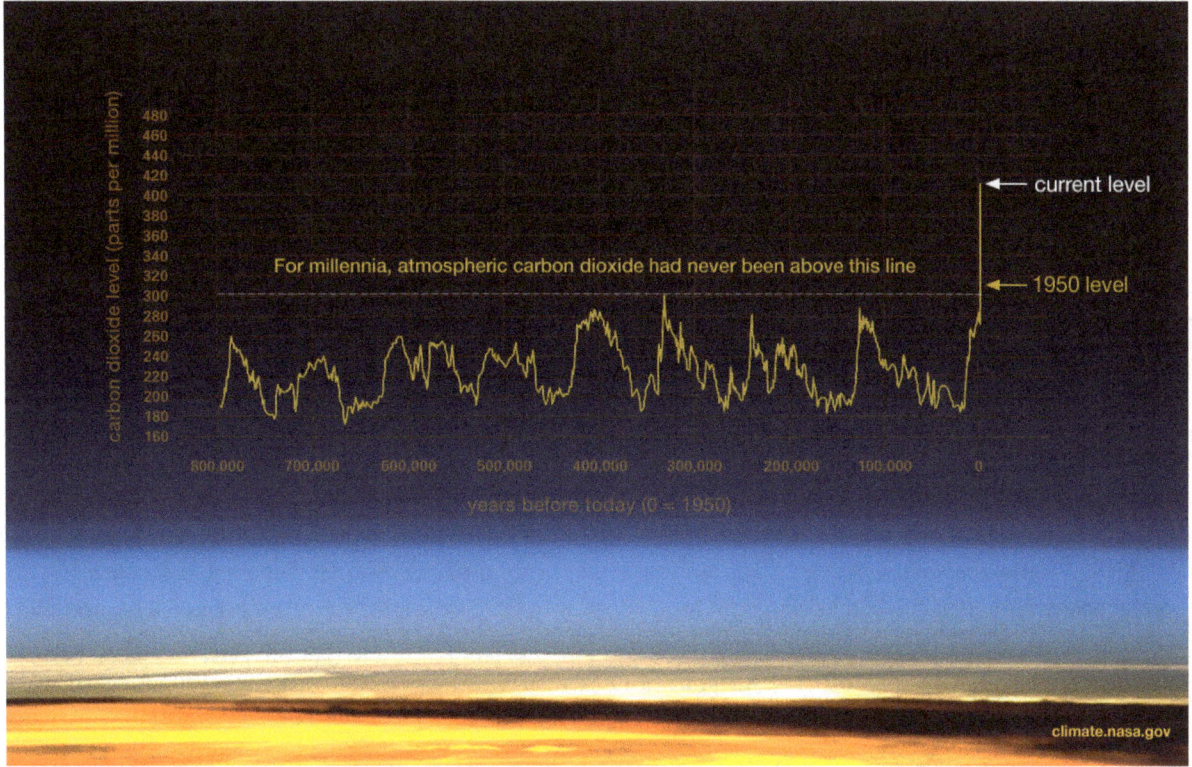

Figure 9.3 This graph, based on the comparison of atmospheric samples contained in ice cores and more recent direct measurements, illustrates how atmospheric CO_2 has fluctuated over time and increased sharply since the Industrial Revolution.

Both local and global climatic/environmental changes have been used to understand parameters affecting our evolution (DeHeinzelin et al. 1999; Kingston 2007). There are numerous hypotheses regarding how climate has driven and continues to drive human evolution. Environmental change acts as an important keystone in hypotheses regarding the onset of several important hominin traits that are seen in early hominins and which are discussed in this chapter. Namely, the environment has been interpreted as:

1. the driving force behind the evolution of bipedalism (terrestrial locomotion on two legs),
2. the changing and diversifying of early hominin diets, and
3. the diversification of multiple early hominin species.

Here, we will explore the five most popular hypotheses.

Savannah Hypothesis (or Aridity Hypothesis)

The hypothesis: This popular theory was first penned by Charles Darwin and supported by anthropologists like Raymond Dart (Darwin 1871; Dart 1925). It suggests that the expansion of the savannah (or less densely forested, drier environments) forced early hominins from an **arboreal** lifestyle (one living in trees) to a terrestrial one where bipedalism was a more efficient form of locomotion (Figure 9.4). This hypothesis stems from the idea that the Last Common Ancestor (LCA) between us and chimpanzees was a knuckle-walking quadruped like chimpanzees and gorillas. However, this idea was supported by little fossil or paleoenvironmental evidence and was later refined as the **Aridity Hypothesis**. The Aridity Hypothesis states that the long-term **aridification** and, thereby, expansion of savannah biomes were drivers in diversification in early hominin evolution (deMenocal and Bloemendal 1995; deMenocal 2004). It advocates particularly for periods of accelerated aridification leading to early hominin speciation events.

The evidence: While early bipedal hominins are often associated with wetter, more closed environments (i.e., not supporting the Savannah Hypothesis), both marine and terrestrial records seem to support general cooling, drying conditions, with isotopic records indicating an increase in grasslands (i.e., colder and wetter climatic conditions) between 8 mya and 6 mya across the African continent (Cerling et al. 2011). This can be contrasted with later climatic changes derived from aeolian dust records (sediments transported to the site of interest by wind), which demonstrate increases in seasonal rainfall between 3 mya and 2.6 mya, 1.8 mya and 1.6 mya, and 1.2 mya and 0.8 mya (deMenocal and Bloemendal 1995; deMenocal 2004).

Interpretation(s): Despite a relatively scarce early hominin record, it is clear that two important factors occur around the time period in which we see increasing aridity. The first factor is the diversification of taxa, where high morphological variation between specimens has led to the naming of multiple hominin genera and species. The second factor is the observation that the earliest hominin fossils appear to have traits associated with bipedalism and are dated to around the drying period (as based on isotopic records). Some have argued that it is more accurately a combination of bipedalism and arboreal locomotion, which will be discussed later. However, the local environments in which these early specimens are found (as based on the faunal assemblages) do not appear to have been dry.

Figure 9.4 The African savannah grew during early hominin evolution. This may have forced early hominins from an arboreal lifestyle to a terrestrial one, where bipedalism was a more efficient form of locomotion.

Turnover Pulse Hypothesis

The hypothesis: In 1985, paleontologist Elisabeth Vbra noticed that in periods of extreme and rapid climate change, **ungulates** (hoofed mammals of various kinds) that had generalized diets fared better than those with specialized diets (Vrba 1988; Vrba 1998). **Specialist** eaters (eating and relying primarily on specific food types) faced extinction at greater rates than their **generalist** (able to eat more varied and variable diets) counterparts because they were unable to adapt to new environments. This meant that specialist eater species were often confined to isolated areas with dwindling resources, whereas generalist eaters were able to move out across the landscape in search of new food sources (Vrba 2000). Thus, periods with extreme climate change would be associated with high **faunal turnover:** that is, the extinction of many species and the speciation, diversification, and migration of many others to occupy various niches.

The evidence: The onset of the **Quaternary Ice Age**, between 2.5 mya and 3 mya, brought extreme global, cyclical **interglacial** and **glacial** periods (warmer, wetter periods with less ice at the poles, and colder, drier periods with more ice near the poles). Faunal evidence from the Turkana basin in East Africa indicates multiple instances of faunal turnover and extinction events, in which global climatic change resulted in changes from closed/forested to open/grassier habitats at single sites (Behrensmeyer et al. 1997; Bobe and Behrensmeyer 2004). Similarly, work in the Cape Floristic Belt of South Africa shows that extreme changes in climate play a role in extinction and migration in ungulates. While this theory was originally developed for ungulates, its proponents have argued that it can be applied to hominins as well. However, the link between climate and speciation is only vaguely understood (Faith and Behrensmeyer 2013).

Interpretation(s): While the evidence of rapid faunal turnover among ungulates during this time period appears clear, there is still some debate around its usefulness as applied to the paleoanthropological record. Specialist hominin species do appear to exist for long periods of time during this time period, yet it is also true that *Homo*, a generalist genus with a varied and adaptable diet, ultimately survives the majority of these fluctuations, and the specialists appear to go extinct.

Forest Hypothesis

The hypothesis: Based on contrasting environmental evidence to the Savannah hypothesis, R. J. Rayner and colleagues (1993) hypothesized that forested environments, rather than savannahs, were a key influence on the development of bipedalism in hominins. Unlike the Savannah Hypothesis, one criterion for this may be that the last common ancestor (LCA) between chimpanzees and us used an arboreal form of bipedal locomotion (i.e., walking along branches using the arms for stability), similar to orangutans, and was not a knuckle-walker like contemporary chimpanzees.

The evidence: Pollen evidence from the site of Makapansgat in South Africa indicated that around the time early hominins occupied the area, it was a closed, wooded environment. Similarly, the earliest evidence for bipedalism occurs in specimens (associated with taxa such as *Orrorin* and *Ardipithecus spp.* as well as *Australopithecus anamensis*) found in sites with evidence of **closed habitats** (Suwa et al. 2009). Furthermore, evidence of knuckle-walking in older hominin species is sorely lacking or highly contested.

Interpretation(s): This hypothesis can be considered in contrast to the Savannah Hypothesis, and it does appear to be evidence based. However, it is worth noting that preservation and resulting fossilization might be better in these kinds of environments, biasing this interpretation of the fossil record. Evidence for knuckle-walking in our more distant ancestors is also highly contested.

Variability Selection Hypothesis

The hypothesis: This hypothesis was first articulated by paleoanthropologist Richard Potts (1998). It links the high amount of climatic variability over the last 7 million years to both behavioral and morphological changes. Unlike previous notions, this hypothesis states that hominin evolution does not respond to habitat-specific changes or to specific aridity or moisture trends. Instead, long-term environmental unpredictability over time and space influenced morphological and behavioral adaptations that would help hominins survive, regardless of environmental context (Potts 1998; Potts 2013). The Variability Selection Hypothesis states that hominin groups would experience varying degrees of natural selection due to continually changing environments and potential group isolation. This would allow certain groups to develop genetic combinations that would increase their ability to survive in shifting environments. These populations would then have a genetic advantage over others that were forced into habitat-specific adaptations (Potts 2013).

The evidence: The evidence for this theory is similar to that for the Turnover Pulse Hypothesis: large climatic variability and higher survivability of generalists versus specialists. However, this hypothesis accommodates for larger time-scales of extinction and survival events.

Interpretation(s): In this way, the Variability Selection Hypothesis allows for a more flexible interpretation of the evolution of bipedalism in hominins, accommodating the discrepancies in evidence between the conflicting Savannah and Forest Hypotheses. This also allows for a more fluid interpretation of the Turnover Pulse Hypothesis, where species turnover is meant to be more rapid. In some ways, this hypothesis accommodates both environmental data and our interpretations of an evolution toward greater variability among species and the survivability of generalists.

Pulsed Variability Selection Hypothesis

The hypothesis: This hypothesis proposes that the East African Rift System (EARS) and changes in deep lakes are key drivers of diversification during early human evolution. EARS first developed about 10 mya and is responsible for the creation of large super lakes (e.g., Lake Baringo and Lake Turkana) within East Africa. The water contents of these lakes were primarily affected by both monsoonal rains and **solar precessional cycles** (cyclical changes in earth's axis rotation- or wobble- that have global climatic effects). According to the Pulsed Variability Selection Hypothesis, human evolution was greatly affected by 200,000-year cyclical changes in aridity and humidity in this region, caused by those global cyclical changes .

The evidence: Proponents of this hypothesis name three extreme humid phases in East Africa at 2.7 mya to 2.5 mya, 1.8 mya to 1.6 mya, and 1 mya to 0.7 mya. During these periods, changes in solar precessional cycles increased the monsoonal system, causing more rain in East Africa, thereby increasing lake sizes. This is documented by the increase of diatomaceous lake sediments during these times. These expanded lakes would act as geographic barriers to hominin populations, allowing for changes and diversification in diet and adaptive behavior to the variable regions, even resulting in (allopatric) speciation (Maslin et al. 2014).

Interpretation(s): High levels of species diversity during these time periods as well as environmental indications of these barriers may allow for an interpretation of allopatric-speciation (i.e., speciation due to geographic barriers) events. However, the degree of interspecific variability and the extent to which these barriers acted as drivers of speciation are still debated.

Paleoenvironment Consolidated Summary

Some of the hypotheses presented in this section pay specific attention to habitat (Savannah and Forest Hypotheses) while others point to large-scale climatic forces (Pulsed Variability and Variability Selection Hypotheses). Some are complementary (Pulsed Variability and Turnover Pulse Hypotheses), whereas others are directly opposed to one another (Savannah and Forest Hypotheses). Some may be interpreted to describe the evolution of traits such as bipedalism (Savannah and Forest Hypotheses), and others more generally explain the diversification of early hominins (Turnover Pulse and Variability Selection Hypotheses). While there is no consensus as to how the environment drove our evolution, it is clear that the environment shaped both habitat and resource availability in ways that would have influenced our early ancestors physically and behaviorally.

DERIVED ADAPTATIONS: BIPEDALISM

The unique form of locomotion exhibited by modern humans, called **obligate bipedalism**, is important in distinguishing our species from the **extant** (living) great apes. The ability to walk habitually upright is thus considered one of the defining attributes of the hominin lineage. We also differ from other animals that walk bipedally (such as kangaroos) in that we do not have a tail to balance us as we move.

The origin of bipedalism in hominins has been debated in paleoanthropology, but at present there are two main ideas:

1. that early hominins descended from trees, and so we were a product of an arboreal last common ancestor (LCA) or
2. that our LCA was a terrestrial quadrupedal knuckle-walking species, more similar to extant chimpanzees.

Most research supports the theory of an arboreal LCA (i.e., idea 1) based on skeletal morphology of early hominin genera that demonstrate adaptations for climbing but not for knuckle-walking. This would mean that both humans and chimpanzees can be considered "derived" in terms of locomotion since chimpanzees would have independently evolved knuckle-walking.

There are many current ideas regarding selective pressures that would lead to early hominins adapting upright posture and locomotion. Many of these selective pressures, as we have seen in the previous section, coincide with a shift in environmental conditions, supported by paleoenvironmental data. In general, however, it appears as though early hominins thrived in forested regions, similar to extant great apes, with dense tree coverage, which would indicate an arboreal lifestyle. As the environmental conditions changed and a savannah/grassland environment became more widespread, the tree cover would become less dense, scattered, and sparse and bipedalism therefore would become more important.

There are several proposed selective pressures for bipedalism:

1. Energy conservation: modern bipedal humans conserve more energy than extant chimpanzees, which are predominantly knuckle-walking quadrupeds when walking over land. While chimpanzees, for instance, are faster than humans terrestrially, they expend large amounts of energy being so. Adaptations to bipedalism include "stacking" the majority of the weight of the body over a small area around the center of gravity (i.e., the head is above the chest, which is above the pelvis, which is over the knees, which is above the feet). This reduces the amount of muscle needed to be engaged during locomotion to "pull us up" and allows us to travel longer distances expending far less energy.
2. **Thermoregulation:** less surface area (i.e., only the head and shoulders) is exposed to direct sunlight during the

hottest parts of the day (i.e., midday). This means that the body is exposed to less heat and has less need to employ additional "cooling" mechanisms such as sweating, which additionally means less water loss.
3. Bipedalism freed up our ancestors' hands such that they could more easily gather food and carry tools or infants. This further enabled the use of hands for more specialized adaptations associated with the manufacturing and use of tools.

These selective pressures are not mutually exclusive, and bipedality could have evolved from a combination of these selective pressures, in ways that increased the chances of early hominin survival.

Skeletal Adaptations for Bipedalism

Humans, as the only obligate bipedal species among primates, have highly specialized adaptations to facilitate this kind of locomotion (Figure 9.5). Many of these adaptations occur within the soft tissue of the body (e.g., muscles and tendons). However, when analyzing the paleoanthropological record for evidence of the emergence of bipedalism, all that remains is the fossilized bone. Interpretations of locomotion are therefore often based on comparative analyses between fossil remains and the skeletons of extant primates with known locomotor behaviors. These adaptations occur throughout the skeleton and are summarized in Table 9.1.

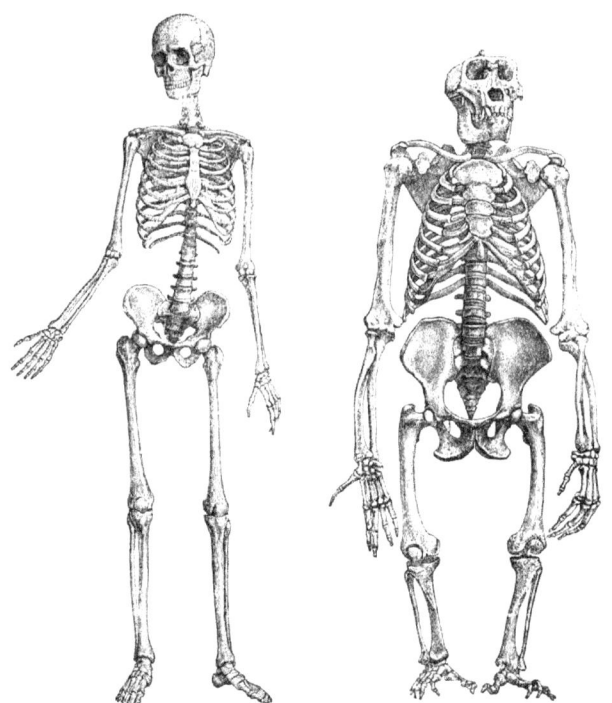

Figure 9.5 Compared to gorillas (right) and other apes, humans (left) have highly specialized adaptations to facilitate bipedal locomotion.

The majority of these adaptations occur in the **postcranium** (the skeleton from below the head) and are outlined in Figure 9.6. In general, these adaptations allow for greater stability and strength in the lower limb, by allowing for more shock absorption, for a larger surface area for muscle attachment, and for the "stacking" of the skeleton directly over the center of gravity to reduce energy needed to be kept upright. These adaptations often mean less flexibility in areas such as the knee and foot.

However, these adaptations come at a cost. Evolving from a non-obligate bipedal ancestor means that the adaptations we have are evolutionary compromises. For instance, the valgus knee (angle at the knee) is an essential adaptation to balance the body weight above the ankle during bipedal locomotion. However, the strain and shock absorption at an angled knee eventually takes its toll, with runners often experiencing joint pain. Similarly, the long neck of the femur absorbs stress and accommodates for a larger pelvis, but it is a weak point, resulting in hip replacements being commonplace among the elderly, especially in cases where the bone additionally weakens through osteoporosis. Finally, the S-shaped curve in our spine allows us to stand upright, relative to the more curved C-shaped spine of an LCA. Yet the weaknesses in the curves lead to pinching of nerves and back pain. Since many of these problems primarily are only seen in old age, they can potentially be seen as an evolutionary compromise.

Region	Feature	Obligate Biped (H. sapiens)	Non-obligate Biped
Cranium	Position of the **foramen magnum**	Positioned inferiorly (immediately under the cranium) so that the head rests on top of the vertebral column for balance and support (head is perpendicular to the ground	Posteriorly positioned (to the back of the cranium). Head is positioned parallel to the ground
Postcranium	Body proportions	Shorter upper limb (not used for locomotion)	Nonhuman apes: Longer upper limbs (used for locomotion)
Postcranium	Spinal curvature	S-curve due to pressure exerted on the spine from bipedalism (**lumbar lordosis**)	C-curve
Postcranium	Vertebrae	Robust lumbar (lower-back) vertebrae (for shock absorbance and weight bearing). Lower back is more flexible than that of apes as the hips and trunk swivel when walking (weight transmission).	Gracile lumbar vertebrae compared to those of modern humans
Postcranium	Pelvis	Shorter, broader bowl-shaped pelvis (for support); very robust. Broad sacrum with large sacroiliac joint surfaces	Longer, flatter, elongated ilia, more narrow and gracile, narrower sacrum, relatively smaller sacroiliac joint surface
Postcranium	Lower limb	In general, longer, more robust lower limbs and more stable, larger joints • Large femoral head and longer neck (absorbs more stress and increases the mechanical advantage). • **Valgus angle** of knee, positions knee over the ankle and keeps the center of gravity balanced over stance leg during stride cycle (shock absorbance). • Distal tibia (lower leg) of humans has a large medial malleolus for stability.	In general, smaller, more gracile limbs with more flexible joints • Femoral neck is smaller in comparison to modern humans and has a shorter neck. • The legs bow outward, there is no valgus angle of the knee (no "knock-knees"). • The distal tibia in chimpanzees is trapezoid (wider anteriorly) for climbing and allows more flexibility.
Postcranium	Foot	Rigid, robust foot, without a midtarsal break. Non-opposable and large, robust big toe (for push off while walking) and large heel for shock absorbance.	Flexible foot, midtarsal break present (which allows primates to lift their heels independently from their feet), opposable big toe for grasping.

Figure 9.6 Skeletal comparisons between modern humans (obligate bipeds) and non-obligate bipeds (e.g., chimpanzees).

Despite relatively few postcranial fragments, the fossil record in early hominins indicates a complex pattern of emergence of bipedalism. Key features, such as a more anteriorly placed foramen magnum, are argued to be seen even in the earliest discovered hominins, indicating an upright posture (Dart 1925). Some early species appear to have a mix of primitive (arboreal) and derived (bipedal) traits, which indicates a mixed locomotion and a more **mosaic evolution** of the trait. Some early hominins appear to, for instance, have bowl-shaped pelvises (hip bones) and angled femurs suitable for bipedalism but also have retained an opposable **hallux** (big toe) or curved fingers and longer arms (for arboreal locomotion). These mixed morphologies may indicate that earlier hominins were not fully obligate bipeds and thus thrived in mosaic environments.

It is also worth noting that, while not directly related to bipedalism per se, other postcranial adaptations are evident in the hominin fossil record from some of the earlier hominins. For instance, the hand and finger morphologies of many of the earliest hominins indicate adaptations consistent with arboreality. These include longer hands, more curved metacarpals and **phalanges** (long bones in the hand and fingers), and a shorter, relatively weaker thumb. This allows for gripping onto curved surfaces during locomotion. The earliest hominins appear to have mixed morphologies for both bipedalism and arborealism. However, among Australopiths, there are indications for greater reliance on bipedalism as the primary form of locomotion. Similarly, adaptations consistent with tool manufacture (shorter fingers and a longer, more robust thumb, in contrast to the features associated with arborealism) have been argued to appear before the genus *Homo*.

Earliest Hominins: Sahelanthropus and Orrorin

We see evidence for bipedalism in some of the earliest fossil hominins, dated from within our estimates of our divergence from chimpanzees. These hominins, however, also indicate evidence for arboreal locomotion.

The earliest dated hominin find (between 6 mya and 7 mya, based on radiometric dating of volcanic tufts) has been argued to come from Chad and is named *Sahelanthropus tchadensis* (Figure 9.7; Brunet et al. 1995). The initial discovery was made in 2001 by Ahounta Djimdoumalbaye and announced in *Nature* in 2002 by a team led by French paleontologist Michel Brunet. The find has a small cranial capacity (360 cc) and has canines smaller than those in extant great apes, yet still larger and pointier than those in humans. This implies strongly that, over evolutionary time, the need for display and dominance among males has reduced, as has our sexual dimorphism. A short cranial base and a foramen magnum (the hole through which the spinal cord enters the cranium) that is more humanlike in positioning have been argued to indicate upright walking. However, the inclusion of *Sahelanthropus* in the hominin family has been debated by researchers, since the evidence for bipedalism is based on cranial evidence alone. Researchers have suggested that in order to conclude if it is a truly bipedal species, we need to find postcranial remains such as a pelvis or a leg bone, which would support the idea of upright walking. An unpublished femur (thigh bone) thought to belong to *Sahelanthropus* was discovered in 2001 and could potentially shed light on this topic once it is fully studied. However, the extent to which this femur is hominin-like is currently unknown.

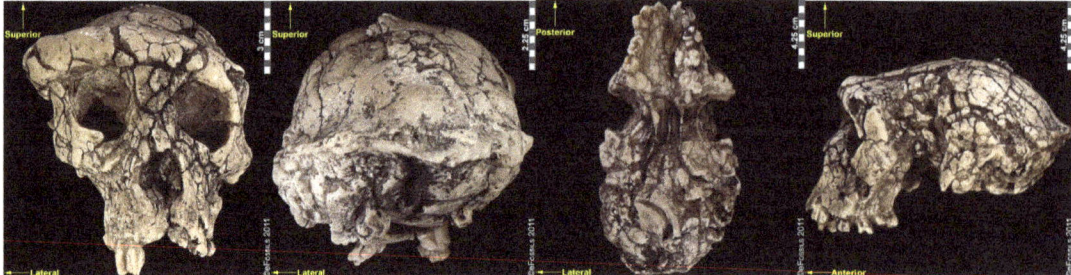

Figure 9.7 Sahelanthropus tchadensis exhibits a set of a set of derived features, including a long, low cranium; a small, ape-sized braincase; and relatively reduced prognathism.

Orrorin tugenensis (Orrorin meaning "original man"; dated to between 6 mya and 5.7 mya) was discovered near Tugen Hills in Kenya in 2000. Smaller **cheek teeth** (molars and premolars) than those in even more recent hominins (i.e., derived), thick enamel, and reduced, but apelike, canines characterize this species. This is the first species that clearly indicates adaptations for bipedal locomotion, with fragmentary leg, arm, and finger bones having been found but few cranial remains. One of the most important elements discovered was a proximal femur, BAR 1002'00. The femur is the thigh bone, and the proximal part is that which articulates with the pelvis—it is very important when studying posture and locomotion. This femur indicates that *Ororrin* was bipedal, and recent studies suggest that it walked in a similar way to later **Pliocene** hominins. Some have argued that features of the finger bones suggest potential tool-making capabilities, although many researchers argue that these features are also consistent with climbing.

Earliest Hominins: The Genus *Ardipithecus*

Another genus, *Ardipithecus*, is argued to be represented by at least two species: *Ardipithecus ramidus* and *Ar. kadabba*.

Ardipithecus ramidus ("ramid" means root in the Afar language) is currently the best known of the earliest hominins (Figure 9.8). Unlike *Sahelanthropus* and *Orrorin*, this species has a large sample size of over 110 specimens from Aramis alone. Dated to 4.4 mya, *Ar. ramidus* was found in Ethiopia (in the Middle Awash region and in Gona). This species was announced in 1994 by American palaeoanthropologist Tim White, based on a partial female skeleton nicknamed "Ardi" (ARA-VP-6/500; White et al. 1994). Ardi demonstrates a mosaic of ancestral and derived characteristics in the postcrania. For instance, she had an opposable big toe (hallux), similar to chimpanzees (i.e., "primitive" or more ancestral), which could have aided in climbing trees effectively. However, the pelvis and hip show that she could walk upright (i.e., it is derived), supporting her hominin status. A small brain (300 cc to 350 cc), midfacial projection, and slight prognathism show retained primitive cranial features, but the cheek bones are less flared and robust than in later hominins.

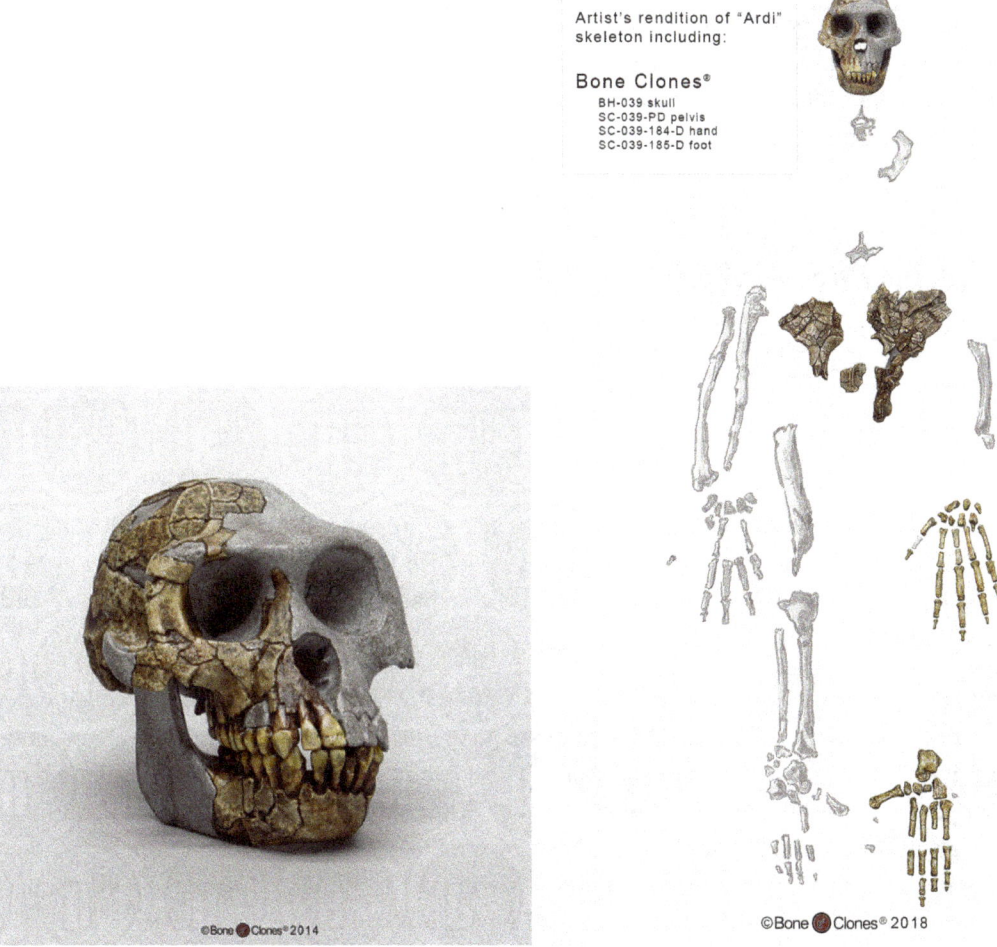

Figure 9.8 Researchers believe that Ardipithecus ramidus was able to walk upright, although not as efficiently as later humans. It possessed the musculature required for tree climbing, and while moving quadrupedally, it likely placed weight on the palms of the hands rather than on the knuckles.

Ardipithecus kadabba (the species name means "oldest ancestor" in the Afar language) is known from localities on the western margin of the Middle Awash region, the same locality where *Ar. ramidus* has been found. Specimens include mandibular fragments and isolated teeth as well as a few postcranial elements from the Asa Koma (5.5 mya to 5.77 mya) and Kuseralee (5.2 mya) Members (well-dated and understood- but temporally separate- volcanic layers in East Africa). This species was discovered in 1997 by paleoanthropologist Dr. Yohannes Haile-Selassie. Originally these specimens were referred to as a subspecies of *Ar. ramidus*. In 2002, six teeth were discovered at Asa Koma and the dental-wear patterns confirmed that this was a distinct species, named *Ar. kadabba*, in 2004. One of the postcranial remains recovered included a 5.2 million-year-old toe bone that demonstrated features that are associated with toeing off (pushing off the ground with the big toe leaving last) during walking, a characteristic unique to bipedal walkers. However, the toe bone was found in the Kuseralee Member, and therefore some doubt has been cast by researchers about its association with the teeth from the Asa Koma Member.

Bipedal Trends in Early Hominins

Trends toward bipedalism are seen in our earliest hominin finds. However, many specimens also indicate retained capabilities for climbing. Trends include a larger, more robust hallux; a more compact foot, with an arch; a robust, long femur, angled at the knee; a robust tibia; a bowl-shaped pelvis; and a more anterior foramen magnum. While the level of bipedality in *Salehanthropus tchadenisis* is debated since there are few fossils and no postcranial evidence, *Orrorin tugenensis* and *Ardipithecus* show clear indications of some of these bipedal trends. However, some retained primitive traits, such as an opposable hallux in *Ardipithecus*, indicate some retention in climbing ability.

DERIVED ADAPTATIONS: EARLY HOMININ DENTITION

The Importance of Teeth

Teeth are abundant in the fossil record, primarily because they are already highly mineralized as they are forming, far more so than even bone. Because of this, teeth preserve readily. And, because they preserve readily, they are well-studied and better understood than many skeletal elements. Even in the sparse hominin (and primate) fossil record, teeth are, in some cases, all we have.

Teeth also reveal a lot about the individual from whom they came. We can tell what they evolved to eat, which other species they may be more closely related to, and even, to some extent, the level of sexual dimorphism, or general variability, within a given species. This is powerful information that can be contained in a single tooth. With a little more observation, the wearing patterns on a tooth can tell us about the diet of the individual in the weeks leading up to its death. Furthermore, the way in which a tooth is formed, and the timing of formation, can reveal information about changes in diet (or even mobility) over infancy and childhood, using isotopic analyses. When it comes to our earliest hominin relatives, this information is vital for understanding how they lived.

The purpose of comparing different hominin species is to better understand the functional morphology as it applies to dentition. In this, we mean that the morphology of the teeth or masticatory system (which includes jaws) can reveal something about the way in which they were used and, therefore, the kinds of foods these hominins ate. When comparing the features of hominin groups, it is worth considering modern analogues (i.e., animals with which to compare) to make more appropriate assumptions about diet. In this way, hominin dentition is often compared with that of chimpanzees, gorillas (our two closest relatives), and/or modern humans.

The most divergent group, however, is humans. Humans around the world have incredibly varied diets. Among hunter-gatherers, it can vary from a honey- and plant-rich diet, as seen in the Hadza in Tanzania, to a diet almost entirely reliant on animal fat and protein, as seen in Inuits in polar regions of the world. We are therefore considered generalists, more general than the largely **frugivorous** (fruit-eating) chimpanzee or the **folivorous** (foliage-eating) gorilla.

One way in which all humans are similar is our reliance on the processing of our food. We cut up and tear meat with tools using our hands, instead of using our front teeth (incisors and canines). We smash and grind up hard seeds, instead of crushing them with our hind teeth (molars). This means that, unlike our ape relatives, we can rely more on developing tools to navigate our complex and varied diets. Our brain, therefore, is our primary masticatory organ. Evolutionarily, partially in response to our increased reliance on our hands and brain, our teeth have reduced in size and our faces are flatter, or more **orthognathic**. Similarly, a reduction in teeth and a more generalist dental morphology could also indicate an increase in softer and more variable foods, such as the inclusion of more meat. These trends begin early on in our evolution. The link has been made between some of the earliest evidence for stone tool manufacture, the earliest members of our genus, and the features that we associate with these specimens.

General Dental Trends in Early Hominins

Several trends are visible in the dentition of early hominins. However, worth noting is that all tend to have the same **dental formula**. The dental formula is a method to characterize how many of the different kinds of teeth are present in the mouth. Going from the most anterior (front) of the mouth, this includes the square, flat **incisors**; the pointy **canines**; the small, flatter **premolars**; and the larger hind **molars**. In many primates, from Old World monkeys to great apes, the typical dental formula is 2:1:2:3. This means that if we divide the mouth into quadrants, each should have two incisors, one canine, two premolars and three molars. In total that is eight teeth a quadrant, for a total of 32 teeth. In humans, this number can be variable. Unlike in other apes, it is not uncommon for people to have only two molars in one or more of their quadrants. One explanation for this is that, because of our processed foods, there are fewer dietary constraints—that is, less pressure to have many teeth for additional processing. Furthermore, with smaller mouths and faces, fewer teeth may be advantageous. All early hominins have the primitive condition shared with other great apes.

The morphology of the individual teeth is where we see the most change. Among primates, large incisors are associated with food procurement or preparation (such as biting small fruits), while small incisors indicate a diet which may contain small seeds or leaves (where the preparation is primarily in the back of the mouth). Most hominins have relatively large, flat, vertically aligned incisors that **occlude** (touch) relatively well, forming a "bite." This differs from, for instance, the orangutan, whose teeth stick out (i.e., are **procumbent**).

While the teeth are often sensitive, evolutionarily speaking, with diet, the canines may be misleading in that regard. We tend to associate pointy, large canines with the ripping required for meat, and the reduction (or, in some animals, the absence) of canines as indicative of more herbivorous diets. In humans, our canines are often a similar size to our incisors and are therefore considered **incisiform** (Figure 9.9). However, our closest relatives all have very long, pointy canines, particularly on their upper dentition. This is true even for the gorilla, which lives almost exclusively on plants, as you have seen in previous chapters. The canines, in these instances, possibly indicate more about social structure and sexual dimorphism than diet.

Early on in human evolution, we see a reduction in canine size. *Sahelanthropus tchadensis* and *Orrorin tugenensis* both have smaller canines than those in extant great apes, yet the canines are still larger and pointier than those in humans or more recent hominins. This implies strongly that, over evolutionary time, the need for display and dominance among males has reduced, as has our sexual dimorphism. In *Ardipithecus ramidus*, there is no obvious difference between male and female canine size, yet they are still slightly larger and pointier than in humans. This implies a less sexually dimorphic social structure in the earlier hominins relative to modern-day chimpanzees and gorillas.

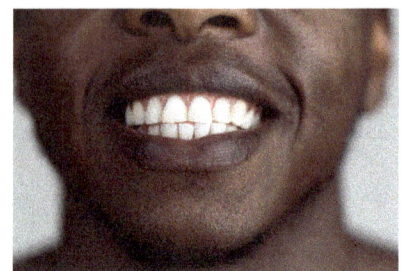

Figure 9.9 In humans, our canines are often a similar size to our incisors.

Along with a reduction in canine size is the reduction or elimination of a canine **diastema**: a gap between the teeth on the mandible that allows room for elongated teeth on the maxilla to "fit" in the mouth. Absence of a diastema is an excellent indication of a reduction in canine size. In animals with large canines (such as baboons), there is also often a **honing P3**, where the first premolar (also known as P3 for evolutionary reasons) is triangular in shape, "sharpened" by the extended canine from the upper dentition. Evidence for this is also seen in some of the early hominins such as *Ardipithecus*, for whom even though the canines are much smaller and almost the same height as the incisors, they are larger than those in more recent hominins.

The hind dentition, such as the bicuspid (two cusped) premolars or the much larger molars, are also highly indicative of a generalist diet in hominins. Among the earliest hominins, the molars are larger than we see in our genus, increasing in size to the back of the mouth and angled in such a way from the much smaller anterior dentition as to give these hominins a **parabolic** (V-shaped) dental arch. This is opposed to our living relatives as well as some of the earliest hominins, such as *Sahelanthropus*, whose molars and premolars are relatively parallel between the left and right sides of the mouth, creating a U-shape.

Among more recent early hominins, the molars are relatively large, larger than those in the earliest hominins and far larger than those in our own genus, *Homo*. Large, short molars with thick **enamel** allow these early cousins of ours to grind away at fibrous, coarse foods, such as sedges, which require plenty of chewing. This is further evidenced in the low **cusps,** or ridges, on the teeth, which are ideal for chewing. In our genus, the hind dentition is far smaller than in these early hominins. Our teeth also have medium-size cusps, which allow for both efficient grinding and tearing/shearing meats.

Understanding the dental morphology has allowed researchers to extrapolate very specific behaviors of early hominins. It is worth noting that while teeth preserve well and are abundant, a slew of other morphological traits additionally provide evidence for many of these hypotheses. Yet there are some traits that are ambiguous. For instance, while there are definitely high levels of sexual dimorphism in *Au. afarensis*, which we will discuss in the next section, the canine teeth are reduced in size, implying that while canines may be useful indicators for sexual dimorphism, it is also worth noting other lines of evidence.

Dental Trends in Early Hominins

Trends among early hominins include a reduction in procumbency, reduced hind dentition (molars and premolars), a reduction in canine size (more incisiform with a lack of canine diastema and honing P3), flatter molar cusps, and thicker dental enamel. All early hominins have the primitive dental formula of 2:1:2:3. These trends are all consistent with a generalist diet, incorporating more fibrous foods.

THE GENUS AUSTRALOPITHECUS

The Australopithecines are a diverse group of hominins comprised of various species. *Australopithecus* is the given group or genus name. It stems from the Latin word *Australo*, meaning "southern," and the Greek word *pithecus*, meaning "ape." Within this section, we will outline these differing species' geological and temporal distributions across Africa, unique derived and/or shared traits, and importance in the fossil record.

Between 3 mya and 1 mya, there seems to be differences in dietary strategy between species of hominins designated as Australopithecines, which is evident from the peculiar size of the molars in one of the groups. This pattern of larger posterior dentition (even relative to the incisors and canines), thick enamel, and cranial evidence for large chewing muscles is far more pronounced in a group known as the robust australopithecines, as opposed to their earlier contemporaries or predecessors, the gracile australopithecines, and certainly larger than those seen in early *Homo*, which emerges during this time. This pattern of incredibly large hind dentition (and very small anterior dentition) has led people to refer to robust australopithecines as **megadont** hominins (Figure 9.10).

Figure 9.10: Robust Australopithecines (left) had large molars and chewing muscles compared to modern humans (right).

This section has been categorized into "gracile" and "robust" Australopithecines, highlighting the morphological differences between the two groups (which many researchers have designated as separate genera: *Australopithecus* and *Paranthropus*, respectively) and then focusing on the individual species. It is worth noting, however, that not all researchers accept these clades as biologically or genetically disparate, with some researchers insisting that the relative gracile and robust features found in these species are due to parallel evolutionary events, toward similar dietary niches.

Despite this genus' ancestral traits and small cranial capacity, all members show evidence of bipedal locomotion. It is generally accepted that *Australopithecus* species display varying degrees of arborealism and bipedality—these individuals were walking on the ground on two legs but were probably still comfortable with climbing trees.

Gracile Australopithecines

The section below describes individual species from across Africa. These species have coined the term "**gracile** australopithecines" because of the less exaggerated, smaller, and less robust features seen in the divergent "**robust**" group. Numerous Australopithecine species have been named, but some are still only based on a handful of fossil finds, whose designations are controversial.

East African Australopithecines

East African Australopithecines are found throughout the EARS, a system running from Malawi to Ethiopia, and include the earliest species associated with this genus. Numerous fossil-yielding sites, such as Olduvai, Turkana, and Laetoli, have excellent, datable stratigraphy, owing to the layers of **volcanic tufts** that have accumulated over millions of years. These tufts may be dated using absolute dating techniques, such as Potassium-Argon dating. This means that it is possible to know a relatively refined date for any fossil if the **context** of that find is known. Similarly, comparisons between the faunal assemblages of these stratigraphic layers have allowed researchers to chronologically identify environmental changes.

The earliest known Australopithecine is dated to 4.2 mya to 3.8 mya. *Australopithecus anamensis* (after "Anam," meaning "lake" from the Turkana region in Kenya; Leakey et al. 1995; Patterson and Howells 1967) is currently found from sites in the Turkana region (Kenya) and Middle Awash (Ethiopia; Figure 9.11). Recently, a 2019 find from Ethiopia, named MRD, after Miro Dora where it was found, was discovered by an Ethiopian herder named Ali Bereino. It is one of the most complete cranial finds of this species (Ward et al. 1999). A small brain size (370 cc), relatively large canines, projecting cheekbones, and primitive earholes show more primitive features as compared to those of more recent Australopithecines. The most important element discovered associated with this species that indicates bipedalism is a fragment of a tibia (shinbone), which demonstrates features associated with weight transfer during bipedal walking. Similarly, the earliest found hominin femur belongs to this species. Primitive traits in the upper limb (such as the humerus) indicate some retained arboreal locomotion. Some researchers suggest that *Au. anamensis* is an intermediate form of the chronospecies that becomes *Au. afarensis*, evolving from *Ar. ramidus*. However, this is debated, with other researchers suggesting morphological similarities and affinities with more recent species instead. Almost 100 specimens, representing over 20 individuals, have been found to date (Leakey et al. 1995; McHenry, 2009; Ward et al. 1999).

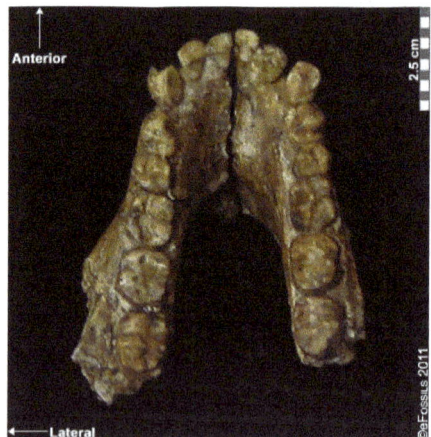

Au. afarensis is one of the oldest and most well-known australopithecine species and consists of a large number of fossil remains. *Au. afarensis* (which means "from the Afar region") is dated to between 2.9 mya and 3.9 mya and is found in sites all along the EARS system, in Tanzania, Kenya, and Ethiopia (Figure 9.12). The most famous individual stemming from this species is a partial female skeleton discovered in Hadar (Ethiopia), which was later nicknamed "Lucy," after the Beatles' song "Lucy in the Sky with Diamonds," which was played in celebration of the find (Johanson et al. 1978; Kimbel and Delezene 2009). This skeleton was found in 1974 by Donald Johanson and dates to approximately 3.2 mya (Figure 9.13). In addition, in 2002 a juvenile of the species was found by Zeresenay Alemseged and given the name "Selam" (meaning "peace," DIK 1-1), though it is popularly known as "Lucy's Child" or as the "Dikika Child"(Alemseged et al. 2006). Similarly, the "Laetoli Footprints" (discussed in Chapter 7; Hay and Leakey 1982; Leakey and Hay 1979) have drawn much attention.

Figure 9.11 As seen in this mandible, Australopithecus anamensis had relatively large canine teeth.

Figure 9.12 Artistic reconstructions of Australopithecus afarensis by artist John Gurche. Female "Lucy" is left and a male is on the right.

The canines and molars of Au. afarensis are reduced relative to great apes but are larger than those found in modern humans (indicative of a generalist diet); in addition, Au. afarensis has a **prognathic** face (the face below the eyes juts anteriorly) and robust facial features that indicate relatively strong chewing musculature (compared with Homo) but which are less extreme than in Paranthropus. Despite a reduction in canine size in this species, large overall size variation indicates high levels of sexual dimorphism in this species.

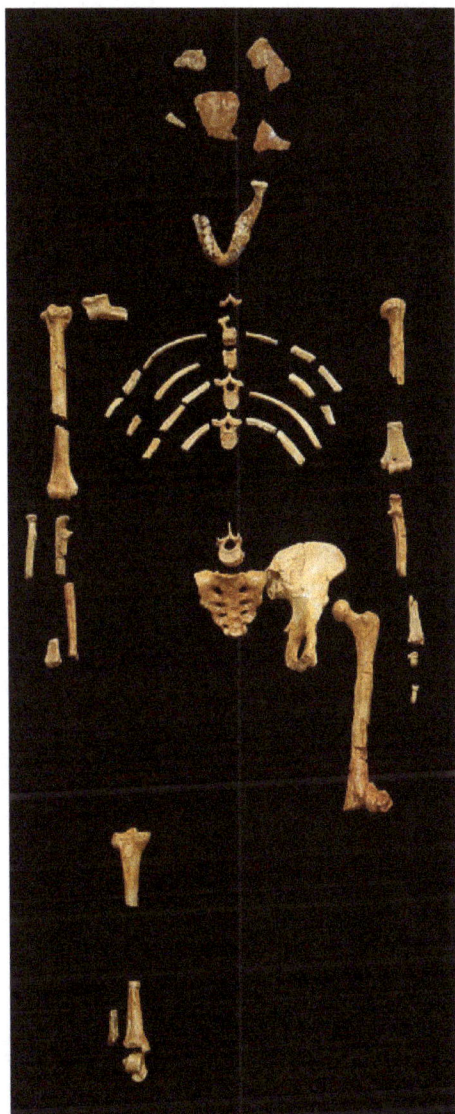

Figure 9.13 The humanlike femoral neck, valgus knee, and bowl-shaped hip seen in the "Lucy" skeleton indicates that Australopithecus afarensis was bipedal.

Skeletal evidence indicates that this species was bipedal, primarily through examining the pelvis and lower limb, which demonstrate a humanlike femoral neck, a valgus knee, and bowl-shaped hip. More evidence of bipedalism is found not in the skeleton but in the footprints of this species. Au. afarensis is associated with the Laetoli Footprints, a 24-meter trackway of hominin fossil footprints preserved in volcanic ash discovered by Mary Leakey in Tanzania and dated to 3.5 mya to 3 mya. This set of prints is thought to have been produced by three bipedal individuals as there are no knuckle imprints, no opposable big toes, and a clear arch is present. The infants of this species are thought to have been more arboreal than the adults, as was discovered through analyses of the foot bones of the Dikika Child dated to 3.32 mya (Alemseged et al. 2006).

Although not found in direct association with stone tools, potential evidence for cut marks on bones, found at Dikika, and dated to 3.39 mya indicates a potential temporal/geographic overlap between meat eating, tool use, and this species. However, this evidence is fiercely debated. Others have associated the cut marks with the earliest tool finds from Lomekwi, Kenya, temporally (3.3 mya) and in close geographic proximity to this species.

Contested Species

Many named species are highly debated and/or newly described. Often these species are argued to have specimens associated with a more variable Au. afarensis or Au. anamensis species. Sometimes these specimens from which these species are named are dated to times, or found in places, when there are "gaps" in the palaeoanthropological record. Often these are argued to represent chronospecies or variants of Au. afarensis. However, it is possible that, with more discoveries, these species definitions will hold.

Australopithecus bahrelghazali (named after the Bahr el Ghazal river valley in the southern region of Borkou-Ennedi Tibesti in Chad, which is not within the EARS system) is dated to within the time period of Au. afarensis (3.6 mya; Brunet et al. 1995). Yet this discovery holds considerable significance in the field as this was the first Australopithecine to be discovered in Chad in central Africa (unlike those in the usual east Africa and South Africa). Researchers argue that the **holotype**, whom discoverers have named "Abel," falls under the range of variation of Au. afarensis and therefore that A. bahrelghazali does not fall into a new species (Lebatard et al. 2008). If "Abel" is a member of Au. afarensis, the geographic range of the species would be extended even further.

On a different note, **Australopithecus deyiremada** (meaning "close relative" in the Ethiopian language of Afar) is dated to 3.5 mya to 3.3 mya and is based on fossil mandible bones discovered in 2011 in Woranso-Mille (in the Afar region of Ethiopia) by Yohannes Haile-Selassie, an Ethiopian paleoanthropologist (Haile-Selassie et al. 2019). The discovery indicated smaller teeth with thicker enamel than seen in Au. afarensis (potentially suggesting a harder diet) and a larger mandible and more projecting cheekbones than in Au. afarensis. The discoverers believe that this was a pivotal find in the palaeoanthropology field as it shows evidence of more than one closely related hominin species occupying the same region at the same temporal period (Haile-Selassie et al. 2015; Spoor 2015). If so, it may also imply that other Au. afarensis specimens have been incorrectly designated and that researchers should attempt to better understand the variability among these species. However, others have argued that this species has been prematurely identified and that more evidence is needed before splitting the taxa, since the variation appears subtle and may be due to slightly different niche occupations between populations over time.

Australopithecus garhi is another species found in the Middle Awash region of Ethiopia. It is currently dated to 2.5 mya and is therefore younger than Au. afarensis. Researchers have suggested it fills in a much-needed temporal "gap" between hominin finds in the region. It has a relatively large cranial capacity (450 cc) and larger hind dentition than seen in other gracile Australopithecines. The discoverers argue that the postcrania is also different (Afsaw et al. 1999), and the femur of a fragmentary partial skeleton (argued to belong to Au. garhi) indicates that this species may be longer limbed than Au. afarensis, although still able to move arboreally. However, this species is not well documented or understood and is based on only several fossil specimens. More astonishingly, crude/primitive stone tools resembling Oldowan (which will be described later) have been found in association with Au. garhi. While lacking some of the features of the Oldowan, this is one of the earliest technologies found in direct association with a hominin.

Kenyanthopus platyops (the name "platyops" refers to its flatter-faced appearance) is a highly contested genus/species designation of a specimen (KNM-WT 40000) from Lake Turkana in Kenya, discovered by Maeve Leakey in 1999 (Figure 9.14). Dated to between 3.5 mya and 3.2 mya, some have suggested this specimen is an Australopithecus, perhaps even Au. afarensis (with a brain size which is difficult to determine, yet appears small), while still others have placed this specimen in Homo (small dentition and flat-orthognathic face). While taxonomic placing of this species is quite divided, the discoverers have argued that this species is ancestral to Homo, in particular to Homo ruldolfensis (Leakey et al. 2001). Some have placed the species itself into the genus Homo, although the cranial capacity and general cranial features are not as derived. Some researchers have additionally associated the earliest tool finds from Lomekwi, Kenya, temporally (3.3 mya) and in close geographic proximity to this species/specimen.

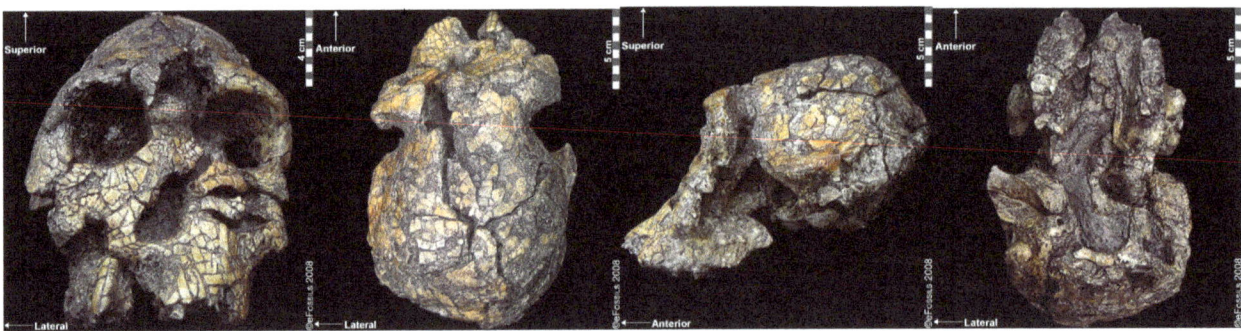

Figure 9.14 This specimen (Kenyanthopus platyops) has small detention, a small brain case, and a relatively flat face. Its genus/species designation remains contested.

South African Australopithecines

Since the discovery of the Taung Child, there have been numerous Australopithecine discoveries from the region known as "The Cradle of Humankind," recently given UNESCO World Heritage Site status as "The Fossil Hominid Sites of South Africa." The limestone caves found in the Cradle allow for the excellent preservation of fossils. Past animals navigating the landscape and falling into cave openings, or caves used as dens by carnivores, led to the accumulation of deposits over millions of years. Many of the hominin fossils we have, encased in **breccia** (hard, calcareous sedimentary rock), are recently exposed from limestone quarries that were mined in the previous century. This means that extracting fossils requires excellent and detailed exposed work, often by a team of skilled technicians.

While these sites have historically been difficult to date, with mixed assemblages accumulated over large time periods, advances in techniques such as uranium-series dating have allowed for greater accuracy. Historically, the excellent faunal record from East Africa has traditionally been used to compare sites based on **relative dating**. In this, the knowledge of environmental/faunal changes and extinction events allows us to know which hominin finds are relatively younger or older than others.

Research Highlight: The Taung Child

The well-known fossil of a juvenile *Australopithecine*, the "Taung Child," was the first early hominin evidence ever discovered and was the first to demonstrate our common human heritage in Africa (Figure 9.15; Dart 1925). The tiny facial skeleton and natural endocast were discovered in 1924 by a local quarryman in the North West Province in South Africa and was painstakingly removed from the surrounding cement-like breccia by Raymond Dart using his wife's knitting needles. When first shared with the scientific community in 1925, it was discounted as being nothing more than a young monkey of some kind. Prevailing biases of the time made it too difficult to contemplate that this small-brained hominin could have anything to do with our own history. The fact that it was discovered in Africa simply served to strengthen this bias.

It was not until adult specimens of the species began to be discovered at Sterkfontein Caves that scientific and public opinion began to be swayed. The most complete of these remains is best known as "Mrs. Ples" and was discovered in 1947 (Broom 1947).

The Taung Child is an excellent example of how understanding the morphology and physiology of teeth can reveal information about our evolution. While many introductory lectures will showcase how the foramen magnum is more anteriorly placed (indicating a head that sits centrally on the body, ideal for bipedalism), Taung Child also shows very human-like dentition. For one, the canine teeth were relatively small compared to other apes. In addition, there was little to no diastema (or gap) between the canines and incisors. The incisors themselves were vertical and close together, and not at an angle to the mouth (procumbent), as seen in other apes. Furthermore, the overall shape of the dental arcade was more rounded, or parabolic. Even though these features were related to deciduous teeth, they were overwhelmingly more human like than those seen in other apes.

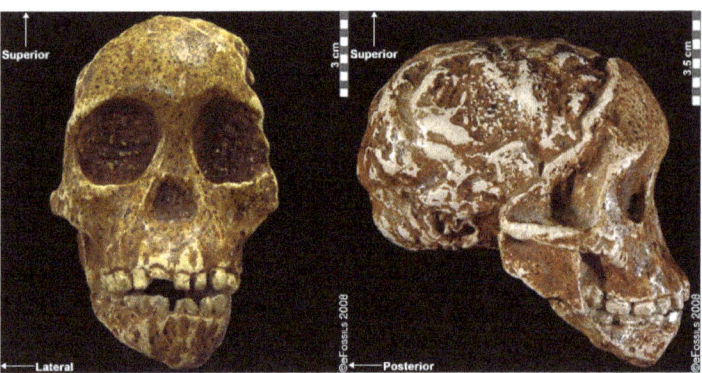

Figure 9.15 The Taung Child has a nearly complete face, mandible, and partial endocranial cast.

The discovery of the Taung Child in 1924 shifted the focus of palaeoanthropological research from Europe to Africa although acceptance of this shift was slow (Dart 1925; Broom 1947). The species with which it is assigned, **Australopithecus africanus** (name meaning "Southern Ape of Africa"), is currently dated to between 3.3 mya and 2.1 mya (Pickering and Kramers 2010), with discoveries from Sterkfontein, Taung, Makapansgat, and Gladysvale in South Africa (Figure 9.16). A relatively large brain (400 cc to 500 cc), small canines without an associated diastema, and more rounded cranium and smaller teeth than *Au. afarensis* indicate some derived traits. Similarly, the postcranial remains (in particular, the pelvis) indicate bipedalism. However, the sloping face and curved phalanges (indicative of retained arboreal locomotor abilities) show some primitive features. Although not in direct association with stone tools, a 2015 study noted that the trabecular bone morphology of the hand was consistent with forceful tool manufacture and use, suggesting potential early tool abilities.

Figure 9.16 An artistic reconstruction of Australopithecus africanus by John Gurche.

Another famous *Au. africanus* skull (the skull of "Mrs. Ples") was previously attributed to *Plesianthropus transvaalensis*, meaning "near human from the Transvaal," the old name for Gauteng Province, South Africa (Broom 1947; Broom 1950). The name was shortened by contemporary journalists to "Ples" (Figure 9.17). Due to the prevailing mores of the time, the assumed female found herself married, at least in name, and has become widely known as "Mrs. Ples." It was later reassigned to *Au. africanus* and is now argued to be a young male rather than an adult female cranium (Thackeray 2000, Thackeray et al. 2002).

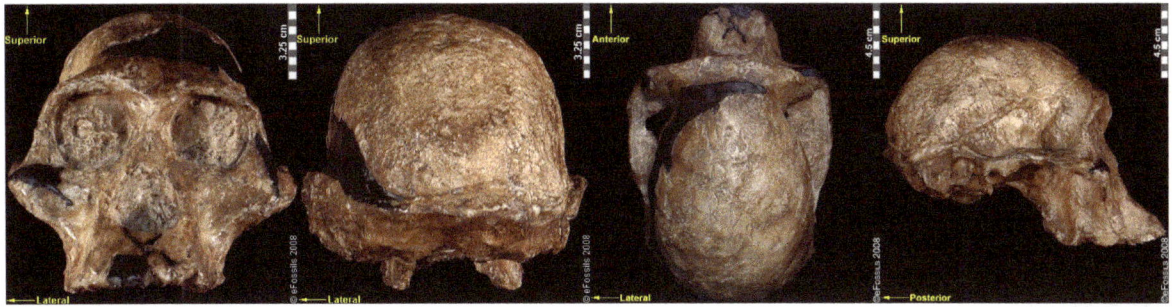

Figure 9.17 The "Mrs. Ples" brain case is small in size (like apes) but has a less prognathic face and its foramen magnum is positioned more like modern humans than in African apes.

In 2008, nine-year-old Matthew Berger, son of paleoanthropologist Lee Berger, noted a clavicle bone in some leftover mining breccia in the Malapa Fossil Site (South Africa). After rigorous studies, the species, **Australopithecus sediba** (meaning "fountain" or "wellspring" in the South African language of Sesotho), was named in 2010 (Figure 9.18; Berger et al. 2010). The first type specimen belongs to a juvenile male, Karabo (MH1), but the species is known from at least six partial skeletons of infants through adult. These specimens are currently dated to 1.97 mya (Dirks et al. 2010). The discoverers have argued that Au. sediba shows mosaic features between Au. africanus and Homo, which potentially indicates a transitional species, although this is heavily debated. These features include a small brain size (Australopithecus-like; 420 cc to 450 cc) but gracile mandible and small teeth (Homo-like). Similarly, the postcranial skeletons are also said to have mosaic features: scientists have interpreted this mixture of traits (such as a robust ankle but evidence for an arch in the foot) as a transitional phase between a body previously adapted to arborealism (tree climbing, particularly in evidence from the bones of the wrist) to one that adapted to bipedal ground walking. Some researchers have argued that Au. sediba shows a modern hand morphology (shorter fingers and a longer thumb), indicating that adaptations to tool manufacture and use may be present in this species.

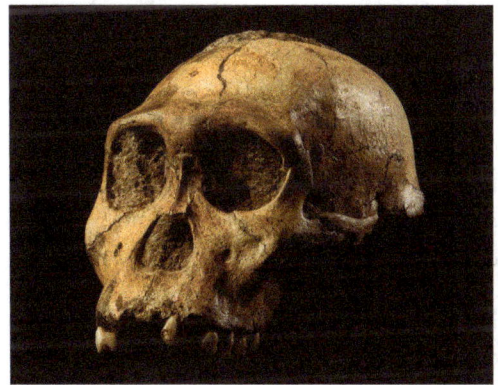

Another famous Australopithecine find from South Africa is that of the nearly complete skeleton now known as "Little Foot" (Clarke 1998; Clarke 2013). Little Foot (StW 573) is potentially the earliest dated South African hominin fossil (3.7 mya, based on radiostopic techniques, although some argue that it is younger than 3 mya; Pickering and Kramers 2010). The name is jokingly in contrast to the cryptid species "bigfoot" and is named because the initial discovery of four ankle bones indicated bipedality. Little Foot was discovered by Ron Clarke in 1994, when he came across the ankle bones while sorting through monkey fossils in the University of Witwatersrand collections (Clarke and Tobias 1995). He asked Stephen Motsumi and Nkwane Molefe to identify the known records of the fossils, which allowed them to find the rest of the specimen within just days of searching the Sterkfontein Caves' Silberberg Grotto. The

Figure 9.18 Australopithecus sediba shows mosaic features between Au. africanus and Homo.

discoverers of Little Foot insist that other fossil finds, previously identified as Au. Africanus, be placed in this new species based on shared primitive traits with older East African Australopithecines (Clarke and Kuman 2019). These include features such as a relatively large brain size (408 cc), robust zygomatic arch, and a flatter midface. Furthermore, the discoverers have argued that the heavy anterior dental wear patterns, relatively large anterior dentition, and smaller hind dentition of this specimen more closely resemble that of Au. anamensis or Au. afarensis.

It has thus been placed in the species **Australopithecus prometheus**. This species name refers to a previously defunct taxon named by Raymond Dart. The name "prometheus" refers to the Greek titan who stole fire from the gods to give to humanity. Raymond Dart believed that the bones he discovered at Makapansgat in South Africa reflected burning when it was later determined that they were in fact Au. africanus remains that had been stained by manganese during fossilization. The species designation was, through analyzing Little Foot, revived by Ron Clarke, who insists that many other fossil hominin specimens have prematurely been placed into *Au. africanus*. Others say that it is more likely that *Au. africanus* is a more variable species and not representative of two distinct species.

Paranthropus "Robust" Australopithecines

In the robust australopithecines, the specialized nature of the teeth and masticatory system, such as flaring zygomatic arches (cheekbone) to accommodate the large temporalis (chewing) muscle, indicated a shift in diet in these taxa. Some argued that the diet of the robust australopithecines was so specific that any change in environment would have accelerated their extinction. The generalist nature of the teeth of the gracile australopithecines, and certainly early *Homo*, would have made these hominins more capable of surviving through and adapting to environmental change. However, some have suggested that the features of the robust australopithecines might have developed more in response to effectively eating **fallback foods** in hard times rather than indicating a lack of adaptability.

Paranthropus is usually referred to by scholars as the "robust" australopithecine, because of its defining distinct morphological features. Features that are closer to those of the assumed ancestral type are referred to as *P. aethiopicus*, and those that have become derived are referred to as both *P. boisei* and *P. robustus* (Strait et al. 1997; Wood and Schroer 2017). These features include a large, broad, dish-shaped face and zygomatic arches that are forward facing, including a large mandible with extremely large posterior dentition. These three species have been grouped together by a majority of scholars as a genus as they share more derived features (are more closely related to each other; or, in other words, are **monophyletic**) than the other australopithecines (Wood 2010; Hlazo 2015; Grine 1988; Strait et al. 1997). Much of the phylogenetic debate (and research, more generally) has revolved around the shared adaptations of these "robust" australopithecines linked to a diet of hard and/or tough foods (Brain 1967; Rak 1988). This includes their large posterior dentition (they are referred to as megadonts), hyper-thick enamel, thick robust jaws, and flared zygomatic arches (Kimbel 2015; Lee-Thorp 2011; Wood 2010).

In terms of diet, the tougher, chewing diets of the robust australopithecines are supported by the extreme morphology of their face and cranium. Similarly, the prognathic faces, which jut out under the eyes in the earlier hominins, are less pronounced than in those of living great apes, yet are more pronounced than in early *Homo*. In contrast, the orthognathic (flat) face of our genus is well suited to accommodate our relatively small generalized teeth and processed diets.

Researchers have mostly reached a consensus to the umbrella term *Paranthropus*. However, there are those who remain cautious/disagree (Constantino and Wood 2004; Constantino and Wood 2007; Wood 2010). As a collective, this genus spans 2.7 mya to 1.0 mya, although the dates of the individual species differ. The genus was first discovered in Kromdraai B, South Africa, by Robert Broom, who first attributed the holotype of specimen TM 1517 (Broom 1938a; Broom 1938b; Broom 1950; Hlazo 2018).

The earliest of the Paranthropus species, *Paranthropus aethiopicus*, is dated to between 2.7 mya and 2.3 mya and is currently found in Tanzania, Kenya, and Ethiopia in the EARS system (Figure 9.19; Walker et al. 1986; Constantino and Wood 2007; Hlazo 2015; Kimbel 2015; White 1988). It is well known because of the "Black Skull" (KNM-WT 17000), so called because of the mineral manganese that stained it black during fossilization (Kimbel 2015). As with all robust Australopithecines, *P. aethiopicus* has the shared derived traits of large, flat premolars and molars; large, flaring zygomatic arches for accommodating large chewing muscles (the temporalis muscle); a sagittal crest for increased muscle attachment of the chewing muscles to the skull; and a robust mandible and supraorbital torus (brow ridge). However, only a few teeth have been found. A proximal tibia indicates bipedality and similar body size to *Au. afarensis*. In recent years, researchers have discovered and assigned a proximal tibia and juvenile cranium (L.338y-6) to the species (Wood and Boyle 2016).

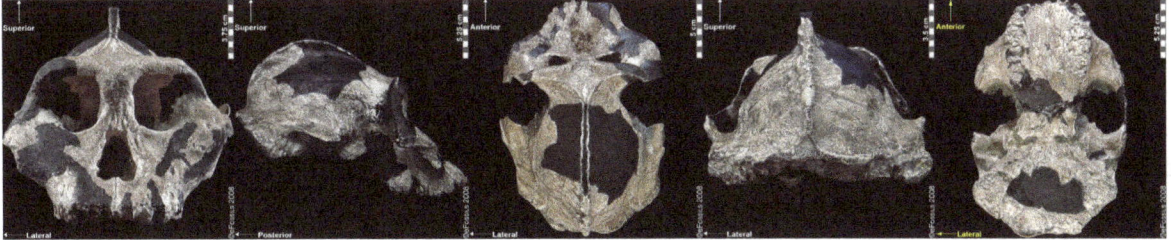

Figure 9.19 The "Black Skull" (Paranthropus aethiopicus) had a large sagittal crest and large, flared zygomatic arches that indicate it had large chewing muscles and a powerful biting force.

Figure 9.20 Artistic reconstruction of a Paranthropus boisei, male, by John Gurche.

First attributed as *Zinjanthropus boisei* (with the first discovery going by the nickname "Zinj" or sometimes "Nutcracker Man"), *Paranthropus boisei* was discovered in 1959 by Mary Leakey (see Figure 9.20 and 9.21; Hay 1990; Leakey 1959). This "robust" australopith species is distributed across countries in East Africa at sites such as Kenya (Koobi Fora, West Turkana, and Chesowanja), Malawi (Malema-Chiwondo), Tanzania (Olduvai Gorge and Peninj), and Ethiopia (Omo River Basin and Konso). The **hypodigm** has been found by researchers to date to roughly 2.4 mya to 1.4 mya. Due to the nature of its exaggerated, larger, and more robust features, *P. boisei* has been termed **hyper-robust**—that is, even more heavily built than other robust forms, with very large, flat posterior dentition (largest of all hominins currently known; Kimbel 2015). Richard Leakey and Bernard Wood have both suggested that *P. boisei* could have made and used stone tools. Tools dated to 2.5 mya in Ethiopia have been argued to possibly belong to this species. Despite the cranial features of *P. boisei* indicating a tough diet of tubers, nuts, and seeds, isotopes indicate a diet high in C4 foods (e.g., grasses, such as sedges). This differs from what is seen in *P. robustus*. Another famous specimen from this species is the Peninj mandible from Tanzania, found in 1964 by Kimoya Kimeu.

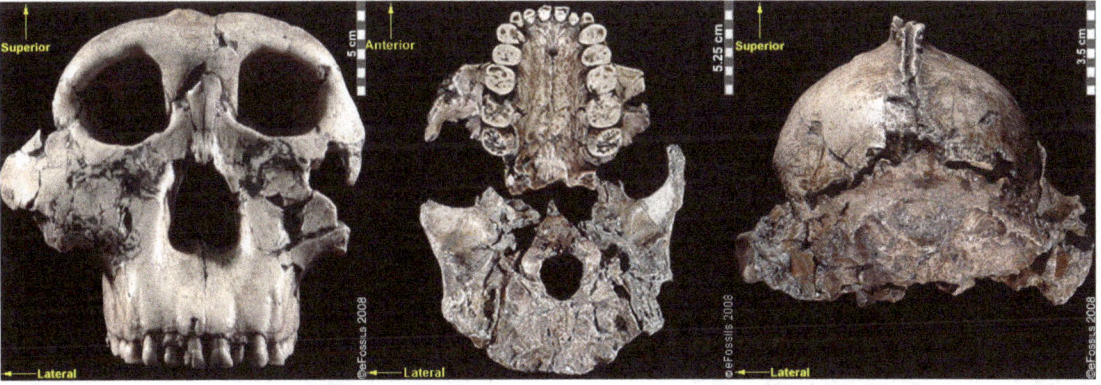

Figure 9.21 "Nutcracker Man" (Paranthropus boisei) had hyper-robust features including very large dentition, flaring zygomatic arches, a broad concave face. It had a powerful and extremely efficient chewing force.

Paranthropus robustus was the first taxon to be discovered within the genus in Kromdraai B by a school boy named Gert Terblanche, and subsequent fossil discoveries were made by researcher Robert Broom in 1938 (Figure 9.22; Broom, 1938a; Broom 1938b; Broom 1950). *Paranthropus robustus* dates approximately to 2.0 mya to 1 mya and is the only taxon from the genus to be discovered in South Africa. It has been found in sites all over the Cradle, such as Kromdraai B,

Early Hominins | 343

Swartkrans, Gondolin, Drimolen, and Coopers Cave. Several of these fossils are fragmentary in nature, distorted, and not well preserved because they have been recovered from quarry breccia using explosives. *P. robustus* features are neither as "hyper-robust" as *P. boisei* nor as primitive as *P. aethiopicus*; instead, they have been described as being less derived, more general features that are shared with both East African species (e.g., the sagittal crest and zygomatic flaring) (Rak 1983; Walker and Leakey 1988). Enamel hypoplasia is also common in this species, possibly because of instability in the development of large, thick-enameled dentition.

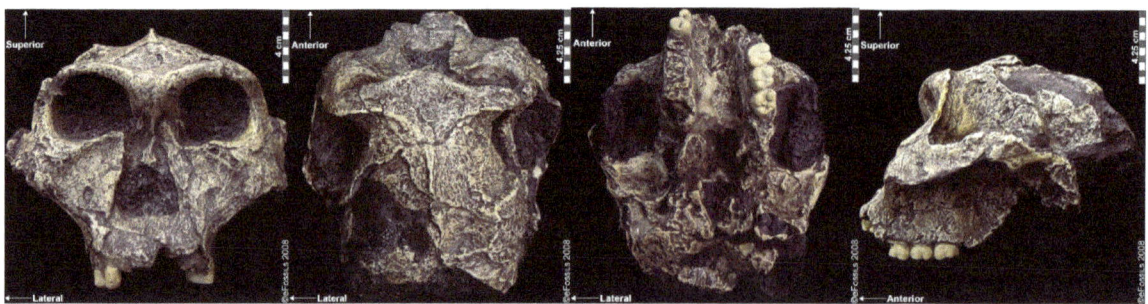

Figure 9.22 Paranthropus robustus had less derived, more general features; it was not as robust as P. boisei and not as primitive as P. aethiopicus. It also appeared to be prone to a tooth defect (enamel hypoplasia), making the enamel thinner and more prone to decay.

Comparisons between Gracile and Robust Australopiths

Comparisons between gracile and robust australopithecines may indicate different phylogenetic groupings but may also indicate parallel evolution in several species. In general, the robust australopithecines have large temporalis (chewing) muscles, as indicated by flaring zygomatic arches, sagittal crests, and robust mandibles (jawbones). Their hind dentition is large (megadont), with low cusps and thick enamel. Within the gracile australopithecines, researchers have debated the relatedness of the species, or even whether these species should be lumped together to represent more variable or polytypic species. Often researchers will attempt to draw chronospecific trajectories, with one taxon evolving into another over time.

EARLY TOOL USE AND TECHNOLOGY

Early Stone Age Technology (ESA)

The **Early Stone Age (ESA)** marks the beginning of recognizable technology as made by our human ancestors. Stone-tool (or **lithic**) technology is defined by the fracturing of rocks and the manufacture of tools through a process called **knapping**. The Stone Age lasted for more than 3 million years and is broken up into chronological periods called the Early (ESA), Middle (MSA), and Later Stone Ages (LSA). Each period is further broken up in different techno-complexes, as explained below. This section focuses on the earliest tools associated with ESA. The ESA spanned the largest technological time period of human innovation from over 3 million years ago to around 300,000 years ago and is associated almost entirely with hominin species prior to modern *Homo sapiens*. As the ESA advanced, stone tool makers (known as **knappers**) began to change the ways they detached **flakes** and eventually were able to shape artifacts into functional tools. These advances in technology go together with the developments in human evolution and cognition, dispersal of populations across the African continent and the world, and climatic changes.

In order to understand the ESA, it is important to consider some definitions. A **techno-complex** is a term encompassing multiple **assemblages** (collections of artifacts) that share similar traits in terms of artifact production and morphology. Not all assemblages are exactly the same within each techno-complex: one can have multiple phases and traditions at different sites (Lombard et al. 2012). However, there is an overarching commonality between them. Within stone tool assemblages, both flakes or **cores** (the rocks from which flakes are removed) are used as tools. **Large Cutting Tools (LCTs)** are tools that are shaped to have functional edges. It is important to note that the information presented here is a small fraction of what is known about the ESA, and there are many ongoing debates and discoveries within the archaeological discipline.

Currently, the oldest known stone tools, which form the techno-complex the Lomekwian, date to 3.3 mya (Harmand et al. 2015; Toth 1985). They were found at a site called Lomekwi 3 in Kenya. This techno-complex is the most recently defined and pushed back the oldest known date for lithic technology. There is only one known site thus far and, due to the age of the site, it is associated with species prior to *Homo*, such as *Kenyanthropus platyops*. Flakes were produced through indirect percussion, whereby the knappers held a rock and hit it against another rock resting on the ground. The pieces are very chunky and do not display the same fracture patterns as seen in later techno-complexes. Lomekwian knappers likely aimed to get a sharp-edged piece on a flake, which would have been functional, although the specific function is currently unknown.

Stone tool use, however, is not only understood through the direct discovery of the tools. Cut marks on fossilized animal bones may illuminate the functionality of stone tools. In one controversial study in 2010, researchers argued that cut marks on a pair of animal bones from Dikika (Ethiopia), dated to 3.4 mya, were from stone tools. The discoverers suggested that they be more securely associated, temporally, with *Au. afarensis*. However, others have noted that these marks are consistent with teeth marks from crocodiles and other carnivores.

The Oldowan techno-complex is far more established in the scientific literature (Leakey 1971). It is called the **Oldowan** because it was originally discovered in Olduvai Gorge, Tanzania, but the oldest assemblage is from Gona in Ethiopia, dated to 2.6 mya (Semaw 2000). The techno-complex is defined as a core and flake industry. Like the Lomekwian, there was an aim to get sharp-edged flakes, but this was achieved through a different production method. Knappers were able to actively hold or manipulate the core being knapped, which they could directly hit using a hammerstone. This technique is known as free-hand percussion, and it demonstrates an understanding of fracture mechanics. It has long been argued that the Oldowan hominins were skillful in tool manufacture.

Because Oldowan knapping requires skill, earlier researchers have attributed these tools to members of our genus, *Homo*. However, some have argued that these tools are in more direct association with hominins in the genera described in this chapter (Figure 9.23).

Invisible Tool Manufacture and Use

The vast majority of our understanding of these early hominins comes from fossils and reconstructed paleoenvironments. It is only from 3 mya when we can start "looking into their minds" and lifestyles by analyzing their manufacture and use of stone tools. However, the vast majority of tool use in primates (and, one can argue, in humans) is not with durable materials like stone. All of our extant great ape relatives have been observed using sticks, or leaves, or other materials for some secondary purpose (to wade across rivers, to "fish" for termites, or to absorb water for drinking). It is possible that the majority of early hominin tool use and manufacture may be invisible to us because of this preservation bias.

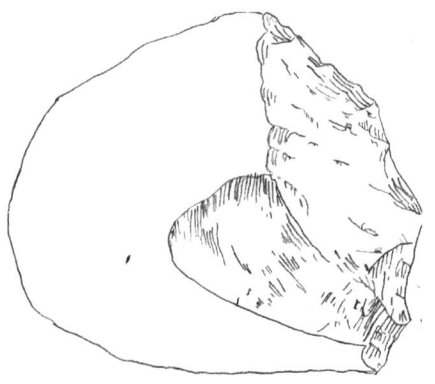

Figure 9.23 Some scholars believe that some genera explored in this chapter were capable of producing more complex stone tools (Oldowan).

HOMININ CHARTS

Hominin	*Sahelanthropus tchadensis*
Dates	7 mya to 6 mya
Region(s)	Chad
Famous discoveries	The initial discovery, made in 2001.
Brain size	360 cc average
Dentition	Smaller than in extant great apes, larger and pointier than in humans. Canines worn at the tips.
Cranial features	A short cranial base and a foramen magnum (hole in which the spinal cord enters the cranium) that is more humanlike in positioning, has been argued to indicate upright walking.
Postcranial features	Currently little published postcranial material.
Culture	N/A
Other	The extent to which this hominin was bipedal is currently heavily debated. If so, it would indicate an arboreal bipedal ancestor of hominins, not a knuckle-walker like chimpanzees.

Hominin	*Orrorin tugenensis*
Dates	6 mya to 5.7 mya
Region(s)	Tugen Hills (Kenya)
Famous discoveries	Original discovery in 2000.
Brain size	N/A
Dentition	Smaller cheek teeth (molars and premolars) than even more recent hominins (i.e., derived), thick enamel, and reduced, but apelike, canines.
Cranial features	Not many found
Postcranial features	Fragmentary leg, arm, and finger bones have been found. Indicates bipedal locomotion.
Culture	Potential toolmaking capability based on hand morphology, but nothing found directly.
Other	This is the earliest species that clearly indicates adaptations for bipedal locomotion.

Hominin	*Ardipithecus ramidus*
Dates	4.4 mya
Region(s)	Middle Awash region and Gona (Ethiopia)
Famous discoveries	A partial female skeleton nicknamed "Ardi" (ARA-VP-6/500).
Brain size	300 cc to 350 cc
Dentition	Little differences between the canines of males and females (small sexual dimorphism).
Cranial features	Midfacial projection, slightly prognathic. Cheekbones less flared and robust than in later hominins.
Postcranial features	Ardi demonstrates a mosaic of ancestral and derived characteristics in the postcrania. For instance, an opposable big toe similar to chimpanzees (i.e., "primitive" or more ancestral), which could have aided in climbing trees effectively. However, the pelvis and hip show that she could walk upright (i.e., it is derived), supporting her hominin status.
Culture	None directly associated
Other	Over 110 specimens from Aramis

Hominin	*Ardipithecus kadabba*
Dates	5.2 mya to 5.8 mya
Region(s)	Middle Awash (Ethiopia)
Famous discoveries	This species discovery in 1997 by Yohannes Haile-Selassie.
Brain size	N/A
Dentition	Larger hind dentition than in modern chimpanzees. Thick enamel and larger canines than in later hominins.
Cranial features	N/A
Postcranial features	A large hallux (big toe) bone indicates a bipedal "push off."
Culture	N/A
Other	Faunal evidence indicates a mixed grassland/woodland environment.

Hominin	*Australopithecus anamensis*
Dates	4.2 mya to 3.8 mya
Region(s)	Turkana region (Kenya), Middle Awash (Ethiopia)
Famous discoveries	A 2019 find from Ethiopia, named MRD.
Brain size	370 cc
Dentition	Relatively large canines compared with more recent Australopithecines.
Cranial features	Projecting cheekbones and primitive earholes.
Postcranial features	Lower limb bones (tibia and femur) indicate bipedality; arboreal features in upper limb bones (humerus) found.
Culture	N/A
Other	Almost 100 specimens, representing over 20 individuals, have been found to date.

Hominin	*Australopithecus afarensis*
Dates	2.9 mya to 3.9 mya
Region(s)	Afar Region, Omo, Maka, Fejej, and Belohdelie (Ethiopia); Laetoli (Tanzania); Koobi Fora (Kenya).
Famous discoveries	Lucy, Selam (Dikika Child), Laetoli Footprints.
Brain size	380 cc to 430 cc
Dentition	Reduced canines and molars relative to great apes, but larger than in modern humans.
Cranial features	Prognathic face, facial features indicate relatively strong chewing musculature (compared with *Homo*), but less extreme than in *Paranthropus*.
Postcranial features	Clear evidence for bipedalism from lower limb postcranial bones. Laetoli Footprints indicate humanlike walking. Dikika Child bones indicate retained primitive arboreal traits in the postcrania.
Culture	None directly; but close in age and proximity to controversial cut marks at Dikika and early tools in Lomekwi.
Other	*Au. afarensis* is one of the oldest and most well-known australopithecine species and consists of a large number of fossil remains.

Hominin	*Australopithecus bahrelghazali*
Dates	3.6 mya
Region(s)	Chad
Famous discoveries	"Abel," the holotype.
Brain size	N//A
Dentition	NA
Cranial features	N/A
Postcranial features	N/A
Culture	N/A
Other	Arguably within range of variation of *Au. afarensis*

Hominin	*Australopithecus deyiremada*
Dates	3.5 mya to 3.3 mya
Region(s)	Woranso-Mille (Afar region, Ethiopia)
Famous discoveries	First fossil mandible bones were discovered in 2011 in the Afar region of Ethiopia by Yohannes Haile-Selassie.
Brain size	N/A
Dentition	Smaller teeth with thicker enamel than seen in *Au. afarensis*, with a potentially hardier diet.
Cranial features	Larger mandible and more projecting cheekbones than in *Au. afarensis*.
Postcranial features	N/A
Culture	N/A
Other	Contested species designation; arguably a member of *Au. afarensis*.

Hominin	*Australopithecus garhi*
Dates	2.5 mya
Region(s)	Middle Awash (Ethiopia)
Famous discoveries	N/A
Brain size	450 cc
Dentition	Larger hind dentition than seen in other gracile Australopithecines.
Cranial features	N/A
Postcranial features	A femur of a fragmentary partial skeleton, argued to belong to *Au. garhi*, indicates this species may be longer-limbed than *Au. afarensis*, although still able to move arboreally.
Culture	Crude/primitive stone tools resembling Oldowan (described later) have been found in association with *Au. garhi*.
Other	This species is not well documented or understood and is based on only a few fossil specimens.

Hominin	*Australopithecus africanus*
Dates	3.3 mya to 2.1 mya
Region(s)	Sterkfontein, Taung, Makapansgat, Gladysvale (South Africa)
Famous discoveries	Taung Child, "Mrs. Ples," Little Foot (?).
Brain size	400 cc to 500 cc
Dentition	Smaller teeth (derived) relative to *Au. afarensis*. Small canines with no diastema.
Cranial features	A rounder skull compared with *Au. afarensis* in East Africa. A sloping face (primitive).
Postcranial features	Similar postcranial evidence for bipedal locomotion (derived pelvis) with retained arboreal locomotion (e.g., curved phalanges–fingers), as seen in *Au. afarensis*.
Culture	None with direct evidence.
Other	A 2015 study noted that the trabecular bone morphology of the hand was consistent with forceful tool manufacture and use, suggesting potential early tool abilities.

Hominin	*Australopithecus sediba*
Dates	1.97 mya
Region(s)	Malapa Fossil Site (South Africa)
Famous discoveries	Karabo (MH1)
Brain size	420 cc to 450 cc
Dentition	Small dentition with Australopithecine cusp-spacing.
Cranial features	Small brain size (*Australopithecus*-like), but gracile mandible (*Homo*-like).
Postcranial features	Scientists have interpreted this mixture of traits (such as a robust ankle but evidence for an arch in the foot) as a transitional phase between a body previously adapted to arborealism (tree climbing, particularly in evidence from the bones of the wrist) to one that adapted to bipedal ground walking.
Culture	None of direct association, but some have argued that a modern hand morphology (shorter fingers and a longer thumb) means that adaptations to tool manufacture and use may be present in this species.
Other	It was first discovered through a clavicle bone in 2008 by nine-year-old Matthew Berger, son of paleoanthropologist Lee Berger.

Hominin	*Australopithecus prometheus*
Dates	3.7 mya (debated)
Region(s)	Sterkfontein (South Africa)
Famous discoveries	"Little Foot" (StW 573)
Brain size	408 cc (Little Foot estimate)
Dentition	Heavy anterior dental wear patterns, relatively large anterior dentition and smaller hind dentition, similar to *Au. afarensis*.
Cranial features	Relatively larger brain size, robust zygomatic arch, and a flatter midface.
Postcranial features	The initial discovery of four ankle bones indicated bipedality.
Culture	N/A
Other	Highly debated new species designation.

Hominin	*Paranthropus aethiopicus*
Dates	2.7 mya to 2.3 mya
Region(s)	West Turkana (Kenya), Laetoli (Tanzania), Omo River Basin (Ethiopia)
Famous discoveries	The 'Black Skull" (KNM-WT 17000)
Brain Size	410 cc
Dentition	*P. aethiopicus* has the shared derived traits of large flat premolars and molars, although few teeth have been found.
Cranial features	Large flaring zygomatic arches for accommodating large chewing muscles (the temporalis muscle), a sagittal crest for increased muscle attachment of the chewing muscles to the skull, and a robust mandible and supraorbital torus (brow ridge).
Postcranial features	A proximal tibia indicates bipedality, and similar size to *Au. afarensis*.
Culture	N/A
Other	The "Black Skull" is so called because of the mineral manganese that stained it black during fossilization.

Hominin	*Paranthropus boisei*
Dates	2.4 mya to 1.4 mya
Region(s)	Koobi Fora, West Turkana, and Chesowanja (Kenya), Malema-Chiwondo (Malawi), Olduvai Gorge and Peninj (Tanzania), and Omo River basin and Konso (Ethiopia)
Famous discoveries	"Zinj," or sometimes "Nutcracker Man" (OH5), in 1959 by Mary Leakey. The Peninj mandible from Tanzania, found in 1964 by Kimoya Kimeu.
Brain size	500 cc to 550 cc
Dentition	Very large, flat posterior dentition (largest of all hominins currently known). Much smaller anterior dentition. Very thick dental enamel.
Cranial features	Indications of very large chewing muscles (e.g., flaring zygomatic arches and a large sagittal crest).
Postcranial features	Evidence for high variability and sexual dimorphism, with estimates of males at 1.37 meters tall and females at 1.24 meters.
Culture	Richard Leakey and Bernard Wood have both suggested that *P. boisei* could have made and used stone tools. Tools dated to 2.5 mya in Ethiopia have been argued to possibly belong to this species.
Other	Despite the cranial features of *P. boisei* indicating a tough diet of tubers, nuts, and seeds, isotopes indicate a diet high in C4 foods (e.g., grasses, such as sedges). This differs from what is seen in *P. robustus*.

Hominin	*Paranthropus robustus*
Dates	2.3 mya to 1 mya
Region(s)	Kromdraai B, Swartkrans, Gondolin, Drimolen, and Coopers Cave (South Africa)
Famous discoveries	SK48 (original skull)
Brain size	410 cc to 530 cc
Dentition	Large posterior teeth with thick enamel, consistent with other Robust Australopithecines. Enamel hypoplasia is also common in this species, possibly because of instability in the development of large, thick enameled dentition.
Cranial features	*P. robustus* features are neither as "hyper-robust" as *P. boisei* or as primitive as *P. aethiopicus*, but have been described as less derived more general features that are shared with both East African species, e.g., the sagittal crest and zygomatic flaring.
Postcranial features	Reconstructions indicate sexual dimorphism.
Culture	N/A
Other	Several of these fossils are fragmentary in nature, distorted, and not well preserved, because they have been recovered from quarry breccia using explosives.

Hominin	*Kenyanthopus platyops*
Dates	3.5 mya to 3.2 mya
Region(s)	Lake Turkana (Kenya)
Famous discoveries	KNM-WT 40000
Brain size	Difficult to determine, but appears within the range of *Australopithecus afarensis*.
Dentition	Small molars/dentition (*Homo*-like characteristic)
Cranial features	Flatter (i.e., orthognathic) face
Postcranial features	N/A
Culture	Some have associated the earliest tool finds from Lomekwi, Kenya, temporally (3.3 mya) and in close geographic proximity to this species/specimen.
Other	Taxonomic placing of this species is quite divided. The discoverers have argued that this species is ancestral to *Homo*, in particular to *Homo ruldolfensis*.

Review Questions

- What is the difference between a "derived" versus a "primitive" trait? Give an example of both, seen in Au. afarensis.
- Which of the paleoenvironment hypotheses have been used to describe early hominin diversity, and which have been used to describe bipedalism?
- Which anatomical features for bipedalism do we see in early hominins? Are these primarily obligate bipeds? Explain.
- Describe the dentition of gracile and robust australopithecines. What might these tell us about their relative diets?
- List the hominin species argued to be associated with stone tool technologies. Are you convinced of these associations? Why/why not?

Key Terms

Arboreal: Related to trees or woodland.

Aridification: Becoming increasingly arid or dry, as related to the climate or environment.

Aridity Hypothesis: The hypothesis that long-term aridification and expansion of savannah biomes were drivers in diversification in early hominin evolution

Assemblage: A collection demonstrating a pattern. Often pertaining to a site or region.

Bipedalism: The locomotor ability to walk on two legs.

Breccia: Hard, calcareous sedimentary rock.

Canines: The pointy teeth just next to the incisors, in the front of the mouth.

Cheek teeth: Or hind dentition (molars and premolars).

Chronospecies: Species that are said to evolve into another species, in a linear fashion, over time.

Clade: A group of species or taxa with a shared common ancestor.

Cladistics: The field of grouping organisms into those of shared ancestry.

Closed habitat: A phrase typically referring to a woodland, or tree-filled, environment.

Context: As pertaining to palaeoanthropology, this term refers to the place where an artifact or fossil is found.

Cores: The remains of a rock that has been flaked or knapped.

Cusps: The ridges or "bumps" on the teeth.

Dental formula: A technique to describe the number of incisors, canines, premolars, and molars in each quadrant of the mouth.

Derived traits: Newly evolved traits that differ from those seen in the ancestor.

Diastema: A gap. In this chapter, this term refers to a tooth gap occurring between the incisors and canines.

Early Stone Age (ESA): The earliest described archaeological period in which we start seeing stone tool technology.

East African Rift System (EARS): This term is often used to refer to the Rift Valley, expanding from Malawi to Ethiopia. This active geological structure is responsible for much of the visibility of the paleoanthropological record in East Africa.

Enamel: The highly mineralized outer layer of the tooth.

Encephalization: Expansion of the brain.

Extant: Currently living–i.e., not extinct.

Fallback foods: Foods that may not be preferred by an animal (e.g., foods that are not nutritionally dense) but that are essential for survival in times of stress or scarcity.

Fauna: The animals of a particular region, habitat, or geological period.

Faunal assemblages: Collections of fossils of other animals found at a site.

Faunal turnover: The rate at which species go extinct and are replaced with new species.

Flake: The piece knocked off of a stone core during the manufacture of a tool, which may be used as a stone tool.

Flora: The plants of a particular region, habitat, or geological period.

Folivorous: Foliage-eating.

Foramen magnum: The large hole (foramen) at the base of the cranium, through which the spinal cord enters the skull.

Fossil: The remains or impression of an organism from the past.

Frugivorous: Fruit-eating.

Generalist: A species that can thrive in a wide variety of habitats and can have a varied diet.

Glacial: Colder, drier periods during an ice age when there is more ice trapped at the poles.

Gracile: Slender, less rugged, or pronounced features.

Hallux: The big toe.

Holotype: A single specimen from which a species or taxon is described or named.

Honing P3: The mandibular premolar alongside the canine (in primates, the P3), which is angled to give space for (and sharpen) the upper canines.

Hominin: A primate category that includes humans and our fossil relatives since our divergence from extant great apes.

Hyper-robust: Even more robust than considered normal in the *Paranthropus* genus.

Hypodigm: A sample (here, fossil) from which researchers extrapolate features of a population.

Incisiform: An adjective referring to a canine that appears more incisor-like in morphology.

Incisors: The teeth in the front of the mouth, used to bite off food.

Interglacial: A period of milder climate in between two glacial periods.

Isotopes: Two or more forms of the same element that contain equal numbers of protons but different numbers of neutrons, giving them the same chemical properties but different atomic masses.

Knappers: The people who fractured rocks in order to manufacture tools.

Knapping: The fracturing of rocks for the manufacture of tools.

Large Cutting Tool (LCT): A tool that is shaped to have functional edges.

Last Common Ancestor (LCA): The hypothetical final ancestor (or ancestral population) of two or more taxa before their divergence.

Lithic: Relating to stone (here to stone tools).

Lumbar lordosis: The inward curving of the lower (lumbar) parts of the spine. The lower curve in the human S-shaped spine.

Lumpers: Researchers who prefer to lump variable specimens into a single species or taxon and who feel high levels of variation is biologically real.

Megadont: An organism with extremely large dentition compared with body size.

Molars: The largest, most posterior of the hind dentition.

Monophyletic: A taxon or group of taxa descended from a common ancestor that is not shared with another taxon or group.

Morphology: The study of the form or size and shape of things; in this case, skeletal parts.

Mosaic evolution: The concept that evolutionary change does not occur homogeneously throughout the body in organisms.

Obligate bipedalism: Where the primary form of locomotion for an organism is bipedal.

Occlude: When the teeth from the maxilla come into contact with the teeth in the mandible.

Oldowan: Lower Paleolithic, the earliest stone tool culture.

Orthognathic: The face below the eyes is relatively flat and does not jut out anteriorly.

Paleoanthropologists: Researchers that study human evolution.

Paleoenvironment: An environment from a period in the Earth's geological past.

Parabolic: Like a parabola (parabola-shaped).

Phalanges: Long bones in the hand and fingers.

Phylogeny: The study of the evolutionary relationships between groups of organisms.

Phylogenetics: The study of phylogeny.

Pliocene: A geological epoch between the Miocene and Pleistocene.

Polytypic: In reference to taxonomy, having two or more group variants.

Postcranium: The skeleton below the cranium (head).

Premolars: The smallest of the hind teeth, behind the canines.

Procumbent: In reference to incisors, tilting forward.

Prognathic: In reference to the face, the area below the eyes juts anteriorly.

Quaternary Ice Age: The most recent geological time period, which includes the Pleistocene and Holocene Epochs and which is defined by the cyclicity of increasing and decreasing ice sheets at the poles.

Relative dating: Dating techniques that refer to a temporal sequence (i.e., older or younger than others in the reference) and do not estimate actual or absolute dates.

Robust: Rugged or exaggerated features.

Site: A place in which evidence of past societies/species/activities may be observed through archaeological or paleontological practice.

Solar precessional cycles: cyclical changes in earth's axis rotation that have global climatic effects.

Specialist: A specialist species can thrive only in a narrow range of environmental conditions or has a limited diet.

Splitters: Researchers who prefer to split a highly variable taxon into multiple groups or species.

Taxa: Plural of taxon, a taxonomic group such as species, genus, or family.

Taxonomy: The science of grouping and classifying organisms.

Techno-complex: A term encompassing multiple assemblages that share similar traits in terms of artifact production and morphology.

Thermoregulation: Maintaining body temperature through physiologically cooling or warming the body.

Ungulates: Hoofed mammals—e.g., cows and kudu.

Volcanic tufts: Rock made from ash from volcanic eruptions in the past.

Valgus knee: The angle of the knee between the femur and tibia, which allows for weight distribution to be angled closer to the point above the center of gravity (i.e., between the feet) in bipeds.

About the Authors

Kerryn Warren, Ph.D.

University of Cape Town, kerryn.warren@gmail.com

Kerryn Warren

Kerryn Warren is a postdoctoral researcher at the University of Cape Town. She lectures on archaeology and human evolution. Her research interests include identifying hybridization in the hominin fossil record, stemming from research from her Ph.D., and understanding the evolution of education in South African schools. She is also currently one of the new "Underground Astronauts" selected to excavate Homo naledi remains from the Rising Star Cave System in the Cradle of Humankind. She is passionate about education and science communication.

Lindsay Hunter, Ph.D.

University of Witwatersrand

Lindsay Hunter

Lindsay Hunter is a trained paleoanthropologist who uses her more than 15 years of experience to make sense of the distant past of our species in ways that can help us to build a better future. She received her master's degree in biological anthropology from the University of Iowa and is completing her Ph.D. in archaeology at the University of the Witwatersrand. She has studied fossil and human bone collections across five continents with major grant support from the National Science Foundation (United States) and the Wenner-Gren Foundation for Anthropological Research. More recently she developed and led the National Geographic "Umsuka" Public Palaeoanthropology Project in South Africa with support from the National Geographic Society and private donors. She now works as the Community Relations and Development Director for the Center for Academic Research and Training in Anthropogeny (CARTA) at UCSD.

Navashni Naidoo, M.Sc.

University of Cape Town

Navashni Naidoo

Navashni Naidoo is a researcher at Nelson Mandela University, lecturing on physical geology. Her research interests include developing paleoenvironmental proxies suited to the African continent, behavioral ecology, and engaging with community-driven archaeological projects. She has excavated at Stone Age sites across South Africa and East Africa.

Silindokuhle Mavuso, M.Sc.

University of Witwatersrand

Silindokuhle Mavuso

Silindokuhle has always been curious about the world around him and how it has been shaped. He is a Ph.D. Candidate at the University of Witwatersrand (Wits) conducting palaeoenvironmental reconstruction and change of the northeastern Turkana Basin's Pleistocene sequence. Silindokuhle begun his education with a B.Sc. (geology, archaeology, and environmental and geographical sciences) from the University of Cape Town before moving to Wits for a B.Sc. Honors (geology and palaeontology) and M.Sc. in geology. During this time, he has gained more training as a Koobi Fora Fieldschool fellow (Kenya) as well as an Erasmus Mundus scholar (France). Silindokuhle is a Plio-Pleistocene geologist with a specific focus on identifying and explaining past environments that are associated with early human life and development through time. He is interested in a wide range of disciplines such as micromorphology, sedimentology, geochemistry, geochronology, and stratigraphy. He has worked with teams from significant eastern and southern African hominid sites including Elandsfontein, Rising Star, Sterkfontein, Gondolin, Laetoli, Olduvai, and Koobi Fora. He plans to extend his knowledge from both parts of the continent to assist the better understanding of how we as humans came to being.

Kimberleigh Tommy, M.Sc.

University of Witwatersrand

Kimberleigh Tommy

Kimberleigh Tommy is currently a Ph.D. candidate in biological anthropology at the Human Variation and Identification Research Unit of the School of Anatomical Sciences at the University of Witwatersrand. Her current research focuses on the evolution and biomechanical implications of bipedal walking through analyses of trabecular bone structure in the joints of the lower limb. Kimberleigh was awarded her Master of Science (M.Sc.) degree with distinction (and no corrections) from the University of the Witwatersrand, specializing in palaeoanthropology and functional morphology in 2018. Her research interests include trabecular structure, functional morphology, primate locomotion, ontogenetic development of gait, biomechanics, and joint pathologies.

Rosa Moll, M.Sc.

University of Witwatersrand

Rosa Moll

Rosa Moll is an archaeology Ph.D. candidate at the University of Witwatersrand. She focuses on Earlier Stone Age core reduction strategies of east Africa and south Africa and received her M.Sc. with distinction in the same field. She is interested in how stool tool technological behaviors correspond with cognitive human evolution. In 2018 she was awarded the Baldwin Fellowship from the Leakey Foundation as part of her Ph.D.

Nomawethu Hlazo, M.Sc.

University of Cape Town

Nomawethu Hlazo

Nomawethu Hlazo is a student at the University of Cape Town currently undergoing her Doctoral Degree. She completed her undergraduate degree in biochemistry and archaeology. Since then her postgraduate studies have focused on the genus *Paranthropus* and the variation that exists between and within species. Following the fossil species, she has concentrated on the study of geometric morphometrics and will follow new techniques such as paleoproteomics to investigate not only shape change but contributions of evolutionary processes and ecological niches occupied by the genus *Paranthropus*. Since the start of her research with *Paranthropus*, she has worked at several sites, not only in the Cradle of Humankind World Heritage Site in South Africa but also in Kenya. Her research has shown that this genus is highly diverse and more variable than we expected. After completion of her master's (with distinction), she has been able to show the contributions of both natural selection and genetic drift and their roles in shaping *Paranthropus* craniomandibular variation.

For Further Exploration

The Smithsonian website hosts descriptions of fossil species, an interactive timeline and much more! It is a highly recommended website. http://humanorigins.si.edu/evidence

The Maropeng Museum website hosts a wealth of information regarding South African Fossil Bearing sites in the Cradle of Humankind. https://www.maropeng.co.za/content/page/human-evolution

This quick comparison between *Homo naledi* and *Australopithecus sediba* from the Perot Museum: https://perot-museum.imgix.net/2019-08-naledi-sediba-quick-comparison.pdf

This explanation of the braided stream by the Perot Museum: https://www.dropbox.com/s/l1d2hv42psj21y9/Braided%20Stream-1920.mp4?dl=0

A collation of 3-D files for visualizing (or even 3-D printing) for homes, schools, and universities: https://www.hetmp.com/

PBS learning materials, including videos and diagrams of the Laetoli footprints, bipedalism, and fossils: https://www.pbslearningmedia.org/resource/tdc02.sci.life.evo.lp_humanevo/human-evolution/

A wealth of information from the Australian Museum website, including species descriptions, family trees, and explanations of bipedalism and diet: https://australianmuseum.net.au/learn/science/human-evolution/

References

Alemseged, Z., F. Spoor, W. H. Kimbel, R. Bobe, D. Geraads, D. Reed, and J. G. Wynn. 2006. "A Juvenile Early Hominin Skeleton from Dikika, Ethiopia." Nature 443 (7109): 296–301.

Asfaw, B., T. White, O. Lovejoy, B. Latimer, S. Simpson, and G. Suwa. 1999. "*Australopithecus garhi*: A New Species of Early Hominid from Ethiopia." Science 284 (5414): 629–635.

Behrensmeyer, A. K., N. E. Todd, R. Potts, and G. E. McBrinn. 1997. "Late Pliocene Faunal Turnover in the Turkana Basin, Kenya, and Ethiopia." Science 278 (5343): 637–640.

Berger, L. R., D. J. De Ruiter, S. E. Churchill, P. Schmid, K. J. Carlson, P. H. Dirks, and J. M. Kibii. 2010. "*Australopithecus sediba*: A New Species of *Homo*-like Australopith from South Africa." Science 328 (5975): 195–204.

Bobe, R. and A. K. Behrensmeyer. 2004. "The Expansion of Grassland Ecosystems in Africa in Relation to Mammalian Evolution and the Origin of the Genus *Homo*." Palaeogeography, Palaeoclimatology, Palaeoecology 207 (3–4): 399–420.

Brain, C. K. 1967. "The Transvaal Museum's Fossil Project at Swartkrans." South African Journal of Science 63 (9): 378–384.

Broom, R. 1938a. "More Discoveries of Australopithecus." Nature 141 (1): 828–829.

———. 1938b. "The Pleistocene Anthropoid Apes of South Africa." Nature 142 (3591): 377–379.

———. 1947. "Discovery of a New Skull of the South African Ape-Man, Plesianthropus." Nature 159 (4046): 672.

———. 1950. "The Genera and Species of the South African Fossil Ape-Man." American Journal of Physical Anthropology 8 (1): 1–14.

Brunet, M., A. Beauvilain, Y. Coppens, E. Heintz, A. H. Moutaye, and D. Pilbeam. 1995. "The First Australopithecine 2,500 Kilometers West of the Rift Valley (Chad)." Nature 378 (6554): 275-273.

Cerling, T. E., J. G. Wynn, S. A. Andanje, M. I. Bird, D. K. Korir, N. E. Levin, W. Mace, A. N. Macharia, J. Quade, and C. H. Remien. 2011. "Woody Cover and Hominin Environments in the Past 6 Million Years." Nature 476: 51e56.

Clarke, R. J. 1998. "First Ever Discovery of a Well-Preserved Skull and Associated Skeleton of *Australopithecus*." South African Journal of Science 94 (10): 460-463.

Clarke, R.J. 2013. "Australopithecus from Sterkfontein Caves, South Africa." In The Paleobiology of Australopithecus, edited by K.E. Reed, J.G. Fleagle, and R.E. Leakey, 105-123. Netherlands: Springer.

Clarke, R. J. and K. Kuman. 2019. "The Skull of StW 573, a 3.67 Ma Australopithecus Prometheus Skeleton from Sterkfontein Caves, South Africa." Journal of Human Evolution 134: 102634.

Clarke, R. J. and P. V. Tobias. 1995. Sterkfontein Member 2 Foot Bones of the Oldest South African Hominid. Science 269 (5223): 521-524.

Constantino, P. J. and B. A. Wood. 2004. Paranthropus Paleobiology. In Miscelanea en Homenae a Emiliano Aguirre, volumen III: Paleoantropologia, edited by E.G. Pérez and S.R. Jara, 136-151. Alcalá de Henares: Museo Arqueologico Regional.

---. 2007. "The Evolution of Zinjanthropus boisei." Evolutionary Anthropology: Issues, News, and Reviews 16 (2): 49-62.

Dart, R. A. 1925. "Australopithecus africanus, the Man-Ape of South Africa." Nature 115: 195-199.

Darwin, Charles. 1871. The Descent of Man: And Selection in Relation to Sex. London: J. Murray.

DeHeinzelin, J., J. D. Clark, T. White, W. Hart, P. Renne, G. WoldeGabriel, Y. Beyene, and E. Vrba. 1999. "Environment and Behavior of 2.5-million-year-old Bouri Hominids." Science 284 (5414): 625-629.

DeMenocal, P. B. D. 2004. "African Climate Change and Faunal Evolution during the Pliocene–Pleistocene." Earth and Planetary Science Letters 220 (1-2): 3-24.

DeMenocal, P. B. D. and J. Bloemendal, J. 1995. "Plio-Pleistocene Climatic Variability in Subtropical Africa and the Paleoenvironment of Hominid Evolution: A Combined Data-Model Approach." In Paleoclimate and Evolution, with Emphasis on Human Origins, edited by E.S. Vrba, G.H. Denton, T.C. Partridge, and L.H. Burckle, 262-288. New Haven: Yale University Press.

Dirks, P. H., J. M. Kibii, B. F. Kuhn, C. Steininger, S. E. Churchill, J. D. Kramers, and G. C. King. 2010. "Geological Setting and Age of Australopithecus sediba from Southern Africa." Science 328 (5975): 205-208.

Faith, J. T. and A. K. Behrensmeyer. 2013. "Climate Change and Faunal Turnover: Testing the Mechanics of the Turnover-Pulse Hypothesis with South African Fossil Data." Paleobiology 39 (4): 609-627.

Grine, F. E. 1988. "New Craniodental Fossils of *Paranthropus* from the Swartkrans Formation and Their Significance in "Robust" Australopithecine Evolution." In Evolutionary History of the "Robust" Australopithecines, edited by F. E. Grine, 223-243. New York: Aldine de Gruyter.

Haile-Selassie, Y., L. Gibert, S. M. Melillo, T. M. Ryan, M. Alene, A. Deino, G. Scott, and B. Z. Saylor. 2015. "New Species from Ethiopia Further Expands Middle Pliocene Hominin Diversity." Nature 521 (7553): 432-433.

Haile-Selassie, Y., S. M. Melillo, A. Vazzana, S. Benazzi, and T. M. Ryan. 2019. "A 3.8-Million-Year-Old Hominin Cranium from Woranso-Mille, Ethiopia." Nature 573 (7773): 214-219.

Harmand, S., J. E. Lewis, C. S. Feibel, C. J. Lepre, S. Prat, A. Lenoble, X. Boë, et al. 2015. "3.3-million-year-old Stone Tools from Lomekwi3, West Turkana, Kenya." Nature 521(7552): 310–316.

Hay, R. L. 1990. "Olduvai Gorge: A Case History in the Interpretation of Hominid Paleoenvironments." In East Africa: Establishment of a Geologic Framework for Paleoanthropology, edited by L. Laporte, 23–37. Boulder: Geological Society of America.

Hay, R. L. and M. D. Leakey. 1982. "The Fossil Footprints of Laetoli." Scientific American 246 (2): 50–57.

Hlazo, N. 2015. "Paranthropus: Variation in Cranial Morphology." Honours thesis, Archaeology Department, University of Cape Town, Cape Town.

---. 2018. "Variation and the Evolutionary Drivers of Diversity in the Genus *Paranthropus*." Master's thesis, Archaeology Department, University of Cape Town, Cape Town.

Johanson, D. C., T. D. White, and Y. Coppens. 1978. "A New Species of the Genus *Australopithecus* (Primates: Hominidae) from the Pliocene of East Africa." Kirtlandia 28: 1–14.

Kimbel, W. H. 2015. "The Species and Diversity of Australopiths. In Handbook of Paleoanthropology, Second Edition, edited by T. Hardt, 2071–2105. Berlin: Springer.

Kimbel, W. H. and L. K. Delezene. 2009. "'Lucy' Redux: A Review of Research on *Australopithecus afarensis*." American Journal of Physical Anthropology 140 (S49): 2–48.

Kingston, J. D. 2007. "Shifting Adaptive Landscapes: Progress and Challenges in Reconstructing Early Hominid Environments." American Journal of Physical Anthropology 134 (S45): 20–58.

Kingston, J. D. and T. Harrison. 2007. "Isotopic Dietary Reconstructions of Pliocene Herbivores at Laetoli: Implications for Early Hominin Paleoecology." Palaeogeography, Palaeoclimatology, Palaeoecology 243 (3–4): 272–306.

Leakey, L. S. B. 1959. "A New Fossil Skull from Olduvai." Nature 184 (4685): 491–493.

Leakey, M. 1971. Olduvai Gorge, Vol. 3. Cambridge: Cambridge University Press.

Leakey, M. G., C. S. Feibel, I. McDougall, and A. Walker. 1995. "New Four-million-year-old Hominid Species from Kanapoi and Allia Bay, Kenya." Nature 376 (6541): 565–571.

Leakey, M. D. and R. L. Hay. 1979. "Pliocene Footprints in the Laetoli Beds at Laetoli, Northern Tanzania." Nature 278 (5702): 317–323.

Leakey, M. G., F. Spoor, F. H. Brown, P. N. Gathogo, C. Kiarie, L. N. Leakey, and I. McDougall. 2001. "New Hominin Genus from Eastern Africa Shows Diverse Middle Pliocene Lineages." Nature 410 (6827): 433–440.

Lebatard, A. E., D. L. Bourlès, P. Duringer, M. Jolivet, R. Braucher, J. Carcaillet, and A. Likius. 2008. "Cosmogenic Nuclide Dating of *Sahelanthropus tchadensis* and *Australopithecus bahrelghazali*: Mio-Pliocene Hominids from Chad." Proceedings of the National Academy of Sciences 105 (9): 3226–3231.

Lee-Thorp, J. 2011. "The Demise of 'Nutcracker Man.'" Proceedings of the National Academy of Sciences 108 (23): 9319–9320.

Lombard, M., L. Wadley, J. Deacon, S. Wurs, I. Parsons, M. Mohapi, J. Swart, and P. Mitchell. 2012. "South African and Lesotho Stone Age Sequence Updated." The South African Archaeological Bulletin 67 (195): 123–144.

Maslin, M. A., C. M. Brierley, A. M. Milner, S. Shultz, M. H. Trauth, and K. E. Wilson. 2014. "East African Climate Pulses and Early Human Evolution." Quaternary Science Reviews 101: 1-17.

McHenry, H. M. 2009. "Human Evolution." In Evolution: The First Four Billion Years, edited by M. Ruse and J. Travis, 256-280. Cambridge: The Belknap Press of Harvard University Press..

Patterson, B. and W. W. Howells. 1967. "Hominid Humeral Fragment from Early Pleistocene of Northwestern Kenya." Science 156 (3771): 64-66.

Pickering, R. and J. D. Kramers. 2010. "Re-appraisal of the Stratigraphy and Determination of New U-Pb Dates for the Sterkfontein Hominin Site." Journal of Human Evolution 59 (1): 70-86.

Potts, R. 1998. "Environmental Hypotheses of Hominin Evolution." American Journal of Physical Anthropology 107 (S27): 93-136.

---. 2013. "Hominin Evolution in Settings of Strong Environmental Variability." Quaternary Science Reviews 73: 1-13.

Rak, Y. 1983. The Australopithecine Face. New York: Academic Press.

---. 1988. "On Variation in the Masticatory System of Australopithecus boisei." In Evolutionary History of the "Robust" Australopithecines, edited by M. Ruse and J. Travis, 193-198. New York: Aldine de Gruyter.

Rayner, R. J., B. P. Moon, and J. C. Masters. 1993. "The Makapansgat Australopithecine Environments." Journal of Human Evolution 24(3): 219-231.

Semaw, S. 2000. "The World's Oldest Stone Artefacts from Gona, Ethiopia: Their Implications for Understanding Stone Technology and Patterns of Human Evolution Between 2.6 Million Years Ago and 1.5 Million Years Ago." Journal of Archaeological Science 27: 1197-1214.

Shipman, Pat. 2002. The Man Who Found the Missing Link: Eugene Dubois and his Lifelong Quest to Prove Darwin Right. New York: Simon & Schuster.

Spoor, F. 2015. "Palaeoanthropology: The Middle Pliocene Gets Crowded." Nature 521 (7553): 432- 433.

Strait, D. S., F. E. Grine, and M. A. Moniz. 1997. A Reappraisal of Early Hominid Phylogeny." Journal of Human Evolution 32 (1): 17-82.

Suwa, G., B. Asfaw, R. T. Kono, D. Kubo, C. O. Lovejoy, and T. D. White. 2009. "The Ardipithecus ramidus Skull and Its Implications for Hominid Origins." Science 326 (5949): 68-68e7.

Thackeray, J. F., Braga, J. Treil, N. Niksch, and J. H. Labuschagne. 2002. "'Mrs. Ples' (Sts 5) from Sterkfontein: An Adolescent Male?" South African Journal of Science 98 (1-2): 21-22.

Thackeray, J. F. 2000. "'Mrs. Ples' from Sterkfontein: Small Male or Large Female?" The South African Archaeological Bulletin, 55: 155-158.

Toth, N. 1985. "The Oldowan Reassessed." Journal of Archaeological Science 12(2): 101-120.

Vrba, E. S. 1988. "Late Pliocene Climatic Events and Hominid Evolution." In The Evolutionary History of the Robust Australopithecines, edited by F. E. Grine, 405-426. New York: Aldine.

---. 1998. "Multiphasic Growth Models and the Evolution of Prolonged Growth Exemplified by Human Brain Evolution." Journal of Theoretical Biology 190(3): 227-239.

---. 2000. "Major Features of Neogene Mammalian Evolution in Africa." In Cenozoic Geology of Southern Africa, edited by T. C. Partridge and R. Maud, 277–304. Oxford: Oxford University Press.

Walker, A. C., R. E. Leakey, J. M. Harris, and F. H. Brown. 1986. "2.5-my *Australopithecus boisei* from West of Lake Turkana, Kenya." Nature 322 (6079): 517–522.

Walker, A. C. and R. E. Leakey. 1988. "The Evolution of *Australopithecus boisei*." In Evolutionary History of the "Robust" Australopithecines, edited by F. E. Grine, 247–258. New York: Aldine de Gruyter.

Ward, C., M. Leakey, and A. Walker. 1999. "The New Hominid Species *Australopithecus anamensis*." Evolutionary Anthropology 7(6): 197–205.

White, T. D. 1988. "The Comparative Biology of 'Robust' Australopithecus: Clues from Content." In Evolutionary History of the "Robust" Australopithecines, edited by F. E. Grine, 449–483. New York: Aldine de Gruyter.

White, T. D., G. Suwa, and B. Asfaw. 1994. "*Australopithecus ramidus*, a New Species of Early Hominid from Aramis, Ethiopia." Nature 371(6495): 306–312.

Wood, B. A. 2010. "Reconstructing Human Evolution: Achievements, Challenges, and Opportunities." Proceedings of the National Academy of Sciences 10(2): 8902–8909.

Wood, B. A. and E. K. Boyle. 2016. "Hominin Taxic Diversity: Fact or Fantasy?" Yearbook of Physical Anthropology 159 (S61): 37–78.

Wood, B. and K. Schroer. 2017. "Paranthropus: Where Do Things Stand?" In Human Paleontology and Prehistory, edited by A. Marom and E. Hovers, 95–107. New York: Springer, Cham.

Acknowledgments

All of the authors in this section are students and early career researchers in paleoanthropology and related fields in South Africa (or at least have worked in South Africa). We wish to thank everyone who supports young and diverse talent in this field and would love to further acknowledge black, African, and female academics who have helped pave the way for us.

Figure Attributions

Figure 9.1 IMG_1696 Great Rift Valley by Ninara is used under a CC BY 2.0 License.

Figure 9.2 Clades original to Explorations: An Open Invitation to Biological Anthropology by Katie Nelson is under a CC BY-NC 4.0 License.

Figure 9.3 CO_2 increase since the Industrial Revolution by NASA, original from Luthi, D., et al.. 2008; Etheridge, D.M., et al. 2010; Vostok ice core data/J.R. Petit et al.; NOAA Mauna Loa CO_2 record is in the public domain and used within NASA guidelines on re-use.

Figure 9.4 African savannah @ Masai Mara (21308330314) by Leo Li from Hong Kong is used under a CC BY 2.0 License.

Figure 9.5 Skeleton of human (1) and gorilla (2), unnaturally sketched by unknown from Brehms Tierleben, Small Edition 1927 is in the public domain.

Figure 9.6 Skeletal comparisons between modern humans and non-obligate bipeds original to Explorations: An Open Invitation to Biological Anthropology is under a CC BY-NC 4.0 License.

Figure 9.7a Sahelanthropus tchadensis: TM 266-01-060-1 anterior view by eFossils is copyrighted and used for noncommercial purposes as outlined by eFossils.

Figure 9.7b Sahelanthropus tchadensis: TM 266-01-060-1 posterior view by eFossils is copyrighted and used for noncommercial purposes as outlined by eFossils.

Figure 9.7c Sahelanthropus tchadensis: TM 266-01-060-1 inferior view by eFossils is copyrighted and used for noncommercial purposes as outlined by eFossils.

Figure 9.7d Sahelanthropus tchadensis: TM 266-01-060-1 lateral left view by eFossils is copyrighted and used for noncommercial purposes as outlined by eFossils.

Figure 9.8a Ardipithecus ramidus Skull by ©BoneClones is used by permission and available here under a CC BY-NC 4.0 License.

Figure 9.8b Artist's rendition of "Ardi" skeleton by ©BoneClones is used by permission and available here under a CC BY-NC 4.0 License.

Figure 9.9 Adult human teeth by Genusfotografen (Tomas Gunnarsson) through Wikimedia Sverige Wikimedia Sverige is used under a CC BY-SA 4.0 License.

Figure 9.10 Paranthropus bonsei compared to Homo sapiens by Constantino, Paul J. is used under a CC BY-SA 4.0 License.

Figure 9.11 Australopithecus anamensis: KNM-KP 29281 occlusal view by eFossils is copyrighted and used for noncommercial purposes as outlined by eFossils.

Figure 9.12a Australopithecus afarensis, "Lucy," adult female. Reconstruction based on AL-288-1 by artist John Gurche, front view close-up. by Smithsonian [exhibit: Reconstructed Faces, What does it mean to be human?] is copyrighted and used for educational and noncommercial purposes as outlined by the Smithsonian.

Figure 9.12b Australopithecus afarensis, adult male. Reconstruction based on AL444-2 by John Gurche by Smithsonian [exhibit: Reconstructed Faces, What does it mean to be human?] is copyrighted and used for educational and noncommercial purposes as outlined by the Smithsonian.

Figure 9.13 Lucy blackbg (AL 288-1, Australopithecus afarensis, cast from Museum national d'histoire naturelle, Paris) by 120 is used under a CC BY-SA 3.0 License.

Figure 9.14a Kenyanthropus platyops KNM WT 40000 anterior view by eFossils is copyrighted and used for noncommercial purposes as outlined by eFossils.

Figure 9.14b Kenyanthropus platyops KNM WT 40000 superior view by eFossils is copyrighted and used for noncommercial purposes as outlined by eFossils.

Figure 9.14c Kenyanthropus platyops KNM WT 40000 lateral left view by eFossils is copyrighted and used for noncommercial purposes as outlined by eFossils.

Figure 9.14d Kenyanthropus platyops KNM WT 40000 inferior view by eFossils is copyrighted and used for noncommercial purposes as outlined by eFossils.

Figure 9.15a *australopithecus africanus*: Taung 1 anterior view by eFossils is copyrighted and used for noncommercial purposes as outlined by eFossils.

Figure 9.15b *australopithecus africanus*: Taung 1 lateral right view by eFossils is copyrighted and used for noncommercial purposes as outlined by eFossils.

Figure 9.16a *Australopithecus africanus* Sts 5 anterior view by eFossils is copyrighted and used for noncommercial purposes as outlined by eFossils.

Figure 9.16b *Australopithecus africanus* Sts 5 posterior view by eFossils is copyrighted and used for noncommercial purposes as outlined by eFossils.

Figure 9.16c *Australopithecus africanus* Sts 5 superior view by eFossils is copyrighted and used for noncommercial purposes as outlined by eFossils.

Figure 9.16d *Australopithecus africanus* Sts 5 lateral right view by eFossils is copyrighted and used for noncommercial purposes as outlined by eFossils.

Figure 9.17 *Australopithecus africanus*. Reconstruction based on STS 5 by John Gurche by Smithsonian [exhibit: Reconstructed Faces, What does it mean to be human?] is copyrighted and used for educational and noncommercial purposes as outlined by the Smithsonian.

Figure 9.18 *Australopithecus sediba*, photo by Brett Eloff, courtesy Profberger and Wits University is used under a CC BY-SA 4.0 License.

Figure 9.19a *Paranthropus aethiopicus*: KNM-WT 17000 anterior view by eFossils is copyrighted and used for noncommercial purposes as outlined by eFossils.

Figure 9.19b *Paranthropus aethiopicus*: KNM-WT 17000 lateral right view by eFossils is copyrighted and used for noncommercial purposes as outlined by eFossils.

Figure 9.19c *Paranthropus aethiopicus*: KNM-WT 17000 superior view by eFossils is copyrighted and used for noncommercial purposes as outlined by eFossils.

Figure 9.19d *Paranthropus aethiopicus*: KNM-WT 17000 posterior view by eFossils is copyrighted and used for noncommercial purposes as outlined by eFossils.

Figure 9.19e *Paranthropus aethiopicus*: KNM-WT 17000 inferior view by eFossils is copyrighted and used for noncommercial purposes as outlined by eFossils.

Figure 9.20 *Paranthropus boisei*, male. Reconstruction based on OH 5 and KNM-ER 406 by John Gurche by Smithsonian [exhibit: Reconstructed Faces, What does it mean to be human?] is copyrighted and used for educational and noncommercial purposes as outlined by the Smithsonian.

Figure 9.21a *Paranthropus boisei*: OH 5 anterior view by eFossils is copyrighted and used for noncommercial purposes as outlined by eFossils.

Figure 9.21b *Paranthropus boisei*: OH 5 inferior view by eFossils is copyrighted and used for noncommercial purposes as outlined by eFossils.

Figure 9.21c *Paranthropus boisei*: OH 5 posterior view by eFossils is copyrighted and used for noncommercial purposes as outlined by eFossils.

Figure 9.22a *Paranthropus robustus*: SK 48 anterior view by eFossils is copyrighted and used for noncommercial purposes as outlined by eFossils.

Figure 9.22b *Paranthropus robustus*: SK 48 superior view by eFossils is copyrighted and used for noncommercial purposes as outlined by eFossils.

Figure 9.22c *Paranthropus robustus*: SK 48 inferior view by eFossils is copyrighted and used for noncommercial purposes as outlined by eFossils.

Figure 9.22d *Paranthropus robustus*: SK 48 lateral left view by eFossils is copyrighted and used for noncommercial purposes as outlined by eFossils.

Figure 9.23 Olduwan Industry Chopper 2 by Emmyanne29 is used under a CC0 1.0 License.

Chapter 10: Early Members of the Genus *Homo*

Bonnie Yoshida-Levine Ph.D., Grossmont College

Learning Objectives

- Describe how early Pleistocene climate change influenced the evolution of the genus *Homo*.
- Identify the characteristics that define the genus *Homo*.
- Describe the skeletal anatomy of *Homo habilis* and *Homo erectus* based on the fossil evidence.
- Assess opposing points of view about how early *Homo* should be classified.
- Describe what is known about the adaptive strategies of early members of the *Homo* genus, including tool technologies, diet, migration patterns, and other behavioral trends.

The boy was no older than 9 when he perished by the swampy shores of the lake. After death, his slender, long-limbed body sank into the mud of the lake shallows. His bones fossilized and lay undisturbed for 1.5 million years. In the 1980s, fossil hunter Kimoya Kimeu, working on the western shore of Lake Turkana, Kenya, glimpsed a dark colored piece of bone eroding in a hillside. This small skull fragment led to the discovery of what is arguably the world's most complete early hominin fossil—a youth identified as a member of the species *Homo erectus*. Now known as Nariokotome Boy, after the nearby lake village, the skeleton has provided a wealth of information about the early evolution of our own genus, *Homo* (see Figure 10.1). Today, a stone monument with an inscription in three languages—English, Swahili, and the local Turkana language—marks the site of this momentous fossil discovery.

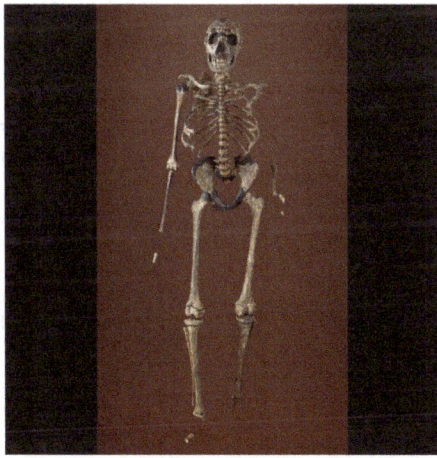 

Figure 10.1 Skeleton of a young male Homo erectus known as "Nariokotome Boy," along with an artist's depiction of how he may have looked during his life. This is the most complete hominin fossil from this time period ever found.

The previous chapter described our oldest human ancestors, primarily members of the genus *Australopithecus* who lived between 2 million and 4 million years ago. This chapter introduces the earliest members of the genus *Homo*, focusing on the species *Homo habilis* and *Homo erectus*.

DEFINING THE GENUS *HOMO*

Since our discipline is fundamentally concerned with what makes us human, defining our own genus takes on special significance for anthropologists. The genus is the next level up from species in the classification system originally devised by Carolus Linnaeus. In the 1758 publication *Systema Naturae*, Linnaeus assigned humans the genus name *Homo*, meaning "person." Under this classification scheme, Linnaeus included several ape species, as well as wild children and mythical humans such as cave-dwelling troglodytes. In the present-day classification, the apes and monster people have long been removed, and our species, *Homo sapiens*, remains as its only living representative. But ever since scientists have acknowledged the existence of extinct species of humans, they have debated which of these display sufficient "humanness" to merit classification in our genus.

When grouping species into a common genus, biologists will consider criteria such as physical characteristics (morphology), evidence of recent common ancestry, and adaptive strategy (use of the environment). However, there is disagreement about which of those criteria should be prioritized, as well as how specific fossils should be interpreted in light of the criteria.

There is general agreement that species classified as *Homo* should share characteristics broadly similar to our species. These include the following:

- a relatively large brain size, indicating a high degree of intelligence;
- a smaller and flatter face;
- smaller jaws and teeth; and
- increased reliance on culture, particularly the use of stone tools, to exploit a greater diversity of environments (adaptive zone).

Some researchers would include larger overall body size and limb proportions (longer legs/shorter arms) in this list. There is also an apparent decline in sexual dimorphism (body-size differences between males and females). While these criteria seem relatively clear-cut, evaluating them in the fossil record has proved more difficult, particularly for the earliest members of the genus. There are several reasons for this. First, many fossil specimens dating to this time period are incomplete and poorly preserved, making them difficult to evaluate. Second, early *Homo* fossils appear quite variable in brain size, facial features, and teeth and body size, and there is not yet consensus about how to best make sense of this diversity. Finally, there is growing evidence that the evolution of the genus *Homo* proceeded in a mosaic pattern: in other words, these characteristics did not appear all at once in a single species; rather, they were patchily distributed in different species from different regions and time periods. Consequently, different researchers have come up with conflicting classification schemes depending on which criteria they think are most important.

In this chapter, we will take several pathways toward examining the origin and evolution of the genus *Homo*. First, we will explore the environmental conditions of the Pleistocene epoch in which the genus *Homo* evolved. Next we will examine the fossil evidence for the two principal species traditionally identified as early Homo: *Homo habilis* and *Homo erectus*. Then we will use data from fossils and archaeological sites to reconstruct the behavior of early members of *Homo*, including tool manufacture, subsistence practices, migratory patterns, and social structure. Finally, we will consider these together in an attempt to characterize the key adaptive strategies of early *Homo* and how they put our early ancestors on the trajectory that led to our own species, *Homo sapiens*.

CLIMATE CHANGE AND HUMAN EVOLUTION

A key goal in the study of human origins is to learn about the environmental pressures that may have shaped human evolution. As indicated in Chapter 7, scientists use a variety of techniques to reconstruct ancient environments. These include stable isotopes, core samples from oceans and lakes, windblown dust, analysis of geological formations and volcanoes, and fossils of ancient plant and animal communities. Such studies have provided valuable information about the environmental context of early *Homo*.

The early hominin species covered previously, such as *Ardipithecus ramidus* and *Australopithecus afarensis*, evolved during the late Pliocene epoch. The Pliocene (5.3 million to 2.6 million years ago) was marked by cooler and drier conditions, with ice caps forming permanently at the poles. Still, Earth's climate during the Pliocene was considerably warmer and wetter than at present.

The subsequent **Pleistocene** epoch (2.6 million years to 11,000 years ago) ushered in major environmental change. The Pleistocene is popularly referred to as the Ice Age. Since the term "Ice Age" tends to conjure up images of glaciers and woolly mammoths, one would naturally assume that this was a period of uniformly cold climate around the globe. But this is not actually the case. Instead, climate became much more variable, cycling abruptly between warm/wet (interglacial) and cold/dry (glacial) cycles. The climate pattern was likely influenced by changes in Earth's elliptical orbit around the sun. As is shown in Figure 10.2, each cycle averaged about 41,000 years during the early Pleistocene; the cycles then lengthened to about 100,000 years starting around 1.25 million years ago. Since mountain ranges, wind patterns, ocean currents, and volcanic activity can all influence climate pattern, climate change had extreme effects on the environment in some regions but less effects on others.

For a present-day example with which you might be familiar, consider the El Niño weather pattern. This is where warming of the Pacific Ocean in the equator region influences rainfall, hurricane frequency, and other weather activity in different parts of the world. During El Niño years, some areas get more rainfall than average and some get less. A recent El Niño in 2017 produced catastrophic flooding along the Peruvian coast, and one in 2015 led to drought and severe bushfires in Australia. If El Niños, despite being a predictable and well-known occurrence, can cause so much disruption to our technologically advanced society, imagine how vulnerable our ancestors must have been to climate change. An adaptive strategy that could buffer against this kind of uncertainty would have been extremely valuable.

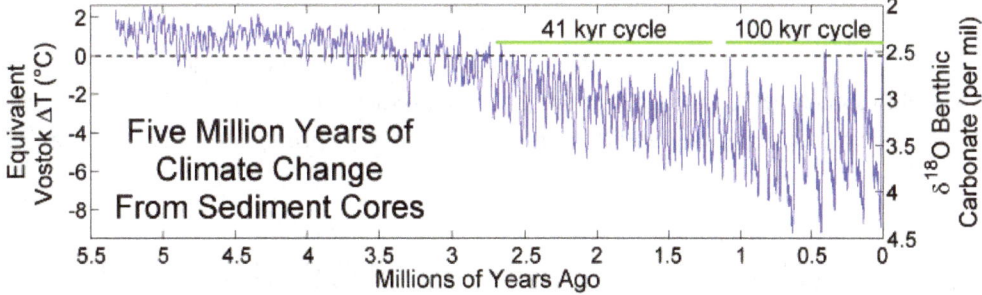

Figure 10.2 Temperature estimates during the last five million years, extrapolated from deep-sea core data. Note both the lower temperatures and the increased temperature oscillations starting at 2.6 million years ago, the start of the Pleistocene epoch. Glacial/interglacial cycles during the early part of the epoch are shorter, each averaging about 41,000 years.

Data on ancient geography and climate help us understand how our ancestors moved and migrated to different parts of the world, and the constraints under which they operated. When periods of global cooling dominated, sea levels were lower as more water was captured as glacial ice. This exposed continental margins and opened pathways between land masses. During glacial periods, the large Indonesian islands of Sumatra, Java, and Borneo were connected to the Southeast Asian mainland, while New Guinea was part of the southern landmass known as greater Australia. There was a land bridge connection between Britain and continental Europe, and an icy, treeless plain known as Beringia connected Northern Asia and Alaska. At the same time, glaciation made some northern areas inaccessible to human habitation. For example, there is evidence that hominin species were in Britain 950,000 years ago, but it does not appear that Britain was continuously occupied during this period. These early humans may have died out or been forced to abandon the region during glacial periods.

In Africa, paleoclimate research has determined that grasslands (shown in Figure 10.3) expanded and shrank multiple times during this period, even as they expanded over the long term (deMenocal 2014). From studies of fossils, paleontologists have been able to reconstruct Pleistocene animal communities and to consider how they were affected by the changing climate. Among the African animal populations, the number of grazing animal species such as antelope increased. Since our early ancestors were also part of this animal community, it is informative to consider how climate change caused changes in the home ranges and migration patterns of animals. Although the African and Eurasian continents are connected by land, the Sahara desert and the mountainous topography of North Africa serve as natural barriers to crossing. But the fossil record shows that animal species moved back and forth between Africa and Eurasia during the Pliocene and Pleistocene epochs. During the early Pleistocene, there is evidence of African mammal species such as baboons, hippos, antelope, and African buffalo migrating out of Africa into Eurasia during periods when drier conditions extended out from Africa into the Middle East (Belmaker 2010).

Figure 10.3 A savanna grassland in East Africa. Habitats such as this were becoming increasingly common during the Pleistocene.

This changing environment was undoubtedly challenging for our ancestors, but it offered new opportunities for hominins to make a living. One solution adopted by some hominins was to specialize in feeding on the new types of plants growing in this landscape. As discussed in the previous chapter, the robust australopithecines probably developed their large molar teeth with thick enamel in order to exploit this particular dietary niche. Chemical analyses of robust australopith teeth show an isotopic signature of a diet where grasses and sedges are prominent, such as papyrus.

Members of the genus *Homo* took a different route. Faced with the unstable African climate and shifting landscape, they evolved bigger brains that enabled them to rely on cultural solutions such as crafting stone tools that opened up new foraging opportunities. This strategy of behavioral flexibility served them well during this unpredictable time and led to new innovations such as increased meat-eating, cooperative hunting, and the exploitation of new environments outside Africa.

HOMO HABILIS: THE EARLIEST MEMBERS OF OUR GENUS

Homo habilis has traditionally been considered the earliest species placed in the genus *Homo*. However, as we will see, there is substantial disagreement among paleoanthropologists about the fossils classified as *Homo habilis*, including whether they come from a single or multiple species, or even whether they should be part of the genus *Homo* at all.

Compared to the australopithecines in the previous chapter, *Homo habilis* has a somewhat larger brain size–an average of 650 cubic centimeters (cc) compared to less than 500 cc for *Australopithecus*. Additionally, the skull is more rounded and the face less prognathic. However, the postcranial remains show a body size and proportions similar to *Australopithecus*.

Known dates for fossils identified as *Homo habilis* range from about 2.5 million years ago to 1.7 million years ago. Recently, a partial lower jaw dated to 2.8 million years from the site of Ledi-Gararu in Ethiopia has been tentatively identified as belonging to the genus *Homo* (Villmoare et al. 2015). If this classification holds up, it would push the origins of our genus back even further.

Discovery and Naming

The first fossils to be named *Homo habilis* were discovered at the site of Olduvai Gorge in Tanzania, East Africa, by members of a team led by Louis and Mary Leakey (Fig. 10.4). The Leakey family had been conducting fieldwork in the area since the 1930s and had discovered other hominin fossils at the site, such as the robust *Australopithecus boisei*. The key specimen, a juvenile individual, was actually found by their 20-year-old son Jonathan Leakey. Louis Leakey invited South African paleoanthropologist Philip Tobias and British anatomist John Napier to reconstruct and analyze the remains. The fossil of the juvenile shown in Figure 10.5 (now known as OH-7) consisted of a lower jaw, parts of the parietal bones of the skull, and some hand and finger bones. Potassium-argon dating of the rock layers showed that the fossil dated to about 1.75 million years. In 1964, the team published their findings in the scientific journal *Nature* (Leakey et al. 1964). As described in the publication, the new fossils had smaller molar teeth that were less "bulgy" than australopithecine teeth. Although the primary specimen was not yet fully grown, an estimate

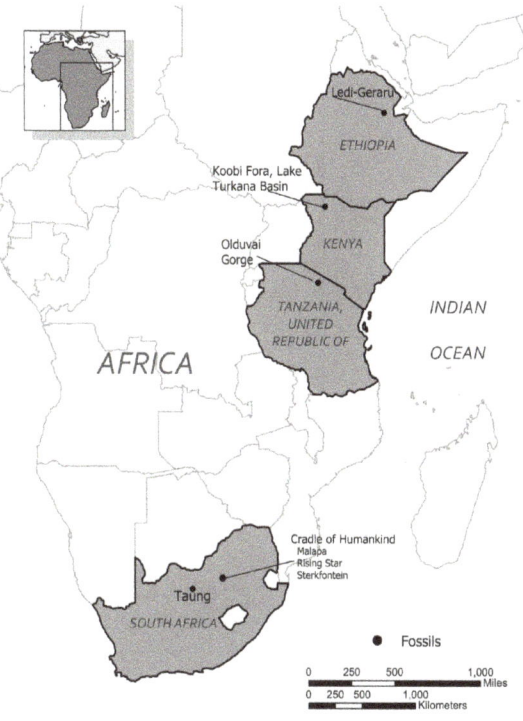

Figure 10.4 Map showing major sites where Homo habilis fossils have been found.

of its anticipated adult brain size would make it somewhat larger-brained than australopithecines such as *A. africanus*. The hand bones were similar to humans' in that they were capable of a precision grip. This increased the likelihood that stone tools found earlier at Olduvai Gorge were made by this group of hominins. Based on these findings, the authors inferred that it was a new species that should be classified in the genus *Homo*. They gave it the name *Homo habilis*, meaning "handy" or "skilled."

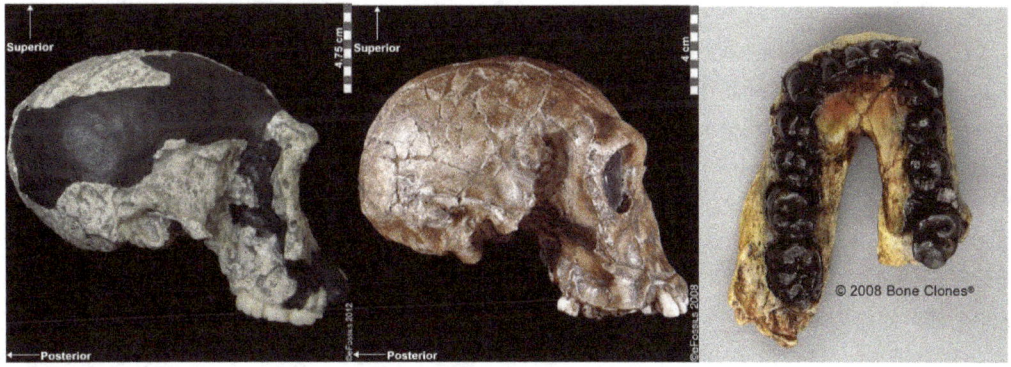

Figure 10.5 Homo habilis fossil specimens. From left to right they are: OH-24 (found at Olduvai Gorge), KNM-ER-1813 (from Koobi Fora, Kenya), and the jaw of OH-7, which was the type specimen found in 1960 at Olduvai Gorge, Tanzania.

Location of Fossils	Dates	Description
Ledi-Gararu, Ethiopia	2.8 mya	Partial lower jaw with evidence of both *Australopithecus* and *Homo* traits; tentatively considered oldest Early *Homo* fossil evidence.
Olduvai Gorge, Tanzania	1.7 mya to 1.8 mya	Several different specimens classified as Homo habilis, including the type specimen found by Leakey, a relatively complete foot, and a skull with a cranial capacity of about 600 cc.
Koobi Fora, Lake Turkana Basin, Kenya	1.9 mya	Several fossils from the Lake Turkana basin show considerable size differences, leading some anthropologists to classify the larger specimen (KNM-ER-1470) as a separate species, *Homo rudolfensis*.
Sterkfontein and other possible South African cave sites	about 1.7 mya	South African caves have yielded fragmentary remains identified as *Homo habilis*, but secure dates and specifics about the fossils are lacking.

Figure 10.6 Key Homo habilis fossil locations and the corresponding fossils and dates.

Controversies over Classification of *Homo habilis*

How Many Species of Homo habilis?

Since this initial discovery, more fossils classified as Homo habilis were discovered in sites in East and South Africa in the 1970s and 1980s (Figure 10.6).. As more fossils joined the ranks of *Homo habilis*, several trends became apparent. First, the fossils were quite variable. While some resembled the fossil specimen first published by Leakey and colleagues, others had larger cranial capacity and tooth size. A well-preserved fossil skull from East Lake Turkana labeled KNM-ER-1470 displayed a larger cranial size along with a strikingly wide face reminiscent of a robust australopithecine. The diversity of the *Homo habilis* fossils prompted some scientists to question whether they displayed too much variation to all remain as part of the same species. They proposed splitting the fossils into at least two groups. The first group resembling the original small-brained specimen would retain the species name *Homo habilis*; the second group consisting of the larger-brained fossils such as KNM-ER-1470 would be assigned the new name of *Homo rudolfensis* (see Figure 10.7). Researchers who favored keeping all fossils in *Homo habilis* argued that sexual dimorphism, adaptation to local environments, or **developmental plasticity** could be the cause of the differences. For example, modern human body size and body proportions are influenced by variations in climates and nutritional circumstances.

Given the incomplete and fragmentary fossil record from this time period, it is not surprising that classification has proved contentious. As a scholarly consensus has not yet emerged on the classification status of early *Homo*, this text will make use of the single (inclusive) *Homo habilis* species designation.

Homo habilis: Homo *or* Australopithecus?

There is also disagreement on whether *Homo habilis* legitimately belongs in the genus *Homo*. Most of the fossils first classified as *Homo habilis* consisted mainly of skulls and teeth. When arm, leg, and foot bones were later found, making it possible to estimate body size, they turned out to be quite small in stature with long arms and short legs. Analysis of the relative strength of limb bones suggested that the species, though bipedal, was much more adapted to arboreal climbing than *Homo erectus* and *Homo sapiens* (Ruff 2009). This has prompted some scientists to question whether *Homo habilis* behaved more like an australopithecine—with a shorter gait and the ability to move around in the trees (Wood and Collard 1999). They also questioned whether the brain size of *Homo habilis* was really that much larger than that of *Australopithecus*. They have proposed reclassifying some or all of the *Homo habilis* fossils into the genus *Australopithecus*, or even placing them into a newly created genus (Wood 2014).

Figure 10.7 Cast of the Homo habilis cranium KNM-ER-1470. This cranium has a wide, flat face, larger brain size, and larger teeth than other Homo habilis fossils, leading some scientists to give it a separate species name, Homo rudolfensis.

Other scholars have interpreted the fossil evidence differently. A recent reanalysis of *Homo habilis/rudolfensis* fossils concluded that they sort into the genus *Homo* rather than *Australopithecus* (Figure 10.8). In particular, statistical analysis performed indicates that the *Homo habilis* fossils differ significantly in average cranial capacity from the australopithecines. They also note that some australopithecine species such as the recently discovered *Australopithecus sediba* have relatively long legs, so body size may not have been as significant as brain- and tooth-size differences (Anton et al. 2014).

Hominin	Homo habilis
Dates	2.5 million years ago to 1.7 million years ago
Region(s)	East and South Africa
Famous Discoveries	Olduvai Gorge, Tanzania; Koobi Fora, Kenya; Sterkfontein, South Africa
Brain Size	650 cc average (range from 510 cc to 775 cc)
Dentition	Smaller teeth with thinner enamel compared to Australopithecus; parabolic dental arcade shape
Cranial Features	Rounder cranium and less facial prognathism than Australopithecus
Postcranial Features	Small stature; similar body plan to Australopithecus
Culture	Oldowan tools

Figure 10.8 Summary features of Homo habilis.

HOMO HABILIS CULTURE AND LIFEWAYS

Early Stone Tools

The larger brains and smaller teeth of early *Homo* are linked to a different adaptive strategy than that of earlier hominins—one dependent on modifying rocks to make stone tools and exploit new food sources. Based on what we know from nonhuman-primate tool use, it is assumed that all hominins used tools of some sort. For example, australopithecines could have used digging sticks to extract the roots and tubers that were part of some species' diets (though tools made from perishable material would leave no trace). As discussed in the previous chapter, stone tools almost certainly predated *Homo habilis* (possibly by *Australopithecus garhi* or the species responsible for the tools from Kenya dating to 3.7 million years ago). However, stone tools become more frequent at sites dating to about 2 million years ago, the time of *Homo habilis* (Roche, Blumenschine, and Shea 2009). This suggests that these hominins were increasingly reliant on stone tools to make a living.

Stone tools are assigned a good deal of importance in the study of human origins. Studying the form of the tools, the raw materials selected, and how they were made and used can provide insight into the thought processes of early humans and how they modified their environment in order to survive. Paleoanthropologists have traditionally classified collections of stone tools into industries, based on their form and mode of manufacture. There is not an exact correspondence between a tool industry and a hominin species; however, some general associations can be made between tool industries and particular hominins, locations, and time periods. The names for the four primary tool industries in human evolution (from oldest to most recent) are the Oldowan, Acheulean, Mousterian, and Upper Paleolithic.

The oldest stone tool industry is the **Oldowan**, named after the site of Olduvai Gorge where the tools were first discovered. The time period of the Oldowan is generally considered to last from about 2.5 mya to 1.6 mya. The tools of this industry are described as "flake and chopper" tools—the choppers consisting of stone cobbles with a few flakes struck off them (Figure 10.9). To a casual observer, these tools might not look much different from randomly broken rocks. However, they are harder to make than their crude appearance suggests. The rock selected as the core must be struck by the rock serving as a hammerstone at just the right angle so that one or more flat flakes are removed. This requires selecting rocks that will fracture predictably instead of chunking, as well as the ability to plan ahead and envision the steps needed to create the finished product. The process leaves both the core and the flakes with sharp cutting edges that can be used for a variety of purposes.

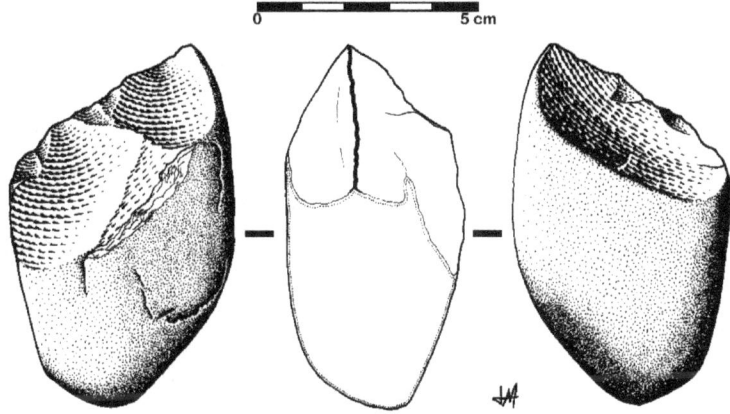

Figure 10.9 Drawing of an Oldowan-style tool. This drawing shows a chopper; the flakes removed from the cores functioned as cutting tools.

Stone Tool Use and the Diet of Early *Homo*

What were the hominins doing with the tools? One key activity seems to have been butchering animals. Animal bones with cutmarks start appearing at sites with Oldowan tools. Studies of animal bones at the site show leg bones are often cracked open, suggesting that they were extracting the marrow from the bone cavities. It is interesting to consider whether the hominins hunted these animals or acquired them through other means. The butchered bones come from a variety of African mammals, ranging from small antelope to animals as big as wildebeest and elephants! It is difficult to envision slow, small-bodied *Homo habilis* with their Oldowan tools bringing down such large animals. One possibility is that the hominins were scavenging carcasses from lions and other large cats. Paleoanthropologist Robert Blumenschine has evaluated the scavenging hypothesis by directly observing the behavior of present-day animal carnivores and scavengers on the African savanna. From this, he inferred that there were scavenging opportunities for Plio-pleistocene hominins. When lions abandon a kill after eating their fill, scavenging animals arrive almost immediately to pick apart the carcass. By the time the slow-footed hominins arrived on the scene, the carcass would be mostly stripped of meat. However, if hominins could use stone tools to break into the leg bone cavities, they could get to the marrow, a fatty, calorie-dense source of protein (Blumenschine 1987).

Reconstructing activities that happened millions of years ago is obviously a difficult undertaking, and there is an active debate among anthropologists about whether scavenging or hunting was more commonly practiced during this time. Regardless of how they were acquiring the meat, all these activities suggest an important dietary shift from the way that the australopithecines were eating. The Oldowan toolmakers were exploiting a new ecological niche that provided them with more protein and calories. And it was not just limited to meat-eating–stone tool use could have made available numerous other subsistence opportunities. A study of microscopic wear patterns on a sample of Oldowan tools indicates that they were used for processing plant materials such as wood, roots or tubers, and grass seeds and stems (Lemorini et al. 2014). In fact, it has been pointed out that the Oldowan toolmakers' cutting ability (whether for the purposes of consuming meat and plants or for making tools, shelters or clothing) represents a new and unique innovation, never seen before in the natural world! (Roche, Blumenschine, and Shea 2009).

Overall, increasing use of stone tools allowed hominins to expand their ecological niche and exert more control over their environment. As we'll see shortly, this pattern continued and became more pronounced with *Homo erectus*.

HOMO ERECTUS: BIOLOGICAL AND CULTURAL INNOVATIONS

After 2 million years ago, a new hominin appeared on the scene. Known as *Homo erectus*, the prevailing scientific view was that this species was much more like us. These hominins were equipped with bigger brains and large bodies with limb proportions similar to our own. Perhaps most importantly, their way of life is now one that is recognizably human, with more advanced tools, hunting, use of fire, and colonizing new environments outside of Africa.

As will be apparent below, new data suggests that the story is not quite as simple. The fossil record for *Homo erectus* is much more abundant than that of *Homo habilis*, but it is also more complex and varied–both with regard to the fossils as well as the geographic context in which they are found. We will first summarize the anatomical characteristics that define *Homo erectus*, and then discuss the fossil evidence from Africa and the primary geographic regions outside Africa where the species has been located.

Homo erectus Anatomy

Compared to *Homo habilis*, *Homo erectus* showed increased brain size, smaller teeth, and a larger body. However, it also displayed key differences from later hominin species including our own.

Although the head of *Homo erectus* was less ape-like in appearance than the australopithecines, neither did it resemble modern humans (Figure 10.10). Compared to *Homo habilis*, *Homo erectus* had a larger brain size (average of about 900 cc compared to 650 cc to 750 cc). Instead of having a rounded shape like our skulls have, the *erectus* skull was long and low like a football, with a receding forehead, and a horizontal ridge called an **occipital torus** that gave the back of the skull a squared-off appearance. The cranial bones are thicker than those of modern humans, and some *Homo erectus* skulls have a slight thickening along the sagittal suture called a **sagittal keel**. Large, shelf-like brow ridges hang over the eyes. The face shows less **prognathism**, and the back teeth are smaller than those of *Homo habilis*. Instead of a pointed chin, like ours, the mandible of *Homo erectus* recedes back.

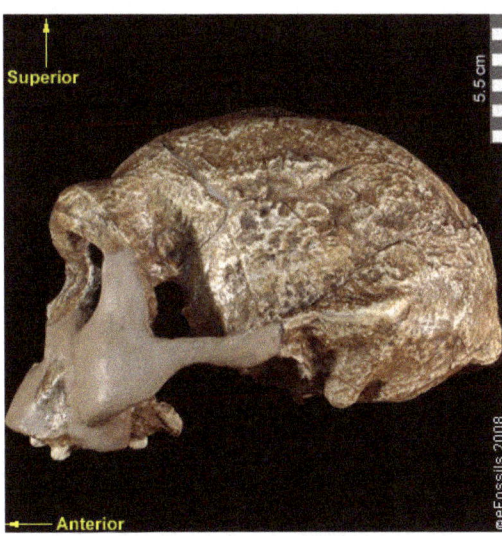

Figure 10.10 Replica of Homo erectus from Java, Indonesia. This cranium (known as Sangiran 17) dates to approximately 1.3 million to 1 million years ago. Note the large brow ridges and the occipital torus that gives the back of the skull a squared-off appearance.

Apart from these distinctive features, significant variation is present between *Homo erectus* fossils from different regions. Scientists have long noted differences between the fossils from Africa and those from Indonesia and China. For example, the Asian fossils tend to have a thicker skull and larger brow ridges than the African specimens, and the sagittal keel described above is more pronounced. *Homo erectus* fossils from the Republic of Georgia (described in the next section) also display distinctive characteristics. As with *Homo habilis*, this diversity has prompted a classification debate about whether or not *Homo erectus* should be split into multiple species. When African *Homo erectus* is characterized as a separate species, it is called *Homo ergaster*, while the Asian variant retains the *erectus* species name because it was discovered first. This text will use the species name *Homo erectus* for both variants.

Homo erectus was thought to have a body size and proportions more similar to modern humans. Unlike *Homo habilis* and the australopithecines, both of whom were small-statured with long arms and short legs, *Homo erectus* shows evidence of being fully committed to life on the ground. This meant long, powerfully muscled legs that enabled these hominins to cover more ground efficiently. Indeed, studies of the *Homo erectus* body form have linked several characteristics of the species to long-distance running in the more open savanna environment (Bramble and Lieberman 2004). Many experts think that hominins around this time had lost much of their body hair, were particularly efficient at sweating, and had darker-pigmented skin—all traits that would support the active lifestyle of such a large-bodied hominin (see Special Topic box).

Much of the information about the body form of *Homo erectus* comes from the Nariokotome fossil of the *Homo erectus* youth, described at the beginning of the chapter (see Figure 10.1). However, *Homo erectus* fossils are turning out to be more varied than previously thought. *Homo erectus* fossils from sites in Africa, as well as from Dmanisi, Georgia, show smaller body sizes than the Nariokotome boy's. Even the Nariokotome skeleton itself has been reassessed to be quite a bit shorter (predicted to be closer to 5 feet 4 inches when fully grown, rather than over 6 feet), although there is still disagreement about which measurement is more accurate. One explanation for the range of body sizes could be adaptation to a range of different local environments, just as humans today show reduced body size in poor nutritional environments (Anton and Snodgrass 2012).

Homo erectus also shows some evidence of a reduction in sexual dimorphism in body size compared to the earlier australopithecines. In other words, *Homo erectus* males were only slightly larger in body size than females. The degree of sexual dimorphism among early hominin species is a contentious issue. It is a difficult characteristic to measure and assess in the fossil record, since fossils have to be complete enough to determine both body size and sex. However, if *Homo erectus* was less sexually dimorphic, it may signify changes in social organization within the species. If you recall from the chapter on primates, highly dimorphic species are those where males compete intensely for mating access to females. Decreased sexual dimorphism suggests that the lifestyle of *Homo erectus* may have been different from that of earlier hominins.

SPECIAL TOPICS: HOW WE BECAME HAIRLESS, SWEATY PRIMATES

As an anthropology instructor, one question about human evolution that students often ask me concerns human body hair—when did our ancestors lose it and why? It is assumed that our earliest ancestors were as hairy as modern-day apes. Today, though, we lack thick hair on most parts of our bodies except in the armpit and pubic regions and on the tops of our heads. Humans actually have about the same number of hair follicles per unit of skin as chimpanzees. But, the hairs on most of our body are so thin as to be practically invisible. When did we develop this peculiar pattern of hairlessness? Which selective pressures in our ancestral environment were responsible for this unusual characteristic?

Many experts believe that the driving force behind our loss of body hair was the need to effectively cool ourselves. Along with the lack of hair, humans are also distinguished by being exceptionally sweaty: we sweat larger quantities and more efficiently than any other primate. Humans have a larger amount of eccrine sweat glands than other primates and these glands generate an enormous volume of watery sweat. Sweating produces liquid on the skin that cools you off as it evaporates. It seems likely that hairlessness and sweating evolved together, as a recent DNA analysis has identified a shared genetic pathway between hair follicles and eccrine sweat gland production (Kamberov et al 2015).

Which particular environmental conditions led to such adaptations? In this chapter, we learned that the climate was a driving force behind many changes seen in the hominin lineage during the Pleistocene. At that time, the climate was increasingly arid and the forest canopy in parts of Africa was being replaced with a more open grassland environment, resulting in increased sun exposure for our ancestors. Compared to the earlier australopithecines, members of the genus Homo were also developing larger bodies and brains, starting to obtain meat by hunting or scavenging carcasses, and crafting sophisticated stone tools.

According to Nina Jablonski, an expert on the evolution of human skin, the loss of body hair and increased sweating capacity are part of the package of traits characterizing the genus Homo. While larger brains and long-legged bodies made it possible for humans to cover long distances while foraging, this new body form had to cool itself effectively to handle a more active lifestyle. Preventing the brain from overheating was especially critical. The ability to keep cool may have also enabled hominins to forage during the hottest part of the day, giving them an advantage over savanna predators, like lions, that typically rest during this time.

When did these changes occur? Although hair and soft tissue do not typically fossilize, there are several indirect methods that have been used to explore this question. One method tracks a human skin color gene. Since chimpanzees have light skin under their hair, it is probable that early hominins also had light skin color. Apes and other mammals with thick fur coats have protection against the sun's rays. As our ancestors lost their fur, it is likely that increased melanin pigmentation was selected for to shield our ancestors from harmful ultraviolet radiation. A recent genetic analysis determined that one of the genes responsible for melanin production originated about 1.2 million years ago (Jablonski 2012).

Another line of evidence tracks the coevolution of a rather unpleasant human companion—the louse. A genetic study identified human body louse as the youngest of the three varieties of lice that infest humans, splitting off as a distinct variety around 70,000 years ago (Kittler, Kayser, and Stoneking 2003). Because human body lice can only spread through clothing, this may have been about the time when humans started to regularly wear clothing. However, the split between human head and pubic lice is estimated to have occurred much earlier, about three million years ago (Reed et al. 2007). When humans lost much of their body hair, lice that used to roam freely around the body were now confined to two areas: the head and pubic region. As a result of this "geographic" separation, the lice population split into two distinct groups.

Other explanations have also been suggested for the loss of human body hair. For example, being hairless has other advantages such as making it more difficult for skin parasites like lice, fleas, and ticks to live on us. Additionally, after bipedality evolved, hairless bodies would also make reproductive organs and female breasts more visible, suggesting that sexual selection may have played a role.

Homo erectus *in Africa*

Although the earliest discoveries of *Homo erectus* fossils were from Asia, the greatest quantity and best-preserved fossils of the species come from East African sites. The earliest fossils in Africa identified as *Homo erectus* come from the East African site of Koobi Fora, around Lake Turkana in Kenya, and are dated to about 1.8 million years ago. Other fossil remains have been found in East African sites in Kenya, Tanzania, and Ethiopia. Other notable African *Homo erectus* finds are a female pelvis from the site of Gona, Ethiopia (Simpson et al 2008), and a cranium from Olduvai Gorge known as Olduvai 9, thought to be about 1.4 million years old with massive brow ridges.

Homo erectus' presence in South Africa is not well documented, though fossils thought to belong to the species have also been uncovered from the famed South African Swartkrans cave site along with stone tools and burned animal bones.

Regional Discoveries Outside Africa

It is generally agreed that *Homo erectus* was the first hominin to migrate out of Africa and colonize Asia and later Europe (although recent discoveries in Asia may challenge this view). Key locations and discoveries of *Homo erectus* fossils, along with the fossils' estimated age are summarized below, and in Figure 10.12.

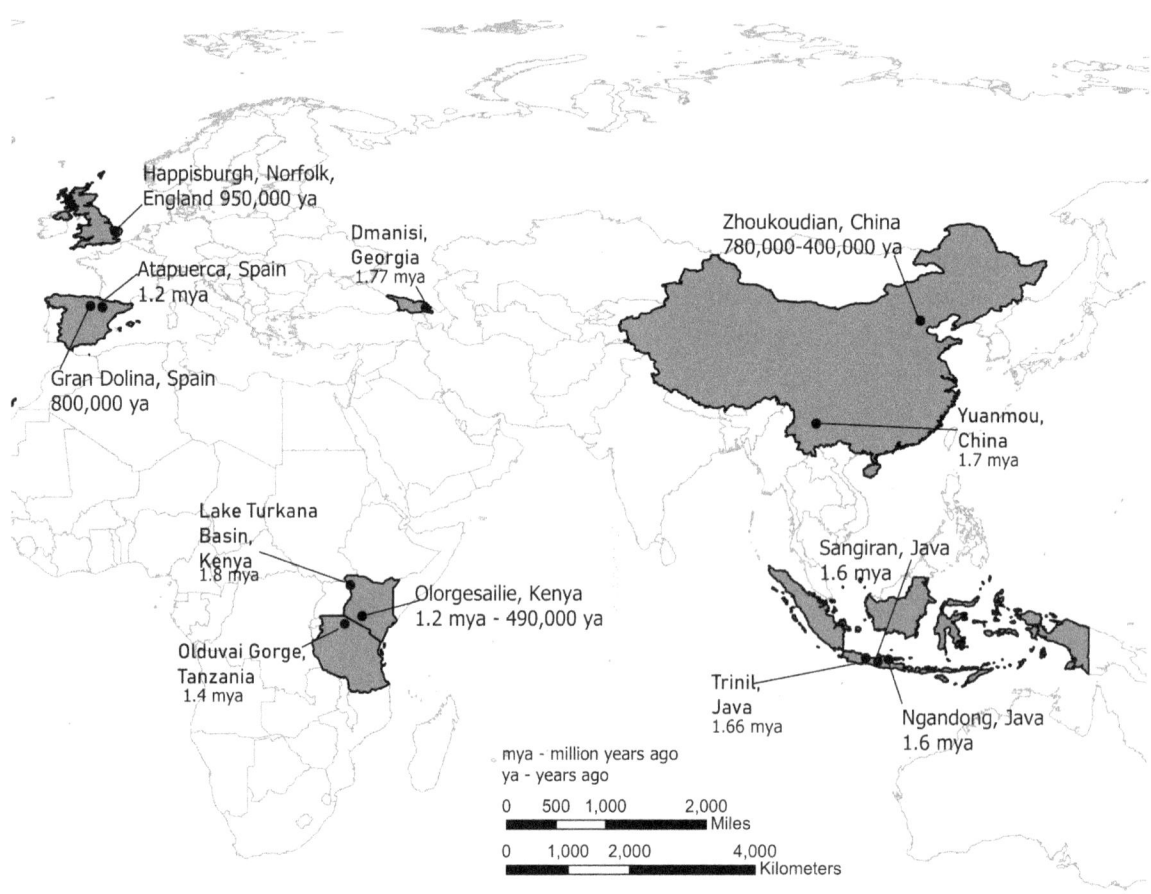

Figure 10.11 Map showing the locations of Homo erectus *fossils around Africa and Eurasia.*

Indonesia

The first discovery of *Homo erectus* was in the late 1800s in Java, Indonesia. A Dutch anatomist named Eugene Dubois searched for human fossils with the belief that since orangutans lived there, it might be a good place to look for remains of early humans. He discovered a portion of a skull, a femur, and some other bone fragments on a riverbank. While the femur looked human, the top of the skull was smaller and thicker than a modern person's. Dubois named the fossil *Pithecanthropus erectus* ("upright ape-man"), popularized in the media at the time as "Java Man." After later discoveries of similar fossils in China and Africa, they were combined into a single species (retaining the *erectus* name) under the genus *Homo*.

Homo erectus has a long history in Indonesia; further discoveries of fossils from Java were dated by argon dating to about 1.6 million to 1.8 million years. A cache of *H. erectus* fossils from the site of Ngandong in Java has yielded very recent dates of 43,000 years, although a more recent study with different dating methods concluded that they were much older—between 140,000 and 500,000 years old. Still, the possible existence of isolated, yet-to-be-discovered hominin populations in the region is of great interest to paleoanthropologists, especially given the discovery of the tiny *Homo floresiensis* fossils discovered on the nearby island of Flores, Indonesia, and the very recent announcement of possible tiny hominin fossils from the island of Luzon in the Philippines.

China

There is evidence of *Homo erectus* in China from several regions and time periods. *Homo erectus* fossils from northern China, collectively known as "Peking Man," are some of the most famous human fossils in the world. Dated to about 400,000–700,000 years ago, they were excavated from the site of Zhoukoudian, near the outskirts of Beijing. Hundreds of bones and teeth, including six nearly complete skulls, were excavated from the cave in the 1920s and 1930s. Much of the fossils' fame comes from the fact that they disappeared under mysterious circumstances. As Japan advanced into China during World War II, Chinese authorities, concerned for the security of the fossils, packed up the boxes and arranged for them to be transported to the United States. But in the chaos of the war, they vanished and were never heard about again. What exactly happened to them is murky—there are several conflicting accounts. Fortunately, an anatomist named Frans Weidenreich who had previously studied the bones had made casts and measurements of the skulls, so this valuable information was not lost. More recent excavations, at Longgushan "Dragon Bone Cave" at Zhoukoudian, of tools, living sites, and food remains, have revealed much about the lifestyle of *Homo erectus* during this time.

Despite this lengthy history of scientific research, China, compared to Africa, was perceived as somewhat peripheral to the study of hominin evolution. Although *Homo erectus* fossils have been found at several sites in China, with dates that make them comparable to those of Indonesian *Homo erectus*, none seemed to approximate the antiquity of African sites. The notable finds at sites like Nariokotome and Olorgesaille took center stage during the 1970s and 80's, as scientists focused on elucidating the species' anatomy and adaptations in its African homeland. In contrast, fewer research projects were focused on East Asian sites (Qiu 2016).

However, isolated claims of very ancient hominin occupation kept cropping up from different locations in Asia. While some were dismissed because of problems with dating methods or stratigraphic context, the 2018 publication of the discovery of stone tools from China dated to 2.1 million years caught everyone's attention. Dated by paleomagnetic techniques that date the associated soils and windblown dust, these tools indicate that hominins in Asia predated those at Dmanisi by at least 300,000 years (Zhu et al. 2018). In fact, the tools are older than any *Homo erectus* fossils anywhere. Since no fossils were found with the tools, it isn't known which species made them, but it opens up the intriguing possibility that hominins earlier than *Homo erectus* could have migrated out of Africa. These exciting new discoveries are shaking up previously held views of the East Asian human fossil record.

Western Eurasia

An extraordinary collection of fossils from the site of Dmanisi in the Republic of Georgia has revealed the presence of *Homo erectus* in Western Eurasia between 1.75 million and 1.86 million years ago. Dmanisi is located in the Caucasus mountains in Georgia. When archaeologists began excavating a medieval settlement near the town in the 1980s and came across the bones of extinct animals, they shifted their focus from the historic to the prehistoric era, but they probably did not anticipate going back quite so far in time! The first hominin fossils were discovered in the early 1990s, and since that time, at least five relatively well-preserved crania have been excavated.

There are several surprising things about the Dmanisi fossils. Compared to African *Homo erectus*, they have smaller brains and bodies. However, despite the small brain size, they show clear signs of *Homo erectus* traits such as heavy brow ridges and reduced facial prognathism. Paleoanthropologists have pointed to some aspects of their anatomy (such as the shoulders) that appear rather primitive, although their body proportions seem fully committed to terrestrial bipedalism. One explanation for these differences could be that the Dmanisi hominins represent a very early form of *Homo erectus* that left Africa before increases in brain and body size evolved in the African population.

Second, although the fossils at this location are from the same geological context, they show a great deal of variation in brain size and in facial features. One skull (Skull 5) has a cranial capacity of only 550 cc, smaller than many *Homo habilis* fossils, along with larger teeth and a protruding face. Scientists disagree on what these differences mean. Some contend that the Dmanisi fossils cannot all belong to a single species because each one is so different. Others assert that the variability of the Dmanisi fossils proves that they, along with all early Homo fossils, including *H. habilis* and *H. rudolfensis*, could *all* be grouped into *Homo erectus* (Lordikipanidze et al. 2013). Regardless of which point of view ends up dominating, the Dmanisi hominins are clearly central to the question of how to define the early members of the genus *Homo*.

Europe

Until recently, there was scant evidence of any *Homo erectus* presence in Europe, and it was assumed that hominins did not colonize Europe until much later than East Asia or Eurasia. One explanation for this was that the harsh ice age climate of Western Europe served as a barrier to living there. However, recent fossil finds from Spain suggest that *Homo erectus* could have made it into Europe over a million years ago. In 2008 a mandible from the Atapuerca region in Spain was discovered, dating to about 1.2 million years ago. A more extensive assemblage of fossils from the site of Gran Dolina in Atapuerca have been dated to about 800,000 years ago. In England in 2013 fossilized hominin footprints of adults and children dated to 950,000 years ago were found at the site of Happisburgh, Norfolk, which would make them the oldest human footprints found outside Africa (Ashton et al. 2014).

At this time, researchers aren't in agreement as to whether the first Europeans belonged to *Homo erectus* proper or to a later descendent species. Some scientists refer to the early fossils from Spain by the species name, *Homo antecessor*.

Region	Sites	Dates	Significance of Fossils
East Africa	East and West Lake Turkana, Kenya; Olduvai Gorge, Tanzania	1.8 to 1.4 mya	Earliest evidence of *H. erectus*; significant variation in skull and facial features.
Western Eurasia	Dmanisi, Republic of Georgia	1.75 mya	Smaller brains and bodies than *H. erectus* from other regions.
Western Europe	Atapuerca, Spain (Sima del Elefante and Gran Dolina caves)	1.2 mya– 400,000 ya	Partial jaw from Atapuerca is oldest evidence of *H. erectus* in Western Europe. Fossils from Gran Dolina (dated to about 800,000 years) sometimes referred to as *H. antecessor*.
Indonesia	Ngandong, Java; Sangiran, Java	1.6 mya	Early dispersal of *H. erectus* to East Asia; Asian *H. erectus* features.
China	Zhoukoudian, China; Loess Plateau (Lantian)	780,000 – 400,000 ya 2.1 mya	Large sample of *H. erectus* fossils and artifacts. Recent evidence of stone tools from Loess Plateau suggests great antiquity of *Homo* in East Asia.

Figure 10.12 Regional comparisons of Homo erectus fossils.

HOMO ERECTUS LIFEWAYS

Now, our examination of *Homo erectus* will turn to its lifeways–how the species utilized its environment in order to survive. This includes making inferences about diet, technology, life history, environments occupied, and perhaps even social organization. As will be apparent, *Homo erectus* shows significant cultural innovations in these areas, some that you will probably recognize as more "human-like" than any of the hominins previously covered.

Tool Technology: Acheulean Tool Industry

In early African sites associated with *Homo erectus*, stone tools such as flakes and choppers identified to the Oldowan Industry dominate. Starting at about 1.5 million years ago, some *Homo erectus* populations began making different forms of tools. These tools–classified together as constituting the **Acheulean** tool industry–are more complex in form and more consistent in their manufacture. Unlike the Oldowan tools, which were cobbles modified by striking off a few flakes, Acheulean toolmakers carefully shaped both sides of the tool. This type of technique, known as bifacial flaking, requires more planning and skill on the part of the toolmaker; he or she would need to be aware of principles of symmetry when crafting the tool. One of the most common tool forms, the handaxe, is shown in Figure 10.13. As with the tool illustrated below, handaxes tend to be thicker at the base and then come to a rounded point at the tip. Besides handaxes, forms such as scrapers, cleavers, and flake tools are present at *Homo erectus* sites.

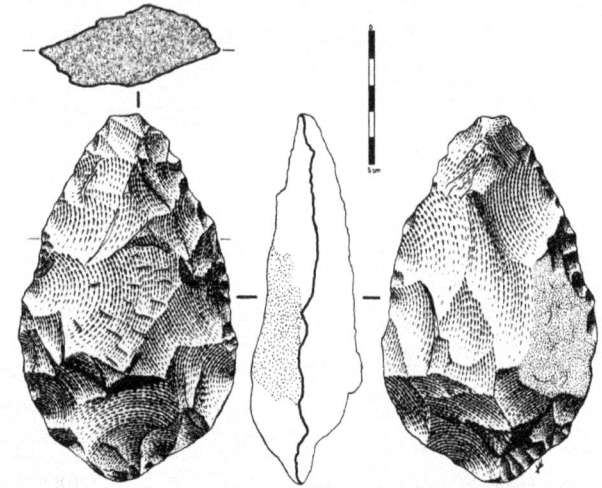

Figure 10.13 Drawing of an Acheulean handaxe. This specimen is from Spain. When drawing a stone tool, artists typically show front and back faces, as well as top and side profiles.

One striking aspect of Acheulean tools is their uniformity. They are more standardized in form and mode of manufacture than the earlier Oldowan tools. For example, the aforementioned handaxes vary in size, but they are remarkably consistent in regard to their shape and proportions. They were also an incredibly stable tool form over time–lasting well over a million years with little change.

Curiously, the Acheulean tools so prominent at African sites are mostly absent in *Homo erectus* sites in East Asia. Instead, Oldowan-type choppers and scrapers are found at those sites. If this technology seemed to be so important to African *Homo erectus*, why didn't East Asian *Homo erectus* also use the tools? One reason could be environmental differences between the two regions. Perhaps the rocks available in Asia weren't of the material suitable for making the Acheulean handaxes. It has been suggested that *Asian Homo erectus* populations used perishable material such as bamboo to make tools. Another possibility is that *Homo erectus* (or even an earlier hominin) migrated to East Asia before the Acheulean technology developed in Africa. The recent discovery of the 2.1 million-year-old tools in China gives credence to this last explanation.

Tool Use and Cognitive Abilities of *Homo erectus*

What (if anything) do the Acheulean tools tell us about the mind of *Homo erectus*? Clearly, they took a fair amount of skill to manufacture. Apart from the actual shaping of the tool, other decisions made by toolmakers can reveal their use of foresight and planning. Did they just pick the most convenient rocks to make their tools, or did they search out a particular raw material that would be ideal for a particular tool? Analysis of Acheulean stone tools suggest that at some sites, the toolmakers selected their raw materials carefully—traveling to particular rock outcrops to quarry stones and perhaps even removing large slabs of rock at the quarries to get at the most desirable material. Such complex activities would require advanced planning. They also likely required cooperation and communication with other individuals, as such actions would be difficult to carry out solo. However, other *Homo erectus* sites lack evidence of such selectivity; instead of traveling even a short distance for better raw material, the hominins tended to use what was available in their immediate area (Shipton et al. 2018).

In contrast to *Homo erectus* tools, the tools of early modern *Homo sapiens* during the Upper Paleolithic display tremendous diversity across regions and time periods. Additionally, Upper Paleolithic tools and artifacts communicate information such as status and group membership. Such innovation and social signaling seem to have been absent in *Homo erectus*, suggesting that they had a different relationship with their tools than did *Homo sapiens* (Coolidge and Wynn 2017). Some scientists assert that these contrasts in tool form and manufacture may signify key cognitive differences between the species, such as the ability to use a complex language.

Subsistence and Diet

In reconstructing the diet of *Homo erectus*, researchers can draw from multiple lines of evidence. These include stone tools used by *Homo erectus*, animal bones and occasionally plant remains from *Homo erectus* sites, and the bones and teeth of the fossils themselves. These data sources suggest that compared to the australopithecines, *Homo erectus* consumed more animal protein. Coinciding with the appearance of *Homo erectus* fossils in Africa are archaeological sites with much more abundant stone tools and larger concentrations of butchered animal bones.

Meat Eating and Increased Brain Size

It makes sense that a larger body and brain would be correlated with a dietary shift to more calorically dense foods. This is because the brain is a very energetically greedy organ. Indeed, our own human brains require more than 20% of one's calorie total intake to maintain. When biologists consider the evolution of intelligence in any animal species, it is often framed as a cost/benefit analysis: In order for large brains to evolve, there has to be a compelling benefit to having them and a way to generate enough energy to fuel them.

One solution that would allow for an increase in human brain size would be a corresponding reduction in the size of the digestive tract (gut). According to the "expensive tissue hypothesis," initially formulated by Leslie Aiello and Peter Wheeler (1995), a smaller gut would allow for a larger brain without the need for a corresponding increase in the organism's metabolic rate. Judging from their skeleton, australopithecines have a wider rib cage and trunk region more similar to apes than humans. It is thought that the australopithecines had large gut sizes similar to today's great apes because they were eating mainly plant foods, which require more gut bacteria to digest. More meat in the diet would allow for a smaller gut and could also fuel the larger brain and body size seen in the genus Homo. Some researchers also believe that body fat percentages increased in hominins (particularly females) around this time, which would have allowed them to be better buffered against environmental disruption such as food shortages (Anton and Snodgrass 2012).

Evidence for Dietary Versatility in Homo erectus

As indicated above, evidence from archaeology and the inferences about Homo erectus body size suggest increased meat eating. How much hunting did Homo erectus engage in compared to the earlier Oldowan toolmakers? Although experts continue to debate the relative importance of hunting versus scavenging, there seems to be stronger evidence of hunting for these hominins. For example, at sites such as Olorgesailie in Kenya (Figure 10.14), there are numerous associations of Acheulean tools with butchered remains of large animals.

However, Homo erectus certainly ate more than just meat. Modern-day hunter-gatherer societies have been used as models for considering the behavior patterns and environmental constraints of our early ancestors. Plant foods make up the bulk of calories for most modern-day hunter-gatherer societies, since they are a much more reliable food source. It would make sense that we would see similar patterns among early hominins.

Studies of the tooth surfaces and microscopic wear patterns on hominin teeth indicate that Homo erectus ate a variety of foods, including some hard, brittle plant foods (Unger and Scott 2009). This would make sense, considering the environment was changing to be more dominated by grasslands in some areas. Roots, bulbs, and tubers (known as underground storage organs) of open savanna plants may have been a primary food source. Indeed, hunter-gatherer groups such as the Hadza of Tanzania rely heavily on such foods, especially during periods when game is scarce. In the unstable environment of the early Pleistocene, dietary versatility would be a definite advantage.

Figure 10.14 Excavations at the site of Olorgesailie, Kenya. Dated from between 1.2 million years ago and 490,000 years ago, Olorgesailie has some of the most abundant and well-preserved evidence of Homo erectus activity in the world. Fossils of large mammals, such as elephants, along with thousands of Acheulean tools, have been uncovered over the decades.

Tool Use, Cooking, and Fire

One key characteristic of the genus Homo is smaller teeth compared to Australopithecus. Why would teeth get smaller? Besides the change in the type of foods eaten, there may have also been changes in how food was prepared and consumed. Think about how you would eat if you didn't have access to cutting tools. What you couldn't rip apart with your hands would have to be bitten off with your teeth—actions that would require bigger, more powerful teeth and jaws.

During this time, stone tools were becoming increasingly important. If hominins were using these tools to cut up, tenderize, and process meat and plants, they wouldn't have to use their teeth so vigorously.

Cooking food could also have contributed to the reduction in tooth and jaw size. In fact, anthropologist Richard Wrangham (2009) asserts that cooking played a crucial role in human evolution. Cooking provides a head start in the digestive process because of how heat begins to break down food before food even enters the body, and it can help the body extract more nutrients out of meat and plant foods such as starchy tubers. According to Wrangham's model, this improved diet had a number of far-reaching consequences for human evolution. Most importantly, it allowed for the larger brain and body size (and smaller gut size) seen in *Homo erectus*.

Obviously cooking requires fire, and the earliest use of fire is a fascinating topic in the study of human evolution. Fire, of course is not limited to humans; it occurs naturally as a result of lightning strikes. Like other wild animals, early hominins must have been terrified of wildfires, but at some point in time learned to control fire and put it to good use. Cooking, warmth, and scaring off wild animals are just some of the benefits of fire. Consider the potential social benefits of having a light source after dark. Rather than just going to sleep, members of the group could repair tools, plan the next day's activities, or socialize—just as you might do sitting around a campfire with family or friends. Isn't it intriguing to think about how such activities might have encouraged the development of language?

Documenting the earliest evidence of fire has been a contentious issue in archaeology because of the difficulty in distinguishing between human-controlled fire and natural burning at hominin sites. Burned areas and ash deposits must have direct associations with human activity to make a case for deliberate fire use. Examples might include the presence of wood ash in caves where trees don't naturally grow, deep ash deposits in hearths lined with stones, or burned pieces of stone tools and butchered animal bones (Gao 2017). Unfortunately, such evidence is rare at ancient hominin sites, which have been profoundly altered by humans, animals, and geological forces over millions of years. Recently, newer methods—including microscopic analysis of burned rock and bone—have revealed clear evidence of fire use at Koobi Fora, Kenya, dating to 1.5 million years ago (Hlubik et al. 2017).

Migration out of Africa

Homo erectus is generally thought to be the first hominin species to leave the continent of Africa and settle in Eurasia in places such as the Republic of Georgia, Indonesia, and northern China. We previously discussed the timing and fossil evidence for the appearance of *Homo erectus* at those sites; now we can address why the species traveled such vast distances to these far-flung regions. To do this, we have to consider what we have learned about the biology, culture, and environmental circumstances of *Homo erectus*. The larger brain and body size of *Homo erectus* were fueled by a diet consisting of more meat, and longer more powerful legs made it possible to walk and run longer distances to acquire food. Since they were eating higher on the food chain, it was necessary for them to extend their home range to find sufficient game. Cultural developments including better stone tools and new technology such as fire gave them greater flexibility in adapting to different environments. Finally, the major Pleistocene climate shift discussed earlier in the chapter certainly played a role. Changes in air temperature, precipitation, access to water sources, and other habitat alteration had far-reaching effects on animal and plant communities; this included *Homo erectus*. If hominins were relying more on hunting, the migration patterns of their prey could have led them increasingly long distances.

Life History

The **life history** of a species refers to its overall pattern of growth, development, and reproduction during its lifetime, with the assumption being that these characteristics have been shaped by natural selection. Our species, *Homo sapiens*, is characterized by a unique life history pattern of slow development, a long period of juvenile dependence, and a long lifespan. Unlike the great apes whose offspring achieve early self-sufficiency, human children are dependent on their parents long after weaning. Additionally, human fathers and grandparents (particularly post-menopausal grandmothers) devote substantial time and energy to caring for their children.

Human behavioral ecologists who study modern hunter-gatherer societies have observed that foraging is no easy business (Figure 10.15). Members of these groups engage in complex foraging techniques that are difficult and take many years to master. An extended juvenile period gives children the time to acquire these skills. It also allows time for large human brains to grow and mature. On the back end, a longer developmental period results in skilled, successful adults, capable of living a long time (Hill and Kaplan 1999). Despite the time and energy demands, females could have offspring at more closely spaced intervals if they could depend on help from fathers and grandmothers (Hawkes et al. 1998).

Figure 10.15 Hadza men practice bowing. Native to Tanzania, the Hadza have retained many traditional foraging practices. Although most do not subsist entirely upon wild foods today, their way of life may shed light on how humans lived for most of their evolutionary history.

What can the study of *Homo erectus* reveal about its life history pattern? Well-preserved fossils such as the Nariokotome boy can provide some insights. We know that apes such as chimpanzees reach maturity more quickly than humans, and there is some evidence that the australopithecines had a growth rate more akin to that of chimpanzees. Scientists have conducted extensive studies of the Nariokotome skeleton's bones and teeth to assess growth and development. On the one hand, examination of the long bone ends (epiphyses) of the skeleton suggested that he was an early adolescent with a relatively large body mass, though growth had not yet been completed. On the other hand, study of the dentition, including measurement of microscopic layers of tooth enamel called **perikymata**, revealed a much younger age of 8 or 9. According to Christopher Dean and Holly Smith (2009), the best explanation for this discrepancy between the dental and skeletal age is that *Homo erectus* had its own distinct growth pattern—reaching maturity more slowly than chimpanzees but faster than *Homo sapiens*. This suggests that the human life history pattern of slow maturation and lengthy dependency was a more recent development. More work remains on refining this pattern for early *Homo*, but it is an important question, as it sheds light on how and when we developed our unique life history characteristics (Figure 10.16).

Hominin	*Homo erectus*
Dates	1.8 million years ago to about 200,000 years ago
Region(s)	East and South Africa; West Eurasia; China and Southeast Asia
Famous Discoveries	Lake Turkana, Olorgesailie, Kenya; Zhoukoudian, China; Dmanisi, Republic of Georgia
Brain Size	Average 900 cc; range between 650 cc and 1,100 cc
Dentition	Smaller teeth than *Homo habilis*
Cranial Features	Long, low skull with robust features including thick cranial vault bones and large brow ridge, sagittal keel, and occipital torus
Postcranial Features	Larger body size compared to *Homo habilis*; body proportions (longer legs and shorter arms) similar to *Homo sapiens*
Culture	Acheulean tools (in Africa); evidence of increased hunting and meat-eating; use of fire; migration out of Africa

Figure 10.16 Summary features of Homo erectus.

THE BIG PICTURE OF EARLY *HOMO*

We are discovering that the evolution of the genus Homo is more complex than what was previously thought. The earlier prevailing view of a simple progression from *Australopithecus* to *Homo habilis* to *Homo erectus* as clearly delineated stages in human evolution just doesn't hold up anymore.

Variability in the Fossil Record of Early *Homo*

As is apparent from the information presented here, there is tremendous variability during this time. While fossils classified as *Homo habilis* show many of the characteristics of the genus *Homo*, such as brain expansion and smaller tooth size, the small body size and long arms are more akin to australopithecines. There is also tremendous variability within the fossils assigned to *Homo habilis*, so there is no consensus on whether it is a single or multiple species of *Homo*, a member of the genus *Australopithecus*, or even a yet-to-be-defined new genus. Similarly, there are considerable differences in skull morphology and body size and form of *Homo erectus*, of which some specimens show more similarity to *Homo habilis* than previously thought.

What does this diversity mean for how we should view early *Homo*? First, there isn't an abrupt break between *Australopithecus* and *Homo habilis* or even between *Homo habilis* and *Homo erectus*. Characteristics we define as *Homo* don't appear as a unified package; they appear in the fossil record at different times. This is known as **mosaic evolution**.

Indeed, fossil finds such as *Australopithecus sediba*, and *Homo naledi* and *Homo floresiensis* discussed in the next chapter, have displayed unexpected combinations of primitive and derived traits.

We can consider several explanations for the diversity we see within early *Homo* from about 2.5 million to 1.5 million years ago. One possibility is the existence of multiple contemporaneous species of early *Homo* during this period. In light of the pattern of environmental instability discussed earlier, it shouldn't be surprising to see fossils from different parts of Africa and Eurasia display tremendous variability. Multiple hominin forms could also evolve in the same region, as they diversified in order to occupy different ecological niches. However, even the presence of multiple species of hominin does not preclude their interacting and interbreeding with one another. As you'll see in the next chapter, sequencing of ancient hominin genomes has led to deeper understanding of genetic relationships between extinct species such as the Neanderthals and Denisovans.

Diversity of brain and body sizes could also reflect developmental plasticity—short-term adaptations within a lifetime (Anton, Potts, and Aiello 2014). These have the advantage of being more flexible than genetic natural selection, which could only occur over many generations. For example, among human populations today, different body sizes are thought to be adaptations to different climate or nutritional environments. Keeping in mind that the climate was intensely variable, wouldn't a more flexible strategy of adaptation be valuable under these conditions?

Trends in the Behavior of Early *Homo*

New discoveries are also questioning old assumptions about the behavior of *Homo habilis* and *Homo erectus*. Just as the fossil evidence doesn't neatly separate *Australopithecus* and *Homo*, evidence of the lifeways of early *Homo* show similar diversity. For example, one of the traditional dividing lines between *Homo* and *Australopithecus* was thought to be stone tools: *Homo* made them; *Australopithecus* didn't. However, the recent discovery of stone tools from Kenya dating to 3.3 million years ago challenges this point of view. Similarly, the belief that *Homo erectus* was the first species to settle outside Africa may now come into question with the report of 2.1 million-year-old stone tools from China. If this find is supported by additional evidence, it may cause a reevaluation of *Homo erectus* being first to leave. Instead, there could have been multiple earlier migrations of hominins such as *Homo habilis* or even *Australopithecus* species.

These various lines of evidence about the genus *Homo* point out the need for a more nuanced view of this period of human evolution. Rather than obvious demarcations between species and their corresponding behavioral advancements, it now looks like many behaviors were shared among species. Earlier hominins that we previously didn't think had the capability could have been doing things like expanding out of Africa or using stone tools. Meanwhile, some other hominins that we had considered more advanced didn't actually have the full suite of "human" characteristics previously expected.

From a student's perspective, all this complexity probably seems frustrating. It would be ideal if the human story were a straightforward, sequential narrative. Unfortunately, it seems that human evolution was not a nice, neat trajectory of increasingly humanlike traits and behaviors; rather, it is emblematic of the untidy but exciting nature of the study of human evolution.

Despite the haziness dominating the early *Homo* narrative, we can identify some overall trends for the million-year period associated with early *Homo*. These trends include brain expansion, a reduction in facial prognathism, smaller jaw and tooth size, larger body size, and evidence of full terrestrial bipedalism. These traits are associated with a key behavioral shift that emphasizes culture as a flexible strategy to adapt to unpredictable environmental circumstances. Included in this repertoire are the creation and use of stone tools to process meat obtained by scavenging and later hunting, a utilization of fire and cooking, and the roots of the human life history pattern of prolonged childhood, cooperation in child raising, and the practice of skilled foraging techniques. In fact, it's apparent that the cultural innovations are driving the biological changes, and vice versa, fueling a feedback loop that will continue during the later stages of human evolution.

> ## Review Questions
>
> - Describe the climate during the early Pleistocene. Explain why climate is important for understanding the evolution of early *Homo*.
> - List the key anatomical characteristics that are generally agreed to define the genus *Homo*.
> - Why has classification of early *Homo* fossils proved difficult? What are some explanations for the variability seen in these fossils?
> - Compare and contrast the Oldowan and Acheulean tool industries.
> - Name some specific behaviors associated with *Homo erectus* in the areas of tool use, subsistence practices, migration patterns, and other cultural innovations.

Key Terms

Acheulean: Tool industry characterized by teardrop-shaped stone handaxes flaked on both sides.

Developmental plasticity: The capability of an organism to modify its phenotype during development in response to environmental cues.

Human behavioral ecology: Study of human behavior from an evolutionary and ecological perspective.

Life history: The broad pattern of a species' life cycle including development, reproduction, and longevity.

Mosaic evolution: Different characteristics evolve at different rates and appear at different stages.

Occipital torus: A ridge on the occipital bone in the back of the skull.

Oldowan: Earliest stone-tool industry consisting of simple flakes and choppers.

Perikymata: Microscopic ridges on the surface of tooth enamel that serve as markers of tooth development.

Pleistocene: Geological epoch dating from 2.6 million years ago to about 11,000 years ago.

Prognathism: Condition where the lower face and jaw protrude forward from a vertical plane.

Sagittal keel: A thickened area along the top of the skull.

About the Author

Bonnie Yoshida-Levine, Ph.D.

Grossmont College, bonnie.yoshida@gcccd.edu

Bonnie Yoshida-Levine is an instructor of anthropology at Grossmont College, where she teaches biological anthropology and archaeology. She received her bachelor's degree in history from the University of California, Los Angeles, and her M.A. and Ph.D. degrees in anthropology from the University of California, Santa Barbara. Her dissertation research focused on the bioarchaeology of early civilizations in north coastal Peru. Bonnie has also collaborated on archaeological field projects in Bolivia and coastal California.

Bonnie Yoshida-Levine

For Further Exploration

Boaz, Noel Thomas, and Russell L. Ciochon. 2004. *Dragon Bone Hill: An Ice-Age Saga of* Homo erectus. New York: Oxford University Press.

Human Evolution by the Smithsonian Institution: http://humanorigins.si.edu/ Produced by the Smithsonian National Museum of Natural History, this website covers many aspects of human evolution including 3-D models of hominin fossils.

Jablonski, Nina G. 2010. "The Naked Truth." *Scientific American* 302 (2): 42–49.

Lewin, Roger, and Robert A. Foley. 2004. *Principles of Human Evolution*. Oxford, UK: Blackwell Publishing.

Stoneking, Mark. 2015. "Of Lice and Men: The Molecular Evolution of Human Lice." Lecture, Center for Academic Research & Training in Anthropogeny, San Diego, California, October 16, 2015. https://carta.anthropogeny.org/events/unique-features-human-skin

Tarlach, Gemma. 2015. "The First Humans to Know Winter." *Discover*, February 26.

Ungar, Peter S. 2017. *Evolution's Bite : A Story of Teeth, Diet, and Human Origins*. Princeton, NJ: Princeton University Press.

Wrangham, Richard. 2009. *Catching Fire: How Cooking Made Us Human*. New York: Basic Books.

References

Aiello, Leslie C., and Peter Wheeler. 1995. "The Expensive-Tissue Hypothesis." *Current Anthropology* 36 (2): 199–221.

Anton, Susan C., Richard Potts, and Leslie C. Aiello. 2014. "Evolution of Early *Homo*: An Integrated Biological Perspective." *Science* 345 (6192) doi: 10.1126/science.1236828

Anton, Susan C., and J. Josh Snodgrass. 2012. "Origins and Evolution of Genus *Homo*: New Perspectives." *Current Anthropology* 53 (S6): S479–S496.

Ashton, Nick, Simon G. Lewis, Isabelle De Groote, Sarah M. Duffy, Martin Bates, Richard Bates, Peter Hoare, Mark Lewis, Simon A. Parfitt, Sylvia Peglar, Craig Williams, and Chris Stringer. 2014. "Hominin Footprints from Early Pleistocene Deposits at Happisburgh, UK." *PLOS ONE* 9 (2): e88329.

Belmaker, Miriam. 2010. "Early Pleistocene Faunal Connections between Africa and Eurasia: An Ecological Perspective." In *Out of Africa I: The First Hominin Colonization of Eurasia*, edited by John G. Fleagle, John J. Shea, Frederick E. Grine, Andrea L. Baden, and Richard E. Leakey, 183–205. Dordrecht: Springer Netherlands.

Blumenschine, Robert, Henry T. Bunn, Valerius Geist, Fumiko Ikawa-Smith, Curtis W. Marean, Anthony G. Payne, John Tooby, J. Nikolaas, and Van Der Merwe. 1987. "Characteristics of an Early Hominid Scavenging Niche [and Comments and Reply]." *Current Anthropology* 28 (4): 383–407.

Bower, Bruce. 2004. "Evolution's Buggy Ride." *Science News* 166 (15): 230–230.

Bramble, Dennis M., and Daniel E. Lieberman. 2004. "Endurance Running and the Evolution of *Homo*." *Nature* 432: 345–352.

Coolidge, Frederick L., and Thomas Grant Wynn. 2017. *The Rise of Homo Sapiens: The Evolution of Modern Thinking*. New York: Oxford University Press.

Dean, M. Christopher, and B. Holly Smith. 2009. "Growth and Development of the Nariokotome Youth, KNM-WT 15000." In *The First Humans—Origin and Early Evolution of the Genus Homo: Contributions from the Third Stony Brook Human Evolution Symposium and Workshop October 3–7, 2006*, edited by Frederick E. Grine, John G. Fleagle, and Richard E. Leakey, 101–120. Dordrecht: Springer Netherlands.

deMenocal, Peter B. 2014. "Climate Shocks." *Scientific American* 311 (3): 48–53.

Dennell, Robin, and Wil Roebroeks. 2005. "An Asian Perspective on Early Human Dispersal from Africa." *Nature* 438 (7071): 1099–1104.

Gao, Xing, Shuangquan Zhang, Yue Zhang, and Fuyou Chen. 2017. "Evidence of Hominin Use and Maintenance of Fire at Zhoukoudian." *Current Anthropology* 58 (Number S16): S267–S277.

Hawkes, Kristen, James F. O'Connell, Nicholas G. Blurton Jones, Helen Alvarez, and Eric L. Charnov. 1998. "Grandmothering, Menopause, and the Evolution of Human Life Histories." *Proceedings of the National Academy of Sciences* 95 (3): 1336–1339.

Hill, Kim, and Hillard Kaplan. 1999. "Life History Traits in Humans: Theory and Empirical Studies." *Annual Review of Anthropology* 28 (1): 397–430.

Hlubik, Sarah, Francesco Berna, Craig Feibel, David Braun, and John W. K. Harris. 2017. "Researching the Nature of Fire at 1.5 Mya on the Site of FxJj20 AB, Koobi Fora, Kenya, Using High-Resolution Spatial Analysis and FTIR Spectrometry." *Current Anthropology* 58 (S16): S243–S257.

Jablonski, Nina G. 2010. "The Naked Truth." *Scientific American* 302 (2): 42–49.

Kamberov, Yana G., Elinor K. Karlsson, Gerda L. Kamberova, Daniel E. Lieberman, Pardis C. Sabeti, Bruce A. Morgan, and Clifford J. Tabin. 2015. "A Genetic Basis of Variation in Eccrine Sweat Gland and Hair Follicle Density." *Proceedings of the National Academy of Sciences* 112 (32): 9932–9937.

Kittler, R., M. Kayser, and M. Stoneking. 2003. "Molecular Evolution of Pediculus Humanus and the Origin of Clothing." *Current Biology* 13 (16): 1414-7.

Leakey, Louis S. B., Phillip V. Tobias, and John R. Napier. 1964. "A New Species of Genus *Homo* from Olduvai Gorge." *Nature* 202: 308-312.

Lemorini, Cristina, Thomas W. Plummer, David R. Braun, Alyssa N. Crittenden, Peter W. Ditchfield, Laura C. Bishop, Fritz Hertel, James S. Oliver, Frank W. Marlowe, Margaret J. Schoeninger, and Richard Potts. 2014. "Old Stones' Song: Use-wear Experiments and Analysis of the Oldowan Quartz and Quartzite Assemblage from Kanjera South (Kenya)." *Journal of Human Evolution* 72: 10-25.

Lordkipanidze, David, Marcia S. Ponce de León, Ann Margvelashvili, Yoel Rak, G. Philip Rightmire, Abesalom Vekua, and Christoph P. E. Zollikofer. 2013. "A Complete Skull from Dmanisi, Georgia, and the Evolutionary Biology of Early *Homo*." *Science* 342 (6156): 326-333.

Qiu, Jane. 2016. "How China Is Rewriting the Book on Human Origins." *Nature* 535: 22-25.

Reed, David L., Jessica E. Light, Julie M. Allen, and Jeremy J. Kirchman. 2007. "Pair of Lice Lost or Parasites Regained: The Evolutionary History of Anthropoid Primate Lice." *BMC Biology* 5 (1):7. doi: 10.1186/1741-7007-5-7.

Roche, Helene, Robert J. Blumenschine, and John J. Shea. 2009. "Origins and Adaptations of Early *Homo*: What Archeology Tells Us." In *The First Humans: Origin and Early Evolution of the Genus Homo*, edited by Frederick E. Grine, John G. Fleagle, and Richard E. Leakey, 135-147. New York: Springer.

Rogers, Alan R., David Iltis, and Stephen Wooding. 2004. "Genetic Variation at the MC1R l Locus and the Time since Loss of Human Body Hair." *Current Anthropology* 45 (1): 105-108.

Ruff, Christopher. 2009. "Relative Limb Strength and Locomotion in *Homo habilis*." *American Journal of Physical Anthropology* 138 (1): 90–100.

Shipton, Ceri, James Blinkhorn, Paul S. Breeze, Patrick Cuthbertson, Nick Drake, Huw S. Groucutt, Richard P. Jennings, Ash Parton, Eleanor M. L. Scerri, Abdullah Alsharekh, and Michael D. Petraglia. 2018. "Acheulean Technology and Landscape Use at Dawadmi, Central Arabia." *PloS one* 13 (7): e0200497–e0200497.

Simpson, Scott W., Jay Quade, Naomi E. Levin, Robert Butler, Guillaume Dupont-Nivet, Melanie Everett, and Sileshi Semaw. 2008. "A Female *Homo erectus* Pelvis from Gona, Ethiopia." *Science* 322 (5904): 1089-1092.

Ungar, Peter S and Robert S. Scott. 2009. "Dental Evidence for Diets of Early *Homo*." In *The First Humans: Origin and Early Evolution of the Genus Homo*, edited by Frederick E. Grine, John G. Fleagle, and Richard E. Leakey, 121-134. New York: Springer.

Villmoare, Brian, William H. Kimbel, Chalachew Seyoum, Christopher J. Campisano, Erin N. DiMaggio, John Rowan, David R. Braun, J. Ramón Arrowsmith, and Kaye E. Reed. 2015. "Early *Homo* at 2.8 Ma From Ledi-Geraru, Afar, Ethiopia." *Science* 347 (6228): 1352-1355.

Wood, Bernard. 2014. "Human Evolution: Fifty Years after *Homo habilis*." *Nature* 508 (7494): 31-33.

Wood, Bernard, and Mark Collard. 1999. "The Changing Face of Genus Homo." *Evolutionary Anthropology* 8 (6): 195–207.

Wrangham, Richard. 2009. *Catching Fire: How Cooking Made Us Human*. New York: Basic Books.

Zhu, Zhaoyu, Robin Dennell, Weiwen Huang, Yi Wu, Shifan Qiu, Shixia Yang, and Zhiguo Rao. 2018. "Hominin Occupation of the Chinese Loess Plateau Since about 2.1 Million Years Ago." *Nature* 559: 608-612.

Acknowledgments

The author gratefully acknowledges funding from the California Community Colleges Chancellor's Office Zero Textbook Cost Degree Grant Program–Implementation Phase 2.

Figure Attributions

Figure 10.1a KNM-WT 15000 Turkana Boy Skeleton by Smithsonian [exhibit: Human Evolution Evidence, Human Fossils, Fossils, KNM-WT 15000] is copyrighted and used for educational and non-commercial purposes as outlined by the Smithsonian.

Figure 10.1b MNP – Turkanajunge 2 by Wolfgang Sauber (photograph) and E. Daynes (sculpture) is used under a CC BY-SA 4.0 License.

Figure 10.2 Five Myr Climate Change by Dragons flight (Robert A. Rohde), based on data from Lisiechi and Raymo (2005), is used under a CC BY-SA 3.0 License.

Figure 10.3 Savanna grasslands of East Africa by International Livestock Research Institute (ILRI)/Elsworth is used under a CC BY-NC-SA 2.0 License.

Figure 10.4 Homo habilis site map original to Explorations: An Open Invitation to Biological Anthropology by Chelsea Barron at GeoPlace, California State University, Chico is under a CC BY-NC 4.0 License.

Figure 10.5a Homo habilis: OH 24 lateral right view by eFossils is copyrighted and used for non-commercial purposes as outlined by eFossils.

Figure 10.5b Homo habilis: KNM-ER 1813 lateral right view by eFossils is copyrighted and used for non-commercial purposes as outlined by eFossils.

Figure 10.5c Homo habilis OH 7 Jaw by ©BoneClones is used by permission and available here under a CC BY-NC 4.0 License.

Figure 10.6 Homo habilis table original to Explorations: An Open Invitation to Biological Anthropology is under a CC BY-NC 4.0 License.

Figure 10.7 Homo rudolfensis Cranium KNM-ER 1470 by ©BoneClones is used by permission and available here under a CC BY-NC 4.0 License.

Figure 10.8 Summary features of Homo habilis original to Explorations: An Open Invitation to Biological Anthropology is under a CC BY-NC 4.0 License.

Figure 10.9 Chopping tool by José-Manuel Benito Álvarez is used under a CC BY-SA 2.5 License.

Figure 10.10 Homo erectus: Sangiran 17 lateral left view by eFossils is copyrighted and used for non-commercial purposes as outlined by eFossils.

Figure 10.11 Homo erectus site map original to Explorations: An Open Invitation to Biological Anthropology by Chelsea Barron at GeoPlace, California State University, Chico is under a CC BY-NC 4.0 License.

Figure 10.12 Regional comparisons of Homo erectus fossils original to Explorations: An Open Invitation to Biological Anthropology is under a CC BY-NC 4.0 License.

Figure 10.13 Hand axe spanish by Locutus Borg has been designated to the public domain (CC0).

Figure 10.14 Elephant Butchery Site Olorgesailie, Kenya by Smithsonian [exhibit: Human Evolution Research, East African Research Projects, Olorgesailie, Kenya] is copyrighted and used for educational and non-commercial purposes as outlined by the Smithsonian.

Figure 10.15 Hadzabe1 by Idobi is used under a CC BY-SA 3.0 License.

Figure 10.16 Summary features of Homo erectus original to Explorations: An Open Invitation to Biological Anthropology is under a CC BY-NC 4.0 License.

Chapter 11: Archaic *Homo*

Amanda Wolcott Paskey, M.A., Cosumnes River College

AnnMarie Beasley Cisneros, M.A., American River College

Learning Objectives

- Describe the unique anatomical and cultural characteristics of archaic *Homo sapiens* in contrast to other hominins.
- Articulate how archaic *Homo sapiens* fossils fit into anatomical evolutionary trends including brain size development, as well as cultural innovations and distribution throughout the Old World.
- Explain how shifting environmental conditions required flexibility of adaptations, both anatomically and culturally, for hominin survival and the potential consequences of a high degree of specialization.
- Recognize that while archaic *Homo sapiens* share similarities, they are characterized by significant regional variation and local adaptation.
- Detail the increased complexity and debates surrounding archaic *Homo sapiens*' classification in light of transitional species, species admixture, etc.

BREAKING THE STIGMA OF THE "CAVEMAN"

Figure 11.1 Popular perceptions of human ancestors at the transition to modern Homo sapiens often take the form of the stereotypical, and inaccurate, "caveman."

What do you think of when you hear the word "caveman"? Perhaps you imagine a character from a film such as *The Croods*, *Tarzan*, or *Encino Man* or from the cartoon *The Flintstones*. Maybe you picture the tennis-playing, therapy-going hairy Neanderthals from Geico Insurance commercials. Or perhaps you imagine comic characters from "The Far Side" or "B.C." comics. Whichever you picture, the character in your mind is likely stooped over with a heavy brow, tangled long locks and other body hair, and clothed in animal skins, if anything. They might be holding a club with a confused look on their face, standing at the entrance to a cave or dragging an animal carcass to a fire for their next meal (see Figure 11.1). You might have even signed up to take this course because of what you knew—or expected to learn—about "cavemen."

These images have long been the stigma and expectation about our ancestors at the transition to modern *Homo sapiens*. Tracing back to works as early as Linnaeus, scientists once propagated and advanced this imagery, creating a clear picture in the minds of early scholars that informed the general public, even through today, that archaic *Homo sapiens*, "cavemen," were somehow distinctly different and much less intelligent than we are now. Unfortunately, this view is incorrect, overly simplistic, and misleading. Understanding what archaic *Homo sapiens* were actually like requires a much more complex and nuanced picture, one that continues to be understood with greater clarity as current research uncovers the lives of our not-too-distant (and not-too-different) ancestors.

The first characterizations of archaic *Homo sapiens* were formed from limited fossil evidence in a time when **ethnocentric** and species-centric perspectives (**anthropocentrism**) were more extensively accepted and entrenched in both society and science. Today, scientists are working from a more complete fossil record from three continents (Africa, Asia, and Europe) and even genetic evidence that informs their analyses and conclusions. The existence of archaic *Homo sapiens* mark an exciting point in our lineage—a point at which many modern traits had emerged and key refinements were on the horizon. Anatomically, we today are not that much different from archaic *Homo sapiens*.

This chapter will examine the environment with which archaic *Homo sapiens* had to contend, one that shaped their, and our, ultimate development. It will also examine the key anatomical traits that define this group of fossils (including the infamous subgroup known as Neanderthals), cultural innovations that aided their adaptation to the changing environment, and their geographic distribution and regional variations. Additionally, it will consider areas of exciting new research that suggest even greater nuance and complexity during this time period. Our understanding of this species and our evolution is complex and exciting and could become even more so as new data is uncovered.

THE CHANGING ENVIRONMENT

While modern climate change is of critical concern today due to its cause (human activity) and pace (unprecedentedly rapid), the existence of global climate change itself is not a recent phenomenon. The climate across the globe has changed, drastically at times, over the course of Earth's existence. The Pleistocene epoch—between 1.8 million years ago (mya) and 11,000 years ago (kya); illustrated in Figure 7.7—was a time of great climatic upheaval. The Middle Pleistocene, roughly between 780 kya and 125 kya, is the time period in which archaic *Homo sapiens* appear in the fossil record—a time that witnessed some of the most drastic climatic changes that have been seen in human existence. During this time period, there were 15 major and 50 minor glacial events in Europe alone!

What exactly is a **glaciation**? When scientists talk about glacial events, they are referring to the climate being in an ice age. This means that the ocean levels were much lower than today, as much of the earth's water was tied up in large glaciers or ice sheets. Additionally, the average temperature would have been much cooler, which would have better supported an Arctic or tundra-adapted plant-and-animal ecosystem in northern latitudes. The most interesting and relevant features of Middle Pleistocene glacial events are the sheer number of them and their repeated bouts—this era alternated between glacial periods and warmer periods, known as **interglacials**. In other words, the world wasn't in an ice age the whole time.

How have scientists determined how many glaciations there were during the Middle Pleistocene and how severe they were? Several lines of evidence help inform our understanding of past climates. One important source is the study of oxygen isotopes preserved in the shells of marine invertebrates called **foraminifera**. Foraminifera incorporate oxygen from seawater during their life. When they die, foraminifera shells fall to the ocean floor and can be preserved as microscopic fossils that are part of the sediment, which can later be sampled and studied in **sediment cores**. Studying these cores has revealed that the oxygen isotope present varies depending on Earth temperatures at the time the foraminifera were alive. During glacial periods, seawater is cooler and one oxygen isotope—^{18}O—is in higher concentrations in seawater (and, as a result, in foraminifera shells) because it is heavier. In contrast, water with the oxygen isotope ^{16}O is lighter and therefore evaporates first, becomes part of precipitate (such as snow), and eventually becomes trapped in glaciers. During interglacials, ^{16}O returns to the ocean in water runoff, resulting in higher ocean and foraminifera concentrations of this oxygen isotope. Recent research with **ice cores** further confirms the length and severity of glacial periods using similar techniques.

The Pleistocene is characterized by shifts in Earth's temperatures and their impact on plant and animal life. The Middle Pleistocene was an even more intense period of fluctuation with frequent and severe glacial and interglacial episodes recorded in marine isotopes, among other data points. You can see the dramatic and increasing fluctuations in temperature, recorded through foraminifera, in the chart (Figure 11.2). The distance between lows and highs demonstrates the severity of temperature shift. Much as the Richter scale represents more intense earthquakes with more dramatic peaks, so too does this chart, which uses dramatic peaks to demonstrate intense temperature swings.

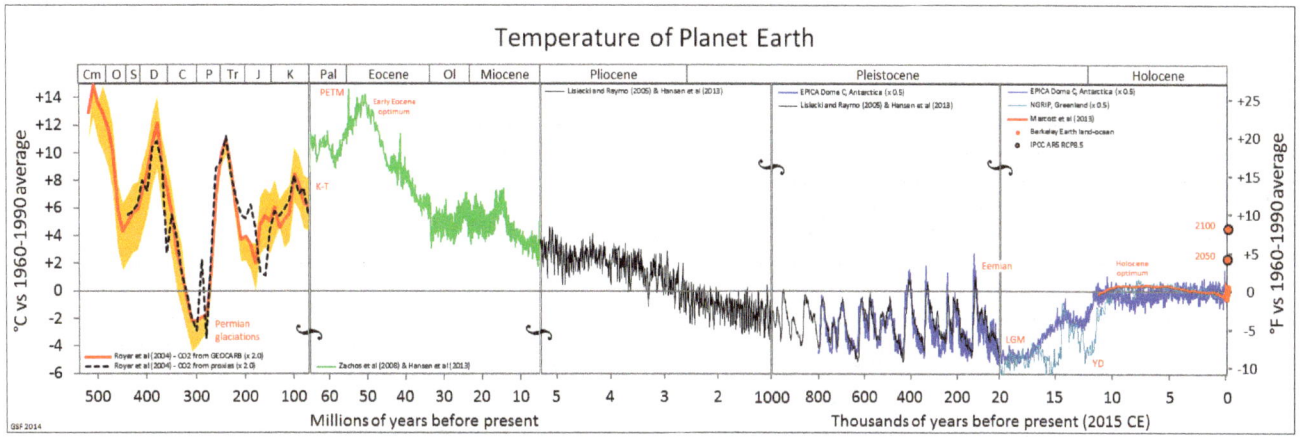

Figure 11.2 The Geologic Timescale and corresponding temperature shifts. Note the wide and rapid shifts during the Pleistocene (the second box from the right). More dramatic fluctuations depict greater severity of temperature shift.

Glacial periods are defined by Earth's average temperature being lower. Worldwide, temperatures are reduced, with cold areas becoming even colder. The water cycle experiences limited runoff as water evaporates from the seas, precipitates (often as snow and ice), and accumulates in glaciers with little precipitation melting as runoff. Over time, continued evaporation with little runoff results in the accumulation of snowpacks and glaciers at the expense of sea level, which is lowered. In simple terms, the water that is normally in the sea is now tied up on land as ice. Huge portions of the landscape may have become inaccessible during glacial events due to the formation of glaciers and massive ice sheets. In Europe, the Scandinavian continental glacier covered what is today Ireland, England, Sweden, Norway, Denmark, and some of continental Europe. Plant and animal communities shifted to lower latitudes along the periphery of ice sheets. Additionally, some new land was opened during glacials. Evaporation with little runoff reduced sea levels by as much as almost 150 meters, shifting coastlines outward by in some instances as much as almost 100 kilometers. Additionally, land became exposed that connected what were previously unconnected continents such as Africa at the Gulf of Aden into Yemen.

Glacial periods also affected equatorial regions and other regions that are today thought of as warmer or at least more temperate parts of the globe, including Africa. While these areas were not covered with glaciers, the impact of increased global glaciation resulted in lower sea levels and expanded coastlines. Cooler temperatures were accompanied by the drying of the climate, which caused significantly reduced rainfall, increased aridity, and the expansion of deserts. It is an interesting question to consider whether the same plants and animals that lived in these regions prior to the ice ages would be able to survive and thrive in this new climate? Plant and animal communities shifted in response to the changing climate, whenever possible.

Rather than a single selective force, the Middle Pleistocene was marked by periods of fluctuation, not just cold periods. Interglacials interrupted glaciations, reversing trends in sea level, coastline, temperature, precipitation, and aridity, as well as glacier size and location. Interglacials are marked by increased rainfall and a higher temperature, which causes built-up ice in glaciers to melt. Interglacials are marked by glacial retreat, which is the shrinking of glaciers and the movement of the glaciers back toward the poles, as we've seen in our lifetime. During interglacials, sea levels increase, flooding some previously exposed coastlines and continental connections. In addition, plant and animal communities shift accordingly, often finding more temperate climates to the north and less arid and more humid climates in the tropics.

Scientists have found that at one site, the Olorgesailie region in southern Kenya, a single location was at various times in the Middle Pleistocene a deep lake, a drought-dried lakebed, small streams, and a grassland. While various animal species would have moved in and out of the area as the climate shifted, some animal species went extinct, and new, often related, species took up residence. The trend, scientists noted, was that animals with more specialized features went extinct and animals with more generalized features, such as animals we see today, survived in this changing climatic time period. For example, a zebra with specialized teeth for eating grass was ultimately replaced by a zebra that could eat grass and other types of vegetation. The exclusively terrestrial fossil baboon *Therapithecus oswaldi* was replaced by *Papio anubis*, the more flexible locomotor baboon that exists in the region today. If this small, localized example shows such a dramatic change in terms of the environment and the plant and animal biocommunities, what would have been the impact on humans?

There is no way humans could have escaped the effects of Middle Pleistocene climate change, no matter what region of the world they were living in. As noted earlier, and as evidenced by what was seen in the other biotic communities, humans would have faced changing food sources as previous sources of food may have gone extinct or moved to a different latitude. Depending on where they were living, fresh water may have been limited. Durial glacials, lower sea levels would have given humans more land to live on, while the interglacials would have reduced the available land through the increase in rainfall and associated sea level rise. Dry land connections between the continents would have made movement from one continent to another by foot easier at times than today, although these passageways were not consistently available through the Middle Pleistocene due to the glacial/interglacial cycle. Finally, as evidenced by the study at the Olorgesailie region in Kenya, during the Middle Pleistocene animal species that were overly specialized to one particular type of environment were less likely to survive when compared to their more generalized counterparts. Evidence suggests that this same pattern may have held true for archaic *Homo sapiens*, in terms of their ability to survive this dramatic period of climate change.

DEFINING CHARACTERISTICS OF ARCHAIC *HOMO SAPIENS*

Archaic *Homo sapiens* share our species name but are distinguished by the term "archaic" as a way of recognizing both the long period of time between their appearance and ours, as well as the way in which human traits have continued to evolve over time—making archaic *Homo sapiens* look slightly different from us today, despite technically being considered the same species. Living throughout the Old World during the Middle Pleistocene, archaic *Homo sapiens* are considered, in many ways, transitional between *Homo erectus* and modern *Homo sapiens* (see Figure 11.3). All archaic *Homo sapiens* share the defining trait of an increased brain size—specifically a brain of at least 1,100 cc and averaging 1,200 cc—but are also characterized by significant regional and temporal (time) variations. Because of these variations, scientists disagree on whether these fossils represent a single, variable species or multiple, closely related species (sometimes called *Homo antecessor*, *Homo heidelbergensis*, *Homo georgicus*, *Homo neanderthalensis*, and *Homo rhodesiensis*). For simplicity we are going to lump them all together under the heading of archaic *Homo sapiens* and discuss them as a unit, with the exception of a particularly unique and well-known population living in Europe and West Asia known as the Neanderthals, which we will examine separately.

Trait	Homo erectus	Archaic Homo sapiens	Anatomically Modern Homo sapiens
Average Brain Size	900 cc	1,200 cc (1,500 cc when including Neanderthals)	1,400 cc
Skull Shape	Long and low Angular	Intermediate	Short and high **Globular**
Forehead	Absent	Emerging	Present
Nasal Region	Projecting nasal bones (bridge of the nose), no midfacial prognathism	Wider nasal aperture and midfacial prognathism	Narrower nasal aperture, no midfacial prognathism
Chin	Absent	Absent	Present
Other Facial Features	Large brow ridge and large projecting face	Intermediate	Small brow ridge and **retracted face**
Other Skull Features	Nuchal torus, sagittal keel, thick cranial bone	Projecting occipital bone, often called occipital bun in Neanderthals; intermediate thickness of cranial bone	Small bump on rear of skull, if anything; thin cranial bone
Dentition	Large teeth, especially front teeth	Slightly smaller teeth; front teeth still large; retromolar gap in Neanderthals	Smaller teeth
Postcranial Features	Robust bones of skeleton	Robust bones of skeleton	More gracile bones of skeleton

Figure 11.3 A comparison of Homo erectus, *archaic* Homo sapiens, *and anatomically modern* Homo sapiens. *This table compares key traits of the crania and postcrania that distinguish these three hominins.*

When comparing *Homo erectus*, archaic *Homo sapiens*, and anatomically modern *Homo sapiens* across several anatomical features, one can see quite clearly that archaic *Homo sapiens* are intermediate in their physical form. This follows the trends first seen in *Homo erectus* for some features and in other features having early, less developed forms of traits more clearly seen in modern *Homo sapiens*. For example, archaic *Homo sapiens* trended toward less angular and higher skulls than *Homo erectus* but had skulls notably not as short and globular in shape and with a less developed forehead than anatomically modern *Homo sapiens*. archaic *Homo sapiens* had smaller brow ridges and a less-projecting face than *Homo erectus* and slightly smaller teeth, although incisors and canines were often about as large as that of *Homo erectus*. Archaic *Homo sapiens* also had a wider **nasal aperture**, or opening for the nose, as well as a forward-projecting midfacial region, known as **midfacial prognathism**. The occipital bone often projected and the cranial bone was of intermediate thickness, somewhat reduced from *Homo erectus* but not nearly as thin as that of anatomically modern *Homo sapiens*. The postcrania remained fairly robust, as well. To identify a set of features that is unique to the group archaic *Homo sapiens* is a challenging task, due to both individual variation—these developments were not all present to the same degree in all individuals—and the transitional nature of their features. Neanderthals will be the exception, as they have several clearly unique traits that make them notably different from modern *Homo sapiens* as well as their closely related archaic cousins.

The one thing that is clear about archaic *Homo sapiens* is that regional variation, first seen in the different *Homo erectus* specimens across Asia and Africa, is clearly present and even more pronounced. While the general features of archaic *Homo sapiens*, identified earlier, are present in the fossils of this time period, there are significant regional differences. The majority of this regional variation lies in the degree to which fossils have features more closely aligned with *Homo erectus* or with anatomically modern *Homo sapiens*.

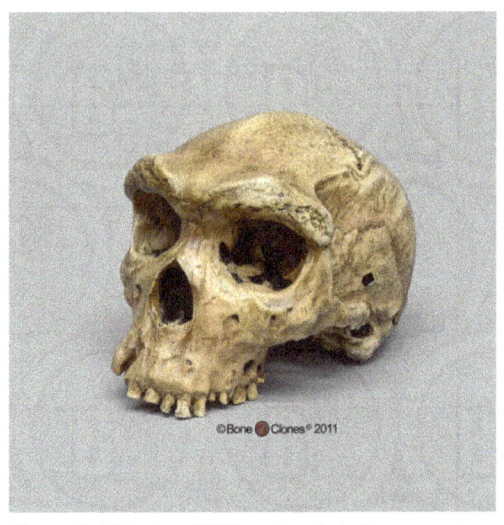

Figure 11.4 "Broken Hill Man" archaic Homo sapiens cranium found at Kabwe in Zambia. One of several individuals found at this site, this cranium reflects common traits associated with archaic Homo sapiens in Africa including a large brain, taller cranium, and many Homo erectus-like features such as massive brow ridges, a large face, and thick cranial bones.

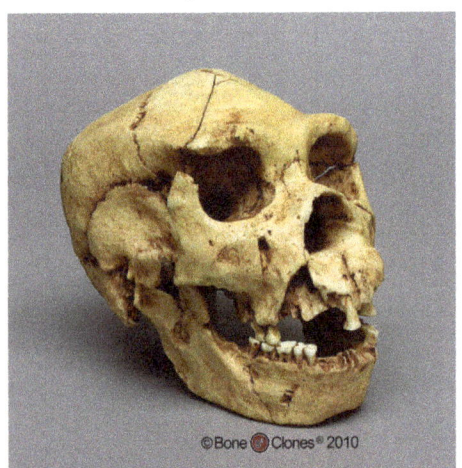

Figure 11.5 Atapuerca 5 archaic Homo sapiens found in northern Spain. One of many fossils found at this site, this fossil is representative of traits seen in archaic Homo sapiens in Europe including thick a cranial bone, enlarged cranial capacity, intermediate cranial height, and a more rounded cranium, as well as increased midfacial prognathism.

To illustrate this point, we will examine three exemplary specimens, one from each of the three continents on which archaic *Homo sapiens* lived. In Africa, "Broken Hill Man," one of several individuals found in the Kabwe lead mine in Zambia, had a large brain (1,300 cc) and taller cranium as well as many *Homo erectus*-like skull features, including massive brow ridges, a large face, and thick cranial bones (Figure 11.4). Conditions for preservation in Asia during the Middle Pleistocene were not as conducive to the fossilization of complete crania; however, many archaic *Homo sapiens* skullcaps have been found. One partial crania from Dali, China, is representative of archaic *Homo sapiens* in Asia, including large and robust features with heavy brow ridges, akin to what is seen in *Homo erectus*, and a large cranial capacity intermediate between *Homo erectus* and anatomically modern *Homo sapiens*. Across Europe, many near-complete archaic *Homo sapiens* crania have been discovered, including one, part of an almost-complete skeleton, found in northern Spain at Atapuerca. Atapuerca 5 (Figure 11.5) has thick cranial bone, an enlarged cranial capacity, intermediate cranial height, and a more rounded cranium than seen previously. Additionally, Atapuerca 5 demonstrates features that foreshadow Neanderthals, including increased midfacial prognathism. After examining some of the fossils, the transitional nature of archaic *Homo sapiens* is clear—their features place them squarely between *Homo erectus* and modern *Homo sapiens*.

Due to the transitional nature of archaic *Homo sapiens*, identifying the time period they are associated with is problematic and complex. Generally, it is agreed upon that archaic *Homo sapiens* lived between 600,000 and 200,000 years ago. But regionally this varies with considerable overlap between *Homo erectus* on the early end of the spectrum and modern *Homo sapiens* and Neanderthals on the latter end. The earliest-known archaic *Homo sapiens* fossils tentatively date to about 600,000 years ago in Africa, whereas archaic *Homo sapiens* fossils in Asia appear around 300,000 years ago and in Europe around 350,000 years ago (and potentially as early as 600,000 years ago). The end point of archaic *Homo sapiens* is also problematic since it largely depends upon when the next subspecies of *Homo sapiens* appears and the classification of highly intermediate specimens. For example, in Africa, the end of archaic *Homo sapiens* is met with the appearance of modern *Homo sapiens*, while in Europe it is the appearance of Neanderthals that is traditionally seen as the end of archaic *Homo sapiens*.

Archaic *Homo sapiens* mark an important chapter in the human lineage, bridging more ancestral forms, such as *Homo erectus*, with modern *Homo sapiens*. During this period of climatic transition and fluctuation, archaic *Homo sapiens* mirror the challenges of their environments. Showing increasing regional variation due to the need for local adaptation, there is no single archetype for this group but, rather, multiple variations; their transitional nature is one of their key defining characteristics.

NEANDERTHALS

One particularly well-known population of archaic *Homo sapiens* are the Neanderthals, named after the site where they were first discovered in the Neander Valley, or "thal" in German, located near Dusseldorf, Germany. Popularly known as the stereotypical "cavemen" examined at the outset of this chapter, recent research is upending long-held beliefs about this group of archaics. As mentioned in the introduction, Neanderthals have long been thought to be dumb brutes who were, behaviorally speaking, not much different from apes. However, today, scientists agree that Neanderthal behavior was increasingly complex and nuanced, far beyond what was exhibited by even other archaic *Homo sapiens* discussed throughout this chapter. We implore you to forget the image of the iconic caveman and have an open mind when exploring the fossil evidence of the Neanderthals.

It is important to understand why Neanderthals are typically separated from other archaic *Homo sapiens*. Unlike the rest of archaic *Homo sapiens*, Neanderthals are easily defined and identified in many ways. There is a clear geographic boundary of where Neanderthals lived: western Europe, the Middle East, and western Asia. The time period for when Neanderthals lived is widely accepted as between 150,000 and 35,000 years ago. Additionally, Neanderthals have a unique and distinct cluster of physical characteristics. While a few aspects of Neanderthals are less clear cut and are shared among some archaic *Homo sapiens*, such as the types of tools they created and used, most attributes of Neanderthals, both anatomically and behaviorally, are unique to them.

As mentioned previously, the geographic distribution of Neanderthals is very specific. Neanderthal fossils, thus far, have been found across a narrow latitude of western Europe, the Middle East, and western Asia. No Neanderthal fossils have ever been discovered outside of this area, including Africa. This is a bit curious, as other archaics seem to have adapted in Africa and then migrated elsewhere, but Neanderthals' regional association makes sense in light of the environment to which they were best adapted. While Neanderthals lived in different ecosystems, including temperate environments, they were very well adapted to extreme cold weather and their geographic distribution includes what would have been some of the coldest habitable locations at the time of their existence.

Neanderthals lived during some of the coldest times during the last Ice Age and at far northern latitudes. This means Neanderthals were living very close to the glacial edge, and not in a more temperate region of the globe, like some of their archaic *Homo sapiens* relatives. Their range likely expanded and contracted along with European glacial events, moving into the Middle East during glacial events when Europe became even cooler, and when the animals they hunted would have moved for the same reason. During interglacials, when Europe warmed a bit, Neanderthals and their prey would have been able to move back into Western Europe.

Many of the Neanderthals' defining physical features are more extreme and robust versions of traits seen in other archaic *Homo sapiens*, clustered in this single population (Figure 11.6). Brain size is one of the Neanderthal features that continues to follow the same patterns as seen with other archaic *Homo sapiens*, namely an enlargement of the cranial capacity. The average Neanderthal brain size is around 1,500 cc, and the range for Neanderthal brains can extend to upwards of 1,700 cc. The majority of the increase in the brain occurs in the occipital region, or the back part of the brain, resulting in a skull that has a large cranial capacity with a distinctly long and low shape that is slightly wider than previous forms at far back of the skull. Modern humans have a brain size comparable to that of Neanderthals; however, our brain expansion occurred in the frontal region of the brain, not the back, as in Neanderthal brains. This difference is also the main reason why Neanderthals lack the vertical forehead that modern humans possess. They simply did not need an enlarged forehead, because their brain expansion occurred in the rear of their brain. Due to cranial expansion, the back of the Neanderthal skull is less angular (as compared to *Homo erectus*) and is more rounded, a feature similar to that of modern *Homo sapiens*.

Another feature that continues the trend noted in previous hominins is the enlargement of the nasal region, or the nose. Neanderthal noses are large and have a wide nasal aperture, which is the opening for the nose. While the nose is only made up of two bones, the nasals, the true size of the nose can be determined by looking at other facial features, including the nasal aperture, and the angle of the nasal and maxillary, or facial bones. In Neanderthals, these indicate a large, forward-projecting nose that appears to be pulled forward away from the rest of the face. This feature is further emphasized by the backward-sloping nature of the cheekbones, or the zygomatic arches. The unique shape and size of the Neanderthal nose is often characterized by the term *midfacial prognathism*—a jutting out of the middle portion of the face, or nose. This is in sharp contrast to the prognathism exhibited by other hominins, who exhibited prognathism, or the jutting out, of their jaws.

The teeth of the Neanderthals follow a similar pattern seen in the archaic *Homo sapiens*, which is an overall reduction in size, especially as compared to the extremely large teeth seen in the genus *Australopithecus*. However, while the teeth have continued to reduce, the jaw size does not keep pace, leaving Neanderthals with an interesting situation. Their jaw is oversized for their teeth, leaving a gap between their final molar and the end of their jaw. This gap is called a **retromolar gap**.

The projecting occipital bone present in other archaic *Homo sapiens* is also more prominent in Neanderthals, extending the trend found in archaics. Among Neanderthals, this projection of bone is easily identified by its bun shape on the back of the skull and is known as an **occipital bun**. This projection appears quite similar to a dinner roll in size and shape. Its purpose, if any, remains unknown.

Continuing the archaic *Homo sapiens* trend, Neanderthal brow ridges are prominent but somewhat smaller in size than those of *Homo erectus* and earlier archaic *Homo sapiens*. In Neanderthals, the brow ridges are also often slightly less arched than those of other archaic *Homo sapiens*.

In addition to extending traits present in archaic *Homo sapiens*, Neanderthals possess several distinct traits. Neanderthal **infraorbital foramina**, the holes in the maxillae or cheek bones through which blood vessels pass, are notably enlarged compared to other hominins. The Neanderthal postcrania are also unique in that they demonstrate increased robusticity in terms of the thickness of bones and body proportions that show a barrel-shaped chest and short, stocky limbs, as well as increased musculature. These body portions are seen across the spectrum of Neanderthals—in men, women, and children.

Many of the unique traits that Neanderthals possess can be attributed to adaptation to the extreme cold environments in which they often lived. Together explained as cold adaptations, these traits are thought to be a response to the cold, dry environments in which Neanderthals lived and which certainly exerted strong selective forces. For example, Bergmann's and Allen's Rules dictate that an increased body mass and short, stocky limbs are common in animals that live in cold conditions. Neanderthals match the predictions of Bergmann's and Allen's Rules perfectly. In addition, the Neanderthal skull also exhibits adaptations to the cold. Neanderthals' large infraorbital foramina allow for larger blood vessels, increasing the volume of blood that is found closest to the skin, which helps to keep the skin warmer. The midfacial prognathism present in Neanderthals indicates that Neanderthals would have had a large nose. This enlarged nose may also have been beneficial to have in cold weather due to longer nasal passages and mucus membranes for cold air to travel through before reaching the lungs. It is very uncomfortable and challenging to breathe and exert oneself in exceptionally cold, dry air. The more time the air spends in the mucus membranes, the warmer and more moist the air will be before it reaches the lungs. The Neanderthals' larger nose has long been thought to have acted as a humidifier, easing physical exertion in their climate, although research on this particular trait continues to be studied and debated.

Distinct Neanderthal Anatomical Features	
Brain Size	1,500 cc average
Skull Shape	Long and low
Brow Ridge Size	Large
Nose Size	Large, with midfacial prognathism
Dentition	Reduced, but large jaw size, creating retromolar gap
Occipital Region	Enlarged occipital region, occipital bun
Other Unique Cranial Features	Large infraorbital foramina
Postcranial Features	Short and stocky body, increased musculature, barrel-shaped chest

Figure 11.6 Neanderthal distinguishing features. This table outlines key features associated with Neanderthals.

In summary, Neanderthal characteristics are a distinct cluster of features, some of which were apparent in previous hominins and others that were unique. Additionally, it is clear that Neanderthals were specially adapted to a particular environment—a very cold one. A classic example of a Neanderthal with all of the characteristics mentioned above is the La Ferrassie 1 Neanderthal, from France. The skeleton is near complete, which is not necessarily unique among Neanderthal fossils as many partially complete remains have been found, but it does provide us with a lot of information. The La Ferrassie 1 Neanderthal, who was male, had a brain size of around 1640cc and had an extremely large nose and infraorbital foramina. Additionally, the brow ridges are marked in size, and the overall skeleton is robust (Figure 11.7).

What are the benefits or the potential challenges Neanderthals could have faced for being highly specialized to one particular environment, when we know their environment and climate were in flux?

Neanderthal Culture and Lifeways

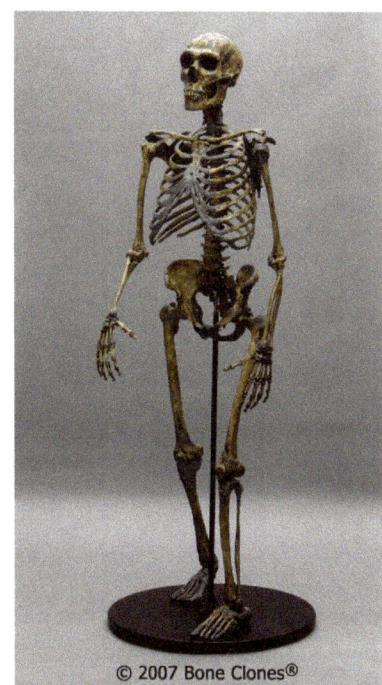

Figure 11.7 La Ferrassie 1 Neanderthal is representative of many classic Neanderthal features including a large brain, large nose, large infraorbital foramina, large brow ridges, and robust postcrania.

One key Neanderthal adaptation was their cultural innovations. Cultural innovation is a key way that hominins adapt to their environment. As you recall, the culture of *Homo erectus* was marked by the development of a bifacial tool, the Acheulean handaxe, which allowed them differential access to meat on animal carcasses when compared to their predecessors. For *Homo erectus*, the Acheulean handaxe allowed more efficient removal of meat and possibly calculated scavenging. The increase in their body and brain size, along with their more effective tools, allowed them to track predators and snatch their kills sometimes even before the predators themselves had even fed.

Acheulean tools represent a significant increase in complexity over Oldowan tools, as they required more time, effort, and skill to shape. Acheulean handaxes were not only worked on two sides, they shared a common shape, which required forethought and advanced planning by their makers. *Homo erectus* would have had a mental template for the desired outcome and, with practice, these tools were likely made quite quickly and could have been made by most individuals. While these tools were a significant step forward in tool production, they were not intended to be kept. *Homo erectus* discarded the tools after use and treated them as a disposable item.

In contrast, Neanderthal tools mark a significant innovation both in tool-making technique and their use. Known as **Mousterian tools**, after the Le Moustier site in southwest France, the Neanderthal's toolkit was truly that—a set of tools with specific applications and unique forms for each desired purpose. Mousterian tools were significantly smaller, thinner, and lighter than Acheulean handaxes and formed a true toolkit. The materials used for Mousterian tools were of higher quality, which allowed for both more precise toolmaking and tool reworking when the tools broke or dulled after frequent reuse. The use of higher-quality materials is also indicative of required forethought and planning to acquire them for tool manufacture. It is noteworthy that the Neanderthals, unlike *Homo erectus*, saved and reused their tools, rather than making new ones each time a tool was needed.

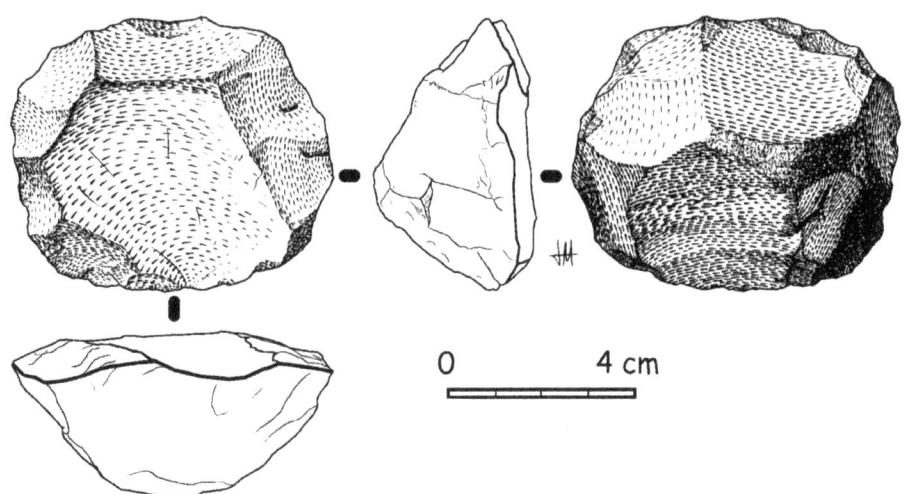

Figure 11.8 The Levallois technique is used to create Mousterian tools. The multistep process involves preparing the core, or raw material, in a specific way that will yield flakes that are roughly uniform in dimension. The flakes are then turned into individual tools.

Mousterian tools are constructed in a very unique manner, utilizing the **Levallois technique** (Figure 11.8), named after the first finds of tools made with this technique, which were discovered in the Levallois-Perret suburb of Paris, France. The Levallois technique is a multistep process that requires preparing the core, or raw material, in a specific way that will yield flakes that are roughly uniform in dimension. The flakes are then turned into individual tools. The preparation of the core is akin to peeling a potato or carrot with a vegetable peeler—when peeling vegetables, you want to remove the skin in long, regular strokes, so that you are taking off the same amount of the vegetable all the way around. In the same way, the Levallois technique requires removing all edges of the **cortex**, or outside surface of the raw material, in a circle before removing the lid. The flakes, which will eventually be turned into the individual tools, can then be removed from the core. The potential yield of tools from one core would be many, as seen in Figure 11.9, compared to all previous tool-making processes, in which one core yielded a single tool.

Figure 11.9 Levallois core and flakes for tool production. Using this technique, one core is used to produce many flakes, each of which can be turned into a tool.

Neanderthal tools were used for a variety of purposes. They would have constructed a tool for each specific task they needed to complete, such as cutting, butchering, woodworking or antler working, and hide working. Additionally, because the Mousterian tools were lighter than previous stone tools, Neanderthals could **haft**, or attach the tool onto a handle, as the stone would not have been too heavy. Neanderthals attached small stone blades onto short wood or antler handles to make knives or other small weapons, as well as attached larger blades onto longer shafts to make spears. New research examining tar-covered stones and black lumps at several Neanderthal sites in Europe suggests that Neanderthals may have been making tar by distilling it from birch tree bark, which could have been used to glue the stone tool onto its handle. If Neanderthals were, in fact, manufacturing tar to act as glue, this would predate modern humans in Africa making tree resin or similar adhesives by nearly 100,000 years! While research on specific applications continues, from just this brief discussion, it should be clear that Neanderthal tool manufacturing was much more complex than previous tool-making efforts, requiring skill and patience to carry out.

With their more sophisticated suite of tools, Neanderthals were better armed for hunting than previous hominins and had very robust bodies with larger muscles. The animal remains in Neanderthal sites show that unlike earlier archaic *Homo sapiens*, Neanderthals were very effective hunters who were able to kill their own prey, rather than relying on scavenging. Oftentimes, this included very large animals like deer, horses, and bovids (relatives of the cow). In fact, isotopes from Neanderthal bones show that meat was a primary and significant component of their diet, similar to that seen in carnivores like wolves (Bocherens et al. 1999). Of course, Neanderthals' diet varied according to the specific environment in which they lived, but according to Christoph Wißin and colleagues (2015), meat comprised up to 80% of their diet.

Though more sophisticated than the tools of earlier hominins, the Neanderthal spear was not the kind of weapon that would have been thrown; rather, it would have been used in a jabbing fashion (Churchill 1998; Kortlandt 2002). This may have required Neanderthals to hunt in groups rather than individually, and it almost certainly meant that they would have had to approach their prey quite closely. Remember, the animals living with Neanderthals were very large-bodied due to their adaptations to cold weather. In addition to large bovids, prey included ibex, seals, rabbits, and pigeons. Though red meat was a critical component of the Neanderthal diet, evidence shows that at times they also ate limpets, mussels, and pine nuts. Tartar examined from Neanderthal teeth in Iraq and Belgium reveal that plant material including wheat, barley, date palms, and tubers were also eaten by Neanderthals and were cooked to make them palatable.

While the new, close-range style of hunting used by Neanderthals was effective, it also had some major consequences. Many Neanderthal skeletons have been found with significant injuries, which could have caused paralysis or severely limited their mobility. Many of the injuries are to the head, neck, or upper-body. Thomas Berger and Erik Trinkaus (1995) conducted a statistical comparative analysis of Neanderthal injuries compared to those recorded in modern day workers' compensation reports and found that the closest match was between Neanderthal injuries and those of rodeo workers. Rodeo professionals have a high rate of head and neck injuries that are similar to the Neanderthals' injuries. What do Neanderthals and rodeo workers have in common? They were both getting very close to large, strong animals, and at times their encounters might have gone awry.

The extensive injuries sustained by Neanderthals are evident in many fossil remains. Shanidar 1 (Figure 11.10), an adult male found at the Shanidar site in northern Iraq and dating to 45,000 ya, has a lifetime of injuries recorded in his bones. Shanidar 1 sustained—and healed from—an injury to his face that would have likely caused blindness. His lower right arm was missing and his right humerus shows severe atrophy, likely due to disuse. This pattern has been interpreted to indicate a substantial injury that required or otherwise resulted in amputation or wasting away of the lower arm. Additionally, Shanidar 1 suffered from severe arthritis in his feet and bony growths in his inner ear that would have significantly impaired his hearing. He also exhibited extensive anterior tooth wear, matching the pattern of wear found among modern populations who use their teeth as a tool. Rather than an anomaly, the type of injuries evident in Shanidar 1 are similar to those found in many other Neanderthal fossils, revealing injuries likely sustained from hunting large mammals as well as demonstrating a long life of physical activity.

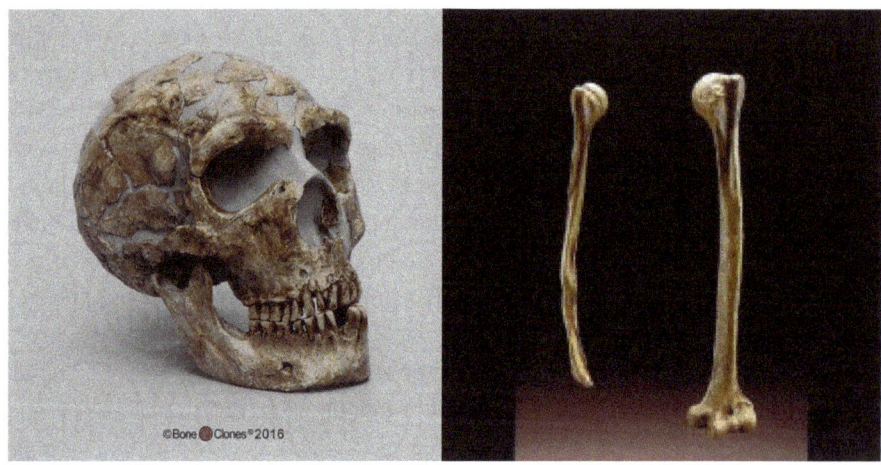

Figure 11.10 Like many other Neanderthals, Shanidar 1 has a lifetime of injuries recorded in his bones. Shanidar 1 sustained—and healed from—an injury to his face that would have likely caused blindness. His lower right arm was missing and his right humerus shows severe atrophy, likely due to disuse.

The pattern of injuries is as significant as the fact that Shanidar 1 and other injured Neanderthals often show evidence of having *survived* their severe injuries. One of the earliest known Neanderthal discoveries—the one on whom misinformed analysis shaped the stereotype of the species for nearly a century—is the La Chapelle-aux-Saints Neanderthal. The La Chapelle Neanderthal had a damaged eye orbit that likely caused blindness and suffered arthritis of the spine. He had also lost of most of his teeth, many of which he had lived without for so long that the mandibular and maxillary bones were partially reabsorbed due to lack of use. The La Chapelle Neanderthal was also thought to be at least in his mid-40s at death, an old age for the rough life of the Late Pleistocene, giving rise to his nickname, "the Old Man." To have survived so long with so many injuries that obviously precluded successful large game hunting, he would have had to have been taken care of by others. Such caretaking behavior is also evident in the survival of other seriously injured Neanderthals, such as Shanidar 1. Long thought to be a hallmark human characteristic, taking care of the injured and elderly, to the extent of even preparing or pre-chewing food for those without teeth, indicates strong social ties among Neanderthals.

The care expressed in taking care of the sick or injured may have been expressed upon death as well. Full Neanderthal skeletons are not uncommon in the fossil record, and many of these skeletons were so well preserved due to having been placed in deliberate burials. These burials appear intentional, as the graves are dug down a bit, and the bodies found in the graves are in specific positions quite distinct from the natural position the body automatically goes into after death during rigor mortis. Neanderthal burials are often in a **flexed position,** or fetal position. Discoveries of pollen in a grave at the Shanidar site in the 1960s led scientists to think that perhaps Neanderthals had deliberately placed flowering plants in the grave, an indication of ritual ceremony or spirituality so common in modern humans. But future investigations have raised some doubt about this conclusion. The pollen may have been brought in by burrowing rodents. Claims of **grave goods** or other ornamentation in burials are similarly debated, although possible.

Some tantalizing evidence for symbolism, and debatably, ritual, is the frequent occurrence of natural pigments, such as **ochre** (red) and manganese dioxide (black) in Neanderthal sites. Such pigments could have been used for art, like some of the spectacular cave paintings produced by modern humans who lived in this area after the Neanderthals. However, how these pigments were actually used by Neanderthals themselves is unclear, as there is very little evidence of art or paintings in Mousterian sites. One exception may be the recent discovery in Spain of a perforated shell that appears to be painted with an orange pigment, which may be some of the best evidence of Neanderthal art and jewelry. However, many pigments also have properties that make them good emulsifiers in adhesive (like for attaching a stone tool to a wooden handle) or useful in tanning hides. So the presence of pigment may or may not be associated with symbolic thought, but it at the very least shows a technological sophistication beyond that exhibited by earlier archaic hominins and clearly counters the old stereotypes of Neanderthals as dumb, thoughtless brutes.

The more recent time period in which Neanderthals lived and extensive excavations completed across Europe allow for a much more complete archaeological record from this time period. Additionally, the increased cultural complexity such as complex tools and ritual behaviors expressed by Neanderthals left a more detailed record than previous hominins. Intentional burials enhanced preservation of the dead and potentially associated ritual behaviors. Such evidence allows for a more complete and nuanced picture of this species.

Figure 11.11 Artistic reconstruction of Neanderthals.

Additional analyses are possible on many Neanderthal finds, due to increased preservation of bone, the amount of specimens that have been uncovered, and the recency in which Neanderthals lived. These additional studies include the examination of dental calculus and even DNA analysis. While limited, some samples of Neanderthal DNA have been successfully extracted and analyzed. Studies thus far have identified specific genetic markers that show some Neanderthals were light-skinned and probably red-haired with light eyes. Genetic analyses, different than the typical hominin reconstruction done with earlier species, allow scientists to further investigate soft tissue markers of Neanderthals and other more recent hominin species. These studies and Neanderthal cultural behavior have given scientists a wealth of information to study and offer striking conclusions regarding Neanderthal traits, their physical appearance, and their culture, as reflected in these artists' reconstructions (Figure 11.11).

The Neanderthals' more complicated behavior likely stems, in part, from their larger brains. Evidence shows that raw materials used by Neanderthals came from distances as far away as 100 km. This could indicate a variety of things regarding Neanderthal behavior, including a limited trade network with other Neanderthal groups, or simply a large area scoured by Neanderthals when collecting raw materials. Additionally, we know that Neanderthals lived in groups and may have relied on their group members for survival. Shanidar 1 and the "Old Man at La Chapelle" would have struggled to acquire and consume food on their own, strongly suggesting that they may have been assisted by relatives of other group members. In other nonhuman primates (like chimpanzees) and earlier hominins, injured individuals would have been left on their own, to either survive or perish.

The impressive cultural innovations and behavioral expansions seen in the Neanderthals would have required at least a basic form of communication in order to function, which suggests to many researchers that Neanderthals spoke. The challenge with this line of research is that speech, itself, of course is not preserved, so indirect evidence must be used to support this conclusion. It is thought that Neanderthals would have possessed some basic speech, as evidenced from a variety of sources, including throat anatomy and genetic evidence. There is only one bone in the human body that could demonstrate if a hominin was able to speak, or produce clear vocalizations like modern humans, and that is the hyoid, a U-shaped bone that is found in the throat and is associated with the ability to precisely control the vocal cords. Very few hyoid bones have been found in the archaeological record; however, a few have been uncovered in Neanderthal burials. The shape of the Neanderthal hyoid is nearly identical to that of modern humans, pointing to the likelihood that they had the same vocal capabilities as modern humans. Genetic evidence has been debated concerning the likelihood of speech. Geneticists have uncovered a possible mutation, the FOXP2 gene, that has been linked to the ability to speak and that both modern humans and Neanderthals possess. However, some scientists counter those findings, indicating that the study's sample size was too small to make sweeping conclusions that the FOXP2 gene is what accounts for human or Neanderthal speech. Finally, scientists have also pointed to the increasingly complex cultural behavior of Neanderthals as a sign that symbolic communication, likely through speech, would have been the only way to pass down the skills needed to make, for example, a Levallois blade or to position a body correctly for intentional burial.

Neanderthal Intelligence

One of the enduring questions about Neanderthals centers on their intelligence, specifically in comparison to modern humans. Brain volume indicates that Neanderthals certainly had a large brain, but it continues to be debated if Neanderthals were of equal intelligence to modern humans. Brain volume, cultural complexity, tool use, and compassion toward their kind all point to an increase in intellect among Neanderthals when compared to previous hominins.

However, there have been several studies that seem to indicate that while Neanderthals did have a large brain volume and were far more advanced than their previous relatives, they may not have been nearly as intelligent as or may have even lacked the intellectual abilities possessed by modern humans. Euluned Pearce and colleagues, from the University of Oxford, noted that based on cranial endocasts, the frontal lobe of Neanderthals and modern humans are almost identical. However, Neanderthal faces and other cranial features were larger. Neanderthals possessed larger eye sockets, and the larger eyes they held would have helped Neanderthals see in the low light levels common for the latitudes at which they lived. Because of the larger eye sockets, the visual cortex—the portion of the brain involved in processing visual information—would have had to have been enlarged, as well. This would have left Neanderthals with less neural tissue for other components of the brain, including those that would have aided them in dealing with expansive social networks, one of the differences that it has been suggested existed between Neanderthals and modern humans.

New research is suggesting additional differences between Neanderthal brains and our own. Research being conducted by geneticist John Blangero and his team from the Texas Biomedical Research Institute are examining genes involved in certain diseases among modern populations. His team has also looked at brain structure and function. Comparing data from the Neanderthal genome against MRI data from his modern study participants, Blangero and his team discovered that some Neanderthal brain components were very different, and smaller, than those in the modern sample. These areas include decreased gray matter surface area, a smaller amygdala, and less white matter. These three regions are important in the processing of information and controlling emotion and motivation, as well as overall brain connectivity. In short, as Blangero stated at the annual meeting of the American Association of Physical Anthropologists in 2014, "Neanderthals were certainly cognitively adept," although their specific abilities may have differed from modern humans' in key areas (qtd. in Wong 2015), a point echoed in other recent genetic studies comparing Neanderthal and anatomically modern human brains (el-Showk 2019).

Finally, scientists are fairly certain that Neanderthal brain development after birth was not the same as that of modern humans. After birth, anatomically modern Homo sapiens babies go through a critical period of brain expansion and cognitive development. It appears that Neanderthal babies' brains did not follow the same developmental pattern. This could also be related to the length of the period of childhood. Modern humans enjoy an extended period of childhood, which, among many things, allows children to engage in imaginative play and develop creativity. Child development studies indicate that children who have extended, undirected play opportunities will be better off academically and socially later in life than their peers who had less play opportunities. Based on their anatomical developments, it appears that Neanderthals had a limited childhood. It has been suggested that this limited time for play and developing a creative mind might have limited adult creativity and how successful they were as a species, in the long run.

The exact nature of Neanderthal intelligence remains under investigation, however. Some studies disagree with the idea that Neanderthal intelligence had limitations compared to our own, noting that there is extensive evidence showing that Neanderthals displayed limb asymmetry. Their tools also have wear marks indicating that they were hand-dominant. It has been established that favoring the right hand is one key marker between modern humans and chimpanzees, and that handedness is likely also related to language development, in the form of bilateral brain development. That Neanderthals likely were hand-dominant as well suggests that they at least had many of the preconditions for human speech and likely experienced similar bilateral brain development to our own.

In addition to cut marks on animal bones, there are marks on Neanderthal teeth that demonstrate hand dominance. Neanderthal upper incisors, or front teeth, show not only wear from using their teeth when preparing hides or cordage but also cut marks that were created by using their teeth as a third limb when eating. The "stuff-and-cut method," noted by David Frayer, would have seen the Neanderthal hold a piece of meat in their teeth and pull it taut with one hand, and then, using their other hand, their dominant one, cut meat off the slab. When looking at 17 Neanderthals and their tooth wear, only two do not show markings made by a right-hand dominant individual. This research suggests another similarity between Neanderthal and modern human brains and their associated intelligence.

THE MIDDLE STONE AGE: NEANDERTHAL CONTEMPORARIES IN AFRICA

While Neanderthals made their home on and adapted to the European and Asian continents, evidence of fossil humans in Africa show they were also adapting to their local environments. These populations in Africa exhibit many more similarities to modern humans than Neanderthals, as well as overall evolutionary success. While the African fossil sample size is smaller and more fragmentary than the number of Neanderthal specimens across Europe and Asia, the African sample is interesting in that it represents a longer time period and larger geographical area. This group of fossils, often represented under the name of "Middle Stone Age," or MSA, dates to between 300,000 and 30,000 years ago across the entire continent of Africa. As with archaic Homo sapiens, there is much variability seen in this African set of fossils. There are also a few key consistent elements: none of them exhibit Neanderthal skeletal features; instead, they demonstrate features that are increasingly consistent with anatomically modern Homo sapiens.

Similarities to Neanderthals and MSA contemporaries in Africa are seen, however, in their behavioral adaptations, including stone tools and other cultural elements. The tools associated with the specimens living in Africa during this time period are, like their physical features, varied. In some parts of Africa, namely Northern Africa, stone tools from this time so closely resemble Neanderthal tools that they are classified as Mousterian. In sub-Saharan Africa, the stone tools associated with these specimens are labeled as Middle Stone Age, or MSA. Some scholars argue that these could also be a type of Mousterian tools, but they are still typically subdivided based on geographical location.

Recall that Mousterian tools were much more advanced than their Acheulean predecessors in terms of how the stone tools were manufactured, the quality of the stones used, and the ultimate use of the stone tools that were made. In addition, recent evidence suggests that MSA tools may also have been heat treated—to improve the quality of the stone tool produced. Evidence for heat treating is seen not only through advanced analysis of the tool itself but also through the residue of fires from this time period. Fire residues show a shift over time from small, short fires fueled by grasses (probably intended for cooking) to larger, more intensive fires that required the exploitation of dry wood, exactly the type of fire that would have been needed for heat treating stone tools.

Other cultural elements seen with specimens dating to the MSA include use of marine (sea-based) resources for their diet, manufacture of bone tools, use of adhesive and compound tools (e.g., hafted tools), shell bead production, engraving, use of pigments (such as ochre), and other more advanced tool-making technology (e.g., microlithics). While many of these cultural elements are also seen to a limited extent among Neanderthals, many of the developments at MSA sites are far more complex than what is demonstrated with Neanderthal sites. Several explanations have been posited to explain this expansion of cultural complexity. It has been suggested that MSA cultural expansion was a response to climate change. It has also been suggested that perhaps the MSA cultural expansion was due to an increased use of language, which triggered increased symbolic thought. Others have suggested that the cultural expansion of the MSA was due to the increase of marine resources in their diet, which included more fatty acids and may have aided their cognitive development. Still others have suggested that the increased cultural complexity was due to an increase in competition and interaction among groups, which spurred competition to innovate with increased cultural complexity. Recent studies suggest that perhaps the best explanation for the marked cultural complexity and diversity demonstrated by MSA cultural artifacts is best explained by the simple fact that they lived in diverse habitats. This would have necessitated a unique set of cultural adaptations for each habitat type (for example, specialized marine tools would have been needed along coastal sites but not at inland locations). Simply put, the most useful adaptation of MSA was their flexibility of behavior and adaptability to their local environment. As noted previously in this chapter, flexibility of behavior and physical traits, rather than specialization, seems to be a feature that was favored in hominin evolution at this time.

WHERE DID THEY GO? THE END OF NEANDERTHALS

While MSA were increasingly successful and ultimately transitioned into modern *Homo sapiens*, Neanderthals disappear from the fossil record by around 35,000 years ago. The main question that lingers, however, is what happened to them. We know, based on genetics, that modern humans come largely from the modern people who occupied Africa around 300,000 to 100,000 years ago, at the same time that Neanderthals were living in the icy portions of northern Europe and Asia. Modern humans expanded out of Africa around 60,000 to 40,000 years ago, rapidly entering areas of Europe and Asia inhabited by Neanderthals and likely other populations of archaic hominins. Despite intense interest and speculation in fictional works about possible interactions between these two groups, there is very little direct evidence of either peaceful coexistence or aggressive encounters. It is clear, though, that these two closely related hominins shared Europe for thousands of years, and recent DNA evidence suggests that they at least occasionally interbred. Geneticists have found traces of Neanderthal DNA (1% to 4%) in modern humans of European and Asian descent that is not present in modern humans from Africa. This is generally interpreted as indicating limited regional interbreeding with Neanderthals. Interestingly, while some studies suggest interbreeding was often problematic for their offspring, gene flow from Neanderthals may have benefited modern *Homo sapiens*. David Enard and Dmitri Petrov (2018) compared sequenced Neanderthal and modern human DNA, observing that the portions of Neanderthal DNA in modern humans of European descent seem to confer defense against viral pathogens that they would have been exposed to as they moved out of Africa.

While some interbreeding likely occurred, as a whole, Neanderthals did not survive. What is the cause for their extinction? This question has fascinated many researchers and several possibilities have been suggested that deserve some exploration. Possibilities include the following:

- The climate began changing considerably from the height of Neanderthal expansion. At the time that Neanderthals were disappearing from the fossil record, the climate went through both cooling and warming periods—each of which posed challenges for Neanderthal survival (Defleur and Desclaux 2019; Staubwasser et al. 2018). It has been argued that as temperatures warmed, large-bodied animals, well adapted to cold weather, moved farther north to find colder environments or face extinction themselves. A shifting resource base could have been problematic for continued Neanderthal existence, especially as additional humans, in the form of modern *Homo sapiens*, began to appear in Europe and were competing with them for a smaller pool of available resources.
- It has been suggested that the eruption of a European volcano 40,000 years ago could have put a strain on available plant resources (Golovanova et al. 2010). The eruption would have greatly affected local microclimates, reducing the overall temperature enough to alter the growing season.
- Possible differences in cognitive development may have limited Neanderthals in terms of their creative problem solving. It has been argued that as much as they were biologically specialized for their environment, the nature of their intelligence might not have offered them the creative problem solving skills to rethink their cultural adaptations and innovate ways to adapt their culture when faced with a changing environment (Pearce, Stringer, and Dunbar 2013).
- There is evidence that suggests reproduction may have posed challenges for Neanderthals. Childbirth was thought to have been at least as difficult for female Neanderthals as anatomically modern *Homo sapiens* (Weaver and Hublin 2009). Female Neanderthals may have become sexually mature at an older age, even older than modern humans. This delayed maturation could have kept the Neanderthal population size small. A recent study has further suggested that male Neanderthals might have had a genetic marker that would have had negative impacts on the longevity of the Neanderthal population (Mendez et al. 2016).
- We would be remiss if we did not point out that the end of Neanderthal existence also overlaps with modern human expansion into northern Europe and Asia. There is no conclusive direct evidence to indicate that Neanderthals and modern humans lived peacefully side by side, nor that they engaged in brutal warfare, but by studying modern societies and the tendencies of modern humans, it has been suggested that modern humans may not have warmly embraced their close but slightly odd-looking cousins when they first encountered them (Churchill et al. 2009). Competition for resources may have been the cause of the Neanderthals' decline (Gilpin, Feldman, and Aoki 2016). It is also completely possible that modern humans gave Neanderthals diseases to which they previously had little to no exposure, causing a mass population decline similar to what happened when the invading Spanish wiped out the Mayan and Aztec populations (Houldcroft and Underdown 2016). Estimates of energy expenditures suggest Neanderthals had slightly higher caloric needs than modern humans (Venner 2018). When competing for similar resources, the slightly greater efficiency of modern humans might have helped them experience greater success in the face of competition—at a cost to Neanderthals.
- Finally, less dramatically yet still significantly, even a small but continuous decrease in fertility would have been enough to result in the extinction of Neanderthals (Degioanni et al. 2019).

As Neanderthal populations were fairly small to begin with (estimated between 5,000 and 70,000 individuals) (Bocquet-Appel and Degioanni 2013), one or a combination of these factors could have easily led to their demise. As more research is conducted, we will likely get a better picture of exactly what led to Neanderthal extinction.

DENISOVANS

While Neanderthals represent one regionally adapted branch of the archaic *Homo sapiens* family tree, recent discoveries in Siberia and the Tibetan Plateau have surprised paleoanthropologists by revealing yet another population that was contemporary with archaic *Homo sapiens*, Neanderthals, and modern *Homo sapiens*. The genetic analysis of a child's finger bone and an adult upper third molar from Denisova Cave in the Altai Mountains in Siberia by a team including Svante Pääbo shocked even the researchers when they discovered that the mitochondrial and nuclear DNA sequences revealed distinct genetic differences from all known archaic populations. Dubbed "Denisovans" after the cave in which the bones were found, this population is more closely related to Neanderthals than modern humans, suggesting the two groups shared an ancestor who split from modern humans first, then the Neanderthal-Denisovan line diverged more recently.

Denisovans share up to 5% of their DNA with modern Melanesians, aboriginal Australians, and Polynesians, and 0.2% of their DNA with other modern Asian populations and Native Americans. Additional studies have suggested two separate instances of interbreeding between humans and Denisovans, whom researchers have yet to classify as a separate species, pending additional information.

Genetic analysis reveals that Denisovans potentially had at least three populations and had genetic adaptations for life at high altitudes, preventing them from developing altitude sickness and hypoxia. Recent publications also suggest that Denisovans shared these genetic adaptations with modern Tibetans through interbreeding 30,000 to 40,000 years ago. Stone tools similar to those found in Siberia have also been found in the Tibetan plateau, suggesting the possibility that Denisovans could have inhabited this extreme environment where the average annual temperature is close to 0°C and the altitude is more than a kilometer (about 4,000 feet) above sea level. Research continues on this population and other archaic populations in the hopes of discovering more DNA evidence that can confirm current hypotheses and clarify our understanding of the complex interactions of archaic groups.

To stay up to date with new discoveries, consider following organizations such as the Smithsonian's Human Origins Program on social media (https://www.facebook.com/smithsonian.humanorigins/).

MODELS OF MODERN HUMAN DISTRIBUTION

There has been much debate in anthropological circles concerning the origin of modern humans and their relationship with other hominin populations. Three competing models have been developed and seek to explain the fossil evidence and what it indicates for modeling human origins.

The first model, the Out-of-Africa Hypothesis, states that modern humans originated in Africa, replacing archaic populations found elsewhere in the Old World. Theorists including Christopher Stringer (1996) argue that each archaic population comprised a separate species, making interbreeding between populations impossible. Admixture resulting from gene flow would not have been possible according to this model.

The second, called the Multiregional Continuity Hypothesis, states that modern *Homo sapiens* are directly derived from *Homo erectus* and evolved in place after *Homo erectus* left Africa and populated areas in Asia and Europe. Milford Wolpoff argues that interbreeding between regions and across regional boundaries contributed to gene flow that maintained *Homo sapiens* as a single species throughout the Old World, despite regional variation.

The third model, dubbed the Assimilation Hypothesis, draws from the strengths of both previous models, attempting to recognize some of the evidence that was not previously addressed and blending the fossil and DNA evidence together into one cohesive view. In this model, modern humans originated in Africa, spreading outward into Asia and Europe and interbreeding with more archaic forms they encountered along the way. For example, while the Out-of-Africa model argues that interbreeding would have been impossible, many fossils have been found with what appear to be a mixture of archaic and more modern traits, suggesting interbreeding between populations, such as Neanderthals and modern humans. DNA evidence increasingly also suggests that, while limited, interbreeding between modern *Homo sapiens* and Neanderthals or modern *Homo sapiens* and Denisovans occured in at least three instances. While this is more interbreeding than allowed under the Out-of-Africa Hypothesis, it is considerably less than modeled in the Multiregional Continuity Hypothesis. The Assimilation Hypothesis, argued by Eric Trinkaus (2006, 2007) and others, represents an attempt to incorporate all lines of evidence, although new research will tell whether it can capture the full complexity revealed in the next generation of hominin studies, such as that revealed by ancient DNA.

SPECIAL TOPIC: ANCIENT DNA

Robyn Humphries, MSc., University of Cape Town

hmprob005@myuct.ac.za

Ancient DNA has provided us with new insights into our evolutionary history that cannot be garnered from the fossil record. It has also assisted with the discovery of the new hominin species the Denisovans, for which little fossil evidence is available. It has helped us better understand the evolution of Neanderthals, Denisovans, and modern humans. Through genomic data and the use of population genetics, we have been able to make some inferences about Neanderthal and Denisovan population structure and relationships within these populations as well as between different groups of hominins. It has also helped to answer some very important questions about what happened when modern humans migrated out of Africa and encountered these European/Asian hominins. Two theories dominated the debate regarding the evolution of modern humans: the multiregional theory and the Out-of-Africa theory. Though it was clear–based on a plethora of evidence–that modern humans evolved in Africa, what happened when our ancestors migrated out of Africa was still questioned. Ancient DNA (aDNA) helped answer this question, indicating that modern humans interacted with other archaic hominins such as Neanderthals and Denisovans. We will discuss all the above in this section.

Sequencing Ancient Genomes

The first successful sequencing of aDNA from an archaic hominin took place in 1997 with the sequencing of mitochondrial DNA (mtDNA) from the Neanderthal-type specimen from Feldhofer Cave. Sequencing of a portion of the mitochondrial genome provided molecular evidence that Neanderthals belonged in a clade separate from modern humans and that they were four times more different from modern humans than modern humans were from each other based on mtDNA data. mtDNA is ideal for sequencing from fossil material because of the abundance of mtDNA when compared to nuclear DNA.

Sequencing of nuclear DNA would not occur until more than ten years later. The first nuclear genomic sequence representing Neanderthals was produced by sequencing three individuals and using their sequences to create a composite draft Neanderthal genome in 2010. The first high-coverage sequence of a single Neanderthal was that of a female Neanderthal who lived in Siberia, which was published in 2014, followed by another high-coverage sequence from a female Neanderthal whose remains were found in the

Vidja cave in Croatia, which was published in 2017. **High-coverage sequences** are produced when the genome has been sequenced multiple times. This is to ensure that the sequences obtained are a true reflection of the genomic sequence and not due to errors that occur during the process of sequencing. If you have many sequences from the same region and there is one sequence that has a slight difference while the other copies are all the same, it is easier to identify the variant as an error.

Collecting and Sequencing aDNA

Ancient DNA can be collected from many different sources including soft tissue such as skin and muscle, hair, paleo feces, soils, and sediments. However, in the case of ancient hominins, they are often collected from bone and teeth. When collecting aDNA, usually around 100 mg to 500 mg of bone powder needs to be collected. Because extraction of aDNA requires destruction of part of the bone, and the morphology of the skeletal element might be informative, care needs to be taken when deciding which part of the bone is sampled. It is advised that multiple samples be taken so that sequencing is repeated to show reproducibility of results. Contamination is an important consideration when it comes to sequencing aDNA; thus, it is best that samples that are used had minimal handling before extraction of DNA.

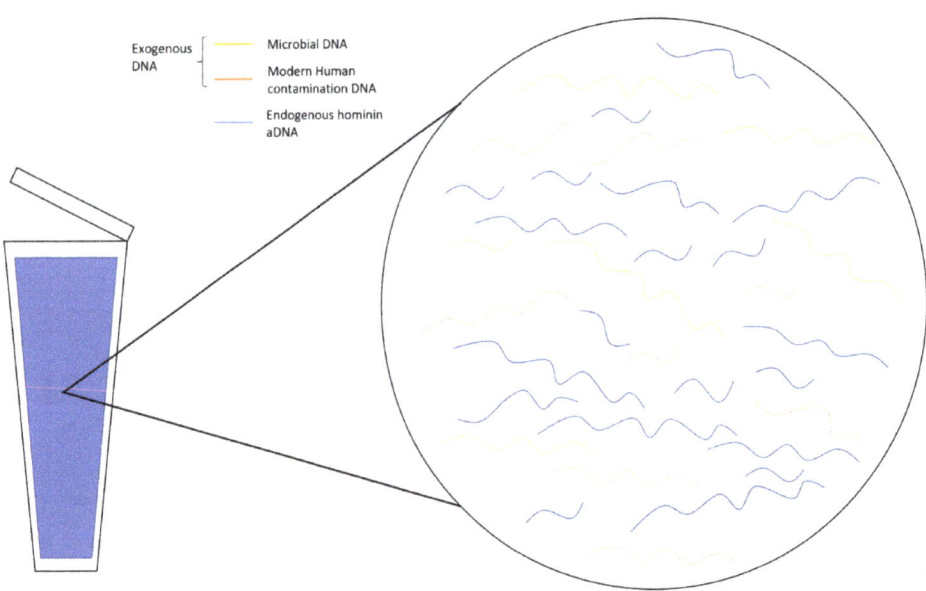

Figure 11.12 An illustration of the different types of DNA you may find after DNA extraction is performed on bone or other samples.

It has taken a lot of time and much trial and error to sequence these ancient genomes because of the fragility of DNA. When sequencing ancient DNA, it is important to consider that aDNA sequences are usually short due to degradation, there are very few copies of the **endogenous aDNA**. Endogenous aDNA is the DNA that comes from the bone and was present in the tissue before decomposition of the body and before the introduction of DNA from other sources, such as microbes or contamination from modern humans, which is known as **exogenous DNA** (Figure 11.12).

There are also modifications that occur to aDNA that are a result of chemical reactions known as deamination. **Deamination** results in Cytosine (C) to Thymine (T) conversions, which are mostly at the 5' end **(5 prime end)** of the DNA fragment. This in turn results in Guanine (G) to Adenine (A) substitutions on the 3' end **(3 prime end)** of the DNA fragment. Thus, there are sequence changes in aDNA that might not reflect the original hominin sequence. These changes can be helpful when differentiating between aDNA and modern human DNA contamination. The environment in which the DNA is preserved also plays a significant role. DNA preserves well in cold conditions such as permafrost, which extends the lifespan of DNA significantly. aDNA has also been recovered from material found in drier environments under special conditions. Factors such as water percolation, salinity, pH, and microbial growth all affect the preservation of aDNA.

In extraction of DNA from modern samples where DNA is still intact, the DNA strands are usually long and this is ideal for sequencing. However, aDNA samples are often composed of small fragments of DNA, usually 100 bp to 300 bp long. Initially this posed a big problem with usual PCR procedures used to sequence DNA. This changed with the advent of high throughput sequencing, which has revolutionized sequencing the genomes of ancient hominins. High throughput sequencing allows for the parallel sequencing of many fragments of DNA in one reaction. It also doesn't require any knowledge of the target sequence. Thus, we can sequence as much of the available aDNA as possible. Because the high throughput sequencing method does not discriminate between endogenous aDNA from hominins and contamination from modern humans and microbial DNA, it is important to either ensure that there is as little contamination as possible or create methods that allow for differentiation between modern human sequences and ancient hominin sequences. Both methods have been used when sequencing hominin aDNA.

The Discovery of the Denisovans

The Denisovans are named after the cave in which they were discovered, the Denisovan Cave in the Altai Region of Siberia. Denisovans were initially identified as a distinct group based on analysis of mtDNA sequences indicating that they had haplotypes outside the range of variation of modern humans and Neanderthals. A **haplotype** is a set of genetic variants located on a single stretch of the genome. This unique combination of variants on a stretch of the genome can be used to differentiate groups who will have different combinations of variants. Some haplotypes may be more similar to one another. The more similar two haplotypes are, the more closely related they are. Dubbed lineage X, the mtDNA sequence showed that Denisovans diverged from modern humans and Neanderthals at around 1 million years ago (mya). The subsequent high-coverage sequence of a Denisovan 3 nuclear genome showed that Denisovans are a sister group to Neanderthals and thus more closely related than indicated by the mtDNA data.

The mtDNA and nuclear DNA provided conflicting data regarding the relationships between Denisovans and Neanderthals. Because mtDNA and nuclear DNA have different patterns of inheritance, they can paint different pictures about the relationships between two groups when used to construct phylogenies. The Denisovans are thought to have a mtDNA sequence that is derived from an ancient hominin group that hybridized with Denisovans and introduced the mtDNA sequence.

Sequences are also available for three other Denisovans, Denisovan 2, 4, and 8. aDNA sequences have been used to estimate the ages of the Denisovans. Using a combination of usual dating methods (such as radio carbon dating and uranium dating) as well as genetic data, it has been determined that Denisovans occupied the Denisovan cave from around 195 kya to 52 kya to 76 kya. DNA can assist with dating because younger sequences will have accumulated more sequence changes from the putative common ancestral sequence than older samples. This is because younger sequences would have had more time over which changes to the DNA sequence through mutation could occur. Thus, it is possible to conclude based on sequence data that Denisovan 2 is 54.2 kya to 99.4 kya older than Denisovan 3 and 20.6 kya to 37.7 kya older than Denisovan 8. Molecular data indicates that Neanderthals and Denisovans separated between 381 kya and 473 kya and that the branch leading to Denisovans and modern humans diverged around 800 kya. Denisovans are also more closely related to another set of fossils found in the cave Sima de los Huesos dated to 480 kya. Thus, the split between Neanderthals and Denisovans must have occurred before 480 kya.

What Can We Learn about Population Structure of the Neanderthals and Denisovans from aDNA

Ancient DNA has helped us understand the demographics of Neanderthals and Denisovans and make inferences about population size and history. The genomic data from Neanderthals indicates that their population was small toward the end of their existence. This is supported by three lines of evidence.

The first is by using **coalescent** methods. This is the process used to determine which population dynamics in the past are most likely to give rise to the genetic sequences we have, allowing us to use genetic sequences to estimate population genetic parameters in the past. It can be used to understand recombination, population subdivision, and variable population size.

The second indicator that Neanderthals and Denisovans had smaller population size is that these groups carried many deleterious genomic variants. Genomic variants are considered deleterious when they are found in protein-coding regions of the genome and the change in genomic sequence translates to a change in amino acid sequence of the protein. Changes in amino acid at a certain section in the protein could affect the functioning of the protein—these types of changes in genomic sequence are known as non-synonymous mutations. **Synonymous mutations** also occur in protein-coding regions of the genome, but the amino acid sequence does not change because of changes in the genomic sequence. Changes in amino acid and subsequent protein sequence can change the protein function and thus are more likely to be deleterious and weeded out by natural selection. The ratio of synonymous to **non-synonymous mutations** can give you an indicator of whether there are more deleterious variants than expected. Denisovans and Neanderthals have a higher ratio of non-synonymous to synonymous mutations when compared to contemporary modern human populations. This is an indicator of a small population size, because if the population were larger, natural selection would have acted on these deleterious variants and weeded them out.

A third indicator of small population size is that the Neanderthals sequenced thus far have low levels of **heterozygosity**, a measure of how many genes within a genome are made up of more than one variant. Each individual has two copies of the same gene: one is inherited from their mother and the other from their father. Variations of the same gene are known as **alleles**, which are versions of the same gene with h different sequences. If the alleles inherited from both parents are the same, the individual is homozygous for that gene;

if the alleles inherited are different, the individual is heterozygous for that gene. Heterozygosity is measured by looking at how many times you happen to find two different alleles within a certain stretch of DNA. When you find many regions on the genome with different alleles, there is a high level of heterozygosity. When you find very few positions where there are two different alleles, this results in a low level of heterozygosity.

Ancient Neanderthal genomes also revealed that there were consanguineous relations between Neanderthals. One Neanderthal female is thought to be the offspring of relations between either half-siblings, an uncle/aunt and niece/nephew, or a grandfather/grandmother and grandson/granddaughter. This was determined by looking at the stretches of **homozygosity** in her genome that were longer than expected and could not be explained by small population size alone.

Denisovans also had low levels of heterozygosity indicating a smaller population size. However, there is no indication yet of inbreeding among the Denisovans, as none of the individuals sequenced thus far show long stretches of homozygosity. Thus, both Denisovans and Neanderthals had small populations size and low levels of genetic diversity when compared to modern humans.

How Sequencing Archaic Genomes Can Help Understand Our Own Unique Evolutionary Trajectory as Modern Humans

Not only did the sequencing of archaic genomes allow us to learn more about Neanderthals and Denisovans, it gave us important insights into our own evolution. Previously the human genome could only be compared to our closest living relatives, the great apes, which helped us identify unique derived genomic changes that occurred in humans since our split from the last common ancestor between chimps and humans. Neanderthal and Denisovan genomes provided another set of comparative samples that could help us identify changes that were unique to modern humans occurring after our split from the last common ancestor with Neanderthals/Denisovans. We now have an opportunity to identify genetic variants that may have contributed to our success as a species.

Hybridization between Hominin Groups

Ultimately aDNA provides us with great insight into interactions between modern humans migrating out of Africa and other hominins that evolved in Europe and Asia. There was speculation that hybridization occurred due to the intermediate morphology of some fossil remains. The following hypothesis was tested: if hybridization between modern humans and Neanderthals occurred, Neanderthals would have more shared genomic variants with some modern human populations than with others. If this was true, hybridization between Neanderthals and humans happened. This comparison showed that Neanderthals shared more genomic variants with Europeans and Asians than with the African individuals. This difference in relatedness was significant. This indicated that there had been hybridization between Neanderthals and modern humans.

From the genetic data, we know that different groups have different amounts of Neanderthal and Denisovan contributions. For example, Europeans have a smaller proportion of Neanderthal-derived genes than East Asians. Thus, there was more admixture into ancestral East Asian populations than into ancestral European populations. This is unexpected because Neanderthals fossils are mostly found in West Asia and Europe. Oceanians (Melanesians, Australian aborigines, and other Southeast Asian islanders) have a higher proportion of their DNA derived from Denisovans. These populations also have longer stretches of Denisovan DNA. Since DNA in chromosomes get exchanged and "break apart" between each generation (in the process known as genetic recombination), this implies that the admixture event between the Denisovan and human ancestors of these populations is more recent than the admixture events between Neanderthals and modern humans. Genomic recombination breaks down introgressed regions (inherited from different species or taxon) into smaller segments in every successive generation, thus longer stretches of introgressed DNA indicates that hybridization occurred more recently.

Initially, some researchers believed that populations outside of Africa had higher proportions of Neanderthal DNA due to population substructure, which existed in the ancestral population before the split between modern humans and Neanderthals. According to these researchers, Eurasian populations retained these ancient sequences by chance, through genetic drift. These would be shared derived genomic sequences between Neanderthals and modern humans outside of Africa. However, studies of the shared regions indicate that these genomic regions are most likely the result of introgression, which is the transfer of genetic information from one species to another because of hybridization between them and repeated backcrossing.

Divergence time is important for determining whether shared sequences are a result of introgression or more ancient substructure. **Divergence time** is a measure of how long two sequences have been changing independently. It is measured by looking at how many differences there are between the two sequences. The longer the two sequences have been changing independently, the more differences they will accumulate, which will result in a longer divergence time. By measuring the divergence time between the introgressed regions in modern human genomes and the Neanderthal sequences, researchers can calculate that the shared sequences are recent as well as date to when the two taxa made secondary contact. This is also well after the initial population split between modern humans and Neanderthals occurred. If they were shared derived genomic sequences, then we would expect longer divergence times between the introgressed Neanderthal genomic sequences in modern humans and the Neanderthal genome. Hybridization has occurred between hominins at different times over the last 100 kya as shown in Figure 11.14.

The Neanderthal and Denisovan genomes would provide definitive proof that there was interaction and interbreeding between humans, Neanderthals, and Denisovans around 44 to 55 kya, with data suggesting that there was an admixture event as far back as 100 kya. There has been gene flow from Neanderthals and Denisovans into modern human populations, between Neanderthals and Denisovans, and from modern humans into Neanderthals.

Because of the climate in Africa, it has been difficult or impossible due to fossilization to extract aDNA from African fossil remains. However, analysis of genomes of modern African populations indicate that there was admixture between modern humans and other hominins within Africa (Figure 11.13). Thus, hybridization is an important part of human evolution and has affected our evolution within and outside of Africa.

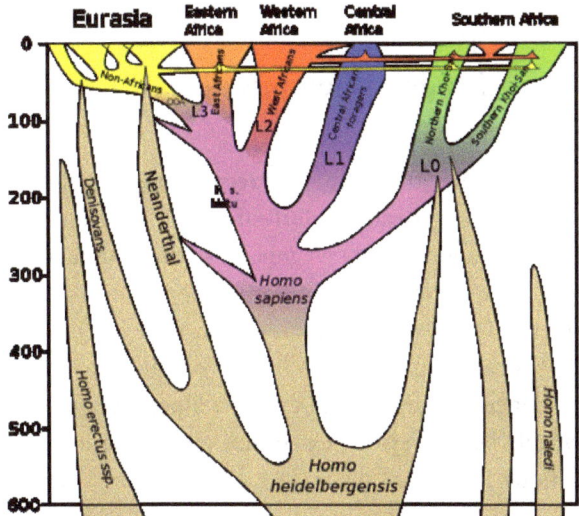

Figure 11.13: Phylogeny showing the relationship between modern humans and other hominins over the last 500 kya. This image is also depicting a number of hybridization events—for example, the genetic contributions that Neanderthals and Denisovans made to modern humans around 50 kya.

The oldest modern human that has been sequenced Ust'-Ishim is from Europe and is dated to around 49 kya. He had a similar amount of Neanderthal-derived genes as modern humans from outside of Africa. Analysis of the genome indicated that the hybridization event resulting in the introgression occurred 50 ky before. The fact that the Ust'-Ishim modern human had longer tracts of Neanderthal-derived DNA than contemporary populations lends support to the idea that Neanderthal-derived DNA in modern humans is due to hybridization. Contemporary modern humans have shorter stretches of Neanderthal-derived genes because there has been a longer period over which the Neanderthal segments of DNA could be broken down by **recombination.**

Thus, there are multiple lines of evidence supporting hybridization between modern humans and Neanderthals/Denisovans. This includes shorter divergence times between introgressed regions in modern-human and Neanderthal sequences, older modern-human sequences having longer tracts of Neanderthal-derived genes and, as discussed below, the sequencing of confirmed hybrids.

Confirmed Fossil Hybrids

When discussing hybrids, there are some important terms to understand. A first-generation hybrid is called an F1 hybrid; it is the direct offspring of two lineages that have been evolving independently over an extended period. A second-generation hybrid (F2) would be the offspring of two F1 hybrids. A backcrossed individual is the result of an F1 or F2 hybrid mating with an individual from one of the parental populations. An example of a backcross would be when a Neanderthal-human hybrid produces offspring with a human; their offspring would be considered a first-generation backcrossed hybrid (B1). Sequencing of aDNA from fossil material has further confirmed that hybridization between different hominins has occurred, supporting the introgression data from recent populations.

The sequencing of Oase 1, a suspected hybrid based on skeletal morphology (what the fossil looked like), showed that it had a Neanderthal ancestor as recently as six to eight generations back. He would thus be considered a backcrossed individual. The recent sequencing of a 13-year-old Denisovan female showed that she was the F1 hybrid offspring of a Neanderthal mother (from whom she inherited Neanderthal mtDNA) and a Denisovan father. She was confirmed to be an F1 hybrid because approximately 50% of her genome was derived from a Neanderthal and 50% from a Denisovan.

These are only two examples of individuals who are confirmed hybrids. Many other remains show some indication of gene flow between hominins.

Neanderthal- and Denisovan-Derived DNA in Modern Genomes

There is variation in how much of the Neanderthal genome is represented in the modern human population. Individuals outside of Africa usually have 1% to 2 % of their genome derived from Neanderthals. Approximately 30% of the Neanderthal genome is represented in modern human genomes. Asian populations usually have a higher proportion of their genome derived from Neanderthals when compared to modern European populations. Additionally, the sequencing of the Denisovan genome indicates that they interacted with the ancestors of modern Oceanic populations. Thus, oceanic populations have around 5% to 6% of their genome derived from Denisovans. There is also evidence that different Denisovans populations may have contributed to Oceanians and East Asians. The available Denisovan sequences are more similar to the Denisovan introgressed genes found in East Asian populations.

Introgressed genes have signatures that allow us to identify them and differentiate them from parts of the genome that are not introgressed. Some of the things to look for when determining if a segment of the genome is introgressed include the following. First, how closely does the segment you are looking at match the Neanderthal/Denisovan sequence compared to contemporary modern human sequences from Africa? If the sequence is more similar to the Neanderthal sequence (i.e., it has less sequence differences from the Neanderthal than the African modern human), it is likely that it is derived from a Neanderthal). Second, what is the divergence time between the allele and the same allele in a Neanderthal? If it is shorter than the divergence time between humans and Neanderthal, then the gene is most likely introgressed. This is expected because if the divergence time is after the split between modern humans and Neanderthals, the most likely explanation for a shorter divergence time is introgression. An example of this can be seen in Figure 11.14. And, third and finally, you need to look at whether the allele is found at higher frequencies in populations outside of Africa.

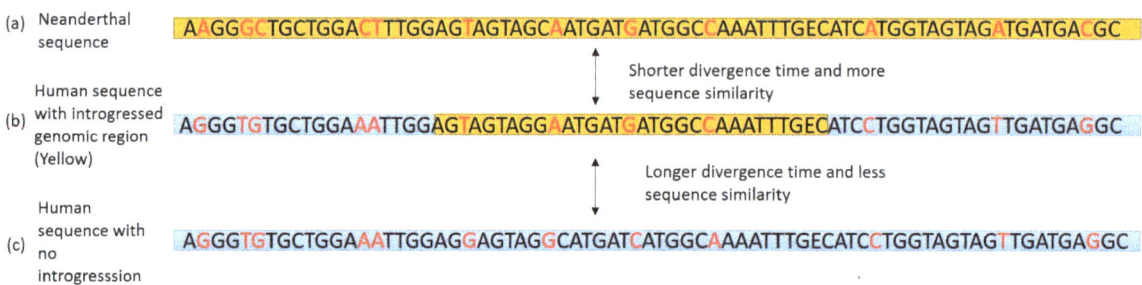

Figure 11.14 An illustration of a (b) introgressed region (in yellow) in a modern human genome and how it compares to the same segment in a (c) modern human with no introgression and an (a) Neanderthal sequence.

What Can We Learn about the Process of Hybridization from Ancient DNA?

Ancient DNA has also allowed us to make certain inferences about the process of hybridization between modern humans and Neanderthals/Denisovans. From looking at the genomes of modern humans, we can see that there are regions of the genome with no Neanderthal and Denisovan genomic variants. These are known as Neanderthal or Denisovan introgression deserts. There are also overlaps between regions in the human genome that are Neanderthal and Denisovan deserts, which might indicate that there were genomic incompatibilities between modern humans and these groups, resulting in those genes being selected against on the modern human genome background. This resulted in strong negative selection against these genomic variants in subsequent generations of hybrids and backcrossed individuals.

We can also infer that hybridization may itself have been a barrier to gene flow because there is a significant reduction in introgression on the X chromosome compared to the other chromosomes. There is also a reduction of introgressed genes around genes that are disproportionately expressed in the testes when compared to other tissue groups. This could indicate that hybridization between modern humans and Neanderthals may have resulted in male hybrid infertility.

Hybridization and Modern Human Evolution

Hybridization provided adaptive advantage to modern humans migrating out of Africa by providing them with advantages in genetic variation. Neanderthals and Denisovans had spent hundreds of thousands of years adapting to the European and Asian environments and thus had genetic variants favorable for inhabiting those regions. Through hybridization, humans were able to acquire favorable genomic variants already selected for, and these variants could rapidly spread through the population. This allowed for faster adaptation because acquiring new variation through mutation alone is much slower and less likely to spread through the population. Some of the adaptive genes that were important include genes associated with immunity, adapting to new diets, adapting to new altitudes as well as genes involved in skin color and hair traits were introgressed. An excellent example of this would be a variant of the EPAS1 gene found at high frequencies in Tibetans, thought to be important for living at high altitudes. This variant of EPAS1 has been shown to be an introgressed gene from Denisovans.

The Future of Genetic Studies

We are continuing to learn how introgressed genes affect modern humans. Combining phenotypic and genetic information Neanderthal derived genes have been associated with diverse traits such as the skin's sensitivity to the sun to excessive blood clotting by certain individuals. Interesting research has also shown that introgressed alleles might produce different gene expression profiles when compared to non-introgressed alleles. However, there is a lot of research that needs to be done to fully understand the effects of introgression on modern populations and how it might have assisted modern humans who migrated out of Africa.

It has also been possible to extract DNA from sediments. However, extractions from sediments will result in extraction of DNA from multiple organisms. To extract the hominin sequences, we will need to use the known sequence information. Known sequences will also assist with differentiating between which hominins are represented in the sediment. This could assist with identifying changes in populations across time. The

> availability of more Neanderthal and Denisovan samples will also help us understand which genetic changes were fixed and defined these populations.

HOW DO THESE FIT IN? *HOMO NALEDI* AND *HOMO FLORESIENSIS*

Relatively recently, some fossils have been unearthed that have significantly challenged our understanding of the hominin lineage. The fossils of *Homo naledi* and *Homo floresiensis* are significant for several reasons but are mostly known for how they don't fit the previously held patterns of hominin evolution. We'll examine present information about both of these fossils, and we ask that you consider the wealth of evidence presented in this chapter and in others to draw your own conclusions regarding the significance and placement of these two unusual fossil species in the hominin lineage.

Homo naledi

Found in 2013 by recreational spelunkers, a collection of bones was uncovered in a deep cave network in Johannesburg, South Africa. The cave system, known as Rising Star, had been well documented by other cavers; however, it appears few people had ever gone as far into the cave as these spelunkers had. Lee Berger, paleoanthropologist at University of Witwatersrand, in Johannesburg, immediately put out a call for what he termed "underground astronauts" to begin recovery and excavation of the fossil materials. Unlike other excavations, Berger and most other paleoanthropologists would not be able to access the site, as it was incredibly difficult to reach, and at some points there was only eight inches of space through which to navigate. The underground astronauts, all petite, slender female anthropologists, were the only ones who were able to access this remarkable site. Armed with small excavation tools and a video camera, which streamed the footage up to the surface, the team worked together and uncovered a total of 1,550 bones, representing at least 15 individuals, as seen in Figure 11.15. Later, an additional 131 bones, including an almost-complete cranium, were found in a nearby chamber of the cave, representing three more individuals (Figure 11.16). Berger called in a team of specialists to participate in what was dubbed "Paleoanthropology Summer Camp." Each researcher specialized in a different portion of the hominin skeleton. With various specialists working simultaneously, more rapid analysis was possible of *Homo naledi* than most fossil discoveries.

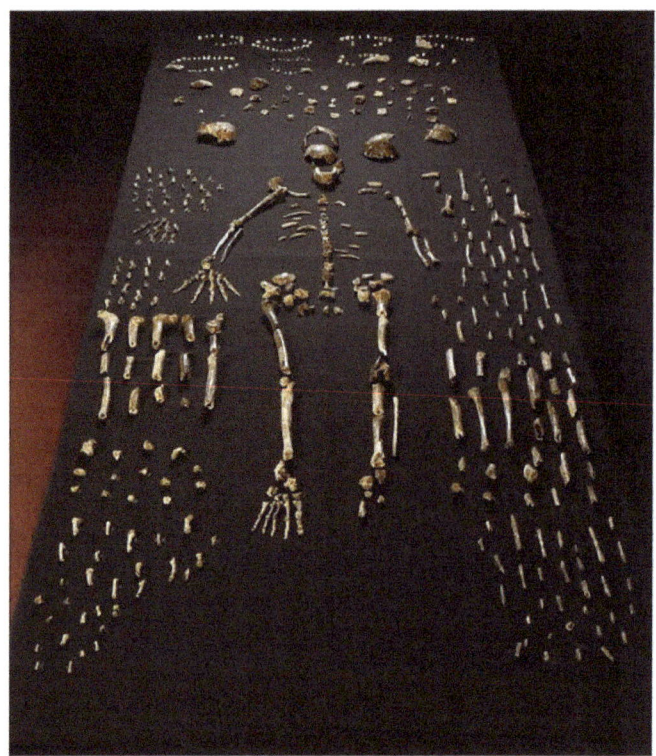

Figure 11.15 A sample of some of the 1,550 bones found representing Homo naledi.

The features of *Homo naledi* are well-documented due to the fairly large sample, which represents individuals of all sexes and a wide range of ages. The skull shape and features are very much like other members of the genus *Homo*, including features such as a sagittal keel and large brow, like *Homo erectus*, and a well-developed frontal lobe, similar to modern humans, yet the brain size is significantly smaller than its counterparts, at approximately 500 cc (560 cc for males and 465 cc for females). The teeth also exhibit features of later members of the genus *Homo*, such as Neanderthals, including a reduction in overall tooth size. *Homo naledi* also had unique shoulder anatomy and curved fingers, indicating similarities to tree-dwelling primates, which is very different from any other hominin yet found. The date on the species, which was obtained some time after the fossils were first analyzed, indicates that *Homo naledi* lived between 335,000 and 236,000 years ago. This has been perhaps the greatest shock of all about *Homo naledi*, as this places this fossil as a contemporary to modern *Homo sapiens*, despite the very primitive features it retains.

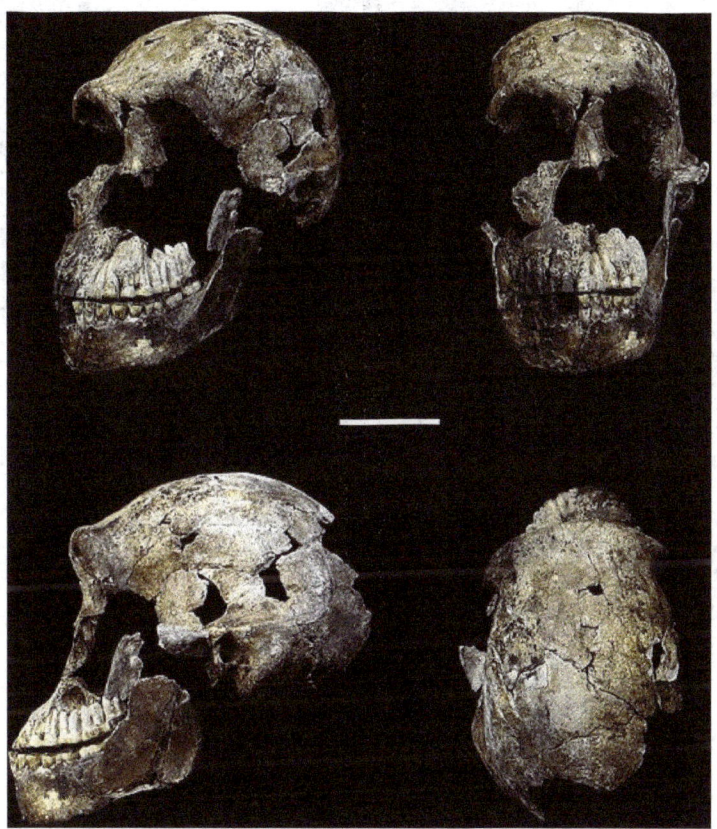

Figure 11.16 Several angles of the nearly complete LES1 Homo naledi skull. The skull shape and features are very much like other members of the genus Homo, including features such as a sagittal keel and large brow like Homo erectus and a well-developed frontal lobe, similar to modern humans. The brain size, however, is significantly smaller than its counterparts, at approximately 500 cc.

Other remarkable aspects of the find is the placement of the *Homo naledi* fossils and what it may suggest. To access the site, approximately 80 m from any known cave entrance or opening, a treacherous route would have had to have been taken—including moving through a portion that is just 25 cm wide at some points, known as "Superman's Crawl." The only way to get through this section is by crawling on your stomach with one arm by your side and the other raised above your head. Past Superman's Crawl, a jagged wall known as the Dragon's Back would have been very difficult to traverse. Below that, a narrow vertical chute would have eventually led down to the area where the fossils were discovered. While geology changes over time and the cave system likely has undergone its fair share, it is not likely that these difficult features arose after *Homo naledi* lived. This has made scientists curious as to how the bones ended up in the bottom of the cave system in the first place. It has been suggested that *Homo naledi* deposited the bones there, one way or another. Another competing idea is that a few individuals may have entered the cave system to escape a predator and then got stuck. To account for the sheer number of fossils, this would have had to happen multiple times. In contrast, if *Homo naledi* did deposit the bones, either through random disposal or intentional burial, this calls into question their symbolic behavior and other cultural traits, including the use of fire, to access a very dark cave system.

Homo floresiensis

Figure 11.17 Liang Bua Cave on the island of Flores, in Indonesia, where a collection of Homo floresiensis specimens were discovered.

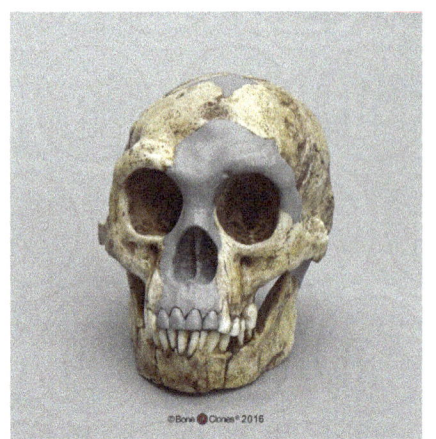

Figure 11.18 Homo floresiensis had a brain that was remarkably small at 400 cc. Recent genetic studies suggest a common ancestor with modern humans that predates Homo erectus.

In a small cave called Liang Bua, on the island of Flores, in Indonesia, a small collection of fossils were discovered beginning in 2003 (Figure 11.17). The fossil fragments represent as many as nine individuals, including a nearly complete female skeleton. The features of the skull are very similar to that of *Homo erectus*, including the presence of a sagittal keel, an arching brow ridges and nuchal torus, and the lack of a chin (Figure 11.18). *Homo floresiensis*, as the new species is called, had a brain size that was remarkably small at 400 cc, and recent genetic studies suggest a common ancestor with modern humans that predates *Homo erectus*.

The complete female skeleton, who was an adult, was approximately a meter tall and would have weighed just under 30 kg, which is significantly shorter and just a few kilograms more than the average, modern young elementary-aged child. A reconstructed comparison between an anatomically modern human and *Homo floresiensis* can be seen in Figure 11.19. The small size of the fossil has earned the species the nickname "the Hobbit." Many questions have been asked about the stature of this species, as all of the specimens found also show evidence of diminutive stature and small brain size. Some explanations include pathology; however, this seems increasingly unlikely as all fossils found thus far demonstrate the same pattern. Another possible explanation lies in a biological phenomena seen in other animal species also found on the island and which date to a similar time period. This phenomenon, called **insular dwarfing**, is due to limited food resources on an island, which can create a selective pressure for large-bodied species to be selected for smaller size, as an island would not have been able to support their larger-bodied cousins for a long period of time. This phenomenon is the cause of other unique species known to have lived on the island at the same time, including the miniature stegadon, a dwarf elephant species.

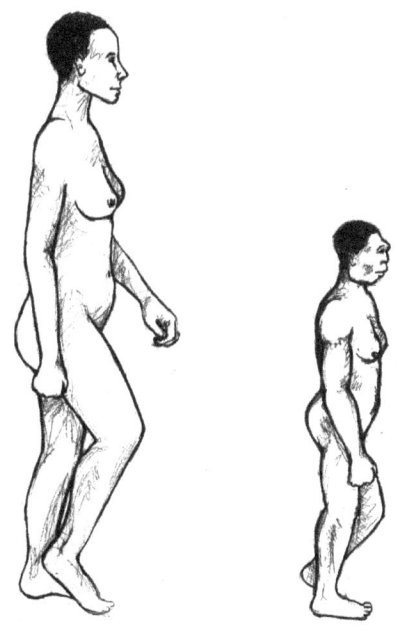

Figure 11.19 A reconstructed comparison between an anatomically modern human and Homo floresiensis. As an adult, Homo floresiensis was approximately 1 meter tall and would have weighed under 30 kg.

Homo floresiensis fossils have been dated to have lived on the island between 100,000 and at least 60,000 years ago. There is ongoing research and debate regarding *Homo floresiensis*' dates of existence, with some researchers concluding that they lived on Flores until perhaps as recently as 17,000 years ago. Stone tools were also uncovered that have dates overlapping with those of the site and are similar in nature to other hominin stone tools found on the island of Flores. *Homo floresiensis* would have hunted a wide range of animals, including the miniature stegadon, giant rats, and other large rodents. Other animals on the island that could have threatened them include the giant komodo dragon. An interesting note about this island chain is that ancestors of *Homo floresiensis* would have had to access the open ocean in order to get there, as the nearest island is almost 10 km away, and there is little evidence to support that a land bridge connecting mainland Asia or Australia to the island would have been present. This would also have limited the number of other animals, including predators as well as human species, that would have had access to the island. Anatomically modern *Homo sapiens* arrived on the island around 30,000 years ago and may have lived there at the same time as *Homo floresiensis*, if some researchers' later dates for *Homo floresiensis*' occupation are correct. The modern population living on the island of Flores today believes that their ancestors came from the Liang Bua cave; however, recent genetic studies have determined they are not related to the *Homo floresiensis* species.

Homo naledi and *Homo floresiensis* are clear outliers when compared to their contemporary hominin species. Each has surprised paleoanthropologists for both their archaic traits in relatively modern times and their unique combination of traits seen in archaic species and modern species of humans. While these finds have been exciting, they have also completely upended the assumed trajectory of the human lineage, causing scientists to re-examine their previously held assumptions about hominin evolution and what it means to be modern. Add this to the developments being made using ancient DNA, other new fossil discoveries, and other innovations in paleoanthropology, and you see that our understanding of archaic *Homo sapiens* and others living during this time period is rapidly developing and changing. This is a true testament to the nature of science and the scientific method!

FOSSIL SPECIES SUMMARIES

Hominin	archaic *Homo sapiens*
Dates	600,000–200,000 years ago (although some regional variation)
Region(s)	Africa, Europe, and Asia
Famous discoveries	Broken Hill (Zambia), Atapuerca (Spain)
Brain size	1,200 cc average
Dentition	Slightly smaller teeth in back of mouth, larger front teeth
Cranial features	Emerging forehead, wide nasal aperture, midfacial prognathism, no chin, projecting occipital region
Postcranial features	Robust skeleton
Culture	Varied regionally, but some continue to use Acheulean handaxe, others adopt Mousterian tool culture
Other	Lots of regional variation in this species

Hominin	Neanderthals
Dates	150,000–35,000 years ago
Region(s)	Western Europe, Middle East, and Western Asia only
Famous discoveries	Shanindar (Iraq), La Chapelle-Aux-Saints (France)
Brian size	1500 cc average
Dentition	Retromolar gap
Cranial features	Large brow ridge, midfacial prognathism, large infraorbital foramina, occipital bun
Postcranial features	Robust skeleton with short and stocky body, increased musculature, barrel chest
Culture	Mousterian tools often constructed using the Levallois technique

Hominin	Denisovans
Dates	100,000–30,000 years ago
Region(s)	Siberia
Famous discoveries	Child's finger bone and adult molar
Brain size	unknown
Dentition	unknown
Cranial features	unknown
Postcranial features	unknown
Culture	unknown
Other	Closely related to Neanderthals (genetically)

Species	Homo naledi
Dates	335,000-235,000 years ago
Region(s)	South Africa
Famous Discoveries	Rising Star Cave
Brain size	500 cc average
Dentition	Reduced tooth size
Cranial features	Sagittal keel, large brow, well-developed frontal region
Postcranial features	unknown
Culture	unknown

Species	Homo floresiensis
Dates	100,000–60,000 years ago, perhaps as recently as 17,000 years ago
Region(s)	Lingua Bua, island of Flores, Indonesia
Famous discoveries	"The Hobbit"
Brian size	400 cc average
Dentition	unknown
Cranial features	Sagittal keel, arching brow ridges, nuchal torus, no chin
Postcranial features	Very short stature (approximately 3.5 ft.)
Culture	Similar to other tools found on the island of Flores

Review Questions

- What physical and cultural features are unique to archaic *Homo sapiens*? How are archaic *Homo sapiens* different in both physical and cultural characteristics from *Homo erectus*?
- Describe the specific changes to the brain and skull first seen in archaic *Homo sapiens*. Why does the shape of the skull change so dramatically from *Homo erectus*?
- What role did the shifting environment play in the adaptation of archaic *Homo sapiens*, including Neanderthals? Discuss at least one physical feature and one cultural feature that would have assisted these groups in surviving the changing environment.
- In your opinion, which of the hypotheses concerning the disappearance of the Neanderthals best incorporates the available evidence? Why?
- What does the regional variation in archaic *Homo sapiens* represent in terms of the broader story of our species' evolution?
- Describe the issues raised by the discoveries of *Homo naledi* and *Homo floresiensis* in the understanding of the story of the evolution of *Homo sapiens*.

Key Terms

5 prime end: A nucleic acid strand that terminates at the chemical group attached to the fifth carbon in the sugar-ring.

3 prime end: A nucleic acid strand that terminates at the hydroxyl (-OH) chemical group attached to the third carbon in the sugar-ring.

Allele: Each of two or more alternative forms of a gene that arise by mutation and are found at the same place on a chromosome.

Anthropocentrism: A way of thinking that assumes humans are the most important species and leads to interpreting the world always through a human lens. Species-centric science and thought.

Coalescent methods: These are models which allow for inference of how genetic variants sampled from a population may have originated from a common ancestor

Cortex: The outside, or rough outer covering, of a rock. Usually the cortex is removed during the process of stone tool creation.

Deamination: The chemical process that results in the conversion of Cytosine to uracil, which results in Cytosine to Thymine conversions during sequencing.

Divergence time: A measure of how long two genomic sequences have been changing independently.

Endogenous aDNA: A form of ancient DNA in which DNA originates from the specimen being examined.

Ethnocentric: Applying negative judgments to other cultures based on comparison to one's own.

Exogenous DNA: DNA that originates from sources outside of the specimen you are trying to sequence.

Flexed position: Fetal position, in which the legs are drawn up to the middle of the body and the arms are drawn toward the body center. Intentional burials are often found in the flexed body position.

Foraminifera: Microscopic single-celled organisms with a shell that are common in all marine environments. The fossil record of foraminifera extends back well over 500 million years.

Glaciation: A glacial period, or time when a large portion of the world is covered by glaciers and ice sheets.

Globular: Round-shaped, like a globe.

Grave goods: Items included with a body at burial. Items may signify occupation or hobbies, social status, or level of importance in the community, or they may be items believed necessary for the afterlife.

Haft: A handle. Also used as a verb—to attach a handle to an item, such as a stone tool.

Haplotype: A set of genetic variants located on a single stretch of the genome. This unique combination of variants on a stretch of the genome can be used to differentiate groups that will have different combinations of variants.

Heterozygosity: A measure of how many genes within a diploid genome are made up of more than one variant for a gene.

High-coverage sequences: These are genomic sequences which have been sequenced multiple times to ensure that the sequence produced is a true reflection of the genomic sequence, and reduce the likelihood that the sequence has sequencing errors as a result of the the sequencing process.

Homozygosity: A measure of how many genes within a diploid genome are made up of more than the same variant for a gene.

Ice core: A colundular sample of ice that is removed from an ice sheet. The annual buildup of snow and ice can be studied and interpreted to better understand climate change, as well as local environmental shifts.

Infraorbital foramina: Small holes on the maxilla bone of the face that allows nerves and blood to reach the skin.

Insular dwarfing: A form of dwarfism that occurs when a limited geographic region, such as an island, causes a large-bodied animal to be selected for a smaller body size.

Interglacial: A warmer period between two glacial time periods.

Introgressed genes: This is the movement of genes from one species to the gene pool of another species through hybridization between the species and backcross into the parental population by hybrid offspring.

Levallois technique: A distinctive technique of stone tool manufacturing used by archaic *Homo sapiens*, including Neanderthals. The technique involves the preparation of a core and striking edges off in a regular fashion around the core. Then a series of similarly sized pieces can be removed, which can then be turned into different tools.

Midfacial prognathism: A forward projection of the nose, or middle facial region. Usually associated with Neanderthals.

Mousterian tools: The stone tool industry of Neanderthals and their contemporaries in Africa and Western Asia. Mousterian tools are known for a diverse set of flake tools, which is different than the large bifacial tools of the Acheulean industry.

Nasal aperture: The opening for the nose visible on a skull. Often pear- or heart-shaped.

Non-synonymous mutations: These are changes that also occur in the protein-coding region of the genome but don't result in a change in amino acid sequence of the protein being produced.

Occipital bun: A prominent bulge or projection on the back of the skull, specifically the occipital bone. This is a feature present only on Neanderthal skulls.

Ochre: A natural clay pigment mixed with ferric oxide and clay and sand. Ranges in color from brown to red to orange.

Recombination: This is the process of exchange of DNA between two strands to produce new sequence arrangements.

Retracted face: A face that is flatter.

Retromolar gap: A space behind the last molar and the end of the jaw. This is a feature present only on Neanderthals. It also occurs through cultural modification in modern humans who have had their third molars, or wisdom teeth, removed.

Sediment core: A colundular sample of soil and sediments that can be analyzed to study plant and animal presence in a location, or more broadly to determine a regional environment.

Synonymous mutations: Mutations that occur in the protein-coding region of the genome and result in a change in the amino acid sequence of the protein produced.

About the Authors

Amanda Wolcott Paskey

Amanda Wolcott Paskey

Amanda Wolcott Paskey is an anthropology professor at Cosumnes River College in Sacramento, California. She earned her B.A. and M.A. in anthropology from the University of California, Davis. Her speciality in anthropology is archaeology; however, she was trained in a holistic program and most of her teaching load is in biological anthropology. She is currently working on analyzing a post-gold rush era archaeological site, in Sacramento, with colleagues and students. This project has given her many opportunities to engage in sharing archaeology with a public audience, including local school children and Sacramentans interested in local history.

AnneMarie Beasley Cisneros

AnneMarie Beasley Cisneros

AnneMarie Beasley Cisneros is an anthropology professor at American River College in Sacramento, California. Trained as a four-field anthropologist, she earned her B.A. and M.A. in anthropology from California State University, Sacramento. She regularly teaches biological anthropology, among other courses, and is currently engaged in applied anthropology work in community development with historically underserved communities. She most recently has particularly enjoyed facilitating her students' involvement in projects serving Sacramento's Latino and immigrant Mexican populations.

About the Special Topic: Ancient DNA Author

Robyn Humphreys

Robyn Humphreys is a biological anthropologist based in the archaeology department at the University of Cape Town. Her MSc focused on the role of hybridization in human evolution. She is now pursuing her Ph.D., which will involve looking at the relationship between archaeologists and communities in relation to research on human remains from historical sites in Cape Town.

For Further Exploration

Anne and Bernard Spitzer Hall of Human Origins–American Museum of Natural History https://www.amnh.org/exhibitions/permanent-exhibitions/anne-and-bernard-spitzer-hall-of-human-origins

"Dawn of Humanity," PBS documentary, 2015

"DNA Clues to Our Inner Neanderthal," TED Talk by Svante Pääbo, 2011. https://www.ted.com/talks/svante_paeaebo_dna_clues_to_our_inner_neanderthal?language=en

"The Dirt" Podcast, Episode 30 "The Human Family Tree (Shrub? Crabgrass? Tumbleweed?), Part 3: Very Humany Indeed"
https://thedirtpod.com/episodes//episode-30-the-human-family-tree-shrub-crabgrass-tumbleweed-part-3

E Fossil games and activities http://www.efossils.org/page/games-and-activities

"Hobbits on Flores, Indonesia" Smithsonian Human Origins http://humanorigins.si.edu/research/asian-research-projects/hobbits-flores-indonesia

Shanindar 3–Neanderthal Skeleton–Smithsonian Human Origins http://humanorigins.si.edu/evidence/human-fossils/shanidar-3-neanderthal-skeleton

Smithsonian's Human Origins Program Facebook page (@smithsonian.humanorigins) https://www.facebook.com/smithsonian.humanorigins/

Paleoartist Brings Human Evolution to Life–Elisabeth Daynés https://www.smithsonianmag.com/science-nature/bringing-human-evolution-life-180951155/

Green, R. E., J. Krause, A. W. Briggs, T. Maricic, U. Stenzel, M. Kircher, et al. 2010. "A Draft Sequence of the Neanderthal Genome." *Science* 328 (5979): 710-722.

Gibbons, A. 2014. "Neanderthals and Moderns Made Imperfect Mates." *Science* 343 (6170): 471–472. doi: 10.1126/science.343.6170.471.

Huerta-Sánchez, E., X. Jin, Z. Bianba, B. M. Peter, N. Vinckenbosch, Y. Liang, et al. 2014. Altitude Adaptation in Tibetans Caused by Introgression of Denisovan-like DNA. *Nature* 512 (7513): 194.

Jeong, C., G. Alkorta-Aranburu, B. Basnyat, M. Neupane, D. B. Witonsky, J. K. Pritchard, C. M. Beatl, and A. Di Rienzo. 2014. "Admixture Facilitates Genetic Adaptations to High Altitude in Tibet." *Nature Communications* 5: 3281. doi: 10.1038/ncomms4281

Krings, M., A. Stone, R. W. Schmitz, H. Krainitzki, M. Stoneking, and S. Pääbo. 1997. "Neanderthal DNA Sequences and the Origin of Modern Humans." *Cell* 90 (1): 19–30.

Krouse, J., Q. Fu, J. M. Good, B. Viola, M. V. Shunkov, A. P. Derevianko, and S. Pääbo. 2010. "The Complete Mitochondrial DNA Genome of an Unknown Hominin from Southern Siberia." *Nature* 464: 894–897.

Prüfer, K., F. Racimo, N. Patterson, F. Jay, S. Sankararaman, S. Sawyer, et al. 2014. "The Complete Genome Sequence of a Neanderthal from the Altai Mountains." *Nature* 505 (7481): 43-49.

Racimo, F., S. Sankararaman, R. Nielsen, and E. Huerta-Sánchez. 2015. Evidence for Archaic Adaptive Introgression in Humans. *Nature Reviews Genetics* 16 (6): 359-371.

Sankararaman, Sriram, et al. "The genomic landscape of Neanderthal ancestry in present-day humans." *Nature* 507.7492 (2014): 354.

Vernot, B., S. Tucci, J. Kelso, J. G. Schraiber, A. B. Wolf, R. M. Gittelman, et al. 2016. "Excavating Neanderthal and Denisovan DNA from the Genomes of Melanesian Individuals." *Science* 352 (6282): 235-239.

References

Atkinson, E. G., A. J. Audesse, J. A. Palacios, D. M. Bobo, A. E. Webb, S. Ramachandran, B. M. Henn. 2018. "No Evidence for Recent Selection at FOXP2 among Diverse Human Populations." Cell 174 (6): 1424-1435.

Berger, T. D, and E. Trinkaus. 1995. "Patterns of Trauma among the Neanderthals." *Journal of Archaeological Science* 22 (6): 841-852.

Bocherens, Hervé, Daniel Billiou, André Mariotti, Marylène Patou-Mathis, Marcel Otte, Dominique Bonjean, and Michel Toussaint. 1999. "Palaeoenvionmental and Palaeodietary Implications of Isotopic Biogeochemistry of Last Interglacial Neanderthal and Mammal Bones in Scladina Cave (Belgium)." *Journal of Archaeological Science* 26 (6): 599-607.

Bocquet-Appel, J. P., and A. Degioanni. 2013. "Neanderthal Demographic Estimates." *Current Anthropology* 54 (S8): S202-S213.

Churchill, S. E. 1998. "Cold Adaptations, Heterochrony, and Neanderthals." *Evolutionary Anthropology* 7: 46-61.

Churchill, S. E., R. G. Franciscus, H. A. McKean-Peraza, J. A. Daniel, and B. R. Warren. 2009. "Shanidar 3 Neanderthal Rib Puncture Wound and Paleolithic Weaponry." *Journal of Human Evolution* 57 (2): 163-178.

Degioanni A., C. Bonenfant, S. Cabut, and S. Condemi. 2019. Living on the Edge: Was Demographic Weakness the Cause of Neanderthal Demise? *PLoS ONE* 14 (5): e0216742.
doi: 10.1371/journal.pone.0216742

Dirks, P. H. G. M., E. M. Roberts, H. Hilbert-Wolf, J. D. Kramers, J. Hawks, A. Dosseto, M. Duval, et al. 2017. "The Age of *Homo naledi* and Associated Sediments in the Rising Star Cave, South Africa." *eLife* 6 (24231). doi: 10.7554/eLife.24231

el-Showk, S. 2019. "Neanderthal Clues to Brain Evolution in Humans." *Nature* 571: S10-S11. doi: 10.1038/d41586-019-02210-6

Enard, D. and D. A. Petrov. 2018. "Evidence that RNA Viruses Drove Adaptive Introgression between Neanderthals and Modern Humans." *Cell* 175 (2): 360-371. doi: 10.1016/j.cell.2018.08.034

Frayer, D. W., M. Lozano, J. M. Bermudez de Castro, E. Carbonell, J.-L. Arsuaga, J. Radovcic, I. Fiore, and L. Bondioli. 2012. "More Than 500,000 Years of Righthandness in Europeans." *Laterality* 17 (1): 51-69.

Gilpin, W., M. W. Feldman, and K. Aoki. 2016. "An Ecocultural Model Predicts Neanderthal Extinction through Competition With Modern Humans." *Proceedings of the National Academy of Sciences* 113 (8): 2134-2139.

Golovanova, L.V., V. B. Doronichev, N. E. Cleghorn, M. A. Koulkova, T. V. Sapelko, and M. S. Shackley. 2010. "Significance of Ecological Factors in the Middle to Upper Paleolithic Transition." *Current Anthropology* 51 (5): 655-691.

Houldcroft, C. J., and S. J. Underdown. 2016. "Neanderthal Genomics Suggests a Pleistocene Time Frame for the First Epidemiologic Transition." *American Journal of Physical Anthropology* 160 (3): 379-388.

Jaouen, K., A. Le Cabec, F. Welker, J. Hublin, M. Soressi, and S. Talamo. 2019. "Exceptionally High δ15N Values in Collagen Single Amino Acids Confirm Neanderthals as High-Trophic Level Carnivores." *Proceedings of the National Academy of Sciences* 116 (11): 4928-4933. doi: 10.1073/pnas.1814087116

Kortlandt, Adriaan. 2002. "Neanderthal Anatomy and the Use of Spears." *Evolutionary Anthropology* 11 (5): 183-184.

Macdonald, K., W. Roebroeks, and A. Verpoorte. 2009. "An Energetics Perspective on the Neanderthal Record." In *The Evolution of Hominin Diets: Integrating Approaches to the Study of Palaeolithic Subsistence*, edited by J.-J. Hublin and M. P. Richards, pp. 211–e220. Dordrecht, Germany: Springer.

Mendez, F. L., G. D. Poznik, S. Castellano, and C. D. Bustamante. 2016. "The Divergence of Neanderthal and Modern Human Y Chromosomes." *American Journal of Human Genetics* 98 (4): 728-734.

Pearce, E., C. M. Stringer, and R. I. M. Dunbar. 2013. "New Insights into Differences in Brain Organizations between Neanderthals and Anatomically Modern Humans." *Proceedings of the Royal Society B: Biological Sciences* 280 (1758): 20130168. doi: 10.1098/rspb.2013.0168

Staubwasser, M., V. Drăguşin, B. P. Onac, S. Assonov, V. Ersek, D. O. Hoffman, and D. Veres. 2018. "Impact of Climate Change on the Transition of Neanderthals to Modern Humans in Europe." *Proceedings of the National Academy of Sciences* 115 (37): 9116–9121. doi: 10.1073/pnas.1808647115

Stringer, C. B. 1996. "Current Issues in Modern Human Origins." In *Contemporary Issues in Human Evolution*, edited by W. E. Meickle, F. C. Howell, and N. G. Jablonski, pp. 115-134. San Francisco: California Academy of Sciences.

Trinkaus, E. 2006. "Modern Human versus Neandertal Evolutionary Distinctiveness," *Current Anthropology* 47, no. 4 (August 2006): 597-620. https://doi.org/10.1086/504165

Trinkaus, E. 2007. "European Early Modern Humans and the Fate of the Neanderthals." PNAS May 1, 2007 104 (18) 7367-7372; https://doi.org/10.1073/pnas.0702214104

Venner, S. J. 2018. "A New Estimate for Neanderthal Energy Expenditure." CUNY Academic Works. https://academicworks.cuny.edu/hc_sas_etds/327

Weaver, T. D., and J. Hublin. 2009. "Neanderthal Birth Canal Shape and the Evolution of Human Childbirth." *Proceedings of the National Academy of Sciences* 106 (20): 8151-8156.

Wißing, C. H. Rougier, I. Crevecoer, M. Germonpré, Y. Naito, P. Semal, and H. Bocherens. 2015. "Isotopic Evidence for Dietary Ecology of Late Neanderthals in Northwestern Europe." *Quaternary International* 411 (A): 327-345. doi: 10.1016/j.quaint.2015.09.091

Wong, K. 2015. "Different yet Alike." *Scientific American* 312, 2, 6 (February 2015) doi:10.1038/scientificamerican0215-6

Acknowledgments

The authors would like to extend their thanks to Cassandra Gilmore and Anna Goldfield for thoughtful and insightful suggestions on this chapter.

Figure Attributions

Figure 11.1 Big head primitive caveman nose man bone cave at Max Pixel has been designated to the public domain (CC0).

Figure 11.2 All paleotemps by Glen Fergus is used under a CC BY-SA 3.0 License.

Figure 11.3 *Homo erectus*, archaic *Homo sapiens*, and anatomically modern *Homo sapiens* table original to Explorations: An Open Invitation to Biological Anthropology is under a CC BY-NC 4.0 License.

Figure 11.4 *Homo heidelbergensis* Cranium Broken Hill 1 (Rhodesian Man) by ©BoneClones is used by permission and available here under a CC BY-NC 4.0 License.

Figure 11.5 *Homo heidelbergensis* Skull Atapuerca 5 by ©BoneClones is used by permission and available here under a CC BY-NC 4.0 License.

Figure 11.6 Neanderthal distinguishing features table original to Explorations: An Open Invitation to Biological Anthropology is under a CC BY-NC 4.0 License.

Figure 11.7 Neanderthal Skeleton Articulated by ©BoneClones is used by permission and available here under a CC BY-NC 4.0 License.

Figure 11.8 Nucléus Levallois La-Parrilla by José-Manuel Benito Álvarez is used under a CC BY-SA 2.5 License,

Figure 11.9 NHM – Levalloiskern by Wolfgang Sauber is used under a CC BY-SA 4.0 License.

Figure 11.10a *Homo neanderthalensis* Shanidar 1 Skull by ©BoneClones is used by permission and available here under a CC BY-NC 4.0 License.

Figure 11.10b Shanidar 1 by Smithsonian [exhibit: Human Evolution Evidence, Human Fossils, Species, *Homo neanderthalensis*] is copyrighted and used for educational and non-commercial purposes as outlined by the Smithsonian.

Figure 11.11 Neandertala homo, modelo en Neand-muzeo (image was taken in the Neanderthal Museum, Mettmann, Germany) by UNiesert is used under a CC BY-SA 3.0 License.

Figure 11.12 DNA extraction by Robyn Humphreys original to Explorations: An Open Invitation to Biological Anthropology is under a CC BY-NC 4.0 License.

Figure 11.13 *Homo sapiens* lineage by Dbachmann is used under a CC BY-SA 4.0 License.

Figure 11.14 Introgressed Neanderthal DNA in a modern human genome by Robyn Humphreys original to Explorations: An Open Invitation to Biological Anthropology is under a CC BY-NC 4.0 License.

Figure 11.15 Dinaledi skeletal specimens (Figure 1) by Berger, Lee R. et al. 2015. "*Homo naledi*, a new species of the genus Homo from the Dinaledi Chamber, South Africa." eLife 2015;4:e09560 (DOI: 10.7554/eLife.09560) is used under a CC BY 4.0 License.

Figure 11.16 LES1 Cranium (Figure 5) by Hawks et al. 2017. "New fossil remains of *Homo naledi* from the Lesedi Chamber, South Africa". eLife 2017;6:e24232. (DOI:10.7554/eLife.24232) is used under a CC BY 4.0 License.

Figure 11.17 *Homo floresiensis* cave by Rosino is used under a CC BY-SA 2.0 License.

Figure 11.18 *Homo floresiensis* Skull (Flores Skull LB1) by ©BoneClones is used by permission and available here under a CC BY-NC 4.0 License.

Figure 11.19 Anatomically modern human and *Homo floresiensis* reconstruction original to Explorations: An Open Invitation to Biological Anthropology by Mary Nelson is under a CC BY-NC 4.0 License.

Chapter 12: Modern *Homo sapiens*

Keith Chan, Ph.D., University of Missouri: Grossmont College and MiraCosta College

Learning Objectives

- Identify the skeletal and behavioral traits that represent modern *Homo sapiens*.
- Critically evaluate different types of evidence for the origin of our species in Africa, and our expansion around the world.
- Understand how the human lifestyle changed when people transitioned from foraging to agriculture.

Figure 12.1 The excavation of an exposed cave at Jebel Irhoud, Morocco, where hominin fossils were found in the 1960s and in 2007. Dating showed that they represent the earliest-known modern Homo sapiens.

The walls of a pink limestone cave exposed to the outside world in the hillside of Jebel Irhoud jutted out of the otherwise barren landscape of the Moroccan desert (Figure 12.1). The year was 2007 and it turned out to be a momentous occasion for science. A fossil unearthed by a team of researchers was barely visible to the untrained eye. Just the fossil cranium's robust brows were peering out of the rock. The find was welcome but not sheer luck: Hominin fossils have been found here since their first accidental discovery by miners in 1960. This research team from the Max Planck Institute for Evolutionary Anthropology was just the latest to explore the prehistoric human presence in this part of North Africa. Excavating near the first discovery, the researchers wanted to learn more about how *Homo sapiens* lived far from East Africa, where we thought our species originated.

The scientists were surprised when they analyzed the cranium, named Irhoud 10, and other fossils. Statistical comparisons with other human crania concluded that the Irhoud face shapes were typical of recent modern humans while the braincases matched ancient modern humans. Based on the findings of other scientists, the team expected these modern *Homo sapiens* fossils to be around 200,000 years old. Instead, dating revealed that the cranium had been buried for around 315,000 years.

Together, the modern-looking facial dimensions and the older date changed the interpretation of our species, modern *Homo sapiens*. Our key evolutionary changes from the archaic *Homo sapiens* of the previous chapter to our species today happened 100,000 years earlier than what we had thought. In addition, the new information suggests that our home region covered more of the vast African continent instead of being concentrated in the east.

This big addition to the study of modern *Homo sapiens* is just one of the latest in this continually advancing area of biological anthropology. Researchers are continually discovering amazing fossils and ingenious ways to collect data and test hypotheses about our past. Through the collective work of scientists, including archaeologists, geneticists, and anatomists, we are building an overall theory or explanation of modern human origins. We will first cover the skeletal changes from archaic *Homo sapiens* to modern *Homo sapiens*. Next, we will track how modern *Homo sapiens* expanded the range of its species around the world. Lastly, we will cover the development of agriculture and how it changed human culture to how we practice it today.

DEFINING MODERNITY

What defines a modern *Homo sapiens* when compared to an archaic *Homo sapiens*, like the ones in the previous chapter? Modern humans, like you and me, have a set of derived traits that are not seen in archaic humans or any other hominin. As with other transitions in hominin evolution, such as increasing brain size and bipedal ability, modern traits do not appear fully formed or all at once. In other words, the first modern *Homo sapiens* was not just born one day from archaic parents. The traits common to modern *Homo sapiens* appeared in a **mosaic** manner: gradually and out of sync with one another. There are two areas to consider when tracking the complex evolution of modern human traits. One is the physical change in the skeleton. The other is behavior inferred from the cranium and material culture.

Skeletal Traits

The skeleton of a modern *Homo sapiens* is less robust than that of an archaic *Homo sapiens*. In other words, the modern skeleton is **gracile**, meaning that the structures are thinner and smoother. Differences related to gracility in the cranium are seen in the braincase, the face, and the mandible. There are also broad differences in the rest of the skeleton.

Cranial Traits

Several elements of the braincase differ between modern and archaic *Homo sapiens*. Overall, the shape is much rounder, or more **globular**, on a modern skull (Lieberman, McBratney, and Krovitz 2002; Neubauer, Hublin, and Gunz 2018; Pearson 2008) (Figure 12.2). You can feel the globularity of the modern human skull on the example built into you. Feel the height of your forehead with the palm of your hand. Viewed from the side, the tall vertical forehead of a modern *Homo sapiens* stands out when compared to the sloping archaic version. This is because the frontal lobe of the modern human brain is larger than the one in archaic humans, and the skull has to accommodate the expansion. The vertical forehead reduces a trait that is common to all other hominins: the brow ridge or **supraorbital torus**. The sides of the braincase also exhibit changes associated with the globular expansion of the brain: the parietal lobes of the brain and the matching parietal bones of the skull both bulge outward more in modern humans. At the back of the skull, the archaic occipital bun is no longer present. Instead, the occipital region of the modern human cranium has a derived tall and smooth curve, again reflecting the globular brain inside. The different priorities in brain regions may also indicate cognitive and behavioral differences between archaic humans and modern humans, discussed in the next section.

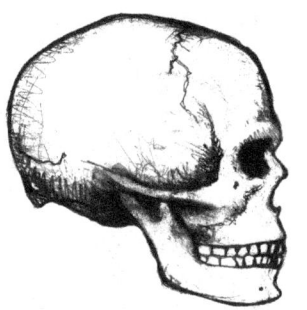 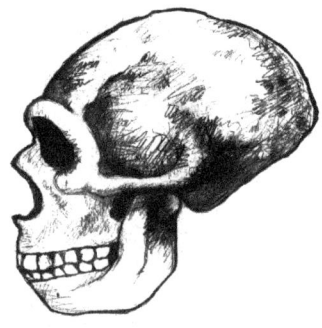

Figure 12.2 Comparison between modern (left) and archaic (right) Homo sapiens skulls. Note the overall gracility of the modern skull, as well as the globular braincase.

The trend of shrinking face size across hominins reaches its extreme with our species as well. The facial bones of a modern *Homo sapiens* are extremely gracile compared to all other hominins (Lieberman, McBratney, and Krovitz 2002). One specific dimension to compare is the thickness of the zygomatic arches, or cheekbones. As with the shrinking of the face leading up to our species, the decreasing reliance on needing large teeth for survival may have been the reason that modern human faces are so gracile in comparison to other humans. Continuing a trend in hominin evolution, technological innovations kept reducing the importance of teeth in reproductive success (Lucas 2007). As natural selection favored smaller and smaller teeth, the surrounding bone holding these teeth also shrank.

Connected to the face, the mandible is also gracile in modern humans when compared to archaic humans and other hominins. Interestingly, our mandibles have pulled back so far from the prognathism of earlier hominins that we gained an extra structure at the most anterior point, called the **mental eminence**. You know this structure as the chin: trace your own chin and feel how it curves forward before swooping posteriorly toward your neck. At the skeletal level, it resembles an upside-down "T" at the centerline of the mandible (Pearson 2008). If you look back at illustrations of other hominins, you will see that they all lack a chin. Instead, their mandibles curve straight back without a forward point. What is the chin for and how did it develop? Flora Gröning and colleagues (2011) found evidence of the chin's importance by simulating physical forces on computer models of different mandible shapes. Their results showed that the chin acts as structural support to withstand strain on the otherwise gracile mandible. In other words, as natural selection favored smaller dentition, the chin developed to maintain structural integrity of the mandible.

Post-Cranial Gracility

The rest of the modern human skeleton is also more gracile than its archaic counterpart. The differences are clear when comparing a modern *Homo sapiens* with a cold-adapted Neanderthal (Sawyer and Maley 2005), but the trends are still present when comparing modern and archaic humans within Africa (Pearson 2000). Overall, a modern *Homo sapiens* post-cranial skeleton has thinner cortical bone, smoother features, and more slender shapes when compared to archaic *Homo sapiens* (Figure 12.3). For example, the modern pelvis has gracile features along its surface and is narrower in overall width. Our elbow and knee joint surfaces are also narrower. Even the individual fingers and toes are more slender in modern humans. Comparing whole skeletons, modern humans have longer limb proportions relative to the length and width of the torso, giving us lankier outlines.

As with the cranial traits, we have to consider the evolutionary process behind postcranial gracility. Why is our skeleton so gracile compared to those of other hominins? Natural selection can drive the gracilization of skeletons in several ways (Lieberman 2015). A slender frame is adapted for the efficient long-distance running ability that started with *Homo erectus*. Furthermore, slenderness is a genetic adaptation for cooling an active body in hotter climates, which aligns with the ample evidence that Africa was the home continent of our species.

Behavioral Modernity

Aside from physical differences in the skeleton, researchers have also tracked clues of behavioral changes from archaic to modern humans. From the anthropology of our species today, we know that we practice a very complex version of culture, with many layers to our language, art, social organization, and technology, among other areas. Did cultural complexity increase gradually or quickly with the first modern humans? This question is being actively investigated. A major obstacle to answering this question is that it is hard to define and measure cultural complexity. Since we cannot directly observe humans of the distant past, we have to infer these measures of human behavior from other types of evidence. Two particularly illuminating areas are archaeology and the analysis of reconstructed brains.

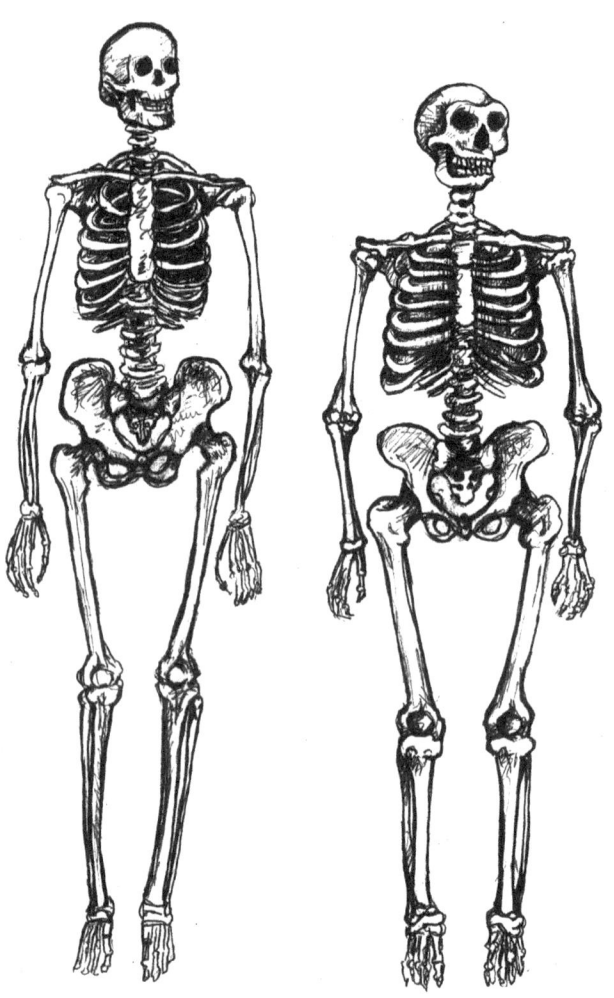

Figure 12.3 Anterior views of modern (left) and archaic (right) Homo sapiens skeletons. The modern human has an overall gracile appearance at this scale as well.

Archaeology tells us much about the behavioral complexity of past humans by interpreting the significance of material culture. In terms of evolved advanced culture, items created with an artistic flair, or as a decorative piece, speak of some abstract thought process (Figure 12.4). The demonstration of difficult artistic techniques and technological skills hints at social learning and cooperation as well. For example, most of your skills were taught to you by a more experienced person, upon which you've developed your own style with practice. Some day you may pass on what you know to someone else using language to convey your knowledge. The same process is believed to have happened with early modern humans in areas such as toolmaking and craftwork, producing the sophisticated material culture that we can now study. According to paleoanthropologist John Shea (2011), one way to track the complexity of past behavior through artifacts is by measuring the variety of tools found together. The more types of tools constructed with different techniques and for different purposes, the more modern the behavior. Turning this view to ourselves, think of all of the tools we have available to us today at a typical hardware store and the cumulative knowledge they represent. This idea of measuring past behavior is promising, but researchers are still working on an archaeological way to measure cultural complexity that is useful across time and place.

Figure 12.4 Carved ivory figure called the Lion-Man of the Hohlenstein-Stadel. It dates to the Aurignacian culture, between 35 and 40 kya. What does this artifact suggest about the culture and technical skill of its artist?

The interpretation of brain anatomy is another promising approach to studying the evolution of human behavior. When looking at the body of work on this topic in modern *Homo sapiens* brains, researchers found a weak association between brain size and test-measured intelligence (Pietschnig et al. 2015). This means that there are more significant factors that affect tested intelligence than just brain size. Additionally, they found no association between intelligence and biological sex. Since the sheer size of the brain is not useful for weighing intelligence, paleoanthropologists are instead investigating the differences in certain brain structures. The differences in organization between modern *Homo sapiens* brains and archaic *Homo sapiens* brains may reflect different cognitive priorities that account for modern human culture. Researchers (e.g., Bruner 2010) have hypothesized that the expanded frontal and parietal lobes in the globular modern human braincases mean that we can do more complex thinking regarding memory and social ability than the Neanderthals could. In contrast, the Neanderthal brain prioritized the visual regions where the occipital bun was located, with fewer neurons in the frontal area for complex thinking. As with the archaeological line of research in the preceding paragraph, this is a very active area of investigation. New discoveries will refine what we know about the human brain and apply that knowledge to studying the distant past.

Taken together, the cognitive abilities in modern humans may have translated into an adept use of tools to enhance survival. The ability to process a new environment, adapt to it with innovative technology, and pass on that knowledge may be the key behind the success of modern *Homo sapiens*. Researchers Patrick Roberts and Brian A. Stewart call this concept the **generalist-specialist niche**: Our species is an expert at living in a wide array of environments, with populations culturally specializing in their own particular surroundings (Roberts and Stewart 2018). The next section tracks how far around the world these skeletal and behavioral traits have taken us.

FIRST AFRICA, THEN THE WORLD

What enabled modern *Homo sapiens* to expand its range further in 300,000 years than *Homo erectus* did in 1.5 million years? The key is the set of derived biological traits from the last section. The gracile frame and neurological anatomy allowed modern humans to survive and even flourish in the vastly different environments they encountered. Based on multiple types of evidence, the source of all of these modern humans, including all of us today, was Africa.

This section traces the origin of modern *Homo sapiens* and the massive expansion of our species across all of the continents except Antarctica by 12,000 years ago. While modern *Homo sapiens* first shared geography with archaic humans, modern humans eventually spread into lands where no human had gone before. Starting with the first-known modern *Homo sapiens*, around 315,000 years ago, we will follow our species from a time called the Middle Pleistocene to the end of the Late Pleistocene. Culturally, we will trace developments from the **Middle Stone Age** through the transition around 50,000 years ago to the **Later Stone Age**, when cultural complexity quickly grew with both technology and artistry. We will end this section right before the next big cultural change, called the Neolithic Revolution.

A few notes on this part of the chapter: It is organized from past to present when possible, though a lot happens simultaneously to our species in that time. Figure 12.5 shows the broad routes that our species took expanding around the world. I encourage you to make your own timeline with the dates in this part to see the overall trends. References are provided to the research leading to the information on key finds. Search for these scientific papers online to see how researchers reach the conclusions presented here.

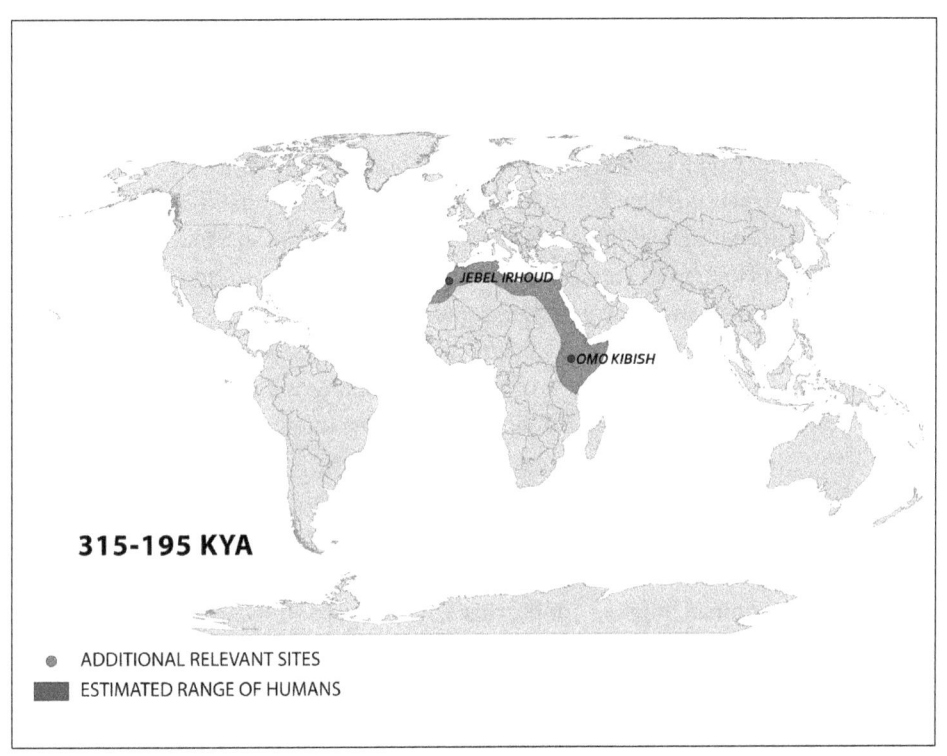

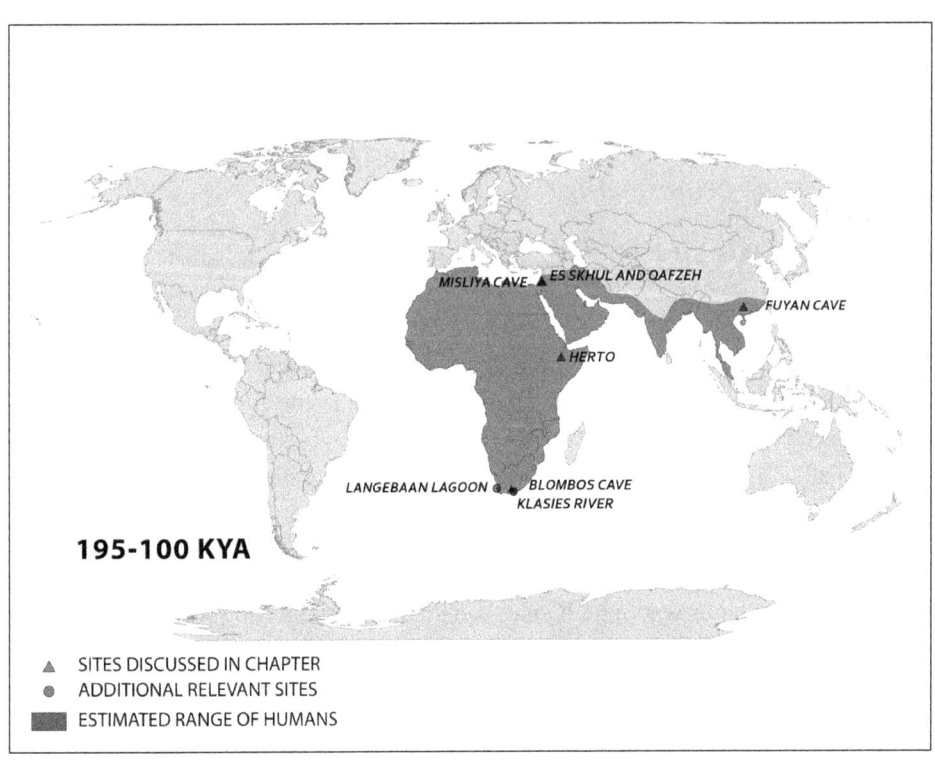

Modern Homo sapiens | 449

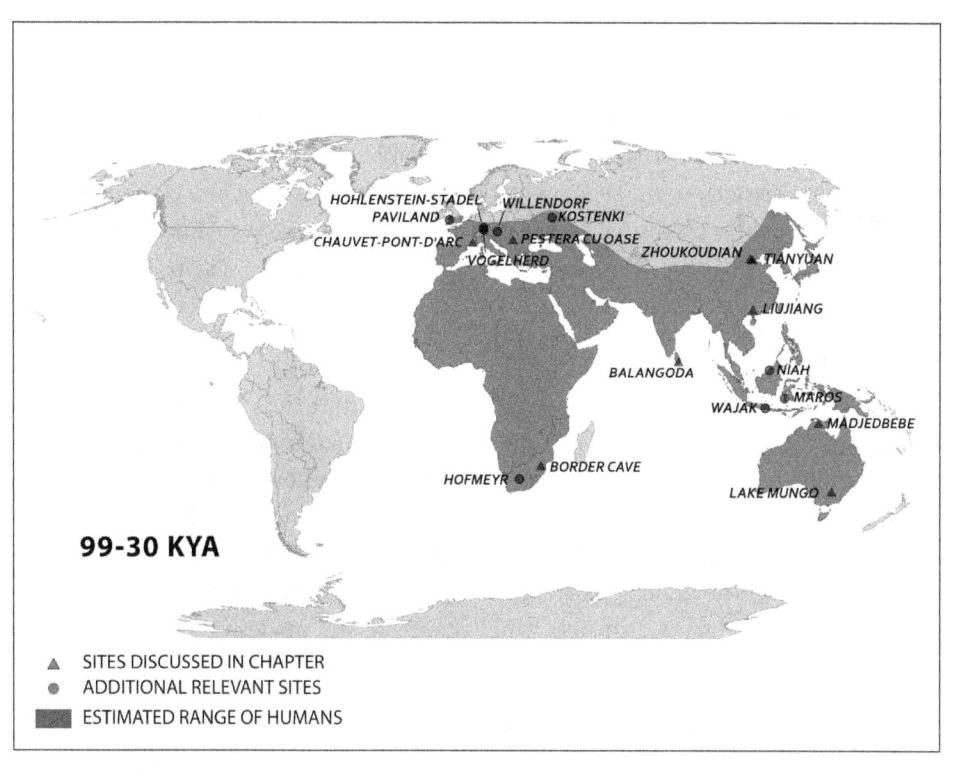

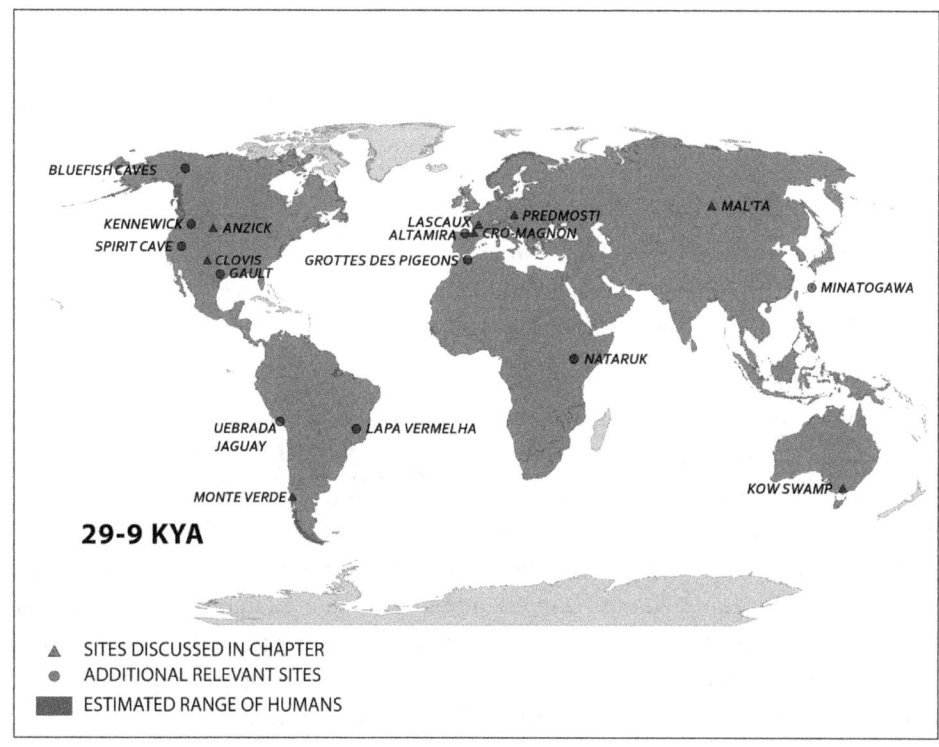

Figure 12.5 Maps depicting the estimated range of modern Homo sapiens through time. The shaded area is based on geographical connections across known sites. Note the growth in area starting in Africa and the oftentimes coastal routes that populations followed.

The Start of Modern *Homo sapiens* in Africa

We start with the ample fossil evidence supporting the theory that modern humans originated in Africa during the Middle Pleistocene, having evolved from African archaic *Homo sapiens*. The earliest dated fossils considered to be modern actually have a mosaic of archaic and modern traits, showing the complex changes from one type to the other. Experts have various names for these transitional fossils, such as **Early Modern Homo sapiens** or **Early Anatomically Modern Humans**. However they are labeled, the presence of some modern traits means that they illustrate the origin of the modern type. Three particularly informative sites with fossils of the earliest modern *Homo sapiens* are Jebel Irhoud, Omo, and Herto.

Recall from the start of the chapter that the most recent finds at Jebel Irhoud are now the oldest dated fossils that exhibit the traits of modern *Homo sapiens*. Besides Irhoud 10, the cranium that was dated to 315,000 years ago (Hublin et al. 2017; Richter et al. 2017), there were other fossils found in the same deposit that we now know are from the same time period. In total there are at least five individuals, representing life stages from childhood to adulthood. These fossils form an image of high variation in skeletal traits. For example, the skull named Irhoud 1 has a primitive brow ridge, while Irhoud 2 and Irhoud 10 do not (Figure 12.6). The braincases are lower than what is seen in the modern humans of today but higher than in archaic *Homo sapiens*. The teeth also have a mix of archaic and modern traits that defy clear categorization into either group.

Research separated by nearly four decades uncovered fossils and artifacts from the Kibish Formation in the Lower Omo Valley in Ethiopia. These Omo Kibish hominins were represented by braincases and fragmented postcranial bones of three individuals found kilometers apart, dating back to 195,000 years ago (Day 1969; McDougall, Brown, and Fleagle 2005). One interesting finding was the variation in braincase size between the two more-complete specimens: While the individual now named Omo I had a more globular dome, Omo II had an archaic-style long and low cranium. In more recent fieldwork, an informative section of the Omo I pelvis was found in a re-excavation in 2001. Analysis by Ashley S. Hammond and colleagues (2017) found that the measurements and observations were in line with modern *Homo sapiens*, although larger in absolute size and robusticity.

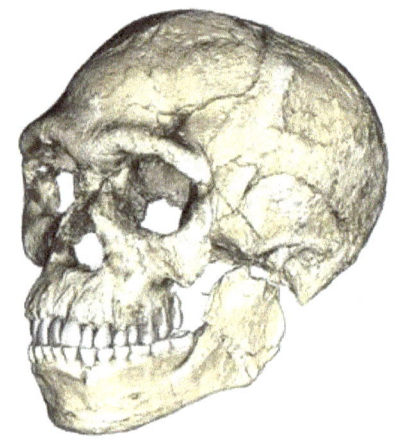

Figure 12.6 Composite rendering of the Jebel Irhoud hominin based on micro-CT scans of multiple fossils from the site. The facial structure is within the modern human range, while the braincase is between the archaic and modern shapes.

Also in Ethiopia, a team led by Tim White (2003) excavated numerous fossils at Herto. There were fossilized crania of two adults and a child, along with fragments of more individuals. The dates ranged between 160,000 and 154,000 years ago. The skeletal traits and stone tool assemblage were both intermediate between the archaic and modern types. Features reminiscent of modern humans included a tall braincase and thinner zygomatic (cheek) bones than those of archaic humans (Figure 12.7). Still, some archaic traits persisted in the Herto fossils. Looking at the face, the supraorbital tori were still prominent. The cranium included an angled occipital bone and was longer than in present-day modern *Homo sapiens*. Statistical analysis by other research teams concluded that at least some cranial measurements fit just within the modern human range (McCarthy and Lucas 2014), favoring categorization with our own species.

Summary of Early Modern H. sapiens in Africa

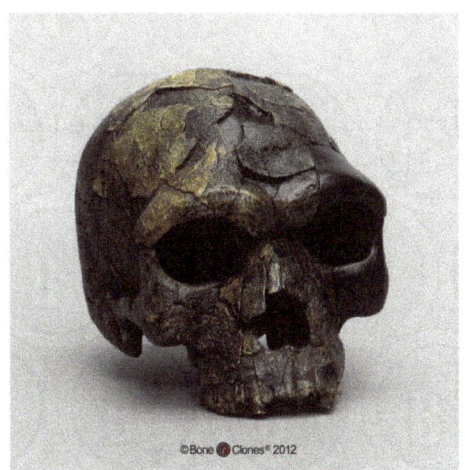

Figure 12.7 *This model of the Herto cranium showing its mosaic of archaic and modern traits.*

The combined fossil evidence paints a picture of diversity in geography and traits. Instead of evolving in just East Africa, the Jebel Irhoud find revealed that early modern *Homo sapiens* had a wide range across Middle Pleistocene Africa. The hypothesis that there was no single original home within Africa for our species is called **African multiregionalism** (Scerri et al. 2018). Supporting this explanation, fossils have different mosaics of archaic and modern traits in different places and even within the same area. The high level of diversity from just these fossils shows that the modern traits took separate paths toward the set we have today. The connections were convoluted, involving fluctuating gene flow among small groups of regional nomadic foragers across a large continent over a long time.

What about behavioral modernity? Jebel Irhoud, Omo, and Herto all bore Middle Stone Age tools of the same flaked style as archaic assemblages, even though they were separated by almost 150,000 years. The apparent stability in technology may be evidence that behavioral modernity was not so developed back then, though there was a high variety of tool types used throughout that time. No clear signs of art dating back this far have been found either. Other hypotheses not related to behavioral modernity could explain these observations. The tool set may have been suitable for thriving in Africa without further innovation. As for the lack of art, maybe works from that time were made with media that deteriorated or perhaps such works were removed by later humans.

While modern *Homo sapiens* lived across Africa, some members eventually left the continent. Generations of these pioneers entered environments far different from what their ancestors experienced in Africa. The next four sections cover evidence of modern *Homo sapiens* in other parts of the Old World and the evidence we have about what they did. We will check back with Africa later in the chapter to see what happened biologically and culturally on the home front amid the expansion.

Expansion into the Middle East and Asia

This section presents key finds showing where modern *Homo sapiens* went after the range of the species first extended out of Africa. These pioneers could have used two connections to the Middle East, or West Asia. From North Africa, they could have crossed the Sinai Peninsula and moved north to the **Levant**, or eastern Mediterranean. Finds in that region show an early modern human presence. Other finds support the **Southern Dispersal model**, with a crossing from East Africa to the southern Arabian Peninsula through the Straits of Bab-el-Mandeb. It is tempting to think of one momentous event in which people stepped off Africa and into the Middle East, never to look back. In reality, there were likely multiple waves of movement producing gene flow back and forth across these regions. The expanding modern human population could have thrived by using resources along the southern coast of the Arabian Peninsula to South Asia, with side routes moving north along rivers. The maximum range of the species then grew across Asia as shown by evidence across the continent.

Modern Homo sapiens *in the Middle East*

Geographically, the Middle East is the ideal place for the African modern *Homo sapiens* population to inhabit upon expanding out of their home continent. In the Eastern Mediterranean coast of the Levant, there is a wealth of skeletal and material culture linked to modern *Homo sapiens*. Recent discoveries from Saudi Arabia further add to our view of human life just beyond Africa.

The Caves of Mount Carmel in present-day Israel have preserved skeletal remains and artifacts of modern *Homo sapiens*, the first-known group living outside Africa. The skeletal presence at Misliya Cave is represented by just part of the left upper jaw of one individual, but it is notable for being dated to a very early time, between 194,000 and 177,000 years ago (Hershkovitz et al. 2018). Later, from 120,000 to 90,000 years ago, fossils of multiple individuals across life stages were found in the caves of Es-Skhul and Qafzeh (Shea and Bar-Yosef 2005). The skeletons had many modern *Homo sapiens* traits, such as globular crania and more gracile postcranial bones when compared to Neanderthals. Still, there were some archaic traits. For example, the adult male Skhul V also possessed what researchers Daniel Lieberman, Osbjorn Pearson, and Kenneth Mowbray (2000) called marked or clear occipital bunning. Also, compared to later modern humans, the Mount Carmel people were more robust. Skhul V had a particularly impressive brow ridge that was short in height but sharply jutted forward above the eyes (Figure 12.8). The high level of preservation is due to the intentional burial of some of

Figure 12.8 This Skhul V cranium model shows the sharp browridges. The contour of a marked occipital bun is barely visible from this angle.

these people. Besides skeletal material, there are signs of artistic or symbolic behavior. For example, the adult male Skhul V had a boar's jaw on his chest. Similarly, Qafzeh 11, a juvenile with healed cranial trauma, had an impressive deer antler rack placed over his torso (Figure 12.9) (Coqueugniot et al. 2014). Perforated seashells colored with **ochre**, mineral-based pigment, were also found in Qafzeh (Bar-Yosef Mayer, Vandermeersch, and Bar-Yosef 2009).

Figure 12.9 This cast of the Qafzeh 11 burial shows the antler's placement over the upper torso. The forearm bones appear to overlap the antler.

One remaining question is, what happened to the modern humans of the Levant after 90,000 years ago? Another site attributed to our species did not appear in the region until 47,000 years ago. Competition with Neanderthals may have accounted for the disappearance of modern human occupation since the Neanderthal presence in the Levant lasted longer than the dates of the early modern *Homo sapiens*. John Shea and Ofer Bar-Yosef (2005) hypothesized that the Mount Carmel modern humans were an initial expansion from Africa but one that failed. Perhaps they could not succeed due to competition with the Neanderthals who had been there longer and had both cultural and biological adaptations to that environment.

Six-hundred kilometers from Mount Carmel, the fossil AW-1 from Al Wusta in Saudi Arabia was just one finger bone, but it greatly enhanced our view of modern *Homo sapiens* just outside Africa. Dating methods converged on a range between 130,000 and 90,000 years ago, overlapping the Skhul and Qafzeh range (Groucutt et al. 2018). The AW-1 bone and its associated stone tools added to evidence of many sites dotted throughout the Arabian Peninsula that contained stone tools but not skeletal remains.

Modern Homo sapiens *of China*

A long history of paleoanthropology in China has found ample evidence of modern human presence. Four notable sites are the caves at Fuyan, Liujiang, Tianyuan, and Zhoukoudian. In the distant past, these caves would have been at least seasonal shelters that unintentionally preserved evidence of human presence for modern researchers to discover.

At Fuyan Cave in Southern China, paleoanthropologists found 47 adult teeth associated with cave formations dated to between 120,000 and 80,000 years ago (Liu et al. 2015). It is currently the oldest-known modern human site in China, though other researchers question the validity of the date range (Michel et al. 2016). The teeth have the small size and gracile features of modern *Homo sapiens* dentition. No lithics have been found in Fuyan Cave.

The fossil Liujiang (or Liukiang) hominin has derived traits that classified it as a modern *Homo sapiens*, though primitive archaic traits were also present. In the skull, which was found nearly complete, the Liujiang hominin had a taller forehead than archaic *Homo sapiens* but also had an enlarged occipital region (Figure 12.10) (Brown 1999). A reconstruction of the brain based on the endocast of the cranium confirmed these trends along with a larger overall volume (Wu et al. 2008). Other parts of the skeleton also had a mix of modern and archaic traits: for example, the femur fragments suggested a slender length but with thick bone walls (Woo 1959). Dating methods suggested an age of around 67,000 years.

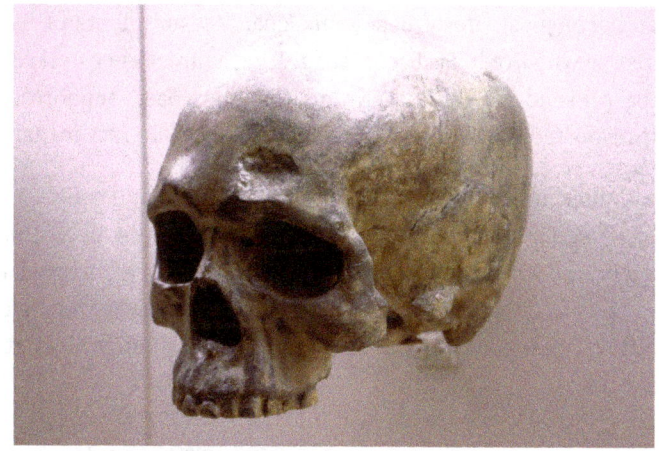

Figure 12.10 The Liujiang cranium shows the tall forehead and overall gracile appearance typical of modern Homo sapiens.

A mandible fragment, teeth, and postcranial skeletal remains of a single adult of indeterminate sex was found by tree farmers in Tianyuan, 50 km from Beijing (Tong 2004). Radiocarbon dating of the bones estimated that they were from 42,000 to 39,000 years ago (Shang et al. 2007). As with other fossils described in this section, researchers noted a few transitional traits between archaic and modern categories, such as deep tooth measurements (the anteroposterior or front-to-back dimension) and a robust tibia. The Tianyuan fossils also had some antemortem tooth loss (which happened during life), osteoarthritis of a left-hand finger joint, and enlargements to muscle attachment sites of the tibia and femur. The evidence pointed to a physically demanding life.

The last Chinese site to describe here is the one that has been studied the longest. In the Zhoukoudian Cave system, where *Homo erectus* and archaic *Homo sapiens* have also been found, there were three crania that fit the modern *Homo sapiens* set of traits (Figure 12.11). These crania were in a part of the cave called the Upper Cave, dating to between 34,000 and 10,000 years ago. The crania were all more globular than that of archaic humans but still lower and longer than later modern humans' (Brown 1999; Harvati 2009). When compared to one another, the three Upper Cave crania showed significant differences from one another. Comparison of cranial measurements to other populations past and present found no connection with modern East Asians. These findings again show that human variation was very different from what we see today.

Figure 12.11 The entrance to the Upper Cave of the Zhoukoudian complex, where crania of three prehistoric modern humans were found.

Other Asian Modern Humans

Other discoveries in Asia show us where modern *Homo sapiens* went after the initial expansion. Sites with evidence of modern human occupation stretch from the island of Sri Lanka north to Siberia. The first modern humans may have followed rivers north to settle in colder regions while still accessing the rich freshwater environment.

The Balangoda hominins refer to around 36 modern humans as far back as 38,000 years ago whose fossils were found in numerous cave sites around Sri Lanka (Kennedy et al. 1987). The name also refers to one particularly well-studied skeleton from the archaeological site of Batadombalena. Measurements of Balangoda Man show a closeness to the modern-day Vedda people who live in Sri Lanka, suggesting a direct ancestral relationship. Ornamentation such as pendants and beads, and the presence of shark teeth far from the coast, supported the presence of modern behavior as they were possibly transported for their aesthetic or symbolic value rather than their practical use.

A double-infant burial dated to 28,000 years ago was found in 1928 at the site of Mal'ta in southern Siberia, north of Mongolia (Raghavan et al. 2014). Researchers named the three- to four-year-old individual MA-1. This burial was decorated with Later Stone Age decorations: a beaded necklace, pendants, and a headband. Other accessories and lithics were buried with the pair. Genetic analysis of MA-1 found a connection with both present-day Western Europeans and Native Americans but not East Asians. This finding hints at the complex routes people took in the expansion of the species.

Summary of Modern H. sapiens in the Middle East and Asia

As in Africa, the finds of the Middle East have shown that humans were biologically diverse and had complex relationships with their environment. Work in the Levant showed an initial expansion north from the Sinai Peninsula that did not last. Away from the Levant, expansion continued. People were present in Saudi Arabia, too, as rainfall increased the amount of habitable land. Local resources were used to make lithics and decorative items.

The early Asian presence of modern *Homo sapiens* was complex and varied as befitting the massive continent. What the evidence shows is that people adapted to a wide array of environments that were far removed from Africa. From the

Levant to Sri Lanka, Siberia, and China, humans with modern anatomy used caves that preserved signs of their presence. Faunal and floral remains found in these shelters speak to the flexibility of the human omnivorous diet as local wildlife and foliage became nourishment. Decorative items, often found as burial goods in planned graves, show a flourishing cultural life.

Eventually, modern humans at the southeastern fringe of the geographical range of the species found their way southeast until some became the first humans in Australia.

Crossing to Australia

Expansion of the first modern human Asians, still following the coast, eventually entered an area called **Sunda** by researchers before continuing on to modern Australia. Sunda was a landmass made up of the modern-day Malay Peninsula, Sumatra, Java, and Borneo. Lowered sea levels connected these places with land bridges, making them easier to traverse. Proceeding past Sunda meant navigating **Wallacea**, the archipelago that includes the Indonesian islands east of Borneo. The name refers to naturalist Sir Alfred Russel Wallace, who noted that organisms from this region differed from those to the west. Prehistorically, there were many **megafauna**, large animals that migrating humans would have used for food and materials such as hides and bones. Further southeast was another prehistoric landmass called **Sahul**, which included New Guinea and Australia as one contiguous continent. This land had never seen hominins or any other primates before modern *Homo sapiens* arrived. Sites along this path offer clues about how our species handled these changes to the local environment to live successfully as foragers.

While no fossil humans have been found at the Madjedbebe rock shelter in the North Territory of Australia, more than 10,000 artifacts found there show both behavioral modernity and variability (Clarkson et al. 2017). They include a diverse array of stone tools and different shades of ochre for rock art, including mica-based reflective pigment (similar to glitter). The ochre were shaped into what the researchers called "crayons" to be held and used to mark other things. There were also plant and animal remains matching the tools used to process them. One notable find in this category is the partial upper jaw of a thylacine, or Tasmanian wolf, which was colored red. These impressive artifacts date as far back as 56,000 years ago, providing the date for the earliest-known presence of humans in Australia.

The skeletal remains at Lake Mungo are the oldest known in the continent. The lake, now dry, was one of a series located along the southern coast of Australia in New South Wales, far from where the first people entered from the north (Barbetti and Allen 1972; Bowler et al. 1970). Two individuals dating to around 40,000 years ago show signs of artistic and symbolic behavior, including intentional burial. The bones of Lake Mungo 1 (LM1), an adult female, were crushed repeatedly, colored with red ochre, and even cremated (Bowler et al. 1970). Lake Mungo 3 (LM3), a tall older male with a gracile cranium but robust postcranial bones, had his fingers interlocked over his pelvic region (Brown 2000).

Kow Swamp, also in southern Australia, contained human crania that looked distinctly different from the ones at Lake Mungo (Durband 2014; Thorne and Macumber 1972). The Kow Swamp crania had extremely robust brow ridges and thick bone walls, but these were paired with globular features on the braincase (Figure 12.12). The frontal bones had extremely linear slopes from the brow to the top of the cranium, resembling intentional cranial modification seen in other parts of the world. If the crania were shaped on purpose, they are another sign of symbolic behavior, as the practice has linked to ideas of group cultural identity. By the time of the Kow Swamp people, between 9,000 and 20,000 years ago, cranial modification may have been a meaningful part of culture in southern Australia.

Summary of Modern H. sapiens in Australia

The presence of the first humans in Australia along the current northern and southern coasts suggests that they used a route that wrapped around the perimeter of the continent. This path allowed access to both coastal and inland resources. Megafauna was a likely source of food and other resources. The mythology of Australian aborigines today has been linked by researchers to extinct life, such as marsupial tapirs and lions. Predation by humans may be why the megafauna became extinct, leaving the oral tradition of their existence.

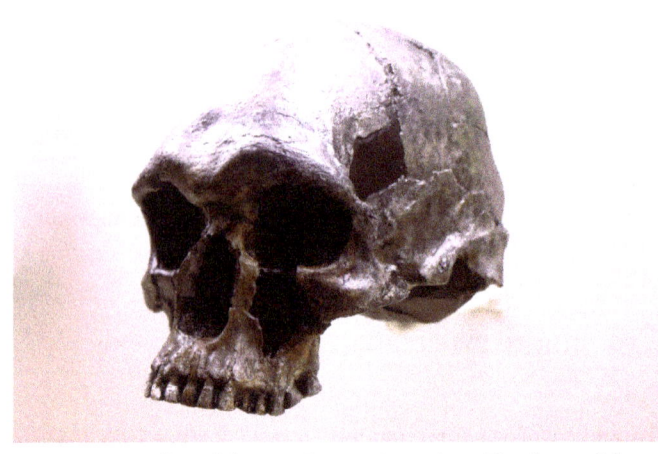

Figure 12.12 Replica of the Kow Swamp 1 cranium. The shape of the braincase could be due to artificial cranial modification. A competing hypothesis is that it reflects the primitive shape of Homo erectus.

The abundant evidence matching the criteria for behavioral modernity shows that the early Australians had a rich artistic and symbolic life. Raw materials must have been transported or traded across long distances in order to make art and color both human and nonhuman skeletal remains. The local varieties of stone tools and art may reflect cultural variation across distant regions of the continent.

The overall view of the first modern humans in Australia from a biological perspective shows a high amount of skeletal diversity. This is similar to the trends seen earlier in Africa, the Middle East, and East Asia. While the Lake Mungo individuals had derived gracile cranial traits, the Kow Swamp crania were measurably more robust.

Northwest to Europe

The first modern human expansion into Europe occurred after other members of our species settled East Asia and Australia. As the evidence from the Levant suggests, modern human movement to Europe may have been hampered by the presence of Neanderthals. Another obstacle was that the colder climate was incompatible with the biology of African modern *Homo sapiens*, which was adapted for exposure to high heat and ultraviolet radiation. Still, by 40,000 years ago, modern *Homo sapiens* had enough of a presence in Europe to leave evidence for researchers to find. This time was also the start of the Later Stone Age or **Upper Paleolithic**, with an expansion in cultural complexity. Connected with the history of science in general, early modern *Homo sapiens* in Europe have been studied for centuries. Due to the bias in research focus favoring Europe, there is a wealth of evidence to explore. Still, there are also eye-opening discoveries in this area today. This section will cover some of the key evidence of early modern human life in Europe, then go over the typologies used to view the cultural changes in this region.

In Romania, the site of Peștera cu Oase (Cave of Bones) had the oldest known remains of modern *Homo sapiens* in Europe, dated to around 40,000 years ago (Trinkaus et al. 2003a). Among the bones and teeth of cave bears, wolves, ibex, and other animals were the fragmented cranium of one person and the mandible of another (the two bones did not fit each other). Both bones have modern human traits similar to the fossils from the Middle East, but they also had Neanderthal traits. Oase 1, the mandible, has a mental eminence but also extremely large molars (Trinkaus et al. 2003b). This mandible has yielded DNA, opening another dimension of study. Surprisingly, DNA from Oase 1 is equally similar to DNA from present-day Europeans and Asians (Fu et al. 2015). This means that Oase 1 was not the direct ancestor of modern Europeans. The Oase 2 cranium has the derived traits of reduced brow ridges along with archaic wide zygomatic cheekbones (Figure 12.13) (Rougier et al. 2007). What the braincase shows is also between the two extremes: an overall globular shape that had a tall but sloped frontal bone and an occipital bun-like protrusion at the other end. No artifacts were found at this site. The assemblage was likely gathered by either carnivores or geological events such as water action since the Oase human bones were found with a high amount of nonhuman remains.

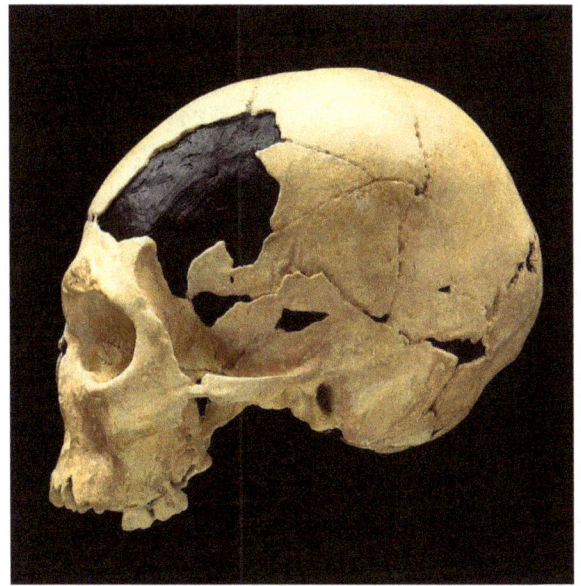

Figure 12.13 This side view of the Oase 2 cranium shows the reduced brow ridges but also occipital bunning that is a sign that modern Homo sapiens interbred with Neanderthals.

The term "Cro-Magnon" has entered public usage as a name for any prehistoric modern European *Homo sapiens*, and maybe any "caveman" of our species, but it technically refers to four adults (three male and one female) and an infant found in the Cro-Magnon rock shelter in France in 1868 (Balzeau et al. 2013). The remains are dated to 28,000 years ago and may all have been intentionally buried along with over 300 pierced seashells and nonhuman skeletal remains. The Cro-Magnon crania are easily identifiable by their rectangular eye orbits, which are more angular than any contemporary (Figure 12.14). Compared to Neanderthal skeletons of the same region, the Cro-Magnons are extremely gracile. The adults also show signs of much pathology, including fused neck vertebrae and healed fractures. The individual Cro-Magnon 1 has skeletal lesions typical of neurofibromatosis type 1, a rare genetic disease that causes tumor growth (Charlier et al. 2018). The combination of disease markers suggest that life for the Cro-Magnons was so physically demanding that it greatly affected the skeleton.

Dating to around 26,000 years ago, Předmostí near Přerov in the Czech Republic was a site where people buried over 30 individuals along with many artifacts. Eighteen individuals were found in one mass burial area, a few covered by the scapulae of woolly mammoths (Germonpré, Lázničková-Galetová, and Sablin 2012). While the recovered human skeletons were destroyed in World War II, finely detailed photographic negatives allowed comparisons to other human groups (Figure 12.15). The Předmostí crania were more globular than those of archaic humans but tended to be longer and lower than in later modern humans (Velemínská et al. 2008). The height of the face was in line with modern residents of Central Europe. One standout trait seen on every mandible on this site was an unusually long length to the mandibular body and jutting chin, resulting in a particular local appearance. Besides the human remains, the site contained the bones of over a thousand mammoths. Some of the mammoth remains were shaped by humans, including a limb bone fragment with a carved abstract female figure. There is also

Figure 12.14 This reconstruction of the Cro-Magnon 1 skull shows the gracility of modern Homo sapiens along with a disease that marked the bone.

skeletal evidence of dog domestication, such as the presence of dog skulls with shorter snouts than in wild wolves (Germonpré, Lázničková-Galetová, and Sablin 2012). In total, Předmostí could have been a settlement dependent on mammoths for subsistence with people participating in artistic behaviors and the artificial selection of early domesticated dogs.

Upper Paleolithic European Material Culture

The sequence of modern Homo sapiens technological change in the Later Stone Age has been thoroughly labeled and dated by researchers working in Europe. The style associated with the start of the Upper Paleolithic is the Aurignacian, starting around 40,000 years ago and ending around 27,000 years ago. Items in this tradition include stone blades as well as beads made from shell, bones, and teeth. Next is the Gravettian, which lasted from 6,000 years to 21,000 years ago. This culture is associated with most of the known curvy female figurines, often assumed to be "Venus" figures. Hunting technology also advanced, such as with the first known boomerang, **atlatl** (spear thrower), and archery. The Solutrean, marked by further innovation in delicate tool work, is the following style from 21,000 to 17,000 years ago. After that time, the Magdalenian tradition spread. This culture further expanded on fine bone tool work, including barbed spearheads and fishhooks (Figure 12.16). The end of the Magdalenian is also the end of the Later Stone Age and the Pleistocene Period. While these labels and time spans apply to Europe, other regions also showed changes in material culture to some of the same types of technology. Uncovering the regional timelines of cultural styles around the world to see these transitions on a global scale is an ongoing goal of paleoanthropologists.

Figure 12.15 This illustration is based upon one of the surviving photographic negatives since the original fossil was lost in World War II. The modern human chin is prominent, as is an archaic occipital bun.

Among the many European sites dating to the Later Stone Age, the famous cave art sites deserve mention. Chauvet-Pont-d'Arc Cave in southern France dates to separate Aurignacian occupations 31,000 years ago and 26,000 years ago. Over a hundred art pieces representing 13 animal species are preserved. Some depicted species are common to European cave art, such as deer and horses. Others are rare, such as rhinos and owls. Two possible human figures are in the deepest gallery of the cave system. Besides the painted figures, the tracks and skulls of cave bears and an ibex were also found in the cave. Another famous French cave with art is Lascaux, which is several thousand years younger at 17,000 years ago in the Magdalenian period. At this site, there are over 6,000 painted figures on the walls and ceiling (Figure 12.17). The paint was made of a mix of mineral pigments in liquid binder made from fat or clay. Scaffolding and lighting must have been used to make the paintings on the walls and ceiling deep in the cave. Overall, visiting Lascaux as a contemporary must have been an awesome experience: trekking deeper in the cave lit only by torches giving glimpses of animals all around as mysterious sounds echoed through the galleries. The professionally lit photographs of today do not give the original context justice, though replicas have been built to simulate the experience for tourists. Both Chauvet and Lascaux have been closed to all but researchers due to the degradation of the art when tourism was allowed.

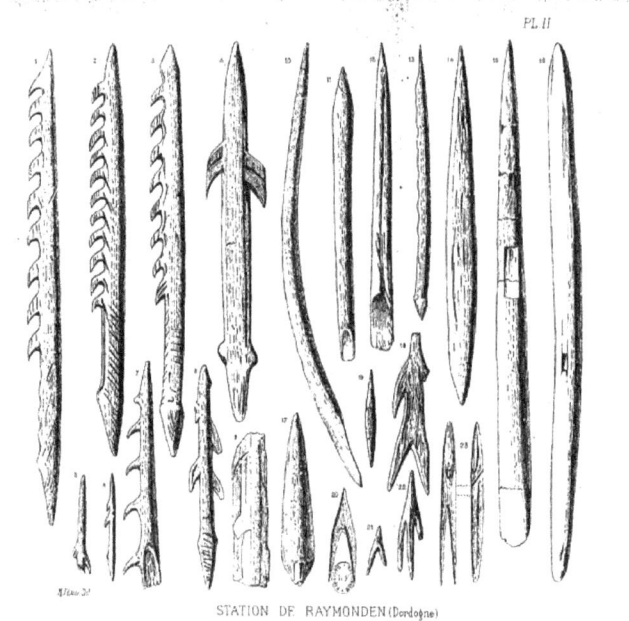

Figure 12.16 This drawing from 1891 shows an array of Magdalenian-style barbed points found in the burial of a reindeer hunter. They were carved from antler.

Figure 12.17 Photograph of just one surface with cave art at Lascaux Cave. The most prominent piece here is the Second Bull, found in a chamber called the Hall of Bulls. Smaller cattle and horses are also visible.

Summary of Modern H. sapiens *in Europe*

Study of Europe in the Upper Paleolithic gives a more detailed view of the general pattern of biological and cultural change linked with the arrival of modern *Homo sapiens*. The modern humans experienced a rapidly changing culture that from our perspective went through four major growths in complexity and refinement. Skeletally, the increasing globularity of the cranium and the gracility of the rest of the skeleton continued, though with unique regional traits, too. The cave art sites showed a deeper use of expression and symbolism, though the exact meaning is unclear. With survival dependent on the surrounding ecology, painting the figures may have connected people to important and impressive wildlife at both a physical and spiritual level. Both reverence for animals and the use of caves for an enhanced sensory experience are common to cultures today and through recorded history.

In the next section we continue our exploration of *Homo sapiens* origins by seeing the genetic evidence of interbreeding between the archaic and modern types, leaving just the latter to continue to the present day.

Distant Relations: Interbreeding with Archaic Humans Outside Africa

As the modern human population grew beyond Africa, they interbred with the archaic *Homo sapiens* who were already there, descendants of the *Homo erectus* populations before them. This statement is different from what many people in the public believe: that modern humans are the direct descendants of the archaic Neanderthals. Instead, the building evidence suggests a more complex connection between archaic and modern humans outside of Africa. This section describes the evidence showing that three *Homo sapiens* groups interbred with one another: modern *Homo sapiens* and two archaic groups, the Neanderthals and the Denisovans (Figure 12.18).

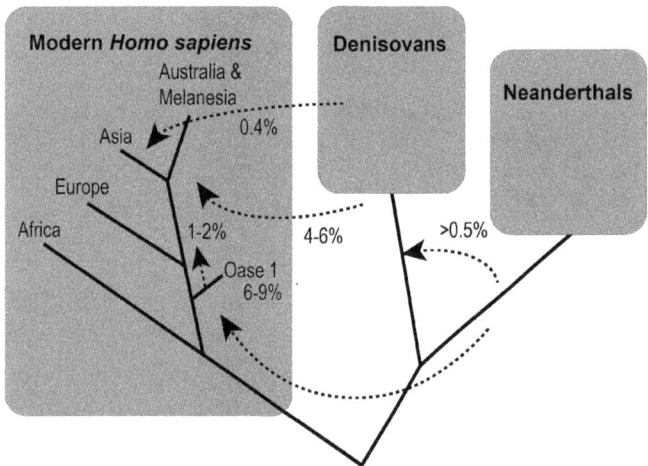

Figure 12.18 This diagram shows the amount of DNA introgression between Neanderthals, Denisovans, and various regional lineages of modern Homo sapiens. The 6–9% Neanderthal DNA found in the modern human Oase 1 was narrowed down to 1–2% in later modern humans. Denisovans share a few percent of their DNA with modern Australasians and Melanesians but just a fraction of a percent with modern East Asians.

Interbreeding with Neanderthals

Since the first finds of Neanderthal remains, researchers have sought evidence of a biological connection with modern Europeans. While there are no sites that show Neanderthals and modern *Homo sapiens* lived together (such as both types of skeletons found together in a common burial), interbreeding has been suggested by the appearance of Neanderthal traits in otherwise modern human skeletons found in their common geographical range. For example, the Oase 2 cranium from Peștera cu Oase and the Skhul V cranium each had a partial occipital bun between the Neanderthal and modern extremes.

A new source of evidence arrived with the invention of ancient DNA (aDNA) analysis, which has built up more evidence of Neanderthal and modern human interbreeding. DNA samples from Neanderthal fossils have been compared to DNA from both prehistoric and present-day modern *Homo sapiens* to trace the amount of gene flow between these groups. The amount of transfer is more indicative of **introgression**, the entrance of small, uneven portions of Neanderthal DNA into modern humans, rather than an even hybridization over time (Dannemann and Racimo 2018; Slatkin and Racimo 2016). The introgression could have been caused by an imbalance in population size: the continually growing modern population with gene flow from Africa could have diluted the incoming Neanderthal DNA to the low percentage seen today. The time spent apart as separate lineages could have caused genetic incompatibility, especially in the Y chromosome (Mendez et al. 2016). Natural selection may also have removed the inherited Neanderthal alleles if they were maladaptive, leaving just the adaptive or neutral variants.

Continuing DNA analyses reveal more details about interbreeding. Geneticist Fu Qiaomei and her team (2015) revealed long sections of Neanderthal DNA in Oase 1, around 6%–9% of the total amount, suggesting a Neanderthal ancestor four to six generations before. Fu also found continuous sections of Neanderthal DNA in the DNA of Russian and Siberian modern humans from around 45,000 years ago, reinforcing the genetic evidence of interbreeding (Fu et al. 2014).

The findings of Neanderthal DNA analysis and comparison with modern human genomes worldwide have revealed surprising details about the interactions between these groups. An unexpected result is that modern Asians have more DNA from Neanderthals than modern Europeans despite the separation in geography (Wall and Yoshihara Caldeira Brandt 2016). Today, non-Africans have around 1%–2% Neanderthal DNA in their genomes, with Asians having more than Europeans. This is a drop from the amount found in Oase 1. One explanation for this finding is that the interbreeding between Neanderthals and modern humans happened in the Middle East before the population split into the modern European and Asian populations. Then Neanderthal DNA introgressed at least a second time just into the Asian population, leaving more in that group.

Interbreeding with Denisovans

Comparison of DNA between the Denisovan archaic humans and modern humans has also produced intriguing information about the interaction between these groups. Denisovan DNA has also introgressed into some modern human populations (Reich et al. 2010; Reich et al. 2011). In this case, neither modern Africans nor Europeans have any Denisovan DNA. There is around 0.4% in modern East Asians. Notably, most modern Tibetans inherited a Denisovan allele that produces an adaptation to high-altitude living (Huerta-Sánchez et al. 2014). The highest amount is in some modern Melanesians and aboriginal Australians, between 4% and 6%. Though the Denisovan sample came from the Altai Mountains in Siberia, the most likely location for the interbreeding based on the DNA evidence was in East Asia or Sunda. The ancestors of the Melanesians and Australians would have received the Denisovan DNA into their genomes there before their descendants expanded to their eventual destinations.

Summary of Archaic Human Genetic Introgression

While the study of skeletal traits suggested archaic-modern interbreeding, the use of DNA analysis provided solid evidence of these events between archaic and modern *Homo sapiens* in Europe and Asia. This is a very active field as the technology keeps improving and more samples are analyzed. A consistent picture is forming, but many of the details concerning the timing and context of interbreeding are still unclear. At this point, we know that three human groups interbred with each other at different times. DNA originating from Neanderthals and Denisovans was found in prehistoric modern humans and is present in some Europeans and Asians of today. The introgressed DNA has affected the traits of our own species and they are just being discovered.

African Developments

We now switch our view back to Africa to see what developments occurred after members of our species first crossed to the Middle East and beyond. Our survey of modern *Homo sapiens* expansion left Africa around 150,000 years ago to see where people pushed the fringes of our geographical range. It is important to remember the species did not all leave Africa together. While modern humans found ways to survive in the Middle East, Asia, Sahul, and Europe, many others remained in Africa. Evidence of what *Homo sapiens* did in Africa from the end of the Middle Stone Age to the Later Stone Age is concentrated in South African sites. There, Blombos Cave and Border Cave show that complex human behavior was also developing in the home continent.

Blombos Cave is located along the present shore of the Cape of Africa facing the Indian Ocean and is notable for having a wide variety of artifacts. The material culture shows that toolmaking and artistry were more complex than previously thought for the Middle Stone Age. Excavations and analysis have been carried out since the 1990s by a research team including Francesco d'Errico, Christopher Henshilwood, and Marian Vanhaeren. In a layer dated to 100,000 years ago, researchers found two intact ochre-processing kits made of abalone shells and grinding stones (Henshilwood et al. 2011). Chemical analysis found the likely ingredients of the ochre-based paint, including crushed bone, animal fat, and charcoal. More ochre fragments, including some marked with notches, were found all throughout the site. The team performed numerous analyses and experiments to show that perforated marine snail shell beads from 75,000 years ago were shaped by people using bone points found in the cave (Figure 12.19) (d'Errico et al. 2005). Together, the evidence shows that the Middle Stone Age occupation at Blombos Cave incorporated resources from a variety of local environments into their culture, from caves (ochre), open land (animal bones and fat), and the sea (abalone and snail shells). This complexity shows a deep knowledge of the region's resources and their use—not just for survival but also for symbolic purposes.

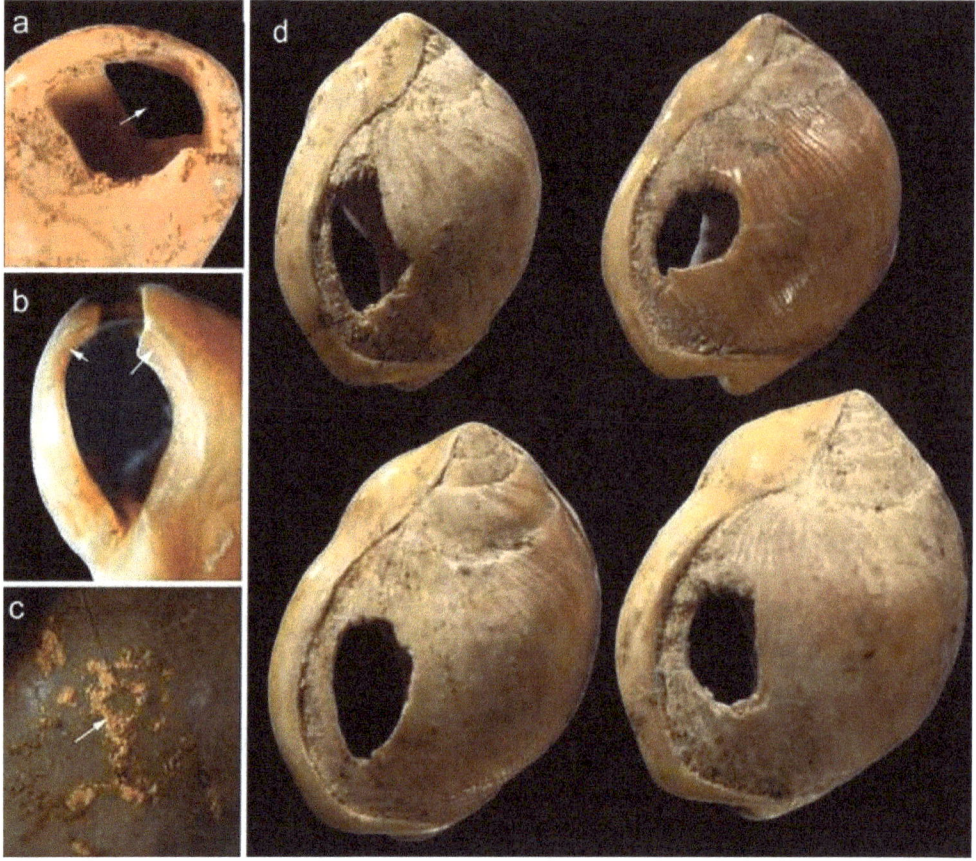

Figure 12.19 Examples of the perforated shell beads found in Blombos Cave, South Africa: (a) view of carved hole seen from the inside; (b) arrows indicate worn surfaces due to repetitive contact with other objects, such as with other beads or a connecting string; (c) traces of ochre; and (d) four shell beads showing a consistent pattern of perforation.

On the eastern coast of South Africa, Border Cave shows new African cultural developments at the start of the Later Stone Age. Paola Villa and colleagues (2012) identified several changes in technology around 43,000 years ago. Stone tool production transitioned from a slower, measured process to one that took less time to finish but made many **microliths**, small stone tools. An adhesive made from tree bark was found on some of the microliths. The researchers hypothesize that hunting technology moved from large crafted spearheads to smaller bone arrow points that were adhered to shafts and even tipped with poison for more effectiveness. Changes in decorations were also found across the Later Stone Age transition. Beads were made from a new resource: fragments of ostrich eggs (d'Errico et al. 2012). Unlike the snail shell beads, which retained the shape of the original structure, ostrich shell beads were shaped into circular forms, resembling present-day breakfast cereal O's. While a subtle difference, these beads show a higher level of altering one's own surroundings and a move from the natural to the abstract in terms of design.

Summary of Continuing Modern H. sapiens in Africa

African culture experienced a long constant phase called the Middle Stone Age until a faster burst of change produced innovation and new styles. The change was not one moment but rather a ramping up in development. Later Stone Age culture introduced elements seen across many cultures, including the construction of composite tools and even the use of strung decorations such as beads. These developments appear in the Later Stone Age of other regions, such as with the Balangoda of Sri Lanka and the Aurignacian tradition of Europe, both mentioned above. Based on the early date of the African artifacts, Later Stone Age culture may have originated in Africa and passed from person to person and region to region, with people adapting the general technique to their local resources and viewing the meaning in their own way.

Unfortunately, information about modern humans in Africa from 40,000 to 12,000 years ago is scarce. In the next section, we will return to the expanding frontier as the first hominins set foot in the Western Hemisphere.

Discovering the Americas

By 20,000 years ago, our species was the only member of Homo left on Earth. Gone were the Neanderthals, Denisovans, and *Homo floresiensis*. The range of modern *Homo sapiens* kept expanding eastward into—using the name given to this area by Europeans much later—the Western Hemisphere. This section will address what we know about the peopling of the Americas, from the first entry to these continents to the rapid spread of prehistoric Native Americans (referred to by researchers without intentional insult as prehistoric **Amerindians**, **Paleoindians**, or **Paleoamericans**) across its lush and varied environments.

The Changing Role of Beringia

Evidence points to a prehistoric land bridge called **Beringia** that allowed people to cross from Asia to North America, just as expansion to Australia was made easier with lowered sea levels that exposed Sunda and Sahul. Beringia connected what is now northeastern Siberia with Alaska. What people did to cross this land bridge is still being investigated. Currently there are two competing models for this event, called the **Ice-Free Corridor model** and the **Coastal Route model**, though the latter has been gaining intriguing evidence.

For most of the 20th century, the accepted theory was that prehistoric northeast Asians (East Asians and Siberians) first expanded across Beringia inland through an ice-free corridor between glaciers that opened into the western Great Plains of the United States, just east of the Rocky Mountains, around 13,000 years ago (Swisher et al. 2013). While life up north in the cold environment would have been harsh, migrating birds and an emerging forest might have provided sustenance as generations expanded through this land (Potter et al. 2018). These residents would have used a stone tool style that developed into the common Clovis style found later in North America.

In recent decades, researchers accumulated evidence against the ice-free corridor as the original path the first Native Americans took. For example, some archaeological sites around the Americas date to a time before the corridor was open. While one site with a date that contradicts the model could be dismissed as an error at first, several more sites were found that brought more scrutiny to the Ice-Free Corridor model. The route between glaciers was available later, and was likely used at that time, but there was already a more accessible path between the hemispheres.

The reconstruction of past geography, climate, and ecology led to the formation of the Coastal Route model that explains how people reached the Americas through Beringia. The new focus is the southern edge of the land bridge instead of its center: About 16,000 years ago, members of our species expanded along the coastline from northeast Asia, east through Beringia, and south down the Pacific Coast of North America while the inland was still sealed off by ice. Archaeologist K. R. Fladmark (1979) brought the Coastal Route model into the archaeological spotlight and researcher Jon M. Erlandson has been at the forefront of compiling support for this theory (Erlandson et al. 2015). Reconstructing the geography and climate of Beringia, the coast would have been free of ice at least part of the year by 16,000 years ago, earlier than when the ice-free corridor was completely opened. Studies of past ecology found that the coastal route would have provided abundant plant and animal resources for most of the path. Besides migrating birds, many useful fish (e.g., salmon), shellfish, mammals (e.g., whales, seals, and otters), and plants (e.g., seaweed) would have been available on the coast. A refinement of this model called the **Kelp Highway hypothesis** focuses on one particular ecosystem found just offshore from Japan, north to Beringia, and south to Baja California. This addition states that subsisting off of resources from kelp forests could have supported the rapid expansion to the Americas and down the coast of the two continents.

Other lines of evidence are also compatible with the Coastal Migration model. One indirect archaeological connection between prehistoric Japan and the Americas is a certain style of stone tool. Coastal tanged or stemmed lithics, which are stone points with a thin projection at the base, have been found in both of these distant regions (Erlandson and Braje 2011). The similarity could indicate a cultural tie. Genetic analysis of Native American DNA also shows shared ancestry with northeast Asians, linking them biologically as well (Raghavan et al. 2014).

While many factors such as reconstructions of climate and ecology indirectly support the Coastal Migration model, the search continues for direct evidence such as archaeological sites along the route. Due to the warming trend since 18,000 years ago that reduced glaciers and raised the sea level, much of the prehistoric coast that would have been occupied by the first coastal migrants to North America is currently over 100 meters underwater (Erlandson et al. 2015).

Researchers are also still determining how many large waves of people made the crossing through either Beringian route. A four-field analysis of modern Native American languages found evidence of three migration events, resulting in three major language groups (Greenberg 1987). Analyzing the DNA of prehistoric and modern peoples, which was not possible in Greenberg's time, researchers found evidence for one large wave of gene flow from Beringia, with major splits once in North America (Raghavan et al. 2015). Smaller waves after the main one could also have moved from Beringia to North America. As far back as 23,000 years ago, people living in Beringia would have had lowered gene flow with northeast Asians and also been unable to expand further east. This concept of a period of genetic isolation based on DNA analysis is called the **Beringia Standstill Model**. It explains the amount of genetic differences between Native Americans and northeast Asians within the time frame of the other evidence.

South through the Americas

However the first modern *Homo sapiens* reached the Western Hemisphere, the spread through the Americas was rapid. Multiple migration waves crossed from North to South America (Posth et al. 2018). Our species took advantage of the lack of hominin competition and the bountiful resources both along the coasts and inland. The Americas had their own wide array of megafauna, which included woolly mammoths, mastodons, camels, horses, ground sloths, giant tortoises, and—a favorite of researchers—a two-meter-tall beaver (Figure 12.20). The reason we cannot find these amazing animals today may be that Paleoindians hunted them all to extinction. Resources gained from these fauna must have been an important part of survival for people over 12,000 years ago (Araujo et al. 2017). Several sites are notable for what they add to our understanding of American prehistory, including interactions with megafauna and other elements of the environment.

Figure 12.20 Lifesize reconstruction of a woolly mammoth at the Page Museum, part of the La Brea Tar Pits complex in Los Angeles, California. Outside of Africa, megafauna such as this went extinct around the time that humans entered their range.

Monte Verde is a landmark site that shows that the human population had expanded down the whole vertical stretch of the Americas to Chile by 14,600 years ago, only a few thousand years after humans first entered the Western Hemisphere from Alaska. The site has been excavated by archaeologist Tom D. Dillehay and his team (2015), revealing fragile material culture that is rarely preserved, including human footprints, animal hides, and wooden tools. Two of the discoveries at Monte Verde relate to the Coastal Migration model. The discovery of nine edible species of seaweed at the site shows familiarity with coastal resources that might have been passed down through generations of experience living near the ocean. A stemmed point, reminiscent of the coastal styles, was also among the lithics at Monte Verde (Figure 12.21).

Named after the town in New Mexico, the Clovis stone tool style is the first example of a widespread culture across much of North America, between 13,400 and 12,700 years ago (Miller, Holliday, and Bright 2013). Instead of a stem-shaped base, Clovis points were fluted with two small projections, one on each end of the base, facing away from the head (Figure 12.22). The stone points found at this site match those found as far as the Canadian border and northern Mexico, and from the west coast to the east coast of the United States. Fourteen Clovis sites also contained the remains of mammoths or mastodons, suggesting that hunting megafauna with these points was an important part of life for the Clovis people. Other Clovis sites show that other types of hunting and gathering were important to people's subsistence, too. After the spread of the Clovis style, it diversified into several regional styles, keeping some of the Clovis form but also developing their own unique touches.

Figure 12.21 A stemmed point (left) and drill fragment (right) found in the same level at Monte Verde. The stemmed point resembles a coastal Andean style called the Paiján and may be evidence supporting the Coastal Route model.

Figure 12.22 Compared to the stemmed point in Figure 12.21, this Clovis point has a drastically different structure. The Clovis point has a wider tip and the base has two small projections instead of a single large stem. This example was carved from chert and found in north central Ohio, dated to around 11 kya.

Only one site has a human burial containing Clovis tools: Anzick in western Montana. The individual, Anzick-1, is a male infant dated to 12,800 years ago (Rasmussen et al. 2014). He was buried with over 100 Clovis stone and bone tools that were coated in ochre. Genetic analysis found that Anzick-1's people were related to all later Native Americans, proving a direct ancestral connection and supporting the model of one large wave of migrants populating the Americas with Paleoindians.

Summary of Modern H. sapiens in the Americas

Research in prehistoric Native American origins found some surprising details, refining older models. Genetically, the migration can be considered one long period of movement, with splits into regional populations. This finding matches the sudden appearance of the homegrown Clovis culture, its rapid expansion, and the radiation of descendant cultures in North America. A few thousand years after arrival into the hemisphere, people had already covered the Americas from north to south.

The peopling of the Americas also had a lot of common elements with the prior spread of humans across Africa, Europe,

Asia, and Australia. In all of these expansions, people explored new lands that tested both the cultural and biological adaptations of the pioneers. Besides stone tool technology, the use of ochre as decoration was seen from South Africa to South America. The coasts and rivers were likely avenues in the movement of people, artifacts, and ideas, outlining the land masses while providing access to varied environments. The presence of megafauna aided human success, but this resource was eventually depleted in many parts of the world.

With our tracing of human expansion across the continents complete, we will see how researchers visualize what we learned about the origin and dispersal of modern *Homo sapiens* from 315,000 to 12,000 years ago.

The Big Picture: The Assimilation Model

How do researchers make sense of all of these modern *Homo sapiens* discoveries that cover over 300,000 years of time and stretch across every continent except Antarctica? How was modern *Homo sapiens* related to archaic *Homo sapiens*? Over the past few decades, paleoanthropologists have engaged in spirited debates based on their interpretation of the data. In the mid- to late 20th century, scientists had split into two competing views. This section describes this episode of paleoanthropology history and how continuing scientific research improves our view of the world.

One competing model was called the **Out of Africa model** or Recent African Origin model. Supporters of this model saw evidence that modern *Homo sapiens* first evolved in Africa, then expanded into the other continents without interaction with the archaic *Homo sapiens* of Europe and Asia (Stringer and Andrews 1988). Researchers on this side noted that the oldest modern *Homo sapiens* fossils were found in Africa, suggesting that that continent was the origin. Genetic analysis found the same conclusion.

The other model was called **Multiregionalism** or the Multiregional Continuity model. The view of the data by scientists on this side was that modern *Homo sapiens* evolved from the archaic humans in Africa, Europe, and Asia simultaneously (Wolpoff 1989). Gene flow would have kept the species cohesive across the great distance while producing local variation as well. The multiregionalist experts pointed to the sharing of traits from *Homo erectus*, through archaic *Homo sapiens*, and then to the modern humans in different parts of the world as supporting their model. For example, in Europe the Oase modern humans possessed Neanderthal-like traits and certain modern humans possess alleles that came from Neanderthals and Denisovans.

Eventually, researchers noticed that both the Out of Africa model and the Multiregionalism model had elements that were supported by data and elements that were not supported. Taking the supported parts of each model and combining them formed an explanation that was more complicated, but explained much more of the scientific evidence. The merging of two models to form a better one suits the name of the improved version: the Assimilation model.

The **Assimilation model** proposes that modern *Homo sapiens* evolved in Africa first and expanded out (from the Out of Africa model) but also interbred with the archaic *Homo sapiens* they encountered outside Africa (from the Multiregionalism model) (Figure 12.23). True multiregionalism occurred just within Africa as the species evolved from a web of interactions between varied groups (Scerri et al. 2018). As the modern human population expanded from Africa, they assimilated the alleles of archaic humans they encountered through interbreeding. The Assimilation model is powerful since it explains why Africa has the oldest modern human fossils, why early modern humans found in Europe and Asia bear a resemblance to the regional archaics, and why traces of archaic DNA can be found in our genomes today (Smith et al. 2017).

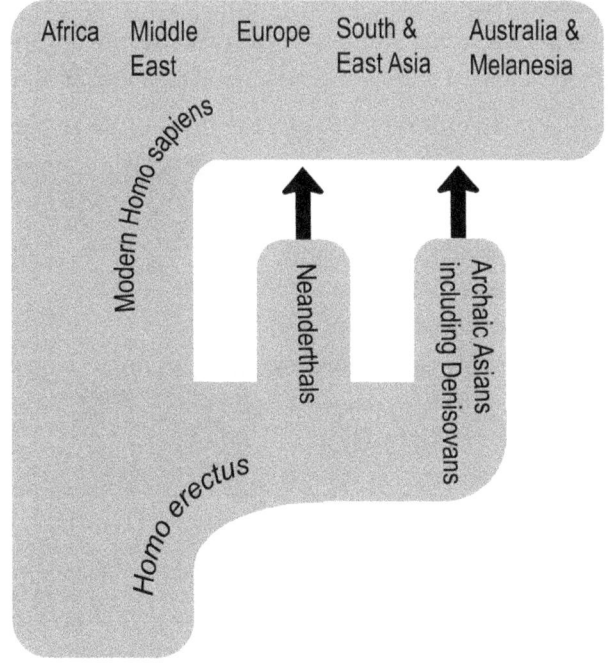

Figure 12.23 This diagram depicts the connections between archaic and modern Homo sapiens of different regions. Having evolved from Homo erectus, the archaic humans expanded from Africa and established the Neanderthal and Denisovan groups. In Africa, the remaining archaic humans evolved the modern set of traits and expanded from the continent as well, encountering and interbreeding with two archaic groups across Europe and Asia.

While scientific progress has produced a model that satisfies the data, there are still a lot of questions for paleoanthropologists to answer regarding our origins. What were the patterns of migration in each part of the world? Why did the archaic humans go extinct? In what ways did archaic and modern humans interact? How large were the past populations? How did biological, cultural, and environmental factors influence the material culture found in different parts of the world? The definitive explanation of how our species started and what our ancestors did is still out there to be found. You are now in a great place to welcome the next discovery about our distant past—maybe you'll even contribute to our understanding as well.

Special Topics: "Cavemen" in Popular Culture

"Cavemen," or our prehistory in general, is a constant presence in western popular culture. From the iconic opening to 2001: A *Space Odyssey* to the less iconic 10,000 B.C., the distant past is a common setting for dramatic stories. The prehistoric experience even gets interactive with games like *Far Cry Primal* where the player can persistence-hunt for food and ride a woolly mammoth (!) (Figure 12.24). The distant past has also been the setting for more comedic stories, such as *The Flintstones* and, recently, *The Croods* with Nicolas Cage.

Why are we interested in the past beyond a scientific understanding? Like feudal times or the Wild West, prehistory may be a setting that is rife for telling stories that excite us. With humanity stripped of the modern conveniences we are used to, situations become more intense. Prehistory takes this trope to the extreme. The viewer/game player is invited to think about what they would do if they had to live more directly off of the environment, unshielded from the dangers of the natural world. Experiencing our imaginings of that time may satisfy parts of our brain that evolved in that situation, just as people accustomed to urban life find enjoyment by camping or sitting around a fire with friends and family. Seeing the portrayal of the prehistoric world may reach those parts of our psychology that feel at home away from our constructed environment.

Figure 12.24 *Screenshot of an action scene from the videogame Far Cry Primal. While the game is set at 12 kya, one faction of humans has distinctly Neanderthal traits (center-left), though none were left by that time in reality. Note touches inspired by research, such as the use of shells for decoration on the protagonist's wrist.*

That said, the portrayal of the past in fiction is rarely accurate. There is a significant lag time between the scientific view of our past and when it reaches mass media. Older works age very poorly. In *Clan of the Cave Bear*, a book from 1980, the Neanderthals have limited emotions and communicate with sign language rather than speaking: two ideas that have not stood the test of time but were core to the story. Even in recent productions, prehistoric people are dim-witted and have limited vocabulary, though the evidence shows that our brains and language abilities are basically the same today as 300,000 years ago. How our media choose to represent the past may say more about our own values and views of ourselves rather than what people were actually like long ago.

As you engage in the next fiction set in our distant past, consider how the presentation differs from the scientific view and why there is this divide. Also, as you enjoy the world that is presented to you, consider that we are not so different from the cavemen. We are the ones born into the world of projectors and streaming media, and we may build on that to create the next medium, but at our core we are the same as the painters of Lascaux and the carvers of prehistoric figurines.

THE CHAIN REACTION OF AGRICULTURE

While it may be hard to imagine today, for most of our species' existence we were nomadic: moving through the landscape without a singular home. Instead of a refrigerator or pantry stocked with food, we procured nutrition and other resources as needed based on what was available in the environment. Instead of collecting and displaying stuff, we kept our possessions at a minimum for mobility. This part gives an overview of how this foraging lifestyle enabled the expansion of our species, then describes the invention of a new way of life, causing a chain reaction of cultural change taking us to the present day and beyond.

The Foraging Tradition

To understand our species is to understand **foraging**, or the search for resources in the environment. This **subsistence strategy**, or method of finding sustenance, sounds unusual to most of us today. Most of us live in cultures that practice another strategy, **agriculture**, where we shape the environment to mass produce what we need. Considering the age of modern *Homo sapiens*, however, we have spent far more time as nomadic foragers than as settled agriculturalists. As such, our traits have evolved to be primarily geared toward foraging. For instance, our efficient bipedalism allows persistence-hunting across long distances as well as movement from resource to resource. Even our psychological tendency toward our ability to form stable relationships with around 150 people (Dunbar 1993) may derive from the foraging lifestyle.

How does human foraging, also known as hunting and gathering, work? Anthropologists have used all four fields to answer this question (see Ember n.d.). Typically, people formed **bands**, or groups of around 50, and rarely over 100. A band's organization would be **egalitarian**, with a flexible hierarchy based on an individual's age, level of experience, and relationship with others. Everyone would have a general knowledge of the skills assigned to their gender roles, rather than specializing in different occupations. A band would move from place to place in the environment, using knowledge of the area to hunt and gather (Figure 12.25). While there were exceptions, women typically gathered plants and hunted small animals while men hunted larger prey where present (Waguespack 2005). The ratio of plant to meat in one's diet would have depended on the local resources. As a location's resources became used up, and as human waste accumulated, the band would travel to another patch (Venkataraman et al. 2017). In the varied environments that humans entered—from savannas to tropical forests, deserts, coasts, and the Arctic circle—people found sustenance needed for survival. Our species's omnivorous and cultural ability led us to excel in the generalist-specialist niche. People could have temporarily altered their environment to be more productive, such as by burning foliage to spur new growth. Besides food sources, people would have known the local areas to find rock and wood suitable for tool production, and ochre for decoration. Bands could have formed trading connections to acquire goods from distant areas. Certain sites could have been gathering spots for local bands to trade, socialize, and worship, though they were not typically large permanent settlements.

Figure 12.25 A present-day San man in Namibia demonstrates hunting using archery. Anthropologists still study the San today to learn about the foraging lifestyle in Africa.

Humans made extensive use of the foraging subsistence strategy, but this lifestyle did have limitations. The ease of foraging depended on the richness of the environment. Due to the lack of storage, resources had to be dependably found when needed. While a bountiful environment would require just a few hours of foraging a day, the level and duration of labor increased greatly in poor or unreliable environments. Labor was also needed to process the acquired resources, contributing to filling the foragers' daily schedule (Crittenden and Schnorr 2017).

The adaptations to foraging found in modern *Homo sapiens* may explain why our species became so successful both within Africa and in the rapid expansion around the world. Overcoming the limitations, each generation at the edge of our species's range would have found it beneficial to expand a little further, keeping contact with other bands but moving into unexplored territory where resources were richer. The cumulative effect would have been the spread of modern *Homo sapiens* across continents and hemispheres.

Why Agriculture?

After hundreds of thousands of years of foraging, some groups of people around 12,000 years ago started to practice agriculture instead. This transition is called the **Neolithic Revolution**, and it occurred at the start of the **Holocene** epoch. The reasons for this global change are still being investigated, but there are two likely causes that may have occurred together: a growing human population and natural global climate change.

Overcrowding could have affected the success of foraging in the environment, leading to the development of a more productive subsistence strategy (Cohen 1977). Foraging works the best with low population densities since each band needs a lot of space to support itself. If too many people occupy the same environment, they would deplete the area faster. The high population could exceed the **carrying capacity**, or number of people a location can reliably support. For instance, what if a band arrived at a grove of nutritious plants they were depending on, but it had already been used by other groups? Then the late arrivals are suddenly in a dire situation without the food they were depending on finding. This situation on a global level due to growing population and limited areas of expansion would have been an increasingly pressing issue after the human expansion through the major continents by 14,600 years ago.

A changing global climate immediately preceded the transition to agriculture, so researchers have also explored a connection between the two events. Since the **Last Glacial Maximum** of 23,000 years ago, the Earth slowly warmed. At 13,000 years ago, the temperature in most of the Northern Hemisphere dropped suddenly in a phenomenon called the **Younger Dryas**. Glaciers returned in Europe, Asia, and North America. In Mesopotamia, which includes the Levant, the climate changed from warm and humid to cool and dry. The change would have occurred over decades, disrupting the usual nomadic patterns and subsistence of foragers around the world. The Younger Dryas lasted until 11,700 years ago, when the climate returned to the long-term warming pattern. The disruption to foragers due to the temperature shift could have been a factor in spurring the transition to agriculture. Researchers Gregory K. Dow and colleagues (2009) believe that foraging bands would have clustered in the new resource-rich places where people started to direct their labor to farming the limited area. Continued practice would prompt innovations such as better tools and increasing productivity. After the Younger Dryas ended, people expanded out of the clusters. As they reinhabited the region, they brought with them a culture in which farming had become the norm, along with the technology and knowledge to succeed with this subsistence strategy (Figure 12.26).

The double threat of the limitation of human continental expansion and the sudden global climate change may have placed bands in peril as more populations outpaced their environment's carrying capacity. Not only had a growing population led to increased competition with other bands, but environments worldwide shifted to create more uncertainty. As people in different areas around the world faced this chaotic situation, they became the independent inventors of agriculture.

Figure 12.26 Rice farmers in the present day using draft cattle to prepare their field.

Agriculture around the World

Due to global changes to the human experience starting from 12,000 years ago, cultures with no knowledge of each other turned toward farming their local resources (Figure 12.27). The switch to agriculture took time and effort with no guarantee of success. Agriculture is a difficult process with fires, floods, droughts, disease, and pests being constant problems to address. Heavy physical labor with no immediate payoff was also needed to shape the landscape in a coordinated way to support agriculture. For example, people had to direct water flow to irrigate constructed fields of crops. The first farmers also engaged in artificial selection of their domesticates to enhance useful traits. The biggest success stories in the face of these obstacles became the primary centers of agriculture (Figure 12.27) (Fuller 2010):

- Mesopotamia: The Fertile Crescent from the Tigris and Euphrates rivers through the Levant was where bands started to domesticate plants and animals around 12,000 years ago. The connection between the development of agriculture and the Younger Dryas was especially strong here. Farmed crops included wheat, barley, peas, and lentils. This was also where cattle, pigs, sheep, and goats were domesticated.
- South and East Asia: Multiple regions across this land had varieties of rice, millet, and soybeans by 10,000 years ago. Pigs were farmed with no connection to Mesopotamia. Chickens were also originally from this region, bred for fighting first and food second.
- New Guinea: An under-appreciated center in Melanesia, agriculture started here 10,000 years ago. Bananas, sugarcane, and taro were native to this island. Sweet potatoes were brought back from voyages to South America around the year C.E. 1,000. No known animal farming occurred here.
- Mesoamerica: Agriculture from Central Mexico to northern South America also occurred from 10,000 years ago; it was also only plant based. Maize was a crop bred from teosinte grass, which has become one of the global staples. Beans, squash, and avocados were also grown in this region.
- The Andes: Starting around 8,000 years ago, local domesticated plants started with squash but later included potatoes, tomatoes, beans, and quinoa. Maize was brought down from Mesoamerica to join the local variety. The main farm animals were llamas, alpacas, and guinea pigs.
- Sub-Saharan Africa: This region went through a change 5,000 years ago called the Bantu expansion. The Bantu agriculturalists were established in West Central Africa and then expanded south and east. Native varieties of rice, yams, millet, and sorghum were grown across this area. Cattle were also domesticated here.
- Eastern North America: This region was the last major independent agriculture center, from 4,000 years ago. Squash and sunflower are the produce from this region that are most known today, though sumpweed and pitseed goosefoot were also farmed. Hunting was still the main source of animal products.

By 5,000 years ago, our species was well within the Neolithic Revolution. From the primary centers, agriculturalists spread to neighboring parts of the world with their domesticates, further expanding the use of this subsistence strategy. For example, the Mesopotamian farmers spread their innovations along the northern coast of the Mediterranean into Europe (Pinhasi, Fort, and Ammerman 2005). The crops of China were brought into the Korean peninsula (Lee 2011). From this point, the human species changed from being primarily foragers to primarily agriculturalists. The revolution took millennia, but it was a true revolution in that the lifestyle of our species was reshaped to something vastly different.

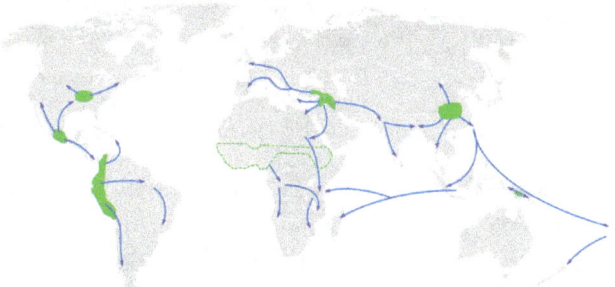

Figure 12.27 Map showing the areas where agriculture was independently invented around the world. The dotted line around sub-Saharan Africa represents a possible range that is still being narrowed by research. Blue arrows show the spread of agriculture from these zones to other regions.

Cultural Effects of Agriculture

The worldwide adoption of agriculture altered the course of human culture and history forever. The foraging lifestyle was incompatible with agriculture, so dependence on the latter required huge changes in how people lived. This section starts by following the human developments that occurred due to agriculture, leading us from 12,000 years ago to the present day. We will also reconnect with modern foragers to see how their lives have changed.

The core change in human culture due to agriculture is the move toward not moving: rather than live a nomadic lifestyle, farmers had to remain in one area to tend to their crops and livestock. The term for living bound to a certain location is **sedentarism**. Remaining in one place led to aspects of life that were uncommon in foragers: the construction of permanent shelters and agricultural infrastructure such as fields and irrigation, plus the development of storage technology such as pottery to preserve extra resources in case of future instability.

The high productivity of successful agriculture sparked further changes (Smith 2009). Since successful agriculture produced a much greater amount of food and other resources per unit of land compared to foraging, the population growth rate skyrocketed. The surplus of a bountiful harvest also provided insurance for harder times, reducing the risk of famine. Changes happened to society as well. With a few farming households producing enough food to feed many others, other people could focus on other tasks. So began specialization into different occupations such as craftspeople, traders, religious figures, and artists, spurring innovation in these areas as people could now devote time and effort toward specific skills. These interdependent people would settle an area together for convenience, causing a rise in the number of dense populations focused around farms, water, and trade routes. The growth of these settlements led to **urbanization**, the founding of cities that became the foci of human interaction.

Figure 12.28 *View of downtown San Diego taken by the author at a shopping complex during a break from jury duty. Here, people live amongst structures that facilitate commerce, government, and art.*

The formation of cities led to new issues that sparked the growth of further specializations, called **institutions**. These were cultural constructs that existed beyond the individual and had wide control over a population. Leadership of these cities became hierarchical with different levels of rank and control. Laws influenced the behavior of citizens, establishing ideal behavior and punishment for deviations. Organized religion also kept followers under a standard set of beliefs and values tied to spirituality. Under leadership, people built impressive **monumental architecture** such as pyramids that embodied the wealth and power of these early cities. Alliances could unite cities, forming the earliest states. In several regions of the world, state organization expanded into empires, wide-ranging political entities that covered a variety of cultures.

Urbanization brought new challenges as well. The concentration of sedentary peoples was ideal for infectious diseases to thrive since they could jump from person to person and even from livestock to person (Armelagos, Brown, and Turner 2005). Urban life also caused sanitation problems as human waste accumulated, adding to the spread of disease. While successful agriculture provided a large surplus of food to thwart famine, the variety of food produced was smaller than what foragers experienced (Cohen and Armelagos 1984; Cohen and Crane-Kramer 2007). The dependence on high-yield crops also caused an overabundance of carbohydrates in the diet of agriculturalists. This shift in nutrition caused another set of diseases to flourish among those who adopted farming as their subsistence strategy: dental issues such as **dental caries** (the cavities that ruin your visit to the dentist) and **malocclusion** (the misalignment of teeth caused by the softness of agricultural diets). The issues with "wisdom teeth" or third molars seen in agricultural cultures today stems from this misalignment between the environment our ancestors adapted to and our lifestyles today.

As the new disease trends show, the adoption of agriculture and the cultural changes that followed were not entirely positive. It is also important to note that this is not an absolutely linear progression of human culture from simple to complex and that higher complexity is not necessarily better than lower complexity. In many cases empires have collapsed and cities have dispersed to low-density bands that no longer saw use in maintaining institutions. However, a global trend has emerged since the adoption of agriculture, wherein population and complexity have increased, leading to the massive and influential nation states of today.

The rise of states in Europe has a direct impact on many of this book's topics. Science started as a European cultural practice by the upper class that became a standardized way to study the world. Education became an institution to provide a standardized path toward producing and gaining knowledge. The scientific study of human diversity, embroiled in the race concept that still haunts us today, was connected to the European slave trade and colonialism.

Also starting in Europe, the Industrial Revolution of the 19th century turned cities into centers of mass manufacturing and spurred the rapid development of inventions. In the technologically interconnected world of today, human society has reached a new level of complexity with **globalization**. In this system, goods are mass produced and consumed in different parts of the world due to worldwide economic factors. Instead of relying on local farms and factories, we now receive our everyday goods from all over the world.

Figure 12.29 This combine harvester can collect and process grain at a massive scale. Our food now commonly come from enormous farms located around the world.

As states based on agriculture and industry keep exerting influence on humanity today, there are people who continue to live a foraging–or mostly foraging–lifestyle. Due to the overwhelming force that agricultural societies could exert, foragers today have been marginalized to live in the least habitable parts of the world (Headland et al. 1989). These are places that are the worst for farmland, such as tropical rainforests, deserts, and the arctic. Foragers can no longer live in the abundant environments that humans would have enjoyed before the Neolithic Revolution. Interactions with agriculturalists are typically imbalanced, with trade and other exchanges heavily favoring the larger group. One of anthropology's important roles today is to intelligently and humanely manage interactions between people of different backgrounds and levels of influence.

The Future of Humanity

This chapter covered what modern *Homo sapiens* has done to get to the present time, but what will our species do far in the future? Just as biological changes accumulated from over 300,000 years ago to today, what will human traits and genetics be like? When posed with these questions, people tend to think of directional selection. Maybe our braincases will be even larger, resembling the large-headed and small-bodied aliens of science fiction (see figure 12.30. Or, our hands could be specialized for interacting with our touch-based technology with less risk of repetitive injury. These ideas do not stand up to scrutiny. Since natural selection is based on adaptations that increase reproductive success, any directional change must be due to a higher rate of producing successful offspring compared to other alleles. Larger brains and more agile fingers would be convenient to possess, but they do not translate into an increase in the underlying allele frequencies.

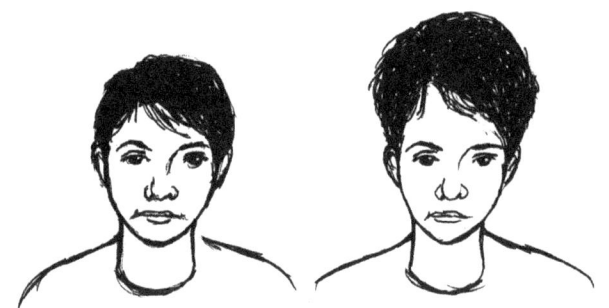

Figure 12.30 Will we evolve toward even more globular brains? Actually, this trend is not likely to continue for our species.

Scientists are hesitant to professionally speculate on the unknowable, and we today will never know what is in store for our species a thousand or a million years from now, but there are trends in human evolution that may carry on into the future. These trends are increased genetic variation and a reduction in regional differences.

Rather than a directional change, genetic variation in our species could expand. Our technology can protect us from extreme environments and pathogens, even if our biological traits are not tuned to handle these stressors. The rapid pace of technological advancement means that biological adaptations will become less and less relevant to reproductive success, so non-beneficial genetic traits will be more likely to remain in the gene pool. Biological anthropologist Jay T. Stock (2008) views environmental stress as needing to defeat two layers of protection before affecting our genetics. The first layer is our cultural adaptations. Our technology and knowledge can cover for many of our biological issues, reducing pressure on one's genotype to be just right to pass to the next generation. The second defense is our flexible physiology, such as our functional adaptations. Only stressors not handled by these powerful responses would then cause natural selection on our alleles. These shields are already substantial, and cultural adaptations will only keep increasing in strength.

The increasing ability to travel far from one's home region means that there will be a mixing of genetic variation on a global level in the future of our species. In recent centuries, gene flow of people around the world has increased, creating admixture in populations that had been separated for tens of thousands of years. For skin color, this means that populations all around the world could exhibit the whole range of skin colors, rather than the current pattern of decreasing melanin pigment farther from the equator. The same trend of intermixing would apply to all other traits, such as blood types. While our genetics will become more varied, the variation will be more intermixed instead of regionally isolated.

Our distant descendants will not likely be dextrous ultra-intellectuals; more likely, they will be a highly variable and mobile species. They will be supported by cultural adaptations that we cannot even imagine, making up for any biological limitations that keep getting passed to the next generation. Technology may even enable the editing of DNA directly, changing these trends. With the uncertainty of our future, these are just the best educated guesses for now. Our future is open and will be shaped little by little by our actions and those of our descendants.

CONCLUSION

Modern *Homo sapiens* is the species that took the hominin lifestyle the furthest to become the only living member of that lineage. This last section of the chapter summarizes what we know about modern *Homo sapiens* traits, origins, and history.

The largest factor that allowed us to persist while other hominins went extinct was likely our advanced ability to culturally adapt to a wide variety of environments. Our species, with its skeletal and behavioral traits, was well suited to be generalist-specialists who successfully foraged across most of the world's environments. The biological basis of this adaptation was our reorganized brain that facilitated innovation in cultural adaptations and intelligence for leveraging our social ties. As the brain's ability increased, it shaped the skull by reducing the evolutionary pressure to have large teeth and robust cranial bones to produce the modern *Homo sapiens* face.

Our ability to be generalist-specialists is seen in the geographical range that modern *Homo sapiens* covered in 300,000 years. In Africa, our species formed from multiregional gene flow that loosely connected archaic humans across the continent. People then expanded out to the rest of the continental Old World and even further to the Americas. Wherever people went, they were enabled and connected by the shared tools and art they crafted.

For most of our species's existence, foraging was the general subsistence strategy within which people specialized to culturally adapt to their local environment. With biologically endowed omnivorousness and mobility, people found ways to extract and process resources, shaping the environment in return. When global fluctuation in climate and a sudden resource uncertainty hit the species, people around the world focused on agriculture to have a firmer control of necessities. The new strategy shifted human history toward exponential growth and innovation to address the drastic shift in lifestyle, leading to our high dependence on cultural adaptations today. We may continue this trend in the future, with global changes to human genetic diversity.

While a cohesive image of our species has formed in recent years, there is still much to learn about our past. The work of many driven researchers shows that there are amazing new discoveries made all the time that refine our knowledge of human evolution. Technological innovations such as DNA analysis enable scientists to approach lingering questions from new angles. The answers we get allow us to ask even more insightful questions that will lead us to the next revelation. Like the pink limestone strata at Jebel Irhoud, previous effort has taken us so far and you are now ready to see what the next layer of discovery holds.

Review Questions

- What are the skeletal and behavioral traits that define modern *Homo sapiens*? What are the evolutionary explanations for its presence?
- What are some creative ways that researchers have learned about the past by studying fossils and artifacts?
- How do the discoveries mentioned in "First Africa, Then the World" fit the Assimilation model?
- What is foraging and what adaptations do we have for this subsistence strategy? Could you train to be a skilled forager?
- What are aspects of your life that come from dependence on agriculture and its cultural effects? Where did the ingredients of your favorite foods originate from?

Key Terms

African multiregionalism: The idea that modern *Homo sapiens* evolved as a complex web of small regional populations with sporadic gene flow among them.

Agriculture: The mass production of resources through farming and domestication.

Amerindian: Term used to refer to the ancient humans of North and South America.

Assimilation model: Current theory of modern human origins stating that the species evolved first in Africa and interbred with archaic humans of Europe and Asia.

Atlatl: A handheld spear thrower that increased the force of thrown projectiles.

Band: A small group of people living together as foragers.

Beringia: Prehistoric landmass that connected Siberia and Alaska. The ancestors of Paleoindians would have crossed this area to reach the Americas.

Beringia Standstill Model: Theory that people were genetically isolated in Beringia before expanding to the Americas.

Carrying capacity: The amount of organisms that an environment could reliably support.

Coastal Route model: Theory that the first Paleoindians crossed to the Americas by following the southern coast of Beringia.

Dental caries: Damage to tooth enamel due to the waste products of built-up bacteria. Known in the general public as cavities.

Early Modern *Homo sapiens*, Early Anatomically Modern Human: Terms used to refer to transitional fossils between archaic and modern *Homo sapiens* that have a mosaic of traits. Humans like ourselves, who mostly lack archaic traits, are referred to as Late Modern *Homo sapiens* and simply Anatomically Modern Humans.

Egalitarian: Human organization without strict ranks. Foraging societies tend to be more egalitarian than those based on other subsistence strategies.

Foraging: Lifestyle consisting of frequent movement through the landscape and acquiring resources with little storage.

Generalist-specialist niche: The ability to survive in a variety of environments by developing local expertise. Evolution toward this niche may have been what allowed modern *Homo sapiens* to expand past the geographical range of other human species.

Globalization: A recent increase in the interconnectedness and interdependence of people facilitated with long-distance networks.

Globular: Having a rounded appearance. Increased globularity of the braincase is a trait of modern *Homo sapiens*.

Gracile: Having a smooth and slender quality; the opposite of robust.

Holocene: The epoch of the Cenozoic Era starting around 12,000 years ago and lasting arguably through the present.

Ice-Free Corridor model: Theory that the first prehistoric Native Americans crossed to the Americas through a passage between glaciers.

Institutions: Long-lasting and influential cultural constructs. Examples include government, organized religion, academia, and the economy.

Introgression: The uneven mixing of DNA over time in which a small amount of outside genetic material is incorporated into a larger genome.

Kelp Highway hypothesis: Addition to the Coastal Route model that focuses on the use of kelp-based environments as a resource.

Last Glacial Maximum: The time 23,000 years ago when the most recent ice age was the most intense.

Later Stone Age: Time period following the Middle Stone Age with a diversification in tool types, starting around 50,000 years ago.

Levant: The eastern coast of the Mediterranean. The site of early modern human expansion from Africa and later one of the centers of agriculture.

Malocclusion: The misalignment of the jaw due to the soft diets of agriculturalists. The healthy development of the jaw, including making room for all of the teeth, depends on experiencing a higher level of physical force than what people experience with farmed and processed foods. The term literally means "bad shutting."

Megafauna: Large prehistoric animals that may have been hunted to extinction by people around the world.

Mental eminence: The chin on the mandible of modern *H. sapiens*. One of the defining traits of our species.

Microlith: Small stone tool found in the Later Stone Age; also called a bladelet.

Middle Stone Age: Time period known for Mousterian lithics that connects African archaic to modern *Homo sapiens*.

Monumental architecture: Large and labor-intensive constructions that signify the power of the elite in a sedentary society. A common type is the pyramid, a raised crafted structure topped with a point or platform.

Mosaic: Composed from a mix or composite of traits.

Multiregionalism: Theory that modern *Homo sapiens* evolved simultaneously in Africa, Asia, and Europe from archaic populations.

Neolithic Revolution: Time of rapid change to human cultures due to the invention of agriculture, starting around 12,000 years ago.

Ochre: Iron-based mineral pigment that can be a variety of yellows, reds, and browns. Used by modern human cultures worldwide since at least 80,000 years ago.

Out of Africa model: Theory that modern *Homo sapiens* expanded from Africa to cover the rest of the world without interacting with archaic humans.

Paleoamerican, Paleoindian: Terms used to refer to the ancient humans of North and South America.

Sahul: Prehistoric landmass connecting New Guinea and Australia.

Sedentarism: Lifestyle based on having a stable home area; the opposite of nomadism.

Southern Dispersal model: Theory that modern *H. sapiens* expanded from East Africa by crossing the Red Sea and following the coast east across Asia.

Subsistence strategy: The method an organism uses to find nourishment and other resources.

Sunda: Asian prehistoric landmass that incorporated modern Southeast Asia.

Supraorbital torus: The bony brow ridge across the top of the eye orbits on many hominin crania.

Upper Paleolithic: Time period considered synonymous with the Later Stone Age.

Urbanization: The increase of population density as people settled together in cities.

Wallacea: Archipelago southeast of Sunda with different biodiversity than Asia.

Younger Dryas: The rapid change in global climate, especially a cooling of the Northern Hemisphere, 13,000 years ago.

About the Author

Keith Chan, Ph.D.

University of Missouri: Grossmont College and MiraCosta College, drkeithcchan@gmail.com, keithcchan.com

Keith Chan

Dr. Keith Chan is an instructor of anthropology at Grossmont College and MiraCosta College in San Diego County. He reached this step of his anthropological path after many memorable experiences across the country and the hemisphere. He earned a bachelor's degree in anthropology from the University of California, Berkeley, in 2001. As a graduate student at the University of Missouri, he traveled to Perú with teams of students to study prehistoric skeletons to understand the lives of prehistoric Andeans. He completed his writing to earn a Ph.D. in 2011. Inspired by many educators in his journey, Dr. Chan turned his career toward teaching anthropology and helping students understand and appreciate humanity.

For Further Exploration

Websites

Ministère de la Culture and Musée d'Archéologie Nationale. "Visit the cave" Lascaux website. http://archeologie.culture.fr/lascaux/en/visit-cave.

SAPIENS. "Evolution." SAPIENS website. https://www.sapies.org/category/evolution/.

Smithsonian Institution. "What does it mean to be human?" Smithsonian National Museum of Natural History website. http://humanorigins.si.edu.

ThoughtCo. "Archaeology." ThoughtCo. Website. https://www.thoughtco.com/archaeology-4133504.

University of California, San Diego. "MOCA Domains." Center for Academic Research & Training in Anthropogeny website. https://carta.anthropogeny.org/moca/domains.

Books

Kolbert, Elizabeth. 2014. The Sixth Extinction: An Unnatural History. New York: Bloomsbury.

Sykes, Bryan. 2002. The Seven Daughters of Eve: The Science That Reveals Our Genetic Ancestry. New York: W. W. Norton & Company.

Articles

Stringer, C. 2016. "The Origin and Evolution of Homo sapiens." Philosophical Transactions of the Royal Society B 371 (1698): doi:10.1098/rstb.2015.0237.

Trinkaus, E. 2018. "One Hundred Years of Paleoanthropology: An American Perspective." American Journal of Physical Anthropology 165 (4): 638-651.

Wheelwright, Jeff. 2015. "Days of Dysevolution." Discover 33-39. http://discovermagazine.com/2015/may/16-days-of-dysevolution.

Wierer, Ursula, Simona Arrighi, Stefano Bertola, Günther Kaufmann, Benno Baumgarten, Annaluisa Pedrotti, Patrizia Pernter, and Jacques Pelegrin. 2018. "The Iceman's Lithic Toolkit: Raw Material, Technology, Typology and Use." PLOS One 13 (6): e0198292. doi:10.1371/journal.pone.0198292.

Documentaries

Brown, Nicholas, dir. 2015. First Peoples. Edmonton: Wall to Wall Television. Amazon Prime Video.

Thompson, Niobe, dir. 2016. Great Human Odyssey. Edmonton: Clearwater Documentary. http://www.pbs.org/wgbh/nova/evolution/great-human-odyssey.html.

References

Araujo, Bernardo B. A., Luiz Gustavo R. Oliveira-Santos, Matheus S. Lima-Ribeiro, José Alexandre F. Diniz-Filho, and Fernando A. S. Fernandez. 2017. "Bigger Kill Than Chill: The Uneven Roles of Humans and Climate on Late Quaternary Megafaunal Extinctions." Quaternary International 431: 216-222.

Armelagos, George J., Peter J. Brown, and Bethany Turner. 2005. "Evolutionary, Historical, and Political Economic Perspectives on Health and Disease." Social Science & Medicine 61 (4): 755-765.

Balzeau, A., D. Grimaud-Hervé, F. Détroit, R. L. Holloway, B. Combès, and S. Prima. 2013. "First Description of the Cro-Magnon 1 Endocast and Study of Brain Variation and Evolution in Anatomically Modern Homo sapiens." Bulletins et Mémoires de la Société d'Anthropologie de Paris 25 (1-2): 1-18.

Bar-Yosef Mayer, Daniella E., Bernard Vandermeersch, and Ofer Bar-Yosef. 2009. "Shells and Ochre in Middle Paleolithic Qafzeh Cave, Israel: Indications for Modern Behavior." Journal of Human Evolution 56 (3): 307-314.

Barbetti, M., and H. Allen. 1972. "Prehistoric Man at Lake Mungo, Australia, by 32,000 Years Bp." Nature 240 (5375): 46-48.

Bowler, J. M., Rhys Jones, Harry Allen, and A. G. Thorne. 1970. "Pleistocene Human Remains from Australia: A Living Site and Human Cremation from Lake Mungo, Western New South Wales." World Archaeology 2 (1): 39-60.

Brown, Peter. 1999. "The First Modern East Asians? Another Look at Upper Cave 101, Liujiang and Minatogawa 1." In Interdisciplinary Perspectives on the Origins of the Japanese, edited by K. Omoto, 105-131. Kyoto: International Research Center for Japanese Studies.

———. 2000. "Australian Pleistocene Variation and the Sex of Lake Mungo 3." Journal of Human Evolution 38 (5): 743–749.

Bruner, Emiliano. 2010. "Morphological Differences in the Parietal Lobes within the Human Genus." Current Anthropology 51 (S1): S77–S88.

Charlier, Philippe, Nadia Benmoussa, Philippe Froesch, Isabelle Huynh-Charlier, and Antoine Balzeau. 2018. "Did Cro-Magnon 1 Have Neurofibromatosis Type 1?" The Lancet 391 (10127): 1259.

Clarkson, Chris, Zenobia Jacobs, Ben Marwick, Richard Fullagar, Lynley Wallis, Mike Smith, Richard G. Roberts, et al. 2017. "Human Occupation of Northern Australia by 65,000 Years Ago." Nature 547 (7663): 306–310.

Cohen, Mark Nathan. 1977. The Food Crisis in Prehistory. Overpopulation and the Origins of Agriculture. New Haven, CT: Yale University Press.

Cohen, Mark Nathan, and George J. Armelagos, eds. 1984. Paleopathology at the Origins of Agriculture. Orlando, FL: Academic Press.

Cohen, Mark Nathan, and Gillian M. M. Crane-Kramer, eds. 2007. Ancient Health: Skeletal Indicators of Agricultural and Economic Intensification. Gainesville, FL: University Press of Florida.

Coqueugniot, Hélène, Olivier Dutour, Baruch Arensburg, Henri Duday, Bernard Vandermeersch, and Anne-Marie Tillier. 2014. "Earliest Cranio-Encephalic Trauma from the Levantine Middle Palaeolithic: 3-D Reappraisal of the Qafzeh 11 Skull, Consequences of Pediatric Brain Damage on Individual Life Condition and Social Care." PLOS ONE 9 (7): e102822.

Crittenden, Alyssa N., and Stephanie L. Schnorr. 2017. "Current Views on Hunter-Gatherer Nutrition and the Evolution of the Human Diet." American Journal of Physical Anthropology 162 (S63): 84–109.

d'Errico, Francesco, Lucinda Backwell, Paola Villa, Ilaria Degano, Jeannette J. Lucejko, Marion K. Bamford, Thomas F. G. Higham, Maria Perla Colombini, and Peter B. Beaumont. 2012. "Early Evidence of San Material Culture Represented by Organic Artifacts from Border Cave, South Africa." Proceedings of the National Academy of Sciences 109 (33): 13214–13219.

d'Errico, Francesco, Christopher Henshilwood, Marian Vanhaeren, and Karen Van Niekerk. 2005. "Nassarius Kraussianus Shell Beads from Blombos Cave: Evidence for Symbolic Behaviour in the Middle Stone Age." Journal of Human Evolution 48 (1): 3–24.

Dannemann, Michael, and Fernando Racimo. 2018. "Something Old, Something Borrowed: Admixture and Adaptation in Human Evolution." Current Opinion in Genetics & Development 53: 1–8.

Day, M. H. 1969. "Omo Human Skeletal Remains." Nature 222: 1135–1138.

Dillehay, Tom D., Carlos Ocampo, José Saavedra, Andre Oliveira Sawakuchi, Rodrigo M. Vega, Mario Pino, Michael B. Collins, et al. 2015. "New Archaeological Evidence for an Early Human Presence at Monte Verde, Chile." PLOS ONE 10 (11): e0141923. doi:10.1371/journal.pone.0141923.

Dow, Gregory K., Clyde G. Reed, and Nancy Olewiler. 2009. "Climate Reversals and the Transition to Agriculture." Journal of Economic Growth 14 (1): 27–53.

Dunbar, R. I. M. 1993. "Coevolution of Neocortical Size, Group Size and Language in Humans." Behavioral and Brain Sciences 16 (4): 681–694.

Durband, Arthur C. 2014. "Brief Communication: Artificial Cranial Modification in Kow Swamp and Cohuna." American Journal of Physical Anthropology 155 (1): 173–178.

Ember, Carol R. N.d. "Hunter-Gatherers." Explaining Human Culture. Human Relations Area Files. http://hraf.yale.edu/ehc/summaries/hunter-gatherers

Erlandson, Jon M., and Todd J. Braje. 2011. "From Asia to the Americas by Boat? Paleogeography, Paleoecology, and Stemmed Points of the Northwest Pacific." Quaternary International 239 (1–2): 28–37.

Erlandson, Jon M., Todd J. Braje, Kristina M. Gill, and Michael H. Graham. 2015. "Ecology of the Kelp Highway: Did Marine Resources Facilitate Human Dispersal from Northeast Asia to the Americas?" The Journal of Island and Coastal Archaeology 10 (3): 392–411.

Fladmark, K. R. 1979. "Routes: Alternate Migration Corridors for Early Man in North America." American Antiquity 44 (1): 55–69.

Fu, Qiaomei, Mateja Hajdinjak, Oana Teodora Moldovan, Silviu Constantin, Swapan Mallick, Pontus Skoglund, Nick Patterson, et al. 2015. "An Early Modern Human from Romania with a Recent Neanderthal Ancestor." Nature 524 (7564): 216–219.

Fu, Qiaomei, Heng Li, Priya Moorjani, Flora Jay, Sergey M. Slepchenko, Aleksei A. Bondarev, Philip L. F. Johnson, et al. 2014. "Genome Sequence of a 45,000-Year-old Modern Human from Western Siberia." Nature 514 (7523): 445–49.

Fuller, Dorian Q. 2010. "An Emerging Paradigm Shift in the Origins of Agriculture." General Anthropology 17 (2): 1, 8–11.

Germonpré, Mietje, Martina Lázničková-Galetová, and Mikhail V. Sablin. 2012. "Palaeolithic Dog Skulls at the Gravettian Předmostí Site, the Czech Republic." Journal of Archaeological Science 39 (1): 184–202.

Greenberg, Joseph H. 1987. Language in the Americas. Palo Alto, CA: Stanford University Press.

Gröning, Flora, Jia Liu, Michael J. Fagan, and Paul O'Higgins. 2011. "Why Do Humans Have Chins? Testing the Mechanical Significance of Modern Human Symphyseal Morphology with Finite Element Analysis." American Journal of Physical Anthropology 144 (4): 593–606.

Groucutt, Huw S., Rainer Grün, Iyad S. A. Zalmout, Nick A. Drake, Simon J. Armitage, Ian Candy, Richard Clark-Wilson, et al. 2018. "Homo sapiens in Arabia by 85,000 Years Ago." Nature Ecology & Evolution 2 (5): 800–809.

Hammond, Ashley S., Danielle F. Royer, and John G. Fleagle. 2017. "The Omo-Kibish I Pelvis." Journal of Human Evolution 108: 199–219.

Harvati, Katerina. 2009. "Into Eurasia: A Geometric Morphometric Reassessment of the Upper Cave (Zhoukoudian) Specimens." Journal of Human Evolution 57 (6): 751–762.

Headland, Thomas N., Lawrence A. Reid, M. G. Bicchieri, Charles A. Bishop, Robert Blust, Nicholas E. Flanders, Peter M. Gardner, Karl L. Hutterer, Arkadiusz Marciniak, and Robert F. Schroeder. 1989. "Hunter-Gatherers and Their Neighbors from Prehistory to the Present." Current Anthropology 30 (1): 43–66.

Henshilwood, Christopher S., Francesco d'Errico, Karen L. van Niekerk, Yvan Coquinot, Zenobia Jacobs, Stein-Erik Lauritzen, Michel Menu, and Renata García-Moreno. 2011. "A 100,000-Year-Old Ochre-Processing Workshop at Blombos Cave, South Africa." Science 334 (6053): 219–222.

Hershkovitz, Israel, Gerhard W. Weber, Rolf Quam, Mathieu Duval, Rainer Grün, Leslie Kinsley, Avner Ayalon, et al. 2018. "The Earliest Modern Humans Outside Africa." Science 359 (6374): 456–459.

Hublin, Jean-Jacques, Abdelouahed Ben-Ncer, Shara E. Bailey, Sarah E. Freidline, Simon Neubauer, Matthew M. Skinner, Inga Bergmann, et al. 2017. "New Fossils from Jebel Irhoud, Morocco, and the Pan-African Origin of Homo sapiens." Nature 546 (7657): 289–292.

Huerta-Sánchez, Emilia, Xin Jin, Asan, Zhuoma Bianba, Benjamin Peter, Nicolas Vinckenbosch, Yu Liang, et al. 2014. "Altitude Adaptation in Tibetans Caused by Introgression of Denisovan-like DNA." Nature 512 (7513): 194–197.

Kennedy, Kenneth A. R., Siran U. Deraniyagala, William J. Roertgen, John Chiment, and Todd Disotell. 1987. "Upper Pleistocene Fossil Hominids from Sri Lanka." American Journal of Physical Anthropology 72 (4): 441–461.

Lee, Gyoung-Ah. 2011. "The Transition from Foraging to Farming in Prehistoric Korea." Current Anthropology 52 (S4): S307–S329.

Lieberman, Daniel E. 2015. "Human Locomotion and Heat Loss: An Evolutionary Perspective." Comprehensive Physiology 5 (1): 99–117.

Lieberman, Daniel E., Brandeis M. McBratney, and Gail Krovitz. 2002. "The Evolution and Development of Cranial Form in Homo sapiens." Proceedings of the National Academy of Sciences 99 (3): 1134–1139.

Lieberman, Daniel E., Osbjorn M. Pearson, and Kenneth M. Mowbray. 2000. "Basicranial Influence on Overall Cranial Shape." Journal of Human Evolution 38 (2): 291–315.

Liu, Wu, María Martinón-Torres, Yan-jun Cai, Song Xing, Hao-wen Tong, Shu-wen Pei, Mark Jan Sier, Xiao-hong Wu, R. Lawrence Edwards, and Hai Cheng. 2015. "The Earliest Unequivocally Modern Humans in Southern China." Nature 526 (7575): 696.

Lucas, Peter W. 2007. "The Evolution of the Hominin Diet from a Dental Functional Perspective." In Evolution of the Human Diet: The Known, the Unknown, and the Unknowable, edited by Peter S. Ungar, Oxford, UK: Oxford University Press.

McCarthy, Robert C., and Lynn Lucas. 2014. "A Morphometric Reassessment of Bou-Vp-16/1 from Herto, Ethiopia." Journal of Human Evolution 74: 114–117.

McDougall, Ian, Francis H. Brown, and John G. Fleagle. 2005. "Stratigraphic Placement and Age of Modern Humans from Kibish, Ethiopia." Nature 433 (7027): 733.

Mendez, Fernando L., G. David Poznik, Sergi Castellano, and Carlos D. Bustamante. 2016. "The Divergence of Neanderthal and Modern Human Y Chromosomes." The American Journal of Human Genetics 98 (4): 728–734.

Michel, Véronique, Hélène Valladas, Guanjun Shen, Wei Wang, Jian-xin Zhao, Chuan-Chou Shen, Patricia Valensi, and Christopher J. Bae. 2016. "The Earliest Modern Homo sapiens in China?" Journal of Human Evolution 101: 101–104.

Miller, D. Shane, Vance T. Holliday, and Jordon Bright. 2013. "Clovis across the Continent." Paleoamerican Odyssey. College Station: Texas A&M University Press. 207–220.

Neubauer, Simon, Jean-Jacques Hublin, and Philipp Gunz. 2018. "The Evolution of Modern Human Brain Shape." Science Advances 4 (1): eaao5961.

Pearson, Osbjorn M. 2000. "Postcranial Remains and the Origin of Modern Humans." Evolutionary Anthropology 9: 229–247.

———. 2008. "Statistical and Biological Definitions of 'Anatomically Modern' Humans: Suggestions for a Unified Approach to Modern Morphology." Evolutionary Anthropology: Issues, News, and Reviews 17 (1): 38–48.

Pietschnig, Jakob, Lars Penke, Jelte M. Wicherts, Michael Zeiler, and Martin Voracek. 2015. "Meta-Analysis of Associations between Human Brain Volume and Intelligence Differences: How Strong Are They and What Do They Mean?" Neuroscience & Biobehavioral Reviews 57: 411–432.

Pinhasi, Ron, Joaquim Fort, and Albert J. Ammerman. 2005. "Tracing the Origin and Spread of Agriculture in Europe." PLOS Biology 3 (12): e410.

Posth, Cosimo, Nathan Nakatsuka, Iosif Lazaridis, Pontus Skoglund, Swapan Mallick, Thiseas C. Lamnidis, Nadin Rohland, et al. 2018. "Reconstructing the Deep Population History of Central and South America." Cell 175 (5): 1185–1197.

Potter, Ben A., James F. Baichtal, Alwynne B. Beaudoin, Lars Fehren-Schmitz, C. Vance Haynes, Vance T. Holliday, Charles E. Holmes, et al. 2018. "Current Evidence Allows Multiple Models for the Peopling of the Americas." Science Advances 4 (8): eaat5473.

Raghavan, Maanasa, Pontus Skoglund, Kelly E. Graf, Mait Metspalu, Anders Albrechtsen, Ida Moltke, Simon Rasmussen, et al. 2014. "Upper Palaeolithic Siberian Genome Reveals Dual Ancestry of Native Americans." Nature 505 (7481): 87–91.

Raghavan, Maanasa, Matthias Steinrücken, Kelley Harris, Stephan Schiffels, Simon Rasmussen, Michael DeGiorgio, Anders Albrechtsen, et al. 2015. "Genomic Evidence for the Pleistocene and Recent Population History of Native Americans." Science 349 (6250): aab3884.

Rasmussen, Morten, Sarah L. Anzick, Michael R. Waters, Pontus Skoglund, Michael DeGiorgio, Thomas W. Stafford Jr., Simon Rasmussen, et al. 2014. "The Genome of a Late Pleistocene Human from a Clovis Burial Site in Western Montana." Nature 506 (7487): 225–229.

Reich, David, Richard E. Green, Martin Kircher, Johannes Krause, Nick Patterson, Eric Y. Durand, Bence Viola, et al. 2010. "Genetic History of an Archaic Hominin Group from Denisova Cave in Siberia." Nature 468 (7327): 1053–1060.

Reich, David, Nick Patterson, Martin Kircher, Frederick Delfin, Madhusudan R. Nandineni, Irina Pugach, Albert Min-Shan Ko, et al. 2011. "Denisova Admixture and the First Modern Human Dispersals into Southeast Asia and Oceania." American Journal of Human Genetics 89 (4): 516–528.

Richter, Daniel, Rainer Grün, Renaud Joannes-Boyau, Teresa E. Steele, Fethi Amani, Mathieu Rué, Paul Fernandes, et al. 2017. "The Age of the Hominin Fossils from Jebel Irhoud, Morocco, and the Origins of the Middle Stone Age." Nature 546 (7657): 293–296.

Roberts, Patrick, and Brian A. Stewart. 2018. "Defining the 'Generalist-Specialist' Niche for Pleistocene Homo sapiens." Nature Human Behaviour 2: 542–550.

Rougier, Helene, Ştefan Milota, Ricardo Rodrigo, Mircea Gherase, Laurenţiu Sarcină, Oana Moldovan, João Zilhão, et al. 2007. "Peştera Cu Oase 2 and the Cranial Morphology of Early Modern Europeans." Proceedings of the National Academy of Sciences 104 (4): 1165–1170.

Sawyer, G. J., and Blaine Maley. 2005. "Neanderthal Reconstructed." The Anatomical Record (Part B: New Anat.) 283 (1): 23–31.

Scerri, Eleanor M. L., Mark G. Thomas, Andrea Manica, Philipp Gunz, Jay T. Stock, Chris Stringer, Matt Grove, et al. 2018. "Did Our Species Evolve in Subdivided Populations Across Africa, and Why Does It Matter?" Trends in Ecology & Evolution.

Shang, Hong, Haowen Tong, Shuangquan Zhang, Fuyou Chen, and Erik Trinkaus. 2007. "An Early Modern Human from Tianyuan Cave, Zhoukoudian, China." Proceedings of the National Academy of Sciences 104 (16): 6573–6578.

Shea, John J. 2011. "Refuting a Myth about Human Origins." American Scientist 99 (2): 128.

Shea, John J., and Ofer Bar-Yosef. 2005. "Who Were the Skhul/Qafzeh People? An Archaeological Perspective on Eurasia's Oldest Modern Humans." Journal of the Israel Prehistoric Society, 451–468.

Slatkin, Montgomery, and Fernando Racimo. 2016. "Ancient DNA and Human History." Proceedings of the National Academy of Sciences 113 (23): 6380-6387.

Smith, Fred H., James C. M. Ahern, Ivor Janković, and Ivor Karavanić. 2017. "The Assimilation Model of Modern Human Origins in Light of Current Genetic and Genomic Knowledge." Quaternary International 450: 126-136.

Smith, Michael. 2009. "V. Gordon Childe and the Urban Revolution: A Historical Perspective on a Revolution in Urban Studies." Town Planning Review 80 (1): 3-29.

Stock, Jay T. 2008. "Are Humans Still Evolving?" EMBO Reports 9 (Suppl 1): S51-S54.

Stringer, Chris B., and Peter Andrews. 1988. "Genetic and Fossil Evidence for the Origin of Modern Humans." Science 239 (4845): 1263-1268.

Swisher, Mark E., Dennis L. Jenkins, Lionel E. Jackson Jr., and Fred M. Phillips. 2013. "A Reassessment of the Role of the Canadian Ice-Free Corridor in Light of New Geological Evidence." Poster Symposium 5B: Geology, Geochronology and Paleoenvironments of the First Americans at the Paleoamerican Odyssey Conference, Santa Fe, New Mexico, October 16-19.

Thorne, A. G., and P. G. Macumber. 1972. "Discoveries of Late Pleistocene Man at Kow Swamp, Australia." Nature 238 (5363): 316.

Tong, Haowen. 2004. "A Preliminary Report on the Newly Found Tianyuan Cave, a Late Pleistocene Human Fossil Site Near Zhoukoudian." Chinese Science Bulletin 49 (8): 853–857.

Trinkaus, Erik, Ştefan Milota, Ricardo Rodrigo, Gherase Mircea, and Oana Moldovan. 2003a. "Early Modern Human Cranial Remains from the Peştera Cu Oase, Romania." Journal of Human Evolution 45 (3): 245-253.

Trinkaus, Erik, Oana Moldovan, Adrian Bîlgăr, Laurenţiu Sarcina, Sheela Athreya, Shara E Bailey, Ricardo Rodrigo, Gherase Mircea, Thomas Higham, and Christopher Bronk Ramsey. 2003b. "An Early Modern Human from the Peştera Cu Oase, Romania." Proceedings of the National Academy of Sciences 100 (20): 11231-11236.

Velemínská, J., J. Brůzek, P. Velemínský, L. Bigoni, A. Sefcáková, and S. Katina. 2008. "Variability of the Upper-Palaeolithic Skulls from Predmostí Near Prerov (Czech Republic): Craniometric Comparison with Recent Human Standards." Homo 59 (1): 1-26.

Venkataraman, Vivek V., Thomas S. Kraft, Nathaniel J. Dominy, and Kirk M. Endicott. 2017. "Hunter-Gatherer Residential Mobility and the Marginal Value of Rainforest Patches." Proceedings of the National Academy of Sciences 114 (12): 3097-3102.

Villa, Paola, Sylvain Soriano, Tsenka Tsanova, Ilaria Degano, Thomas F. G. Higham, Francesco d'Errico, Lucinda Backwell, Jeannette J. Lucejko, Maria Perla Colombini, and Peter B. Beaumont. 2012. "Border Cave and the Beginning of the Later Stone Age in South Africa." Proceedings of the National Academy of Sciences 109 (33): 13208-13213.

Waguespack, Nicole M. 2005. "The Organization of Male and Female Labor in Foraging Societies: Implications for Early Paleoindian Archaeology." American Anthropologist 107 (4): 666-676.

Wall, Jeffrey D., and Deborah Yoshihara Caldeira Brandt. 2016. "Archaic Admixture in Human History." Current Opinion in Genetics & Development 41: 93-97.

White, Tim D., Berhane Asfaw, David DeGusta, Henry Gilbert, Gary D. Richards, Gen Suwa, and F. Clark Howell. 2003. "Pleistocene Homo sapiens from Middle Awash, Ethiopia." Nature 423 (6941): 742-747.

Wolpoff, Milford H. 1989. "Multiregional Evolution: The Fossil Alternative to Eden." The Human Revolution-Behavioral and Biological Perspective on the Origin of Modern Humans. 62–108. Princeton: Princeton University Press.

Woo, Ju-Kang. 1959. "Human Fossils Found in Liukiang, Kwangsi, China." Vertebrata PalAsiatica 3 (3): 109–118.

Wu, XiuJie, Wu Liu, Wei Dong, JieMin Que, and YanFang Wang. 2008. "The Brain Morphology of Homo Liujiang Cranium Fossil by Three-Dimensional Computed Tomography." Chinese Science Bulletin 53 (16): 2513–2519.

Acknowledgments

I could not have undertaken this project without the help of many who got me to where I am today. I extend sincere thank yous to the many colleagues and former students who have inspired me to keep learning and talking about anthropology. Thank you also to all who are involved in this textbook project. The anonymous reviewers truly sparked improvements to the chapter. Lastly, the staff of Starbucks #5772 also contributed immensely to this text.

Figure Attributions

Figure 12.1 View looking south of the Jebel Irhoud (Morocco) site by Shannon McPherron, Max Planck Institute for Evolutionary Anthropology Leipzig, is used under a CC BY-SA 2.0 License.

Figure 12.2 Modern human and Neanderthal original to Explorations: An Open Invitation to Biological Anthropology by Mary Nelson is under a CC BY-NC 4.0 License.

Figure 12.3 Modern and archaic Homo sapiens skeletons original to Explorations: An Open Invitation to Biological Anthropology by Mary Nelson is under a CC BY-NC 4.0 License.

Figure 12.4 Loewenmensch1 by Dagmar Hollmann is used under a CC BY-SA 3.0 License.

Figure 12.5 Maps depicting the estimated range of modern *Homo sapiens* through time original to Explorations: An Open Invitation to Biological Anthropology by Elyssa Ebding at GeoPlace, California State University, Chico is under a CC BY-NC 4.0 License.

Figure 12.6 A composite reconstruction of the earliest known Homo sapiens fossils from Jebel Irhoud (Morocco) based on micro computed tomographic scans by Philipp Gunz, Max Planck Institute for Evolutionary Anthropology Leipzig, is used under a CC BY-SA 2.0 License.

Figure 12.7 Homo sapiens idaltu BOU-VP-16/1 Herto Cranium by ©BoneClones is used by permission and available here under a CC BY-NC 4.0 License.

Figure 12.8 Homo sapiens Skull Skhul 5 by ©BoneClones is used by permission and available here under a CC BY-NC 4.0 License.

Figure 12.9 Moulage de la sépulture de l'individu "Qafzeh 11" (avec ramure de cervidé), homme de Néandertal (Collections du Muséum national d'histoire naturelle de Paris, France) by Eunostos has been modified (cropped and color modified) and is used under a CC BY-SA 4.0 License.

Figure 12.10 Liujiang cave skull-a. Homo Sapiens 68,000 Years Old (Taken at the David H. Koch Hall of Human Origins at the Smithsonian Natural History Museum) by Ryan Somma from Occoquan, USA has been modified (color modified) and is used under a CC BY-SA 2.0 License.

Figure 12.11 Zhoukoudian Upper Cave by Mutt is used under a CC BY-SA 4.0 License.

Figure 12.12 Kow Swamp1-Homo sapiens by Ryan Somma from Occoquan, USA, under a CC BY-SA 2.0 License has been modified (background cleaned and color modified) and is available here under a CC BY-NC 4.0 License.

Figure 12.13 Oase 2 by Smithsonian National Museum of Natural History [exhibit: Human Evolution Evidence, Human Fossils] has no known copyright restrictions and has been modified (sharpened) and is available here under a CC BY-NC 4.0 License.

Figure 12.14 Cro-Magnon 1 Skull by ©BoneClones is used by permission and available here under a CC BY-NC 4.0 License.

Figure 12.15 Předmostí 9 by J. Matiegka (1862-1941) is in the public domain and has been modified (sharpened) and is available here under a CC BY-NC 4.0 License.

Figure 12.16 La station quaternaire de Raymonden (…)Hardy Michel bpt6k5567846s (2) by M. Féauxis [original by Michel Hardy (1891)] is in the public domain.

Figure 12.17 Lascaux cave (document 108435) Prehitoric Sites and Decorated Caves of the Vézère Valley (France) by Francesco Bandarin, © UNESCO, has been modified (color modified) and is used under a CC BY-SA 3.0 License.

Figure 12.18 Current Estimates of Arhcaic-Modern Admixture original to Explorations: An Open Invitation to Biological Anthropology by Keith Chan and Katie Nelson is under a CC BY-NC 4.0 License.

Figure 12.19 BBC-shell-beads by Chenshilwood (Chris Henshilbood & Francesco d'Errico) at English Wikipedia is used under a CC BY-SA 3.0 License.

Figure 12.20 Woolly Mammoth (La Brea Tar Pits & Museum) by Keith Chan is under a CC BY-NC 4.0 License.

Figure 12.21 Fig 9. Paijan-like projectile point of rhyolite recovered from a late Pleistocene level at the CH-I site (Unit 6, Level 51 cm; see S6a Fig) by Dillehay et al. (2015). New Archaeological Evidence for an Early Human Presence at Monte Verde, Chile. PLOS ONE, 10(11), e0141923. doi:10.1371/journal.pone.0141923 is used under a CC BY 4.0 License.

Figure 12.22 Clovis Point (15.2012.25) by Smithsonian National Museum of Natural History [Department of Anthropology; Cooper Hewitt, Smithsonian Design Museum] has no known copyright restrictions.

Figure 12.23 Assimilation Model original to Explorations: An Open Invitation to Biological Anthropology by Keith Chan and Katie Nelson is under a CC BY-NC 4.0 License.

Figure 12.24 Image from video game FarCry Primal by Keith Chan is under a CC BY-NC 4.0 License.

Figure 12.25 San hunter with bow and arrow by Charles Roffey has been modified (color modified) and is used under a CC BY-NC-SA 2.0 License.

Figure 12.26 Plowing muddy field using cattle by IRRI Photos (International Rice Research Institute) has been modified (color modified) and is used under a CC BY-NC-SA 2.0 License.

Figure 12.27 Centres of origin and spread of agriculture by Joe Roe is used under a CC BY-SA 3.0 License.

Figure 12.28 Downtown San Diego (October 13, 2016) by Keith Chan is under a CC BY-NC 4.0 License.

Figure 12.29 Combine CR9060 by Hertzsprung is used under a CC BY-SA 3.0 License.

Figure 12.30 Hypothetical image of future human evolution original to Explorations: An Open Invitation to Biological Anthropology by Mary Nelson is under a CC BY-NC 4.0 License.

Chapter 13: Race and Human Variation

Michael B. C. Rivera, Ph.D., University of Cambridge

> *Learning Objectives*
>
> - Review the illustrious and (at times) troubling history of "race" concepts.
> - Recognize human diversity and evolution as the thematic roots of our discipline.
> - Critique earlier "race" concepts based on overall human diversity being lower compared to other species and human genetic variation being greater within a population than between populations.
> - Explain how biological variation in humans is distributed clinally and in accordance with both isolation-by-distance and Out-of-Africa models.
> - Identify phenotypic traits that reflect selective and neutral evolution.
> - Relate a more nuanced view of human variation with today's ongoing bioanthropological research, implications for biomedical studies, applications in forensic anthropology, and sociopolitical/economic concerns.

Humans exhibit biological diversity. Cognitively, humans also have a natural desire to categorize objects and other humans in order to make sense of the world around them. Since the birth of the discipline of **biological anthropology**, we have been interested in studying how humans vary biologically and what the sources of this variation are. Before we tackle these big problems, this first begs the question: Why *should* we study human diversity?

There are certainly academic reasons for studying **human diversity**. First, it is highly interesting and important to consider the evolution of our species and how our biological variation may be similar to (or different from) that of other species of animals (e.g., other primates and apes). Such investigation can give us clues as to how unique we are as a biological organism in relation to the rest of the animal kingdom. Second, anthropologists study modern human diversity to understand how different biological traits developed over evolutionary time. If we are able to grasp the evolutionary processes that produce and affect diversity, we can make more accurate inferences about evolution and adaptation among our hominin ancestors, complementing our study of fossil evidence and the archaeological record. Third, as will be discussed in more detail later on, it is important to consider that biological variation among humans has biomedical, forensic, and sociopolitical implications. For these reasons, the study of human variation and evolution has formed the basis of anthropological inquiry for centuries and continues to be a major source of intrigue and inspiration for scientific research conducted today.

An even more important role of the biological anthropologist is to improve *public* understanding of human evolution and diversity, outside of academic circles. Terms such as **race** and **ethnicity** are used in everyday conversations and in formal settings within and outside academia. The division of humankind into smaller, discrete categories is a regular occurrence in day-to-day life. This can be seen regularly when governments acquire census data with a heading like "geographic origin" or "ethnicity." Furthermore, such checkboxes and drop-down lists are commonly seen as part of the identifying information required for surveys and job applications.

According to the Oxford English Dictionary (2018), *race* is a term that should be used to describe one or more of the following:

- a major division of the human species based on particular physical characteristics;
- the biological origin of a group of people, or ancestry;
- the fact or condition of belonging to a racial division or group, or the social qualities associated with this;
- a group of people sharing the same culture and language;
- any group of people or things with a common feature or features;
- a population within a species that is distinct in some way, especially a subspecies.

So many various definitions for one word already suggests that perhaps the concepts or meanings behind biological diversity are complicated. Even though the terms *race* and *ethnicity* are used often in commonplace settings, there is no consensus among biological anthropologists as to what races are, whether they even exist, and, if they do, how the term should be applied to the human species meaningfully. If biological anthropologists cannot reach a consensus on how to view human diversity, how can we possibly expect there to be a clear perspective on the nature and causes of biological variation outside of scientific academia? Ideas about ethnicity that people hold have huge social and political impacts, and notions of race have been part of the motivation behind various forms of **racism** and **prejudice** today, as well as many wars and genocides throughout history. This is how the role of the biological anthropologist becomes crucial in the public sphere, as we may be able to debunk myths surrounding human diversity and shed light on how human variation is actually distributed worldwide for the non-anthropologists around us (Figure 13.1). Recent work in anthropological genetics has revealed the similarities amongst humans on a molecular level and the relatively few differences that exist between populations that one might be tempted to see as significantly distinctive.

Figure 13.1 Humans are biologically and culturally diverse. (Top left: Hadzabe members in Tanzania; top right: Inuit family in traditional seal and caribou clothing; bottom left: Andean man in traditional dress in Peru; bottom right: Dr. Jane Goodall.)

Science communication and education that centers upon race and our species' variation is interesting and important. Throughout this chapter, I will highlight how humans cannot actually be divided into discrete "races," because most traits instead vary on a continuous basis and human biology is, in fact, very **homogenous** compared to the greater genetic variation we observe in other closely related species. The reason we know this now is thanks to technological developments that have taken place over the last 50 or so years. Molecular anthropology, or anthropological genetics, revolutionized and continues to add new layers to our understanding of human biological diversity and the evolutionary processes that gave rise to the patterns of variation we observe in contemporary populations. The study of human variation has not always been unbiased, and thinkers and scientists have always worked in their particular sociohistorical context. For this reason, this chapter opens with a brief overview of race concepts throughout history, many of which relied on unethical and unscientific notions about different human groups.

THE HISTORY OF "RACE" CONCEPTS

"Race" in the Classical Era

The earliest classification systems used to understand human diversity are evidenced by ancient manuscripts, scrolls, and stone tablets recovered through archaeological, historical, and literary research. The Ancient Egyptians had the *Book of Gates*, dated to the New Kingdom between 1550 B.C.E. and 1077 B.C.E (Figure 13.2). In one part of this tome dedicated to depictions of the underworld, scribes used pictures and hieroglyphics to illustrate a division of Egyptian people into the four categories known to them at the time: the Aamu (Asiatics), the Nehesu (Nubians), the Reth (Egyptians), and the Themehu (Libyans). Though not rooted in any scientific basis like our current understandings of human variation today, the Ancient Egyptians believed that each of these groups were made of a distinctive category of people, distinguishable by their skin color, place of origin, and even behavioral traits.

Figure 13.2 (from left to right) Depicting a Berber (Libyan), a Nubian, an Asiatic (Levantine), and an Egyptian, copied from a mural of the tomb of Seti I.

The Roman philosopher Pliny the Elder (23–79 C.E.) also wrote about different groupings of people in his encyclopedia *Naturalis Historia* (Figure 13.3). In his opinion, all people fit under one of three categories: civilized peoples, barbarians, and monstrous individuals. Pliny the Elder's work was deeply problematic. He believed that only Europeans were civilized and not monstrous-looking, while other groups of people lacked the ideal character and appearance. In both the cases of the *Book of Gates* and *Naturalis Historia*, the worldviews of those who wrote these volumes were also limited by how few and infrequent their encounters were with peoples elsewhere around the world—that is, those not residing in Europe, the Near East, or northern Africa. When faced with only the level of biological diversity they could see around them, distinguishing factors identified by these prominent thinkers relied simply on readily visible phenotypic traits, such as body size, skin color, and facial shape.

C. PLINII SECUNDI
NATURALIS
HISTORIÆ,
TOMUS PRIMUS.
Cum Commentariis & adnotationibus HERMOLAI BARBARI, PINTIANI, RHENANI, GELENII, DALECHAMPII, SCALIGERI, SALMASII, Is. VOSSII, & Variorum.
Accedunt praeterea variae Lectiones ex MSS. compluribus ad oram Paginarum accurate indicatae.
Item JOH. FR. GRONOVII Notarum Liber Singularis ad Illustrem Virum *Johannem Capelanum.*
MOVENDO
LUGD. BATAV. ROTERODAMI. } Apud HACKIOS, A°. 1669.

Figure 13.3 Front page of Pliny the Elder's Naturalis Historia.

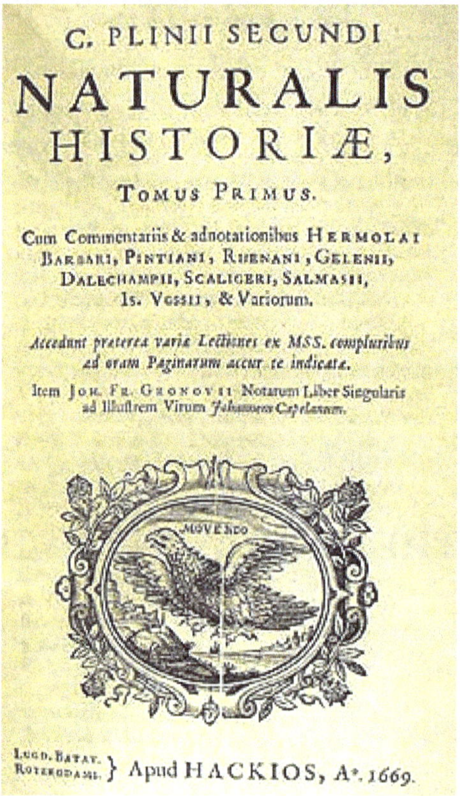

The most well-known of early documents is perhaps the Bible, where it is written that all humankind descends from one of three sons of Noah: Shem (the ancestor to all olive-skinned Asians), Japheth (the ancestor to pale-skinned Europeans), and Ham (the ancestor to darker-skinned Africans). Similar to the Ancient Egyptians, these distinctions were based on behavioral traits and skin color. More recent work in historiography and linguistics suggest that the branches of "Hamites," "Japhethites," and "Shemites" may also relate to the formation of three independent language groups some time between 1000 and 3000 B.C.E. With the continued proliferation of Christianity, this concept of approximately three racial groupings lasted until the Middle Ages and spread as far across Eurasia as crusaders and missionaries ventured at the time.

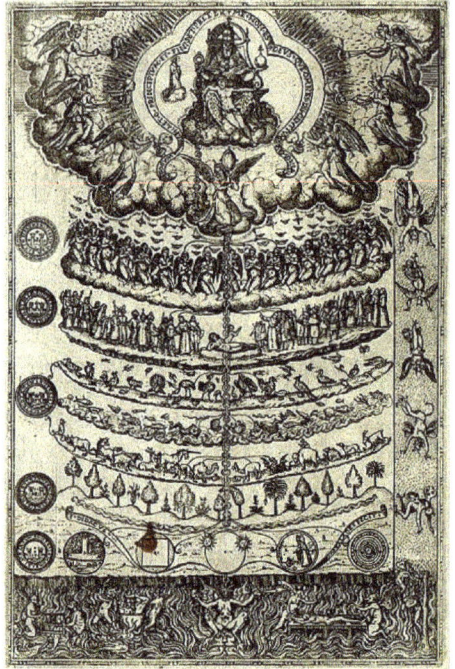

Figure 13.4 The Great Chain of Being from the Rhetorica Christiana by Fray Diego de Valades (1579).

Finally, there is also the "Great Chain of Being," conceived by ancient Greek philosophers like Plato (427–348 B.C.E.) and Aristotle (384–322 B.C.E.). They played a key role in laying the foundations of empirical science, whereby observations of everything from animals to humans were noted with the aim of creating taxonomic categories. Aristotle describes the Great Chain of Being as a ladder along which all objects, plants, animals, humans, and celestial bodies can be mapped in an overall hierarchy (in the order of existential importance, with humans placed near the top, just beneath divine beings) (Figure 13.4). Where he writes about humans, Aristotle expressed the belief that certain people are inherently (or genetically) more instinctive rulers, while others are more natural fits for the life of a worker or slave. Nowadays, based on research by biological anthropologists, we currently recognize that these early systems of classification and hierarchization are unhelpful in studying human biological diversity. Both behavioral traits and physical traits are coded for by multiple genes each, and how we exhibit those traits based on our genetics can vary significantly even between individuals of the same population.

"Race" during the Scientific Revolution

The 1500s and 1600s saw the beginnings of the "**Scientific Revolution**" in European societies, with thinkers like Copernicus, Galileo, and Da Vinci publishing some of their most important findings. While by no means the first or only scholars globally to use observation and experimentation to understand the world around them, early scientists living at the end of the medieval period in Europe increasingly employed more experimentation, quantification, and rational thought in their work. This is the main difference between the work of the ancient Egyptians, Romans, and Greeks, and that of workers like Isaac Newton and Carl Linnaeus in the 1600s and 1700s.

Linnaeus is the author of *Systema Naturae* (1758), in which he classified all plants and animals he could observe under the first formalized naming system known as **binomial nomenclature** (i.e., how all organisms can be named by their genus and species, such as *Homo sapiens* or *Pan troglodytes*) (Figure 13.5). What was most anthropologically notable about Linnaeus's taxonomy was that he was one of the first to group humans with apes and monkeys, after noting the anatomical similarities between humans and nonhuman primates. Linnaeus viewed the world in line with **essentialism**, a concept which dictates that there are a unique set of characteristics that organisms of a specific kind *must* have—organisms would fall outside taxonomic categorizations if they lacked any of the required criteria.

Figure 13.5 Carl Linnaeus.

Despite these useful contributions to the biological sciences, Linnaeus still subdivided the human species into four varieties, with overtly racist categories based on skin color and "inherent" behaviors. According to him, Africans are all "black-skinned" and ruled by an erratic nature; Native Americans are "red" in skin tone and ruled by habit; Asians are "yellow-" or "brown-skinned" and ruled by belief; and Europeans are "white" and regulated by custom. These standards for categorization imply that Europeans are governed by carefully considered culture and custom, unlike the unthinking Asians and Indigenous Americans in his framework who normally act out of "habit" or "belief." Moreover, Linnaeus's traditional ranking also places sub-Saharan, dark-skinned Africans inferior to the other three. Wrongly so, European scientists during this period were not aware of their own biases skewing their interpretations of biological diversity. The conclusions and claims they came to, consciously or subconsciously, often fit such an age when the superiority of European cultures over others was a pervasive idea throughout these scientists' social and political lives.

Figure 13.6 Discovery of the Mississippi by Spanish colonialist explorer Hernando DeSoto in 1541 (painted in 1853 by William H. Powell).

Occurring alongside this Scientific Revolution was also the "**Age of Discovery**." Although much of Eurasia was linked by spice and silk trading routes, the European colonial period between the 1400s and 1700s was marked by many new and intentionally violent encounters overseas (Figure 13.6). When Europeans arrived by ship on the shores of continents that were already inhabited, it was their first meeting with the indigenous peoples of the Americas and Australasia, who looked, spoke, and behaved differently from peoples with whom they were familiar. Building on the idea of species and "subspecies," natural historians of this time invented the term *race*, from the French *rasse* meaning "local strain." The idea behind this terminology was rooted in the observation that geography plays a significant role in producing the biological traits we observe today. Naturalists like Comte de Buffon and Johann Blumenbach did believe that all people have a single origin, but they also believed that differences in environment could lead to biological changes between different groups of people (i.e., races). However, as they had no understanding of genetics, they were incorrect in assuming that factors such as skin color could change in a single lifetime depending on climate and diet and, essentially, behavior. Again, while drawing links between external physical characteristics and behavior is not scientific, differences in both were used to justify the **Othering** of "nonwhite" cultures. Establishing "otherness" and "inferiority" in other people's cultures was necessary at the time for colonialists to enforce European domination and the subordination of non-European people. Without genetic technologies, little was known at the time about the hereditary or evolutionary basis of skin color having little to do with innate differences between various "races."

Another such scientist at the time, Johann Friedrich Blumenbach (1752–1840), classified humans into five races based on his observations of cranial form variation as well as skin color. He thus dubbed the "original" form of the human cranium the "Caucasian" form, with the idea that the ideal climate conditions for early humans would have been in the Caucasus region near the Caspian Sea. The key insight Blumenbach presented was that human variation in any particular trait should be more accurately viewed as falling along a gradation (Figure 13.7). While some of his theories were correct according to what we observe today with more knowledge in genetics, workers like him and Buffon believed erroneously that human "subspecies" were "degenerated" or "transformed" varieties of an ancestral Caucasian or European race. According to them, the Caucasian cranial dimensions were the least changed over human evolutionary time, while the other skull forms represented geographic variants of this "original." As will be discussed in greater detail later in this chapter, we have genetic and craniometric evidence for sub-Saharan Africa being the origin of the human species instead. Based on work that shows how most biological characteristics are coded for by nonassociated genes, it is not reasonable to draw links between individuals' personalities and their skull shapes.

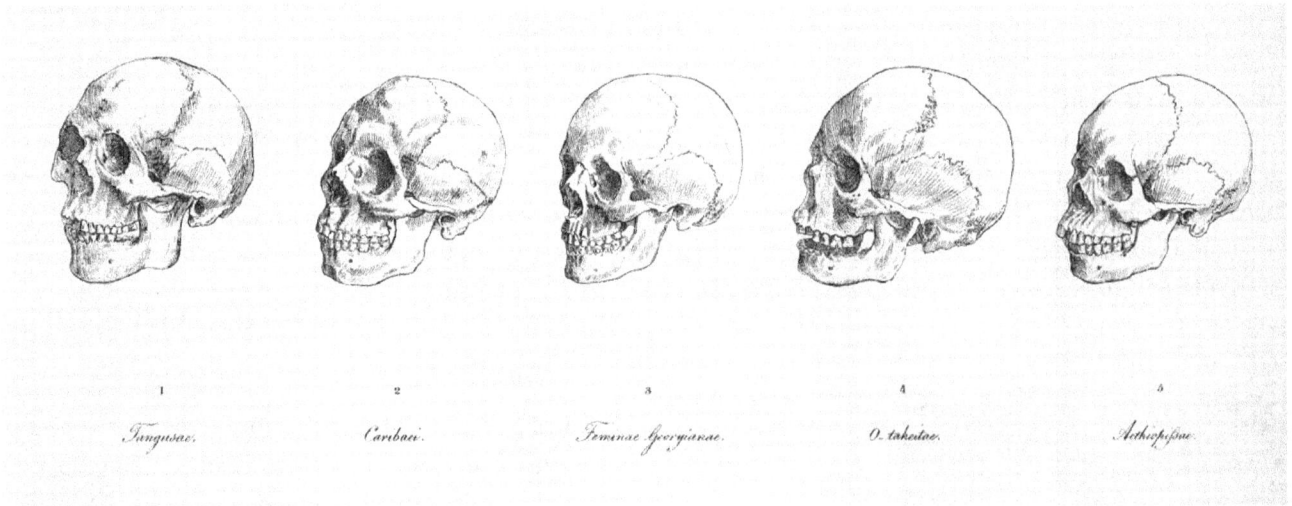

Figure 13.7 Five skull drawings representing specimens for Blumenbach's "Mongolian," "American," "Caucasian," "Malayan," and "Aethiopian" races.

"Race" and the Dawn of Scientific Racism

Between the 1800s and mid-1900s, and contrary to what you might expect, an increased use of scientific methods to justify racial schemes developed in scholarship. Differing from Blumenbach and Buffon's views in earlier centuries, which saw all humans as environmentally deviated from one "original" humankind, classification systems after 1800 became more **polygenetic** (viewing all people as having separate origins) rather than **monogenetic** (viewing all people as having a single origin). Instead of moving closer to our modern-day understandings of human diversity, there was increased support for the notion that each race was created separately and with different attributes (intelligence, temperament, and appearance).

The 1800s were an important precursor to modern biological anthropology as we know it, given that the scientific measurement of human physical features (anthropometry) truly became popularized then. However, whether it was skin color, skull shape, or observations of behavior being analyzed as the data, empirical studies in the 1800s pushed the idea even further that Europeans were culturally and biologically superior. The leading figures in craniometry at this time, focusing on measurements of the skull, were also linked heavily with powerful individuals and wealthy sociopolitical institutions and financial bodies. Therefore, polygenetic ways of thinking were particularly influenced by sociohistorical and economic factors at the time. Theories in support of hierarchical racial schemes certainly helped continue the exploitative and unethical transatlantic slave trade between the 1500s and 1800s by justifying the transport and enslavement of African people on a "scientific" basis.

While considered one of the pioneers of American "physical" anthropology, Samuel George Morton (1799–1851) was a scholar who had a large role in 1800s scientific racism. By measuring cranial size and shape, he calculated that "Caucasians," on average, have greater cranial volumes than other groups, such as the Native Americans and "Negros." Today, we know that cranial size variation depends on such factors as Allen's and Bergmann's rules, which give the more likely explanation for the largest heads being found in people living among colder regions (i.e., Europeans) being climatic adaptation (Beals et al. 1984). In colder environments, it is advantageous for those living there to have larger and rounder heads because they conserve heat more effectively than slenderer heads (Beals et al. 1984).

Morton went on to write in his publication *Crania Americana* (1839) a number of views that fit with a concept called **biological determinism**. The idea behind biological determinism is that an association exists between people's physical characteristics and their behavior, intelligence, ability, values, and morals. If the idea is that some groups of people are *essentially* superior to others in cognitive ability and temperament, then it is easier to justify the unequal treatment of certain groups based on outward appearances. Based on his cranial measurements and observations of human nature, Morton claimed that Europeans were the most intelligent and "well-proportioned," while Asians were not fit for leadership and had short attention spans, Native Americans were slow in acquiring knowledge and fond of war, and Africans were superstitious, uninventive, and "barbarous."

Another such problematic thinker was Paul Broca (1824–1880), after which a region of the frontal lobe related to language use is named (Broca's area). Influenced by Morton, he likewise claimed that internal skull capacities could be linked with skin color and cognitive ability. Considering his data taken from different parts of the globe, Broca thought that factors such as gender, education, and social status could have an influence on brain size for different groups, purporting that men had larger brains than women and that "eminent" men were superior to men of "mediocre talent." He went on to justify the European colonization of other global territories by purporting it was noble for a biologically more "civilized" population to improve the "humanity" of more "barbaric" populations. Today, these theories of Morton, Broca, and others like them are known to have no scientific basis. If we could speak with them today, they would likely try to emphasize that their conclusions were based on empirical evidence and not *a priori* reasoning. However, we now can clearly see that their reasoning was biased and affected by prevailing societal views at the time.

"Race" and the Beginnings of Physical Anthropology

In the early 20th century, we saw a number of new figures coming into the science of human variation and shifting the theoretical focuses within. Most notably, these included Aleš Hrdlička and Franz Boas.

Aleš Hrdlička (1869–1943) was a Czech anthropologist who moved to the United States. In 1903, he established the physical anthropology section of the National Museum of Natural History (Figure 13.8). In 1918, he founded the *American Journal of Physical Anthropology*, one of the foremost scientific journals disseminating bioanthropological research still today. As part of his work and the scope of the journal, he differentiated "**physical anthropology**" from other kinds of anthropology–he wrote that physical anthropology is "the study of racial anatomy, physiology, and pathology" and "the study of man's variation" (Hrdlička 1918). In some ways, although the scope and technological capabilities of biological anthropologists have changed significantly, Hrdlička established an area of inquiry that has continued and prospered for over a hundred years.

Figure 13.8 Aleš Hrdlička (1869–1943), a Czech anthropologist who founded the American Journal of Physical Anthropology.

Franz Boas (1858–1942) was a German American anthropologist who established the four-field anthropology system in the United States and founded the American Anthropological Association in 1902. He argued that the scientific method should be used in the study of human cultures and the comparative method for looking at human biology worldwide. Boas's specialization was in the study of skull dimensions with respect to race. After a long-term research project, he demonstrated how cranial form was highly dependent on cultural and environmental factors and that human behaviors were influenced primarily not by genes but by social learning. He wrote in one essay for the journal *Science*: "While individuals differ, biological differences between races are small. There is no reason to believe that one race is by nature so much more intelligent, endowed with great willpower, or emotionally more stable than another, that the difference would materially influence its culture" (Boas 1931:6). This conclusion directly contrasted with the theories of the past that relied on biological determinism. Biological anthropologists today have found evidence that corroborates Boas's explanations: societies do not exist on a hierarchy or gradation of "civilizedness" but instead are shaped by the world around them, their demographic histories, and the interactions they have with other groups.

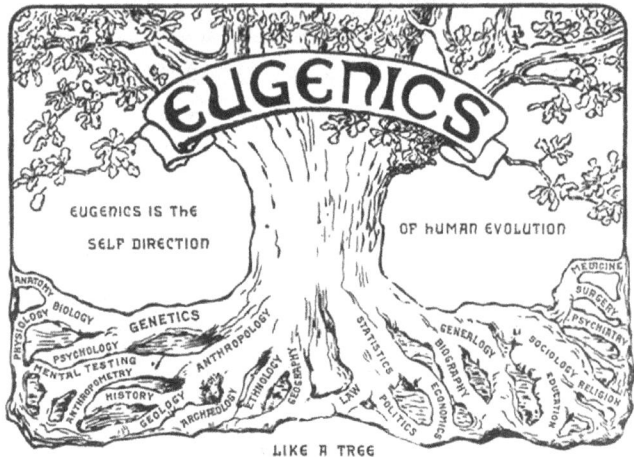

Figure 13.9 Logo of the Second International Exhibition of Eugenics held in 1921.

The first half of the 1900s still involved some research that was essentialist and focused on proving racial determinism. Anthropologists like Francis Galton (1822–1911) and Earnest A. Hooton (1887–1954) created the field of **eugenics** as an attempt to formalize the social scientific study of "fitness" and "superiority" among members of 19th-century Europe. As a way of "dealing with" criminals, diseased individuals, and "uncivilized" people, eugenicists recommended prohibiting parts of the population from being married and sterilizing these members of society so they could no longer procreate (Figure 13.9). They instead encouraged "reproduction in individual families with sound physiques, good mental endowments, and demonstrable social and economic capability" (Hooton 1936). In the 1930s, Nazi Germany used this false idea of there being "pure races" to highly destructive effect. The need to be protected against admixture from "unfit" groups was their justification for their blatant racism and purging of citizens that fell under their subjective criteria.

Shortly after World War II and the Nazi Holocaust, the full extent of essentialist, eugenicist thinking became clear.

Social constructions of race, and the notion that you could predict psychological or behavioral traits based on external appearance, had become unpopular both within and outside the discipline. It was up to those in the field of physical anthropology at the time to separate physical anthropology from race concepts that supported unscientific and socially damaging agendas. This does not mean that there are no physiological or behavioral differences between different members of the human species. However, going forward, a number of physical anthropologists saw human biological variation as more complicated than simple **typologies** could describe.

HUMAN VARIATION IN BIOLOGICAL ANTHROPOLOGY TODAY

"Populations" Instead of "Races"

After 1950, replacing the concept of "race" as a unit of diversity was the "**population**." This was outlined by those pioneering the "new physical anthropology," such as Sherwood Washburn, Theodosius Dobzhansky, and Julian Huxley, who borrowed this way of framing human groups from contemporary population geneticists (Figure 13.10). "Races" were then defined simply as populations that differ in the frequency of some gene or genes. And, on the other hand, a "population" is a group of individuals potentially capable of or actually interbreeding due to shared geographic proximity, language, ethnicity, culture, and/or values. Put another way, a population is a *local* interbreeding group with reduced gene flow between themselves and other groups of humans. Members of the same population may be expected to share many genetic traits (and, as a result, many phenotypic traits that may or may not be visible outwardly).

Figure 13.10 Theodosius Dobzhansky, an important scientist who formulated the 20th-century "modern synthesis" reconciling Charles Darwin's theory of evolution and Gregor Mendel's ideas on heredity.

Figure 13.11 Julian Huxley (1942).

Thinking of humans in terms of populations was part of Julian Huxley's (1942) "Modern Synthesis"—so named because it helped to reconcile two fundamental principles about evolution that had not been made sense of together before (Figure 13.11). As discussed in Chapter 3, Gregor Mendel (1822–1884) was able to show that inheritance was mediated by discrete particles (or genes) and not blended in the offspring. However, it was difficult for some 19th-century scientists to accept this model of genetic inheritance at the time because much of biological variation appeared to be continuous and not particulate (take skin color or height as examples). In the 1930s, it was demonstrated that traits could be polygenic and that multiple alleles could be responsible for any one phenotypic trait, thus producing the continuous variation in traits such as eye color that we see today. Thus, Huxley's "Modern Synthesis" outlines not only how human populations are capable of exchanging genes at the microevolutionary level but also how multiple alleles for one trait (polygenic exchanges) can cause gradual macroevolutionary changes.

Human Variation Is Clinal/Continuous (Not Discrete)

Human diversity cannot be broken into discrete "races," because most physical traits vary on a continuous or "clinal" basis. One obvious example of this is how human height does not only come in three values ("short," "medium," and "tall") but instead varies across a spectrum of vertical heights achievable by humans all over the world. (However, this is with the only difference being the huge divergence in how factors like body size and traits such as skin color have been viewed and used sociopolitically as a way of separating people throughout history.) The need to shift from typological "race" categories to a more nuanced understanding of continuously variable populations was realized by anthropologists working in the 1960s and 1970s who shifted their focus toward the study of individual traits rather than the study of groups (populations, races). Systematic evaluations of global biological variation in humans only began then, when large numbers of genetic loci for large numbers of samples were sampled from human populations distributed worldwide. It was during the 1960s that "**clines**" in human genetic variation were first identified.

Frank B. Livingstone (1928–2005) wrote: "There are no races, only clines" (1962). A *cline* is a gradation in the frequency of an allele/trait between populations living in different geographic regions. In order to study human traits that are clinally distributed, it is often required to perform genetic testing to uncover the true frequencies of an allele or trait across a certain geographic space. One easily visible example of a clinal distribution seen worldwide is the patterning of human variation in skin color. Whether in southern Asia, sub-Saharan Africa, or Australia, dark brown skin is found. Paler skin tones are found in higher-latitude populations such as those who have lived in areas like Europe, Siberia, and Alaska for millennia. Skin color is easily observable as a phenotypic trait exhibiting **continuous variation**.

A clinal distribution still derives from genetic inheritance, but clines often correspond to some gradually changing environmental factor. Clinal patterns arise when selective pressures in one geographic area differ from those in another as well as when people procreate and pass on genes together with their most immediate neighbors. There are several mechanisms, selective and neutral, that can lead to the clinal distribution of an allele or a biological trait. **Natural selection** is the mechanism that produced a global cline of skin color, whereby darker skin color protects equatorial populations from high amounts of UV radiation; there is a transition of lessening pigmentation in individuals that reside further and further away from the tropics (Jablonski 2004; Jablonski and Chaplin 2000) (Figure 13.12). The ability and inability to digest lactose (milk sugar) among different world communities varies according to differential practices and histories of milk and dairy product consumption (Gerbault et al. 2011; Ingram et al. 2009). Where malaria seems to be most prevalent as a disease stressor on human populations, a clinal gradient of increasing sickle cell anemia experience toward these regions has been studied extensively by genetic anthropologists (Luzzatto 2012). Sometimes culturally defined mate selection based on some observable trait can lead to clinal variation between populations as well.

Figure 13.12 *Global map of indigenous skin colors.*

Two neutral microevolutionary processes that may produce a cline in a human allele or trait are **gene flow** and **genetic drift**. The ways in which neutral processes can produce clinal distributions is seen clearly when looking at clinal maps for different blood groups in the human ABO blood group system (Figure 13.13). For instance, scientists have identified an east-to-west cline in the distribution of the blood type B allele across Eurasia. The frequency of B allele carriers decreases gradually westward when we compare the blood groups of East and Southeast Asian populations with those in Europe. This shows how populations residing nearer to one another are more likely to interbreed and share genetic material (i.e., undergo gene flow). We also see 90%–100% of native South American individuals, as well as between 70%–90% of Aboriginal Australian groups, carrying the O allele (Mourant et al. 1976). These high frequencies are likely due to random genetic drift and founder effects, in which population sizes were severely reduced by the earliest O allele-carrying individuals migrating into those areas. Over time, the O blood type has remained predominant.

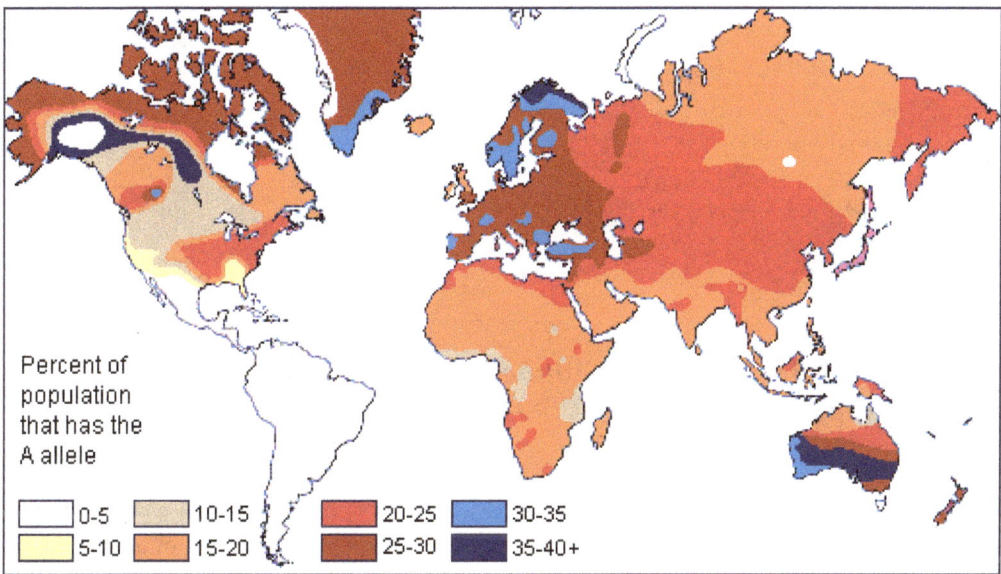

Figure 13.13a Global distribution of blood group A.

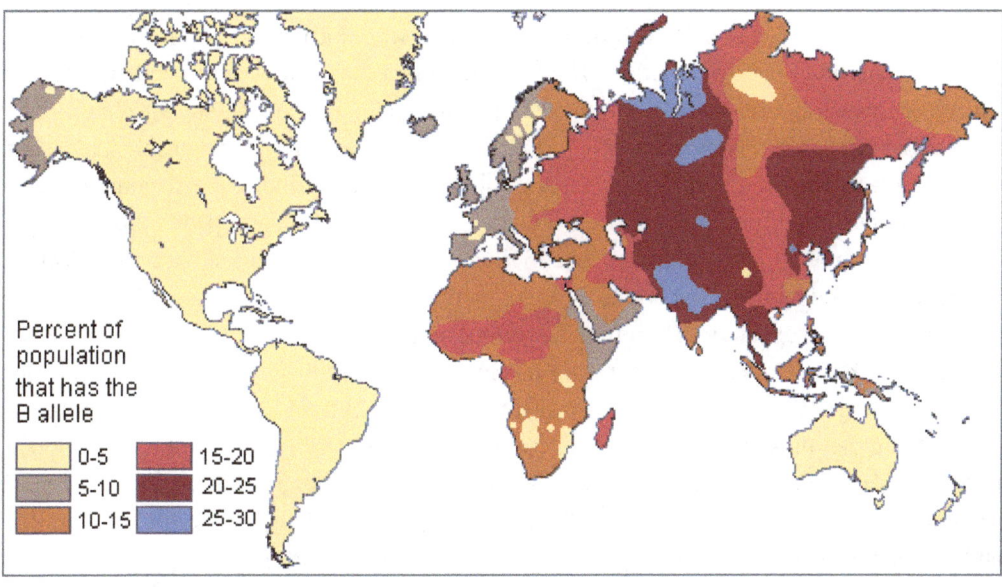

Figure 13.13b Global distribution of blood type B.

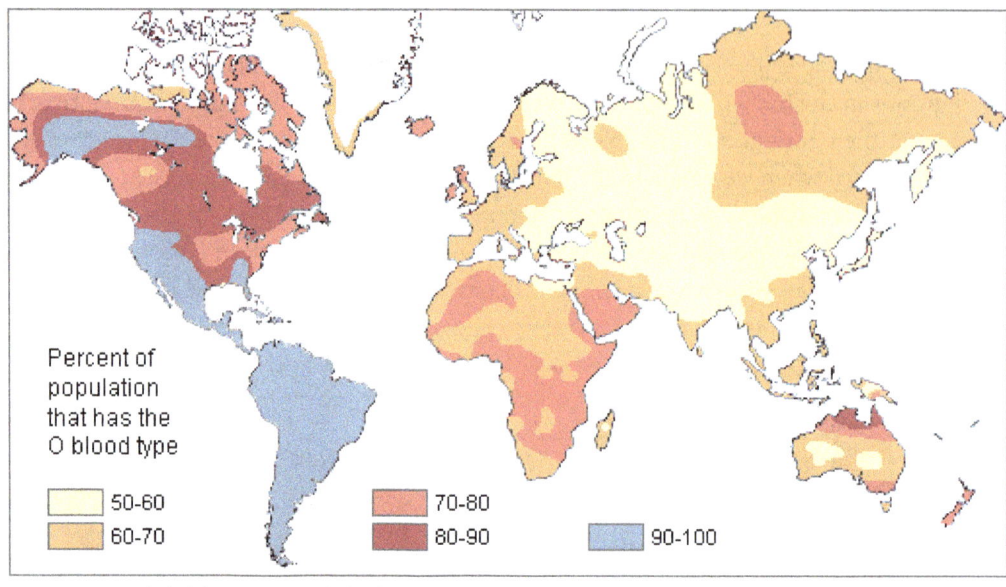

Figure 13.13c Global distribution of blood type O.

The Apportionment of Human Variation: Genetic Diversity Is Greater Within-Group Than Between-Groups

One problem with race-based classifications is they relied on an erroneous idea that people within a typological category were more similar to each other than they were to people in other groups. In other words, "race" concepts were predicated on the notion that individuals with particular characteristics would share more similar genes with each other within a particular "race" and share less with individuals of other "races" possessing different traits and genetic makeups. However, since around 50 years ago, scientific studies have shown that the majority of human genetic differences worldwide exist *within* groups (or "races") individually rather than *between* groups.

Richard Lewontin (1929–) is a biologist and evolutionary geneticist who authored a paper evaluating where the total genetic variation in humans lies. This article, titled "The Apportionment of Human Diversity" (Lewontin 1972), addressed the following question: On average, how genetically similar are two randomly chosen people from the same group when compared to two randomly chosen people from different groups? Lewontin studied this problem by using genetic data. He obtained data for a large number of different human populations worldwide using 17 genetic markers (including alleles that code for various important enzymes and proteins, such as blood-group proteins). The statistical analysis he ran used a measure of human genetic differences in and among populations known as the fixation index (F_{ST}). Technically, F_{ST} can be defined as the proportion of total genetic variance within a *subpopulation* relative to the total genetic variance from an *entire population*. Therefore, F_{ST} values range from 0 to 1 (or, sometimes you will see this stated as a percentage between 0% and 100%). The closer the F_{ST} value of a population (e.g., the world's population) approaches 1, the higher the degree of genetic differentiation among subpopulations relative to the overall population. In his paper, Lewontin (1972) identified that most of human genetic differences (85.4%) were found within local subpopulations (e.g., the Germans or Easter Islanders), whereas 8.3% were found between populations within continental human groups, and 6.3% were attributable to traditional "race" groups (e.g., "Caucasian" or "Amerind"). These findings have been important for scientifically rejecting the existence of biological races (Long and Kittles 2008).

In 2002, another landmark article by Noah Rosenberg and colleagues (2002) explored worldwide human genetic variation using an even-greater genetic data set. They used 377 highly variable markers in the human genome and sampled from 1,056 individuals representative of 52 populations. The markers chosen for study were not ones that code for any expressed genes. Because these regions of the human genome were made of unexpressed genes, we may understand these markers as neutrally derived (as opposed to selectively derived) as they do not code for functional advantages or disadvantages. These neutral genetic markers likely reflect an intricate combination of regional **founder effects** and population histories. Analyses of these neutral markers allowed scientists to identify that a majority of global genetic variance (93%–95%) can be accounted for by within-population differences at the 377 genetic loci, while only a small proportion of genetic variance (3%–5%) can be attributed to differences among major groups (Rosenberg et al. 2002). Like Lewontin's (1972) findings, this lends support to the theory that distinct biological races do not exist, even though misguided concepts of race may still have real social and political consequences.

Biological Data Fit Isolation-By-Distance and Out-of-Africa Models

One further note is that while the world's population may be genetically divided into "groups," "subsets," "clumps," or "clusters" that reflect some degree of genetic similarity, it is more likely that these identifiable clusters reflect genetic or geographic distances—either with gene flow facilitated by proximity between populations or impeded by obstacles like oceans or environmentally challenging habitats (Rosenberg et al. 2005). Sometimes, inferred clusters using multiple genetic loci are interpreted by non-geneticists literally as "ancestral populations." However, it would be wrong to assume from these genetic results that highly differentiated and "pure" ancestral groups ever existed. These groupings reflect differences that have arisen over time due to clinal patterning, genetic drift, and/or restricted or unrestricted gene flow (Weiss and Long 2009). The clusters identified by scientists are arbitrary and the parameters used to split up the global population into groups is subjective and dependent on the particular questions or distinctions being brought into focus (Relethford 2009).

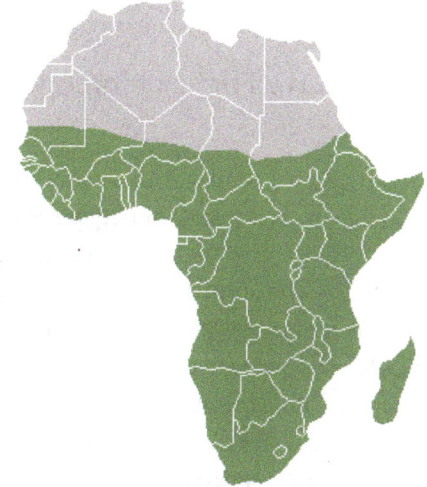

Figure 13.14 Sub-Saharan Africa (shaded dark/green).

Additionally, research on worldwide genetic diversity has shown that human variation decreases with increasing distance from sub-Saharan Africa, where there is evidence for this vast region being the geographical origin of anatomically modern humans (Liu et al. 2006; Prugnolle et al. 2005) (Figure 13.14). Genetic differentiation decreases in human groups the further you sample data from relative to sub-Saharan Africa because of serial founder effects (Relethford 2004). Over the course of human colonization of the rest of the world outside Africa, populations broke away in expanding waves across continents into western Asia, then Europe and eastern Asia, followed by Oceania and the Americas. As a result, founder events occurred whereby genetic variation was lost, as the colonization of each new geographical region involved a smaller number of individuals moving from the original larger population to establish a new one (Relethford 2004). The most genetic variation is found across populations residing in different parts of sub-Saharan Africa, while other current populations in places like northern Europe and the southern tip of South America exhibit some of the least genetic differentiation relative to all global populations.

Besides fitting nicely into the **Out-of-Africa model**, worldwide human genetic variation conforms to an **isolation-by-distance model**, which predicts that genetic similarity between groups will decrease exponentially as the geographic distance between them increases. This is because of the greater and greater restrictions to gene flow presented by geographic distance, as well as cultural and linguistic differences that occur as a result of certain degrees of isolation. Since genetic data conform to isolation-by-distance and Out-of-Africa models, these findings support the abolishment of "race" groupings. This research demonstrates that human variation is continuous and cannot be differentiated into geographically discrete categories. There are no "inherent" or "innate" differences between human groups; instead, variation derives from some degree of natural selection, as well as neutral processes like **population bottlenecking** (Figure 13.15), random **mutations** in the DNA, genetic drift, and gene flow through between-mate interbreeding.

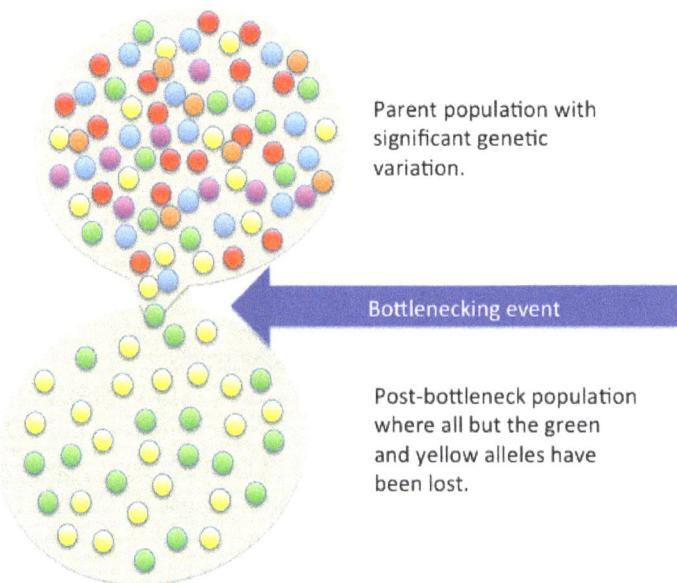

Figure 13.15 The founder effect is a change in a small population's gene pool due to a limited number of individuals breaking away from a parent population.

Humans Have Higher Homogeneity Compared to Many Other Species

An important fact to bear in mind is that humans are 99.9% identical to one another. This means that the apportionments of human diversity discussed above only concern that tiny 0.1% of difference that exists between all humans globally. Compared to other mammalian species, including the other great apes, human diversity is remarkably lower. This may be surprising given that the worldwide human population has already exceeded seven billion, and, at least on the surface level, we appear to be quite phenotypically diverse. Molecular approaches to human and primate genetics tells us that external differences are merely superficial. For a proper appreciation of human diversity, we have to look at our closest relatives in the primate order and mammalian class. Compared to chimpanzees, gibbons, and even gray wolves and giant pandas, humans have remarkably low average genome-wide **heterogeneity**.

Figure 13.16 Chimpanzee (Pan troglodytes).

When we look at chimpanzee genetic diversity, it is fascinating that western, central, eastern, and Cameroonian chimpanzee groups have substantially more genetic diversity between them than large global samples of human DNA (Bowden et al. 2012) (Figure 13.16). This is surprising given that all of these chimpanzee groups live relatively near one another in Africa, while measurements of human genetic diversity have been conducted using samples from entirely different continents. First, geneticists suppose that this could reflect differential experiences of the founder effect between humans and chimpanzees. Because all non-African human populations descended from a small number of anatomically modern humans who left Africa, it would be expected that all groups descended from that smaller ancestral group would be similar genetically. Second, our species is really young, given that we have only existed on the planet for around 150,000 to 300,000 years. This gave humans little time for random genetic mutations to occur as genes get passed down through genetic interbreeding and meiosis. Chimpanzees, however, have inhabited different **ecological niches**, and less interbreeding has occurred between the four chimpanzee groups over the past six to eight million years compared to the amount of gene flow that occurred between worldwide human populations (Bowden et al. 2012).

Recent advances have now enabled the attainment of genetic samples from the larger family of great apes and the evaluation of genetic diversity among bonobos, orangutans, and gorillas alongside that of chimpanzees and humans (Prado-Martinez et al. 2013). Collecting such data and analyzing primate genetic diversity has been important not only to elucidate how different ecological, demographic, and climatic factors have shaped our evolution but also to inform upon conservation efforts and medical research. Genes that may code for genetic susceptibilities to tropical diseases that affect multiple primates can be studied through genome-wide methods. Species differences in the genomes associated with speech, behavior, or cognition could tell us more about how human individuals may be affected by genetically derived neurological or speech-related disorders and conditions (Prado-Martinez et al. 2013; Staes et al. 2017). In 2018, a great ape genomic study also reported genetic differences between chimpanzees and humans related to brain cell divisions (Kronenberg et al. 2018). From these results, it may be inferred that cognitive or behavioral variation between humans and the great apes might relate to an increased number of cortical neurons being formed during human brain development (Kronenberg et al. 2018). Comparative studies of human and nonhuman great ape genetic variation highlight the complex interactions of population histories, environmental changes, and natural selection between and within species. When viewed in the context of overall great ape diversity, we may reconsider how variable the human species is relatively and how unjustified previous "race" concepts really were.

Phenotypic Traits That Reflect Neutral Evolution

Most human traits are non-concordant. "**Non-concordance**" is a term used to describe how biological traits vary independent of each other–that is, they don't get inherited in a correlative manner with other genetically controlled traits. For example, if you knew an individual had genes that coded for tall height, you would not be able to predict if they are lighter-skinned or have red hair. Depending on the trait being observed, different patterns of phenotypic variation may be found within and among groups worldwide. In this subsection, some phenotypic traits that reflect the aforementioned patterns of genetic variation will be discussed.

Figure 13.17 *Human skulls in Tana Toraja (Indonesia), common scenery in public graves.*

Looking beyond genetic variation briefly, recent studies have revisited biological anthropology's earlier themes of externally observable traits, such as skull shape (Figure 13.17). In the last 20 or so years, anthropologists have evaluated the level to which human cranial shape diversity reflects the results from genetic markers, such as those used previously to fit against Out-of-Africa models (Relethford 2004) or those used in the apportionment of human diversity between and within groups (Lewontin 1972; Rosenberg et al. 2002). Using larger sample sizes of cranial data collected from thousands of skulls worldwide and a long list of cranial measurements, studies demonstrate a similar decrease in diversity with distance from Africa and show that a majority of cranial variation occurs within populations rather than between populations (Betti et al. 2009; Betti et al.

2010; Manica et al. 2007; Relethford 2001; von Cramon-Taubadel and Lycett 2008). The greatest cranial diversity is found among skulls of sub-Saharan African origin, while the least variation is found among populations inhabiting places like Tierra del Fuego at the southern tip of Argentina and Chile. While ancient and historical thinkers previously thought "race" categories could reasonably be determined based on skull dimensions, modern-day analyses using more informative sets of cranial traits simply show that migrations out of Africa and the relative distances between populations can explain a majority of worldwide cranial diversity (Betti et al. 2009).

Figure 13.18 Diagram of the bony labyrinth in the inner ear.

This same patterning in phenotypic variation has even been found in studies examining shape variation of the pelvis (Betti et al. 2013; Betti et al. 2014), the teeth (Rathmann et al. 2017), and the human **bony labyrinth** of the ear (Ponce de León et al. 2018) (Figure 13.18). The skeletal morphology of these bones still varies worldwide, but a greater proportion of that variation can still be attributed to the ways in which human populations migrated across the world and exchanged genes with those closer to them rather than those further away. Human skeletal variation in these parts of the body is continuous and non-discrete. Given the important functions of the cranium and these other skeletal parts, we may infer that the genes that underpin their development have been relatively conserved by neutral evolutionary processes such as genetic drift and gene flow. It is also important to note that while some traits such as height, weight, cranial dimensions, and body composition are determined, in part, by genes, the underlying developmental processes behind these traits are underpinned by complex polygenic mechanisms that have led to the continuous spectrum of variation in such variables among modern-day human populations.

Phenotypic Traits That Reflect Natural Selection

Even though 99.9% of our DNA is the same between all humans worldwide, and many traits reflect neutral processes, there are parts of that remaining 0.1% of the human genome that code for individual and regional differences. Similarly to craniometric analyses that have been conducted in recent decades, human variation in skin color has also been reassessed using new methods and in light of greater knowledge of biological evolution.

New technologies allow scientists to use color photometry to sample and quantify the visible wavelength of skin color, in a way 19th- and 20th-century readers could not. In one report, it was found that 87.9% of global skin color variation can be attributed to genetic differences *between* groups, 3.2% to those among local populations within regions, and 8.9% *within* local populations (Relethford 2002). This apportionment differs significantly and is the reverse situation found in the distribution of genetic differences we see when we examine genetic markers such as blood type–related alleles. However, this pattern of human skin color worldwide is not surprising, given that we now understand that past selection has occurred for darker skin near the equator and lighter skin at higher latitudes (Jablonski 2004; Jablonski and Chaplin 2000). While most genetic diversity reflects neutral variation due to population migrations, geographic isolation, and restricted gene flow dynamics, some human genetic/phenotypic diversity is best explained as local adaptation to environmental conditions (i.e., selection). Given that skin color variation is atypical compared to other genetic markers and biological traits, this, in fact, goes against earlier "race" typologies. This is because recent studies ironically show how so much of genetic variation relates to neutral processes, while skin color does not. It follows that skin color *cannot* be viewed as useful in making inferences about other human traits.

On top of social implications, the quantification and interpretation of human variation has important medical and clinical applications (National Research Council Committee on Human Genome Diversity 1997). For instance, large-scale genomic studies sampling from human populations distributed worldwide have produced detailed knowledge on variation in disease resistance or susceptibility between and within populations. If we think about drug companies who develop medicines for African American patients particularly, the genetic diversity in predispositions to disease and/or good health is likely higher among people of African descent than these pharmaceutical businesses have taken into account. Through targeted sampling of various world groups, clinical geneticists may also identify genetic risk factors of certain common disorders such as chronic heart disease, asthma, diabetes, autoimmune diseases, and behavioral disorders. Having an understanding of population-specific biology is crucial in the development of therapies, medicines, and vaccinations, as not all treatments may be suitable for for every human, depending on their genotype. During diagnosis and treatment, it is important to have an evolutionary perspective on gene-environment relationships in patients. Typological concepts of "race" are not useful, given that most racial groups (whether self-identified or not) popularly recognized lack homogeneity and are, in fact, variable. **Cystic fibrosis**, for instance, occurs in all world populations but can often be underdiagnosed in populations of African ancestry because it is thought of as a "white" disease (Yudell et al. 2016).

Figure 13.19 *The Forensic Anthropology Lab at the National Museum of Natural History, Smithsonian Institute, Washington, D.C.*

Lastly, assignments of "race" to human remains is a common practice in forensic anthropology, especially in the United States and other worldwide contexts where bones are recovered and associated with criminal investigations (Figure 13.19). Forensic anthropologists have ascribed "race" or ancestry to sets of skeletons thanks to scientific research that has attempted to divide up different human groups into culturally constructed categories based on biologically "discrete" assortments (Sauer 1992). Rather than focusing on the neutral or selective *causes* of human biological variation, the concentration in forensic anthropology centers upon how *probabilistic* it may be to assign bones of certain dimensions to one of several identified racial categories. Forensic anthropologists do not agree with the typological "race" concepts of the past but, instead, root their racial categorization in methods of probability estimation (Sauer 1992). Based on many samples of skeletons from different world regions, statistical tests (such as discriminant function analysis) allow them to distinguish how *likely* certain skeletal dimensions may predict geographic **ancestry**.

It is important to remember that while it is possible to determine geographic origin (or ancestry) based on skull morphology, again, the amount of craniometric distinctiveness required to distinguish whether a cranium belongs to one group or another will make for arbitrary decisions (Relethford 2009). Individuals can vary in their skeletal dimensions by continental origin, country origin, regional origin, sex, age, environmental factors, and the time period in which they lived, making it difficult to assign individuals to particular categories in a completely meaningful way (Ousley et al. 2009). When forensic reports and scientific journal articles give an estimation of ancestry, it is crucial to keep in mind that responsible assignments of ancestry will be done through robust statistical testing and stated as a probability estimate. Today, we also live in a more globalized world where a skeletal individual may have been born originally to parents of two separate traditional racial categories. In contexts of great heterogeneity within populations, this definitely adds difficulty to the work of forensic scientists and anthropologists preparing results for the courtroom.

TALKING ABOUT HUMAN BIOLOGICAL VARIATION GOING FORWARD

To conclude, utilizing *races* to describe human biological variation is not accurate or productive. Using a select few hundred genetic loci, or perhaps a number of phenotypic traits, it may be possible to assign individuals to a geographic ancestry. However, what constitutes a bounded genetic or geographical grouping is both arbitrary and potentially harmful owing to ethical and historical reasons (see Chapter 3 for more on the issues with commercial ancestry tests, for example). The discipline of biological anthropology has moved past typological frameworks that shoehorn continuously variable human populations into discrete and socially constructed subsets. Improvements in the number of markers, the genetic technologies used to study variation, and the number of worldwide populations sampled have led to more nuanced understandings of human diversity. It is of utmost importance that scientists and non-scientists, in theory, have each of the following clarified:

1. Today, we refer to different local human groups as "populations." What constitutes a population is carefully defined in scientific reports based on some geographical, linguistic, or cultural criteria and some degree of relativity to other closely or distantly related human groups.
2. Humans have significantly less genetic diversity than other primates and mammals, and all human beings on Earth share 99.9% of their overall DNA. Some of the remaining 0.1% of human variation varies on a clinal or continuous basis, such as can be seen when looking at ABO blood type **polymorphisms** worldwide.
3. Many biological characteristics in humans are actually determined non-concordantly and/or polygenically. Therefore, superiority or inferiority in human behavior or body form cannot justifiably be linked to fixed and innate differences between groups.
4. Genetic distances are correlated with geographic distances among the global human population. This is especially apparent when we consider that genetic diversity is highest in sub-Saharan Africa, and average genetic heterogeneity decreases in populations further away from the African continent in accordance with the migratory history of anatomically modern *Homo sapiens*.
5. The effects of gene flow, genetic drift, and population bottlenecking are reflected in some phenotypic traits, such as cranial shape.
6. Other traits, like skin color and lactase persistence, we recognize to be the product of many millennia of natural selective pressures influencing human biology from the external environment.

When taken altogether, genetic analyses of human diversity do not support 20th-century (or even earlier) concepts of race. In discussions about human diversity, each of these genomic results help clarify for all conversationalists how biological variation is distributed across the human population today. Taking care to think about and debate the nature of human variation is important, because although the effects and events that produced genetic differences among groups occurred in the ancient past, sociocultural concepts about race and ethnicity continue to have real social, economic, and political consequences in the modern era.

Beyond talking about diversity in the university setting, it is important that teachers, researchers, and students of anthropology recognize and assume the responsibility of influencing public perspectives of human diversity. Race-based classification systems were developed during the colonial era, transatlantic slave trade, and Scientific Revolution by some of the earliest scholars whom we may call the first "anthropologists" and students of humankind's variation. Unfortunately, some of their ideas put forward have persisted and evolved into present-day lived realities. Some of today's politicians and socioeconomic bodies have racially charged agendas that promote racism or certain kinds of economic or racial inequalities. As anthropologists, we must acknowledge that while human "races" are not a biological reality, their status as a (misguided) social construction does have real consequences for many people (Antrosio 2011). In other words, while "race" is a sociocultural invention in some people's minds, the treatment different individuals receive due to their perceived "race" can have significant financial, emotional, sociopolitical, and physiological costs. But assuming a "color-blind" position when it comes to the topics of "race" and ethnicity (especially in political discussions) is actually counterproductive since the negative social consequences of modern "race" ideas could be ignored, making it harder to examine and address instances of discrimination properly (Wise 2010). Rather than shy away from these topics, we can use our scientific findings to establish socially relevant and biologically accurate ideas concerning human diversity. Today, research into genetic and phenotypic differentiation among and within various human populations continues to expand in its scope, its technological capabilities, its sample sizes, and its ethical concerns. It is thanks to such scientific work done in the past few decades that we now have a deeper understanding not only of how humans vary but also of how we are biologically a rather homogenous, intermixing world population.

SPECIAL TOPIC: MY EXPERIENCES AS A MINORITY ACADEMIC OF COLOR

Figure 13.20 Michael B. C. Rivera in Hong Kong.

My name is Michael, and I am a researcher in biological anthropology (Figure 13.20). What strikes me as most interesting to investigate is human biological diversity today and the study of past human evolution. What I am really curious about is how we can use human skeletons to infer how people adapt to coastal environments. Relying on aquatic foods near rivers, lakes, and the sea is interesting because we have found evidence for positive effects of coastal living on dietary health and many unique adaptations in bones and teeth when living near rivers and beaches. I also really enjoy talking to students and non-scientists about our work, through teaching, science communication events, and writing book chapters like this one! I grew up in Hong Kong, a city in southern China. My father is from the Philippines and my mother is from Hong Kong, which makes me a mixed Filipino-Chinese academic. When I attended international schools in my youth, I saw that kids my age came in all shapes, sizes, and colors. It was not until I left Hong Kong that I realized people with my skin tone were somewhat rarer in British universities I attended.

Biological anthropology is not taught extensively back home in Hong Kong, but my initial motivation to enter this field was a great TV show called *Bones*. This TV series was about a brilliant anthropologist who examined human remains for the Smithsonian Institute in Washington, D.C., identified the individuals they belonged to through scientific analyses of bones and teeth, and told the stories of the deceased who could not tell their own. I went to the United Kingdom to earn my bachelor's, master's, and doctorate degrees. During my studies, I was taught about human genetics, apes and monkeys, forensics, human cultural and behavioral diversity, and the story of human evolution that began six million to eight million years ago. It was fascinating to me that we could answer important questions about human variation and history using scientific methods. While I was at university, I did not have many minority academic role models to look up to. Today, I look around and see other academics of color during conferences and perhaps one or two others around the places at which I work. I am inspired by all my colleagues who advocate for greater representation and diversity in universities (whether they are minority academics or not). I admire many of my fellow researchers who are underrepresented and do a great job of representing minority groups through their cutting-edge research and quality teaching at the undergraduate and graduate levels. The study of anthropology has really highlighted for me that we share a common humanity and history. Being somebody who is "mixed race" and Asian likely played a key role in steering me toward a discipline that studies human diversity. As this chapter hopefully shows, there is a lot about race and ethnicity to discuss in terms of the discipline's history and current understandings of human biological diversity. Some scientific and technological advancements today are unfortunately misused for reasons to do with money, politics, or the continuation of fairly antiquated ideas. It is my belief, alongside many of my friends and fellow anthropologists, that science should be more about empathy toward all members of our species and contributing to the intellectual and technological nourishment of society. After speaking to many members of the public, as well as my own undergraduate students, I have received lovely messages from other individuals of color expressing thanks and appreciation for my presence and understanding as a fellow minority and mentor figure. This is why anthropology needs more diversity and to make room for more personal routes into the discipline. All paths to anthropology are valuable and valid. I would encourage anyone to study anthropology as it really is a field for understanding and celebrating the intricacies of human diversity.

Review Questions

- How is the genetic variation of the human species distributed worldwide?
- What evolutionary processes are responsible for producing genotypic/phenotypic diversity within and between human populations?
- Should we continue to attribute any value in "race" concepts older than 1950, based on our current understandings of human biological diversity?
- How should we communicate scientific findings about human biological variation more accurately and responsibly to those outside the anthropological discipline?

Key Terms

Age of Discovery: A period between the late 1400s and late 1700s when European explorers and ships sailed extensively across the globe in pursuit of new trading routes and territorial conquest.

Ancestry: Biogeographical information about an individual, traced either through the study of an individual's genome, skeletal characteristics, or some other form of forensic/archaeological evidence. Anthropologists carry out probabilistic estimates of ancestry. They attribute sets of human remains to distinctive "ancestral" groups using careful statistical testing and should report ancestry estimations with statistical probability values.

Binomial nomenclature: A system of naming living things developed by Linnaeus in the 1700s using a scientific name made up of two Latin- or Greek-form words, with the first name capitalized and representative of an organism's genus and the second name indicating an organism's species (e.g., *Homo sapiens*, *Australopithecus afarensis*, *Pongo tapanuliensis*, etc.).

Biological anthropology: A subdiscipline of anthropology concerned with the biological origins, ecology, evolution, and diversity of humans and other primates. This term is increasingly preferred to *physical anthropology*, as many in the field now uncomfortably associate this original name (coined by Aleš Hrdlička) with the ways in which questions of human variation were studied in decades past and the sociohistorical context that made anthropology problematic before 1950 (see Warren 2018).

Biological determinism: The erroneous concept that an individual's behavioral characteristics are innate and determined by genes, brain size, or other physiological attributes, and with no influence of social learning or the environment around the individual during development.

Bony labyrinth: A system of interconnected canals within the auditory (ear- or hearing-related) apparatus, located in the inner ear and responsible for balance and the reception of sound waves.

Cline: A gradient of physiological or morphological change in a single character or allele frequency among a group of species across environmental or geographical lines (e.g., skin color varies clinally, as, over many generations, human groups living nearer the equator have adapted to have more skin pigmentation).

Continuous/clinal variation: Variation that exists between individuals and cannot be measured using distinct categories. Instead, differences between individuals within a population in relation to one particular trait are measurable along a smooth, continuous gradient.

Cystic fibrosis: A genetic disorder in which one defective gene causes overproduction and buildup of mucus in the lungs and other bodily organs, most common in northern Europeans (but also in other world populations more rarely).

Ecological niche: The position or status of an organism within its community and/or ecosystem, resulting from the organism's structural and functional adaptations (e.g., bipedalism, omnivory, lactose digestion, etc.).

Essentialism: A belief or view that an entity, organism, or human grouping has a specific set of characteristics that are fundamentally necessary to its being and classification into definitive categories.

Ethnicity: A complex term used commonly in an interchangeable way with the term *race* (see below).

Eugenics: A set of beliefs and practices that involves the controlled selective breeding of human populations with the hope of improving their heritable qualities, especially through surgical procedures like sterilization and legal rulings that affect marriage rights for interracial couples.

Founder effect: See population bottlenecking below.

Gene flow: A neutral (or nonselective) evolutionary process that occurs when genes get shared between populations.

Genetic drift: A neutral evolutionary process in which allele frequencies from generation to generation due to random chance.

Heterogeneity: The quality of being diverse genetically.

Homogenous: The quality of being uniform genetically.

Human diversity/differentiation/variation: Group differences involving variation in biology, physiology, body chemistry, behavior, and culture.

Isolation-by-distance model: A model that predicts a positive relationship between genetic distances and geographical distances between pairs of populations.

Monogenic: Characterized as being controlled by a single gene (or, in other words, one pair of alleles). Sickle cell anemia and cystic fibrosis are examples of disorders that are monogenically caused.

Monogenetic: Pertaining to the idea that the origin of a species is situated in one geographic region or time (as opposed to *polygenetic*).

Mutation: A gene alteration in the DNA sequence of an organism. As a random, neutral evolutionary process that occurs over the course of meiosis and early cell development, gene mutations are possible sources of diversity in any given human gene pool. Genetic mutations that occur in more than 1% of a population are termed *polymorphisms*.

Natural selection: An evolutionary process whereby certain traits are perpetuated through successive generations, likely owing to the advantages they give organisms in terms of chances of survival and/or reproduction.

Non-concordance: The fact of genes or traits not varying with one another and instead being inherited independently.

Othering: In postcolonial anthropology, we now understand "othering" to mean any action by someone or some group that establishes a division between "us" and "them" in relation to other individuals or populations. This could be based on linguistic or cultural differences, and it has largely been based on external characteristics throughout history.

Out-of-Africa model: A model that suggests that all humans originate from one single group of *Homo sapiens* in (sub-Saharan) Africa who lived between 100,000 and 315,000 years ago and who subsequently diverged and migrated to other regions across the globe.

Physical anthropology: See *biological anthropology* above.

Polygenetic: Having many different ancestries, as in older theories about human origins that involved multiple traditional groupings of humans evolving concurrently in different parts of the world before they merged into one species through interbreeding and/or intergroup warfare. These earlier suggestions have now been overwhelmed by insurmountable evidence for a single origin of the human species in Africa (see the "Out-of-Africa model").

Polymorphism: A genetic variant within a population (caused either by a single gene or multiple genes) that occurs at a rate of over 1% among the population. Polymorphisms are responsible for variation in phenotypic traits such as blood type and skin color.

Population: A group of humans living in a particular geographical area, with more local interbreeding within-group than interbreeding with other groups. A limited or restricted amount of gene flow between populations can occur due to geographical, cultural, linguistic, or environmental factors.

Population bottlenecking (or founder effect): An event in which genetic diversity is significantly reduced owing to a sharp reduction in population size. This can occur when environmental disaster strikes or as a result of human activities (e.g., genocides or group migrations). An important example of this loss in genetic variation occurred over the first human migrations out of Africa and into other continental regions.

Prejudice: An unjustified attitude toward an individual or group not based on reason, whether that is positive and showing preference for one group of people over another or negative and resulting in harm or injury to others.

Race: The identification of a group based on a perceived distinctiveness that makes that group more similar to each other than they are to others outside the group. This may be based on cultural differences, genetic parentage, physical characteristics, behavioral attributes, or something arbitrarily and socially constructed. As a social or demographic category, perceptions of "race" can produce effects that have real and serious consequences for different groups of people. This is despite the fact that biological anthropologists and geneticists have demonstrated that all humans are genetically homogenous and that more differences can be found within populations as opposed to between them in the overall apportionment of human biological variation.

Racism: Any action or belief that discriminates against someone based on perceived differences in race or ethnicity, and the characteristics, qualities, or abilities believed to be specific to a race that is inferior to another in some way.

Scientific Revolution: A period between the 1400s and 1600s when substantial shifts occurred in the social, technological, and philosophical sense, when a scientific method based on the collection of empirical evidence through experimentation was emphasized and inductive reasoning used to test hypotheses and interpret their results.

Typology: An assortment system that relies on the interpretation of qualitative similarities or differences in the study of variation among objects or people. The categorization of cultures or human groups according to "race" was performed with a typological approach in the earliest practice of anthropology, but this practice has since been discredited and abandoned.

About the Author

Michael B. C. Rivera

University of Cambridge, mbcr2@alumni.cam.ac.uk

The Arch and Anth Podcast, archandanthpodcast@gmail.com

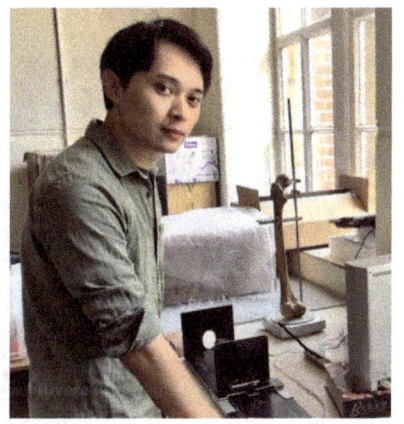

Michael B. C. Rivera

Michael B. C. Rivera is a biological anthropologist and human bioarchaeologist, studying the transition into agriculture in coastal environments. His recently completed doctoral thesis brought together human skeletal biology, palaeopathology, and prehistoric archaeology to investigate the lives of ancient people on the northeastern European coastline. Being from Hong Kong and a student of human biological variation, Michael is also an advocate for greater inclusion, diversity, and equality in academia. Additionally, as a believer in the value of science communication, and of the value of the discipline to greater society, he launched The Arch and Anth Podcast in May 2019, which disseminates scientific knowledge in a fun, educational, and informal interview-style audio format.

References

Antrosio, Jason. 2011. "'Race Reconciled': Race Isn't Skin Color, Biology, or Genetics." *Living Anthropologically Website*. https://www.livinganthropologically.com/biological-anthropology/race-reconciled-debunks-race/.

Beals, Kenneth L., Courtland L. Smith, Stephen M. Dodd, J. Lawrence Angel, Este Armstrong, Bennett Blumenberg, Fakhry G. Girgis, et al. 1984. "Brain Size, Cranial Morphology, Climate, and Time Machines [and Comments and Reply]." *Current Anthropology* 25 (3): 301–330.

Betti, Lia, François Balloux, William Amos, Tsunehiko Hanihara, and Andrea Manica. 2008. "Distance from Africa, Not Climate, Explains Within-Population Phenotypic Diversity in Humans." *Proceedings of the Royal Society B: Biological Sciences* 276 (Issue 165B): 809–814. doi:10.1098/rspb.2008.1563.

Betti, Lia, François Balloux, Tsunehiko Hanihara, and Andrea Manica. 2010. "The Relative Role of Drift and Selection in Shaping the Human Skull." *American Journal of Physical Anthropology* 141 (1): 76–82. doi:10.1002/ajpa.21115.

Betti, Lia, Noreen von Cramon-Taubadel, Andrea Manica, and Stephen J. Lycett. 2013. "Global Geometric Morphometric Analyses of the Human Pelvis Reveal Substantial Neutral Population History Effects, Even across Sexes." *PloS ONE* 8 (2): e55909. doi:10.1371/journal.pone.0055909.

———. 2014. "The Interaction of Neutral Evolutionary Processes with Climatically Driven Adaptive Changes in the 3D Shape of the Human Os Coxae." *Journal of Human Evolution* 73 (August): 64–74. doi:10.1016/j.jhevol.2014.02.021.

Boas, Franz. 1931. "Race and Progress." *Science* 74 (1905): 1–8.

Bowden, Rory, Tammie S. MacFie, Simon Myers, Garrett Hellenthal, Eric Nerrienet, Ronald E. Bontrop, Colin Freeman, Peter Donnelly, and Nicholas I. Mundy. 2012. "Genomic Tools for Evolution and Conservation in the Chimpanzee: *Pan troglodytes ellioti* Is a Genetically Distinct Population." *PLoS Genetics* 8 (3): e1002504. doi:10.1371/journal.pgen.1002504.

Gerbault, Pascale, Anke Liebert, Yuval Itan, Adam Powell, Mathias Currat, Joachim Burger, Dallas M. Swallow, and Mark G. Thomas. 2011. "Evolution of Lactase Persistence: An Example of Human Niche Construction." *Philosophical Transactions of the Royal Society B* 366 (1566): 863–877. doi:10.1098/rstb.2010.0268.

Hooton, Earnest A. 1936. "Plain Statements about Race." *Science* 83 (2161): 511–513.

Hrdlička, Aleš. 1918. "Physical Anthropology: Its Scope and Aims; Its History and Present Status in America. A: Physical Anthropology; Its Scopes and Aims." *American Journal of Physical Anthropology* 1 (1): 3–23.

Huxley, Julian. 1942. *Evolution: The Modern Synthesis*. London: Allen and Unwin.

Ingram, Catherine J. E., Charlotte A. Mulcare, Yuval Itan, Mark G. Thomas, and Dallas M. Swallow. 2009. "Lactose Digestion and the Evolutionary Genetics of Lactase Persistence." *Human Genetics* 124 (6): 579–591. doi:10.1007/s00439-008-0593-6.

Jablonski, Nina G. 2004. "The Evolution of Human Skin and Skin Color." *Annual Review of Anthropology* 33 (1): 585–623. doi:10.1146/annurev.anthro.33.070203.143955.

Jablonski, Nina G., and George Chaplin. 2000. "The Evolution of Human Skin Coloration." *Journal of Human Evolution* 39 (1): 57–106. doi:10.1006/jhev.2000.0403.

Kronenberg, Zev N., Ian T. Fiddes, David Gordon, Shwetha Murali, Stuart Cantsilieris, Olivia S. Meyerson, Jason G. Underwood, et al. 2018. "High-Resolution Comparative Analysis of Great Ape Genomes." *Science* 360 (6393): eaar6343. doi:10.1126/science.aar6343.

Lewontin, Richard. 1972. "The Apportionment of Human Diversity." *Evolutionary Biology* 6: 381–398. Eds. Dobzhansky, Theodosius, Hecht, Max K., Steere, William C. Springer, New York, NY

Linnaeus, Carl. 1758. *Systema Naturae*. http://www.cabdirect.org/abstracts/20057000018.html.

Liu, Hua, Franck Prugnolle, Andrea Manica, and François Balloux. 2006. "A Geographically Explicit Genetic Model of Worldwide Human-Settlement History." *American Journal of Human Genetics* 79 (2): 230–237.

Livingstone, Frank B. 1962. "On the Nonexistence of Human Races." *Current Anthropology* 3 (3): 279–281.

Long, Jeffery C., and Kittles, Rick A. 2003. "Human Genetic Diversity and the Nonexistence of Biological Races." *Human Biology* 75 (4): 449–471.

Luzzatto, Lucio. 2012. "Sickle Cell Anaemia and Malaria." *Mediterranean Journal of Hematology and Infectious Diseases* 4 (1). doi:10.4084/MJHID.2012.065.

Manica, Andrea, William Amos, François Balloux, and Tsunehiko Hanihara. 2007. "The Effect of Ancient Population Bottlenecks on Human Phenotypic Variation." *Nature* 448 (7151): 346–348. doi:10.1038/nature05951.

Mourant, A. E., Ada C. Kopeć, and Kazimiera Domaniewska-Sobczak. 1976. *The Distribution of the Human Blood Groups and Other Polymorphisms*. 2nd edition. Oxford: Oxford University Press.

Morton, Samuel George. 1839.*Crania Americana, or, A comparative view of the skulls of various aboriginal nations of North and South America*. Philadelphia: J. Dobson.

National Research Council (U.S.) Committee on Human Genome Diversity. 1997. *Evaluating Human Genetic Diversity*. Washington, D.C.: National Academies Press

Ousley, Stephen D., Richard L. Jantz, and Donna Freid. 2009. "Understanding Race and Human Variation: Why Forensic Anthropologists Are Good at Identifying Race." *American Journal of Physical Anthropology* 139 (1): 68–76. doi:10.1002/ajpa.21006.

Oxford English Dictionary. 2018. 3rd edition. Oxford: Oxford University Press.

Ponce de León, Marcia S., Toetik Koesbardiati, John David Weissmann, Marco Millela, Carlos S. Reyna-Blanco, Gen Suwa, Osamu Kondo, Anna-Sapfo Malaspinas, Tim D. White, and Christoph P. E. Zollikofer. 2018. "Human Bony Labyrinth Is an Indicator of Population History and Dispersal from Africa." *Proceedings of the National Academy of Sciences* 115 (16): 4128–4133. doi:10.1073/pnas.1808125115.

Prado-Martinez, Javier, Peter H. Sudmant, Jeffrey M. Kidd, Heng Li, Joanna L Kelley, Belen Lorente-Galdos, Krishna R. Veeramah, et al. 2013. "Great Ape Genetic Diversity and Population History." *Nature* 499 (7459): 471–475. doi:10.1038/nature12228.

Prugnolle, Franck, Andrea Manica, and François Balloux. 2005. "Geography Predicts Neutral Genetic Diversity of Human Populations." *Current Biology* 15 (5): 159–160.

Rathmann, Hannes, Hugo Reyes-Centeno, Silvia Ghirotto, Nicole Creanza, Tsunehiko Hanihara, and Katerina Harvati. 2017. "Reconstructing Human Population History from Dental Phenotypes." *Scientific Reports* 7: 12495. doi:10.1038/s41598-017-12621-y.

Relethford, John H. 2001. "Global Analysis of Regional Differences in Craniometric Diversity and Population Substructure." *Human Biology* 73 (5): 629–636. doi:10.1353/hub.2001.0073.

———. 2002. "Apportionment of Global Human Genetic Diversity Based on Craniometrics and Skin Color." *American Journal of Physical Anthropology* 118 (4): 393–398. doi:10.1002/ajpa.10079.

———. 2004. "Global Patterns of Isolation by Distance Based on Genetic and Morphological Data." *Human Biology* 76 (4): 499–513. doi:10.1353/hub.2004.0060.

———. 2009. "Race and Global Patterns of Phenotypic Variation." *American Journal of Physical Anthropology* 139 (1): 16–22. doi:10.1002/ajpa.20900.

Rosenberg, Noah A., Saurabh Mahajan, Sohini Ramachandran, Chengfeng Zhao, Jonathan K. Pritchard, and Marcus W. Feldman. 2005. "Clines, Clusters, and the Effect of Study Design on the Inference of Human Population Structure." *PLoS Genetics* 1 (6): e70. doi:10.1371/journal.pgen.0010070.

Rosenberg, Noah A., Jonathan K. Pritchard, James L. Weber, Howard M. Cann, Kenneth K. Kidd, Lev A. Zhivotovsky, and Marcus W. Feldman. 2002. "Genetic Structure of Human Populations." *Science* 298 (5602): 2381–2385.

Sauer, Norman J. 1992. "Forensic Anthropology and the Concept of Race: If Races Don't Exist, Why Are Forensic Anthropologists So Good at Identifying Them?" *Social Science and Medicine* 34 (2): 107–111. doi:10.1016/0277-9536(92)90086-6.

Staes, Nicky, Chet C. Sherwood, Katharine Wright, Marc de Manuel, Elaine E. Guevara, Tomas Marques-Bonet, Michael Krützen, et al. 2017. "FOXP2 Variation in Great Ape Populations Offers Insight into the Evolution of Communication Skills." *Scientific Reports* 7 (1): 1–10. doi:10.1038/s41598-017-16844-x.

von Cramon-Taubadel, Noreen, and Stephen J. Lycett. 2008. "Brief Communication: Human Cranial Variation Fits Iterative Founder Effect Model with African Origin." *American Journal of Physical Anthropology* 136 (1): 108–113. doi:10.1002/ajpa.20775.

Warren, Kerryn A. 2018. "AAPA Name Change." *Bone and Evolution*, April 4. https://bonevolution.wordpress.com/2018/04/04/aapa-name-change/.

Weiss, Kenneth M., and Jeffrey C. Long. 2009. "Non-Darwinian Estimation: My Ancestors, My Genes' Ancestors." *Genome Research* 19: 703–710. doi:10.1101/gr.076539.108.19.

Wise, Tim. 2010. *Colorblind: The Rise of Post-Racial Politics and the Retreat from Racial Equity*. San Francisco: City Lights.

Yudell, Michael, Dorothy Roberts, Rob DeSalle, and Sarah Tishkoff. 2016. "Taking Race out of Human Genetics." *Science* 351 (6273): 564–565. doi:10.1126/science.aac4951.

Figure Attributions

Figure 13.1a Tanzania – Hadzabe hunter (14533536392) by A_Peach from Berlin, Germany, is used under a CC BY 2.0 License.

Figure 13.1b Inuit-Kleidung 1 by Ansgar Walk is used under a CC BY-SA 3.0 License.

Figure 13.1c Andean Man by Cacophony is used under a CC BY-SA 4.0 License.

Figure 13.1d Jane Goodall GM byFloatjon is used under a CC BY-SA 3.0 License.

Figure 13.2 Egyptian races Drawing (1772-1846) by an unknown artist after a mural of the tomb of Seti I, Copy by Heinrich von Minutoli (1820), is in the public domain.

Figure 13.3 Naturalishistoria from the front page of Pliny the Elder's Naturalis Historia is in the public domain.

Figure 13.4 Great Chain of Being 2 by Didacus Valades (Diego Valades) is in the public domain.

Figure 13.5 Carl von Linné by Alexander Roslin artist QS:P170,Q315102 is in the public domain.

Figure 13.6 Discovery of the Mississippi by William Henry Powell artist QS:P170,Q3568696 (photograph courtesy Architect of the Capitol) is in the public domain.

Figure 13.7 Blumenbach's five races by Johann Friedrich Blumenbach is in the public domain.

Figure 13.8 (Ales Hrdlicka) SIA2009-4246 by Unknown photographer is in the public domain.

Figure 13.9 Eugenics congress logo scanned from Harry H. Laughlin, The Second International Exhibition of Eugenics held September 22 to October 22, 1921, is in the public domain.

Figure 13.10 Dobzhansky no Brasil em 1943 by Unknown photographer is in the public domain.

Figure 13.11 Julian Huxley 1-2 by Unknown photographer is in the public domain.

Figure 13.12 Skin color by S25454541 is used under a CC BY-SA 4.0 License.

Figure 13.13a Map of blood group a by Muntuwandi at en.wikipedia is used under a CC BY-SA 3.0 License.

Figure 13.13b Map of blood group b by Muntuwandi at en.wikipedia is used under a CC BY-SA 3.0 License.

Figure 13.13c Map of blood group o Based on diagrams from http://anthro.palomar.edu/vary/vary_3.htm reproduced from A. E. Mourant et.al., The Distribution of the Human Blood Groups and Other Polymorphisms, 2nd ed. (1976) is used under a CC BY-SA 3.0 License.

Figure 13.14 Sub-Saharan-Africa by Ezeu has been designated to the public domain (CC0).

Figure 13.15 Bottleneck effect by Tsaneda is used under a CC BY 3.0 License.

Figure 13.16 Chimpanzee IV (13968482163) by Chi King is used under a CC BY 2.0 License.

Figure 13.17 Human skulls by 22Kartika is used under a CC BY-SA 3.0 License.

Figure 13.18 Bony labyrinth by Selket (5 February 2007, UTC) has been designated to the public domain (CC0).

Figure 13.19 Forensic Anthropology Lab by Pp391 is used under a CC BY-SA 3.0 License.

Figure 13.20 Michael B. C. Rivera in Hong Kong original to Explorations: An Open Invitation to Biological Anthropology is under a CC BY-NC 4.0 License.

Chapter 14: Human Variation: A Human Adaptive Approach

Leslie E. Fitzpatrick, Ph.D., Mercyhurst University

Learning Objectives

- Describe how specific patterns of human adaptation are correlated to natural selection processes.
- Summarize the role of solar radiation in variations of human skin tone. In your explanation, include information as to why reduced pigmentation leading to lighter skin colors is advantageous for populations indigenous to northern latitudes.
- Compare and contrast the various genetic mutations present in Tibetan, Andean, and Ethiopian populations that allow them to survive at high altitudes.
- Define the relationship between specific genetic mutations in some human populations and certain infectious diseases, such as the sickle-cell trait mutation and malarial infection.

In the previous chapters of this text, we explored the role of evolutionary forces in human evolution as well as the basics of genetic variation. Within this framework, we now shift our focus toward examining the numerous challenges our species has faced throughout its evolutionary odyssey as well as how we have met those trials. Genetic variability within and between modern populations of humans has been influenced by years of evolutionary forces, most notably natural selection and genetic drift. As early humans left Africa and spread across the globe, they faced numerous challenges related to their new environments. Beyond genetically influenced changes in physiology as a result of evolution, humans have developed lifestyle strategies to cope with and even thrive in a wide range of habitats. The ways populations of humans met such challenges, coupled with their geographic separation throughout the majority of the last two centamillenia, have led to the many forms of adaptation in our species. This chapter focuses on the complexities of modern human variation through the lens of human evolutionary history.

STRESS AND HOMEOSTASIS

All organisms, including humans, must maintain a baseline of normal functions within their cells, tissues, and organs to survive. This constancy of internal functions is referred to as **homeostasis**; however, homeostatic regulation may be challenged by a variety of both external and internal factors. These stimuli are referred to as **stressors**, exposure to which leads to a period in which there is a potential for the disruption of homeostasis. Within limits, all organisms have evolved certain physiological mechanisms to respond to stressors in an effort to maintain homeostasis. For example, some organisms, such as dogs, will develop a thicker coat of fur during cooler periods and they will shed this additional fur during warmer periods. This cyclical fur development linked to seasonal weather changes is but one way that these organisms maintain their homeostasis. The range of changes in the physiology (function), morphology (form), and/or behavior of organisms in response to their environments and the potential stressors of those environments is regulated by its **phenotypic plasticity**. A special case of phenotypic plasticity, **polyphenism**, is broadly defined as the ability of a single genotype within the organism to produce multiple phenotypes when exposed to different environmental conditions or stressors. Changes to the organism's physiology, morphology, and/or behavior that are linked to its underlying phenotypic plasticity may result in changes that are merely temporary or those that are permanent. With respect to human phenotypic plasticity as well as evolutionary history, there are several primary mechanisms that have led to variations among individuals and between populations. These mechanisms, which are referred to as **adjustments** (behavioral, acclimatory, and developmental) and **adaptations**, are explained in detail in the following sections.

ADJUSTMENTS AND ADAPTATIONS

Adjustments

The term "adjustment" refers to an organism's non-genetic way of coping with the stressors of its environment. Although adjustments themselves are non-genetic in nature, the ability of an organism to experience or develop an adjustment is based in its phenotypic plasticity, which is linked to its evolutionarily guided genetic potential. Adjustments occur exclusively on the individual level. As such, different individuals within a population may experience a wide range of possible adjustments in response to a similar stressor. In general, the three main forms of adjustment are: behavioral, acclimatory, and developmental.

Behavioral Adjustments

When you are cold, do you reach for a blanket? When you are warm, do you seek out shelter cooled by an air-conditioning system? If so, you have likely been influenced to do so by the culture in which you were raised. As noted earlier in the text, the term "culture" refers to a collection of shared, learned behaviors among individuals within a discrete population. **Behavioral adjustments** are regarded as cultural responses to environmental stressors. These adjustments are temporary in nature and, since they are nongenetic, must be constantly altered to meet novel situations posed by the environment. For example, through the use of a specialized mixture of gases for breathing, an apparatus for the delivery of the gases, protective clothing, and gear to increase visibility, divers are able to reach extraordinary depths (in excess of 300 meters below the surface) within the water. The deeper a diver descends, the more atmospheric pressure the diver experiences

Figure 14.1 Notice the lack of full spectrum color in this photo of a deep-water diver and the diver's use of specialized equipment, such as a breathing apparatus to deliver gases for respiration, bodysuit to ensure thermal regulation, and flashlight to increase visibility in the low-light setting.

resulting in increased levels of potentially toxic byproducts of respiration within the body. In addition, with increased depth there is a decrease in the ambient temperature of the water as well as a decrease in the availability of light within the visible spectrum. Deep-water divers are well-versed in the environmental stressors of open waters and employ a variety of strategies based on behavioral adjustments to meet such demands. From wearing protective clothing to assist with maintaining the body's core temperature to waiting at a specific depth for a prescribed period of time to facilitate the expulsion from the body of nitrogen gas that may have accumulated within the bloodstream, divers employ numerous behavioral adjustments to ensure their safety dive after dive (Figure 14.1). Without these culturally mediated behavioral adjustments, a deep-water diver's first dive would be their last.

In many developing countries, the use of refrigeration for the storage of perishable food products is uncommon; therefore, individuals within these cultures have developed a variety of behavioral adjustment strategies related to food preparation to address the possibility of food spoilage. Through a cross-cultural analysis of spice use in recipes, Sherman and Billing (1999) determined that cultures closest to the equator, where temperatures are hotter, tend to use both a greater number and a wider variety of plant-based spices with bacteria-inhibiting phytochemical properties (e.g., garlic and onion) in their recipes than cultures located further from the equator. The antimicrobial properties of the spices permits the consumption of foods, particularly animal-based protein sources, for a period of time beyond that which would be considered safe. There are some acclimatory adjustment benefits to the use of some pungent spices as well, which are explored in the following section.

Acclimatory Adjustments: Thermal Stressors

Acclimatory adjustments are temporary, reversible changes in an organism's physiology in response to environmental stressors. Although they are regarded as non-genetic in nature, the range of acclimatory adjustments an organism is capable of producing to accommodate a given stressor is linked to its underlying phenotypic plasticity and duration and severity of the stressor.

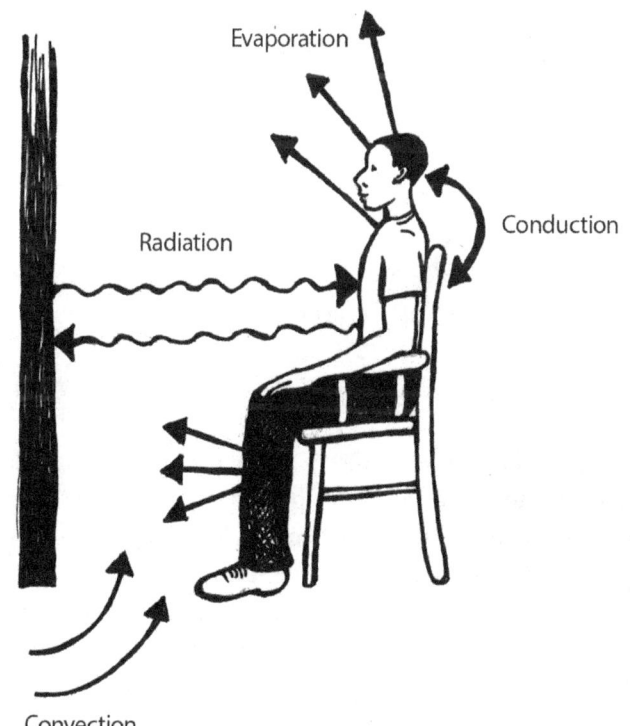

Figure 14.2 *Various thermodynamic mechanisms related to heat gain and loss in the human body.*

Before we discuss how varying ambient temperatures affect the human body, we must detail the thermodynamic mechanisms through which heat may be gained or lost. There are four pathways for the loss of heat within the human body: conduction, convection, evaporation, and radiation (Figure 14.2).

Through **conduction** processes, heat will move from a warmer body to a cooler one through direct contact. An example of this is when you accidentally touch a hot cooktop with your hand and the heat is transferred from the cooktop to your skin.

With **convection**, when a warm body is surrounded by a cooler fluid (e.g. air or water) heat will be transferred from the warmer body to the cooler fluid. This is why we will often employ the behavioral adjustment of wearing multiple layers of clothing during the winter in an effort to prevent heat loss to the cooler atmosphere. Conversely, if your body temperature is cooler than that of the air surrounding you, your body will absorb heat.

Depending on your physical condition, most people will begin to sweat around 37.2°C to 37.7°C (98.9°F – 99.9°F). Sweating is an example of **evaporation**, which occurs when a liquid, such as the water within our bodies, is converted to a gas. Phase conversions, such as those underlying the evaporative processes of transforming liquids to gases, require energy. In evaporation, this energy is in the form of heat, and the effect is to cool the body.

The final mechanism for heat loss within the human body is **radiation**, through which energy in the form of electromagnetic waves is produced at a wavelength that typically lies below that which is visible to the human eye. Although humans gain and lose heat from their bodies through radiation, this form of heat transfer is not visible. Humans are capable of losing and gaining heat through conduction, convection, and radiation; however, heat may not be gained through evaporation.

As the ambient temperature decreases, it becomes increasingly difficult for the human body to regulate its core temperature, which is central to the maintenance of homeostasis. The **hypothalamus** is a small portion of the human brain located near its base. It is responsible for numerous functions, including the regulation of body temperature. As measured orally, normal human body temperature averages 37°C (98.6°F). When an individual's body temperature falls below 34.4°C (93.9°F), the hypothalamus becomes impaired leading to issues with body temperature control. A total loss of the ability to regulate body temperature occurs around 29.4°C (84.9°F), which may result in death. When the ambient temperature (e.g. air temperature) falls below the critical temperature of 31°C (87.8°F), a nude human body that is at rest will respond with a series of physiological changes to preserve homeostasis (Figure 14.3).

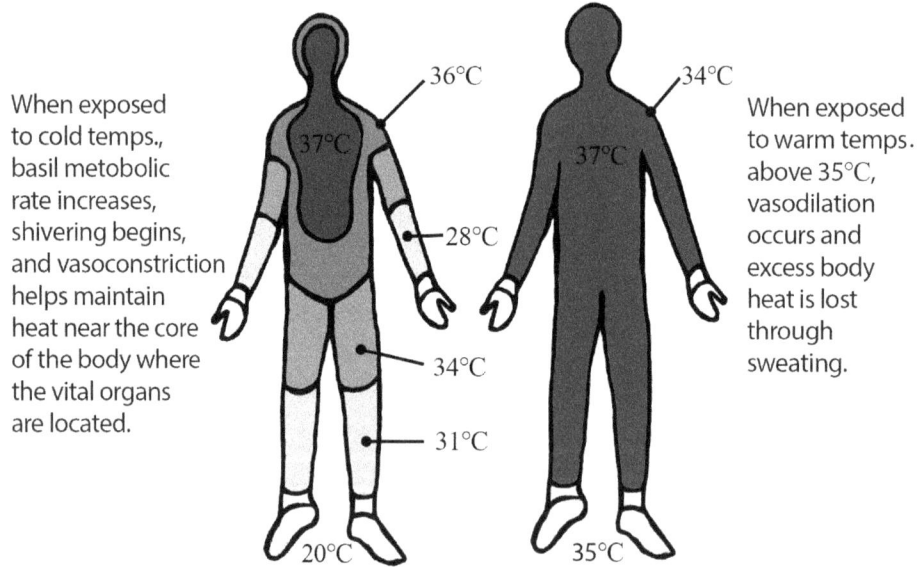

Figure 14.3 Example of overall body heat maintenance in cold and warm ambient environments.

In response to colder temperatures, the human body experiences two main types of physiological responses: those that increase the production of heat within the body and those that seek to retain the body's heat. The production of heat within the body is accomplished through short-term increases in the body's basal metabolic rate. This rate is a measure of the energy required to maintain necessary body processes while the body is in a resting state. As the body's basal metabolic rate increases, an individual must consume greater quantities of energy-providing nutrients to maintain the increase. Of course, such increases may not continue forever as they are energetically expensive. As with all acclimatory adjustments, an increase in the basal metabolic rate is merely temporary.

Another form of a temporary heat-generating acclimatory adjustment to cold stress is the physiological response of shivering. Shivering results when the hypothalamus stimulates increased muscular activity that leads to an elevation of the muscular metabolism. Much like the increased muscular metabolism that occurs during periods of strenuous exercise, the elevation of muscular metabolism rates during shivering leads to higher rates of body heat generation.

Other physiological mechanisms the body uses to assist with the maintenance of temperature related to homeostasis involve the preservation of heat already contained within the body. Of these mechanisms, the most notable is the constriction of peripheral capillaries in the skin through a process called **vasoconstriction**. The decreased surface area of the capillaries through vasoconstriction results in less heat reaching the surface of the skin where it would be dissipated into the atmosphere. In addition, vasoconstriction leads to the maintenance of heat near the core of the body where the vital organs are located. This is one of the reasons that an individual may experience cold-related injuries, such as frost-bite leading to tissue necrosis (tissue death) in regions of the body that are most distant from the core (e.g. fingers, toes, nose, ears, cheeks, chin, etc.).

Just as cold stress presents challenges to maintaining homeostasis within the body with respect to temperature, heat does as well. In hot climates, the body will begin to absorb extra heat from its surroundings (through conduction, convection, and radiation) resulting in potential heat-related disorders, such as heat exhaustion. When the human body is exposed to ambient temperatures above 35°C (95°F), excess body heat will be lost primarily through evaporative processes, specifically through sweating. All humans, regardless of their environment, have approximately the same number of sweat glands within their bodies. Over time, individuals living in hot, arid environments will develop more sensitive forms of sweat glands resulting in the production of greater quantities of sweat. In an effort to prevent dehydration due to this form of acclimatory adjustment, there will be an additional reduction in the volume of urine produced by the individual.

As noted in the previous section, some cultural groups, particularly those in equatorial regions, add pungent spices to their foods to inhibit the colonization of bacteria (Sherman and Billing 1999). Although the addition of spices to foods to decrease spoilage rates is a behavioral adjustment, the application of some forms of peppers triggers an acclimatory adjustment process as well. Compounds referred to as capsaicinoids are the secondary byproducts of chili pepper plants' metabolism. Capsaicinoids are produced by the plants to deter their consumption by some forms of fungi and mammals. When mammals, such as humans, consume the capsaicinoids from chili peppers, a burning sensation may occur within their mouths and along their digestive tracts. This burning sensation is the result of the activation of capsaicin receptors along the body's nerve pathways. Although the peppers themselves may be at ambient temperature so their consumption is technically not causing any form of body temperature increase, the human body perceives the pepper as elevating its core temperature due to the activation of the capsaicin receptors. Even though the body's temperature has not actually been elevated due to the consumption of capsaicin, the hypothalamus will react as if it has, which leads to the initiation of sweating processes in an attempt to lower body temperature and maintain homeostasis. The increased piquancy (application of pungent spices to food) as a means of inhibiting food-borne bacterial colonization in warm climates, as well as spices' ability to trigger sweating processes as a method for cooling the body, is an example of the intersection between behavioral and acclimatory adjustments that may be utilized by individuals within certain populations.

In addition to increased sweat production in the body as a means of regulating internal body temperature to maintain homeostasis, **vasodilation** may occur (Figure 14.4). Vasodilation occurs when there is an expansion of the capillaries within the skin leading to a more effective transfer of heat from within the body to the exterior to allow conductive, convective, radiative, and evaporative (sweating) processes to occur.

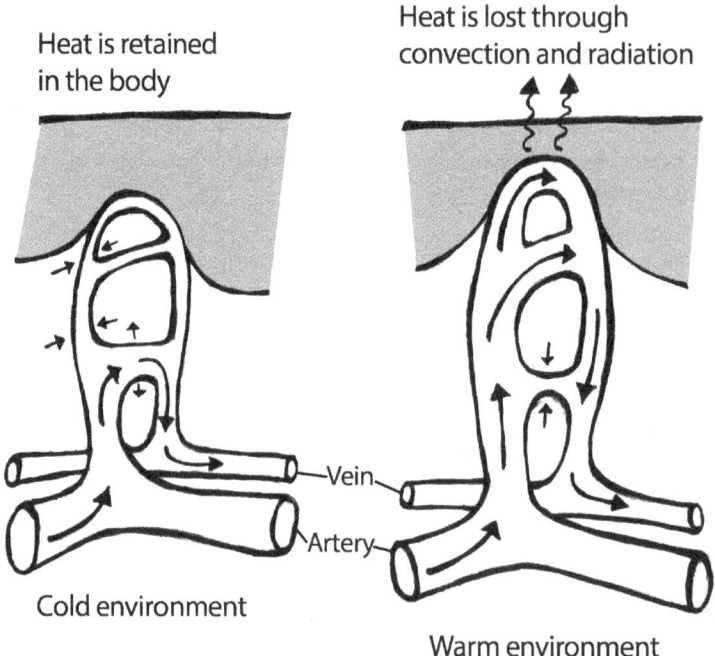

Figure 14.4 This image features an illustration of the vasoconstriction processes that occur within the peripheral vascular system when an individual is exposed to cold ambient temperatures and the vasodilation that occurs in warmer environments.

Physiologically-based acclimatory adjustments to hot, dry climates may be complemented by behavioral adjustments as well. For example, individuals in such climates may limit their physical activity during the times of day when the temperature is typically the hottest. Additionally, these individuals may wear loose fitting clothing that covers much of their skin. The looseness of the clothing allows for air to flow between the clothing and the skin to permit the effective evaporation of sweat. Although it may seem counterintuitive to cover one's body completely in a hot climate, the covering of the skin keeps the sun's rays from directly penetrating the skin and elevating the body's core temperature.

Acclimatory Adjustments: Altitudinal Stressors

The challenges posed by thermal conditions are but one form of environmental stressor humans must face. High-altitude environments, which are defined as altitudes in excess of 2400 meters above sea level (m.a.s.l.) or 7874 feet above sea level (f.a.s.l.), pose additional challenges to the maintenance of homeostasis in humans. Some of the main stressors encountered by those living within high-altitude environments include: decreased oxygen availability, cold temperatures, low humidity, high wind speed, a reduced nutritional base, and increased solar radiation levels. Of these challenges, the most significant is the decreased availability of oxygen.

To visualize how altitude affects the availability of oxygen, imagine two balloons that are each filled with the same quantity of oxygen molecules. One of these balloons is positioned at sea-level and the other is placed high upon a mountain peak. For the balloon at sea level, there is more atmospheric pressure pressing down on the molecules within this balloon. This leads to the oxygen molecules within the sea level balloon being forced into a more compact organization. In contrast, the mountain peak balloon has less atmospheric pressure pressing down on it. This leads to the oxygen molecules within that balloon spreading out from each other since they are not being forced together quite as strongly. This example highlights the availability of oxygen molecules in each breath than we take in low- versus high-altitude environments. At 5,500 m.a.s.l. (approximately 18,000 f.a.s.l.), the atmospheric pressure is approximately 50% of its value at sea level (Peacock 1998). At the peak of Mount Everest (8,900 m.a.s.l. or approximately 29,200 f.a.s.l.), the

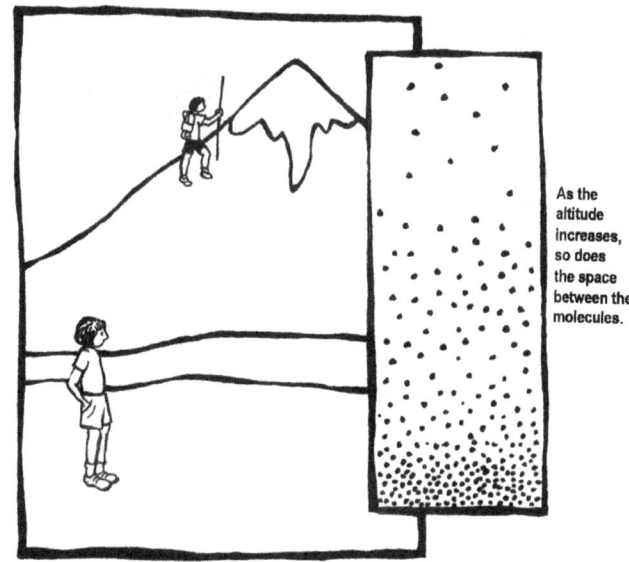

Figure 14.5 As altitude increases, atmospheric pressure decreases, which allows for more space between air molecules.

atmospheric pressure is equivalent to only about 30% of their sea level amounts (Peacock 1998) (Figure 14.5).

Due to the decreased availability of oxygen at higher altitudes, certain acclimatory adjustments are required to ensure the maintenance of homeostasis for individuals other than those who were gestated, born, and raised at high altitude. For these people, their rate of breathing will increase to permit greater quantities of air containing oxygen into the lungs when they ascend into higher altitude environments. An increased speed and depth of breathing, which is referred to as **hyperpnea**, is not sustainable indefinitely; thus, the rate of breathing begins to decrease as the person becomes acclimatized to the altitude. During the initial phases of high-altitude-related hyperpnea, the heart will begin to beat faster but the stroke volume (the amount of blood pushed through during each beat) will decrease slightly. In addition, the body will divert energy from non-critical bodily functions, such as digestive processes.

Once the atmospheric oxygen reaches the alveoli (small air sacs) in the lungs, it diffuses (spreads) across the alveolar membrane and enters **erythrocytes** (red blood cells). When the oxygen reaches the erythrocytes, it will loosely bind with hemoglobin, which is an iron-rich protein. It is within the alveoli that the oxygen combines with the hemoglobin. When the erythrocytes carrying the hemoglobin-binded oxygen molecules reach the capillaries where the partial pressure of oxygen is relatively low, the oxygen will be released by the hemoglobin so that it is free for diffusion into body cells. High-altitude-related hyperpnea leads to an increase in the pH of the blood, which makes the blood more alkaline. An increase in the alkalinity of blood is directly related to the partial pressures of oxygen and carbon dioxide in the bloodstream (Shah et al. 2006).

Similar to the acclimatory adjustments related to thermal conditions (e.g., shivering or sweating), those related to high altitude may not be sustained permanently due to their energetically expensive nature. Over a period of days or weeks, the human body will begin to compensate for the increases in respiration as well as pH through the urinary excretion of bicarbonate (a metabolic byproduct). In addition, to assist with the transportation of oxygen in the absence of decreased respiration, there will be an increase in the following: **hematocrit** (percentage volume of erythrocytes in the blood), myoglobin (oxygen- and iron-binding protein in muscle tissues), red blood cell mass, pulmonary artery pressure, and quantity of capillaries in the skeletal muscular tissue.

Although the long-term acclimatory adjustments that an individual from low altitude experiences in a high-altitude environment may permit them to reside there successfully, reproduction within such settings is frequently complicated. With increased altitude comes an increased risk of miscarriage, lower birth weights, and higher infant mortality rates. As the mother's body seeks to preserve its own homeostasis when faced with challenges related to high-altitude living, there is often a decreased rate and volume of blood flow to the uterus as compared to a pregnant woman of similar physiological condition at a lower altitude (Moore et al. 1998). Of course, a decreased rate and volume of uterine blood flow results in a decrease in the amount of oxygen that will be passed through the uterus and placenta to the developing fetus. In addition, women who experience pregnancy at higher altitudes are more prone to developing preeclampsia (severe elevation of blood pressure), which is linked to increased rates of both fetal and maternal death (Moore et al. 1998) (Figure 14.6).

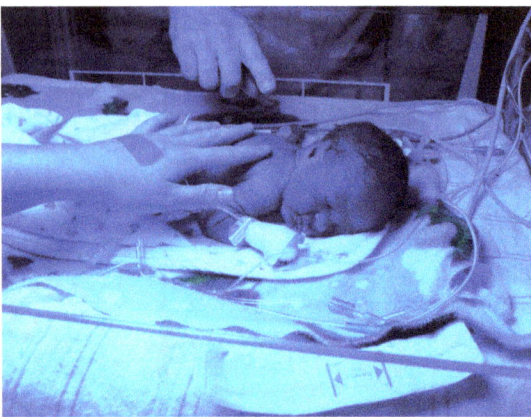

Figure 14.6 Premature infant born at 30 weeks, 4 days gestation to a mother with altitudinal-induced preeclampsia. Blue light assists the infant's liver with processing high levels of bilirubin.

Developmental Adjustments

Although there are often significant challenges for a mother gestating a fetus at high altitude, individuals who are native to such environments experience a form of adjustment referred to as a **developmental adjustment**. Developmental adjustments occur only in individuals who spent their developmental period (i.e. childhood and adolescence) within a high-altitude environment and they do not apply to those who moved into these environments in the post-developmental (i.e., adult) phase. Furthermore, the degree of developmental adjustment within an individual is directly related to their underlying phenotypic plasticity (polyphenism) as well as the amount of time during the crucial growth and development period the individual resides within the challenging environment. Although humans have the remarkable capacity to develop and survive within environments that are not overly conducive to the successful maintenance of homeostasis, there are definitely physiological costs associated with this ability.

Figure 14.7 Quechua woman from high-altitude region of the Peruvian Andes.

In general, high-altitude natives tend to grow more slowly and physically mature later than their low-altitude counterparts (Figure 14.7). Decreased growth and maturity rates are linked not only to the increased physiological demands placed on the body due to the decreased partial pressure of oxygen but to decreases in the quality of the nutritional base at higher altitudes. Increased terrain complexity, elevated solar radiation levels, and higher wind speeds coupled with decreased temperatures and lower humidity levels at higher altitudes leads to difficulties with growing and maintaining crops and raising livestock. Overall, there is a decreased quality in the available nutritional base as altitude increases, which is correlated to a lack of the nutrients necessary to ensure proper physiological growth and development in humans. Thus, even though individuals may be able to develop and grow within high-altitude environments, they may not reach their full genetically mediated growth potential as they would in a lower-altitude environment.

The heart and lung capacity of individuals who are lifelong residents of high-altitude environments is larger than for individuals from lower-altitude regions. In addition, the high-altitude individuals are more efficient than those from low altitudes at diffusing oxygen from the bloodstream to the body's various tissues. Of course, as noted previously, the developmental adjustments that an individual may experience are defined by their underlying genetic composition (phenotypic plasticity) and researchers have begun to discover some of the genetic factors that appear to be unique to certain populations of humans who have resided in high-altitude environments for significant periods of time. The time frame necessary for natural selection processes to act upon the underlying genetic composition of a population is on the order of many millennia; thus, the physiological changes to indigenous high-altitude populations on a whole are best described in the following section on adaptations.

Not all developmental adjustments are linked to environmental pressures such as climate or altitude; rather, some of these adjustments are correlated to sociocultural or behavioral practices. As noted earlier, some behavioral adjustments permit individuals to maintain homeostasis in challenging environments (e.g., wearing heavy clothing layers to maintain body temperature in cold weather). Other behavioral adjustments, many of which are based on sociocultural principles, may affect the physiological appearance of an individual when they are practiced consistently during the development and growth phases.

Sudden infant death syndrome (SIDS) has no definitive cause; however, the American Academy of Pediatrics published a report in 1992 linking SIDS to infants (under the age of one) sleeping on their stomachs. The "Back to Sleep" campaign championed by the American Academy of Pediatrics helped educate members of the medical community as well as the public that the best sleep position for infants is on their backs. Per the American Academy of Pediatrics Task Force on Infant Sleep Position and Sudden Infant Death Syndrome (2000: 1,245), between 1992 and 2000 the frequency of infants being placed on their stomachs to sleep decreased from more than 70% to less than 20% and the SIDS rate decreased by more than 40%.

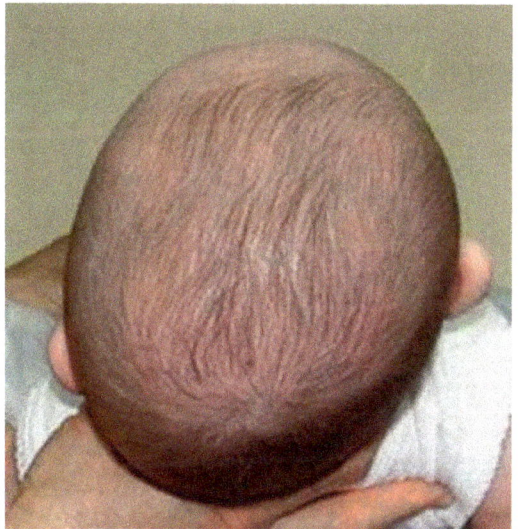

Figure 14.8 Infant with positional plagiocephaly. Notice the irregular shape of the posterior (back) of the skull.

Placing infants on their backs to sleep has led to decreased infant mortality (death) rates due to SIDS; however, it has led to an unintended consequence: infant cranial deformation. The cranial deformations experienced by infants who sleep solely on their back tend to manifest in one of two forms: brachycephaly and plagiocephaly (Roby et al. 2012). With positional brachycephaly, the back of the infant's head appears rather uniformly flattened due to repetitive contact with a flat surface, such as a crib mattress or car seat back. In cases of positional plagiocephaly, the back of the infant's head appears asymmetrically flattened (Figure 14.8). This asymmetry is typically due to an uneven distribution of mechanical forces resulting from the manner in which the infant's head is in contact with a flat surface. The forms of cranial deformation resulting from sleep positioning do not affect the infant's brain development. For many individuals, the appearance of the deformation is minimized during later development. Still, some individuals will maintain the pattern of cranial deformation acquired during their infancy throughout their lives. The unintentional cranial deformation resulting from placing infants on their backs to sleep as a means of preventing SIDS-related deaths is a physiological indicator of a behavioral adjustment.

Adaptations

As we have just explored, survival and reproduction at high altitudes present numerous physiological challenges for most humans, but what if there were some humans who were specially adapted to life at high altitudes? The behavioral, acclimatory, and developmental adjustments discussed above are all related to the phenotypic plasticity of the individual; however, most adjustments are temporary in nature and they affect a single individual rather than all individuals within a population. But, what if the physiological changes were permanent? What if they affected all members of a population rather than just a single individual? The long-term, micro-evolutionary (i.e., genetic) changes that occur within a population in response to an environmental stressor are referred to as an **adaptation**. From an evolutionary standpoint, the term "adaptation" refers to a phenotypic trait (i.e., physiological/morphological feature or behavior) that has been acted upon by natural selection processes to increase a species' ability to survive and reproduce within a specific environment. Within the field of physiology, the term "adaptation" refers to traits that serve to restore homeostasis. The physiology-based interpretation of adaptations presumes that all traits serve a purpose and that all adaptations are beneficial in nature; however, this may be a fallacy, since some traits may be present without clear evidence as to their purpose. As such, during the following discussion of various forms of adaptations in human populations, we will focus our attention to phenotypic traits with an evidence-based purpose.

Adaptation: Altitudinal Adaptation

As mentioned in the previous section, there is genomic research supporting the evolutionary selection of certain phenotypes and their corresponding genotypes within indigenous high-altitude populations across the globe. The following discussion focuses on three high-altitude indigenous populations from Tibet, the Andes, and Ethiopia (Figure 14.9). Although these populations share many common genetic traits based on relatively similar evolutionary histories influenced by similar environmental stressors, there is support for local genetically based adaptation as well, based on different genes being acted upon by environmental stressors that may be unique to Tibet, the Andes, and Ethiopia (Bigham 2016).

Figure 14.9 Highlighted regions feature (from left to right) the Andean, Simian (Ethiopian), and Tibetan Plateau high-altitude regions.

Tibetan populations have resided in the Tibetan Plateau and Himalayan Mountain regions at elevations exceeding 4,000 m.a.s.l. (13,100 f.a.s.l.) for at least the past 7,400 years (Meyer et al. 2017). A gene referred to as EPAS1 is involved in the regulation of red blood cell (and hemoglobin) production as well as catecholamine homeostasis. Catecholamines are hormones (e.g., epinephrine) secreted as part of the sympathetic nervous system's acute stress ("fight-or-flight") response. An acute stress response typically includes an increase in: heart rate, blood pressure, and blood glucose levels. Long-term elevation of catecholamines in the body may lead to hypertension (elevated blood pressure), increased blood pH levels, the development of a form of cardiovascular disease leading to narrowing of the arteries (atherosclerosis), and blood clots. In the short term, an acclimatory adjustment leading to the increase of catecholamines and hemoglobin production by the hypoxia (low-oxygen level)-induced activation of the EPAS1 gene may assist individuals from lower altitudes as they ascend to significantly higher altitudes; however, such increases may not be maintained for long before they cause damage to the body. For indigenous high-altitude populations of Tibet, a mutation in the EPAS1 gene inhibits increased red blood cell production and assists with catecholamine regulation. The red blood cell count of high-altitude Tibetans with the EPAS1 point mutation is about the same as for individuals residing at sea level.

Interestingly, individuals in populations from the high-altitude Andean Altiplano of Peru and Bolivia, such as the Quechua and Aymara, lack the EPAS1 point mutation, so their red blood cell counts are relatively elevated compared with the Tibetan populations. In addition, populations from the Andean Altiplano also have an increased arterial oxygen saturation and low, hypoxia-induced breathing pattern (minor hyperventilation) as compared to their Tibetan counterparts (Bigham 2016). Populations indigenous to the Semien Plateau of Ethiopia, such as the Oromo and Amhara, share a similar but not identical EPAS1 point mutation with the Tibetan population (Bigham 2016). This suggests that the EPAS1 mutations occurred independently from each other; however, their effects are still similar in that they permit the Tibetan and Ethiopian populations to survive at high altitudes. Not all adaptations are related to life in high-altitude environments, however. In the following sections, we will address two more general examples of adaptation in human populations: variations in skin color and differences in body build.

Adaptation: Skin Tone Basics

When you think about your own skin tone and compare it to members of your family, do you all possess exactly the same shade? Are some members of your family darker than others? What about your friends? Your classmates? Skin tone occurs along a continuum, which is a reflection of the complex evolutionary history of our species. The expression of skin tone is regulated primarily by both melanin and hemoglobin. **Melanin** is a dark brown-black pigment that is produced by the oxidation of certain amino acids (e.g., tyrosine, cysteine, phenylalanine) in the melanocytes. **Melanocytes** are specialized cells located in the base layer (stratum basale) of the skin's epidermis as well as several other areas within the body (Figure 14.10). Within the melanocytes, melanin is produced in the special organelle called a melanosome. Melanosomes serve as sites for the synthesis, storage, and transportation of melanin. Melanosomes transport the melanin particles through cellular projections to epidermal skin cells (keratinocytes) as well as to the base of the growing hair root (root sheath portion). In the eye, however, melanin particles produced by the melanosomes remain present within the iris (iridial melanocytes) and are not transported beyond their origin location. The two main forms of melanin related to skin, hair, and eye color are eumelanin and pheomelanin. All humans contain both eumelanin and pheomelanin within their bodies; however, the relative expression of these two forms of melanin determines an individual's overall coloring. Eumelanin is a brown-to-black colored melanin particle and pheomelanin is more pink-to-red. Individuals with darker skin or hair color have a greater expression of eumelanin than those with lighter-colored skin and blonde or red hair.

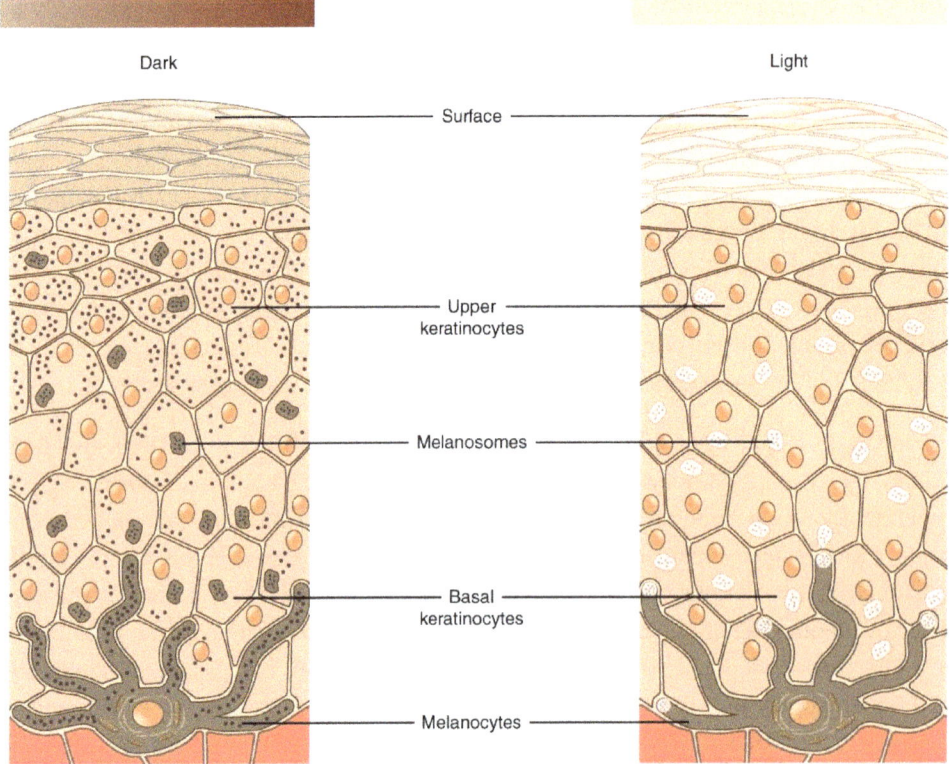

Figure 14.10 Diagram featuring the relative numbers of melanocytes and melanosomes in light and dark shades of skin tone.

SPECIAL TOPIC: SKIN TONE GENETIC REGULATION

The melanocortin 1 receptor (MC1R) gene acts to control which types of melanin (eumelanin or pheomelanin) are produced by melanocytes. The MC1R receptor is located on the surface of the melanocyte cells (Quillen et al. 2018). Activation of the MC1R receptors may occur through exposure to specific environmental stimuli or due to underlying genetic processes. Inactive or blocked MC1R receptors results in melanocytes producing pheomelanin. If the MC1R gene receptors are activated, then the melanocytes will produce eumelanin. Thus, individuals with activated MC1R receptors tend to have darker pigmented skin and hair than individuals with inactive or blocked receptors.

The alleles of another gene, the major facilitator, superfamily domain-containing protein 12 (MFSD12) gene, affect the expression of melanocytes in a different way than the MC1R gene. Instead of affecting the activation of melanocyte receptors, the MFSD12 alleles indirectly affect the membranes of melanocyte lysosomes (Quillen et al. 2018). The melanocyte's lysosomes are organelles containing digestive enzymes, which ultimately correlate to varying degrees of pigmentation in humans. Variations in the membranes of the melanocyte lysosomes ultimately correlate to differing degrees of pigmentation in humans.

Ancestral MFSD12 allele variants are present in European and East Asian populations and are associated with lighter pigmentation of the skin (Crawford et al. 2017; Quillen et al. 2018). In addition, this ancestral variant is also associated with Tanzanian, San, and Ethiopian populations of Afro-Asiatic ancestry (Crawford et al. 2017; Quillen et al. 2018). In contrast, the more-derived (i.e. more recent) allele variants that are linked to darker skin tones are more commonly present in East African populations, particularly those of Nilo-Saharan descent (Crawford et al. 2017; Quillen et al. 2018). The notion that ancestral alleles of MFSD12 are associated with lighter skin pigmentation is in opposition to the commonly accepted idea that our pigmentation was likely darker throughout early human evolution (Crawford et al. 2017; Quillen et al. 2018). Due to the complexity of the human genome, MFSD12 and MC1R are but two examples of alleles affecting human skin tone. Furthermore, there is genetic evidence suggesting that certain genomic variants associated with both darker and lighter skin color have been subject to directional selection processes for as long as 600,000 years, which far exceeds the evolutionary span of *Homo sapiens sapiens* (Crawford et al. 2017; Quillen et al. 2018). So, evolutionary processes may lead to skin becoming more darkly pigmented as well as more lightly pigmented.

Adaptation: Melanogenesis

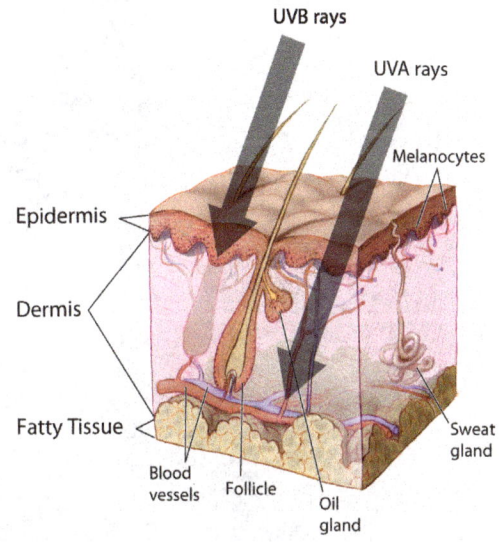

Figure 14.11 Penetration of skin layers by UVA and UVB rays.

Although all humans have approximately the same number of melanocytes within the epidermis, the production of melanin by these melanocytes varies. There are two forms of melanogenesis (the process through which melanocytes generate melanin): basal and activated. As discussed previously, the expression of eumelanin and pheomelanin by the melanocytes is genetically regulated through the expression of specific receptors (e.g., MC1R) or other melanocyte components (e.g., MFSD12). **Basal melanogenesis** is dependent upon an individual's inherent genetic composition and is not influenced by external factors. **Activated melanogenesis** occurs in response to ultraviolet radiation (UV) exposure, specifically UV-B (short UV wave) exposure. Increased melanogenesis in response to UV-B exposure serves to provide protection to the skin's innermost layer called the hypodermis, which lies below the epidermis and dermis (Figure 14.11). Melanin in the skin, specifically eumelanin, effectively absorbs UV-B radiation from light meaning that it will not reach the hypodermal layer. This effect is often more apparent during periods of the year when individuals tend to be outside more and the weather is warmer, which leads to those individuals donning fewer protective garments. The exposure of skin to sunlight is, of course, culturally mediated with some cultures encouraging the covering of skin at all times.

As previously noted, hemoglobin is an iron-rich protein that binds with oxygen in the bloodstream. For individuals with lighter-colored skin, blood vessels near the surface of the skin and the hemoglobin contained within those vessels is more apparent than in individuals with darker skin. The visible presence of hemoglobin coupled with the pink-to-red tone of the pheomelanin leads to lighter-skinned individuals having a pale pink skin tone. Individuals with lighter skin more readily absorb UV radiation as their basal melanin expression is directed more toward the production of pheomelanin than eumelanin. But, why are there so many variations in skin tone in humans? To answer this question, we now turn toward an exploration of an evolutionary-based adaptation of skin tone as a function of the environment.

Adaptation: Evolutionary Basis for Skin Tone Variation

Skin cancer is a significant concern for many individuals with light skin tone as the cumulative exposure of the epidermis and underlying skin tissues to UV radiation may lead to the development of abnormal cells within those tissues leading to malignancies. Although darker-skinned individuals are at risk for skin cancer as well, they are less likely to develop it due to increased levels of melanin, specifically eumelanin, in their skin. Even though skin cancer is a serious health concern for some individuals, most skin cancers occur in the post-reproductive years; therefore, it is improbable that evolutionary forces favoring varying melanin expression levels are related to a selective pressure to avoid such cancers. Furthermore, if avoiding skin cancer were the primary factor driving the evolution of various skin tones, then it reasons that everyone would have the most significant expression of eumelanin possible. So, why do we have different skin tones (Figure 14.12)? The term **cline** refers to the continuum or spectrum of gradations (i.e., levels or degrees) from one extreme to another. With respect to skin tone, the various tonal shades occur clinally with darker skin being more prevalent near the equator and gradually decreasing in tone (i.e., decreased melanin production) in more distant latitudes. For individuals who are indigenous to equatorial regions, the increased levels of melanin within their skin provides them with a measure of protection against both sunburn and sunstroke as the melanin is more reflective of UV radiation than hemoglobin. In cases of severe sunburn, eccrine glands are affected, resulting in an individual's ability to sweat being compromised. As sweat is the body's most effective means of reducing its core temperature to maintain homeostasis, damage to the eccrine glands may lead to numerous physiological issues related to heat that may ultimately result in death.

Even though avoiding severe sunburn and sunstroke is of great importance to individuals within equatorial regions, this is likely not the primary factor driving the evolutionary selection of darker skin within these regions. It has been proposed that the destruction of **folic acid**, which is a form of B-complex vitamin, by UV radiation may have led to the selection of darker skin in equatorial regions. For pregnant women, low levels of folic acid within the body during gestation may lead to defects in the formation of the brain and spinal cord of the fetus. This condition, which is referred to as spina bifida, often significantly reduces the infant's chances of survival without medical intervention. In men, low levels of folic

Evolution of Skin Color Variation

HAIR AND SKIN
Once hominins lost most of their body hair they likely had dark pigmented skin. In environments with high UV radiation, dark skin protected early humans against skin damage.

FOLATE & UV RAYS
UV rays penetrate the skin and can break down folate in the blood stream. Folate is necessary for sperm production and for fetal development.

LEAVING AFRICA
Once some humans left Africa, they encountered environments with different levels of UV radiation. New selective pressures began to shape human skin color among these groups.

VITAMIN D
In low UV environments, people with dark skin could not synthesize enough vitamin D resulting in rickets and other health problems. People with dark skin had a lower chance of survival in most of these environments.

SELECTIVE PRESSURES
Vitamin D, folate and changing UV environments were the selective pressures that resulted in the development of a variety of skin colors in different populations throughout the world.

Figure 14.12 Evolutionary basis for human skin color variation.

acid within the body lead to an inhibition in the production of sperm. Thus, in geographic regions with high UV radiation levels (i.e., equatorial regions), there appears to be an evolutionarily driven correlation between darker skin and the maintenance of fertility.

If darker skin tone is potentially correlated to more successful reproduction, then why do lighter shades of skin exist? One hypothesis is that there is a relationship between lighter skin tone and vitamin D synthesis within the body. When skin is exposed to the UV-B radiation waves in sunlight, a series of chemical reactions occur within the epidermis leading to the production of vitamin D3. Before the body can use vitamin D3, it must travel to the liver and then to the kidneys where it is converted into different forms of bioactive molecules. Ultimately, it is converted into the bioactive molecule calcitriol (Vukić et al. 2015). Within the human body there are numerous cell types with binding receptors for calcitriol, so it is capable of adhering to the DNA of those cells (Snoddy et al. 2016). Calcitriol serves as a regulator in cellular-replication processes within the body, including those for pancreatic, breast, colon, and kidney cells (Snoddy et al. 2016). Insufficient calcitriol is associated with an increased risk of: some forms of cancer (colon, prostate, etc.), autoimmune diseases (multiple sclerosis, lupus, type I diabetes, etc.), cardiovascular diseases, and infections (e.g., tuberculosis, influenza) (Snoddy el al. 2016; Chaplin and Jablonski 2009). Deficiencies in calcitriol production and absorption within the human body may be linked to underlying genetic factors, such as a mutation in the vitamin D receptors present in some of the body's cells (Chaplin and Jablonski 2009). Alternatively, it may be linked to inadequate exposure to the UV-B rays necessary to stimulate calcitriol production or to a nutritional deficiency in vitamin D-rich foods. Regardless of the cause of the deficiency, individuals with a calcitriol (vitamin D3) deficiency may also be at risk for the development of certain skeletal abnormalities in addition to the previously mentioned health issues.

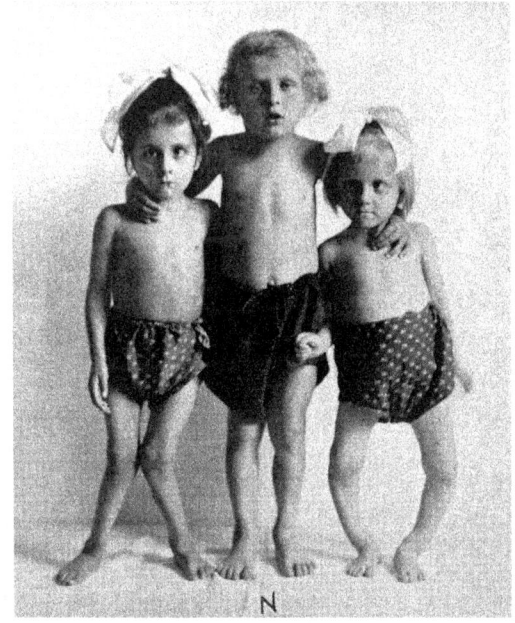

Figure 14.13 Children with rickets in various developmental stages.

Vitamin D is required for the absorption of certain nutrients, such as calcium and phosphorus, in the small intestine. These nutrients are among those that are critical for the proper growth and maintenance of bone tissue within the body. In the absence of adequate minerals, particularly calcium, bone structure and strength will be compromised leading to the development of rickets during the growth phase. Rickets is a disease affecting children during their growth phase and is characterized by inadequately calcified bones that are softer and more flexible than normal. Individuals with rickets will develop a true bowing of their femora, which may affect their mobility (Figure 14.13). In addition, deformation of pelvic bones in women may occur as a result of rickets leading to complications with reproduction. In adults, a deficiency in vitamin D will often result in osteomalacia, which is a general softening of the bones due to inadequate mineralization. This softening is the result of impaired bone metabolism that is primarily linked to insufficient levels of bioavailable vitamin D, calcium, and phosphate. In addition, it may be linked to inadequate absorption of calcium in the bloodstream. As noted, a variety of maladies may occur due to the inadequate production or absorption of vitamin D, as well as the destruction of folate within the human body; so, from an evolutionary perspective, natural selection should favor a skin tone that is best suited to a given environment.

In general, the trend related to lighter skin pigmentation further from the equator follows a principle called **Gloger's Rule**. This rule states that within the same species of mammals the more heavily pigmented individuals tend to originate near the equator while lighter-pigmented members of the species will be found in regions further from the equator. Gloger's Rule applies latitudinally; however, it does not appear to hold for certain human populations near the poles. Specifically, the Inuit people (Figure 14.14), who are indigenous to regions near the North Pole and currently reside in portions of Canada, Greenland, Alaska, and Denmark. The Inuit have a darker skin tone that would not be anticipated under the provisions of Gloger's Rule. The high reflectivity of light off of snow and ice, which is common in polar regions, necessitates the darker skin tone of these individuals to prevent folic acid degradation just as it does for individuals within equatorial regions. The consumption of vitamin D-rich foods, such as raw fish, permits the Inuit to reside at high latitudes with darker skin tone while preventing rickets.

Figure 14.14 Inuit family, 1917.

Genome studies have identified a number of genes (TYR, OCA2/HERC2, TYRP1, SLC45A2, HPS6i, etc.) related to the expression of melanin and pigmentation presentation in humans. Compared to the exceptionally large number of genes within the human genome, those regulating the expression of melanin are relatively few and appear on distinct loci. The genes at these loci are generally pleiotropic in nature, so there is a relatively predictable patterning in skin, hair, and eye color combinations (Sturm and Duffy 2012). For example, some populations that are indigenous to higher latitude regions tend to have lighter skin, hair, and eye color than their counterparts from equatorial regions. Still, since the genes affecting skin, hair, and eye color are actually independent, it is possible that variations may produce many phenotypic combinations. Turning again to our example of individuals indigenous to higher latitudes, it is theoretically possible to encounter an individual with dark hair, light-toned skin, and blue eyes within this region due to the variability of phenotypic combinations.

Adaptation: Shape and Size Variations

In addition to natural selection playing a role in the determination of melanin expression related to skin tone, which is correlated to the environment, it plays a significant role in the determination of the shape and size of the human body. As previously discussed, the most significant thermodynamic mechanism of heat loss from the body is radiation. At temperatures below 20°C (68°F), the human body loses around 65% of its heat to radiative processes; however, the efficiency of radiation as a means of heat reduction is correlated to the overall body shape and size of the individual. There is a direct correlation between the ratio of an object's surface area to mass and the amount of heat that may be lost through radiation. For example, two metal objects of identical composition and mass are heated to the same temperature. One object is a cube and the other is a sphere. Which object will cool the fastest? Geometrically, a sphere has the smallest surface area per unit mass of any three-dimensional object, so the sphere will cool more slowly than the cube. In other words, the smaller the ratio of the surface area to mass an object has, the more it will retain heat.

With respect to the cube in our example, mass increases by the cube, but surface area may increase only by the square, so size will affect the mass to surface area ratio. This, in general, holds true for humans, as well.

In regions where temperatures are consistently cold, the body shape and size of the individuals who are indigenous to the area tend to be more compact. These individuals have a relatively higher body mass to surface area (i.e., skin) than their counterparts from equatorial regions where the average temperatures are considerably warmer. Individuals from hot climates, such as the Fulani (Figure 14.15a) of West Africa, have limbs that are considerably longer than those of individuals from cold climates, such as the Inuit of Greenland (Figure 14.15b). Evolutionarily, the longer limbs of individuals from equatorial regions (e.g., the Fulani) provide a greater surface area (i.e., lower body mass to surface area ratio) for the dissipation of heat through radiative processes. In contrast, the relatively short limbs of Arctic-dwelling people, such as the Inuit, allows for the retention of heat as there is a decreased surface area through which heat may radiate away from the body.

Figure 14.15a The Fula people of Burkina Faso (pictured here in 1974) are from a tropical environment where the rapid dispersal of heat is necessary to maintain homeostasis.

Figure 14.15b These Inuit people from Greenland live in an arctic environment where the conservation of heat in the body's core is of critical importance.

As described above, there are certain trends related to the general shape and size of human bodies in relation to the thermal conditions. To better describe these trends, we turn to a couple of general principles that are applicable to a variety of species beyond humans. **Bergmann's Rule** predicts that as average environmental temperature decreases, populations are expected to exhibit an increase in weight and a decrease in surface area (Figure 14.16a). Also, within the same species of homeothermic animals, the relative length of projecting body parts (e.g., nose, ears, and limbs) increases in relation to the average environmental temperature (Figure 14.16b). This principle, referred to as **Allen's Rule**, notes that longer, thinner limbs are advantageous for the radiation of excess heat in hot environments and shorter, stockier limbs assist with

Figure 14.16a These organisms are representative of Bergmann's rule. The animal on the left depicts an ungulate from a cooler environment with increased body weight and decreased surface area, compared to the slender ungulate on the right.

the preservation of body heat in cold climates. A measure of the crural index (crural index=tibia length [divided by] femur length) of individuals from various human populations provides support for Allen's Rule since this value is lower in individuals from colder climates than it is for those from hot climates. The crural indices for human populations varies directly with temperature, so individuals with higher crural index values are generally from regions with a warmer average environmental temperature. Conversely, the crural indices are lower for individuals from regions where there are colder average temperatures.

Figure 14.16b These animals are representative of Allen's rule. Note the shorter limbs and ears of the rabbit on the left that you might find in cold temperatures. Note the length of the ears on the rabbit on the right that you might find in a warm climate. Rabbits do not sweat like humans, heat is dissipated primarily through their ears.

Nasal shape and size (Figure 14.17) is another physiological feature that is affected by way of an individual's ancestors' environments. The selective role of climate in determining human nasal variation is typically approached by dividing climates into four adaptive zones: hot-dry, hot-wet, cold-dry, and cold-wet (Maddux et al. 2016). One of the principal roles of the nasal cavity is to condition (i.e., warm and humidify) ambient air prior to its reaching the lungs. Given that function of the nasal cavity, it is anticipated that different nasal shapes and sizes will be related to varying environments. In cold-dry climates, an individual's nasal cavity must provide humidification and warmth to the dry air when breathing in through the nose (Noback et al. 2011). Also, in that type of climate, the nasal cavity must conserve moisture and minimize heat loss during when the individual exhales through the nose (Noback et al. 2011). From a physiological stress perspective, this is a stressful event.

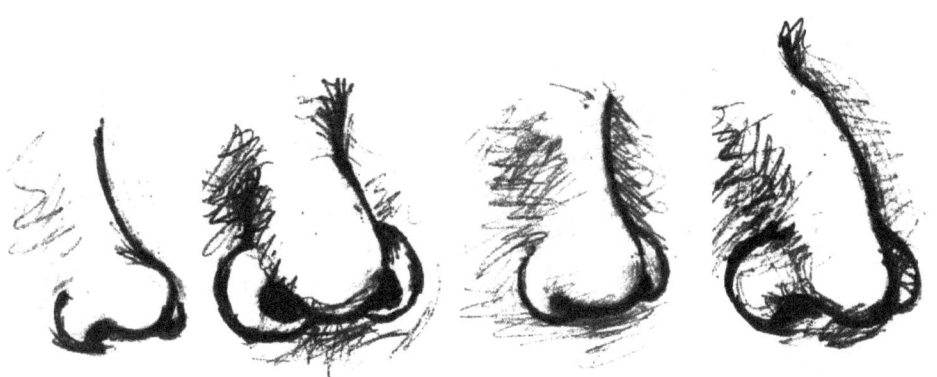

Figure 14.17 Human nasal morphological variation as influenced by four major climate-based adaptive zones: hot-dry, hot-wet, cold-dry, and cold-wet. Note that images are presented left-to-right in relation to the climate-based adaptive zones, respectively.

Conversely, in hot-wet environments, there is no need for the nasal cavity to provide additional moisture to the inhaled air nor is there a need to warm the air or to preserve heat within the nasal cavity (Noback et al. 2011). So, in hot-wet climates, the body is under less physiological stress related to the inhalation of ambient air than in cold-dry climates. As with most human morphological elements, the shape and size of the nasal cavity occurs along a cline. Due to the environmental stressors of cold-dry environments requiring the humidification and warming of air through the nasal cavity, individuals indigenous to such environments tend to have taller (longer) noses with a reduced nasal entrance (nostril opening) size (Noback et al. 2011). This general shape is referred to as leptorrhine, and it allows for a larger surface area within the nasal cavity itself for the air to be warmed and humidified prior to entering the lungs (Maddux et al. 2016). In addition, the relatively small nasal entrance of leptorrhine noses serves as a means of conserving moisture and heat (Noback et al. 2011). Individuals indigenous to hot-wet climates tend to have platyrrhine nasal shapes, which are shorter with broader nasal entrances (Maddux et al. 2016). Since individuals in hot-wet climates do not need to humidify and warm the air entering the nose, their nasal tract is shorter and the nasal entrance wider to permit the effective cooling of the nasal cavity during respiratory processes.

Adaptation: Infectious Disease

Throughout our evolutionary journey, humans have been exposed to numerous infectious diseases. In the following section, we will explore some of the evolutionary-based adaptations that have occurred in certain populations in response to the stressors presented by select infectious diseases. One of the primary examples of natural selection processes acting on the human genome in response to the presence of an infectious disease is the case of the relationship between the sickle-cell anemia trait and malaria.

Malaria is a zoonotic disease (type of infectious disease naturally transmitted between animals and humans; covered in more detail in Chapter 16: Human Biology and Health) caused by the spread of the parasitic protozoa from the genus *Plasmodium* (Figure 14.18). These unicellular, eukaryotic protozoa are transmitted through the bite of a female *Anopheles* mosquito. During the bite process, the protozoan parasites that are present within an infected mosquito's saliva will enter the bloodstream of the individual where they will be transported to the liver. Within the liver, the parasites multiply and will eventually be released into the bloodstream where they will infect erythrocytes. Once inside the erythrocytes, the parasites will reproduce until they exceed the cell's storage capacity, causing it to burst and release the parasites into the bloodstream once again. This replication cycle will continue as long as there are viable erythrocytes within the host to infect.

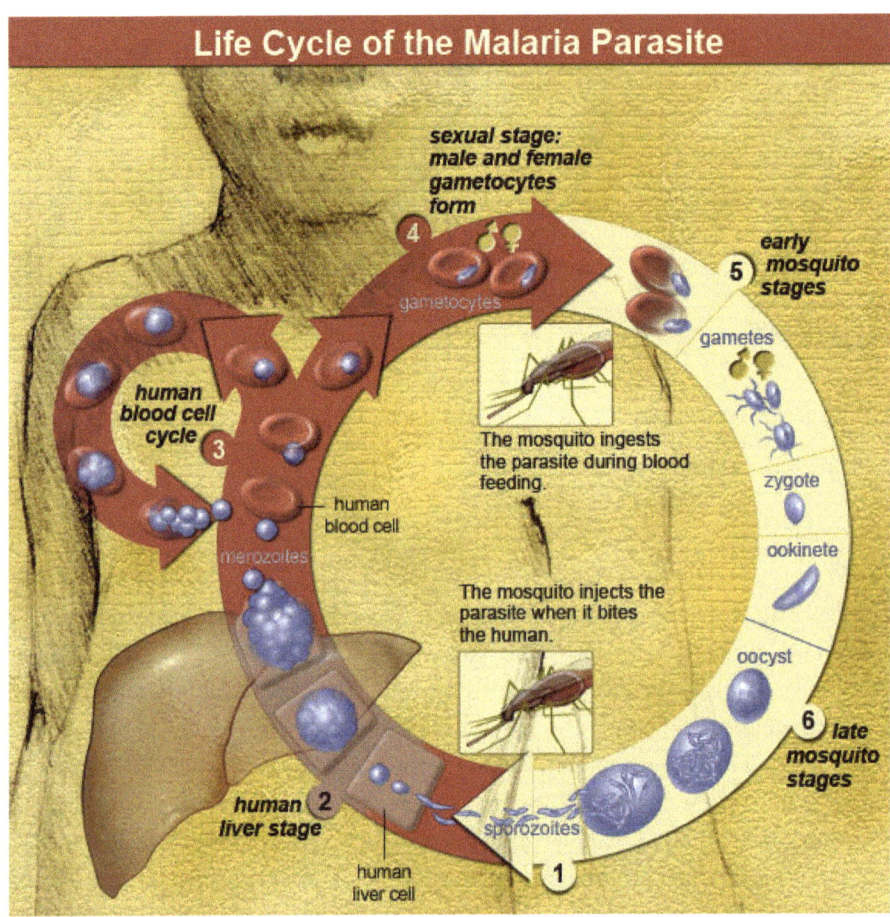

Figure 14.18 Life cycle of the malaria parasite.

General complications from malaria infections include: enlargement of the spleen (due to destruction of infected erythrocytes), lower number of thrombocytes (also called platelets, required for coagulation/clotting of blood), high levels of bilirubin (a byproduct of hemoglobin breakdown in the liver) in the blood, jaundice (yellowing of the skin and eyes due to increased blood bilirubin levels), fever, vomiting, retinal (eye) damage, and convulsions (seizures). According to the World Health Organization, in 2016 there were 445,000 deaths from malaria globally with the highest percentage of those deaths occurring in Africa (91%) and Southeast Asia (6%) (World Health Organization 2017). In sub-Saharan Africa, where incidents of malaria are the highest in the world, 125 million pregnancies are affected by malaria, resulting in 200,000 infant deaths (Hartman et al. 2013). Pregnant women who become infected during the gestational process are more likely to have low-birthweight infants due to prematurity or growth restriction inside the uterus (Hartman et al. 2013). After birth, infants born to malaria-infected mothers are more likely to develop infantile anemia (low red blood cell counts), a malaria infection that is not related to the maternal malarial infection, and they are more likely to die than infants born to non-malaria-infected mothers (Hartman et al. 2013).

For children and adolescents whose brains are still developing, there is a risk of cognitive (intellectual) impairment associated with some forms of malaria infections (Fernando et al. 2010). Given the relatively high rates of morbidity (disease) and mortality (number of deaths) associated with malaria, it leads to reason that this disease may have served as a selective pressure during human evolution. Support for natural selection related to malaria resistance is related to genetic mutations associated with sickle cell, thalassemia, glucose-6-phosphate dehydrogenase (G6PD) deficiency, and the absence of certain antigens (molecules capable of inducing an immune response from the host) on erythrocytes. For the purposes of this text, we will focus our discussion on the relationship between sickle cell disease and malaria.

Sickle cell disease is a group of genetically inherited blood disorders characterized by an abnormality in the shape of the hemoglobin within erythrocytes. It is important to note that there are multiple variants of hemoglobin, including, but not limited to: A, D, C, E, F, H, S, Barts, Portland, Hope, Pisa, and Hopkins. Each of these variants of hemoglobin may result in various conditions within the body; however, for the following explanation we will focus solely on variants A and S.

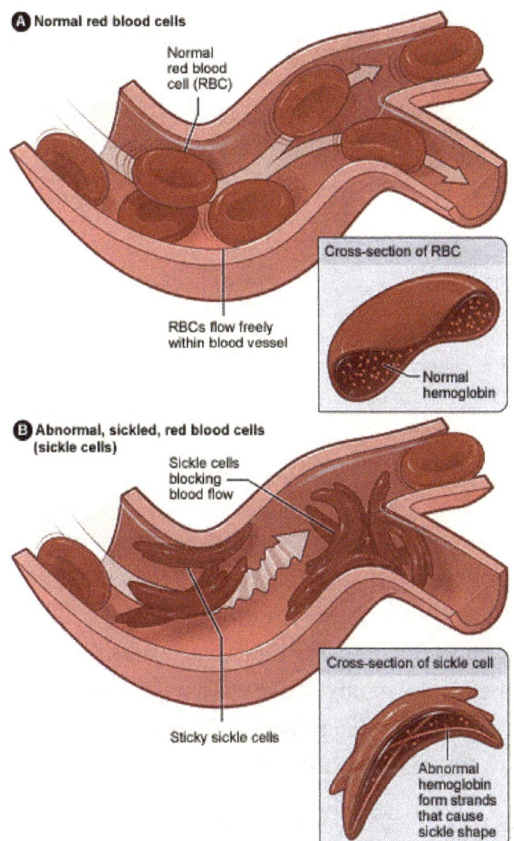

Figure 14.19 Normal and sickled erythrocytes.

Individuals who inherit a mutated gene (hemoglobin with a sickled erythrocyte variety, HbS) on chromosome 11 from both parents will develop sickle cell anemia, which is the most severe form of the sickle cell disease family (Figure 14.19). The genotype of an individual with sickle cell anemia is HbSS; whereas, an individual without sickle cell alleles has a genotype of HbAA representing two normal adult hemoglobin type A variants. Manifestations of sickle cell anemia (HbSS) range from mild to severe with some of the more common symptoms being: anemia, blood clots, organ failure, chest pain, fever, and low blood oxygen levels. In high-income countries with advanced medical care, the median life expectancy of an HbSS individual is around 60 years; however, in low-income countries where advanced medical care is scarce, as many as 90% of children with sickle cell disease perish before the age of five (Longo et al. 2017).

Considering that advanced medical care was not available during much of human evolutionary history, it stands to reason that the majority of individuals with the HbSS genotype died before the age of reproduction. If that is the case though, why do we still have the HbS variant present in modern populations? As covered earlier in this textbook, the genotype of an individual is composed of genes from both biological parents. In the case of an individual with an HbSS genotype, the sickle cell allele (HbS) was inherited from each of the parents. For individuals with the heterozygous genotype of HbSA, they have inherited both a sickle cell allele (HbS) and a normal hemoglobin allele (HbA). Heterozygous (HbSA) individuals who reside in regions where malaria is endemic may have a selective advantage. They will experience a sickling of some, but not all, of their erythrocytes. Unlike an individual with the HbSS genotype, someone with HbSA may experience some of the symptoms listed above; however, they are generally less severe.

As noted earlier, the mechanism through which *Plasmodium* protozoan parasites replicate involves human erythrocyte cells. However, due to their sickled shape, as well as the presence of an abnormally shaped protein within the cell, the parasites are unable to replicate effectively in the erythrocyte cells coded for by the HbS allele (Cyrklaff et al. 2011). An individual who has an HbSA genotype and an active malaria infection will become ill with the disease to a lesser extent than someone with an HbAA genotype. Although normal erythrocytes (regulated by the HbA allele) allow for the replication of the parasite, the parasites will not be able to replicate in HbS erythrocytes of the heterozygote. So, individuals with the HbSA genotype are more likely to survive a malaria infection than an individual who is HbAA. Although individuals with the HbSA genotype may endure some physiological complications related to the sickling of some of their erythrocytes, their morbidity and mortality rates are lower than they are for HbSS members of the population. The majority of individuals who are heterozygous or homozygous for the HbS trait have ancestors who originated in sub-Saharan Africa, India, Saudi Arabia, regions in South and Central America, the Caribbean, and the Mediterranean (Turkey, Greece, and Italy) (Centers for Disease Control and Prevention 2017) (Figure 14.20).

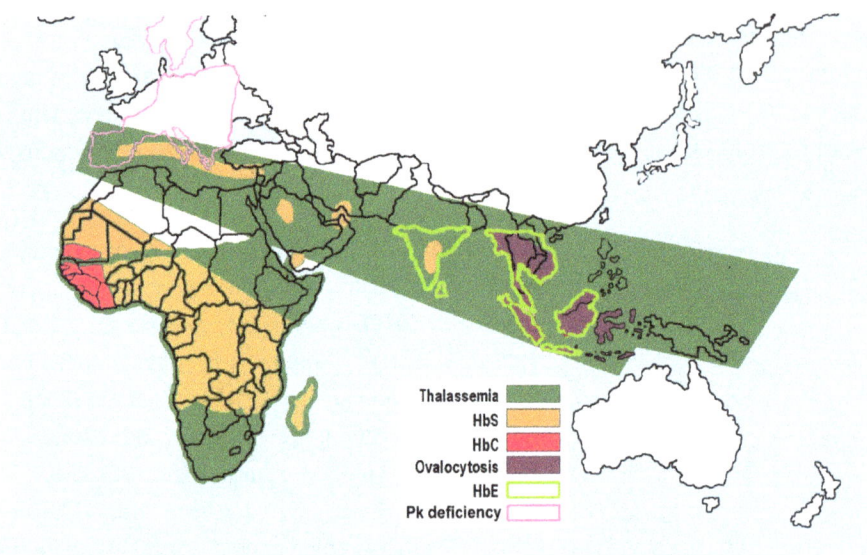

Figure 14.20 Distribution of sickle cell and associated erythrocytic abnormalities for Africa and Asia.

With respect to the history of these regions, during the early phases of settlement horticulture was the primary method of crop cultivation. Typically performed on a small scale, horticulture is based on manual labor and relatively simple hand tools rather than the use of draft animals or irrigation technologies. Common in horticulture is *swidden*, or the cutting and burning of plants in woodland and grassland regions. The swidden is the prepared field that results following a slash-and-burn episode. This practice fundamentally alters the soil chemistry, removes plants that provide shade, and increases the areas where water may pool. This anthropogenically altered landscape provides the perfect breeding ground for the *Anopheles* mosquito, as it prefers warm, stagnant pools of water (Figure 14.21).

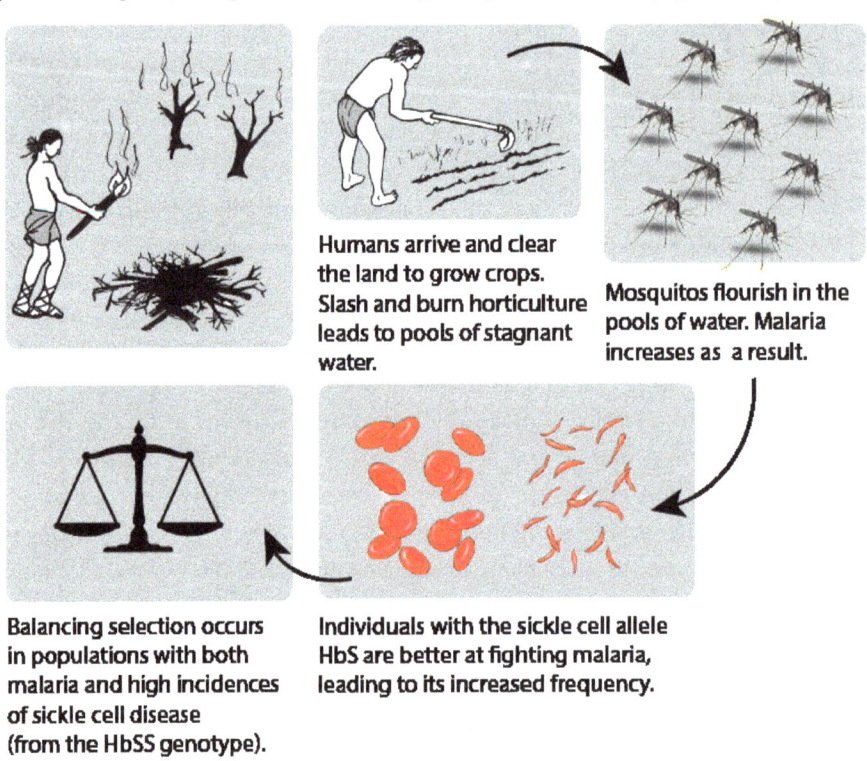

Figure 14.21 The effects of human horticultural activities on the balancing selection of populations in relation to sickle cell disease genotype variants.

Human Variation: An Adaptive Significance Approach | 537

Although swidden agriculture was historically practiced across the globe, it became most problematic in the regions where the *Anopheles* mosquito is endemic. These areas have the highest incidence rates of malaria infection. Over time, the presence of the *Anopheles* mosquito and the *Plasmodium* parasite that it transmitted acted as a selective pressure, particularly in regions where swidden agricultural practices were common, toward the selection of individuals with some modicum of resistance against the infection. In these regions, HbSS and HbSA individuals would have been more likely to survive and reproduce successfully. Although individuals and populations are far more mobile now than they have been throughout much of history, there are still regions where we can see higher rates of malaria infection as well as greater numbers of individuals with the HbS erythrocyte variant. The relationship between malaria and the selective pressure for the HbS variant is one of the most prominent examples of natural selection in the human species within recent evolutionary history.

Adaptation: Lactase Persistence

With the case of sickled erythrocytes and their resistance to infection by malaria parasites, there is strong support for a cause-and-effect-style relationship linked to natural selection. Although somewhat less apparent, there is a correlation between lactase persistence and environmental challenges. Lactase-phlorizin hydrolase (LPH) is an enzyme that is primarily produced in the small intestine and permits the proper digestion of lactose, a disaccharide (composed of two simple sugars: glucose and galactose) found in the milk of mammals. Most humans will experience a decrease in the expression of LPH following weaning, leading to an inability to properly digest lactose. Generally, LPH production decreases between the ages of two and five and is completely absent by the age of nine (Dzialanski et al. 2016). For these individuals, the ingestion of lactose may lead to a wide variety of gastrointestinal ailments including abdominal bloating, increased gas, and diarrhea. Although the bloating and gas are unpleasant, the diarrhea caused by a failure to properly digest lactose can be life-threatening if severe enough due to the dehydration it can cause. Some humans, however, are able to produce LPH far beyond the weaning period.

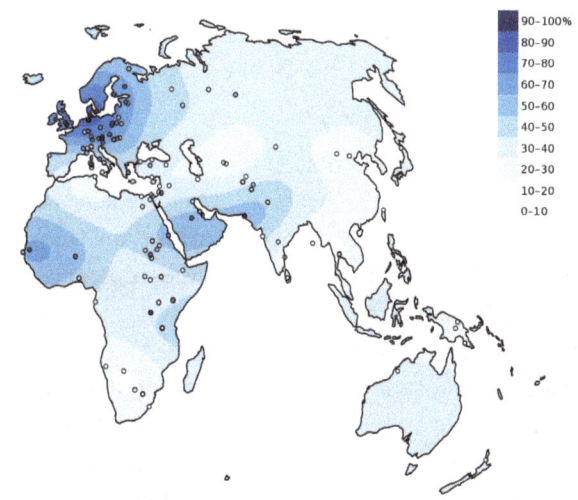

Individuals who continue to produce LPH have what is referred to as the **lactase persistence** trait. The lactase persistence trait is encoded for a gene called LCT, which is located on human chromosome 2 (Ranciaro et al. 2014; see also Chapter 3). From an evolutionary and historical perspective, this trait is most commonly linked to cultures that have practiced cattle domestication (Figure 14.22). For individuals in those cultures, the continued expression of LPH may have provided a selective advantage. During periods of environmental stress, such as a drought, if an individual is capable of successfully digesting cow's milk, they have a higher chance of survival than someone who suffers from diarrhea-linked dehydration due to a lack of LPH. Per Tishkoff et al., the "frequency of lactase persistence is high in northern European populations (more than 90% in Swedes and Danes), decreases in frequency across southern Europe and the Middle East (less than 50% in Spanish, French, and pastoralist Arab populations), and is low in non-pastoralist Asian and African populations (less than 1% in Chinese, less than 5% to 20% in West African agriculturalists)" (2007: 248). Although the frequency of the lactase persistence trait is relatively low among African agriculturalists, it is high among

Figure 14.22 Interpolated map depicting the percentage of adults with the lactase persistence genotype in indigenous populations of the Old World. Circles denote sample locations.

pastoralist populations that are traditionally associated with cattle domestication, such as the Tutsi and Fulani, who have frequencies of 90% and 50%, respectively (Tishkoff et al. 2007).

Cattle domestication began around 11,000 years ago in Europe (Beja-Pereira et al. 2006) and 7,500 to 9,000 years ago in the Middle East and North Africa (Tishkoff et al. 2007). Based on human genomic studies, it is estimated that the mutation for the lactase persistence trait occurred around 2,000 to 20,000 years ago for European populations (Tishkoff et al. 2007). For African populations, the lactase persistence trait emerged approximately 1,200 to 23,000 years ago (Gerbault et al. 2011). This begs the question: Is this mutation the same for both populations? It appears that the emergence of the lactase persistence mutation in non-European populations, specifically those in East Africa (e.g., Tutsi and Fulani), is a case of **convergent evolution**. With convergent evolution events, a similar mutation may occur in species of different lineages through independent evolutionary processes. Based on our current understanding of the genetic mutation pathways for the lactase persistence trait in European and African populations, these mutations are not representative of a shared lineage. In other words, just because a person of European origin and a person of African origin can each digest milk due to the presence of the lactase-persistence trait in their genotypes, it does not mean that these two individuals inherited it due to shared common ancestry.

Is it possible that the convergent evolution of similar lactase-persistence traits in disparate populations is merely a product of genetic drift? Or is there evidence for natural selection? Even though 23,000 years may seem like a long time, it is but a blink of the proverbial evolutionary eye. From the perspective of human evolutionary pathways, mutations related to the LCT gene have occurred relatively recently. Similar genetic changes in multiple populations through genetic drift processes, which are relatively slow and directionless, fail to accumulate as rapidly as have lactase-persistence traits (Gerbault et al. 2011). The widespread accumulation of these traits in a relatively short period of time supports the notion that an underlying selective pressure must be driving this form of human evolution. Although to date no definitive factors have been firmly identified, it is thought that environmental pressures are likely to credit for the rapid accumulation of the lactase-persistence trait in multiple human populations through convergent evolutionary pathways.

Human Variation: Our Story Continues

From the time that the first of our species left Africa, we have had to adjust and adapt to numerous environmental challenges. The remarkable ability of human beings to maintain homeostasis through a combination of both nongenetic (adjustments) and genetic (adaptations) means has allowed us to occupy a remarkable variety of environments from high-altitude mountainous regions to the tropics near the equator. From adding piquant, pungent spices to our foods as a means of inhibiting food-borne illnesses due to bacterial growth to donning garments specially suited to local climates, behavioral adjustments have provided us with a nongenetic means of coping with obstacles to our health and well-being. Acclimatory adjustments, such as sweating when we are warm in an attempt to regulate our body temperature or experiencing increased breathing rates as a means of increasing blood oxygen levels in regions where the partial pressure of oxygen is low, have been instrumental in our survival with respect to thermal and altitudinal environmental challenges. For some individuals, developmental adjustments that were acquired during their development and growth phases (e.g., increased heart and lung capacities for individuals from high-altitude regions) provide them with a form of physiological advantage not possible for someone who ventures to such an environmentally challenging region as an adult. Genetically-mediated adaptations, such as variations in the pigmentation of our skin, have ensured our evolutionary fitness across all latitudes.

Will the human species continue to adjust and adapt to new environmental challenges in the future? If past performance is any measure of future expectations, then the human story will continue as long as we do not alter our environment to the point that the plasticity of our behavior, physiological, and morphological boundaries is exceeded. In the following chapters, you will explore additional information about our saga as a species. From the concept of race as a sociocultural construct to our epidemiological history, the nuances of evolutionary-based human variation are always present and provide the basis for understanding our history and our future as a species.

Review Questions

- Detail at least two examples of how natural selection has influenced human variation. Specifically, what was the selective pressure that may have led to a preference for a specific trait and how is that trait related to an increased level of fitness?
- Why is reduced pigmentation of the skin advantageous for individuals from northern latitudes? What role does darker skin pigmentation serve for individuals near the equator? What is the relationship between skin pigmentation and fitness?
- What are some of the risks associated with pregnancy at high altitude? Compare and contrast the various genetic mutations of the indigenous Tibetan, Andean, and Ethiopian high-altitude populations. In your answer, specifically address the issue of pregnancy at high altitudes.
- What is the relationship between the sickle cell mutation and the *Plasmodium* parasite? Would having the HbSA genotype still be advantageous in a region where such parasites are not common? Why or why not?

Key Terms

Acclimatory adjustments: Processes by which an individual organism adjusts to maintain homeostasis in response to environmental challenges.

Activated melanogenesis: Increase in melanin production in response to ultraviolet radiation (UV) exposure.

Adaptation: alteration in population-level gene frequencies related to environmentally induced selective pressures; leads to a greater level of fitness for a population related to a specific environment.

Adjustment: Non-genetic-based ways in which organisms adjust to environmental stressors.

Allen's Rule: Due to thermal adaptation, homeothermic animals have body volume-to-surface ratios that vary inversely with the average temperature of their environment. In cold climates, the anticipated ratio is high and it is low in warm climates.

Basal melanogenesis: Genetically-mediated, non-environmentally influenced base melanin level.

Behavioral adjustments: An individual's culturally mediated responses to an environmental stressor in an effort to maintain homeostasis.

Bergmann's Rule: For a broadly distributed monophyletic group, species and populations of smaller size tend to be found in environments with warmer climates and those of larger size tend to be found in ones that are colder.

Cline: A continuum of gradations (i.e., degrees or levels) of a specific trait.

Conduction: Mechanism of heat transfer between objects through direct contact.

Convection: Movement of heat away from a warm object to the cooler surrounding fluid (i.e., gas or liquid).

Convergent evolution: Evolutionary process where organisms that are not closely related independently evolve similar traits as a product of adaptation to similar evolutionary parameters.

Erythrocyte: Red blood cell; most common form of blood cell—principle means of transporting oxygen throughout the circulatory system.

Evaporation: Mechanism of heat transfer where liquid is transformed into a gas utilizing energy (e.g., heat).

Folic acid: Form of B complex vitamin necessary for proper fetal development.

Gloger's Rule: For mammals of the same species, those with more darkly pigmented forms tend to be found closer to the equator and those with lighter forms are found in regions further from the equator.

Hematocrit: Volume percentage of red blood cells within the blood.

Homeostasis: Condition of optimal functioning for an organism.

Hyperpnea: Increased depth and rate of respiration.

Hypothalamus: Small portion of the human brain responsible for body temperature regulation.

Lactase persistence: Genetic mutation permitting the continued production of lactase-phlorizin hydrolase enzyme in the small intestine past the weaning period.

Melanin: Black-brown pigment produced by melanocytes; one of the primary pigments in skin.

Melanocytes: Specialized cells that produce melanin.

Phenotypic plasticity: Ability of one genotype to produce more than one phenotype dependent on environmental conditions.

Polyphenism: Multiple discrete phenotypes from an organism's genotype in response to the environment; a special form of phenotypic plasticity.

Radiation: Mechanism of heat transfer involving electromagnetic energy being emitted from an object.

Sickle cell disease: A group of genetically inherited blood disorders characterized by an abnormality in the shape of the hemoglobin within erythrocytes (red blood cells).

Stressor: Any stimulus resulting in an imbalance in an organism's homeostatic balance.

Vasoconstriction: Narrowing of the blood vessels due to contractions of the muscular vessel walls.

Vasodilation: Dilation of the blood vessels due to relaxation of the muscular vessel walls.

About the Author

Leslie Fitzpatrick, Ph.D.

Mercyhurst University, Lfitzpatrick@mercyhurst.edu

Leslie Fitzpatrick

Leslie Fitzpatrick is an Assistant Professor in the Department of Biological Anthropology and Applied Forensic Sciences at Mercyhurst University in Erie, Pennsylvania. She earned a Ph.D. in Anthropology from the University of Wyoming (2017), an M.A. in Anthropology from Georgia State (2012), and a B.S. in Mechanical Engineering from Georgia Tech (2000). Her primary research focus is the stable-isotope analysis of human remains as a means of interpreting past mobility and diet profiles for both modern and archaeological populations. In addition to her work in the classroom and laboratory, she has worked as a bioarchaeologist at field sites in Germany, Spain, Croatia, Mexico, Peru, and throughout the United States.

References

American Academy of Pediatrics, Task Force on Infant Sleep Position and Sudden Infant Death Syndrome. 2000. "Changing concepts of sudden infant death syndrome: implications for infant sleeping environment and sleep position." Pediatrics 105: 650–656, 116 (5): 1,245.

Beja-Pereira, Albano, David Caramelli, Carles Lalueza-Fox, Cristiano Vernesi, Nuno Ferrand, Antonella Casoli, Felix Goyache, Luis J. Royo, et. all., 2006. "The origin of European cattle: evidence from modern and ancient DNA." PNAS 103 (21): 8,113–8,118.

Bigham, Abigail W. 2016. "Genetics of Human Origin and Evolution: High-Altitude Adaptations." Current Opinion in Genetics & Development 41: 8–13.

Centers for Disease Control and Prevention. 2017. "Data & Statistics on Sickle Cell Disease." Centers for Disease Control and Prevention website, August 9. https://www.cdc.gov/ncbddd/sicklecell/data.html.

Chaplin, George, and Nina G. Jablonski. 2009. "Vitamin D and the Evolution of Human Depigmentation." American Journal of Physical Anthropology 139 (4): 451–461.

Crawford, Nicholas G., Derek E. Kelly, Matthew E. B. Hansen, Marcia H. Beltrame, Shaohua Fan, Shanna L. Bowman, Ethan Jewett, et.all., 2017. "Loci associated with skin pigmentation identified in African populations." Science 358 (6,365): 1–49.

Cyrkalff, Marek, Cecilia P. Sanchez, Nicole Kilian, Curille Bisseye, Jacques Simpore, Friedrich Frischknecht, and Michael Lanzer. 2011. "Hemoglobins S and interfere with actin remodeling in Plasmodium falciparium-infected erythrocytes." Science 334 (6,060): 1,283–1,286.

Dzialanski, Zbigniew, Michael Barany, Peter Engfeldt, Anders Magnuson Lovisa A. Olsson, and Torbjörn K. Nilsson. 2016.

"Lactase persistence versus lactose intolerance: Is there an intermediate phenotype?" Clinical Biochemistry 49 (2,016): 248. 252.

Fernando, Sumadya D., Chaturaka Rodrigo, and Senaka Rajapakse. 2010. "The 'hidden' burden of malaria: cognitive impairment following infection." Malaria Journal 9 (366): 1–11.

Gerbault, Pascale, Anke Liebert, Yuval Itan, Adam Powell, Mathias Currat, Joachim Burger, Dallas M. Swallow, and Mark G. Thomas. 2011. "Evolution of lactase persistence: an example of human niche construction." Philosophical Transactions of the Royal Society B: Biological Sciences 366 (1,566): 863–877.

Hartman, T. K., S. J. Rogerson, and P. R. Fischer. 2013. "The impact of maternal malaria on newborns." Annals of Tropical Paediatrics 30 (4): 271-282.

Longo, Dan L., Frédéric B. Piel, Martin H. Steinberg, and David C. Rees. 2017. "Sickle Cell Disease." The New England Journal of Medicine 376 (16): 1,561-1,573.

Maddux, Scott D., Todd R. Yokley, Bohumil M. Svoma, and Robert G. Franciscus. 2016. "Absolute Humidity and the Human Nose: A Reanalysis of Climate Zones and Their Influence on Nasal Form and Function." American Journal of Physical Anthropology 161 (2): 309–320.

Meyer, M. C., M. S. Alexander, Z. Wang, D. L. Hoffmann, J. A. Dahl, D. Degering, W. R. Haas and F. Schlütz. 2017. "Permanent human occupation of the central Tibetan Plateau in the Early Holocene." Science 355 (6,320): 64-67.

Moore, Lorna G, Susan Niermeyer, and Stacy Zamudio. 1998. "Human Adaptation to High Altitude: Regional and Life-Cycle Perspectives." Yearbook of Physical Anthropology 41: 25-64.

Noback, Marlijn L., Katerina Harvati, and Fred Spoor. 2011. "Climate-Related Variation of the Human Nasal Cavity." American Journal of Physical Anthropology 145 (4): 599–614.

Peacock, A. J. 1998. "ABC of Oxygen: Oxygen at High Altitude." BMJ 317 (7,165): 1,063–1,066.

Quillen, Ellen E., Heather L. Norton, Esteban J. Parra, Frida Loza-Durazo, Khai C. Ang, Florin Mircea Illiescu, Laurel N. Pearson, Mark D. Shriver, Tina Lasisi, Omer Gokcumen, Izzy Starr, Yen-Lung Lin, Alicia R. Martin, and Nina G. Jablonksi. 2018. "Shades of complexity: New perspectives on the evolution and genetic architecture of human skin." American Journal of Physical Anthropology 1-23.

Ranciaro, Alessia, Michael C. Campbell, Jibril B. Hirbo, Wen-Ya Ko, Alain Froment, Paolo Anagnostou, Maritha J. Kotze, Muntaser Ibrahim, Thomas Nyambo, Sabah A. Omar, and Sarah A. Tishkoff. 2014. "Genetic Origins of Lactase Persistence and the Spread of Pastoralism in Africa." American Journal of Human Genetics 94 (4): 496-510.

Roby, Brianne Barnett, Marsha Finkelstein, Robert J. Tibesar, and James D. Sidman. 2012. "Prevalence of Positional Plagiocephaly in Teens Born after the 'Back to Sleep' Campaign." Otolaryngology–Head and Neck Surgery 146 (5): 823-828.

Shah, Mark B., Darren Braude, Cameron S. Crandall, Heemun Kwack, Lisa Rabinowitz, Thomas A. Cumbo, Buddha Basnyat, and Govin Bhasyall. 2006. "Changes in Metabolic and Hematologic Laboratory Values With Ascent to Altitude and the Development of Acute Mountain Sickness in Nepalese Pilgrims." Wilderness and Environmental Medicine 17 (3): 171-177.

Sherman, Paul W., and Jennifer Billing. 1999. "Darwinian Gastronomy: Why We Use Spices." BioScience 49 (6): 453-463.

Snoddy, Anne Marie E., Hallie R. Buckley, and Siân E. Halcrow. 2016. "More than Metabolic: Considering the Broader Paleoepidemiological Impact of Vitamin D Deficiency in Bioarchaeology." American Journal of Physical Anthropology

160 (2): 183–196.Sturm, Richard A., and David L. Duffy. 2012. "Human Pigmentation Genes Under Environmental Selection." Genome Biology 13 (248): 1–15.

Tishkoff, Sarah A., Floyd A. Reed, Alessia Ranciaro, Benjamin F. Voight, Courtney C. Babbitt, Jesse S. Silverman, Kweli Powell, Holly M. Mortensen, Jibril B. Hirbo, Maha Osman, Muntaser Ibrahim, Sabah A. Omar, Godfrey Lema, Thomas B. Nyambo, Jilur Ghori, Suzannah Bumpstead, Jonathan K. Pritchard, Gregory A. Wray, and Panos Deloukas. 2007. "Convergent adaptation of human lactase persistence in Africa and Europe." Nature Genetics 39 (1): 31–40.

Vukić, Maja, Antonio Neme, Sabine Seuter, Noora Saksa, Vanessa D. F. de Mello, Tarji Nurmi, Matti Uusitupa, Tomi-Pekka Tuomainen, Jyrki K. Virtanen, and Carsten Carlberg. 2015. "Relevance of Vitamin D Receptor Target Genes for Monitoring the Vitamin D Responsiveness of Primary Human Cells." PLoS One, San Francisco 10 (4): 1–15.

World Health Organization. 2017. "Key points: World malaria report 2017." World Health Organization website, November 29. http://www.who.int/malaria/media/world-malaria-report-2017/en/.

Figure Attributions

Figure 14.1 Deep water diver by Leslie E. Fitzpatrick is under a CC BY-NC 4.0 License.

Figure 14.2 Mechanisms of heat transfer original to Explorations: An Open Invitation to Biological Anthropology by Mary Nelson is under a CC BY-NC 4.0 License.

Figure 14.3 Body heat maintenance in cold and warm original to Explorations: An Open Invitation to Biological Anthropology by Mary Nelson is under a CC BY-NC 4.0 License.

Figure 14.4 Vasoconstriction and vasodilation original to Explorations: An Open Invitation to Biological Anthropology by Mary Nelson is under a CC BY-NC 4.0 License.

Figure 14.5 Atmospheric pressure original to Explorations: An Open Invitation to Biological Anthropology by Mary Nelson is under a CC BY-NC 4.0 License.

Figure 14.6 Premature infant by Leslie E. Fitzpatrick is under a CC BY-NC 4.0 License.

Figure 14.7 Quechua Woman in Peru by Alexander Fiebrandt (Alecconnell at de.wikipedia) is under a CC BY-SA 2.0 DE License.

Figure 14.8 Плагиоцефалия (Plagiocephaly) by Medical advises at http://larece.ru/?p=27115 is under a CC BY-SA 3.0 License.

Figure 14.9 World Map of HVR adaptation in high altitude populations by Chkuu is used under a CC BY-SA 4.0 License.

Figure 14.10 Skin Pigmentation (Anatomy and Physiology, Figure 5.8) by OpenStax is used under a CC BY 4.0 License.

Figure 14.11 Penetration of skin layers by UVA and UVB rays a derivative work original to Explorations: An Open Invitation to Biological Anthropology by Katie Nelson is under a CC BY-NC 4.0 License. [Includes Skin Anatomy by NIH National Cancer Institute, public domain].

Figure 14.12 Evolutionary basis for human skin color variation original to Explorations: An Open Invitation to Biological Anthropology by Katie Nelson is under a CC BY-NC 4.0 License.

Figure 14.13 Rachitis, stages of development for children (slide numbers 7181 and 7182; photo number: M0003399) by Wellcome Collection is under a CC BY 4.0 license.

Figure 14.14 Eskimo Family NGM-v31-p564 by George R. King [original from National Geographic Magazine, Volume 31 (1917)] is in the public domain.

Figure 14.15a COLLECTIE TROPENMUSEUM Fulani vrouwen en kinderen putten water uit de waterput van Santaba TMnr 20010199 (Fulani women and children draw water from the Santaba water well) by Tropenmuseum, part of the National Museum of World Cultures is used under a CC BY-SA 3.0 License.

Figure 14.15b Greenland 1999 (01) by vadeve has been designated to the public domain (CC0).

Figure 14.16a Bergmann's Rule original to Explorations: An Open Invitation to Biological Anthropology by Mary Nelson is under a CC BY-NC 4.0 License.

Figure 14.16b Allen's Rule original to Explorations: An Open Invitation to Biological Anthropology by Mary Nelson is under a CC BY-NC 4.0 License.

Figure 14.17 Human nasal morphological variation original to Explorations: An Open Invitation to Biological Anthropology by Mary Nelson is under a CC BY-NC 4.0 License.

Figure 14.18 Malaria parasite life cycle-NIAID by NIH National Institute of Allergy and Infectious Diseases is in the public domain.

Figure 14.19 Sickle cell 01 by The National Heart, Lung, and Blood Institute (NHLBI) is in the public domain.

Figure 14.20 Red Blood Cell abnormalities by Armando Moreno Vranich has been designated to the public domain (CC0).

Figure 14.21 Sickle cell disease a derivative work original to Explorations: An Open Invitation to Biological Anthropology by Katie Nelson is under a CC BY-NC 4.0 License. [Includes two illustrations by Mary Nelson; Sickle cell anemia by Pkleong at English Wikibooks, public domain (CC0), modified (labels removed background erased).]

Figure 14.22 Lactose tolerance in the Old World by Joe Roe is used under a CC BY 4.0 License.

Chapter 15: Bioarchaeology and Forensic Anthropology

Ashley Kendell, Ph.D., D-ABMDI, California State University, Chico

Alex Perrone, M.A., California State University, Chico

Colleen Milligan, Ph.D., California State University, Chico

Learning Objectives

- Define and differentiate bioarchaeology and forensic anthropology as subfields of biological anthropology.
- Describe the seven steps carried out during skeletal analysis.
- Outline the four major components of the biological profile.
- Contrast the four categories of trauma.
- Explain how to identify the different taphonomic agents that alter bone.
- Discuss ethical considerations for both bioarchaeology and forensic anthropology.

Bioarchaeology and forensic anthropology are both subfields of biological anthropology. While the goals of each subfield are different, each relies on skeletal analysis to gain information about humans, both past and present. This chapter will provide a general overview of the analysis of human skeletal remains, as it applies to both bioarchaeology and forensic anthropology.

BIOARCHAEOLOGY

In 2010 Hurricane Earl reached the Caribbean Island of Antigua. The storm brought strong winds and heavy rainfall to the island. After the storm calmed, accumulated water drained back out to the ocean, carving a channel through one of the beaches at English Harbor as it went. Out of the newly created channel, human bones were exposed. Although they had been buried for many years, the remains belonged to 18th-century British sailors who had died from Yellow Fever while stationed in the Caribbean. While no headstones were present to divulge information about each person buried on the beach, a large amount of evidence was still accessible through the analysis of each skeleton as well as the information garnered from the **burial context**. To gather more information about each of the individuals buried on the beach, the bones were examined, and a detailed analysis was carried out of the positions of the skeletons, the burial depth, whether clothing material such as buttons were found with each set of remains, and whether it appeared that the sailors were buried in coffins. In addition, the sex, age, and other individualizing characteristics were estimated through careful analysis of the bones themselves.

The remains uncovered by Hurricane Earl in Antigua became part of a bioarchaeological study. **Bioarchaeology** is the study of human remains excavated from archaeological sites. Bioarchaeologists glean information about each set of human remains by examining the skeleton and by considering the archaeological context in which the skeleton was recovered. Through this type of detailed skeletal analysis, bioarchaeologists obtain information about each individual skeleton, which can include age, sex, height, ancestry, disease, diet, and behavior. For a broader understanding of past peoples, bioarchaeologists look at skeletal trends on a population level. They gather data on groups of individuals to reveal both biological and cultural patterns within and between samples. In this way, bioarchaeological samples can contribute to our knowledge of the demographics and lifeways of past populations.

In the example of the buried remains on the beach in Antigua, Dr. Matthew Brown, a bioarchaeologist, examined the historic remains individually and then was able to combine the information from each individual to discern patterns within the entire sample of burials. For example, all of the skeletons belonged to males, not surprising considering that the beach was a burial site for British sailors. Dr. Brown also discovered that not all of the sailors were buried in the same manner. During the excavation, degraded wood fragments and rusted nails were uncovered in some of the burials. The wood and metal materials were consistent with those used to make coffins, leading him to suspect some of the sailors were buried in coffins. In other instances, no wood or nails were found but, instead, the bodies were positioned with their arms and legs tucked in close to the torso, with their hands positioned tightly together in the area of the pelvis. This was likely indicative of a hammock burial. A hammock burial would have served as a relatively easy way to inter a sailor who died in his hammock on board the ship. The hammock could be removed from the ship, carried onto the beach, and placed in a grave with minimal effort.

Bioarchaeologists like Dr. Brown help us understand information about past populations and the degree of social complexity found within each society. This information can help determine what types of food were consumed and how consumption patterns changed over time in one area. Or it may help us ascertain the scale of interpersonal violence that occurred during culture contact. Other research questions that bioarchaeology addresses revolve around physiological stress from disease or from malnutrition, daily activity, injuries, or growth patterns of individuals.

SPECIAL TOPIC: BIOARCHAEOLOGY IN ACTION

In this short clip, an excerpt from the BBC documentary Nelson's Caribbean Hell-hole: An Eighteenth-Century Navy Graveyard Uncovered (2013), Dr. Brown discusses the excavation of a skeleton of a British sailor: https://www.bbc.co.uk/programmes/p0187q6r.

FORENSIC ANTHROPOLOGY

Much like bioarchaeologist Dr. Brown in Antigua examined the skeletons of the British sailors, forensic anthropologists analyze the human skeleton to gain information regarding an individual who is deceased. However, one of the major differences between the two subfields of biological anthropology is that in **forensic anthropology** researchers specifically conduct their analysis on recently deceased individuals (typically within the last 50 years) and within the context of the law—in other words, as part of a criminal investigation. This means that forensic anthropologists can assist law enforcement agencies in several different ways, including aiding in the identification of human remains whether they are complete, fragmentary, burned, scattered, or decomposed. Additionally, forensic anthropologists can help determine what happened to the deceased at or around the time of death as well as what processes acted on the body after death (for example, whether the remains were scattered by animals, whether they were buried in the ground, or whether they remained on the surface as the soft tissue decomposed).

Many times, because of their expertise in identifying human skeletal remains, forensic anthropologists are called to help with outdoor search-and-recovery efforts, such as locating remains scattered across the surface or carefully excavating and documenting buried remains. In other cases, forensic anthropologists recover remains after natural disasters or accidents, such as fire scenes, and can help identify whether each bone belongs to a human or an animal. Forensic anthropology spans a wide scope of contexts involving the law, including incidences of mass disasters, genocide, and war crimes.

A point that can be somewhat confusing for students is that although the term *forensic* is included in this subfield of biological anthropology, there are many forensic techniques that are not included in the subfield. Almost exclusively, forensic anthropology deals with skeletal analysis. While this can include the comparison of antemortem (before death) and postmortem (after death) radiographs to identify whether remains belong to a specific person, or using photographic superimposition of the cranium, it does not include analyses beyond the skeleton. For example, blood spatter analysis, DNA analysis, fingerprints, and material evidence collection do not fall under the scope of forensic anthropology.

So, what can forensic anthropologists glean from bones alone? Forensic anthropologists can address a number of questions about a human individual based on their skeletal remains. Some of those questions include: How old was the person? Was the person biologically male or female? How tall was the person? What happened to the person at or around their time of death? Were they sick? The information from the skeletal analysis can then be matched with missing persons records, medical records, or dental records, aiding law enforcement agencies with identifications and investigations.

INITIAL SKELETAL ANALYSIS

While bioarchaeology and forensic anthropology have different goals and purposes, they both rely on skeletal analysis to reveal information about the deceased. Whether they aim to determine more information regarding an individual deceased for thousands of years (bioarchaeologists) or one who died within the last year (forensic anthropologists), they carry out the same basic steps as part of their analysis. They begin with seven steps or questions:

- Is it bone?
- Is it human?
- Is it modern or archeological?
- How many individuals are present or what is the minimum number of individuals (MNI)?
- Who is it?
- Is there evidence of trauma before or around the time of death?
- What happened to the remains after death?

Is It Bone?

One of the most important steps in any skeletal analysis starts with determining whether or not material suspected to be bone is in fact bone. Though it goes without saying that a forensic anthropologist or bioarchaeologist would only carry out analysis on bone, this step is not always straightforward. Whole bones are relatively easy to identify, determining whether or not something is bone becomes more challenging once it becomes fragmentary. For example, at high heat such as that seen on fire scenes, bone can break into pieces. During a house fire with fatalities, firefighters watered down the burning home. After the fire was extinguished, the sheetrock (used to construct the walls of the home) was drenched and crumbled. The crumbled sheetrock was similar in color and form to burned, fragmented bone, therefore mistakable for human remains (Figure 15.1). Forensic anthropologists on scene were able to separate the bones from the construction material, helping to confirm the presence of bone and hence the presence of individual victims of the fire. In this case, forensic anthropologists were able to recognize the anatomical and layered structure of bone and were able to distinguish it from the uniform and unlayered structure of sheetrock.

Figure 15.1 Example of burned sheetrock. Burned sheetrock used as building material appears similar to human bone but can be differentiated by the fact that it is the same density throughout.

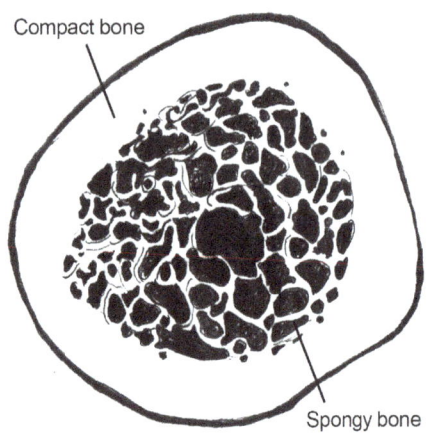

Figure 15.2 caption: Cross section of human long bone with compact and spongy bone layers visible.

As demonstrated by the example above, both the macrostructure (visible with the naked eye) and microstructure (visible with a microscope) of bone are helpful in bone identification. Bones are organs in the body made up of connective tissue. The connective tissue is hardened by a mineral deposition, which is why bone is rigid in comparison to other connective tissues such as cartilage (Tersigni-Tarrant and Langley 2017, 82–83; White and Folkens 2005, 31). In a living body, the mineralized tissue does not make up the only component of bone–there is also blood, bone marrow, cartilage, and other types of tissues. However, in dry bone, two distinct layers of the bone are the most helpful for identification. The outer layer is made up of densely arranged osseous (bone) tissue called **compact (cortical) bone**. The inner layer is comprised of much more loosely organized, porous bone tissue whose appearance resembles that of a sponge, hence the name **spongy (trabecular) bone**. Knowing that most bone contains both layers helps with the macroscopic identification of bone (Figures 15.2, 15.3). For example, a piece of coconut shell might look a lot like a fragment of a human skull bone. However, closer inspection will demonstrate that coconut shell only has one very dense layer, while bone has both the compact and spongy layers.

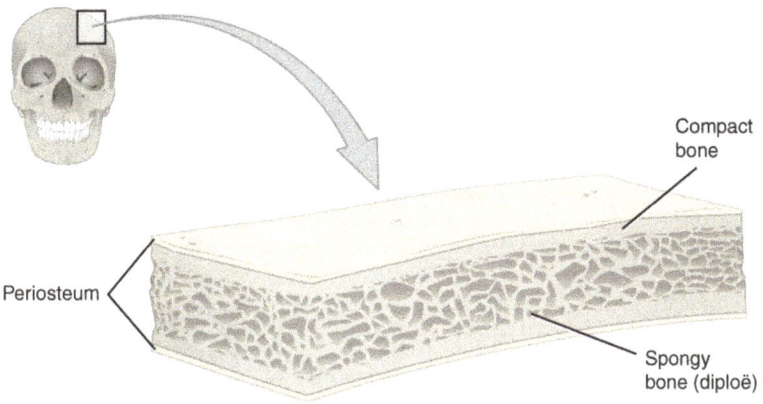

Figure 15.3 Cross-section of human cranial bone.

Cranial anatomy is slightly different as compared to that of a long bone in cross section. The compact (cortical) bone layers sandwich the spongy (trabecular) bone. One layer of compact bone forms the very outer surface of the skull and the other lines the internal surface of the skull.

The microscopic identification of bone relies on knowledge of **osteons**, or bone cells (Figure 15.4). Under magnification, bone cells are visible in the outer, compact layer of bone. The bone cells are arranged in a concentric pattern around blood vessels for blood supply. The specific shape of the cells can help differentiate, for example, a small piece of PVC (white plastic) pipe from a human bone fragment (Figure 15.5).

Figure 15.4 Bone microstructure (osteons).

Figure 15.5 Fragments of plastic PVC pipe, such as those seen in this photo, may be mistaken for human bone.

Is It Human?

Once it can be determined that an object is bone, the next logical step is to identify whether the bone belongs to a human or an animal. Bioarchaeologists must make this determination each time they come across remains at an archaeological site. Forensic anthropologists are faced with this question in everyday practice because human versus nonhuman bone identification is one of the most frequent requests they receive from law enforcement agencies.

There are many different ways to distinguish human versus nonhuman bone. The morphology (the shape/form) of human bone is a good place for students to start. Identifying the 206 bones in the adult human skeleton and each bone's distinguishing features (muscle attachment sites, openings and grooves for nerves and blood vessels, etc.) is fundamental to skeletal analysis.

Nevertheless, there are many animal bones and human bones that look similar. For example, the declawed skeleton of a bear paw looks a lot like a human hand, pig molars appear similar to human molars, and some smaller animal bones might be mistaken for those of an infant. To add to the confusion, fragmentary bone may be even more difficult to identify as human or nonhuman. However, several major differences between human and nonhuman vertebrate bone help distinguish the two.

Bioarchaeologists and forensic anthropologists pay special attention to the density of the outer, compact layer of bone in both the cranium and in the long bones. Human cranial bone has three distinctive layers. The spongy bone is sandwiched between the outer (ectocranial) and inner (endocranial) compact layers. In most other mammals, the distinction between the spongy and compact layers is not always so definite. Secondly, the compact layer in nonhuman mammal long bones can be much thicker than observed in human bone. Due to the increased density of the compact layer, nonhuman bone tends to be heavier than human bone (Figure 15.6).

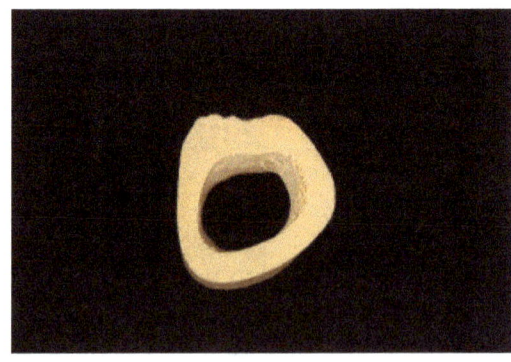

Figure 15.6 The compact layer of this animal bone is very thick with almost no spongy bone visible.

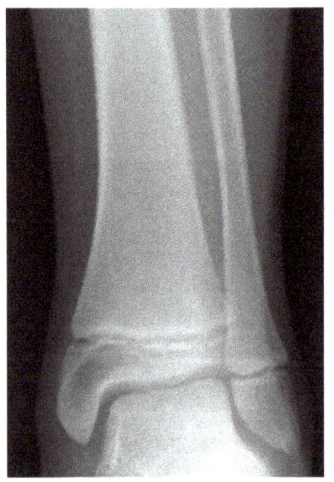

Figure 15.7 In this x-ray of a subadult's ankle with the epiphyses of the tibia and fibula visible. The gap between the shaft of the bone and the end of the bone (epiphysis) is the location of the growth plate. Therefore, the growth plate gap is what separates the shafts from the epiphyses in the image.

The size of a bone helps determine whether it belongs to a human. Adult human bones are larger than subadult or infant bones. However, another major difference between human adult bones and those of a young individual or infant human can be attributed to development and growth of the **epiphyses** (ends of the bone). The epiphyses of human subadult bones are not fused to the shaft (Figure 15.7). Therefore, if a bone is small and it is suspected to belong to a human subadult or infant, the epiphyses would not be fused. Many small animal bones appear very similar in form compared to adult human bone, but they are much too small to belong to an adult human. Yet they can be eliminated as subadult or infant bones if the epiphyses are fused to the shaft.

Is It Modern or Archaeological?

As discussed earlier, bioarchaeologists are concerned with human remains from archaeological contexts, while forensic anthropologists work with modern cases that fall within the scope of law enforcement investigations. Accordingly, it is important to determine whether discovered human remains are archaeological or forensic in nature.

In many instances, bioarchaeologists work at known archaeological sites. Nevertheless, every bioarchaeologist and forensic anthropologist should begin their analysis by reviewing the context in which the remains were discovered. This will help them understand a great deal about the remains, including determining whether they are bioarchaeological or forensic in nature as well as considering legal and ethical issues associated with the collection, analysis, and storage of human remains (see "Ethics and Human Rights" section of this chapter for more information).

The "context" refers to the relationship the remains have to the immediate area in which they were found. The context includes the specific place where the remains were found, the soil or other organic matter immediately surrounding the remains, and any other objects or artifacts in close proximity to the body. For example, imagine that a set of remains has been located during a house renovation. The remains are discovered below the foundation. Do the remains belong to a murder victim? Or was the house built on top of an ancient burial ground? Observing information from the surroundings can help determine whether the remains are archaeological or modern. How long ago was the foundation of the house erected? Are there artifacts in close proximity to the body, such as clothing or stone tools? These are questions about the surroundings that will help determine the relative age of the remains.

Clues directly from the skeleton may also indicate whether the remains are archaeological or modern. For example, tooth fillings can suggest that the individual was alive recently (Figure 15.8). In fact, filling material has changed over the decades, and the specific type of material used to fix a cavity can be matched with specific time periods. Gold was used in dental work in the past, but more recently composite (a mixture of plastic and fine glass) fillings have become more common.

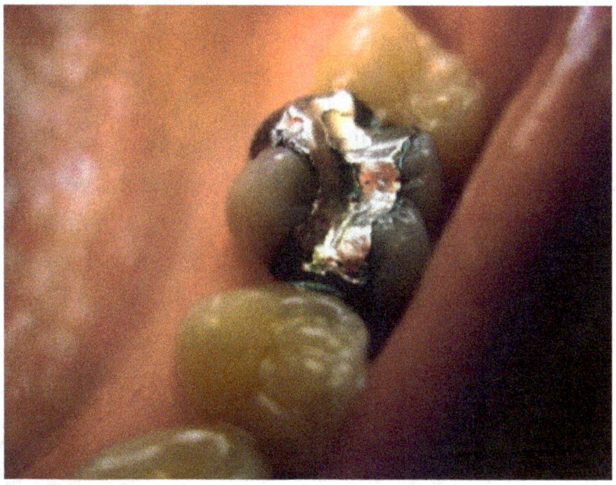

How Many Individuals Are Present?

Figure 15.8 A human tooth with a filling.

What Is MNI?

Another assessment that an anthropologist can perform is the calculation of the number of individuals in a mixed burial assemblage. Because not all burials consist of a single individual, it is important to be able to estimate the number of individuals in both an archaeological and forensic context. Quantification of the number of individuals in a **burial assemblage** can be done through the application of a number of methods, including the following: the Minimum Number of Individuals (MNI), the Most Likely Number of Individuals (MLNI), and the Lincoln Index (LI). The most commonly used method in physical anthropology, and the focus of this section, is determination of the MNI.

The MNI presents "the minimum estimate for the number of individuals that contributed to the sample" (Adams and Konigsberg 2008, 243). Many methods of calculating MNI were originally developed within the field of zooarchaeology for use on calculating the number of individuals in faunal or animal assemblages (Adams and Konigsberg 2008, 241). What MNI calculations provide is a lowest possible count for the total number of individuals contributing to a skeletal assemblage. Traditional methods of calculating MNI include separating a skeletal assemblage into categories according to the individual bone and the side the bone comes from and then taking the highest count per category and assigning that as the minimum number.

Before beginning MNI calculations, however, it is important to make sure that all elements in the assemblage belong to the same species. If an assemblage contains both human and faunal (animal) elements, the assemblage should be divided into two separate groups. In a forensic context, it is likely that an MNI calculation is only necessary for the human skeletal remains. However, in an archaeological assemblage, it may be useful to calculate MNI for both the human and faunal remains. Faunal remains can contribute to a greater understanding of lifeways in past populations. For example, the age and sex profile of the animals at a site might be indicative of domestication. Large numbers of young male cattle bones and adult female cattle bones may indicate that the males were killed young while females were kept into adulthood. This pattern is consistent with cattle selection for captivity: adult males can be dangerous and aggressive, so they are killed young. On the other hand, females produce milk and are kept into adulthood.

Why Calculate MNI?

The determination of MNI is critical in both bioarchaeological and forensic contexts, as it allows anthropologists to establish an approximate number of deceased individuals within a burial assemblage (Adams and Konigsberg 2008). However, it must be recognized that unless a skeletal assemblage has a near-100% recovery rate for at least one type of skeletal element, the MNI will not provide an accurate estimate for the original number of individuals contributing to the burial assemblage (Adams and Konigsberg 2008, 243).

Determination of MNI is most applicable in cases of mass graves or **commingled burials** (Figure 15.9). The term *commingled* is applied to any burial assemblage in which individual skeletons are not separated into separate burials. Commingled assemblages occur in cases of familial burials (e.g., multiple family members buried in a single grave plot) and mass graves, possibly the result of genocide. However, it is important to remember that in any forensic context, MNI should be referenced and an MNI of one should be substantiated by the fact that there was no repetition of elements associated with the case.

Figure 15.9 Commingled human remains.

CONSTRUCTING THE BIOLOGICAL PROFILE

Who Is It?

"Who is it?" is one of the first questions that law enforcement officers ask when they are faced with a set of skeletal remains. Likewise, when human bones are found as part of archaeological fieldwork, the remains present the opportunity to learn more about the individuals who lived in the past. In order to answer this question, "who is it?", bioarchaeologists and forensic anthropologists construct a biological profile (White and Folkens 2005, 405). A **biological profile** is an individual's identifying characteristics, or biological information, which include the following: sex, age, stature, ancestry, skeletal variation, trauma, and pathology.

Although the biological profile is constructed by forensic anthropologists and bioarchaeologists using the same methodology, the estimations of these skeletal characteristics, or attributes, form the framework for different kinds of questions. Forensic anthropologists typically construct a biological profile to help positively identify a deceased person. In some cases, bioarchaeologists match information about a known individual in the past to remains found in an archaeological context, but they generally construct a biological profile to learn more about people's everyday lives. For example, bioarchaeologists may focus on indicators of pathological conditions in bone to assess the level of stress or disease that affected a particular individual or population. Likewise, bioarchaeologists might assess ancestry to understand more about migration patterns, population history, or relatedness among groups. For an additional example, see the search for, excavation, and analysis of King Richard III's remains in the box below.

SPECIAL TOPIC: THE SEARCH FOR THE LOST GRAVE OF KING RICHARD III

For an interesting overview of the search for the grave of the English King Richard III, as well as the discovery of the skeletal remains and the subsequent osteological analysis to help identify the remains as King Richard III's, see *The Discovery of Richard III* at: https://www.le.ac.uk/richardiii/.

The following section will lay out each component of the biological profile and briefly review standard methodology used for each.

Estimating Sex

Estimation of sex is often one of the first things considered when establishing a biological profile because several other parts, such as age and stature estimations, rely on an estimation of sex to make the calculations more accurate.

Estimations of sex look at differences in both morphological (form or structure) and metric (measured) traits in individuals. When assessing morphological traits, the skull and the pelvis are the most commonly used areas of the skeleton for estimations. These differences are related to sexual dimorphism usually varying in the amount of robusticity seen between males and females. **Robusticity** deals with strength and size; it is frequently used as a term to describe a large size or thickness. In general, males will show a greater degree of robusticity than females. For example, the length and width of the mastoid process, a bony projection located behind the opening for the ear, is typically larger in males. The mastoid process is an attachment point for muscles of the neck, and this bony projection tends to be wider and longer in males. In general, cranial features tend to be more robust in males (Figure 15.10).

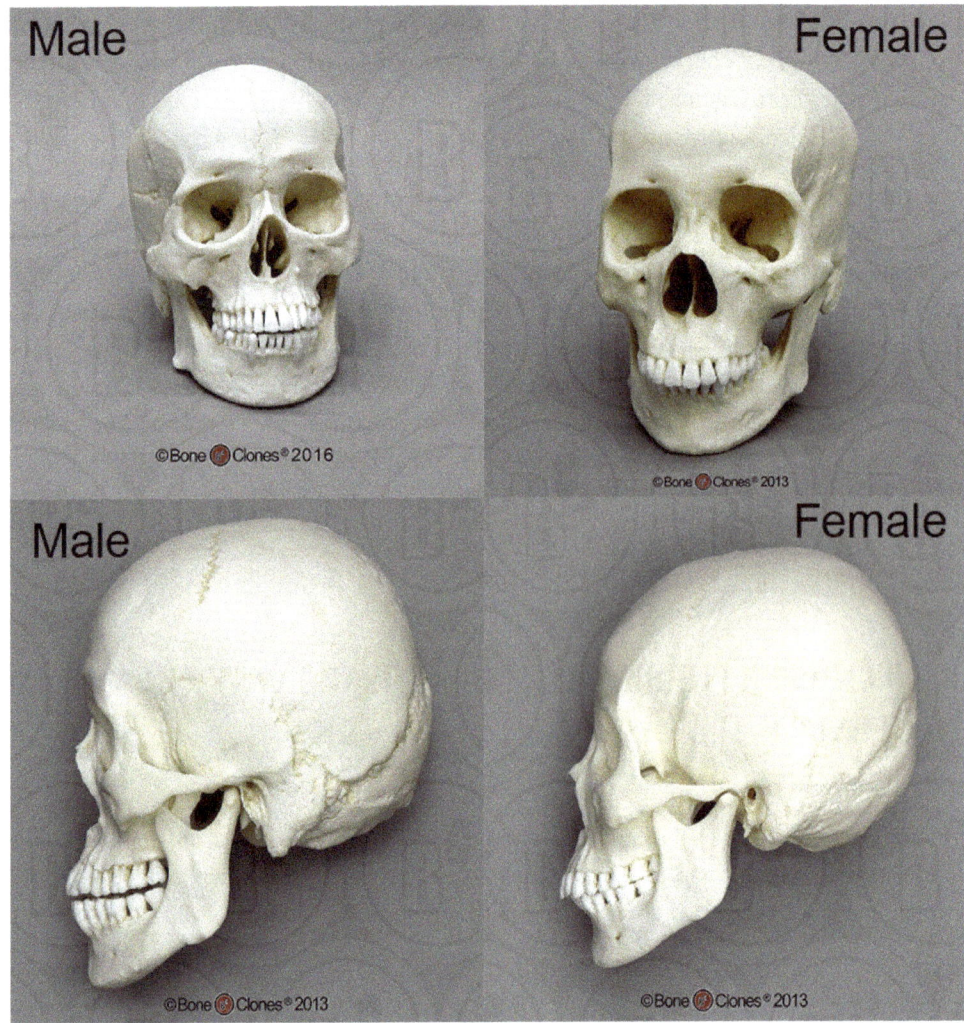

Figure 15.10 Anterior and lateral view of a male and female cranium.

When considering the pelvis, the features associated with the ability to give birth help distinguish females from males. During puberty, estrogen causes a widening of the female pelvis to allow for the passage of a baby. Several studies have identified specific features or bony landmarks associated with the widening of the hips, and this section will discuss one such method. The Phenice Method (Phenice 1969) is traditionally the most common reference used to assess morphological characteristics associated with sex. The Phenice Method specifically looks at the presence or absence of (1) a ventral arc, (2) the presence or absence of a sub-pubic concavity, and (3) the width of the medial aspect of the ischiopubic ramus (Figure 15.11). When present, the ventral arc, a ridge of bone located on the ventral surface of the pubic bone, is indicative of female remains. Likewise the presence of a sub-pubic concavity and a narrow medial aspect of the ischiopubic ramus is associated with a female sex estimation. Assessments of these features, as well as those of the skull (when both the pelvis and skull are present), are combined for an overall estimation of sex.

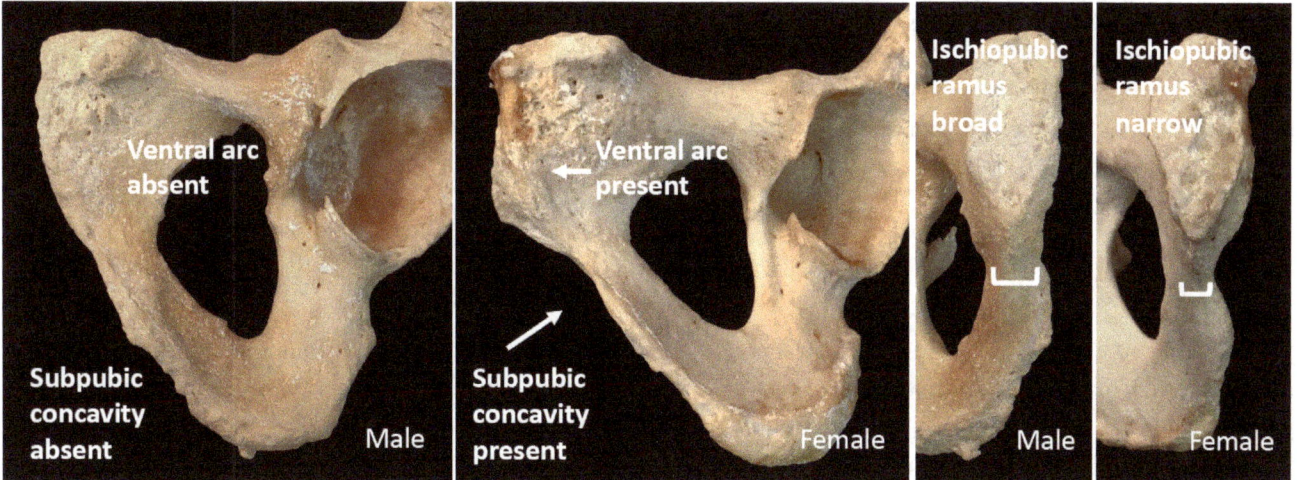

Figure 15.11 Features associated with the Phenice Method.

Metric analyses are also used in the estimation of sex. Measurements taken from every region of the body can contribute to estimating sex through statistical approaches that assign a predictive value of sex. These approaches can include multiple measurements from several skeletal elements in what is called multivariate (multiple variables) statistics. Other approaches consider a single measurement, such as the diameter of the head of the femur, of a specific element in a univariate (single variable) analysis (Berg 2017, 152–156).

It is important to note that, although forensic anthropologists and bioarchaeologists usually begin assessment of biological profile with sex, there is one major instance in which this is not appropriate. The case of two individuals found near Willits, California, on July 8, 1979, is one example that demonstrates the effect age has on the estimation of sex. The identities of the two individuals found in Willits were unknown; therefore, law enforcement sent them to a lab for identification. A skeletal analysis determined that the remains represented one adolescent male and one adolescent female, both younger than 18 years of age. This information did not match with any known missing children at the time.

In 2015, the cold case was reanalyzed, and DNA samples were extracted. The results indicated that the remains were actually those of two girls who went missing in 1978. The girls were 15 years old and 14 years old at the time of death. It is clear that the 1979 results were incorrect, but this mistake also provides the opportunity to discuss the limitations of assessing sex from a subadult skeleton.

Assessing sex from the human skeleton is based on biological and genetic traits associated with females and males. These traits are linked to differences in sexual dimorphism and reproductive characteristics between females and males. The link to reproductive characteristics means that most indicators of biological sex do not fully manifest in prepubescent individuals, making estimations of sex unreliable in younger individuals (SWGANTH 2010b). This was the case in the example of the 14-year-old girl. When examined in 1979, her remains were misidentified as male because she had not yet fully developed female pelvic traits.

Sex vs. Gender

Biological sex is a different concept than **gender**. While biological anthropologists can estimate sex from the skeleton, estimating an individual's gender would require a greater context as gender is culturally defined rather than biologically defined. Take for example an individual who identifies as transgender. This is an individual who has a gender identity that is different from their biological sex. The gender identity of any individual depends on factors related to self-identification, situation, or context, and cultural factors. While in the U.S. we have historically thought of sex and gender as binary concepts (male or female), many cultures throughout the world recognize several possible gender identities. In this sense, gender is seen as a continuous or fluid variable rather than a fixed one.

Estimating Ancestry

Ancestry is another component of the biological profile. As noted previously, ancestry can aid law enforcement in their identification of missing persons and can help bioarchaeologists understand many different things about individuals and populations living in the past, such as migration patterns and population distance. Biological ancestry today is often incorrectly labeled as race and generally refers to the individual's **phenotype** (outward appearance). Within the field of anthropology, ancestry estimation has a contentious history, and early attempts at racial classification were largely based on the erroneous assumption that an individual's phenotype was correlated with their innate intelligence and abilities (see Chapter 13 for a more in-depth discussion of the history of the race concept). **Biological ancestry** refers to the underlying genetic differences between modern populations. In any other organism/living thing, groups divided according to the biological race concept would be defined as a separate species. The major issue with applying the biological race concept to humans is that there are not enough differences between any two populations to separate on a genetic basis. In other words, *biological races do not exist in human populations*. However, the concept of race has been perpetuated and upheld by sociocultural constructs of race (see Chapter 13).

The conundrum for forensic anthropologists is the fact that while races do not exist on a biological level, we still recognize and categorize others based on their phenotype. Clearly, our phenotype is an important factor in not only how we are viewed by others but also how we identify ourselves. Also, when a person is reported missing, the information that is collected by law enforcement and sometimes entered into a missing person's database includes age, biological sex, stature, and "race." Therefore, the more information a forensic anthropologist can provide regarding the individual's physical characteristics, the more he or she can help to narrow the search. As an exercise, create a list of all of the women you know who are between the ages of 18 and 24 and approximately 5′ 4″ to 5′ 9″ tall. You probably have several dozen people on the list. Now, consider how many females you know who are between the ages of 18 and 24, approximately 5′ 4″ to 5′ 9″ tall, and are Vietnamese. Your list is going to be significantly shorter. That's how missing persons searches go as well. The more information you can provide regarding a decedent's phenotype, the fewer possible matches law enforcement are left to investigate. This is how ancestry has become an indispensable part of the biological profile.

In an effort to combat the erroneous assumptions tied to the race concept, forensic anthropologists have attempted to reframe this component of the biological profile. The term *race* is no longer used in casework and teaching. Instead, employing the word *ancestry* is a more appropriate way to describe an individual's phenotype, because we are largely shaped by the environments surrounding our recent ancestral origins. In other words, our phenotype lends clues to the environment for which our ancestors were best adapted (for additional information, see Chapters 13 and 14).

Because human populations vary in their phenotype due to environmental forces, forensic anthropologists are able to use morphological traits to predict the ancestral origins of an unidentified individual. In general, anthropologists are able to divide humans into broad geographically discrete groups, including (but not limited to) the following: European, African, Asian, Native American, and Hispanic. Traditionally, ancestry assessment was accomplished through a visual inspection of morphological variants of the skull (morphoscopics), primarily focused on elements of the facial skeleton, including the nose, eyes, and cheek bones (Figure 15.12). However, in an effort to reduce subjectivity, nonmetric cranial traits are now assessed within a statistical framework to help anthropologists better interpret their distribution among living populations (Hefner and Linde 2018). Based on the observable traits, a macromorphoscopic analysis will allow the practitioner to create a statistically validated prediction of geographic origin. In essence, forensic anthropologists are using human variation in the estimation of geographic origin, by referencing documented frequencies of nonmetric skeletal indicators, or macromorphoscopic traits.

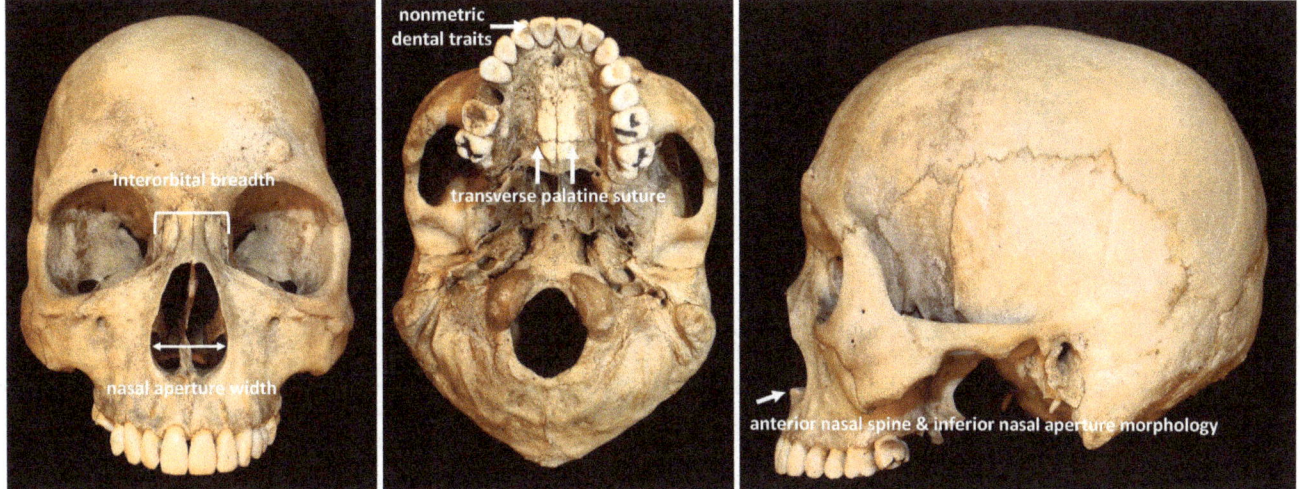

Figure 15.12 Skeletal traits commonly used in a morphological assessment of ancestry.

Finally, ancestry can also be determined through metric analyses. The computer program Fordisc is an anthropological tool used to estimate different components of the biological profile, including ancestry, sex, and stature. When using Fordisc, skeletal measurements are input into the computer software and the program employs multivariate statistical classification methods, including discriminant function analysis, to generate a statistically validated prediction for the geographic origin of unknown remains. Fordisc will also tell the analyst the likelihood of the prediction being correct, as well as how typical the metric data is for the assigned group.

Estimating Age

Estimating age from the skeleton relies on the measurement of two basic physiological processes: (1) growth and development and (2) degeneration (or aging). From fetal development on, our bones and teeth grow and change at a predictable rate. This provides for relatively accurate age estimates. After our bones and teeth cease to grow and develop, the bone begins to undergo structural changes, or degeneration, associated with aging. This does not happen at such predictable rates and, therefore, results in less accurate or larger age-range estimations.

During growth and development stages, two primary methods used for estimations of age of subadults (those under the age of 18) are **epiphyseal union** and **dental development**. **Epiphyseal union,** or **epiphyseal fusion**, refers to the appearance and closure of the epiphyseal plates between the primary centers of growth in a bone and the subsequent centers of growth (refer to Figure 15.7). Prior to complete union, the cartilaginous area between the primary and secondary centers of growth is also referred as the growth plates (Schaefer et al. 2009). Different areas of the skeleton have documented differences in the appearance and closure of epiphyses, making this a reliable method for aging subadult remains (SWGANTH 2013).

As an example of its utility in the identification process, epiphyseal development was used to identify two subadult victims of a fatal fire in Flint, Michigan, in February 2010. The remains represented two young girls, ages three and four. Due to the intensity of the fire, the subadult victims were differentiated from each other through the appearance of the patella, the kneecap. The patella is a bone that develops within the tendon of the quadriceps muscle at the knee joint. The patella begins to form around three to four years of age (Cunningham et al. 2016, 407–409). In the example above, radiographs of the knees showed the presence of a patella in the four-year-old girl and the absence of a clearly discernible patella in the three-year-old.

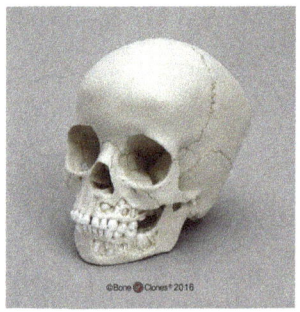

Figure 15.13 Dental development in a subadult.

Dental development begins during fetal stages of growth and continues until the complete formation and eruption of the adult third molars (if present). The first set of teeth to appear are called deciduous or baby teeth. Individuals develop a total of 20 deciduous teeth, including incisors, canines, and molars. These are generally replaced by adult dentition as an individual grows (Figure 15.13). A total of 32 teeth are represented in the adult dental arcade, including incisors, canines, premolars, and molars. When dental development is used for age estimations, researchers use both tooth-formation patterns and eruption schedules as determining evidence. For example, the crown of the tooth forms first followed by the formation of the tooth root. During development, an individual can exhibit a partially formed crown or a complete crown but a partially formed root. The teeth generally begin the eruption process once the crown of the tooth is complete. The developmental stages of dentition are one of the most reliable and consistent aging methods for subadults (Langley et al. 2017, 176–177).

Degenerative changes in the skeleton typically begin after 18 years of age, with more prominent changes developing after an individual reaches middle adulthood (commonly defined as after 35 years of age in osteology). These changes are most easily seen around joint surfaces of the pelvis, the cranial vault, and the ribs. In this chapter, we focus on the pubic symphysis surfaces of the pelvis and the sternal ends of the ribs, which show metamorphic changes from young adulthood to older adulthood. The **pubic symphysis** is a joint that unites the left and right halves of the pelvis. The surface of the pubic symphysis changes during adulthood, beginning as a surface with pronounced ridges (called billowing) and flattening with a more distinct rim to the pubic symphysis as an individual ages. As with all metamorphic age changes, older adults tend to develop lipping around the joint surfaces as well as a breakdown of the joint surfaces. The most commonly used method for aging adult skeletons from the pubic symphysis is the Suchey-Brooks method (Brooks and Suchey 1990; Katz and Suchey 1986). This method divides the changes seen with the pubic symphysis into six phases based on macroscopic age-related changes to the surface. Figure 15.14 provides a visual of the degenerative changes that typically occur on the pubic symphysis.

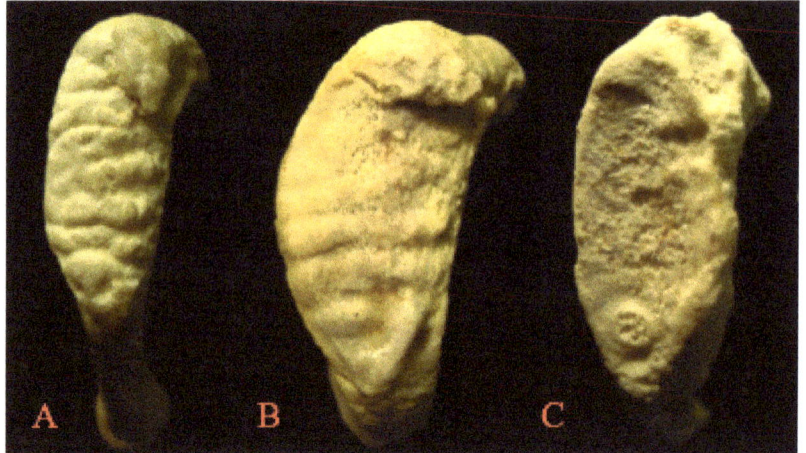

Figure 15.14 Examples of degenerative changes to the pubic symphysis: (A) young adult; (B) middle adult; (C) old adult.

The sternal end of the ribs, the **anterior** end of the rib that connects via cartilage to the sternum, is also used in age estimations of adults. This method, first developed by M. Y. İşcan and colleagues, looks at both the change in shape of the sternal end but also the quality of the bone (İşcan et al. 1984; İşcan et al. 1985). The sternal end first develops a billowing appearance in young adulthood. The bone typically develops a wider and deeper cupped end as an individual ages. Older adults tend to exhibit bony extensions of the sternal end rim as attaching cartilage ossifies. Figure 15.15 provides a visual of the degenerative changes that typically occur in sternal rib ends.

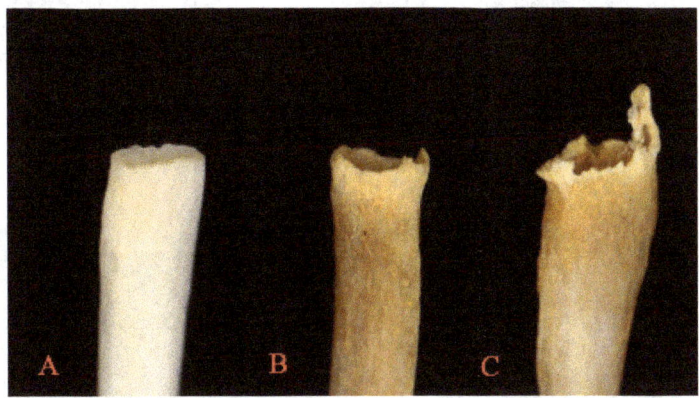

Figure 15.15 Examples of degenerative changes to the sternal rib end: (A) young adult; (B) middle adult; (C) old adult.

Estimating Stature

Stature, or height, is one of the most prominently recorded components of the biological profile. Our height is recorded from infancy through adulthood. Doctor's appointments, driver's license applications, and sports rosters all typically involve a measure of stature for an individual. As such, it is also a component of the biological profile nearly every individual will have on record. Bioarchaeologists and forensic anthropologists use stature estimation methods to provide a range within which an individual's biological height would fall. **Biological height** is a person's true anatomical height. However, the range created through these estimations is often compared to **reported stature**, which is typically self-reported and based on an approximation of an individual's true height (Ousley 1995).

In June 2015, two men were shot and killed in Granite Bay, California, in a double homicide. Investigators were able to locate surveillance camera footage from a gas station where the two victims were spotted in a car with another individual believed to be the perpetrator in the case. The suspect, sitting behind the victims in the car, hung his right arm out of the window as the car drove away. The search for the perpetrator was eventually narrowed down to two suspects. One suspect was 5′ 8″ while the other suspect was 6′ 4″, representing almost a foot difference in height between the two. Forensic anthropologists were given the dimensions of the car (for proportionality of the arm) and were asked to calculate the stature of the suspect in the car from measurements of the suspect's forearm hanging from the window. Approximate lengths of the bones of the forearm were established from the video footage and used to create a predicted stature range. Stature estimations from skeletal remains typically look at the correlation between the measurements of any individual bone and the overall measurement of body height. In the case above, the length of the right forearm pointed to the taller of the two suspects who was subsequently arrested for the homicide.

Certain bones, such as the long bones of the leg, contribute more to our overall height than others and can be used with mathematical equations known as regression equations. **Regression methods** examine the relationship between variables such as height and bone length and use the correlation between the variables to create a prediction interval (or range) for estimated stature. This method for calculating stature is the most commonly used method (SWGANTH 2012). Figure 15.16 shows the measurement of the bicondylar length of the femur for stature estimations.

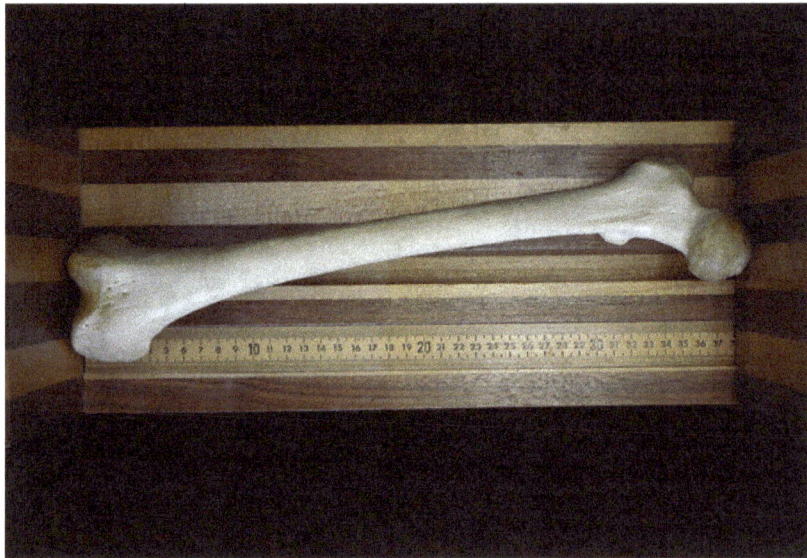

Figure 15.16 Image of measurement of the bicondylar length of the femur, often used in the estimation of living stature.

Identification Using Individualizing Characteristics

One of the most frequently requested analyses within the forensic anthropology laboratory is assistance with the identification of unidentified remains. While all components of a biological profile, as discussed above, can assist law enforcement officers and medical examiners to narrow down the list of potential identifications, a biological profile will not lead to a **positive identification**. The term *positive identification* refers to a scientifically validated method of identifying previously unidentified remains. Presumptive identifications, however, are not scientifically validated; rather, they are based on circumstances or scene context. For example, if a decedent is found in a locked home with no evidence of forced entry but the body is no longer visually identifiable, it may be presumed that the remains belong to the homeowner. Hence, a presumptive identification.

The medicolegal system ultimately requires that a positive identification be made in such circumstances, and a presumptive identification is often a good way to narrow down the pool of possibilities. Biological profile information also assists with making a presumptive identification based on an individual's phenotype in life (e.g., what they looked like). As an example, a forensic anthropologist may establish the following components of a biological profile: white male, between the ages of 35 and 50, approximately 5´ 7 " to 5´ 11 " . While this seems like a rather specific description of an individual, you can imagine that this description fits dozens, if not hundreds, of people in an urban area. Therefore, law enforcement can use the biological profile information to narrow their pool of possible identifications to include only white males who fit the age and height outlined above. Once a possible match is found, the decedent can be identified using a method of positive identification.

Positive identifications are based on what we refer to as individualizing traits or characteristics, which are traits that are unique at the individual level. For example, brown hair is not an individualizing trait as brown is the most common hair color in the U.S. But, a specific pattern of dental restorations or surgical implants can be individualizing, because it is unlikely that you will have an exact match on either of these traits when comparing two individuals.

A number of positive methods are available to forensic anthropologists, and for the remainder of this section we will discuss the following methods: comparative medical and dental radiography and identification of surgical implants.

Comparative medical and dental radiography is used to find consistency of traits when comparing antemortem records (medical and dental records taken during life) with images taken postmortem (after death). Comparative medical radiography focuses primarily on features associated with the skeletal system, including trabecular pattern (internal structure of bone that is honeycomb in appearance), bone shape or cortical density (compact outer layer of bone), and evidence of past trauma or skeletal pathology. Other individualizing traits include the shape of various bones or their features, such as the frontal sinuses (Figure 15.17).

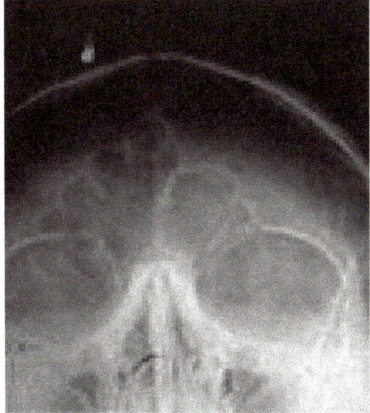

Figure 15.17 Example of the unique shape of the frontal sinus.

Comparative dental radiography focuses on the number, shape, location, and orientation of dentition and dental restorations in antemortem and postmortem images. While there is not a minimum number of matching traits that need to be identified for an identification to be made, the antemortem and postmortem records should have enough skeletal or dental consistencies to conclude that the records did in fact come from the same individual (SWGANTH 2010a). Consideration should also be given to population-level frequencies of specific skeletal and dental traits. If a trait is particularly common within a given population, it may not be a good trait to utilize for positive identification.

Figure 15.18 Image of joint replacement in the right shoulder.

Surgical implants or devices can also be used for identification purposes (Figure 15.18). These implements are sometimes recovered with human remains. One of the ways forensic anthropologists can use surgical implants to assist in decedent identification is by providing a thorough analysis of the implant and noting any identifying information such as serial numbers, manufacturer symbols, and so forth. This information can then sometimes be tracked directly to the manufacturer or the place of surgical intervention, which may be used to identify unknown remains (SWGANTH 2010a).

TRAUMA ANALYSIS

Types of Trauma

Within the field of anthropology, **trauma** is defined as an injury to living tissue caused by an extrinsic force or mechanism (Lovell 1997:139). Forensic anthropologists can assist a forensic pathologist by providing an interpretation of the course of events that led to skeletal trauma. Within the field of bioarchaeology, trauma analyses may contribute to a deeper understanding of past lifeways and interpersonal relationships. Within this section, the different types of trauma will be briefly outlined. Next, the timing of the injury (e.g., did trauma occur before, at or around, or after the time of death) will be discussed. Finally, the section will conclude with a discussion of how trauma interpretation is performed in the forensic anthropology laboratory.

Typically, traumatic injury to bone is classified into one of four categories, defined by the trauma mechanism. A trauma mechanism refers to the force that produced the skeletal modification and can be classified as (1) sharp force, (2) blunt force, (3) projectile, or (4) thermal (burning). Each type of trauma, and the characteristic pattern(s) associated with that particular categorization, will be discussed below.

First, let's consider *sharp-force trauma*, which is caused by a tool that is edged, pointed, or beveled—for example, a knife, saw, or machete (SWGANTH 2011). The patterns of injury resulting from sharp-force trauma include linear incisions created by a sharp, straight edge; punctures; and chop marks (Figure 15.19; SWGANTH 2011). When observed under a microscope, an anthropologist can often determine what kind of tool created the bone trauma. For example, a power saw cut will be discernible from a manual saw cut.

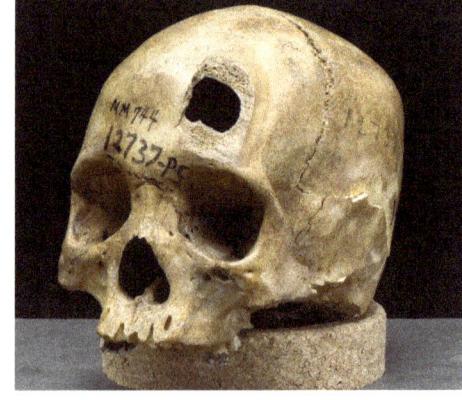

Figure 15.19 Example of sharp-force trauma (sword wound) to the frontal bone.

Second, *blunt-force trauma* is defined as "a relatively low-velocity impact over a relatively large surface area" (Galloway et al. 1999, 5). Blunt-force injuries can result from impacts from clubs, sticks, fists, and so forth. Blunt-force impacts typically leave an injury at the point of impact but can also lead to bending and deformation in other regions of the bone. Depressions, fractures, and deformation at and around the site of impact are all characteristics of blunt-force impacts (Figure 15.20). As with sharp-force trauma, an anthropologist attempts to interpret blunt-force injuries, providing information pertaining to the type of tool used, the direction of impact, the sequence of impacts, if more than one, and the amount of force applied.

Figure 15.20 Example of multiple blunt force impacts to the left parietal and frontal bones.

Third, *projectile trauma* refers to high-velocity trauma, typically affecting a small surface area (Galloway et al. 1999, 6). Projectile trauma results from fast-moving objects such as bullets or shrapnel. It is typically characterized by penetrating defects or embedded materials (Figure 15.21). When interpreting injuries resulting from projectile trauma, an anthropologist can often offer information pertaining to the type of weapon used (e.g., rifle vs. handgun), relative size of the bullet (but not the caliber of the bullet), the direction the projectile was traveling, and the sequence of injuries if there are multiple present.

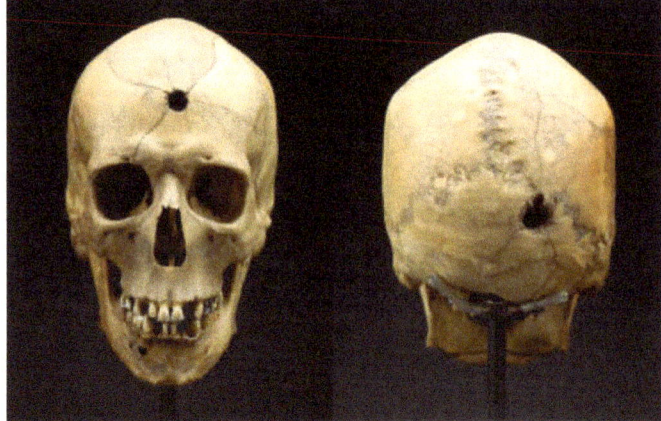

Figure 15.21 Example of projectile trauma with an entrance wound to the frontal bone and exit wound visible on the occipital.

Finally, *thermal trauma* is a bone alteration that results from bone exposure to extreme heat. Thermal trauma can result in cases of house or car fires, intentional disposal of a body in cases of homicidal violence, plane crashes, and so on. Thermal trauma is most often characterized by color changes to bone, ranging from yellow to black (charred) or white (calcined). Other bone alterations characteristic of thermal trauma include delamination (flaking or layering due to bone failure), shrinkage, fractures, and heat-specific burn patterning. When interpreting injuries resulting from thermal damage, an anthropologist can differentiate between thermal fractures and fractures that occurred before heat exposure, thereby contributing to the interpretation of burn patterning (e.g., was the individual bound or in a flexed position prior to the fire).

While there are characteristic patterns associated with the four categories of bone trauma, it is also important to note that these bone alterations do not always occur independently of different trauma types. An individual's skeleton may present with multiple different types of trauma, such as a projectile wound and thermal trauma. Therefore, it is important that the anthropologist recognize the different types of trauma and interpret them appropriately.

Timing of Injury

Another important component of any anthropological trauma analysis is the determination of the timing of injury (e.g., when did the injury occur). Timing of injury is traditionally split into one of three categories: **antemortem** (before death), **perimortem** (at or around the time of death), and **postmortem** (after death). This classification system differs slightly from the classification system used by the pathologist because it specifically references the qualities of bone tissue and bone response to external forces. Therefore, the perimortem interval (at or around the time of death) means that the bone is still fresh and has what is referred to as a green bone response, which can extend past death by several weeks or even months. For example, in cold or freezing temperatures a body can be preserved for extended periods of time increasing the perimortem interval, while in desert climates decomposition is accelerated, thereby significantly decreasing the postmortem interval (Galloway et al. 1999, 12). Antemortem injuries (occurring well before death and not related to the death incident) are typically characterized by some level of healing, in the form of a fracture callus or unification of fracture margins. Finally, postmortem injuries (occurring after death, while bone is no longer fresh) are characterized by jagged fracture margins, resulting from a loss of moisture content during the decomposition process (Galloway et al. 1999, 16). In general, all bone traumas should be classified according to the timing of injury, if possible. This information will help the medical examiner or pathologist better understand the circumstances surrounding the decedent's death, as well as events occurring during life and after the final disposition of the body.

The Role of the Forensic Anthropologist in Trauma Analysis

Within the medicolegal system, forensic anthropologists are often called upon by the medical examiner, forensic pathologist, or coroner to assist with an interpretation of trauma. The forensic anthropologist's main focus in any trauma analysis is the underlying skeletal system—as well as, sometimes, cartilage. Analysis and interpretation of soft tissue injuries fall within the purview of the medical examiner or pathologist. It is also important to note that the main role of the forensic anthropologist is to provide information pertaining to skeletal injury to assist the medical examiner/pathologist in their final interpretation of injury. Forensic anthropologists do not hypothesize as to the cause of death of an individual. Instead, a forensic anthropologist's report should include a description of the injury (e.g., trauma mechanism, number of injuries, location, timing of injury); documentation of the injury, which may be utilized in court testimony (e.g., photographs, radiographs, measurements); and, if applicable, a statement as to the condition of the body and state of decomposition, which may be useful for understanding the depositional context (e.g., how long has the body been exposed to the elements; was it moved or in its original location; are any of the alterations to bone due to environmental or faunal exposure instead of intentional human modification).

BONE PATHOLOGY

While there is a wide range of variation within the human skeletal system, bone development can also occur pathologically. Bone pathology can occur when there is excessive bone growth (osteoblastic activity or bone building) or bone is destroyed unnecessarily (osteoclastic activity or bone breakdown). Osteoblastic (bone building) and osteoclastic (bone destruction or breakdown) activities are normal processes of bone development, growth, and maintenance; however, when bone growth or breakdown exceeds what is necessary, the bony change can be classified as pathological, resulting in a bone pathology.

Types of Bone Pathology

For the purposes of this chapter, we will focus on both osteoblastic and osteoclastic pathologies of the human skeleton. In addition to considering whether a pathology is osteoclastic or osteoblastic, it is also important to classify a pathology according to its origin. Bone pathologies can be classified in a number of ways, including:

- congenital: occurring in the developmental period, often hereditary;
- traumatic: resulting from extrinsic factors and forces;
- degenerative: causing the degeneration or breakdown of bone tissue;
- infectious: resulting from bacterial, viral, or fungal agents;
- circulatory: resulting from a disruption in the relationship between the skeletal and circulatory system;
- metabolic: resulting from nutrient deficiencies;
- endocrinological: caused by hormonal imbalances; and
- neoplastic: related to abnormal growth, both benign and malignant, of bone tissue.

For the remainder of this section, we will focus on six different bone pathologies: (1) osteosarcoma, (2) osteogenesis imperfecta, (3) rickets, (4) achondroplasia, (5) Paget's disease of bone, and (6) diffuse idiopathic skeletal hyperostosis (DISH).

Osteosarcoma

Osteosarcoma is a type of neoplastic bone pathology. Characterized by malignant tumors that begin within bone tissues, osteosarcoma is a primary bone cancer (meaning it begins directly in bone tissue, rather than spreading to bone from other body tissues). Malignant tumors associated with osteosarcoma usually occur during growth and development and are observed most often in adolescents and young adults (Ortner and Putschar 1981, 384). Tumors are most frequently observed near the ends of long bones (Figure 15.22; Ortner and Putschar 1981, 384).

Osteogenesis Imperfecta

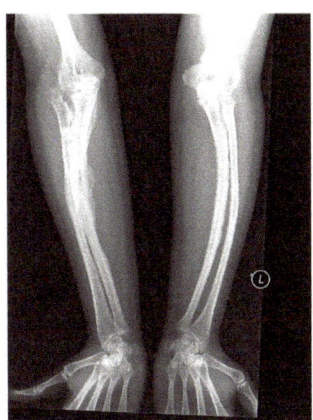

Figure 15.23 X-ray of the forearms of an individual with osteogenesis imperfecta (note the presence of multiple healing fractures).

Osteogenesis Imperfecta (OI) is a congenital bone pathology characterized by bones with low collagen content, leading to frequent fracturing (Ortner and Putschar 1981, 337). However, OI can also occur as a result of a spontaneous mutation. The disease is characterized by multiple fractures throughout the skeleton, particularly in the long bones (Figure 15.23). Depending on the type of OI, the disease is either manifest at birth or during childhood or adolescence (Ortner and Putschar 1981, 337). In addition to their susceptibility to easily fractured bones, individuals with OI are typically shorter in stature and may be subject to fracturing of tooth enamel and premature tooth loss (Ortner and Putschar 1981, 337).

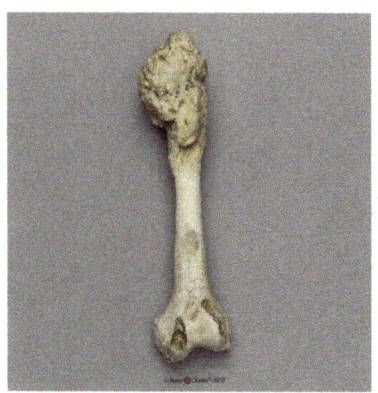

Figure 15.22 Osteosarcoma on a left human femur.

Rickets

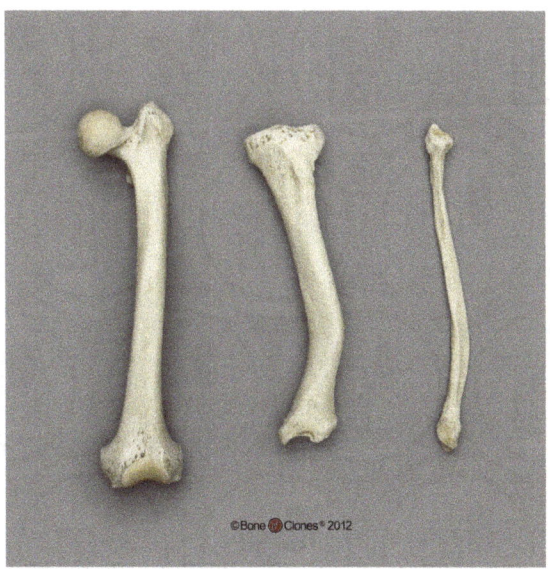

Figure 15.24 Example of rickets in long bones of the leg.

Rickets is a metabolic bone pathology resulting from a Vitamin D deficiency in childhood (Ortner and Putschar 1982, 273). Vitamin D is essential to the mineralization of bone tissue and is characterized by a wide variety of cranial and postcranial changes, including the following: asymmetrical deformities of the skull, bowing of the long bones, vertebral compression fractures, and a smaller, thicker pelvis (Figure 15.24; Ortner and Putschar 1981, 273–278).

Achondroplasia

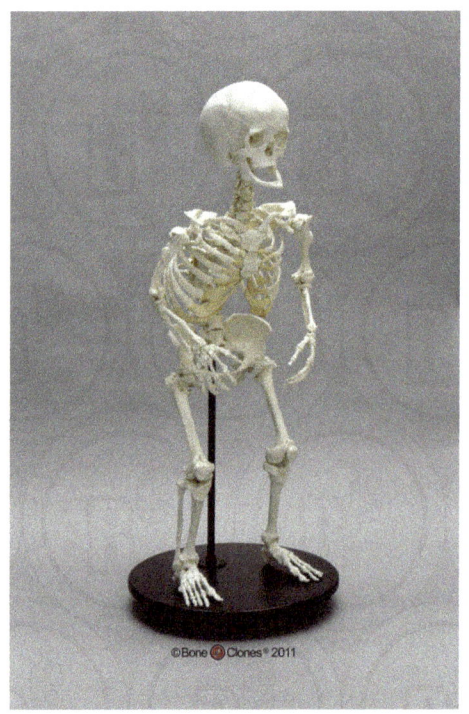

Figure 15.25 A cast of a complete skeleton of an adult female skeleton with achondroplasia.

Achondroplasia is a congenital bone pathology resulting from an abnormality in the conversion of cartilage to bone and is the most common form of dwarfism (Ortner and Putschar 1981, 329). The skeletal manifestations of achondroplasia are most apparent in the long bones comprising the arms and legs, while the trunk is of relatively normal proportions in individuals with achondroplasia (Figure 15.25). On average, males with achondroplasia are approximately 4´ 4˝ tall and females are approximately 4´ 1˝ tall (NIH 2019).

Paget's Disease of Bone

Paget's disease of bone is a disease of unknown origin that causes bones to grow larger and weaker over time (NIH 2019). The disease is marked by both osteoblastic and osteoclastic activity, with excessive osteoclastic resorption followed by osteoblastic proliferation leading to unnecessary amounts of new woven bone (Ortner and Putschar 1981, 309). The disease typically does not appear until the fourth or fifth decade of life and is more common in males than females (Ortner and Putschar 1981, 309). Paget's disease of bone can affect any bone, but the most commonly affected elements include the spine, pelvis, skull, and legs. The frequency of osteosarcoma is also higher among individuals with Paget's disease of bone (NIH 2019).

Diffuse Idiopathic Skeletal Hyperostosis (DISH)

DISH is a bone pathology characterized by a hardening (calcification or buildup of calcium salts) of the ligaments and tendons of the vertebral column. While DISH is observed in other areas of the skeleton, the vertebral column is the most frequently affected region. DISH is more prevalent in males than females and typically is observed in older adults (50-plus years) (NIH 2019). Recent medical research suggests that DISH results from abnormal osteoblastic activity in the spine, leading to excessive bone growth (NIH 2019).

TAPHONOMY

What Happened to the Remains After Death?

The majority of the skeletal analysis process revolves around the identity of the deceased individual. However, there is one last, very important question bioarchaeologists and forensic anthropologists should ask: What happened to the remains after death? Generally speaking, processes that alter the bone after death are referred to as taphonomic changes.

The term *taphonomy* was originally used to refer to the processes through which organic remains mineralize, also known as fossilization. Within the context of biological anthropology, the term *taphonomy* is better defined as the study of what happens to human remains after death. Initial factors affecting a body after death include processes such as decomposition and scavenging by animals. However, taphonomic processes encompass much more than the initial period after death. For example, plant root growth can leach minerals from bone, leaving a distinctive mark. Sunlight can bleach human remains, leaving exposed areas whiter than those which remained buried. Water can wear the surface of the bone until it becomes smooth.

Some taphonomic processes can help a forensic anthropologist estimate the relative amount of time human remains have been exposed to the elements. For example, root growth through a bone would certainly indicate a body was buried for more than a few days. Forensic anthropologists must be very careful when attempting to estimate time since death based on taphonomic processes as environmental conditions can greatly influence the rate at which taphonomic processes progress. For example, in cold environments, tissue may decay slower than in warm, moist environments.

The study of the decomposition and placement of an individual's body in the grave can also help bioarchaeologists understand more about how the body was placed and treated, and if there were any rituals that took place during the burial. For example, ochre, a mineral used as a pigment in paintings and dyes throughout human history, can stain bone and be an indication of ceremonial practice related to burial. Likewise, corrosion of different kinds of metals placed as grave goods or used as material in coffins can stain bone. For example, in a sample of medieval and post-medieval Spanish and Basque skeletons from the Cathedral of Santa Maria, Kimberly Hopkinson and colleagues (2008) noted a bright green to turquoise staining in some of the skeletons' teeth. The researchers believe that the staining was due to an ancient Greek practice of placing a coin in the mouth of the deceased to serve as the payment for the ferryman of Hades, Charon, who transported the deceased across the river that divided the world of the living from that of the dead. Hopkinson and colleagues determined that as the copper component of the bronze coins reacted with acid, it stained the teeth and surrounding bone, leaving evidence of the ancient Greek burial practice.

Both bioarchaeologists and forensic anthropologists must contend with taphonomic processes that affect the preservation of bones. For example, high acidity in the soil can break down human bone to the point of crumbling. In addition, when noting trauma, they must be very careful not to confuse postmortem (after death) bone damage with trauma.

A short description and photographic examples of several different types of taphonomic processes are shown below.

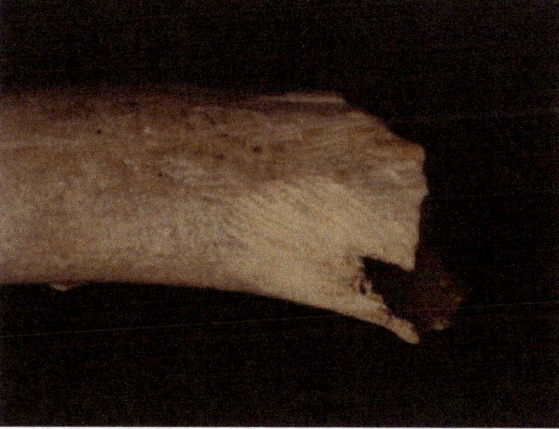

Figure 15.26 Rodent gnawing.

Rodent gnawing: When rodents, such as rats and mice, chew on bone, they leave sets of parallel grooves. The shallow grooves are etched by the rodent's incisors (Figure 15.26).

Figure 15.27 Carnivore damage.

Carnivore damage: Like rodents, carnivores leave destructive dental marks on bone. Tooth marks may be visible be in form of pit marks or punctures from the canines, as well as extensive gnawing or chewing of the ends of the bones to retrieve marrow (Figure 15.27).

Figure 15.28 Burned bone.

Burned bone: Fire causes observable damage to bone. Temperature and the amount of time bone is heated affect the appearance of the bone. Very high temperatures can crack bone and result in white coloration. Color gradients are visible in between high and lower temperatures, with lower temperatures resulting in black coloration from charring. Cracking can also reveal information about the directionality of the burn (Figure 15.28).

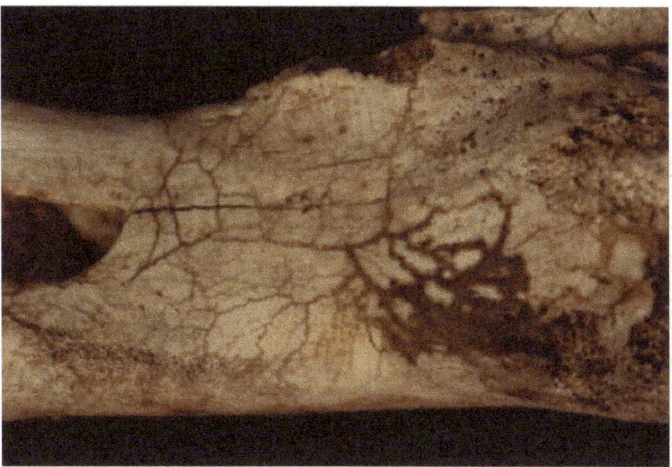

Figure 15.29 Root etching.

Root etching: Plants can alter bone. Specifically, plant roots can etch the outer surface of the bone, leaving grooves where the roots attached as they leached nutrients. During this process, the plant's roots secrete acid that breaks down the surface of the bone (Figure 15.29).

Figure 15.30 Weathering.

Weathering: Many different environmental conditions affect bone. River transport can smooth the surface of the bone due to water abrasion. Sunlight can bleach the exposed surface of bone. Dry and wet environments or the mixture of both types of environments can cause cracking and exfoliation of the surface. Burial in different types of soil can cause discoloration, and exposure can cause degreasing (Figure 15.30).

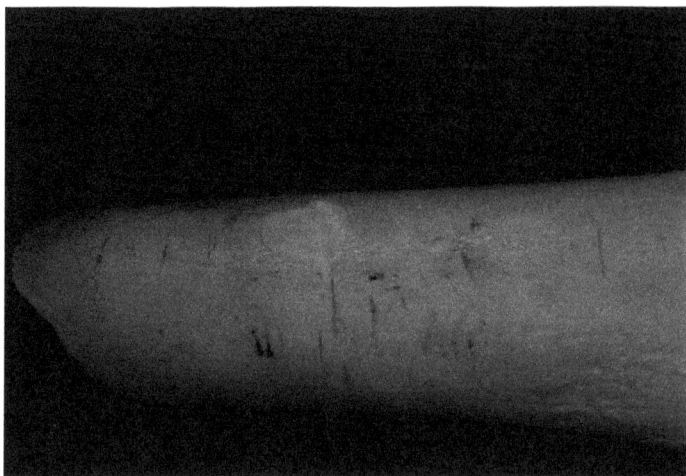
Figure 15.31 Cut marks.

Cut marks: Humans also alter bone by cutting, scraping, or sawing it directly or in the process of removing tissue. The groove pattern—that is, the depth and width of the cuts—can help identify the tool used in the cutting process (Figure 15.31).

ETHICS AND HUMAN RIGHTS

Working with human remains requires a great deal of consideration and respect for the dead. Forensic anthropologists and bioarchaeologists have to think about the ethics beyond our use of human remains for scientific purposes. How do we conduct casework in the most respectable manner possible? This section will discuss several ethical issues to consider when contemplating a career in forensic anthropology and bioarchaeology. While there are a wide range of ethical considerations within both subfields, this chapter will focus on two major categories: working with human remains and acting as an expert within the medicolegal system.

Working with Human Remains

Forensic anthropologists and bioarchaeologists work with human remains in a number of contexts, including casework, excavation, research, and teaching. When working with human remains, it is always important to use proper handling techniques. To prevent damage to skeletal remains, bones should be handled over padded surfaces. Skulls should never be picked up by placing fingers in the eye orbits, foramen magnum (hole at the base of the skull for entry of the spinal cord), or through the zygomatic arches (cheekbones). Human remains, whether related to casework, fieldwork, donated skeletal collections, or research, were once living human beings. It is important to always bear in mind that work with remains should be ingrained with respect for the individual and his or her relatives. In addition to fieldwork, casework, and teaching, anthropologists are often invited to work with remains that come from a bioarchaeological context or from a human rights violation. While this discussion of ethics is not comprehensive, two case examples will be provided below in which an anthropologist must consider the ethical standards outlined above.

NAGPRA

NAGPRA stands for the Native American Grave Protection and Repatriation Act, a federal law enacted in 1990 (NAGPRA 1990). NAGPRA provides protections and establishes repatriation procedures for Native American and Native Hawaiian remains, cultural items, and sacred objects. Human remains and associated artifacts, curated in museum collections and federally funded institutions, are subject to three primary provisions outlined by the NAGPRA statute: (1) protection for Native graves on federal and private land; (2) recognition of tribal authority on such lands; and (3) the requirement that all Native skeletal remains and associated artifacts be inventoried and culturally affiliated groups be consulted concerning decisions related to ownership and final disposition (Rose et al. 1996). NAGPRA legislation was enacted to ensure ethical consideration and treatment of Native remains and, in many cases, has improved dialogue between scientists and Native groups.

SPECIAL TOPIC: NATIVE AMERICAN GRAVES PROTECTION AND REPATRIATION ACT (NAGPRA)

- For more information on NAGPRA, visit:https://www.usbr.gov/nagpra/.
- For the text of the law, visit: https://www.nps.gov/history/local-law/FHPL_NAGPRA.pdf.

Modern Human Rights Violations

Forensic anthropologists may also be called to participate in criminal investigations involving human rights violations. Anthropological investigations may include assistance with identifications, determination of the number of victims, and trauma analyses. In this role, forensic anthropologists play an integral part in promoting human rights, preventing future human rights violations, and providing the evidence necessary to prosecute those responsible for past events. A few ethical considerations for the forensic anthropologist involved in human rights violations include the use of appropriate standards of identification, presenting reliable and unbiased testimony, and maintaining preservation of evidence. For a more comprehensive history of forensic anthropological contributions to human rights violation investigation, see Ubelaker 2018.

Acting as an Expert in the Medicolegal System

In addition to the ethical considerations involved with working with human skeletal remains, forensic anthropologists must abide by ethical standards when they act as experts within the medicolegal system. The role of the forensic anthropologist within the medicolegal system is primarily to provide information to the medical examiner or coroner that will aid in the identification process or determination of cause and manner of death. Forensic anthropologists also may be called to testify in a court of law. In this capacity, forensic anthropologists should always abide by a series of ethical guidelines that pertain to their interpretation, presentation, and preservation of evidence used in criminal investigations. First and foremost, practitioners should never misrepresent their training or education. When appropriate, outside opinions and assistance in casework should be requested (e.g., consulting a radiologist for radiological examinations or odontologist for dental exams). The best interest of the decedent should always take precedence. All casework should be conducted in an unbiased way, and financial compensation should never be accepted if it is incentive to take a biased stance regarding casework. All anthropological findings should be kept confidential, and release of information is best done by the medical examiner or coroner. Finally, while upholding ethical standards for oneself, a forensic anthropologist is also expected to report any perceived ethical violations committed by his or her peers.

Ethical standards for the field of forensic anthropology are outlined by the Organization of Scientific Area Committees (OSAC) for Forensic Science, administered by the National Institute of Standards and Technology (NIST). OSAC and NIST recently began an initiative to develop standards that would strengthen the practice of forensic science both in the United States and internationally. OSAC's main objective is to "strengthen the nation's use of forensic science by facilitating the development of technically sound forensic science standards and by promoting the adoption of those standards by the forensic science community" (NIST n.d.). Additionally, OSAC promotes the establishment of best practices and other guidelines to ensure that forensic science findings and their presentation are reliable and reproducible (OSAC 2018).

Review Questions

- What kinds of questions can bioarchaeologists answer from studying human skeletal remains?
- What is the main difference between bioarchaeology and forensic anthropology? (Hint: consider the age of the remains.)
- What are the seven primary steps involved in a skeletal analysis?
- What are the major components of a biological profile? Why are forensic anthropologists often tasked with creating biological profiles for unknown individuals?
- What are the four major types of skeletal trauma?
- What is taphonomy, and why is an understanding of taphonomy often critical in forensic anthropology analyses?
- What are some of the ethical considerations faced by forensic anthropologists and bioarchaeologists?

Key Terms

Antemortem trauma: Trauma occurring before death.

Anterior: Toward the front.

Bioarchaeology: The study of human remains excavated from archaeological sites .

Biological ancestry: Refers to the underlying genetic differences between modern populations.

Biological height: A person's true anatomical height.

Biological profile: An individual's identifying characteristics or biological information, commonly including sex, age, ancestry, and stature.

Burial assemblage: A set of human remains and associated artifacts associated with a single burial context.

Burial context: The circumstances surrounding the formation of a burial assemblage, an understanding of which can help inform our understanding and interpretation of the burial.

Commingled burials: Burial assemblages in which individual skeletons are not separated into discrete burials.

Compact (cortical) bone: The outer layer of bone, made up of densely arranged osseous (bone) tissue.

Dental development: The gradual replacement of deciduous (baby) teeth with adult teeth.

Epiphyseal union (or epiphyseal fusion): The appearance and closure of the epiphyseal plates between the primary centers of growth in a bone and the subsequent centers of growth.

Epiphyses: Ends of the bone, where growth occurs.

Forensic anthropology: The analysis of the skeletal remains of recently deceased individuals (typically within the last 50 years) within the context of the law—or, in other words, as part of a criminal investigation.

Gender: Culturally dependent identity of male or female.

Osteon: Primary structural unit of compact bone.

Perimortem trauma: Trauma occurring at or around the time of death.

Phenotype: A set of outwardly observable characteristics for an individual.

Positive identification: A scientifically validated method of identifying previously unidentified remains.

Postmortem trauma: Trauma occurring after death.

Pubic symphysis: A joint that joins the left and right halves of the pelvis anteriorly.

Regression methods: Mathematical analysis that examines the relationship between dependent and independent variables.

Reported stature: Self-reported height.

Robusticity: Strength relative to size.

Spongy (trabecular) bone: The inner layer of bone comprised of loosely organized porous bone tissue whose appearance resembles that of a sponge.

Trauma: An injury to living tissue caused by an extrinsic force or mechanism. (See Lovell 1997, 139.)

About the Authors

Ashley Kendell

California State University, Chico, akendell@csuchico.edu

Ashley Kendell

Dr. Ashley Kendell is currently an assistant professor and forensic anthropologist at Chico State. Prior to beginning her position at Chico State, she was a visiting professor at the University of Montana and the forensic anthropologist for the state of Montana. Dr. Kendell obtained her doctorate from Michigan State University, and her research interests include skeletal trauma analysis and digitization and curation methods for digital osteological data. She is also a Registry Diplomate of the American Board of Medicolegal Death Investigators. Throughout her doctoral program, she worked as a medicolegal death investigator for the greater Lansing, Michigan, area and was involved in the investigation of over 200 forensic cases.

Alex Perrone

California State University, Chico, aperrone1@mail.csuchico.edu

Alex Perrone

Alex Perrone is a lecturer in anthropology and biological sciences at California State University, Chico, and a lecturer in anthropology at Butte Community College. She is also the Supervisor of the Human Identification Laboratory in the Department of Anthropology at California State University, Chico. Her research interests include bioarchaeology, paleopathology, forensic anthropology, skeletal biology, California prehistory, and public health. She has worked on bioarchaeological and archaeological projects in Antigua, California, Hawaii, Greece, and the UK, and was an archaeological technician for the USDA Forest Service. She assists with training courses for local and federal law enforcement agencies and assists law enforcement agencies with the recovery and analysis of human remains.

Colleen Milligan

California State University, Chico, cfmilligan@csuchico.edu

Colleen Milligan

Dr. Colleen Milligan is a physical anthropologist with research interests in bioarchaeology, skeletal biology, and forensic anthropology. She has been a Fellow with the Department of Homeland Security and has assisted in forensic anthropology casework and recoveries in the State of Michigan and California. She has also assisted in community outreach programs in forensic anthropology and forensic science, as well as recovery training courses for local, state, and federal law enforcement officers. She is a certified instructor through Peace Officers Standards and Training (POST). Dr. Milligan serves as the current co-director of the Chico State Human Identification Laboratory.

References

Adams, Bradley J., and Lyle W. Konigsberg, eds. 2008. *Recovery, Analysis, and Identification of Commingled Remains*. Totowa, NJ: Humana Press.

Berg, Gregory E. 2017. "Sex Estimation of Unknown Human Skeletal Remains." In *Forensic Anthropology: A Comprehensive Introduction, Second edition*, edited by Natalie R. Langley and MariaTeresa A. Tersigni-Tarrant, 143–159. Boca Raton, FL: CRC Press.

Brooks, S., and J. M. Suchey. 1990. "Skeletal Age Determination Based on the Os Pubis: A Comparison of the Acsádi-Nemeskéri and Suchey-Brooks Methods." *Human Evolution* 5 (3): 227–238.

Cunningham, Craig, Louise Scheuer, and Sue Black. 2016. *Developmental Juvenile Osteology, Second edition*. London: Elsevier Academic Press.

Galloway, Alison. Broken Bones: Anthropological Analysis of Blunt Force Trauma. 1999. Springfield, IL: Charles C. THomas Publisher, LTD.

Hefner, Joseph T., and Kandus C. Linde. 2018. *Atlas of Human Cranial Macromorphoscopic Traits*. San Diego: Academic Press.

Hopkinson, Kimberly A., Sarah M. Yeats, and G. Richard Scott. 2008. "For Whom the Coin Tolls: Green Stained Teeth and Jaws in Medieval and Post-Medieval Spanish Burials." *Dental Anthropology* 21 (1): 12–17.

Katz, Darryl, and Judy Myers Suchey. 1986. "Age Determination of the Male Os Pubis." *American Journal of Physical Anthropology* 69 (4): 427–435.

Langley, Natalie R., Alice F. Gooding, and MariaTeresa Tersigni-Tarrant. 2017. "Age Estimation Methods." In *Forensic Anthropology: A Comprehensive Introduction, Second edition*, edited by Natalie R. Langley and MariaTeresa A. Tersigni-Tarrant, 175–191. Boca Raton, FL: CRC Press.

Lovell, Nancy C. 1997. "Trauma Analysis in Paleopathology." *Yearbook of Physical Anthropology* 104 (S25): 139–170.

İşcan, M. Y., S. R. Loth, and R. K. Wright. 1984. "Age Estimation from the Rib by Phase Analysis: White Males." *Journal of Forensic Sciences* 29 (4): 1094–1104.

———. 1985. "Age Estimation from the Rib by Phase Analysis: White Females." *Journal of Forensic Sciences* 30 (3): 853–863.

Native American Graves Protection and Repatriation Act (NAGPRA) 1990 (25 U.S. Code 3001 et seq.)

Nelson's Caribbean Hell-hole: An Eighteenth-Century Navy Graveyard Uncovered. 2013. BBC Documentary. https://www.bbc.co.uk/programmes/p0187q6r.

NIH U.S. National Library of Medicine. 2019. "Genetics Home Reference: Achondroplasia." Last modified February 5, 2019. https://ghr.nlm.nih.gov/condition/achondroplasia.

NIH. Genetic and Rare Diseases Information Center. Last modified October 13, 2017. https://rarediseases.info.nih.gov

NIST (National Institute of Standards and Technology). N.d. "The Organization of Scientific Area Committees for Forensic Science." https://www.nist.gov/topics/organization-scientific-area-committees-forensic-science.

Ortner, Donald J., and Walter G. J. Putschar. 1981. *Identification of Pathological Conditions in Human Skeletal Remains*. Washington, D.C.: Smithsonian Institution Press.

Ousley, Stephen. 1995. "Should We Estimate Biological or Forensic Stature?" *Journal of Forensic Sciences*. 40, no. 5: 768–773.

Phenice, T. W. 1969. "A Newly Developed Visual Method of Sexing the Os Pubis." *American Journal of Physical Anthropology* 30 (2): 297–302.

Rose, Jerome C., Thomas J. Green, and Victoria D. Green. 1996. "NAGPRA Is Forever: Osteology and the Repatriation of Skeletons." *Annual Review of Anthropology* 25: 81–103.

Schaefer, Maureen, Sue Black, and Louise Scheuer. *Juvenile Osteology: A Laboratory and Field Manual*. 2009. San Diego: Elsevier Academic Press.

Scientific Working Group for Forensic Anthropology (SWGANTH). 2010a. "Personal Identification." Last modified June 3, 2010. https://www.nist.gov/sites/default/files/documents/2018/03/13/swganth_personal_identification.pdf.

Scientific Working Group for Forensic Anthropology (SWGANTH). 2010b. "Sex Assessment." Last modified June 3, 2010. https://www.nist.gov/sites/default/files/documents/2018/03/13/swganth_sex_assessment.pdf.

Scientific Working Group for Forensic Anthropology (SWGANTH). 2011. "Trauma Analysis." Last modified May 27, 2011. https://www.nist.gov/sites/default/files/documents/2018/03/13/swganth_trauma.pdf.

Scientific Working Group for Forensic Anthropology (SWGANTH). 2012. "Stature Estimation." Last modified August 2, 2012. https://www.nist.gov/sites/default/files/documents/2018/03/13/swganth_stature_estimation.pdf.

Scientific Working Group for Forensic Anthropology (SWGANTH). 2013. "Age Estimation." Last modified January 22, 2013. https://www.nist.gov/sites/default/files/documents/2018/03/13/swganth_age_estimation.pdf.

Tersigni-Tarrant, MariaTeresa A., and Natalie R. Langley. 2017. "Human Osteology." In *Forensic Anthropology: A Comprehensive Introduction, Second edition*, edited by Natalie R. Langley and MariaTeresa A. Tersigni-Tarrant, 81–109. Boca Raton, FL: CRC Press.

Ubelaker, Douglas H. 2018. "A History of Forensic Anthropology." Special issue: Centennial Anniversary Issue of AJPA, *American Journal of Physical Anthropology* 165 (4): 915–923.

White, Tim D., and Pieter A. Folkens. 2005. *The Human Bone Manual*. Burlington, MA: Elsevier Academic Press.

Figure Attributions

Figure 15.1 Example of burned sheetrock by Alex Perrone original to Explorations: An Open Invitation to Biological Anthropology is under a CC BY-NC 4.0 License.

Figure 15.2 Cross section of human long bone original to Explorations: An Open Invitation to Biological Anthropology by Mary Nelson is under a CC BY-NC 4.0 License.

Figure 15.3 Anatomy of a Flat Bone (Anatomy & Physiology, Figure 6.3.3 byOpenStax is used under aCC BY 4.0 License.

Figure 15.4 Bone (248 12) Bone cross section by Doc. RNDr. Josef Reischig, CSc. is used under a CC BY-SA 3.0 License.

Figure 15.5 Example of PVC pipe by Alex Perrone original to Explorations: An Open Invitation to Biological Anthropology is under a CC BY-NC 4.0 License.

Figure 15.6 Animal bone cross section by Alex Perrone original to Explorations: An Open Invitation to Biological Anthropology is under a CC BY-NC 4.0 License.

Figure 15.7 Tib fib growth plates by Gilo1969 at English Wikipedia is used under a CC BY 3.0 License.

Figure 15.8 Filling by Kauzio has been designated to the public domain (CC0).

Figure 15.9 Spanish Civil War – Mass grave – Estépar, Burgos by Mario Modesto Mata is used under a CC BY-SA 4.0 License.

Figure 15.10 Anterior and lateral view of a male and female cranium by Ashley Kendell a derivative work original to Explorations: An Open Invitation to Biological Anthropology is under a CC BY-NC 4.0 License. [Includes Human Female Asian Skull and Human Male Asian Skull by ©BoneClones used by permission.]

Figure 15.11 Features associated with the Phenice Method by Colleen Milligan original to Explorations: An Open Invitation to Biological Anthropology is under a CC BY-NC 4.0 License.

Figure 15.12 Skeletal traits commonly used in a morphological assessment of ancestry by Colleen Milligan original to Explorations: An Open Invitation to Biological Anthropology is under a CC BY-NC 4.0 License.

Figure 15.13 5-year-old Human Child Skull with Mixed Dentition Exposed by ©BoneClones is used by permission and available here is under a CC BY-NC 4.0 License.

Figure 15.14 Example of the progression of degenerative changes to the pubic symphysis a derived work by Ashley Kendell original to Explorations: An Open Invitation to Biological Anthropology is under a CC BY-NC 4.0 License. [Original photos by Dr. Julie Fleischman used by permission.]

Figure 15.15 Examples of degenerative changes to the sternal rib end by Alex Perrone original to Explorations: An Open Invitation to Biological Anthropology is under a CC BY-NC 4.0 License.

Figure 15.16 Measurement of the bicondylar length of the femur by Alex Perrone original to Explorations: An Open Invitation to Biological Anthropology is under a CC BY-NC 4.0 License.

Figure 15.17 Frontal bone sinuses by Alex Khimich is used under a CC BY-SA 4.0 License.

Figure 15.18 Shoulder replacement by Smithsonian [exhibit: Written in Bone, Today's Bones] has no known copyright restrictions.

Figure 15.19 Skull sword trauma by the National Institutes of Health, Health & Human Services [19th Century Collection, National Museum of Health and Medicine, Armed Forces Institute of Pathology, Washington, D.C. From exhibition "Visible Proofs: Forensic Views of the Body" U.S. National Library of Medicine] is in the public domain.

Figure 15.20 Skull hammer trauma by the National Institutes of Health, Health & Human Services [19th Century Collection, National Museum of Health and Medicine, Armed Forces Institute of Pathology, Washington, D.C. From exhibition "Visible Proofs: Forensic Views of the Body" U.S. National Library of Medicine] is in the public domain.

Figure 15.21 Trauma: Gunshot Wounds by Smithsonian [exhibit: Written in Bone, How Bone Biographies Get Written] has no known copyright restrictions.

Figure 15.22 Human Left Femur, Osteosarcoma by ©BoneClones is used by permission and available here is under a CC BY-NC 4.0 License.

Figure 15.23 Osteogenesis Imperfecta Type V by ShakataGaNai is used under a CC BY-SA 4.0 License.

Figure 15.24 Human Femur, Tibia and Fibula, Rickets by ©BoneClones is used by permission and available here is under a CC BY-NC 4.0 License.

Figure 15.25 Human Female Achondroplasia Dwarf Skeleton, Articulated by ©BoneClones is used by permission and available here is under a CC BY-NC 4.0 License.

Figure 15.26 Rodent gnawing by Alex Perrone original to Explorations: An Open Invitation to Biological Anthropology is under a CC BY-NC 4.0 License.

Figure 15.27 Carnivore damage by Alex Perrone original to Explorations: An Open Invitation to Biological Anthropology is under a CC BY-NC 4.0 License.

Figure 15.28 Burned bone by Alex Perrone original to Explorations: An Open Invitation to Biological Anthropology is under a CC BY-NC 4.0 License.

Figure 15.29 Root etching by Alex Perrone original to Explorations: An Open Invitation to Biological Anthropology is under a CC BY-NC 4.0 License.

Figure 15.30 Weathering by Alex Perrone original to Explorations: An Open Invitation to Biological Anthropology is under a CC BY-NC 4.0 License.

Figure 15.31 Cut marks by Alex Perrone original to Explorations: An Open Invitation to Biological Anthropology is under a CC BY-NC 4.0 License.

Chapter 16: Contemporary Topics: Human Biology and Health

Joylin Namie, PhD, Truckee Meadows Community College

> *Learning Objectives*
>
> - Describe what is meant by a "mismatch" between our evolved biology and contemporary lifestyles and how this is reflected in modern disease patterns.
> - Describe diet and physical activity patterns among preagricultural hunter-gatherers.
> - Describe changes in subsistence, diet, and activity patterns that occurred as a result of the transition to food production and how these affected health among early agriculturalists.
> - Explain what is meant by an epidemiological transition and describe the major transitions in patterns of disease among humans that have occurred throughout human evolution.
> - Explain what is meant by examining health issues from an ecological perspective.
> - Discuss examples of contemporary evolution.

When is the last time you needed to do research for an upcoming paper? I bet you started by looking for information online. How did you go about your search? Which websites looked promising? Which ones did not entice you to click past the home page? Once you found one you thought might be useful, how much time did you spend searching for information? At what point did you decide to leave that site and move on? I would wager money that you never once thought your behavior had anything do with human evolution, but it does.

Although we may not often stop to think about it, our evolutionary past is reflected in many aspects of modern life. The ways we "forage" for information on the internet mimics the ways we once foraged for food during our several-million-year history as hunter-gatherers (Chin et al. 2015). Humans are visual hunters (Lieberman 2006). We practice optimal foraging strategy, meaning we make decisions based on energy return for investment (McElroy and Townsend 2009). When we search for information online, we locate a "patch," in this case a website or research article, then quickly scan the contents to discern how many resources it has that we can use. Like our hominin ancestors, we spend more time in "patches" with abundant resources and abandon sites quickly and move on once we have exhausted the available goods. As with internet searches, our evolutionary past is also reflected in the kinds of landscapes we find appealing, the foods that taste good to us, why we break a sweat at the gym, and why we have to go to the gym at all (Bogin 1991; Dutton 2009; Lieberman 2015). Many of the health problems facing humans in the 21st century also have their beginnings in the millions of years we roamed the earth as foragers.

This chapter addresses contemporary health issues from an evolutionary perspective. It begins with a review of diet, activity patterns, and causes of **morbidity** and **mortality** among our preagricultural ancestors, which form the foundation for the ways our bodies function today. This is followed by a discussion of the health consequences of the transition to agriculture, marking the first of three major **epidemiological transitions** experienced by humankind. It then hones in on health conditions that have become all too familiar to those of us living in modern, industrialized societies, including **obesity**, diabetes, heart disease, **osteoarthritis**, **cancer**, and the impact of stress on health. The environments in which we now live and the choices we make put a strain on biological systems that came about in response to selective pressures in our past. Furthermore, the transitions happened too quickly for natural selection to keep up (Stearns et al. 2008).

PREAGRICULTURAL HUMANS

Diet

Higher primates, including humans, may be the species with the longest list of nutritional requirements (Bogin 1991). This is likely due to the fact that we evolved in environments where there was a high diversity of species but low densities of any given species. Humans require 45–50 essential nutrients for growth, maintenance, and repair of cells and tissues. These include protein, carbohydrates, fats, vitamins, minerals, and water. As a species, we are (or were) highly active with high metabolic demands. Humans are not **autotrophic**. We cannot manufacture our own nutrients. Doing so is metabolically expensive, meaning it takes a lot of energy to accomplish it. If the surrounding environment can provide those nutrients, it makes evolutionary sense to obtain them from outside the body, rather than spending energy producing them, as green plant species do (National Geographic Society n.d.). Given our nutritional requirements and caloric needs, it is not surprising that humans are **omnivorous** and evolved to choose foods that are dense in essential nutrients. One of the ways we identified high-calorie resources in our evolutionary past was through taste, and it is no accident that humans find sweet, salty, fatty foods appealing.

The human predisposition toward sugar, salt, and fat is innate (Farb and Armelagos 1980). This is reflected in receptors for sweetness found in every one of the mouth's ten thousand taste buds (Moss 2013). This tuning toward sweet makes sense in an ancestral environment where sweetness signaled high-value resources like ripe fruits. Likewise, "the long evolutionary path from sea-dwelling creatures to modern humans has given us salty body fluids, the exact salinity of which must be maintained" (Farb and Armelagos 1980), drawing us to salty-tasting things. Cravings for fat, another high-calorie resource, are also inborn, with some archaeological evidence suggesting that hominins may have been collecting bones for their fatty marrow, which contains two essential fatty acids necessary for brain development (Richards 2002), rather than for any meat remaining on the surface (Bogin 1991).

Archaeological and bone chemistry studies of preagricultural populations indicate that Paleolithic peoples ate a wider variety of foods than many people eat today (Armelagos et al. 2005; Bogin 1991; Larsen 2014; Marciniak and Perry 2017). Foragers took in more protein, less fat, much more fiber, and far less sodium than modern humans typically do (Eaton et al. 1988). Changes in tooth and intestinal morphology illustrate that animal products were an important part of human diets from the time of *Homo erectus* onward (Baltic and Boskovic 2015; Richards 2002; Wrangham 2009). These animal products consisted of raw meat scavenged from carnivore kills and marrow from the leftover bones. It is not possible to discern from current archaeological evidence when cooking began. The "cooking hypothesis" proposed by Richard Wrangham (2009) argues that *H. erectus* was adapted to a diet of cooked food, and phylogenetic studies comparing body mass, molar size, and other characteristics among nonhuman and human primates support this conclusion (Organ et al. 2011). However, the first documented archaeological evidence of human-controlled use of fire is dated to one million years ago, roughly a million years after the first appearance of *H. erectus* (Berna et al. 2012). Whenever cooking became established, it opened up a wider variety of both plant and animal resources to humans and led to selection for gene variants linked to reductions in the musculature of the jaw and thickness of tooth enamel (Lucock et al. 2014). However, the protein, carbohydrates, and fats preagricultural peoples ate were much different from those we eat today. Wild game, for example, lacked the antibiotics, growth hormones, and high levels of cholesterol and saturated fat associated with industrialized meat production today (Walker et al. 2005). It was also protein dense, providing only 50% of energy as fat (Lucock et al. 2014), and not prepared in ways that increase cancer risk, as modern meats often are (Baltic and Boskovic 2015).

Meats cooked well done over high heat and/or over an open flame, including hamburgers and barbecued meats, are highly carcinogenic due to compounds formed during the cooking process (Trafialek and Kolanowski 2014). Processed meats that have been preserved by smoking, curing, salting, or by adding chemical preservatives such as sodium nitrite (e.g., ham, bacon, pastrami, salami) have been linked to cancers of the colon, lung, and prostate (Abid et al. 2014) (See Figure 16.1). Nitrites/nitrates have additionally been linked to cancers of the ovaries, stomach, esophagus, bladder, pancreas, and thyroid (Abid et al. 2014). In addition, studies analyzing the diets of 103,000 Americans for up to 16 years indicate that those who ate grilled, broiled, or roasted meats more than 15 times per month were 17% more likely to develop high blood pressure than those who ate meat fewer than four times per month, and participants who preferred their meats well done were 15% more likely to suffer from **hypertension** than those who preferred their meats rare (Liu 2018). A previous study of the same cohort indicated "independent of consumption amount, open-flame and/or high-temperature cooking for both red meat and chicken is associated with an increased risk of Type 2 diabetes among adults who consume animal flesh regularly" (Liu et al. 2018). Although cooking, especially of meat (Wrangham 2009), has been argued to be crucial to cognitive and physical development among hominins, there has clearly been an evolutionary trade-off between the ability to preserve protein and the health risks humans experience due to consumption of cooked meat and exposure to chemical preservatives.

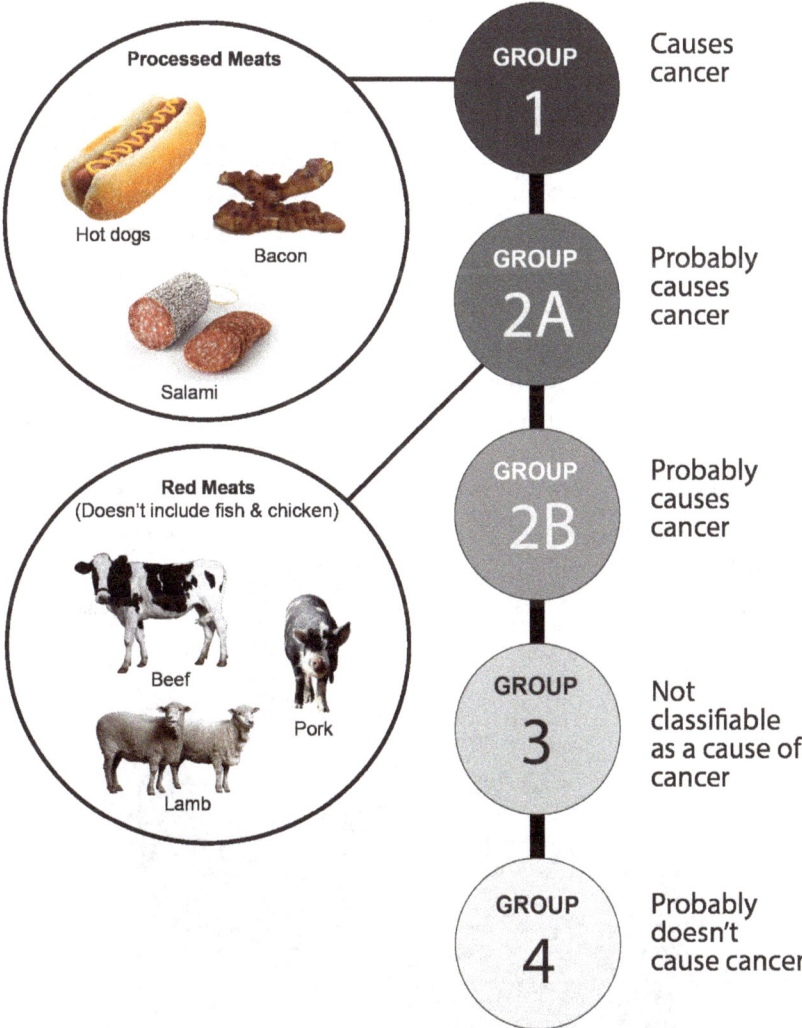

Figure 16.1 Positive associations have been observed between meat consumption and some types of cancer. The International Agency for Research on Cancer (2018) categorized these four groupings of cancer risk.

Although carbohydrates represent half of the diet on average for both ancient foragers and modern humans, the types of carbohydrates are very different. Ancient foragers ate fresh fruits, vegetables, grasses, legumes, and tubers, rather than the processed carbohydrates common in industrialized economies (Moss 2013). Their diets also lacked the refined white sugar and corn syrup found in many modern foods that, in themselves, contribute to the development of **Metabolic Syndrome** and diabetes (Pontzer et al. 2012).

Physical Activity Patterns

How do we know how active our ancestors really were? Hominin morphology and physiology provide us with clues. Consider our ancestral environment of sub-Saharan Africa. It was hot and dry, and close to the equator, meaning the sun was brighter and at a more direct angle than it is for many human populations today. This made the transition to bipedalism very important to survival. When the sun is at its highest in the sky, a bipedal human exposes only 7% of its surface area to maximal radiation, approximately one-third of the maximally exposed area of a similarly sized quadruped (Lieberman 2015). In a savannah environment where predators roamed in the cool of the night, it would have been evolutionarily advantageous for small, bipedal hominins to forage in the heat of the day, especially in an open habitat without the safety of trees. As early hominins were primarily scavengers who likely needed to travel to find food, heat-dissipating mechanisms would have been strongly favored.

Humans have four derived sets of adaptations for preventing hyperthermia (overheating): (1) fur loss and an increased ability to sweat (versus panting); (2) an external nose, allowing for nasal regulation of the temperature and humidity of air entering the lungs; (3) enhanced ability to cool the brain; and (4) an elongated, upright body. These adaptations suggest an evolutionary history of regular, strenuous physical activity. Some scholars have gone so far as to argue that, beginning with *H. erectus*, there are skeletal markers of adaptations for endurance running (Lieberman 2015; Richards 2002). The relevant morphological changes include modifications in the arches of the feet, a longer Achilles tendon, a nuchal ligament and ear canals that help maintain balance while running, shoulders decoupled from the head allowing rotation of the torso independently from the pelvis and head, and changes to the gluteus maximus. It is argued these modifications would have provided benefits for running, but not walking, and that *H. erectus* may have been running prey to the point of exhaustion before closing in for the kill (Lieberman 2015). This conclusion is controversial, with other scholars pointing to a lack of evidence for the necessary cognitive and projectile-making abilities among the genus *Homo* that far back in time (Pickering and Bunn 2007). Whether our ancestors were walking or running, they were definitely engaged in significant amounts of physical activity on a daily basis. They had to be or they would not have survived. As Robert Malina and Bertis Little (2008) point out, prolonged exertion and motor skills (*e.g.*, muscular strength, tool making, and, eventually, accuracy with projectiles) are important determinants of success and survival in preindustrial societies.

Figure 16.2 Hadza foragers hunting on foot.

Research with modern foraging populations, although controversial, can also offer clues to ancient activity patterns. Criticisms of such research include sampling bias due to the fact that modern foragers occupy marginal habitats and that such societies have been greatly influenced by their association with more powerful agricultural societies. Modern foragers may also represent an entirely new human niche that appeared only with climatic changes and faunal depletion at the end of the last major glaciation (Marlowe 2005). Despite these issues, the ethnographic record of foragers provides the only direct observations of human behavior in the absence of agriculture (Lee 2013). From such studies, we know hunter-gatherers cover greater distances in single-day foraging bouts than other living primates, and these treks require high levels of cardiovascular endurance (Raichlen and Alexander 2014). Recent research with the Hadza in Tanzania, one of the last remaining foraging populations, indicates that they walk up to 11 kilometers (6.8 miles) daily while hunting or in search of gathered foods (Pontzer et al. 2012), engaging in moderate-to-vigorous physical activity for over two hours each day–meeting the U.S. government's weekly requirements for physical activity in just two days (Raichlen et al. 2016) (See Figure 16.2). The fact that humans were physically active in our evolutionary past is also supported by the fact that regular physical exercise has been shown to be protective against a variety of health conditions found in modern humans, including **cardiovascular disease** (Raichlen and Alexander 2014) and Alzheimer's dementia (Mandsager et al. 2018), even in the presence of brain pathologies indicative of cognitive decline (Buchman et al. 2019).

Infectious Disease

Population size and density remained low throughout the Paleolithic, limiting morbidity and mortality from infectious diseases, which sometimes require large populations to sustain epidemics. Our earliest ancestors had primarily two types of infections to contend with (Armelagos 1990). The first were organisms that adapted to our prehominin ancestors and have been problems ever since. Examples include head lice, pinworms, and yaws. A second set of diseases were **zoonoses**, diseases that originate in animals and mutate into a form infectious to humans. A contemporary example is the Human Immunodeficiency Virus (HIV) that originated in non-human primates and was likely passed to humans through the butchering of hunted primates for food (Sharp and Hahn 2011). Zoonoses that could have infected ancient hunter-gatherers include tetanus and **vector-borne diseases** transmitted by flies, mosquitoes, fleas, midges, and ticks. Many of these diseases are slow acting, chronic, or latent, meaning they can last for weeks, months, or even decades, causing low levels of sickness and allowing victims to infect others over long periods of time. Survival or cure does not result in lasting immunity with survivors returning to the pool of potential victims. Such diseases often survive in animal reservoirs, reinfecting humans again and again (Wolfe et al. 2012). A recent study of bloodsucking insects preserved in samples of amber dating from 15 to 100 million years ago indicate they carried microorganisms that today cause diseases such as filariasis, sleeping sickness, river blindness, typhus, Lyme disease, and malaria (Poinar 2018). Such diseases may have been infecting humans throughout our evolutionary history, and they may have had significant social and economic impacts on small foraging communities because they more often infected adults, who provided the food supply (Armelagos et al. 2005).

Health Profiles

Given their diets, levels of physical activity, and low population densities, the health profiles of preagricultural humans were likely better than those of many modern populations. This assertion is supported by comparative research conducted with modern foraging and industrialized populations. Measures of health taken from 20th-century foraging populations demonstrate excellent aerobic capacity, as measured by oxygen uptake during exertion, and low body-fat percentages, with triceps skinfold measurements half those of white Canadians and Americans. Serum cholesterol levels were also low, and markers for diabetes, hypertension, and cardiovascular disease were missing among them (Eaton et al. 1988; Raichlen et al. 2016). Life expectancies among our ancient ancestors are difficult to determine, but an analysis of living foragers by Michael Gurven and Hillard Kaplan (2007:331) proposed that, "for groups living without access to modern healthcare, public sanitation, immunizations, or an adequate or predictable food supply, at least one-fourth of the population is likely to live as grandparents for 15–20 years." Based on their analysis, the maximum lifespan among our ancestors was likely seventy years of age, just two years less than average global life expectancy in 2016 (WHO 2018a).

HEALTH CONSEQUENCES OF THE TRANSITION TO AGRICULTURE AND ANIMAL DOMESTICATION

The shift from foraging to food production occurred relatively recently in our evolutionary history (Larsen 2014), and there are indications our biology has not yet caught up (Pritchard 2010). Beginning around 12,000 BCE in several parts of the globe, humans began to move to a diet based on domesticated plants and animals (Armelagos et al. 2005). This involved manipulating the natural landscape to facilitate intensive food production, including the clearing of forest and construction of wells, irrigation canals, and ditches, exposing humans to water-borne illnesses and parasites, and attracting mosquitos and other vectors of disease to human settlements. The heavy, repetitive physical labor of early agricultural production resulted in negative impacts on articular joints, including osteoarthritis (Larsen 2014). At the same time, nutritional diversity became restricted, focused on major cereal crops that continue to dominate agricultural production today, including corn, wheat, and rice (Jain 2012). This represented a major shift in diet from a wide variety of plant and animal foods to dependence on starchy carbohydrates, leading to increases in dental caries (cavities), reductions in stature and growth rates, and nutritional deficiencies (Larsen 2014). Domesticated animals added new foods to the human diet, including meat that was higher in fat and cholesterol than wild game as well as dairy products (Lucock et al. 2014). Agriculture provided the means to produce a storable surplus for the first time in human history, allowing some individuals to grow and consume more than others, leading to the beginnings of economic inequality (Harris 1989). Social hierarchies led to the unequal distribution of the basic resources for healthy living, concentrating infectious disease among the poor and malnourished (Zuckerman et al. 2014), a situation that continues to plague humanity today (Marmot 2005).

Sedentism and a rise in population density accompanied the move to agriculture, increasing the risk of infectious disease. Agriculture often provided enough calories, if not enough nutrition, to increase fertility. That is, although diets were worse and people unhealthier, populations continued to grow, even in the midst of high levels of child and maternal mortality and short life expectancies (Omran 2005). Hygiene became an issue as large settlements increased the already-difficult problem of removing human wastes and providing uncontaminated water (Armelagos et al. 2005). Domesticated animals, including cattle, sheep, goats, pigs, chickens, and horses, provided reservoirs of zoonotic pathogens, which affected farmers more than foragers, as farmers were in closer proximity to their animals on a daily basis (Marciniak and Perry 2017). Many of these diseases became major killers of humankind, including influenza, tuberculosis, malaria, plague, syphilis, and smallpox, functioning as selective pressures in and of themselves (Cooling 2015). As these diseases encountered large human populations, malnourished and concentrated in early settlements, they caused major epidemics that traveled along newly established routes for trade, warfare, and colonization.

EPIDEMIOLOGICAL TRANSITIONS

Changes in diet and physical-activity patterns associated with agriculture, in conjunction with increased population densities and exposure to zoonoses, resulted in what is known as an epidemiological transition, a shift in the causes of morbidity and mortality among humankind (Omran 1971). The first epidemiological transition from foraging to food production resulted in increases in dental caries, nutritional deficiencies, infectious disease, and skeletal conditions like osteoarthritis, as well as decreases in growth and height (Larsen 2014). A second epidemiological transition occurred following the Industrial Revolution in Western Europe and the United States when socioeconomic, political, and cultural conditions contributed to improved standards of living, hygiene, and nutrition that minimized the effects of infectious disease, after which people began to experience the **Noncommunicable Diseases (NCDs)** that are the focus of the remainder of this chapter (Omran 2005). With the addition of immunizations and other public health initiatives, modified forms of this transition remain ongoing in many low- and middle-income countries (Zuckerman et al. 2014), with several now facing a **"double burden"** of disease, with poor, often rural, populations falling prey to infectious diseases, while more affluent citizens are victims of chronic illnesses. A third epidemiological transition is now underway as infectious diseases, some of them novel, others re-emergent, and others even multi-drug resistant, have once again become major health concerns (Harper and Armelagos 2010; Zuckerman et al. 2014). These include Ebola, HIV/AIDS, tuberculosis, malaria, dengue, Lyme disease, and West Nile virus, all zoonoses that initially spread to humans through contact with animals. These diseases are increasing their geographic ranges due to climate change, economic development, and deforestation (Baer and Singer 2009).

Patterns of morbidity and mortality continue to shift across the globe. As with the first epidemiological transition resulting from the adoption of large-scale agriculture, such shifts can be the direct, if unintended, result of human interactions with the environment. For example, there has been a well-documented rise in chronic inflammatory diseases (CIDs) in recent decades in developed countries (Versini et al. 2015). This includes increased rates of allergic conditions like asthma, as well as autoimmune diseases like rheumatoid arthritis, multiple sclerosis, Crohn's disease, and inflammatory bowel disease. This has coincided with the decrease in infectious disease associated with the second epidemiological transition, and the two are related. The "hygiene hypothesis" postulates the rise in CIDs is a result of limited exposure to nonlethal environmental pathogens in utero and early childhood (Zuckerman and Armelagos 2014). Modern human societies have become so sanitized that we are no longer exposed to microorganisms that stimulate the development of a healthy immune system (Versini et al. 2015). "In effect, the lifestyle changes–sanitary improvements, pasteurization, use of antibiotics, and improved hygiene–that contributed to the second transition may have produced a substantial trade-off in health and quality of life, with developed nations exchanging a high burden of infectious disease for a higher burden of CIDs" (Zuckerman et al. 2014).

Similarly, the re-emergence of infectious disease, the third epidemiological transition, reflects the continuing relationship between humans, animals, and pathogens. Over 60% of **Emerging Infectious Diseases (EIDs)** between 1940 and 2004 have been of zoonotic origin, with over 70% stemming from human contact with wildlife (Jones et al. 2008). The global bushmeat trade currently devastating Africa's wildlife is a continuing source of Ebola infection (Asher 2017), as well as the original source of HIV and viruses related to leukemia and lymphoma among humans (Zuckerman et al. 2014). Further, new strains of avian (bird) flu, some with mortality rates as high as 60% among human victims (WHO n.d.), are transmitted to humans through poultry production and contact with wild birds; these pose a looming global threat of epidemic disease (Davis 2005). Lastly, the use of antibiotics in commercial meat production is directly related to the rise of drug-resistant strains of previously controlled infectious diseases. An estimated 80% of antibiotics in the U.S. are used to promote growth and prevent infection in livestock, and drug-resistant bacteria from these animals are transmitted to humans through meat consumption (Ventola 2015).

These examples illustrate continuing interaction between humans, our evolved biology, and the physical and cultural environments in which we live. The remainder of this chapter will focus on selected noncommunicable diseases and the social, cultural, and environmental factors that contribute to their **prevalence** in modern, industrialized economies. We begin with the health condition that affects all of the others–obesity.

OBESITY

According to the World Health Organization (2017b), 1.9 billion of the world's people are overweight and 650 million of these are obese. In the United States, 70% of Americans are overweight, and 40% of these meet the criteria for obesity. For the first time in human history, most of the world's population lives in countries where overweight and obesity kill more people than hunger does (see Figure 16.3). Improvements in public health and food production have allowed a greater number of people to live past childhood and to have enough food to eat. This does not include everyone. Many people still struggle with poverty, hunger, and disease, even in the wealthiest of nations, including the United States. On a global scale, however, many people not only have enough food to survive but also to gain weight—and, notably, enough extra weight to cause significant health problems. Several aspects of life in modern, industrialized societies contribute to the obesity crisis.

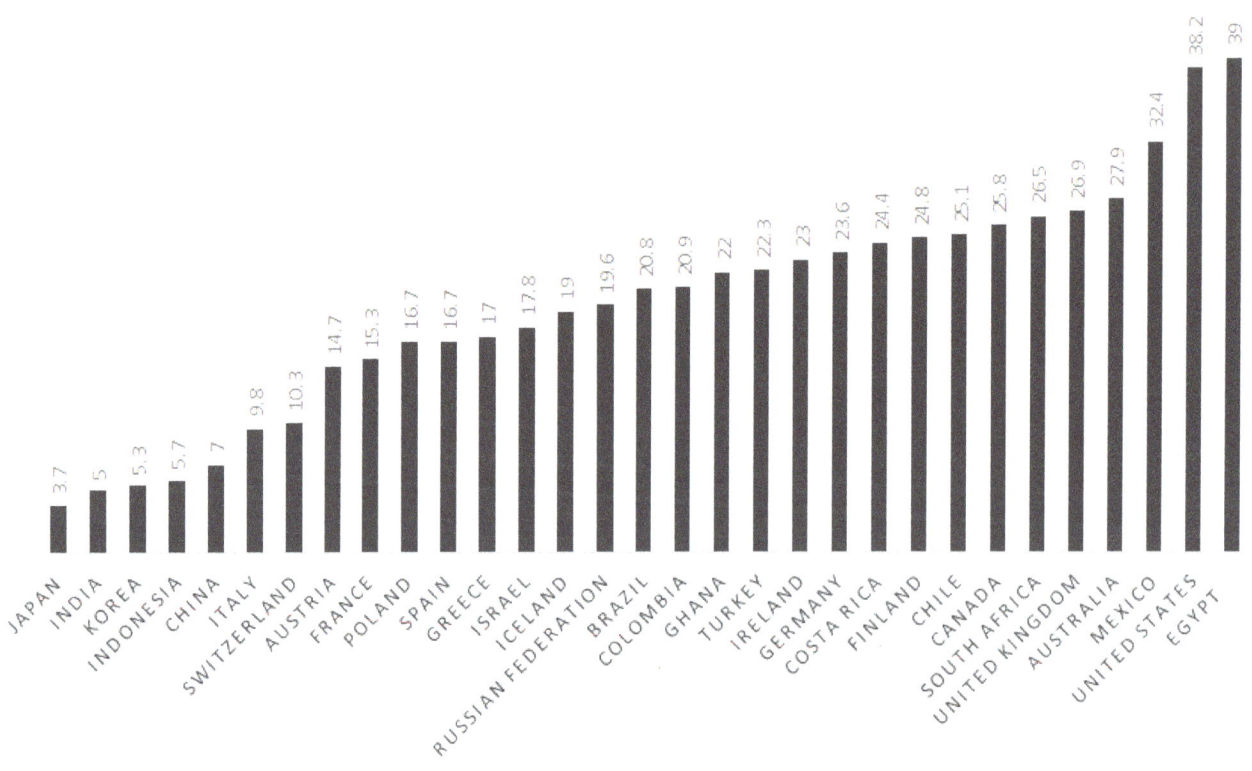

Figure 16.3 Obesity rates by country, 2017.

Causes of Obesity

Although studies show differences in daily energy expenditure between modern foraging and farming populations in comparison with industrialized peoples, the major contributor to obesity in Western populations is energy intake (Pontzer et al. 2012). Many people not only eat too much but too much of the wrong things. Biological anthropologist Leslie Lieberman (2006) argues that contemporary humans continue to rely on cues from foraging strategies in our evolutionary past that are now counterproductive in the **obesogenic** environments in which we now live.

Examine your own eating habits in the context of how humans once hunted and gathered. We relied on visual cues to find food, often traveling long distances to obtain it, then transporting it back to our home base. There we may have had to process it, by hand, to render it edible. Think of how much less energy it takes to find food now. If we have the financial resources, we can acquire big energy payoffs by simply sitting at home and using an app on our mobile phone to place an order for delivery. And, voila! High-calorie (if not highly nutritious) food arrives at our door within minutes. Should we venture out for food, search time is reduced by signage and advertising directing us toward high-density "patches" where food is available 24 hours a day. These include vending machines, gas stations, and fast-food outlets. Travel time is minimal and little human energy is used in the process (Lieberman 2006).

Foods are also prepackaged and prepared in ways that allow us to eat large quantities quickly. Think French fries or chicken nuggets, which we can easily eat with our hands while doing other things, like driving or watching television, rendering eating mindless and allowing us to take in food faster than our **endocrine systems** can let us know we are getting full. Modern "patches" offer low-fiber, calorie-dense resources, which allows us to eat larger quantities, a problem already encouraged by our larger portion sizes (Lieberman 2006). Processed foods are also engineered to appeal to hominin preferences for sweet tastes and fatty, creamy textures (Moss 2013). Remember from earlier chapters that natural selection favored depth perception, color vision, grasping hands, and coordinated eye-hand movements as general primate traits. Advertising and packaging now use our color vision against us, attracting us to products with little nutritional value and playing to our evolutionary predisposition toward variety. Remember those 50 different nutrients we require? That variety is now presented to us in the form of 55 different flavors of Oreo cookies (Cerón 2017), which we take out of the package and dip in milk using our hand-eye coordination and depth perception.

Even if we are ostensibly eating the same things our ancestors did, these foods may not be all that much alike. Take potatoes, for example. One medium-sized, plain, baked potato is a healthy food, especially if we eat the skin too. It contains 110 calories, 0 grams of fat, 26 grams of carbohydrates, and 3 grams of protein, plus 30% of the U.S. Recommended Daily Allowance (RDA) of vitamin C, 10% of vitamin B6, 15% of potassium, and no sodium (http://www.potatogoodness.com). In contrast, a medium order of McDonald's fries, which takes the potato and adds salt and fat, contains 340 calories, 16 grams of fat, 44 grams of carbohydrates, 4 grams of protein, and 230 mg of sodium (http://www.mcdonalds.com). Potato chips take food processing to a whole new level, removing even more nutrition and adding a host of additional ingredients, including oils, preservatives, and artificial flavorings and colors (Moss 2013). Let us use Ruffles Loaded Bacon and Cheddar Potato Skins Potato Chips, one of the top new flavors of 2018, as an example (St. Pierre 2018). The number of ingredients increases from one to 11 to 35 as we move from the potato to the potato chip, moving further from nature with each step (Figure 16.4). It should be noted that the nutritional information for the potato chips is based on a serving size of 11 chips, an amount likely smaller than many people eat. Our bodies also do not react to fries and chips the same way they do to potatoes. Added fat and calories translate into overweight and obesity. Sodium contributes to hypertension. And, artificial flavorings and colorings, including the Yellow 5 and Yellow 6 in the chips, have been linked to cancer, as well as allergies and hyperactivity in children (CSPI 2010). Many sweet, fatty, salty foods like fries and chips are cheap and easily available, which is why many people choose to eat them (Moss 2013). The price of a medium-sized order of McDonald's fries as of this writing is US$1.79, and the potato chips are $2.98 for an 8.5-ounce bag. A single potato prewrapped for microwaving is available in many supermarkets for US$1.99 but requires travel to a market and access to a microwave and eating utensils, making it less convenient.

	Baked Potato [baked, skin on, plain]	**French Fries** [medium order]	**Potato Chips** [1 oz. serving of 11 chips]
Calories	110	340	160
Calories from fat	0	144	90
Fat	0 g	16 g	10 g
Carbohydrates	26 g	44 g	15 g
Protein	3 g	4 g	2 g
Sodium	0 g	230 mg	170 mg
Dietary fiber	2 g	4 g	1 g
Sugars	1 g	0 g	1 g
Cholesterol	0 g	0 g	0 g
Ingredients	Potato	Potatoes, Vegetable Oil (Canola Oil, Soybean Oil, Hydrogenated Soybean Oil, Natural Beef Flavor [Wheat and Milk Derivatives]*, Citric Acid [Preservative]), Dextrose, Sodium Acid Pyrophosphate (Maintain Color), Salt.	Potatoes, Vegetable Oil (Sunflower, Corn, and/or Canola oil), Bacon & Cheddar Loaded Potato Skins Seasoning (Maltodextrin [Made from Corn], Salt, Cheddar Cheese [Milk, Cheese Cultures, Salt, Enzymes], Sour Cream [Cultured Cream, Skim Milk], Whey, Dried Onion, Monosodium Glutamate, Natural Flavor [including Natural Smoke Flavor], Skim Milk, Corn Oil, Canola Oil, Sugar, Buttermilk, Yeast Extract, Romano Cheese [Part-Skim Cow's Milk, Cheese Cultures, Salt Enzymes], Whey Protein Concentrate, Dextrose, Spice, Citric Acid, Lactic Acid, Artificial Color [Yellow 5 Lake, Yellow 5, Yellow 6, Yellow 6 Lake], Butter [Cream, Salt], Sodium Caseinate, Garlic Powder, Blue Cheese [Milk, Cheese Cultures, Salt, Enzymes], and Bacon Fat.

Figure 16.4 The potato in three modern forms.

Not only have we transformed the food supply and our eating in ways that are detrimental to our health, but these changes have been accompanied by reductions in physical activity. **Sedentarism** is built into contemporary lifestyles. Think of how much time you spent sitting down today. Some of it may have been in class or at work, some may have been driving a car or perhaps binge-watching your favorite show, playing a video game, or checking in on social media. An inactive lifestyle is almost dictated by the digital age (Lucock et al. 2014). Levels of physical activity in many countries are now so low that large portions of the population are completely sedentary, including 28% of Americans (Physical Activity Council 2018). For a species whose biology evolved in an environment where walking, lifting, and carrying were part of daily life, this is unhealthy and often leads to weight gain.

Obesity varies by gender, age, geography, and, to some degree, ethnicity (Brown 1991). In general, women tend to gain weight easier than men, but fat distribution is different between them. Women tend to put on weight in the thighs and hips, while men gain weight around their abdomen. The latter is a much greater health risk (Akil and Ahmad

2011). Weight gain also varies across the lifespan, with infants and toddlers tending toward chubbiness then becoming slimmer until adolescence and the onset of puberty (Lucock et al. 2014). This pattern is the result of selective pressure to maintain energy for brain development in early life, then again later on for reproduction. There is also the "thrifty gene" hypothesis: the idea that natural selection favored genotypes that clung to every calorie available to protect against the constant threat of food shortages throughout our evolutionary history, and that this was a species-wide adaptation (Neel 1962).

Figure 16.5 Participants of a walk against diabetes and for general fitness around Nauru airport.

More recent genetic research indicates there are multiple genetic variants that influence weight gain, and they are not spread evenly across or within human populations. Tuomo Rankinen and colleagues (2006) identified 127 genes associated with obesity, of which 22 were supported by research indicating that they contributed to positive energy balance and weight gain. Claude Bouchard (2007) went further, identifying five categories of obesity-promoting genotypes. These include genotypes that promote sedentarism, result in low metabolism, and lead to poor regulation of appetite and satiety and a propensity to overeat. An example of the impact such genotypes can have in an environment of plenty is found among the population of the Micronesian island of Nauru. Historically, the island was geographically isolated and the food supply was unpredictable. These conditions favored genotypes that promoted the ability to rapidly build up and store fat in times of food availability. In Nauruans, there are two genetic variations favoring weight gain and insulin resistance, and both are associated with obesity and Type 2 diabetes. One variant is also associated with higher diastolic blood pressure. One of these variants is also found in Pima Indians in the United States, where it is associated with a high **Body Mass Index (BMI)** and Type 2 diabetes, although it is not associated with the same outcomes in Japanese and British subjects (de Silva et al. 1999). The other variant was also analyzed in Finnish and South Indian populations, neither of whom experienced the same outcome as Nauruans. This suggests these alleles may act as modifying genes for Type 2 diabetes in some population groups (Baker et al. 1994). Unfortunately, Nauruans are one of those groups. Eventually, they became wealthy through phosphate mining on the island, gaining access to a calorie-rich Western diet of imported foods and developing a sedentary lifestyle. This resulted in rates of Type 2 diabetes as high as 30–40% of Nauruans over the age of 15, which became the leading cause of death (Lucock et al. 2014), something Nauruans are taking seriously (See Figure 16.5).

Factors other than biology influence which populations carry and express a genetic predisposition toward obesity and which populations carry but do not express it. The Pima Indians, for example, were seriously impacted by U.S. government policies that affected water rights, forcing the population away from subsistence farming to dependence on government commodities and convenience food. This resulted in a significant loss of physical activity and sedentarism, as well as malnutrition and obesity. Those living on the reservation continue to experience hardship due to high rates of unemployment and poverty, as well as depression, sometimes made worse by alcoholism. In the absence of these pressures, the Pima were diabetes free for centuries prior, even though they relied on agriculture for subsistence, suggesting genetics alone is not responsible for high rates of obesity and diabetes in current populations (Smith-Morris 2004).

Obesity also has an epigenetic component. You learned about epigenetics in Chapter 3. With regard to obesity, epigenetics is counterintuitive in that mothers who do not take in enough calories during pregnancy often give birth to babies who grow up to be fat. What takes place is that the fetus receives signals from the mother through the placenta and intrauterine environment about environmental conditions during pregnancy, in this case food insecurity. These signals encourage the turning on and off of genes related to metabolism, for example. This alters the phenotype of the fetus so that if the child is born into an environment where food is readily available, it will put on weight rapidly whenever possible, falling prey to obesity and related diseases later in life. What is worse is that if the child is a girl, her own eggs are formed in utero with the same genetic changes coded in, meaning she will pass along this same genetic predisposition to gain weight to her children. Hence, a biological propensity toward obesity can continue across generations (Worthman and Kuzara 2005). This same mechanism operates in populations born into poverty that are now growing into plenty. Epigenetic changes to genes that promote weight gain are argued to be partly responsible for the rapid rise in obesity and diabetes in recent years in developing countries gaining access to Western diets (Stearns et al. 2008).

Obesity and overweight put a tremendous strain on several biological systems of the body, including the circulatory, endocrine, and skeletal systems, contributing to hypertension, heart disease, **stroke**, diabetes, and osteoarthritis (See Figure 16.6). Obesity also elevates the risk of cancers of the breast, endometrium, kidney, colon, esophagus, stomach, pancreas, and gallbladder (National Institutes of Health 2017; Vucenik and Stains 2012). Diabetes, one of the fastest growing health conditions around the globe (WHO 2016) and one tightly connected to obesity and overweight, is the focus of the following Special Topics feature.

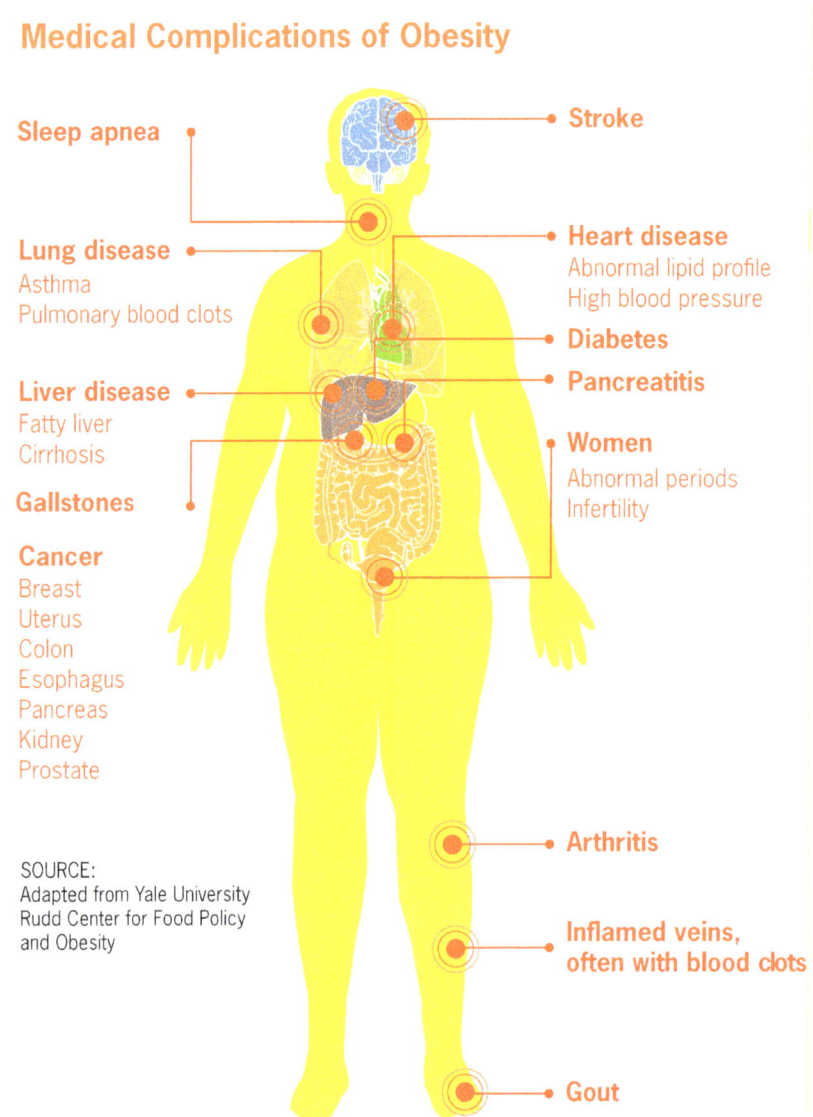

Figure 16.6 *Medical Complications of Obesity.*

SPECIAL TOPIC: DIABETES

Diabetes Mellitus is an endocrine disorder characterized by excessively high blood glucose levels (Martini et al. 2013). According to a report released by the World Health Organization, the number of people living with diabetes is growing in all regions of the world. Rates of diabetes have nearly doubled in the past three decades, largely due to increases in obesity and sugary diets (WHO 2016). One in 11 people around the world, 435 million people, now have diabetes, including over 30 million Americans. In the United States, the disease is rising fastest among millennials (those ages 20-40) (BCBSA 2017), and one in every two adults with diabetes is undiagnosed (IDF 2018). Obesity and diabetes are linked: that is, obesity causes a diet-related disease (diabetes) because of humans' evolved metabolic homeostasis mechanism, which is mismatched to contemporary energy environments (Lucock et al. 2014).

To function properly, cells need a steady fuel supply. Blood sugar is the primary fuel for most cells in the body, and the body produces the hormone **insulin** to help move energy into cells that need it. Insulin functions like a key, turning on insulin receptors located on the surface of the cell. The receptor then activates glucose transporters (GLUTs) that do the work of hauling glucose (blood sugar) out of your bloodstream and into your cells (McKee and McKee 2015; see Figure 16.7). Foods that most readily supply glucose to your bloodstream are carbohydrates, especially starchy foods like potatoes or sweet,

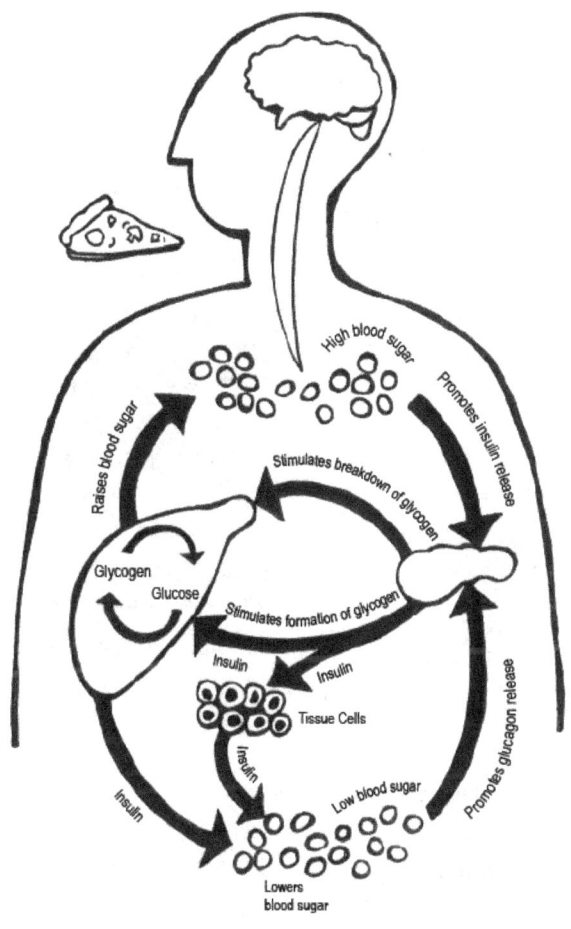

Figure 16.7 Glucose metabolism is the body's evolved mechanism by which we turn food into energy for bodily functions. Carbohydrates are eaten and broken down into simple sugars (e.g., glucose). Glucose enters the bloodstream from the intestines, and the increase in glucose stimulates the pancreas to release insulin into the bloodstream. Insulin deposits glucose in the muscles and fat cells, where it is stored and used for energy.

sugary foods like candy and soda. The body can also convert other types of foods, including protein-rich foods (e.g., lean meats) and fatty foods (e.g., vegetable oils and butter), into blood sugar in the liver via gluconeogenesis. Insulin's main job is to tell your cells when to take up glucose. The cell also has to listen to the signal and mobilize the glucose transporters. This not only allows your cells to get the energy they need, but it also keeps blood sugar from building up to dangerously high levels when you are at rest. Muscles can use glucose without insulin when you are exercising; it does not matter if you are insulin resistant or if you do not make enough insulin. When you exercise, your muscles get the glucose they need, and, in turn, your blood glucose level goes down. If you are insulin resistant, resistance goes down when you exercise and your cells use glucose more effectively (Leontis n.d.).

This system is efficient, but there are limits. Keep in mind that, like the rest of our biology, it evolved during several million years when sugar was hard to come by and carbohydrates took the form of fresh foods with a low **glycemic index (GI)**. Our ancestors were also active throughout the day, taking pressure off of the endocrine system. Now, sedentary lifestyles and processed-food diets cause many of us to take in more calories—and especially more carbohydrates—than our bodies can handle. The fact is, there is only so much blood sugar your cells can absorb. As soaring rates of diabetes show, many modern populations are taxing those limits. After years of being asked by insulin to take in more glucose than they can use, cells eventually stop responding (McKee and McKee 2015). This is called Type 2 diabetes or insulin resistance, which accounts for 90–95% of diabetes cases in the United States. People with Type 1 diabetes do not produce insulin (O'Keefe Osborn 2017; see Figure 16.8).

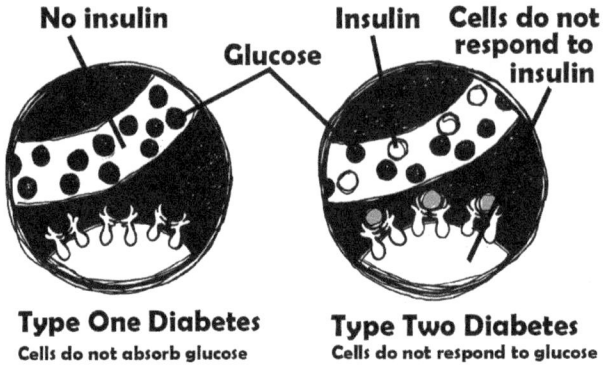

Figure 16.8 Type 1 and Type 2 Diabetes.

Type 2 diabetes is a progressive metabolic condition that occurs over time when our evolved biological mechanism that turns food into energy is derailed by the obesogenic environments in which we live. This is compounded by a sedentary lifestyle. Think about how living in a college environment contributes to the development of diabetes. How much time do you spend sitting each day? How many sugary—and often cheap—carbohydrates are within easy reach? Making simple changes now can head off health complications later. Carrying an apple or orange in your backpack instead of a candy bar and walking or biking instead of driving can make a big difference.

CARDIOVASCULAR DISEASE

Cardiovascular disease (CVD)—which includes coronary heart disease, hypertension (high blood pressure), and stroke—is the leading cause of death globally, and heart disease remains the number one cause of death in the United States (American Heart Association 2018). Risk factors for cardiovascular disease include diet, obesity/overweight, diabetes, and physical inactivity, as well as smoking and alcohol consumption. The connections between these factors and heart disease may not seem obvious and will be addressed here beginning with diet. Diets high in saturated fat and cholesterol can lead to atherosclerosis, a condition in which fat and cholesterol form plaque inside the arteries, eventually building up and hardening to the point that blood flow is blocked. Too much salt in the diet leads to fluid retention, which increases blood volume and thereby blood pressure, taxing the heart. Obesity/overweight contribute to cardiovascular disease directly through increases in total blood volume, cardiac output, and cardiac workload. In other words, the heart has to work much harder if one is overweight (Akil and Ahmad 2011).

Obesity also relates to CVD indirectly through elevation of blood pressure (hypertension) and diabetes. High levels of blood glucose from diabetes can damage blood vessels and the nerves that control the heart and blood vessels. Physical activity also alters the likelihood of having heart disease, both directly and indirectly. Regular exercise of moderate to vigorous intensity strengthens the heart muscle and allows capillaries, tiny blood vessels in your body, to widen, improving blood flow. Regular exercise can also lower blood pressure and cholesterol levels and manage blood sugar levels, all of which reduce the risk of CVD. Alcohol consumption can raise blood pressure and triglyceride levels, a type of fat found in the blood. Alcohol also adds extra calories, which may cause weight gain, especially around the abdomen, which is directly associated with risk of a heart attack (Akil and Ahmad 2011). Cigarette smoking also increases the risk of coronary heart disease. Nicotine increases blood pressure; in addition, cigarette smoke causes fatty buildup in the main artery in the neck and thickens blood, making it more likely to clot. It also decreases levels of HDL ("good") cholesterol (American Heart Association 2014). Even secondhand smoke can have an adverse effect if exposure occurs on a regular basis. Chronic psychological stress also elevates the risk of heart disease (Dimsdale 2008). The repeated release of stress hormones like adrenaline elevates blood pressure and may eventually damage artery walls. The human **stress response** and its connections to health and disease are discussed in more detail below.

OSTEOARTHRITIS

The appearance of osteoarthritis in skeletal remains from the Neolithic has been attributed to the repetitive loading of articular joints due to the manual labor associated with early agricultural production (Larsen 2014). In modern populations, overweight and obesity are major contributing factors to arthritis, due not only to the overloading of joints that comes with excess weight (Guilak 2011) but also to the action of fat cells that generate low-level inflammation in response to high levels of glucose in the blood (Issa and Griffin 2012). Meaning, diabetes is a risk factor for osteoarthritis (Berenbaum 2011). A high percentage of obese individuals with knee osteoarthritis are sedentary, suggesting lack of physical activity may increase susceptibility to inflammation (Issa and Griffin 2012). Again, excess body weight and lack of physical activity are a mismatch for Stone Age bodies making their way in the space age (Eaton et al. 1988).

CANCER

Cancer is the second-leading cause of death globally, causing one in every six deaths and killing nearly nine million people in 2015 (WHO 2018b). Lifetime cancer risk in developed Western populations is now one in two, or 50% (Greaves 2015). Approximately one-third of deaths from cancer are due to behavioral and dietary factors, including high Body Mass Index (BMI), low fruit and vegetable intake, lack of physical activity, and the use of tobacco and alcohol. Depending on the type of cancer and one's own genetic inheritance, these factors can increase cancer risk from 2- to 100-fold (Greaves 2015). Cancer is the result of interactions between a person's genes and three categories of external agents: physical carcinogens (e.g., ultraviolet radiation), chemical carcinogens (e.g., tobacco smoke, asbestos), and biological carcinogens, such as infections from certain viruses, bacteria, or parasites (WHO 2018b). Obesity is also a risk factor for cancer, including of the breast, endometrium, kidney, colon, esophagus, stomach, pancreas, and gallbladder (National Institutes of Health 2017; Vucenik and Stains 2012).

Cancer has been regarded as a relatively recent affliction for humans that became a problem after we encountered exposure to modern carcinogens and lived long enough to express the disease (David and Zimmerman 2010). Given the long history that humans share with many oncogenic (cancer-causing) parasites and viruses (Ewald 2018), and the recent discovery of cancer in the metatarsal bone of a 1.8-million-year-old hominin (Odes et al. 2016), this view is being challenged (See Special Topics). The difficulties of identifying cancer in archaeological populations are many. Most cancer occurs in soft tissue, which rarely preserves, and fast-growing cancers would likely kill victims before leaving evidence in bone. It is also difficult to distinguish cancer from benign growths and inflammatory disease in ancient fossils, and there is often post-mortem damage to fossil evidence from scavenging and erosion. In light of these challenges, Paul Ewald (2018) suggests using other lines of evidence to discern the prevalence of cancer in ancient humans, including examining the history of cancer-causing parasites and viruses. His complete analysis is beyond the scope of this chapter, but one example of a virus you may be familiar with will serve to illustrate the concept.

SPECIAL TOPIC

Earliest evidence of cancer in hominins: Using 3-D images, South African researchers diagnosed a type of cancer called osteosarcoma in a toe bone belonging to a human relative who died in Swartkrans Cave between 1.6 and 1.8 million years ago. https://news.nationalgeographic.com/2016/07/oldest-human-cancer-disease-origins-tumor-fossil-science/

Human papillomavirus (HPV) is the most common sexually transmitted infection in the United States, and 79 million Americans, most in their late teens and early twenties, are infected with HPV (CDC 2017). HPVs are transmitted through sexual activity and can cause cancers of the cervix, vulva, vagina, penis, or anus. It can also cause cancer in the back of the throat, including at the base of the tongue and tonsils. The Centers for Disease Control recommends all 11–12 year olds, both girls and boys, get two doses of the HPV vaccine to protect against diseases, including cancers, caused by HPV. One such disease is cervical cancer, the fourth-leading cause of death for women in the world, and the second most common cause of death by cancer (surpassed only by breast cancer) for women ages 15–44 (Bruni et al. 2017). There are over 100 different strains of HPV, but Types 16 and 18 cause 70% of all cervical cancers (Bruni et al. 2017). Type 16 is the most oncogenic of the HPVs, and it has been present in the genus *Homo* for half a million years, suggesting cervical cancer and other cancers caused by HPV may have been too (Ewald 2018).

Behavioral or "lifestyle" choices have an impact on cancer risk. Breast cancer is one example. It is the most common cancer in women worldwide, but **incidence** of new cases varies from 19.3 per 100,000 women in Eastern Africa to 89.7 per 100,000 women in Western Europe (WHO 2018b). These differences are attributable to cultural changes among women in Western, industrialized countries that are a mismatch for our evolved reproductive biology. Age at **menarche**, the onset of menstrual periods, has dropped over the course of the last century from 16 to 12 years of age in the U.S. and Europe, with some girls getting their periods at nine or ten years old and developing breasts as young as eight years old (Greenspan and Deardorff 2014). A World Health Organization study involving data from 34 countries in Europe and North America suggests the primary reason for the increase in earlier puberty is obesity, with differences in Body Mass Index (BMI) accounting for 40% of individual- and country-level variance (Currie et al. 2012). Exposure to hormone-disrupting chemicals in utero and childhood may also be a factor (Greenspan and Deardorff 2014). As with other aspects of health discussed in this chapter, social and economic factors also influence earlier puberty, with girls who grow up in homes without their biological father twice as likely to experience early puberty, as is the case for girls who experience childhood trauma and/or grow up in a home with a depressed mother (Greenspan and Deardorff 2014). There is also ethnic variation in early puberty, with African American and Latina girls much more likely to experience puberty at younger ages. These factors combine in that African American and Latina girls are more likely to be overweight or obese and to grow up in low-income neighborhoods, where they are more likely to be exposed to environmental pollutants. Early puberty in girls has been associated with increased risk of breast cancer, ovarian cancer, obesity, diabetes, and raised triglycerides in later life (Pierce and Hardy 2012). In addition, there are negative social consequences, with girls who develop early more likely to experience anxiety, depression, poor body image, and eating disorders (Greenspan and Deardorff 2014).

At the same time, age at puberty is dropping for girls in Western nations and age at birth of the first child is later, on average at 26 years old (Mathews and Hamilton 2016). Women are also having fewer children, two on average (Gao 2015), with 15% of women choosing to remain childless (Livingston 2015). Rates of breastfeeding have risen in recent decades but drop to only 27% of infants once babies reach 12 months of age (CDC 2014). Nearly one-third of women also take oral contraceptives or use another hormonal method of birth control (Jones and Dreweke 2011). In contrast, data from modern foraging populations (Eaton et al. 1994) indicate age at menarche is around 16 years old, age at birth of the first child is 19, breastfeeding on-demand continues for three years for each child, and the number of live births to women who survive to age 60 averages six. These differences relate to elevated risk for reproductive cancers among women in developed countries.

Other than an established genetic risk (e.g., BRCA gene), the primary risk factor for breast cancer is exposure to estrogen. For women living in modern, industrialized economies, this exposure now often comes from women's own ovaries rather than from external environmental sources (Stearns et al. 2008). There is nothing biologically normal about regular monthly periods. Women in cultures without contraception are pregnant or lactating (breastfeeding) for much of their reproductive lives, resulting in 100 or so menstrual cycles per lifetime. In contrast, Western women typically experience 400 or more (Strassmann 1997). This is partly due to younger ages at menarche. From menarche to the birth of a woman's first child can be 14 years or longer in modern, Western populations, after which breastfeeding, if undertaken at all, lasts for a few weeks or months and is not on-demand, negating the natural birth control provided by frequent lactation. Women may also choose to use oral contraceptives or other hormonal methods to control reproduction. In their current form, these drugs induce a monthly period. Age at menopause (the cessation of menstrual cycles) is constant at 50–55 years old across human populations. For Western women, this translates into forty years of nearly continuous menstrual cycling between menarche and menopause. Each month the body prepares for a pregnancy that never occurs, increasing cell divisions that put women at risk for cancers of the breast, endometrium, ovaries, and uterus (Strassmann 1999). Obesity adds to this risk, as obese women have greater proportions of bioavailable estrogen (Eaton et al. 1994). In obese and overweight postmenopausal women, adipose (fat) tissues are the main source of estrogen biosynthesis. Thus, weight gain during the postmenopausal stage means higher exposure to estrogen and greater risk of cancer (Ali 2014). Factors associated with reduced risk of reproductive cancers are late menarche, early first birth, high numbers of pregnancies, early menopause, and breastfeeding.

Again, humans cannot return to our evolutionary past, and there are important social and economic reasons for delaying pregnancy and having fewer children. These include achieving educational and career goals, leading to greater earning power and a reduction in the gender pay gap, as well as more enduring marriages and a decrease in the number of women needing public assistance (Sonfield et al. 2013). There are also cultural means by which we might reduce the risk of reproductive cancers that do not involve increases in family size. These include reformulating hormonal contraceptives with enough estrogen to maintain bone density and stave off osteoporosis, but reducing the number of menstrual periods over the reproductive lifespan (Stearns et al. 2008). Reducing fat intake may also lower serum estrogen concentrations, while high-fat diets have been shown to contribute to breast tumor development. High-fiber diets are also beneficial in decreasing intestinal resorption of estrogenic hormones. Exercise also appears protective, with studies of former college athletes demonstrating risks of breast, uterine, and ovarian cancers later in life two to five times lower than those of non-athletes (Eaton et al. 1994).

SPECIAL TOPIC: THE PALEO DIET

Given the impact of diet on every health condition discussed so far in this chapter, you may be considering changing what you eat. But what diet to follow? Given your interest in human evolution, have you ever wondered about the Paleo diet? Popularized by the 2002 book, *The Paleo Diet: Lose Weight and Get Healthy by Eating the Food You Were Designed to Eat*, by professor of nutrition and exercise physiology Loren Cordain, the Paleo diet is an eating plan based on the idea that eating like our ancestors is protective against weight gain, metabolic disorders, and other maladies of modern life. Its publication spawned an entire industry of diets, exercise plans, cookbooks, and other products based on the "Paleolithic prescription."

Recommendations of the Paleo diet include eating high amounts of protein, fewer carbohydrates, more fiber, certain fats, and foods rich in plant phytochemicals, vitamins, minerals, and antioxidants. Sounds good so far, but let's dive a little deeper. Protein in the Paleo diet consists of lean meats (including organ meats), fish, and seafood. And not industrially produced versions of these. The meat should be grass- not grain-fed, and the fish should be wild caught, not farmed. All fruits are included in the diet, but only non-starchy vegetables make the cut, meaning no tubers like potatoes. The recommended carbohydrates have a low Glycemic Index, meaning they are more slowly digested and metabolised causing a lower, slower rise in blood glucose and insulin levels. There are also no cereals, no legumes (beans), no dairy products, no processed foods, no refined sugars (including honey), and no added salt. The primary fats in the diet are monounsaturated, polyunsaturated, and omega-3 fats, rather than the trans fats and saturated fats most often found in contemporary diets (Cordain 2002).

Particular attention is given to counteracting what many people think of as high-protein foods. Hamburger, eggs, and cheese, which are 24%, 34%, and 28% protein, respectively, are off the list, as opposed to skinless turkey breast (94% protein) and shrimp (90%). There is also the idea that current Western diets are more acidic than alkaline, reducing calcium levels in the body by promoting excretion of calcium in the urine. Cereals, dairy products, legumes, meat, fish, eggs, and salty processed foods elevate acid loads in the body, while fruits and non-starchy vegetables produce net alkaline loads. The diet advises eating 35% of your daily calories as fruits and veggies to balance out the high recommended protein intake. These recommendations are based on the premise that this represents a typical diet of hunter-gatherers in our ancient past before the transition to agriculture. Given what you have learned about human evolution from this text, what might be some problems with this assumption? How about with the diet itself?

To begin, there is no such thing as *the* Paleo diet. Hominins occupied a variety of ecological niches, with corresponding variety in what they ate (Lucock et al. 2014), including wide variation in their consumption of meat (Wrangham 2009). There is also archaeological evidence and dietary analysis of teeth demonstrating that hominin foragers ate cooked grains as far back as two million years ago (Zuk 2013). Although modern foragers are not an analogue for the past, they vary widely in their dietary intake. Meat forms 99% of the traditional Inuit diet (McElroy and Townsend 2009), while the diet of the !Kung of sub-Saharan Africa is mostly vegetarian (Lee 2013). In the case of the Inuit, they have genetic mutations related to the processing of omega-3 fatty acids that allow them to live on such a high-protein, high-fat diet without the cardiovascular disease and metabolic issues found in other populations (Fumagalli et al. 2015). Similarly, some pastoral populations became lactase persistent over time, allowing their members to digest milk as adults (Crow and Kimura 1970), and there are genotypes favored among peoples with high-starch diets that improve the digestion of starches (Marciniak and Perry 2017) and promote resistance to infectious disease (Lucock et al. 2014). Clearly, not all humans ate the same things, and natural selection favored genotypes that allowed populations to survive as they encountered new food sources and their diets changed. The modern Paleo diet also does not take into account the difficulty of procuring the lean protein that it recommends in the absence of hunting it yourself. Furthermore, it leaves out fermented foods, like pickled vegetables, yogurt, and cheeses, that contribute to a healthy microbiome (Graber 2014), something researchers are coming to find is essential to health (Shreiner et al. 2015).

What, then, to eat? As with Paleo diets, what humans eat today varies by geography, economics, and cultural preferences, among other factors. The burgeoning science of nutrigenomics hopes to one day be able to provide each individual with a customized diet based on analysis of your own DNA, lifestyle, and disease risk (Neeha and Kinth 2013). Until that time, World Health Organization dietary recommendations for the prevention of chronic diseases like cardiovascular disease, diabetes, and cancer emphasize diets that are low in saturated fat, salt, and sugar, high in fiber, and feature lean proteins (including nuts and fish) and carbohydrates from whole grains, legumes (beans), fresh fruits, and vegetables (WHO 2018c). Fiber, in particular, has been shown to be protective. Epidemiological and clinical studies demonstrate that intake of dietary fiber from plants and whole grains is inversely related to obesity, Type 2 diabetes, colon cancer, and cardiovascular disease (Lattimer and Haub 2010). Newer research suggests diets high in fiber also boost immune function, mood, and cognition (Kaczmarczyk et al. 2012).

Can these recommendations be met with a vegetarian or vegan diet? Research suggests this is the case, if one is conscientious and knowledgeable about the combination and timing of foods to obtain essential nutrients (McEvoy et al. 2012; Woo et al. 2014). Research introduced earlier in this chapter regarding the negative health effects of cooked meats suggests that eating meat four times per month or less, eating it rare, and avoiding processed meats altogether, is less likely to result in cancer, diabetes, and hypertension (Abid et al. 2014; Liu 2018; Liu et al. 2018; Trafialek and Kolanowski 2014). Additionally, according to the EAT-Lancet Commission on healthy diets from sustainable food systems, global consumption of foods such as red meat and sugar will have to decrease by half to make sure the Earth will be able to feed a growing population of 10 billion people by 2050. At the same time, people will need to double the amount of plant-based foods they eat, including nuts, fruits, vegetables, and legumes (Willett et al. 2019).

STRESS

Have you ever been "stressed out" in class? Say you're in a large lecture hall with a hundred other people, or even in a small class where you don't know anyone. You're not sure about something the professor just said and you would really like to ask about it, so you start to raise your hand. Does your heart begin to pound and your mouth get dry? Do you sometimes get so nervous you choose to catch up with a classmate after lecture instead? If so, you are not alone. Fear of speaking in public is one of the most common social phobias (APA 2013). It has been estimated that 75% of all people experience some degree of anxiety or nervousness when it comes to public speaking (Hamilton 2011), and surveys have shown that most people fear public speaking more than they fear death (Croston 2012).

We have evolution to thank for this.

Humans, like other primates, are social animals. Being part of a group helped us to survive predation, get enough to eat, and successfully raise our young. When faced with standing up in front of a group, or even speaking up in class, we break into a sweat because we are afraid of rejection. Psychologist Glenn Croston (2012) writes, "The fear is so great because we are not merely afraid of being embarrassed or judged. We are afraid of being rejected from the social group, ostracized and left to defend ourselves all on our own. We fear ostracism still so much today it seems, fearing it more than death, because not so long ago getting kicked out of the group probably really was a death sentence." Hence, it is no surprise that public speaking triggers a stress response among much of humankind.

The human nervous system evolved in a context where quick responses to perceived threats presented an evolutionary advantage. The "fight or flight" response with which we are all familiar was honed during millions of years when threats more often took the form of an approaching lion than an approaching deadline. Our body's response, however, is triggered by a wide variety of stressors that produce the same general pattern of hormonal and physiological adjustments (Martini et al. 2013). In today's world, the system is often stuck in the "on" position due to the constant pressures of modern life, and this is a significant influence on health and disease.

The human stress response involves the **Central Nervous System** acting in concert with the **endocrine** and **circulatory systems**. It includes three phases: alarm, resistance, and exhaustion (Martini et al. 2013). The alarm phase is the automatic, short-term response to a crisis, the "fight or flight" response you might have experienced when thinking about raising your hand in class. Epinephrine is the dominant hormone of this phase. Its secretion stimulates activation of the sympathetic nervous system, including sudden increases in heart rate, respiration, mental alertness, sweat gland excretion, and energy use. If the stress-inducing situation lasts more than a few hours, the body shifts to the resistance phase. Glucocorticoids are the dominant hormones of this phase, which involves mobilizing the body's metabolic reserves to maintain the energy levels necessary for the brain to function during continued stress. A side effect of glucocorticoids is suppression of inflammation and the immune response, and cardiovascular damage can occur from elevations in blood pressure and blood volume from the action of ADH (antidiuretic hormone) and aldosterone (a hormone that regulates salt and water in the body). The resistance phase can be maintained for weeks or months, but eventually homeostatic regulation breaks down and leads to the exhaustion phase. If corrective actions are not taken, organs begin to fail, and death follows (Martini et al. 2013).

The negative effects of sustained, elevated cortisol levels on health are well documented. These include higher levels of infectious disease and slowed growth in childhood (Flinn and England 2003) and increased incidence of heart disease, obesity, and diabetes in adults (Worthman and Kuzara 2005). As opposed to what might have been the case in our evolutionary past, many causes of sustained stress in contemporary societies are psychosocial rather than physical threats. These can include an unhappy marriage or frustrations at work (Dimsdale 2008). Stressors can also be more subtle. For example, a recent review of research into the effects of stress on health indicated internalized racism was a significant stressor that was positively associated with alcohol consumption, psychological distress, overweight, abdominal obesity, and higher fasting-glucose levels among minority groups (Williams and Mohammed 2013). Chronic everyday discrimination is also positively associated with coronary artery calcification, elevated blood pressure, giving birth to lower-birth-weight infants, cognitive impairment, poor sleep, visceral fat, and mortality. These effects have been shown to increase morbidity and mortality among members of affected groups.

Epigenetics can also be a factor in how a person is able to deal with stressful situations. Maternal experiences of stress during pregnancy have the potential to permanently alter the physiology of mothers' offspring, especially the hypothalamic-pituitary-adrenal (HPA) axis. The HPA axis regulates metabolism, blood pressure, and the immune response, and these alterations can predispose prenatally stressed individuals to suffer metabolic, cardiovascular, and mental disorders in adulthood (Palma-Gudiel et al. 2015). These experiences carry across generations, with children of Holocaust survivors who experienced PTSD demonstrating similar changes in neurochemistry in the absence of a sustained, traumatic event, as did infant offspring of mothers who developed PTSD during pregnancy after witnessing the traumatic events of 9/11 (Yehuda and LeDoux 2007). Clearly, stress has a profound impact on human health and is one more example of a biological system that is maladaptive in many modern contexts.

SYNDEMICS AND THE ECOLOGICAL MODEL

It is important to recognize that disease risk is not spread evenly within or between populations. Diseases also combine and interact to create a **syndemic**, where the coexistence of two or more conditions exacerbates the effects of one or all conditions. One example is coinfection with HIV and *Mycobacterium tuberculosis*, which is associated with more rapid disease progression, worse symptoms, and a higher pathogenic load than during a single infection with either agent (Singer et al. 2017). Syndemic risk also includes social, political, economic, and environmental factors that increase risk for the clustering of two or more diseases (Singer et al. 2017; Singer and Clair 2003). One of the first syndemics identified involved substance abuse, violence, and AIDS (SAVA), in which the inner-city health crisis around HIV/AIDS was related to other conditions, including tuberculosis, sexually transmitted infections, hepatitis, cirrhosis, infant mortality, drug abuse, suicide, and homicide. These were, in turn, connected to poverty, homelessness, unemployment, poor nutrition, lack of social support, and social and ethnic inequality (Singer et al. 2017). Together, these factors and others, like health policy and unequal access to health care, form an **ecological model** of health and disease, a more holistic way of viewing health issues and their solutions than focusing solely on biology and medical intervention (Sallis et al. 2008).

A historical example will serve to illustrate these concepts. You will remember the discussion of the first epidemiological transition from earlier in this chapter. This involved a rise in infectious disease following human adoption of agriculture as a primary subsistence strategy. This transition took place in the Old World and was fueled by zoonotic pathogens that infected humankind following the domestication of cattle, pigs, horses, sheep, goats, chickens, and other species. During the thousands of years following that transition, epidemics repeatedly occurred among Old World populations resulting in periods of crisis mortality, when large numbers of people died. This was followed by population recovery as survivors, who often became immune to reinfection, produced new generations to be infected during the next epidemic (Omran 2005). This same set of interactions did not, however, occur in the New World, where species that might have developed into domesticated animals equivalent to horses and cattle were wiped out at the end of the last Ice Age, when humans are hypothesized to have migrated to the New World across an exposed land bridge in the Arctic (Diamond 1997). These extinctions may have been the result of hunting or climate change or a combination of both. What is important to note is that the land bridge disappeared as sea levels rose at the end of the Ice Age, isolating the Americas until European contact in the 15th century. This isolation was to have severe consequences for Native Americans.

When Columbus "discovered" the New World in 1492, he unleashed one of the first waves of infectious disease that decimated Native American populations in the centuries to follow (Crosby 2003), eventually killing 90% of the population, an estimated 20 million people (Diamond 1997). The devastation of native communities was the result of a combination of factors. One was the very different histories of Europe and the Americas. With no history of animal domestication beyond dogs, turkeys, ducks, guinea pigs, llamas, and alpacas, Native Americans did not fall prey to zoonotic pathogens that produced highly contagious infectious diseases, leaving them with no resistance. Also, in spite of their profound differences in culture, language, subsistence, and political and economic systems, Native Americans were genetically very much alike (Crosby 2003). This was due to the small number of individuals who crossed the land bridge, which then closed, leaving them in genetic isolation for 10,000 years or more. This meant there was not a high degree of variation for natural selection to act upon in the midst of the severe evolutionary pressure of smallpox and other infectious diseases introduced by Europeans. Native Americans had also not benefited from the technological developments associated with warfare in the Old World, including steel swords, guns, and fighting on horseback, that had been perfected over centuries of conflict (Diamond 1997). European conquest also toppled existing political and social systems already crippled by epidemics of disease, leading to social disorder and cultural and economic disruption. To compound the situation, European colonization included the enslavement and forced labor of native populations to serve European interests, resulting in injury, starvation, and other mistreatment and leading to further loss of life. This complex of epidemiological, technological, social, political, and economic factors (a syndemic) combined to nearly exterminate Native Americans in the centuries following European contact, but this need not have been the case. Alfred Crosby (2003) points out that although epidemics among immunologically unprepared populations produce high mortality rates, some individuals survive, and the population will recover if left alone. He reminds us that,

> Europe, for instance, lost one-third of its population to the Black Death in the fourteenth century and recovered in time. If the Black Death had been accompanied by the arrival of Genghis Khan's hordes, miraculously plague-proof, the story would have been very different. It might have been similar to what happened when European settlers followed on the heels of smallpox and other infections previously unknown to American Indians. [Crosby 2003:xxii]

Unfortunately, syndemics did not begin or end with European colonization of the New World. Interactions between disease and income inequality, education, discrimination, warfare, migration, climate change, and a host of other factors continue to affect humans today, causing health disparities that lead to differences in morbidity and mortality within and across nations (Singer and Baer 2012; see Figure 16.9).

United States	Worldwide
1. Heart disease	1. Heart disease
2. Cancer	2. Stroke
3. Accidents	3. Chronic Obstructive Pulmonary Disease
4. Chronic lower respiratory diseases	4. Lower respiratory infections
5. Stroke	5. Alzheimer disease and dementia
6. Alzheimer's disease	6. Lung cancer
7. Diabetes	7. Diabetes mellitus
8. Influenza and pneumonia	8. Road injury
9. Kidney disease	9. Diarrheal diseases
10. Suicide	10. Tuberculosis

Figure 16.9 Top ten causes of death in the U.S. and worldwide.

Although a full discussion of global health disparities is beyond the scope of this chapter, a brief discussion of asthma in the United States can shed light on several common factors that contribute to inequalities in health today. Nearly 20 million people in the U.S. suffer from asthma, over a third of whom are children under 18 years of age (CDC 2017). Childhood-asthma prevalence doubled from 1980 to 1995, then increased slowly from 2001 to 2010, leveling off in 2013. Rates of asthma are highest among African American and Latino children (Akinbami et al. 2016). Among Latinos, Puerto Ricans have the highest lifetime asthma rate (16.9%), more than three times the rate for Mexican Americans (Singer and Baer 2012). Given that most adult asthma has its origins in early life, discovering the causes of childhood asthma and preventing it has become a major public health focus (Beasley et al. 2015).

A range of factors contribute to the development of asthma in childhood. These include genetics and family history, as well as exposure to stress and being born into a single-parent family. Other factors include being a low-birth-weight baby or being born prematurely. Living in an urban environment, being exposed to indoor and outdoor air pollution, including cigarette smoke, is also a contributor. Certain childhood infections (e.g., pertussis), antibiotics use, and exposure to environmental toxins like mold are also associated with asthma. Diets high in trans-fatty acids and salt, especially fast-food, also contribute to the development of asthma. Sedentarism, high BMI, overweight, and obesity are also factors, with incidence increased by 20% in overweight children and doubled for obese kids (Chen et al. 2012). There are also gender differences associated with the obesity-asthma connection, with boys experiencing higher rates until age 13 and asthma becoming more prevalent in girls post-puberty (Beasley et al. 2015). The mechanisms behind this are unknown but may include anatomical differences in lung capacity, sleep disorders, body fat distribution, and inflammation (Chen et al. 2012). In keeping with the hygiene hypothesis, children exposed to dogs or farm animals in early childhood, including before age one, are less likely to develop asthma (Fall et al. 2015), especially children in urban environments where they may have less frequent contact with the natural environment (Dunn 2018).

Differences in prevalence of childhood asthma between ethnic groups within a population are not mainly because of genetic differences but, rather, because of differences in exposure to environmental and lifestyle factors (Beasley et al. 2015). Given this, let us examine the case of African American and Latino children in light of the risk factors just described. Working-class people and people of color in the U.S. are more likely to live in close proximity to freeways and environmental threats like petrochemical plants and waste incinerators. They are also more likely to live in poverty and in areas with high rates of crime and violence, which elevate stress levels, as does racial discrimination (Singer and Baer 2012). African American children are also far more likely than other groups in the U.S. to grow up in female-headed households, with 72% now being born to single mothers (Washington 2010), many of whom live in poverty and lack access to health care (Pearl 2015). Accurate diagnosis and treatment are key to management of childhood asthma, yet many children of color remain undiagnosed, in part because of lack of regular check-ups. One study conducted among Puerto Ricans in Chicago found prevalence of asthma among Puerto Rican children jumped to 34% when counting cases of possible asthma based on reports of patient symptoms rather than a physician's diagnosis (Joseph et al. 1996). Another study, conducted in New York City, demonstrated that Puerto Rican children were more likely to miss school because of asthma than other ethnic groups in the same neighborhoods, and that low-income Latino families with children with asthma were less likely to have training, education, and resources to manage their child's asthma (Findley et al. 2003). A 2002 study of over 1,000 American children and their families found that Latino and African American children were less likely to be prescribed the standard treatment for asthma and that Latino children received fewer inhaled steroids than white children (Ortega et al. 2002). Clearly, there are multiple factors contributing to health disparities in asthma for American children of different ethnic backgrounds, suggesting an ecological approach is necessary for addressing the problem.

Currently, there is no cure for asthma and no vaccine against it. Instead, public health efforts have largely focused on diagnosis, treatment, and education in place of prevention (Beasley et al. 2015). Given the sheer number of risk factors involved, some scholars have begun to question whether prevention is even possible. Richard Beasley and colleagues

(2015:1078) explain: "Public health efforts will need to focus on reducing environmental tobacco exposure, reducing indoor and outdoor air pollution and occupational exposures, reducing childhood obesity and encouraging a diet high in vegetables and fruit, improving fetal and maternal health, encouraging breastfeeding, promoting childhood vaccinations, and reducing social inequalities." These challenges serve to remind us to take an ecological approach to health and disease. As humans, we all have our biology and genetics with which to contend, but we often do so in the midst of very different life circumstances.

ARE WE STILL EVOLVING?

Given the current global burden of non-communicable diseases like heart disease, cancer, and diabetes discussed in this chapter, many students ask why humans have not yet evolved in response. First, the health conditions highlighted here do not typically have repercussions on reproductive success, meaning natural selection cannot act to favor one genotype over another to protect against them. There also may not have been sufficient time for natural selection to act (Stearns et al. 2008). The cultural transformation of our food supply and lifestyle came about quickly. The transition from foraging to farming took place beginning 12,000 years ago, industrial food production came about in the last 200 years, and technologies like television, the internet, and social media that promote sedentarism are less than 75 years old—one human lifetime. Even under the strongest selective pressure, evolution takes many generations. For example, the mutation that led pastoral populations to be able to digest fresh milk likely took 8,000 years, or 325 generations, to reach a frequency of 90% (Crow and Kimura 1970). This does not mean, however, that humans have stopped evolving. As a species, we continue to respond to selective pressures biologically and culturally. This portion of the chapter will focus on contemporary examples of human evolution.

Before beginning, let's remind ourselves of the modern definition of *evolution*, which is a change in allele frequencies across generations in a given population for a particular trait. We must also review the conditions necessary for natural selection to operate on a trait. First, the trait must be heritable, meaning it is transmitted genetically from generation to generation. Non-inherited traits are learned and include things like cultural preferences for certain types of foods or who we think it is best to marry. Not only must a trait be heritable, there must also be variation of the trait in human populations and the trait must influence reproductive success. Three examples of traits that meet these criteria are immunity to HIV, height, and wisdom teeth (Andrews et al. 2011).

AIDS is a potentially fatal infectious disease caused by the Human Immunodeficiency Virus (HIV), a zoonosis believed to be derived from Simian Immunodeficiency Viruses (SIVs) found in chimpanzees and monkeys, most likely transmitted to humans through the butchering of infected animals (Sharp and Hahn 2011). In total, 35 million people have died from AIDS-related illnesses since the start of the global epidemic in the 1980s. There were 36.7 million people around the world living with AIDS as of 2016, including 1.8 million new cases and 1 million deaths in that year alone (UNAIDS 2018). A disease causing this level of morbidity and mortality represents a major selective pressure, especially given that infection can occur before birth (Goulder et al. 2016), having an affect on future reproductive success.

The majority of people in the world are highly susceptible to HIV infection, but some are not. There are individuals who are homozygous for a rare, recessive allele at the CCR5 locus who are immune. Heterozygotes who inherit a single copy of this allele are more resistant to infection and the disease takes longer to progress in the event they are infected. The mechanism by which the allele prevents infection involves a 32-base pair deletion in the DNA sequence of the CCR5 gene, creating a non-functioning receptor on the surface of the cell that prevents HIV from infecting the cell. The allele is inherited as a simple Mendelian trait, and there is variation in its prevalence, ranging as high as 14% of the population in northern Europe and Russia (Novembre et al. 2005; see Figure 16.8). What is interesting about the allele's geographic distribution is that it does not map onto parts of the world with the highest rates of HIV infection (UNAIDS 2018), suggesting that AIDS was not the original selective pressure favoring this allele (Figure 16.10 and Figure 16.11).

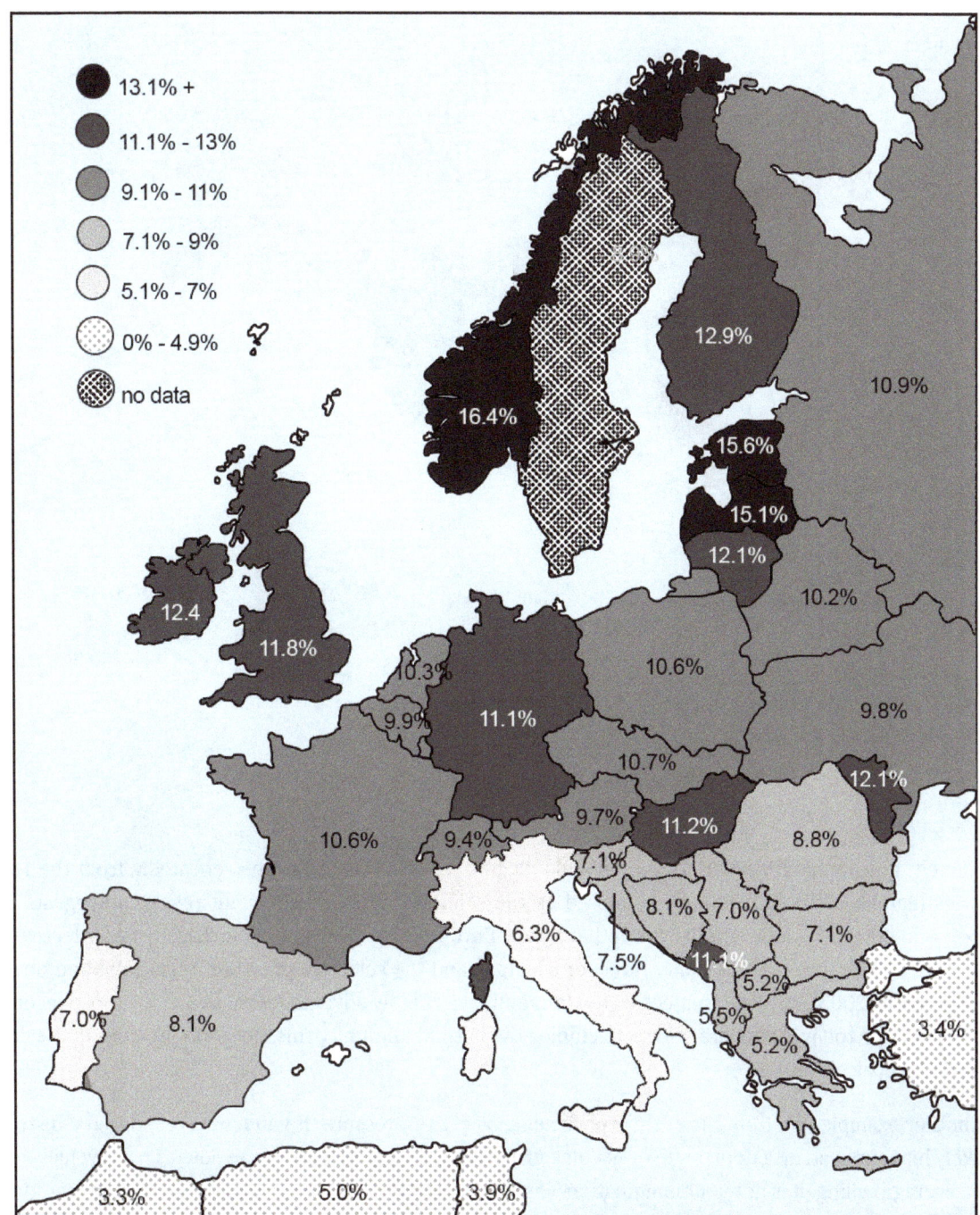

Figure 16.10 Map of CCR5-delta32 allele distribution.

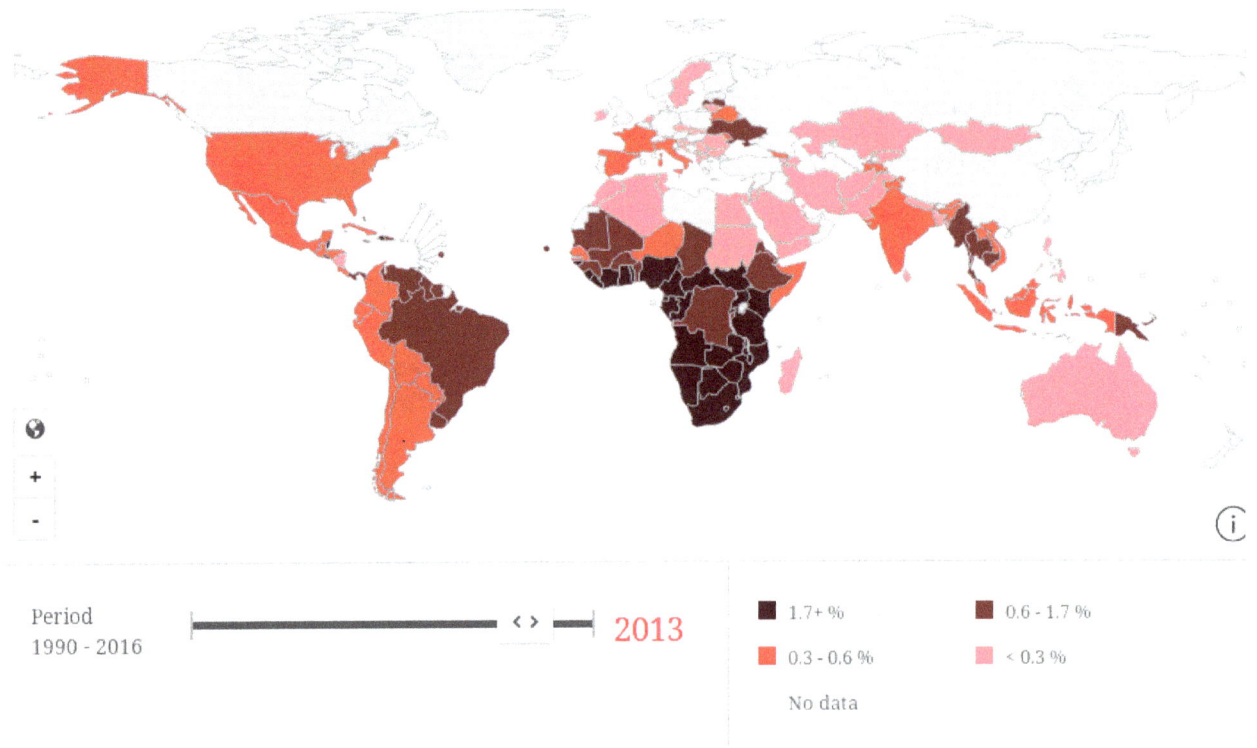

Figure 16.11 Map of global HIV infection.

Given its current geographic distribution, the bubonic plague, which ravaged Europe repeatedly from the 14th to the 19th centuries (Pamuk 2007), was initially proposed as the selective agent. Subsequent research suggests smallpox, which killed up to 400,000 people annually in 18th-century Europe (Hays 2005), was more likely the selective pressure (Novembre et al. 2005). Given the mortality rates for smallpox and the selective pressure it has exhibited on humanity for centuries (Crosby 2003), an allele that conferred immunity was highly advantageous, as it is for those faced with the threat of HIV infection today. There are efforts to employ the natural immunity this mutation provides in the creation of an AIDS vaccine (Lopalco 2010).

Height is another example of a trait currently experiencing selective pressure. If you have ever toured a historical site, you have likely hit your head on a doorframe or become claustrophobic trying to squeeze down a narrow hallway under a lower-than-average ceiling. It is not your imagination. Humans have gotten taller in recent centuries. In fact, the average height of people in industrialized nations has increased approximately 10 centimeters (about four inches) in the past 150 years. This increase has been attributed to improvements in nutrition, sanitation, and access to medical care (Hatton 2014). But this is only part of the story.

Height is highly heritable. Studies indicate 80% of variation in height within populations is due to genetics, with 697 different genetic variances identified as having an effect on adult stature (Devuyst 2014). Multiple studies also demonstrate a positive relationship between height and reproductive success for men (Andrews et al. 2011). This is primarily due to sexual selection and nonrandom mating, namely women's preferences for taller men, which may explain why height is one characteristic men often lie about on dating websites (Guadagno et al. 2012). Sexual selection also plays out with regard to economic success in Western cultures, with taller men more likely to be in higher-level positions that pay well. Research demonstrates an inch of height is worth an additional $789 per year in salary, meaning a man who is six feet tall will earn on average $5,525 more per year than an identical man who is five foot five (Gladwell

2007). Over the course of a thirty-year career, this adds up to hundreds of thousands of dollars, likely allowing the taller man to attract more potential mates and increase his reproductive success.

Wisdom teeth are also undergoing evolutionary pressure. Have you or anyone in your family had their wisdom teeth removed? It can be a painful and expensive process, and it is a common experience in Western nations. Conversely, do you know anyone whose wisdom teeth never came in? That is fairly common in other populations, suggesting evolutionary pressure favoring the absence of wisdom teeth has been culturally influenced. According to research by physical anthropologists, the oldest fossil evidence of skulls missing third molars was found in China and is 300,000 to 400,000 years old, suggesting the earliest mutation selecting against the eruption of wisdom teeth arose in Asia (Main 2013). Since that time, jaws have continued to decrease in size to the point they often cannot accommodate third molars, which can become impacted, painful, and even infected, a condition physical anthropologist Alan Main argues might have interfered with the ability to survive and reproduce in ancestral populations (Main 2013). As we have learned, a mutation that positively influences reproductive success—such as being born without the trait to develop wisdom teeth in an environment where food was cooked before eating—would likely be selected for over time. Evidence in modern humans suggests this is the case, with 40% of modern Asians and 45% of Native Alaskans and Greenlanders (populations descended from Asian populations) lacking wisdom teeth. The percentage among those of European descent ranges from 10 to 25% and for African Americans is 11% (Main 2013). Earlier chapters in this text emphasize that directional selection progresses along a particular path until the environment changes and a trait is no longer advantageous. In the case of wisdom teeth, the ability of modern dentistry to preempt impaction through surgery may, in fact, be what is preventing natural selection from doing away with wisdom teeth altogether.

FOOD FOR THOUGHT

This chapter focused on health conditions prevalent in contemporary, industrialized societies that are due, in part, to the mismatch between our evolved biology and modern cultural and physical environments. Obesity is at the root of it all. Claude Bouchard (2007) identified factors contributing to the global epidemic of obesity and the diseases associated with it. These are the built environment and the social environment, which together form the obesogenic environment in which unhealthy behaviors are encouraged. This chapter will close by examining each of these in a college context.

Figure 16.12 Students walking around campus.

In terms of the built environment, consider your campus or neighborhood from an evolutionary perspective. To what degree does the construction of the space lend itself to physical activity as part of daily life? Is your campus constructed in such a way that it promotes the use of automobiles at the expense of walking or biking? If driving is necessary, is parking available close to the buildings or do you need to walk a fair distance from the parking lot to your destination? Do the buildings have stairs or ramps or is it necessary to take the elevator? Is it possible to negotiate safely around campus or the neighborhood on foot or by bike in all weather? After dark? How about the classrooms and computer labs? Do they have standing or treadmill desks as options? Does your class schedule encourage walking from building to building between classes, or are most courses in your major scheduled in the same location? I regularly have students who sit in the same room for hours, not even changing desks, while instructors rush from place to place. Most college majors also lack a physical activity requirement, leaving it up to students to incorporate exercise into already-busy schedules (See Figure 16.12).

Sociocultural factors that contribute to obesity include food advertising, ubiquitous fast-food and junk food options, and social pressure to consume, all of which are present on college campuses. Although nutritional options on campuses have improved in recent years, many students find eating healthy in the dining halls and dorms challenging (Plotnikoff et al. 2015), and students who live off campus fare even worse (Small et al. 2013). There are also parties and other social events, a normal part of college life, that often involve unhealthy food and encourage behaviors like alcohol consumption and smoking. Give some thought to the social atmosphere on your campus and the ways in which it may contribute to obesity. My own freshman orientation involved a succession of pizza parties, ice cream socials, and barbecues, followed by late-night runs to the nearest fast-food outlet. The purpose of these events was to encourage people to make friends and feel comfortable living away from home, but the foods served were not healthy, and there was social pressure to join in and be part of the group. Such activities set students up for the "freshman fifteen" and then some. They also reinforce the idea that being social involves eating (and sometimes drinking and/or smoking).

Sedentarism and inactivity are also built into the academics of college life. Digital technology is a significant contributor to obesity. Students use laptops and cell phones to take notes, complete their work outside of class, and access social media. There are also video games, virtual reality headsets, and streaming television and movies for entertainment. The built environment of college already necessitates that students sit in class for hours each day, then sit at computers to complete work outside of class. The social environment enabled by digital technology encourages sitting around for entertainment. It is telling that we call it "binge watching" when we spend hours watching our favorite shows. Doing so often involves eating, as well as multiple exposures to food advertising embedded in the shows themselves. In these many ways, college contributes to the development of obesogenic behaviors that can have negative health ramifications long after college is over (Small et al. 2013).

In the U.S., the greatest increase in obesity is among young adults aged 18–29 years, a significant percentage of whom are college students (Plotnikoff et al. 2015). Analyses of college students' behavior across semesters shows consumption of fruits and vegetables drops over time, as does the amount of physical activity, while consumption of sugar-sweetened beverages and fast-food goes up, leading to weight gain at nearly six times the rate of the general public (Small et al. 2013). Realizing this, many colleges and universities have instituted programs to encourage healthier eating and more physical activity among students (Plotnikoff et al. 2015). Some schools have even done away with collegiate sports, which often serve a small percentage of students, in favor of campus-wide efforts at getting everyone active (Tierney 2013). Investigate the options on your campus and take advantage of opportunities. We cannot change our biology, but we can certainly change our habits.

Review Questions

- Geographer, historian, and author Jared Diamond (1987) once referred to agriculture as "the worst mistake in the history of the human race." Given what you have learned about the health consequences of the domestication of plants and animals for humans, how would you respond to his statement?
- Why do humans like foods that are "bad" for them? Describe the evolutionary underpinnings of our tastes for sugar, salt, and fat.
- How might understanding contemporary disease from an evolutionary perspective benefit medical practitioners in treating their patients?
- Given the size of the world population today, humanity could not return to foraging for subsistence.

> What can we do to promote healthier food consumption on a world scale? How might we build changes into our physical environments to counter the health risks associated with modern diet and activity patterns?
> - Several risk factors for conditions like heart disease, diabetes, and cancer are referred to as "lifestyle factors," implying these are behavioral choices people make that put them at risk. These include unhealthy eating, lack of physical activity, smoking, and alcohol consumption. To what degree is unhealthy behavior structured by environment? For example, how does being a college student influence your eating habits, physical activity patterns, smoking, and consumption of alcohol?
> - Who benefits from the global obesity epidemic? Think about the following industries and institutions: How might the medical establishment profit from obesity? The fitness industry? The diet industry? Fashion? Pharmaceutical companies? Food manufacturers? Advertisers?
> - Can you think of any human traits in addition to height, wisdom teeth, and immunity from HIV that might be undergoing selection? How would you go about investigating those traits to find out if this is true?

Key Terms

Autotrophic: Autotrophic organisms are capable of producing their own food using inorganic substances such as light, water, carbon dioxide or chemical energy.

Body Mass Index (BMI): A person's weight in kilograms divided by the square of their height in meters. The most widely used measure for identifying obesity. The formula using kilograms and meters (or centimeters) is: weight (kg) / [height (m)]^2. The formula using pounds and inches is: 703 x weight (lbs) / [height (in)]^2.

Cancer: A collection of related diseases in which some of the body's cells begin to divide without stopping and spread into surrounding tissues.

Cardiovascular Disease (CVD): A disease of the heart and blood vessels, often related to atherosclerosis, CVD is a condition in which a substance called plaque builds up in the walls of the arteries, blood vessels that carry blood away from the heart, compromising the flow of blood to the heart or brain.

Central Nervous System: The complex of nerve tissues stemming from the brain and spinal cord that controls the activities of the body.

Circulatory system: The biological system that circulates blood around the body via the heart, arteries, and veins, delivering oxygen and nutrients to organs and cells and carrying waste products away.

Diabetes Mellitus: An endocrine disorder in which high glucose (blood sugar) levels occur over a prolonged period of time. Blood glucose is your body's main source of energy and comes from the food you eat. Insulin, a hormone made by the pancreas, helps glucose from food get into your cells to be used for energy. Sometimes your body does not make enough—or any—insulin (Type 1 diabetes) or does not take up insulin well (Type 2 diabetes). Glucose then stays in your blood and does not reach your cells.

"Double Burden": Refers to parts of the world in which there is a prevalence of chronic disease (e.g.,. cancer, heart disease) while, at the same time, there are also high rates of infectious disease due to poverty, malnutrition, poor sanitation, and lack of access to health care, often accompanied by high rates of maternal and child mortality.

Ecological model: Ecological models of health and disease emphasize environmental and policy contexts of behavior, while incorporating social and psychological influences, rather than focusing on individual behaviors. These models encompass multiple levels of influence and can lend themselves to more comprehensive health interventions.

Emerging Infectious Diseases (EIDs): Infections that have recently appeared within a population or those whose incidence or geographic range is rapidly increasing or threatens to increase in the near future. Examples include Ebola, Zika, SARS, and avian (bird) flu.

Endocrine system: Those organs in the body whose primary function is the production of hormones.

Epidemiological transition: A transformation in patterns of disease (morbidity) and death (mortality) among a population.

Glucose metabolism: The body's evolved mechanism by which we turn food into energy for bodily functions.

Glycemic Index (GI): A system that ranks foods on a scale from 1 to 100 based on their effect on blood-sugar levels. Carbohydrates with a low GI value (55 or less) are more slowly digested and metabolised causing a lower, slower rise in blood glucose and insulin levels.

Hypertension: High blood pressure. Blood pressure is the force exerted by the blood against the walls of the blood vessels. In a blood pressure reading, the top number (usually higher) refers to the systolic pressure, the amount of pressure in your arteries during the contraction of your heart muscle when your heart beats. The bottom number is the diastolic pressure when your heart muscle is resting between beats. Hypertension can lead to severe health complications and increases the risk of heart attack and stroke.

Incidence: The rate at which new cases of a disease occur in a population over a given period of time.

Insulin: A hormone produced in the pancreas that regulates the amount of glucose in the blood. Lack of insulin or the inability to absorb insulin causes diabetes.

Metabolic Syndrome: A cluster of conditions, including increased blood pressure, high blood sugar, excess body fat around the waist, and abnormal cholesterol levels that occur together, increasing the risk of heart disease, stroke, and diabetes. Lifestyle changes like losing weight, regularly exercising, and making dietary changes can help prevent or reverse metabolic syndrome.

Menarche: The first occurrence of menstruation.

Morbidity: The number of cases of disease per unit of population occurring over a unit of time.

Mortality: The number of deaths attributable to a particular cause per unit of population over a unit of time.

Noncommunicable Diseases (NCDs): Also known as chronic diseases, NCDs tend to be of long duration and are the result of a combination of genetic, physiological, environmental, and behavior factors. The main types of NCDs are cardiovascular diseases (like heart attacks and stroke), cancers, chronic respiratory diseases (such as chronic obstructive pulmonary disease and asthma), and diabetes.

Obesity: A medical condition in which excess body fat has accumulated to the point that it has adverse effects on health. The most widely used measure for identifying obesity is the Body Mass Index (BMI), a person's weight in kilograms divided by the square of their height in meters. A measure of 30 kg/m^2 is considered obese and 25–29 kg/m^2 overweight. Distribution of body fat also matters. Fat in the abdominal region has a stronger association with Type

2 diabetes and cardiovascular disease, meaning waist to hip ratio and waist circumference are also important indicators of obesity-related health risk.

Obesogenic: Promoting excessive weight gain. For example, an environment in which tasty, cheap food filled with excess calories is abundant.

Omnivorous: Able to eat and digest foods of both plant and animal origins.

Osteoarthritis: Refers to the degeneration of joint cartilage and underlying bone, causing pain and stiffness. In the absence of previous injury, it is most common in modern populations from middle age onward.

Prevalence: The proportion of individuals in a population who have a particular disease or condition at a given point in time.

Sedentism: Living in groups settled permanently in one place.

Sedentarism: A way of life characterized by much sitting and little physical activity.

Stress response: A predictable response to any significant threat to homeostasis. The human stress response involves the central nervous system and the endocrine system acting together. Sudden and severe stress incites the "flight or flight" response from the autonomic nervous system in conjunction with hormones secreted by the adrenal and pituitary glands, increasing our heart rate and breathing and releasing glucose from the liver for quick energy.

Stroke: A stroke occurs when a blood vessel leading to the brain is blocked or bursts, preventing that part of the brain from receiving blood and oxygen, leading to the death of cells in that part of the brain.

Syndemic: The aggregation (grouping together) of two or more diseases or health conditions in a population in which there is some level of harmful biological or behavioral interface that exacerbates the negative health effects of any or all of the diseases involved. Syndemics involve the adverse interaction of diseases of all types, including infections, chronic non-communicable diseases, mental health problems, behavioral conditions, toxic exposure, and malnutrition.

Vector-borne diseases: Human illnesses caused by parasites, viruses, and bacteria that are transmitted by mosquitoes, flies, ticks, mites, snails, and lice.

Zoonoses: Diseases that can be transmitted from animals to humans.

About the Author

Joylin Namie

Truckee Meadows Community College, jnamie@tmcc.edu

Joylin Namie

Dr. Joylin Namie teaches courses in biological and cultural anthropology at Truckee Meadows Community College. Her research interests are in the areas of food, gender, media, and health. She began her career interviewing women in Costa Rica regarding beliefs about breast cancer and investigating the ways these affected engagement with cancer screening. She then moved to food studies, publishing on a variety of topics, including the cultural reasons mothers feed their children junk food, how images of successful athletes are used to market unhealthy foods as "fuel" for athletic pursuits, and feminine representation in sports nutrition advertising. She enjoys collaborating with students, including exploring plastic surgery among Latter-day Saint (Mormon) women in Utah, which resulted in a documentary film and an article that won the award for best paper in Social Science from the Utah Academy of Sciences, Arts, and Letters. She also co-researched and co-authored an article with students on the ways Mormon masculinity promotes involvement with child-feeding. In addition to teaching and research, Dr. Namie's favorite things in life are competing in sports and traveling, often with her dog, Brooklyn, who has run behind her mountain bike everywhere from Vermont to Vancouver Island.

For Further Exploration

Lents, Nathan H. 2018. *Human Errors: A Panorama of Our Glitches, from Pointless Bones to Broken Genes.* Boston: Houghton Mifflin Harcourt.

Stearns, Stephen C., and Jacob C. Koella, eds. 2008. *Evolution in Health and Disease.* Second Edition. United Kingdom: Oxford University Press.

Zuk, Marlene. 2013. *Paleofantasy: What Evolution Really Tells Us About Sex, Diet, and How We Live.* New York: W.W. Norton & Company.

References

Abid, Zaynah, Amanda J. Cross, and Rashmi Sinha. 2014. "Meat, Dairy, and Cancer." *The American Journal of Clinical Nutrition* 100, Issue Supplement 1 (1): 386S–393S.

Akil, Luma, and H. Anwar Ahmad. 2011. "Relationships between Obesity and Cardiovascular Diseases in Four Southern States and Colorado." *Journal of Health Care for the Poor and Underserved* 22 (Suppl. 4): 61–72.

Akinbami, Lara J., Alan E. Simon, and Lauren M. Rossen. 2016. "Changing Trends in Asthma Prevalence among Children." *Pediatrics* 137 (1). doi:10.1542/peds.2015-2354.

Ali, Aus Tariq. 2014. "Reproductive Factors and the Risk of Endometrial Cancers." *International Journal of Gynecological Cancer* 24 (3): 384–393.

American Heart Association. 2014. "Smoking & Cardiovascular Disease (Heart Disease)." Last modified February 17, 2014. https://docs.google.com/ document/d/1iMgccSz67i37839NhIAPGQlwsWA3VGtSKtejlrGN_LI/edit.

———. 2018. "Heart Disease and Stroke Statistics 2017 At-a-Glance." Last modified January 31, 2018. https://healthmetrics.heart.org/wp-content/uploads/2018/02/At-A-Glance-Heart-Disease-and-Stroke-Statistics-2018.pdf.

American Psychiatric Association (APA). 2013. *Diagnostic and Statistical Manual of Mental Disorder*. Fifth Edition: DSM-5. Washington, DC: APA.

Andrews, Tessa M., Steven T. Kalinowski, and Mary J. Leonard. 2011. "Are Humans Evolving? A Classroom Discussion to Change Students' Misconceptions Regarding Natural Selection." *Evolution: Education and Outreach* 4 (3): 456–466.

Armelagos, George. 1990. "Health and Disease in Populations in Transition." In *Disease in Populations in Transition*, edited by Alan C. Swedlund and George J. Armelagos, 127–144. New York: Bergin & Garvey.

Armelagos, George J., Peter J. Brown, and Bethany Turner. 2005. "Evolutionary, Historical and Political Economic Perspectives on Health and Disease." *Social Science and Medicine* 61 (4): 755–765.

Asher, Claire. 2017. "Illegal Bushmeat Trade Threatens Human Health and Great Apes." *Mongabay*, April 6. https://news.mongabay.com/2017/04/illegal-bushmeat-trade-threatens-human-health-and-great-apes/.

Baer, Hans, and Merrill Singer. 2009. *Global Warming and the Political Ecology of Health: Emerging Crises and Systemic Solutions*. Walnut Creek, CA: Left Coast Press.

Baker, W.A., G.A. Hitman, K. Hawrami, M.I. McCarthy et al. 1994. "Apolipoprotein D Gene Polymorphism: A New Genetic Marker for Type 2 Diabetic Subjects in Nauru and South India." *Diabetic Medicine* 11 (10): 947–952.

Baltic, Milan Z., and Marija Boskovic. 2015. "When Man Met Meat: Meat in Human Nutrition from Ancient Times Till Today." *Procedia Food Science* 5: 6–9.

Beasley, Richard, Alex Semprini, and Edwin A. Mitchell. 2015. "Risk Factors for Asthma: Is Prevention Possible?" *The Lancet* 386 (9998): 1075–1085.

Berenbaum, Francis. 2011. "Diabetes-induced Osteoarthritis: From a New Paradigm to a New Phenotype." *Annals of the Rheumatic Diseases* 70 (8). doi:10.1136/ard.2010.146399.

Berna, Francesco, Paul Goldberg, Liora Kolska Horwitz, James Brink, Sharon Holt, Marion Bamford, and Michael Chazan. 2012. "Microstratigraphic Evidence of In Situ Fire in the Acheulean Strata of Wonderwerk Cave, Northern Cape Province, South Africa." *Proceedings of the National Academy of Sciences* 109: E1215e–E1220.

Blue Cross Blue Shield Association (BCBSA). 2017. "Diabetes and the Commercially Insured U.S. Population." *The Health of America Report*, August 1. https://www.bcbs.com/the-health-of-america/reports/diabetes-and-commercially-insured-us-population.

Bogin, Barry. 1991. "The Evolution of Human Nutrition." In *The Anthropology of Medicine: From Culture to Method*, edited by Lola Romanucci-Ross, Daniel E. Moerman, and Laurence R. Tancredi, 158–195. New York: Bergin & Garvey.

Bouchard, Claude. 2007. "The Biological Predisposition to Obesity: Beyond the Thrifty Genotype Scenario." *International Journal of Obesity* 31: 1337–1339.

Brown, Peter J. 1991. "Culture and the Evolution of Obesity." *Human Nature* 2 (1): 31–57.

Bruni, L., L. Barrionuevo-Rosas, G. Albero, B. Serrano et al. 2017. "Human Papillomavirus and Related Diseases in the World." Summary Report 27, July. ICO/IARC Information Centre on HPV and Cancer (HPV Information Centre). http://www.hpvcentre.net/statistics/reports/XWX.pdf.

Buchman, Aron S., Lei Yu, Robert S. Wilson, Andrew Lim, Robert J. Dawe, Chris Gaiteri, Sue E. Leurgans, Julie A. Schneider, and David A. Bennett. 2019. "Physical Activity, Common Brain Pathologies, and Cognition in Community-Dwelling Older Adults." *Neurology* 98 (2). doi:10.1212/WNL.0000000000006954.

Center for Science in the Public Interest (CSPI). 2010. Food Dyes: A Rainbow of Risk. Washington, DC: Center for Science in the Public Interest.

Centers for Disease Control and Prevention (CDC). 2014. Breastfeeding Report Card: United States/2014. Atlanta, GA: Centers for Disease Control and Prevention.

———. 2016. "Leading Causes of Death." National Center for Health Statistics. https://www.cdc.gov/nchs/fastats/leading-causes-of-death.htm.

——— 2017. "Human Papillomavirus." Genital HPV Infection–Fact Sheet. Atlanta, GA: Centers for Disease Control and Prevention.

———. 2017. "Asthma." National Center for Health Statistics. https://www.cdc.gov/nchs/fastats/asthma.htm.

Cerón, Ella. 2017. "Here's Every Oreo Flavor Ever Created." *TeenVogue.com*, June 19. https://www.teenvogue.com/story/every-oreo-flavor-ranked.

Chen, Yang, Yi-Lun Lee, and Guang-Hui Dong. 2012. "Gender Difference of Childhood Overweight and Obesity in Predicting the Risk of Incident Asthma: A Systematic Review and Meta-Analysis." *Obesity Reviews* 14 (3): 222–231. doi:10.1111/j.1467-789X.2012.01055.x

Chin, Jessie, Brennan R. Payne, Wai-Tat Fu, Daniel G. Morrow, and Elizabeth A. L. Stine-Morrow. 2015. "Information Foraging across the Life Span: Search and Switch in Unknown Patches." *Topics in Cognitive Science* 7 (3): 428–450.

Cooling, Laura. 2015. "Blood Groups in Infection and Host Susceptibility." *Clinical Microbiology Reviews* 28 (3): 801–870.

Cordain, Loren. 2002. *The Paleo Diet: Lose Weight and Get Healthy by Eating the Food You Were Designed to Eat*. Hoboken, NJ: John Wiley & Sons.

Crosby, Alfred W., Jr. 2003. The Columbian Exchange: Biological and Cultural Consequences of 1492. 30th Anniversary Edition. Westport, CT: Praeger Publishers.

Croston, Glenn. 2012. "The Thing We Fear More Than Death: Why Predators Are Responsible for Our Fear of Public Speaking." *Psychology Today* blog, November 29. https://www.psychologytoday.com/us/blog/the-real-story-risk/201211/the-thing-we-fear-more-death.

Crow, James F., and Motoo Kimura. 1970. *An Introduction to Population Genetics Theory*. New York: Harper and Row.

Currie, Candace, Naman Ahluwalia, Emmanuelle Godeau, Saoirse Nic Gabhainn, Pernille Due, and Dorothy B. Mille . 2012. "Is Obesity at Individual and National Level Associated with Lower Age at Menarche? Evidence from 34 Countries in the Health Behaviour in School-Aged Children Study." *Journal of Adolescent Health* 50 (6): 621–626.

David, A. Rosalie, and Michael Zimmerman. 2010. "Cancer: An Old Disease, A New Disease or Something In Between?" *Nature Reviews: Cancer* 10 (10): 728–733.

Davis, Mike. 2005. *The Monster at Our Door: The Global Threat of Avian Flu.* New York: Owl Books.

de Silva, A. M., K. R. Walder, T. J. Aitman, T. Gotoda, A. P. Goldstone, A. M. Hodge, M. P. de Courten, P. Z. Zimmet, and G. R. Collier. 1999. "Combination of Polymophisms in OB-R and the OB Gene Associated with Insulin Resistance in Nauruan Males." *International Journal of Obesity* 23 (8): 816–822.

Devuyst, Olivier. 2014. "High Time for Human Height." *Peritoneal Dialysis International* 34 (7): 685–686.

Diamond, Jared. 1987. "The Worst Mistake in the History of the Human Race." *Discover*, May: 64–66.

———. 1997. *Guns, Germs, and Steel: The Fates of Human Societies.* New York: W. W. Norton.

Dimsdale, Joel E. 2008. "Psychological Stress and Cardiovascular Disease." *Journal of the American College of Cardiology* 51 (13): 1237–1246.

Dunn, Robb. 2018. *Never Home Alone: From Microbes to Millipedes, Camel Crickets, and Honeybees, the Natural History of Where We Live.* New York: Basic Books.

Dutton, Denis. 2009. *The Art Instinct: Beauty, Pleasure, and Human Evolution.* New York: Bloomsbury.

Eaton, S. Boyd, Melvin Konner, and Marjorie Shostak. 1988. "Stone Agers in the Fast Lane: Chronic Degenerative Diseases in Evolutionary Perspective." *American Journal of Medicine* 84 (4): 739–749.

Eaton, S. Boyd, Malcolm C. Pike, Roger V. Short, Nancy C. Lee, James Trussell, Robert A. Hatcher, James W. Wood, et al. 1994. "Women's Reproductive Cancers in Evolutionary Context." *The Quarterly Review of Biology* 69 (3): 353–367.

Ewald, Paul W. 2018. "Ancient Cancers and Infection-Induced Oncogenesis." *International Journal of Paleopathology* 21: 178–185. http://dx.doi.org/10.1016/J.ijpp.2017.08.007.

Fall, Tove, Cecilia Lundholm, Anne K. Orkqvist, Katja Fall et al. 2015. Early Exposure to Dogs and Farm Animals and the Risk of Childhood Asthma. JAMA Pediatrics 169 (11). doi: 10.1001/jamapediatrics.2015.3219.

Farb, Peter, and George Armelagos. 1980. *Consuming Passions: The Anthropology of Eating.* New York: Washington Square Press.

Findley, Sally, Katherine Lawler, Monisha Bindra, Linda Maggio, Madeline M. Penachio, and Christopher Maylahn. 2003. "Elevated Asthma and Indoor Environmental Exposures among Puerto Rican Children of East Harlem." *Journal of Asthma* 40 (5): 557–569.

Flinn, Mark V., and Barry G. England. 2003. "Childhood Stress: Endocrine and Immune Responses to Psychosocial Events." In *Social and Cultural Lives of Immune Systems: Theory and Practice in Medical Anthropology and International Health*, edited by James M. Wilce Jr., 105–146. London: Routledge.

Fumagalli, Matteo, Ida Moltke, Niels Grarup, Fernando Racimo, Peter Bjerregaard, Marit E. Jørgensen, Thorfinn S. Korneliussen, et al. 2015. "Greenlandic Inuit Show Genetic Signatures of Diet and Climate Adaptation." *Science* 349 (6254): 1343–1347.

Gao, George. 2015. "Americans' Ideal Family Size Is Smaller Than It Used to Be." Pew Research Center, May 8. http://www.pewresearch.org/fact-tank/2015/05/08/ideal-size-of-the-american-family/.

Gladwell, Malcolm. 2007. *Blink: The Power of Thinking Without Thinking.* New York: Back Bay Books.

Goulder, Philip J., Sharon R. Lewin, and Ellen M. Leitman. 2016. "Paediatric HIV Infection: The Potential for Cure." *Nature Reviews Immunology* 16: 259–271.

Graber, Cynthia. 2014. "Michael Pollan Explains What's Wrong with the Paleo Diet." Mother Jones, January 17. https://www.motherjones.com/environment/2014/01/michael-pollan-paleo-diet-inquiring-minds/.

Greaves, Mel. 2015. "Evolutionary Determinants of Cancer." *Cancer Discovery* 5 (8): 806–820.

Greenspan, Louise, and Julianna Deardorff. 2014. *The New Puberty: How to Navigate Early Development in Today's Girls.* New York: Rodale.

Guadagno, Rosanna E., Bradley M. Okdie, and Sara A. Kruse. 2012. "Dating Deception: Gender, Online Dating, and Exaggerated Self-Presentation." *Computers in Human Behavior* 28 (2): 642–647.

Guilak, Farshid. 2012. "Biomechanical Factors in Osteoarthritis." *Best Practice & Research: Clinical Rheumatology* 25 (6): 815–823.

Gurven, Michael, and Hillard Kaplan. 2007. "Longevity among Hunter-Gatherers: A Cross-Cultural Examination." *Population and Development Review* 33 (2): 321–365.

Hamilton, Cheryl. 2011. *Communicating for Results, a Guide for Business and the Professions, Ninth Edition.* Belmont, CA: Thomson Wadsworth.

Harper, Kristin, and George Armelagos. 2010. "The Changing Disease-Scape in the Third Epidemiological Transition." *International Journal of Environmental Research and Public Health* 7 (2): 675–697.

Harris, Marvin. 1989. "Life Without Chiefs." *New Age Journal*, November/December: 42–45, 205–209.

Hatton, Tim. 2014. "Why Did Humans Grow Four Inches in 100 Years? It Wasn't Just Diet." The Conversation, May 1. https://theconversation.com/why-did-humans-grow-four-inches-in-100-years-it-wasnt-just-diet-25919.

Hays, J. N. 2005. Epidemics and Pandemics: Their Impacts on Human History. Santa Barbara, CA: ABC-CLIO, Inc.

International Diabetes Federation (IDF). 2018. *IDF Diabetes Atlas.* Eighth Edition. http://www.diabetesatlas.org/key-messages.html.

Issa, Rital, and Timothy M. Griffin. 2012. "Pathobiology of Obesity and Osteoarthritis: Integrating Biomechanics and Inflammation." *Pathobiology of Aging and Age-Related Diseases* 2 (1). https://doi.org/10.3402/pba.v2i0.17470.

Jain, H. K.. 2012. "Transition to Twenty-First Century Agriculture: Change of Direction." *Agricultural Research* 1 (1): 12–17.

Jones, Kate E., Nikkita G. Patel, Mark A. Levy, Adam Storeygard, Deborah Balk, John L. Gittleman, and Peter Daszak. 2008. "Global Trends in Emerging Infectious Disease." *Nature* 451 (7181): 990–993.

Jones, Rachel K., and Joerg Dreweke. 2011. Countering Conventional Wisdom: New Evidence on Religion and Contraceptive Use. Report, April 2011. New York: Guttmacher Institute.

Joseph, Christine L. M., Betsy Foxman, Frederick E. Leickly, Edward Peterson, and Dennis Ownby. 1996. "Prevalence of Possible Undiagnosed Asthma and Associated Morbidity among Urban Schoolchildren." *Journal of Pediatrics* 129 (5): 735–742.

Kaczmarczyk, Melissa M., Michael J. Miller, and Gregory G. Freund. 2012. "The Health Benefits of Dietary Fiber: Beyond the Usual Suspects of Type 2 Diabetes Mellitus, Cardiovascular Disease and Colon Cancer." *Metabolism: Clinical and Experimental* 61 (8): 1058–1066.

Larsen, Clark Spencer. 2014. "Foraging to Farming Transition: Global Health Impacts, Trends, and Variation." In *Encyclopedia of Global Archaeology*, edited by Claire Smith, 2818–2824. New York: Springer.

Lattimer, James M., and Mark D. Haub. 2010. "Effects of Dietary Fiber and Its Components on Metabolic Health." *Nutrients* 2 (12): 1266–1289.

Lee, Richard B. 2013. *The Dobe Ju/'hoansi*. Fourth Edition. Belmont, CA: Wadsworth/Cengage Learning.

Leontis, Lisa M. N.d. "Type 2 Diabetes and Exercise: Exercise Makes It Easier to Control Your Diabetes." https://www.endocrineweb.com/conditions/type-2-diabetes/type-2-diabetes-exercise.

Lieberman, Daniel E. 2015. "Human Locomotion and Heat Loss: An Evolutionary Perspective." *Comprehensive Physiology* 5(1): 99–117.

Lieberman, Leslie Sue. 2006. "Evolutionary and Anthropological Perspectives on Optimal Foraging in Obesogenic Environments." *Appetite* 47 (1): 3–9.

Liu, Gang. 2018. "Abstract P184: Meat Cooking Methods and Risk of Hypertension: Results From Three Prospective Cohort Studies." *Circulation* 137 (Suppl. 1): AP184.

Liu, Gang, Geng Zong, Kana Wu, Yang Hu, Yanping Li, Walter C. Willett, David M. Eisenberg, Frank B. Hu, and Qi Sun. 2018. "Meat Cooking Methods and Risk of Type 2 Diabetes: Results From Three Prospective Cohort Studies." *Diabetes Care* 41 (5): 1049–1060.

Livingston, Gretchen. 2015. "Childlessness." Pew Research Center, May 7. http://www.pewsocialtrends.org/2015/05/07/childlessness/.

Lopalco, Lucia. 2010. "CCR5: From Natural Resistance to a New Anti-HIV Strategy." *Viruses* 2 (2): 574–600.

Lucock, Mark D., Charlotte E. Martin, Zoe R. Yates, and Martin Veysey. 2014. "Diet and Our Genetic Legacy in the Recent Anthropocene: A Darwinian Perspective to Nutritional Health." *Journal of Evidence-Based Complementary and Alternative Medicine* 19 (1): 68–83.

Main, Douglas. 2013. "Ancient Mutation Explains Missing Wisdom Teeth." Live Science, March 13. https://www.livescience.com/27529-missing-wisdom-teeth.html.

Malina, Robert M., and Bertis B. Little. 2008. "Physical Activity: The Present in the Context of the Past." *American Journal of Human Biology* 20 (4): 373–391.

Mandsager, Kyle, Serge Harb, and Paul Cremer. 2018. "Association of Cardiorespiratory Fitness with Long-term Mortality among Adults Undergoing Exercise Treadmill Testing." *JAMA Network Open* 1 (6): e183605. doi:10.1001/jamanetworkopen.2018.3605.

Marciniak, Stephanie, and George H. Perry. 2017. "Harnessing Ancient Genomes to Study the History of Human Adaptation." *Nature Reviews Genetics* 18: 659–674.

Marlowe, Frank W. 2005. "Hunter-Gatherers and Human Evolution." *Evolutionary Anthropology* 14 (2): 54–67.

Marmot, Michael. 2005. "Social Determinants of Health Inequality." *The Lancet* 365 (9464): 1099–1104.

Martini, Frederic H., William C. Ober, Edwin F. Bartholomew, and Judi L. Nath. 2013. *Visual Essentials of Anatomy & Physiology*. Boston, MA: Pearson.

Mathews, T.J., and Brady E. Hamilton. 2016. "Mean Age of Mothers Is on the Rise: United States, 2000-2014." National Center for Health Statistics (CHS) Data Brief. No. 232. https://www.cdc.gov/nchs/data/databriefs/db232.pdf.

McElroy, Ann, and Patricia Townsend. 2009. *Medical Anthropology in Ecological Perspective*. Fifth Edition. Boulder, CO: Westview Press.

McEvoy, Claire T., Norman Temple, and Jayne V. Woodside. 2012. "Vegetarian Diets, Low-Meat Diets and Health: A Review." *Public Health Nutrition* 15 (12): 2287–2294.

McKee, Trudy, and James R. McKee. 2015. *Biochemistry: The Molecular Basis of Life*. Sixth Edition. Oxford, UK: Oxford University Press.

Moss, Michael. 2013. *Salt, Sugar, Fat: How the Food Giants Hooked Us*. New York: Random House.

National Geographic Society. N.d. Resource Library: Encyclopedic Entry (n.d.), s.v., "Autotroph." National Geographic Society. https://www.nationalgeographic.org/encyclopedia/autotroph/.

National Institutes of Health (NIH). 2017. "Obesity and Cancer Fact Sheet." Last modified January, 2017. https://www.cancer.gov/about-cancer/causes-prevention/risk/obesity/obesity-fact-sheet.

Neeha, V. S., and Priyamvadah Kinth. 2013. "Nutrigenomics Research: A Review."*Journal of Food Science and Technology*, 50 (3): 415–428.

Neel, James V. 1962. "Diabetes Mellitus: A 'Thrifty' Genotype Rendered Detrimental by 'Progress'?" *American Journal of Human Genetics* 14 (4): 353–362.

Novembre, John, Alison P. Galvani, and Montgomery Slatkin. 2005. "The Geographic Spread of the CCR5 Δ32 HIV-Resistance Allele." *PLoS Biology* 3 (11): e339.

Odes, Edward J., Patrick S. Randolph-Quinney, Maryna Steyn, Zach Throckmorton, Jacqueline S. Smilg, Bernhard Zipfel, Tanya N. Augustine, et al. 2016. "Earliest Hominin Cancer: 1.7-Million-Year-Old Osteosarcoma from Swartkrans Cave, South Africa." *South African Journal of Science* 112 (7–8): 1–5.

O'Keefe Osborn, Corinne. 2017. "Type 1 and Type 2 Diabetes: What's the Difference?" Healthline Newsletter, August 24. https://www.healthline.com/health/Difference-between-type-1-and-type-2-diabetes.

Omran, Abdel R. 1971. "The Epidemiological Transition: A Theory of the Epidemiology of Population Change." *Milbank Memorial Fund Quarterly* 49 (4): 509–538.

———. 2005. "The Epidemiological Transition: A Theory of the Epidemiology of Population Change." *The Milbank Quarterly* 83 (4): 731–757.

Organ, Chris, Charles L. Nunn, Zarin Machanda, and Richard W. Wrangham. 2011. "Phylogenetic Rate Shifts in Feeding Time during the Evolution of Homo." *Proceedings of the National Academy of Sciences* 108 (35): 14555-14559.

Ortega, Alexander Neil, Peter J. Gergen, A. David Paltiel, Howard Bauchner, Kathleen D. Belanger, and Brian P. Leaderer. 2002. "Impact of Site of Care, Race, and Hispanic Ethnicity on Medication Use for Childhood Asthma." *Pediatrics* 109 (1): E1.

Palma-Gudiel, H., A. Córdova-Palomera, E. Eixarch, M. Deuschle, and L. Fañanás. 2015. "Maternal Psychosocial Stress during Pregnancy Alters the Epigenetic Signature of the Glucocorticoid Receptor Gene Promoter in Their Offspring: A Meta-Analysis." *Epigenetics* 10 (10): 893–902.

Pamuk, Şevket. 2007. "The Black Death and the Origins of the 'Great Divergence' across Europe, 1300–1600." *European Review of Economic History* 11 (3): 289–317.

Pearl, Robert. 2015. "Why Health Care Is Different if You're Black, Latino, or Poor." *Forbes*, March 5. https://www.forbes.com/sites/robertpearl/2015/03/05/healthcare-black-latino-poor/#1ab6e3807869.

Physical Activity Council. 2018. 2018 Participation Report. http://www.physicalactivitycouncil.com/pdfs/current.pdf.

Pickering, Travis Rayne, and Henry T. Bunn. 2007. "The Endurance Running Hypothesis and Hunting and Scavenging in Savanna-Woodlands." *Journal of Human Evolution* 53 (4): 434–438.

Pierce, Mary, and Rebecca Hardy. 2012. "Commentary: The Decreasing Age of Puberty– As Much a Psychosocial as Biological Problem?" *International Journal of Epidemiology* 41 (1): 300–302.

Plotnikoff, Ronald C., Sarah A. Costigan, Rebecca L. Williams, Melinda J. Hutchesson, Sarah G. Kennedy, Sara L. Robards, Jennifer Allen, Clare E. Collins, Robin Callister, and John Germov. 2015. "Effectiveness of Interventions Targeting Physical Activity, Nutrition and Healthy Weight for University and College Students: A Systematic Review and Meta-analysis." *International Journal of Behavioral Nutrition and Physical Activity* 12 (1): 1–10.

Poinar, George. 2018. "Vertebrate Pathogens Vectored by Ancient Hematophagous Arthropods." *Historical Biology*, November 7. doi:10.1080/08912963.2018.1545018.

Pontzer, Herman, David A. Raichlen, Brian M. Wood, Audax Z. P. Mabulla, Susan B. Racette, and Frank W. Marlowe. 2012. "Hunter-Gatherer Energetics and Obesity." *PLoS ONE* 7 (7): e40503. doi:10.1371/journal.pone.0040503.

Pritchard, Jonathan K. 2010. "How We Are Evolving." *Scientific American* 303 (4): 4047.

Raichlen, David A., and Gene E. Alexander. 2014. "Exercise, APOE Genotype, and the Evolution of the Human Lifespan." *Trends in Neurosciences* 37 (5): 247–255.

Raichlen, David A., Herman Pontzer, Jacob A. Harris, Audax Z. P. Mabulla, Frank W. Marlowe, J. Josh Snodgrass, Geeta Eick, J. Colette Berbesque, Amelia Sancilio, Brian M. Wood. 2016. "Physical Activity Patterns and Biomarkers of Cardiovascular Disease Risk in Hunter-Gatherers." *American Journal of Human Biology* 29 (2): e22919. https://doi.org/10.1002/ajhb.22919.

Rankinen, Tuomo, Aamir Zuberi, Yvon C. Chagnon, S. John Weisnagel, George Argyropoulos, Brandon Walts, Louis Pérusse, and Claude Bouchard. 2006. "The Human Obesity Gene Map: The 2005 Update." *Obesity* 14 (4): 529–644.

Richards, M. P. 2002. "A Brief Review of the Archaeological Evidence for Palaeolithic and Neolithic Subsistence." *European Journal of Clinical Nutrition* 56 (12): 1270–1278.

Sallis, James F., Neville Owen, and Edwin B. Fisher. 2008. "Chapter 20: Ecological Models of Health Behavior." In *Health Behavior and Health Education: Theory, Research, and Practice*, edited by Karen Glanz, Barbara K. Rimer, and K. Viswanath, 465–485. Fourth Edition. San Francisco, CA: Jossey-Bass.

Sharp, Paul M., and Beatrice H. Hahn. 2011. "Origins of HIV and the AIDS Pandemic." *Cold Springs Harbor Perspectives in Medicine* 1 (1): a006841.

Shreiner, Andrew B., John Y. Kao, and Vincent B. Young. 2015. "The Gut Microbiome in Health and Disease." *Current Opinion in Gastroenterology* 31 (1): 69–75.

Singer, Merrill, and Hans Baer. 2012. "Health Disparity, Health Inequality." In *Introducing Medical Anthropology: A Discipline in Action*, Second edition, edited by Merrill Singer and Hans Baer, 175–205. Lanham, MD: AltaMira.

Singer, Merrill, and Scott Clair. 2003. "Syndemics and Public Health: Reconceptualizing Disease in Bio-Social Context." *Medical Anthropology Quarterly* 17 (4): 423–441.

Singer, Merrill, Nicola Bulled, Bayla Ostrach, and Emily Mendenhall. 2017. "Syndemics and the Biosocial Conception of Health." *Lancet* 389 (10072): 941–950.

Small, Meg, Lisa Bailey-Davis, Nicole Morgan, and Jennifer Maggs. 2013. "Changes in Eating and Physical Activity Behaviors across Seven Semesters of College: Living On or Off Campus Matters." *Health Education and Behavior* 40 (4): 435–441.

Smith-Morris, Carolyn M. 2004. "Reducing Diabetes in Indian Country: Lessons from the Three Domains Influencing Pima Diabetes." *Human Organization* 63 (1): 34–46.

Sonfield, Adam, Kinsey Hasstedt, Megan L. Cavanaugh, and Ragnar Anderson. 2013. *The Social and Economic Benefits of Women's Ability to Determine Whether and When to Have Children*. New York: Guttmacher Institute. https://www.guttmacher.org/report/social-and-economic-benefits-womens-ability-determine-whether-and-when-have-children.

Stearns, Stephen C., Randolph M. Nesse, and David Haig. 2008. "Introducing Evolutionary Thinking into Medicine." In *Evolution in Health and Disease*, edited by Stephen C. Stearns and Jacob C. Koella, 3–15. United Kingdom: Oxford University Press.

St. Pierre, Danielle. 2018. "The 15 Best Potato Chips for Every Flavor Craving." *Best*, April 6. Retrieved June 13, 2018 from https://www.bestproducts.com/eats/food/g972/best-potato-chips/.

Strassmann, Beverly I. 1997. "The Biology of Menstruation in Homo Sapiens: Total Lifetime Menses, Fecundity, and Nonsynchrony in a Natural-Fertility Population." *Current Anthropology* 38 (1): 123–129.

———. 1999. "Menstrual Cycling and Breast Cancer: An Evolutionary Perspective." *Journal of Women's Health* 8 (2): 193–202.

Tierney, Mike. 2013. "At Spelman, Dropping Sports in Favor of Fitness." *New York Times*, April 13. https://www.nytimes.com/2013/04/14/sports/at-spelman-dropping-sports-in-favor-of-fitness.html.

Trafialek, Joanna, and Wojciech Kolanowski. 2014. "Dietary Exposure to Meat-Related Carcinogenic Substances: Is There a Way to Estimate the Risk?" *International Journal of Food Sciences and Nutrition* 65 (6): 774–780.

UNAIDS. 2018. "Fact Sheet: Latest Statistics on the AIDS Epidemic." http://www.unaids.org/en/resources/fact-sheet.

Ventola, C. Lee. 2015. "The Antibiotic Resistance Crisis: Part I: Causes and Threats." *Pharmacy & Therapeutics* 40 (4): 277–283.

Versini, M., Jeandel, P., Bashi, T., Bizzaro, G., Blank, M., and Shoenfeld, Y. 2015. "Unraveling the Hygiene Hypothesis of Helminthes and Autoimmunity: Origins, Pathophysiology, and Clinical Applications." BMC Medicine, 13: 81. https://doi.org/10.1186/s12916-015-0306-7.

Vucenik, Ivana, and Joseph P. Stains. 2012. "Obesity and Cancer Risk: Evidence, Mechanisms, and Recommendations." Special issue, "Nutrition and Physical Activity in Aging, Obesity, and Cancer," *Annals of the New York Academy of Sciences* Volume 1271:: 37–43.

Walker, Polly, Pamela Rhubart-Berg, Shawn McKenzie, Kristin Kelling, and Robert S. Lawrence. 2005. "Public Health Implications of Meat Production and Consumption." *Public Health Nutrition* 8 (4): 348–356.

Washington, Jesse. 2010. "Blacks Struggle with 72% Unwed Mothers Rate." NBCNEWS.com, November 7. http://www.nbcnews.com/id/39993685/ns/health-womens_health/t/blacks-struggle-percent-unwed-mothers-rate/#.XEETH89KjBJ.

Willett, Walter, Johan Rockström, Brent Loken, Marco Springmann, Tim Lang, Sonja Vermeulen, Tara Garnett, et al.

2019. "Food in the Anthropocene: The EAT–Lancet Commission on Healthy Diets from Sustainable Food Systems." *The Lancet*, January 16. http://dx.doi.org/10.1016/S0140-6736(18)31788-4.

Williams, David R., and Selina A. Mohammed. 2013. "Racism and Health I: Pathways and Scientific Evidence." *American Behavioral Scientist* 57 (8). https://www.ncbi.nlm.nih.gov/pmc/articles/PMC3863357/.

Wolfe, Nathan, Claire P. Dunavan, and Jared Diamond. 2012. "Origins Of Major Human Infectious Diseases." In *Institute of Medicine: Improving Food Safety Through a One Health Approach: Workshop Summary*. Washington, DC: National Academies Press. A16. https://www.ncbi.nlm.nih.gov/books/NBK114494/.

Woo, Kam S., Timothy C.Y. Kwok, and David S. Celermajer. 2014. "Vegan Diet, Subnormal Vitamin B-12 Status and Cardiovascular Health." *Nutrients* 6 (8): 3259–3273.

World Health Organization (WHO). 2016. *Global Report on Diabetes*. http://apps.who.int/iris/bitstream/handle/10665/204871/9789241565257_eng.pdf.

———. 2017a. "Global Health Estimates 2016: Deaths by Cause, Age, Sex, by Country and by Region, 2000–2016." Geneva: WHO.

———. 2017b. "Obesity and Overweight." Fact Sheet. Last modified October 2017. http://www.who.int/mediacentre/factsheets/fs311/en/.

———. 2018a. Global Health Observatory (GHO) Data. "Life Expectancy." http://www.who.int/gho/mortality_burden_disease/life_tables/situation_trends/en.

———. 2018b. "Cancer." Fact Sheet. Last modified February 2018. http://www.who.int/news-room/fact-sheets/detail/cancer.

———. 2018c. "Healthy Diet." Fact Sheet. Last modified October 2018. https://www.who.int/news-room/fact-sheets/detail/Healthy-diet.

———. n.d. "Influenza." Accessed January 7, 2019 from https://www.who.int/influenza/human_animal_interface/avian_influenza/h5n1_research/faqs/en/.

Worthman, Carol M., and Jennifer Kuzara. 2005. "Life History and the Early Origins of Health Differentials." *American Journal of Human Biology* 17 (1): 95–112.

Wrangham, Richard. 2009. *Catching Fire: How Cooking Made Us Human*. New York: Basic Books.

Yehuda, Rachel, and Joseph LeDoux. 2007. "Response Variation Following Trauma: A Translational Neuroscience Approach to Understanding PTSD." *Neuron* 56 (1): 19–32.

Zuckerman, Molly K., and George J. Armelagos. 2014. "The Hygiene Hypothesis and the Second Epidemiologic Transition." In *Modern Environments and Human Health: Revisiting the Second Epidemiologic Transition*, edited by Molly K. Zuckerman, 301-320. Hoboken, NJ: Wiley-Blackwell.

Zuckerman, Molly Kathleen, Kristin Nicole Harper, Ronald Barrett, and George John Armelagos. 2014. "The Evolution of Disease: Anthropological Perspectives on Epidemiologic Transitions." Special issue, "Epidemiological Transitions: Beyond Omran's Theory," *Global Health Action* 7(1): 23303. doi:10.3402/gha.v7.23303.

Zuk, Marlene. 2013. *Paleofantasy: What Evolution Really Tells Us About Sex, Diet, and How We Live*. New York: W. W. Norton.

Figure Attributions

Figure 16.1 Carcinogenic Meats a derivative work original to Explorations: An Open Invitation to Biological Anthropology by Katie Nelson is under a CC BY-NC 4.0 License. [Includes Hot dog PNG image by unknown, CC BY-NC 4.0; Rasher of Bacon by unknown, public domain (CC0); Salami aka by André Karwath Aka, CC BY-SA 2.5; Cow PNG image by unknown, CC BY-NC 4.0; sheep PNG image by unknown, CC BY-NC 4.0; Pig on white background by unknown, public domain (CC0).]

Figure 16.2 Hadazbe returning from hunt by Andreas Lederer has been modified (cropped) and is used under a CC BY 2.0 License.

Figure 16.3 Obesity rates by country original to Explorations: An Open Invitation to Biological Anthropology by Katie Nelson is under a CC BY-NC 4.0 License. Based on data from Obesity Update. 2017. *Organisation for Economic Co-operation and Development (OECD) Health Statistics.*

Figure 16.4 The potato in three modern forms a derivative work original to Explorations: An Open Invitation to Biological Anthropology by Joylin Namie and Katie Nelson is under a CC BY-NC 4.0 License. [Includes Potato by unknown, public domain (CC0); McDonalds-French-Fries-Plate by Evan-Amos, public domain (CC0); Potato chips bowl by unknown, public domain (CC0).]

Figure 16.5 Participants of a walk against Diabetes and for general fitness around Nauru airport by Lorrie Graham, Department of Foreign Affairs and Trade is used under a CC BY 2.0 License.

Figure 16.6 Medical complications of obesity by the Centers for Disease Control and Prevention (CDC) is in the public domain.

Figure 16.7 Glucose metabolism original to Explorations: An Open Invitation to Biological Anthropology by Mary Nelson is under a CC BY-NC 4.0 License.

Figure 16.8 Type 1 and Type 2 Diabetes original to Explorations: An Open Invitation to Biological Anthropology by Mary Nelson is under a CC BY-NC 4.0 License.

Figure 16.9 Top ten causes of death in the U.S. and worldwide original to Explorations: An Open Invitation to Biological Anthropology by Joylin Namie is under a CC BY-NC 4.0 License. Based on data from Centers for Disease Control and Prevention (2016) and World Health Organization (2018).

Figure 16.10 Map of CCR5-delta32 allele distribution original to Explorations: An Open Invitation to Biological Anthropology by Katie Nelson is under a CC BY-NC 4.0 License. [Includes Europe Map Western Political 32847, unknown, Pixabay License; data from Solloch, Ute V., Kathrin Lang, Vinzenz Lange, and Irena Böhme. 2017. "Frequencies of gene variant CCR5-Δ32 in 87 countries based on next-generation sequencing of 1.3 million individuals sampled from 3 national DKMS donor centers." *Human Immonology,* 78 (11-12).]

Figure 16.11 HIV-world-map-UNAIDS by UNAIDS has been designated to the public domain (CC0).

Figure 16.12 Row four man woman people walking together 3755342 by MaxPixel has been designated to the public domain (CC0).

PART II
APPENDICES

Appendix A

Jason M. Organ, Ph.D., Indiana University School of Medicine

Jessica N. Byram, Ph.D., Indiana University School of Medicine

Learning Objectives

- Identify anatomical position and anatomical planes, and use directional terms to describe relative positions of bones.
- Describe the gross structure and microstructure of bone as it relates to bone function.
- Describe types of bone formation and remodeling, and identify (by name) all of the bones of the human skeleton.
- Distinguish major bony features of the human skeleton like muscle attachment sites and passages for nerves and/or arteries and veins.
- Identify the bony features relevant to estimating age, sex, and ancestry in forensic and bioarchaeological contexts.
- Compare human and chimpanzee skeletal anatomy.

Anthropology is the study of people, and the skeleton is the framework of the person. So while all subdisciplines of anthropology study human behavior (culture, language, etc.) either presently or in the past, biological anthropology is the only subdiscipline that studies the human body specifically. And the fundamental core of the human (or any vertebrate) body is the skeleton. Osteology, or the study of bones, is central to biological anthropology because a solid foundation in osteology makes it possible to understand all sorts of aspects of how people have lived and evolved. For example, bones from archaeological sites can be used to understand what animals people ate; fossilized bones can tell us how human and other primate locomotion has changed through time; and bones can give us clues to how modern and ancient humans died, whether by natural causes or in the context of forensic investigations. This appendix will introduce the reader to the basics of anatomical terminology and will then describe the different regions and bones of the skeleton with an emphasis on those structures that have evolved dramatically in humans compared to our closest living relatives: chimpanzees. It will also highlight some (but not all) of the features of the skeleton (e.g., bumps and grooves on bones) used in a forensic context to estimate the age and sex of recovered remains.

ANATOMICAL TERMINOLOGY

Scientists have adopted standardized terminology to describe the position of the body as well as the location and movements of different body parts relative to one another. The terminology used throughout this appendix is consistent with the most recent edition of Terminologia Anatomica: International Anatomical Terminology (Federative Committee on Anatomical Terminology 1998). Below you will find descriptions of standard anatomical position, directional terms, anatomical planes, and skeletal movements (i.e., movements possible where two bones articulate through a joint).

When a body is in **anatomical position**, it is situated as if the individual is standing upright; with head, eyes, and feet pointing forward (anteriorly, see below); and with arms at the side and palms facing forward. In anatomical position, the bones of the forearm are not crossed (Figure A.1).

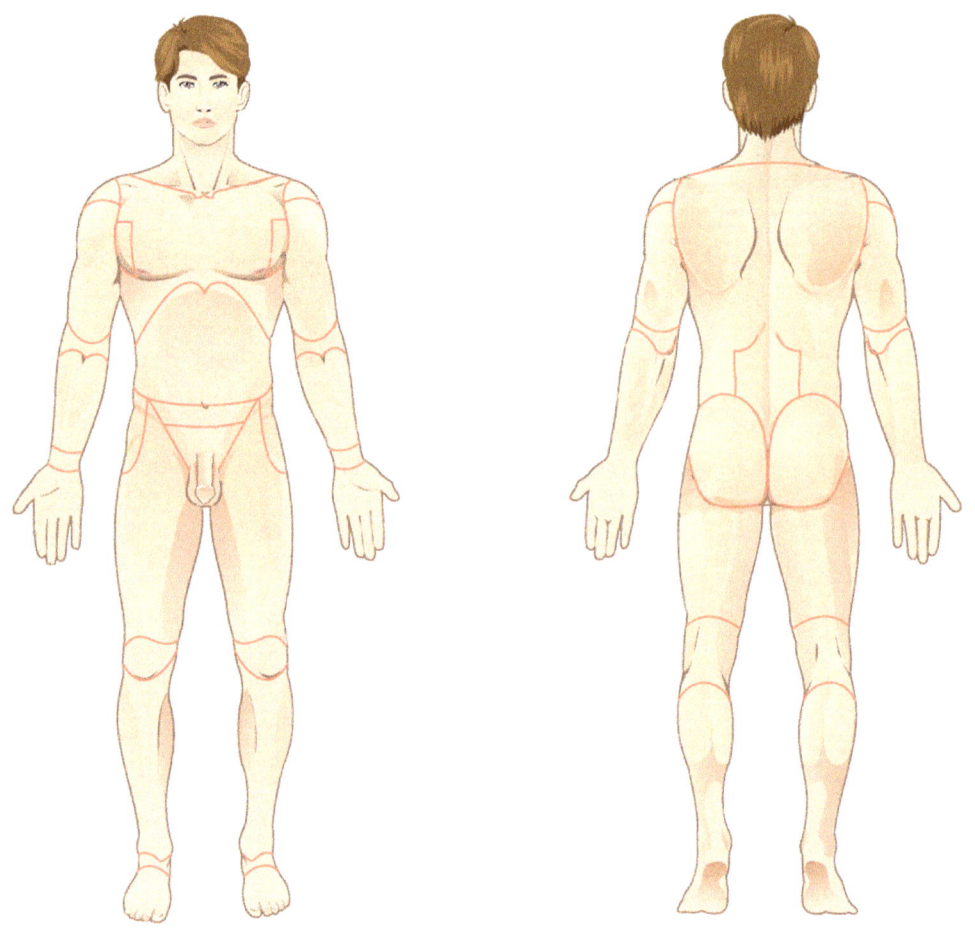

Figure A.1. The human body is shown in anatomical position in an (left) anterior view and a (right) posterior view.

With the body in anatomical position, the position of specific organs (e.g., bones) can be described as situated within specific anatomical planes (Figure A.2). These imaginary planes bisect the body into equal or subequal halves, depending on which plane is described. **Coronal (frontal) planes** divide the body vertically into anterior (front) and posterior (back) halves. **Transverse planes** divide the body horizontally into superior (upper) and inferior (lower) halves. **Sagittal planes** divide the body vertically into left and right halves. The plane that divides the body vertically into equal left and right halves is called the **midsagittal plane**. The midsagittal plane is also called the median plane because it is in the midline of the body. If the left and right halves of the body are divided unequally (i.e., the right "half" is larger than the left "half" or vice versa), we call that dividing plane a **parasagittal plane**. There are potentially an infinite number of parasagittal planes that can be drawn to divide the body into unequal right and left "halves."

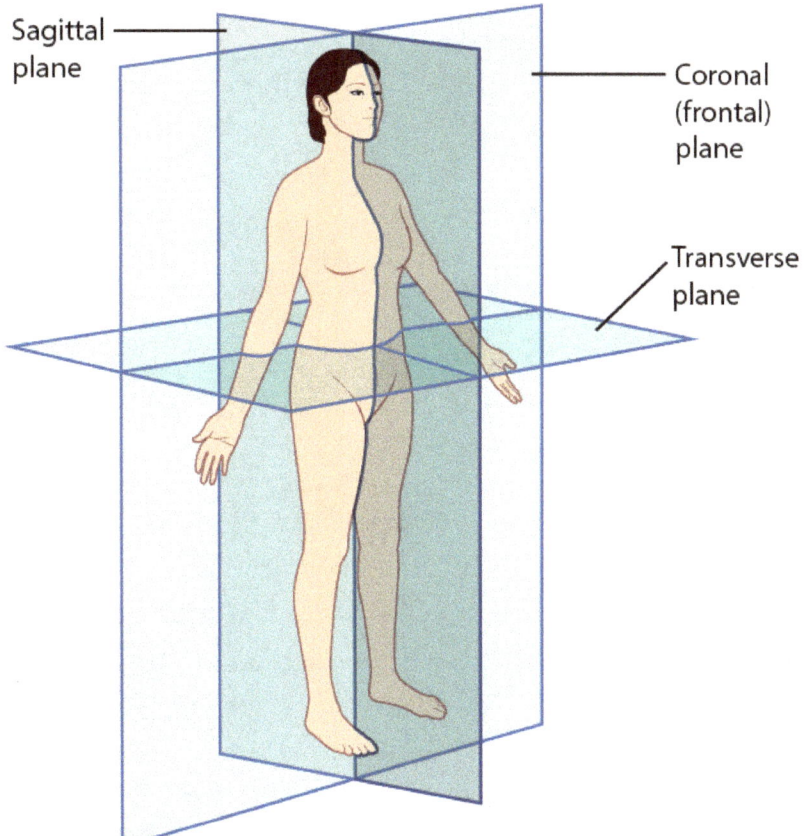

Figure A.2. The three planes most commonly used in anatomical and medical imaging are the sagittal, frontal (or coronal), and transverse planes.

Directional Terms

When describing the position of one body part (in this case, a bone) relative to another, scientists use precisely defined directional terms. Each of the directional terms described below refers to the body in anatomical position. This is an important point because once the position of one bone is established relative to another, that directional term is the same, regardless of whether the body remains in anatomical position (e.g., the skull is always superior to the vertebrae, even if the individual is lying down).

A bone or skeletal feature that is **anterior** (or **ventral**) is located toward the front of the body and a bone that is **posterior** (or **dorsal**) is located toward the back of the body (Figure A.3). For example, the sternum (breastbone) is anterior to the vertebral column ("backbone"). A **medial** bone is located closer to the midline (midsagittal plane) than a bone that is lateral, or located further from the midline. For example, the thumb is lateral to the index finger. A structure that is **proximal** is closer to the trunk of the body (usually referring to limb bones) than a **distal** structure, which is further from the trunk of the body. For example, the femur (thigh bone) is proximal to the tibia (leg bone). Finally, structures that are **superior** (or **cranial**) are located closer to the head than structures that are **inferior** (or **caudal**). For example, the rib cage is superior to the pelvis, and the foot is inferior to the knee. Typically, the terms "cranial" and "caudal" are used in reference to the non-human, quadrupedal skeleton, whereas "superior" and "inferior" are used in reference to the human skeleton.

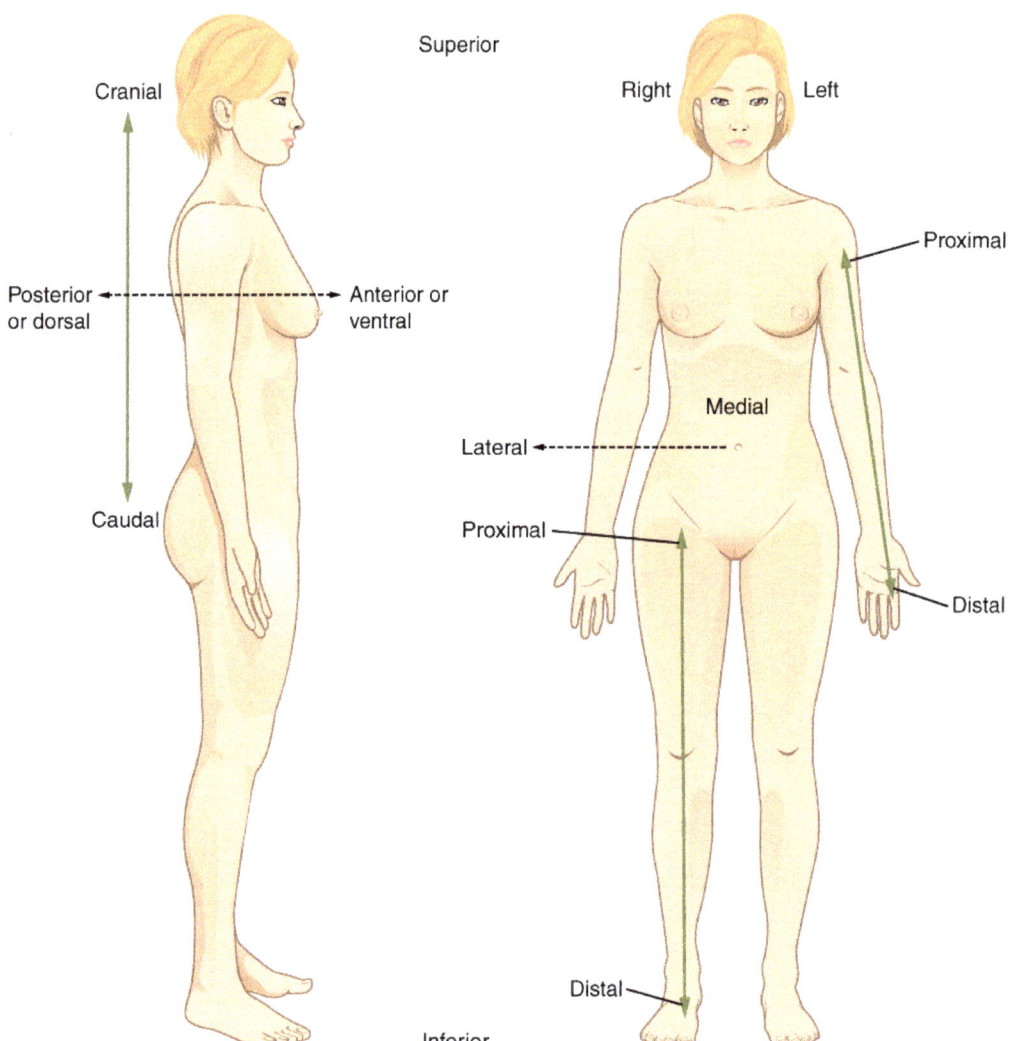

Figure A.3. Paired directional terms are shown as applied to the human body.

SKELETAL FORM AND FUNCTION

Structure and Material of Bone

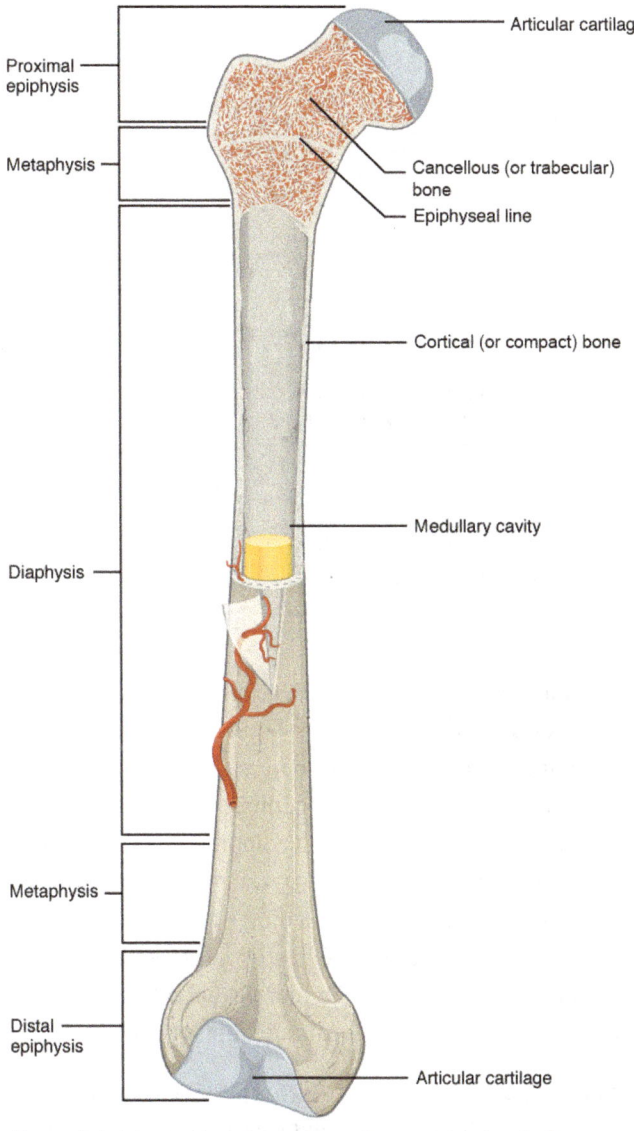

Figure A.4. *A typical long bone shows the gross anatomical characteristics of bone.*

Bone is a composite of organic (collagen) and inorganic (mineral, e.g., hydroxyapatite, a calcium phosphate salt) materials with incredible strength in compression so it can support the body under the force of gravity. When bone is mature (fully mineralized as opposed to juvenile and undermineralized), it comprises an outer dense region of bone called **cortical** (or compact) bone and an inner spongy region of bone called **cancellous** (or trabecular) bone (Figure A.4). However, the interfaces between the organic and inorganic materials, as well as the cortical and cancellous regions, are subject to changing stresses. Each time we move our muscles, our bones are subjected to a combination of bending, twisting, compression, and tension. This results in the formation of microscopic cracks that weaken the bone and may result in complete bone fracture. Bone cells called **osteocytes** have special properties that allow them to sense when these microcracks form. Osteocytes then signal **osteoclast cells** to remove the cracked bone and **osteoblast cells** to lay down new bone—a process known as skeletal remodeling. **Osteogenic cells** are stem cells that are able to differentiate into osteoblasts (Figure A.5).

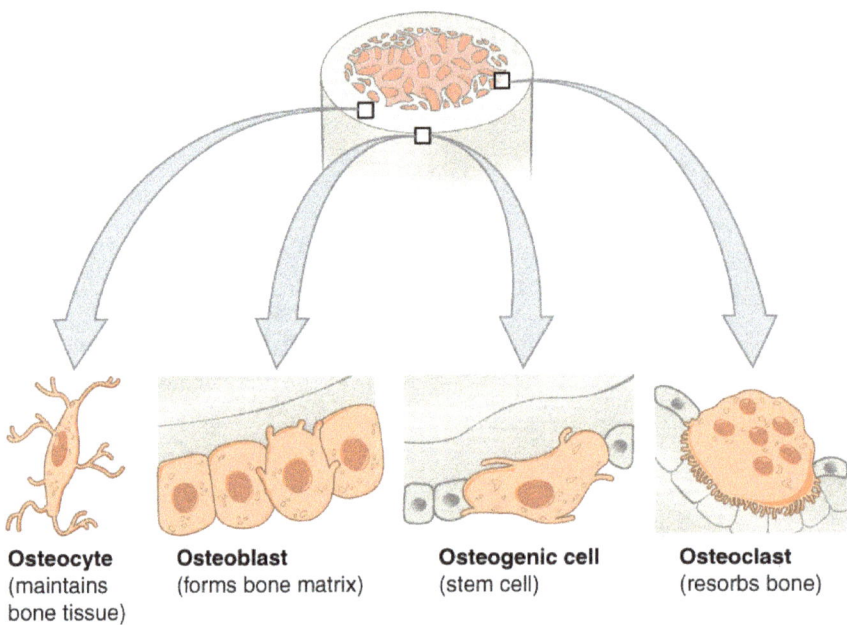

Figure A.5. Four types of cells are found within bone tissue. Osteogenic cells are stem cells that develop into osteoblasts. Osteoblasts lay down new bone while osteoclasts remove bone. Osteoblasts that get trapped in calcified matrix become osteocytes.

Bone Shape

Different bones have different shapes that largely relate to their specific function within the skeletal system. Additionally, the ratio of cortical to cancellous bone, and which muscles are attached to the bone and how, affect the shape of the whole bone. Generally there are five recognized bone shapes: long bones, short bones, flat bones, sesamoid bones, and irregular bones. **Long bones** are longer than they are wide and consist of three sections: diaphysis, epiphysis, and metaphysis (Figure A.4). The **diaphysis** of a long bone is simply the shaft of the bone, and it comprises mostly cortical bone with a thin veneer of internal cancellous bone lining a **medullary cavity**. At both the proximal and distal ends of every long bone, there is an **epiphysis**, which consists of a thin shell of cortical bone surrounding a high concentration of cancellous bone. The epiphysis is usually coated with hyaline (or articular) cartilage to facilitate joint articulation with other bones. The junction between diaphysis and epiphysis is the **metaphysis**, which has a more equal ratio of cortical to cancellous bone. Examples of long bones are the humerus, the femur, and the metacarpals and metatarsals.

The other bone shapes are simpler. **Short bones** are defined as being equal in length and width, and they possess a mix of cortical and cancellous bone (Figure A.6). They are usually involved in forming movable joints with adjacent bones and therefore often have surfaces covered with hyaline cartilage. Examples of short bones are the carpals of the wrist and the tarsals of the ankle.

Flat bones, as their name suggests, are flat and consist of two layers of thick cortical bone with an intermediate layer of cancellous bone called a diploe. Examples of flat bones are most of the bones of the skull, such as the frontal and parietal bones, as well as all parts of the sternum (Figure A.6). Sometimes bones develop within the tendon of a muscle in order to reduce friction on the joint surface and to increase leverage of the muscle to move a joint. These types of bones are called **sesamoid bones**, and these include the patella (or knee cap) and the pisiform (a bone of the wrist).

Irregular bones are bones that don't fit into any of the other four categories. The shapes of these bones are often more complex than the others, and examples include the vertebrae and certain bones of the skull, like the ethmoid and sphenoid bones (Figure A.6).

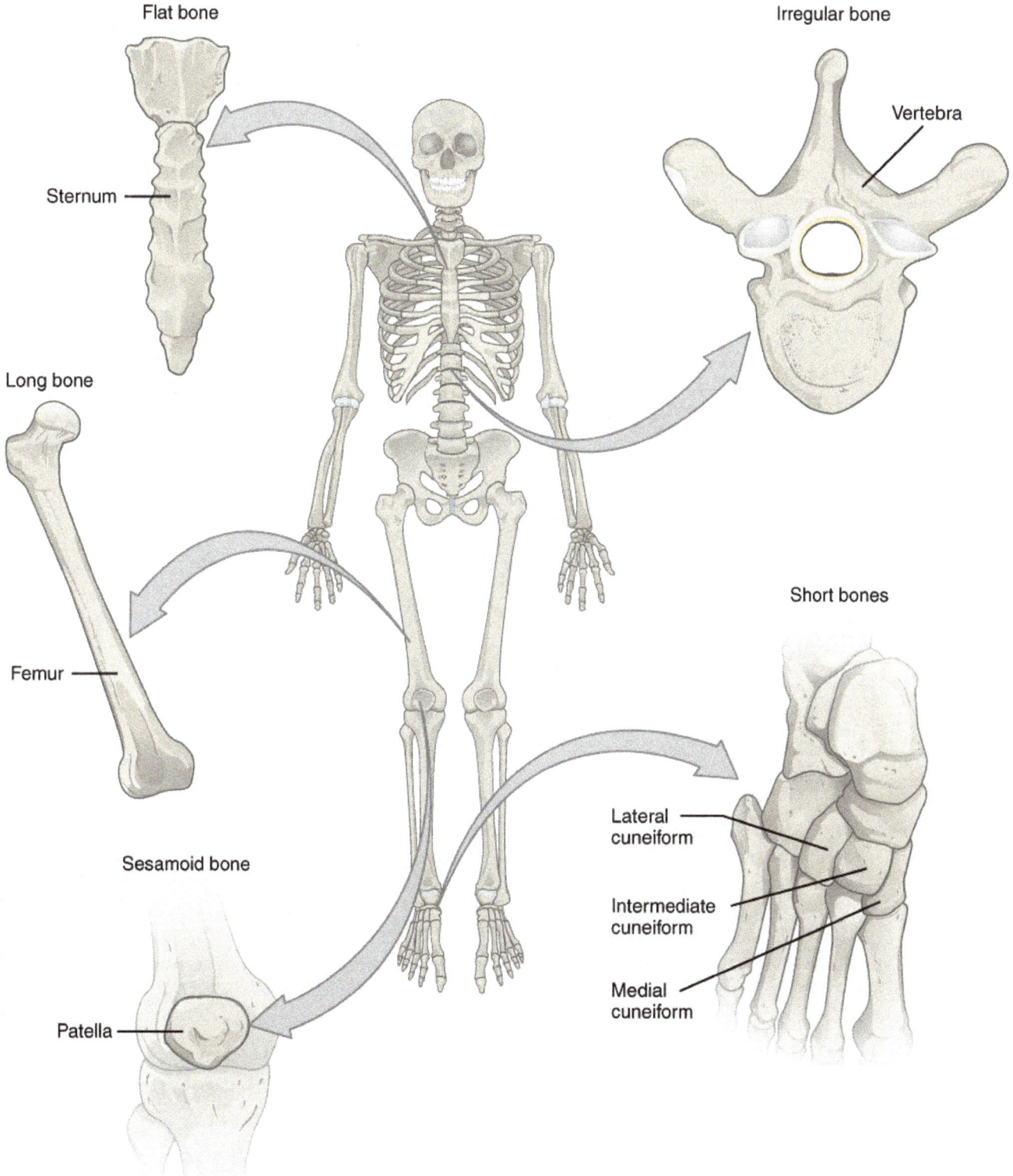

Figure A.6. Bones are classified according to their shape and include long, short, flat, sesamoid, and irregular bones.

Osteology | 629

Bone Formation

Bone develops via one of two mechanisms: intramembranous or endochondral bone formation. **Intramembranous bone formation** occurs when connective tissue mesenchymal (stem) cells aggregate and differentiate into osteoblasts, which then begin to synthesize new bone along the aggregated connective tissue cells (Figure A.7). Intramembranous bone formation is the mechanism by which most bones of the skull develop as well as the clavicle (collar bone). When osteoblasts develop from an intermediate cartilage "model" that is then replaced by bone, instead of developing directly from the mesenchymal cells, the mechanism is described as **endochondral bone formation** (Figure A.8). Endochondral bone formation is the mechanism by which most bones of the skeleton develop (Burr and Organ 2017).

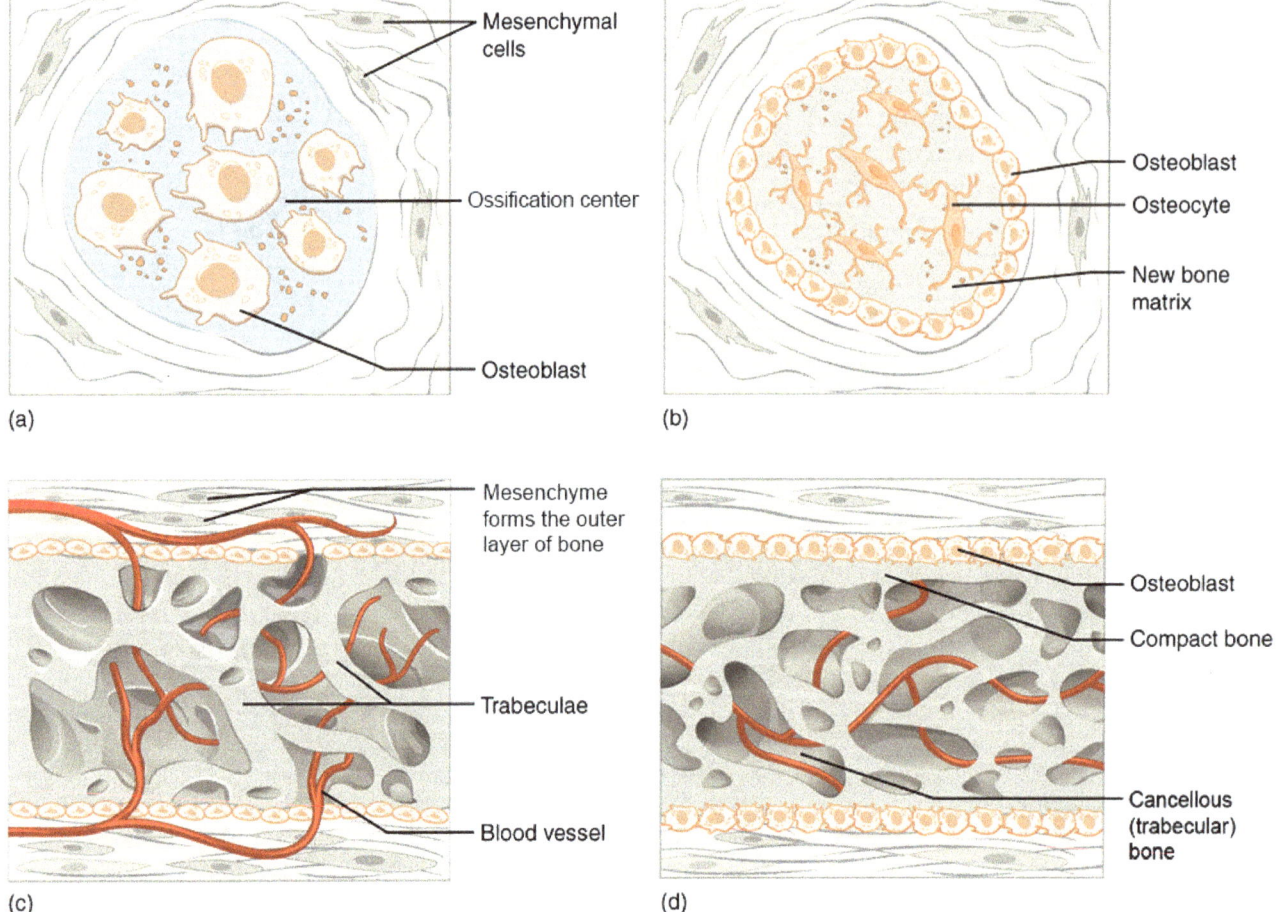

Figure A.7 Intramembranous ossification begins when mesenchymal cells group into clusters. These clusters contain osteoblasts, which lay down the initial trabecular bone. Compact bone develop superficial to the trabecular bone, and the initial structure of the bone is complete.

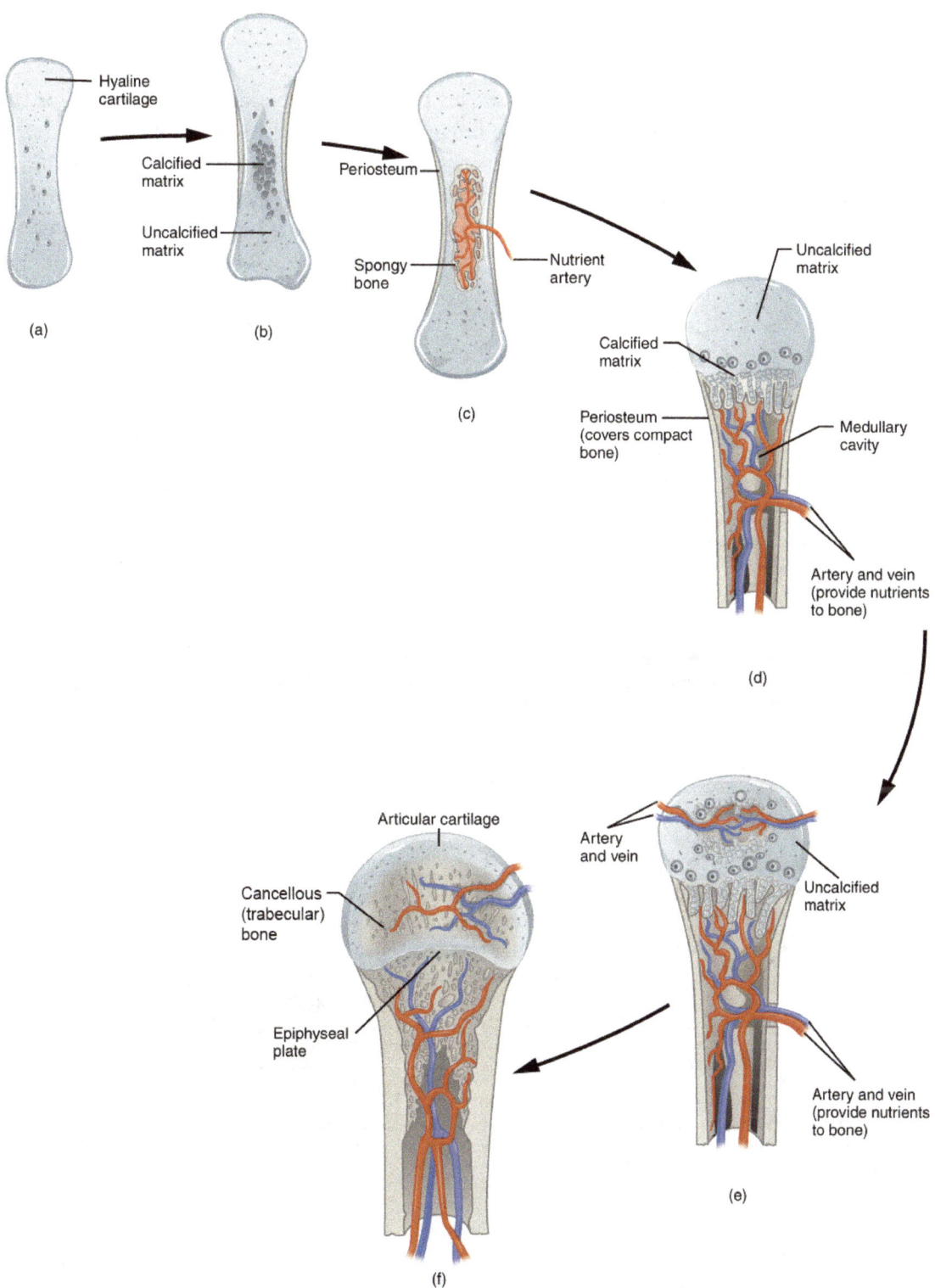

Figure A.8 Endochondral ossification begins when mesenchymal cells differentiate into cartilage cells which lay down a cartilage model of the future bony skeleton. Cartilage is then replaced by bone, except at the (epiphyseal) growth plates (which fuse at the end of postnatal growth) and the hyaline (articular) cartilage on the joint surface.

Bone Function

Bone performs both metabolic and mechanical functions for the body. On the metabolic side, bone is required to maintain mineral (i.e., calcium) homeostasis and for the production of red and white blood cells (Figure A.9), which develop in the cavity and the cancellous region of the metaphysis and epiphysis. But it is undeniable that the mechanical functions of bone are primary because bone is critically responsible for protecting internal organs, providing support against the force gravity, and serving as a network of rigid levers for muscles to act upon during movement.

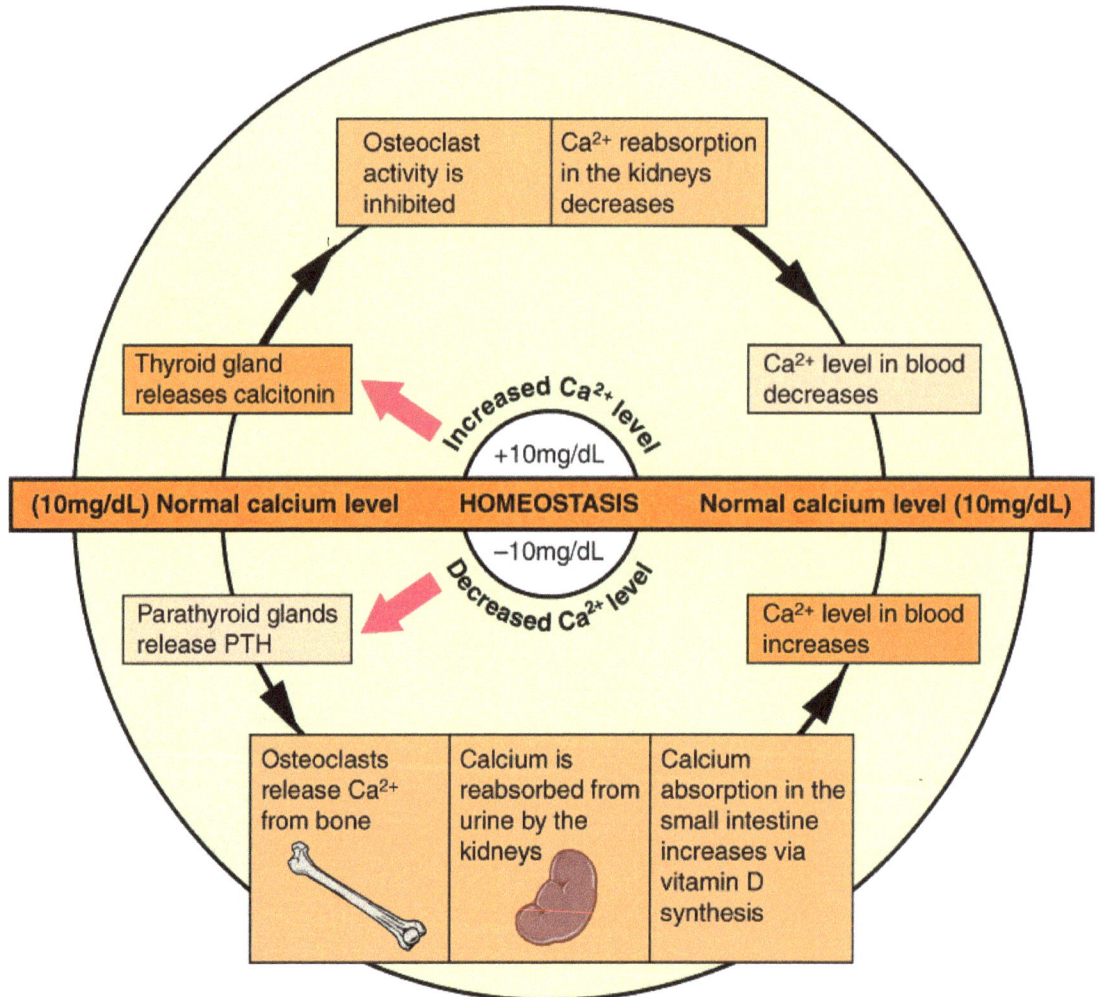

Figure A.9 The body regulates calcium homeostasis with two pathways; one is signaled to turn on when blood calcium levels drop below normal and one is the pathway that is signaled to turn on when blood calcium levels are elevated.

HUMAN SKELETAL SYSTEM

The skeletal system is divided into two regions: axial and appendicular (Figure A.10). The **axial skeleton** consists of the skull, vertebral column, and the thoracic cage formed by the ribs and sternum (breastbone). The **appendicular skeleton** comprises the pectoral girdle, the pelvic girdle, and all the bones of the upper and lower limbs (White and Folkens 2000).

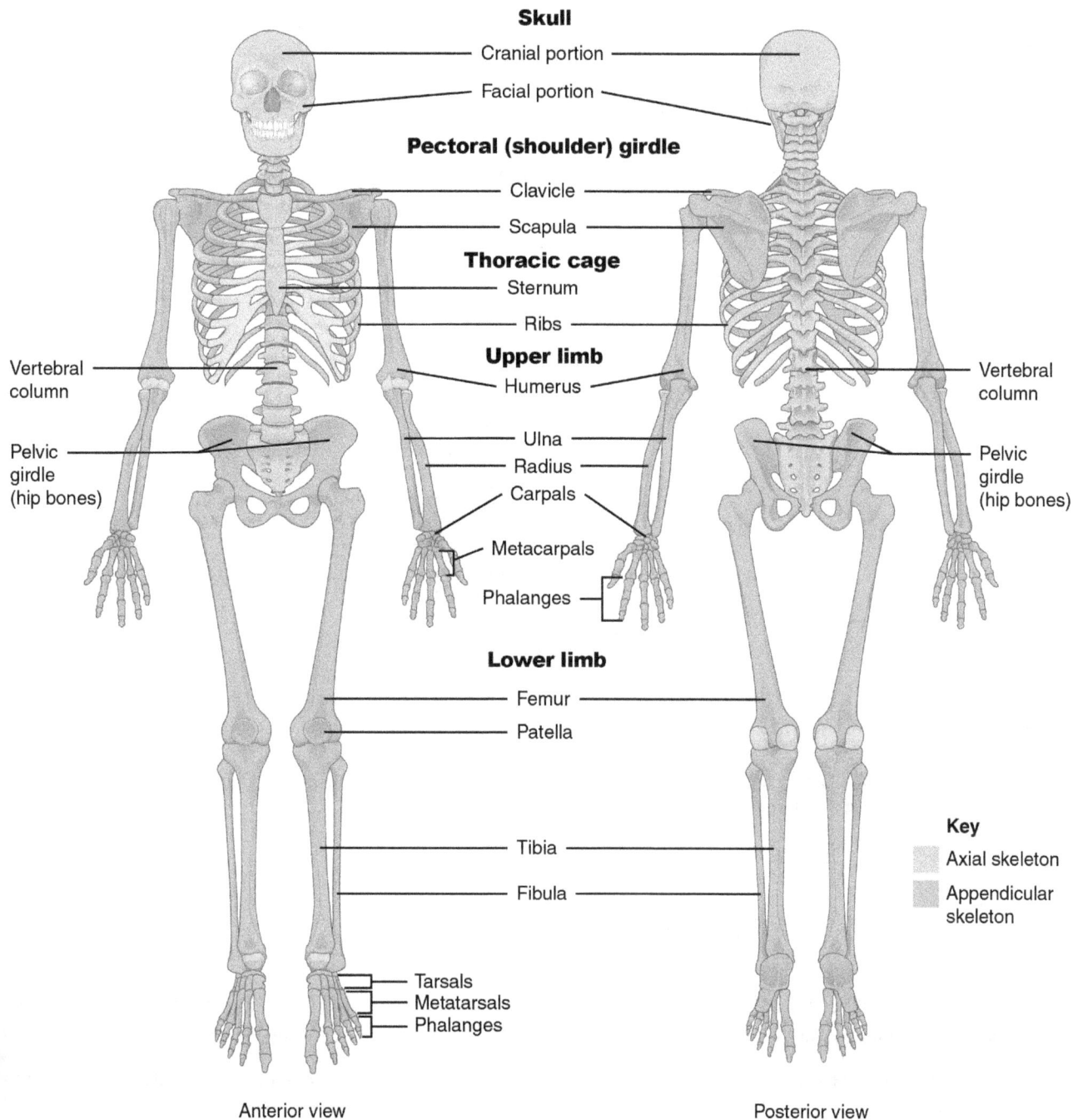

Figure A.10 *The axial skeleton consists of the skull, vertebral column, and the thoracic cage. The appendicular skeleton is made up of all bones of the upper and lower limbs.*

Axial Skeleton

Skull

The skull comprises numerous bones (some paired and others that are unpaired) and is divided into two major portions:

Osteology | 633

the **mandible** (or lower jaw) and the **cranium** (the remainder of the skull). The cranium is further subdivided into the **neurocranium** (or cranial vault), which houses the brain, and the **viscerocranium** (or facial skeleton; Figure A.11). Where two bones of the cranium come together, they form articulations called **cranial sutures**, which fuse (or close) with increasing age and can be used as a broad estimate of age at death. Degree of suture closure is scored at several anatomical landmarks and compiled to produce an age estimate. The remainder of this section lists the bones of the skull by region and details some of the landmarks examined in forensic contexts.

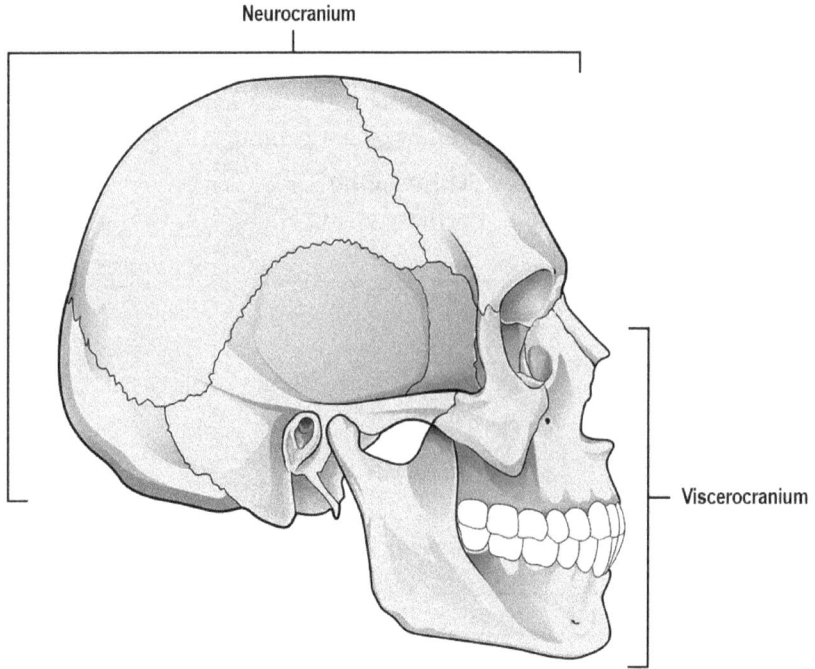

Figure A.11 The skull consists of the cranium and the mandible. The cranium is further divided into the neurocranium and viscerocranium.

Bones and Some Features of the Neurocranium

- **Frontal:** an unpaired bone consisting of two parts: a superior, vertically oriented portion called the squama and an inferior, horizontally oriented portion that forms the roof of the **orbit** (eye socket; Figures A.12 and A.13).
    - **The coronal suture** is the articulation between the frontal bone and the two parietal bones posterior and lateral to the frontal.
    - The frontal bone develops initially as two separate bones that fuse together during growth. Occasionally this fusion is incomplete, resulting in a **metopic suture** that persists between the two halves (left and right) of the frontal bone (White and Folkens 2005).
    - The **glabella** is a bony projection between the brow ridges. The glabella in females tends to be flat while rounded and protruding in males.
    - The **supraorbital margin** is the upper edge of the orbit. The thickness of the edge can be used as an indicator of sex. A thin, sharp border is indicative of a female while a blunt, thick border suggests a male.

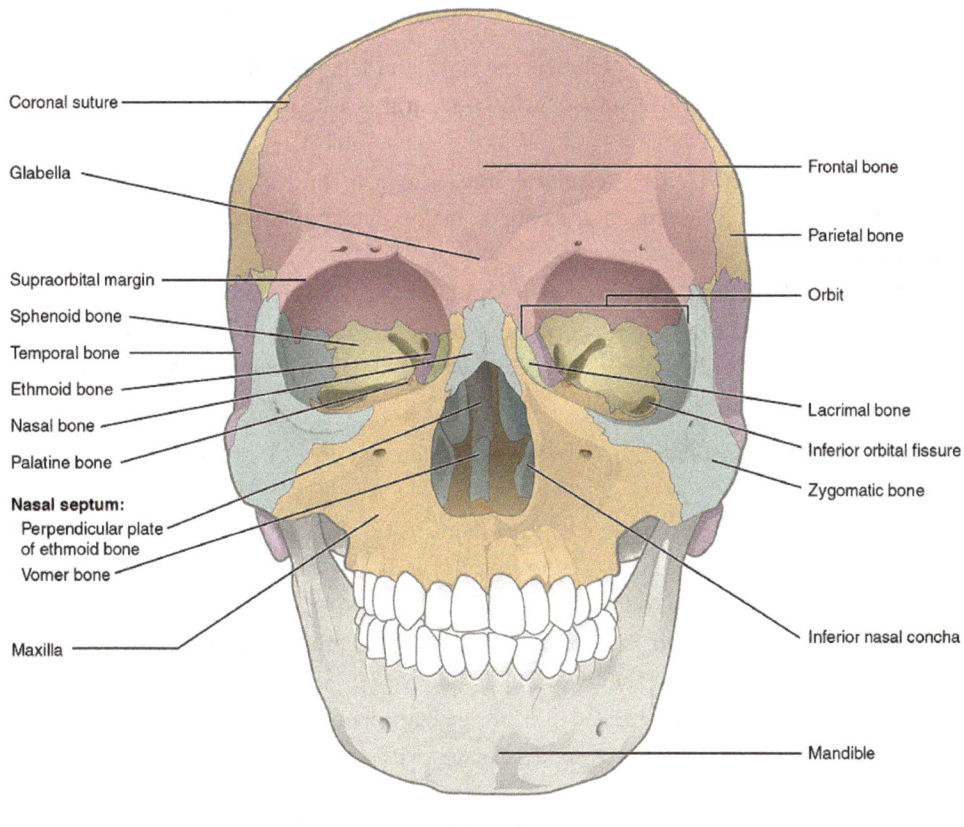

Figure A.12 Anterior view of the skull.

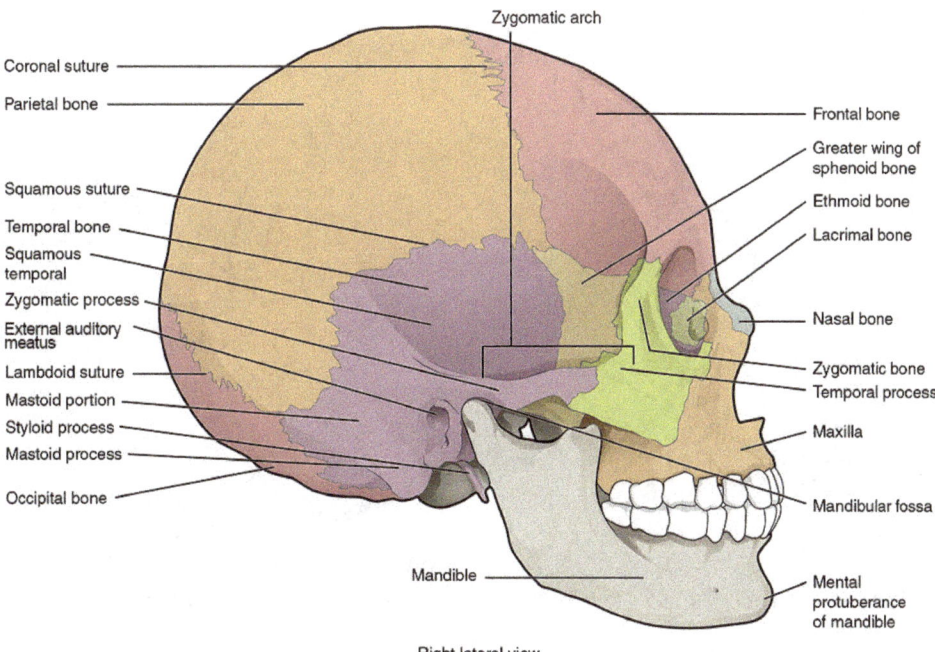

Figure A.13 Lateral view of the skull.

Osteology | 635

- **Parietal:** Paired bones that form the majority of the roof and sides of the neurocranium (Figures A.12 and A.13).
  - The **sagittal suture** is the articulation between the right and left parietal bones. It extends from the coronal suture anteriorly to the lambdoidal suture, which separates the parietal bones from the occipital bone posteriorly.
  - Each parietal bone is marked by two **temporal lines** (superior and inferior), which are anterior-posterior arching lines that serve as attachment sites for a major chewing muscle (temporalis) and its associated connective tissue.
- **Temporal:** Paired bones on the lateral side of the neurocranium that are divided into two portions: squamous (or flat) portion that forms the lateral side of the neurocranium and the petrous (or rock-like) portion that houses the special sense organs of the ear for hearing and balance as well as the three tiny bones of the middle ear: incus, malleus, and stapes (Figures A.13, A.14, and A.15).
  - The **squamosal suture** is the articulation between the squamous portion of the temporal bone and the inferior border of the parietal bone.
  - The **mastoid process** is a prominent attachment site for several muscles including the large sternocleidomastoid muscle. As such, it is often used to estimate sex in that males tend to have longer and wider mastoid processes compared to females (Bass 2005).
  - The **styloid process** is a thin, pointed, inferior projection of the temporal bone that serves as an attachment site for several muscles and a ligament of the throat.
  - The **zygomatic process of the temporal** is a thin, arch-like process that originates from the squamous portion of the temporal bone. The zygomatic process articulates with the temporal process of the zygomatic bone to form the **zygomatic arch** (or cheekbone).
  - **The temporal fossa** is the depression in the temporal bone where the mandibular condyle (see below, under mandible) articulates to form the temporomandibular (or jaw) joint.

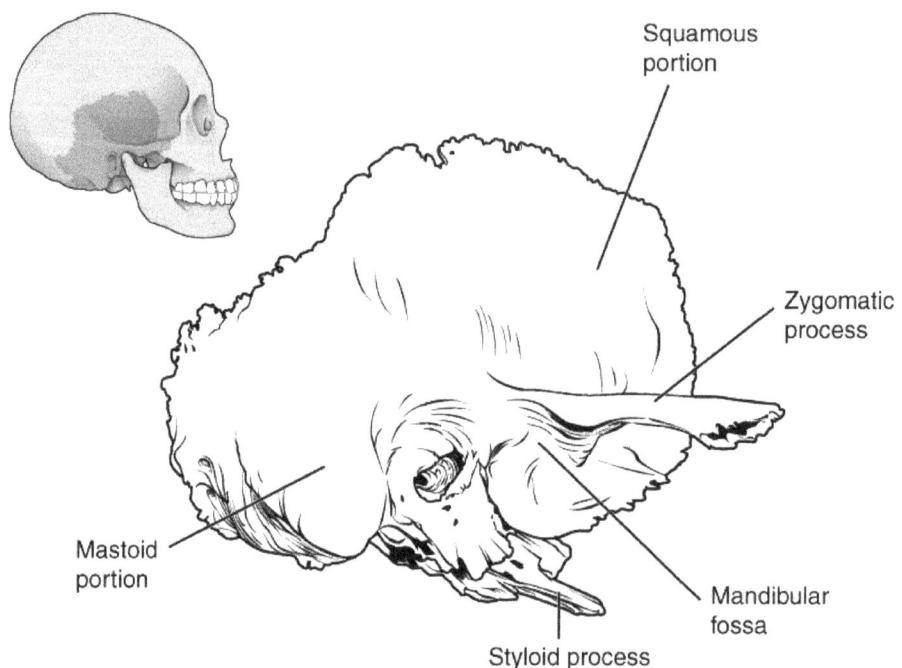

Figure A.14 *A lateral view of the isolated temporal bone shows the squamous portion.*

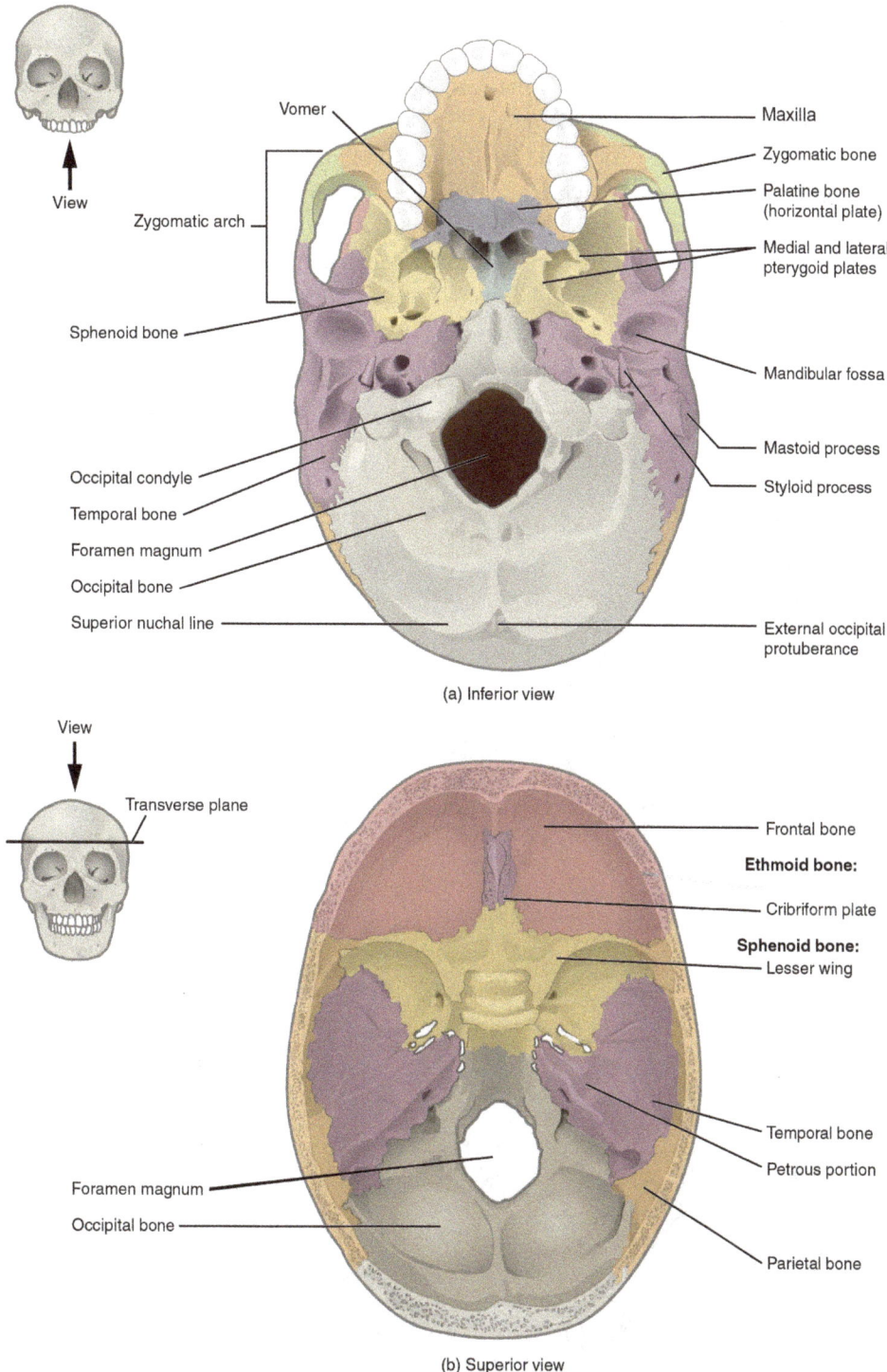

Figure A.15 (a) The base of the cranium (b) The floor of the cranial cavity.

- **Occipital**: Unpaired bone that forms the posterior and inferior portions of the neurocranium (Figures A.13 and A.15).
  - The **lambdoidal suture** is the articulation between the occipital bone and the two parietal bones. It resembles the shape of the Greek letter lambda.
  - The **external occipital protuberance** (EOP) is a robust attachment of the nuchal ligament. When viewed

Osteology | 637

laterally, males tend to have a discernible projection or hook, whereas in females, the occipital is typically smooth.
- The **nuchal lines** are parallel ridges that meet on the midline at the EOP. These prominent muscle attachment sites tend to be more robust and projecting in males.
- The occipital bone contains a large circular opening called the **foramen magnum**, which provides a space for passage of the brainstem/spinal cord from the neurocranium into the vertebral canal of the spine.

- **Sphenoid**: Unpaired, butterfly-shaped bone that forms the central portion of the bottom of the neurocranium. The sphenoid is divided into several regions, including the body, greater wings, lesser wings, and pterygoid processes (with pterygoid plates; see Figures A.15 and A.16). This bone is critical to supporting the brain and several nerves and blood vessels supplying this region.
  - **Pterygoid plates** are flat projections of the pterygoid processes that serve as attachment sites for chewing muscles and muscles of the throat.

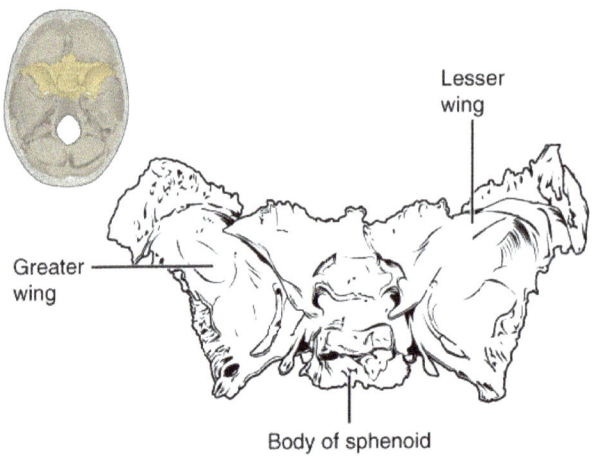

(a) Superior view

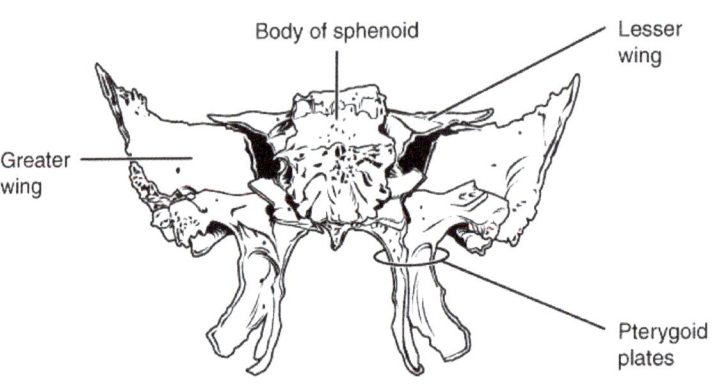

(b) Posterior view

Figure A.16 Shown in isolation in (a) superior and (b) posterior views, the sphenoid forms the central portion of the neurocranium. The sphenoid has multiple openings for the passage of nerves and blood vessels.

- **Ethmoid**: Unpaired bone consisting of a median vertical plate that forms part of the bony nasal septum and a horizontal plate (cribriform plate) with many small foramina (holes) that transmit olfactory nerves (special sense of smell; Figure A.17).

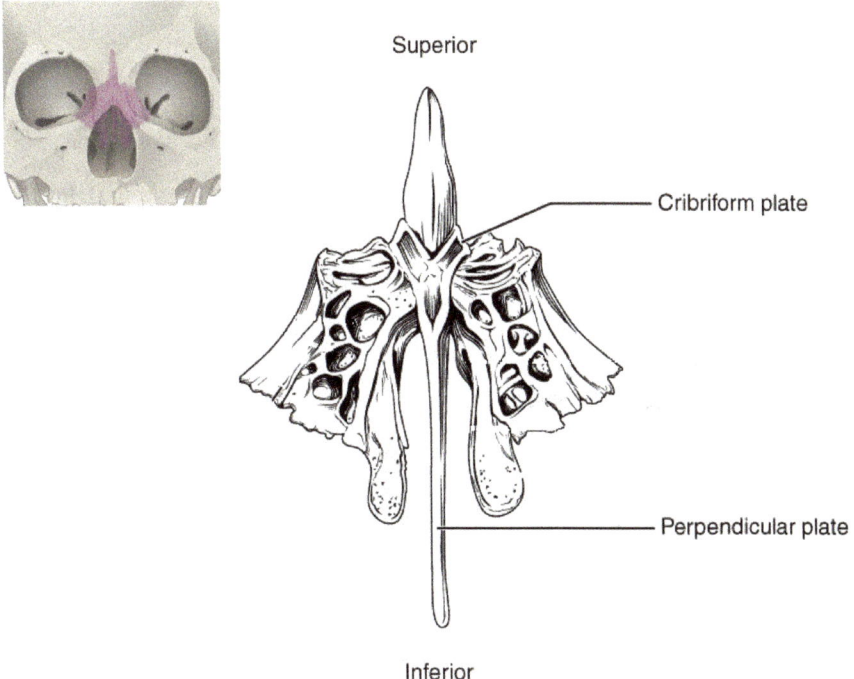

Figure A.17 *The unpaired ethmoid bone is located at the midline within the central skull. It forms the upper nasal septum and contains foramina to convey olfactory nerves.*

Bones of the Viscerocranium

- **Maxilla**: Paired bones that form the upper jaw, support the upper teeth, and form the inferior margin of the cheek (Figures A.12, A.13, A.15, and A.18).
  - The **nasal spine** is a thin projection on the midline at the inferior border of the nasal aperture. Length of the nasal spine has been used as a subjective trait to determine ancestry, with those exhibiting long nasal spines to be more likely of European ancestry.
  - The **zygomatic process of the maxilla** is the portion of the bone that articulates with the zygomatic bone to form the anterior portion of the zygomatic arch.

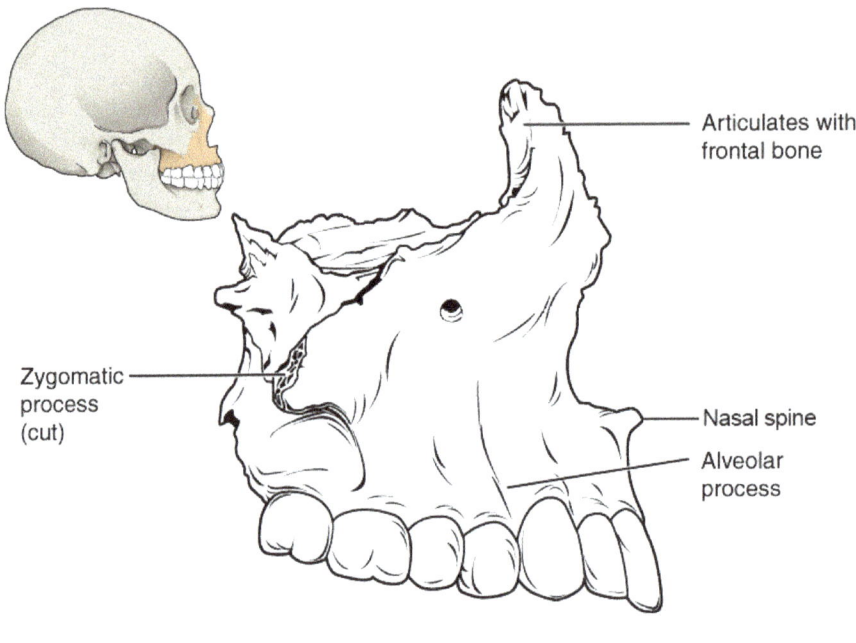

Figure A.18 *The maxilla forms the upper jaw and supports the upper teeth.*

- **Nasal**: Small, paired, flat, rectangular bones that form the bridge of the nose (Figure A.19).
  - **Nasal aperture** is the anterior opening into the nasal cavity. As a forensic trait, it is described as low and wide in those of African ancestry and tall and narrow in those of European ancestry.
- **Zygomatic**: Paired bones that form the anterolateral portion of the cheekbone and contribute to the lateral and inferior wall of the orbit (Figure A.19).
  - The **temporal process of the zygomatic** is the portion of the bone that articulates with the temporal bone to form the anterior portion of the zygomatic arch.
- **Palatine**: Paired L-shaped bones that form the posterior portion of the roof of the mouth, floor of the orbit, and the floor and lateral walls of the nasal cavity (Figures A.15 and A.19).
- **Lacrimal**: Small, flat, paired bones that form the anterior portion of the medial wall of the orbit (Figure A.19).

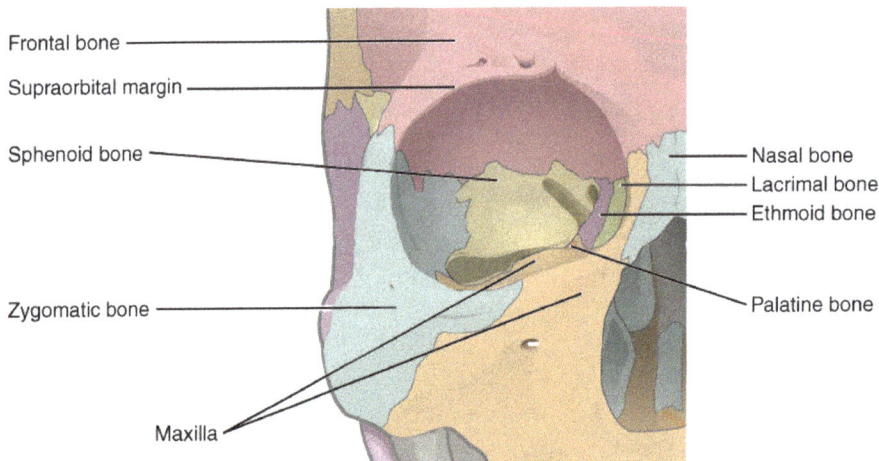

Figure A.19 *Seven skull bones contribute to the walls of the orbit: frontal, zygomatic, maxilla, lacrimal, ethmoid, palatine, and sphenoid.*

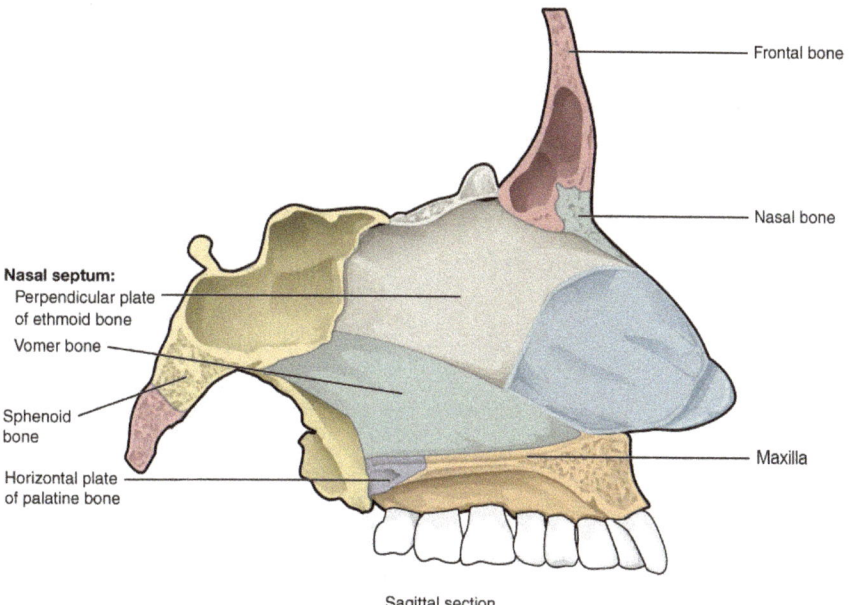

Figure A.20 *The nasal septum is formed by the perpendicular plate of the ethmoid bone and the vomer bone.*

- **Vomer**: Unpaired thin bone that forms the inferior portion of the bony nasal septum. It articulates with the ethmoid superiorly (Figure A.20).
- **Inferior nasal concha**: Paired bones that project and curl like a scroll from the lateral wall of the nasal cavity (Figure A.21).

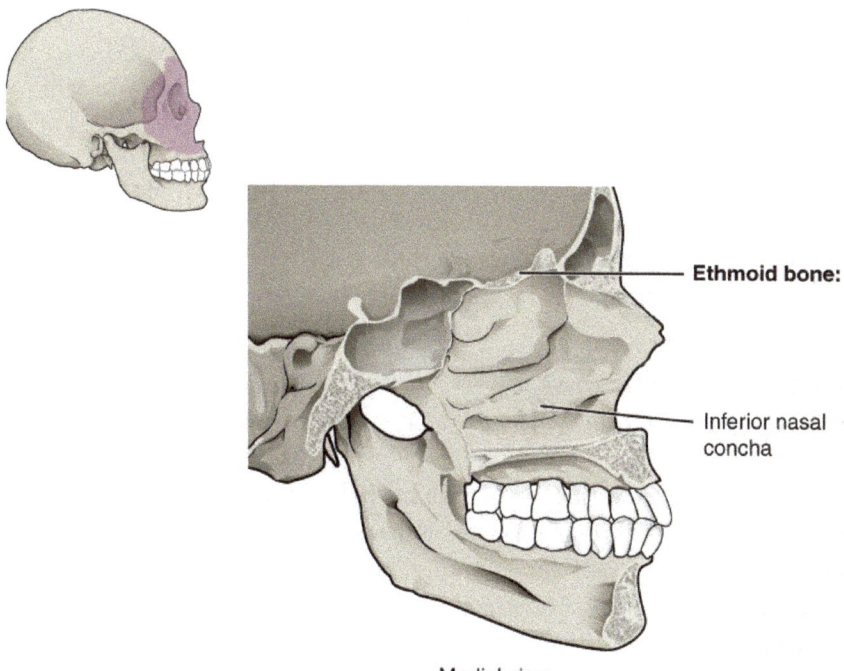

Figure A.21 *Inferior nasal concha scroll from the lateral wall of the nasal cavity.*

- **Hyoid**: Unpaired U-shaped bone that sits in the neck inferior to the mandible. The hyoid is the only bone of the skeleton that does not articulate with another bone. Instead, it is encased in a sling of muscles that move the larynx (voice box), pharynx, and tongue (Figure A.22).

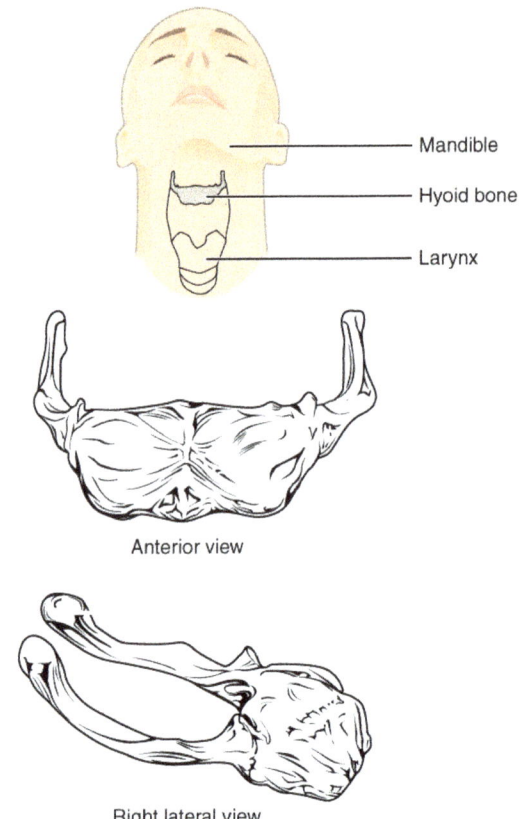

Figure A.22 The hyoid bone is located in the upper neck and does not join with any other bone. It provides attachments for muscles that move the tongue, larynx, and pharynx.

- **Mandible**: Unpaired bone with a horizontal (and anteriorly arched) body and a vertical ramus that articulates with the temporal fossa to form the temporomandibular (jaw) joint. The body of the mandible houses the lower teeth (Figure A.13 and A.23).
    - The **mental protuberance (eminence)** is the most anteriorly projecting point on the mandible—the so-called "chin." A prominent projection is likely to indicate a male, while a smooth mental region likely indicates a female.
    - The **ramus** of the mandible projects superiorly from the body of the mandible and ascends to one of two features on the superior aspect: coronoid process or mandibular condyle.
    - The **coronoid process** is a bony projection off the anterior and superior aspect of the mandibular ramus. The inferior attachment of the temporalis muscle (a chewing muscle) attaches here.
    - The **mandibular condyle**, a rounded projection off the posterior and superior aspect of the mandibular ramus, articulates with the temporal fossa of the temporal bone at the temporomandibular (TMJ) joint.
    - The **gonial (mandibular) angle** is the rounded posteroinferior border of the mandible. It tends to be smooth in females with a more obtuse angle but is laterally flared in males and closer to a right angle in shape.

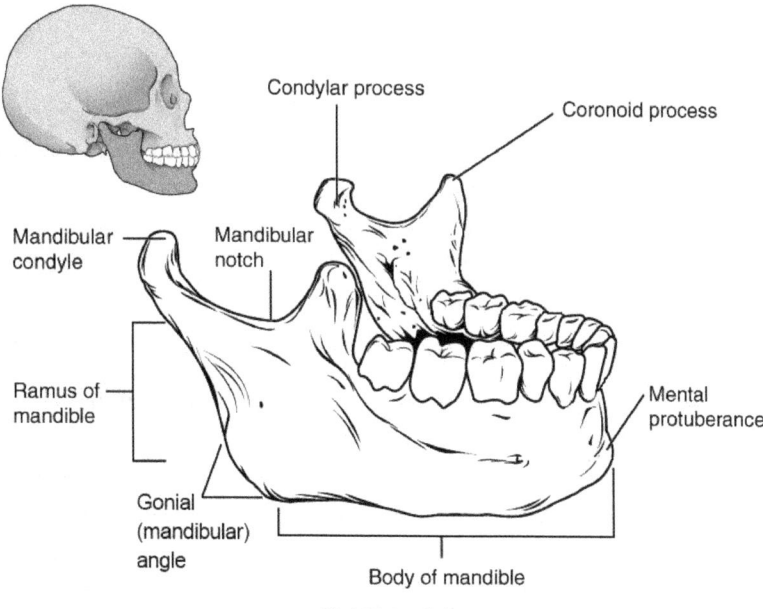

Figure A.23 *The mandible articulates with the temporal fossa to form the temporomandibular joint.*

- **Teeth**: Adults normally have 32 teeth, distributed among four quadrants of the mouth (upper left, upper right, lower left, lower right). In each quadrant, there are eight teeth: two incisors (central and lateral), one canine, two premolars, and three molars. Each of these types of teeth has a different shape that reflects its function during chewing:

  - **Incisors** are flat and shovel shaped and are used to bite into a food item.
  - **Canines** are conical, with a single pointed cusp used to puncture a food item.
  - **Premolars** have two rounded cusps and are used to grind and mash a food item.
  - **Molars** have five flatter cusps and are used to grind food prior to swallowing.

The teeth have their own set of directional terms that help differentiate the different parts of the tooth. For example, the anterior portion of the tooth is called mesial, while the posterior portion of the tooth is called distal. In the case of teeth in the front of the mouth, mesial refers to the aspect toward the midline of the body; distal refers to the aspect away from the midline. Similarly, the side of the tooth facing the lips is called the buccal surface and the side facing the tongue is called the lingual surface. Finally, we can talk about the occlusal surface of the tooth, which is the surface that comes in contact with food or the teeth from the other jaw when the jaw is closed. Sometimes the occlusal surface of the incisors is called the incisal surface.

Vertebral Column

The adult vertebral column consists of 32–33 individual vertebrae, divided into five regions: cervical, thoracic, lumbar, sacral, and coccygeal. This section will review the features of a general vertebra and then will describe the unique features of vertebrae in each of the five regions.

General Structure of a Vertebra

A typical vertebra consists of an anteriorly situated **body**—the main weight-bearing element of the vertebra—and a posteriorly projecting **vertebral arch** (Figure A.24). The vertebral arch consists of the paired **pedicles** and paired laminae. The pedicle connects the **transverse process** (a laterally projecting process that serves as an attachment site for muscles and ligaments) to the vertebral body; the **lamina** connects the **spinous process** (a posteriorly projecting process that serves as an attachment site for muscles and ligaments) to the transverse process. Projecting inferiorly off the vertebral arch is the **inferior articular process**, and projecting superiorly off the vertebral arch is the **superior articular process**. Between the vertebral body anteriorly and the vertebral arch posteriorly is an open space called the **vertebral foramen**.

Adjacent vertebrae articulate with one another through two major types of joints: **intervertebral disc joints** between adjacent vertebral bodies and **zygapophyseal (facet) joints** between the inferior articular process of one vertebra and the superior articular process of the vertebra immediately inferior to it. When all vertebrae are articulated into a column, the adjacent vertebral foramina form the **vertebral canal**, through which the spinal cord travels from the foramen magnum of the occipital bone to approximately the level of the second lumbar vertebra. At the level of each vertebra, the spinal cord gives us a pair (left and right) of spinal nerves that exit between adjacent vertebrae through the intervertebral foramen formed by adjacent vertebral arches. Even though the spinal cord ends in the lumbar region, the spinal nerves emanating from the spinal cord continue all the way to the sacrum (sometimes to the coccyx), culminating in a total of 30–31 pairs of spinal nerves.

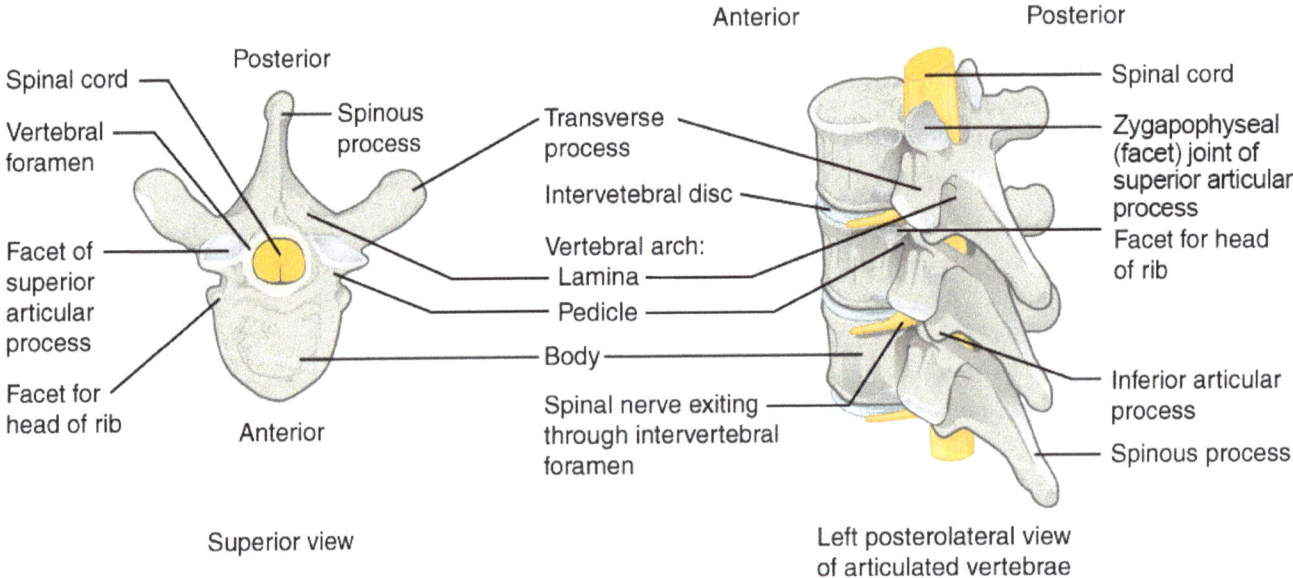

Figure A.24 *A typical vertebra consists of a body and a vertebral arch. The arch is formed by the paired pedicles and paired laminae. Arising from the vertebral arch are the transverse, spinous, superior articular, and inferior articular processes. The vertebral foramen provides for passage of the spinal cord. Each spinal nerve exits through an intervertebral foramen, located between adjacent vertebrae.*

Regional Differences in Vertebral Shape

In the **cervical region** of the vertebral column, there are seven vertebrae (named C1–C7 from superior to inferior; Figure A.25). The first two cervical vertebrae are unique from each other and all other cervical vertebrae, and they get special names: atlas (C1) and axis (C2). The atlas lacks a vertebral body (having only two large articular facets for articulation with the occipital bone of the skull: the **atlanto-occipital joint** for nodding the head) and does not have a spinous process. The axis is notable for the superiorly projecting **dens** (or **odontoid process**), which articulates with the atlas to create the **atlanto-axial joint** for head rotation. Otherwise, a **typical cervical vertebra** has a small vertebral body, a bifid (split) spinous process, a transverse process with a transverse foramen on it for passage of the vertebral artery and vein, and a triangular-shaped vertebral foramen.

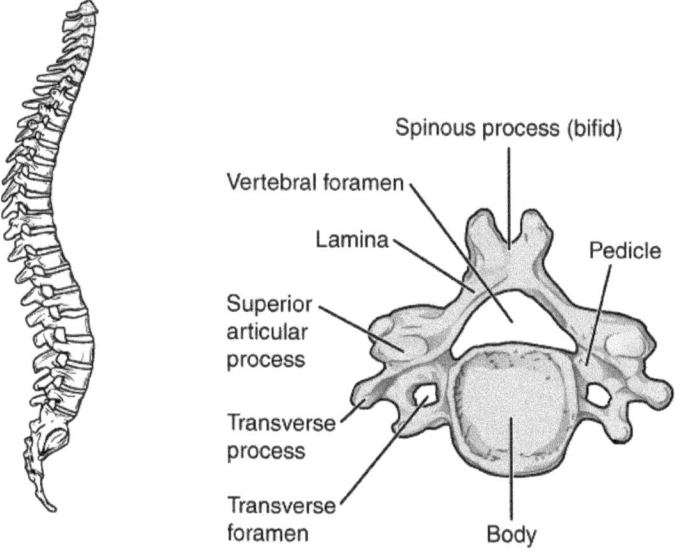

Structure of a typical cervical vertebra

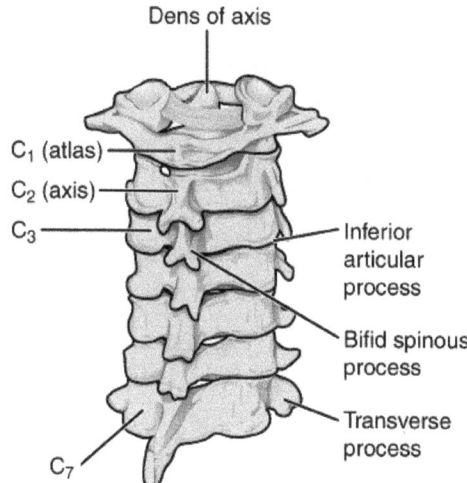

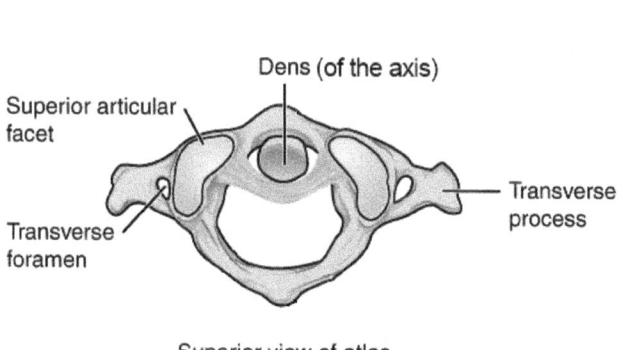

Superior view of atlas

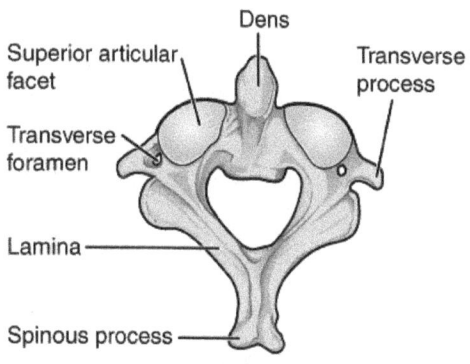

Superior view of axis

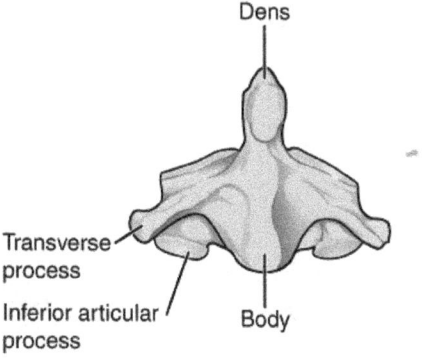

Anterior view of axis

Figure A.25 A typical cervical vertebra has a small body, a bifid spinous process, transverse processes that have a transverse foramen, and a triangular vertebral foramen. The atlas (C1 vertebra) does not have a body or spinous process. The axis (C2 vertebra) has the upward projecting dens, which articulates with the atlas.

Osteology | 645

The vertebrae in the other regions of the spinal column are less variable in shape than the cervical region vertebrae. There are 12 **thoracic region** vertebrae (T1–T12), and they can be easily distinguished from the vertebrae in other regions because they have **articular facets on their vertebral bodies** for articulation with the head of a rib, as well as **articular facets on the transverse process** for articulation with the rib tubercle (Figure A.26). In particular, the vertebral bodies of T2–T9 have two pairs of articular facets called **demifacets** (superior and inferior), for articulation with multiple ribs; T1 and T10–T12 have single facets for articulation with a single rib. All five **lumbar region** vertebrae (L1–L5) are distinguished by their large vertebral body and rounded spinous process (Figure A.27). Finally, there is the **sacrum**, which is a bone of the pelvis that forms from the fusion of all five **sacral region** vertebrae (S1–S5), and there is the **coccyx**, which comprises three to four fused **coccygeal region** vertebrae that form the tailbone (Figure A.28). All great apes (including humans) lack an external tail; the coccygeal vertebrae are homologs of the external tail vertebrae in other primates and mammals (Organ 2017). Homologs are anatomical features that have the same evolutionary origin but do not necessarily have identical structure or function (i.e., the wings of bats and the arms of humans are homologous).

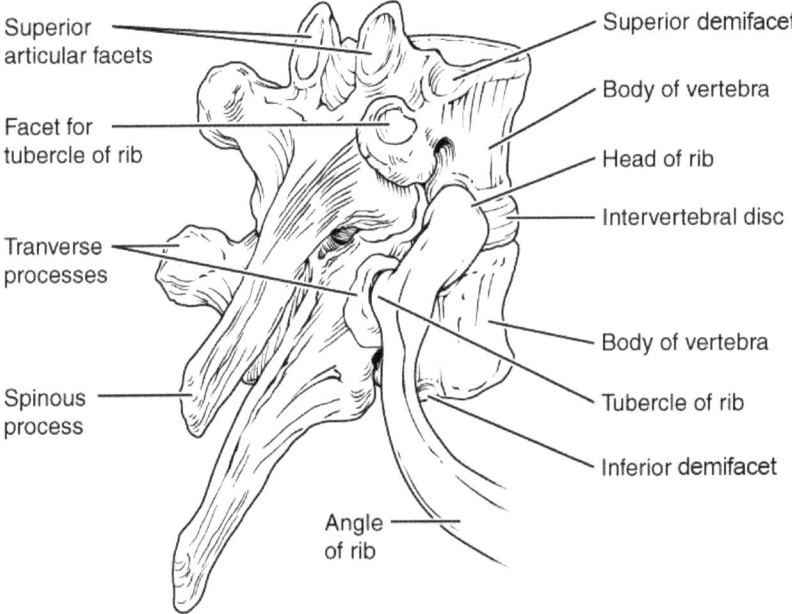

Figure A.26 Thoracic vertebrae have superior and inferior articular facets on the vertebral body for articulation with the head of a rib, and a transverse process facet for articulation with the rib tubercle.

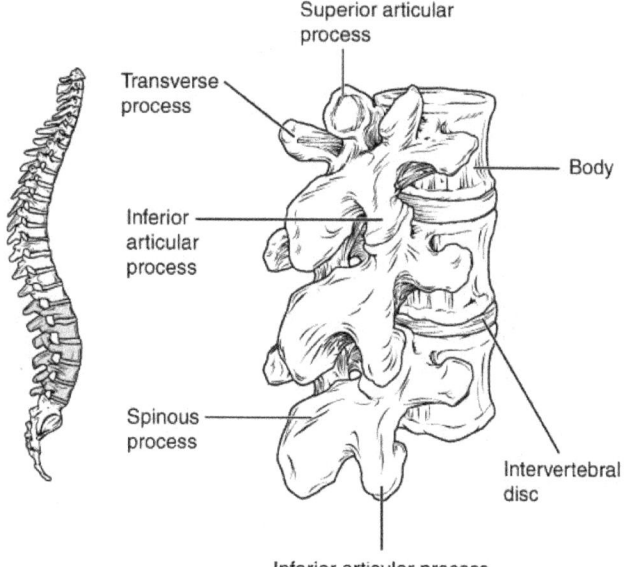

Figure A.27 Lumbar vertebrae are characterized by having a large, thick body and a short, rounded spinous process.

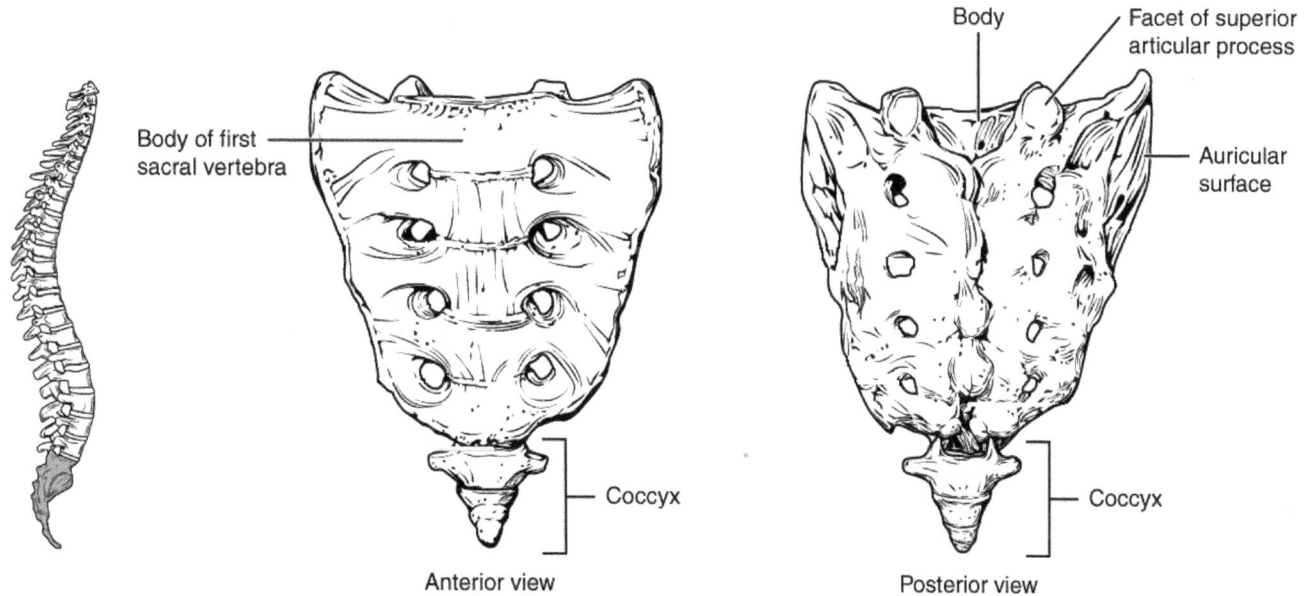

Figure A.28 The sacrum is formed from the fusion of five sacral vertebrae, whose lines of fusion are indicated by the transverse ridges. The coccyx is formed by the fusion of three to four coccygeal vertebrae.

Curvatures of the Vertebral Column

The adult spine is curved in the midsagittal plane in four regions of the vertebral column (cervical, thoracic, lumbar, and sacral; Figure A.29). During the fetal period of development, the vertebral column develops an anteriorly concave curvature called a **kyphosis**. But during the postnatal period, when an infant learns to hold its head up and then again when it learns to walk, it develops secondary curvatures called **lordoses** (singular: lordosis) that are posteriorly concave in the cervical and lumbar vertebral regions, while the kyphoses remain in the thoracic and sacral regions. The end result is an S-shaped curvature to our spine that enables us to keep our head and torso above our center of mass (near our pelvis) while walking around on two legs.

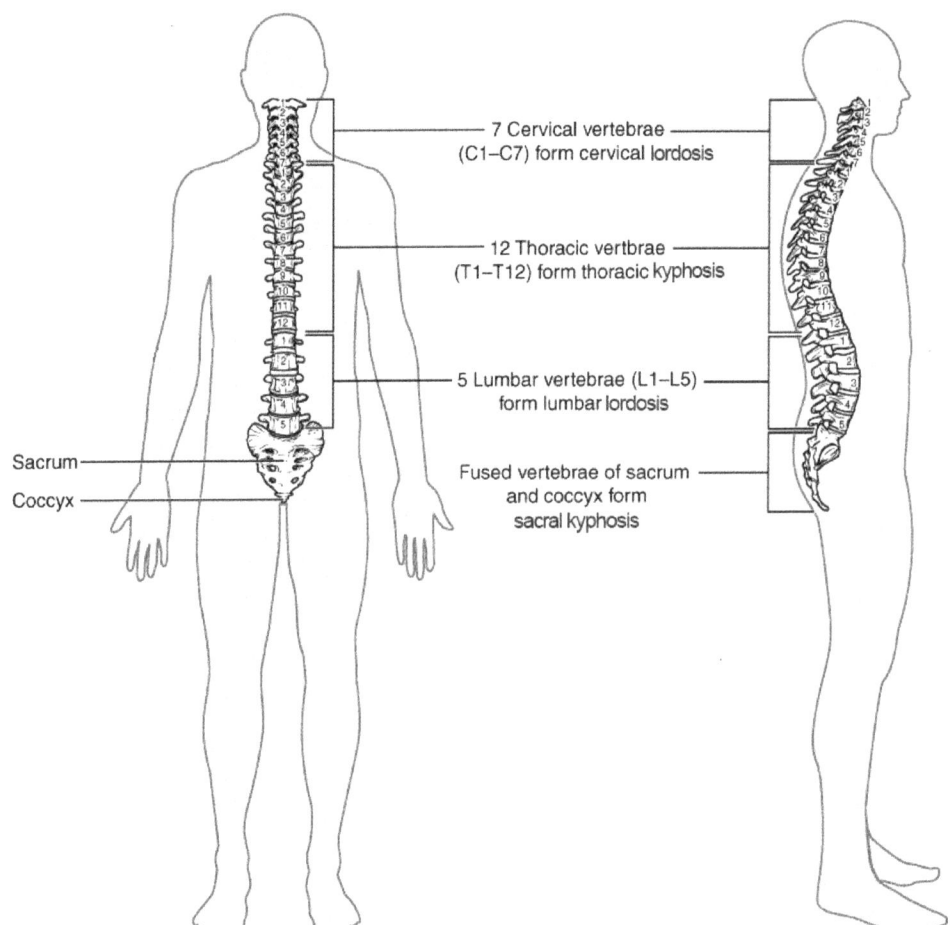

Figure A.29 *The adult vertebral column is curved in the midsagittal plane, with two primary curvatures (thoracic and sacral kyphoses) and two secondary curvatures (cervical and lumbar lordoses).*

Thoracic Cage

The thoracic cage is formed from the sternum and the 12 ribs and their cartilages (costal cartilages), and the 12 thoracic vertebrae with which the ribs articulate (Figure A.30). The **sternum** comprises the **manubrium** (superior portion), the **body of the sternum**, and the **xiphoid process**. Each rib has a head and neck (with rib tubercle) at the vertebral end of the rib as well as a flattened shaft that extends to articulate with the sternum. All ribs articulate with the vertebral column at two points: the transverse process facet (**rib tubercle**) and vertebral body articular facet (**head of rib**). But articulations between the ribs and the sternum vary, where some ribs (1–7, the "true ribs") attach directly to the sternum via their costal cartilages, other ribs (8–10, the "false ribs") attach indirectly to the sternum via the costal cartilage of the rib above, and some ribs (11–12, the "floating ribs") do not attach to the sternum at all. With increasing age, the **sternal end** of the rib becomes thinner and irregularly shaped compared to the smooth, rounded shape seen in young adults.

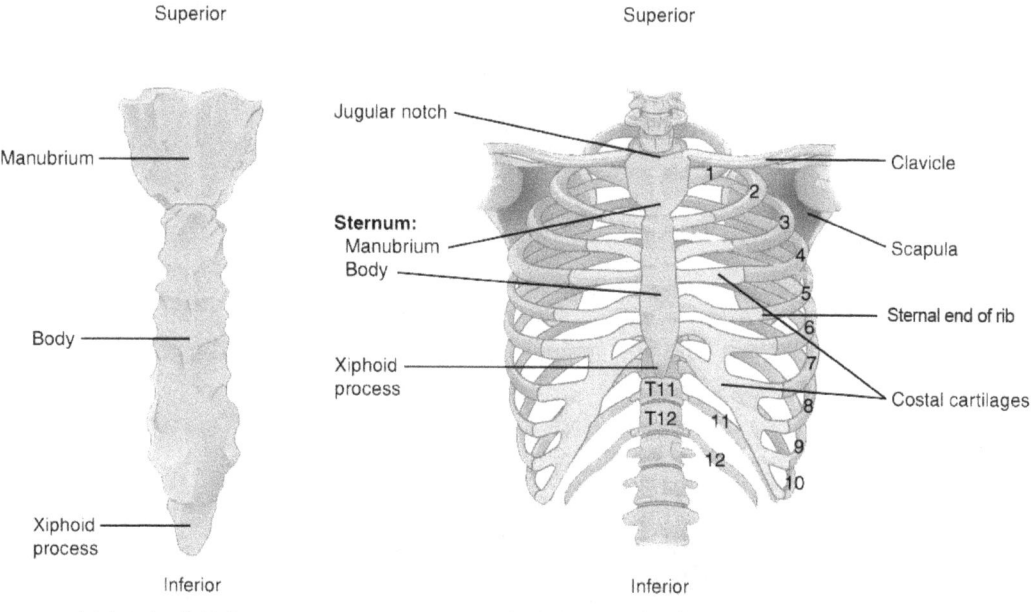

Figure A.30 *The thoracic cage is formed by the (a) sternum and (b) 12 pairs of ribs with their costal cartilages. The ribs are anchored posteriorly to the 12 thoracic vertebrae. The sternum consists of the manubrium, body, and xiphoid process. The ribs are classified as true ribs (1–7) and false ribs (8–12). The last two pairs of false ribs are also known as floating ribs (11–12).*

Appendicular Skeleton

Pectoral Girdle

The pectoral girdle consists of the **clavicle** and the **scapula**, and it serves as the proximal base of the upper limb as well as the anchor for the upper limb to the axial skeleton. The clavicle is an S-shaped bone, and it forms the strut that connects the scapula to the sternum (Figure A.31). The scapula is a large, flat bone with **three angles** (superior, inferior, and lateral) and **three borders** (medial, lateral, and superior). The lateral angle is noteworthy because it serves as the articulation for the head of the humerus of the upper limb at the **glenoid cavity** (or **glenoid fossa**; Figure A.32). The borders and the anterior and posterior surfaces of the scapula are sites of muscle attachment. The scapula also has three important projections for muscle and ligament attachments: the **coracoid process** anteriorly and superiorly; the **acromion**, which articulates with the lateral end of the clavicle; and the **spine** on the posterior aspect of the scapula.

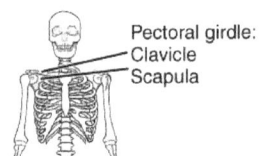

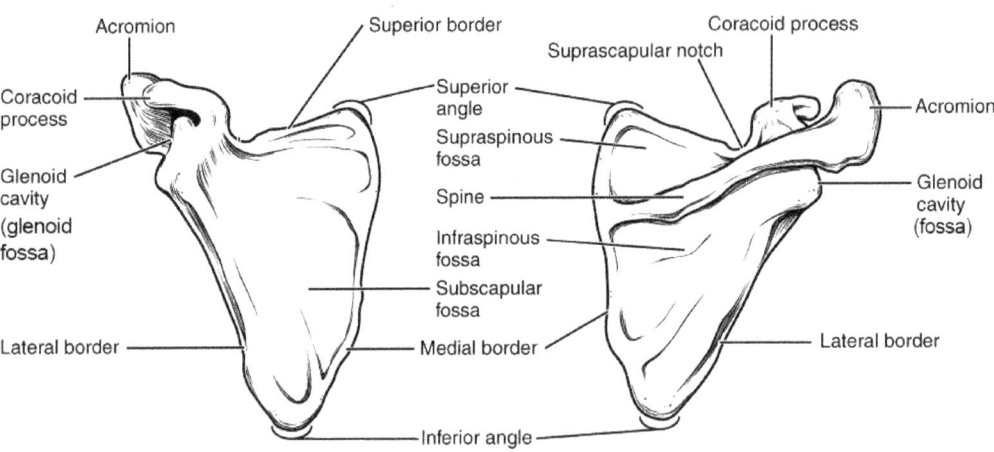

Figure A.32 The scapula is shown from its anterior (deep) side and its posterior (superficial) side.

Upper Limb

The bones of the upper limb skeleton include the humerus, radius, ulna, eight carpal (wrist) bones, five metacarpal (hand) bones, and 14 phalanges (finger bones). Each of these bones is described below along with several of the prominent features.

The **humerus** is the bone of the arm. On the proximal epiphysis of the humerus are attachment sites for muscles of the rotator cuff (**greater tubercle** and **lesser tubercle**). A major shoulder muscle (deltoid muscle) attaches to the humerus along the lateral aspect of the diaphysis at the **deltoid tuberosity**. On the distal epiphysis of the humerus, the **medial epicondyle** is an attachment site for muscles that flex the forearm, and the **lateral epicondyle** is an attachment site for muscles that extend the forearm (Figure A.33).

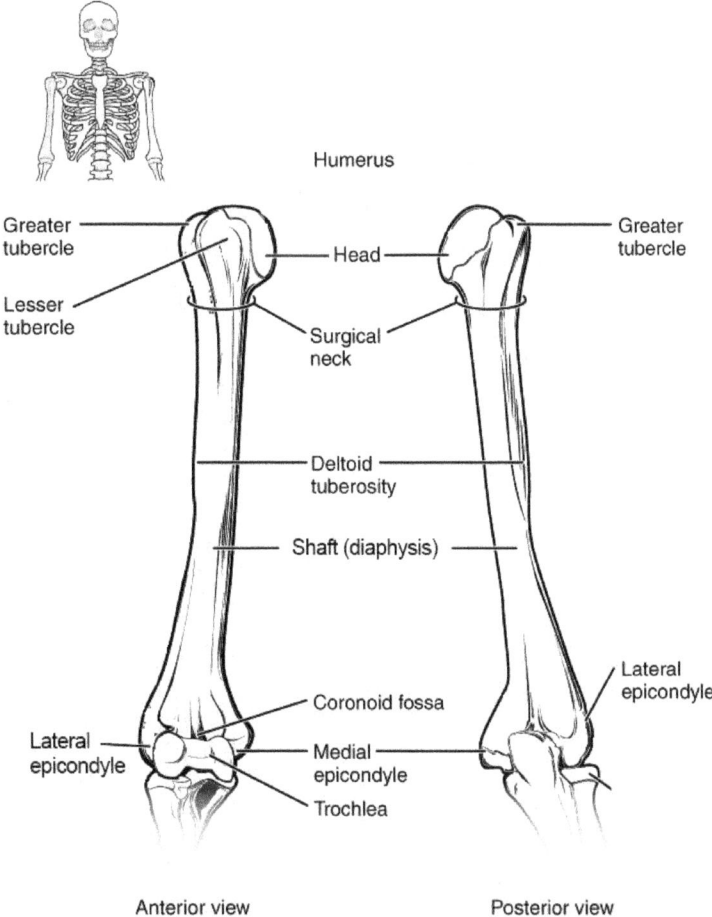

Figure A.33 The humerus is the single bone of the upper arm region. It articulates with the radius and ulna bones of the forearm to form the elbow joint.

There are two bones of the forearm, attached to each other by a thick connective tissue interosseous membrane: the radius and the ulna (Figure A.34). The **radius** is lateral to the ulna in anatomical position (this is called supination of the forearm), but it crosses over the ulna when the wrist is rotated so that the thumb points medially (this is called pronation of the forearm). On the proximal end of the radius is the **radial tuberosity**, an attachment site for the biceps brachii muscle that will help supinate and flex the forearm; on the distal end of the radius is the **styloid process**, an attachment site for ligaments of the wrist. The **ulna** also has a **styloid process**, but unlike the one on the radius it does not have a relevant function. Instead, the important processes on the ulna are located proximally, and they include the **olecranon process** for the attachment of the triceps brachii muscle (a muscle that extends the forearm and arm) and the **coronoid process** for the attachment of the brachialis muscle (a muscle that flexes the forearm).

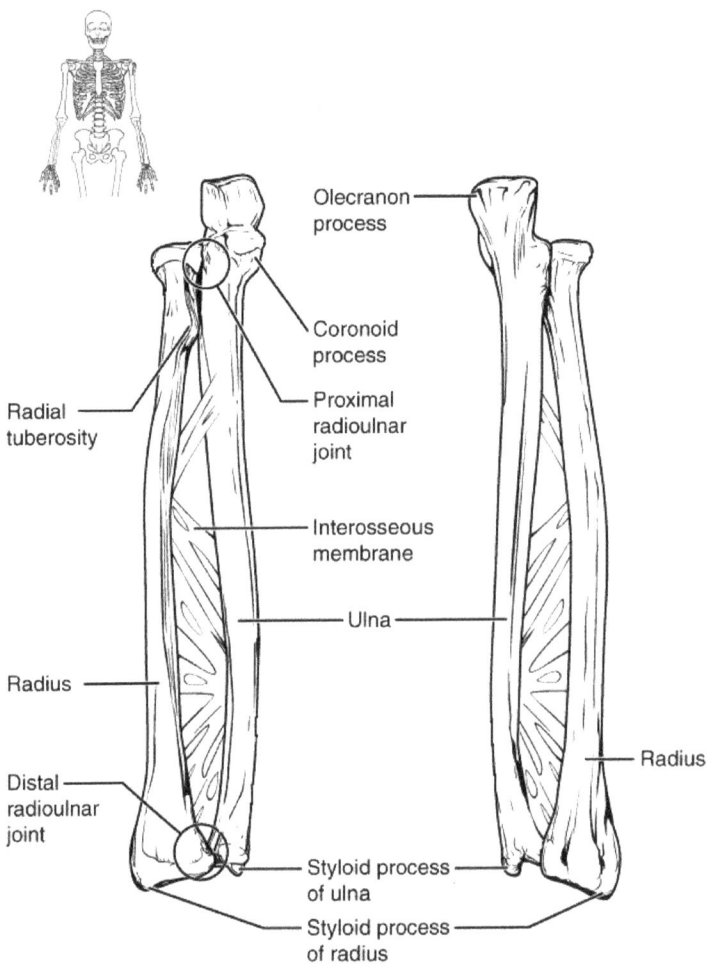

Figure A.34 The ulna is located on the medial side of the forearm, and the radius is on the lateral side. These bones are attached to each other by an interosseous membrane.

There are eight **carpal bones** that comprise the wrist, and they are organized into two rows: proximal and distal (Figure A.35). The proximal row of carpals (from lateral to medial) includes the **scaphoid**, **lunate**, **triquetrum**, and **pisiform**. The distal row (from lateral to medial) includes the **trapezium**, **trapezoid**, **capitate**, and **hamate** with its distinctive hamulus (hook) for muscle and ligament attachments. Distal to the carpal bones are the digital rays, each of which contains a **metacarpal** (hand) bone and three **phalanges** (**proximal**, **middle**, and **distal**) or finger bones. The exception to this rule is the thumb, which has fewer phalanges (proximal and distal, but no middle) than the other digits.

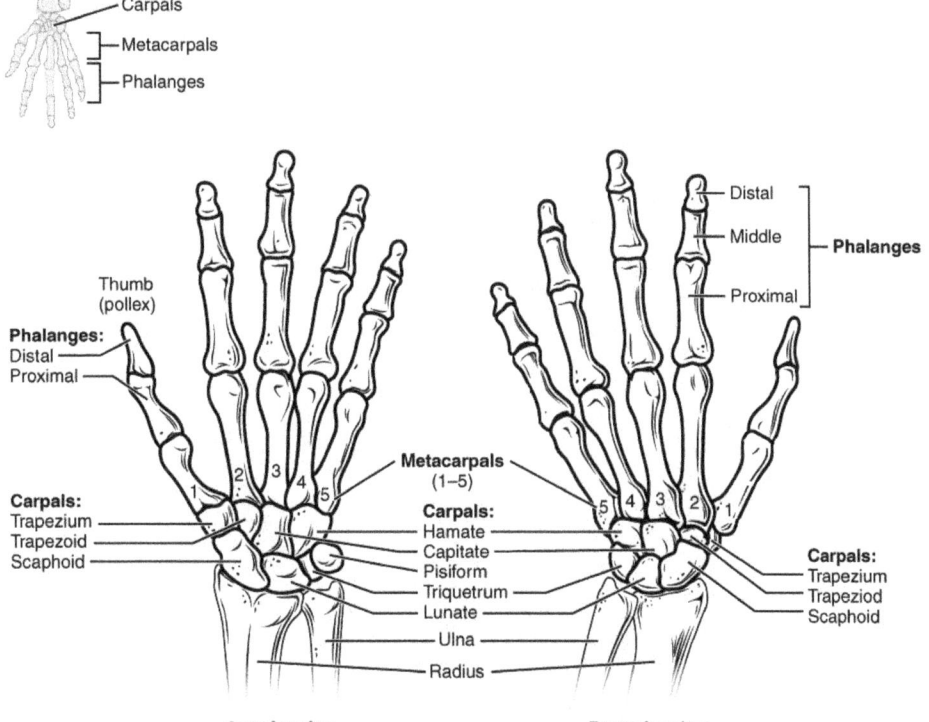

Figure A.35 The eight carpal bones form the base of the hand. These are arranged into proximal and distal rows of four bones each. The five metacarpal bones form the palm of the hand. The thumb and fingers contain a total of 14 phalanges.

Pelvic Girdle

The pelvic girdle consists of the two **os coxae** and the **sacrum** that articulates with both, and it serves as the proximal base and anchor of the lower limb to the axial skeleton. Each os coxa comprises three bones that fuse together during growth: ilium, ischium, and pubis. These three bones fuse in a region called the **acetabulum**, which is the socket for the ball-and-socket hip joint (Figure A.36). The **ilium**, the flared superior portion of the pelvis, is the largest bone of the os coxa and serves as a major site of attachments for muscles from the abdomen, back, and lower limb. The ilium has several important features including the **auricular surface**, the surface where the ilium articulates with the sacrum. The auricular surface is used to estimate age at death as the surface progressively deteriorates with increasing age to appear coarse and porous. The **greater sciatic notch** is a large notch in the ilium that allows for several structures to leave the pelvis and enter the lower extremity, including the sciatic nerve. In females, the notch tends to be symmetrical whereas in males it tends to curve posteriorly (Nawrocki et al. 2018).

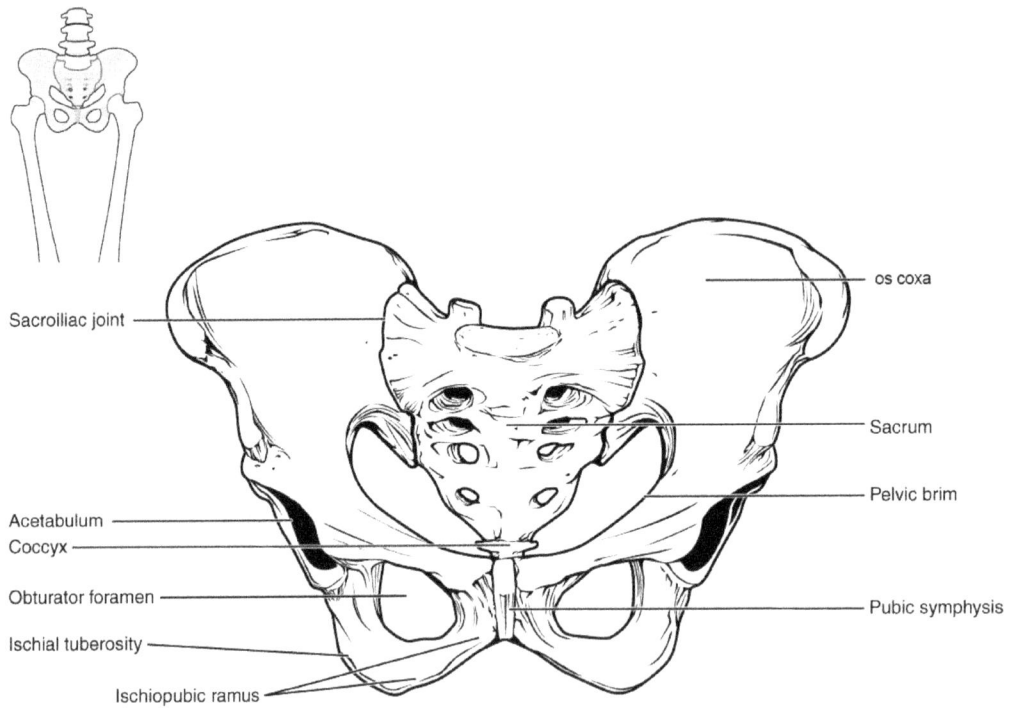

Figure A.36 The pelvic girdle consists of two os coxae and the sacrum. It serves to anchor the axial skeleton to the lower limb.

The **ischium** forms the posterior and inferior portion of the os coxa. There are two significant projections of note on the ischium: the **ischial spine** and tuberosity. The ischial spine is the attachment point for a major pelvic ligament and is located inferior to the greater sciatic notch of the ilium. The **ischial tuberosity** is the proximal attachment site for the hamstring muscles of the lower limb.

The anterior and medial portions of the os coxa are formed by the **pubis**. The pubis is a useful bone with which to sex a skeleton in a forensic context (Bass 2005; Buikstra and Ubelaker 1994). The **body** is the superior and medial portion of the pubis (Figure A.37). The body tends to be rectangular in cross-section in females and triangular in males. The bony projection that unites the ischium and pubis anteriorly is called the **ischiopubic ramus**. Females tend to display a thin and sharp ramus on the medial surface while the surface in males tends to be broad and blunt. The joint that unites the two pubic bones in the front of the pelvis is called the **pubic symphysis**, which is a structure commonly used in age estimation. In young adults, the surface is billowed, but it transitions to being smooth and porous with increasing age. The **subpubic concavity** is a depression inferior to the ischiopubic ramus. Females tend to exhibit a concavity while males tend to be straight. Finally, the large opening encircled by the pubis and ischium is called the **obturator foramen**. The shape of the foramen in females has been described as triangular while it is more likely to appear oval in males (Bass 2005).

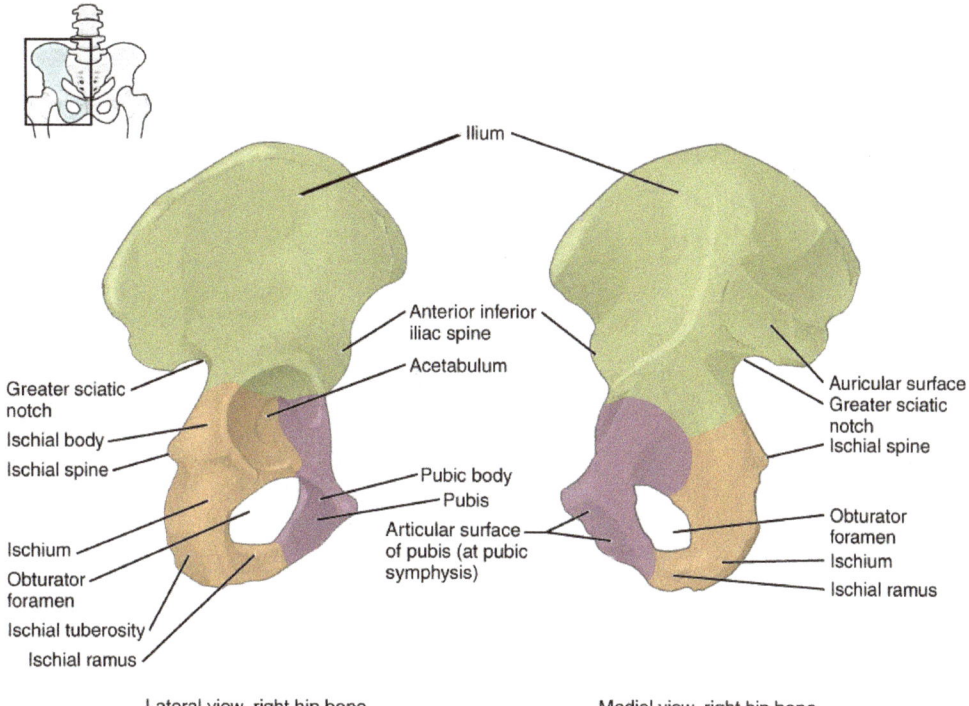

Figure A.37 The os coxae consist of three bones that fuse during development. The ilium forms the large, fan-shaped superior portion, the ischium forms the posteroinferior portion, and the pubis forms the anteromedial portion.

Lower Limb

The bones of the lower limb skeleton include the femur, patella, tibia, fibula, seven tarsal (ankle) bones, five metatarsal (foot) bones, and 14 phalanges (toe bones). Each of these bones is described below along with several of the prominent features.

The femur is the bone of the thigh. On the proximal epiphysis of the femur are attachment sites for major hip and thigh muscles on the **greater trochanter, lesser trochanter,** and **gluteal tuberosity** (Figure A.38). The raised ridge on the posterior aspect of the femoral diaphysis is called the **linea aspera**, and it is a major attachment site for the quadriceps femoris muscles and other muscles, and it terminates distally by splitting into **medial and lateral epicondyles**, additional sites of muscle attachment. The distal epiphysis of the femur is marked by two rounded **condyles** that articulate with the proximal part of the tibia. The anterior surface of the distal femur articulates with the **patella** (kneecap), a bone that develops within the tendon of the quadriceps femoris muscle to enhance the function of the muscle. The patella does not articulate with the tibia.

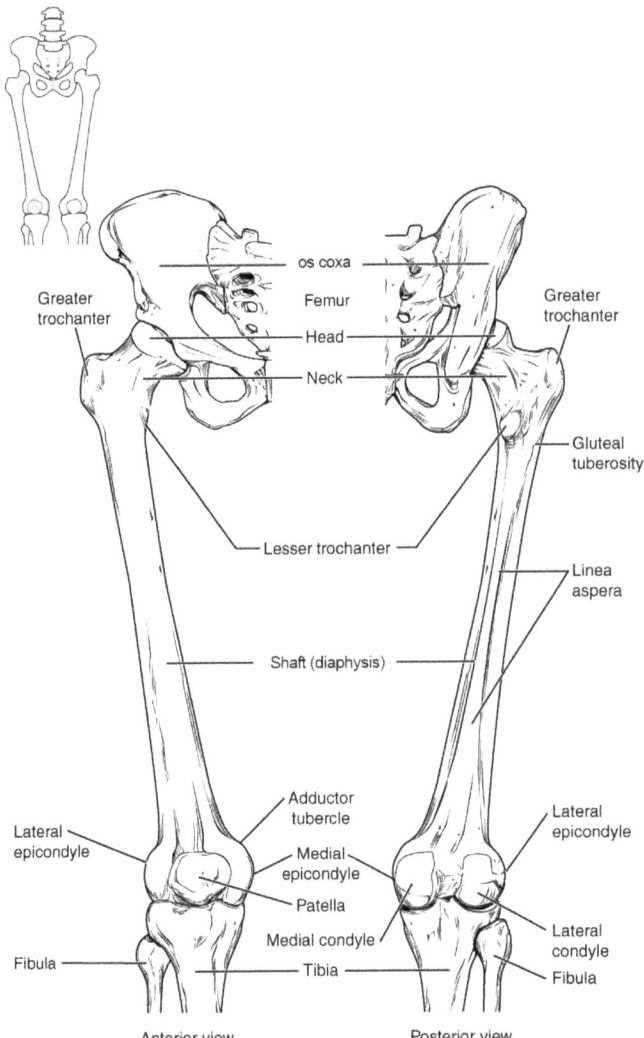

Figure A.38 *The femur is the bone of the thigh that articulates superiorly with the os coxa at the hip joint, and inferiorly with the tibia at the knee joint. The patella only articulates with the distal end of the femur.*

There are two bones of the leg: **tibia** and **fibula**. The tibia is the robust, medial bone of the leg, and it is connected to the laterally positioned fibula by an interosseous membrane like in the forearm (Figure A.39). The proximal epiphysis of the tibia has two articular facets called **tibial condyles** that articulate with the femoral condyles. On the anterior surface of the proximal tibia is a raised projection called the **tibial tuberosity**, where the quadriceps muscle tendon attaches distally after containing the patella. On the distal epiphysis of the tibia is the **medial malleolus**, which articulates with the talus in the ankle joint. The **lateral malleolus** is a feature of the distal end of the fibula; the proximal end of the **fibula** articulates with the lateral portion of the proximal tibia.

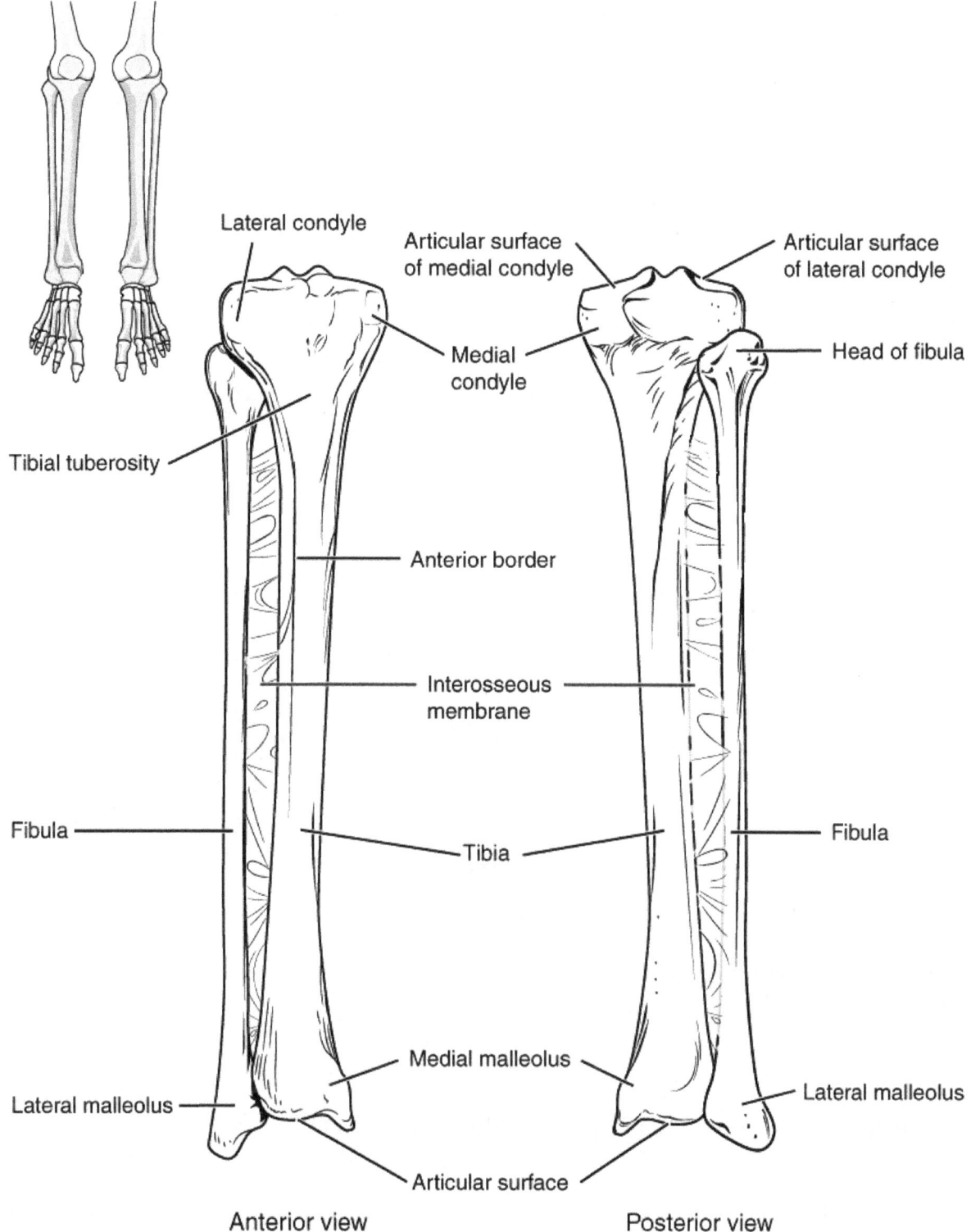

Figure A.39 The tibia is the larger, weight-bearing bone located on the medial side of the leg. It is connected to the laterally-positioned fibula by an interosseous membrane.

There are seven **tarsal bones** that comprise the ankle (Figure A.40). The **talus** is the most superior of the tarsals, and it articulates with the distal tibia and distal fibula superiorly and with the calcaneus inferiorly. The **calcaneus** is the heel of the foot; it is the largest of the tarsals. On the posterior-most aspect of the calcaneus is the **calcaneal tuberosity**, which is the attachment site for the Achilles tendon of the posterior leg. Distal to the talus is the medially positioned navicular, the three **cuneiform bones** (**medial**, **intermediate**, and **lateral**), and the laterally positioned **cuboid**. Distal to the tarsals are the digital rays, each of which contains a **metatarsal** (foot) bone and three **phalanges** (**proximal**, **middle**, and **distal**) or toe bones. The exception to this rule is the big toe, which has fewer phalanges (proximal and distal, but no middle) than the other digits.

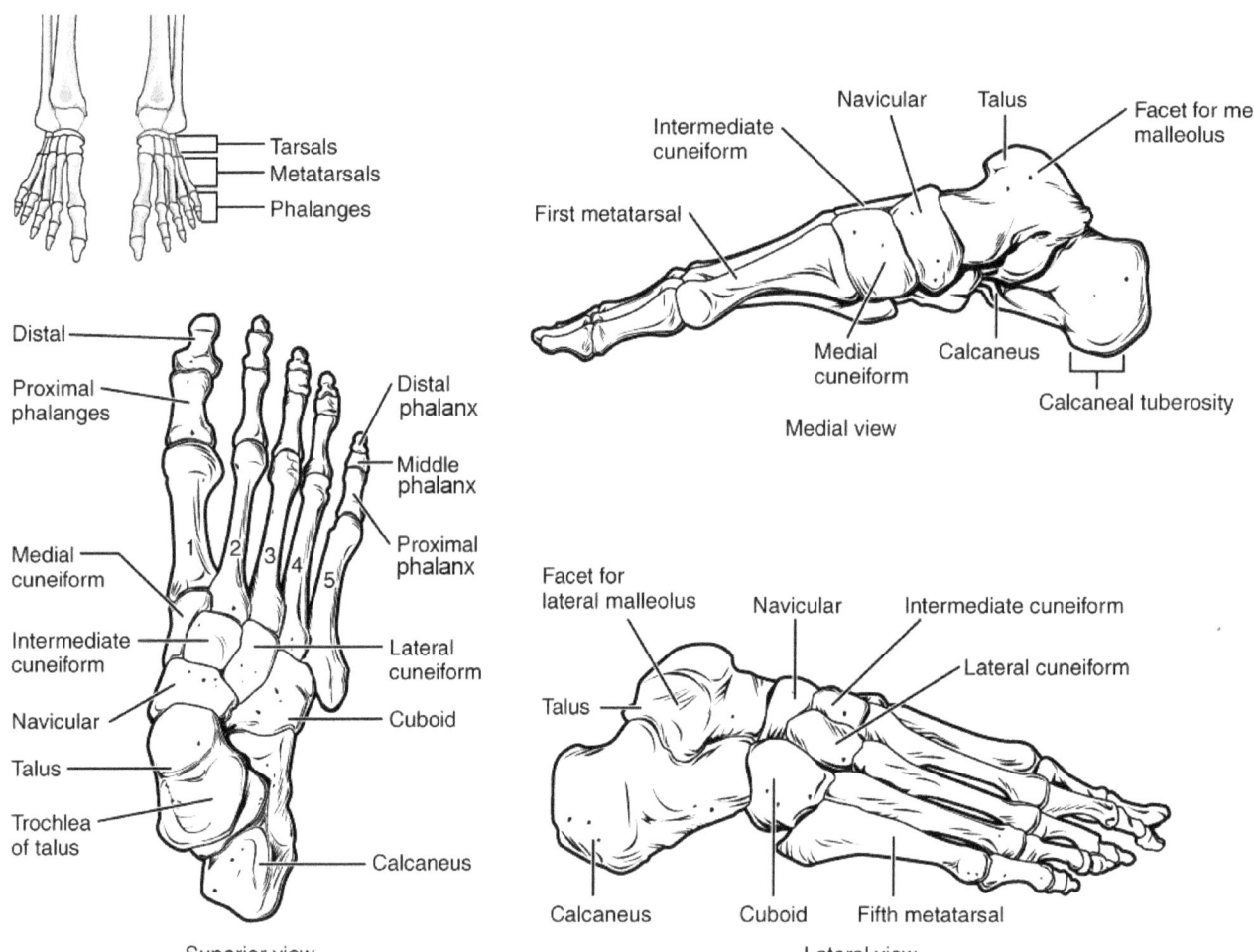

Figure A.40 The bones of the foot are divided into three groups. The posterior foot is formed by the seven tarsal bones. The mid-foot has the five metatarsal bones. The toes contain 14 phalanges.

STATURE ESTIMATION FROM ADULT SKELETONS

In forensic contexts, it makes sense that scientists would want to estimate the height of the individual whose remains were recovered. It also is reasonable that bioarchaeologists would want to estimate stature (height), because body size is one of the most important variables in assessing physiological processes like heart rate and metabolic rate. Stature estimation equations have been developed in bioarchaeological and forensic contexts that rely on measuring length of bones like the cranium, vertebrae, long bones of the limbs, and so forth. These measurements are then input into these equations and stature can be estimated from the resulting solution (Auerbach and Ruff 2010; Lundy 1988).

DIFFERENCES BETWEEN ADULT AND SUBADULT SKELETONS

The adult skeleton consists of 206 bones. Each of these bones develops from a number of centers of ossification. It is estimated, then, that a baby is born with approximately 450 bones that grow from their centers of ossification and eventually become the 206 bones of the adult skeleton. For example, a typical long bone (e.g., tibia) has three centers of ossification: one primary center, the diaphysis; and two secondary centers, the epiphyses. In between epiphysis and diaphysis is an epiphyseal growth plate of cartilage that will remain unfused until postnatal growth is complete after puberty (and for some bones, well into adulthood). There is a relatively well documented order in which bones of the subadult postcranial skeleton reach full fusion, which is used as the basis for age estimation in forensic contexts (Bass 2005; White and Folkens 2000).

Similarly, the sutures between cranial bones in children are unfused, which allows skull growth to coincide with brain growth and provides a basis for age estimation based on suture fusion. The skulls of babies are marked by several **fontanelles** (soft spots), which are areas of the skull filled with membrane that has not been replaced with bone through intramembranous ossification.

Finally, the age of the subadult skeleton can be estimated based on teeth. All mammals develop two sets of teeth: deciduous (baby) teeth and permanent (adult) teeth; humans are no exception. Permanent human teeth were described immediately above. It is worth spending a few words to describe deciduous human teeth. At birth, humans usually display no teeth, but by about six months of age, the deciduous lower central incisors usually appear (see Bass 2005). When the complete sequence of deciduous teeth has erupted, there are five teeth in each quadrant: two incisors, one canine, and two molars. Deciduous incisors and canines are eventually replaced by their adult counterparts; deciduous molars are replaced by adult premolars, and there is no deciduous precursor to adult molars. The eruption patterns of deciduous and adult teeth is well documented and is used as in forensic contexts to estimate age (Bass 2005).

COMPARATIVE SKELETAL ANATOMY

Over the last six to seven million years, humans have been evolving to become more efficient at walking around on two limbs (bipedal locomotion), resulting in skeletal anatomy that is divergent from our closest living relative, the chimpanzee (Pan troglodytes). These differences can be seen in both the axial and appendicular skeletons. In the axial skeleton, for example, the foramen magnum in humans is more anteriorly positioned than that of chimpanzees, which places the vertebral column directly underneath the skull as opposed to behind it as it is in chimpanzees and other quadrupedal mammals. Chimpanzees also do not have an S-shaped curvature to their vertebral column; they simply retain the gentle primary kyphosis developed during the fetal period. Furthermore, they actually have one fewer lumbar vertebrae compared to humans, which results in a stiffer lower back.

As far as differences in the appendicular skeleton are concerned, the shape of the pelvic girdle is dramatically different in humans, where the ilium flares out laterally compared to the posterior flare of the ilium in chimpanzees. This reorganization of the pelvis has changed the function of two muscles, gluteus medius and gluteus minimus, from hip extensors in chimpanzees to hip abductors in humans. The angle of the femoral diaphysis is more oblique in humans because one of the demands of efficient bipedal locomotion is that humans require their knees to remain under their center of mass when they are standing on one limb during walking; in chimpanzees, the knees are not moved under their center of mass, so the femoral diaphysis is nearly vertical in orientation from the hip to the knee joint. In addition, humans have oversized hip and knee joints for their body size compared to chimpanzees, likely because they require more surface area to keep from damaging joint surfaces when they support their entire body mass on a single limb during walking. Chimpanzees spend more time engaging in climbing behavior than humans do, and they are known to have glenoid fossae and scapulae that are oriented more superiorly than humans, which allows them to support their body weight better on their upper limbs than humans can. Finally, the phalanges of the hand and foot are less anteroposteriorly curved in humans than they are in chimpanzees, and instead of having an opposable big toe like chimpanzees, humans have a big toe that is in line with the other digits and more efficient for bipedal locomotion.

Review Questions

- Which bony features of the pelvic girdle are relevant to estimating age and/or sex in forensic and bioarchaeological contexts? Give specific examples of how these features differ among sexes.
- What is the mechanistic difference between endochondral and intramembranous bone formation?
- Which bones articulate with the calcaneus? Which bones articulate with the humerus?
- Which elements of the skeleton belong to the axial skeleton versus the appendicular skeleton?
- Describe the axial and appendicular skeletal differences between humans and chimpanzees.

About the Authors

Jason M. Organ, Ph.D.

Indiana University School of Medicine

Jason M. Organ

Jason M. Organ, Ph.D., is an assistant professor of Anatomy, cell biology, & physiology at the Indiana University School of Medicine and Co-editor and Writer for the Public Library of Science (PLOS) Science Communication Blog, where he advocates for the importance of storytelling and empathy in science communication. Dr. Organ earned his M.A. in anthropology from the University of Missouri and his Ph.D. in functional anatomy & evolution from Johns Hopkins University School of Medicine. He has published over 30 peer-reviewed research papers on evolutionary and mechanical adaptations of bone and muscle in scientific journals and over 40 peer-reviewed teaching modules in digital human anatomy references. Dr. Organ recently completed a three-year term as an elected member of the Board of Directors of the American Association for Anatomy (AAA), where he advocated for the importance of effective science communication and public outreach at the association level, with an emphasis on connecting with policy makers to ensure sufficient federal funding for science. In 2018, Jason received the prestigious AAA Basmajian Award for excellence in teaching gross anatomy and outstanding accomplishments in biomedical research and scholarship in education. Follow Dr. Organ on Twitter: @OrganJM

Jessica N. Byram, Ph.D.

Indiana University School of Medicine

Jessica N. Byram, Ph.D., is an assistant professor of Anatomy, cell biology, & physiology at the Indiana University School of Medicine (IUSM). Jessica earned her M.S. in human biology with a focus in forensic anthropology from the University of Indianapolis and her Ph.D. in anatomy education at IUSM. Jessica is the director of the anatomy education track Ph.D. program at IUSM. Her research interests include medical professionalism, investigating professional identity formation in medical students and residents, and exploring how to improve the learning environments at medical institutions.

Jessica N. Byram

References

Auerbach, Benjamin M., and Christopher B. Ruff. 2010. "Stature Estimation Formulae for Indigenous North American Populations." American Journal of Physical Anthropology 141 (2): 190–207.

Bass, William. 2005. Human Osteology: A Laboratory and Field Method. Springfield, IL: Charles C. Thomas.

Buikstra, Jane E., and Douglas H. Ubelaker. 1994. Standards for Data Collection From Human Skeletal Remains. Arkansas Archaeological Survey Research Series, 44. Fayetteville, AR: Arkansas Archeological Survey.

Burr, David B., and Jason M. Organ. 2017. "Postcranial Skeletal Development and Its Evolutionary Implications." In Building Bones: Bone Formation and Development in Anthropology, edited by Christopher J. Percival and Joan T. Richtsmeier, 148–174. Cambridge, UK: Cambridge University Press.

Federative Committee on Anatomical Terminology (FCAT). 1998. Terminologia Anatomica: International Anatomical Terminology. Stuttgart, Germany: Georg Thieme Verlag.

Lundy, J. K. 1988. "A Report on the Use of Fully's Anatomical Method to Estimate Stature in Military Skeletal Remains." Journal of Forensic Sciences 33 (2): 534–539.

Nawrocki, Stephen P., Krista E. Latham, Thomas Gore, Rachel M. Hoffman, Jessica N. Byram, and Justin Maiers. 2018. "Using Elliptical Fourier Analysis to Interpret Complex Morphological Features in Global Populations." In New Perspectives in Forensic Human Skeletal Identification, edited by Krista E. Latham, Eric J. Bartelink, and Michael Finnegan, 301–312. London: Elsevier/Academic Press.

Organ, Jason M. 2017. "Vertebral Column." Amirsys Anatomy Reference Center. Salt Lake City: Elsevier. https://app.anatomyreferencecenter.com/

White, Tim D., and Pieter A. Folkens. 2000. Human Osteology, 2nd Edition. New York: Academic Press.

———. 2005. The Human Bone Manual. London: Elsevier.

Figure Attributions

Figure A.1 Regions of the Human Body (Anatomy & Physiology, Figure 1.12) by OpenStax has been modified (labels removed) and is used under a CC BY 4.0 License.

Figure A.2 Planes of the Body (Anatomy & Physiology, Figure 1.14) by OpenStax has been modified (some labels modified) and is used under a CC BY 4.0 License.

Figure A.3 Directional Terms Applied to the Human Body (Anatomy & Physiology, Figure 1.13) by OpenStax is used under a CC BY 4.0 License.

Figure A.4 Anatomy of a Long Bone (Anatomy & Physiology, Figure 6.7) by OpenStax has been modified (some labels modified or removed) and is used under a CC BY 4.0 License.

Figure A.5 Bone Cells (Anatomy & Physiology, Figure 6.11) by OpenStax is used under a CC BY 4.0 License.

Figure A.6 Classifications of Bones (Anatomy & Physiology, Figure 6.6) by OpenStax is used under a CC BY 4.0 License.

Figure A.7 Intramembranous Ossification (Anatomy & Physiology, Figure 6.16) by OpenStax has been modified (some labels modified or removed) and is used under a CC BY 4.0 License.

Figure A.8 Endochondral Ossification (Anatomy & Physiology, Figure 6.17) by OpenStax has been modified (some labels modified or removed) and is used under a CC BY 4.0 License.

Figure A.9 Pathways in Calcium Homeostasis (Anatomy & Physiology, Figure 6.24) by OpenStax is used under a CC BY 4.0 License.

Figure A.10 Axial and Appendicular Skeleton (Anatomy & Physiology, Figure 7.2) by OpenStax is used under a CC BY 4.0 License.

Figure A.11 Parts of the Skull (Anatomy & Physiology, Figure 7.3) by OpenStax has been modified (some labels modified or removed) and is used under a CC BY 4.0 License.

Figure A.12 Anterior View of Skull (Anatomy & Physiology, Figure 7.4) by OpenStax has been modified (some labels removed) and is used under a CC BY 4.0 License.

Figure A.13 Lateral View of Skull (Anatomy & Physiology, Figure 7.5) by OpenStax has been modified (some labels removed) and is used under a CC BY 4.0 License.

Figure A.14 Temporal Bone (Anatomy & Physiology, Figure 7.7) by OpenStax has been modified (some labels removed) and is used under a CC BY 4.0 License.

Figure A.15 External and Internal Views of Base of Skull (Anatomy & Physiology, Figure 7.8) by OpenStax has been modified (some labels modified or removed) and is used under a CC BY 4.0 License.

Figure A.16 Sphenoid Bone (Anatomy & Physiology, Figure 7.10) by OpenStax has been modified (some labels removed) and is used under a CC BY 4.0 License.

Figure A.17 Ethmoid Bone (Anatomy & Physiology, Figure 7.12) by OpenStax has been modified (some labels removed) and is used under a CC BY 4.0 License.

Figure A.18 Maxillary Bone (Anatomy & Physiology, Figure 7.14) by OpenStax has been modified (some labels modified or removed) and is used under a CC BY 4.0 License.

Figure A.19 Bones of the Orbit (Anatomy & Physiology, Figure 7.16) by OpenStax has been modified (some labels removed) and is used under a CC BY 4.0 License.

Figure A.20 Nasal Septum (Anatomy & Physiology, Figure 7.17) by OpenStax has been modified (some labels modified or removed) and is used under a CC BY 4.0 License.

Figure A.21 Lateral Wall of Nasal Cavity (Anatomy & Physiology, Figure 7.13) by OpenStax has been modified (some labels removed) and is used under a CC BY 4.0 License.

Figure A.22 Hyoid Bone (Anatomy & Physiology, Figure 7.19) by OpenStax has been modified (some labels removed) and is used under a CC BY 4.0 License.

Figure A.23 Isolated Mandible (Anatomy & Physiology, Figure 7.15) by OpenStax has been modified (some labels modified or removed) and is used under a CC BY 4.0 License.

Figure A.24 Parts of a Typical Vertebra (Anatomy & Physiology, Figure 7.23) by OpenStax has been modified (some labels removed) and is used under a CC BY 4.0 License.

Figure A.25 Cervical Vertebra (Anatomy & Physiology, Figure 7.25) by OpenStax has been modified (some labels removed) and is used under a CC BY 4.0 License.

Figure A.26 Rib Articulation in Thoracic Vertebrae (Anatomy & Physiology, Figure 7.27) by OpenStax has been modified (some labels removed) and is used under a CC BY 4.0 License.

Figure A.27 Lumbar Vertebrae (Anatomy & Physiology, Figure 7.28) by OpenStax is used under a CC BY 4.0 License.

Figure A.28 Sacrum and Coccyx (Anatomy & Physiology, Figure 7.29) by OpenStax has been modified (some labels removed) and is used under a CC BY 4.0 License.

Figure A.29 Vertebral Column (Anatomy & Physiology, Figure 7.20) by OpenStax has been modified (some labels modified or removed) and is used under a CC BY 4.0 License.

Figure A.30 Thoracic Cage (Anatomy & Physiology, Figure 7.32) by OpenStax has been modified (some labels modified or removed) and is used under a CC BY 4.0 License.

Figure A.31 Pectoral Girdle (Anatomy & Physiology, Figure 8.3) by OpenStax has been modified (some labels modified or removed) and is used under a CC BY 4.0 License.

Figure A.32 Scapula (Anatomy & Physiology, Figure 8.4) by OpenStax has been modified (some labels modified or removed) and is used under a CC BY 4.0 License.

Figure A.33 Humerus and Elbow Joint (Anatomy & Physiology, Figure 8.5) by OpenStax has been modified (some labels modified or removed) and is used under a CC BY 4.0 License.

Figure A.34 Ulna and Radius (Anatomy & Physiology, Figure 8.6) by OpenStax has been modified (some labels removed) and is used under a CC BY 4.0 License.

Figure A.35 Bones of the Wrist and Hand (Anatomy & Physiology, Figure 8.7) by OpenStax has been modified (some labels removed) and is used under a CC BY 4.0 License.

Figure A.36 Pelvis (Anatomy & Physiology, Figure 8.12) by OpenStax has been modified (some labels modified or removed) and is used under a CC BY 4.0 License.

Figure A.37 The Hip Bone (Anatomy & Physiology, Figure 8.13) by OpenStax has been modified (some labels removed) and is used under a CC BY 4.0 License.

Figure A.38 Femur and Patella (Anatomy & Physiology, Figure 8.16) by OpenStax has been modified (some labels modified or removed) and is used under a CC BY 4.0 License.

Figure A.39 Tibia and Fibula (Anatomy & Physiology, Figure 8.18) by OpenStax has been modified (one label removed) and is used under a CC BY 4.0 License.

Figure A.40 Bones of the Foot (Anatomy & Physiology, Figure 8.19) by OpenStax has been modified (some labels modified or removed) and is used under a CC BY 4.0 License.

Appendix B

Mary P. Dinsmore, M.S., Ph.D. candidate, University of Wisconsin–Madison

Ilianna E. Anise, B.A., Ph.D. student, University of Wisconsin–Madison

Rebekah J. Ellis, B.A., M.S., University of Wisconsin–Madison

Amanda J. Hardie, M.A., Ph.D. candidate, University of Wisconsin–Madison

Jacob B. Kraus, B.A., Ph.D. student, University of Wisconsin–Madison

Karen B. Strier, Ph.D., University of Wisconsin–Madison

> *Learning Objectives*
>
> - Understand the current conservation status of the world's primates and the criteria that researchers and conservationists use to make these assessments.
> - Recognize the many threats that negatively impact primate survival.
> - Understand how these threats uniquely affect primates because of characteristics like slow growth rates, long interbirth intervals, strong social bonds, and cultural behavior.
> - Become aware of the many ways in which primates are significant to ecological processes, our understanding of human evolution, human cultures, and local economies.
> - Learn about ways that people, wherever they may live, can work to protect primates.

We are field primatologists interested in understanding primates in their natural environments and in contributing to their conservation. Our research focuses on a diversity of primate species that occur in a wide range of habitats throughout the tropics; however, these species and their habitats are subject to many similar threats. As human populations continue to grow (Figure B.1), primates are being pushed out of their natural home ranges and are being forced to occupy increasingly smaller and more isolated patches of land. Humans and primates are sharing more spaces with one another, making it easier for primates to be hunted or captured and for diseases to spread from humans to primates (and vice versa). Even when primates are not directly threatened by human activities, human-induced climate change is altering local ecosystems at an alarming rate. Local political instability exacerbates all of these problems. Our research causes us to think about these issues on a daily basis. Understanding how these threats affect the primates we study is a very important part of what we do. Ultimately, the research of field primatologists like us is important for documenting the status of wild primate populations, as well as for understanding how they respond to these threats and for gaining insights into the kinds of efforts that can help to improve their chances of survival in an uncertain future.

This appendix begins with a review of the current status of primates and the criteria used in these assessments. We then describe the major threats to primates, explain why primates are important, and consider what can be done to improve their chances. We conclude with a brief consideration of the future for primates.

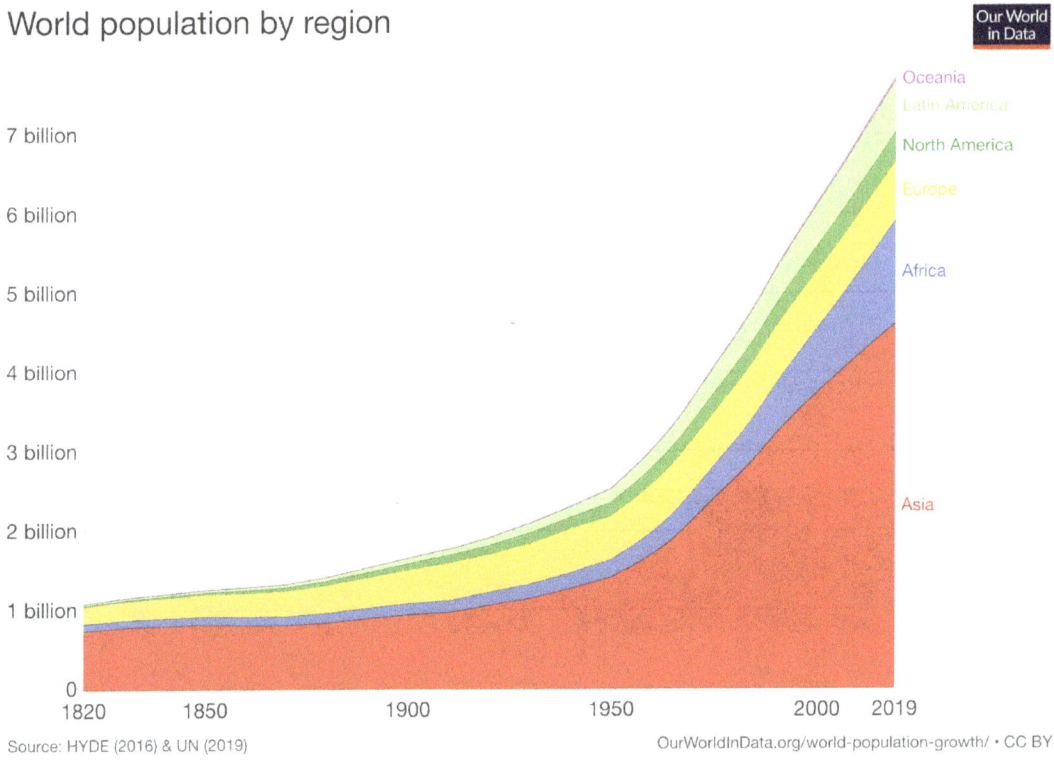

Figure B.1 World population growth by region. Global populations are projected to exceed 11 billion people by 2100 (UN Population Division 2017).

CURRENT CONSERVATION STATUS OF NONHUMAN PRIMATES

Diversity of Primates

The order Primates is one of the most diverse groups of mammals on the planet, with 504 species in 79 different genera currently recognized (Figure B.2; Estrada et al. 2017). Recently new genera, species, and subspecies of nonhuman primates (henceforth, simply "primates") have been recognized, in some cases as a result of new discoveries and new data, but also because of revisions to taxonomic classification systems based on different species concepts (Groves 2014; Lynch Alfaro et al. 2012; Rylands and Mittermeier 2014).

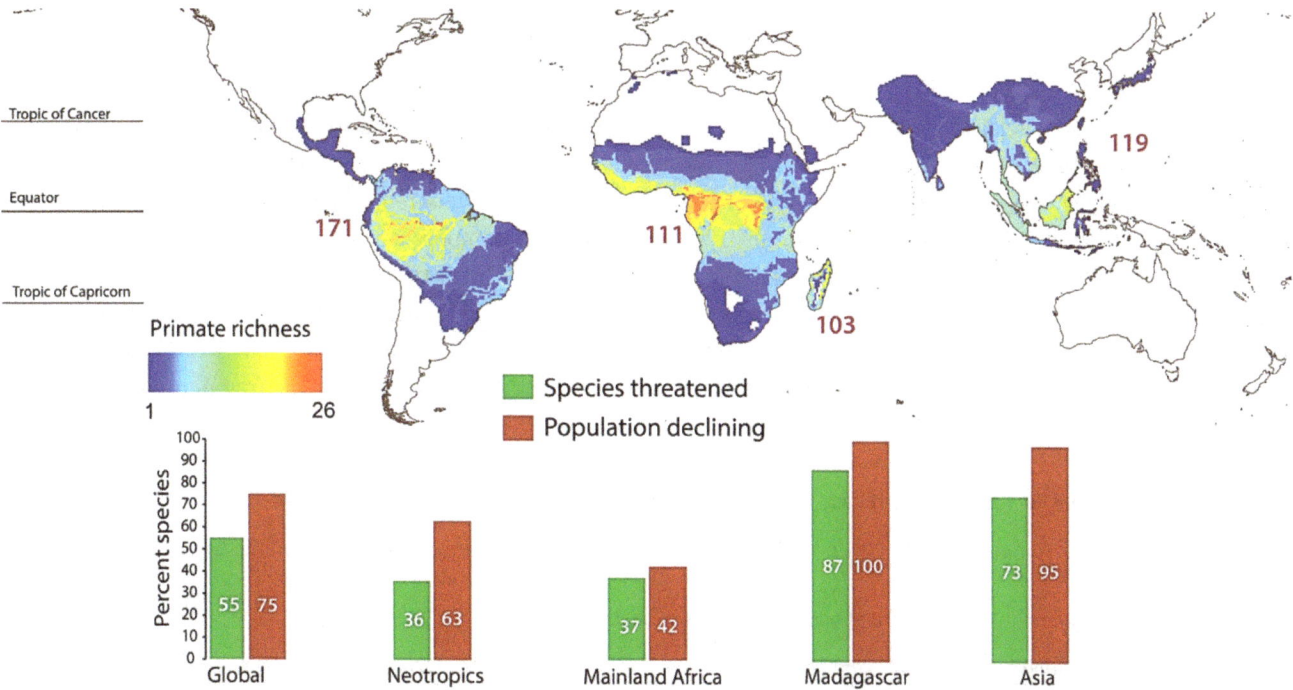

Figure B.2 *The global distribution and species richness of primates and the percentage of those threatened with extinction and declining populations. The numbers next to each geographic area indicate the current species present in that location. The bars below show the percentage of species threatened with extinction (in green) and the percentage of species with declining populations in each region (in red).*

Figure B.3 *Mountain gorilla (Gorilla beringei beringei) in Bwindi Impenetrable National Park, Uganda. Mountain gorillas are classified as endangered and are only found in the Virungas area of Rwanda and the Democratic Republic of Congo and the Bwindi forest of Uganda (Hickey et al. 2018; Kalpers et al. 2003). This species has suffered tremendously due to habitat destruction, poaching, political unrest, and war (Kalpers et al. 2003).*

Wild primates occur in 90 countries around the world, but two-thirds of all species are found in only four countries: Brazil, Madagascar, Democratic Republic of Congo, and Indonesia (Estrada et al. 2017; Estrada et al. 2018). An estimated 60% of primate species are threatened with extinction and 75% are experiencing population declines (Estrada et al. 2017, see Figure B.2). Yet despite these discouraging statistics, there are a growing number of populations recovering as a result of research and conservation efforts. For example, the population of mountain gorillas (Figure B.3) initially studied by Dian Fossey in Rwanda in 1967 has increased from 250 gorillas in 1981 to 339 in 2008 as a result of ongoing research and conservation efforts that include highly controlled ecotourism (Robbins et al. 2011). Similarly, one population of northern muriqui monkeys (Figure B.4) inhabiting a small privately owned forest fragment in southeastern Brazil's Atlantic Forest increased from about 50 individuals to nearly 350 individuals as a result of increased habitat protection over the course of the Muriqui Project of Caratinga, a long-term field study initiated more than 35 years ago by one of the authors of this appendix (Strier and Mendes 2012).

Figure B.4 *A female northern muriqui (Brachyteles hypoxanthus) with infant at the Feliciano Miguel Abdala Private Natural Heritage Reserve outside of Caratinga, Brazil. Muriquis are found exclusively in the Atlantic Forest of southeastern Brazil. The destruction and fragmentation of these forests have caused this species to be listed as Critically Endangered (Strier et al. 2017). Although still threatened, the continued efforts of the Muriqui Project of Caratinga have brought this species back from the brink of extinction.*

International Union for the Conservation of Nature (IUCN)

In conservation, it is crucial to have a global standard to assess and recognize the conservation status of species. The International Union for the Conservation of Nature (IUCN) formed the Red List for Threatened Species in 1994 to determine species extinction risks (IUCN 2017). Scientists submit assessments of species to the IUCN, which are subsequently categorized based on the size and distribution of species' numbers and available habitat. The categories range from "data deficient," when not enough is known, to "least concern," "near threatened," "vulnerable," "endangered," "critically endangered," "extinct in the wild," and "extinct." Threatened species are classified as "vulnerable," "endangered," or "critically endangered," with the most critically endangered species being those whose numbers are fewer than 250 mature individuals and continuing to decline or whose habitats are severely fragmented (Figure B.5; IUCN 2017).

Critically Endangered (CR): Facing an extremely high risk of extinction in the wild due to any of the following:

A. Reduction in population size of 80%–90% over the last ten years or three generations, depending on the causes and reversibility of the reductions;

B. Extent of occurrence <100 km2 or area of occupancy <10 km2 or both;

C. Population size estimated to number fewer than 250 mature individuals and to be declining or unevenly distributed;

D. Population size estimated to number fewer than 50 mature individuals;

E. Probability of extinction within ten years or three generations is at least 50%.

Endangered (EN): Facing a very high risk of extinction in the wild due to any of the following:

A. Reduction in population size of 50%–70% over the last ten years or three generations, depending on the causes and reversibility of the reductions;

B. Extent of occurrence <5000 km2 or area of occupancy <500 km2 or both;

C. Population size estimated to number fewer than 2,500 mature individuals and to be declining or unevenly distributed;

D. Population size estimated to number fewer than 250 mature individuals;

E. Probability of extinction within 20 years or five generations is at least 20%.

Vulnerable (VU): Facing a high risk of extinction in the wild due to any of the following:

A. Reduction in population size of 30%–50% over the last ten years or three generations, depending on the causes and reversibility of the reductions;

B. Extent of occurrence <20,000 km2 or area of occupancy <2000 km2 or both;

C. Population size estimated to number fewer than 10,000 mature individuals and to be declining or unevenly distributed;

D. Population size estimated to number fewer than 1,000 mature individuals;

E. Probability of extinction within 100 years is at least 10%.

Figure B.5 International Union for Conservation of Nature (IUCN) Criteria for Threatened Taxa. Updated from Strier 2011a. Source: Simplified and condensed from IUCN Species Survival Commission, 2012.

The IUCN has a committee specifically dedicated to primates, the IUCN Species Survival Commission (SSC) Primate Specialist Group. This group collaborates with the International Primatological Society (IPS), Conservation International (CI), and the Bristol Zoological Society (BZS) every two years to publish "Primates in Peril: The World's 25 Most Endangered Primates." These lists are created at IPS open meetings and are intended to focus attention on all endangered primates by highlighting the plights of some of the most critically endangered (Schwitzer et al. 2017).

Identifying Priorities in Primate Conservation

It is important to consider extinction risk in making conservation decisions, thus the IUCN Red list and the "Primates in Peril" reports are factors in deciding how to allocate resources and funding. Some primate species are found only in biodiversity hot spots, or areas that contain high levels of species diversity and include primates that are endemic to the area and genetically unique (Sechrest et al. 2002). Hot spots are often considered conservation priorities because protecting these areas can result in the protection of large numbers of species. In addition, some conservation organizations focus on highly charismatic primate species (e.g., primates that are large, closely related to humans, or well-known from zoos, such as the golden lion tamarin) to garner attention and resources for conservation (Figure B.6). However, dramatic declines of charismatic species indicate that charisma is not enough (Estrada et al. 2017). For example, it is estimated that the population of Bornean orangutans (*Pongo pygmaeus*) decreased by 100,000 individuals between 1999 and 2015, despite being very popular with the general public (Voigt et al. 2018). In making conservation decisions, primatologists may also consider the importance of genetically unique primates, such as the aye-aye (*Daubentonia madagascariensis*), the last remaining species within its genus in order to preserve evolutionary history (Strier 2011a).

THREATS TO PRIMATES

Hunting, Poaching, and Wildlife Trade

Figure B.6 A male Bornean orangutan (*Pongo pygmaeus*). This species' large size and close genetic relatedness to humans often make them appealing to the public, categorizing them as a "charismatic species." Such charismatic animals may garner more resources for conservation. In species like the Critically Endangered Bornean orangutan, whose habitat is highly threatened, this attention can be crucial to their survival (Ancrenaz et al. 2016).

Hunting represents one of the most critical threats to primates (Figure B.7). Bushmeat, which is the meat of wild animals, has historically been a staple diet in many societies. However, human population growth and economic development have increased the commercialization of bushmeat hunting, thereby increasing its impact (Estrada et al. 2017). The increased availability and use of shotguns has also dramatically increased the volume of carcasses that hunters capture (Cronin et al. 2015). Across 89 markets in Nigeria and Cameroon, John Fa and colleagues (2015) calculated that almost 150,000 primate carcasses (from at least 16 different species) were sold annually. In one market on the Liberia/Ivory Coast border, Ryan Covey and Scott McGraw (2014) estimated that the carcasses of nearly 9,500 primates (from at least nine different species) were sold per year, resulting in an almost 3% annual reduction in the local primate population.

Not all primates are hunted specifically for food. Biomedical researchers use primates as models for understanding human biology and as test subjects for the development of vaccines, drugs, and hormones (Conaway 2011). Many of these experiments require large numbers of primates; therefore biomedical facilities often require a continuous supply of primates. To support the international demand for biomedical research test subjects, rhesus macaques (*Macaca mulatta*) in northern and central India experienced a 90% decline in populations over a 28-year period, from 1959 to 1986 (Southwick and Siddiqi 1988). Between 2007 and 2008, a single biomedical laboratory purchased roughly 4,000 nocturnal monkeys for over 100,000 USD through a network of 43 traders across Brazil, Colombia, and Peru (Maldonado et al. 2009).

Aside from biomedical research, captured primates are both legally and illegally sold to pet owners, zoos, tourist centers, and circuses. In Peru, it is estimated that, as recently as 2015, hundreds of thousands of primates are illegally traded every year, comparable to levels of trade prior to a 1973 national ban on primate exportation (Shanee et al. 2017). Once captured, primates may spend over a week in transit from a rural village to a coastal market. To make the transportation of primates more manageable, common trafficking strategies include sedation, asphyxiation, electrocution, and the removal of teeth. As these conditions severely affect the health of the trafficked primates, many perish during the journey while others die within the hands of authorities. Out of the 77 greater slow lorises (*Nycticebus coucang*) confiscated from a single wildlife trader in Indonesia, 22 died from either trauma or from the severity of their wounds (Fuller et al. 2018). Even when primates are successfully confiscated from wildlife traders, it is not uncommon for authorities to either resell or gift these animals to friends and family (Shanee et al. 2017).

Figure B.7 A female gelada (Theropithecus gelada) with a snare around its neck in central Ethiopia. Many rural hunters prefer to hunt using snare traps, which can be easily constructed and offer a more affordable and accessible alternative to firearms (Noss 1998; Tumusiime et al. 2010). Snare traps are constructed out of wire nooses anchored to trees or the ground. Snares are designed to tighten around prey as they struggle to free themselves. Though larger primates are sometimes able to detach snares from their anchored positions, the snare often remains wrapped around the affected body part and can result in loss of circulation, infection, and mutilation (Yersin et al. 2017).

To help curb illegal trafficking of animals, the Convention on International Trade in Endangered Species of Wild Fauna and Flora (CITES) was established in 1973 and ratified in 1975. Under this treaty, the 183 participating countries work together to both regulate the international trade of wildlife and to prevent the overexploitation of wild populations. While only some primates are listed as endangered or threatened under the Endangered Species Act (ESA), all primates are listed under CITES. According to the CITES database, more than 450,000 live primates were traded over the past 15 years (CITES n.d.). However, as the CITES database only includes information formally reported by each country, the real number of primates involved is likely to be much higher.

Habitat Loss, Fragmentation, and Degradation

The geographic distribution of many primate species has been severely limited by habitat loss. A recent analysis showed human demands for agricultural land threaten 76% of primate species, followed by demands for logging (60%) and livestock farming (31%) (Estrada et al. 2017). Habitat loss is not new and has affected the distribution of some primate species for thousands of years. Since the Bronze Age, for example, increases in human land use throughout China have been associated with corresponding decreases in suitable habitats for golden snub-nosed monkeys (*Rhinopithecus roxellana*) (Wang et al. 2014). However, our ever-growing need for food, water, and other natural resources has drastically decreased primate habitats globally (Figure B.8). From 2000 to 2013, roughly 220,000 km2 of tropical forest have been completely deforested in the Brazilian Amazon alone (Tyukavina et al. 2017). Since the start of oil palm development in Indonesia's Ketapang District in 1994, over 65% of habitats without government protection have been allocated to the oil palm industry (Carlson et al. 2012). Even within protected areas, primate habitats are rapidly declining. In South Asia, 36% of surveyed protected areas had more than half of their habitat modified for human use, many of which experienced near-total habitat transformation (Clark et al. 2013). One of these protected areas, the Borajan Reserve Forest in India, saw a more than two-thirds reduction in suitable habitat within a three-year period, resulting in severe population declines for five primate species (Srivastava et al. 2001).

Figure B.8 Cattle graze in a newly formed papaya plantation, which was once forested land in Montagne des Français, Madagascar. Forests are cleared throughout the tropics for both large-scale commercial agricultural as well as for subsistence farming. Conversion for agricultural expansion alone accounts for nearly 75% of all tropical deforestation (Hosonuma et al. 2012). While some primates may still be able to utilize these agricultural matrix environments for foraging and resting, it may put them in danger because of potential heightened human-wildlife conflict.

Habitat fragmentation compounds the effects of habitat loss. Whereas habitat loss reduces the total area in which primates can survive, habitat fragmentation divides large, contiguous primate habitats into smaller isolated patches (Figure B.9). The construction of road networks cutting through savannas, forests, and other primate habitats is a key driver of this fragmentation. Within the next half-century, over 25,000,000 km of new roads are expected to be built, many of which in developing nations through primate habitats (Laurance et al. 2014). By fragmenting habitats, it becomes increasingly challenging for primates (particularly arboreal primates) to disperse between isolated habitat patches. While only 0.1% of black-and-white snub-nosed monkey (*Rhinopithecus bieti*) habitat was lost to the construction of China National Highway 214, movement between habitat patches on either side of the highway was reduced by over 20% (Clauzel et al. 2015). In the long run, habitat fragmentation can force primate populations into genetic bottlenecks, which occur when populations become so small that genetic diversity in them is severely reduced. In the forest fragments of Manaus, Brazil, groups of pied tamarins (*Sanguinus bicolor*) that historically formed one biological population were found to harbor only a subset of the genetic diversity previously exhibited in the region (Farias et al. 2015). Furthermore, primates living in fragments with scarce resources experience elevated levels of stress, which can also have long-term consequences on the health of individuals and populations (Rimbach et al. 2014).

Figure B.9 Forest cleared for cattle ranching in the province of Manabí, Ecuador. Cattle ranching is currently the main driver of deforestation in South American countries (Steinweg et al. 2016). Landholders clear and burn primary forests to convert them into cattle pastures, and when yield begins to decline, they typically move to another old-growth forest and the cycle begins again. Not surprisingly, tropical forests are disappearing faster than any other biome (Aide et al. 2013; Wright 2005). Halting deforestation through community-based conservation programs is one of the main objectives of many non-governmental organizations, such as Proyecto Washu in Ecuador.

Figure B.10 An industrial-sized truck leaves the Montagne des Français region in Madagascar, with dozens of bags of charcoal in tow to be delivered to a nearby town. Much of sub-Saharan Africa still relies on charcoal and other fuelwoods as a main source of energy for cooking and heating. Fuelwood collection and charcoal production are the main proximate drivers of forest degradation throughout Africa (Hosonuma et al. 2012). Degradation and forest loss can lead to a suite of harmful effects for primates living in these regions.

Aside from habitat loss, other drivers of habitat degradation may affect primate populations. For example, streams can carry toxic chemicals used for agriculture into local habitats where they are either directly or indirectly consumed by primates. In Uganda, chimpanzees (*Pan troglodytes*) living within the Sebitoli Forest have been spotted with facial and limb deformities that are suspected of being related to their exposure to pesticides and herbicides used by local tea farmers (Krief et al. 2017). Additionally, invasive species that outcompete native species and alter habitats can affect primate behaviors. In Madagascar, southern bamboo lemurs (*Hapalemur meridionalis*) spent less time feeding in forests dominated by invasive Melaleuca trees (*Melaleuca quinquenervia*) than in forests without these trees (Eppley et al. 2015). Lastly, the use of fuelwood and charcoal is still widely used throughout sub-Saharan Africa as a means to produce heat and energy for cooking (Figure B.10).

Climate Change

Current State

Climate change is one of the most devastating threats facing primates because it compounds preexisting threats, such as habitat degradation and fragmentation. In a little over a century, the earth has seen temperatures rise by 0.85°C globally, with each decade being warmer than the last (IPCC Climate Change 2014). The resulting changes that occur, many of which are just beginning to be documented, can be unpredictable and cause a range of consequences for biodiversity. Increasingly frequent regional droughts, especially in the Southern Hemisphere, not only affect resource abundance but also create a cascade of other ecosystem disturbances that contribute to increased carbon dioxide production (Zhao and

Running 2010). In Kibale National Park, Uganda, Jessica Rothman and colleagues (2015) found that the increasing carbon dioxide levels associated with climate change decreased the nutritional value of leaves, an important food resource for many primates.

Climate change is associated with volatile and unpredictable weather patterns. El Niño Southern Oscillation events (ENSO) influence weather patterns across the globe. Although ENSO events have been occurring for thousands of years, climate change is causing them to occur more frequently and with greater intensity (Wiederholt and Post 2010). The warm air and unpredictable rains that come with an ENSO event can negatively affect food resource abundance. Primates whose diets include high quantities of fruit experience the effects of fruit shortages most strongly (Campos et al. 2015). Madagascar, a primate hot spot and country with high levels of anthropogenic disturbance, is a prime example of how the increased intensity and frequency of climatic events such as ENSO can have consequences for primates (Figure B.11). Amy Dunham and colleagues (2008) found that even the folivorous Milne-Edwards' sifaka (*Propithecus edwarsi*), found within Ranomafana National Park in southeastern Madagascar, would experience severely reduced populations within three generations if ENSO events continued at the current frequency.

Figure B.11 *An old-growth tree is uprooted after Cyclone Enawo made landfall in northeast Madagascar in March 2017. Ocean surface temperatures are increasing as a result of anthropogenic climate change, which may cause stronger tropical storms. These storms often result in dramatic alterations to ecosystems, changing vegetation composition by damaging trunks and branches of trees (Dinsmore et al. 2018). These changes in habitat structure can in turn have repercussions for primates living in these regions, driving them to alter feeding, moving, and reproductive patterns.*

Rapidly changing climate also causes other extreme weather events in primate areas. Due to climate change, hurricanes and cyclones are occurring more frequently. Several studies have looked at the effects on primate populations before and after hurricanes (e.g., Ratsimbazafy 2006; Schaffner et al. 2012; Zimmerman and Kovich 2007). A population of howler monkeys in Belize (*Alouatta pigra*) experienced population reduction and reduced reproduction after a hurricane hit. This response lasted more than three years (Behie and Pavelka 2005; Pavelka and Chapman 2006). However, not all primates are as vulnerable to the effects of major storms. In Kirindy Mitea National Park in western Madagascar, Verreaux's sifakas (*Propithecus verreauxi*) did not suffer reduced population or reproduction, despite a reduction in their food supply following a cyclone (Lewis and Rakontondranaivo 2011). The different responses of these species to catastrophic events is likely related to differences in their behavioral flexibility, such as adjusting the types of foods consumed and the amount of time spent resting, feeding, moving, and socializing by each species (Strier 2017) and evolutionary adaptability (Wright 1999).

Large-Scale Change

On a large scale, the deleterious effects of climate change can make primates' current environments inhospitable. Most primates are adapted to live in tropical environments and many have specialized diets. Climate change alters the flowering and fruiting seasons of many plants, requiring a great deal of dietary flexibility from the organisms that rely on their production (Anderson et al. 2012). Many primates are not capable of this adjustment and would need to shift their habitat range to cope. Unfortunately, habitat loss and fragmentation make these range shifts impossible for many species without human assistance in the form of translocations. Primates have relatively slow life-histories, often producing only one offspring at a time, and their extended juvenile period results in slow evolutionary adaptation to change (Campos et al. 2017). To cope with the large-scale effects of climate change, primates must rely on behavioral flexibility and aid from humans. Primates are projected to have some of the most restricted ranges due to climate change (Schloss et al. 2012), forcing them to utilize a variety of possible, non-preferred habitats

Small-Scale Change

On a small or local scale, the effects of climate change are more fine-tuned and can differ depending on the species. For example, spider monkeys (Ateles geoffroyi yucatanensis) exhibited behavioral plasticity after two hurricanes hit Mexico, spending more time resting, feeding on leaves, and in smaller subgroups than they did before the hurricanes (Schaffner et al. 2012). Critically endangered species, such as the northern sportive lemur (Lepilemur septentrionalis), are more vulnerable to catastrophic weather events because in small populations the loss of just a few individuals can have major impacts (Figure B.12) (Dinsmore et al. 2016). Species that are not threatened or that have large, intact ranges are not likely to be greatly affected by localized climatic conditions, but they may nonetheless experience local devastation and even extinction (Strier 2017).

Disease

Disease is especially intertwined with climate change and has increasingly become a critical threat to primates (Nunn and Altizer 2006). Shifting temperatures, unpredictable precipitation, crowding in fragmented habitats, and increased human contact can contribute to increased disease transmission among primates (Nunn and Gillespie 2016). Mosquito populations, which are vectors of diseases that affect humans and nonhuman primates like Zika virus, yellow fever, and malaria, often thrive in this type of environment and have expanded in recent years (Lafferty 2009). Disease outbreaks have the potential to severely reduce primate populations. In 2016 and 2017, a large yellow fever outbreak devastated several populations of the brown howler monkey (Alouatta guariba) endemic to the Atlantic forest of Brazil (Fernandes et al. 2017). Ebola outbreaks have similarly diminished populations of African apes; in 2003 and 2004, an outbreak killed up to 5,000 endangered western gorillas (Gorilla gorilla) (Bermejo et al. 2006) and severely reduced populations of chimpanzees (Pan troglodytes) (Leroy et al. 2004) in Gabon and the Republic of Congo.

Figure B.12 A northern sportive lemur (Lepilemur septentrionalis) rests in a tree at Montagne des Français, Madagascar. A Critically Endangered species, the nocturnal northern sportive lemur is estimated to have a population of only ~50 individuals that are restricted to one forest fragment in northern Madagascar. For small populations like the northern sportive lemur, the impacts of climate change can be exacerbated. However, non-governmental organizations, such as Madagascar Biodiversity Partnership (MBP), work with species like the northern sportive lemur to increase their populations and minimize such impacts. MBP has been working at Montagne des Français to monitor northern sportive lemurs and initiate reforestation efforts since 2012.

Human encroachment into primate habitats as a result of agricultural expansion, resource extraction, or even through irresponsible eco-tourism or research practices can introduce novel pathogens into both human and nonhuman primate populations (Strier 2017). Due to our close shared lineage, many diseases are communicable between humans and primates, such as Ebola, HIV, tuberculosis, herpes, and other common ailments. Close contact and primate handling are often the most direct ways in which these diseases are transmitted. However, poor hygiene practices, improper waste disposal, and primate provisioning contribute to disease susceptibility in primates (Wallis and Lee 1999). For example, two groups of olive baboons (Papio cynocephalus anubis) living in the Masai Mara Game Reserve in Kenya contracted tuberculosis from foraging at contaminated garbage dumps near the tourist lodge (Tarara et al. 1985). Similarly, in Gombe National Park, Tanzania, there is evidence that contact with humans and their domesticated animals in nearby villages caused an outbreak of polio in chimpanzees (Pan troglodytes) (Williams et al. 2008). Transmission of diseases through increased human contact can have devastating effects on primate populations that have not built any resistance (Laurance 2015).

Extinction Vortex

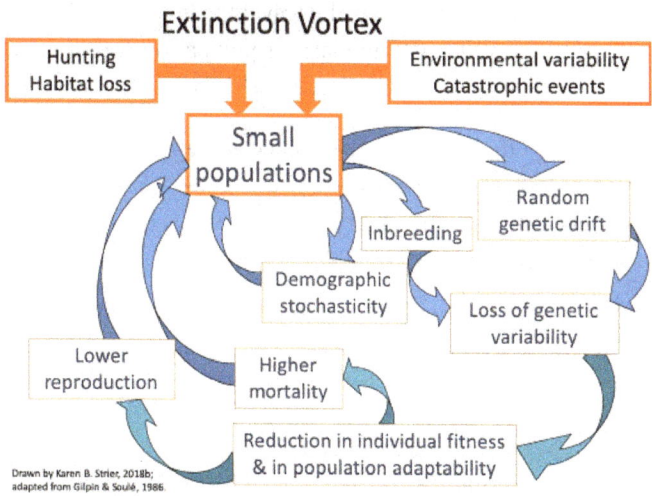

Figure B.13 A model of the extinction vortex. The extinction vortex shows the threats and pressures that work simultaneously to threaten populations. These pressures are often exacerbated by the compounding effects they have on each other. Once a population has entered the vortex, this cascade of events can prevent recovery, resulting in extinction.

The many threats facing primates that we have listed here are completely interrelated. As such, they tend to interact with one another, creating what is known as an extinction vortex (Figure B.13; Gilpin and Soulé 1986). Habitat fragmentation and loss, hunting, climate change, and disease compound to reduce primate populations at a greater rate than when acting alone. Small populations living in isolated fragments of habitat are disconnected from the rest of their species and are therefore more vulnerable to inbreeding effects. Daniel Brito and colleagues (2008) found that many populations of the critically endangered northern muriqui (*Brachyteles hypoxanthus*) residing in the remaining fragments of the Atlantic Forest would experience genetic decay with possibility of extinction over the next 50 generations if management practices were not put into place. Slow life histories resulting in long interbirth intervals push many species of primates farther into the extinction vortex. Shifting demographics can have dire consequences for primates, thrusting them into a cycle that is hard to break once entered. With the continued presence of threats, many species have a difficult time recovering (Brook et al. 2008; Strier 2011a).

PRIMATE SIGNIFICANCE

Ecological Significance of Primates

Primates play a key role within their ecosystems, often acting as important contributors to forest community structure by aiding in seed dispersal and pollination of angiosperms and other plant species. Variability in traits such as diet, gut anatomy, and movement patterns influence the spatial landscape of dispersed seeds (Russo and Chapman 2011). Frugivorous primates that range widely are considered the greatest contributors to the dispersal of seeds, as they often either swallow seeds whole, as is common for most Neotropical frugivorous primates (Figure B.14), or spit seeds out, as is common for primates with cheek pouches in Africa and Asia. These primates can contribute greatly to the diversification and regeneration of forest communities by traveling long distances after consumption and depositing seeds away from the parent plant within heterogeneous landscapes (Strier 2017; Terborgh 1983). Frugivory and seed dispersal are critical plant-animal relationships (Russo 2017). Bach Thanh Hai and colleagues (2018) found that yellow-cheeked crested gibbons (*Nomascus gabriellae*) in Southeast Asia were the most effective seed disperser for the Pacific walnut tree. Gibbons dispersed seeds via consumption anywhere from 4 m to 425 m from the parent tree. Seeds defecated by gibbons had higher germination and success rates than those spit by macaques in the same forest.

Some species of primate may also act as pollinators for local plant species. These primates are attracted to the nectar and flowers of the plant, which often leave pollen on their faces and fur, subsequently spreading pollen to conspecifics when the primate moves to a new location. Jeremy Hogan and colleagues (2016) suggest that white-faced capuchins

(*Cebus capucinus imitator*) may have a beneficial effect on certain plant species in Costa Rica. Other primates may have co-evolved a plant-pollinator relationship. Data indicate that the black and white ruffed lemur (*Varecia variegata*) is reliant on the nectar of the traveler's palm (*Ravenala madagascariensis*) during specific times of the year, allowing pollen to stick to the ruff of their necks. This, along with the notion that no other species visit the travel's palm during certain times of the year, indicate that this plant species may be dependent on nonflying mammals for pollination (Kress et al. 1994).

By acting as seed dispersers and pollinators, primates can aid in the reproductive success, regeneration, and diversification of plants within their ecosystems. The significance of these relationships is only becoming more apparent as habitats continue to be fragmented and destroyed. As habitats dwindle, the ability to regenerate healthy forest systems is crucial to the health and survival of tropical forest systems worldwide (Stier 2017).

Bioanthropological Significance of Primates

Figure B.14 Fecal matter with seeds from the large-bodied northern muriqui (*Brachyteles hypoxanthus*). When primates consume fruit, they often swallow seeds whole. This photo shows several intact seeds within feces, after ingestion. Primates are often effective seed dispersers because of the long distances they travel and the fertilizing properties of their dung.

The study of non-human primates has been an integral component of anthropology for many decades. Even before Sherwood Washburn advocated in The New Physical Anthropology (1951) that primates could be studied as living reference for hominin behaviors, anthropologists like Margaret Mead recognized that studies of wild primates could contribute to biological and sociocultural anthropology in many ways (Strier 2011b). Primatology in Japan, the U.S., and Europe grew out of a desire to better understand ourselves. Thus, research in the 1960s and 1970s largely focused on species such as chimpanzees (*Pan* spp.) or baboons (*Papio* spp.) that are closely related to humans phylogenetically or live in environments similar to those occupied by early hominins (Haraway 1991; Strum and Fedigan 1999; Washburn 1973). Since those early days, biological anthropological primatology has broadened to include primates from around the world (Strier 2003, 2018a). The inclusion of diverse taxa from what were then-understudied regions challenged notions of "typical" primate behavior, such as the idea that aggression was the main mechanism for maintaining hierarchical social relationships (Strier 1994).

Anthropologists draw broadly from primate studies to explore the many facets of human behavior and evolution. For example, studies demonstrating the tool-using capabilities of wild chimpanzees (*Pan troglodytes*) and capuchin monkeys (*Sapajus* spp., formerly *Cebus* spp.) show that similar ecological pressures and intelligence contribute to tool-using behaviors, rather than just phylogenetic relatedness to humans (Fragaszy et al. 2004; Inoue-Nakamura and Matsuzawa 1997). Similarly, studies of modern primate morphology are frequently used to assess how locomotor style or behaviors (such as foraging) are related to anatomy, and this knowledge can then be used to assess the skeletal and dental anatomy of fossil hominins. Studies of microscopic wear patterns, for example, use living primates as analogues to understand wear patterns generated by different food items as well as the rapidity with which changes to these patterns can occur (Teaford and Oyen 1989; Ungar and Sponheimer 2011). Living nonhuman primates provide a comparative sample with which we deepen our understanding of the evolutionary mechanisms that shaped human evolution.

Cultural Significance of Primates

For as long as our species has existed, groups of people have lived alongside nonhuman primates and engaged with them in varying ways (Fuentes 2012). The development and expansion of the field of ethnoprimatology, the study of the human–nonhuman primate interface, has encouraged researchers from sociocultural anthropology and primatology to investigate these points where primates and humans interact and influence each other in surprising ways (Fuentes 2012; Sponsel 1997). Primates are viewed by many as exceptional animals for the ways in which they reflect elements of humanness, stimulating many thousands of people to observe their exhibits at zoos and sanctuaries throughout the world. However, the significance of these animals to diverse cultures goes beyond anthropocentrism and touches on aspects of ecology, religion, and social systems. Primates are common figures in religion and myth, appearing sometimes as gods or deities themselves (e.g., the Hindu deity Hanuman) and sometimes as mediators between the human and spirit realms (Alves et al. 2017; Peterson 2017; Wheatley 1999). Primates have additional cultural significance as figures in folklore and legend, and they are often ascribed human-like characteristics in many of these narratives (Cormier 2017). These stories often inform local taboos that may discourage the consumption of particular species or deforestation of particular areas (Osei-Tutu 2017; Roncal et al. 2018; Sicotte 2017).

The role that primates play in human cultures is complex and varies significantly with local history, religious practice, and economies. Among the Awa Guajá of eastern Amazonia, for example, primates are considered a part of the humans' extended kin network and are protected as such, yet they also constitute an important source of dietary protein and are hunted regularly (Cormier 2003). In other primate habitat countries, such as Bali, primates play a significant role in religious practice. Long-tailed macaques (*Macaca fascicularis*) in Bali are frequently found in the forests surrounding Hindu temples and will consume offerings left by residents and tourists once festivals or rituals are concluded (Fuentes 2010; Wheatley 1999). These macaques are seen by some as mediators between the natural world and the spiritual world that transports offerings from one realm to another (Wheatley 1999). Investigating how local residents view primates—for example, whether species are considered sacred or not—is a vital component of conservation programs in these areas (Peterson and Riley 2017). Studying the interface between human and nonhuman primates, and what factors (e.g., local religious practices, taboos, etc.) influence these interactions can lead to more holistic conservation planning and implementation.

Economic Significance of Primates

One of the most promising ways that primates can benefit people is through the potential to stimulate local economies from ecotourism. Ecotourism differs from traditional tourism in three main ways: it focuses on nature-based attractions, it provides learning opportunities, and its tourism management practices adhere to economic and ecological sustainability (Fennell and Weaver 2005). Primates are charismatic megafauna, meaning that they are large animals (oftentimes mammals) that elicit mass appeal. They have the possibility to draw tourists, which can in turn bring revenue to lower-income communities found near primate habitats. This attraction from tourists, along with revenue-sharing, can then stimulate local populations to have more positive attitudes toward protected areas and become more invested in the well-being and protection of primates and their habitats (Archabald and Naughton-Treves 2001).

Perhaps one of the greatest success stories of nature-based tourism revolves around the mountain gorillas (*Gorilla beringei beringei*) of Rwanda. After internal conflict plagued Rwanda during the 1990s, the Virungas area developed gorilla-based tourism as a means to aid in socioeconomic development and to bring stability to the region. This process not only helped to increase mountain gorilla populations but was also able to generate enough income to cover the operation costs of three national parks (Maekawa et al. 2013). Research indicated that low-income individuals living around Parc National des Volcans in Rwanda could garner direct income as well as nonfinancial benefits (such as the development of schools and hospitals) from gorilla tourism in the region (Spencely et al. 2010). Although ecotourism has the potential to alleviate poverty situations for local populations and aid in the overall sustainability of natural habitats, it can also bring a suite of new problems to areas. It can overcrowd national parks and over-habituate primates (Figure B.15), increase potential disease transfer between humans and primates, and exacerbate corruption, which often pulls money away from local communities (Hvenegaard 2014; Muehlenbein et al. 2010).

Figure B.15 Bonnet macaques (Macaca radiata) being fed by tourists. Food sharing and other forms of direct contact between humans and primates provide opportunities for disease transmission. Despite most ecotourists understanding the dangers of human-primate contact, according to a recent survey over half would still opt to touch or feed primates if possible (Muehlenbein 2017). Though nature-based tourism may have benefits for local communities (Spencely et al. 2010), a better understanding of what drives tourists to engage with primates is necessary to minimize direct human-primate interactions.

WHAT CAN BE DONE?

Role of Research

Systematic and long-term research studies provide some of the most foundational and necessary information for the conservation of endangered primates (Kappeler and Watts 2012). Research provides critical data on essential and preferred feeding resources, life history parameters and reproduction rates, territoriality, the carrying capacity of habitats, and solitary or group social dynamics. Within the last few decades, researchers have also begun to stress the acute need for studies investigating how various primates are responding to human disturbances; how climate change is affecting the behavior, range, and habitat of these species; and the significance of primate biodiversity hotspots (Brown and Yoder 2015; Chapman and Peres 2001; Estrada et al. 2018). Understanding these aspects will provide crucial information for practitioners to make the most effective and species-specific conservation decisions.

Long-term studies on primate species provide some of the most conclusive information on changes occurring to populations in the face of anthropogenic disturbances and climate change. They also provide a suite of direct and indirect conservation contributions to endangered species, and the continual monitoring of populations can deter deleterious anthropogenic actions, allowing for population growth and forest regeneration. For example, the Northern Muriqui Project of Caratinga in Minas Gerais, Brazil, has documented growth of both the muriqui population and the regeneration of the forest via secondary succession (Strier 2010). The project has also invested in future research and conservation by training more than 65 Brazilian students, as well as providing stable jobs for local people, stimulating the local community, and alleviating reliance on forest products for income and survival (Strier 2010; Strier and Boubli 2006; Strier and Mendes 2012). Several other long-term primate studies all over the world have seen similar positive impacts and conservation successes including work in Beza Mahafaly Special Reserve, Berenty Reserve, and Ranomafana National Park, Madagascar; Lomas Barbudal and Santa Rosa National Park, Costa Rica; Khau Yai National Park, Thailand; Amboseli National Park, Kenya; Gombe Stream National Park, Tanzania; Kibale National Park, Uganda, among many others (Kappeler and Watts 2012).

The implementation of novel research techniques can also aid in the conservation of primates and their ecosystems. The use of high-resolution camera traps have become widespread and invaluable in their ability to aid primatologists and conservationists in surveying rare populations, establishing population counts, and assessing behavior (Pebsworth and LaFleur 2014). Camera traps also have the potential to aid in ethical considerations, photographing illegal activities such as poaching. Research is also imperative for making important decisions regarding translocations and reintroductions of animals. Without knowledge of the species' social ecology, demography, and unique learned behaviors—also known as primate traditions or cultures—successful translocations and reintroductions from captive populations would not be possible. Researchers and conservationists must recognize these dynamics when making the difficult decision to reintroduce or move populations and factor in how these dynamics may shift or affect the resident population after management. The most notable case of effective translocation and reintroduction is that of the golden lion tamarin (*Leontopithecus rosalia*). Over 30 zoos contributed 146 captive-born individuals to be reintroduced into Brazil, providing essential information on nutrition and health that aided in reintroduction strategies. Additionally, in 1994, isolated individuals in forest fragments were successfully translocated into protected regions in order to increase gene flow, which through the exchange of genes, introduces more genetic variation into the next generation (Kierulff et al. 2012).

Nongovernmental Organizations (NGOs) and Community-Based Conservation Work

Conservation NGOs have a long-standing history of working to save endangered species from going extinct. These organizations often target primates for their work because of their ability to act as umbrella species, supporting the conservation of many species found within their ecosystems. Over the past 30 years, conservation NGOs have begun to move away from a preservation-based mindset that focused on excluding humans from using protected areas. The 1990s ushered in a shift toward community-based conservation (CBC), which instead aimed to work with local people living near targeted natural environments to reduce human-wildlife conflict and establish sustainable practices (Horwich and Lyon 2007). CBC has shown success in terms of reducing hunting and deforestation in many regions including the Manas Biosphere Reserve in Assam, India, as well as in the cloud forests of Peru from the work of the Yellow Tailed Woolly Monkey Project (Horwich et al. 2012; Shanee et al. 2007). Although CBC has seen conservation successes, many warn that it should not be a panacea for all conservation goals but, rather, one mechanism among many when attempting to conserve endangered species (Reibelt and Nowack 2015; Scales 2014).

Reforestation is widely becoming one of the most practical ways in which NGOs aid in primate conservation. Organizations often collaborate with communities to establish nurseries to grow saplings, which can then be transplanted strategically to reforest certain parts of primate habitats or create habitat corridors between forest fragments. Madagascar Biodiversity Partnership, an NGO with four field sites throughout Madagascar, has planted over 1,850,000 trees from 2010 to June of 2018 (Edward E. Louis Jr., personal communication, 05/24/2018). These efforts have been shown to be successful, as lemurs have been observed in reforested regions where they had previously not been seen.

What Can Readers of This Book Do?

It may be difficult to imagine how an individual living thousands of miles away can aid in the conservation of primates and their habitats, but in fact there are several small steps that people all over the world can take to make a difference. Many local zoos contribute to in situ conservation work as well as maintain species survival plans in order to increase diversity among zoo populations. We recommend readers visit their local zoos to learn about what actions zoos take to aid in the conservation of primates and how they can get involved in these activities.

One tangible action that can be done is to reduce the purchasing of products that contain non-sustainable ingredients. The demand for cheap oil has increased in recent years for commercial products such as peanut butter, chocolate, soaps, and shampoos, among many others. As such, palm oil plantations have expanded into wildlife habitat throughout Southeast Asia, especially in Borneo and Sumatra, the last remaining habitats of orangutans (*Pongo* spp.) and many other species of primates. This, coupled with other local pressures such as hunting and peat fires, resulted in the IUCN upgrading the Borneo orangutan's (*Pongo pygmaeus*) conservation status to Critically Endangered in 2016. They were also included in the 25 most endangered primates list for the first time (Husson et al. 2016). Although data suggest that orangutans will nest within agroindustrial environments, they will only do so with natural forest patches nearby (Ancrenaz et al. 2014). Reducing individual consumption of palm oil or choosing sustainable oil products can help reduce the overall demand; it can drive producers to commit to more environmentally friendly practices. This can hopefully slow the conversion of naturally forested landscapes into agroindustrial environments.

With the proliferation of social media, the desirability to photograph animals in close proximity has greatly increased (Pearce and Moscardo 2015). We recommend that readers who visit native primate environments resist engaging with primates in an attempt to take "selfies" with animals. Repeated encounters with travelers and tourists can overhabituate primates and put them in danger of contracting (and transmitting) diseases (Geffroy et al. 2015). Paying for photos with primates can also exacerbate the illegal pet trade because local people will be incentivized to harvest primate infants from wild populations, adversely affecting primate densities and social group dynamics. While it may be popular to try to take the most engaging "selfie" with a wild animal, it is best to just admire these animals from afar (Figure B.16).

Figure B.16 Students on a field course observe and record data on primates in the canopy at El Zota field station in Costa Rica. Field courses are a great way to learn how to safely observe animals in the wild while gaining hands-on experience collecting behavioral, ecological, and conservation data.

Lastly, readers can aid in primate conservation by resisting sharing YouTube (or other) videos depicting primates in nonnative habitats. Often times videos of primates engaging with humans spark the popularity of these animals as pets. The desire for these animals can lead to an influx in illegal pet harvesting and trading, the mistreatment of wild animals in domestic settings, and the belief that these animals are not endangered since others own them as pets (Nekaris et al. 2013). After a video depicting a pygmy slow loris (*Nycticebus pygmaeus*) being "tickled" went viral in 2009, and another depicting a slow loris eating rice went viral in 2012, international confiscations of slow lorises increased (Nekaris et al. 2013). Awareness, coupled with the resistance to share these "cute" videos, can help reduce the market for primates to be captured for the illegal pet trade.

For those interested in gaining hands-on experience with primates, we recommend visiting Primate Info Net, where a list of field school opportunities and professional, educational, and volunteer positions are posted regularly. These listings can be found at: http://pin.primate.wisc.edu/jobs/list/avail

FUTURE PERSPECTIVES

As anthropogenic and natural disturbances continue to intensify in range and scale, the future status of the world's primates is increasingly dire. However, researchers, conservationists, and the general public are attempting to understand how primates respond to these disturbances, what actions can be done to mitigate further disturbances, how to establish sustainable relationships between humans and primates, and what small actions can be done in their own lives to aid these processes.

Regardless of our cultural or political views, we think it is valid to ask ourselves as researchers, conservationists, and students: What is the value of Earth's biological diversity, and what are our obligations to nonhuman primates, our closest living ancestors? Although scientists and conservationists often argue that there is inherent value in maintaining the world's biodiversity, we propose that primates have a special significance that goes beyond their intrinsic contribution to biodiversity. The concept that species and systems can provide a suite of benefits to humans is known as ecosystem services (Cardinale et al. 2012; Kremen 2005). These services are often classified into four categories: provisioning (e.g., food), regulating (e.g., water quality regulating), cultural (e.g., recreation and aesthetic), and supporting services (e.g., nutrient cycling) (Harrison et al. 2014; Mace et al. 2011; Millennium Ecosystem Assessment 2005). Following this approach, we propose that understanding the value of primates and their habitats in terms of their ecological, bioanthropological, cultural/historical, and economic contributions can aid in the long-term conservation of these endangered species. Recognizing the connections and continuities between ourselves and other primates is the first critical step toward caring about their future and making it part of our own.

Review Questions

- What criteria do researchers and conservationists use to identify the conservation status of primate populations and species?
- What are the main threats facing primates today, and how do the combined impacts of these threats uniquely affect primates?
- What do you think a world without primates would look like? Consider their unique significance and the various roles they play in ecology, human evolutionary and cultural history, and local economies. How would the absence of primates affect ecosystems, other animals, and humans?
- Considering all the other problems in the world today, should primate conservation be a high priority? What are the arguments to support prioritizing primate conservation?
- How can you contribute to primate conservation in your everyday life?

About the Authors

Mary P. Dinsmore, M.S., Ph.D. candidate

University of Wisconsin–Madison

Mary P. Dinsmore

Mary P. Dinsmore is a Ph.D. candidate in the Department of Environment and Resources at the University of Wisconsin–Madison and a member of the Strier Lab. Mary's interest in primatology began when she was working as a research assistant in Peru with saddleback tamarins (Saguinus fuscicollis) and in Madagascar with greater bamboo lemurs (Prolemur simus). It was during these experiences that she saw firsthand the immense impacts that humans had on primate habitat and became interested in human-wildlife conflict and conservation. Her dissertation work explores the consequences of anthropogenic and natural disturbances on the habitat and behavior of the northern sportive lemur (Lepilemur septentrionalis). She has received funding for this work from the Primate Action Fund of Conservation International and African Studies Department of

UW–Madison. Mary received her BS and BA from the University of Portland in 2009 and her MS from the University of Wisconsin–Madison in 2014. She currently teaches study abroad with Broadreach Global Adventures as well as throughout the academic year in the Department of Integrative Biology at UW–Madison.

Ilianna E. Anise, B.A., Ph.D. student

University of Wisconsin–Madison

Ilianna E. Anise

Ilianna E. Anise is a Ph.D. student in the Integrative Biology department at the University of Wisconsin–Madison. She is a member of the Strier Lab, studying primate behavioral ecology and conservation. Ilianna's current research focuses on studying vigilance and risk in black-horned capuchin monkeys (*Sapajus nigritus*) in southeast Brazil. She holds an Advanced Opportunity Fellowship and has received funding from the Department of Integrative Biology. Ilianna received her BA in biology and environmental science from Drew University. She found her passion for fieldwork while participating in a small mammal demography research project as an undergraduate student. At UW–Madison, Ilianna is a teaching assistant for an animal biology lab course and enjoys sharing her love of animals with students.

Rebekah J. Ellis, B.A., M.S.

University of Wisconsin–Madison

Rebekah J. Ellis

Rebekah J. Ellis is a Ph.D. student in the Department of Anthropology at the University of Wisconsin–Madison. She is a member of the Strier Lab. Rebekah received her BA in anthropology and psychology from the University of Texas at Austin. She has studied the behavior of neotropical primates at field sites in Eastern Costa Rica and the Ecuadorian Amazon. At UW–Madison, Rebekah has assisted in teaching an introductory course covering the subdisciplines of cultural, archeological, and biological anthropology. She currently holds a Foreign Language and Area Studies Fellowship. Her research utilizes social network analysis to explore the social behavior of neotropical primates.

Amanda J. Hardie, M.A., Ph.D. candidate

University of Wisconsin–Madison

Amanda J. Hardie

Amanda J. Hardie is a Ph.D. Candidate in Anthropology at the University of Wisconsin–Madison and a member of the Strier Lab. Amanda received her BA in Anthropology at the University of North Carolina-Charlotte, after attending Central Piedmont Community College. Amanda's research focuses on the dynamic interactions between primates and the environment, and she currently works in Brazil studying the behavior and diet of brown howler monkeys in the Atlantic Forest. She has received funding from the Department of Anthropology, a Foreign Language Area Studies Fellowship, and the National Geographic Society.

Jacob B. Kraus, B.A., Ph.D. student

University of Wisconsin-Madison

Jacob B. Kraus is a Ph.D. student and teaching assistant in the Department of Integrated Biology at the University of Wisconsin–Madison and a member of the Strier Lab. His interest in primatology began while studying the ecology and behavior of Gelada monkeys (Theropithecus gelada) as a field assistant for the Guassa Gelada Research Project (GGRP) in Ethiopia. He is broadly interested in the behavioral thermoregulation strategies that primates, and other social mammals, employ in high-altitude habitats. Jacob's current research is focused on how the sociality of Yunnan snub-nosed monkeys (*Rhinopithecus bieti*) affects their microhabitat selection and grooming behaviors. He has been funded by the Department of Integrative Biology. Jacob received his BA in Biology from Reed College. Prior to attending UW-Madison, Jacob interned at the Smithsonian Conservation Biology Institute (SCBI), where he worked on various remote sensing and habitat survey projects.

Jacob B. Kraus

Karen B. Strier, Ph.D.

University of Wisconsin-Madison

Karen B. Strier is Vilas Research Professor and Irven DeVore Professor of Anthropology at the University of Wisconsin–Madison. After graduating from Swarthmore College in 1980, she received her MA in 1981 and her PhD in 1986 in Anthropology from Harvard University. She is an international authority on the endangered northern muriqui monkey, which she has been studying in the Brazilian Atlantic forest since 1982. Her pioneering, long-term field research has been critical to conservation efforts on behalf of this species, and has been influential in broadening comparative perspectives on primate behavioral and ecological diversity. She is a fellow of the U.S. National Academy of Sciences, the American Academy of Arts and Sciences, and the American Association for the Advancement of Science. She was awarded an Honorary Doctorate of Science from the University of Chicago, and Distinguished Primatologist Awards from the American Primatological Society and the Midwestern Primate Interest Group. She has received various research, teaching, and service awards from the University of Wisconsin–Madison and has been honored with Lifetime Honorary Memberships from the Brazilian Primatological Society and the Latin American Primatological Society, and with Honorary Citizenship of the city of Caratinga, in Minas Gerais, Brazil. She has authored or coauthored more than 100 publications, in addition to working on various coauthored and edited volumes and two single-authored books, Faces in the Forest: The Endangered Muriqui Monkeys of Brazil (1992) and Primate Behavioral Ecology, 5th edition (2017). Since 2016, she has served as the elected President of the International Primatological Society.

Karen B. Strier

References

Aide, T. Mitchell, Matthew L. Clark, H. Ricardo Grau, David López-Carr, Marc A. Levy, Daniel Redo, Martha Bonilla-Moheno, George Riner, María J. Andrade-Núñez, and María Muñiz. 2013. "Deforestation and Reforestation of Latin America and the Caribbean (2001–2010)." Biotropica 45 (2): 262–271. doi: 10.1111/j.1744-7429.2012.00908.x.

Alves, Rômulo Romeu Nóbrega, Raynner Rilke Duarte Barboza, and Wedson de Medeiros Silva Souto. 2017. "Primates in

Mythology." In The International Encyclopedia of Primatology, edited by Agustín Fuentes, 1149–1154. Hoboken, NJ: John Wiley and Sons. doi: 10.1002/9781119179313.wbprim0173.

Ancrenaz, M., M. Gumal, A. J. Marshall, E. Meijaard, S. A. Wich, and S. Husson. 2016. Pongo pygmaeus (errata version published in 2018). The IUCN Red List of Threatened Species 2016. doi: 10.2305/IUCN.UK.2016-1.RLTS.T17975A17966347.

Ancrenaz, Marc, Felicity Oram, Laurentius Ambu, Isabelle Lackman, Eddie Ahmad, Hamisah Elahan, Harjinder Kler, Nicola K. Abram, and Erik Meijaard. 2014. "Of Pongo, Palms, and Perceptions: A Multidisciplinary Assessment of Bornean Orangutans Pongo pygmaeus in an Oil Palm Context." Oryx 49 (3): 465–472. doi: 10.1017/S0030605313001270.

Anderson, Jill T., David W. Inouye, Amy M. McKinney, Robert I. Coulatti, and Tom Mitchell-Oldes. 2012. "Phenotypic Plasticity and Adaptive Evolution Contribute to Advancing Flowering Phenology in Response to Climate Change." Proceedings of the Royal Society B 279 (1743): 3843–3852. doi: 10.1098/rspb.2012.1051.

Archabald, Karen, and Lisa Naughton-Treves. 2001. "Tourism Revenue-Sharing around National Parks in Uganda: Early Efforts to Identify and Reward Local Communities." Environmental Conservation 28 (2): 135–149. doi: 10.1017/S0376892901000145.

Behie, Alison M., and Mary S. M. Pavelka. 2005. "The Short-Term Effects of a Hurricane ?on the Diet and Activity of Black Howlers (Alouatta pigra) in Monkey River, Belize." Folia Primatologica 76 (1): 1–9. doi: 10.1159/000082450.

Bermejo, Magdalena, Jose Domingo Rodriguez-Teijeiro, German Illera, and Peter D. Walsh. 2006. "Ebola Outbreak Killed 5,000 Gorillas." Science 314 (5805): 1564. doi: 10.1126/science.1133105.

Brito, Daniel, Carlos E. V. Grelle, and Jean Phillipe Boubli. 2008. "Is the Atlantic Forest Protected Area Network Efficient in Maintaining Viable Populations of Brachyteles hypoxanthus?" Biodiversity and Conservation 17 (13): 3255–3268. doi: 10.1007/s10531-008-9427-z.

Brook, Barry W., Navjot S. Sodhi, and Corey J. A. Bradshaw. 2008. "Synergies among Extinction Drivers under Global Change." Trends in Ecology and Evolution 23 (8): 453–460. doi: 10.1016/j.tree.2008.03.011.

Brown, Jason L., and Anne D. Yoder. 2015. "Shifting Ranges and Conservation Challenges for Lemurs in the Face of Climate Change." Ecology and Evolution 5 (6): 1131–1142. doi: 10.1002/ece3.1418.

Campos, Fernando A., Katharine M. Jack, and Linda M. Fedigan. 2015. "Climate Oscillations and Conservation Measures Regulate White-Faced Capuchin Population Growth and Demography in a Regenerating Tropical Dry Forest in Costa Rica." Biological Conservation 186: 204–213. doi: 10.1016/j.biocon.2015.03.017.

Campos, Fernando A., William F. Morris, Susan C. Alberts, Jeanne Altmann, Diane K. Brockman, Marina Cords, Anne Pusey, Tara S. Stoinski, Karen B. Strier, and Linda M. Fedigan. 2017. "Does Climate Variability Influence the Demography of Wild Primates? Evidence from Long-Term Life-History Data in Seven Species." Globe Change Biology 23 (11): 1–15. doi: 10.1111/gcb.13754.

Cardinale, B. J., J. Emmett Duffy, Andrew Gonzalez, David U. Hopper, Charles Perrings, Patrick Venail, Anita Narwani, et al. 2012. "Biodiversity Loss and Its Impact on Humans." Nature 486 (7401): 59–67. doi: 10.1038/nature11148.

Carlson, Kimberly M., Lisa M. Curran, Dessy Ratnasari, Alice M. Pittman, Britaldo S. Soares-Filho, Gregory P. Asner, Simon N. Trigg, David A. Gaveau, Deborah Lawrence, and Herman O. Rodrigues. 2012. "Committed Carbon Emissions, Deforestation, and Community Land Conversion from Oil Palm Plantation Expansion in West Kalimantan, Indonesia." Proceedings of the National Academy of Sciences 109 (19): 7559–7564. doi: 10.1073/pnas.1200452109.

Chapman, Colin A., and Carlos A. Peres. 2001. "Primate Conservation in the New Millennium: The Role of Scientists." Evolutionary Anthropology 10 (1): 16–33. doi: 10.1002/1520-6505(2001)10:1<16::AID-EVAN1010>3.0.CO;2-O.

CITES. N.d. "CITES Trade Database." Accessed July 22, 2018. https://trade.cites.org/en/cites_trade/#

Clark, Natalie E., Elizabeth H. Boakes, Philip J. K. McGowan, Georgina M. Mace, and Richard A. Fuller. 2013. "Protected Areas in South Asia Have Not Prevented Habitat Loss: A Study Using Historical Models of Land-Use Change." PLoS ONE 8 (5):e65298. doi: 10.1371/journal.pone.0065298.

Clauzel, Celine, Deng Xiqing, Wu Gongsheng, Patrick Giraudoux, and Li Li. 2015. "Assessing the Impact of Road Developments on Connectivity across Multiple Scales: Application to Yunnan Snub-Nosed Monkey Conservation." Biological Conservation 192: 207-217. doi: 10.1016/j.biocon.2015.09.029.

Conaway, Eileen. 2011. "Bioidentical Hormones: An Evidence-Based Review for Primary Care Providers." The Journal of the American Osteopathic Association 111 (3): 153–164.

Cormier, Loretta A. 2003. Kinship with Monkeys: The Guajá Foragers of Eastern Amazonia. New York: Columbia University Press.

———. 2017. "Primates in Folklore." In The International Encyclopedia of Primatology, edited by Agustín Fuentes, 1139-1146. Hoboken, NJ: John Wiley and Sons. doi: 10.1002/9781119179313.wbprim0285.

Covey, Ryan, and W. Scott McGraw. 2014. "Monkeys in a West African Bushmeat Market: Implications for Cercopithecid Conservation in Eastern Liberia." Tropical Conservation Science 7 (1): 115–125. doi: 10.1177/194008291400700103.

Cronin, Drew T., Stephen Woloszynek, Wayne A. Morra, Shaya Honarvar, Joshua M. Linder, Mary Katherine Gonder, Michael P. O'Connor, and Gail W. Hearn. 2015. "Long-term Urban Market Dynamics Reveal Increased Bushmeat Carcass Volume Despite Economic Growth and Proactive Environmental Legislation on Bioko Island, Equatorial Guinea." PLoS ONE 10 (7): e0134464. doi: 10.1371/journal.pone.0134464.

Dinsmore, Mary P., Edward E. Louis Jr., Daniel Georges Randriamahazomana, Ali Hachim, John R. Zaonarivelo, and Karen B. Strier. 2016. "Variation in Habitat and Behavior of the Northern Sportive Lemur (Lepilemur septentrionalis) at Montagne des Français, Madagascar." Primate Conservation 30: 73–88.

Dinsmore, Mary P., Karen B. Strier, and Edward E. Louis Jr. 2018. "The Impacts of Cyclone Enawo and Anthropogenic Disturbances on the Habitat of Northern Sportive Lemurs (Lepilemur septentrionalis) in Northern Madagascar." American Journal of Physical Anthropology 165 (2): 68.

Dunham, Amy E., Elizabeth M. Erhart, Deborah J. Overdorff, and Patricia C. Wright. 2008. "Evaluating Effects of Deforestation, Hunting, and El Nino Events on a Threatened Lemur." Biological Conservation 141 (1): 287–297. doi: 10.1016/j.biocon.2007.10.006.

Eppley, Timothy M., Giuseppe Donati, Jean Baptiste Ramanamanjato, Faly Randriatafika, Laza N. Andriamandimbiarisoa, David Rabehevitra, Robertin Ravelomanantsoa, and Jörg U. Ganzhorn. 2015. "The Use of an Invasive Species Habitat by a Small Folivorous Primate: Implications for Lemur Conservation in Madagascar." PLoS ONE 10 (11): e0140981. doi: 10.1371/journal.pone.0140981.

Estrada, Alejandro, Paul A. Garber, Russell A. Mittermeier, Serge Wich, Sidney Gouveia, Ricardo Dobrovolski, K. A. I. Nekaris, et al. 2018. "Primates in Peril: The Significance of Brazil, Madagascar, Indonesia, and the Democratic Republic of the Congo for Global Primate Conservation." PeerJ 6: e4869. doi: 10.7717/peerj.4869.

Estrada, Alejandro, Paul A. Garber, Anthony B. Rylands, Christian Roos, Eduardo Fernandez-Duque, Anthony Di Fiore, K.

Anne-Isola Nekaris, et al. 2017. "Impending Extinction Crisis of the World's Primates: Why Primates Matter." Science Advances 3(229): 1–16. doi: 10.1126/sciadv.1600946.

Fa, John E., Jesus Olivero, Miguel A. Farfán, Ana L. Márquez, Jesús Duarte, Janet Nackoney, Amy Hall, et al. 2015. "Correlates of Bushmeat in Markets and Depletion of Wildlife." Conservation Biology 29 (3): 805–815. doi: 10.1111/cobi.12441.

Farias, Izeni P., Wancley G. Santos, Marcelo Gordo, and Tomas Hrbek. 2015. "Effects of Forest Fragmentation on Genetic Diversity of the Critically Endangered Primate, the Pied Tamarin (Saguinus Bicolor): Implications for Conservation." Journal of Heredity 106 (S1): 512–521. doi: 10.1093/jhered/esv048.

Fennell, David, and David Weaver. 2005. "The Ecotourium Concept and Tourism-Conservation Symbiosis." Journal of Sustainable Tourism 13(4): 373–390. doi: 10.1080/09669580508668563.

Fernandes, Natalia C.C.A., Mariana Sequetin Cunha, Juliana Mariotti Guerra, Rodrigo Albergaria Ressio, Cinthya dos Santos Cirqueira, Silvia D'Andretta Iglezias, Julia de Carvalho, Emerson L.L. Aruajo, Jose-Luiz Catao-Dias, and Josue Diaz-Delgado. 2017. "Outbreak of Yellow Fever among Nonhuman Primates, Espirito Santo, Brazil, 2017." Emerging Infectious Diseases 23 (12): 2038–2041. doi: 10.3201/eid2312.170685.

Fragaszy, Dorothy, Patrícia Izar, Elisabetta Visalberghi, Eduardo B. Ottoni, and Marino Gomes de Oliveira. 2004. "Wild Capuchin Monkeys (Cebus libidinosus) Use Anvils and Stone-Pounding Tools." American Journal of Primatology 64 (4): 359–366. doi: 10.1002/ajp.20085.

Fuentes, Agustín. 2010. "Natural Cultural Encounters in Bali: Monkeys, Temples, Tourists, and Ethnoprimatology." Cultural Anthropology 25 (4): 600–624. doi:10.1111/j.1548-1360.2010.0170.x

———. 2012. "Ethnoprimatology and the Anthropology of the Human-Primate Interface." Annual Review of Anthropology 41: 101–117. doi: 10.1148/annurev-anthro-092611-145808.

Fuller, Grace, Wilhelmina Frederica Eggen, Wirdateti Wirdateti, and K. A. I. Nekaris. 2018. "Welfare Impacts of the Illegal Wildlife Trade in a Cohort of Confiscated Greater Slow Lorises, Nycticebus Coucang." Journal of Applied Animal Welfare Science 21 (3): 224–238. doi: 10.1080/10888705.2017.1393338.

Geffroy, Benjamin, Diogo S.M. Samia, Eduardo Bessa, and Daniel T. Blumstein. 2015. "How Nature-Based Tourism Might Increase Prey Vulnerability to Predators." Trends Ecology and Evolution (Amst) 30 (12): 755–765.

Gilpin, Michael E., and Michael E. Soulé. 1986. "Minimum Viable Populations: Processes of Species Extinction." In Conservation Biology: The Science of Scarcity and Diversity, edited by Michael E. Soulé, 19–34. Sunderland, UK: Sinauer and Associates.

Groves, Colin P. 2014. "Primate Taxonomy: Inflation or Real?" Annual Review of Anthropology 43: 27–36. doi: 10.1146/annurev-anthro-102313-030232.

Hai, Bach Thanh, Jin Chen, Kim R. McConkey, and Salindra K. Dayananda. 2018. "Gibbons (Nomascus gabriellae) Provide Key Seed Dispersal for the Pacific Walnut (Dracontomelon dao), in Asia's Lowland Tropical Forest." Acta Oecologica 88: 71–79. doi: 10.1016/j.actao.2018.03.011.

Haraway, Donna. 1991. Simians, Cyborgs, and Women: The Reinvention of Nature. New York: Routledge.

Harrison, P. A., P. M. Barry, G. Simpson, J. R. Haslett, M. Blicharska, M. Bucur, R. Dunford, et al. 2014. "Linkages between Biodiversity Attributes and Ecosystem Services: A Systematic Review." Ecosystem Services 9: 191–203. doi: 10.1016/j.ecoser.2014.05.006.

Hickey, J. R., A. Basabose, K. V. Gilardi, D. Greer, S. Nampindo, M. M. Robbins, and T .S. Stoinski. 2018. Gorilla beringei ssp. beringei. The IUCN Red List of Threatened Species 2018. doi: 10.2305/IUCN.UK.2018-2.RLTS.T39999A17989719.

Hogan, Jeremy D., Amanda D. Melin, Krisztina N. Mosdossy, and Linda M. Fedigan. 2016. "Seasonal Importance of Flowers to Costa Rican Capuchins (Cebus capucinus imitator): Implications for Plant and Primate." American Journal of Anthropology 161 (4): 591-602. doi: 10.1002/ajpa.23059.

Horwich, Robert H., and Jonathan Lyon. 2007. "Community Conservation: Practitioners' Answer to Critics." Oryx 41(3): 376-385. doi: 10.1017/S0030605307001010.

Horwich, R. H., J. Lyon, and A. Bose. 2012. "Preserving Biodiversity and Ecosystems: Catalyzing Conservation Contagion." In Deforestation around the World, edited by P. Moutinho, 283-318. Rijeka, Croatia: InTech.

Hosonuma, Noriko, Martin Herold, Veronique de Sy, Ruth S. de Fries, Maria Brockhaus, Louis Verchot, Arild Angelsen, and Erika Romijn. 2012. "An Assessment of Deforestation and Forest Degradation Drivers in Developing Countries." Environmental Research Letters 7 (4). doi: 10.1088/1748-9326/7/4/044009.

Husson, Simon J., Marc Ancrenaz, Elizabeth J. Macfie, Sri Suci Utami-Atmoko, and Serge A. Wich. 2016. "Bornean Orangutan." In Primates in Peril: The 25 Most Endangered Primates 2016-2018, edited by C. Schwitzer, R. A. Mittermeier, A. B. Rylands, F. Chiozza, E. A. Williamson, E. J. Macfie, J. Wallis, and A. Cotton, 75-78. IUCN SSC Primate Specialist Group (PSG), International Primatological Society (IPS), Conservation International (CI), and Bristol Zoological Society, Arlington, Virginia.

Hvenegaard, Glen. 2014. "Economic Aspects of Primate Tourism Associated with Primate Conservation." In Primate Tourism: A Tool for Conservation? edited by Anne E. Russon and Janette Wallis, 259-277. Cambridge, UK: Cambridge University Press.

Inoue-Nakamura, Noriko, and Tetsuro Matsuzawa. 1997. "Development of Stone Tool Use by Wild Chimpanzees (Pan troglodytes)." Journal of Comparative Psychology 111 (2): 159-173.

IPCC. 2014: "Climate Change 2014: Synthesis Report. Contribution of Working Groups I, II, and III to the Fifth Assessment Report of the Intergovernmental Panel on Climate Change", edited by Core Writing Team, R. K. Pachauri and L. A. Meyer,151. Geneva, Switzerland: IPCC.

IUCN. 2012. "IUCN Red List Categories and Criteria: Version 3.1." Technical Report, 32. Gland, Switzerland and Cambridge, UK: IUCN.

IUCN. 2017. "The IUCN Red List of Threatened Species: Version 13." Available: http://www.iucnredlist.org, accessed March 3, 2017.

Kalpers, José, Elizabeth A. Williamson, Martha M. Robbins, Alastair Mcneilage, Augustin Nzamurambaho, Ndakasi Lola, and Ghad Mugiri. 2003. "Gorillas in the Crossfire: Population Dynamics of the Virunga Mountain Gorillas over the Past Three Decades." Oryx 37 (3): 326-337. doi: 10.1017/S0030605303000589.

Kappeler, Peter M., and David P. Watts. 2012. Long-term Field Studies of Primates. New York: Springer.

Kierulff, M. C. M., C. R. Ruiz-Miranda, P. Procopio de Oliveira, B. B. Beck, A. Martins, J. M. Dietz, D. M. Rambaldi, and A. J. Baker. 2012. "The Golden Lion Tamarin Leontopithecus rosalia: A Conservation Success Story." International Zoo Yearbook 46 (1): 36-45. doi: 10.1111/j.1748-1090.2012.00170.x.

Kremen, Claire. 2005. "Managing Ecosystem Services: What Do We Need to Know about Their Ecology?" Ecology Letters 8 (5): 468-479. doi: 10.1111/j.1461-0248.2005.00751.x.

Kress, John, George E. Schatz, Michael Andrianifahanana, and Hilary Simons Morland. 1994. "Pollination of Ravenala madagascariensis (Strelitziaceae) by Lemurs in Madagascar: Evidence for an Archaic Coevolution System?" American Journal of Botany 81 (5): 542–551. doi: 10.1002/j.1537-2197.1994.tb15483.x.

Krief, Sabrina, Philippe Berny, Francis Gumisiriza, Régine Gross, Barbara Demeneix, Jean Baptiste Fini, Colin A. Chapman, Lauren J. Chapman, Andrew Seguya, and John Wasswa. 2017. "Agricultural Expansion as Risk to Endangered Wildlife: Pesticide Exposure in Wild Chimpanzees and Baboons Displaying Facial Dysplasia." Science of the Total Environment 598: 647–656. doi: 10.1016/j.scitotenv.2017.04.113.

Lafferty, Kevin D. 2009. "The Ecology of Climate Change and Infectious Diseases." Ecology 90 (4): 888–900. doi: https://doi.org/10.1890/08-0079.1.

Laurance, William F., Gopalasamy Reuben Clements, Sean Sloan, Christine S. O'Connell, Nathan D. Mueller, Miriam Goosem, Oscar Venter, et al. 2014. "A Global Strategy for Road Building." Nature 513 (7517): 229–232. doi: 10.1038/nature13717.

Laurance, William F. 2015. "Emerging Threats to Tropical Forests." Annals of the Missouri Botanical Garden 100 (3): 159–169. doi: 10.3417/2011087.

Leroy, Eric M., Pierre Rouquet, Pierre Formenty, Sandrine Souquiere, Annelisa Kilbourne, Jean-Marc Froment, Magdalena Bermejo, et al. 2004. "Multiple Ebola Virus Transmission Events and Rapid Decline of Central African Wildlife." Science 303 (5656): 387–390. doi: 10.1126/science.1092528.

Lewis, Rebecca, and F. Rakontondranaivo. 2011. "The Impact of Cyclone Fanele on Sifaka Body Condition and Reproduction in the Tropical Dry Forest of Western Madagascar." Journal of Tropical Ecology 27 (4): 429–432. doi: 10.1017/S0266467411000083.

Lynch Alfaro, Jessica W., José de Sousa E. Silva Jr., and Anthony B. Rylands. 2012. "How Different Are Robust and Gracile Capuchin Monkeys? An Argument for the Use of Sapajus and Cebus." American Journal of Primatology 74 (4): 273–286. doi: 10.1002/ajp.22007.

Mace, Georgina M., Ken Norris, and Alastair H. Fitter. 2011. "Biodiversity and Ecosystem Services: A Multilayered Relationship." Trends in Ecology and Evolution 27 (1): 19–26. doi: 10.1016/j.tree.2011.08.006.

Maekawa, Miko, Annette Lanjouw, Eugene Rutagarama, and Douglas Sharp. 2013. "Mountain Gorilla Tourism Generating Wealth and Peace in Post-Conflict Rwanda." Natural Resources Forum 37 (2): 127–137. doi: 10.1111/1477-8947.12020.

Maldonado, Angela M., Vincent Nijman, and Simon K. Bearder. 2009. "Trade in Night Monkeys Aotus Spp. in the Brazil-Colombia-Peru Tri-Border Area: International Wildlife Trade Regulations Are Ineffectively Enforced." Endangered Species Research 9 (2): 143–149. doi: 10.3354/esr00209.

Millenium Ecosystem Assessment. 2005. Ecosystems and Human Well-Being: Synthesis. Washington, DC: World Resources Institute.

Muehlenbein, Michael P. 2017. "Primates on Display: Potential Disease Consequences beyond Bushmeat." American Journal of Physical Anthropology 162 (S63): 32–43. doi: 10.1002/ajpa.23145.

Muehlenbein, Michael P., Leigh A. Martinez, Andrea A. Lemke, Laurentius Ambu, Senthilvel Nathan, Sylvia Alsisto, Rosman Sakong. 2010. "Unhealthy Travelers Present Challenges to Sustainable Primate Ecotourism." Travel Medicine and Infectious Disease 8 (3): 169–175. doi: 10.1016/j.tmaid.2010.03.004.

Nekaris, Anne-Isola, Nicola Campbell, Tim G. Coggins, E. Johanna Rode, and Vincent Nijman, 2013. "Tickled to Death:

Analysing Public Perceptions of 'Cute' Videos of Threatened Species (Slow Loris – Nycticebus spp.) on Web 2.0 Sites." PLoS ONE 8(7): e69215. doi: 10.1371/journal.pone.0069215.

Noss, Andrew J. 1998. "The Impacts of Cable Snare Hunting on Wildlife Populations in the Forests of the Central African Republic." Conservation Biology 12 (2): 390–398.

Nunn, Charles L., and Sonia Altizer. 2006. Infectious Diseases in Primates. Oxford, UK: Oxford University Press.

Nunn, Charles L., and Thomas R. Gillespie. 2016. "Infectious Disease and Primate Conservation." In An Introduction to Primate Conservation, edited by Serge A. Wich and Andrew J. Marshall, 157–174. Oxford, UK: Oxford University Press.

Osei-Tutu, Paul. 2017. "Taboos as Informal Institutions of Local Resource Management in Ghana: Why They Are Complied With or Not." Forest Policy and Economics 85 (1): 114–123. doi: 10.1016/j.forpol.2017.09.009.

Pavelka, Mary S. M., and Colin A. Chapman. 2006. "Population Structure of Black Howlers (Alouatta pigra) in Southern Belize and Responses Hurricane Iris." In New Perspectives on the Study of Mesoamerican Primates: Distribution, Ecology, Behavior, and Conservation, edited by Alejandro Estrada, Paul A. Garber, Mary S. M. Pavelka, and LeAndra Luecke, 143–163. New York: Springer.

Pearce, John, and Gianna Moscardo. 2015. "Social Representations of Tourist Selfies: New Challenges for Sustainable Tourism." In BEST EN Think Tank X, The Environment-People Nexus in Sustainable Tourism: Finding the Balance, 59–73. BEST EN Think Tank XV, 17–21 June 2015, Skukuza, Mpumalanga, South Africa.

Pebsworth, Paula A., and Marni LaFleur. 2014. "Advancing Primate Research and Conservation through the Use of Camera Traps: Introduction to the Special Issue." International Journal of Primatology 35 (5): 825–840. doi: 10.1007/s10764-014-9802-4.

Peterson, Jeffrey V. 2017. "Primates in World Religions (Buddhism, Christianity, Hinduism, Islam)." In The International Encyclopedia of Primatology, edited by Agustín Fuentes, 1171–1177. Hoboken, NJ: John Wiley and Sons. doi: 10.1002/9781119179313.wbprim0122.

Peterson, Jeffrey V., and Erin P. Riley. 2017. "Sacred Monkeys? An Ethnographic Perspective on Macaque Sacredness in Balinese Hinduism." In Ethnoprimatology: A Practical Guide to Research at the Human-Nonhuman Primate Interface, edited by Kerry M. Dore, Erin P. Riley, and Agustín Fuentes, 206–218. Cambridge, UK: Cambridge University Press.

Ratsimbazafy, J. 2006. "Diet Composition, Foraging, and Feeding Behavior in Relation to Habitat Disturbance: Implications for the Adaptability of Ruffed Lemurs (Varecia v. editorium) in Manombo Forest, Madagascar." In Lemurs: Ecology and Adaptation, edited by L. Gould and M. L. Sauther, 403–422. New York: Springer.

Reibelt, L. M., and J. Nowack. 2015. "Editorial: Community-Based Conservation in Madagascar, the 'Cure-All' Solution? Madagascar Conservation & Development. 10 (1): 3–5. doi: 10.4314/mcd.v10i1.S1.

Rimbach, Rebecca, Andrés Link, Andrés Montes-Rojas, Anthony Di Fiore, Michael Heistermann, and Eckhard W. Heymann. 2014. "Behavioral and Physiological Responses to Fruit Availability of Spider Monkeys Ranging in a Small Forest Fragment." American Journal of Primatology 76 (11): 1049–1061. doi: 10.1002/ajp.22292.

Robbins, Martha M., Markye Gray, Katie A. Fawcett, Felicia B. Nutter, Prosper Uwingeli, Innocent Mburanumwe, Edwin Kagoda, et al. 2011. "Extreme Conservation Leads to Recovery of the Virunga Mountain Gorillas." PLoS ONE 6 (6): e19788. doi: 0.1371/journal.pone.0019788.

Roncal, Carla Mere, Mark Bowler, and Michael P. Gilmore. 2018. "The Ethnoprimatology of the Maijuna of the Peruvian Amazon and Implications for Primate Conservation." Journal of Ethnobiology and Ethnomedicine 14 (19). doi: 10.1186/s13002-018-0207-x.

Rothman, Jessica M., Colin A. Chapman, Thomas T. Struhsaker, David Raubenheimer, Dennis Twinomugesha, and Peter G. Waterman. 2015. "Long-term Declines in Nutritional Quality of Tropical Leaves." Ecology 96 (3): 873–878. doi: 10.1890/14-0391.1.

Russo, Sabrina E. 2017. "Seed Dispersal." In The International Encyclopedia of Primatology, edited by Agustín Fuentes, 1265–1269. Hoboken, NJ: John Wiley and Sons.

Russo, Sabrina, and Colin Chapman. 2011. "Primate Seed Dispersal: Linking Behavioral Ecology with Forest Community Structure." In Primates in Perspective, edited by Christina Campbell, Agustín Fuentes, Katherine McKinnon, Simon Bearder, and Rebecca Stumpf, 523–534. New York: Oxford University Press.

Rylands, Anthony B., and Russell A. Mittermeier. 2014. "Primate Taxonomy: Species and Conservation." Evolutionary Anthropology 23 (1): 8–10. doi: 10.1002/evan.21387.

Scales, I. R. 2014. "The Future of Biodiversity Conservation and Environmental Management in Madagascar: Lessons from the Past and Challenges ahead." In Conservation and Environmental Management in Madagascar, edited by I. R. Scales, 342–360. London: Routledge.

Schaffner, Colleen M., Luisa Rebecchini, Gabriel Ramos-Fernandez, Laura G. Vick, and Fillipo Aureli. 2012. "Spider Monkeys (Ateles geoffroyi yucatenensis) Cope with the Negative Consequences of Hurricanes through Changes in Diet, Activity Budget, and Fission-Fusion Dynamics." International Journal of Primatology 33 (4): 922–936. doi: 10.1007/s10764-012-9621-4.

Schloss, Carrie A., Tristan A. Nuñez, and Joshua J. Lawler. 2012. "Dispersal Will Limit Ability of Mammals to Track Climate Change in the Western Hemisphere." PNAS 109 (22): 8606–8611. doi: 10.1073/pnas.1116791109.

Schwitzer, Christoph, Russell A. Mittermeier, Anthony B. Rylands, Federica Chiozza, Elizabeth A. Williamson, Elizabeth J. Macfie, Janette Wallis, and Alison Cotton, eds. 2017."Primates in Peril: The World's 25 Most Endangered Primates 2016-2018." Arlington, VA: IUCN SSC Primate Specialist Group (PSG), International Primatological Society (IPS), Conservation International (CI), and Bristol Zoological Society.

Sechrest, W., Thomas M. Brooks, Gustavo A. B. da Fonseca, William R. Konstant, Russel A. Mittermeier, Andy Purvis, Anthony B. Rylands, and John L. Gittleman. 2002. "Hot Spots and the Conservation of Evolutionary History." Proceedings of the National Academy of Sciences 99 (4): 2067–2071. doi: 10.1073/pnas.251680798.

Shanee, Noga, A. Patricia Mendoza, and Sam Shanee. 2017. "Diagnostic Overview of the Illegal Trade in Primates and Law Enforcement in Peru." American Journal of Primatology 79 (11): 1–12. doi: 10.1002/ajp.22516.

Shanee, N., S. Shanee, and A. M. Maldonado. 2007. "Conservation Assessment and Planning for the Yellow-Tailed Woolly Monkey (Oreonax flavicauda) in Peru." Wildlife Biology in Practice. 3 (2): 73–82. doi: 10.2461/wbp.2007.3.9.

Sicotte, Pascale. 2017. "Social Taboos." In The International Encyclopedia of Primatology, edited by Agustín Fuentes, 1319–1321. Hoboken, NJ: John Wiley and Sons. doi: 10.1002/9781119179313.wbprim0117.

Southwick, Charles H., and M. Farooq Siddiqi. 1988. "Partial Recovery and a New Population Estimate of Rhesus Monkey Populations in India." American Journal of Primatology 16 (3): 187–197.

Spenceley, Anna, Straton Habyalimana, Ritah Tusabe, and Donnah Mariza. 2010. "Benefits to the Poor from Gorilla Tourism in Rwanda." Development Southern Africa 27 (5): 647–662. doi: 10.1080/0376835X.2010.522828.

Sponsel, Leslie E. 1997. "The Human Niche in Amazonia: Explorations in Ethnoprimatology." In New World Primates: Ecology, Evolution, and Behavior, edited by W. Kinzey, 143–165. New York: Aldine de Gruyter.

Srivastava, Arun, Jayanta Das, Jihosuo Biswas, Pranab Buzarbarua, Prabal Sarkar, Irwin S. Bernstein, and Surendra Mal Mohnot. 2001. "Primate Population Decline in Response to Habitat Loss: Borajan Reserve Forest of Assam, India." Primates 42 (4): 401-406. doi: 10.1007/BF02629631.

Steinweg, Tim, Barbara Kuepper, and Gabriel Thoumi. 2016. Economic Drivers of Deforestation. Washington, DC: Chain Reaction Research. http://chainreactionresearch.com/wp-content/uploads/2016/08/economic-drivers-of-deforestation-crr-160803-final1.pdf

Strier, Karen B. 1994. "Myth of the Typical Primate." American Journal of Physical Anthropology 37 (S19): 233-271. doi: 10.1002/ajpa.13303700609.

---. 2003. "Primatology Comes of Age: 2002 AAPA Luncheon Address." Yearbook of Physical Anthropology 46: 2-13.

---. 2010. " Long-term Field Studies: Positive Impacts and Unintended Consequences." American Journal of Primatology 72 (9): 772-778. doi: 10.1002/ajp.20830.

---. 2011a. "Conservation." In Primates in Perspective, edited by Christina Campbell, Agustín Fuentes, Katherine C. MacKinnon, Simon K. Bearder, and Rebecca M. Stumpf, 664-675. New York: Oxford University Press.

---. 2011b. "Why Anthropology Needs Primatology." General Anthropology 18 (1): 1-8.

---. 2017. Primate Behavioral Ecology: Fifth Edition. New York: Routledge.

---. 2018a. "Primate Social Behavior." American Journal of Physical Anthropology 165 (4): 801-812.

---. 2018b. "What Climate Change Means for Primates and Primatology." Paper presented at the 87th Annual Meeting of American Association of Physical Anthropologists, Austin, Texas, April 11-14, 2018.

Strier, Karen B. and Jean Philippe Boubli. 2006. "A History of Long-term Research and Conservation of Northern Muriquis (Brachyteles hypoxanthus) at the Estação Biológica de Caratinga/RPPN-FMA." Primate Conservation 20: 53-63. doi: 10.1896/0898-6207.20.1.53.

Strier, Karen B. and Sérgio L. Mendes. 2012. "The Northern Muriqui (Brachyteles hypoxanthus): Lessons on Behavioral Plasticity and Population Dynamics from a Critically Endangered Species." In Long-term Field Studies of Primates, edited by Peter M. Kappeler and David P. Watts, 125-140. Berlin, Heidelberg: Springer.

Strier, Karen B., Carla B. Possamai, Fernanda P. Tabacow, Alcides Pissinatti, Andre M. Lanna, Fabiano Rodrigues de Melo, Leandro Moreira, et al. 2017. "Demographic Monitoring of Wild Muriqui Populations: Criteria for Defining Priority Areas and Monitoring Intensity." PLoS ONE: 12 (12): e0188922. doi: 10.1371/journal.pone.0188922.

Strum, Shirley C., and Linda M. Fedigan. 1999. "Theory, Method, Gender, and Culture: What Changed Our Views of Primate Society." In The New Physical Anthropology: Science, Humanism, and Critical Reflection, edited by S. C. Strum, D. G. Lindburg, and D. A. Hamburg, 67-105. New Jersey: Prentice Hall.

Tarara, R., M. A. Suleman, R. Sapolsky, M. J. Wabomba, and J. G. Else. 1985. "Tuberculosis in Wild Olive Baboons (Papio cynocephalus anubis) in Kenya." Journal of Wildlife Diseases 21 (2): 137-140. doi: 10.7589/0090-3558-21.2.137.

Teaford, Mark F., and Ordean J. Oyen. 1989. "In Vivo and In Vitro Turnover in Dental Microwear." American Journal of Physical Anthropology 80 (4): 447-600. doi: 10.1002/ajpa.1330800405.

Terborgh, J. 1983. Five New World Primates: A Study in Comparative Ecology. Princeton: Princeton University Press.

Tumusiime, David Mwesigye, Gerald Eilu, Mnason Tweheyo, Mnason Tweheyo, and Fred Babweteera. 2010. "Wildlife

Snaring in Budongo Forest Reserve, Uganda." Human Dimensions of Wildlife 15 (2): 129-144. doi: 10.1080/10871200903493899.

Tyukavina, Alexandra, Matthew C. Hansen, Peter V. Potapov, Stephen V. Stehman, Kevin Smith-Rodriguez, Chima Okpa, and Ricardo Aguilar. 2017. "Types and Rates of Forest Disturbance in Brazilian Legal Amazon, 2000-2013." Science Advances 3 (4): 1-16. doi: 10.1126/sciadv.1601047.

UN Population Division. 2017. "World Population Prospects: The 2017 Revision." Accessed January 2, 2019. https://esa.un.org/unpd/wpp/publications/files/wpp2017_keyfindings.pdf.

Ungar, Peter S., and Matt Sponheimer. 2011. "The Diets of Early Hominins." Science 334 (6053): 190-193.

Voigt, Maria, Serge A Wich, Marc Ancrenaz, Erik Meijaard, Nicola Abram, Graham L. Banes, Gail Campbell-Smith, et al. 2018. "Global Demand for Natural Resources Eliminated More Than 100,000 Bornean Orangutans." Current Biology 28 (5): 761-769. doi: 10.1016/j.cub.2018.01.053.

Wallis, Janette, and D. Rick Lee. 1999. "Primate Conservation: The Prevention of Disease Transmission." International Journal of Primatology 20 (6): 803-826. doi: 10.1023/A:1020879700286.

Wang, Chengliang, Xiaowei Wang, Xiaoguang Qi, Songtao Guo, Haitao Zhao, Wei Wei, and Baoguo Li. 2015. "Influence of Human Activities on the Historical and Current Distribution of Sichuan Snub-Nosed Monkeys in the Qinling Mountains, China." Folia Primatologica 85 (6): 343-357.

Washburn, Sherwood L. 1951. "Section of Anthropology: The New Physical Anthropology." Transactions of the New York Academy of Sciences 13 (7): 298-304.

———.1973. "The Promise of Primatology." American Journal of Physical Anthropology 38 (2): 177-182.

Wheatley, Bruce P. 1999. The Sacred Monkeys of Bali. New York: Waveland.

Wiederholt, Ruscena, and Eric Post. 2010. "Tropical Warming and the Dynamics of Endangered Primates." Biology Letters. 6 (2): 257-260. doi: 10.1098/rsbl.2009.0710.

Williams, J. M., E. V. Lonsdorf, M. L. Wilson, J. Schumacher-Stankey, J. Goodall, and A. E. Pusey. 2008. "Causes of Death in the Kasekela Chimpanzees of Gombe National Park, Tanzania." American Journal of Primatology 70 (8): 766-777. doi: 10.1002/ajp.20573.

Wright, Patricia. 1999. "Lemur Traits and Madagascar Ecology: Coping with an Island Environment." Yearbook of Physical Anthropology 42: 31-72. doi: 10.1002/(SICI)1096-8644(1999)110:29+<31::AID-AJPA3>3.0.CO;2-0.

Wright, S. Joseph. 2005. "Tropical Forests in a Changing Environment." Trends in Ecology and Evolution 20 (10): 553-560. doi: 10.1016/j.tree.2005.07.009.

Yersin, Harmony, Caroline Asiimwe, Maarten J. Voordouw, and Klaus Zuberbühler. 2017. "Impact of Snare Injuries on Parasite Prevalence in Wild Chimpanzees (Pan Troglodytes)." International Journal of Primatology 38 (1): 21-30. doi: 10.1007/s10764-016-9941-x.

Zhao, Maosheng, and Steven W. Running. 2010. "Drought-Induced Reduction in Global Terrestrial Net Primary Production from 2000 through 2009." 2010. Science 329 (5994): 940-943. doi: 10.1126/science.1192666.

Zimmerman, Julie K. H., and Alan P. Covich. 2007. "Damage and Recovery of Riparian Sierra Palms after Hurricane Georges: Influence of Topography and Biotic Characteristics." Biotropica 39 (1): 43-49. doi: 10.1111/j.1744-7429.2006.00237.x.

Acknowledgments

We are grateful to the University of Wisconsin-Madison for the various sources of funding that enabled us to write this Appendix, including Teaching Assistantships from the departments of Integrative Biology (to MPD and JBK) and Anthropology (to RJE and AJH), an Advanced Opportunity Fellowship (to IEA), and a Vilas Research Professorship (to KBS). We are grateful to our new lab member, Irene Duch Latorre, for her photograph and helpful additions as well as to Kadie Callingham for the use of her photograph. We thank the editors of this volume for inviting our contribution and for the helpful comments that they and an anonymous reviewer provided.

Figure Attributions

Figure B.1 World population by region by Our World in Data [Source HYDE (2016) & UN (2019)] accessed August 5, 2019 is used under a CC BY 4.0 License.

Figure B.2 Global primate species richness, distributions, and the percentage of species threatened and with declining populations (Figure 1) by Estrada et al. [Original: 2017 "Impending Extinction Crisis of the World's Primates: Why Primates Matter." Science Advances 3 (229): 1–16. doi:10.1126/sciadv.1600946] is used under a CC BY 4.0 License.

Figure B.3 Mountain Gorilla Bwindi by Rod Waddington is used under a CC BY-SA 2.0 License.

Figure B.4 A female northern muriqui (*Brachyteles hypoxanthus*) with infant at the Feliciano Miguel Abdala Private Natural Heritage Reserve outside of Caratinga, Brazil by Amanda J. Hardie, courtesy of Projeto Muriqui de Caratinga, is used by permission and available here under a CC BY-NC 4.0 License.

Figure B.5 International Union for Conservation of Nature (IUCN) Criteria for Threatened Taxa by Mary P. Dinsmore et al., updated from Strier 2011, with data simplified and condensed from IUCN Species Survival Commission (2012), is under a CC BY-NC 4.0 License.

Figure B.6 Bornean Orangutan Wide Face by Eric Kilby is used under a CC BY-SA License.

Figure B.7 A female gelada (Theropithecus gelada) with a snare around its neck in central Ethiopia by Kadie Callingham is used by permission and available here under a CC BY-NC 4.0 License.

Figure B.8 Cattle graze in papaya plantation, once forested land, in Montagne des Français, Madagascar by Mary P. Dinsmore is under a CC BY-NC 4.0 License.

Figure B.9 Forest cleared for cattle-ranching in the province of Manabí, Ecuador by Irene Duch-Latorre, courtesy of Proyecto Washu, is used by permission and available here under a CC BY-NC 4.0 License.

Figure B.10 An industrial-sized truck with charcoal leaves Montagne des Français region, Madagascar by Mary P. Dinsmore is under a CC BY-NC 4.0 License.

Figure B.11 Old-growth tree uprooted after Cyclone Enawo, Madagascar by Mary P. Dinsmore is under a CC BY-NC 4.0 License.

Figure B.12 A northern sportive lemur (*Lepilemur septentrionalis*), Montagne des Français, Madagascar by Mary P. Dinsmore is under a CC BY-NC 4.0 License.

Figure B.13 A model of the extinction vortex drawn by Karen B. Strier (AAPA 87th Annual Meeting, 11–14 April 2018), adapted from Gilpin and Soulé (1986), is available here under a CC BY-NC 4.0 License.

Figure B.14 Fecal matter with seeds from the large-bodied northern muriqui (*Brachyteles hypoxanthus*) by Amanda J. Hardie, courtesy of Projeto Muriqui de Caratinga, is used by permission and available here under a CC BY-NC 4.0 License.

Figure B.15 Tourists feeding monkeys ATR P1180869 by T. R. Shankar Raman is used under a CC BY-SA 4.0 License.

Figure B.16 Students in the canopy at El Zota field station, Costa Rica, by Mary P. Dinsmore, courtesy of Broadreach Global Summer Adventures, Inc. is used by permission and available here under a CC BY-NC 4.0 License.

Appendix C

Kristin Snopkowski, Ph.D., Boise State University

Learning Objectives

- Define human behavioral ecology.
- Describe the types of behaviors that human behavioral ecologists study.
- Explain why humans share food.
- Identify how human behavioral ecology contributes to contemporary world issues.

Figure C.1 Aftermath of the 2004 Asian Tsunami in Sri Lanka.

On December 26, 2004, an earthquake in the Indian Ocean resulted in a tsunami that killed over 200,000 people in at least a dozen different countries (Editors of Encyclopaedia Britannica 2018; see Figure C.1). In the aftermath, 30% of American households donated an estimated $2.78 billion to help the victims (The Center on Philanthropy at Indiana University 2008). At the same time, despite being one of the wealthiest countries in the world, the United States has over a million children who experience homelessness each year (National Center for Homeless Education 2017). Why is it that sometimes humans work together to help those in need, but at other times, humans struggle to solve basic problems? The field of Human Behavioral Ecology seeks to understand this and many other questions to learn why humans behave the way they do. **Human Behavioral Ecology** is the field of anthropology that explores how evolutionary history and ecological factors combine to influence human behavior.

HUMAN BEHAVIORAL ECOLOGY

Evolutionary History

Natural selection is the force of evolution whereby individuals with heritable traits that result in greater survival and reproduction have more offspring than individuals without those traits. By having more offspring (specifically, offspring who themselves survive and reproduce), these heritable traits become more common in future generations. As an example, hominin brain size has increased dramatically over the past two million years. Our ancestors with larger brains were better able to survive and reproduce than those with smaller brains, possibly because they were better able to acquire food or navigate the social complexities of living in a large group (Dunbar 1998; Parker and Gibson 1979).

Human behavioral ecology uses the theory of evolution by natural selection to understand how modern behaviors were advantageous in our **evolutionary history**. For most of human history, humans lived as hunter-gatherers, meaning they collected or hunted food; they typically resided in small communities with individuals related through blood or marriage; and they had no access to modern medicines or other modern conveniences. It is useful to think about this environment—which is much different than how humans live today—to help us understand how current behaviors may have evolved. For example, humans today enjoy consuming food high in fats and sugars (see Chapter 16; see Figure C.2). In the past, eating fatty and sugary food was a good survival strategy since food was limited in a hunter-gatherer's environment, and these foods contained a lot of calories. Over time, those individuals who sought out these foods were probably better able to survive and reproduce, resulting in a population of people today who have preferences for these foods. In modern environments, where food is abundant, this preference has likely contributed to the obesity epidemic, which increases people's risk of cardiovascular diseases and no longer improves people's ability to survive and reproduce.

Figure C.2 Sample of sweets to celebrate Diwali, a Hindu festival of lights.

Ecology

In addition to evolutionary history, the field of human behavioral ecology also focuses on the influence of ecology. **Ecology** is defined as one's physical environment, including types of resources, predators, terrain, and weather, as well as one's social environment, including the behaviors of other individuals and cultural rules. For example, if one lives in an environment where there are abundant fruit trees, then one's diet likely includes fruit. Since fruits are easy to acquire, children can engage in food gathering at young ages. In contrast, in environments like the Arctic, where there are fewer plant resources, the diet focuses more on hunting and fishing. Since these skills take longer to acquire, children may only be able to contribute to their own subsistence at older ages. One's environment influences the behaviors in which individuals engage, such as children's foraging.

Another component of ecology is one's social environment, including cultural rules. Throughout the world, different cultures have quite different norms of behavior. For instance, in some societies marriages are required to be monogamous, meaning that a marriage is between just two individuals. This is a cultural norm in American society, and it is illegal to violate this rule. In other societies, marriages can occur between one man and several wives or one woman and several husbands, referred to as polygyny and polyandry respectively. If you are in a society where monogamy is the rule, then this will influence people's behavior, as each individual knows that they can only marry one other individual at a time. This may influence who they choose to be their partner. In polygynous cultures, the age difference between husbands and wives tends to be larger than it is in monogamous cultures, as the men who are able to attract additional wives tend to have high status or wealth and are typically older than the women who are available for marriage. One's environment (both physical and social) influences one's behavioral options, and human behavioral ecologists examine how one's ecology influences people's behavior. In Figure C.3, we see a visual depiction of the field of human behavioral ecology, using evolutionary history and ecology (physical environment plus culture) to explain modern human behavior.

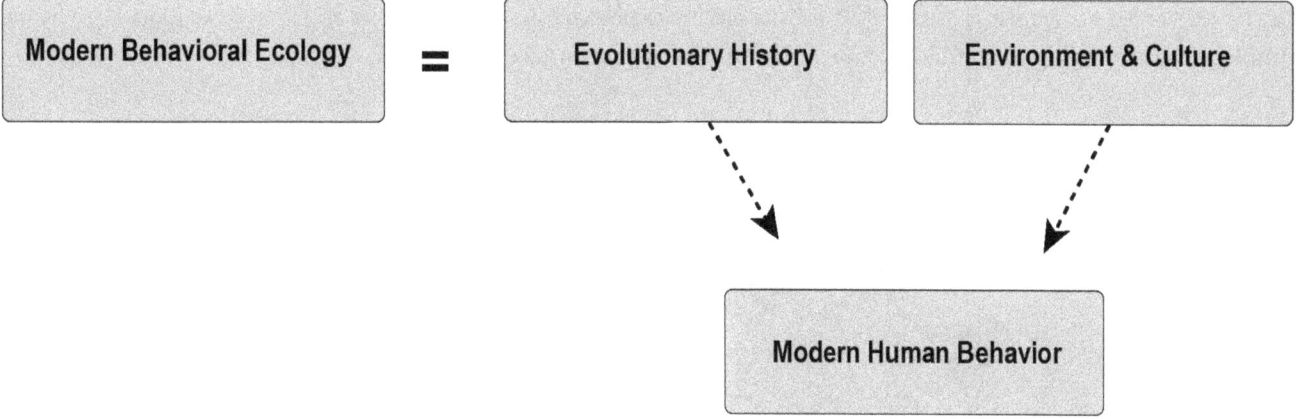

Figure C.3 Human behavioral ecology.

Both Genes and Environment Influence Behavior

While physical characteristics (like height) are clearly heritable, we also know that they depend on the environment. When children grow up with poor nutrition and do not ingest enough calories, their growth is stunted. At the same time, if your parents are both tall, then you are more likely to be tall as well. Physical traits are the result of both genes and environment. Behavior is the same–dependent on both genes and environment. While there are no genes for specific behaviors, behavioral tendencies do show some level of heritability. Personality disorders, for instance, may be partially heritable, but it also depends on the environment in which a child is raised–for example, where there is child neglect or sexual abuse, there is a corresponding increased risk of personality disorders (Johnson et al. 1999).

Human behavioral ecologists assume that even though there are not genes for specific behaviors, genes may influence behavioral tendencies. Additionally, behaviors are flexible and people use information from the environment to determine how they should behave. For example, the *ability* to cooperate has evolved over evolutionary time, but whether or not an individual cooperates in a particular instance likely depends on the situation. Research shows that people are more likely to cooperate if (1) their behavior is known to others (that is to say their identity is *not* anonymous), (2) it will improve their reputation, or (3) they will be punished for not cooperating (Andreoni and Petrie 2004; Fehr and Fischbacher 2003; Milinski, Semmann, and Krambeck 2002).

HOW CAN HUMAN BEHAVIORAL ECOLOGY HELP US UNDERSTAND ALTRUISM?

Altruism is defined as providing a benefit to someone without expecting anything in return. A perfect example is donating money to tsunami victims. From an evolutionary perspective, it seems that providing benefits to others would be disadvantageous for one's own survival and reproduction, as resources given to others are resources that cannot be used for oneself. But people do engage in altruistic behaviors, so how can the field of human behavioral ecology help us understand this behavior? We will use the example of food sharing to think about different ways human behavioral ecologists have examined this question. In many small-scale hunter-gatherer societies, people share food extensively with other people living in their communities. This sharing is most widespread when the item is a hunted animal, which can typically feed many people. Just as giving away money seems counterintuitive, so does giving away food. So, why do people in these foraging communities share so much food with each other?

Kin Selection

Figure C.4 Lao family eating together.

One of the first explanations for why humans share food is that they are sharing with their close family members. **Kin selection** proposes that individuals help kin, even at a cost to themselves, because this help is directed at individuals with whom they share genes (Hamilton 1964). If we think of evolution from a *gene's eye view*, then individuals should care about passing on their genes. Since family members share genes, this may explain why kin help one another. Figure C.4 shows a Lao family eating together. It is very common around the world for families to share food with one another. In many small-scale societies, people share food with family members but also with those who are not family members. Kin selection helps explain some food sharing, but it doesn't explain all food sharing.

Reciprocal Altruism

Another potential explanation for why humans share food is that they are engaging in **reciprocal altruism**, meaning that an individual shares food today with the expectation of repayment at some point in the future (Trivers 1971). This can work well, unless the person who receives the help chooses not to reciprocate in the future. In this case, the original sharer does not obtain anything in return. To maintain these relationships, it is important that individuals have the opportunity to share with one another repeatedly and that if one person chooses not to reciprocate, the original sharer terminates their sharing. Reciprocal altruism is even more likely to occur if the value of the food is greater to the person receiving the food than the person sharing the food. For instance, imagine that you have an entire pizza. After you eat several slices, you are no longer hungry and the next piece of pizza has little value to you. In contrast, if

Figure C.5 Jakun hunting party.

you are hungry, receiving a slice of pizza from a friend would mean a lot to you. In this case, the person giving a piece of pizza after already eating their fill is giving away something of little value, but the person receiving a slice of pizza when they are hungry is receiving something with substantial value. If the following week, the roles are reversed, then in both cases, the person receiving the food has received something of greater value than has the person who gave it away. This makes sense in the case of sharing hunted meat as well. When hunters kill an animal, it is typically a large animal with a lot of meat. In environments without refrigeration technology, leftover meat has little value as it is likely to spoil. In contrast, sharing that meat with hungry community members has a lot of value to those receiving the meat. Then, at some point in the future, the person who received the meat may successfully hunt and share with others. Figure C.5 displays an indigenous hunting party from Malaysia. Food is widely shared in small-scale societies, particularly when the item is large in size and when there is a lot of uncertainty around when the next successful hunt will occur (Gurven 2004). But, as with other skilled activities, some individuals are better hunters than others and acquire more meat than others consistently, so why would highly skilled hunters give more food to low-skilled hunters than will be reciprocated? Again, reciprocal altruism is one piece of the story but cannot explain all sharing behavior.

The "Show-Off" Hypothesis

Another possible explanation for why people share food, particularly meat in small-scale societies, is because they want to display their skills as a hunter to their community, termed the **show-off hypothesis** (Hawkes 1991). As a social species, an individual's success relies on what others think of them. Providing resources to the community may help attract mates, friends, and allies. Those that share are likely to be viewed as good cooperators and worth having around. Among the Melanesian Meriam Islanders, evidence shows that turtle hunting during the breeding season, which is highly risky and unpredictable, is only done by unmarried males (Bliege Bird and Bird 1997). Turtle hunting during the nesting season, which is relatively easy and low risk, is done by males of all ages. This suggests that unmarried males engage in risky hunting to signal their skills as a hunter and cooperator. Again, while some sharing behavior may be best explained by a desire to *show off*, it cannot explain all sharing behavior.

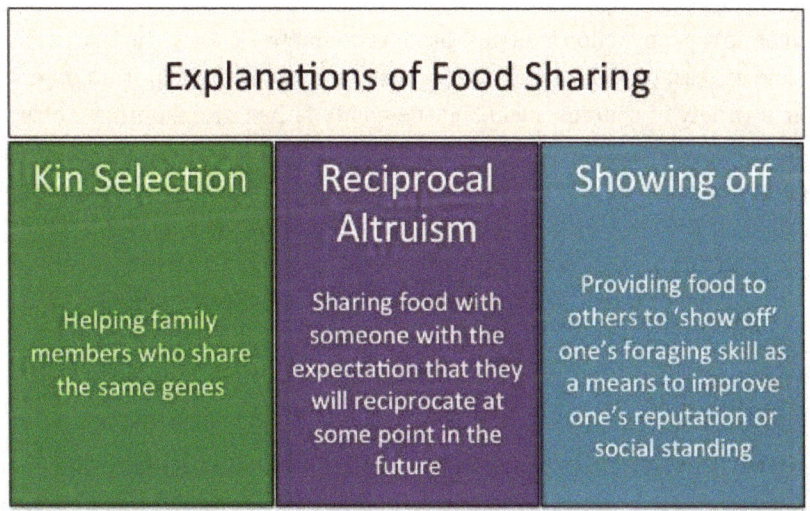

Figure C.6 Explanations of food sharing.

Examining these three explanations of sharing behavior (see Figure C.6)–kin selection, reciprocal altruism, and "showing off"–helps explain a lot of sharing seen around the world, but donating money to tsunami victims is still hard to understand. Most Americans were not related to the victims of the tsunami and they probably do not expect reciprocation. It is possible that people were doing it to *show off*, although it seems unlikely that many people used it as a means to improve their reputation. While some charitable giving may be explained by the tax incentives, the donations to the tsunami victims were so extensive that it seems unlikely to be the main explanation. People commonly state that they donate because "it makes them feel good." While helping others does make people feel good, this likely evolved because those that had the feel-good sensation helped others–like their kin–resulting in greater survival and reproduction. The "feel good" sensation is a **proximate mechanism**, the immediate explanation, while human behavioral ecology seeks to understand the **ultimate explanation**, or deep evolutionary reason that this trait led to increased survival and reproduction. In the case of donating money to people living on the other side of the world, our modern environment (allowing us to help people living so far away) may lead us to act in ways that were adaptive in our evolutionary past but that may not improve our survival or reproduction today.

At the same time, we struggle to solve the problem of homelessness across the United States. Using evolutionary theory may help us understand why people are unable to come together to eliminate this problem. Eradicating homelessness would be costly, would require the cooperation of lots of individuals (no single individual or small group can solve it on their own), and would be ongoing. This type of long-lasting commitment to help unrelated strangers may be difficult to acquire from large enough numbers of people to make an impact.

MAIN RESEARCH AREAS OF HUMAN BEHAVIORAL ECOLOGY

Throughout this appendix, we have been discussing one of the main research areas in Human Behavioral Ecology: cooperation and sharing. There are two other main areas of research for Human Behavioral Ecologists: production and reproduction. Production research explores how people acquire the resources that they need. Some research in this area has examined which items people choose to include in their diets and how long people spend foraging. This research has shown that people do not simply acquire any food resource in their environment; instead they make strategic decisions based on the food options available and the possible nutrients gained. Research on reproduction includes an examination of how people choose mates, make reproductive choices, invest in children, and acquire help to raise offspring. This line of research has shown that human mothers need help from others to raise offspring, and this help can come from a variety of sources, including the child's father, grandmothers, older siblings, grandfathers, or others (Hrdy 2009; Sear and Mace 2008). This is quite different from our non-human primate relatives, for whom almost all child care is given by mothers. These research areas capture many behaviors we faced in our evolutionary history: How did we get food, how did we distribute that food once we got it, and how did we make mating and reproductive decisions? All of the topics examined in the field of human behavioral ecology are closely linked to survival and reproduction inherent to evolution by natural selection and understanding how the environment influences decision making.

What Are the Common Misunderstandings about Human Behavioral Ecology?

There are a few common misperceptions about human behavioral ecology that make some people skeptical of this type of research. Some critiques have argued that studying the evolution of human behavior is problematic because of **biological determinism**, the idea that all behaviors are innate, determined by our genes. If behaviors are innate, then we cannot hold people accountable for their actions. But this is a misunderstanding. As mentioned previously, both genes and the environment influence behavior. Individuals may have a tendency to behave in a particular way, but behaviors are flexible. Also, there is no guarantee that everyone behaves in perfectly optimal ways. Over evolutionary time, those who acted more optimally in the past will have more offspring than those who did not, but in each generation we have variation in genotypes, phenotypes, and behaviors upon which selection can act.

Another common misconception is that by studying human behavior, human behavioral ecologists are providing justifications for those behaviors. The **naturalistic fallacy** describes the incorrect belief that what occurs in nature is what *ought to be*. This is a fallacy because it is absolutely *not* the goal of researchers in this field. For instance, some researchers study human violence. It is wrong to assume that by studying violence, the researchers believe that violence is an acceptable behavior or is justifiable. It is easy to slip into this misconception. For instance, while studying mating behavior, researchers may try to understand why some people cheat on their partners. Understanding what environmental factors might increase the likelihood of cheating is *not* providing an excuse for the behavior.

HOW CAN HUMAN BEHAVIORAL ECOLOGY HELP US UNDERSTAND THE WORLD?

While it may seem that the field of human behavioral ecology is more concerned about our evolutionary past than our present, there are many contemporary issues that human behavioral ecology can help us solve. One area that human behavioral ecologists have focused on is reproductive decisions. Around the world, people are choosing to have fewer children than in the past. Some countries are still dealing with overpopulation, but an even larger number are dealing with population aging and depopulation. Understanding how people decide how many children to have is an important area of research in today's world (Colleran and Snopkowski 2018). Researchers have also used evolutionary theory to improve handwashing rates around the world (Curtis 2013), reduce the obesity epidemic (Pepper and Nettle 2014), reduce conflict (de Waal 2000), and improve cooperation (Boyd and Richerson 1992).

Review Questions

- Human behavioral ecologists focus on what two main factors as influencing behavior?
- What are the three main explanations for why people in small-scale societies share food extensively?
- Describe the environment that represents most of human history.
- What are two misconceptions about human behavioral ecology?
- What contemporary world issues can human behavioral ecology help us solve?

Key Terms

Altruism: Providing a benefit to someone else at a cost to oneself, without expecting future reciprocation.

Biological determinism: Behaviors are determined exclusively by genes.

Ecology: The physical and social environment, including food resources, predators, terrain, weather, social rules, behavior of other people, and cultural rules.

Evolutionary history: An understanding of how traits (including behaviors) may be the result of natural selection in our hominin past.

Human Behavioral Ecology: The field of anthropology that explores how ecological factors and evolutionary history combine to influence how humans behave.

Kin selection: A type of natural selection whereby people help relatives, which can evolve because people are helping other individuals with whom they share genes.

Naturalistic fallacy: The incorrect belief that what occurs is what ought to be.

Proximate explanation: The mechanism that is immediately responsible for an event.

Reciprocal altruism: Helping behavior that occurs because individuals expect that any help they provide will be reciprocated in the future.

Show-off hypothesis: Individuals provide benefits to others because it improves their reputation and social status.

Ultimate explanation: An explanation for an event that is further removed than a proximate explanation but that provides a greater insight or understanding. In human behavioral ecology, ultimate explanations usually describe how a behavior is linked to reproduction and survival.

About the Author

Kristin Snopkowski

Boise State University, kristinsnopkowski@boisestate.edu

Kristin Snopkowski

Kristin Snopkowski is a human behavioral ecologist and associate professor of anthropology at Boise State University. Her research examines reproductive decisions, including how many children people choose to have, how other family members influence those decisions, and the interaction between females and males in negotiating these decisions. She has conducted field work in Bolivia, interviewing women about their reproductive choices, and has been analyzing data sets from around the world to understand how environmental factors influence these decisions worldwide.

For Further Exploration

Barrett, Louise, Robin Dunbar, and John Lycett. 2002. *Human Evolutionary Psychology*. Princeton: Princeton University Press.

Low, Bobbi S. 2015. *Why Sex Matters: A Darwinian Look at Human Behavior*. Princeton: Princeton University Press.

Cronk, Lee and Beth L. Leech. 2013. *Meeting at Grand Central: Understanding the Social and Evolutionary Roots of Cooperation*. Princeton: Princeton University Press.

References

Andreoni, James, and Ragan Petrie. 2004. "Public Goods Experiments without Confidentiality: A Glimpse into Fund-Raising." *Journal of Public Economics* 88 (7-8): 1605-1623. doi:10.1016/S0047-2727(03)00040-9.

Bliege Bird, R. L., and D.W. Bird. 1997. "Delayed Reciprocity and Tolerated Theft." *Current Anthropology* 38 (1): 49-78.

Boyd, Robert, and Peter J. Richerson. 1992. "Punishment Allows the Evolution of Cooperation (or Anything Else) in Sizable Groups." *Ethology and Sociobiology* 13 (3): 171-195.

Colleran, Heidi, and Kristin Snopkowski. 2018. "Variation in Wealth and Educational Drivers of Fertility Decline across 45 Countries." *Population Ecology* 60: 155-169. doi:10.1007/s10144-018-0626-5.

Curtis, Valerie. 2013. *Don't Look, Don't Touch, Don't Eat*. Chicago: University of Chicago Press.

de Waal, Frans B. M. 2000. "Primates—A Natural Heritage of Conflict Resolution." *Science* 289 (5479): 586-590. doi:10.1126/science.289.5479.586.

Dunbar, Robin I. M. 1998. "The Social Brain Hypothesis." *Evolutionary Anthropology* 6 (5): 178-190.

Editors of Encyclopaedia Britannica. 2018. "Indian Ocean Tsunami of 2004." *Encyclopaedia Britannica*. https://www.britannica.com/event/Indian-Ocean-tsunami-of-2004.

Fehr, Ernst, and Urs Fischbacher. 2003. "The Nature of Human Altruism." *Nature* 425 (6960): 785-791.

Gurven, Michael. 2004. "Reciprocal Altruism and Food-Sharing Decisions among Hiwi and Ache Hunter-Gatherers." *Behavioral Ecology and Sociobiology* 56 (4): 366-380. doi:10.1007/s00265-004-0793-6.

Hamilton, W. D. 1964. "The Genetical Evolution of Social Behaviour I & II." *Journal of Theoretical Biology* 7 (1): 1-52.

Hawkes, Kristen. 1991. "Showing off: Tests of an Hypothesis about Men's Foraging Goals." *Ethology and Sociobiology* 12 (1): 29-54.

Hrdy, Sarah Blaffer. 2009. *Mothers and Others: The Evolutionary Origins of Mutual Understanding*. Cambridge, MA: The Belknap Press of Harvard University Press.

Johnson, Jeffrey G., Patricia Cohen, Jocelyn Brown, Elizabeth M. Smailes, and David P. Bernstein. 1999. "Childhood Maltreatment Increases Risk for Personality Disorders During Early Adulthood." *Archives of General Psychiatry* 56 (7): 600-606. doi:10.1001/archpsyc.56.7.600.

Milinski, Manfred, Dirk Semmann, and Hans Jürgen Krambeck. 2002. "Reputation Helps Solve the 'Tragedy of the Commons.'" *Nature* 415 (6870): 424-426.

National Center for Homeless Education. 2017. *Federal Data Summary: School Years 2013-2014 to 2015-2016*. https://nche.ed.gov/downloads/data-comp-1314-1516.pdf.

Parker, Sue Taylor, and Kathleen Rita Gibson. 1979. "A Developmental Model for the Evolution of Language and Intelligence in Early Hominids." *Behavioral and Brain Sciences* 2 (3): 367-381. doi:10.1017/S0140525X0006307X.

Pepper, Gillian V., and Daniel Nettle. 2014. "Out-of-Control Mortality Matters: The Effect of Perceived Uncontrollable Mortality Risk on a Health-Related Decision." *PeerJ* 2: e459. doi:10.7717/peerj.459.

Sear, Rebecca, and Ruth Mace. 2008. "Who Keeps Children Alive? A Review of the Effects of Kin on Child Survival." *Evolution and Human Behavior* 29 (1): 1-18. doi:10.1016/j.evolhumbehav.2007.10.001.

The Center on Philanthropy at Indiana University. 2008. "Key Findings about Charitable Giving." https://philanthropy.iupui.edu/files/research/copps_2005_key_findings.pdf.

Trivers, Robert L. 1971. "The Evolution of Reciprocal Altruism." *The Quarterly Review of Biology* 46 (1): 35–57. doi:10.1086/406755.

Acknowledgments

Thanks to Sheryl Millard, Steven Menicucci, two anonymous reviewers, and the editors for helpful feedback on previous drafts of this section.

Figure Attributions

Figure C.1 Pictures from bus 13 by Sarvodaya Shramadana is used under a CC BY 2.0 License.

Figure C.2 Diwali sweets India 2009 by robertsharp is used under a CC BY 2.0 License.

Figure C.3 Human Behavioral Ecology by Katie Nelson original to Explorations: An Open Invitation to Biological Anthropology is under a CC BY-NC 4.0 License.

Figure C.4 Lao Mangkong family eats together by BigBrotherMouse is used under a CC BY-SA 3.0 License.

Figure C.5 Jakun Hunting Party Blowpipe Malaysia Mongoloid by Walter William Skeat, Charles Otto Blagden is in the public domain.

Figure C.6 Explanations of food sharing table by Kristin Snopkowski original to Explorations: An Open Invitation to Biological Anthropology is under a CC BY-NC 4.0 License.

CPSIA information can be obtained
at www.ICGtesting.com
Printed in the USA
LVHW052033130821
695224LV00011B/624